Contents

Preface		ix
List of Abbreviations		xi
Introduction		1
BERNARD COMRIE, UNIVERSITY OF SOUTHERN CALIFORNIA		
1 Indo-European Languages		31
PHILIP BALDI, PENNSYLVANIA STATE UNIVERSITY		
2 Germanic Languages		68
JOHN A. HAWKINS, UNIVERSITY OF SOUTHERN CALIFORNIA		
3 English		77
EDWARD FINEGAN, UNIVERSITY OF SOUTHERN CALIFORNIA		
4 German		110
JOHN A. HAWKINS, UNIVERSITY OF SOUTHERN CALIFORNIA		
5 Dutch		139
JAN G. KOOIJ, UNIVERSITY OF LEIDEN		
6 Danish, Norwegian and Swedish		157
EINAR HAUGEN, HARVARD UNIVERSITY		
7 Latin and the Italic Languages		180
R.G.G. COLEMAN, UNIVERSITY OF CAMBRIDGE		
8 Romance Languages		203
JOHN N. GREEN, UNIVERSITY OF BRADFORD		
9 French		210
MARTIN HARRIS, UNIVERSITY OF ESSEX		
10 Spanish		236
JOHN N. GREEN, UNIVERSITY OF BRADFORD		
11 Portuguese		260
STEPHEN PARKINSON, UNIVERSITY OF OXFORD		

	12 Italian	279
	NIGEL VINCENT, UNIVERSITY OF MANCHESTER	
	13 Rumanian	303
	GRAHAM MALLINSON, MONASH UNIVERSITY	
14	Slavonic Languages	322
	BERNARD COMRIE, UNIVERSITY OF SOUTHERN CALIFORNIA	
	15 Russian	329
	BERNARD COMRIE, UNIVERSITY OF SOUTHERN CALIFORNIA	
	16 Polish	348
	GERALD STONE, UNIVERSITY OF OXFORD	
	17 Czech and Slovak	367
	DAVID SHORT, UNIVERSITY OF LONDON	
	18 Serbo-Croat	391
	GREVILLE CORBETT, UNIVERSITY OF SURREY	
19	Greek	410
	BRIAN D. JOSEPH, OHIO STATE UNIVERSITY	
20	Indo-Aryan Languages	440
	GEORGE CARDONA, UNIVERSITY OF PENNSYLVANIA	
	21 Sanskrit	448
	GEORGE CARDONA, UNIVERSITY OF PENNSYLVANIA	
	22 Hindi-Urdu	470
	YAMUNA KACHRU, UNIVERSITY OF ILLINOIS AT URBANA-CHAMPAIGN	
	23 Bengali	490
	M.H. KLAIMAN, CALIFORNIA STATE UNIVERSITY FULLERTON	
24	Iranian Languages	514
	J.R. PAYNE, UNIVERSITY OF MANCHESTER	
	25 Persian	523
	GERNOT L. WINDFUHR, UNIVERSITY OF MICHIGAN	
	26 Pashto	547
	D.N. MACKENZIE, UNIVERSITY OF GÖTTINGEN	
27	**Uralic Languages**	567
	ROBERT AUSTERLITZ, COLUMBIA UNIVERSITY	
	28 Hungarian	577
	DANIEL ABONDOLO, UNIVERSITY OF LONDON	
	29 Finnish	593
	MICHAEL BRANCH, UNIVERSITY OF LONDON	

THE WORLD'S
MAJOR
LANGUAGES

THE WORLD'S MAJOR LANGUAGES

EDITED BY
BERNARD COMRIE

ROUTLEDGE
London

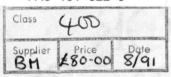
First published in 1987
Reprinted with revisions and additions in 1989 by Routledge
11 New Fetter Lane, London EC4P 4EE

British Library Cataloguing in Publication Data

The World's major languages.
  1. Language and languages
  I. Comrie, Bernard
  400   P121
  ISBN 0–415–04516–9

Typeset in 10 on 12pt Times by Computype, Middlesex
Printed and bound in Great Britain by Mackays, Chatham, Kent

30 Turkish and the Turkic Languages   619
JAKLIN KORNFILT, SYRACUSE UNIVERSITY

31 Afroasiatic Languages   645
ROBERT HETZRON, UNIVERSITY OF CALIFORNIA SANTA BARBARA

32 Semitic Languages   654
ROBERT HETZRON, UNIVERSITY OF CALIFORNIA SANTA BARBARA
33 Arabic   664
ALAN S. KAYE, CALIFORNIA STATE UNIVERSITY FULLERTON
34 Hebrew   686
ROBERT HETZRON, UNIVERSITY OF CALIFORNIA SANTA
BARBARA

35 Hausa and the Chadic Languages   705
PAUL NEWMAN, INDIANA UNIVERSITY

36 Tamil and the Dravidian Languages   725
SANFORD B. STEEVER, CENTRAL INDIAN INSTITUTE OF LANGUAGES

37 Tai Languages   747
DAVID STRECKER, CINCINNATI
38 Thai   757
THOMAS JOHN HUDAK, UNIVERSITY OF KENTUCKY

39 Vietnamese   777
ĐÌNH-HOÀ NGUYỄN, SOUTHERN ILLINOIS UNIVERSITY
AT CARBONDALE

40 Sino-Tibetan Languages   797
SCOTT DELANCEY, UNIVERSITY OF OREGON
41 Chinese   811
CHARLES N. LI AND SANDRA A. THOMPSON,
BOTH UNIVERSITY OF CALIFORNIA SANTA BARBARA
42 Burmese   834
JULIAN K. WHEATLEY, CALIFORNIA STATE UNIVERSITY FRESNO

43 Japanese   855
MASAYOSHI SHIBATANI, KOBE UNIVERSITY

44 Korean   881
NAM-KIL KIM, UNIVERSITY OF SOUTHERN CALIFORNIA

45 Austronesian Languages   899
ROSS CLARK, UNIVERSITY OF AUCKLAND
   46 Malay (Indonesian and Malaysian)   913
     D.J. PRENTICE, UNIVERSITY OF LEIDEN
   47 Tagalog   936
     PAUL SCHACHTER, UNIVERSITY OF CALIFORNIA LOS ANGELES

48 Niger-Kordofanian Languages   959
DOUGLAS PULLEYBLANK, UNIVERSITY OF SOUTHERN CALIFORNIA
   49 Yoruba   971
     DOUGLAS PULLEYBLANK, UNIVERSITY OF
     SOUTHERN CALIFORNIA
   50 Swahili and the Bantu Languages   991
     BENJI WALD, NATIONAL CENTER FOR BILINGUAL
     RESEARCH USA

Language Index   1015

Preface

This work represents the fruits of the collaboration of 44 scholars with international reputations ranging across a broad spectrum of the world's languages.

Perhaps the most controversial problem that I, as editor, have had to face has been the choice of languages to be included. My main criterion has, admittedly, been a very subjective one: what languages do I think the volume's readership would expect to find included? In answering this question I have, of course, been guided by more objective criteria, such as the number of speakers of individual languages, whether they are official languages of independent states, whether they are widely used in more than one country, whether they are the bearers of long-standing literary traditions. These criteria often conflict — thus Latin, though long since deprived of native speakers, is included because of its immense cultural importance — and I bear full responsibility, as editor, for the final choice. I acknowledge that the criterion of readership expectation has led me to bias the choice of languages in favour of European languages, although over half of the volume is devoted to languages spoken outside Europe.

The notion of 'major language' is obviously primarily a social characterisation, and the fact that a language is not included in this volume implies no denigration of its importance as a language in its own right: every human language is a manifestation of our species' linguistic faculty and any human language may provide an important contribution to our understanding of language as a general phenomenon. In the recent development of general linguistics, important contributions have come from the Australian Aboriginal languages Walbiri (Warlpiri) and Dyirbal (Jirrbal). My own research work has concentrated largely on languages that do not figure in this volume, such as Huichol of Mexico and Maltese of the Mediterranean, and as I write these lines I am about to embark on a year's field-work on Wiyaw, the language of some 1,000 New Guinea Highlanders. Other editors might well have come up with different selections of languages, or have used somewhat different criteria. When linguists learned in 1970 that the last speaker of Kamassian, a Uralic language originally spoken in Siberia, had kept her language alive for decades in her prayers — God being the only other speaker of her language — they may well have wondered whether, for this person, *the* world's major language was not Kamassian.

Contributors were presented with early versions of my own chapters on Slavonic languages and Russian as models for their contributions, but I felt it inappropriate to lay down strict guidelines as to how each individual chapter should be written, although I did ask authors to include at least some material on both the structure of their language and its social background. The main criterion that I asked contributors to follow was: tell the reader what you consider to be the most interesting facts about your language. This has necessarily meant that different chapters highlight different phenomena, e.g. the chapter on English the role of English as a world language, the chapter on Arabic the writing system, the chapter on Turkish the grammatical system. But I believe that this variety has lent strength to the volume, since within the space limitations of what has already grown to be quite a sizable book it would have been impossible to do justice in a more comprehensive and homogeneous way to each of over 50 languages and language families.

Editorial support in the preparation of this work was provided by the Division of Humanities of the University of Southern California, through the research fund of the Andrew W. Mellon Professorship, which I held during 1983–4, and by the Max Planck Institute for Psycholinguistics (Nijmegen, The Netherlands), where I was a visiting research worker in the summer of 1984. I am particularly grateful to Jonathan Price for his continuing willingness to consult with me on all details of the preparation of the volume.

For the 1989 reprint, a number of minor errors have been corrected and bibliographical material has been updated.

Bernard Comrie
Los Angeles

Abbreviations

abilit.	abilitative	conj.	conjunction
abl.	ablative	conjug.	conjugation
abstr.	abstract	conjv.	conjunctive
acc.	accusative	cont.	contemplated
acr.	actor	cop.	copula
act.	active	cp	class prefix
act.n.	action nominal	crs.	currently relevant state
adj.	adjective	Cz.	Czech
adv.	adverb	Da.	Danish
Alb.	Albanian	dat.	dative
Am.	American	dbl.	double
anim.	animate	decl.	declension
aor.	aorist	def.	definite
Ar.	Arabic	dent.	dental
Arm.	Armenian	deriv. morph.	derivational morpheme
art.	article	de-v.	deverbal
Ashk.	Ashkenazi(c)	dir.	direct
asp.	aspirated	disj.	disjunctive
AT	actor-trigger	Dor.	Doric
athem.	athematic	drc.	directional
aux.	auxiliary	DT	dative-trigger
Av.	Avestan	du.	dual
ben.	beneficiary	dur.	durative
BH	Biblical Hebrew	d.v.	dynamic verb
BN	B-Norwegian	E.	Eastern
Boh.	Bohemian	Eng.	English
BP	Brazilian Portuguese	ENHG	Early New High German
Br.	British		
BT	beneficiary-trigger	EP	European Portuguese
c.	common	erg.	ergative
Cast.	Castilian	ex.	existential-possessive
Cat.	Catalan	f.	feminine
caus.	causative	fact.	factive
cc	class concord	foc.	focus
Cent.	Central	Fr.	French
cl.	class(ifier)	fut.	future
clit.	clitic	g.	gender
comp.	comparative	gen.	genitive

ger.	gerund(ive)	neg.	negative
Gk.	Greek	NHG	New High German
Gmc.	Germanic	nm.	nominal
Go.	Gothic	NN	N-Norwegian
gr.	grade	nom.	nominative
GR	Gallo-Romance	noms.	nominalisation
gutt.	guttural	NP	New Persian
H	High	nt.	neuter
Hier. Hitt.	Hieroglyphic Hittite	Nw.	Norwegian
Hitt.	Hittite	O.	Oscan
hon.	honorific	OArm.	Old Armenian
IE	Indo-European	obj.	object
imper.	imperative	obl.	oblique
imperf.	imperfect(ive)	OBs.	Old Burmese
inanim.	inanimate	Oc.	Occitan
incl.	inclusive	OCS	Old Church Slavonic
indef.	indefinite	OE	Old English
indic.	indicative	OFr.	Old French
indir.	indirect	OFri.	Old Frisian
infin.	infinitive	OHG	Old High German
inst.	instrumental	OIc.	Old Icelandic
intr.	intransitive	OIr.	Old Irish
inv.	inversion particle	OIran.	Old Iranian
irr.	irrational	OLat.	Old Latin
It.	Italian	OLith.	Old Lithuanian
IT	instrument-trigger	ON	Old Norse
i.v.	intransitive verb	OP	Old Persian
L	Low	opt.	optative
lab.	labial	OPtg.	Old Portuguese
Lat.	Latin	orig.	original(ly)
Latv.	Latvian	OS	Old Saxon
LG	Low German	OV	object–verb
lig.	ligature	p.	person
lingu.	lingual	pal.	palatal
lit.	literally	part.	participle
Lith.	Lithuanian	pass.	passive
loc.	locative	pat.	patient
m.	masculine	PDr.	Proto-Dravidian
MBs.	Modern Burmese	perf.	perfect(ive)
ME	Middle English	pers.	person
med.	medio-passive	PGmc.	Proto-Germanic
MH	Middle Hebrew	PIE	Proto-Indo-European
MHG	Middle High German	PIt.	Proto-Italic
mid.	middle	Pkt.	Prakrit
MidFr.	Middle French	pl.	plural
ModE	Modern English	Po.	Polish
ModFr.	Modern French	pos.	position
MoH	Modern Hebrew	poss.	possessive
Mor.	Moravian	prep.	preposition
MP	Middle Persian	prepl.	prepositional
n.	noun	pres.	present
necess.	necessitative	pret.	preterit

prim.	primary	st.	standard
prog.	progressive	su.	subject
pron.	pronoun	subj.	subjunctive
PT	patient-trigger	sup.	superlative
Ptg.	Portuguese	s.v.	stative verb
Q	question	SVO	subject–verb–object
rat.	rational	Sw.	Swedish
recip.	reciprocal	tap.	tense/aspect pronoun
refl. pron.	reflexive pronoun	tg.	trigger
rel.	relative	them.	thematic
rep.	reported	Tk.	Turkish
res.	result	Toch.	Tocharian
Ru.	Runic	top.	topic
Rum.	Rumanian	tr.	transitive
Rus.	Russian	transg.	transgressive
Sard.	Sardinian	t.v.	transitive verb
SCr.	Serbo-Croat	U.	Umbrian
sec.	secondary	v.	verb
Seph.	Sephardi(c)	v.n.	verbal noun
sg.	singular	vd.	voiced
S-J	Sino-Japanese	Ved.	Vedic
Skt.	Sanskrit	VL	Vulgar Latin
Slk.	Slovak	vls.	voiceless
SOV	subject–object–verb	VO	verb–object
Sp.	Spanish	voc.	vocative
spec.	species	VSO	verb–subject–object

* The asterisk is used in discussion of historical reconstructions to indicate a reconstructed (non-attested) form. In synchronic discussions, it is used to indicate an ungrammatical item; (*X) means that inclusion of X makes the item ungrammatical; *(X) means that omission of X makes the item ungrammatical.

In the chapters on Tamil and Vietnamese, a subscript numeral n after a word in the English translation indicates that that word glosses the nth word in the Tamil or Vietnamese example.

In the chapters on the Romance languages, capitals are used to represent Latin or reconstructed Proto-Romance forms.

INTRODUCTION

Bernard Comrie

1 Preliminary Notions

How many languages are there in the world? What language(s) do they speak in India? What languages have the most speakers? What languages were spoken in Australia, or in California before European immigration? When did Latin stop being spoken, and when did French start being spoken? How did English become such an important world language? These and other similar questions are often asked by the interested layman. One aim of this volume — taking the Introduction and the individual chapters together — is to provide answers to these and related questions, or in certain cases to show why the questions cannot be answered as they stand. The chapters concentrate on an individual language or group of languages, and in this Introduction I want rather to present a linking essay which will provide a background against which the individual chapters can be appreciated.

After discussing some preliminary notions in this section, section 2 of the Introduction provides a rapid survey of the languages spoken in the world today, concentrating on those not treated in the subsequent chapters, so that the reader can gain an overall impression of the extent of linguistic diversity that characterises the world in which we live. Since the notion of 'major language' is primarily a social notion — languages become major (such as English), or stop being major (such as Sumerian) not because of their grammatical structure, but because of social factors — section 3 discusses

1

some important sociolinguistic notions, in particular concerning the social interaction of languages.

1.1   How Many Languages?

Linguists are typically very hesitant to answer the first question posed above, namely: how many languages are spoken in the world today? Probably the best that one can say, with any hope of not being contradicted, is that at a very conservative estimate some 4,000 languages are spoken today. Laymen are often surprised that the figure should be so high, but I would emphasise that this is a conservative estimate. But why is it that linguists are not able to give a more accurate figure? There are several different reasons conspiring to prevent them from doing so, and these will be outlined below.

One is that many parts of the world are insufficiently studied from a linguistic viewpoint, so that we simply do not know precisely what languages are spoken there. Our knowledge of the linguistic situation in remote parts of the world has improved dramatically in recent years — New Guinea, for instance, has changed from being almost a blank linguistic map to the stage where most (though still not all) of the languages can be pinpointed with accuracy: since perhaps as many as one fifth of the world's languages are spoken in New Guinea, this has radically changed any estimate of the total number of languages. But there are still some areas where uncertainty remains, so that even the most detailed recent index of the world's languages, Voegelin and Voegelin (1977), lists several languages with accompanying question marks, or queries whether one listed language might in fact be the same as some other language but under a different name.

A second problem is that it is difficult or impossible in many cases to decide whether two related speech varieties should be considered different languages or merely different dialects of the same language. With the languages of Europe, there are in general established traditions of whether two speech varieties should be considered different languages or merely dialect variants, but these decisions have often been made more on political and social grounds rather than strictly linguistic grounds.

One criterion that is often advanced as a purely linguistic criterion is mutal intelligibility: if two speech varieties are mutually intelligible, they are different dialects of the same language, but if they are mutually unintelligible, they are different languages. But if applied to the languages of Europe, this criterion would radically alter our assessment of what the different languages of Europe are: the most northern dialects and the most southern dialects (in the traditional sense) of German are mutually unintelligible, while dialects of German spoken close to the Dutch border are mutually intelligible with dialects of Dutch spoken just across the border. In fact, our criterion for whether a dialect is Dutch or German relates in large measure to social factors — is the dialect spoken in an area where Dutch is the standard language or where German is the standard language? By the same criterion, the three nuclear Scandinavian languages (in the traditional sense), Danish, Norwegian and Swedish, would turn out to be dialects of one language, given their mutual intelligibility. While this criterion is often applied to non-European languages (so that nowadays linguists often talk of the Chinese languages rather than the Chinese dialects, given the mutual unintelligibility of, for instance, Mandarin and Cantonese), it seems unfair that it should not be applied consistently to European languages as well.

While native speakers of English are often surprised that there should be problems in delimiting languages from dialects — since present-day dialects of English are in general mutually intelligible (at least with some familiarisation), and even the language most closely related genetically to English, Frisian, is mutually unintelligible with English — the native speaker of English would be hard put to interpret a sentence in Tok Pisin, the English-based pidgin of much of Papua New Guinea, like *sapos ol i karamapim bokis bilong yumi, orait bai yumi paitim as bilong ol* 'if they cover our box, then we'll spank them', although each word, except perhaps *i*, is of English origin ('suppose all ?he cover-up-him box belong you-me, all-right by you-me fight-him arse belong all').

In some cases, the intelligibility criterion actually leads to contradictory results, namely when we have a dialect chain, i.e. a string of dialects such that adjacent dialects are readily mutually intelligible, but dialects from the far ends of the chain are not mutually intelligible. A good illustration of this is the Dutch-German dialect complex. One could start from the far south of the German-speaking area and move to the far west of the Dutch-speaking area without encountering any sharp boundary across which mutual intelligibility is broken; but the two end points of this chain are speech varieties so different from one another that there is no mutual intelligibility possible. If one takes a simplified dialect chain A – B – C, where A and B are mutually intelligible, as are B and C, but A and C are mutually unintelligible, then one arrives at the contradictory result that A and B are dialects of the same language, B and C are dialects of the same language, but A and C are different languages. There is in fact no way of resolving this contradiction if we maintain the traditional strict difference between language and dialects, and what such examples show is that this is not an all-or-nothing distinction, but rather a continuum. In this sense, it is impossible to answer the question how many languages are spoken in the world.

A further problem with the mutual intelligibility criterion is that mutual intelligibility itself is a matter of degree rather than a clearcut opposition between intelligibility and unintelligibility. If mutual intelligibility were to mean 100 per cent mutual intelligibility of all utterances, then perhaps no two speech varieties would be classified as mere dialect variants; for instance, although speakers of British and American English can understand most of one another's speech, there are areas where intelligibility is likely to be minimal unless one speaker happens to have learned the linguistic forms used by the other, as with car (or auto) terms like British *boot, bonnet, mudguard* and their American equivalents *trunk, hood, fender*. Conversely, although speakers of different Slavonic languages are often unable to make full sense of a text in another Slavonic language, they can usually make good sense of parts of the text, because of the high percentage of shared vocabulary and forms.

Two further factors enter into the degree of mutual intelligibility between two speech varieties. One is that intelligibility can rise rapidly with increased familiarisation: those who remember the first introduction of American films into Britain often recall that they were initially considered difficult to understand, but increased exposure to American English has virtually removed this problem. Speakers of different dialects of Arabic often experience difficulty in understanding each other at first meeting, but soon adjust to the major differences between their respective dialects, and Egyptian Arabic, as the most widely diffused modern Arabic dialect, has rapidly gained in intelligibility throughout the Arab world. This can lead to 'one-way intelligibility', as when speakers of, say, Tunisian Arabic are more likely to understand Egyptian Arabic than vice versa, because Tunisian Arabic speakers are more often exposed to Egyptian Arabic than vice versa. The second factor is that intelligibility is to a certain extent a social and psychological phenomenon: it is easier to understand when you want to understand. A good example of this is the conflicting assessments different speakers of the same Slavonic language will often give about the intelligibility of some other Slavonic language, correlating in large measure with whether or not they feel well-disposed to speakers of the other language.

The same problems as exist in delimiting dialects from languages arise, incidentally, on the historical plane too, where the question arises: at what point has a language changed sufficiently to be considered a different language? Again, traditional answers are often contradictory: Latin is considered to have died out, although its descendants, the Romance languages, live on, so at some time Latin must have changed sufficiently to be deemed no longer the same language, but a qualitatively different language. On the other hand, Greek is referred to in the same way throughout its attested history (which is longer than that of Latin and the Romance languages combined), with merely the addition of different adjectives to identify different stages of its development (e.g. Ancient Greek, Byzantine Greek, Modern Greek). In the case of the history of the English language, there is even conflicting terminology: the oldest attested stages of English can be referred to either as Old English (which suggests an earlier stage of Modern English) or as Anglo-Saxon (which suggests a different language that is the ancestor of English, perhaps justifiably so given the mutual unintelligibility of Old and Modern English).

A further reason why it is difficult to assess the number of languages spoken in the world today is that many languages are on the verge of extinction. While it has probably been the case throughout mankind's history that languages have died out, the historically recent expansion of European population to the Americas and Australia has resulted in a greatly accelerated rate of language death among the indigenous languages of these areas. Perusal of Voegelin and Voegelin (1977) will show a number of languages as 'possibly extinct' or 'possibly still spoken', plus an even greater number of languages with only a handful of speakers — usually of advanced age — so that a language may well be dying out somewhere in the world as I am writing these words. When a language dies, this is sometimes an abrupt process, such as the death of a fluent speaker who happened to have outlived all other speakers of the language; more typically, however, the community's facility with the language decreases, as more and more functions are taken over by some other language, so that what they speak, in terms of the original language of the community, is only a part of that language. Many linguists working on Australian Aboriginal languages have been forced, in some cases, to do what has come to be called 'salvage linguistics', i.e. to elicit portions of a language from someone who has neither spoken nor heard the language for decades and has perhaps only a vague recollection of what the language was like.

1.2 Language Families and Genetic Classification
One of the basic organisational principles of this volume, both in section 2 of the Introduction and in the arrangement of the individual chapters, is the organisation of languages into language families. It is therefore important that some insight should be provided into what it means to say that two languages belong to the same language family (or equivalently: are genetically related).

It is probably intuitively clear to anyone who knows a few languages that some languages are closer to one another than are others. For instance, English and German are closer to one another than either is to Russian, while Russian and Polish are closer to one another than either is to English. This notion of similarity can be made more precise, as is done for instance in the chapter on the Indo-European languages below, but for the moment the relatively informal notion will suffice. Starting in the late eighteenth century, a specific hypothesis was proposed to account for such similarities, a hypothesis which still forms the foundation of research into the history and relatedness of languages. This hypothesis is that where languages share some set of features in common, these features are to be attributed to their common ancestor. Let us take some examples from English and German.

In English and German we find a number of basic vocabulary items that have the same or almost the same form, e.g. English *man* and German *Mann*. Likewise, we find a number of bound morphemes (prefixes and suffixes) that have the same or almost the same form, such as the genitive suffix, as in English *man's* and German *Mann(e)s*. Although English and

German are now clearly different languages, we may hypothesise that at an earlier period in history they had a common ancestor, in which the word for 'man' was something like *man* and the genitive suffix was something like -*s*. Thus English and German belong to the same language family, which is the same as saying that they share a common ancestor. We can readily add other languages to this family, since a word like *man* and a genitive suffix like -*s* are also found in Dutch, Frisian, and the Scandinavian languages. The family to which these languages belong has been given the name Germanic, and the ancestor language is Proto-Germanic. It should be emphasised that the proto-language is not an attested language — although if written records had gone back far enough, we might well have had attestations of this language — but its postulation is the most plausible hypothesis explaining the remarkable similarities among the various Germanic languages.

Although not so obvious, similarities can be found among the Germanic languages and a number of other languages spoken in Europe and spreading across northern India as far as Bangladesh. These other languages share fewer similarities with the Germanic languages than individual Germanic languages do with one another, so that they are more remotely related. The overall language family to which all these languages belong is the Indo-European family, with its reconstructed ancestor language Proto-Indo-European. As is discussed in more detail in the chapter on Indo-European languages, the Indo-European family contains a number of branches (i.e. smaller language families, or subfamilies), such as Slavonic (including Russian and Polish), Iranian (including Persian and Pashto), and Celtic (including Irish and Welsh). The overall structure is therefore hierarchical: the most distant ancestor is Proto-Indo-European. At an intermediate point in the family tree, and therefore at a later period of history, we have such languages as Proto-Germanic and Proto-Celtic, which are descendants of Proto-Indo-European but ancestors of languages spoken today. Still later in history, we find the individual languages as they are spoken today or attested in recent history, such as English or German as descendants of Proto-Germanic and Irish and Welsh as descendants of Proto-Celtic. One typical property of language change that is represented accurately by this family-tree model is that, as time goes by, languages descending from a common ancestor tend to become less and less similar. For instance, Old English and Old High German (the ancestor of Modern German) were much closer to one another than are the modern languages — they may even have been mutually intelligible, at least to a large extent.

Although the family-tree model of language relatedness is an important foundation of all current work in historical and comparative linguistics, it is not without its problems, both in practice and in principle. Some of these will now be discussed.

We noted above that with the passage of time, genetically related languages will grow less and less similar. This follows from the fact that, once two languages have split off as separate languages from a common ancestor, each will innovate its own changes, different from changes that take place in the other language, so that the cumulative effect will be increasing divergence. With the passage of enough time, the divergence may come to be so great that it is no longer possible to tell, other than by directly examining the history, that the two languages do in fact come from a common ancestor. The best established language families, such as Indo-European or Sino-Tibetan, are those where the passage of time has not been long enough to erase the obvious traces of genetic relatedness. (For language families that have a long written tradition, one can of course make use of earlier stages of the language, which contain more evidence of genetic relatedness). In addition, there are many hypothesised language families for which the evidence is not sufficient to convince all, or even the majority, of scholars. For instance, the Turkic language family is a well-established language family, as is each of the Uralic, Mongolian and Tungusic families. What is controversial, however, is whether or not these individual families are related as members of an even larger family. The possibility of an Altaic family, comprising Turkic, Mongolian, and Tungusic, is rather widely accepted, and some scholars would advocate increasing the size of this family by adding some or all of Uralic, Korean and Japanese.

The attitudes of different linguists to problems of this kind have been characterised as an opposition between 'splitters' (who require the firmest evidence before they are prepared to acknowledge genetic relatedness) and 'clumpers' (who are ready to assign languages to the same family on the basis of quite restricted similarities). I should, incidentally, declare my own splitter bias, lest any of my own views that creep in be interpreted as generally accepted dogma. The most extreme clumper position would, of course, be to maintain that all languages of the world are genetically related, although there are less radical positions that are somewhat more widely accepted, such as the following list of sixteen stocks, where a stock is simply the highest hierarchical level of genetic relatedness (just as a language family has branches, so families would group together to form stocks): Dravidian, Eurasiatic (including, inter alia, Uralic and Altaic), Indo-European, Nilo-Saharan, Niger-Kordofanian, Afroasiatic, Khoisan, Amerind (all indigenous languages of the Americas except Eskimo-Aleut and Na-Dene), Na-Dene, Austric (including Austro-Asiatic, Tai and Austronesian), Indo-Pacific (including all Papuan languages and Tasmanian), Australian, Sino-Tibetan, Ibero-Caucasian (including Basque and Caucasian), Ket, Burushaski – this schema still operates, incidentally, with two language isolates (Ket and Burushaski), i.e. languages not related to any other language, and retains a number of established language families as distinct (Dravidian, Indo-European, Nilo-Saharan, Niger-Kordofanian, Afro-asiatic, Khoisan, Australian, and Sino-Tibetan). In the survey of the distribution of languages of the world in section 2, I have basically retained my own splitter position, although for areas of great linguistic diversity and great controversy surrounding genetic relations (such as New Guinea and South America) I have simply refrained from detailed discussion.

While no linguist would doubt that some similarities among languages are due to genetic relatedness, there are several other possibilities for the explanation of any particular similarity, and before assuming genetic relatedness one must be able to exclude, at least with some degree of plausibility, these other possibilities. Unfortunately, in a great many cases it is not possible to reach a firm and convincing decision. Let us now examine some of the explanations other than genetic relatedness.

First, two languages may happen purely by chance to have some feature in common. For instance, the word for 'dog' in Mbabaram, an Australian Aboriginal language, happens to be *dog*. This Mbabaram word is not, incidentally, a borrowing from English, but is the regular development in Mbabaram of a Proto-Australian form something like **gudaga* (it is usual to prefix reconstructed forms with an asterisk). If anyone were tempted to assume on this basis, however, that English and Mbabaram are genetically related, examination of the rest of Mbabaram vocabulary and grammar would soon quash the genetic relatedness hypothesis, since there is otherwise minimal similarity between the two languages. In comparing English and German, by contrast, there are many similarities at all levels of linguistic analysis. Even sticking to vocabulary, the correspondence *man*: *Mann* can be matched by *wife* : *Weib*, *father* : *Vater*, *mother* : *Mutter*, *son* : *Sohn*, *daughter* : *Tochter*, etc. Given that other languages have radically different words for these concepts (e.g. Japanese *titi* 'father', *haha* 'mother', *musuko* 'son', *musume* 'daugher'), it clearly can not be merely the result of chance that English and German have so many similar items. But if the number of similar items in two languages is small, it may be difficult or impossible to distinguish between chance similarity and distant genetic relatedness.

Certain features shared by two languages might turn out to be manifestations of language universals, i.e. of features that are common to all languages or are inherently likely to occur in any language. Most discussions of language universals require a fair amount of theoretical linguistic background, but for present purposes I will take a simple, if not particularly profound, example. In many languages across the world, the syllable *ma* or its reduplicated form *mama* or some other similar form is the word for 'mother'. The initial syllable *ma* enters into the Proto-Indo-European word for 'mother' which has given English *mother*, Spanish *madre*, Russian *mat´*, Sanskrit *mātā*. In Mandarin Chinese, the equivalent word is *mā*, while in Wiyaw (Harui) (Papua New Guinea) it is *mam*. Once again, examination of other features of Indo-European languages, Chinese and Wiyaw would soon dispel any possibility of assigning Chinese or Wiyaw to the Indo-European language family. Presumably the frequency across languages of the syllable *ma* in the word for 'mother' simply reflects the fact that this is typically one of the first syllables that babies articulate clearly, and is therefore interpreted by adults as the word for 'mother'. (In the South Caucasian language Georgian, incidentally, *mama* means 'father' — and 'mother' is *deda* — so that there are other ways of interpreting baby's first utterance.)

Somewhat similar to universals are patterns whereby certain linguistic features frequently cooccur in the same language, i.e. where the presence of one feature seems to require or at least to foster the presence of some other feature. For instance, the study of word order universals by Greenberg (1963) showed that if a language has verb-final word order (i.e. if 'the man saw the woman' is expressed literally as 'the man the woman saw'), then it is highly probable that it will also have postpositions rather than prepositions (i.e. 'in the house' will be expressed as 'the house in') and that it will have genitives before the noun (i.e. the pattern 'cat's house' rather than 'house of cat'). Thus, if we find two languages that happen to share the features: verb-final word order, postpositions, prenominal genitives, then the cooccurrence of these features is not evidence for genetic relatedness. Many earlier attempts at establishing wide-ranging genetic relationships suffer precisely from failure to take this property of typological patterns into account. Thus the fact that Turkic languages, Mongolian languages, Tungusic languages, Korean and Japanese share all of these features is not evidence for their genetic relatedness (although there may, of course, be other similarities, not connected with recurrent typological patterns, that do establish genetic relatedness). If one were to accept just these features as evidence for an Altaic language family, then the family would have to be extended to include a variety of other languages with the same word order properties, such as the Dravidian languages of southern India and Quechua, spoken in South America.

Finally, two languages might share some feature in common because one of them has borrowed it from the other (or because they have both borrowed it from some third language). English, for instance, borrowed a huge number of words from French during the Middle Ages, to such an extent that an uncritical examination of English vocabulary might well lead to the conclusion that English is a Romance language, rather than a Germanic language. The term 'borrow', as used here, is the accepted linguistic term, although the terminology is rather strange, since 'borrow' suggests a relatively superficial acquisition, one which is moreover temporary. Linguistic borrowings may run quite deep, and there is of course no implication that they will ever be repaid. Among English loans from French, for instance, there are many basic vocabulary items, such as *very* (replacing the native Germanic *sore*, as in the biblical *sore afraid*). Examples from other languages show even more deep-seated loans: the Semitic language Amharic — the dominant and official language of Ethiopia — for instance, has lost the typical Semitic word order patterns, in which the verb precedes its object and adjectives and genitives follow their noun, in favour of the order where the verb follows its object and adjectives and genitives precede their noun; Amharic is in close contact with Cushitic languages, and Cushitic languages typically have the order object-verb, adjective/genitive-noun, so that Amharic has in fact borrowed these word orders from neighbouring Cushitic languages.

It seems that whenever two languages come into close contact, they will borrow features from one another. In some cases the contact can be so intense among the languages in a given area that they come to share a significant number of common features, setting this area off from adjacent languages, even languages that may happen to be more closely related genetically to languages within the area. The languages in an area of this kind are often said to belong to a sprachbund (German for 'language league'), and perhaps the most famous example of a sprachbund is the Balkan sprachbund, whose members (Modern Greek, Albanian, Bulgarian (with Macedonian), Rumanian) share a number of striking features not shared by closely related languages like Ancient Greek, other Slavonic languages (Bulgarian is Slavonic), or other Romance languages (Rumanian is Romance). The most striking of these features is loss of the infinitive, so that instead of 'give me to drink' one says 'give me that I drink' (Modern Greek *ðos mu na pjo*, Albanian *a-më të pi*, Bulgarian *daj mi da pija*, Rumanian *dă-mi să beau*; in all four languages the subject of the subordinate clause is encoded in the inflection of the verb).

Since we happen to know a lot about the history of the Balkan languages, linguists were not deceived by these similarities into assigning a closer genetic relatedness to the Balkan languages than in fact holds (all are ultimately members of the Indo-European family, though from different branches). In other parts of the world, however, there is the danger of mistaking areal phenomena for evidence of genetic relatedness. In South-East Asia, for instance, many languages share very similar phonological and morphological patterns: in Chinese, Thai and Vietnamese words are typically monosyllabic, there is effectively no morphology (i.e. words do not change after the manner of English *dog*, *dogs* or *love*, *loves*, *loved*), syllable structure is very simple (only a few single consonants are permitted word-finally, while syllable-initially consonant clusters are either disallowed or highly restricted), and there is a phonemic tone (thus Mandarin Chinese *mā*, with a high level tone, means 'mother', while *mǎ*, with a falling-rising tone, means 'horse'), and moreover there are a number of shared lexical items. For these reasons, it was for a long time believed that Thai and Vietnamese were related genetically to Chinese, as members of the Sino-Tibetan family. More recently, however, it has been established that these similarities are not the result of common ancestry, and Thai and Vietnamese are now generally acknowledged not to be genetically related to Chinese. The similarities are the results of areal contact. The shared vocabulary items are primarily the result of intensive Chinese cultural influence, especially on

Vietnamese. The tones and simple syllable structures can often be shown to be the result of relatively recent developments, and indeed in one language that is incontrovertibly related to Chinese, namely Classical Tibetan, one finds complex consonant clusters but no phonemic tone, i.e. the similarities noted above are neither necessary nor sufficient conditions for genetic relatedness.

In practice, the most difficult task in establishing genetic relatedness is to distinguish between genuine cognates (i.e. forms going back to a common ancestor) and those that are the result of borrowing. It would therefore be helpful if one could distinguish between those features of a language that are borrowable and those that are not. Unfortunately, it seems that there is no feature that can absolutely be excluded from borrowing. Basic vocabulary can be borrowed, so that for instance Japanese has borrowed the whole set of numerals from Chinese, and even English borrowed its current set of third person plural pronouns (*they*, *them*, *their*) from Scandinavian. Bound morphemes can be borrowed: a good example is the agent suffix *-er* in English, with close cognates in other Germanic languages; this is ultimately a loan from the Latin agentive suffix *-ārius*, which has however become so entrenched in English that it is a productive morphological device applicable in principle to any verb to derive a corresponding agentive noun.

At one period in the recent history of comparative linguistics, it was believed that a certain basic vocabulary list could be isolated, constant across languages and cultures, such that the words on this list would be replaced at a constant rate. Thus, if one assumes that the retention rate is around 86 per cent per millennium, this means that if a single language splits into two descendant languages, then after 1,000 years each language would retain about 86 per cent of the words in the list from the ancestor language, i.e. the two descendants would then share just over 70 per cent of the words in the list. In some parts of the world, groupings based on this 'glottochronological' method still form the basis of the only available detailed and comprehensive attempt at establishing genetic relations. It must be emphasised that the number of clear counter-examples to the glottochronological method, i.e. instances where independent evidence contradicts the predictions of this approach, is so great that no reliance can be placed on its results.

It is, however, true that there are significant differences in the ease with which different features of a language can be borrowed. The thing that seems most easily borrowable is cultural vocabulary, and indeed it is quite normal for a community borrowing some concept (or artifact) from another community to borrow the foreign name along with the object. Another set of features that seem rather easily borrowable are general typological features, such as word order: in addition to the Amharic example cited above, one might note the fact that many Austronesian languages spoken in New Guinea have adopted the word order where the object is placed before the verb, whereas almost all other Austronesian languages place the object after the verb; this change occurred under the influence of Papuan languages, almost all of which are verb-final. Basic vocabulary comes next. And last of all one finds bound morphology. But even though it is difficult to borrow bound morphology, it is not impossible, so in arguments over genetic relatedness one cannot exclude *a priori* the possibility that even affixes may have been borrowed.

2   Distribution of the World's Languages

In this section, I wish to give a general survey of the distribution of the languages of the world, in terms of their genetic affiliation. I will therefore be talking primarily about the distribution of language families, although reference will be made to individual languages where appropriate. The discussion will concentrate on languages and language families not covered in individual chapters, and at appropriate places I have digressed to give a brief discussion of some interesting structural or sociological point in the language being treated.

2.1   Europe

Europe, taken here in the traditional cultural sense rather than in the current geographical sense of 'the land mass west of the Urals', is the almost exclusive preserve of the Indo-European family. This family covers not only almost the whole of Europe, but also extends through Armenia (in the Caucasus), Iran and Afghanistan into Soviet Central Asia (Tadzhikistan), with the easternmost outpost of this strand the Iranian language Sarikoli, spoken just inside China. Another strand spreads from Afghanistan across Pakistan, northern India and southern Nepal, to end with Bengali in eastern India and Bangladesh; an off-shoot from northern India, Sinhalese, is spoken in Sri Lanka, and the language of the Maldives is the closely related Maldivian.

In addition, the great population shifts that resulted from the voyages of exploration starting at the end of the fifteenth century have carried Indo-European languages to many distant lands. The dominant languages of the Americas are now Indo-European (English, Spanish, Portuguese, French), as is the dominant language of Australia and New Zealand (English). While in some countries these languages are spoken by populations descended primarily from European settlers, there are also instances where a variety of the European language is spoken by a population of a different origin, perhaps the best known example being the creolised forms of European languages (especially English, French and Portuguese) spoken by the descendants of African slaves in the Caribbean. It should be noted that these population shifts have not led exclusively to the spread of European languages, since many languages of India, both Indo-European and

Dravidian, have also extended as a by-product, being spoken now by communities in the Caribbean area, in East Africa and in the South Pacific (especially Fiji).

Of the few European languages not belonging to the Indo-European family, mention may first be made of Basque, a language isolate, with no established genetic relations to any other language. It is spoken in the Pyrenees on both sides of the French-Spanish border. Basque is perhaps most noted for its ergative construction, whereby instead of having a single case (nominative) for both subjects of intransitive verbs and subjects (agents) of transitive verbs, with a different case (accusative) for objects (patients) of transitive verbs, Basque uses one case (absolutive) for both intransitive subjects and objects of transitive verbs, and a different case (ergative) for subjects of transitive verbs, as in the following sentences from the Labourdin dialect:

Martin ethorri da. 'Martin came.'
Martinek haurra igorri du. 'Martin sent the child.'

In the first sentence, *Martin* is intransitive subject, and stands in the absolutive (no inflection); in the second sentence, *Martin-ek* is transitive subject, and therefore stands in the ergative (suffix *-ek*), while *haurra* 'child' is transitive object, and therefore stands in the absolutive, with no inflection.

Some other languages of Europe belong to the Uralic family. These include Hungarian, Finnish, Estonian and Lappish, to which can be added a number of smaller languages closely related to Finnish and Estonian. Other members of the Uralic family are spoken on the Volga and in northern Eurasia on both sides of the Urals, stretching as far as southern Siberia.

Turkish as spoken in the Balkans represents the Turkic family in Europe, but this family is primarily an Asian family, and will be treated in the next section. The same is true of Afroasiatic, represented in Europe by Maltese.

2.2 Asia

Having just mentioned Turkish, we may now turn to the Turkic family, which is spoken in Turkey, parts of the Caucasus, some areas on the Volga, most of Soviet Central Asia (and stretching down into northwestern Iran), and large parts of southern Siberia, with one off-shoot, Yakut, in northeastern Siberia. Turkic is perhaps to be joined in a single language family (Altaic) with the Mongolian and Tungusic families. The Mongolian languages are spoken predominantly in Mongolia and northern China, though there are also isolated Mongolian languages in Afghanistan (Moghol) and just to the north of the Caucasus mountains (Kalmyk); the main member of the family is the language Mongolian (sometimes called Khalkha, after its principal dialect), which is the official language of Mongolia. The Tungusic languages are spoken by numerically small population groups in Siberia and the Soviet Far East, spreading over into Mongolia and especially northeastern China. The Tungusic language best known to history is Manchu, the native language of the dynasty that ruled China from 1644 to 1911; the Manchu language is, however, now almost extinct, having been replaced by Chinese. Whether Korean or Japanese can be assigned to the Altaic Family is a question of current debate, as is the possible genetic link between Uralic and Altaic.

This is a convenient point at which to discuss a number of other languages spoken in northern Asia. All are the languages of small communities (a few hundred or a few thousand). They are sometimes referred to collectively as Paleosiberian (or Paleoasiatic), although this is not a genetic grouping. Three of them are language isolates: Ket, spoken on the Yenisey river; Yukaghir, spoken on the Kolyma river; and Nıvkh (Gilyak), spoken at the mouth of the Amur river and on Sakhalin island. The small Chukotko-Kamchatkan family comprises the indigenous languages of the Chukotka and Kamchatka peninsulas: Chukchi, Koryak, Kamchadal (Itelmen); it has been suggested that they may be related to Eskimo-Aleut, which is treated in section 2.5 on the Americas. Finally, we may mention here Ainu, now spoken by a few individuals in Hokkaido, the most northerly Japanese island, and apparently a language isolate.

One of the geographic links between Europe and Asia, the Caucasus, has since antiquity been noted for the large number of clearly distinct languages spoken; indeed it was referred to by the Arabs as the 'mountain of tongues'. Some of the languages spoken in the Caucasus belong to other families (e.g. Armenian and Ossete to Indo-European, Azerbaidjani to Turkic), but there are in addition a number of languages with no known affiliations to languages outside the Caucasus: these are the Caucasian languages. Even the internal genetic relations of the Caucasian languages are the subject of debate. While some scholars accept the genetic relatedness of all Caucasian languages, at least as a working hypothesis, many work rather with three or four distinct families, whose only common feature would be that they happen to be spoken in the Caucasus and not to be related to any of the larger language families. The South Caucasian or Kartvelian family includes Georgian, the Caucasian language with the largest number of speakers (over three million) and the only Caucasian language to have a long-standing literary tradition (dating back to the fifth century). The North-West Caucasian languages are found on and close to the Black Sea coast, though also in Turkey as a result of emigration since the mid-nineteenth century; one Caucasian language, Ubykh, is spoken exclusively in Turkey and is virtually extinct even there, but is noteworthy for the large number of its consonant phonemes – for a long time it was considered the world record-holder. The remaining groups are the North-Central Caucasian languages, which are sometimes considered a subgroup of the North-East Caucasian languages, and the North-East Caucasian languages; several of the North-

East Caucasian languages are spoken only in a single village, a reflection of the difficulties of communication in this mountainous region.

Turning now to southwestern Asia, we may consider the Afroasiatic family, which, as its name suggests, is spoken in both Asia and Africa. In Asia its main focus is the Arab countries of the Middle East, although Hebrew and Aramaic are also Afroasiatic languages of Asia, belonging to the Semitic branch of Afroasiatic. In addition Arabic is, of course, the dominant language of North Africa, where Afroasiatic is represented not only by a number of other Semitic languages (those of Ethiopia, the major one being Amharic), but also by Berber, the Cushitic languages of the Horn of Africa (including Somali, the official language of Somalia), and the Chadic languages of northern Nigeria and adjacent areas (including Hausa). One branch of Afroasiatic formerly spoken in Africa, Egyptian (by which is meant the language of ancient Egypt, not the dialect of Arabic currently spoken in Egypt), is now extinct.

In South Asia (the traditional 'Indian subcontinent'), four language families meet. Indo-European languages, more specifically languages of the Indo-Aryan branch of Indo-European, dominate in the north, while the south is the domain of the Dravidian languages (although some Dravidian languages are spoken further north, in particular Brahui, spoken in Pakistan). The northern fringe of the subcontinent is occupied by Sino-Tibetan languages, to which we return below. The fourth family is the Austro-Asiatic or Munda-Mon-Khmer family. The languages in this family with most speakers are actually spoken in South-East Asia: Vietnamese in Vietnam and Khmer (Cambodian) in Cambodia (Kampuchea), and they are the only languages of the family to have the status of official languages. Languages of the family are scattered from central India eastwards into Vietnam. In India itself, the Austro-Asiatic language with most speakers is Santali. The assignment of some languages to Austro-Asiatic is controversial (e.g. Nicobarese, and the Jakun, Sakai and Semang languages of the Malay peninsula), and it is only relatively recently that the assignment of Vietnamese to this family has gained widespread acceptance. In addition, there is one language isolate, Burushaski, spoken in northern Pakistan, while the genetic affiliations of the languages of the Andaman Islands remain unclear.

We have already introduced a number of South-East Asian languages, and may now turn to the other two families represented in this area: Tai (more accurately: Kadai (Kam-Tai)) and Sino-Tibetan. While the Kadai group of languages, which includes Thai (Siamese) and Lao, was earlier often considered a branch of Sino-Tibetan, this view has now been largely rejected; Kam-Tai languages are spoken in Thailand, Laos, southern China and also in parts of Burma and Vietnam. Sino-Tibetan contains the language with the largest number of speakers in the world today, Chinese (and this remains true even if one divides Chinese into several different languages, in which case Mandarin occupies first position). The other Sino-Tibetan languages form the Tibeto-Burman branch, which includes Tibetan and Burmese, in addition to a vast number of languages spoken predominantly in southern China, Burma, northern India and Nepal. Whether the Miao-Yao languages, spoken in southern China and adjacent areas, are now generally held not to belong to the Sino-Tibetan family.

In East Asia there are also two language isolates, Korean and Japanese, whose genetic affiliations to each other or to other languages (such as Altaic) remain the subject of at times heated debate.

The Austronesian family (formerly called Malayo-Polynesian), though including some languages spoken on the Asian mainland, such as Malay of the Malay peninsula and Cham spoken in Cambodia and Vietnam, are predominantly languages of the islands stretching eastwards from the South-East Asian mainland: even Malay-Indonesian has more speakers in insular South-East Asia than on the Malay peninsula. Austronesian languages are dominant on most of the islands from Sumatra in the west to Easter Island in the east, including the Philippines, but excluding New Guinea (where Austronesian languages are, however, spoken in many coastal areas); Malagasy, the language of Madagascar, is a western outlier of the family; Austronesian languages are also indigenous to Taiwan, though now very much in the minority relative to Chinese.

2.3 New Guinea and Australia

The island of New Guinea, which can be taken linguistically together with some of the smaller surrounding islands, is the most differentiated area linguistically in the whole world. Papua New Guinea, which occupies the eastern half of the island, contains some 750 languages for a total population of only slightly more than three million, meaning that the average language has just over 4,000 speakers. In many of the coastal areas of New Guinea, Austronesian languages are spoken, but the other languages are radically different from these Austronesian languages. These other languages are referred to collectively as either 'non-Austronesian languages of New Guinea' or as 'Papuan languages', though it should be realised that this is a negatively characterised term, rather than a claim about genetic relatedness. Though some progress has been made in classifying the Papuan languages genetically, the results of this research must be regarded as extremely tentative: there are not enough good descriptions of individual languages to provide a reliable basis for comparative work, and many of the claims made to date rest primarily on glottochronological methods.

One syntactic property that is widespread among the Highland Papuan languages is worthy of note, namely switch reference. In a language with a canonical switch reference system, a sentence may (and typically does) consist of several clauses, of which only one is an independent clause (i.e. could occur on its own as a free-standing sentence), all the others being dependent; each dependent clause is marked according to whether or not its subject is the same as or different from the subject of the clause on which it is dependent. The examples below are from Usan:

Ye nam su-ab, isomei. 'I cut the tree and went down.'
Ye nam su-ine, isorei. 'I cut the tree and it fell down.'

The independent verbs, *isomei* and *isorei*, are respectively first person singular and third person singular. The dependent verbs, *su-ab* and *su-ine*, have respectively the suffix for same subject and the suffix for different subject. In the first example, therefore, the subjects of the two clauses are the same (i.e. I cut the tree and I went/fell down), while in the second sentence they are different (i.e. I cut the tree and some other entity — from the context only the tree is available – went/fell down). The words *ye* and *nam* mean respectively 'I' and 'tree'. One effect of switch reference is that the speaker of a language with switch reference must plan a discourse ahead to a much greater extent than is required by languages lacking switch reference, since in switch reference languages it is nearly always the case that the dependent clause precedes the independent clause, i.e. in clause *n* one has to mark the coreference relation that holds between the subject of clause *n* and the subject of clause *n* + 1. This should, incidentally, serve to dispel any lingering notions concerning the primitiveness or lack of grammar in the languages of other societies. Although switch reference is found in many other parts of the world (e.g. in many Amerindian languages), it is particularly characteristic of the languages of the New Guinea Highlands.

Nearly all the Aboriginal languages of Australia, which numbered some 200 at the time of contact with Europeans, are now generally accepted to be genetically related. The genetic relatedness is not always readily apparent, since quite sweeping sound changes have often altered the shape of words, but it is often possible to show how the regular operation of sound changes, well attested in a large number of lexical items, has given rise to the observed diversity: for instance, Mbabaram *dog* 'dog', discussed in section 1.2, is a regular development from Proto-Australian **gudaga*, with regular loss of the final vowel and regular loss of the initial syllable, with umlaut of the remaining vowel by the vowel of the first syllable before its loss (i.e. *a* was rounded to *o* under the influence of the *u*). Only two Australian languages seem to be unrelated to the Australian family, namely Tiwi (spoken on Bathurst and Melville islands, and separated from the mainland languages during several millennia) and Djingili (on the Barkly Tableland).

The Australian languages overall are characterised by an unusual consonant system, from the viewpoint of the kinds of consonant systems that are found most frequently across the languages of the world. Most Australian languages have no fricatives, and no voice opposition among their stops. However, they distinguish a large number of places of articulation, especially in terms of lingual articulations: thus most languages have, in addition to labial and velar stops, all of palatal, alveolar, and retroflex stops, while many languages add a further series of phonemically distinct dentals. The same number of distinctions is usually found with the nasals, and some languages extend this number of contrasts in the lingual stops to the laterals as well. One result of this is that Europeans usually fail to perceive (or produce, should they try to do so) phonemic oppositions that are crucial in Aboriginal languages, while conversely Aboriginals fail to perceive or produce phonemic oppositions that are crucial in English (such as the distinction among *pit*, *bit*, *bid*).

One Australian language, Dyirbal, spoken in the Cairns Rain Forest in northern Queensland, has played an important role in recent discussions of general linguistic typology, and it will be useful to make a short digression to look at the relevant unique, or at least unusual, features of Dyirbal — though it should be emphasised that these features are not particularly typical of Australian languages overall.

In English, one of the pieces of evidence for saying that intransitive and transitive subjects are just subtypes of the overall notion 'subject' is that they behave alike with respect to a number of different syntactic processes. For instance, a rule of English syntax allows one to omit the subject of the second conjunct of a coordinate sentence if it is coreferential with the subject of the first conjunct, i.e. one can abbreviate the first sentence below to the second one:

I hit you and I came here.
I hit you and came here.

It is not possible to carry out a similar abbreviation of the next sentence below, since its subjects are not coreferential, even though the object of the first conjunct is coreferential with the subject of the second conjunct:

I hit you and you came here.

In the above examples, the first clause is transitive and the second clause intransitive, but the notion of subject applies equally to both clauses, If we think not so much of grammatical labels like subject and object, but rather of semantic labels like agent and patient, then we can say that in English it is the agent of a transitive clause that behaves as subject. In the corresponding Dyirbal sentences, however, it is the patient that behaves as subject, as can be seen in the following sentences:

Ngaja nginuna balgan, ngaja baninyu. 'I hit you and I came here.'
Ngaja nginuna balgan, nginda baninyu. 'I hit you and you came here.'
Ngaja nginuna balgan, baninyu. 'I hit you and you came here.'

In these sentences, *ngaja* is the nominative form for 'I', while *nginuna* is the accusative form for 'you'; the verbs are *balgan* 'hit' (transitive) and *baninyu* 'come here' (intransitive). In the third sentence, where the intransitive subject is omitted, it must be interpreted as coreferential with the patient, not the agent, of the first clause. In section 2.1 mention was made of ergativity in connection with Basque case marking. These Dyirbal examples show that Dyirbal has ergativity in its syntactic system: patients of transitive verbs, rather than agents of transitive verbs, are treated as subjects, i.e. are treated in the same way as intransitive subjects. Note that in this sense Dyirbal grammar is certainly different from English grammar, but it is no less well-defined.

Another unusual feature of Dyirbal is sociolinguistic. In many, if not all languages there are different choices of lexical item depending on differences in social situation, such as the difference between English *father* and *dad(dy)*. What is unusual about Dyirbal is that a difference of this kind exists for every single lexical item in the language. Under certain circumstances, in particular in the presence of a taboo relative (e.g. a parent-in-law), every lexical item of ordinary language (Guwal) must be replaced by the corresponding lexical item from avoidance style (Jalnguy). No doubt in part for functional reasons, to ease the memory load, it is usual for several semantically related words of Guwal to correspond to a single Jalnguy word, as when the various Guwal names for different species of lizard are all subsumed by the one Jalnguy word *jijan*.

The surviving textual materials in the Tasmanian languages, extinct since the end of the nineteenth century, are insufficient in scope or reliability to allow any accurate assessment of the genetic affiliations of these languages — certainly none is immediately apparent.

Because of their small number of speakers and geographic restrictedness, no indigenous languages of New Guinea or Australia are included in this volume.

2.4 Africa

Africa north of the Sahara is the preserve of Afroasiatic languages, which have already been treated in section 2.2. This section will therefore concentrate on the sub-Saharan languages, though excluding languages introduced into Africa by external colonisation (though one such language, Afrikaans, a descendant of colonial Dutch, is a language of Africa by virtue of its geographic distribution), and also Malagasy, the Austronesian language of Madagascar.

Until quite recently, ideas on the classification of sub-Saharan languages were almost as diffuse as those on the classification of languages of New Guinea or the Americas. One language family, Bantu, was recognised early on, spoken over most of eastern and southern Africa. It was suspected that many of the languages of West Africa might be related to one another, and it was recognised that the Khoisan languages, spoken in the southwestern corner of Africa, were probably a single family. This near-chaos was reduced to order in large measure by the efforts of Joseph H. Greenberg, who posited a four-way classification of the languages of Africa: in the north, the Afroasiatic family; in the north-east of sub-Saharan Africa, the Nilo-Saharan family; in the southwest corner of Africa, the Khoisan family (with two outliers, Sandawe and Hatsa, in Tanzania) — the Khoisan languages are noted for having click sounds as part of their regular phoneme inventory. The whole of the rest of the continent, from the Atlantic to the Indian Ocean, is covered by the Niger-Kordofanian (or Congo-Kordofanian) family (Greenberg 1966); Bantu is a sub-sub-sub-subgroup of this family. In general, Greenberg's classification has gained widespread acceptance, in particular the division into four major families, although some of the details remain controversial (see, for instance, the chapter on Niger-Kordofanian languages for proposed revisions to the internal classification of this family).

2.5   The Americas

The classification of the indigenous languages of the Americas is problematic. While a number of families have been established on the basis of criteria acceptable to all or most scholars, in many other cases groupings have been proposed that meet with only limited approval, such as Na-Dene (including Athapaskan-Eyak), Hokan, Penutian. A new classification of the Amerindian languages has been proposed by Greenberg (1987), but his suggestion that all indigenous languages of the Americas other than Eskimo-Aleut and Na-Dene form a single family remains highly controversial. In what follows, rather than attempting to give a comprehensive listing of all families and language isolates, I have concentrated instead on some of the more widespread established families and on some of the other languages with relatively large numbers of speakers. No indigenous language of the Americas satisfied my criteria for an individual chapter in this volume; the closest would be Quechua, with some six million speakers, and Guarani, with over a million speakers, primarily in Paraguay, where it has achieved social status as an expression of Paraguayan identity, alongside the official language, Spanish.

Two population groups of North America are not ethnically Amerindian, namely the Eskimos and Aleuts. The Eskimo-Aleut family contains two branches, Aleut and Eskimo. Eskimo is properly a number of different languages rather than a single language, and is spoken from the eastern tip of Siberia in the west through Alaska and northern Canada to Greenland in the east; in Greenland it is, under the name Greenlandic, an official language.

Another language family centred in Alaska is the Athapaskan family (more properly: Athapaskan-Eyak, with inclusion of the Athapaskan languages and the single language Eyak as the two branches of the family). Most of the Athapaskan languages are spoken in Alaska and northwestern

Canada, though the Athapaskan language with most speakers, Navaho
(Navajo), is spoken in Arizona and adjacent areas. Navaho is the indigenous
language of North America (Canada and the USA) with the largest number
of speakers, over 100,000.

Among the other major families of North America are Iroquoian (around
Lakes Ontario and Erie), Siouan (the Great Plains), and Algonquian (much
of the northeastern USA and eastern and central Canada, though also
extending into the Great Plains with Arapaho and Cheyenne). One
interesting feature of the Algonquian languages to which it is worth devoting
a short digression is obviation. In Algonquian languages, a distinction is
made between two kinds of third person, namely proximate and obviative,
so that where English just has one set of third person pronouns (e.g. *he*, *she*,
it, *they*) and morphology (e.g. the third person singular present tense ending
-s), Algonquian languages distinguish two sets. In a given text span (which
must be at least a clause, but may be longer than a sentence), one of the third
person noun phrases is selected as proximate (the one which is in some sense
the most salient at that part of the text), all other third person participants
are obviative. In the remainder of the text span, the proximate participant is
always referred to by proximate morphology, while other participants are
referred to by obviative morphology. In this way, the ambiguity of English
sentences like *John saw Bill as he was leaving* (was it John that was leaving,
or Bill?) is avoided. The following examples are from Cree:

Naapeew atim-wa waapam-ee-w, ee-sipwehtee-t. 'The man saw the dog as he (the
man) was leaving.'
Naapeew atim-wa waapam-ee-w, ee-sipwehtee-yit. 'The man saw the dog as it (the
dog) was leaving.'

In both sentences, 'the man' is proximate (indicated by the absence of any
affix on *naapeew* 'man'), and 'the dog' is obviative (indicated by the suffix
-wa on *atim-wa* 'dog'). The morphology of the verb *waapam-ee-w* 'he sees
him' indicates that the agent is proximate and the patient obviative (this is
important, since the word order can be varied). The prefix *ee-* on the second
verb indicates that it is subordinate ('conjunct', in Algonquianist terminology). In the first sentence, the suffix *-t* on this second verb indicates a
proximate subject, i.e. the subject must be the proximate participant of the
preceding clause, namely *the man*. In the second sentence, the suffix *-yit*
indicates an obviative subject, i.e. the subject of this verb must be an
obviative participant of the preceding clause, in this sentence the only
candidate being *the dog*.

Another important family, Uto-Aztecan, includes languages spoken in
both North America (the South-West) and Central America. Its Aztecan
branch includes Nahuatl, whose dialects have in total around a million
speakers. The ancestor of the modern dialects, Classical Nahuatl, was the
language of the Aztec civilisation which flourished in Central Mexico before

the arrival of the Spanish. Spoken to the south of Nahuatl entirely within Central America, the Mayan family has an equally glorious past, because of its association with the ancient Mayan civilisation. Mayan languages, several of which have around a quarter of a million speakers (Kekchi, Mam, Yucatec, Quiché, Cakchiquel) are spoken in southern Mexico and Guatemala, with some overspill into neighbouring Central American countries.

The major families of South America include Carib, Arawakan and Tupi. These language families do not occupy geographically continuous areas: Carib languages are spoken to the north of the Amazon, and predominate in the eastern part of this region; Arawakan languages, once also spoken in the West Indies, dominate further west and are also found well south of the Amazon; while Tupi languages are spoken over much of Brazil south of the Amazon and Paraguay. One Tupi language, Guarani, has, as noted above, been adopted almost as the national language of Paraguay. Hixkaryana, a Carib language spoken by just over a hundred people on the Nhamundá river, a tributary of the Amazon, has become famous in recent linguistic literature as the first clear attestation of a language in which the word order is object-verb-subject, as in the following sentence:

Toto yonoye kamara. 'The jaguar ate the man.'

In Hixkaryana, *toto* means 'man', *kamara* means 'jaguar', while the verb *yonoye* has the lexical meaning 'eat' and specifies that both subject and object are third person singular. Since there is no case marking on the nouns, and since the verb morphology is compatible with either noun as subject or object, the word order is crucial to understanding this Hixkaryana sentence (which cannot mean 'the man ate the jaguar'), just as the different subject-object-verb word order is crucial in English (Derbyshire 1977).

The South American language with the largest number of speakers, Quechua, is of uncertain genetic affiliation: it is widely claimed to be related to the neighbouring Aymara language, as the Quechumaran family, which is in turn, though less widely, claimed to be related to a number of small languages as the Andean family. Different dialects of Quechua are not always mutually intelligible, so on this criterion Quechua should perhaps be considered a language family rather than a single language (but see the discussion in section 1.1). Quechua was the language of the Inca civilisation, centred on Cuzco in what is now Peru, and the spread of the language is due both to Inca colonisation and to the use of Quechua as a lingua franca by the early Spanish colonists. It is spoken over much of Peru and Bolivia, with extensions into neighbouring countries.

3   The Social Interaction of Languages

As was indicated in the Preface, the notion of 'major language' is defined in social terms, so it is now time to look somewhat more consistently at some notions relating to the social side of language, in particular the social interaction of languages. Whether a language is a major language or not has nothing to do with its structure or with its genetic affiliation, and the fact that so many of the world's major languages are Indo-European is a mere accident of history.

First, we may look in more detail at the criteria that serve to define a language as being major. One of the most obvious criteria is the number of speakers, and certainly in making my choice of languages to be given individual chapters in this volume number of speakers was one of my main criteria. However, number of speakers is equally clearly not the sole criterion.

An interesting comparison to make here is between Chinese (or even more specifically, Mandarin) and English. Mandarin has far more native speakers than English, yet still English is generally considered a more useful language in the world at large than is Mandarin, as seen in the much larger number of people studying English as a second language than studying Mandarin as a second language. One of the reasons for this is that English is an international language, understood by a large number of people in many different parts of the world; Mandarin, by contrast, is by and large confined to China, and even taking all Chinese dialects (or languages) together, the extension of Chinese goes little beyond China and overseas Chinese communities. English is not only the native language of sizable populations in different parts of the world (especially the British Isles, North America, Australia and New Zealand) but is also spoken as a second language in even more countries, as is discussed in more detail in the chapter on English. English happens also to be the language of some of the technologically most advanced countries (in particular of the USA), so that English is the basic medium for access to current technological developments. Thus factors other than mere number of speakers are relevant in determining the social importance of a language.

Indeed, some of the languages given individual chapters in this volume have relatively few native speakers. Some of them are important not so much by virtue of the number of native speakers but rather because of the extent to which they are used as a lingua franca, as a second language among people who do not share a common first language. Good examples here are Swahili and Malay. Swahili is the native language of a relatively small population, primarily on the coast of East Africa, but its use as a lingua franca has spread through much of East Africa (especially Kenya and Tanzania), and even stretches into parts of Zaire. Malay too is the native language of relatively few people in western Malaysia and an even smaller number in Indonesia, but its adoption as the lingua franca and official language of both countries has raised the combined first and second language speakers to well over a hundred million. In many instances, in my choice of languages I have been guided by this factor rather than by raw statistics. Among the Philippine languages, for instance, Cebuano has more native speakers than Tagalog, but I selected Tagalog because it is both the national language of the Philippines and used as a linga franca across much of the country. Among the Indonesian languages, Javanese has more native speakers than Malay and is also the bearer of an old culture, but in terms of the current social situation Malay is clearly the dominant language of this branch of Austronesian. A number of other Indo-Aryan languages would surely have qualified for inclusion in terms of number of speakers, such as Marathi, Rajasthani, Panjabi, Gujarati, but they have not been assigned individual chapters because in social terms the major languages of the northern part of South Asia are clearly Hindi-Urdu and Bengali.

Another important criterion is the cultural importance of a language, in terms of the age and influence of its cultural heritage. An example in point is provided by the Dravidian languages, where Telugu actually has more speakers than Tamil; Tamil, however, is the more ancient literary language, and for this reason my choice rested with Tamil. I am aware that many of these decisions are in part subjective, and in part dangerous: as I emphasised in the Preface, the thing furthest from my mind is to intend any slight to speakers of languages that are not considered major in the contents of this volume.

Certain languages are major even despite the absence of native speakers, as with Latin and Sanskrit. Latin has provided a major contribution to all European languages, as can be seen most superficially in the extent to which words of Latin origin are used in European languages. Even those languages that have tried to avoid the appearance of Latinity by creating their own vocabulary have often fallen back on Latin models: German *Gewissen* 'conscience', for instance, contains the prefix *ge-*, meaning 'with', the stem *wiss-*, meaning 'know', and the suffix *-en* to form an abstract noun — an exact copy of the Latin *con-sci-entia*; borrowings that follow the structure rather than the form in this way are known as calques or loan translations. Sanskrit has played a similar role in relation to the languages of India, including Hindi. Hebrew is included not because of the number of its speakers — as noted in the chapter on Hebrew, this has never been large — but because of the contribution of Hebrew and its culture to European and Middle Eastern society.

A language can thus have influence beyond the areas where it is the native or second language. A good example to illustrate this is Arabic. Arabic loans form a large part of the vocabulary of many languages spoken by Islamic peoples, even of languages that are genetically only distantly related to Arabic (e.g. Hausa) or that are genetically totally unrelated (e.g. Turkish,

Persian and Urdu). The influence of Arabic can also be seen in the adoption of the Arabic writing system by many Islamic peoples. Similarly, Chinese loan words form an important part of the vocabulary of some East Asian languages, in particular Vietnamese, Japanese and Korean; the use of written Chinese characters has also spread to Japan and Korea, and in earlier times also to Vietnam.

It is important to note also that the status of a language as a major language is far from immutable. Indeed, as we go back into history we find many significant changes. For instance, the possibility of characterising English as the world's major language is an innovation of the twentieth century. One of the most important shifts in the distribution of major languages resulted from the expansion of European languages, especially English, Spanish, Portuguese, and to a lesser extent French as a result of the colonisation of the Americas: English, Spanish and Portuguese all now have far more native speakers in the New World than in Britain, Spain or Portugal. Indeed, in the Middle Ages one would hardly have imagined that English, confined to an island off the coast of Europe, would have become a major international language.

In medieval Europe, Latin was clearly the major language, since, despite the lack of native speakers, it was the lingua franca of those who needed to communicate across linguistic boundaries. Yet the rise of Latin to such preeminence — which includes the fact that Latin and its descendants have ousted virtually all other languages from southwestern Europe — could hardly have been foreseen from its inauspicious beginnings confined to the area around Rome. Equally spectacular has been the spread of Arabic, in the wake of Islamic religious zeal, from being confined to the Arabian peninsula to being the dominant language of the Middle East and North Africa.

In addition to languages that have become major languages, there are equally languages that have lost this status. The earliest records from Mesopotamia, often considered the cradle of civilisation, are in two languages: Sumerian and Akkadian (the latter the language of the Assyrian and Babylonian empires); Akkadian belongs to the Semitic branch of Afroasiatic, while Sumerian is as far as we can tell unrelated to any other known language. Even at the time of attested Sumerian inscriptions, the language was probably already approaching extinction, and it continued to be used in deference to tradition (as with Latin in medieval Europe). The dominant language of the period was to become Akkadian, but in the intervening period this too has died out, leaving no direct descendants. Gone too is Ancient Egyptian, the language of the Pharaohs. The linguistic picture of the Mediterranean and Middle East in the year nought was very different from that which we observe today.

Social factors and social attitudes can even bring about apparent reversals in the family-tree model of language relatedness. At the time of the earliest texts from Germany, two distinct Germanic languages are recognised: Old Saxon and Old High German. Old Saxon is the ancestor of the modern Low German (Plattdeutsch) dialects, while Old High German is the ancestor of the modern High German dialects and of the standard language. Because of social changes — such as the decline of the Hanseatic League, the economic mainstay of northern Germany — High German gained social ascendancy over Low German. Since the standard language, based on High German, is now recognised as the standard in both northern and southern Germany, both Low and High German dialects are now considered dialects of a single German language, and the social relations between a given Low German dialect and standard German are in practice no different from those between any High German dialect and standard German.

One of the most interesting developments to have arisen from language contact is the development of pidgin and creole languages. A pidgin language arises from a very practical situation: speakers of different languages need to communicate with one another to carry out some practical task, but do not speak any language in common and moreover do not have the opportunity to learn each other's languages properly. What arises in such a situation is, initially, an unstable pidgin, or jargon, with highly variable structure — considerably simplified relative to the native languages of the people involved in its creation — and just enough vocabulary to permit practical tasks to be carried out reasonably successfully. The clearest examples of the development of such pidgins arose from European colonisation, in particular from the Atlantic slave trade and from indenturing labourers in the South Pacific. These pidgins take most of their vocabulary from the colonising language, although their structures are often very different from those of the colonising language.

At a later stage, the jargon may expand, particularly when its usefulness as a lingua franca is recognised among the speakers of non-European origin, leading to a stabilised pidgin, such as Tok Pisin, the major lingua franca of Papua New Guinea. This expansion is on several planes: the range of functions is expanded, since the pidgin is no longer restricted to uses of language essential to practical tasks; the vocabulary is expanded as a result of this greater range of functions, new words often being created internally to the pidgin rather than borrowed from some other language (as with Tok Pisin *maus gras* 'moustache', literally 'mouth grass'); the structure becomes stabilised, i.e. the language has a well defined grammar.

Throughout all of this development, the pidgin has no native speakers. The next possible stage (or this may take place even before stabilisation) is for the pidgin to 'acquire native speakers'. For instance, if native speakers of different languages marry and have the pidgin as their only common language, then this will be the language of their household and will become the first language of their children. Once a pidgin has acquired native speakers, it is referred to as a creole. The native languages of many inhabitants of the Caribbean islands are creoles, for instance the English-based creole of Jamaica, the French-based creole of Haiti, and the Spanish-and/or Portuguese-based creole Papiamentu (Papiamento) of the Netherlands Antilles (Aruba, Bonaire and Curaçao). At an even later stage, social improvements and education may bring the creole back into close contact with the European language that originally contributed much of its vocabulary. In this situation, the two languages may interact and the creole, or some of its varieties, may start approaching the standard language. This gives rise to the so-called post-creole continuum, in which one finds a continuous scale of varieties of speech from forms close to the original creole (basilect) through intermediate forms (mesolect) up to a slightly regionally coloured version of the standard language. Jamaican English is a good example of a post-creole continuum.

No pidgin or creole language has succeeded in gaining sufficient status or number of speakers to become one of the world's major languages, but pidgin and creole languages provide important insights into the processes that arise from natural language contact. And while it would probably be an exaggeration to consider any of the word's major languages a creole, it is not unlikely that some of the processes that go to create a pidgin or a creole have been active in the history of some of these languages — witness, for instance, the morphological simplification that has attended the development from Old English to Modern English, or from Latin to the modern Romance languages.

A few centuries ago, as we saw above, it would have been difficult to predict the present-day distribution of major languages in the world. It is equally impossible to predict the future. In terms of number of native speakers, it is clear that a major shift is underway in favour of non-European languages: the rate of population increase is much higher outside Europe than in Europe, and while some European languages draw some benefit from this (such as Spanish and Portuguese in Latin America), the main beneficiaries are the indigenous languages of southern Asia and Africa. It might well be that a later version of this volume would include fewer of the European languages that are restricted to a single country, and devote more space to non-European languages. Another factor is the increase in the range of functions of many non-European languages: during the colonial period European languages (primarily English and French) were used for most official purposes and also for education in much of Asia and Africa, but the winning of independence has meant that many countries have turned more to their own languages, using these as official language and medium of education. The extent to which this will lead to increase in their status as major languages is difficult to predict — at present, access to the frontiers of scholarship and technology is still primarily through European languages, especially English; but one should not forget that the use of English, French and German as vehicles for science was gained only through a prolonged struggle against what then seemed the obvious language for such writing: Latin. (The process may go back indefinitely: Cicero was criticised for writing philosophical treatises in Latin by those who thought he should have used Greek.) But at least I hope to have shown the reader that the social interaction of languages is a dynamic process, one that is moreover exciting to follow.

Bibliography

Recent comprehensive indexes of the world's languages, with genetic classification, are Voegelin and Voegelin (1977) and Grimes (1984), both of which favour broad genetic groupings; the same is true of Ruhlen (1987), which provides an overall genetic classification for the languages of the world, though with due attention to alternative, including less bold, proposals. For sources that also give information on the structure of at least some of the languages and language families included, reference may be made to Meillet and Cohen (1926; 1952). The latter is now out of print, and is being replaced by a completely new series of volumes under the general editorship of Perrot (1981–). Another series of volumes each dealing with a particular language family or geographical area is the Cambridge Language Surveys series, in which so far volumes have appeared on Australia (Dixon 1980), the Soviet Union (Comrie 1981a), Meso-America (Suárez 1983), and New Guinea (Foley 1986); further volumes are in preparation.

Readers wanting to delve deeper into problems of genetic classification should consult a good introduction to historical and comparative linguistics, such as Bynon (1977). For discussions of language universals and typology, reference may be made to Comrie (1981b) and Foley and Van Valin (1984).

The standard reference on language contact is Weinreich (1953), while Todd (1984) is a useful introduction to pidgins and creoles.

References

Bynon, T. 1977. *Historical Linguistics* (Cambridge University Press, Cambridge)

Comrie, B. 1981a. *Languages of the Soviet Union* (Cambridge University Press, Cambridge)

—— 1981b. *Language Universals and Linguistic Typology* (Basil Blackwell, Oxford and University of Chicago Press, Chicago)

Derbyshire, D.C. 1977. 'Word Order Universals and the Existence of OVS Languages', *Linguistic Inquiry*, vol. 8, pp. 590–8

Dixon, R.M.W. 1980. *The Languages of Australia* (Cambridge University Press, Cambridge)

Foley, W.A. 1986. *The Papuan Languages of New Guinea* (Cambridge University Press, Cambridge)

—— and R.D. Van Valin, Jr. 1984. *Functional Syntax and Universal Grammar* (Cambridge University Press, Cambridge)

Greenberg, J.H. 1963. 'Some Universals of Grammar with Particular Reference to the Order of Meaningful Elements', in J.H. Greenberg (ed.), *Universals of Language* (MIT Press, Cambridge, Mass.), pp. 73–112

—— 1966. *The Languages of Africa* (Indiana University, Bloomington and Mouton, The Hague)

—— 1987. *Language in the Americas* (Stanford University Press, Stanford)

Grimes, B.F. (ed.) 1984. *Languages of the World: Ethnologue*, 10th edition (Wycliffe Bible Translators, Dallas)

Meillet, A. and M. Cohen (eds.) 1926 (1st ed.) 1952 (2nd ed.). *Les Langues du monde* (Champion, Paris)

Perrot, J. (ed.) 1981–. *Les Langues dans le monde ancien et moderne* (Éditions du Centre National de la Recherche Scientifique, Paris)

Ruhlen, M. 1987. *A Guide to the World's Languages*, vol. 1: *Classification* (Stanford University Press, Stanford)

Suárez, J. 1983. *The Meso-American Languages* (Cambridge University Press, Cambridge)

Todd, L. 1984. *Modern Englishes: Pidgins and Creoles* (Basil Blackwell, Oxford)

Voegelin, C.F. and F.M. 1977. *Classification and Index of the World's Languages* (Elsevier, New York)

Weinreich, U. 1953. *Languages in Contact* (Mouton, The Hague)

1 INDO-EUROPEAN LANGUAGES

Philip Baldi

1   Introduction

By the term *Indo-European* we are referring to a family of languages which by about 1000 BC were spoken over a large part of Europe and parts of southwestern and southern Asia. Indo-European is essentially a geographical term: it refers to the easternmost (India) and westernmost (Europe) expansion of the family at the time it was proven to be a linguistic group by scholars of the eighteenth and nineteenth centuries (the term was first used in 1813). Of course modern expansion and migrations which have taken Indo-European languages to Africa, Hawaii, Australia and elsewhere around the world now suggest another name for the family, but the term *Indo-European* (German *Indogermanisch*) is now well rooted in the scholarly tradition.

Claiming that a language is a member of a linguistic family is quite different from establishing such an assertion using proven methods and principles of scientific analysis. During the approximately two centuries in which the interrelationships among the Indo-European languages have been systematically studied, techniques to confirm or deny genetic affiliations between languages have been developed with great success. Chief among these methods is the comparative method, which takes shared features among languages as its data and provides procedures for establishing proto-forms. The comparative method is surely not the only available approach, nor is it by any means foolproof. Indeed, other methods of reconstruction, especially the method of internal reconstruction and the method of typological inference, work together with the comparative method to achieve reliable results. But since space is limited and the focus of this chapter is Indo-European and not methods of reconstruction, we will restrict ourselves here to a brief review of the comparative method using only data from Indo-European languages.

When we claim that two or more languages are genetically related, we are at the same time claiming that they share common ancestry. And if we make such a claim about common ancestry, then our methods should provide us with a means of recovering the ancestral system, attested or not. The initial

Table 1.1: Some Basic Indo-European Terms

A. NUMERALS

	one	two	three	four
Skt.	ćka-	dvá, dváu	tráya-	catvára-
Gk.	oînos 'ace'	dú(w)o	treîs	téttares, téssares
Lat.	ūnus	duo	trēs	quattuor
Hitt.		dā-	*trijaš (gen.)	
Toch. A		wu	tre	śtwar
B		we	trai	ś(t)wār
OIr.	oïn, ōcn	dāu, dō	trī	ceth(a)ir
Go.	ains	twai	þreis	fidwōr
OCS	inŭ	dŭva	trĭje	četyre
Lith.	víenas	dù	trỹs	keturì
Arm.		erku	erek'	č'ork'
Alb.	njё	dü	tre, tri	katёr

B. ANIMAL NAMES

	mouse	wolf		cow		sheep	
Skt.	múṣ-	vŕ̥ka-		gó-		ávi-	
Gk.	mûs	lúkos		boûs		ó(w)is	
Lat.	mūs	lupus		bōs		ovis	
Hitt.							
Toch. A				ko			
B				kau			
OIr.		olc 'evil'		bō		ōi	
Go.	mūs	wulfs	OIc.	kŷr	OHG	ouwi	
					'threshing floor'		
OCS	myší	vlŭkŭ		gumŭno		ovĭca	
Lith.		vìlkas	Latv.	gùovs	Lith.	avìs	
Arm.	mukn			kov		hoviw 'shepherd'	
Alb.	mī	ulk					

C. BODY PARTS

	foot	heart	eye	tongue
Skt.	pád-		ákṣi-	jihvá
Gk.	poús (gen. podós)	kardíā	ópsomai 'I will see'	
Lat.	pēs (gen. pedis)	cor (gen. cordis)	oculus	lingua
Hitt.	pat-	kard-		
Toch. A	pe		ak	kāntu
B	pai		ek	kantwo
OIr.	ïs 'below'	cride	enech	teng
Go.	fōtus	haírtō	augō	tuggō
OCS	pěší 'on foot'	srĭdĭce	oko	językŭ
Lith.	pãdas 'sole'	širdìs	akìs	liežùvis
Arm.	otn	sirt	akn	lezu
Alb.	(pёr)posh 'under'		sü	

D. KINSHIP TERMS

	mother	father	sister		brother	
Skt.	mātár-	pitár-	svásar-		bhrátar-	'member of a
Gk. (Dor.)	mátēr	patēr	éor (voc.)	(Dor.)	phrátēr <	brotherhood'
Lat.	mātcr	pater	soror		frāter	
Hitt.						
Toch. A	mācar	pācar			pracar	
B	mācer	pācer			procer	
OIr.	māthir	athir	siur		brāth(a)ir	
OIc.	mōðir	Go. fadar	swistar		brōþar	
OCS	mati		sestra		bratrŭ, bratŭ	
Lith.	mótė 'woman'		sesuõ		brólis	
Arm.	mayr	hayr	k'oyr		ełbayr	
Alb.	motrё					

	five	*six*	*seven*	*eight*	*nine*
	páñca	şáṭ-	saptá-	aṣṭá(u)	náva-
	pénte, pémpe	héks	heptá	oktō	enné(w)a
Hier.	quīnque	sex	septem	octō	novem
Hitt. <	paⁿta		šipta-		
	pěñ	säk	şpät	okät	ñu
	piś	şkas	şuk(t)	okt	ñu
	cöic	sē	secht	ocht	noī
	fimf	saíhs	sibun	ahtau	niun
	pęṭī	šestī	sedmī	osmī	devęṭī
	penkì	šсšì	septynì	aštuonì	devynì
	hing	vec'	evt'n	ut'	inn
	pesě	gjashtë	shtatë	tetë	nëntë

	pig	*dog*	*horse*
	sūkará-	śván-	áśva-
		hūs	kúōn	híppos
		sūs	canis	equus
		ku	yuk
	suwo	ku	yakwe
		cū	ech
	swein	hunds OE	coh
	svinija		
Latv.	suvēns, sivēns Lith.	šuō (OLith.)	csvà, aśvà, 'mare'
	'young pig'	šun	
	thi		

Table 1.1 continued over.

Table 1.1 cont'd:

E. GENERAL TERMS	full	race, kind	month	die, death
Skt.	pūrṇá-	jána-	mās-	mṛtá-
Gk.	plḗrēs	génos	mēn	ámbrotos 'immortal'
Lat.	plēnus	genus	mēnsis	mortuus
Hitt.				merta
Toch. A			mañ	
B			meñc	
OIr.	lān	gein 'birth'	mī	marb
Go.	fulls	kuni	mēna, mēnōþs	maúrþr
OCS	plŭnŭ		měsęcĭ	mīrǫ, mrěti
Lith.	pìlnas		měnuo	miřti
Arm.	li	cin 'birth'	amis	
Alb.	plot		muai	

demonstration of relatedness is the easy part; establishing well-motivated intermediate and ancestral forms is quite another matter. Among the difficulties are: which features in which of the languages being compared are older? which are innovations? which are borrowed? how many shared similarities are enough to prove relatedness conclusively, and how are they weighted for significance? what assumptions do we make about the relative importance of lexical, morphological, syntactic and phonological characteristics, and about directions of language change?

All of these questions come into play in any reconstruction effort, leaving us with the following assumption: if two or more languages share a feature which is unlikely to have arisen by accident, borrowing or as the result of some typological tendency or language universal, then it is assumed to have arisen only once and to have been transmitted to the two or more languages from a common source. The more such features are discovered and securely identified, the closer the relationship.

In determining genetic relationship and reconstructing proto-forms using the comparative method, we usually start with vocabulary. Table 1.1 contains a number of words from various Indo-European languages which will demonstrate a common core of lexical items too large and too basic to be explained either by accident or borrowing. A list of possible cognates which is likely to produce a maximum number of common inheritance items, known as the basic vocabulary list, provides many of the words we might investigate, such as basic kinship terms, pronouns, basic body parts, lower numerals and others. From these and other data we seek to establish sets of equations known as correspondences, which are statements that in a given environment X phoneme of one language will correspond to Y phoneme of another language *consistently* and *systematically* if the two languages are descended from a common ancestor.

In order to illustrate the comparative method we will briefly and selectively choose a few items from tables 1.1 and 1.2, restricting our data to fairly clear cases.

old		vomit
sána-	'last	vámiti
hénos	year's'	eméó
senex		vomō

| sen | | |
| sineigs | OIc. | vāma 'sickness' |

| sēnas | | vémti |
| hin | | |

---

	mouse		mother		nine
Skt.	mū́ṣ-		mātár-		náva
Gk.	mūs	(Dor.)	mā́tēr		enné(w)a
Lat.	mūs		māter		novem
Go.	mūs	OIc.	mōðir	Go.	niun

	dead		dog		race, kind
Skt.	mṛtá-		śvắn-		jána-
Gk.	ámbrotos 'immortal'		kúōn		génos
Lat.	mortuus		canis		genus
Go.	maúrþr 'murder'		hunds		kuni

	'I am'		vomit		old
Skt.	ásmi		vámiti		sána-
Gk.	eimí		eméō		hénos 'last year's'
Lat.	sum		vomō		senex
Go.	im	OIc.	vāma 'sickness'	Go.	sineigs

We will first look only at the nasals *m* and *n*. Lined up for the comparative method they look like this:

	mouse	mother	nine	dead	dog	race, kind	I am	vomit	old
Skt.	m-	m-	-n-	-m-	-n	-n-	-m-	-m-	-n-
Gk.	m-	m-	-nn-	-m(b)-	-n	-n-	-m-	-m-	-n-
Lat.	m-	m-	-n-	-m-	-n-	-n-	-m	-m-	-n-
Gmc.	m-	m-	-n-	-m-	-n-	-n-	-m	-m-	-n-

Before we begin reconstructing we must be sure that we are comparing the appropriate segments. It is clear that this is the case in 'mouse', 'mother', 'dog', 'race, kind', 'I am', 'vomit' and 'old', but less clear in 'nine' and 'dead'. What of the double *n* in Gk. *enné(w)a*? A closer look reveals that *en-* is a prefix; thus, the first *n* is outside the equation. Similarly with *ámbrotos* 'immortal': the *á-* is a prefix meaning 'not' (=Lat. *in-*, Go. *un-*, etc.), and the *b* results from a rule of Greek in which the sequence *-mr-* results in *-mbr-*, with epenthetic *b* (cf. Lat. *camera* > Fr. *chambre*). So the *m*'s do indeed

Table 1.2: Inflectional Regularities in Indo-European Languages

A. Examples of Verb Inflection

	I am	*he, she is*
Skt.	ásmi	ásti
Gk.	eimí	estí
Lat.	sum	est
Hitt.	ešmi	ešzi
Toch. A		
B		ste
OIr.	am	is
Go.	im	ist
OCS	jesmŭ	jestŭ
OLith.	esmì	ēsti
Arm.	em	ē
Alb.	jam	ёshtë

B. Examples of Noun Inflection

tooth

	Skt.	Gk.	Lat.	Go.	Lith.
Sg.					
nom.	dán	odőn	dēns	*tunþus	dantìs
gen.	datás	odóntos	dentis	*tunþáus	dantiẽs
dat.	daté	odónti	dentī	tunþáu	dañčiui
acc.	dántam	odónta	dentem	tunþu	dañtį
abl.	datás		dente		
loc.	datí				dantyjè
inst.	datā́				dantimì
voc.	dan	odőn	dēns	*tunþu	dantiẽ
Pl.					
nom.	dántas	odóntes	dentēs	*tunþjus	dañtys
gen.	datā́m	odóntōn	dentium	tunþiwē	dantṹ
dat.	dadbhyás	odoũsi	dentibus	tunþum	dantìms
acc.	datás	odóntas	dentēs	tunþuns	dantìs
abl.	dadbhyás		dentibus		
loc.	datsú				dantysè
inst.	dadbhís				dantimìs
voc.	dántas	odóntes	dentēs	*tunþjus	dañtys

C. Examples of Pronoun Inflection

I, me

	Skt.	Gk.	Lat.	Hitt.	Go.	OCS
nom.	ahám	egő	ego	uk	ik	azŭ
gen.	máma(me)	emoũ(mou)	meī	ammēl	meina	mene
dat.	máhyam(me)	emoí(moi)	mihī	ammuk	mis	mĭně(mi)
acc.	mā́m(mā)	emé(me)	mē(d)	ammuk	mik	mene(mę)
abl.	mat		mē(d)	ammēdaz		
loc.	máyi			ammuk		mĭně
inst.	máyā					mŭnojǫ

C. Examples of Pronoun Inflection – *continued*
  you (sg.)

	Skt.	Gk.	Lat.	Hitt.	Go.	OCS
nom.	tvám	sú	tū	zik	þu	ty
gen.	táva(te)	soú(sou)	tuī, tīs	tuēl	þeina	tebe
dat.	túbhyam(te)	soí(soi)	tibī	tuk	þus	tebě(ti)
acc.	tvā́m(tvā)	sé(se)	tē(d)	tuk	þuk	tebe(tę)
abl.	tvát		tē(d)	tuēdaz		
loc.	tváyi			tuk		tebě
inst.	tváyā					tobojǫ

Note: Forms in parentheses are enclitic variants.

align, leaving us with a consistent set of *m* and *n* correspondences:

m : m : m : m   n : n : n : n

These alignments represent the horizontal or comparative dimension. Next we 'triangulate' the segments, adding the vertical, or historical dimension:

m : m : m : m   n : n : n : n

Finally, after checking all the relevant data and investigating their distributional patterns, we make a hypothesis concerning the proto-sound. In these two cases there is only one reasonable solution, namely **m* and **n*:

*m   *n
m : m : m : m   n : n : n : n

At this stage of the analysis we are claiming that **m* > (develops into) *m* and **n* > *n* in the various daughter languages.

Neat correspondences such as these are more the exception than the rule in historical-comparative linguistics. It is far more common to find sets in which only a few of the members have identical segments. But the method of comparative reconstruction, when supplemented with sufficient information about the internal structure of the languages in question, can still yield replicable results. Consider the following data from table 1.1, supplemented by some additional material:

	six	old	race, kind (gen. case)	be
Skt.	ṣáṭ	sána-	jánasas	ástu 'let him be!'
Gk.	héks	hénos 'last year's'	géneos (génous)	éō (ð) 'I might be'
Lat.	sex	senex	generis	erō 'I will be'
Go.	saíhs	sineigs	(OCS slovese 'word')	ist 'he/she is'

We are concentrating here on the correspondences which include *s*, *h*, and *r*. In 'six' and 'old' we have the set *s* : *h* : *s* : *s* initially (cf. also 'seven' and 'pig'). In final position we find Ø : *s* : *s* : *s* in 'six' and 'old' (cf. also 'one', 'three', 'mouse' and 'wolf', among others). And in medial position we have *s* : Ø : *r* : *s* in 'race, kind' (gen.) and 'be'. What is or are the proto-sound(s)?

A brief look at the languages in question takes us straight to *s for all three correspondences. *s > *h* in Greek initially (weakens), and disappears completely medially, yielding a phonetically common pattern of *s* > *h* > Ø (cf. Avestan, Spanish). Final Ø in the Sanskrit examples is only the result of citing the Sanskrit words in their root forms; the full nominative forms (as in the other languages) would contain *s* as well (e.g. *jánas*, *sánas*, etc.). And the medial Latin *r* is the result of rhotacism, whereby Latin consistently converts intervocalic *s* to *r* (cf. *es-* 'be', *erō* 'I will be'; (nom.) *flōs* 'flower' (gen.) *flōris*).

From these few, admittedly simplified examples we see that the comparative method, when supplemented by adequate information about the internal structure of the languages in question and by a consideration of all the relevant data, can produce consistent and reliable reconstructions of ancestral forms. It is with such methods that Proto-Indo-European has been reconstructed.

2   The Languages of the Indo-European Family

The Indo-European languages are classified into eleven major groups (ten if Baltic and Slavonic are considered together as Balto-Slavonic). Some of these groups have many members, while some others have only one. Of the eleven major groups, nine have modern spoken representatives while two, Anatolian and Tocharian, are extinct.

2.1   Indo-Iranian
The Indo-Iranian group has two main subdivisions, Indo-Aryan (Indic) and Iranian. The similarities between the two subdivisions are so consistent that there is no question about the status of Indo-Iranian intermediate between Proto-Indo-European and the Indic and Iranian subgroups. The Indo-Aryan migrations into the Indian area took place some time in the second millennium BC.

2.1.1   Indo-Aryan (or Indic)
(See separate chapter.)

2.1.2   Iranian
(See separate chapter.)

2.2   Hellenic
(See chapter on Greek.)

2.3   Italic
(See chapter on Latin and the Italic languages.)

2.4   Anatolian
The Anatolian languages were unknown to modern scholars until archaeological excavations during the first part of this century in Boğazköy, Turkey, yielded texts which were written primarily in Hittite, the principal language of the Anatolian group. The texts, which date from approximately the seventeenth to the thirteenth centuries BC, were written in cuneiform script and contained not only Hittite, but Akkadian and Assyrian as well. Decipherment proceeded quickly and it was claimed by B. Hrozný in 1915 that the Hittite in the texts was an Indo-European language. It was later shown that Hittite contained a large number of archaic features not found in other Indo-European languages, which resulted in revised reconstructions of the proto-language. Now totally extinct, the Anatolian group contains, in addition to Hittite, Luwian, Palaic, Lydian and Lycian, the last three surviving only in fragments.

2.5   Tocharian
Around the turn of this century a large amount of material written in an unknown language was discovered in the Chinese Turkestan (Tarim Basin) region of Central Asia. The language represented in these texts is now known as Tocharian, and is unquestionably of the Indo-European group. The documents are chiefly of a religious nature, but also contain commercial documents, caravan passes and medical and magical texts. There are two dialects of Tocharian: Tocharian A, also known as East Tocharian or Turfan, and Tocharian B, also known as West Tocharian or Kuchean. The texts found in Chinese Turkestan are all from the period AD 500 to 1000, so this language has not played the same role as other twentieth-century discoveries like Hittite and Mycenaean Greek in the shaping of reconstructed Proto-Indo-European.

2.6   Celtic
The Celtic languages are largely unknown until the modern period, though it is clear from inscriptional information and place and river names that Celtic languages were once spread over a fairly wide section of Europe in the pre-Christian era. The Celtic languages are commonly classified into two groups: the Goidelic or Gaelic group, made up of Irish, Scots Gaelic and the extinct

Manx, and the Brythonic or Brittanic group, made up of Welsh, Breton and the extinct Cornish. The oldest records of Celtic are some sepulchral inscriptions from the fourth century AD, and Old Irish manuscripts which date from the late seventh to early eighth century AD.

Many specialists believe that the Celtic and Italic languages have a remote relationship intermediate between the disintegration of Proto-Indo-European and the establishment of the separate Celtic and Italic groups. The 'Italo-Celtic' topic recurs periodically in Indo-European studies.

2.7   Germanic
(See separate chapter.)

2.8   Slavonic
(See separate chapter.)

2.9   Baltic
This highly conservative group of Indo-European languages has played a significant role in Indo-European studies. Despite the fact that the oldest useful recorded material from Baltic dates from the mid-fourteenth century AD, Baltic has preserved many archaic features, especially in morphology, which scholars believe existed in Proto-Indo-European.

Only two Baltic languages are spoken today, Lithuanian and Latvian (or Lettish). Many others are now extinct, including Semigallian, Selonian, Curonian, Yotvingian and Old Prussian. Old Prussian is the most important of these; it became extinct in the early eighteenth century, but provides us with our oldest written documentation of the Baltic group.

The Baltic languages are considered by many specialists to be in a special relationship with the Slavonic languages. Those who follow such a scheme posit a stage intermediate between Proto-Indo-European and Baltic and Slavonic called Balto-Slavonic.

2.10   Armenian
Spoken now predominantly in Soviet Armenia, Armenian was probably established as a language by the sixth century BC. The first records of the language are from the fifth century AD, and it shows considerable influence from Greek, Arabic, Syriac and especially Persian. In fact, so extreme is the foreign influence on Armenian that it was at first thought to be a radical dialect of Persian rather than a language in its own right. Written in an alphabet developed in the fifth century, the language is quite conservative in many of its structural features, especially inflectional morphology and, by some recent accounts, consonantal phonology.

2.11   Albanian
The remote history of Albanian is unknown, and although there are

references to Albanians by Greek historians in the first century AD, we have no record of the language until the fifteenth century. Much influenced by neighbouring languages, Albanian has proven to be of marginal value in the reconstruction of Proto-Indo-European. There are two principal dialects of Albanian: Gheg, spoken in the north and in Yugoslavia, and Tosk, spoken in southern Albania and various colonies in Greece and Italy.

In addition to these eleven major groups, there remain a number of 'minor' Indo-European languages which are known only in fragments, glosses, inscriptions and other unpredictable sources. Though there is some dispute about the Indo-European character of some of these languages, scholars generally agree on the following as Indo-European: Ligurian (Mediterranean region), Lepontic (possibly affiliated with Celtic), Sicel (possibly affiliated with Italic), Raetic, Thraco-Phrygian (frequently connected with Armenian and Albanian), Illyrian (especially prevalent along the Dalmatian coast), Messapic (with uncertain Italic or Albanian connections), and Venetic (probably connected with Italic). None of these languages exists in sufficient material detail to be of systematic value in the reconstruction of Proto-Indo-European.

3 The Structure of Proto-Indo-European

There have been many attempts to reconstruct Proto-Indo-European from the evidence of the daughter languages. The discoveries of Hittite, Tocharian and Mycenaean Greek in this century have modified the data base of Indo-European studies, so it is not surprising that there have been frequent changes in views on Proto-Indo-European. Also, there have been a refinement of technique and an expansion of knowledge about language structure and language change which have modified views of the proto-language. In this section we will briefly review past and present thinking on Proto-Indo-European phonology, and we will then discuss commonly held positions on the morphological and syntactic structure of the proto-language.

3.1 Phonology

3.1.1 Segmental Phonology

The first systematic attempt to reconstruct the sound system of Proto-Indo-European was by A. Schleicher in the first edition of his *Compendium der vergleichenden Grammatik der indogermanischen Sprachen* in 1861. Using the sound correspondences worked out by his predecessors, Schleicher proposed the consonant system as in table 1.3 (from the 1876 ed., p. 10). Schleicher's vowel system was based primarily on the pattern found in Sanskrit whereby 'basic vowels' are modified by strengthening processes

Table 1.3: Schleicher's Reconstructed System

| | unaspirated | | aspirated | spirants | | nasals | r |
	vls.	vd.	vd.	vls.	vd.	vd.	vd.
gutt.	k	g	gh				
pal.					j		
lingu.							r
dent.	t	d	dh	s		n	
lab.	p	b	bh		v	m	

which the Indian grammarians called *guṇa* 'secondary quality' and *vṛddhi* 'growth, increment'. By these processes a basic three-vowel system is changed by the prefixation of *a* as follows (1876:11):

Basic Vowel	First Increment	Second Increment
a	a + a → aa	a + aa → āa
i	a + i → ai	a + ai → āi
u	a + u → au	a + au → āu

This system is not identical to the Sanskrit system; it is, however, patterned on it.

Schleicher's system soon gave way to the model proposed by the Neogrammarians, a group of younger scholars centred at Leipzig who had quite different views about Proto-Indo-European, and about language change generally, from their predecessors. The Neogrammarian system is embodied in the classic work of K. Brugmann, as in table 1.4 (1903:52).

Brugmann's system is much more elaborate than Schleicher's in almost every respect: there are more occlusives, more fricatives, diphthongs, etc. But probably the most significant difference is in the vowel system. Brugmann proposes a six short, five long vowel system which is much more like that of Greek or Latin than that of Sanskrit. This change was brought about by the discovery that a change had taken place whereby Sanskrit collapsed PIE *ĕ, *ŏ, *ă into ă (cf. Lat. *sequor*, Gk. *hépomai*, Skt. *sáce* 'I follow' (*e*); Lat. *ovis*, Gk. *óis*, Skt. *ávi-* 'sheep' (*o*); Lat. *ager*, Gk. *agrós*, Skt. *ájra-* 'field, plain' (*a*)). From this it could be seen that Sanskrit was not to be considered closest to the proto-language in all respects.

The Neogrammarian system, which in modified form still finds adherents today, was put to the test by the theories of Saussure and the findings of Kuryłowicz and others. Based on the irregular behaviour of certain sounds in the daughter languages, Saussure proposed that Proto-Indo-European had contained sounds of uncertain phonetic value which he called 'coefficients sonantiques'. According to Saussure, these sounds were lost in the daughter languages but not before they left traces of their former presence on the sounds which had surrounded them. For example, there is no regular explanation for the difference in vowel length between the two

Table 1.4: Brugmann's Reconstructed System

Consonants

Occlusives:	p	ph	b	bh	(labial)				
	t̰	th	d	dh	(dental)				
	k̂	k̂h	ĝ	ĝh	(palatal)				
	q	qh	g	gh	(velar)				
	qu̯	qu̯h	gu̯	gu̯h	(labio-velar)				
Fricatives:	s	sh	z	zh	þ	þh	ð	ðh	(j)
Nasals:	m	n	n̂	ŋ					
Liquids:	r	l							
Semi-vowels:	i̯	u̯							

Vowels (Brugmann 1903:67, 89, 122-38)

A.	Vowels:	e	o	a	i	u	ə		
		ē	ō	ā	ī	ū			
B.	Diphthongs:	ei̯	oi̯	ai̯	əi̯		eu̯	ou̯	au̯	əu̯
		ēi̯	ōi̯	āi̯			ēu̯	ōu̯	āu̯	
C.	Syllabic Liquids and Nasals:	l̥	r̥	m̥	n̥	n̥̂	ŋ̥		
		l̥̄	r̥̄	m̥̄	n̥̄	n̥̂̄	ŋ̥̄		

forms of Gk. *hístāmi* 'I stand' and *stătos* 'stood'. Saussure theorised that originally the root had been **steA* (A = a coefficient sonantique). The A had coloured the *e* to *a* and had lengthened it to *ā* in *hístāmi* before disappearing. The major changes ascribed to the action of these sounds include changing *e* to *o*, *e* to *a* and lengthening preceding vowels.

This new theory, based on abstract principles, was put to use to explain a wide range of phonological and morphological phenomena in various Indo-European languages. It came to be called the 'laryngeal theory', since it is thought that these sounds may have had a laryngeal articulation. Proposals were made to explain facts of Indo-European root structure, ablaut relations (see section 3.2.2) and other problems. Many proposals concerning the exact number of laryngeals, and their effects, were made. Some scholars worked with one, others with as many as ten or twelve. It remained an unverifiable theory until 1927, when Kuryłowicz demonstrated that Hittite preserved laryngeal-like sounds (written as *ḫ* or *ḫḫ*) precisely in those positions where Saussure had theorised they had existed in Proto-Indo-European. Some examples: Hitt. *ḫanti* 'front': Lat. *ante*; Hitt. *ḫarkiš-* 'white': Gk. *argés*; Hitt. *palḫiš* 'broad': Lat. *plānus*; Hitt. *meḫur* 'time': Go. *mēl*; Hitt. *u̯aḫanzi* 'they turn': Skt. *vāya-* 'weaving'; Hitt. *newaḫḫ-* 'renew': Lat. *novāre*.

The empirical confirmation that Hittite provided for Saussure's theories led to a complete reworking of the Proto-Indo-European sound system. We may take the system proposed by W. Lehmann as representative of these developments as in table 1.5 (1952:99):

Table 1.5: Lehmann's Reconstructed System

Obstruents:	p	t	k	k^w
	b	d	g	g^w
	b^h	d^h	g^h	g^{wh}
		s		
Resonants:	m	n		
	w	r	l	y
Vowels:		e	a	o $_c$
	i·	e·	a·	o· u·
Laryngeals:		x	γ	h ʔ

There are many differences between Lehmann's system and that of Brugmann. Note in particular the postulation of only one fricative, *s*, the lack of phonemic palatals, diphthongs, voiceless aspirates and shwa. These were all given alternative analyses, partly based on the four laryngeals which Lehmann assumed.

Recent criticisms of the Lehmann system (and others of its generation) centre on the typological naturalness of the overall system. While faithful to the comparative method, such a system seems to be in conflict with known patterns of phonological structure in attested languages. One problem lies in

Table 1.6: Szemerényi's Reconstructed System

Obstruents:	p	p^h	b	b^h
	t	t^h	d	d^h
	(k′	k'^h	g′	g'^h?)
	k	k^h	g	g^h
	k^w	k^{wh}	g^w	g^{wh}
	s	h		
Resonanants:	y	w		
	m	n		
	l			
	r			

Syllabic Liquids and Nasals: ņ   m̦   ņ̄   m̦̄
                                l̥   r̥   l̥̄   r̥̄

Vowels and Diphthongs:

i		u	ī		ū			
e ə o			ē	ō		ei	oi	eu ou
a			ā				ai	au

One to three laryngeals

the presence of the voiced aspirate stops without a corresponding series of voiceless aspirates. A principle of typological inference stipulates that the presence of a marked member of a correlative pair implies the presence of the unmarked member of that pair. Thus *bh* ⊃ *ph*. And as T. Gamkrelidze puts it (1981:591): 'Reconstructed systems should be characterized by the same regularities which are found in any historical system.'

Partly in response to such objections (which had been voiced earlier by both Jakobson and Martinet), O. Szemerényi proposed the system in table 1.6 (1980:142). Pursuing the dicta of typological structure and dependency, many scholars have recently begun a new approach to Indo-European sound structure. The focus of the new work has been the obstruent system of Proto-Indo-European, which has long presented problems to Indo-European scholars. Chief among the problems are the following:

(a) The traditional system without voiceless aspirates is in violation of certain markedness principles. But the solution of Szemerényi (and the Neogrammarians) to have a voiceless aspirated series only begs the question, since only one language (Sanskrit) has the four-way distinction of voiced/voiceless, aspirated/unaspirated. Thus the elaborate Proto-Indo-European system seems to rely far too heavily on Sanskrit, and is unjustified for the other groups.

(b) There has always been a problem with **b*. It is extremely rare, and those few examples which point to **b* (e.g. Lith. *dubùs*, Go. *diups* 'deep') are by no means secure.

(c) There are complicated restrictions on the cooccurrence of obstruents in Proto-Indo-European roots (called 'morpheme' or 'root structure' conditions) which are only imperfectly handled with traditional reconstructions. They are that a root cannot begin and end with a plain voiced stop, and a root cannot begin with a plain voiceless stop and end with a voiced aspirate, or vice versa.

(d) Plain voiced stops as traditionally reconstructed almost never occur in reconstructed inflectional affixes, in which Proto-Indo-European was rich. This is a distributional irregularity which canot be explained under the traditionally reconstructed system.

(e) It has long been a curiosity to Indo-European scholars that both Germanic and Armenian underwent similar obstruent shifts (the Germanic one came to be celebrated as 'Grimm's Law', and forms the backbone of much pre- and post-Neogrammarian thinking on sound change):

'Grimm's Law' and the Armenian Consonant Shift

PIE					Gmc.				Arm.			
*p	t	k	k^w	>	f	þ	h	h^w	h(w)	th	s	kh
*b	d	g	g^w	>	p	t	k	k^w/k	p	t	c	k
*bh	dh	gh	gh^w	>	b	d	g	g^w/g	b	d	z(j)	g

In the new reconstruction of the obstruent system, the pattern in the occlusives is based on a three-way distinction of voiceless stops/voiced aspirates/glottalised stops (see Hopper 1981, Gamkrelidze 1981, Gamkrelidze and Ivanov 1984). The traditional plain voiced stops are now interpreted as glottalised stops (ejectives).

Typologically Reconstructed Obstruents

	I *Glottalised*	*II* *Voiced Aspirates/* *Voiced Stops*	*III* *Voiceless Aspirates/* *Voiceless Stops*
Labial	(p')	b^h/b	p^h/p
Dental	t'	d^h/d	t^h/t
Velar	k'	g^h/g	k^h/k
Labio-velar	k'^{w}	g^{wh}/g^w	k^{wh}/k^w

The allophonic distribution of these segments has been a matter of some debate, and indeed each Indo-European language seems to have generalised one allophone or another, or split allophones, according to differing circumstances.

This new system provides phonetically natural solutions to the five problems posed above:

(a) The system with the three-way distinction above violates no naturalness condition or typological universal. In fact, it is a system found in modern Armenian dialects. Under this view, Indo-Iranian is an innovator, not a relic area.

(b) The near absence of **b* now finds a simple solution. In systems employing glottalised stops, the labial member is the most marked. Thus this gap, unexplained by traditional views, is no longer anomalous.

(c) The complicated morpheme structure restrictions turn out to be fairly simple: two glottalised stops cannot occur in the same root; furthermore, root sounds must agree in voicing value.

(d) The absence of plain voiced stops in inflections turns out to be an absence of glottalics in the new reconstruction. Such a situation is typologically characteristic of highly marked phonemes such as glottalised sounds (Hopper 1981:135).

(e) Under the new system the parallel Germanic and Armenian consonant 'shifts' turn out to reflect archaisms rather than innovations. All the other groups have undergone fairly regular phonological changes which can be efficiently derived from the system just outlined.

As Bomhard has insightfully pointed out (1984), we must recognise different periods in the development of the various Indo-European groups.

Thus any attempt to arrive at an airtight, uniform reconstruction of Proto-Indo-European fails to recognise the unevenness of the records and the fact that some of the languages undoubtedly split off from Proto-Indo-European long before others did. This is especially true with Hittite, whose extreme archaism suggests that if it is not a 'sister' of Proto-Indo-European, it is at least a daughter that split off from Proto-Indo-European long before the latter started to disintegrate. It is for these reasons that Proto-Indo-European phonology continues to be a matter of debate.

3.1.2 Ablaut

In the oldest stages of Proto-Indo-European, verbs and probably nouns as well were differentiated in their various classes by a modification of the root-vowel rather than by the addition of suffixes to invariant bases, which we find predominating in later stages of the language. This type of vowel modification or alternation is known as 'ablaut' or 'vowel gradation'.

Vowel gradation patterns were based on the interplay of both vowel quality (qualitative ablaut) and vowel quantity or length (quantitative ablaut). The main alternations were between the basic root-vowel, usually *e*, called the 'normal grade', alternating with *o* ('*o*-grade'), zero (Ø) ('zero-grade') and lengthening plus change (lengthened *ō*-grade). In what follows I will treat the two ablaut types separately, though it should be emphasised that this is one system, not two. They are separated here because the daughter languages typically generalised either the qualitative or quantitative system, or eliminated ablaut altogether.

Qualitative Ablaut

The primary qualitative relations were based on the vowels $e \sim o \sim \emptyset$ ($ei \sim oi \sim i; er \sim or \sim r̥; en \sim on \sim n̥$, etc.). Different forms of a morpheme were represented by different ablaut grades. This system is rather well

	e-grade		*o-grade*		*Ø-grade*	
Gk.	pét-omai	'I fly'	pot-é	'flight'	e-pt-ómēn	'I flew'
Gk.	ékh-ō	'I have'	ókhos	'carriage'	é-skh-on	'I had'
Lat.	sed-eō	'I sit'	sol-ium (<*sod-ium)	'throne'		
Lat.	reg-ō	'I rule'	rog-us(?)	'funeral-pyre'		
Lat.	teg-ō	'I cover'	toga	'a covering'		
Gk.	leíp-ō	'I leave'	lé-loip-a	'I left'	é-lip-on	'I left'
Lat.	fīdō (<*feidō)	'I trust'	foedus	'agreement'	fidēs	'trust'
Gk.	peíth-ō	'I persuade'	pé-poith-a	'I trust'	é-pith-on	'I persuaded'
Gk.	dérk-omai	'I see'	dé-dork-a	'I saw'	é-drak-on	'I saw'
Gk.	pénth-os	'grief'	pé-ponth-a	'I suffered'	é-path-on	'I suffered'

represented in Greek, but is recoverable in nearly every Indo-European language to one degree or another. (Note: $e \sim o \sim \emptyset$ alternation is not the only series, nor does this account consider the many interactions between vowel length and quality.)

Quantitative Ablaut

Quantitative ablaut patterns are based on the alternations of 'normal', 'lengthened', and 'reduced' varieties of a vowel, e.g. $o : \bar{o} : \emptyset; e : \bar{e} : \emptyset; a : \bar{a} : \emptyset$. While represented vestigially in a wide number of Indo-European languages, (cf. Lat. *pēs*, gen. *pedis* 'foot'; *vōx* 'voice, *vocō* 'I call'; Gk. *patér*, *patrós* (gen.), *patéra* (acc.) 'father'), the quantitative system is most systematically represented in Sanskrit. This is the system which the Indian grammarians described in terms of *guṇa* and *vṛddhi* increments (though in a different order). Quantitive vowel alternation, in conjunction with the qualitative type, provided an important means of morphological marking in Proto-Indo-European, providing a basis for distinguishing different grammatical representations of a morpheme.

Normal Grade (=guṇa)	Lengthened Grade (=vṛddhi)	Reduced Grade
pát-ati 'he falls'	*pāt*-áyati 'he causes to fall'	pa*pt*-imá 'we fell'
kar-tr̥- 'doer'	*kār*-yá 'business'	*kr̥*-tá- 'done'
deś-á- (*e < ai*) 'region'	*daiś*-ika- (*ai < āi*) 'local'	*díś*- 'region, direction'

3.1.3 Accent

Because of the widely different accentual patterns found in the daughter languages, reconstructing the accent of Proto-Indo-European is a hazardous undertaking. Developments in all the descendant groups except for Sanskrit and Greek seem to be innovative, thus forcing us to rely heavily on our interpretations of accent in these two languages.

The best accounts of Proto-Indo-European accent suggest that it was a pitch accent system. Every word (except clitics, which were unaccented) had one and only one accented syllable which received high pitch accent. The accent was 'free' in that it could fall on any syllable in a word, its specific position being conditioned by morphological considerations; accent was one means of marking grammatical categories in Proto-Indo-European. (For a parallel, cf. Eng. *rébel* (n.): *rebél* (v.); *cónflict* (n.): *conflíct* (v.).)

For example, some noun cases are typically accented on the inflections, while others are accented on the root for 'foot'. Here we see that the nominative and accusative cases, the so-called 'strong cases', have root accent, while the genitive and dative (and instrumental) have inflectional accent, indicating that accent is interacting with case markers to indicate grammatical function.

Root/Inflectional Accent (Nouns)

	Gk.	Skt.
nom.	poús	pā́t
acc.	póda	pā́dam
gen.	podós	padás (gen./abl.)
dat.	podí	padé
		padí (loc.)

Similarly, some verbal forms are accented on roots, some on inflections:

Root/Inflectional Accent (Verbs)

	Pres.	Perf.	Perf. Pl.	Part.
Skt. 'turn'	vártāmi	vavárta	vavṛtimá	vṛtanáḥ
OE 'become'	weorþe	wearþ	wurdon	worden

The original nature of the Sanskrit accent in the various morphological categories is confirmed by the evidence of Germanic, which, though it has root-initial accent throughout, treated certain obstruent forms differently (þ, ð (d)) depending on whether the accent originally preceded (þ) or followed (ð (d)) the sound in question (Verner's Law). For further evidence, cf. the following forms for 'point out, show':

Skt. didéśa (1st sg. perf.): OE tāh OHG zeh (<*dedóika)
    didiśimá (1st pl. perf.):   tigon zigum (<*dedikıné)

3.2 Morphology

As we mentioned in the preceding discussion, the unevenness of historical records and huge chronological gaps among many of the languages (e.g. 3,000 years between Hittite and Lithuanian) pose special problems for the reconstruction of phonology. These same problems exist in the reconstruction of morphology, perhaps even more dramatically because of the much larger inventory of morphological elements. Many of the older, well-documented languages, especially Latin, Greek and Sanskrit, have very complex morphologies: they have well-developed case systems in nouns, adjectives and pronouns; they have finely marked gender and number categories with fixed concord relations. In the verb they have elaborate systems of tense, voice, mood and aspect, as well as number markers and even gender concord in some forms, all marked with complex morphological formatives.

Many Indo-European languages reflect this complex morphology to one degree or another: Baltic, Slavonic, Celtic, Armenian and, in part, Tocharian, in addition to Latin, Greek and Sanskrit. But many of the other languages of which we have adequate records show much less morphological complexity, with fewer formal categories and distinctions; and it is not only the modern ones. Hittite, Germanic, Tocharian (in part) and Albanian do not agree with the other groups in morphological complexity.

What does the analyst do? Traditionally, scholars have reconstructed the largest composite system which the data allow. Thus reconstructed Proto-Indo-European has assumed all the features of the attested languages. When a particular language shows a given feature, this is evidence for the prior existence of that feature. And when a given language does not show that feature, it is assumed that the feature has been lost, or that it has merged with another feature in that language. This preference for over-differentiated proto-systems reflects a methodological bias on the part of linguists (and not only Indo-Europeanists) to postulate rules of loss or deletion from full forms rather than to assume rules of accretion or addition from impoverished forms. In short, it is easier to assume a specific something and make it disappear than it is to assume nothing and specify when it develops into a specific something.

The fact is that the highly complex morphological systems of Sanskrit, Greek, Latin, Baltic and Slavonic must have come from somewhere! There is no justifiable reason to assume that Proto-Indo-European emerged full-blown with no history of its own. We must keep this in mind as we proceed.

3.2.1   Nominal and Pronominal Morphology
Traditionally, Proto-Indo-European is considered to be an inflecting language which uses case markers to indicate grammatical relations between nominal elements and other words in a sentence, and to indicate gender and number agreement between words in phrases. Of all the Indo-European languages, Sanskrit has the most detailed nominal morphology. It has eight cases (nominative, vocative, accusative, genitive, ablative, dative, locative and instrumental), three genders (masculine, feminine and neuter), and three numbers (singular, plural and dual). No other Indo-European language has such detailed nominal morphology: Old Church Slavonic, Lithuanian and (by some accounts) Old Armenian have seven cases, and Latin has six. But Greek, Old Irish and Albanian have only five; Germanic has only four, and Hittite may have had as few as four. In gender categories most of the groups have the three mentioned above, but Hittite and a few others have no such system, nor is there any reason to believe they ever did. The same is true with number: Sanskrit, Greek and Old Irish, for example, show the three-way singular/plural/dual distinction, and there are apparent relics of it in Latin and Hittite. Do we assume that it was lost in those groups which do not show it, or do we assume that it never developed in those languages?

This is not the place to debate the history of Indo-European noun inflection or the philosophy of reconstruction. So, following Shields (1981) we will give a brief chronological overview of what *might* have been the developmental stages in the prehistory of Proto-Indo-European. In this way one might be able to imagine how various languages might have broken off from the main stock during the formation of Proto-Indo-European. We must not think of Proto-Indo-European as a single monolithic entity, uniform and dialect-free, which existed at a certain time in a single place before it began to disintegrate. Rather, we must recognise that this language was itself the product of millennia of development. As Ivanov puts it (1965:51):

> Within the limits of the case systems of the Indo-European languages it is possible to distinguish chronological layers of various epochs beginning with the pre-inflectional in certain forms of the locative and in compound words ... right up to the historical period when the case systems were being formed ... Between these two extreme points one must assume a whole series of intermediate points. (Quoted from Schmalstieg 1980:46.)

Shields postulates the following five stages in the development of Proto-Indo-European:

Stage I. In this, the formative period of the language, Proto-Indo-European might have been an isolating language, like Chinese, in which words were monosyllabic roots and there was no complex morphology. At this point there was probably no distinction between nouns and verbs, and no agreement or concord. The lack of agreement or concord in compounds like Gk. *akrópolis* (not *akrápolis*) 'high or upper city' and *logopoiós* (not *logompoiós*) 'prose-writer' attests to this stage. Gender was based on a distinction between animate, inanimate and natural agents.

Stage II. During this period Proto-Indo-European became an ergative system, i.e. one in which the subject of a transitive verb is in a different case from the subject of an intransitive verb, and in which the object of a transitive verb is in the same case as the subject of an intransitive verb (in English it would be something like *I* (subject) *see* (trans.) *her* (object), but *her* (subject) *falls* (intrans.)). Evidence for this stage comes from noun inflection patterns in different gender categories in various languages, as well as occasional irregular subject patterns in some languages in which oblique cases serve as subjects. At this time there were only two cases, the agent case in *∅ or *r, and the absolutive case in *N. Through the development of a concord relationship between verbal suffixes and noun suffixes, Proto-Indo-European starts to develop into a nominative/accusative language.

Stage III. The oblique cases start to develop, primarily from the fusion of adverbs and particles onto noun stems. Nominative and vocative functions become generalised, and gender distinctions start to develop. As the ergative marker develops into a generalised subject marker, the language changes into a nominative/accusative type, where the subjects of transitive and intransitive verbs are the same (cf. Eng. *He sees Bill*: *He falls*).

Stage IV. Dative, instrumental, locative and genitive/ablative functions start to emerge as separate entities. The dual number starts to develop, and the gender distinction (found in Hittite) based on the animate/inanimate distinction first appears. Gender and number agreement within phrases as well as concord between nouns and verbs becomes fixed. This is now close to traditionally reconstructed Proto-Indo-European.

Stage V. This is a period of highly accelerated dialect division, and the beginning of the disintegration of Proto-Indo-European. New endings and formal markers develop within various groups, with formal and functional differentiations of case forms. The feminine gender emerges.

The preceding summary, based on Shields's 1981 speculations, provides us with a brief but provocative account of the prehistory of Proto-Indo-European. We will now proceed to a discussion of the traditional system as reconstructed in the nineteenth and twentieth centuries. This system represents one, surely very late, stage of Proto-Indo-European from which some, but not all of the daughter languages descended. In this context it has validity as the most probable system based on the comparative method.

Proto-Indo-European nouns and adjectives were inflected in three genders, three numbers and eight cases. Through a comparison of the various languages we arrive at the following reconstruction of case endings (Szemerényi 1980:146):

Reconstructed Case Endings

	Sg.	Pl.	Du.
Nom.	-s, -∅	-es	
Voc.	-∅	-es	-e, -ī/-i
Acc.	-m/-m̥	-ns/-n̥s	
Gen.	-es/-os/-s	-om/-ōm	-ous? -ōs?
Abl.	-es/-os/-s; -ed/-od	-bh(y)os, -mos	-bhyō, -mō
Dat.	-ei	-bh(y)os, -mos	-bhyō, -mō
Loc.	-i	-su	-ou
Inst.	-e/-o, -bhi/-mi	-bhis/-mis, -ōis	-bhyō, -mō

These endings represent a composite set of possibilities for the Proto-Indo-European noun; no single form reflects them all. The structure of the noun was based on the following scheme: a *root*, which carried the basic lexical meaning, plus a *stem*, which marked morphological class, plus an *ending*, which carried grammatical information based on syntactic function. Thus a word like Lat. nom. sg. m. *lupus* (OLat. *lupos*) 'wolf' would be *lup + o + s*. Generally we recognise consonantal and vocalic stem nouns. Some examples of consonantal stems are **ped* 'foot' (Skt. *pád-*, Gk. (gen.) *podós*, Lat. (gen.) *pedis*); **edont-/*dont-/*dent-* 'tooth' (Skt. *dánt-*, Gk. (gen.) *odóntos*, Lat. (gen.) *dentis*); **ĝhom-* 'man' (Lat. *homo*, Go. *guma*); **māter* 'mother' (Skt. *mātár-*, Gk. *mḗtēr*, Lat. *māter*); **gonos/*genos-* 'race' (Skt.

(gen.) *jánasas*, Gk. (gen.) *géneos* (< *génesos*), Lat. (gen.) *generis* (< *genesis*)).

To illustrate some of the vocalic stems we may cite the *i*-stem form *egnis/ *ognis* 'fire' (Skt. *agní-*, Lat. *ignis*) or *potis* 'master' (Skt. *páti-*, Gk. *pósis*, Lat. *potis*); an *-eu-* diphthongal stem like *dyeu-* 'sky, light' (Skt. nom. *dyāús*, Gk. *Zeús*, Lat. *diēs, -diūs*); and finally the *o*-stem *wĺkʷos* 'wolf ' (Skt. *vŕ̥ka-*, Gk. *lúkos*, Lat. *lupus*).

The Proto-Indo-European adjective followed the same declensional pattern as the noun. Adjectives were inflected for gender, number and case, in agreement with the nouns which they modified. Some adjectives are inflected in masculine, feminine and neuter according to m. *-o* stem, f. *-ā* stem and nt. *-om* patterns, as in *newos*, *newā*, *newom* 'new' (cf. Skt. *návas*, *návā*, *návam*, Gk. *né(w)os*, *né(w)ā*, *né(w)on*, Lat. *novus, nova, novum*). Other adjectival forms have identical masculine and feminine forms, but separate neuter (cf. Lat. *facilis, facile* 'easy'), and still others have all three identical in some cases (cf. Lat. *ferens* 'carrying' (< *ferentis*)).

Adjectives were compared in three degrees, as in English *tall, taller, tallest*. Comparative forms are typically derived from positive forms through the suffixation of *-yes*, *-yos* (cf. Lat. *seniōr* 'older' (*senex*), Skt. *sánya* 'older' (*sána-*), and with *-tero-* (cf. Gk. *ponērós* 'wicked', comp. *ponēróteros*). Superlatives are often found with the suffixes *-isto-* and *-samo-*, though there are others. Some examples: Gk. *béltistos*, Go. *batista* 'best', Skt. *náviṣṭha-* 'newest' (*náva-*). For *-samo-*, cf. Lat. *proximus* 'nearest', *maximus* 'greatest', OIr. *nessam* 'next'. As with Gk. *béltistos*, Go. *batista*, adjectival comparison was occasionally carried out with suppletive forms, cf. Lat. *bonus, melior, optimus* 'good, better, best'.

Proto-Indo-European distinguished many different types of pronouns. A short sample of personal pronouns is given in table 1.2. Pronouns followed the same general inflectional patterns as nouns, though they have their own set of endings for many of the case forms, except personal pronouns, which are almost entirely different from nouns and did not mark gender. In addition to the personal pronouns 'I/we', 'you/you' (*eĝ(h)om, eĝṓ/*wei, *n̥smés; *tū, *tu/*yūs, *usmés*), Proto-Indo-European also had demonstrative pronouns with the form (m.) *so*, (f.) *sā*, (nt.) *tod* and *is, *ī, *id*. These also served the function of third person pronouns in many of the Indo-European languages. The first of these is represented in Skt. *sa, sā, tad*, Go. *sa, so, þata* and Gk. *ho, hē, tó*. The latter Proto-Indo-European demonstrative forms are represented in Lat. *is, ea, id* and in various forms in Sanskrit and Germanic such as Skt. nom. sg. nt. *id-ám*, acc. sg. m. *im-ám*, f. *im-ā́m*, and Go. acc. sg. *in-a*, nom. pl. m. *eis*, acc. pl. *ins*.

Interrogative and relative pronouns are also well represented, though it is not possible to reconstruct a single relative. From a PIE (anim.) *kʷis*, (inanim.) *kʷid*, which had either interrogative or indefinite meaning, we find Lat. *quis, quis, quid*, Gk. *tís, tís, tí*, Hitt. *kwis, kwit*, Skt. *kás, kā́, kim*, and a number of variants of this stem with interrogative or indefinite meaning. In Italic, Tocharian, Hittite, Celtic and Germanic the root *k^wis, *k^wid also functioned as a relative pronoun (as does Eng. *who*). In Indo-Iranian, Greek and Slavonic a different form *yos, *$yā$, *yod served the relative function (cf. Skt. *yás*, *yá̄*, *yád*, Gk. *hós*, *hḗ*, *hó*). There is also a recoverable reflexive form *sew-, *sw (OCS *sę*, Lat. *se*, Go. *si-k*).

3.2.2   Verb Morphology

The Proto-Indo-European verb presents the analyst with many of the same problems as the noun. The various daughter languages show wide variation in formal categories and inflectional complexity; some of the ancient classical languages, especially Greek, Latin and Sanskrit, have highly diversified formal structure characterised by intricate relations of tense, mood, voice and aspect. Others, like Hittite and Germanic, have fairly simple morphological systems with few formal distinctions. We can contrast formal complexity by the following simple chart.

Verbal Categories

	Voices	Moods	Tenses
Greek	3	4	7
Sanskrit	3	4	7
Hittite	2	2	2
Gothic	2	3	2

As with the noun, we may take several paths to a reconstructed system. We can propose a full Proto-Indo-European system with losses and syncretisms in Hittite and Gothic, we may propose a simple Proto-Indo-European system with additive, accretionary developments in Greek and Sanskrit, or we may assume different periods of development and break-off from the parent language. Accepting this final alternative in effect prohibits us from reconstructing a single system which will underlie the others, but this is surely the most reasonable course. All we can do, then, is to present one version, surely quite late, of the Proto-Indo-European verbal system as traditionally reconstructed, recognising that many unanswered questions remain which are outside the scope of this chapter.

The classical reconstruction of the Proto-Indo-European verbal system posits two voices, four moods and from three to six tenses. In addition, there were person and number suffixes and a large number of derivational formatives by which additional categories were formed. The verb structure is as follows:

Voice refers to the relationship of the subject to the activity defined by the verb, i.e. whether the subject is agent, patient or both. In Proto-Indo-European there were two voices, active and medio-passive. An active verb is one in which the subject is typically the agent, but is not directly affected by the action (e.g. *John called Bill*). Medio-passive is a mixed category which includes the function of middle (= reflexive) and passive. When the subject of the verb is both the agent and the patient, the verb is in the middle voice (e.g. Gk. *ho paîs loúetai* 'the boy washes himself', Skt *yájate* 'he makes a sacrifice for himself'). When the subject of the verb is the patient, but there is a different agent, the verb is in the passive voice (e.g. Gk. *ho paîs loúetai hupò tês mētrós* 'the boy is washed by his mother'). In general, the various Indo-European languages generalised either the middle or the passive function from the Proto-Indo-European medio-passive. For example, in Sanskrit the middle function dominates, the passive being late and secondary. In Greek the middle and passive are morphologically identical in all but the future and aorist tenses, with the middle dominating. Italic and Celtic have mostly passive use, though there are ample relics of the middle in deponent verbs like Lat. *loquitur* 'he speaks', OIr. *-labrathar* 'who speaks', as well as Lat. *armor* 'I arm myself', Lat. *congregor* 'I gather myself', and others. Germanic has no traces of the middle, and Hittite has a medio-passive with largely middle function.

Mood describes the manner in which a speaker makes the statement identified by the verb, i.e. whether he believes it is a fact, wishes it, doubts it or orders it. In Proto-Indo-European there were probably four moods: indicative, optative, conjunctive (known more commonly as subjunctive), and imperative. With the indicative mood the speaker expresses statements of fact. Indicative is sometimes marked by a vowel suffix (thematic class) and sometimes not (athematic class), e.g. Skt. *rud-á-ti*, Lat. *rud-e-t* 'he cries' (thematic); Skt. *ás-ti*, Lat. *es-t* 'he is' (athematic). The optative mood is used when the speaker expresses a wish or desire, and is also marked by a vowel which depends on the vowel in the indicative, e.g. OLat. *siet*, Gk. *eíē*, Skt. *syát* 'let him be'. The conjunctive is used when the speaker is expressing doubt, exhortation or futurity. Its theme vowel depends on the vowel of the verb in the indicative, though it is commonly with *e/o* ablaut. Some examples are Lat. *erō* 'I will be', *agam, agēs* 'I, you will/might drive', Gk. *íomen* 'let us go'. The final mood is the imperative, which is used when the speaker is' issuing a command. The imperative was formed from the bare verbal stem, without a mood-marking vowel as with the other three. Imperatives are most common in the second person, though they are found in the first and third as well. Examples are (second person) Gk. *phére*, Skt. *bhára*, Lat. *fer* 'carry' (sg.) and *phérete, bhárata, ferte* (pl.). There were other imperative suffixes as well which need not concern us here.

Tense refers to the time of the action identified by the verb. The original Proto-Indo-European verb was probably based on aspectual rather than temporal relations (aspect refers to the type of activity, e.g. momentary, continuous, iterative, etc.), but traditionally these have been interpreted as tenses. We usually identify three tense stems, the present, the aorist and the perfect. The present identifies repeated and continuing actions or actions going on in the present (= imperfective aspect): Lat. *sum*, Gk. *eimí*, Skt. *ásmi* 'I am', or Lat. *fert*, Gk. *phérei*, Skt. *bhárati* 'he carries'. The aorist stem (= perfective aspect) marks actions that did or will take place only once, e.g. Gk. *égnōn* 'I recognised', Skt. *ádāt* 'he gave', Gk. *édeikse* 'he showed', Skt. *ánaiṣam* 'I led'. The final stem is the perfect stem (= stative aspect), which describes some state pertaining to the subject of the verb. Examples are Skt. *véda*, Gk. *oîda*, Go. *wáit* 'I know'.

The exact internal structure of the various tense systems is extremely complicated. A number of formal types exist, including stems characterised by ablaut, reduplication, prefixation (augment), infixation and a wide variety of derivational suffixes. An interesting fact is that though tense was not directly and explicitly marked in Proto-Indo-European, most of the daughter languages generalised tense as the defining characteristic of their respective verbal systems.

In addition to the tense, voice and mood categories, the Proto-Indo-European verb carried at the end of the verbal structure a set of endings which indexed first, second or third person and singular, plural or dual number. There were different sets of endings for different voices, tense stems and moods. Here we list only the principal 'primary' and 'secondary' endings; they are identical except for the final *-i*, an earlier particle which marks the primary endings. These endings were originally used with specific tenses and moods, but have been largely generalised in the daughter languages.

Verbal Endings

	Primary	Secondary
1st sg.	-mi (Skt. bhárāmi)	-m (Lat. sum)
2nd sg.	-si (Skt. bhárasi)	-s (OLat. ess)
3rd sg.	-ti (Skt. bhárati)	-t (Lat. est)
3rd pl.	-nti (Skt. bháranti)	-nt (Lat. sunt)

We can schematise the overall structure of the Proto-Indo-European verb as follows:

The Structure of the Indo-European Verb

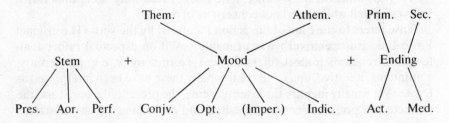

A few examples:

Lat.	am	ā	s	'you love'	(Pres. indic. 2nd pers. sg. act.)
	am	ē	s	'you might love'	(Pres. subj. 2nd pers. sg. act.)
	am	ā	ris	'you are loved'	(Pres. indic. 2nd pers. sg. pass.)
	am	ē	ris	'you might be loved'	(Pres. subj. 2nd pers. sg. pass.)
Gk.	paideú	ei	s	'you teach'	(Pres. indic. 2nd pers. sg. act.)
	paideú	ē	s	'you might teach'	(Pres. subj. 2nd pers. sg. act.)
	paideú	oi	s	'may you teach'	(Pres. opt. 2nd pers. sg. act.)
Skt.	bhár	a	ti	'he carries'	(Pres. indic. 3rd pers. sg. act.)
	á neṣ		vahi	'we two led ourselves'	(Aor. indic. 1st pers. du. mid.)
	sunu		yắma	'we might press'	(Pres. opt. 1st pers. pl. act.)

Besides the finite verb forms which we have been discussing, Proto-Indo-European also made use of a number of derivative forms which were non-finite, i.e. they did not stand as independent tensed predications. We include here a number of infinitive forms, which were originally noun forms in various oblique cases (mostly accusative and dative) and became reanalysed as part of the verbal system: cf. Skt. *dātum* (acc.), *dātavē* (dat.) 'to give'. There were also participial formations represented in most of the languages from Proto-Indo-European formations in *-nt- (e.g. Go. *bairands*, Skt. *bháran-*, Lat. *ferens* 'carrying'), as well as others in *-wes- (cf. Skt. *vidvás-* 'knowing'), *meno- (cf. Gk. *hepómenos* 'following'), and *-to- (cf. Lat. *amātus* 'loved'). These secondary formations, as well as a number of others such as gerunds, gerundives, supines and other verbal nouns, are widely represented and used throughout the Indo-European family.

3.3 Syntax

The reconstruction of syntax has lagged far behind the reconstruction of the phonological, morphological and lexical structures of Proto-Indo-European. This is initially surprising in light of the central role played by syntax and syntactic theory in modern linguistics. There are many reasons for this lag. Among them are the following:

(a) The lack of native speakers. Modern linguistics draws its data from the speech and intuitions of native speakers, but of course a reconstructed language has no such data source.

(b) The abstractness of syntax. Phonological, morphological and lexical units are far more concrete units than rules or patterns of syntax. Fewer theoretical notions are required in order to isolate concrete units, whereas in syntax, nothing exists pretheoretically. Syntax is an abstract set of principles, requiring abstract theories before even data organisation can begin.

(c) The structure of the descendant languages. The Indo-European daughter languages are of a highly inflecting type, and carry out a great deal of their 'syntax' in morphological expressions. Consider the difference between (1) and (2) in English:

(1) The boy sees the girl.
(2) The girl sees the boy.

The Latin equivalents to these sentences can have the words arranged in any order without affecting the agent/patient relations:

(1′) i Puer puellam videt.
     Boy   girl   sees
   ii Puellam puer videt.
     Girl   boy   sees
   iii Videt puer puellam.
     Sees   boy   girl
           etc.

(2′) i Puella puerum videt.
     Girl   boy   sees
   ii Puerum puella videt.
     Boy   girl   sees
   iii Videt puella puerum.
     Sees   girl   boy
           etc.

From these few examples we can readily see that the morphology/syntax division in inflected languages is quite a different matter from the same division in a language like English.

(d) The data. The Indo-European languages on which the reconstruction of Proto-Indo-European is based are simply not uniform enough to allow a straightforward account of syntactic patterns. The problem is no greater, and no less, than that found in phonology and morphology.

We will move now to a brief and highly selective review of some major features of Proto-Indo-European syntax. Because the citation of examples is extremely complicated, I will limit the data to the bare minimum.

3.3.1 Word Order

Late Proto-Indo-European was most likely a subject–object–verb (SOV) language with attendant adjective + noun (*good boy*), genitive + noun (*John's hat*), standard + marker + adjective (*John than bigger*) order, postpositions (*the world over*), and the preposing of relative clauses (*the who I saw man*). The reconstruction of these structural patterns is based on principles of typological inference developed largely by W. Lehmann (e.g. 1974), who extended the concepts of word order harmony formulated by J. Greenberg (1963) to historical syntax. According to these principles, there are major structural configurations in languages which are harmonious or compatible with each other. They take the form of statements like the following: if a language has some property P, then it will also have some property Q. For example, if a language is SOV in its basic sentence pattern, it will also have postpositions; if it is SVO, it will have prepositions.

Lehmann has put such 'implicational universals' to work in the reconstruction of Proto-Indo-European word order patterns. For example, Hittite, Vedic Sanskrit and Tocharian are SOV; Latin is predominantly SOV (Homeric Greek is apparently alternately SVO/SOV). Concentrating on Hittite, we find that it has postpositions and adjective + noun order, and dominant genitive + noun and relative clause + noun order. This seems to be ample evidence for an SOV Proto-Indo-European, a conclusion which is augmented by the existence of SOV-harmonic forms in otherwise SVO languages like relic postpositions in Slavonic and Baltic, as well as large numbers of formulaic postpositions in the Italic languages which, though they are mostly SOV, become SVO by the time of Vulgar Latin. The archaic-like nature of the frozen postpositions in Latin *mēcum* 'with me', *tēcum* 'with you' (not *cum mē, *cum tē*, as expected; cf. *cum puellā* 'with the girl') or English expressions like *the world over* can be taken as evidence for early SOV structure, even in languages which show a move toward SVO structures. Discovering such patterns and drawing inferences for reconstruction depends crucially on the assumption that such marked structures as the Latin postpositions are indeed archaisms and not innovations.

There has been much criticism of the typological approach to syntax. For one thing, it has been noted that inflected languages have much freer word order possibilities than do languages like English, which rely on word order for marking grammatical function. According to this view, the word order issue is a false one, since word order serves mainly secondary functions like marking topic or focus relations

Another problem with the typological approach is the fact that the pure types are very rare (in the Indo-European family only Celtic is consistent, and it is VSO!). But the typological method has a built-in escape: languages which are internally inconsistent, like English with its SVO but adjective + noun structures, are said to be in transition from one type to another; the process is not yet complete. This begs the issue, because languages are always in such a transitional state. In other words, Greenberg's observations should be regarded as interesting tendencies and frequentalia, and should not be elevated to the status of explanatory devices. Furthermore, there is ample evidence that such implicational universals do not serve as reliable predictors of future syntactic change in a language.

Finally there is the matter of method. Typological inferences often are based on data being used in two directions, viz. if a language is SOV, one expects postpositions. And if a language is SVO but a stray postposition is found, one assumes that it must have been SOV at one time. There is also the issue of 'marked' vs. 'unmarked' structures. Determining that a language is SOV or SVO when both are present in the data requires a judgement that one of the structures is more natural, more basic, more regular than the other. The problem with ancient languages with no native speakers is that judgements about marked/unmarked structures often reduce to simple frequency counts, and this is not adequate.

3.3.2   Ergative–Nominative/Accusative Structure

It is clear from the daughter languages that late Proto-Indo-European was of the nominative/accusative type. That is, the agent of the verb was inflected in the nominative case, and the patient or goal was inflected in the accusative: cf. Lat. *Marc-us amat puell-am* 'Marcus loves the girl'. But as we saw in our discussion of early Proto-Indo-European noun morphology, there is significant evidence that Proto-Indo-European was at one time of the ergative type, i.e. a language in which the subject of a transitive verb is in a different case from the subject of an intransitive verb. There are many instances throughout the early Indo-European languages of agents in the genitive case: cf. OArm. *ēr nora* (gen.) *hraman aṙeal* 'he (of him) had received a promise', Lat. *attonitus serpentis* 'astonished by the serpent'. There are other cases where the real object of a verb of perception is in the accusative while the producer of the perceived act is in the genitive: cf. Skt. *vắcam* (acc.) *śṛṇóti* 'he hears a voice' vs. *devásya* (gen.) *śṛṇóti* 'he hears a god'. These agentive genitives may at one time have been the subjects of intransitive verbs with genitive agents, as would be found with ergative languages. As Proto-Indo-European developed its complex nominal and verbal morphology, these genitives were reinterpreted as objects of transitive verbs and are now considered simply irregular formations. Schmalstieg (esp. 1980) has found traces of ergative syntax in a number of Indo-European dialects.

3.3.3   Some Syntactic Characteristics of Proto-Indo-European

Proto-Indo-European made use of a simple phrase structure principle by which the verb was the only obligatory constituent of a sentence. The subject of the verb was in the nominative, the object in the accusative and a number of other grammatical functions were served by the remaining cases. Verb structures could be expanded with case expressions of time, place-to, place-in, place-from, goal, possession and a number of other qualifiers. Conjunction of both noun phrases and other constituents was possible, including sentence conjunction. Simple sentences could be extended by the use of cases, adverbs and particles to indicate circumstance, purpose, result or manner. Particles were used to introduce different types of clauses (e.g. subordinate, interrogative, relative, co-ordinate). The modality of a sentence, as well as tense and aspect, were expressed inflectionally, though they may have been originally marked only by particles. Finally, there is evidence for a well-developed noun-compounding system, represented chiefly by Sanskrit.

As a final note to the structure of Proto-Indo-European, it may be useful to take a brief look at a version of a reconstructed Proto-Indo-European sentence. This sentence is from Lehmann and Zgusta's (1979:462) reinterpretation of Schleicher's famous Indo-European fairy tale, which was written in 1868.

Owis	ekwōskʷe
Sheep	horses-and

Gʷərēi	owis,	kʷesyo	wl̥hnā	ne	ēst
Hill-on	sheep,	of whom	wool	not	is

ekwōns	espeket,	oinom	ghe	gʷr̥um
horses	he-saw,	one	emph. prt.	heavy

wog̑hom	weg̑hontm̥,	oinomkʷe	meg̑am
load	pulling,	one-and	great

bhorom	oinomkʷe	g̑hm̥enm̥	ōku	bherontm̥
burden	one-and	man	swiftly	carrying.

'The sheep and the horses

On a hill, a sheep which had no wool saw horses, one pulling a heavy load, one carrying a great burden and one (carrying) quickly a man.'

4 Aspects of Proto-Indo-European Culture and Civilisation

When we reconstruct a proto-language, we are by implication also reconstructing a proto-culture and civilisation. But linguistic evidence alone is not sufficient to provide a complete picture of a proto-culture; it must be supplemented by information from archaeology, history, folklore, institutions and other sources. The question 'Who were the Proto-Indo-Europeans?' has been studied ever since the Indo-European family was established. Where was their homeland, when were they a unit, and what was the nature of their culture?

Many different areas of the world have been suggested for the Proto-Indo-European homeland. Central Asia was an early favourite because of the strong Biblical tradition that this was the home of mankind; the Baltic region, Scandinavia, the Finnic area, Western Europe, the Babylonian Empire, southern Russia, the Mediterranean region and a number of other places have been advanced as possibilities. The reason such a wide variety of views exists lies not only in the complexity and ambiguity of the issues, but also in the trends of the times and the prejudices of individual investigators, many of whom have been motivated by racial or ethnic considerations rather than scientific method. For example, many of the early researchers, lacking the insights of modern anthropology, believed that the obviously strong and warlike Indo-European people could only have been blond, blue-eyed Aryans who must have originated in Northern Europe, and not Asia or the Baltic region, for example. Such a confusion of the matters of race, culture and language, fuelled by religious prejudice and scientific immaturity, produced the many speculations on the homeland issue.

A famous argument about the homeland was made by Thieme (1953, summarised in 1958). Using the word for 'salmon' *$la\hat{k}s$ (Eng. *lox* < Yiddish *laks*), Thieme argued that these fish fed only in the streams of northern Europe in the Germano-Baltic region during Indo-European times. Since *$la\hat{k}s$ is recoverable with the meaning 'salmon' in Germanic and Baltic and 'fish' in Tocharian, this distribution suggests a northern homeland. In Indo-Iranian a form Skt. *lakṣá* 'one hundred thousand' is interpreted by Thieme as an extension of the uncountable nature of a school of salmon. Thieme concludes that the existence of this root in Indo-Iranian and Tocharian, where salmon are unknown, confirms the Germano-Baltic region as the original homeland.

Thieme uses similar argumentation with the reconstructed words for 'turtle' and 'beech tree'. There is a botanical beech line where the beech flourished about 5,000 years ago, as well as an area which defines the limits of the turtle at the time. Finding these roots in a number of Indo-European languages where the physical objects are unknown suggests the north European region again.

Of course the problem with such argumentation is that the botanical evidence for the beech line of 5,000 years ago is not conclusive. Also, it is well known that speakers frequently transfer old names to new objects in a new environment, as American speakers of English have done with the word *robin*. Thus the root *bhāgo-* may have been used to designate trees other than the beech in some dialects.

This brief review provides us with some background to consider current thinking on the 'Indo-European Problem' (Mallory 1973). The most widely held view is that of M. Gimbutas, who has argued in a number of research articles (e.g. 1970) that the Proto-Indo-European people were the bearers of the so-called Kurgan or Barrow culture found in the Pontic and Volga steppes of southern Russia, east of the Dnieper River, north of the Caucasus, and west of the Ural mountains. The Kurgan culture (from Russian *kurgan* 'burial mound') is typified by the tumuli, round barrows or 'kurgans', which are raised grave structures from the Calcolithic and Early Bronze Age periods. Evidence from the Kurgan archaeological excavations gives clear evidence of animal breeding, and even the physical organisation of houses accords with the reconstructed Proto-Indo-European material. For example, Go. *waddjus* 'wall' is cognate with Skt. *vāya-* 'weaving', which reflects the wattled construction of walls excavated from the Kurgan sites.

Kurgan culture is divided into three periods, beginning in the fifth millennium BC. The Indo-Europeanisation of the Kurgan culture took place during the Kurgan II period, roughly 4000–3500 BC. Kurgan sites from this period have been found in the north Pontic region, west of the Black Sea in the Ukraine, Rumania, Yugoslavia and Eastern Hungary. During the Kurgan III period (c. 3500–3000 BC), Kurgan culture spread out across Central Europe, the entire Balkan area and into Transcaucasia, Anatolia and northern Iran. Eventually, it also spread into northern Europe and the upper Danube region. During the final period, Kurgan IV, waves of expansion carried the culture into Greece, West Anatolia and the eastern Mediterranean.

According to Gimbutas, the archaeological evidence attesting to the domesticated horse, the vehicle, habitation patterns, social structure and religion of the Kurgans is in accord with the reconstruction of Proto-Indo-European, which reflects a linguistic community from about 3000 BC.

In a recent work (Renfrew, 1987) it has been proposed that the older Indo-European languages were spoken as early as the seventh millenium BC in eastern Anatolia, and that they spread from there gradually throughout Europe through the introduction of farming. This view, which is based primarily on the archaeological record and a demographic model of processual spread, fits with the independently formulated linguistic speculations of Gamkrelidze and Ivanov (1984), who place the original Indo-Europeans in the same region, though a few millenia later.

Salient lexical items which give insight into Proto-Indo-European culture can be cited. In the remaining space we will note those items which are particularly useful in developing a view of Proto-Indo-European culture.
Physical Environment. Words for day, night, the seasons, dawn, stars, sun, moon, earth, sky, snow and rain are plainly recoverable. A number of arboreal units have been identified and successfully reconstructed. Words for horse, mouse, bear, wolf, eagle, owl, turtle, salmon, beaver, otter, dog, cattle, sheep, pig, goat, wasp, bee and louse can also be reliably postulated. It is interesting that no single word for river or ocean can be established.
Family Organisation and Social Structure. According to Friedrich (1966:29), Proto-Indo-European culture had patriarchal, patrilocal families that probably lived in small houses and adjacent huts. Villages were small, distant and presumably exogamous. There is excellent evidence for patriliny, and cross-cousin marriage was probably not permitted. Kinship terms are reconstructible for father, mother, brother, sister, son, daughter, husband's in-laws and probably grand-relatives. The word for husband means 'master' and the wife was probably 'a woman who learns through marriage'. Evidence for Proto-Indo-European patriarchal kinship comes not only from the lexicon, but also from epic songs, legal tracts and ethnological sources from the various ancient Indo-European languages.

There is widespread evidence of a word for tribal king, giving some indication that government was established.

Technology. The Indo-European languages confirm the technological advancements of the proto-culture. Evidence from farming and agricultural terms indicates small-scale farmers and husbandmen who raised pigs, knew barley, and had words for grain, sowing, ploughing, grinding, settlement and field or pasture. We can also safely reconstruct words for arrow, axe, ship, boat, gold, wagon, axle, hub and yoke, showing a rather advanced people with knowledge of worked metals and agriculture.

Religion and Law. From lexical, legal and other sources we find clear indications of a religious system among the Proto-Indo-European people. There is a word for god, and a designation for a priest; words for worship, prayer, praise, prophesy and holy give clear indications of organised religion. There is lexical evidence and evidence from ancient institutions for legal concepts such as religious law, pledge, justice and compensation.

Bibliography

General overviews of the Indo-European languages include Lockwood (1972) and Baldi (1983). Meillet (1937) is a lucid exposition of the principles of Indo-European linguistics, while Szemerényi (1980) is currently the most authoritative handbook.

For recent developments in the conception of Proto-Indo-European phonology, reference may be made to Lehmann (1952) and to the more recent suggestions by Gamkrelidze (1981) and Hopper (1981). Lehmann's often highly controversial statements on Proto-Indo-European syntax may be found in Lehmann (1974).

Pokorny (1951–9) sets the standard in Indo-European etymology and lexicography, while Buck (1951) is a resource of synonyms arranged by semantic class. For particular semantic areas in relation to Proto-Indo-European culture, see Friedrich (1966) and Thieme (1953; 1958). For the relation between the Proto-Indo-Europeans and the Kurgan culture, see Gimbutas (1970).

References

Baldi, P. 1983. *An Introduction to the Indo-European Languages* (Southern Illinois University Press, Carbondale)

Bomhard, A.R. 1984. *Toward Proto-Nostratic* (John Benjamins, Amsterdam)

Brugmann, K. 1903. *Kurze vergleichende Grammatik der indogermanischen Sprachen* (Trübner, Strassburg)

Buck, C.D. 1951. *A Dictionary of Selected Synonyms of the Principal Indo-European Languages* (University of Chicago Press, Chicago)

Friedrich, P. 1966. 'Proto-Indo-European Kinship', *Ethnology*, vol. 5, pp. 1–36

Gamkrelidze, T.V. 1981. 'Language Typology and Language Universals and Their Implications for the Reconstruction of the Indo-European Stop System', in Y.L. Arbeitman and A.R. Bomhard (eds.), *Bono Homini Donum: Essays in Historical Linguistics in Memory of J. Alexander Kerns* (John Benjamins, Amsterdam), pp. 571–609

—— and V.V. Ivanov. 1984. *Indoevropejskij jazyk i indoevropejcy* (Tbilisi State University, Tbilisi)

Gimbutas, M. 1970. 'Proto-Indo-European Culture: The Kurgan Culture During the

Fifth, Fourth, and Third Millennia B.C.', in G. Cardona, H.M. Hoenigswald and A. Senn (eds.), *Indo-European and Indo-Europeans* (University of Pennsylvania Press, Philadelphia), pp. 155–97

Greenberg, J.H. 1963. 'Some Universals of Grammar with Particular Reference to the Order of Meaningful Elements', in J.H. Greenberg (ed.), *Universals of Language* (MIT Press, Cambridge, Mass.), pp. 73–113

Hopper, P. 1981. ' "Decem" and "Taihun" Languages: An Indo-European Isogloss', in Y.L. Arbeitman and A.R. Bomhard (eds.), *Bono Homini Donum: Essays in Historical Linguistics in Memory of J. Alexander Kerns* (John Benjamins, Amsterdam), pp. 133–42

Ivanov, V.V. 1965. *Obščeindoevropejskaja, praslavjanskaja i anatolijskaja jazykovye sistemy* (Nauka, Moscow)

Kuryłowicz, J. 1927. 'ə indo-européen et ḫ hittite', in *Symbolae Grammaticae in Honorem Ioannis Rozwadowski* (Drukarnia Uniwersytetu Jagiellońskiego, Cracow), pp. 95–104.

Lehmann, W.P. 1952. *Proto-Indo-European Phonology* (University of Texas Press, Austin)

—— 1974. *Proto-Indo-European Syntax* (University of Texas Press, Austin)

—— and L. Zgusta. 1979. 'Schleicher's Tale After a Century', in Bela Brogyanyi (ed.), *Festschrift for Oswald Szemerényi on the Occasion of his 65th Birthday* (John Benjamins, Amsterdam), pp 455–66.

Lockwood, W.B. 1972. *A Panorama of Indo-European Languages* (Hutchinson University Library, London)

Mallory, J. 1973. 'A Short History of the Indo-European Problem', *Journal of Indo-European Studies*, vol. 1, pp. 21–65.

Meillet, A. 1937. *Introduction à l'étude comparative des langues indo-européennes*, 8th ed. (reprinted by University of Alabama Press, University, Alabama, 1964)

Pokorny, J. 1951–9. *Indogermanisches etymologisches Wörterbuch* (Francke, Bern and Munich)

Renfrew, C. 1987. *Archaeology and Language* (Jonathan Cape, London)

Schleicher, A. 1876. *Compendium der vergleichenden Grammatik der indogermanischen Sprachen* (Böhlau, Weimar)

Schmalstieg, W.R. 1980. *Indo-European Linguistics: A New Synthesis* (Pennsylvania State University Press, University Park)

Shields, K. 1981. *Indo-European Noun Inflection: A Developmental History* (Pennsylvania State University Press, University Park)

Szemerényi, O. 1980. *Einführung in die vergleichende Sprachwissenschaft*, 2nd ed. (Wissenschaftliche Buchgesellschaft, Darmstadt)

Thieme, P. 1953. 'Die Heimat der indogermanischen Gemeinsprache', in *Abhandlungen der geistes- und sozialwissenschaftlichen Klasse* (Akademie der Wissenschaften und Literatur, Wiesbaden), pp. 535–610

—— 1958. 'The Indo-European Language', *Scientific American*, vol. 199, no. 4, pp. 63–74

2 Germanic Languages

John A. Hawkins

The Germanic languages currently spoken fall into two major groups: North Germanic (or Scandinavian) and West Germanic. The former group comprises: Danish, Norwegian (i.e. both the Dano-Norwegian Bokmål and Nynorsk), Swedish, Icelandic, and Faroese. The latter: English (in all its varieties), German (in all its varieties, including Yiddish), Dutch (including Afrikaans) and Frisian. The varieties of English are particularly extensive and include not just the dialectal and regional variants of the British Isles, North America, Australasia, India and Africa, but also numerous English-based pidgins and creoles of the Atlantic (e.g. Jamaican Creole and Pidgin Krio) and the Pacific (e.g. Hawaiian Pidgin and Tok Pisin). When one adds to this list the regions of the globe in which Scandinavian, German and Dutch are spoken, the geographical distribution of the Germanic languages is more extensive than that of any other group of languages. In every continent there are countries in which a modern Germanic language (primarily English) is extensively used or has some official status (as a national or regional language). Demographically there is an estimated minimum of 440 million speakers of Germanic languages in the world today, divided as follows: North Germanic (including speakers in the USA), 18.55 million (Danish 5.1 million, Norwegian 4.3 million, Swedish 8.9 million, Icelandic and Faroese 250,000); West Germanic apart from English, 128.4 million (German worldwide 103 million, Dutch and Afrikaans 25 million, Frisian 400,000); English worldwide, at least 300 million (comprising at least 250 million native speakers and at least 50 million second language speakers).

There is a third group of languages within the Germanic family that needs to be recognised: East Germanic, all of whose members are now extinct. These were the languages of the Goths, the Burgundians, the Vandals, the Gepids and other tribes originating in Scandinavia that migrated south occupying numerous regions in western and eastern Europe (and even North Africa) in the early centuries of the present era. The only extensive records we have are from a fourth-century Bible translation into Gothic. The Goths had migrated from southern Sweden around the year nought into the area around what is now Gdańsk (originally Gothiscandza). After AD 200 they moved south into what is now Bulgaria, and later split up into two groups, Visigoths and Ostrogoths. The Visigoths established new kingdoms in southern France and Spain (AD 419–711), and the Ostrogoths in Italy (up till AD 555). These tribes were subsequently to become absorbed in the local populations, but in addition to the Bible translation they have left behind numerous linguistic relics in the form of place names (e.g. *Catalonia*, originally 'Gothislandia'), personal names (e.g. *Rodrigo* and *Fernando*, compare Modern German *Roderich* and *Ferdinand*), numerous loanwords (e.g. Italian-Spanish *guerra* 'war'), and also more structural features (such as the Germanic stress system, see below). In addition, a form of Gothic was still spoken on the Crimean peninsula as late as the eighteenth century. Eighty-six words of Crimean Gothic were recorded by a Flemish diplomat in 1562, who recognised the correspondence between these words and his own West Germanic cognates.

The earliest records that we have for all three groups of Germanic languages are illustrated in figure 2.1. These are runic inscriptions dating back to the third century AD and written (or rather carved in stone, bone or wood) in a special runic alphabet referred to as the Futhark. This stage of the language is sometimes called Late Common Germanic since it exhibits

Figure 2.1: The Earliest Written Records in the Germanic Languages (taken from Kufner 1972)

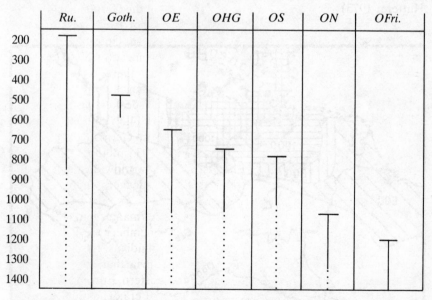

minimal dialect differentiation throughout the Germanic-speaking area. Further evidence of early Germanic comes from words cited by the classical writers such as Tacitus (e.g. *rūna* 'rune') and from some extremely early Germanic loanwords borrowed by the neighbouring Baltic languages and Finnish (e.g. Finnish *kuningas* 'king'). The runic inscriptions, these early citations and loans, the Gothic evidence and the method of comparative reconstruction applied to both Germanic and Indo-European as a whole provide us with such knowledge as we have of the Germanic parent language, Proto-Germanic.

There is much uncertainty surrounding the origin and nature of the speakers of Proto-Germanic, and even more uncertainty about the speakers of Proto-Indo-European. It seems to be agreed, however, that a Germanic-speaking people occupied an area comprising what is now southern Sweden, southern Norway, Denmark and the lower Elbe at some point prior to 1000 BC, and that an expansion then took place both to the north and to the south. Map 2.1 illustrates the southward expansion of the Germanic peoples in the period 1000 to 500 BC. But a reconstruction of the events before 1000 BC is rather speculative and depends on one's theory of the 'Urheimat' (or original homeland) of the Indo-European speakers themselves (see pages 63–65). At least two facts suggest that the pre-Germanic speakers migrated to their southern Scandinavian location sometime before 1000 BC and that they encountered there a non-Indo-European-speaking people from whom linguistic features were borrowed that were to have a substantial impact on

Map 2.1: Expansion of the Germanic People 1000–500 BC (adapted from Hutterer 1975)

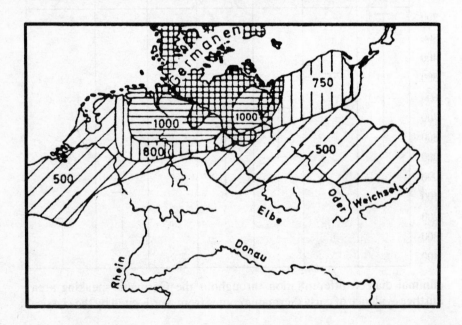

the development of Proto-Germanic from Proto-Indo-European: first, fully one third of the vocabulary of the Germanic languages is not of Indo-European origin (see pages 74–5); second, if a substrate language is to have any influence at all on a superimposed language one would expect to see this influence primarily in the lexicon and the phonology (the latter because of the special difficulty inherent in acquiring non-native speech sounds), and indeed the consonantal changes of the First Sound Shift (see below) are unparalleled in their extent elsewhere in Indo-European and suggest that speakers of a fricative-rich language with no voiced stops made systematic conversions of Indo-European sounds into their own nearest equivalents and that these eventually became adopted by the speech community as a whole.

The major changes that set off Proto-Germanic from Proto-Indo-European are generally considered to have been completed by at least 500 BC. In the phonology these were the following: the First (or Germanic) Sound Shift; several vowel shifts; changes in word-level stress patterns; and reductions and losses in unstressed syllables.

The First Sound Shift affected *all* the voiceless and voiced stops of Proto-Indo-European and is illustrated in figure 2.2.

Figure 2.2: The First (Germanic) Sound Shift (adapted from Krahe 1948)

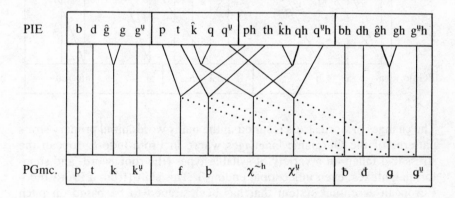

Proto-Indo-European had a voiceless and a voiced series of consonants, each of which could be unaspirated or aspirated, and within each series there was a bilabial, a dental, a palatal, a velar and a labio-velar (labialised velar) stop, as shown. Proto-Germanic abandoned the palatal/velar distinction throughout, and collapsed the unaspirated and aspirated series of voiceless stops. Unaspirated voiced stops shifted to their voiceless counterparts (see, for example, Lat. *decem*, Eng. *ten*), voiceless stops shifted to voiceless fricatives (e.g. Lat. *tres*, Eng. *three*), and aspirated voiced stops shifted to voiced fricatives (most of which subsequently became voiced stops). The dotted line in figure 2.2 indicates the operation of what is called 'Verner's Law'. Depending on the syllable that received primary word stress, the voiceless fricatives of Germanic would either remain voiceless or become voiced. For example, an immediately following stressed syllable would induce voicing, cf. Go. *fadar* 'father' pronounced with [ð] rather than [θ], from PIE **pətér*, cf. Skt. *pitár-*, Gk. *patér*.

The vowel shifts are illustrated in figure 2.3. Short *a*, *o* and *ə* were collapsed into Germanic *a* (compare Lat. *ager*, Go. *akrs* 'field, acre'; Lat. *octo* (PIE **oḱtō*), Go. *ahtau* 'eight'; PIE **pəter*, Go. *fadar* 'father'). The syllabic liquids and nasals of Proto-Indo-European became *u* plus a liquid or nasal consonant. Long *ā* and *ō* collapsed into *ō* (Lat. *frāter*, Go. *brōþar* 'brother'; Lat. *flōs* (PIE **bhlōmen*), Go. *blōma*, 'flower, bloom'), and the number of diphthongs was reduced as shown.

Figure 2.3: Germanic Vowel Shifts (from Krahe and Meid 1969)

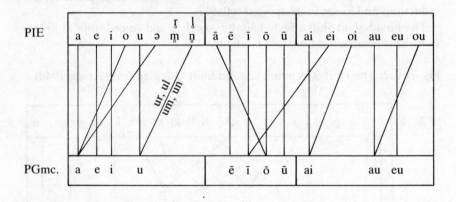

The changes in word stress resulted in the many word-initial primary stress patterns of the Germanic languages where in Proto-Indo-European the stress had fallen on a variety of syllable types (the root, word- and stem-forming affixes, even inflectional endings). This shift (from a Proto-Indo-European accentual system that has been argued to be based on pitch originally, i.e. high versus low tones) is commonly assumed to have occurred after the First Sound Shift, since the operation of Verner's Law presupposes variable accentual patterns of the Indo-European type that were subsequently neutralised by the reassignment of primary stress. Thus, both PIE **bhráter* 'brother' and **pətér* 'father' end up with primary stress on the initial syllable in Go. *brōþar* and *fádar*, and yet the alternation between voiceless [θ] in the former case and voiced [ð] in the latter bears testimony to earlier accentual patterns. Had the stress shifted first, both words should have changed *t* in the same way. A major and lasting consequence of initial stress was the corresponding reduction and loss of unstressed syllables. This process was well underway in predialectal Germanic and was to continue after the separation of the dialects. Indo-European final -*t* was regularly dropped (Lat. *velit*, Go. *wili* 'he will/wants'), and final -*m* was either dropped or reduced to -*n* (OLat. *quom*, Eng. *when*). Final short vowels were dropped (Gk. *oīda* 'I see', Go. *wait* 'I know'), and final long vowels were reduced in length.

The extremely rich morphology of Proto-Indo-European was reduced in Proto-Germanic. The Proto-Indo-European noun distinguished three genders (masculine, feminine, neuter), three numbers (singular, plural, dual) and eight cases (nominative, vocative, accusative, genitive, dative, ablative, instrumental and locative). The three genders were preserved in Germanic, but special dual inflections disappeared (though residual dual forms survive in the pronominal system of the early dialects). The eight cases were reduced to four: the original nominative, accusative, and genitive preserved their forms and functions; the vocative was collapsed with the nominative; the dative, instrumental and locative (and to some extent the ablative) were united in a single case, the Germanic dative, though occasional instrumental forms are attested; and some uses of the ablative were taken over by the genitive.

Proto-Indo-European nouns were also divided into numerous declensional classes depending on the final vowel or consonant of the stem syllable, each with partially different inflectional paradigms. These paradigms survive in Germanic, though some gained, and were to continue to gain, members at the expense of others (particularly the PIE *o*-class (Gmc. *a*-class) for masculine and neuter nouns, and the PIE *ā*-class (Gmc. *ō*-class) for feminine nouns). The inflectional paradigm for masculine *a*-stems in the earliest Germanic languages is illustrated in the chart given here.

The Inflectional Paradigm for Germanic Masculine *a*-Stems. Germanic *a*-stems exemplified by Gothic *dags* 'day' and cognates in the other Germanic dialects derive from Indo-European *o*-stems (cf. Latin *lupus*, earlier *lupos* 'wolf').

		Go.	ON	OE	OS	OHG
Sg.	Nom.	dags	dagr	dæg	dag	tag
	Gen.	dagis	dags	dæges	dages	tages
	Dat.	daga	dege	dæge	dage	tage
	Acc.	dag	dag	dæg	dag	tag
	Voc.	dag	(=Nom.)	(=Nom.)	(=Nom.)	(=Nom.)
	Inst.	–	–	dæge	dagu	tagu
Pl.	Nom.	dagōs	dagar	dagas	dagos	taga
	Gen.	dagē	daga	daga	dago	tago
	Dat.	dagam	dǫgom	dagum	dagum	tagum
	Acc.	dagans	daga	dagas	dagos	taga

The syncretism of the case system was accompanied by an expansion in the use of prepositions in order to disambiguate semantic distinctions that had been carried more clearly by the morphology hitherto.

The pronouns of Germanic correspond by and large to those of Indo-European, except for the reduction in the number of dual forms.

As regards the adjective, Germanic innovated a functionally productive distinction between 'strong' and 'weak' inflections, which is still found in Modern German (cf. pages 124–5) for illustration). Proto-Indo-European adjectival morphology was fundamentally similar to that for nouns. The Germanic strong adjective inflections were formed from a fusion of pronominal inflections with the declensional paradigm for nouns and adjectives ending in a stem vowel, while the weak adjective inflections were those of nouns and adjectives with *n*-stems. Strong and weak adjectives in the early dialects carried a meaning difference similar to that of the indefinite versus definite articles of the modern Germanic languages, and it is no accident that adjectives within indefinite versus definite noun phrases are typically strong and weak respectively in German today.

Proto-Indo-European verbal morphology was considerably reduced in Germanic. The Proto-Indo-European medio-passive voice was lost (except for a few relics in Gothic and Old English), and only the active survives. Distinct subjunctive and optative forms were collapsed, and only two of several tense and aspect distinctions were maintained in the Germanic present versus past tenses. Separate verb agreement inflections for dual subjects survive only (partially) in Gothic and Old Norse. A special innovation of Germanic involved the development of a systematic distinction between strong and weak verbs. The former (exemplified by Eng. *sing/sang/sung*) exploit vowel alternations, or 'ablaut' (see pages 49–50), in distinguishing, for example, past from present tense forms, the latter use a suffix containing a dental element without any vowel alternation (e.g. Eng. *love/loved*). The verbal morphology of Proto-Germanic has been maintained in all the modern Germanic languages (though the number of strong verbs has been reduced in favour of weak ones), and in addition new periphrastic forms have evolved for the tenses (e.g. perfect and pluperfect) and voices (the passive) that were lost in the transmission from Proto-Indo-European to Proto-Germanic.

The Germanic lexicon, like the phonology and morphology, reveals clearly the Indo-European origin of Germanic. Yet, as pointed out earlier, a full one third of Germanic lexical items cannot be derived from Proto-Indo-European. These items, far from being peripheral, belong to the very core of the basic vocabulary of Common Germanic. They constitute a particularly high proportion of the following semantic fields: seafaring terms; terms for warfare and weaponry; animal names (particularly fish) and terms for hunting and farming; communal activities and social institutions and titles. Examples (taken from English alone) are: *sea, ship, strand, keel, boat, rudder*, *mast*, *ebb*, *steer*, *sail*, *north*, *south*, *east*, *west*; *sword*, *shield*, *helmet*, *bow*; *carp*, *eel*, *calf*, *lamb*, *bear*, *stork*; *thing* (originally a communal meeting), *king*, *knight*. Other fundamental terms that belong here are: *drink*, *leap*, *bone*, *wife*, and many others. Common Germanic also took numerous loanwords from neighbouring Indo-European peoples, especially from Latin, though also from Celtic. The Latin loans reveal the strong influence of Roman culture on the early Germanic peoples in areas such as agriculture (cf. Eng. *cherry*/Lat. *ceresia*, *plum*/*pluma*, *plant*/*planta*, *cheese*/ *caseus*), building and construction (*street*/*strata*, *wall*/*vallum*, *chamber*/ *camera*), trade (*pound*/*pondo*, *fishmonger*/*mango* (= slave-trader), *mint*/ *moneta*), warfare (*camp*/*campus*). Most of the days of the week are loan translations from the Latin (e.g. *Sunday*/*solis dies*, etc.).

There is much less certainty about the syntax of Proto-Germanic, though the word order of the earliest inscriptions (Late Common Germanic) has been quite extensively documented by Smith (1971). He establishes that the basic position of the verb was clause-final (62 per cent of the clauses he investigated were verb-final, with 19 per cent verb-second and 16 per cent verb-first). Within the noun phrase, however, the predominant order of adjectival modifiers and of possessive and demonstrative determiners is after the noun, and not before it, as in many OV languages. In the earliest West Germanic dialects, by contrast, the verb is correspondingly less verb-final, and modifiers of the noun are predominantly preposed.

The precise manner in which the proto-language split up into the three groups (North, East and West) is a question of long-standing dispute. With the exception of the earliest runic inscriptions, the tripartite division is already very clearly established in the earliest records of figure 2.1: each of the groups has undergone enough characteristic innovations to justify both the existence of the group itself and the assumption of a period of separate linguistic development for the languages involved following migration from the homeland. But whether these innovations point to the existence of, for instance, a West Germanic parent language which split off from Proto-Germanic and from which all the later West Germanic dialects are descended, or whether the innovations are the result of contact and borrowing between geographically proximate tribes speaking increasingly distinct dialects whose common point of departure was the Germanic parent language itself, is almost impossible to tell. Some scholars argue against the assumption of a West Germanic parent language on the grounds that a threefold dialect grouping within West Germanic (into North Sea Germanic, Rhine-Weser Germanic, and Elbe Germanic — also called respectively Istveonic, Ingveonic and Erminonic) can be reconstructed back as early as the second century AD. The runic inscriptions of this early period do not lend credence to such an early dialect split, however.

Bibliography

For the Indo-European background, reference may be made to Krahe (1948), especially for phonology and morphology. For the phonology and morphology of the early Germanic languages, an excellent summary is Krahe and Meid (1969). Bach (1965), while primarily concerned with German, includes in part I a valuable summary of early Germanic language and history with extensive further references. Hutterer (1975) is an excellent compendium of the history of all the Germanic languages and of the cultures of their speakers.

A useful summary and discussion of word order is Smith (1971), which is discussed by Hawkins (1983) in relation to synchronic word order universals and derivative predictions for language change. Van Coetsem and Kufner (1972) contains many valuable and up-to-date papers in English on the phonology, morphology and syntax of Proto-Germanic, on the position of Germanic within Indo-European as a whole and on the reconstruction of developments within Germanic prior to the first records; it includes Kufner's (1972) summary and synthesis of the divergent theories concerning subgroupings within Germanic.

References

Bach, A. 1965. *Geschichte der deutschen Sprache* (Quelle and Meyer, Heidelberg)

Hawkins, J.A. 1983. *Word Order Universals* (Academic Press, New York)

Hutterer, C.J. 1975. *Die germanischen Sprachen: ihre Geschichte in Grundzügen* (Akadémiai Kiadó, Budapest)

Krahe, H. 1948. *Indogermanische Sprachwissenschaft* (Walter de Gruyter, Berlin)
—— and W. Meid. 1969. *Germanische Sprachwissenschaft*, 2 vols. (Walter de Gruyter, Berlin)

Kufner, H.L. 1972. 'The Grouping and Separation of the Germanic Languages', in Van Coetsem and Kufner (1972)

Smith, J.R. 1971. 'Word Order in the Older Germanic Dialects' (PhD dissertation, University of Illinois, available from University Microfilms, Ann Arbor, Mich.)

Van Coetsem, F. and H.L. Kufner (eds.) 1972. *Toward a Grammar of Proto-Germanic* (Max Niemeyer, Tübingen)

3 English

Edward Finegan

1 Introduction

At least to the extent that ability to read a language presupposes considerable familiarity with its structures, readers of *The World's Major Languages* may be assumed to have more than a nodding acquaintance with English. English is, moreover, a widely studied language and has received significant attention from linguists in recent decades and from distinguished grammarians since the last century. It thus seems appropriate in this essay to discuss English in terms not altogether parallel to those in which other languages, perhaps less familiar, might best be described. In somewhat more detail than is possible at present for most other languages, this essay will describe the structural variation that characterises English functionally and socially, as well as some of the better-known historical and regional variation.

Section 2 describes the status of English throughout the world, along with its social history and its contact with other languages in the past. Section 3 offers a historical sketch of the lexicon, phonology, morphology and syntax of English, followed by a brief account of orthographic practices. Finally, section 4 treats regional, social and functional variation in present-day English. While this programme for describing English may differ somewhat from the treatment of other languages in this book, it is hoped that this emphasis will be most useful to readers.

2 Status of English

2.1 Current Status of English

Though Chinese is spoken by a greater number of people, English is spoken around the globe and has wider dispersion than any other language. From its earlier home within what is now called the United Kingdom (with 56 million speakers), English has spread to nearby Ireland (three and a half million), across the Atlantic to America (where some 232 million people speak English in the United States, with perhaps as many as 24 million additional speakers in Canada), and across the world to Australia and New Zealand (with about 17 million English speakers between them).

English is the sole official language in more than two dozen other countries: Ghana, Liberia, Nigeria, Uganda and Zimbabwe in Africa; Jamaica, the Bahamas, Dominica and Barbados in the Caribbean; and Vanuatu, Fiji and the Solomon Islands in the Pacific, to name a sample. Elsewhere it shares official status with one or more languages in a score of nations, including Tanzania (with Swahili), Cameroon (French), South Africa (Afrikaans), Singapore (Chinese, Malay and Tamil), the Philippines (Filipino, i.e. Tagalog), Western Samoa (Samoan), Kiribati (Gilbertese), India (where it is an associate official language alongside Hindi) and Pakistan (Urdu). In still other nations, English holds no official status only because its widespread use in government (often alongside an indigenous tongue) and in trade is taken for granted. The two Pacific island nations of Tonga (with 100,000 residents) and Tuvalu (with 9,000) exemplify this situation, as does the United States, where no official language is designated.

Substantial portions of the populations of the United States and Canada speak English as a second language, many of them immigrants, but others born within their boundaries and raised in families and neighbourhoods struggling to preserve the language and culture of ancestral lands. One recognised example is that of French speakers in Canada, who constitute a majority only in Quebec province but whose influence is so strong nationally that Canada is officially a bilingual nation. Less well known is the fact that speakers of languages other than English are sufficiently numerous in the United States to warrant using more than a hundred languages of instruction in various primary and secondary schools throughout the land. Los Angeles is a sufficiently bilingual city that balloting materials for all elections are printed in Spanish and English, while the trilingual ballots in San Francisco permit voting in English, Spanish or Chinese. This suggests that a good many residents of the United States speak English as a second language (an estimated 34 million in 1970, including nearly 26 million American born, of whom a third had American-born parents). The same is true, though to a lesser extent, in England. Elsewhere in the world, Nigeria, Ghana and Uganda each have almost two million speakers of English as a second language, while the Philippines has more than 11 million. Likewise, the millions who speak English in Pakistan and India have learned it, for the most part, not in their infancy but as a second language, a lingua franca for governmental and educational functions.

Beyond its uses as a first and second language in ordinary intercourse, English is now established as the lingua franca of much scholarship, particularly of a scientific and technical nature. In addition, throughout the world there are English-speaking universities in which instruction and textbooks use English as the principal medium, though class discussion frequently reflects the greater ease of communication possible in the local vernacular or the national language.

Reflective of the widespread dissemination of English and perhaps of an extraordinary adaptability is the fact that Nobel Prizes in literature have been awarded to more writers using English than any other language, and that these laureates have been citizens of Australia, Ireland and India, as well as the United States and Britain. Finally, it can be pointed out that – along with Arabic, Chinese, French, Russian and Spanish – English is an official language of the United Nations.

2.2   Possible Reasons for Widespread Use of English

The widespread use of English around the globe is often attributed to social prestige and the need for English in technological advancement, as well as to the simplicity of English inflections and the cosmopolitan character of its vocabulary. While these latter grammatical and lexical features do indeed characterise English, they are influential only when coupled with complex social, historical and economic factors, for other languages and other peoples share them, though with different effect.

Among the reasons sometimes suggested for the extension of English (and one or two other widely dispersed languages) is the spread of technology, for the diffusion of American technologies during the twentieth century likewise diffused English words for those technological bits and bytes. So, too, in other arenas, where the artifacts of culture have borne English words with them in their travels, from jeans to discos, not to mention the intangible but ubiquitous *OK*.

Needless to say, English words cropping up in alien lands have not always been welcome. Troubling such watchdog institutions as the *Académie française*, Anglo-Americanisms like *weekend* and *drugstore* have been banned in France, while German guardians balked at the introduction of words like *Telefon* for the native *Fernsprecher*, though the latter compound has now fallen almost completely into disuse. Elsewhere, people are more open to English loanwords. The Japanese, for example, have drafted the words *beesubooru* 'baseball', *booringu* 'bowling' and *futtobooru* 'football', along with the games they name, trading them (so to speak) for *judo*, *jujitsu* and *karate*, which have joined the English team.

Further contributing to the popularity of English may be its inflectional structure, for compared to languages like German and Russian, English exhibits a remarkable inflectional simplicity. Assuming, as many linguists would, that a language simple at one level will be compensatorily complex elsewhere in order to carry out equivalent communicative tasks, it is difficult to assess the impetus of grammatical simplicity of any kind on the spread of a language. To be sure, English inflections are tidy and relatively easy to learn compared with heavily inflected languages and those that have other complex morphological variations. English nouns, to cite a central example, generally have only two variants in speech, a marked variant for possessive singulars and all plurals, an unmarked one for all other functions. Aside from a few exceptions like *teeth* and *oxen*, plurals are formed by adding /-s/ or /-z/ or /-əz/ to the singular, according to certain straightforward conditions detailed below (page 92). As for possessives, the rules are identical to those for the plural, except that there are no exceptions. Further, English exhibits no variation of adjectives for number, gender, or case, there being but one form each in the positive (*tall*, *beautiful*, *old*), comparative (*-er*) and superlative (*-est*) degrees, the latter two alternating under specified circumstances with the equivalent analytical forms with *more* and *most*. Verbs are only minimally inflected, with suffixes for third person singular concord; for present participle (in *-ing*); for past tense (in /-t/, /-d/, /-əd/); and for past participle (frequently in *-en*). In all, there are but eight productive inflectional suffixes in present-day English: two on nouns, four on verbs and two for adjectives. There are no inflectional prefixes or infixes.

Breadth of vocabulary is the most often cited reason for its acceptance around the globe, and English is indeed lexically rich. *Webster's Third New International Dictionary* (1961) boasts that it contains some 450,000 words; still, an eight-page supplement of new words and meanings was appended to the 1966 printing, and that was expanded to sixteen pages in 1971. When a free-standing supplement appeared in 1976, Merriam-Webster called it *6,000 Words* to reflect the extent of new meanings and new words that had become established in the intervening fifteen years (from *ablator* 'a material that provides thermal protection by ablating' to *zonked* 'being under the influence of alcohol or a drug'). *9,000 Words* appeared in 1983. A supplement to the great *Oxford English Dictionary* (*OED*) is in process of completion, three of four projected volumes already in print (1972, 1976, 1982), the fourth (beginning with the word *sea*) appearing in 1986. This supplement is intended to update the *OED* with words and senses of words that arose during the decades of publication between 1884 and 1928, and since then. When the first volume of the supplement appeared, editor R. W. Burchfield estimated the supplement would contain about 50,000 main word entries. Already, however, in the three existing volumes (up to the word *Scythism*), as many as 49,750 main words have been treated, not a negligible number for a word list intended as a supplement to another dictionary completed only about half a century earlier. Further, the inability of the dictionary makers to predict the number of words to be treated as late as the appearance of the first volume (up to the letter G) is indicative of the current growth rate of the lexicon.

As further evidence of the abundance of the English word stock, we can point to the fact that the number of synonyms (or near synonyms) for many words is quite large, each suggesting some variation on the semantic core. Almost any thesaurus can provide upwards of forty synonyms for the adjective *inebriated* and more than a dozen for the noun *courtesy*, to offer examples from just two parts of speech (without intending to suggest the relative richness of these two notions in the English-speaking world).

English also boasts a distinctively cosmopolitan vocabulary, having borrowed extensively from other Germanic tongues and especially from the Romance languages Latin and French, but absorbing tens of thousands of words from scores of languages over the centuries. From earliest times English has revealed a remarkable magnetism for loanwords, in foods and toponymics of course, but in every other arena of human activity as well. Some indication of the cosmopolitan nature of the English lexicon is suggested by words like *alcove*, *alcohol* and *harem* (from Arabic), *tycoon* and *ikebana* (Japanese), *taboo* (Tongan), some 10,000 words of French origin added during Middle English and an even larger influx from Latin during the Renaissance. (On the French borrowings, Jespersen (1938) and Baugh and Cable (1978) are useful references; on the Latin, Serjeantson (1935).) Recent borrowings reveal an extraordinary range of donor languages, more than seventy-five in number. French provides most items by far, followed by Japanese, Spanish, Italian, Latin, Greek, German, Yiddish, Russian, Chinese, Arabic, more than two dozen African languages and more than three dozen other languages from all parts of the globe.

Maps of the English-speaking parts of the globe are dotted with borrowings from many sources. A map of the City of Los Angeles, to cite the host of the 1984 international Olympiad, exhibits hundreds of street names of Spanish origin (from *La Cienega* to *Los Feliz*) and bears a Spanish name itself. Elsewhere in the USA, place-names like *Mississippi* and *Minnesota* are borrowed from Amerindian languages, while *Kinderhook*, *Schuylerville* and *Watervliet*, all in New York State, are taken from Dutch.

Names for such popular foods as *taco*, *burrito*, *chili* and *guacamole* (from Mexican Spanish), *hamburger*, *frankfurter*, *liverwurst* and *wiener schnitzel* (German), *teriyaki* and *sukiyaki* (Japanese), *chow mein* and *foo yong* (Cantonese), *kimchi* (Korean), *pilaf* (Persian and Turkish), *falafel* (Arabic) and a thousand others indicate the catholic tastes of English speakers both gustatorily and linguistically. Playing a special role, French culinary words have leavened the English lexicon used in kitchens around the world: *hors d'œuvre*, *quiche*, *pâté*, *fondue*, *flambé*, *soufflé*, *sauté*, *carrot*, *mayonnaise*, *bouillon*, *flan*, *casserole*, and the ubiquitous *à la*, as in *à la mode* and *à la carte*, are illustrative. A wide stripe of other languages is represented by the following familiar culinary words: *semolina* (Italian), *chocolate* (Nahuatl, via Spanish and French), *coleslaw* (Dutch), *chutney* (Hindi), *moussaka* (Greek), *bamboo* (Malay), *gazpacho* (Spanish), *yoghurt* (Turkish), *kebob* (Arabic), *caviar* (Persian, via Turkish, Italian and French), *pepper* (Latin), *whiskey* (Irish), *maize* (Taino – an Arawakan language – via Spanish) and *blintz* and *knish* (both Ukrainian, via Yiddish).

Another reason that has been suggested to help explain the spread of English is the fact that its most common words are of such simple structure.

At least in America, 88 of the hundred most frequently written words are monosyllables, from *the* ranking first, to *down* (ranking 100th); among the next most frequent hundred are another 68 monosyllabic words. Of those that are not monosyllables among the first two hundred, all but five are disyllabic, while *American* is the solitary word with more than three syllables. Were similar information available for a wide range of languages, it might be clear that languages generally abbreviate words of frequent use in accordance with Zipf's law. English, however, has had the additional historical impetus that most disyllabic words ending in an unstressed syllable became monosyllabic in early Modern English, as described below.

One final explanation recently offered by some scholars for the diffusion of English lies in the supposed nature of the relationships between grammatical structures and the processing mechanisms for comprehension. Though not universally accepted nor empirically verified, this explanation relies on the fact that English is an SVO language, with subjects preceding verbs preceding objects. The claim is that SVO languages are perceptually simpler than languages whose basic orders are SOV or VSO. It is pointed out that, even granted their sociological and political statuses, it is noteworthy that Chinese, French, Russian and Spanish, all of which are SVO, are languages of wide diffusion, as is the spoken form of Arabic that is spreading. The perceptual advantage of SVO languages is the ready identification of subjects and objects, which are separated (by verbs) in SVO but not SOV or VSO languages. It might also be mentioned that English tends to have topics in sentence-initial position (though to a lesser degree than many other languages); given its preference for SVO word order, subject and topic will often coincide, a coincidence that apparently enhances processibility, especially when the subject is also the semantic agent.

2.3 English and Its Social History

Needless to say, English did not always hold so lofty a position among the world's languages as it holds today. Even in England, to which we trace its beginnings as an independent tongue, English had competitors at times. In America, too, despite its new robustness, it was not always clear that the United States and Canada would be English-speaking countries. Even today, encroachments by Spanish and French on the status of English in North America are vigorous.

English derives from the West Germanic branch of the Indo-European family of languages. It is most closely related to the Low German dialects in northern Germany and to Dutch and Frisian, sharing with them the characteristic absence of the Second, or High, German Sound Shift, occurring around AD 600 and markedly differentiating the phonology of the West Germanic varieties of the highland south from those of the lowland north. (See pages 113–114). Geographically separated from the Continent since the middle of the fifth century, English would not have been subject to this shift, but its origins in the northernmost part of the Germanic-speaking area would also have spared it.

It was in AD 449, according to Bede's *Ecclesiastical History of the English People* (completed in 731), that bands from the three Germanic tribes of Angles (after whom England and its language were named), Saxons and Jutes began leaving the area known today as northern Holland and Germany and southern Denmark. These Teutons sailed to Britain, which had been deserted by the Romans forty years earlier, to assist the Celtic leader Vortigern, who had called upon them to help repulse the invading Picts and Scots from the north of England. Preferring Britain to their continental homelands, the Teutons settled, driving the hapless Celts into remote corners, where their descendants remain to this day – in Scotland in the north and in Cornwall and Wales in the south-west and west.

Surviving the Roman occupation of the British Isles there remain but few linguistic relics of Latin origin, including the second element of such place names as *Lancaster*, *Manchester* and *Rochester* (from Latin *castra* 'camp'). This influence of Latin through Celtic transmission was the slightest of several Latin influences on the English lexicon. As for direct Celtic influence on the early Germanic settlers, it is slight, noticeable only in place-names like *Dover*, *Kent*, *York*, possibly *London*, and a few other toponymics like the river names *Avon*, *Thames* and *Trent*. The missionary activities of St. Columba, who in 563 established an Irish monastery on the island of Iona off the coast of Scotland, introduced a few Celtic words like *cross* and perhaps *curse* into the English word stock.

It is not until the end of the seventh century that we have written records of the Germanic language spoken in England and not until the reign of King Alfred (871–99) that we have 'Englisc' recorded in quantity. In 597, St. Augustine (not the bishop of Hippo famous for his fifth-century *Confessions* and *City of God*) christianised the English people, giving them scores of Latin words like *abbot*, *altar*, *angel*, *cleric*, *priest* and *psalm* in the religious sphere and *grammatical*, *master*, *meter*, *school* and *verse* in learned arenas.

At the end of the eighth century and during the ninth, a series of invasions from the Scandinavian cousins of the Anglo-Saxons brought a secondary Germanic influence into the English lexicon, though it does not vigorously manifest itself in the written record until after the eleventh century. Sporadic raids started in 787, with monasteries sacked and pillaged at Lindisfarne in 793 and Jarrow (Bede's monastery) in 794. In the year 850, as many as 350 ships carried Danish invaders up the Thames. At length, after King Alfred defeated these Vikings in 878 and signed the Treaty of Wedmore with Guthrum, who agreed to become Christian, there followed a period of integration during which bilingualism prevailed in the Danelaw, an area governed by Danish practices and including Northumbria, East Anglia, and half of central England.

This intermingling of the two closely allied groups brought an influx of more than 900 everyday words into English from the Scandinavian tongues, including the verbs *take, give* and *get* and such homely nouns as *gift, egg, skirt, skill, skin* and *sky*. In addition, about 1,400 Scandinavian place-names pepper English maps, besides some 600 ending in *-by* (as in *Derby, Rugby*), 600 in *-thorp* or *-thwaite* and another hundred or so in *-toft*, all Scandinavian. Besides this toponymic evidence, the close relationship between the Scandinavians and the English is suggested by the possibility that both pronoun and verb in the phrase *they are* derive not from OE *hīe sindon* but from Scandinavian sources; it is confirmed by the observation that the verbs *take, give, get* are among the ten most frequently occurring lexical verbs in English, to judge by their currency in American writing (see the discussion of the Brown University Corpus of Present-Day Edited American English in sections 3.1, 4.3 and 4.4 below).

In the development of the English language, the most significant historical event is the invasion by the Normans in 1066. In that year, William, Duke of Normandy, crossed the Channel and with his French-speaking retinues established an Anglo-Norman kingdom in England. During the following century and a half, one could not have confidently predicted the reemergence of English and its eventual triumph over French in all domains. Only a series of extraordinary social events contributed definitively to reestablishing a Germanic tongue emblematic of England.

After 1066, the Normans established themselves in the court, in the church and her monasteries, throughout the legal system and the military and in all other arenas of power and wealth. The upper class spoke only French, while English remained chiefly on peasant tongues. Naturally, between such extremes of the social scale a significant number of bilinguals eventually used English and French, but for generations England was ruled by French-speaking monarchs, unable to understand the language of many subjects and unable to be understood. Only when King John lost Normandy to King Philip of France in 1204 did the knot between England and the Anglo-Norman language start to come undone. Following other political and military antagonisms, the linguistic tide turned.

Finally, a plague known as 'The Black Death' struck England in 1348, wiping out perhaps 30 per cent of the population and increasing the value of every peasant life. This shifted the lower (English-speaking) classes to positions of greater appreciation and enhanced value for their work, and along with their own rise in stature came their language. In 1362, the Statute of Pleading was passed by Parliament, mandating that all court proceedings, which had been conducted solely in French since the Norman conquest, should thenceforth be in English. By about 1300 all the inhabitants of England knew English, and French had begun to fall into disuse. During the fourteenth century, English again became the language of England and of her literature. (Details of this story are conveniently found in *A History of the English Language* (Baugh and Cable 1978).)

Literature in English is known since Old English times. *Beowulf*, an heroic poem of some 3,000 lines, is still studied even in secondary schools (though usually in translation). While the surviving *Beowulf* manuscript dates probably from the late tenth century, the poem itself is likely to have been composed in the eighth. In addition, there survive other texts, including poetry (from the end of the seventh century), translations of the Bible, chronicles and religious writings particularly from the time of Alfred. Besides several known translations, including Boethius' *Consolation of Philosophy*, Alfred is thought by some to have translated Bede's *History* from Latin, and he is credited with establishing the practice of maintaining the Anglo-Saxon Chronicles. Alfred reigned from Wessex and his kingdom was thus within the West Saxon dialect area, making it the basis for the study of Old English today even though it is not the ancestor of the London dialect of Chaucer that became the basis of modern standard English.

Less was written in English between 1066 and the thirteenth century, but English language traditions remained vital enough for the fourteenth century to produce Chaucer (1340–1400) and his *Canterbury Tales*, an extraordinary work still enjoyed for its earthy, humorous narrative and its poetic skill. From quite early times English has been robust in its literary manifestation, except for the period of dominance by Anglo-Norman from which it nevertheless emerged a great literary language, lexically enriched and inflectionally simplified in part from that subordination to French.

3   English Structure and its History

English is usually divided into three major historical periods: Old English, dating from either the arrival of the Germanic tribes in 449 or the earliest documents, about 700, to about 1100 (shortly after the Norman conquest); Middle English from about 1100 to 1500; and, from 1500, Modern English, including an early Modern English period between 1500 and 1700. These dates are necessarily arbitrary, for English did not develop at the same rate in all regions nor at all levels of the grammar. These dates are in fact more appropriate to a phonological than a grammatical history, for Modern English morphology and syntax were established essentially in their current form by about 1400, the year of Chaucer's death.

Old English had four principal dialect areas: Northumbrian, Mercian, Kentish and West Saxon; most extant texts are in West Saxon. In Middle English, Mercian is divided into West Midland and East Midland dialects, and East Midland, which incorporated features of other dialects, gave rise to standard Modern English. In the treatment to follow, little attention is given to Middle English for two reasons. First, it represents a transitional period whose general nature can be inferred from knowledge of Old English and Modern English. Second, Middle English is far more diverse in its regional dialects than is susceptible to straightforward, brief exposition. Looked at overall, Middle English is a language in extraordinary flux. The geographical and chronological details of this unusually complex state of affairs can be traced in Mossé (1952).

3.1   Lexicon

Although the English word stock, enriched by compounding of native elements and by influxes of foreign borrowings, has always been abundant, the mechanisms for enriching it have shifted dramatically in the course of history. The Old English lexicon was almost purely Germanic, with traces of Latin and Celtic influence. This lexicon largely shared etymons with the other Germanic languages and like them developed its word stock chiefly by compounding (which is still a vital source of new words in German and English), as well as by prefixing and suffixing. Compounding was especially frequent and imaginative in Old English poetry, and the resulting kennings, illustrated here from *Beowulf*, enhanced poetic resources: *seġlrād* 'sail road' and *hrōnrād* 'whale road' for sea, and *bānhūs* 'bone house' for body. Old English nouns productively suffixed *-dōm*, *-hād*, *-ere*, and *-scipe* (to cite four with reflexes in Modern English), as in *wīsdōm* 'wisdom', *cildhād* 'childhood', *wrītere* 'writer' and *frēondscipe* 'friendship'. Verbs commonly prefixed *ā-*, *be-*, *for-*, *fore-*, *ge-*, *mis-*, *of-*, *ofer-*, *on-*, *tō-*, *un-*, *under-*, and *wiþ-*. As Baugh and Cable (1978) note, Old English could create from *settan* 'to set' all the following: *āsettan* 'place', *besettan* 'appoint', *forsettan* 'obstruct', *foresettan* 'place before', *gesettan* 'people, garrison', *ofsettan* 'afflict', *onsettan* 'oppress', *tōsettan* 'dispose', *unsettan* 'put down', and *wiþsettan* 'resist'. It could prefix *wiþ-* to fifty different verbs, only one of which (*withstand*) survives in Modern English (*withdraw* and *withhold* originating in Middle English).

The Norman invasion gave new impetus to the borrowing practices of English, for when English reemerged in the thirteenth century it did so in a context in which anybody who was anybody spoke French and in which many of the elite did not speak English. From then on, besides smithing with native elements, English imported gleefully from the languages with which it came into contact, and the character of its lexicon became irrevocably international. Baugh and Cable report that 40 per cent of all French words in English were borrowed between 1250 and 1400, the period during which English came again to be used for official and learned purposes. From this flood of more than 10,000 French words inundating Middle English, 75 per cent remain in use.

By no means did the Normans introduce the practice of lexical borrowing. Earlier, English had borrowed from the Celtic tongues and from Latin, and during the ninth and tenth centuries from its Viking cousins, as we saw. Still, the Normans substituted borrowing for the more characteristic English word-smithing practices of affixing and compounding, which had formerly been the most productive springs of new words and have become so again in the twentieth century, as shown by the *OED* Supplement or Merriam-Webster's list of *9,000 Words* added to English since 1961.

A brief look at the lexical character of Modern English texts may be useful here. Until recently, it would have been difficult to describe accurately the size and character of the Modern English lexicon, but the advent of computers and the development of standard corpora have made the beginnings of that task manageable. The data presented in this section are derived from the Standard Corpus of Present-day English, a structured sample of edited American English appearing in print in 1961. Commonly referred to as the Brown Corpus, it comprises slightly more than a million words, representing 500 samples of about 2,000 words each, taken from 15 prose genres, both informational and imaginative. (The composition of the corpus is described in Kučera and Francis (1967) and in Francis and Kučera (1982), from which, along with Kučera (1982), the data here cited are reported. The similarly structured British sample is known as the Lancaster-Oslo/Bergen corpus and is discussed in Johansson (1982).)

The Brown Corpus contains 61,805 different word forms, or types, belonging to 37,851 lemmas. A lemma is a set of word forms, all of which are inflectional variants or spelling variants of the same base word; thus, the lemma *GET* comprises the word forms *get* (and *git*), *gets*, *got* (and *gotta*), *gotten*, *getting* (and *gettin'*). Extrapolating these figures to an infinite sample would yield about 170,000 lemmas in English, excluding proper nouns and highly specialised and technical terms. Remarkably, just 2,124 lemmas (comprising 2,854 word forms) constitute 80 per cent of the corpus tokens. Approximately another 22,000 word forms occur once each; these so-called *hapax phenomena* account for 58 per cent of the lemmas. This fact gives some hint as to the range of the English lexicon, for the most frequently occurring words are grammatical (i.e., function) words, not lexical words (cf. sections 4.3 and 4.4)

The most common lexical lemmas are the verb *say* at rank 33 and the noun *man* at rank 44. The next most common lexical verbs (with their rank) are *go* (47), *take* (58), *come* (60), *see* (61), *get* (62), *know* (63) and *give* (72). The most common nouns after *man* are *time* (46), *year* (54), *state* (64) and *day* (75). The only adjective among the 75 most common lemmas is *new* at rank 56. Kučera (1982) points out that since content words are the least predictable textual elements, knowing the 2,124 lemmas that account for 80 per cent of the corpus would fall far short of leading to comprehension approximating 80 per cent.

The figures presented here are valid, strictly speaking, only for American written English, although it would be surprising if the broad outlines were far different for British writing. To the extent that speech and writing diverge, differences may be anticipated between these figures and those that would characterise speech samples, whether British or American. A corpus of spoken British English is being compiled under the auspices of the Survey of English Usage at University College London and is being computerised at the University of Lund in Sweden. No plan exists at present to develop a standard corpus of American speech, though the American Dialect Society has recently pointed to the need for one. (The distribution of different word classes across genres will be described in sections 4.3 and 4.4.)

3.2 Phonology

Throughout its history, English exhibits striking instability in its system of vowels, while its consonants have remained relatively fixed especially since the fourteenth century. Old English, Middle English and Modern English all exhibit considerable vocalic variation from dialect to dialect, while the consonants show negligible synchronic variation from region to region. Socially significant heterogeneity, on the other hand, affects both consonants and vowels, as described in section 4.2.

Because the evolution of unstressed vowels has played a pivotal role in the development of English morphology and grammar, their history is central to our discussion. The most pregnant phonological feature of the earliest stages of English is the characteristic Germanic stress placement on the first or root syllable. From before the settlement of England, the language of the Angles, Saxons and Jutes suffered certain phonological reductions that differentiate it from High German (e.g. loss of nasals preceding /f/, /θ/, /s/, with compensatory lengthening of the preceding vowel; compare German *Mund* and *Gans* with English *mouth* and *goose*). Such correspondences between High and Low German stressed vowels only begin to suggest the wholesale reductions that were to affect English unstressed vowels and as a consequence the entire inflectional system.

While Gothic (known to us from several centuries earlier than Old English) apparently preserves both long and short vowels in its inflections, Old English exhibits only short vowels, and syncretism among these inflections is apparent starting in late Old English, especially in the Northumbrian dialect. While early Old English had a relatively elaborate inflectional system, the characteristic Germanic stress placement began to effect reductions of such magnitude in unstressed vowels that inflectional suffixes were reduced in late Old English and Middle English essentially to the bare system of Modern English. In particular, unstressed /u/, /a/, /e/ and /o/ fell together into *e* [ə]. Coupled with the merging of final /-m/ and /-n/ in /-n/, the collapse of unstressed vowels and subsequent loss of final inflectional /-n/ and then of final [ə] led to the virtual elimination of all inflectional suffixes except those with final *-s* and *-þ*. This sequence of phonological levellings explains the plural and genitive forms of Modern English nouns, as well as third person singular verbs in orthographic *-s* and past tenses in *-d*.

When we turn to stressed vowels, their history is complicated by the substantial dialectal variation of Old English and the shifting locus of literary standards until the fifteenth century. Still, the extensive diphthongisation and monophthongisation that characterise Old English occur throughout the history of English. When American southerners pronounce *ride* as [raːd], they evidence the same kind of monophthongisation (or smoothing) that took place in late Old English when *sēon* became *seen* 'to see' and *heorte* became *herte* 'heart'.

Today, between fourteen and sixteen phonemic vowels exist in different regional varieties of standard English, including the three diphthongs /ay/, /aw/, and /oy/ (the last of which was borrowed from Anglo-Norman). Similar regional variation exists throughout the English-speaking world. (A detailed treatment of stressed vowels is available by period in Pyles and Algeo (1982) and by sound in Kurath (1964); both cite additional references.) No discussion of English historical phonology can ignore the dramatic shifting of long vowels that occurred in the fifteenth and sixteenth centuries, between Chaucer's death in 1400 and the birth of Shakespeare in 1564. This so-called Great Vowel Shift altered the pronunciation of every long vowel and diphthongised the two high vowels /iː/ and /uː/ to their Modern English reflexes /ay/ and /aw/. Charted in figure 3.1, this shift is responsible for the discrepancy in pronunciation of orthographic vowels between English and the Romance languages. Traditional English spellings were propagated with Caxton's introduction of printing into England in 1476, preceding the completion of the shift.

Figure 3.1: The English Vowel Shift (also called Great Vowel Shift)

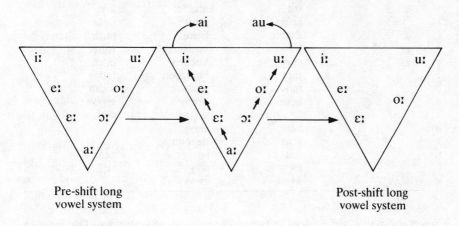

Pre-shift long
vowel system

Post-shift long
vowel system

Source: Bynon 1977

Subsequent to the Vowel Shift, early ModE /eː/ (< ME /ɛː/) came to be pronounced /i/, thus merging with earlier raised /eː/ and producing two sets of ModE /i/ words, those from OE /eː/ as in *sweet* and *see*, and those from

OE /ɛː/ as in *sheaf*, *beacon*, and *sea*. The raising tendency exhibited in the Vowel Shift continues today, where it is sometimes regionally distinctive and sometimes socially marked.

As to consonants, the English system has remained relatively stable throughout its history, and the inventory of phonemes has changed only slightly since about 1400, although certain allophones have been lost and phonotactic constraints have been altered somewhat. The Modern English spelling of *know* and *knife* is indicative of earlier pronunciations, for Old English allowed initial clusters of /hl-/ as in *hlāf* 'loaf', /hr-/ as in *hring* 'ring' and /kn-/ as in *cniht* 'knight', all of which are now prohibited.

In table 3.1 is a list of Modern English consonant phonemes, followed by words illustrating word-initial, word-medial, and word-final occurrence.

Table 3.1: Modern English Consonants

Phoneme	Initial	Medial	Final
p	pat	caper	tap
b	bat	labour	tab
t	tap	button	bat
d	dad	ladder	pad
k	cad	sicker	talk
g	gab	dagger	gag
f	file	beefy	thief
v	vile	saving	crave
θ	thin	author	breath
ð	then	weather	breathe
s	sin	mason	kiss
z	zebra	posit	pose
š	shame	lashes	push
ž		measure	rouge
č	chin	kitchen	pitch
ǰ	jury	bludgeon	fudge
m	moon	dummy	room
n	noon	sunny	spoon
ŋ		singer	sing
h	hen	ahoy	
y	year	beyond	
r	red	berry	deer
l	lot	silly	mill
w	wind	away	

Several notable differences between the consonant systems of Old English (not illustrated here) and Modern English can be mentioned. The members of the three Modern English voiced and voiceless fricative pairs (/f/–/v/, /θ/–/ð/, /s/–/z/) were allophones of single phonemes in Old English, the voiced phones occurring between other voiced sounds, the voiceless phones occurring initially, finally and in clusters with voiceless obstruents. Relics of the Old English allophonic distribution remain in the morphophonemic alternants *wife/wives*, *breath/breathe* and *house/houses*, where the second word in each pair, disyllabic in Old English, voiced the intervocalic fricative. Significantly, initial /ð/ in Modern English is limited to the function words *the*, *this*, *that*, *these*, *those*, *they* and *them*, *there* and *then*, *thus*, *thence*, *though* and *thither*, with initial voiceless /θ/ in Old English later becoming voiced by assimilation when unstressed, as these words often are. Similarly, /θ/ does not occur medially in any native words, though it can be found in borrowings. During the Middle English period, with the baring of the voiced phones word-finally when the syncreted inflections disappeared, the allophones achieved phonemic status, contrasting in most environments; there may also have been some Anglo-Norman influence, though not so much as is sometimes claimed.

Modern English /n/ and /ŋ/ were also non-distinctive variants in Old English, becoming phonemic during the late Middle English or early Modern English period. Of the Old English allophones of /h/, both [x] and [ç] have disappeared, leaving only [h]. In addition, /g/ had two Old English allophones, ModE [g] and a fricative [g] occurring intervocalically but now lost.

Finally, the gap existing in Old English and Middle English where one might expect a voiced palatal fricative /ž/ to parallel native /š/ was filled about 1600 when /ž/ arose by assimilation of /zy/ from earlier /zi/ (as in *glazier*, *lesion* and *vision*) and /ziu/ (as in *measure* and *usual*). More recently, word-final /ž/ has been borrowed directly from French in words like *mirage*, *prestige* and *rouge* (though /ǰ/ is also often heard). /ž/ is the only Modern English consonant not fully native to the English inventory, for the /zy/ cluster from which it arose entered English mainly in French and Latin loanwords. (This alien sound also developed in American English in words like *Asia(n)*, *emersion* and *version*, where British English has /š/; /ž/ sometimes also occurs in American English in words like *transients* and phrases like *as yet* and *all these years*.) The uneven distribution in the pattern of Modern English consonants apparent in table 3.1 reflects the historical development of these sounds.

3.3   Morphology

Old English morphology was considerably more complex than that of Middle English and Modern English – similar, if such comparisons are useful, to that of Latin or Russian. As a consequence of the extensive phonological reductions and mergers described in section 3.2 above, extensive syncretism of the Old English distinctive inflections occurred, and the inflectional morphology of Modern English is scanty, with a mere eight inflections surviving. Only pronouns preserve anything resembling the complexity of Old English, while adjectives and the definite article preserve the least. We shall describe the Old English and Modern English pronominal and adjectival systems, with brief discussions of nouns, verbs and the definite article.

3.3.1 Nouns

Old English had several noun declensions, both strong (from Indo-European vowel stems) and weak (from Indo-European consonant, i.e. *-n*, stems). To each noun was assigned a grammatical gender irrespective of its natural gender (although for human nouns there is a notable fit between grammatical and natural gender). Nouns were inflected generally for four cases in the singular, three in the plural (where the nominative and accusative are identical). Given here are paradigms of the nouns *stān* 'stone', *dēor* 'animal', *lār* 'learning' and *fōt* 'foot'.

	a-stems		o-stems	athematics
	M.	Nt.	F.	M.
Singular				
Nominative	stān	dēor	lār	fōt
Accusative	stān	dēor	lāre	fōt
Genitive	stānes	dēores	lāre	fōtes
Dative	stāne	dēore	lāre	fēt
Plural				
Nom./Acc.	stānas	dēor	lāra	fēt
Genitive	stāna	dēora	lāra	fōta
Dative	stānum	dēorum	lārum	fōtum

From the *stān* declension come the productive Modern English genitive singular in *-s* and all the productive plurals, while the *fōt* declension has yielded the few nouns (like *foot*, *goose* and *tooth*; *louse* and *mouse*; and *man*) whose plurals, generalised from the nominative and accusative, exploit a functional vowel alternation instead of the common suffix in *-s*. This palatal mutation was caused by earlier assimilation of the stem vowels to suffixes. Modern English relic phrases like 'a ten-foot pole' derive from the Old English genitive plural (translated roughly 'a pole of ten feet'), whose form *fōta* has the reflex *foot*. From the *dēor* declension come Modern English uninflected plurals like *deer* and *sheep*.

There were other noun declensions in Old English with variations according to the phonological characteristics of the stems at various periods in their development (and there was considerable dialectal variation over the centuries of Old English). The only productive forms of the genitive singular and of the plural in Modern English are the much reduced reflexes of the masculine *a*-stems, like which many older nouns have been analogically reformed and all new nouns are inflected. Both the plural and the genitive morphemes have the same three phonologically conditioned allomorphs, which by dissimilation have /-əz/ after stems ending in /s, z, š, ž, č, ǰ/, and by assimilation /-s/ after stems ending in other voiceless consonants and /-z/ after voiced segments. The plural and genitive morphemes exhibit syncretism (as in *boys'*), except when the plural noun is marked by a stem change, as in *women's*, *children's*, *geese's*.

3.3.2 Verbs

Like the other Germanic languages, Old English and its reflexes exhibit two types of verbs, called strong and weak by Jakob Grimm. While weak verbs (characteristically Germanic) exhibit a dental suffix ([d] or [t]) in the preterit tense, strong verbs show an internal vowel change (characteristically Indo-European ablaut). Old English had seven classes of strong verbs, with scattered reflexes surviving today, though starting even in Old English many strong verbs have become weak, while others have been reformed analogically. Many Old English strong verbs have developed regular Modern English forms, with past tense and past participle suffixes in /-t/ or /-d/. Listed here are the principal parts (infinitive, past singular, past plural and past participle) for each Old English verb class.

I.	rīdan 'ride'	rād/ridon	geriden
II.	sēoðan 'boil'	sēað/sudon	gesoden
III.	bindan 'bind'	band/bundon	gebunden
IV.	beran 'bear'	bær/bǣron	geboren
V.	giefan 'give'	geaf/gēafon	gegiefen
VI.	standan 'stand'	stōd/stōdon	gestanden
VII.	feallan 'fall'	fēoll/fēollon	gefeallen

From these principal parts can be formed the two tenses (present and preterit) in the indicative and subjunctive moods. A typical weak verb conjugation is provided here, where it will be apparent that while the present indicative exhibits three singular forms and one plural, the subjunctive contrasts only singular and plural forms. The twelve distinct forms of an Old English weak verb have been reduced to four in Modern English.

		Indicative	*Subjunctive*
Pres. Sg.	1	dēme	
	2	dēmst/dēmest	dēme
	3	dēmþ/dēmeþ	
Pl.		dēmaþ	dēmen
Pret. Sg.	1	dēmde	
	2	dēmdest	dēmde
	3	dēmde	
Pl.		dēmdon	dēmden
Gerund		tō dēmenne/dēmanne	
Pres. Part.		dēmende	
Past Part.		dēmed	

The simplicity of the Old English verbal system is striking; inflectionally, it is a mere shadow of its Indo-European predecessors. By way of contrast, recall that Latin is inflected for active and passive voice, for perfective and imperfective aspects and for present, preterit and future tenses, as well as for several moods. On the other hand, the Old English verb is also a far cry from the considerable periphrastic complexity of its modern counterpart in tense and aspect.

3.3.3   Articles

Though its use is complicated and in large measure pragmatically determined, the Modern English definite article is formally simple, having only the single orthographic shape *the* with two standard phonological variants, [ði] before vowels and [ðə] elsewhere. As shown in the chart, the Old English demonstrative (forerunner of today's definite article) was formally complex, inflected for five cases (including the instrumental) and three genders in the singular, and for three cases in the plural without gender distinctions.

	Singular			*Plural*
	M.	F.	Nt.	M./F./Nt.
Nom.	sē	sēo	þæt	þā
Acc.	þone	þā	þæt	þā
Gen.	þæs	þære	þæs	þāra
Dat.	þǣm	þære	þǣm	þǣm
Inst.	þȳ	þære	þȳ	

The initial consonant of the nominative masculine singular *sē* and feminine singular *sēo* differed from all other forms, which begin with [θ], orthographic *þ-*. Thus, Modern English *the* has no direct Old English etymon, being reformed analogically from the forms with inital [θ] and influenced by parallel Scandinavian forms introduced in the late eighth and the ninth centuries. By Middle English *þe* had become the invariant definite article in the north, and its use soon spread to all dialects. Chaucer uses only *the*. (Voicing of the initial segment occurred because the customary lack of stress on *the* encouraged assimilation to the vocalic nucleus).

Such a history is somewhat surprising for what is by far the most common word in Modern English: *the* occurs twice as often as *of*, its nearest competitor, and about twice as often as all forms of the verb *be* combined; *the* accounts for almost seven per cent of all tokens in the Brown Corpus. Remarkable also is the history of the indefinite article *a/an*, the fifth most common lemma in the Brown Corpus, which also did not exist as such in Old English. Like Modern English indefinite plurals, Old English indefinites were frequently unmarked, except that *sum* 'a certain' and *ān* 'one' appear sometimes for emphasis and are declined like adjectives.

3.3.4   Adjectives

Like the definite article, Old English adjectives were formally much more complex than those of Modern English. They were inflected to agree with their head noun in gender, number and case in 'strong' and 'weak' declensions. With the highly inflected demonstratives or possessive pronouns, the weak declension occurred (ending in -*an* in the genitive, dative and instrumental singular and the nominative and accusative plural for all genders and the masculine and neuter accusative singular; the remaining forms ending in -*a*, -*e*, -*ra* and -*um*). In all other instances, including predicative usage, Old English required the more varied strong declension. Both strong and weak adjectival paradigms are given here.

Strong Declension

| | *Singular* | | | *Plural* | | |
	M.	F.	Nt.	M.	F.	Nt.
Nom.	gōd	gōd	gōd	gōde	gōda	gōd
Acc.	gōdne	gōde	gōd	gōde	gōda	gōd
Gen.	gōdes	gōdre	gōdes	gōdra	gōdra	gōdra
Dat.	gōdum	gōdre	gōdum	gōdum	gōdum	gōdum
Inst.	gōde	gōdre	gōde			

Weak Declension

| | *Singular* | | | *Plural* |
	M.	F.	Nt.	M./F./Nt.
Nom.	gōda	gōde	gōde	gōdan
Acc.	gōdan	gōdan	gōde	gōdan
Gen.	gōdan	gōdan	gōdan	gōdra (-ena)
Dat.	gōdan	gōdan	gōdan	gōdum

Nothing remains of the inflectional system of Old English adjectives, which, except for comparative and superlative forms, occur in Modern English in a single shape, as in *tall*, *old* and *beautiful*. The form is invariant regardless of the number and case of the modified noun, and irrespective of attributive or predicative functions.

3.3.5 Pronouns
Personal Pronouns
The Modern English pronominal paradigm maintains more of its earlier complexity than any other form class. It is given in the chart alongside its Old English counterpart, with which it can be readily compared.

| | Old English | | | | | Modern English | | | | |
| | *1st* | *2nd* | *3rd Person* | | | *1st* | *2nd* | *3rd Person* | | |
Singular			M.	F.	Nt.					
Nom.	ic	þū	hē	hēo	hit	I	you	he	she	it
Acc.	mē	þē	hine	hīe	hit	me	you	him	her	it
Gen.	mīn	þīn	his	hiere	his	mine	yours	his	hers	its
Dat.	mē	þē	him	hiere	him	me	you	him	her	it

Dual

Nom.	wit	git	
Acc.	unc	inc	
Gen.	uncer	incer	
Dat.	unc	inc	

Plural

Nom.	wē	gē	hīe		we	you	they
Acc.	ūs	ēow	hīe		us	you	them
Gen.	ūre	ēower	hiera		ours	yours	theirs
Dat.	ūs	ēow	him		us	you	them

As is apparent, the dual number is altogether missing from Modern English, as are distinct singular and plural forms in the second person. Certain varieties of Modern English have evolved second person plural forms but they are either regionally marked (*y'all* in the American South) or socially stigmatised (*yous* [yuz] or [yɪz] in metropolitan New York City and *y'uns* in Western Pennsylvania and the Ohio Valley).

Relative Pronouns
In Old English, an invariant particle *þe* served to mark relative clauses; it was often compounded with a form of the demonstrative *sē*, *sēo*, *þæt*, as in *sē þe* masculine and *sēo þe* feminine 'who'. The forms of *sē* also occur alone as relatives, as in *ānne æðeling sē wæs Cyneheard hāten* 'a prince who was called Cyneheard'. Old English relatives are also sometimes marked by *þe* and an appropriate form of the personal pronoun, as with *him* in:

nis   nū   cwicra nān   þe   ic him modsefan minne durre āsecgan
there isn't now   alive   no one REL   I   him mind   my   dare speak
'There is no one alive now to whom I dare speak my mind.'

Middle English favoured solitary *that* as a relative pronoun, the Old English indeclinable *þe* surviving only into early Middle English. In the fifteenth century, *which* (from Old English interrogative *hwylc* 'which') appears as a relative, alternating with *that*. Modern English relative *that*, which is thus a functionally adapted reflex of the Old English demonstrative, is the relative with broadest pronominal application, anaphoric for noun phrases in nominative and oblique cases other than the possessive, though its use is now limited to restrictive clauses. The Modern English relatives *who/whom/whose* and *which* derive from Old English interrogative pronouns and can be used with restrictive and nonrestrictive clauses. *Whose* (< ME *whōs* by analogy to *whō* < OE *hwā* and to *whōm* < OE *hwām*) ultimately derives from the Old English interrogative pronoun *hwæs*. *Who*, *whose* and *whom* are late developments; while Chaucer occasionally used relative *whose* and *whom*, relative *who* did not come into widespread use until the sixteenth century.

3.4 Syntax

Old English is considered a synthetic language; it relies chiefly on inflectional morphology to indicate the grammatical relations among sentence constituents and (to a lesser extent) the semantic roles of noun phrases. Noun phrases exhibit concord in gender, number and case among the demonstrative/definite article, adjective and noun, with gender a grammatical rather than semantic category, and with adjectives declined either strong or weak as described above. Verbs are inflected for person, number and tense (present and preterit) in indicative and subjunctive moods, the subjunctive occurring far more frequently than in Modern English. Passive voice is signalled periphrastically with the verbs *wesan* 'to be' or *weorþan* 'to become' and a past participle; infinitives are also sometimes employed passively, and the verb *hātan* 'be called' is generally used with passive force.

As to its word order, late Old English exhibits patterns similar in many respects to those of Modern English. Both are characterised by a strong preference for SVO, which Modern English exploits in both independent and subordinate clauses, whereas Old English, like Modern German, prefers verb-final subordinate clauses. While SOV patterns occur in almost 30 per cent of Old English sentences, the twelfth century witnessed the development of an almost exclusively SVO pattern (according to J. Smith, as reported in Hawkins 1983). Old English negative sentences introduced by the particle *ne* favour verb-second position, producing a VS order as in the first clause of *ne geseah ic næfre þā burg, ne ic þone sēaþ nāt* 'I have never seen that city, nor do I know the well'. The characteristic negative concord of Old English is also apparent in this example (*ne/næfre* in the first clause; *ne/nāt* in the second, where *nāt* is a contraction of *ne wāt* from *witan* 'to know'). Clauses introduced by *þā* 'then' or *hēr* 'here, in this year' also commonly exhibit verb-second order, as in *þā cwæþ sēo hell tō Satane* 'then hell said to Satan'; *þā andswarode Satanas and cwæð ...* 'then Satan answered and said ...'; *þā gegaderode Ælfred cyning his fierd* 'then King Alfred gathered his army'; *hēr gefeaht Ecgbryht cyning wiþ fīf and þritig sciphlæsta æt Carrum* 'in this year King Ecgbryht fought against thirty-five shiploads at Charmouth'.

Within Old English noun phrases, the order of elements is usually determiner–adjective–noun, as in Modern English: *sē gōda mann* 'the good man'. Genitives usually precede nouns (far more frequently than in Modern English), as in *folces weard* 'people's protector', *mæres līfes man* 'a man of splendid life' and *fōtes trym* 'the space of a foot'. It has been calculated that the percentage of postnominal genitives increased from about 13 per cent in the year 1035 to 85 per cent in 1300 (also by J. Smith, as reported in Hawkins 1983). Though prepositions usually precede nominals, with pronouns they often follow, as in *sē hālga Andreas him tō cwæþ...* 'St Andrew said to him ...'. Adjectives too are almost uniformly prenominal (*sē foresprecena here* 'the aforementioned army'), but modifiers can be postnominal, as in these isolated examples cited by Quirk and Wrenn (1955: 88–9): *wadu weallendu* 'surging waters'; *ēþel þysne* 'this country'; *wine mīn Unferð* 'my friend Unferð'. Relative clauses generally follow their head nouns.

To a greater degree than Modern English, Old English exhibits a preference for parataxis over hypotaxis, for much Old English prose and poetry was written as a series of loosely associated independent clauses, often linked solely by a form of *and*, with the relationships among succeeding clauses left unspecified. While certain genres of informal speech exhibit considerable parataxis in Modern English, writing and most spoken genres exploit a high degree of hypotaxis, with logical relationships among the clauses of a discourse explicitly marked by subordinating conjunctions (*that*, *as*, *if*, *than* and *like* being the most common exemplars). While coordinating conjunctions are nearly twice as frequent as subordinators in the running texts of the Brown Corpus, a good portion are presumably phrasal rather than clausal coordinators.

Denied the richness of its earlier inflectional signposts, Modern English has developed into an analytical language, more like Chinese than Latin and the other early reflexes of Indo-European. With nouns inflected only for possessive case, word order is now the chief signal of grammatical relations, displacing the earlier inflectional morphology to such an extent that even the fuller pronominal inflections are subordinate to the grammatical relations signalled by word order; thus, an utterance like *her kicked he* may be understood as *she kicked him*.

Why English should have advanced farther along the path to analyticity than other Germanic languages is uncertain, though a basis for the explanation is likely to be found in the thoroughgoing contact between the Danes and the English after the ninth century, in French ascendance over English for so many secular and religious purposes in early Middle English, and in the preservation of the vernacular chiefly in folk speech for several generations in the eleventh and twelfth centuries. Decades before the Norman conquest (almost a century earlier in Northumbria), those inflectional reductions started that are everywhere apparent when English reemerges, and they were doubtless more advanced in speech than extant texts indicate. The syncretism spread as word-order patterns became fixed. Thus, phonological reductions undermined the inflectional morphology and, as flexion grew less able to signal grammatical relations and semantic roles, word order and the deployment of prepositions (which had somewhat redundantly borne certain aspects of meaning) came to bear those communicative tasks less redundantly; gradually, the freer word order of Old English yielded to the relatively fixed orders of Modern English, whose linear arrangements are the chief carrier of grammatical relations.

Perhaps spurred by the virtual absence of inflectional differentiation in its nouns, Modern English syntax has evolved to permit unusually free interplay among grammatical relations and semantic roles. With nouns marked only for genitive case, and pronouns additionally for objective case, Modern English exercises minimal inflectional constraint on subject noun phrases, which are consequently free to represent an exceptionally wide range of participant roles. Besides being agents (as in sentence (a)), subjects may be patients (b), instruments (c), benefactives (d), experiencers (e), locatives (f), temporals (g) and so on; dummy subjects, empty of any semantic content, also occur as in (h):

(a) The janitor (agent) opened the door.
(b) The door (patient) opened.
(c) His first record (instrument) expanded his audiences from friends and neighbours to thousands of strangers.
(d) The youngest jockey (benefactive) took the prize.
(e) Serge (experiencer) heard his father whispering.
(f) Chicago (locative) is cold in winter.
(g) The next day (temporal) found us on the road to Alice Springs.
(h) It became clear that the government had jailed him there.

In representing pragmatic structure, Modern English exploits neither morphology (as Japanese *wa* indicates topic) nor simple fronting to mark focus. In both morphology and word order, sentences like *Nobody expected revolution* are neutral with respect to focus. Spoken English exploits sentence stress to signal focus on particular constituents. In writing, where intonation is unavailable and the constraints on syntax imposed by real-time processing of speech are greatly reduced, English has available a range of syntactic processes to carry out pragmatic functions; these include passivisation, clefting and pseudo-clefting. In the archetypal focusing of noun phrases that is apparent in questions, English does front, of course, as in *who(m) did he choose?*, *what did she win?* and *what did they do?* Likewise, in relative clauses the relativised noun phrase is fronted irrespective of its grammatical relation within the clause and its participant role in the semantic structure; in other words, noun phrases of any type can be relativised. In example (i) below, the fronted relativised pronoun *that* is semantically a recipient functioning grammatically as an indirect object; in (j), the relative pronoun is a patient functioning as a direct object.

(i) She's the teacher that I gave the book to.
(j) The president vetoed the bill that his party endorsed.

The remarkable flexibility of English syntax in carrying out pragmatic functions permits an unusual degree of discrepancy between surface form and semantic structure. Thus, the syntactic processes known as subject-to-object raising (illustrated in (k)), subject-to-subject raising (l), and object-to-subject raising (m) all reduce the isomorphism between surface syntactic structure and underlying semantic structure.

(k) The coach wanted her to win the race.
(l) The economy seems to be sluggish.
(m) An incumbent is always tough to beat.

In (k), the underlying subject of the subordinate verb *win* appears as a surface object of the verb *wanted*. In (l), the underlying subject of *to be sluggish* becomes the surface subject of *seems*. In (m), the underlying object of *to beat* serves as the surface subject of the predicate *is ... tough*. As a comparison with the treatments of syntax in the chapters on Russian and German will indicate, the syntactic flexibility of English is not universal in the languages of the world. In its syntax, English is an exceptionally versatile language.

3.5 Orthography

Modern English orthographical practice is more out of harmony with the spoken language than that of many other languages, including Spanish, German and Old English. The spelling practices in vogue today reflect scribal practices from earlier than the introduction of printing into England when William Caxton established his press in Westminster in 1476. Since then the language has evolved phonologically, but the almost static spelling practices have not kept pace despite attempts by prominent reformers like Noah Webster (whose dictionaries popularised many of the characteristic spelling differences between American and British orthography) and George Bernard Shaw (who caustically observed that English permitted *ghoti* to be pronounced /fɪš/, the *gh* as in *cough*, the *o* as in *women*, and the *ti* as in *nation*). No wonder that English spelling holds the distinction of being the most chaotic in the world.

Still, there are advantages to the relative distance between orthography and speech in that written English is remarkably uniform throughout the world, and printed material can be distributed internationally without adaptation. Further, because English morphophonemics exhibits considerable variation in the pronunciation of the same morpheme in different environments, a closer correspondence of written to spoken forms would deprive readers of the immediate association apparent between words like *nation* and *nation+al* (with /e/–/æ/ alternation) and *electric* and *electric+ity* (with /k/–/s/), to cite just one vowel and one consonant alternation.

4   Present-day English and its Variation

4.1   Regional Varieties and the Question of Standards

As described earlier, English is widely diffused from its earlier home in England to nearby Scotland and Ireland, across the Atlantic to Canada and the United States, and across the world to Australia and New Zealand; it is vigorous in parts of Asia and Africa as well. In addition, it is spoken in isolated enclaves like the Falkland Islands, Bermuda and Tristan da Cunha. Various pidgins, creoles and creole-based varieties also exist, including Krio, spoken as a lingua franca throughout Sierra Leone in West Africa, and the American variety known as Black English, which is thought by some to be creole-based.

There are several varieties of standard English throughout the world, in addition to many more non-standard varieties. One widely accepted view is that the standard varieties can be divided roughly into two types, British and (North) American. To the latter belong the varieties spoken by educated speakers in Canada and the United States, while British English comprises the standard varieties spoken principally in England, Ireland, Wales, Scotland, Australia, New Zealand and South Africa. The differences that exist among the standard varieties are largely matters of pronunciation and lexicon, though even the latter are not very apparent in public written discourse. Thus, English is not governed by a uniform standard of speaking around the globe. Throughout England and the other English-speaking nations, there is considerable variation, notable in non-standard varieties but plentiful in the standard varieties as well.

Occasional proposals to establish national academies for English have been consistently rebuffed, and any suggestion of an international academy would almost certainly meet with international ridicule. Both regionally within countries and across national boundaries, enormous variation is tolerated especially in the pronunciation of vowels. Excepting principally the pronunciation of /r/ in words like *barn*, *corn* and *hour*, consonants tend to vary socially rather than regionally, as we shall see below. There is also considerable lexical variation especially in folk speech, and in some places it inspires strong local pride. With the advent of televised speech-making and with press conferences broadcast worldwide, such diversity as might be expected to crop up lexically has all but vanished from the public remarks of national leaders, though the same cannot be said of pronunciation. Grammatically, few differences are to be noted in the public speech of political leaders, and these are minor and generally understood across national boundaries (cf. *Cambridge are* (Br.)/*is* (Am.) *ahead by two points*; *she is in hospital* (Br.)/*in the hospital* (Am.)).

While national and regional standards of pronunciation exist, there is broad tolerance of variation. RP (Received Pronunciation), the variety pronounced on the BBC, is spoken only by an estimated three to five per cent of the people of England, according to Trudgill and Hannah (1982: 2). In the United States, considerable latitude exists in standard pronunciation, although a 'network standard' (essentially inland northern) has dominated broadcasting until hints of regional origin (especially southern) appeared recently in the pronunciation of national news broadcasters. And at least to American ears, the 'accents' of several recent presidents have been notably distinct from one another, Carter speaking a marked southern dialect, Kennedy exhibiting a signal Boston accent, and Ford and Reagan the relatively widespread inland northern variety. Yet one could not have distinguished among their written speeches (rhetorical style and political stance aside).

In contrast to speech, standards of writing are very strong and permit surprisingly little variation in grammar, lexicon and orthography. In the major centres of publishing within America, as in England, no regional variation exists except that Canada follows British precedent in certain matters, American increasingly in others. Further, as many publishing houses maintain offices on both sides of the Atlantic, there exists only slight (and diminishing) international variation in a few familiar spellings such as *check*/*cheque* and *color*/*colour* (the first of each pair popularised in America by Noah Webster) and in certain lesser known matters of punctuation that are transparent to readers around the globe.

English writing is relatively remote from the variation and vagaries of its speechways. As *The New York Times* and *Los Angeles Times*, published 3,000 miles apart, exhibit no regional linguistic differences, so only slight variation arises in the 3,000 miles between the language of, say, *The Economist* of London and *Time* magazine of New York (again ignoring politics and style). Established printing conventions and a lengthy multi-national grammatical and lexicographic tradition combine to mute the variation characteristic of English speechways and keep it from impeding written communication across dialect boundaries, whether intra-national or international.

4.2 Social Variation

Recent inquiry into synchronic alternation within particular communities has shown that much of what had previously been judged free variation is in fact significant. In New York City, for example, the occurrence of post-vocalic /r/ in words like *car*, *bear*, *beard*, and *fourth* had been thought non-significant. No difference in meaning was attributed to pronunciations with and without /r/. Labov (1972) demonstrated, however, that meaning does attach to such variation and marks social groups and social circumstances. The notion of linguistic 'significance' was thus broadened beyond semantics to encompass social meaning about language users and the uses to which they put language in their social interactions.

Investigating the usage of /r/ among four groups of New York City residents of ranked socioeconomic status, Labov observed increasing degrees of /r/-pronunciation by successively higher ranked groups. Thus, Upper Middle Class respondents exhibited more /r/ than Lower Middle Class respondents, who in turn exhibited more than Working Class respondents, and these last used more /r/ than Lower Class respondents. In addition, each group pronounced more /r/ as attention paid to speech was increased in various styles. Through several graded speech styles (casual style, interview style, reading of passages and reading of word lists), respondents in all socioeconomic groups increased the percentage of /r/ pronounced.

Similar patterns were recorded for other sounds: the *th* in words like *thirty*, *through*, *fourth*, which varies between [θ] and [t]; the *th* of words like *this*, *those*, *breathe*, which varies between [ð] and [d] (the infamous 'dis', 'dat', 'dem' and 'dose'); and the vowels in the word sets comprising *soft*, *bought*, *law*, etc. and *bad*, *care*, etc. These sounds all showed systematic variation: standard pronunciations occurred more frequently in groups of higher socioeconomic status and in styles with increased attention paid to speech.

Research carried out by Trudgill (1974) in Norwich, England, revealed similar patterns. In Norwich, variation in both syntactic and phonological expression was shown to be related to social structure – the socioeconomic status of speakers and the circumstances of use. Trudgill divided his subjects into five Groups: Middle Middle Class (MMC), Lower Middle Class (LMC), Upper Working Class (UWC), Middle Working Class (MWC), and Lower Working Class (LWC). As in New York, the greatest linguistic boundary in Norwich occurs between the Middle and Working Classes (i.e. between LMC and UWC). In table 3.2 are the figures for alternation between final [n] and [ŋ] in the suffix *-ing* for New York City and Norwich residents. For both socioeconomic status and speaking style, the patterns of distribution are strikingly parallel in the two cities.

Table 3.2: Per cent of Pronunciation of *-ing* Suffix as /in/ for Three Styles and Several Socioeconomic Status Groups in Norwich and New York City

	Norwich			New York City		
	A	B	C	A	B	C
I	28	3	0	5	4	0
II	42	15	10	32	21	1
III	87	74	15	49	31	11
IV	95	88	44	80	53	22
V	100	98	66			

Note: A= Casual Speech; B=Careful or Formal Speech; C=Reading Style. Roman numerals refer to socioeconomic groups: Norwich: I=MMC; II=LMC; III=UWC; IV=MWC; V=LWC; New York City: I=UMC; II=LMC; III=WC; IV=LC. Source: Labov 1972 : 239; Trudgill 1974:92

On the basis of evidence from these and other studies, parallel patterns of distribution may be expected for phonological variables wherever similar social structures are found. It is likely that comparable morphological and syntactic variation also exists, though evidence to date is scanty. Further, what holds true of variation in English may characterise other speech communities as well.

4.3   Variation across Modes: Writing and Speaking

Considerable attention has been focused recently on identifying similarities and differences between written and spoken English. In efforts to uncover what influence mode itself may exercise in the deployment of linguistic features, researchers have investigated, for example, whether speech or writing is more complex in sentence structure. Exploring other possible dimensions of comparison, attempts have been made to determine which mode is more nominal, which more verbal; how reliance on context differs and how pragmatic focus is signalled differently; in what ways the syntactic constraints imposed by the exigencies of real-time speech processing are altered in writing, creating degrees of integration of expression; how coherence is established in each mode; and so on. Findings based on a single dimension differ depending on choice of measures and selection of texts. Perplexingly, conclusions have been contradictory.

The use of computerised corpora and certain statistical techniques has demonstrated that the differences between speech and writing cannot be adequately characterised using any single dimension such as 'complexity' or 'reliance on context' or 'integration vs. fragmentation'. Biber (1988) shows that a multi-dimensional construct is needed to account for the distribution of textual features that have been explored as markers of mode. He characterises three of the needed textual dimensions as 'Interactive vs. Edited Text', 'Abstract vs. Situated Content' and 'Reported vs. Immediate Style'. Each dimension is defined by a set of empirically identified cooccurring lexical and syntactic features that function to characterise similarities among texts in a fashion suggested by the name of the dimension.

Along the dimension called 'Abstract vs. Situated Content', for example, a text is placed relative to other texts by the degree to which it exploits the features defining this dimension: nominalisations, prepositions, passives and *it*-clefts, as opposed to place and time adverbs, relative pronoun deletion and subordinator *that* deletion. The same text is independently situated along the 'Interactive vs. Edited' dimension by the degree to which it exploits a different set of defining features: *wh*- and other questions, *that* and *if*-clauses, final prepositions, contractions, the pronouns *I*, *you* and *it*, general emphatics (*just*, *really*, *so* + adjective), a low type/token ratio and shorter words. A third dimension representing 'Reported vs. Immediate Style' characterises measures of past tense markers, third person pronouns, perfect aspect and an absence of adjectives.

The resulting model can be perceived as a multi-dimensional space throughout which texts are distributed according to their exploitation of the feature sets characterising each dimension. From the above, it may be apparent that texts cannot be differentiated along a single dimension of 'complexity' (to take one commonly discussed construct) because the cluster of linguistic features representing complexity do not in fact cooccur significantly in the same texts. Nominalisations and passives, for example, differentiate texts according to their content (as abstract vs. situated), while *that*-clauses, *if*-clauses, relative clauses and other subordinate clauses differentiate texts by degrees of interaction and planning (or 'editing') – irrespective of differentiation with respect to content. Thus, 'complexity' does not comprise a set of textual features with a unified function and hence cannot serve as a linear gauge for comparing texts.

4.4 Register Variation

The computerised corpora used in the analysis of spoken and written English have also proved fruitful in the analysis of register, or situational, variation. Characteristics of various genres in the Standard Corpus of Present-Day Edited American English will be discussed here, although these findings are indicative of other possibilities for analysing styles of individual authors, historical periods and so on. Counts of textual features and inferences about structure that can be drawn from them promise enhanced understanding of textual variation of every kind.

The fifteen genres of the Brown Corpus can be grouped into informational (INFO) and imaginative (IMAG) prose. From an analysis of the distribution of form classes across these subdivisions, Francis and Kučera (1982) document that function words are the least contextualised word classes; that is, articles, coordinating conjunctions, infinitival *to*, determiners (*this*, *some*) and prepositions are the most evenly distributed classes across all genres of prose. Least evenly distributed, on the other hand, are nominative

Table 3.3: Normalised Ratio Values for Some Word Classes

Numerals	2.23
Adjectives	1.43
Common nouns	1.36
Prepositions	1.29
Subordinating conjunctions	1.06
The verb *BE*	1.03
Coordinating conjunctions	0.99
Modal verbs	0.88
All verbs	0.78
Main verbs	0.75
Adverbs	0.64
The verb *HAVE*	0.60
The word *not*	0.52
The verb *DO*	0.43
Pronouns	0.40
Interjections	0.11

and objective personal pronouns, adverbs/particles and past tense in main verbs.

To compare relative distributions, Francis and Kučera (1982) developed a normalised ratio value (NR). An NR of 1.00 for a particular word class would indicate a proportionate distribution of exemplars in INFO and IMAG genres. Values higher than 1.00 indicate proportionately greater representation in INFO, values less than 1.00 a higher proportion in IMAG prose. NR values for several word classes are presented in table 3.3. From these figures it is apparent that certain word classes are about evenly distributed across INFO and IMAG genres; witness coordinating and subordinating conjunctions, with scores close to 1.00. At the extremes of distribution, not surprisingly, are interjections (NR = 0.11), which occur almost exclusively in IMAG, while numerals (NR = 2.23) occur lopsidedly in INFO.

With nouns, prepositions and adjectives all exceeding the norm of 1.00 by more than 20 per cent, INFO is markedly more nominal than IMAG, while IMAG prose, with verbs and adverbs falling more than 20 per cent below the norm, is markedly more verbal in its character. The distribution of pronouns represented by a score of 0.40 suggests that pronominal anaphora provides a major signal of textual cohesion in imaginative prose, as Francis and Kučera (1982) point out.

Over the past several decades, sentence length has been a frequent object of study not least because of the assumption that it indexes structural complexity and therefore comprehensibility. All the INFO genres in the Brown Corpus exhibit mean sentence-lengths greater than the corpus mean of 18.4 words, while all the IMAG genres exhibit sentence-lengths less than the corpus mean. This pattern was initially interpreted as demonstrating that INFO genres were characterised by sentences of greater complexity than IMAG genres. Since those initial calculations were made, however, every token in the corpus has been given an identifying grammatical tag. This enables more valid estimates of complexity based on the number of predications per sentence and of words per predication. As it happens, the corpus averages 2.64 predications per sentence. The nine INFO genres range from 2.59 to 2.93, with the three genres of Press-Reportage, Press-Reviews and Skills/Hobbies falling slightly below the corpus mean. The IMAG genres, on the other hand, range from 2.23 predications per sentence for Science Fiction to 2.82 for Humour, which thus ranks well above the corpus mean. Thus, informational prose genres are not structurally more

Table 3.4

	INFO	IMAG	CORPUS
Words per sentence	21.06	13.38	18.40
Predications per sentence	2.78	2.38	2.64
Words per predication	7.57	5.62	6.96

complex than imaginative prose but deploy more words per predication. In fact, all INFO genres exhibit more words per predication than the corpus mean of 6.96, while all genres of IMAG prose rank below the corpus mean. The data in table 3.4 from Francis and Kučera (1982) summarise these findings.

Francis and Kučera present frequency figures for all 87 tags and an additional 92 combinations of tags for all 15 genres. Exploration of other patterns of variation is possible with large-scale corpora and with tagging procedures and other algorithms for identifying membership in grammatical and lexical categories. The possibilities that such approaches suggest for studying stylistic variation of many kinds are only beginning to be recognised. The findings that are emerging from corpora-based studies also present challenges to theorists – for example, to explain the relationship between the psychological, or processing, functions of textual features on the one hand and the social value that attaches to such functionally conditioned distributions on the other. As the notion of 'significance' was earlier broadened beyond semantics to encompass social meaning, a still further extension may be useful in understanding the regularity of distributions emerging from corpora-based studies of English.

Bibliography

The standard grammar for the modern language is Quirk et al. (1985); Huddleston (1984) is another excellent source, more directed towards problems of linguistic analysis.

Jespersen (1938) is a classic history of English. Pyles and Algeo (1982) is a well balanced treatment of both internal and external history, accompanied by a superb workbook, while Baugh and Cable (1978) is excellent for the external history of the language. For vocabulary, Serjeantson (1935) may be consulted in addition. Grammars of Old English include Quirk and Wrenn (1955), strong on phonology and morphology, and Mitchell and Robinson (1986), strong on syntax, while Mossé (1952) is the standard work for Middle English.

Detailed sociolinguistic studies of English are available in Labov (1972) and Trudgill (1974). Greenbaum (1985) is a collection of essays by more than thirty scholars on the 'state' of the language. Mencken (1963) deals with the development of American English, while Ferguson and Heath (1981) is a collection of 23 essays with an essentially ethnographic and sociolinguistic approach to the former and current languages in the USA (not only English); Trudgill (1984) is a companion volume, similar in scope, for the British Isles. Changing attitudes towards standard English are discussed by Finegan (1980), and Trudgill and Hannah (1982) deal with cross-national variation within standard English, especially British versus American.

Among works concerned with computerised corpora and their use in stylistic research, important references are Kučera and Francis (1967), Francis and Kučera (1982), Johansson (1982) and Biber (1988).

Acknowledgement

I am indebted to John Algeo, Niko Besnier and Douglas Biber for useful comments on an earlier draft of this chapter.

References

Baugh, A. C. and T. Cable. 1978. *A History of the English Language*, 3rd ed. (Prentice-Hall, Englewood Cliffs, N.J.)

Biber, D. 1988. *Variation across Speech and Writing* (Cambridge University Press, Cambridge)

Bynon, T. 1977. *Historical Linguistics* (Cambridge University Press, Cambridge)

Ferguson, C. A. and S. B. Heath. 1981. *Language in the USA* (Cambridge University Press, Cambridge)

Finegan, E. 1980. *Attitudes Toward English Usage: The History of a War of Words* (Teachers College Press, Columbia University, New York)

Francis, W. N. and H. Kučera. 1982. *Frequency Analysis of English Usage: Lexicon and Grammar* (Houghton Mifflin, Boston)

Greenbaum, S. (ed.) 1985. *The English Language Today* (Pergamon Institute of English, Oxford)

Hawkins, J. A. 1983. *Word Order Universals* (Academic Press, New York)

Huddleston, R. 1984. *Introduction to the Grammar of English* (Cambridge University Press, Cambridge)

Jespersen, O. 1938. *Growth and Structure of the English Language*, 9th ed. (Basil Blackwell, Oxford)

Johansson, S. (ed.) 1982. *Computer Corpora in English Language Research* (Norwegian Computing Centre for the Humanities, Bergen)

Kučera, H. 1982. 'The Mathematics of Language', in *The American Heritage Dictionary*, 2nd college ed. (Houghton Mifflin, Boston), pp. 37-41

—— and W. N. Francis. 1967. *Computational Analysis of Present-Day American English* (Brown University Press, Providence, R.I.)

Kurath, H. 1964. *A Phonology and Prosody of Modern English* (University of Michigan Press, Ann Arbor)

Labov, W. 1972. *Sociolinguistic Patterns* (University of Pennsylvania Press, Philadelphia)

Mencken, H. L. 1963. *The American Language: An Inquiry into the Development of English in the United States*, 4th ed. and two supplements, abridged, with annotations and new material by Raven I. McDavid, Jr. (Alfred A. Knopf, New York)

Mitchell, B. and F.C. Robinson. 1986. *A Guide to Old English*, 4th ed. (Basil Blackwell, Oxford)

Mossé, F. 1952. *A Handbook of Middle English*, translated by J. A. Walker (The Johns Hopkins Press, Baltimore)

—— 1959. *Manuel de l'anglais du moyen âge des origines au XIVe siècle* (Aubier Montaigne, Paris)

Pyles, T. and J. Algeo. 1982. *The Origins and Development of the English Language*, 3rd ed. (Harcourt Brace Jovanovich, New York)

Quirk, R. and C. L. Wrenn. 1955. *An Old English Grammar* (Methuen, London and Holt, Rinehart and Winston, New York)

—— S. Greenbaum, G. Leech and J. Svartvik. 1985. *A Comprehensive Grammar of the English Language* (Longman, London)

Serjeantson, M. S. 1935. *A History of Foreign Words in English* (reprinted Routledge and Kegan Paul, London, 1961)

Trudgill, P. 1974. *The Social Differentiation of English in Norwich* (Cambridge University Press, Cambridge)

―――― (ed.) 1984. *Language in the British Isles* (Cambridge University Press, Cambridge)

―――― and J. Hannah. 1982. *International English: A Guide to Varieties of Standard English* (Edward Arnold, London)

Wrenn, C. L. 1959. *The English Language* (Methuen, London)

4 German

John A. Hawkins

1 Historical Background

German, together with English, Dutch and Frisian, is a member of the West Germanic group within the Germanic branch of Indo-European. It is currently used by over 94 million speakers within Europe, and has official national·language status (either alone or in conjunction with other languages) in the following countries: the Federal Republic of Germany (61.3 million users); the German Democratic Republic (16.8 million); Austria (7.5 million); Switzerland (4.2 million); Luxembourg (330,000 users of the Letzebuergesch dialect); Liechtenstein (15,000); and also Namibia (formerly German South West Africa; at least 25,000). Bordering on the official German-language areas there are some sizable German-speaking minorities in Western Europe: Alsace-Lorraine (1.5 million users); South Tirol (200,000); and Belgium (150,000). There are also an estimated two million people in Eastern Europe with German as their mother tongue: the Soviet Union (1.2 million); Rumania (400,000); Hungary (250,000); Czechoslovakia (100,000); Poland (20,000); and Yugoslavia (20,000).

Outside Europe, German is an ethnic minority language in numerous countries to which Germans have emigrated. The extent to which German is still used by these groups varies, and in all cases there is gradual assimilation to the host language from one generation to the next. Nonetheless, an estimated minimum of nine million people currently consider German their mother tongue in countries such as the following: USA (6.1 million according to the 1970 census); Brazil (1.5 million); Canada (561,000); Argentina (400,000); Australia (135,000); South Africa (50,000); Chile (35,000); and Mexico (17,000). As many as four million of the German speakers outside the official German-speaking countries speak Yiddish, or Judaeo-German, which has undergone strong lexical influence from Hebrew and Slavonic.

The current political borders of the German-speaking countries of Europe are shown in map 4.1. Map 4.2 gives an indication of the major regional dialects. There are three main groupings of these dialects: Low

110

German in the north (comprising North Lower Saxon, Westphalian etc.); Central German (comprising Middle Franconian, Rhine Franconian, Thuringian etc.); and Upper German in the south (comprising Swabian, Alemannic etc.). The major basis for the threefold division involves the

Map 4.1: The German-speaking Countries

Map 4.2: Dialects and Dialect Groups (adapted from Clyne 1984)

NORTH SEA

Westphalian

North Lower Saxon

East Low German

Brandenburgisch

Thuringian

Upper Saxon

Silesian

East Central German

Middle Franconian

Rhine Franconian

East Franconian

Franconian

Pfälzisch

Alsatian

Swabian

Alemannic

Bavarian—Austrian

- - - Border between the Federal Republic of Germany and the German
      Democratic Republic
-·-· Boundary between Low German and Central German dialects
······· Boundary between Central German and Upper German dialects

extent to which the Second Sound Shift of the Old High German period was carried out (cf. below for discussion of the historical periods of German). It changed voiceless stops *p*, *t*, *k* to voiceless fricatives *f*, *s*, *x* ([ç] or [x]) and affricates *pf*, *ts*, *kx*; and voiced stops *b*, *d*, *g* to voiceless stops *p*, *t*, *k*. The Low German dialects (as well as Dutch, Frisian and English) were unaffected by these changes. The Central German dialects carried them out in varying degrees, and Upper German carried them out (almost) completely. The following pairs of words provide examples:

Low German *p*ad, Upper German *Pf*ad (English *p*ath)
Low German ski*p*, Upper German Schi*ff* (English shi*p*)
Low German hei*t*, Upper German hei*ss* (English ho*t*)
Low German i*k*, Upper German i*ch* (English I)
Low German bö*k*, Upper German Bu*ch* (English boo*k*)
Low German, Central German *K*uh, Swiss German *Ch*ue (English *c*ow)
Low German *b*äk, Upper German (Bavarian) *P*ach (English *b*rook)
Low German *d*ör, Upper German *T*ür (English *d*oor)
Low German *g*enuch, Upper German (Bavarian) *k*enug (English enough)

The increasing realisation of these changes within the Central German dialects is illustrated for some representative words involving the *p*, *t*, *k* shifts in map 4.3. The gradual conversion of these voiceless stops to the corresponding fricatives or affricates follows the progression shown below, and hence there are dialects of German whose pronunciation of these words corresponds to each of the lines, with Low German shifting at most *ik* to *ich* and Upper German completing all the shifts:

'I'	'make'	'village'	'that'	'apple'	'pound'	
ik	maken	dorp	dat	appel	pund	Low German
ich	maken	dorp	dat	appel	pund	
ich	machen	dorp	dat	appel	pund	
ich	machen	dorf	dat	appel	pund	
ich	machen	dorf	das	appel	pund	Central German
ich	machen	dorf	das	apfel	pund	
ich	machen	dorf	das	apfel	pfund	Upper German

The term High German is used to subsume Central and Upper German (both of which underwent the Second Sound Shift to some extent at least) as opposed to Low German.

There are also numerous other linguistic features which now distinguish the dialects of map 4.2 (see the references listed in the bibliography for discussion of these). In addition to these regional dialects many scholars now

Map 4.3: Isoglosses Resulting from the Second Sound Shift (Map adapted from T. Bynon. *Historical Linguistics*, Cambridge University Press, Cambridge (1977))

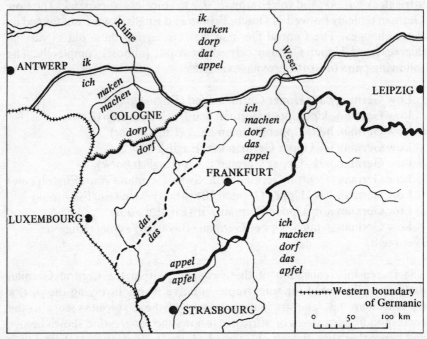

distinguish four national varieties of German, corresponding to the four major political areas in which German is spoken (the Federal Republic, the German Democratic Republic, Austria and Switzerland) on account of various supra-regional and supra-dialectal norms that are accepted as standard in each. The standard languages of the two Germanies, however, differ but little from one another and are both founded on a pre-1945 standard.

This standard emerged much later than the corresponding standard languages of England and France, on account of the political and cultural fragmentation of the German-speaking regions of Europe. There was no centre comparable to London or Paris that could impose its variety as the dominant one, so each region employed its own form of German at least until the sixteenth century. Prior to this point there had been a supra-regional 'compromise language' in the south (*das gemeyne Deutsch*), while in the north Low German enjoyed a privileged status until the seventeenth century as the commercial language of the Hanseatic League and was even used as a lingua franca throughout northern Europe. The basis for the emerging standard language in the fifteenth and early sixteenth centuries, however, was East Central German (see map 4.2). This variety of German was itself a compromise that had arisen as a result of the contact between speakers of numerous dialects following the extensive migration of Germans in the Middle Ages, as they occupied hitherto Slavonic-speaking areas. East Central German was therefore intrinsically well suited to becoming a standard language, and its subsequent acceptance by the remainder of the German-speaking population can be attributed to numerous external factors: the invention of the printing press (1450), which made possible publication on a large scale, the most influential printed work being Luther's translation of the Bible written in East Central German (1522–34) and deliberately intended to be accessible to all German speakers; the use of German instead of Latin for legal records (c. 1400), and the influential and normative role of East Central German legal writing in particular; and the rise of the cities, which attracted people from various regions and increased trade and commerce, making the need for a common language all the more urgent.

The emerging standard gradually permeated both the northern Low German-speaking regions and the south, and during the seventeenth and eighteenth centuries slowly penetrated into Austria and Switzerland as well. However, it was only in the nineteenth century that the phonological norms were finally set. By this time Prussia had become the dominant political force in all the German-speaking areas of Europe except for Switzerland and the Austro-Hungarian Empire, first through a customs union (the *Zollverein*), and then in 1871 through political unification. But prior to its expansion Prussia was originally a northern Low German-speaking state, whose speakers had learnt High German as a second language. With the spread of the emerging High German standard to the north, northern speakers tended to accentuate a close relationship between phonemes and graphemes. And with minor modifications this North German pronunciation of the originally High German standard became the norm for standard German pronunciation or *Bühnendeutsch* (stage German), both in Germany proper, and later in Austria and Switzerland as a result of an agreement concluded between the three countries in 1899. Today, television and radio announcers in Munich, Stuttgart and Baden-Baden sound much the same as their North German counterparts. Despite the 1899 agreement, however, the same does not hold true for Austrian and Swiss announcers. But as far as the written language is concerned, there is now a widespread consensus among the German-speaking countries.

The historical evolution of High German is divided into the following stages: Old High German (OHG), covering the runic inscriptions from the sixth century AD and written texts from the eighth century to 1050; Middle High German (MHG) from 1050 to 1350; Early New High German (ENHG) from 1350 to 1650; and thereafter New High German (NHG) proper.

The Old High German texts are primarily religious writings and translations (from Latin) produced in the monasteries of Central and Upper Germany. Some of the main linguistic changes that separate Old High German from Proto-Germanic are: the Second Sound Shift; numerous vocalic sound changes, including the monophthongisation (in certain environments) of Gmc. *ai* > *ē* and *au* > *ō*, the diphthongisation of Gmc. closed *ē* > *ea* or *ia* and *ō* > *oa*, *ua* or *uo* (depending on the dialect) and the beginnings of *i*-umlaut revealed orthographically in the conversion of *a* > *e* before *i*, *ī*, *j*; the development of a definite article out of a demonstrative determiner; and the emergence of new periphrastic verbal constructions for the passive, future, perfect and pluperfect. In late Old High German some morphological syncretism sets in, anticipating Middle High German, but otherwise Old High German contains a very richly differentiated morphology for nouns, adjectives, determiners, pronouns and verbs.

Middle High German is the language of the great German poets of the late Middle Ages (Walther von der Vogelweide, Wolfram von Eschenbach, Gottfried von Strasburg etc.). The two most characteristic phonological differences between Old High German and Middle High German are: the weakening and partial loss of vowels in unstressed syllables; and the spread of *i*-umlaut (or at least of its graphic representation). Both short vowels *a, e, i, o, u* and long vowels *ā, ē, ī, ō, ū* could be reduced to schwa [ə] (orthographic *e*) or lost altogether: compare OHG *wola* 'well' (adv.), *aro* 'eagle', *beran* 'to bear', *salida* 'bliss' with the corresponding MHG *wol(e)*, *ar(e)*, *bërn*, *sælde*. The *i*-umlauting is responsible for the front rounded vowels of Modern German (see section 2) which became phonemic with the reduction of the *i*-umlaut environment that had triggered their presumably allophonic variation hitherto (e.g. OHG *mūsi* > MHG *miuse* [mü:sə]). The reduction of unstressed syllables is also responsible for widespread syncretism in morphological paradigms as hitherto distinct vowels became reduced to [ə]. Otherwise the morphological paradigms of Middle High German remain much as they were in Old High German, and retain the lexical members and forms characteristic of the latter. Increasingly, however, the phonologically induced syncretism led to uncertainty as more and more words adopted morphological forms that originally belonged to other paradigms. These analogical formations eventually led to widespread restructuring in the morphology, but only in the Early New High German period. Among syntactic changes in Middle High German the replacement of the Old High German negative morpheme *ne* 'not' by *nicht* (etymologically 'no thing') is one of the more striking, as is the further expansion in the uses of the definite article. And in the area of the lexicon, the strong influence of French courtly society is reflected in numerous loanwords. Some of these were not to survive (e.g. *garzūn* 'page' and *tjost* 'joust') but many have, e.g. *Abenteuer* 'adventure', *fein* 'fine', *Lanze* 'lance', *Melodie* 'melody', *Tanz* 'dance', *Tournier* 'tournament'.

The Early New High German period saw numerous important changes throughout the grammar. In the phonology, short open syllables, for example, underwent either vowel or consonant lengthening (e.g. MHG [ligən] > NHG [liːgən], [hamər] > [hammər]); MHG [ə] was lost altogether in numerous environments (in some dialects much more than others) e.g. *legete > legte* 'laid'; the Middle High German diphthongs *ie, üe, uo* became long monophthongs *iː, üː, uː* (in Central but not Upper German, which retains the diphthongs), MHG *biegen* > [biːgən] 'bend', *küene > kühn* 'bold', *ruofen > rufen* 'call'; the Middle High German long closed vowels *iː, üː, uː* were correspondingly diphthongised to *ei, öu (eu), ou* (again subject to dialectal differentiation), MHG *zīt > Zeit*, [lütə] > *Leute, hūs > Haus*. There were profound restructurings in the morphology. For example, new plural paradigms for nouns evolved and expanded to compensate for the vowel reductions in unstressed syllables, particularly umlauted plurals: compare MHG *vogel/vogele* 'bird/birds' with NHG *Vogel/Vögel*. This process went even further in certain dialects with the result that one still hears today *Täg, Ärm, Hünd* in lieu of the standard *Tage* 'days', *Arme* 'arms' and *Hunde* 'dogs', while certain earlier distinct dialectal variants such as *Worte/Wörter* 'words' have both become standard German, though with slightly different meanings (words within a continuous text as opposed to individual words). Another plural suffix that was greatly expanded is *-er*, as in *Kind/Kinder* 'child/children', and also the *-en* suffix. The verb morphology also underwent some reductions, including a certain levelling of alternations in strong verbs (see section 3) and also a levelling of the Middle High German consonantal alternation between *ich was* 'I was' and *wir wāren* 'we were'. In the syntax, Early New High German was the period in which the characteristic verb position of Modern German was fixed: final position in subordinate clauses, second and first position in main clauses (see section 4). This had been the basic tendency in earlier periods as well, but there had been much more variation, especially in Middle High German, during which there were numerous postposings of constituents to the right of the verb in hitherto verb-final structures. Prenominal participial relative clause constructions are first attested in this period: *die von dem Bauer geschlachtete Kuh* 'the by the farmer killed cow', i.e. 'the cow which was killed by the farmer'. Certain postposed adjectives and possessive determiners (*den vater almechtigen* 'the father almighty') were replaced by prenominal orders. And there were widespread changes involving subordinate conjunctions: certain conjunctions died out (*wande, wan* 'because'); new ones emerged (e.g. *während* 'while', *falls* 'in the event that'); and the use of *daß* 'that' alone was frequently replaced by more semantically specific and precise forms such as *so daß* 'with the result that', *damit* 'in order that', *weil* 'because', etc.

With the completion of the Early New High German period (1650) we reach what is essentially Modern German. The precise phonological norms of the standard were still to be set (see above), but morphology and syntax

Table 4.1: The Lord's Prayer

Old High German	Modern German	English
East Franconian, Tatian, c. 830		Authorised Version, 1611
Fater unser thu thar bist in himile,	Vater unser, du bist da im Himmel.	Our father which art in heauen
si giheilagot thin namo,	Geheiligt werde Dein Name.	hallowed be thy name.
queme thin rihhi,	Dein Reich komme.	Thy kyngdome come.
si thin uuillo,	Dein Wille geschehe,	Thy will be done
so her in himile ist so si her in erdu;	wie er im Himmel geschieht, so geschehe er auf Erden.	in earth, as it is in heauen.
unsar brot tagalihhaz gib uns hiutu,	Unser tägliches Brot gib uns heute.	Giue vs this day our daily bread.
inti furlaz uns unsara sculdi,	Und vergib uns unsere Sünden,	And forgiue vs our debts,
so uuir furlazemes unsaren sculdigon;	wie wir unseren Schuldigern vergeben.	As we forgiue our debtors.
inti ni gileitest unsih in costunga,	Und du mögest uns nicht in Versuchung führen,	And lead vs not into temptation,
uzouh arlosi unsih fon ubile.	sondern erlöse uns von Bösem.	but deliuer vs from euill.

now undergo only minor modifications compared with the changes that have been outlined. It is instructive to get a sense of the extent of some of these changes by comparing a short text in Old High German with its Modern German translation. The text is the Lord's Prayer, see table 4.1, as it appeared in the East Franconian Tatian of c. 830. Alongside it is a New High German translation and also the English of the Authorised Version of 1611.

2 Phonology

The segmental phonemes of Modern Standard German (consonants and vowels) are set out in table 4.4. Twenty-one consonant phonemes are normally distinguished. Each of these is illustrated in the minimal pairs of table 4.2, in word-initial, word-medial and word-final position. The blanks in the table indicate that the consonant in question does not occur in the relevant position in a word.

Table 4.2: Minimal Pairs for German Consonant Phonemes

/p/	/pasə/	passe	/raupən/	Raupen	/riːp/	rieb
/b/	/bas/	Baß	/raubən/	rauben		
/t/	/tasə/	Tasse	/baːtən/	baten	/riːt/	riet
/d/	/das/	das	/baːdən/	baden		
/k/	/kasə/	Kasse	/haːkən/	Haken	/ziːk/	Sieg
/g/	/gasə/	Gasse	/haːgən/	Hagen		
/f/	/fasə/	fasse	/höːfə/	Höfe	/raif/	reif
/v/	/vas/	was	/löːvə/	Löwe		
/s/	/sateⁿ/	Satin	/raisən/	reißen	/rais/	Reis
/z/	/zats/	Satz	/raizən/	reisen		
/š/	/šats/	Schatz	/raušən/	rauschen	/rauš/	Rausch
/ž/	/žeːniː/	Genie	/raːžə/	Rage		
/ç/	/çiːna/	China	/raiçən/	reichen	/raiç/	reich
/x/			/rauxən/	rauchen	/raux/	Rauch
/h/	/hasə/	hasse				
/m/	/masə/	Masse	/hemən/	hemmen	/ram/	Ramm
/n/	/nasə/	nasse	/henən/	Hennen	/ran/	rann
/ŋ/			/heŋən/	hängen	/raŋ/	rang
/l/	/lasə/	lasse	/koːlə/	Kohle	/vil/	will
/r/	/rasə/	Rasse	/boːrə/	bohre	/vir/	wirr
/j/	/jakə/	Jacke	/koːjə/	Koje		

One of the most striking things about the minimal pairs in table 4.2 is the absence of any voiced obstruents (stops and fricatives) in word-final position, i.e. /b d g v z ž/. This is no accident. Voiced obstruents are regularly converted to their voiceless counterparts in syllable-final position, i.e. before a syllable break. Such syllable breaks occur in three types of positions: at the end of a word, e.g. /liːp/ *lieb* 'dear'; at the end of part of a compound word, e.g. /liːp+oigəln/ *liebäugeln* 'to make eyes at'; and before suffixes beginning with a consonant, e.g. /liːp+liŋ/ *Liebling* 'darling'. By contrast, the voiced /b/ occurs in syllable-initial position in forms such as /liː+bən/ *lieben* 'to love' and /liː+bər/ *lieber* 'rather', and so does not get devoiced. Devoicing also takes place in consonant clusters before /t/ and /s/: /liːpt/ *liebt* 'loves', /liːpst/ *liebst* 'lovest'. Notice that the orthography retains the voiced stop in these examples, thereby representing the morphological relatedness between the different forms of the same stem.

The status of /ç/ and /x/ in German is a matter of some dispute. The velar fricative /x/ occurs only after central and back vowels, and never in initial position. The palatal /ç/ occurs after front vowels, after the consonants /n l r/, and in word-initial position. This looks like a classic case of complementary distribution which should lead us to analyse these fricatives as allophones of the same phoneme. But there is an exception. The German diminutive suffix spelled *-chen* occurs as /çən/ in all positions, even after central and back vowels, and hence /ç/ sometimes stands in contrast with /x/: /tauçən/ *Tauchen* ('little rope') versus /tauxən/ *tauchen* ('to dive'); /kuːçən/ *Kuhchen* ('little cow') versus /kuːxən/ *Kuchen* ('cake').

Another problem involves the status of the affricates [pf] and [ts], created by the Second Sound Shift. Are these unit phonemes or clusters of two phonemes? They are historically derived from unit phonemes and minimal pairs are readily found which suggest that they retain this status. Nonetheless, German (like English) has numerous other clusters of stop plus fricative, and there seems to be no clear basis for distinguishing [pf] and [ts] from these: e.g. /ps/ in /gips/ *Gips* 'plaster', /pš/ in /hüpš/ *hübsch* 'pretty', /tš/ in /doitš/ *deutsch* 'German' and /ks/ in /zeks/ *sechs* 'six'.

The phoneme /r/ has a complicated set of allophones and is subject to a certain variation in pronunciation among speakers. When /r/ is followed by a vowel, as in /roːt leːrə besərə/ *rot* 'red', *leere* '(I) empty', *bessere* 'better (pl.)' (i.e. whether or not it is also preceded by a vowel), most speakers pronounce it as a uvular trill or fricative (phonetic symbol [ʀ]), although some use an apico-alveolar trill or flap (phonetic symbol [ř]). When /r/ is not followed by a vowel, its pronunciation varies depending on whether the vowel which does precede it is long, short or /ə/. After a long vowel, /r/ is always a non-syllabic [ᵊ], much like the /ʌ/ of English *but*. The word *leer* /leːr/ 'empty' is phonetically [leᵊ]. After unstressed /ə/, the /r/ and /ə/ combine to give syllabic [ʌ]. The word *besser* /besər/ 'better' is phonetically [besʌ]. After a short vowel, /r/ may either be a non-syllabic [ᵊ] again or else it may be pronounced as a uvular trill or fricative or as an apico-alveolar trill or fricative, like an /r/ which precedes a vowel. There are therefore three possible pronunciations for a word like *irrt* /irt/ 'errs': [iᵊt] [iʀt] and [iřt].

There are 19 separate vowel phonemes of German (including three diphthongs), exemplified in the minimal pairs of table 4.3. The vowels written with umlauts /üː ü öː ö/ are front rounded vowels resulting from *i-*

Table 4.3: Minimal Pairs for German Vowel Phonemes

/iː/	bieten	Stiele	ihn	ihre
/i/	bitten	Stille	in	irre
/üː/	Güte	fühle	kühn	führe
/ü/	Mütter	fülle	dünn	Dürre
/uː/	Rute	Buhle	Ruhm	Fuhre
/u/	Kutte	Bulle	Rum	murre
/eː/	beten	stehle	wen	zehre
/e/	Betten	Stelle	wenn	zerre
/öː/	Goethe	Höhle	tönt	höre
/ö/	Götter	Hölle	könnt	dörre
/oː/	rote	Sohle	Sohn	bohre
/o/	Rotte	solle	Bonn	Lorre
/ɛː/	bäte	stähle	wähne	währe
/ə/	gesagt	bitte	wartete	bessere
/aː/	rate	fahle	Bahn	Haare
/a/	Ratte	falle	Bann	harre
/ai/	leite	Feile	Bein	
/oi/	Leute	heule	neun	eure
/au/	Laute	faule	Zaun	

mutation in Old and Middle High German. The colon is a length symbol used for distinguishing the long versus short pairs /iː/ versus /i/, etc. (though see below). There are also articulatory phonetic differences associated with these length distinctions, which are indicated approximately in table 4.4. The short /i ü u/ are lower and more central than /iː üː uː/, the short /e ö o/ are also lower and more central than /eː öː oː/, and /a/ is higher and more central than /aː/. The three diphthongs involve glides from one tongue position to another: in /ai/ the tongue begins in low central position and glides towards a position which is higher and further front; in /oi/ the tongue begins in lower mid back rounded position gliding also towards a position higher and further front; and with /au/ the tongue begins in low central position and glides towards a position higher and further back.

The important difference between long and short vowels in German is more accurately described as a difference of tense versus lax articulation. Tense vowels are produced with greater muscular energy than lax vowels, and it is this that causes them to be articulated in more extreme positions in the vocal tract. The reason for considering the tense/lax opposition more fundamental is that the additional feature of length is found only in stressed syllables: all the examples in table 4.3 involve stressed syllables in which the tense vowels are long (those with a colon), and the lax vowels are short (those without). But in unstressed syllables, it is often possible to perceive a tense/lax distinction, and yet both sets of vowels are now short. There are perceptible differences between tense /iː/ in /diːneː/ *Diner* and lax /i/ in /difuːs/ *diffus*, in both of which the stress falls on the second syllable, and yet both *i* vowels are technically short. Similarly, the unstressed initial syllables of /koːlumbus/ *Kolumbus* and /koleːgə/ *Kollege* differ in tense versus lax articulation of the *o*, but both vowels are again short. In more informal and faster speech, even this tense/lax distinction disappears in unstressed syllables. Nonetheless, the distinctiveness of tense versus lax vowels is not restricted to stressed syllables, whereas the long versus short distinction is. Notice finally that the /ə/ of German occurs only in unstressed syllables.

Table 4.4: Segmental Phonemes of German

Consonants

	Bilabial		Labio-dental		Dental-alveolar		Palato-alveolar		Palatal	Velar		Glottal
Stops	p	b			t	d				k	g	
Fricatives			f	v	s	z	š	ž	ç		x	h
Nasals	m					n					ŋ	
Laterals					l	r						
Semi-vowels									j			

Vowels

	Front					Central	Back	
High	iː		(üː)					(uː)
		i		(ü)			(u)	
Mid	eː		(öː)					(oː)
		e		(ö)	ɛː	ə	(o)	
Low						a		
						aː		

Plus: diphthongs ai, oi, au

Note: ( ) designates lip-rounding

3 Morphology

Despite the morphological syncretism of the Early New High German period (see section 1), the inflectional morphology of Modern German is very rich and preserves major features of the Old High German system. Few among the other modern Germanic languages have a morphology of comparable richness. The biggest changes involved the inflectional paradigms for nouns. The Proto-Indo-European and Proto-Germanic system of classification according to the phonology of the stem (which is still evident in, for example, Russian, see the chapter in this volume) was destroyed and new paradigms evolved. Nouns are now classified according to their inherent gender (masculine, feminine or neuter) and according to their plural forms. The major plural allomorphs are: suffixed -e (*Tier/Tiere* 'animal'), -er (*Kind/Kinder* 'child'), -Ø (*Fenster/Fenster* 'window'), -en (*Frau/Frauen* 'woman'), -s (*Kino/Kinos* 'cinema'), stem vowel mutation plus -e (*Stadt/Städte* 'city'), stem vowel mutation plus -er (*Mann/Männer* 'man') and stem vowel mutation alone (*Mutter/Mütter* 'mother'). The noun phrase as a whole distinguishes separate case inflections for nominative, accusative, genitive and dative in both singular and plural, but these are now only residually marked on the noun itself (because of the reduction of unstressed syllables) and are primarily carried by preceding determiners and adjectives. However, the dative plural of all nouns still exhibits an -(e)n suffix, the genitive singular of most masculine and neuter nouns an -(e)s suffix, and the dative singular of many masculine and neuter nouns an optional -e suffix.

The full set of morphological distinctions carried by the German noun phrase (i.e. gender, number and case) can be illustrated by considering the sequence of definite article + noun in the chart given here.

Definite Article and Noun Inflections

	Singular			Plural
	M.	F.	Nt.	All genders
Nom.	d*er* Mann	d*ie* Frau	d*as* Haus	d*ie* Männer
	'the man'	'the woman'	'the house'	'the men'
Acc.	d*en* Mann	d*ie* Frau	d*as* Haus	d*ie* Männer
Gen.	d*es* Mann*es*	d*er* Frau	d*es* Haus*es*	d*er* Männer
Dat.	d*em* Mann(*e*)	d*er* Frau	d*em* Haus(*e*)	d*en* Männer*n*

The definite article assumes just six forms: *der*, *den*, *des*, *dem*, *das* and *die* (morphologically analysable as two bound morphemes *d+er*, *d+en* etc.). Since gender distinctions are inherent in the noun, and since plurality is richly marked on the noun itself, the most important function of the determiner is to mark case. Individual definite article forms can be used in more than one case function without risk of intolerable ambiguity: *der* followed by a masculine singular noun is a nominative; followed by a feminine singular noun a genitive or dative; and followed by a noun with plural marking a genitive; etc. The expressive power of these definite article case distinctions is identical to that of all other sequences of determiner + noun, and also to determiner + adjective + noun and Ø + adjective + noun sequences as well. The weakest distinction is between nominative and accusative, which is marked only by the *der/den* alternation in the masculine singular. However, the nominative is fully distinguishable in all genders and numbers from the genitive, and is also fully distinguishable from the dative.

The accusative is also fully distinguishable from both genitive and dative. The genitive is in turn distinct from the dative, except for feminine singular nouns.

An adjective following the definite article receives case inflections according to the weak paradigm, with -*e* or -*en* endings, as shown in the chart of adjective inflections.

Adjective Inflections

Weak Adjective Inflections

Singular			Plural
M.	F.	Nt.	All genders
Nom. der gute Mann	die gute Frau	das gute Haus	die guten Männer
'the good man'	'the good woman'	'the good house'	'the good men'
Acc. den guten Mann	die gute Frau	das gute Haus	die guten Männer
Gen. des guten Mannes	der guten Frau	des guten Hauses	der guten Männer
Dat. dem guten Mann(e)	der guten Frau	dem guten Haus(e)	den guten Männern

Strong Adjective Inflections

Singular			Plural
M.	F.	Nt.	All genders
Nom. guter Wein	gute Milch	gutes Obst	gute Äpfel
'good wine'	'good milk'	'good fruit'	'good apples'
Acc. guten Wein	gute Milch	gutes Obst	gute Äpfel
Gen. guten Weines	guter Milch	guten Obstes	guter Äpfel
Dat. gutem Wein	guter Milch	gutem Obst	guten Äpfeln

Mixed Weak and Strong Adjective Inflections

Singular			Plural
M.	F.	Nt.	All genders
Nom. kein guter Mann	keine gute Frau	kein gutes Haus	keine guten Häuser
'no good man'	'no good woman'	'no good house'	'no good houses'
Acc. keinen guten Mann	keine gute Frau	kein gutes Haus	keine guten Häuser
Gen. keines guten Mannes	keiner guten Frau	keines guten Hauses	keiner guten Häuser
Dat. keinem guten Mann	keiner guten Frau	keinem guten Haus	keinen guten Häusern

Other determiners requiring weak adjective endings are: *dieser* 'this', *jener* 'that', *welcher* 'which', *jeder* 'each', *alle* 'all'. It will be apparent that these adjective inflections do not increase the expressive power of the German case system, compared with the definite article + noun inflections. When an adjective + noun sequence has no preceding determiner (with indefinite mass nouns and plurals), the same case distinctions can be carried by adjective inflections of the strong paradigm, also shown in the chart of adjective inflections. These strong adjective inflections (-*er*, -*en*, -*es*, -*em*,

-e) are practically identical in form and distribution to the bound morphemes of the definite article, and the expressive power of the whole paradigm is again identical to the definite article + noun inflections. Indefinite count nouns in the singular require the indefinite article *ein* 'a'. This determiner, together with *kein* 'no' and the possessives *mein* 'my', *dein* 'your', *sein* 'his', etc., is itself inflected more or less like the definite article, but requires accompanying adjective inflections which are a mixture of weak (*-en*, *-e*) and strong (*-er*, *-e*, *-es*). The chart of adjective inflections illustrates this mixed adjective paradigm following *kein*.

Personal Pronouns

Singular

	1st	2nd (familiar)	3rd M.	F.	Nt.
Nom.	ich	du	er	sie	es
Acc.	mich	dich	ihn	sie	es
Gen	meiner	deiner	seiner	ihrer	seiner
Dat.	mir	dir	ihm	ihr	ihm

Plural

	1st	2nd familiar	3rd polite: s. & pl.	sie
Nom.	wir	ihr	Sie	sie
Acc.	uns	euch	Sie	sie
Gen.	unser	euer	Ihrer	ihrer
Dat.	uns	euch	Ihnen	ihnen

German personal pronouns exhibit a rich set of case distinctions, as shown in the chart of personal pronouns. All four cases are fully distinct in the singular for first, second (familiar) and masculine third persons, while feminine and neuter third person forms are identical only in the nominative and accusative. In the plural the four cases are on each occasion represented by three separate forms. In the first and second (familiar) persons accusative and dative fall together, and in the second (polite) and third persons nominative and accusative fall together. Relative and interrogative pronouns are also case-marked. The relative pronoun, for example, is identical in form to the definite article, except for all the genitives and the dative plural (the relative pronoun having *dessen* instead of *des*, *deren* instead of *der*, and *denen* instead of *den*).

The existence of a productive case system sets German off from the other Germanic languages except for Icelandic and Faroese. As regards the use of the cases, the most important factor which determines the assignment of case to a noun phrase is the nature of the 'governing category', loosely, the category which forms an immediate constituent with this noun phrase and which determines the syntactic type of the resulting phrase. Thus, a preposition combines with a noun phrase to make a prepositional phrase and it assigns a case to this noun phrase; a verb combines with a noun phrase to make a verb phrase and assigns case to this noun phrase; and so on. Different prepositions assign accusative case, dative case or genitive case, as illustrated below:

(a) durch das Zimmer; für mich. (acc.)
    'through the room; for me'
(b) aus dem Hause; mit mir. (dat.)
    'out of the house; with me'
(c) an die/der Wand; auf den/dem Stuhl. (acc./dat.)
    'on the wall; on the chair'
(d) trotz des Wetters; während des Jahres. (gen.)
    'despite the weather; during the year'

The case alternation in (c) carries a difference in meaning: *auf den Stuhl* with an accusative noun phrase signals motion towards the place in question, as in 'the cat jumped on(to) the chair'; *auf dem Stuhl* with a dative designates a location without a change in state, e.g. 'the cat was lying on the chair'.

An adjective within an adjective phrase may also assign case to a noun phrase. Different adjectives assign accusative, dative or genitive case, as in:

(a) Ich bin ihn los. (acc.)
    'I am him rid', i.e. 'I am rid of him.'
(b) Sie ist ihrem Vater ähnlich. (dat.)
    'She is her father similar', i.e. 'similar to her father.'
(c) Er ist dieser Taten schuldig. (gen.)
    'He is these deeds guilty', i.e. 'guilty of these deeds.'

A head noun within a noun phrase assigns genitive case to a modifying possessor noun phrase:

der Hut der Anna; Annas Hut.
'the hat of the Anna; Anna's hat'

The most complex governing category is the verb. The single argument of a one-place predicate (verb or predicate adjective) is most typically in the nominative case, as below, though both accusative and dative are found in so-called 'impersonal constructions':

(a) Ich schlafe. Ich friere. (nom.)
    'I am sleeping. I am freezing.'
(b) Mich hungert. Mich friert. (acc.)
    'Me hungers. Me freezes', i.e. 'I am hungry; I am freezing.'
(c) Mir ist warm. (dat.)
    'Me is warm', i.e. 'I am warm.'

These impersonal constructions were more frequent in earlier stages of

German, but they still exist in the modern language. With two-place predicates, one argument is in the nominative case (the subject), but the second argument may be accusative, dative or genitive, depending on the choice of verb. Most verbs take the accusative (and these noun phrases then behave syntactically as direct objects), a not inconsiderable number take the dative and just a handful take the genitive (only one or two of which are really productive in modern usage):

(a) Ich liebe dich. Er sieht meinen Vater. (nom.-acc.)
    'I love you. He sees my father'.
(b) Er hilft mir. Sie antwortete ihrem Vater. (nom.-dat.)
    'He is helping me. She answered her father.'
(c) Sie bedarf des Trostes. Er ermangelt der nötigen Kraft. (nom.-gen.)
    'She needs consolation. He lacks the requisite strength.'

In three-place predicate constructions consisting of a verb and three (prepositionless) noun phrases the most common case assignments are nominative–accusative–dative, followed by nominative–accusative–genitive, with just a handful of nominative–accusative–accusative:

(a) Ich schrieb meinem Vater einen Brief. Das rate ich dir. (nom.-acc.-dat.)
    'I wrote my father a letter.   That advise I you (to do).'
(b) Man enthob ihn seines Amtes. Er schämt sich seines Sohnes. (nom.-acc.-gen.)
    'One relieved him (of) his office. He shames himself (of) his son.'
(c) Er lehrt mich eine Sprache. Er hieß mich einen Toren. (nom.-acc.-acc.)
    'He is teaching me a language. He called me a fool.'

As in the other Germanic languages, many verbs also take prepositional phrases with characteristic prepositions when expanding on their minimally present argument noun phrases, e.g.:

(a) Ich denke oft *an* dich.
    'I think often *of* you.'
(b) Ich danke dir *für* deinen Brief.
    'I thank you *for* your letter.'

Not all case assignment in German is determined by a governing category in this way. For example, there are productive case contrasts in sentence time adverbials such as those shown below, in which the accusative refers to a specified (definite) time, and the genitive to an unspecified (indefinite) time:

(a) Er kam *letzten Freitag*. (acc.)
    'He came last Friday.'
(b) *Eines Tages* kam er. (gen.)
    'One day came he.'

Finally, the major morphological distinctions carried by the verb are illustrated in the chart of verb inflections.

Verb Inflections

	WEAK		STRONG	
Infinitive				
	sag+*en* 'to say'		trag+*en* 'to bear'	
Participles				
Present	sag+*end*		trag+*end*	
Past	*ge*+sag+*t*		*ge*+trag+*en*	
Imperative				
2nd Sg.				
(familiar)	sag+*(e)*		trag+*(e)*	
2nd Pl.				
(familiar)	sag+*t*		trag+*t*	
Polite form	sag+*en* Sie		trag+*en* Sie	

Present

	Indicative	*Subjunctive*	*Indicative*	*Subjunctive*
ich (1st)	sag+*e*	sag+*e*	trag+*e*	trag+*e*
du (2nd)	sag+*st*	sag+*st*	träg+*st*	trag+*st*
er, sie, es (3rd)	sag+*t*	sag+*e*	träg+*t*	trag+*e*
wir (1st)	sag+*en*	sag+*en*	trag+*en*	trag+*en*
ihr (2nd)	sag+*t*	sag+*t*	trag+*t*	trag+*t*
sie (3rd),				
Sie (2nd)	sag+*en*	sag+*en*	trag+*en*	trag+*en*

Past

	Indicative	*Subjunctive*	*Indicative*	*Subjunctive*
ich (1st)	sag+*te*	sag+*te*	trug	trüg+*e*
du (2nd)	sag+*test*	sag+*test*	trug+*st*	trüg+*st*
er, sie, es (3rd)	sag+*te*	sag+*te*	trug	trüg+*e*
wir (1st)	sag+*ten*	sag+*ten*	trug+*en*	trüg+*en*
ihr (2nd)	sag+*tet*	sag+*tet*	trug+*t*	trüg+*t*
sie (3rd),				
Sie (2nd)	sag+*ten*	sag+*ten*	trug+*en*	trüg+*en*

As in all the other Germanic languages, two basic classes of verb need to be distinguished: weak (exemplified by *sagen* 'to say') and strong (exemplified by *tragen* 'to bear'). The strong class undergoes vowel alternations in the stem (so-called 'ablaut') in addition to taking inflectional affixes for person and number agreement, etc. The number of strong verbs has been historically on the decline and there has been a certain levelling and redistribution of vowel alternants among the different tense and person categories that these alternants distinguish (especially in Early New High German), but Modern German still has a large class of strong verbs which includes some of the most common verbs in the language (*geben* 'to give', *essen* 'to eat', *liegen* 'to lie', *sehen* 'to see', *riechen* 'to smell', *gießen* 'to pour', *fliegen* 'to fly', *schreiben* 'to write', *sprechen* 'to speak', *fallen* 'to fall', *fahren* 'to travel', and many others). The weak class does not undergo such vowel alternations and takes (partially different) inflectional affixes for person and number agreement.

Proceeding down the chart of verb inflections, the German infinitive marker is an *-en* suffix attached to the stem. The present participle is formed by adding the suffix *-end*. The past participle consists of a *-t* suffix for weak verbs and an *-en* suffix for strong verbs, with a *ge-* prefix for both in cases where the first syllable of the stem is stressed. If the first syllable is not stressed (e.g. *bemérken* 'to notice'), this initial *ge-* is omitted (*bemérkt* 'noticed' not **gebemérkt*). There are three imperative forms with identical morphologies for weak and strong verbs, as shown. German has only two simple tenses, present and past, both inherited from Proto-Germanic and shared with other Germanic languages. Numerous compound tenses are formed from combinations of *haben* 'to have', *sein* 'to be' and *werden* 'to be/ become' plus past participle or infinitive, e.g. the perfect (*ich habe gesagt* 'I have said'), pluperfect (*ich hatte gesagt* 'I had said'), future (*ich werde sagen* 'I will say'), future perfect (*ich werde gesagt haben* 'I will have said') and so on. These compounds were fixed in the Old High German period. The person and number agreement suffixes of the present tense are identical for weak and strong verbs: four suffixes (*-e, -st, -t, -en*) are divided among the six grammatically distinguishable types of subjects that the verb agrees with (first, second and third persons singular, first, second and third persons plural). For stems ending in various (primarily dental) consonants, e.g. *-t* in *wart+en* 'to wait', an epenthetic *e* appears before the *-st* and *-t* suffixes (compare *sag+st/wart+est* and *sag+t/wart+et*). A special form for the subjunctive exists only in the third person singular (*er sage* as opposed to *er sagt*); otherwise subjunctive and indicative are identical (though productive paradigms for a distinct present subjunctive do exist for *sein* 'to be', the modal auxiliaries and one or two other verbs). The past tense indicative inflections for weak verbs all contain an initial *t-*, and differ in several respects from the corresponding strong verb indicative inflections, as shown. The past subjunctive of weak verbs is identical to the indicative, but the past subjunctive of strong verbs exhibits numerous contrasts with the indicative: first and third persons singular show *-e* rather than *-Ø* and the stem vowel is umlauted wherever possible.

4 Syntax

One of the most interesting features of Modern German syntax, in comparison with other languages, is its word order (particularly the position of the verb). Within the Germanic language family, German is striking for the extent to which it has remained conservative, preserving structural properties of both Old High German and the Germanic parent language itself. The Scandinavian languages and English, by contrast, have undergone more extensive syntactic changes in the same time period, with Dutch being intermediate between German and English. The present summary will accordingly illustrate some of the basic features of German verb position, and will outline some of the major syntactic differences which now distinguish German from one of the more radical Germanic languages, namely English.

There are three major positions of the verb in German clauses: final position, second position (i.e. the verb is the second clause-level constituent) and first position. The basic rule is: final position in subordinate clauses; second and first position in main clauses. A more precise statement, however, must first distinguish between finite and non-finite (i.e. infinitival and participial) verb forms. In subordinate clauses containing a finite verb (and, optionally, any additional non-finite verbs), all verb forms are final (in the order non-finite before finite), e.g.:

(a) Ich weiß, daß Heinrich die Frau *liebt*.
     'I know that Henry the woman *loves*', i.e. 'loves the woman.'
(b) Ich glaube, daß mein Vater vor einigen Tagen nach London *gefahren ist*.
     'I believe that my father several days ago to London *travelled has*.'

In non-finite subordinate clauses, non-finite verbs are again final:

Ich freue mich darauf, abends in der Wirtschaft Bier *zu trinken*.
'I am looking forward to-it, evenings in the pub beer *to drink*', i.e.
'I am looking forward to drinking beer in the pub in the evenings.'

And so they are even in main clauses, although the finite verb now stands in second position (a-b) or first position (c-d):

(a) Heinrich *liebt* die Frau.
     'Henry *loves* the woman.'
(b) Mein Vater *ist* vor einigen Tagen nach London *gefahren*.
     'My father *has* several days ago to London *travelled*.'
(c) *Liebt* Heinrich die Frau?
     'Loves Henry the woman?' i.e. 'Does Henry love the woman?'
(d) *Ist* mein Vater vor einigen Tagen nach London *gefahren*?
     '*Has* my father several days ago to London *travelled*?'

German verb compounds consisting of a separable element (e.g. an adjective, particle, even a prepositional phrase or a noun phrase) in conjunction with a verb provide further examples of verb-final structures. The separable element assumes the same position as a non-finite verb form, and hence German main clauses frequently end in a verbal satellite constituent, such as *tot* 'dead' from the compound *totschlagen* 'to beat dead':

Der König *schlug* den Feigling *tot*.
'The king *beat* the coward *dead*.'

In subordinate clauses, satellite and verb stand together, and the verb alone, not the whole verbal complex, provides the domain for the attachment of infinitival *zu* 'to':

(a) Ich weiß, daß der König den Feigling *totschlug*.
'I know that the king the coward *dead-beat*', i.e. 'beat the coward dead.'
(b) Ich freue mich darauf, den Feigling *totzuschlagen*.
'I look forward to-it, the coward *dead-to-beat*.'

The final position of verbal forms in the above structures is not rigidly adhered to, however. Various constituents can stand to the right of the verb, and the frequency with which they do so is a matter of style: postposings are more frequent in informal, conversational German; and less frequent in formal, written German. There are strict rules governing which constituents can be postposed and which cannot. Direct objects, for example, cannot be postposed over the verbal satellite *über* 'across' (from *übersetzen* 'set across') in the following example, regardless of style:

(a) Man *setzte* die Urlauber in einem Boot *über*.
'One set the holidaymakers in a boat across'
(b) * Man *setzte* in einem Boot *über* die Urlauber.
'One set in a boat across the holidaymakers'

Nor can obligatory adjuncts (or strictly subcategorised constituents) move to rightmost position, as exemplified in the ungrammatical (b) in which the obligatorily present prepositional phrase has been postposed behind the infinitive *verleiten* 'to lead (astray)':

(a) Die Gelegenheit *wird* ihn bestimmt zu einem voreiligen Schritt *verleiten*.
'The opportunity will him certainly to a rash move lead', i.e. 'will certainly encourage him to make a rash move.'
(b) * Die Gelegenheit *wird* ihn bestimmt *verleiten* zu einem voreiligen Schritt.
'The opportunity will him certainly lead to a rash move.'

The constituents which can move are in general: (1) those which are heavy, i.e. which are long in terms of number of words, and complex in their internal structure; and (2) those which are more loosely integrated into the interpretation of ᵗhe sentence, e.g. optional adverbial constituents which can serve as 'afterthoughts'. With regard to (1), notice that non-subject embedded finite clauses in German *must* be postposed behind a 'final' verb form:

(a) * Er *hatte* daß er nicht lange leben würde *gewußt*.
'He had that he not long live would known.'

(b) Er *hatte gewußt*, daß er nicht lange leben würde.
'He had known, that he not long live would.'

With infinitival embeddings (which are typically shorter than finite clauses), the postposing is regularly optional rather than obligatory:

(a) Er *hatte* die Frau zu gewinnen *gehofft*.
'He had the woman to win hoped', i.e. 'He had hoped to win the woman.'
(b) Er *hatte gehofft*, die Frau zu gewinnen.
'He had hoped, the woman to win.'

As an example of (2), consider:

(a) Ich erzähle dir gleich, was ich bei Müllers *gehört habe*.
'I tell you right-away, what I at the Müllers (place) heard have.'
(b) Ich erzähle dir gleich, was ich *gehört habe* bei Müllers.
'I tell you right-away, what I heard have at the Müllers (place).'

The verb-second structures of the main clauses allow a wide variety of constituents to occupy first position, not just a subject. Some typical examples are given below, involving various fronted adverbials (a-d), non-subject noun phrases (e-f), a verb phrase (g), non-finite verb forms (h-i), an adjective (j) and an embedded clause (k):

(a) Möglicherweise *hat* Heinrich uns *vergessen*.
'Possibly has Henry us forgotten', i.e. 'Possibly Henry has forgotten us.'
(b) Gestern *sind* wir ins Theater *gegangen*.
'Yesterday have we to-the theatre gone.'
(c) In München *wohnt* der Mann.
'In Munich resides the man.'
(d) Schön singt die Opernsängerin.
'Beautifully sings the opera singer.'
(e) Den Hund *sieht* die Katze.
'The dog (acc.) sees the cat (nom.)', i.e. 'The cat sees the dog.'
(f) Dem Mann *habe* ich das Buch *gegeben*.
'The man (dat.) have I the book (acc.) given.'
(g) Das Auto zu reparieren *hat* der Junge *versucht*.
'The car to repair has the boy tried', i.e. 'The boy has tried to repair the car.'
(h) *Gewinnen müssen* wir.
'Win must we', i.e. 'Win we must.'
(i) *Bestraft muß* er werden.
'Punished must he be.'
(j) Dumm *bin* ich nicht.
'Stupid am I not.'
(k) Daß er oft lügt *wissen* wir alle.
'That he often lies know we all.'

Only one constituent can typically precede the verb in these constructions. A slight exception is provided by structures such as *gestern abend auf der*

Party fehlte Heinrich 'yesterday evening at the party was-missing Henry', in which two thematically related constituents precede, *gestern abend* and *auf der Party*. But normally this is not possible. The most normal position for the subject in the above verb-second structures is immediately after the verb, though it can sometimes stand further to the right as well.

All of the structures just given are semantically declarative statements. Verb-first structures, by contrast, occur in a variety of primarily non-declarative sentence types, including yes-no questions (see above). Other verb-first structures are: imperatives (a), exclamations (b), and counterfactual and conditional clauses (c-d):

(a) *Bringen* Sie das Buch herein!
     'Bring you the book in-here.'
(b) *Bist* du aber schmutzig!
     'Are you ever dirty.'
(c) *Hätte* ich nur Zeit, ich würde Ihnen helfen.
     'Had I only time, I would you help.'
(d) *Kommt* er, so sehe ich ihn.
     'Comes he, then see I him', i.e. If he comes, then I will see him.'

Modern colloquial German also exhibits a verb-first pattern in 'dramatic' narrative style :

Kommt da plötzlich jemand hereingeschneit.
'Comes then suddenly someone bursting-in', i.e. 'Then suddenly someone comes bursting in.'

This pattern was more productive in earlier stages of the language.

The verb-second and verb-first structures of German main clauses have close parallels in all the modern Germanic languages. Even English, which has gone furthest in the direction of fixing SVO, employs a verb-first rule in an almost identical set of environments to German, and it has numerous subject-verb inversion rules creating verb-second structures in a significant number of the environments that we have seen for German (see Hawkins 1986: chs. 11 and 12 for a summary).

Before leaving the topic of word order, notice that the positioning of other sentence-level constituents in German apart from the verb is relatively free. Within the other major phrasal categories, however (the noun phrase, the adjective phrase, the prepositional phrase), the ordering of daughter constituents is just as fixed as in English.

With its rich inflectional morphology, verb-final structures and word order freedom, Modern German preserves syntactic features that were common to all the older West Germanic languages. Modern English, by contrast, has essentially lost its case morphology on nouns (as well as other inflectional morphology), has fixed basic SVO word order, and permits less sentence-level word order freedom. Modern English syntax also differs from that of

Modern German in other significant ways. Most of these are the result of English having effected changes which were either not carried out, or carried out to a much lesser extent, in German. We shall conclude with a very brief enumeration of some more of these contrasts.

English has larger and semantically broader classes of subject and direct object noun phrases than German, i.e. the quantity and semantic type of noun phrases that undergo rules sensitive to these grammatical relations is greater in English than in German. For example, many direct objects of English correspond to dative-marked noun phrases in German, which are arguably not direct objects since they cannot be converted to passive subjects. Compare the English sentences below with their German translations and with the corresponding passive sentences:

(a) She loves the man/him.
(b) Sie liebt *den Mann/ihn*. (acc.)

(a) She helped the man/him.
(b) Sie half *dem Mann/ihm*. (dat.)

(a) The man/He is loved.
(b) Der Mann/Er wird geliebt.

(a) The man/He was helped.
(b) *Der Mann/Er wurde geholfen.

The accusative-marked (and semantically prototypically patient) noun phrases of German in these constructions correspond to English direct objects and are also direct objects in German. But the dative (and semantically recipient) argument of *helfen* 'to help' also corresponds to a direct object in English, though it is not itself a direct object in German. The case syncretism of English has collapsed the distinct classes of noun phrases in German into a larger class of direct objects, with consequences for both the productivity of various syntactic operations, and for the semantic breadth or diversity of the direct object relation.

Grammatical subjects in English also constitute a larger and semantically more diverse class. English frequently has subjects with non-agentive semantic roles where these are impossible in German, as the following selection shows:

(a) *The king* visited his people. (Su. = agent)
(b) *Der König* besuchte sein Volk.

(a) *My guitar* broke a string. (Su. = locative; cf. *on my guitar...*)
(b) *Meine Gitarre* (zer)riß eine Saite.

(a) *This hotel* forbids dogs. (Su. = locative; cf. *in this hotel...*)
(b) *Dieses Hotel* verbietet Hunde.

(a) *A penny* once bought 2 to 3 pins. (Su = instrumental; cf. *with a penny...*)
(b) **Ein Pfennig* kaufte früher 2 bis 3 Stecknadeln.

(a) *This advertisement* will sell us a lot. (Su. = instrumental; cf. *with this ad...*)
(b) **Diese Anzeige* verkauft uns viel.

Related to this contrast is the existence of a productive set of raising rules in English, creating derived subjects and objects. These operations are either non-existent or extremely limited in German, as the following literal German translations of the English structures show. The English sentences (a-c) exemplify subject-to-subject raising, i.e. *John* is the original subject of *to be ill* and is raised to become subject of *seems*, etc.; (d-e) involve subject-to-object raising, whereby *John* has been raised to become direct object of *believe*, etc.; and (f-h) give examples of object-to-subject raising (or tough movement), in which the original object of *to study* has been raised to become subject of *is easy*, etc.:

(a) John seems to be ill.
(b) John happens to be ill.
(c) John ceased to be ill.

(a) Johann scheint krank zu sein.
(b) *Johann geschieht krank zu sein.
(c) *Johann hörte auf krank zu sein.

(d) I believe John to be ill.
(e) I understand him to be stupid.

(d) *Ich glaube Johann krank zu sein.
(e) *Ich verstehe ihn dumm zu sein.

(f) Linguistics is easy to study.
(g) Literature is pleasant to study.
(h) History is boring to study.

(f) Die Linguistik ist leicht zu studieren.
(g) *Die Literatur ist angenehm zu studieren.
(h) *Die Geschichte ist langweilig zu studieren.

Related to these more productive clause-external raising rules in English is the fact that the extraction of *wh* elements out of subordinate clauses is also more productive in English than in German. For example, German can typically not extract out of finite subordinate clauses:

That is the prize which I hope (that you will win △).

*Das ist der Preis, den ich hoffe (daß du △ gewinnen wirst).

Nor can German extract out of a prepositional phrase, thereby stranding a preposition, whereas such extraction and stranding is typically optional in English:

(a) The woman who I went to the movies PP(with △).
(b) The woman PP(with whom) I went to the movies.

(a) *Die Frau, der ich ins Kino PP(mit △) ging.
(b) Die Frau, PP(mit der) ich ins Kino ging.

The (b) versions of these sentences involve a fronting (or 'pied piping') of the whole prepositional phrase, rather than extraction out of it. German also has a productive verb phrase pied piping rule which is without parallel in English:

(a) *The man VP(to kill whom) I have often tried
(b) The man who I have often tried VP(to kill △).

(a) Der Mann VP(den zu töten) ich öfters versucht habe
(b) Der Mann, den ich VP(△ zu töten) öfters versucht habe; OR
    Der Mann, den ich öfters versucht habe VP(△ zu töten)

Finally, numerous deletions which are possible in English are blocked in German, in part because the case system of German renders non-identical deletion targets which are identical in English. An example is given below, in which the leftmost occurrence of *the king* can delete in English, whereas the accusative-marked *den König* in German is not identical to the dative *dem König* and cannot be deleted by this latter:

(a) Fred saw *the king* and thanked *the king*.
(b) Fred saw   and thanked *the king*.

(a) Fritz sah *den König* und dankte *dem König*.
(b) *Fritz sah   und dankte *dem König*.

Deletions are also more restricted in German for other reasons as well. For example, deletions, like the extractions discussed above, cannot strand a preposition, even when the relevant noun phrases have identical cases:

(a) He is the father of *the boy* and the friend of *the boy*.
(b) He is the father of   and the friend of *the boy*.

(a) Er ist der Vater von *dem Jungen* und der Freund von *dem Jungen*.
(b) *Er ist der Vater von   und der Freund von *dem Jungen*.

Deletion of a relative pronoun is also impossible in German, but possible in English:

(a) The woman who(m) I love is coming tonight.
(b) The woman   I love is coming tonight.

(a) Die Frau, die ich liebe, kommt heute abend.
(b) *Die Frau   ich liebe   kommt heute abend.

Summarising, we have the following overall typological contrasts between English and German:

German	English
More grammatical morphology	Less grammatical morphology
More word order freedom	Less word order freedom
Less semantic diversity of grammatical relations	More semantic diversity of grammatical relations
Less raising	More raising
Less extraction	More extraction
More pied piping	Less pied piping
Less deletion	More deletion

Bibliography

Among numerous grammars of German written in English, Russon (1967) is the best concise traditional statement. For phonology, reference may be made to Moulton (1962), while Hawkins (1986) contains a survey of the major areas of syntactic and morphological contrast between German and English. In German, Althaus et al. (1973a) includes a valuable summary of major areas of German grammar, with extensive further references; Bierwisch (1963) is the first detailed generative treatment of the syntax of the German verb and of numerous related rules, and is still considered a classic.

Althaus et al. (1973b) includes an excellent summary of dialect differences among German regions, the major historical changes in the different periods of both High and Low German and the current status of German in countries where German is not a national language, with extensive further references throughout. Bach (1965) is a standard reference work on the history of the German language, with extensive further references, while Lockwood (1968) is an excellent summary of the major syntactic changes from Old High German to New High German. Keller (1961) is a useful summary of numerous dialects. Clyne (1984) is a most useful discussion of the sociolinguistic situation in those countries in which German is the national language or one of the national languages.

References

Althaus, H.P., H. Henne and H.E. Wiegand. 1973a. *Lexicon der germanistischen Linguistik. Studienausgabe I* (Max Niemeyer Verlag, Tübingen)
—— 1973b. *Lexicon der germanistischen Linguistik. Studienausgabe II* (Max Niemeyer Verlag, Tübingen)

Bach, A. 1965. *Geschichte der deutschen Sprache* (Quelle and Meyer, Heidelberg)

Bierwisch, M. 1963. *Grammatik des deutschen Verbs* (=Studia Grammatica 2) (Akademieverlag, Berlin)

Clyne, M. 1984. *Language and Society in the German-speaking Countries* (Cambridge University Press, Cambridge)

Hawkins, J.A. 1986. *A Comparative Typology of English and German: Unifying the Contrasts* (University of Texas Press, Austin, and Croom Helm, London)

Keller, R.E. 1961. *German Dialects. Phonology and Morphology with Selected Texts* (Manchester University Press, Manchester)

Lockwood, W.B. 1968. *Historical German Syntax* (Clarendon Press, Oxford)

Moulton, W.G. 1962. *The Sounds of English and German* (University of Chicago Press, Chicago)

Russon, L.J. 1967. *Complete German Course for First Examinations* (Longman, London)

5 Dutch

Jan G. Kooij

1 Introduction

Modern Standard Dutch is the official language of the Netherlands and one of the official languages of Belgium. In the two countries together, the number of speakers is approximately 20 million. The official Dutch name of the language is *Nederlands*. It is sometimes called *Hollands*, after the most influential province, and the variety of Dutch that is spoken in Belgium is often, incorrectly, referred to as Flemish (*Vlaams*). Frisian (Dutch *Fries*) is a separate language spoken in the north-east of the Netherlands and is in some respects closer to English than to Dutch. *Afrikaans*, the language of part of the white and mixed-race population of the Republic of South Africa, is derived from Dutch dialects but is now regarded as a separate language. Dutch is also the official language of administration in Surinam (formerly Dutch Guyana) and in the Dutch Antilles but it is not widely spoken there. Some Dutch is still spoken in Indonesia. Dutch-based creole languages have never had many speakers, and the language known as *Negerhollands* ('Negro Dutch') on the Virgin Islands has become virtually extinct. Both Sranan, the English-based creole spoken by a large number of inhabitants of Surinam, and Papiamentu, a Spanish-based creole spoken in the Antilles, have been influenced by Dutch, and Sranan increasingly so. Afrikaans also shows definite features of creolisation.

The word *Dutch* derives from Middle Dutch *Diets* or *Duuts*, the name for the (Low) German vernacular; somewhat confusingly for speakers of English, *Duits* is now the Dutch name for (High) German.

Dialect variation in the Dutch language area is considerable, and a number of geographical dialects are not mutually intelligible. Ever since compulsory education was introduced uniformity in speaking and writing has increased, though less so in the Belgian area than in the Netherlands. The process of standardisation still continues. The large majority of inhabitants have a fair command of the standard language, but in some areas in the north, the east and the south a number of people are virtually bilingual. Language variation is politically insignificant in the Netherlands, but the situation in Belgium is more complex. After the establishment of the

139

boundaries of the Dutch Republic in the seventeenth century, the prestige of Dutch in the southern provinces that are now part of Belgium rapidly declined. Its official recognition next to French has been the subject of bitter controversies, and the language situation is still an important factor in political and cultural life. The boundary between the Dutch-speaking area and the French-speaking area runs from west to east just south of Brussels. In the south-east of the country lives a small German-speaking minority. Minority languages in the Netherlands include Chinese (mostly the Cantonese dialect), Bahasa Indonesia and other forms of Malay, Sranan and, more recently, Turkish and North African dialects of Arabic.

2   History and Typology

Dutch belongs to the West Germanic branch of the Germanic languages and is based on Low Franconian dialects spoken in the south of the present language area. Compared to the two other major West Germanic languages, English and German, Dutch is in fundamental respects closer to German. Like English, however, it has lost most of the original Germanic noun morphology, and the proximity of the Romance language area is apparent from the presence of a sizable Romance vocabulary in the Dutch lexicon. Some characteristic differences and similarities among Dutch, English and German are the following.

(a) Germanic [g] went to [x]: Dutch *goed* [xut] vs. English *good*, German *gut*,

(b) Short back vowel before [l] plus consonant went to [au]: Dutch *oud* vs. English *old*, German *alt*,

(c) Initial [sk] went to [sx]: Dutch *schip* vs. English *ship*, German *Schiff*, and in other positions [sk] went to [s]: Dutch *vis* vs. English *fish*, German *Fisch* with [š],

(d) Final devoicing of obstruents: Dutch *pond*, German *Pfund* with final [t] vs. English *pound*,

(e) Initial voicing of fricatives: Dutch *zien*, German *sehen* with initial [z] vs. English *see*,

(f) Predominance of older plural endings over the more recent ending *-s*: Dutch *boeken*, German *Bücher* vs. English *books*,

(g) No grammatical umlaut: Dutch *dag–dagelijks*, English *day–daily* vs. German *Tag–täglich*,

(h) No initial [š] in consonant clusters: Dutch *steen*, English *stone* vs. German *Stein* [štain],

(i) No affricates and fricatives from original plosives [p], [t], [k]: Dutch *pond*, English *pound* vs. German *Pfund*; Dutch *tien*, English *ten* vs. German *zehn*; Dutch *maken*, English *make* vs. German *machen*.

The latter feature Dutch shares with Low German, which was once a major literary language in the German-speaking area (see page 114).

From the period of Old Dutch or Old Low Franconian (*Oud Nederlands*) only a few texts have survived, mainly fragments of psalms translated into the vernacular. From the period of Middle Dutch (*Middelnederlands*, 1100–1500) a considerable number of literary and non-literary texts have been preserved and edited; most of these are written in the dialects of the leading southern provinces, Flanders and Brabant. By the time that Modern Dutch (*Nieuw Nederlands*) developed, the language had already lost most of its case distinctions and flectional morphology, though some of it was still represented in the orthography. The modern standard language is based on the dialects spoken in and around Amsterdam, since by that time political and cultural leadership had gravitated to the northern provinces; pronunciation was influenced considerably by the speech of immigrants from the Brabant area after the fall of Antwerp in 1585. Typical features of the developing standard pronunciation were the fixation of the diphthongised long [i] as [ɛɪ] rather than [ɑɪ], Dutch *rijden* vs. English *ride* and German *reiten*, and the diphthongisation of original Germanic [u] to [ʌü], Dutch *huis* vs. English *house*, German *Haus*. Diphthongisation also affected French loans: compare English *brewery* and Dutch *brouwerij* with final [ɛɪ], English *flute* and Dutch *fluit* with [ʌü]. Another recent feature in the phonology is the weakening of intervocalic [d] to [j] in inflected forms: *goed*, 'good', inflected form *goede* or *goeie*; many of these forms coexist as formal vs. informal variants.

As elsewhere in Europe, the writing of grammars in the native language began in the period of the Renaissance; the main focus of the older grammarians was proper usage, standardisation and orthography. The most important early contribution to the scholarly study of Dutch and its relationships with the surrounding languages was made by the Amsterdam linguist Lambert ten Kate (1723). Not until the nineteenth century did Dutch universities introduce chairs for the study of the Dutch language and for Dutch philology and lexicography. There is no Language Academy, but the foundation of a Council for the Dutch Language (Raad voor de Nederlandse Taal) in which the Netherlands and Belgium participate has now been agreed upon.

The uniformisation of the orthography was accomplished in the nineteenth century on the initiative of the central government. The basic rules for the present orthography were laid out in 1863 by De Vries and Te Winkel. They are mildly etymological, for instance the diphthong [ɛɪ] is spelled either *ij* or *ei* according to its history. The spelling of inflected forms of nouns and verbs follows the morphology rather than the phonology. So, the stem *vind* 'find', pronounced [ʋɪnt] is spelled with final *-d* because of the infinitive *vinden*, and the form *hij vindt* 'he finds', also pronounced [ʋɪnt] is spelled with final *-dt* because of *loop* 'walk', *hij loopt* 'he walks'. This aspect of the system has been challenged but it has never been changed. Otherwise, Dutch orthography follows the principle that distinct sounds are represented by different letters of the Roman alphabet, with the additional convention that a long vowel in closed syllables is represented by two letters and a short vowel by one: *aap* 'monkey' and *stap* 'step'; in open syllables, the difference between long vowels and short vowels is indicated by single and double consonants, respectively: *apen* 'monkeys' vs. *stappen* 'steps'. The spelling of vowels is less conservative than in English because the major developments in the standardisation of the pronunciation were taken into account. Peculiar features of Dutch orthography are the use of the letter *ij*, which is considered a single letter, for diphthongised [i] as in *rijden* 'ride', and the use of *oe* for the monophthong [u] as in *boek*, *Oeganda* vs. German *Buch*, *Uganda*. The spelling of the Romance vocabulary has been rationalised to some extent, as appears from Dutch *fotografie* vs. English *photography*, but proposals for further adaptation, e.g. *k* instead of *c* in *collectie* 'collection' have met with resistance, especially in Belgium.

3   Phonology

Tables 5.1 and 5.2 show the distinctive segmental phonemes of standard Dutch. Dutch has a comparatively simple consonant system. The main distinctive features are place of articulation, manner of articulation and

Table 5.1: Vowel Phonemes of Dutch, Schematised

	Front		Centralised	Back
High	i	ü		u
Mid	e, ɪ	ö	œ, ə	ɔ, o
	ɛ			ɑ
Low			a	
Diphthongs	ɛɪ		ʌü	ɑu

Table 5.2: Consonant Phonemes of Dutch

	Obstruents		Nasals	Liquids	Glides
	Plosive	Fricative			
Labial	p, b	f, v	m		ʋ
Alveolar	t, d	s, z	n	l	
Palatal					j
Velar	k, -	x, ɣ	ŋ		
Uvular				ʀ	
Glottal					h

presence vs. absence of voicing. The language has no affricates, and no palatal obstruents. Labial fricatives and [ʋ] are labio-dental and all fricatives are strident. Nasals and liquids are never syllabic. [ʀ] is mostly uvular and not often rolled with the tip of the tongue; in most positions, it is distinctly audible: *water* [ʋatǝʀ] 'water', *hard* [haʀt] 'hard'. The [l] is more velarised than it is in German. In some dialects in the south-west, initial [h] is dropped: *oek* [uk] instead of *hoek* [huk], 'corner'. Palatalisation is mostly restricted to alveolars before [j] or non-syllabic [i̯]: [t̯] in *kat+je* 'cat (diminutive)' and [š] in *sociaal* 'social'. Nasalisation of vowels before nasal consonants is absent: *hond* 'dog' is [hɔnt], not [hɔ̃nt] and *hond+je* 'dog (diminutive)' is [hɔɲt̯jǝ] not [hɔ̃ɲt̯jǝ]. It is also avoided in French loans: *plafond* 'ceiling' is [plafɔ́n] rather than [plafɔ̃].

The voiced-voiceless opposition is phonetically quite distinct in plosives, but not in fricatives. For many speakers, the difference between *s/z* and *f/v* is one of tenseness rather than one of voicing. The difference between the voiceless and voiced velar fricatives has become almost allophonic: voiced (or lax) after long vowels word-medially, and voiceless elsewhere. A few exceptions to this regularity are historical and are indicated by the orthography: *lachen* 'laugh' [laxǝn] vs. *vlaggen* 'flags' [ɣlaɣǝn]. The realisation of the velar fricative as [ç] as in German *ich* 'I', or as voiced [ɣ] in word-initial position is regarded as dialectal, more particularly as 'southern'. In the non-native vocabulary, the word-medial alveolar fricative is predictably voiced after long vowels: *televisie*, 'television', *Indonesië* 'Indonesia', *NASA* 'id'. Voiced word-initial fricatives are only minimally distinct from the voiceless fricatives that were reintroduced into the language in loanwords: *fier* 'proud' (from French *fière*) [fiːʀ] vs. *vier* 'four' [ʋiːʀ]. Voiced [g] is lacking because it changed to [x], also in French loans: *galant* 'gallant' [xalánt].

The vowel system of Dutch is somewhat more complex. The opposition long-short is important in the lexicon and in the morphology: *maan* 'moon' vs. *man* 'man'; *boos* 'angry' vs. *bos* 'woods'; *veel* 'much' vs. *vel* 'skin'; *vies* 'dirty' vs. *vis* 'fish'. High vowels are tense rather than long, but pair with long vowels in the phonological system. Dutch has a full set of rounded front vowels.

Non-low back vowels are rounded. Long [a] is central and very open, but its pronunciation differs considerably across the language area. Long [e] is closed, and diphthongal: [eʲ], but long [o] is markedly less diphthongal than its counterpart in English. Short vowels, except schwa, cannot occur in word-final position. Long variants of the short vowels occur before [ʀ], as in *deur* [dœːʀ] 'door' vs. *deuk* [dök] 'dent', and also in loanwords, e.g. *militair* 'military (adj.)', [militέːʀ] vs. *ver* [vɛʀ] 'far'. The unstressed vowel and epenthetic vowel [ǝ] is not always phonetically distinguishable from short [œ] but is clearly a separate phoneme in the system. The pronunciation of the three rising diphthongs varies, but the very open varieties, e.g. [ɑɪ] for [ɛɪ] are socially stigmatised, and so are the non-diphthongised varieties that occur in the larger cities in the western part of the country, e.g. Amsterdam [ɛː] for [ɛɪ] in [fɛːn] *fijn*, 'fine', and The Hague [œː] for [ʌü] in [dœːn] *duin* 'dune'.

One of the most typical features of Dutch pronunciation, which it shares with German, is the devoicing of all obstruents in word-final and syllable-final position. This led to morphological contrasts such as *kruis–kruisen* 'cross–crosses' vs. *huis–huizen* 'house–houses', *hees–hese* 'husky–id., inflected form' vs. *vies–vieze* 'dirty–id., inflected form' and *eis–eisen* 'to demand' vs. *reis–reizen* 'to travel'. That the rule is still operative can be seen from the pronunciation of foreign words like *Sidney* [sɪtni], *Rizla* [ʀɪsla]. Its effects can be undone through regressive voicing assimilation at morpheme boundaries and in sandhi position: *huisdeur* 'front door' is pronounced [hʌüzdœːʀ] and *Mazda* is pronounced [mɑzda]. But when the second of two adjacent obstruents is a fricative, voicing assimilation is progressive: *huisvuil* 'garbage' is [hʌüsfʌül], and *badzout* 'bathing salts' is [bɑtsɑut].

Another typical feature is the insertion of [ə] in non-homorganic consonant clusters in word-final position and at morpheme boundaries: *melk* 'milk' [mɛlək], *arm* 'arm' [ɑʀəm], *hopeloos* 'hopeless' [hopəlos]. A 'linking phoneme' [ə] also occurs in some compounds: *geitemelk* 'goat milk'. This is a characteristic difference between the pronunciation and the lexicons of Dutch and German: Dutch *mogelijk* 'possible', German *möglich*; Dutch *adelaar* 'eagle', German *Adler*. Glottalisation of initial vowels hardly occurs in Dutch and glides are inserted automatically between vowels except after [a]: *douane* 'customs' [duwánə], *theater* 'theatre' [tejátəʀ], compare German [teʔáːtɐ] 'id'. (Re)syllabification is pervasive, and V(C)C-V sequences will preferably be restructured to V(C)-CV, so that the word *gást+àrbeid+er* 'immigrant worker' will be pronounced [χás-tɑʀ-bɛɪ-ɑəʀ]. Geminates disappeared from the language, but can occur at morpheme boundaries and in sandhi position: *uit+trekken* 'to pull out' [ʌütːʀɛkən] vs. *uit+rekken* 'stretch' [ʌütʀɛkən]. Word-final -*n* after schwa is dropped in almost all contexts, so that for most speakers the difference between singular and plural has been reduced to a difference between Ø ending and -*e* ending: *straat–straten* 'street–streets', [stʀat]–[stʀatə]. This situation has been reinforced by a historical rule that deleted word-final schwa in nouns: Dutch *zon* 'sun', German *Sonne*; as a result of this rule, a large majority of native nouns end in a consonant. That this rule is no longer operative can be seen from the pronunciation of loans like English *score* [skóːʀə] and French *elite* [elítə]. Deletion of final [t] in consonant clusters is determined by complex morphological, phonological, and stylistic factors, but it is standard in the formation of diminutives: *lucht+je* 'smell (diminutive)' is pronounced [lœxjə].

Word stress in Dutch is lexical, which means that the location of main stress is unpredictable to a high degree. In words without internal morphological structure main stress tends to be on the (pre)final syllable, and there is a complex interaction between the distribution of stresses, vowel length and syllable weight. Compare *kóning* 'king' [kónɪŋ] and *koníjn* 'rabbit' [konέɪn]. All vowels can be stressed except schwa, unstressed vowels are often reduced but not in word-final position: *banáan* 'banana' [bɑnán], [bənán] but *Amérika* 'America' [ɑmérɪkɑ]. In the Romance vocabulary, Dutch has preserved (pre)final stress; as a consequence, there are systematic differences between the pronunciation of these words in Dutch and the pronunciation of their English cognates: *relátion–relátie* [ʀelátsi] but: *rélative–relatiéf* [ʀèlatíf], *sócial–sociáal* [sošjál]. Most suffixes of Romance origin have kept their stress in Dutch, including the verbal suffix *-eer* that was formed from the original French infinitive ending: *organiseer* 'organise' [ɔʀxaniʒé·ʀ]. Secondary stress on these words is predictably on the initial syllable when main stress is final. In contrast with the pattern of derived Romance words, most native suffixes and early Latin loans have lost their stress. Main stress in complex native words is usually on the stem: *lángzaam* 'slow' – *lángzaamheid* 'slowness', *árbeid* 'work' – *árbeider* 'worker', *vriend* 'friend' – *vríendelijk* 'friendly'. Nominal and verbal compounds normally have primary stress on the first element and secondary stress on the second element: *húisdeùr* 'front door', *uítvoèr* 'export', *ínleìd* 'introduce'. In some classes of derived forms, especially adjectives, main stress shifts to the last syllable preceding the suffix: *ínleìd–inleídend* 'introductory'.

Sentence intonation in Dutch is more 'flat' than the sentence intonation of (British) English. The typical intonation pattern for the Dutch declarative sentence involves two basic contours: a Low declining contour at the beginning and at the end, and a High declining contour in the middle. What is perceived as 'accent' is the result of either a rise towards the High contour or a fall from the High contour: *die **jongen** schrijft een **brief*** 'that boy is writing a letter'.

4 Morphology

Since Dutch lost most of its inflectional endings and case endings in the course of its history, its morphology, in that respect, is closer to English than it is to German. Compare the nominal paradigms for the phrase 'the day' in the chart given here. Case distinctions have been preserved to some extent

Nominal Paradigms

	Middle Dutch	*Modern Dutch*	*Modern German*
Singular			
Nom.	die dach	de dag	der Tag
Acc.	dien dach	de dag	den Tag
Gen.	des daghes	(van) de dag	des Tages
Dat.	dien daghe	(aan) de dag	dem Tag(e)

Plural

Nom.	die daghe		de dagen	die Tage
Acc.	die daghe		de dagen	die Tage
Gen.	der daghe	(van)	de dagen	der Tage
Dat.	dien daghen	(aan)	de dagen	den Tagen

in the forms of pronouns and in some relic forms such as *'s nachts* 'at night'. The basic distinction in both the nominal and the verbal paradigms, however, is the distinction between singular and plural. In the regular (or 'weak') verbal paradigm, singular forms are differentiated for person in the following way: first person stem + Ø, second and third person stem + *t*. As in the nominal paradigms, the contrast between stem-final voiced consonants and stem-final voiceless consonants is neutralised in the singular forms and not consistently represented in the orthography.

Verbal Paradigms

	'travel'	*'demand'*	*'find'*	*'put'*
Stem	reiz-	eis-	vind-	zet-
1st	reis	eis	vind	zet
Sg. 2nd	reist	eist	vindt	zet
3rd	reist	eist	vindt	zet
Pl.	reizen	eisen	vinden	zetten
Infinitive	reizen	eisen	vinden	zetten
Past part.	gereisd	geëist	gevonden	gezet

The basic tense opposition in verbs is between past and non-past. Past forms in regular verbs are made by adding *-de/-te* to the stem, and *-den/-ten* for the plural. Like English and German, Dutch has retained a number of 'strong' verbs where the past is formed by vowel change: *ik vond–I found–ich fand*. Regular past participles are formed by adding the prefix *ge-* and the suffix *-d/ -t*; strong verbs and a few others have the suffix *-en*. The auxiliaries of the perfect tense are *hebben* 'have' or *zijn* 'be'. Transitive verbs take *hebben*, but intransitives are split into two classes: *ik lach–ik heb gelachen* 'I laugh, I have laughed' and *ik val–ik ben gevallen* 'I have fallen'. The perfect tense is largely aspectual, and the future tense with the auxiliary *zullen* expresses modality rather than tense. The auxiliary of the passive voice is *worden*, but the perfect of the passive takes *zijn* 'be'. The phrase *de deur is gesloten* can be interpreted either as 'the door has been closed (by somebody)' or as 'the door is shut'.

The personal pronouns have subject forms and object forms, and full forms and reduced forms in both categories; see the chart of personal pronouns. In the spoken language, full forms have become almost emphatic and the reduced forms are commonly used. The neuter pronoun *het* is pronounced [ət]; *het* [hɛt] is used in the orthography. After prepositions, it is obligatorily replaced by the adverbial pronoun *er*: **ik denk aan het / ik denk*

Personal Pronouns

		Subject forms		Object forms	
		Full forms	Reduced forms	Full forms	Reduced forms
	1st	ik	'k	mij	me
Sg.	2nd	jij, u	je, -	jou, u	je, -
	3rd	hij, zij	-ie, ze	hem, haar	'm, 'r
		(het)	't	(het)	't
	1st	wij	we	ons	-
Pl.	2nd	jullie, u	-	jullie, u	-
	3rd	zij	ze	(hen), hun	ze

er aan 'I think of it'. The clitic pronoun *-ie* and reduced object pronouns cannot be preposed in the sentence: *ik heb 'm niet gezien* 'I haven't seen him', but not *'m heb ik niet gezien*. In the third person, there is strong interaction between personal pronouns and demonstratives, as can be seen from the following sequence of sentences:

Waar is *Jan? Die* komt vandaag niet. *Hij* is ziek; ik geloof dat-*ie* griep heeft.
'Where is John? He is not coming today. He is sick; I think he has the flu.'

The third person plural object pronoun *hen* was artificially introduced into the language and is hardly used; the pronoun *hun* occurs mostly after prepositions: *aan hun* 'to them'. In some dialects it is also used as a subject pronoun: *hun hebben 't gedaan* 'they did it'. A third person reflexive pronoun, *zich*, was introduced under the influence of German. Its syntactic distribution is notoriously complex, and many geographical and social dialects of Dutch still use *hem* instead of *zich*: *Jan heeft geen jas bij zich/ bij'm* 'John doesn't have a coat with him'.

The difference between the polite form of address *u* (pronounced [ü]) and the informal forms *jij/jullie* is comparable to the difference between German *Sie* and *du* and French *vous* and *tu*. As everywhere, the sociology of their usage is complicated. Southern forms of Dutch have different forms of address which include the older pronouns *gij/ge*.

In spite of the strong simplification of the nominal and pronominal paradigms, or, maybe, because of these developments, the gender system of Dutch is actually quite complex. Its major features may be summarised as follows:

(1) Nouns are divided into two classes: nouns with common gender, which take the definite determiner *de*, and nouns with neuter gender, which take the definite determiner *het*. In the plural, the determiner is *de* for both classes. In noun phrases with the indefinite determiner *een*, adjectives that modify a *de* word have the inflected form, and adjectives that modify a *het* word have the uninflected form. Compare the chart of gender distinctions in nouns.

Gender Distinctions in Nouns

	'the big city'	*'the big house'*
Sg. def.	de grote stad	het grote huis
Sg. indef.	een grote stad	een groot huis
Pl. def.	de grote steden	de grote huizen

(2) Nouns belonging to the *de* class are distinguished as masculine and feminine. For instance, words with the ending *-ing* are feminine and require the anaphoric pronoun *zij/ze*. For many speakers in the western area, however, the masculine/feminine distinction is no longer alive, or is felt to be a distinction of natural gender. Anaphoric reference to words denoting a non-human object by the pronouns *hij/hem* or *zij/haar* is sometimes avoided, as in the example: *wat vond je van die lezing? ik vond het vervelend* 'what did you think of that lecture? I found it boring'. In the Belgian area, the masculine/feminine gender distinction is very much alive.

(3) Normally, grammatical gender overrides natural gender, as appears from the usage of the relative pronouns *die* and *dat: de stad, die* 'the town which' vs. *het huis, dat* 'the house which' but also *de jongen, die* 'the boy who' vs. *het jongetje dat* 'the boy (diminutive) that'. However, when relative pronouns are combined with prepositions, the form of the relative pronoun is determined by the distinction human/non-human and not by the distinction between *de* words and *het* words. Compare: *de man, met* **wie** *ik gesproken heb* 'the man with whom I have been speaking' vs. *de stad* **waar** *ik geen kaart van had* 'the city of which I did not have a map'. In the spoken language, sentences like *de man waar ik mee gesproken heb* are not at all uncommon, and they are another indication that the gender system and the system of pronominal reference are unstable. The adverbial pronouns *er*, *daar*, *waar*, which replace the pronouns *het*, *dat*, *wat* in combination with prepositions are the only elements that allow prepositions to be stranded, as appears from the examples above. A sentence like *de man wie ik mee gesproken heb* is incorrect.

Both flection and derivation are predominantly suffixal. With respect to derivation (word formation), many native suffixes were originally elements with independent meanings that they lost in the course of history, and it would seem that, in the present-day language, some elements are going the same way: *rijk* 'rich', *arm* 'poor'; *zuurstofrijk* 'having much oxygen', *zuurstofarm* 'having little oxygen'. Most native suffixes also lost their stress, but some retained their stress and occur in compound-like derivations such as *vriendelijk+heid* 'friendliness' (German *-heit*), *verklaar+baar* 'explainable' (German *-bar*) and *werk+loos* 'unemployed' (German *-los*). Romance suffixes are often fully stressed, as shown in the section on phonology, but the morphological structure of the Romance vocabulary is by and large opaque. The main reason for this is that Dutch formed its own verbal stems on the basis of the original French infinitive: *demonstreer* 'demonstrate'.

Consequently, the common element in related nominal and verbal forms is a 'root' that cannot occur as an independent element: *demonstr+eer* 'demonstrate', *demonstr+atie* 'demonstration'. This is atypical for native word formation.

The Romance vocabulary also has a highly involved morphophonology, whereas native word formation in Dutch typically has not. With few exceptions, non-native affixes cannot be attached to native stems, but native affixes can be attached to non-native stems. For instance, a number of Romance verbs ending in *-eer* have both a Romance and a native nominalisation: *realis + atie* as well as *realis + eer + ing* 'realisation'. But a formation like English *reopen* would be totally impossible (the correct form is *heropen*, with the native prefix *her-*) though the prefix *re-* does occur, e.g. in *constructie* 'construction', *reconstructie* 'reconstruction'. All in all, it appears that the Romance vocabulary has been much less integrated into Dutch than it has been into English, and that both phonologically and morphologically it is still very much [-native], in spite of the fact that a number of Romance words are actually quite common, also in the spoken language.

A much discussed feature of Dutch morphology is the system of diminutives. The diminutive suffix is, actually, one of the few really productive derivational suffixes of the modern language. The basic form of the suffix is *-tje*, the variants are *-je* (after obstruents), *-etje* (in some cases after liquids and nasals); *-pje* and *-kje* are assimilated variants of *-tje*. So we have: *ei–eitje* 'egg', *aap–aapje* 'monkey', *man–mannetje* 'man', *maan–maantje* 'moon', *koning–koninkje* 'king' and *raam–raampje* 'window'. Diminutives are very frequent, and semantically they express a whole range of negative as well as positive attitudes and feelings besides the basic meaning of 'small'. A much used variant of the *-je* forms in the spoken language (after consonants except [t]) is *-ie*: *meisje–meissie* 'girl'. The same paradigm, with the additional ending *-s* is used to form adverbs from certain adjectives: *zacht* 'soft', *zachtjes* 'softly'; *bleek* 'pale', *bleekjes* 'somewhat pale'.

Prefixation is, generally speaking, more transparent and more productive than suffixation and the phonological boundary between prefix and stem is more distinct as well. The prefix *be-* is used to form transitive verbs from intransitives, as in *spreken* 'speak', *bespreken* 'discuss', and can also be used to form verbs from nouns: *dijk* 'dike', *bedijken* 'to put a dike around —'. The prefix *ver-* has a causative meaning in some verbs: *hitte* 'heat (noun)' – *verhitten* 'heat (transitive)', *breed* 'large, broad' – *verbreden* 'enlarge, broaden', but a more complex meaning in other verbs: *draaien* 'turn' – *verdraaien* 'turn into another direction; twist'.

Dutch is like German in that it still exploits a large number of the Indo-European compounding devices. Some of the more familiar types are compounds with nouns as heads: *huisdeur* (noun noun) 'house door; front door', *breekpunt* (noun noun) 'breaking point', *hoogspanning* (adjective noun) 'high voltage' and compounds with verbs as heads: *pianospelen* (noun verb) 'play the piano', *losmaken* (adjective verb) 'make loose, loosen, untie' and *uitvoeren* (particle verb) 'export'. The second group represents the so-called separable compounds. In independent clauses, the complements are separated from the verb as in: *dit land voert bananen uit* 'this country exports bananas'. This type of incorporation, which is actually on the boundary of morphology and syntax, is extremely common and a number of these formations have acquired specialised meanings: *afmaken* 'finish, kill', *zwartmaken* 'blacken, spoil somebody's reputation'. Another special class of compounds are the so-called derivational compounds. On the surface, these formations have the shape of a compound plus derivational suffix, but there is no corresponding non-derived compound, and for some formations, there is no corresponding non-composite derivation either. Some examples: *langslaper* 'somebody who sleeps long' (**langslaap*, but, possibly, *lang* + *slaper*); *werknemer* 'employee' (**werkneem*, and hardly *werk* + *?nemer*); *loslippig* 'talkative' (**loslip*, nor *los* + **lippig*); *driewieler* 'vehicle on three wheels' (**driewiel*, nor *drie* + **wieler*). Here too, it would seem, morphology borders on syntax: one way to account for these words is to assume that they are phrasal at an underlying level: *langslaper* 'somebody who sleeps long'; *loslippig* 'the property of having loose lips', and that they arise through incorporation rather than through simple concatenation of independent elements.

Though some rules of word formation lead to complex forms, it would be wrong to conclude that Dutch is the type of language that allows for fairly unlimited combination of stems and affixes. On the contrary, there are severe, and as yet ill-understood restrictions on affixation and on compounding. Repeated application of compounding rules also has its limitations: compounds of the type *zitkamertafeltje* 'sitting-room-table-diminutive' or *autoverkoopcijfers* 'car-sales-figures' are not very common, and often avoided in favour of more analytical constructions like *cijfers van de autoverkoop*.

5 Syntax

The syntax of Dutch is of the familiar nominative-accusative type. Subject and object are the major grammatical relations. Since the case distinctions have been lost, objects are bare noun phrases and other grammatical relations are expressed by prepositional phrases. Grammatical subjects, including the subjects of passives, agree with the finite verb in person and number and the subject also plays a dominant role in various anaphoric processes, e.g. reflexive pronouns often can only refer to the subject of the sentence. The prominent role of the subject in Dutch is particularly clear from the use of the dummy subject *het* and the use of the dummy subject *er* in impersonal passives, as well as from the fact that subjects in declarative sentences cannot easily be omitted. Compare:

Het is vervelend dat Wim niet komt. 'It is annoying that Bill is not coming'.
Er wordt gedanst. 'There is dancing.'
*(Er) komt niemand. '(There) comes no one.'

In declarative sentences, the subject precedes the finite verb; in questions, requests and certain types of conditionals the finite verb is sentence-initial: *komt Wim vanavond?* 'Is Bill coming tonight?' Question words are sentence-initial, and when a non-subject is preposed, the subject moves to the position after the finite verb: *wat doe je?* 'what are you doing?'.

All this is, indeed, familiar from many other European languages. Nevertheless, Dutch as well as German, Afrikaans and Frisian differ in their surface syntax from both English and, to a lesser extent, the Scandinavian languages in a number of ways, and some of these differences are more than superficial. The prominent features of the Dutch declarative clause can be summarised as follows:

(a) In independent clauses, the finite verb is in second position.

(b) In clauses where the finite verb is an auxiliary, the main verb (whether infinitive or participle) is placed at the end of the clause. The nominal object and any other nominal complement of the verb precede the main verb.

(c) In independent clauses with more than one auxiliary, all verbs except the finite verb are placed at the end of the clause.

(d) In dependent clauses, the finite verb is placed at the end of the clause as well.

(e) In independent clauses, almost any type of constituent can be preposed to sentence-initial position without special emphasis or so-called comma intonation. Compare:

Wim   heeft het boek aan Marietje gegeven.
Het boek   heeft Wim aan Marietje gegeven.
(Aan) Marietje heeft Wim het boek gegeven.
'Bill has given the book to Mary.'

And, with some emphasis:

Mòoi is het níet.
'Beautiful is it not' i.e. 'It is not exactly beautiful.'
Gelàchen hebben we wél.
'Laughed have we modal' i.e. 'We certainly laughed!'

So, it appears that the Dutch independent clause is both verb-second and verb-final. Most grammarians assume that, at a somewhat more abstract level of representation, the Dutch clause is verb-final, and that the second position of the finite verb in the independent clause is 'derived'. It can actually be shown that in the unmarked case, the ordering of constituents proceeds from right to left with the final position of the main verb as the focal point:

Wim heeft   gisteren met een schroevedraaier   het slot opengemaakt.
Bill has   yesterday with a screwdriver   the lock open made
'Bill (has) opened the lock with a screwdriver yesterday'.

Another conclusion is that the Dutch independent clause is not subject-initial but verb-second. The ordering of constituents in those sentences where the subject is not in sentence-initial position is more adequately and more easily accounted for, not by assuming the traditional rule of subject-verb inversion, but by assuming that one constituent has to be preposed to the position before the finite verb. If no other constituent appears in that position, the grammatical subject fills it 'by default'. Preposing is blocked in the dependent clause, but peripheral adverbials can precede the subject in such clauses: *omdat morgen gelukkig de winkels open zijn* 'because tomorrow fortunately the shops open are'.

These constraints on the position of the verb and of its nominal complement developed relatively late in the history of the language and they seem to have been fixed not before the beginning of the period of Modern Dutch. Sentences with a more random word order, including dependent clauses with verb-object order can easily be attested in medieval texts. In the course of the process, Dutch developed another construction that shows a complement ordered to the left of its head, namely, preposed participial modifiers in the noun phrase: *de door de regering genomen beslissing*, 'the by the government taken decision'. The rise of this pattern was probably facilitated by the existence of noun phrases with prenominal adjectives, which is still the basic pattern in all Germanic languages. It should be added that the construction is more typical of the written language than of the spoken language where it can hardly compete with the regular, postnominal relative clause: *de beslissing die de regering genomen heeft* 'the decision that the government has taken'.

As a result of these developments and their codification into the standard language, Dutch, like German, is more of a hybrid in terms of word order typologies than most other Germanic languages are. The noun phrase bears witness to this as well. As we already saw, both prenominal and postnominal modifiers do occur. The genitive construction is predominantly postnominal: *het boek van die man* 'the book of that man', but there is a residue of the prenominal genitive when the 'possessor' is a proper name: *Wim's boek* 'Bill's book', but not *die man's boek*. Interestingly, Dutch developed another genitive construction that is similar to the prenominal genitive, and quite common in the spoken language though not always accepted in the formal style: *die man z'n boek (ligt op tafel)* 'that man his book (is on the table)'. Also adpositions have a somewhat ambiguous position in Dutch syntax. Prepositions are clearly the unmarked case: *in de tuin* 'in the garden'. But postpositions are common, though not always required, when the phrase expresses direction rather than location:

> Wim liep de tuin in. 'Bill walked into the garden.'

Here, too, positing a verb-final position at a more remote level of description is of some explanatory value. Compare:

> Het regende toen Wim de tuin in liep
> it rained   as   Bill the garden into walked
> 'It rained as Bill walked into the garden.'

It is plausible that these postpositions are, at least in origin, complements to the verb. In not a few cases, they can be interpreted both ways. The sentence *Wim zwom de rivier over* 'Bill swam the river across' can be paraphrased both as: 'Bill swam across the river' and as 'Bill crossed the river swimming'. The high frequency of so-called separable verbal compounds, or verb particle constructions, that was noted in the section on morphology may thus be explained through the syntax.

The modal verbs of Dutch are main verbs rather than auxiliaries. They have regular inflection, and they take clausal complements just like other verbs do. In sentences that combine several predicates, all verbs are strung together at the end of the clause. This phenomenon, known as clause union or verb raising manifests itself in different ways in different West Germanic languages (and is absent in English). Dutch sides with German in the curious fact that the expected past participle of non-finite auxiliaries is replaced with the infinitive. This does not occur in (West) Frisian:

> Dutch   dat hij het boek heeft *kunnen* lezen
>   that he the book has   can   read
>   'that he has been able to read the book'
> German   daß er das Buch hat lesen *konnen*
> Frisian   dat er it boek lêze *kent* hat

But Dutch differs from German in that the usual ordering of the modals with respect to the main verb in verbal clusters is the exact mirror image, which is more clear from a comparison of the following sentences:

> Dutch   dat hij het boek moet kunnen lezen
>   that he the book must can read
>   'that he must be able to read the book'
> German   daß er das Buch lesen können muß

And the verbal cluster in Dutch can separate the main verb from its complement, something which does not occur in standard German and is also avoided in many varieties of Dutch in Belgium:

dat hij het boek *uit* moet   kunnen *lezen*
that he the book out must can   read
'that he should be able to finish reading the book'

The order main verb–auxiliary is to be expected in a language where the verb phrase is basically OV; the reverse ordering in the verbal cluster of Dutch has, consequently, been interpreted as a tendency to move away from OV ordering. In sequences of a single auxiliary and a main verb, Dutch has an option: *omdat hij het boek heeft gelezen / omdat hij het boek gelezen heeft* 'because he has read the book'. It is a subject of debate among Dutch grammarians and dialectologists whether the main verb–auxiliary order is a Germanism or whether it is the more natural one.

Apart from the fixed positions of the finite verb and the main verb, the Dutch clause shows considerable freedom of constituent ordering. That freedom is exploited for the foregrounding or backgrounding of information and for embedding the sentence in its context. Preposing is one way to achieve this. Calculations on a fair sample of the written language have shown that less than fifty per cent of declarative clauses are subject-initial. Also, definite nominal objects can easily be moved to a position right after the finite verb, and prepositional phrases can be moved to a position after the main verb:

Wim heeft *dat slot* gisteren met een schroevedraaier opengemaakt.
Wim heeft gisteren dat slot opengemaakt *met een schroevedraaier.*

The latter rule also applies to prepositional phrases that are complements of noun phrases:

Ik heb gisteren *een vogel* gezien *met een hele lange staart.*
I have yesterday a bird seen with a very long tail
'I saw a bird with a very long tail yesterday.'

In the German grammatical tradition this phenomenon is known as *Ausklammerung* ('Exbraciation') and it has sometimes been interpreted as a way to avoid difficulties that might be caused by the long distance between the finite verb and its complement in independent clauses. However, the rule applies equally well in dependent clauses where the finite verb and its complement are adjacent. Postposing a nominal complement remains fully ungrammatical and can be achieved only by dislocation and the use of a resumptive pronoun:

Wim heeft '*t* gisteren met een schroevedraaier opengemaakt, *dat slot.*
'Bill has it yesterday with a screwdriver open made, that lock.'

The sentence-initial position is also available for topicalisation of elements
from the dependent clause, with more restrictions than in some of the
Scandinavian languages but, it would seem, with fewer restrictions than in
standard German.

Die man die jij zei dat je niet — kende is de minister-president.
'That man that you said you didn't know — is the prime minister.'

That topicalisation by preposing is a pervasive feature of Dutch syntax also
appears from the occurrence, in the spoken language, of an incorrect
construction that can be regarded as a form of 'repeated topicalisation':

Toen hebben ze *die man* hebben ze gearresteerd.
then have they that man have they arrested

Sentence-initial anaphoric elements are commonly omitted, as in *waar is
Wim? (Dat) weet ik niet,* 'where is Bill? (That) I don't know'. This
phenomenon is easiest described as deletion of a topic, which would
reinforce the view that the Dutch independent clause is topic-first rather
than subject-first.

Summarising, Dutch has an absolute constraint on the order of the verb
and its nominal complement, and a strong tendency towards ordering
complements to the left of their heads in general, but other features of its
syntax indicate that it is, nevertheless, far from being a consistent OV
language. It is, therefore, not surprising that the concept of the verb phrase
is essential for an adequate description of its syntax, whereas the usefulness
of such a concept has been seriously doubted for classical OV languages like
Japanese.

Bibliography

There are no good comprehensive grammars of Dutch published in English, but
some practical grammars for foreign students are available. Den Hertog (1903–4) is
by far the best grammar of the Dutch language, in spite of the fact that it is now more
than 75 years old, and is modern in its treatment of syntax. Geerts et al. (1984) is a
practical and descriptive grammar of the present-day language written by a team of
Dutch and Belgian linguists; it is meant for the general public, and is important for its
wide coverage of facts. Zonneveld et al. (1980) is a collection of recent articles on
various aspects of Dutch phonology, and contains a useful bibliography compiled by
Zonneveld.

Franck (1910) is the best available grammar of the older stages of the language.
Van Loey (1970) is the standard reference work for the development of Dutch in the
context of Germanic, but some sections have been enlarged so often that it would be

better if the whole book were rewritten. Van Haeringen (1960) is a critical and comprehensive survey of the study of Dutch in the Netherlands and abroad, by one of the outstanding scholars in the field.

References

Den Hertog, C.H. 1903–4. *Nederlandse Spraakkunst*, 3 vols., 2nd ed. (Amsterdam, reprinted with an introduction by H. Hulshof, Versluys Amsterdam, 1972–3)

Franck, J. 1910. *Mittelniederländische Grammatik mit Lesestücken und Glossar* (Tauchnitz, Leipzig, reprinted Gysbers and van Loon, Arnhem, 1967).

Geerts, G., W. Haeseryn, J. de Rooij and M.C. van den Toorn (eds.) 1984. *Algemene Nederlandse Spraakkunst* (Groningen and Leuven, Wolters)

Van Haeringen, C.B.1960. *Netherlandic Language Research: Men and Works in the Study of Dutch*, 2nd ed. (E. J. Brill, Leiden)

Van Loey, A. 1970. *Schönfeld's Historische Grammatica van het Nederlands*, 8th ed. (Thieme and Co., Zutphen)

Zonneveld, W., F. Van Coetsem and O.W. Robinson (eds.) 1980. *Studies in Dutch Phonology* (Martinus Nijhoff, The Hague)

6 Danish, Norwegian and Swedish

Einar Haugen

1 Introduction

Non-Scandinavians are occasionally astonished to hear Danes, Norwegians and Swedes conversing, each in their own language, without interpreters. The fact that some degree of mutual intelligibility exists between these languages, which we shall refer to as the mainland Scandinavian languages, has led some to suggest that together they should really be regarded as only one language. While for some purposes it is convenient to bracket them together, it is hardly correct to speak of only one Scandinavian or Nordic tongue. Such a practice would require a rather restricted definition of the term 'language'. It would neglect those aspects that are not purely linguistic, but are also social and political. To call them 'dialects' is only historically true, i.e. in that they have branched off from a once common Nordic.

In speaking of them as 'languages', we take into account the facts as Scandinavians themselves also see them: that they constitute separately developed norms of writing and speaking. Each language has an officially accepted form, taught in schools, used by journalists and authors, required for government officials, enshrined in grammars and dictionaries and spoken at least by educated members of the nation. They are, in short, what linguists refer to as 'standardised', making them standard languages. This is indisputably true of Danish and Swedish. The fact that Norwegian is spoken and written in two somewhat deviating forms only means that we must distinguish two standard Norwegian languages. These will here be referred to as B-Norwegian (BN), for Norwegian *bokmål* 'book language', formerly *riksmål* 'national language', and as N-Norwegian (NN), for Norwegian *nynorsk* 'New Norwegian', formerly *landsmål* 'country language'. The names used in Norway are misnomers resulting from political conflict and compromise.

In reckoning here with only four mainland languages, we are setting aside what we may call the *insular* Scandinavian languages *Faroese* (in the Faroe Islands) and *Icelandic* (in Iceland). Danish is still one of the two official languages in the Faroes and in Greenland. Swedish is official not only in Sweden, but also alongside Finnish in Finland, although today only 5 or 6

157

per cent of the population speak it natively. We exclude Finnish from this account, since it is wholly unrelated to the Indo-European languages that surround it. It belongs to the Finno-Ugric family, as does Samic, formerly called Lappish, the dialectally divided speech of the Sami (Lapps), who inhabit the far north of Scandinavia and nearby Russia. Greenlandic, a variety of Eskimo (Inuit), is also spoken within Scandinavia, as are Romany (Gypsy) and along the south Danish border some German. The following account is thus limited to the central, mainland Scandinavian of Indo-European descent, the standard languages of the Scandinavian heartland.

2   Historical Background

The earliest written evidence of language in this area is epigraphic, i.e. consisting of inscriptions from about AD 200, mostly quite short. They were written in an alphabet known as a futhark from the sounds of its first six letters. The letters are called runes and the type of writing is runic. The earliest centres of its use are in the Danish peninsula of Jutland, which may also be its place of origin. The 24 runes of the futhark (also known as the 'older' futhark) are clearly based on a classical alphabet, most likely the Latin, but differently ordered and named. Designed for carving in wood, it is mostly preserved on more permanent objects of stone and metal. It was never used for writing on parchment, although it was in use down to c. AD 800, when it was replaced by a shorter 16-rune 'younger' futhark. Although the latter appeared in several regional variations, it steadfastly maintained the number sixteen well into the modern period.

The Older Futhark

ᚠᚢᚦᚨᚱ ᚲᚷᚹ:ᚺᚾ ᛁ ᛃ ᛇ ᛈ ᛉ ᛊ : ᛏ ᛒ ᛖ ᛗ ᛚ ᛜ ᛞ ᛟ
f u þ a r k g w : h n i j ė p z s : t b e m l ng d o

The Younger Futhark

ᚠ ᚢ ᚦ ᚨ ᚱ ᚴ : ᚼ ᚾ ᛁ ᛅ ᛋ : ᛏ ᛒ ᛘ ᛚ ᛦ
f u þ a̧ r k : h n i a s : t b m l R

The earliest runic material, though scanty, is sufficient to assure us that at this time the inhabitants of Scandinavia were of Germanic speech. These inscriptions are in fact the earliest written evidences of any Germanic language, earlier than the extinct East Germanic Gothic or the West Germanic Old English, Old Saxon, Old High German, Old Low Franconian or Old Frisian. The Proto-Scandinavian of the earliest inscriptions constitutes the North Germanic ancestor of the present-day Scandinavian languages.

The line of descent is best (if somewhat roughly) visualised as a branching tree, starting from a hypothetical Common Scandinavian and ending on the bottom line with the present-day languages properly called 'Scandinavian'.

Figure 6.1: The Scandinavian Languages

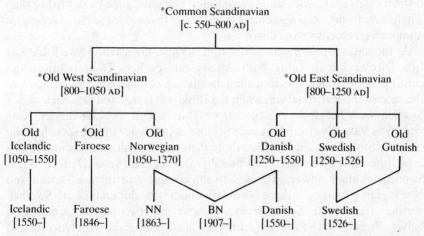

The dates are only approximations. We shall here be dealing with the last four, Danish (Da.), B-Norwegian (BN), N-Norwegian (NN), and Swedish (Sw.). Occasionally it will be convenient to group both Norwegian languages together as 'Norwegian' (Nw.). 'Old Norse' is a commonly used term for a normalised form of Old Icelandic and Old Norwegian, used in the publication of reading texts.

In its medieval, handwritten form there is a large body of Scandinavian writing on parchment or paper. This skill was brought to Scandinavia by Christian missionaries and monks at the end of the Viking Age (AD 750–1050), when the Scandinavians were weaned from their worship of Odin and Thor. The missionaries also taught them the Latin alphabet, significantly adapted to suit the language forms then in use. Traditions of writing gradually grew up, reflecting the practices of Latin orthography, but also innovative.

The most extensive, as well as the most notable of this writing, intellectually, historically and as literature, was that part of it produced by Icelanders in the language which Norway and Iceland then still shared. Among its monuments are the collection of pagan mythical and heroic poems called *The Elder Edda*, the handbook of poetics by Snorri Sturluson (1178–1241) known as *The Younger Edda*, and a multitude of so-called *Sagas*, more or less historical tales from Norwegian and Icelandic life in the pagan and post-pagan period. The Icelanders functioned as recorders of tradition for all Scandinavia, and their work is today claimed as part of the heritage of all the Nordic nations. Symbolic is the use of words like 'Viking' and 'Saga', which enter into everyone's stereotyped conceptions of the Scandinavian countries. Today there is a deep cleft between the language of Iceland (and the Faroes) and those of the mainland. Whereas Icelandic and Faroese have retained nearly all the morphological categories of Proto-Germanic, the mainland languages have retained only the genitive as a distinct case (apart from some archaisms), and have gone even further than English by losing verb agreement completely (except for some obsolescent number agreement in Swedish).

As the dates for their standardisation suggest, Danish and Swedish differ from Norwegian in being both unitary and earlier. Their political and cultural development assured their languages of independent status from the time of the Reformation, when the Bible was translated into each. After Sweden won her independence from Danish rule in 1526 under King Gustavus Vasa, a written language in close dependence on the speech of the court in Stockholm and of the whole central Swedish area around it was established, even to some extent deliberately deviant from Danish. When Swedish military power extended to the conquest of former Danish and Norwegian provinces, these also fell under the dominance of Swedish writing. Henceforth Scandinavia was split into two clearly demarcated halves, Sweden with Finland facing the Baltic, Denmark with Norway and the islands facing the Atlantic.

Denmark, with a language taking shape around Copenhagen (and neighbouring Lund), also got its own Lutheran church and its own Bible, which it succeeded in imposing on Norway as well. Four centuries of Danish dominion (c. 1380–1814) taught Norwegians to write Danish, but not to follow all the newer developments in speech. After an independence gradually won through rupture of the Danish union in 1814 and the Swedish in 1905, the Norwegians found themselves with a cultivated spoken language which, though written like Danish, was spoken with Norwegian sounds and shot through with elements from the folk language. It was a 'Dano-Norwegian' that is still the dominant language, but now written according to its Norwegian pronunciation and known as *bokmål*. The major break with Danish orthography took place in 1907 and was followed by further radical changes in 1917 and 1938. Hence B-Norwegian is shown above as being descended both from Old Norwegian (via speech) and Old Danish (via writing). The father of its spelling reforms was Knud Knudsen (1812–95), schoolmaster and language reformer.

N-Norwegian (known today as *nynorsk*) also goes back to the efforts of a single man, the self-taught linguist and language reformer Ivar Aasen (1813–96). His work was done from 1836 to 1873, including a definitive grammar (1864) and a dictionary (1873). His N-Norwegian was a reconstructed form, a standard based on the spoken dialects, which he was the first to investigate. He was guided also by the Danish and Swedish standards and by Old Norse, which led him to build on the more conservative dialects of western Norway. His norm has been considerably modernised by later users and grammarians, but has won only about one sixth of the school districts of the country. Even so, it must be taken seriously as the standard of a not inconsiderable section of the Norwegian people, including many authors, scholars and institutions.

The consequence of these historical and social developments has been that the old division of Scandinavia into a western and eastern half has been replaced by a much more complex overlapping. Norwegian has had its form returned to a closer relation to Swedish, geographically natural; while at least B-Norwegian has retained a great deal of its cultivated lexicon from Danish. The present-day relation may be seen as a right triangle, with the hypotenuse between Danish and Swedish. Speaking very generally, B-Norwegian (and to some extent even N-Norwegian) has its lexicon common with Danish, but phonology common with Swedish. When Norwegians and Swedes communicate orally, they can tell what word is being spoken, though they may be uncertain of its meaning. When Norwegians and Danes communicate, they have to listen hard to be sure which word the other is using, but once they get that, they usually know what it means. Or as one wit has put it: Norwegian is Danish spoken in Swedish.

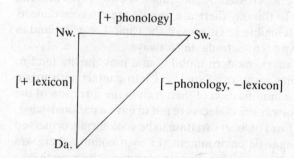

Even though the present-day norms of writing were established with the help of the printing press, at the time of the Reformation, they were not spread to the common people until the nineteenth century, with the establishment of universal public school systems.

3   The Common Heritage

The degree of intelligibility that does exist in Scandinavia today, as well as the obstacles that have led to what I have called 'semi-communication' within the area, have their origin in two major factors: (1) a basic common ancestry in the Old Scandinavian languages; and (2) common influences from outside the area. We do not know how unified Proto-Scandinavian really was; its unity may be an artifact of linguistic reconstruction. There are striking basic similarities that immediately identify the Scandinavian languages, some of them unique, others shared with other Germanic languages. On the other hand, we can follow, at least since the beginning of the manuscript tradition, many of the differential choices made in the course of time. We can also see how the influence of such foreign languages as Greek, Latin, Low German, High German, French, and today English has been incorporated into Scandinavian often giving the same results in each language, but at times also quite different results. Since there has always been some communication within the area, influences of all kinds have spread from one country to the other. It will be noted that the languages listed as providing most of the outside influence are all of the West European type. It is striking that in spite of a certain contact with Celtic languages in the west and with Slavonic languages in the east, very few influences are detectable from these.

The loss of unity in this area is reflected in the growth of dialectal differences both within the countries and between them. Before the standard had been popularised, the mostly rural population split into local and regional dialects. Local communities functioned as closed societies, whether as in Denmark and southern Sweden they were villages, or as in Norway and northern Sweden they were parishes with individual farms. The area turned into a mosaic of dialects, criss-crossed by geographical differences that can be mapped as isoglosses. To this day there are remote areas whose dialects are partly or wholly unintelligible to citizens of the capital, e.g. Jutland in Denmark, Dalecarlia in Sweden, Setesdal in Norway.

For the most part, however, modern mobility and mass media tend to reduce the gap by bringing many rural speakers into contact with urban dialects, often leading to a modification of their own in the direction of the standard. Especially in Norway the dialects are felt to have a national value, a charming and diverting form of local variation to be ecologically protected as part of a vanishing linguistic environment. In each country there are institutes devoted to dialectology. Recent years have seen the growth of a sociolinguistic awareness of speech variation, including the full spectrum from rural dialects and working-class speech to elite and formal varieties.

4   Accent: Stress and Tone

Dynamic stress is distributed over words and sentences in patterns similar to those of other Germanic languages, in degrees varying from primary to weak (also called 'unstressed'). The basic rule of dynamic stress on the first syllable, inherited from Germanic, is still the major rule, but it is now preserved in full only in Icelandic. On the mainland, as in German and English, the rule has been broken to permit a large number of loanwords with stress on the last or penultimate syllable. Post-initial stress may be taken as a marker of 'foreignness' in such words: Da. Nw. Sw. *natu´r* 'nature', *natu´rlig* 'natural'; Nw. *gemytt´* 'temper', *gemytt´lig* 'good natured' (Da. Sw. *gemy´t*, *gemy´tlig*) (note that stress is marked with an accent at the end of the stressed syllable). Differences between the languages may require one to check on one's neighbours with the help of a dictionary: e.g. *egentlig* 'really' is Sw. [ejen´tli], but Nw. [e´gentli], from German *eigentlich*. Verb-particle phrases also have definite, language-specific rules: Danish and Swedish usually stress the particle, Norwegian often the verb, as in Da. *stå opp´*/ Sw. *stå upp´*/ vs. Nw. *stå`-opp* 'get up'.

Compounds usually have primary stress on the first member, secondary or reduced stress on the second, e.g. Da. *kal´veste,g* [-stai,]/BN. *kal`veste,k*/ Sw. *kal`vste,k* 'veal roast'. Again there are exceptions, as in Da./BN *hushold´ning*/ Sw. *hu`shållning* 'housekeeping'. Especially confusing are occasional place-names, like Da. *København´n* [-hau´n], Nw. *Kristiansan´d*, Sw. *Drottninghol´m*.

Parallel to similar developments in English and German, the mainland Nordic languages have over the centuries undergone an extensive process of *stress reduction* in the less conspicuous syllables, reflected especially in the quality of vowels and in the inflectional system. While Old Scandinavian regularly had unstressed syllables containing the vowels -*i*/-*e*, -*u*/-*o* and -*a*, the modern languages have mostly levelled the three to one, -*e* (pronounced [ə]) in Danish and B-Norwegian, to -*e* and -*a* (and an occasional -*o*) in Swedish and N-Norwegian. It is unclear whether the phonological or the morphological development is primary here, but the result is part of a general trend from a more to a less inflected language, i.e. from a synthetic to an analytic language.

The most striking feature of the Scandinavian accentual system is its preservation of a distinction that probably arose in Common Scandinavian, namely its two contrasting prosodemes, which we shall here designate as 'Accent 1' and 'Accent 2'. In most forms of Norwegian and Swedish and in some Danish dialects, these are realised as tonemes, i.e. musical differences that are regularly associated with the primary dynamic stress and are heard as rising or falling word melodies. The difference is significant in poly-syllables, where minimal pairs are common (Accent 1 is marked by an acute, Accent 2 by a grave marker): Nw. *huset* 'the house' [hʉ´sə] vs. *huse* 'to house' [hʉ`sə], *fin´ner* 'finds' vs. *fin`ner* 'finder'; Sw. *bu´ren* 'the cages' vs. *bu`ren* 'borne', *nub´ben* 'the tack' vs. *nub`ben* 'the drink'. The distinction goes back to a difference in Common or Old Scandinavian between monosyllables (with Accent 1) and polysyllables (with Accent 2). Every stressed syllable gets one of the two accents.

In standard Danish the distinction of accent is similar in distribution, but very different in phonetic realisation. Here Accent 1 is realised as a glottal catch or glottalisation, known in Danish as *stød* 'thrust'. It occurs in words that in Old Norse were monosyllables, e.g. *finder* 'finds' [fin?ɔ] from ON *finnr*, not in old polysyllables, e.g. *finder* 'finder' from ON *finnari*. There are some special factors in the Danish case, e.g. in the effect of certain consonants in preventing *stød* in monosyllables. While the rules in each case are complex, their similarity to the Norwegian-Swedish situation is so great that scholars agree they are connected. It is not certain which is primary, but most scholars have assumed that the tonemes are primary and the glottalisation secondary.

5   Vowels

Each language has nine basic vowels, the five Latin vowels *a, e, i, o, u* plus four additional ones: *y* (high front round), Da. Nw. *ø*/Sw. *ö* (mid front round), Da. Nw. *æ*/Sw. *ä* (low front unround) and *å* (mid to low back round; in Da. Nw. formerly written *aa*). The last three are placed at the end of the alphabet: Da. Nw. *æ, ø, å*, Sw. *å, ä, ö*.

All the vowels can be either *long* (tense) or *short* (lax). In Norwegian and Swedish length depends on the following consonant: in stressed syllables vowels are long before short (single) consonants and finally; elsewhere they are short, cf. Nw. Sw. *tak* [taːk] 'roof, ceiling' vs. Nw. *takk*, Sw. *tack* [takː] 'thanks'. This inverse syllabic relationship does not apply in Danish, which lacks long consonants. Hence Nw./Sw. *takk/tack* 'thanks' is written *tak* in Danish, but still with a short vowel. Before a vowel the consonant may be written double to mark the preceding vowel as short, but the consonant is pronounced short: *takke* 'to thank' [tagˊə]. In Danish the symbol *ø* has two values, not distinguished in spelling, its usual mid round front value of [ø] and a lower variety, especially before *r*: [œ].

The vowel qualities are less distorted from the old Latin values of the letters than in English, but even so they have done some shifting. If we visualise the relationship in terms of a traditional vowel diagram, we can say that in Danish they have moved clockwise, in Norwegian and Swedish counterclockwise: see figure 6.2.

Figure 6.2: Vowel Shifts in Danish, Norwegian and Swedish

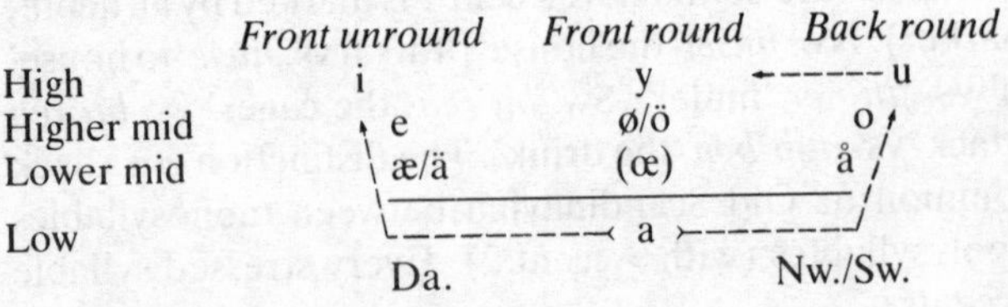

	Front unround	*Front round*	*Back round*
High	i	y	◄‑‑‑‑‑u
Higher mid	↖ e	ø/ö	o ↗
Lower mid	↖ æ/ä	(œ)	å ↗
Low	◄‑‑‑‑‑‑‑‑‑‑‑‑‑◄ a ►‑‑‑‑‑‑‑‑►		
	Da.		Nw./Sw.

In Danish the *a* has been fronted, bringing it closer to *æ*, *æ* has moved towards *e* and *e* towards *i*. But in Norwegian and Swedish *a* has moved closer to *å*, being backed and rounded, while *å* has moved toward *o* and *o* to *u*, and *u* has been fronted and rounded to become almost an *y*. To a Norwegian and a Swede the Da. *ja* sounds like *jæ/jä*, while to a Dane the Nw./Sw. *ja* sounds like *jå*.

Only N-Norwegian has retained the Old Norse diphthongs in full, now written *au* [æʉ], *ei* [æi], *øy* [œy]: *laus* 'loose', *bein* 'leg, bone', *løysa* 'loosen'. In Danish and Swedish (and conservative B-Norwegian) these are monophthongs: *løs/lös*, *ben*, *løse/lösa*. B-Norwegian has acquired some diphthongs in recent reforms, e.g. *bein*, *øy* 'island'. Some are found in loanwords, e.g. BN *feide* 'feud', *mausoleum* 'mausoleum', *føye* 'yield; join'. Others are BN *oi* in *boie* 'buoy', *ai* in *kai* 'quay', *ui* in *hui* 'whee'. In Danish and Swedish these are considered vowel plus consonant, e.g. Da. *fejde/* Sw. *fejd*, Da. *føje*, Da. *bøje*/Sw. *boj*, Da./Sw. *kaj*, Da./Sw. *huj*. Further examples are:

Da.	BN	NN	Sw.
sten 'stone'	sten/stein	stein	sten
høre 'hear'	høre	høyra	höra
rød 'red'	rød	raud	röd

6 Consonants

The symbols of the Latin alphabet are taught in full, but the following are largely limited to proper names, foreign words and place-names: *c q w x z*. In 1801 Sweden adopted a policy of nativising many of these by replacing *c* with *k* (*kapital* 'capital') or *s* (*siffra* 'cipher'), *qu* with *kv* (*kvantum* 'quantity'), *w* with *v* (*valross* 'walrus'), *z* with *s* (*sebra* 'zebra'). Only *x* was regularly retained (*lax* 'salmon'). In 1917 Norway followed suit, going a step further, e.g. adopting *s* for *c* in *sirkus* 'circus' and *sigar* 'cigar' as well as *ks* for *x*: *laks* 'salmon'. Denmark has been more conservative, except for adopting *ks* for *x* (but keeping *x*, e.g. in *sex*, if only to distinguish it from *seks* 'six').

Certain phonemes are written as clusters (like English *sh*, *th*, *ng* etc.). Thus Nw./Sw. [š] may be *sj* (Nw. *sjel*/Sw. *själ* 'soul'), *skj* (Nw. *skjorte*/Sw. *skjorta* 'shirt') or just *sk* before front vowels (Nw./Sw. *ski* [šiː] 'ski', Sw. *sköld* 'shield' but Nw. *skjold*). Similarly [ç] may be spelled *tj* or *kj* (Nw. *tjue*/ Sw. *tjugo* 'twenty', Nw. *kjole* 'dress'/Sw. *kjol* 'skirt') or just *k* before front vowels (BN *kirke*/NN *kyrkje*/Sw. *kyrka* 'church'). These fricatives (or affricates) of Norwegian and Swedish are results of the palatalisation of velar stops, a process not shared by standard Danish, although many Danish dialects have them. Further examples are:

Da.	BN	NN	Sw.
skære 'cut'	skjære	skjera	skära
kysse 'kiss'	kysse	kyssa	kyssa

A feature of modern Scandinavian is the absence of voiced sibilants [z ž dž], lost in Common Scandinavian. But they retain traces of an ancient 'hardening' of the medial sequences -*jj*- and -*ww*-, giving forms like Da. *æg*/ Nw. *egg*/Sw. *ägg* for German *Ei* (English *egg* is a Viking-age borrowing from Norse). A much later development was the trend in Danish and adjacent areas of Norwegian and Swedish to voice short fortis stops *p t k* to *b d g* after vowels. In Danish proper this development went even farther, turning *d* and *g* into spirants or even vocalic glides, a development not reflected in the spelling. The result of this and a general Danish devoicing of the lenis consonants is to make Danish word endings extremely difficult for other Scandinavians to hear correctly:

Da.	BN	NN	Sw.
ta*be* [taːb̥ə] 'lose'	ta*pe*	ta*pa*	ta*ppa*
bi*de* [biːðə] 'bite'	bi*te*	bi*ta*	bi*ta*
le*ge* [lajə] 'play'	le*ke*	lei*ka*	le*ka*

While most of Norwegian and Swedish has retained the Germanic (and Indo-European) *r* as a tongue-tip trill (or tap), Danish has adopted the French and German uvular *r* [ʀ], weakening it usually to a vocalic glide. This insidious sound has spread also into many areas of southern and western Norway and Sweden, still not including either Oslo or Stockholm. But both countries show a widespread weakening of the trills before dentals, resulting in a set of retroflex consonants of Indic type: *rt* [ʈ], *rs* [ʂ], *rl* [ɭ], *rn* [ɳ], *rd* [ɖ]. The same dialects have a so-called 'thick' (cacuminal) flap derived from *rð* and *l* [ɫ] that is virtually unique among the world's languages; though it is universal in the dialects of eastern Norway and north-central Sweden, it is not accepted in elite circles.

7   Morphology

The mainland languages show a parallel and remarkably similar development from the highly synthetic language of Germanic and Old Scandinavian to an analytic, i.e. greatly reduced, formal grammar. Its movement has been in the same direction as Low German and English. The only remaining case is a possessive -*s* that is really a generalised group genitive (see below). Most plural nouns now end in -*r*, and verbs lack markers for person or number of the subject. Definite and indefinite articles, unknown in Proto-Germanic, have developed. Various ways of marking formality of address have arisen, mostly in imitation of German practices.

7.1   Nouns

These still have gender distinction, in which neuter (nt.) is the most stable. In Danish and Swedish and traditional B-Norwegian, masculine (m.) and feminine (f.) have merged into a common (c.) gender having the markers of the masculine. Only in N-Norwegian and folk-oriented B-Norwegian is the feminine retained, in the latter only for certain words or styles. The genders are marked only by accompanying articles, adjectives and referential (anaphoric) pronouns, but are in part also reflected in the forms of the plural.

Plural classes

Eng.		*Da.*		*BN*		*NN*		*Sw.*	
m.	'day'	dag	dage	dag	dager	dag	dagar	dag	dagar
	'park'	park	parker	park	parker	park	parker	park	parker
m.f.	'sun'	sol	sole	sol	soler	sol	soler	sol	solar
m.	'shoe'	sko	sko	sko	sko	sko	skor	sko	skor
m.f.	'goose'	gås	gæs	gås	gjess	gås	gjæs	gås	gäss
m.	'brother'	broder	brødre	bror	brødre	bror	brør	bror	bröder
m.	'cock'	hane	haner	hane	haner	hane	hanar	hane	hanar
m.f.	'song'	vise	viser	vise	viser	vise	viser	vise	visor
nt.	'house'	hus	huse	hus	hus	hus	hus	hus	hus
nt.	'kingdom'	rige	riger	rike	riker	rike	rike	rike	riken
nt.	'ear'	øre	ører (obs. øren)	øre	ører	øyra	øyro	öra	öron

N-Norwegian and Swedish show rudimentary remains of older declensions; all four retain old umlaut classes (like English *geese, feet, men* etc.). Possessive *-s* is regularly suffixed (without an apostrophe unless the word ends in *s*): Da. *dags, dagens, dages, dagenes,* but *gås'.* It is often avoided in favour of compounds or prepositional phrases: Da. *dagsverk* 'day's work', *ord for dagen* 'a word for the day, the day's word'. As in English it can be added to any noun phrase (the so-called group genitive), e.g. Da. *kongen af Danmarks brystsukker* 'the King of Denmark's cough drops.' Formal Swedish rejects this genitive, preferring *kungens av Danmark bröstsocker,* but general usage is the same as in Danish and Norwegian.

7.2 Articles
As in English, nouns can appear either with or without articles, depending on context and meaning. The definite articles are historically earlier, and the indefinite articles are a development of the late Middle Ages (that never reached Iceland). Usage is similar to that of English, though for instance abstracts like 'love' and 'hate' usually are definite (Da. *kærligheden/* BN *kjærligheten/*NN *kjærleiken/*Sw. *kärleken* 'love').

The definite article is an interesting and characteristic feature of all Scandinavian languages (aside from some dialects in west Jutland). There are actually two, one suffixed to the noun and one preceding adjectives (which we will discuss below under adjectives). Originally a separate word *inn* m. (*in* f., *it* nt.) 'that, yon', it was already in Old Norse attached to the noun and became a morphological suffix. To illustrate its uses we take some of the same words as in the previous table and include the indefinite article, which is an unstressed form of the word for 'one'; it is used only in the singular, except for an occasional Swedish form *ena* 'some'.

Articles: Indef. sg., def. sg., and def. pl.

	Da.		*BN*		*NN*		*Sw.*	
m.	en dag	en park	en dag	en park	ein dag	ein park	en dag	en park
	dag*en*	park*en*	dag*en*	park*en*	dag*en*	park*en*	dag*en*	park*en*
	dag*ene*	park*ene*	dag*ene*	park*ene*	dag*ane*	park*ene*	dag*arna*	park*erna*
m.f.	en gås	en vise	en gås	en vise	ei gås	ei vise	en gås	en vis*a*
	gås*en*	vis*en*	gås*a/-en*	vis*a/-en*	gås*a*	vis*a*	gås*en*	vis*an*
	gæss*ene*	vis*erne*	gjess*ene*	vis*ene*	gjæs*ene*	vis*ene*	gäss*ena*	vis*orna*
nt.	et hus	et rige	et hus	et rike	eit hus	eit rike	ett hus	ett rike
	hus*et*	rig*et*	hus*et*	rik*et*	hus*et*	rik*et*	hus*et*	rik*et*
	hus*ene*	rig*erne*	hus*ene*	rik*ene*	hus*a*	rik*a*	hus*en*	rik*ena*

In Norwegian the suffixed *-t* of the neuter singular is silent.

7.3 Adjectives

There are no case endings, but unlike English, there are still gender, definiteness and plurality markers. Gender appears only by the addition of *-t* in the neuter indefinite singular. Definiteness is shown by adding *-e* (Sw. *-a/-e*), plurality by adding *-e* (Sw. *-a/-e*). Definiteness is expressed by the article *den* m.f., *det* nt., *de* (NN *dei*) pl. It may also be dictated by such determiners as the demonstratives *denne* m. f., *dette* nt., *disse* (NN *desse*) pl. 'this, these' and the possessive adjectives (*min* 'my' etc.). The general pattern is displayed in the following chart:

Eng.	*Da.*	*BN*	*NN*	*Sw.*
'a big goose'	en stor gås	en stor gås	ei stor gås	en stor gås
'big geese'	stor*e* gæs	stor*e* gjess	stor*e* gjæser	stor*a* gäss
'a big house'	*et* stor*t* hus	*et* stor*t* hus	ei*t* stor*t* hus	*ett* stor*t* hus
'big houses'	stor*e* hus	stor*e* hus	stor*e* hus	stor*a* hus
'the big goose'	den stor*e* gås	den stor*e* gås*en*	den stor*e* gås*a*	den stor*a* gås*en*
'the big geese'	de stor*e* gæs	de stor*e* gjess*ene*	dei stor*e* gjæs*ene*	de stor*a* gäss*ena*
'the big house'	det stor*e* hus	det stor*e* hus*et*	det stor*e* hus*et*	det stor*a* hus*et*
'the big houses'	de stor*e* hus	de stor*e* hus*ene*	dei stor*e* hus*a*	de stor*a* hus*en*

In Swedish *de* is often replaced in speech by *dom*. The suffix *-a* may be replaced by *-e* with masculine nouns, e.g. *min gamle far* (but *min gamla mor*).

In all the languages the definite form (known as 'weak') may be used without a preceding article (a) in set phrases and in place and personal names, e.g. BN *siste natten* 'the last night', Sw. *Stora Torget* 'The Big Market Place', Da./Nw. *lille Harald* 'little Harold'; and (b) as a vocative in phrases of address: Da. *kære ven*/Nw. *kjære venn*/Sw. *kära vän* 'dear friend'.

There is a marked internal difference in the use of what is usually known as the 'double definite', i.e. the use of both definite articles in the same phrase. As shown in the chart above, this usage is avoided in Danish, but is common in Norwegian and Swedish, in N-Norwegian even required.

The definite article with an adjective is used in noun functions: common gender about animates, neuter gender about inanimates: Nw. *den unge* 'the young one (person)', *de unge* 'the young (people)', *det nye* 'the new (idea, thing etc.)'.

Comparison occurs in three degrees: positive, comparative and superlative. It is formed in one of four ways: (a) regular, by adding Da./BN *-ere*, NN/Sw. *-are* to the positive to form the comparative, and Da./BN *-est(e)*, NN/Sw. *-ast(e)* to form the superlative; (b) umlauting, by vowel change and adding *-re* and *-st(e)*; (c) analytic, by using the words for 'more' and 'most' as modifiers (Da./BN *mer*, NN *meir*, Sw. *mer(a)*, and *mest* for all the languages); (d) suppletion, e.g. *mange*/Sw. *många* 'many' – *fler*, NN *fleir* 'more' (in number). Further examples of (a) and (b):

	Da.		BN		NN		Sw.	
Positive	klar	ung	klar	ung	klår	ung	klar	ung
Comp.	klar*ere*	yng*re*	klar*ere*	yng*re*	klår*are*	yng*re*	klar*are*	yng*re*
Sup.	klar*est*	yng*st*	klar*est*	yng*st*	klår*ast*	yng*st*	klar*ast*	yng*st*

7.4 Adverbs

Most of these are morphologically unmarked and may be classed as particles. But two groups are visibly marked: (1) adverbs derived from adjectives; these are always identical with the neuter indefinite singular of the latter, i.e. they (mostly) add *-t*: e.g., *godt*, Sw. *gott* from *god* 'good' means 'well'; *stort* from *stor* 'big' means 'greatly' etc.; (2) adverbs derived from simple adverbs of motion by adding *-e* (Sw. also *-a*), making them adverbs of place (often with a change of stem); the most important are:

Eng.	Da.		BN		NN		Sw.	
'up'	op	opp*e*	opp	opp*e*	opp	opp*e*	upp	upp*e*
'down'	ned	ned*e*	ned	ned*e*	ned	ned*e*	ned	ner*e*
'out'	ud	ud*e*	ut	ut*e*	ut	ut*e*	ut	ut*e*
'in'	ind	ind*e*	inn	inn*e*	inn	inn*e*	in	inn*e*
'home'	hjem	hjemm*e*	hjem	hjemm*e*	heim	heim*e*	hem	hemm*a*
'away'	bort	bort*e*	bort	bort*e*	bort	bort*e*	bort	bort*a*

In their locative sense these can be compared, e.g. Da. *indre* 'inner', *inderst* 'innermost' etc.

7.5 Pronouns

The structure is much the same as in English, aside from the second person and the reflexives. In the following chart only the informal second person is listed; the honorific will be discussed below.

Personal pronouns: synopsis of 1–3 person sg. and pl., subject and object

	Da.		BN		NN		Sw.	
1p.	jeg mig	vi os	jeg meg	vi oss	eg meg	vi oss	jag mig	vi oss
2p.	du dig	I jer	du deg	dere	du deg	de dykk	du dig	ni er
3p.m.	han ham	de dem	han ham	de dem	han honom	dei	han honom	de dem
3p.f.	hun hende		hun henne		ho henne		hon henne	

The inanimate pronoun is *den* common gender and *det* neuter gender 'it' in all languages; but in N-Norwegian it is replaced in anaphoric use by the appropriate masculine and feminine pronouns (i.e. *han/ho*).

The possessives in the first and second persons are declined like strong adjectives (e.g. for Da. *min* c., *mit* nt., *mine* pl.). Possessive pronouns:

	Da.		BN		NN		Sw.	
1p.	min	vor(es)	min	vår	min	vår	min	vår
2p.	din	jeres	din	deres	din	dykkar	din	er
3p.m.	hans	deres	hans	deres	hans	deira	hans	deras
3p.f.	hendes		hennes		hennar		hennes	
Refl.	sin		sin		sin		sin	

The reflexive pronoun is Da./Sw. *sig*, Nw. *seg* in the third person but identical with the objective form of the pronouns in the first and second persons. Danish restricts the reflexive to the third person singular. It is a peculiarity of Scandinavian that the third person reflexive is in syntactic complementation with the personal. The reflexive is restricted to possessors that are also the subject of the clause in which they occur: *han tok sin hatt* 'he took his (own) hat' vs. *han tok hans hatt* 'he took his (somebody else's) hat'.

English 'you' corresponds to *du* in informal conversations, e.g. in families, among friends and close colleagues and among rural people. But in urban settings and between strangers more formal modes of address have been common. In Danish and B-Norwegian the formal pronouns are identical with the third person plural, capitalised when written: *De, Dem, Deres*. In N-Norwegian and Swedish they are identical with the second person plural: NN *Dykk, Dykk, Dykkar*; Sw. *Ni, Er, Er*. However, in Swedish the *ni* has acquired a touch of condescension, and politeness requires the use of the third person, often including the title: *Vad önskar professoren?* 'What does the professor (i.e., you) want?' The awkwardness of this mode of address became obvious after World War II, and the solution has been a general adoption of *du*, followed in part in Norway (less in Denmark).

7.6 Verbs
The mainland languages have developed a common morphology, eliminating person and number while retaining the distinctions of tense, including complex tense forms. A verb is adequately described if we know its

'principal parts', i.e. the infinitive (also used as citation form), the preterit and the perfect participle (used in complex tenses).

Strong verbs are characterised by vowel changes in the stem and the absence of a suffix in the preterit. We list the seven main classes: 1 'bite'; 2 'enjoy'; 3 'find'; 4 'bear'; 5 'give'; 6 'go'; 7 'cry'.

	Da.			*BN*		*NN*			*Sw.*			
1	bide	bed	bidt	bite	bet	bitt	bita	beit	bite	bita	bet	bitit
2	nyde	nød	nydt	nyte	nøt	nytt	nyta	naut	note	njuta	njöt	njutit
3	finde	fandt	fundet	finne	fant	funnet	finna	fann	funne	finna	fann	funnit
4	bære	bar	båret	bære	bar	båret	bera	bar	bore	bära	bar	burit
5	give	gav	givet	gi	gav	gitt	gje	gav	gjeve	giva	gav	givit
6	fare	for	faret	fare	for	faret	fara	for	fare	fara	for	farit
7	græde	græd	grædt	gråte	gråt	grått	gråta	gret	grete	gråta	gråt	gråtit

These are only examples; there is great variation in the verbs of each class. In the infinitive N-Norwegian can have -*e* for -*a*. N-Norwegian forms its present by dropping the final vowel and when possible changing the stem to its umlaut form, e.g. *fer* from *fara*, *kjem* from *koma*. The others add -(*e*)*r* and change to Accent 1 (*fa´rer*, *kom´mer*), except that Swedish drops all suffixes after *r* or *l* (*far* 'go(es)', *stjäl* 'steal(s)'). In the perfect participle N-Norwegian may have -*i* for -*e*; Swedish has -*e*- for -*i*- when the perfect participle is used adjectivally.

Weak verbs form preterits by adding a dental (-*d*-, -*t*-, -*dd*-, lost in N-Norwegian class 1) with a following vowel that is not in the perfect participle. Class 3 is special for Norwegian/Swedish; the Danish verbs of the same type belong to class 1. We list the main classes below: 1 'throw'; 2a 'choose'; 2b 'judge'; 3 'believe'. In Swedish the perfect participle may end in -*d* for -*t* when used adjectivally: *kastad* for *kastat*.

	Da.			*BN*		*NN*			*Sw.*			
1	kaste	kastede	kastet	kaste	kastet	kastet	kasta	kasta	kasta	kasta	kastade	kastat
2a	vælge	valgte	valgt	velge	valgte	valgt	velja	valde	valt	välja	valde	valt
2b	dømme	dømte	dømt	dømme	dømte	dømt	døma	dømde	dømd	döma	dömde	dömt
3	(tro)	troede	troet	tro	trodde	trodd	tru	trudde	trudd	tro	trodde	trott

Modal verbs are a special group by means of which certain nuances of meaning may be signalled when they are used as auxiliaries (usually with an infinitive verb). As elsewhere in Germanic, most of them are preterit-present verbs, i.e. their present forms are old preterits, and their preterits are newly modelled after the weak verbs. We list only 'can', 'must', 'shall' and 'will' in the present and preterit:

Da.		*BN*		*NN*		*Sw.*	
kan	kunne	kan	kunne	kan	kunne	kan	kunde
må	måtte	må	måtte	må	måtte	måste	måste
skal	skulle	skal	skulle	skal	skulle	skall	skulle
vil	ville	vil	ville	vil	ville	vill	ville

The middle voice is a specially Scandinavian form, now signalled by -s (NN -st) added to many verb forms. Originally a reflexive, it is now used also to form passives, reciprocals and deponents (i.e. active verbs with passive form). An example of each type (here taken from B-Norwegian) follows:

(a) passive: *sangen synges* 'the song is being sung' or 'the song gets sung'
(b) reciprocal: *vi møtes i morgen* 'we will meet tomorrow'
(c) reflexive: *jeg trivs her* 'I enjoy myself here'
(d) deponent: *han synes godt om stedet* 'he thinks well of the place'

These are all in competition with differently structured phrases:

(a) *sangen blir sunget*
(b) *vi møter kl. 10* 'we meet at 10 o'clock'
(c) *jeg liker meg her*
(d) *han tror godt om stedet*

Similar contrasts can be shown for all the languages: the middle voice is highly restricted ('marked'), while the more analytic phrases are relatively unrestricted.

The passive is, as shown above, normally analytic, consisting of an auxiliary (Da. *blive*/BN *bli*/Sw. *bliva*/NN *verta*) plus the perfect participle.

The perfect and the pluperfect are formed by 'have' in the present and preterit tense plus the perfect participle. Except in Swedish (and to some extent in Norwegian) verbs of motion (going, becoming) require the auxiliary 'be'.

Da.	BN	NN	Sw.
har set 'have seen'	har sett	har sett	har sett
havde set 'had seen'	hadde sett	hadde sett	hade sett
er kommet 'have come'	er kommet	er kome	har kommit
var kommet 'had come'	var kommet	var kome	hade kommit

Other verb forms are:

(a) the imperative, formed by dropping the unstressed vowel of the infinitive (except Swedish and N-Norwegian weak class 1: Sw. *kasta*! 'throw!', NN *vakne*! 'awake!');

(b) the present participle, used only adjectivally, formed by adding -*ende* to the verb stem in Danish/B-Norwegian, -*ande* in N-Norwegian/Swedish, except in Swedish after long vowels: *kommande* 'coming', *boende* 'living';

(c) the subjunctive (optative), formed by adding -*e* to the stem of the present, which is used chiefly in set phrases of greeting or cursing: BN *kongen leve* '(long) live the king', *fanden steike* 'may the devil roast (him, me)'. A preterit is found in contrary-to-fact conditional sentences, usually identical in form to the regular preterit: BN *om jeg var...* 'if I were'. However, Swedish (and N-Norwegian) have certain relic forms of the old subjunctive: *om jag vore...* 'if I were' (NN *um eg vøre...*). These are also in competition with analytic forms using auxiliaries: *om jag skulle vara...*

8   Syntax

Only a few of the more significant features will be listed here.

8.1   Basic Word Order

An independent declarative sentence has the same subject-verb-object (SVO) order as English. But the absence of 'do' and 'is' as auxiliaries means that in the present and preterit there are no divided verb forms: Da. *hun kører bilen* 'she drives/does drive/is driving the car'.

8.2   Inversion

In questions the order of subject and verb is simply reversed: Da. *kører hun bilen?* 'does she drive/is she driving the car?'. The same inversion occurs after an initial adverb: Da. *i dag kører hun bilen* 'today she is driving the car'. If the adverb is in its usual position, after the object, sentence order is basic: *hun kører bilen i dag* 'she is driving the car today'.

8.3   Sentence Adverbs

An important subgroup of adverbs, which function as modifiers of the whole sentence, follow the verb immediately, usually in the order modals–negatives: Da. *hun kører jo bilen i dag* 'she is, you know, driving the car today'; *hun kører ikke bilen i dag* 'she is not driving the car today'; *hun kører jo ikke bilen i dag* 'she is not driving the car today, you know'. When the sentence is inverted, the negative follows a pronoun subject, but precedes a noun subject: *kører hun ikke bilen i dag?* vs. *kører ikke min søster bilen i dag?* 'isn't she driving the car today?' vs. 'isn't my sister driving the car today?'

8.4   Subordination

Subordinate clauses have (contrary to German) the same SVO order as independent clauses, except that sentence adverbs then normally precede the verb: *hvis hun ikke kører bilen i dag...* 'if she isn't driving the car today...' In some cases the same word may be either an adverb or a conjunction, e.g. *da* 'then' or 'when'. In such a case the following word order signals the difference: *da kørte hun bilen* 'then she drove the car' vs. *da hun kørte bilen...* 'when she drove the car...'

8.5   Relative Clauses

Relative clauses have subordinate order and are usually introduced by *som* (or in Danish also by *der* when it is the subject). This is not a pronoun but a particle, which cannot be preceded by a preposition. Hence prepositions come at the end of the clause, contrary to an English practice consecrated by some English grammarians: *det var bilen (som) hun kørte i* 'that was the car (which) she rode in'. When the relative particle is the object of the subordinate verb, it may be omitted (as in English).

8.6   Imperatives
Imperatives mostly appear without a subject, since this is understood to be 'you'. But the subject may be expressed, as a vocative: *kør bilen ind, Jørgen!* 'drive the car in, Jørgen!' There are of course more polite ways of formulating requests, e.g. with modal auxiliaries or with subjunctives.

8.7   Impersonal Sentences
Impersonal sentences are rather more common than in English, especially in so-called 'cleft' sentences. These have *det* as formal subject, whoever may be the real ('underlying') subject: *det er hun/hende som kører bilen i dag* 'it is she/her who is driving the car today'. 'Cleaving' is used to give emphasis.

8.8   Indefinite Subject
Basically subjectless sentences fill the subject slot with *det* 'it', as in *det regner* 'it's raining', *det sner/snør/snöar* 'it's snowing'. Norwegian and Swedish use *det* also as an equivalent of English 'there', e.g. *det kommer en bil* 'there's a car coming; a car is coming'. Here Danish (and older B-Norwegian) prefers *der*.

8.9   Conditional Clauses
These may be explicitly introduced by *om* 'if' in all languages, Da./BN *dersom*, *hvis*, Sw. *därest*, *ifall* 'in case'. But the conjunction may be dropped if the clause inverts subject and verb: *kommer bilen i dag...* 'if the car comes today...' One cannot tell if this is a question or a conditional until one hears the conclusion.

8.10   Prepositions
Prepositions can govern clauses and infinitives: Da. *efter at ha kørt bilen...* 'after having driven the car...'; *efter at hun hadde kørt bilen...* 'after she had driven the car...'

8.11
Norwegian has the option of letting possessives either precede or follow the noun, the latter requiring the definite form of the noun: *min bil* 'my car' (more emphatic) vs. *bilen min*.

8.12
Swedish (and some Norwegian dialects) keep the verb together with a

conjoined adverbial particle, while Danish and B-Norwegian separate them: Sw. *vill du köra in´bilen* vs. Da. *vil du køre bilen ind´* 'will you drive the car in?'.

8.13

Only Swedish can omit the perfect auxiliary in a subordinate clause: *jag vet inte om han (har) lämnat staden* 'I don't know if he has left the city'.

8.14

The inferential perfect is a characteristic Scandinavian construction. Normally the perfect is used as in English, not as in German, to mark past events without specified time, but with ongoing effects. If time is specified, it is implied that the statement is an inference rather than an observed fact: *hun har kørt bilen i går* 'she has driven the car yesterday', i.e. '(I suppose that) she must have etc.'.

8.15   The exclamatory preterit

This is a common use of that tense to express a taste or opinion: *det var da en køn bil!* 'that was a lovely car!' i.e. 'that is a lovely car!'. This may be said as one is looking at it, but the experience is made more emphatic by placing it in the past.

8.16   Durative expressions

In the absence of a special 'progressive' verb form like English 'is going', the Scandinavian languages often make use of a verb of motion or position, followed by 'and' and the corresponding tense of the main verb: Da. *jeg sidder og spiser* 'I sit and eat', i.e. 'I am eating'; BN *han stod og spekulerte* 'he stood and speculated', i.e. 'he was speculating (about something)'; Sw. *hon låg och drömde* 'she lay and dreamt', i.e. 'she lay dreaming'. Verbs available for this usage are those that indicate coming, going, sitting, standing and lying.

8.17   Modal adverbs

Certain adverbs, which have regular meanings when stressed, become vague sentence modifiers when unstressed. The chief examples are Da./BN *da* 'then', *dog* 'yet', *jo* 'yes', *nok* 'enough', *vel* 'well', Da. *nu*/BN *nå*/NN *no*; corresponding to Sw. *då*, *dock*, *ju*, *nog*, *väl*, *nu*. They suggest the speaker's degree of assurance or doubt, roughly 'you see', 'after all', 'of course', 'I suppose', 'no doubt' etc.

9   Lexicon

The word stock of any language reflects the needs over time of its speakers and writers and the state of their culture. As suggested above, the similarity and the divergence of the Scandinavian languages mirror their common as well as their separate historical experiences. The lexicon is enshrined in the dictionaries of each language, including massive historical dictionaries. Bilingual dictionaries are also numerous, especially for such familiar languages as English, French and German, and even some intra-Scandinavian.

The origin of the lexicon is multifarious, but overwhelmingly West European, as one can see by consulting the etymological dictionaries. The 'native' stock, i.e. the original Germanic with later native creations, is the bread-and-butter part of the lexicon. The Nordic languages were well equipped to deal with their natural environment of sea, land and mountains in all its variations from the plains of Denmark to the highlands of Norway and the forests of Sweden. Their location as the population closest to the North Pole has left its mark.

The earliest outside influence that is still perceptible was that of the Roman traders who taught them such words as 'buy' (*købe/kjøpe/køypa/köpa*) and 'wine' (*vin*) from Latin *caupo* and *vinum*. They were followed in due course by Roman-trained missionaries who brought them such originally Greek words as 'church' (*kirke/kirke/kjørkja/kyrka*) and 'priest' (*prest*, Sw. *präst*) from *kuriakon* and *presbuteros* and Latin words like 'dean, provost' (*prost*) and 'mass' (*messe*, Sw. *mässa*) from *prōpositus* and *missa*. Actually, there were various intermediaries, such as Old English and Old High (and Low) German, often hard to distinguish. Scandinavia was at the end of a West European chain of transmission of Catholic Christian vocabulary, most of which was common European property.

But the chief source of Scandinavian loans in the later Middle Ages was northern Germany, where the dominant language was Low German. The distance between Low German and the Nordic languages was small, since both were Germanic and had not undergone the High German Sound Shift. One may even suspect that with a little effort they could converse, at least on everyday topics. In any event, thousands of Low German loanwords flooded the North during the period from 1250 to 1500. Low German was the language not only of the powerful Hanseatic League, the trading towns of northern Germany, but also of the North German princes, who often sat on Scandinavian thrones. Cities like Bergen in Norway, Kalmar and Stockholm in Sweden and of course Copenhagen in Denmark were heavily settled by German merchants and craftsmen.

Some Old Norse words were even displaced by Low German loans, e.g. *vindauga* 'window' in Swedish by LG *fenster > fönster*, *vōna* 'hope' by LG *hopen >* Da. *håbe*/BN *håpe*/Sw. *hoppas* (but NN *vona*). Prefixes and suffixes attached to Low German words were also adopted, e.g. *be-, ent-, vor-* and *-heit, -ness, -ske*. Old Scandinavian had a very restricted set of affixes, which were greatly expanded by Low German influence.

At the time of the Reformation (in the sixteenth century) the source of influence changed to High German, the language of Luther's Bible, which became normative for the now converted Scandinavians. Translations of the Bible were modelled on Luther's, giving a heavy freight of German loans. As late as the seventeenth century the Swedish grammarian Samuel Columbus could still write that German and Swedish were sister languages, so that Swedes were justified in taking over words from German. The eighteenth century saw a shift in the direction of French influence, but also a clarification of the independence of the northern languages. A Nordic purism arose, leading to the replacement of French words like *passion* with *lidenskab*, though the latter was ultimately modelled on German *Leidenschaft*. The rediscovery of Old Scandinavian, specifically of Old Icelandic literature, led to a Nordic renaissance.

The nineteenth and even more the twentieth century brought on the Industrial Revolution and with it the rise of English to the status of a world language. Its proximity to Scandinavia and involvement in Nordic affairs made it the source of a new era of influence. Rejection of German led to an adulation of English that changed the attitudes of a whole generation in Scandinavia. An influence already apparent in the 1930s, often transmitted by sailors, merchants and tourists, now led to a flood of military, scientific and literary, as well as generally popular culture, terms. English, once a remote and inaccessible language to most Scandinavians, quickly became a medium not only of information and insight, but a possibly insidious influence on popular thinking and speech.

Only Sweden had a traditional language academy, the Swedish Academy (founded 1786), which still publishes under its ægis a guide to the spelling (and in part the pronunciation) of 'correct' Swedish. But in modern times each country has established special committees or commissions charged with the care of its language. In 1978 a cooperative Nordic Language Secretariat was established under the auspices of the Nordic Council of Ministers. Like its member organisations, the secretariat has only advisory powers. But it is hoped that it will prove to be a useful forum for the discussion of language problems in the area. Aside from issues of correctness, a major concern is for the development and coordination of technical terminology.

Since each language has developed its own lexicon, often along different principles, there are many discrepancies both in words and meanings. These add spice to intra-Scandinavian contacts, but rarely lead to basic misunderstandings.

Differences are either semantic or lexical.

(a) Semantic differences in historically identical words, often called false friends, reflect preferences for one nuance over another. Thus *rar* from Latin *raris*, cognate with English 'rare', means 'good, fine, sweet' in Danish and Swedish, but 'queer, strange' in Norwegian: the 'rare' may be regarded either positively or negatively. *Rolig*, a native word cognate with German *ruhig*, means 'quiet' in Danish and Norwegian, but 'funny, amusing' in Swedish. *Affär*, from French *affaire*, means 'store, place of business' in Swedish, while Danish and Norwegian *affære* means 'affair', as in English. *Anledning*, from German *Anleitung* 'guidance', means 'cause, reason' in Swedish, but 'opportunity, occasion' in Danish/Norwegian. *Blöt* is a native word meaning 'wet' in Swedish (as *blaut* in N-Norwegian), but Da. *blød*/BN *bløt* means 'soft, weak' (with a more recent meaning of 'soft-headed').

(b) Lexical differences may be due to the extinction of a word in one language or to borrowing from a different source. In Swedish a common word for 'poet' is *skald*, an Old Norse word revived in modern times; in Danish and Norwegian it is used only about Old Norse times, the usual word being *digter/dikter* from German *Dichter* (which Swedish also has as *diktare*). While the words for 'man' and 'woman' are much the same, 'boy' and 'girl' are markedly deviant: Da. *dreng*/BN *gutt*/NN *gut*/Sw. *pojke* 'boy' and Da. *pige*/BN *pike*/NN *jente*/Sw. *flicka* 'girl'. Slang is a part of language that reflects innovation most readily and that is often local; in Swedish it has given rise to terms little known in the other languages, e.g. *kille* 'boy', *kul* 'fun' etc. There are also areas of clothing or vegetation that may surprise neighbours: a '(man's) suitcoat' is Sw. *kavaj*, Da./Nw. *jakke*; an 'overcoat' is Sw. *rock*, Da. *frakke* (Nw. *frakk*). Berries are differently named, e.g. what Swedish calls *hallon* 'raspberry', *smultron* 'strawberry', *hjortron* 'cloudberry', *krusbär* 'gooseberry' and *vinbär* 'currant' will be known in Danish and Norwegian as *bringebær*, *jordbær*, *multe(r)*, *stikkelsbær*, and *ribs/rips*. And so forth.

Bibliography

For more detailed surveys of Scandinavian, with comprehensive bibliographies, the reader is referred to Haugen (1976), a survey of the successive periods of the languages' history with extensive background and illustrative material — an updated German translation by Magnús Pétursson, under the title *Die skandinavischen Sprachen*, has been published by Helmut Buske, Hamburg — and Haugen (1982), a more concentrated survey of the history, organised by linguistic levels and emphasising linguistic rules of historical change.

For descriptive grammars, the best sources are in the original languages: Diderichsen (1957) for Danish; Næs (1972) for B-Norwegian; Beito (1970) for N-Norwegian; Thorell (1973) and Collinder (1974) for Swedish. An outline Norwegian grammar (both B-Norwegian and N-Norwegian) in English is contained in Haugen (1964), while Haugen and Chapman (1982) is a pedagogical grammar of Norwegian in English.

Haugen (1966) is a detailed account of language planning in relation to Norwegian.

References

Beito, O. 1970. *Nynorsk grammatikk* (Det Norske Samlaget, Oslo)

Collinder, B. 1974. *Svensk språklära* (C.W.K. Gleerup, Stockholm)

Diderichsen, P. 1957. *Elementær dansk grammatik* (Gyldendal, Copenhagen)

Haugen, E. 1964. *Norsk-engelsk ordbok/Norwegian-English Dictionary: With a Historical and Grammatical Introduction* (University of Wisconsin Press, Madison; 3rd ed., Universitetsforlaget, Oslo, 1984)

—— 1966. *Language Conflict and Language Planning: The Case of Modern Norwegian* (Harvard University Press, Cambridge, Mass.)

—— 1976. *The Scandinavian Languages: An Introduction to Their History* (Faber and Faber, London)

—— 1982. *Scandinavian Language Structures: A Comparative Historical Survey* (Max Niemeyer, Tübingen and University of Minnesota Press, Minneapolis)

—— and K.G. Chapman. 1982. *Spoken Norwegian*, 3rd ed. (Holt, Rinehart and Winston, New York)

Næs, O. 1972. *Norsk grammatikk*, 3rd ed. (Fabritius, Oslo)

Thorell, O. 1973. *Svensk grammatikk* (Esselte Studium, Stockholm)

7 Latin and the Italic Languages

R.G.G. Coleman

1 Introduction

Latin is the chief representative of the Italic group of Indo-European languages. The most important of the others were Oscan, which was spoken over most of Southern Italy in the last four centuries BC and is attested in substantial inscriptions from Avella and Banzi, and Umbrian, which was spoken further north and survives almost exclusively in a series of liturgical inscriptions from Gubbio dating from 350 to 50 BC. A large number of the Oscan and Umbrian texts are in native alphabets, ultimately derived like those of Latin and Etruscan from the Greek alphabet. Some are in the Latin alphabet, and collation of the two graphic systems provides valuable insights into the phonology of the two languages. In this chapter words attested in the native alphabets appear in capitals, those in the Latin alphabet in lower case.

Neither Oscan nor Umbrian is as closely related to Latin as Faliscan, a language attested in a small number of inscriptions from near Città Castellana. Of the non-Italic languages spoken in Italy after 500 BC Venetic in the far north-east was closely related to Italic; Etruscan, which is attested, again epigraphically, over a large area of central and northern Italy, was totally unrelated. Although Oscan was still in use at Pompeii until AD 79, Latin had long since become the written language of all Italy. Some dialects of Latin were partly shaped by the native languages, but it is doubtful whether the latter survived long into the Christian era. In this chapter Oscan and Umbrian phenomena will be treated only in relation to Latin as providing evidence for the Italic complex within which Latin must historically be placed.

For Latin phonology the most valuable source is the spellings, both standard and deviant, and the diachronic changes in spelling that are discernible in the numerous inscriptions recorded from about 500 BC onwards and the manuscripts of contemporary texts written on papyrus and subsequently on other soft materials. The manuscripts of literary texts from antiquity, usually written centuries after their composition, provide fuller testimony for morphology, syntax and lexicon. Among these texts are treatises on the language itself and on rhetoric. These are especially important as revealing the criteria, derived mostly from Greek theory, by which the norms of classical usage were formulated and applied in the period 150 BC–AD 150.

At all periods alongside the formal registers of the written documents there was the Latin spoken by the illiterate majority. Vulgar Latin had of course its own diachrony and, as it spread with the expansion of Roman power, must have acquired the dialectal variations from which the Romance languages emerged. It is partially recoverable from the written documents whose spelling, grammar and lexicon deviate in the direction of Romance from the standard Latin that can be established for the period concerned. Many of these deviations are identifiable with or can be directly linked to the asterisked reconstructions of Proto-Romance. The conservative traditions of the schools of grammar and rhetoric did not entirely immunise classical usage against vulgar infiltration. However, they did ensure that by the ninth century AD written Latin and the diverse spoken forms of Latin had ceased to be registers of one language, coexisting in a state of diglossia like Greek *katharévusa* and *dēmotikḗ*, but were now quite separate, if closely related, languages. Caesar and Livy would have recognised the Latin of Nithard's *Historiae* as a form of their own language; they would have found his citations of the Strassburg oaths as baffling in the *romana lingua* as in the *teudisca*. Latin was to survive for another thousand years after that as a vehicle for liturgy and learned discourse, but in a state of suspended animation dependent upon transfusions from the ancient models. These guaranteed it a homogeneity in time and space, in marked contrast to the independently live and divergent Romance languages.

2 Phonology

The Italic word accent was fixed and not phonemic. In Proto-Italic it is generally thought to have been a stress accent falling on the initial syllable. That this situation continued into the independent history of the languages is confirmed by the fact that both vowel raising ('weakening') in early Latin and syncope in Oscan and Umbrian affected only non-initial syllables. By about 250 BC the rule of the penultimate was established in Latin: in words of more than two syllables the accent was on the penultimate unless it contained a short unchecked vowel (i.e. in an open syllable), in which case the accent retreated to the antepenult. The range of possibilities is illustrated by:

fác 'make!' fácis 'you make' fácilēs 'easy' (nom. pl.)
              fēcit 'he made'   fēcístis 'you made' (pl.)
              fáctō 'made' (abl.) factū́rō 'about to make' (abl.)

The Latin grammarians borrowed from the Greeks the terminology of tonic accentuation, but although some educated native speakers may have affected Greek practice, the frequency of syncope in spoken Latin of all periods and the shortening of the unaccented vowels in *uólō*, *míhī* and later *dícō*, etc. show that the accent remained one of stress.

Table 7.1: The Segmental Phonemes of Latin in the Classical Period (c. 150 BC–AD 150)

Vowels

i		u
e		o
	a	

all ± length

Diphthongs: ae   au   oe   eu   ui

Consonants:

	Stop tense	lax	Fricative	Nasal	Lateral	Semi-vowels
Labial	p	b		m		w
Labio-dental			f			
Dental	t	d		n	l	
Alveolar			s			r
						j
Velar	k	g				
Labio-velar	kʷ					
Glottal			h			

The relative frequency and distribution of Latin short vowels had been affected by the raising that took place in non-initial syllables before 250 BC. The raising was higher in unchecked than in checked vowels; e.g. **défacites > déficitis* 'you fail' vs. **défactos > défectus* 'feeble', **homones > hominis* 'of the man' vs. **fácondom > fácundum* (acc.) 'eloquent'. /i/ and /u/ became more frequent as a result. Syncope, the terminal point in raising, occurred in all periods of spoken Latin: prehistorically in *reppulī* 'I drove back' (< **repepolai*, cf. *pepulī* 'I drove') and in *mēns* 'mind' (< *mentis*); later in *postus* for *positus* 'placed', *caldus* for *calidus* 'hot', *oclus* for *oculus* 'eye'.

Vowel length was phonemic in Latin, e.g. *leuis* 'light', *lēuis* 'smooth'; *rosa* (nom.), *rosā* (abl.) 'rose'. It was never marked systematically in writing, though sporadic devices are found, in Latin (mostly diacritics) as in Oscan (gemination) and Umbrian (addition of *h*). (The long vowels of classical Latin words cited in this chapter are marked diacritically.) /e·/ and /o·/ came to be raised: hence from the first century AD onwards deviant spellings like *filix*, *flus* for *fēlīx*, *flōs*. Eventually the ten vowels were reduced in many areas of Vulgar Latin to seven:

i·   i   e·   e   a   a·   o   o·   u   u·

i̦   ẹ   ę   a   ǫ   ọ   u̦

with length merely a concomitant of stress.

There was a general tendency to monophthongise diphthongs: early Latin *deicō* 'I say', *oino(m)* 'one', *ious* 'law' > *dīcō*, *ūnum*, *iūs* by 150 BC. Only /ae/ (< early Latin /ai/), /au/ and the rare /oe eu ui/ survived in the classical period. In some dialects of central Italy /ae/ and /au/ were monophthongised by the second century BC, e.g. *cedre*, *plostrum*, for standard *caedere* 'to cut', *plaustrum* 'cart', and the [ɛ] pronunciation of *ae* was standard by the fourth century AD. The monophthongisation in *cecīdit* (< *cecaidet*) and *accūsō* 'I accuse' (< *adcausō*) implies a form of raising, /ai/ > /ei/, /au/ > /ou/. The result was again to increase the frequency of high vowels, specifically /i·/ and /u·/.

The Oscan vowel system differs in two principal respects from the Latin one. Firstly it was asymmetrical, with three front vowels /i̦ i e/ and only two back /u̦ ọ/ in addition to /a/. The raising of /e·/ and /o·/, which came relatively late in Latin, had occurred prehistorically in both Oscan and Umbrian. But in Oscan, whereas the resultant /i̦·/ was distinguished from existing /i·/, as in *LÍGATÚÍS* 'to the ambassadors' (< *lēgatois*) vs. *SLAAGID* 'from the place' (< *stlāgīd*), the corresponding raised back vowel merged with /u·/ as in *FRUKTATIUF* 'profit' (< *frūktātiōns*). The raising of /o/ to [ọ] as in *PÚD* 'which' (< *kʷod*, cf. the allograph *pod*) merely increased the asymmetry of the system.

Secondly all but one of the Proto-Italic diphthongs were retained until the latest records of Oscan. Thus *DEÍVAÍ* 'to the goddess', *AVT* 'but', *ÚÍTTIUF* (nom.) 'use', but *LÚVKEÍ* 'in the grove' with /ou/ < */eu/; cf. Lat. *dīuae*, *aut*, *ūsiō*, *lūcī*.

The Umbrian vowel system was more symmetrical. Somewhat like Attic Greek it included two pairs of middle-to-high long vowels, recoverable from the Latin allographs, e.g. *TUTE*, *tote* 'to the people' with /ǫ·/ and /ẹ·/ (< *toutai*) and *HABETU*, *habitu* 'let him have' with /ẹ·/ and ọ·/ (< *habētōd*). In monophthongisation Umbrian was further advanced even than Latin, as the following correspondences illustrate: O. *PRAÍ* = Lat. *prae* = U. *PRE* 'before'; O. *DIÚVEÍ* = Lat. *Iouī* = U. *IUVE* 'to Jupiter'; O. *AVT* = Lat. *aut* = U. *UTE* 'but'; u-stem gen. sg. O. */castr/ous* = Lat. */trib/ūs* = U. */trif/or*.

Although neither Oscan nor Umbrian orthography reveals evidence of short vowel raising, the frequency of syncope in non-initial syllables implies its presence; e.g. O. *actud*, U. *AITU* < *agtōd* < *agetōd* 'let him act'; cf. Lat. *agitō*; O. *MEDDÍSS* < *medodikes* (nom. pl.) 'magistrates'. U. *ANTAKRES* < *antagreis* (abl.) 'intact' (cf. Lat. *integrīs*) and similar spellings must be presumed archaisms.

The Oscan and Umbrian consonant systems were very similar to Latin. The chief divergences will be noted in what follows.

The inherited velar stops /k/ and /g/ were retained in Italic generally. In Oscan and Latin palatalisation of [g] before [j] occurred prehistorically; e.g. O. *mais* 'more', Lat. *maiius* 'bigger' < **magjos* (adj. nt.) beside *magis* 'more' < **magios*. Umbrian shows palatalisation before front vowels, e.g. *šesna* 'dinner' (the native alphabet has a separate letter, transliterated as Ç, representing [tʃ] or [ʃ]), cf. O. *KERSNÚ*, Lat. *cēna*; *muieto*, cf. Lat. *mūgītus* 'a roar'.

The Oscan dialect of Banzi shows palatalisation of [tj] and [dj] (< [ti di]) before vowels: *bansae* 'at Bantia', *zicolom* 'day' < **diēklom*, and it was in this context that the Latin shift began. Lat. *peiius* 'worse' (< **pedjos*) certainly, *Iouī* 'to Jupiter' like O. *IUVEÍ*, U. *IUVE*, (< **djowei*) possibly, provides evidence for a prehistoric tendency. Instances exactly parallel to Oscan are attested in the second century AD: *terciae* for *tertiae* 'third' (Rome), *oze* for *hodiē* 'today' (Algeria). By the fifth century AD the grammarians report the pronunciation of *iūstitia* with [tsia] as normal. Secure Latin examples comparable to U. *šesna* do not occur before the fifth and sixth centuries AD: *intcitamento* 'encouragement' for *incitāmentō* (Italy), *dissesit* 'left' for *discessit* (Algeria), *septuazinta* 'seventy' for *septuāgintā* (Spain). They are abundant in Lombard and Merovingian documents of the seventh and eighth centuries.

The inherited labio-velars **/kʷ/ and **/gʷ/ were replaced by /p/ and /b/ in Oscan and Umbrian. In Latin they merged with /kw/ and /gw/. Thus *equus* 'horse' < PIt. **ekwos*, *quid* 'what?' < **kʷid*, cf. O. *PÍD*, U. *PEŘE* < **pid-i* with the distinctive Umbrian affricate reflex of intervocalic /d/. It is probable that Lat. *qu* represents /kʷ/ rather than /kw/, almost certain that *gu* represents [gw]. Inherited **/gʷ/ > Lat. /w/ except after a nasal: PIt. **gʷīwos* > *uīuus* 'alive', cf. O. *BIVUS* (nom. pl.), **snigʷm* > *niuem* (acc. sg.) 'snow' but **ongʷen* > *unguen* 'ointment', cf. U. *UMEN* (< **omben*).

The labial glide /w/, which was distinguished graphically from *u* in Oscan and Umbrian, was represented by *u* in Latin. Its phonemic status is guaranteed by rare pairs like *uoluī* with /wi·/ 'I rolled' and *uoluī* with /ui·/ 'I wished'. In some areas /w/ > [β] as early as the first century AD, e.g. *baliat* for *ualeat* 'farewell!' at Pompeii. By the third century AD consonantal *u*, formerly transliterated as ου in Greek, was frequently rendered by β. Whereas the earliest Germanic borrowings from Latin show [w], later ones prefer a labio-dental fricative: e.g. OE *wīn*, *weall* < *uīnum* 'wine', *uallum* 'fence', but *fers* < *uersus* 'verse'. The invention of *double u* in the eighth century AD to represent Germanic [w] indicates that the value of Latin consonantal *u* was now [v]. Hence Latin borrowings from Germanic have *w* or *gu* for Germanic [w], e.g. Go. *wadi* 'pledge' > *wadium* (seventh century AD), OHG *werra* 'strife' > *werra/guerra* (ninth century AD).

The palatal glide /j/ was not distinguished graphically in any Italic language. Its phonemic status is guaranteed not by any minimal opposition with /i/ but by pattern congruity in *iam*, *tam* etc. Invervocalic /j/ was regularly [jj]. Secure evidence of an affricate pronunciation [dz] or [dʒ] for /j/ occurs in *Zanuario* (Pozzuoli, fourth century AD) and *Genoarias* (Arles, sixth century AD) for *Ianuar-*.

/f/ and /h/ were more frequent in Oscan and Umbrian than in Latin, often occurring non-initially in uncompounded words. Thus O. *MEFIAÍ* (loc. sg.), cf. Lat. *medius* 'middle' (< **medhio-*); U. *rufru*, cf. Lat. *rubrōs* (acc. pl.) 'red' (< **ₔ₁rudhro-*); U. *VITLAF*, cf. Lat. *uitulās* 'calves' (< **-āns*); O. *FEÍHÚSS* (acc.) 'walls', cf. Lat. *figulus* 'potter' (< **dh(e)igh-*); U. *REHTE*, cf. Lat. *rēctē* 'rightly'. (The diachronic complex that produces the idiosyncratic pattern of reflexes of the Proto-Indo-European voiced aspirates */bh dh gh gʷh/, partially exemplified in some of these forms, is a notable witness to the existence of a unified Proto-Italic.) /h/ was unstable in both Latin and Umbrian. Initially it is ignored in classical versification and there was learned debate about the correct forms of *ūmor* 'moisture' and *harēna* 'sand'; cf. U. *heritu ERETU* 'let him choose'. Medially /h/ is often lost in Latin, e.g. *praehibeō* > *praebeō* 'I provide', *nihil* > *nīl* 'nothing' and, when it remains, it merely marks hiatus, e.g. *ahēnus/aēnus* 'brazen', U. *AHESNES* (abl. pl.); cf. O. *STAHÍNT* 'they stand' (< **stāint*). In Vulgar Latin /h/ disappeared almost completely.

Final /m/ was often omitted in Umbrian and early Latin, e.g. U. *PUPLU* for *PUPLUM* 'people' (acc.), Lat. *oino* for **oinom* 'one' (acc.); rarely in Oscan, except at Pompeii, e.g. *VÍA* for *VÍAM* 'road'. In classical versification it fails to prevent the elision of vowels: *făcĭlem ēssĕ* with [em] > [e]; cf. *făcĭle ēssĕ*. However, *făcĭlem dărĕ* contrasts with *făcĭlĕ dărĕ*, which implies either [em] > [e·] or an assimilation [emd] > [end]. In Vulgar Latin final /m/ was almost totally lost. Hence the homophony of *facilem* and *facile*, *bonum* (acc. sg.) and *bonō* (dat., abl. sg.), with [um] > [ų] > [ǫ].

The frequency of /s/ was much reduced by rhotacism in Latin and Umbrian. In the latter both intervocalic and final /s/ were affected. Thus *FURENT* < **bhusenti* 'they will be', Lat. *foret* but O. *FUSÍD*, both < **bhusēt* (3 sg. subj.); *dequrier* (earlier *TEKURIES* dat. pl.) cf. Lat. *decuria* 'ten-man group'. In Latin final /r/ for /s/ occurs only by paradigmatic analogy; e.g. *honor*, *honōrem* replacing *honōs*, *honōrem* (acc.).

In early Latin final /s/ preceded by a short vowel was apparently lost before consonants but retained before vowels. Together with the normal treatment of final /m/ this would have given the following variants for 'the master's son':

nom. (filius): fīlius erī, fīliu dominī
acc. (filium): fīliu erī, fīlium dominī

This pattern underlies the graphic and metrical data of the period 250–180 BC. Both *-s* and *-m* were restored in standard orthography by the early second century BC, but final -s, unlike -m, always counts as a consonant in classical versification: fīlĭŭs ĕrī, fīlĭŭs dŏmĭnī. Vulgar Latin, like Umbrian earlier, shows frequent loss of final consonants, e.g. of /t/ in VL ama 'he loves', U. HABE 'he has', but in contrast to e.g. U. SESTE for sestes 'you set up' it seems to have kept final /s/ in all regions until at least the sixth century AD and only in eighth-century documents from Italy does -s begin to disappear on a large scale.

There was a tendency in most periods of Latin to reduce all but a small range of consonant clusters by the assimilation or omission of one or more components or by anaptyxis. Thus */sn/ in nix 'snow' < *snigʷs and cēna 'dinner', cf. U. šesna, O. KERSNU; */ns/ in uiās 'roads' < *-āns, cf. O. VÍASS, U. VITLAF 'calves' with /f/ < */ns/, and in mēnsis 'month', sedēns 'sitting', where early Latin usually has s, cf. U. MENZNE (< *mensenei loc.) with [ents], ZEŘEF (< *sedens). Paradigmatic analogy restored /n/ in sedens: sedentem (acc.), and a spelling pronunciation [e·ns] was standard in classical speech; but /n/ was never restored in Vulgar usage and spellings like mesis were widespread in late Latin. Initial and final clusters were the more vulnerable, e.g. /gn/ in nātus, early Lat. gnātus 'son' but cognātus 'relative'; */tl/ simplified in lātus 'raised', but in piāculum 'sacrifice' (cf. U. pihaclu (abl.) < *piātlo-) /t/ has been assimilated to the velar allophone of /l/ and resultant /kl/ has undergone anaptyxis; /kt/ simplified in lac 'milk' but retained in lactis (gen.). As the preceding examples show, Oscan and Umbrian, though they have the same general tendency, often diverge in detail: thus O. ARAGETU (abl.) beside Lat. argentō 'silver', ÚPSANNAM 'which is to be done' beside Lat. operandam, MEDDÍSS 'magistrate' beside Lat. iūdex 'judge', U. acnu (acc.) beside O. AKENEÍ (loc.), Lat. annus 'year'.

3 Morphology and Syntax

The case system of Italic was typologically close to Proto-Indo-European. The cases were fusional, encoding the categories of case, number and partly gender. The noun morphology was organised in six paradigms, exemplified from Latin in the chart given opposite. All save (4) and (5) are shared with adjectives, and all reflect Proto-Indo-European paradigms except (5), which seems to have developed in Proto-Italic; cf. U. RI (dat.-abl.) with Lat. reī, rē.

The diachrony of these paradigms as a whole is notable in two respects. Firstly the i-stems (3b) became progressively more unlike the u-stems (4), to which in Proto-Indo-European they were structurally parallel. This process had not gone so far in Oscan and Umbrian as in Latin, where the cases exhibited for turris represent the most conservative form of the paradigm attested, and the distinctive (3b) cases were gradually replaced by those of (3a). Prehistorically assimilation had been in the opposite direction; cf.

Classical Latin Nominal Paradigms

	1	2	3(a)	3(b)	4	5
Sg. Nom.	ui-a 'road'	popul-us 'people'	lēx 'law'	turr-is 'tower'	trib-us 'tribe'	r-ēs 'thing'
Voc.	-a	-e	lēx	-is	-us	-ēs
Acc.	-am	-um	lēg-em	-im	-um	-em
Gen.	-ae	-ī	-is	-is	-ūs	-ēī
Dat.	-ae	-ō	-ī	-ī	-uī	-ēī
Abl.	-ā	-ō	-e	-ī	-ū	-ē
Loc.	[Rōm-ae 'at Rome']	[hum-ī 'on the ground']	[rūr-e 'in the country']	[Septembr-ī 'in September']	–	[di-ē 'on the day']
Pl. Nom. ⎫ Voc. ⎭	ui-ae	popul-ī	lēg-ēs	turr-ēs	trib-ūs	r-ēs
Acc.	-ās	-ōs	-ēs	-īs	-ūs	-ēs
Gen.	-ārum	-orum	-um	-ium	-uum	-ērum
Dat. ⎫ Abl. ⎬ Loc. ⎭	-īs	-īs	-ibus	-ibus	-ibus	-ēbus

nom. pl. *hominēs* 'men' for *-ĕs*, reflected in O. *HUMUNS*; abl. pl. *legibus*, O. *ligis* as if < *lēg-ifs* < *-ibhos*; cf. U. *homonus* < *-ufs*, with anaptyctic *u*, < *-bhos*.

Secondly there were in Latin from an early date doublets belonging to (1) and (5), e.g. *māteria/-ēs* 'timber' and to (2) and (4), e.g. *senātus* 'senate' and *pīnus* 'pine tree'. This led to the wholesale transfer of nouns in Vulgar Latin from (4) and (5) to (2) and (1) respectively and thus to the elimination of the former pair.

The dual number has not survived in Italic noun or verb morphology. The distinction between singular and plural remained systematic.

There are three genders in Italic: masculine, feminine and neuter. The category is systematically encoded in adjectives and partly in pronouns. Hence, while most nouns in (1) and (5) are feminine, (2) and (4) masculine, there are exceptions, and these are recoverable only from concordant pronouns and adjectives. predicative or attributive; e.g. *nauta est ualidus* 'the sailor is strong', *ille diēs* 'that day' (m.); *humus dūra* 'the hard ground', *haec tribus est* 'this is the tribe' (f.). The neuter gender is usually marked in nouns as well as adjectives but only in the nominative and accusative: *bellum* 'war' (sg.), *maria* 'seas' (pl.). Sex is signalled systematically by the gender of adjectives: *rēx bonus* 'the good king', *honestae mulierēs* 'virtuous women'; but the masculine acts as common gender: *hominēs sunt ualidī* 'humans are strong'. Inanimate nouns are assigned to all three genders; e.g. *flūmen lātum* (nt.) but *fluuius lātus* (m.) 'broad river', *silua dēnsa* (f.) but *nemus dēnsum* (nt.) 'thick forest'. The neuter is the unmarked form of adjectives and pronouns: *facile est dēscendere* 'to go down is easy', cf. *facilis est dēscēnsus* 'the descent is easy' (m.).

Many of the specific case forms are cognate in the different languages even when sound changes have obscured their identity, as in O. *HÚRZ* 'grove' with /ts/ < *-tos* beside Lat. *hortus* (2 nom. sg.) 'garden' and U. *TRIF* 'three' < *trins* (3b acc. pl.), beside Lat. *trīs*. Divergences occur of course; e.g. in paradigm (2) nom. pl. Lat. *Nōlāni, Iguuīnī* with *-ī* < PIE pronominal *-oi* contrast with O. *NÚVLANÚS* 'Nolans', U. *iiouinur* 'Iguvines' < PIE nominal *-ōs*. In addition to the interaction between (3a) and (3b) already noted, (3a) abl. sg. shows Lat. *lēge*, U. *KAPIŘE* 'bowl' with *-e* < PIE loc. *-i* against O. *ligud* < *lēgōd* with the ablative form of (2).

The most remarkable divergence occurs in what is otherwise a very homogeneous paradigm throughout Italic, namely in the genitive singular of (2). PIE *-osio*, reconstructed from Ancient Greek and Indo-Iranian, is directly attested in Faliscan *Kaisiosio* 'Caesius', and in *Valesiosio* 'Valerius' on an inscription, possibly Volscian, from Southern Lazio. Oscan and Umbrian have *-eis*: *SAKARAKLEÍS* 'temple', *popler* 'people'. This was originally the (3b) form, which has also spread to (3a), as in *MEDÍKEÍS* 'magistrate'. Latin *-ī* has cognates in the Venetic and Celtic genitive singular forms, e.g. OIr. *maqi* 'son's'. It reflects either *-iə₂*, for which cf. Vedic *devī́* 'goddess' (< 'belonging to a god, *deváḥ*') or *-ie*, the suffix which was inflected to form adjectives like Latin *patrius* 'belonging to a father, *pater*' and Vedic *divyáḥ* 'belonging to the sky, *dyáuḥ*'.

It will be observed in the chart of nominal paradigms that, although there are fourteen possible cases, no paradigm has more than eight (*populus, lēx*) or fewer than six (*rēs*) distinctive forms. The pattern of syncretism, however, varies from one paradigm to another and the only general syncretism is in the dative-locative-ablative plural. This is also one of the maximally differentiated cases, along with the accusative singular and genitive plural, which have distinctive forms in every paradigm. Least marked are the vocative, the case of second person address, and the locative, which signals position in space or time. The vocative is distinguished only in (2) singular, the declension to which most male personal and family names belong. The locative is more distinct morphologically and more active functionally in both Oscan and Umbrian, e.g. O. *AKENEÍ* but Lat. *annō* (abl.) 'in the year'; U. *MANUVE* but Lat. *in manū* (abl.) 'in the hand'; O. *eizeic uincter* 'he is convicted in this', cf. *in hāc rē conuincitur*. In Latin it is reserved for physical location and subject to severe lexical constraints, e.g. *Rōmae* but *in urbe, in Italiā, humī* 'on the ground' but *in solō*.

The syncretism of the Proto-Indo-European case system had already begun in Proto-Italic with the merging of comitative and ablative cases. Thus early Lat. *dedit meretōd* 'he gave with justification', O. *com preiuatud actud* 'let him plead together with the defendant' (Lat. *cum reō agitō*), where the case forms reflect the Proto-Indo-European ablative. In the plural, as we have remarked, this syncretism also absorbed locative and dative functions; e.g. O. *FIÍSÍAÍS* 'at the festival', Lat. *fēriīs*, *LÍGATÚÍS* 'to the ambassadors', Lat. *lēgātīs*.

A number of Indo-European languages show the apparently independent development of phrases composed of nominal + participle in an appropriate case to signal the temporal location or attendant circumstances of a verbal action or state; e.g. the 'absolute' use of the locative (and genitive) in Sanskrit, and the genitive (and accusative) in Ancient Greek. The corresponding Italic construction has the comitative ablative: O. *lamatir toutad praesentid* 'the penalty is to be exacted with the people being present', Lat. *populō praesente*; U. *ESTE PERSKLUM AVES ANZERIATES ENETU* 'this sacrifice, with the birds having been examined, he is to begin', Lat. *auibus obseruātīs inītō*. Frequent in Latin is the parallel nominal + (predicative) adjective or noun: *auibus secundīs* 'with the birds (being) auspicious', *auibus magistrīs* 'with the birds (being) instructors'. The detachment of the construction from its original comitative meaning is reflected by several developments in the classical period, notably the extension to future participles and to active participles of transitive verbs along with their complements; e.g. *sortītīs cōnsulibus prōuinciās* 'the consuls having been allotted their provinces', *oppugnātūrīs hostibus castra* 'the enemy being about to attack the camp'. The incorporation of prepositional phrases within the ablative phrase itself, as in *rēbus ad profectiōnem comparātīs* 'things being prepared for the departure', and the replacement of the head noun by a clause or phrase, as in *quor praetereātur dēmōnstrātō* 'why it is omitted having been demonstrated' and *cognitō uīuere Ptolemaeum* 'that Ptolemy was alive having been discovered', also added to the internal complexity of the construction. The term 'ablative absolute' is appropriate once it has become the equivalent of a full adverbial clause, *quom cognōuisset uīuere Ptolemaeum* 'when he discovered that Ptolemy...', etc. Not surprisingly, once the case orientation was lost, the ablative came to be replaced in Vulgar Latin by the nominative or accusative; cf. *reliquias recollectas tumulum tibi constitui* 'having gathered up your remains, I set up a grave for you' (fourth century AD, Africa), *coiux moriens non fuit alter amor* 'your husband dying, there was no second love' (sixth century AD, Rome).

There are several distinctively Latin idioms in which a case usage is transferred from verbal to nominal dependency. For instance, the purposive use of the dative in *trīs uirōs ēlēgēre lītibus iūdicandīs* 'three men they chose for deciding law suits' → *trēs uirī lītibus iūdicandīs*; *sēmen sātui parāuī* 'I prepared the seed for sowing' → *sātui sēmen* 'seed for sowing'. A half-way stage is the so-called predicative dative, e.g. *auxiliō tibi est* 'he is of assistance (dat.) to you' ← *adest auxiliō tibi* 'he is here for assistance to you'. Similarly the comitative use of the ablative in *singulārī industriā labōrāuit* 'she worked with exceptional industry' → *mulier singulārī industriā* 'a woman of exceptional industry', the so-called ablative of description.

Prepositions originally defined the case meanings more precisely and hence could accompany more than one case, but they came to usurp more and more of the meaning of the phrase and so to be restricted to a single case. Thus the use of the simple accusative with directional verbs survived as an archaism in a few nouns, e.g. Lat. *Rōmam uēnit* 'he came to Rome', *domum rediī* 'I returned home'; but it was generally replaced by prepositional phrases: O. *ANT PÚNTTRAM* 'up to the bridge', cf. Lat. *ante pontem* 'in front of the bridge'; U. *SPINAM-AŘ* 'to the column', cf. *ad spīnam* 'to the spine'.

The encroachment of prepositional phrases on the simple case is well exemplified in the Latin ablative. The ablative functions of the case and those derived from them, e.g. agency, normally have prepositions except with certain words. Thus *parentibus caret* 'of his parents he is deprived' but *ab eīs sēparātus* 'from them separated', *ab eīs dēsertus* 'by them deserted'. Regularly without prepositions are for instance *cōnsule nātus* 'of a consul begotten', *melle dulcius* 'than honey sweeter'. The comitative function normally has prepositions where the accompaniment is physical: *cum agricolīs labōrābat* 'with farmers he was working' vs. *magnā (cum) cūrā* 'with great care'. The instrumental function acquires prepositions only in post-classical documents; e.g. *dē gladiō percussus* 'by a sword struck'.

Prepositional phrases also encroached upon the functions of other cases. In Oscan and Umbrian the preposition (or rather postposition) *en* 'in' was sometimes attached to the locative, as in O. *HÚRTÍN* 'in the grove', Lat. *in hortō* 'in the garden', *exaisc-en ligis* 'in these laws', Lat. *in hīs lēgibus*.

By analogy with the plural forms the ablative singular also came to be used in locative functions with prepositions, which were, however, generally omitted when the noun was temporal. Thus O. *ÚP SAKARAKLÚD* 'at the temple' beside *SAKARAKLEÍ* (loc.), *meddixud* beside *MEDIKKIAÍ* 'in the magistracy'. In Latin, apart from the lexical group referred to above — *Rōmae, domī* etc. — the locative case had been entirely replaced by the ablative: *in templō, in magistrātū* and *eō tempore* 'at that time'. In Vulgar Latin even the temporal nouns acquired prepositions.

Prepositional ablative phrases in Latin also encroached upon the genitive case: e.g. *iūdicātus dē capite* for *capitis* 'judged on a capital charge' (cf. O. *dat castrid* for *castrous zicolum deicum* 'for a capital charge the day to name') and especially *maior pars ex hostibus* 'the greater part of the enemy', *dīmidium dē praedā* 'half of the loot' beside the genitives *hostium* and *praedae*. Similarly *ad* + accusative phrases encroached upon the dative. The original distinctions between *ad haec respondit* 'in the face of these (arguments) he replied' and *hīs respondit* 'to these persons he replied' and between *ad rēgem id mīsī* 'to (in the direction of) the king it I sent' and *rēgī id dedī* 'to the king it I gave' became blurred, and in post-classical Latin the

Vulgar generalisation of prepositional phrases leads to occasional uses like *ad hōs respondit, ad rēgem id dedī.*

Some of the phonetic changes remarked in section 2 eroded important distinctions in the Latin case paradigms. Thus the disappearance of final /m/, the loss of distinction between /a/ and /a·/ and the merging of /u/ and /o·/ produced homophony between *lēgem* (acc.) and *lēge* (abl.) in paradigm (3a), between *populum* (acc.) and *populō* (dat., abl.) in (2) and between *uia* (nom.), *uiam* (acc.) and *uiā* (abl.) in (1). The plural inflections, being more distinctively marked, were less vulnerable. However, the combined effect of grammatical and phonetic changes was a steady reduction of the cases in Vulgar Latin, until of the four surviving paradigms three had three cases, the fourth, (3b), only two:

Sg.	Nom.	*vi̯a	*pǫpǫlǫs	*lęss	*tǫrręs
	Obl.	-a	-ǫ	*lęgę	-ę
Pl.	Nom.	-ę	-i̯	-ģes	-ęs
	Obl.	-as	-ǫs	-ģes	-ęs

(ģ = a palatalised reflex of /g/)

Pronominal morphology was idiosyncratic to particular languages in both its lexical forms and its inflections, though many of the cases are identical with nouns of (1) and (2). Vulgar Latin developed articles from the deictic pronoun *ille* 'that one' and the cardinal number *ūnus* 'one', the former perhaps partly under Greek influence. This was an innovation in Italic.

The comparison of adjectives was signalled morphologically. Comparatives were formed with inherited *-ios-*; e.g. Lat. *maiior* < **magjōs* (: *magnus* 'big'), O. *mais* < **magjos* (nt.), and its allomorph **-is-* + **-tero-* in Oscan and Umbrian, e.g. U. *MESTRU* < **magisterā* (f. nom.), cf. Lat. *magister* 'master'. Superlative forms were more varied. Inherited were **-mo-* in **supmo-* > Lat. *summum*, U. *somo* (acc.) 'highest', **-t(m̥)mo-* in Lat. *ultimam*, O. *ÚLTIUMAM* (f. acc.), **-is(m̥)mo-* in **magismmo-* > Lat. *maximās*, O. *maimas* (f. acc. pl.). Unique to Latin is **-is-smmo-* as in *strēnuissimus* 'most vigorous'. The analytic exponents *magis/plūs strēnuus*, *maximē strēnuus*, etc. encroached, especially in Vulgar Latin.

The Italic verbal inflections too were fusional, encoding the categories of tense, (past, present, future), aspect (imperfective, perfective), mood (indicative, subjunctive, imperative), number (singular, plural), person (first, second, third) and voice (active and medio-passive). Typologically this system was close to Proto-Indo-European. The specific innovations were the creation of a future tense, the merging of perfect and unmarked (aorist) aspectual distinctions in a new perfective, the absorption of optative into subjunctive and of dual into plural, and the decline of the middle functions of the medio-passive.

Minimal oppositions can be illustrated from Latin:

	imperfect:	dīcēbat	'he was saying'
dīcit 'he says' present indicative singular third person active	perfect:	dīxit	'he said'
	subjunctive:	dīcat	'let him say'
	plural:	dīcunt	'they say'
	second person:	dīcis	'you say'
	passive:	dīcitur	'he is said'

all of which are exactly paralleled in Oscan and Umbrian.

There are three Italic participles: (a) the inherited -*nt*- acts as imperfective active; e.g. U. *ZEŘEF* = Lat. *sedēns* 'sitting' (nom. sg.); (b) the inherited -*to*- verbal adjective signalling state, which was originally neutral as to voice, as in U. *TAÇEZ* 'silent' = Lat. *tacitus* beside *tacēre* 'to be silent', *ÇERSNATUR* 'having dined' (nom. pl.), cf. Lat. *cēnāti* beside *cēnāre* 'to dine', became the medio-passive perfect participle; e.g. O. *scriftas* 'written' (nom. pl.), Lat. *scrīptae* beside *scrībere* 'to write', and *indūtus* 'having put on' beside *induere* 'to clothe'; (c) a prospective passive in -*ndo*-, the gerundive, peculiar to Italic; e.g. O. *ÚPSANNAM* 'to be done' (acc. sg.), U. *anferener* 'to be carried about' (gen. sg.); cf. Lat. *operandam, ferendī*. Latin also has a prospective active participle, e.g. *dictūrus* 'about to say'.

There are infinitives, reflecting verbal noun case forms, e.g. *dīcere* < **deikesi* (*s*-stem loc. sg.); *dīcī* < **deikei* (loc. of **deikom* or dat. of **deiks*) and O. *DEÍKÚM* (the corresponding accusative). Latin developed a systematic marking of tense and voice in the infinitives, starting with the arbitrary assignment of **deikesi* to present active, **deikei* to present passive and the extension of **-si* from the present active to form a perfect active **deix-is-si* (> *dīxisse*). The system was completed by an assortment of makeshift analytic formations.

Apart from the verb 'to be' (Lat. *esse*, O. *ezum* U. *erom*) and, at least in Latin, 'to go' (*īre*) and 'to wish' (*uelle*, with its compounds), the Italic verb was organised into four conjugations, classified according to the present infinitive and first person singular present indicative, as in the chart of Latin verb conjugations.

Conjugation (3a) reflects inherited thematic-stem verbs, e.g. *agere*, O. *acum*, cf. Gk. *ágein* 'to lead', together with a few verbs from the Proto-Indo-European athematic class, e.g. *iungō* 'I join', cf. Ved. *yunájmi, sistō* 'I set up', U. *SESTU*, cf. Gk. *hístāmi*. The transfer of the latter probably began in the plural, with the remodelling of **iungmos, *sistamos* (cf. Ved. *yunjmāḥ*, Gk. *hístamen*) etc. (1) also contains some athematic reflexes, e.g. *fārī* 'to speak', cf. Gk. *phāmí* 'I say', and *stāre* 'to stand', which was formed from the aorist, cf. Gk. *éstān* 'I stood'. But its largest constituency is denominative formations, originally from declension (1), e.g. *cūrāre*, O. *KURAIA* (3 sg. subj.), North O. *coisatens* (3 pl. perf.) all from **koisā* (> Lat. *cūra*), but extended to other declensions, e.g. Lat. *termināre* from the (2)-noun *terminus*, O. *TEREMNATTENS* (3 pl. perf.) from a (3a)-neuter attested in *TEREMENNIÚ* (nom. pl.). In fact it was to this conjugation that all new

Latin Verb Conjugations

Infin.	1	2	3a	3b	4
	cūrāre	monēre	dīcere	facere	uenīre
	'to care'	'to warn'	'to say'	'to make'	'to come'

		1	2	3a	3b	4
Sg.	1	cūr-ō	mon-eō	dīc-ō	fac-iō	uen-iō
	2	-ās	-ēs	-is	-is	-īs
	3	-at	-et	-it	-it	-it
Pl.	1	-āmus	-ēmus	-imus	-imus	-īmus
	2	-ātis	-ētis	-itis	-itis	-ītis
	3	-ant	-ent	-unt	-iunt	-iunt

denominatives and loan-verbs were assigned; e.g. *iūdicāre* from *iūdex* 'judge', cf. O. *medicatud* (abl. part.) 'having been judged', *aedificāre* 'to build' from **aedifex*, *baptizāre* from Gk. *baptízein*, *guardāre/wardāre* from Go. *wardōn* 'to keep watch'.

Conjugation (2) absorbed the Proto-Indo-European stative formant in **-ē-*, e.g. *uidēre* 'to see', the causative **-ejo-*, e.g. *moneō* 'I warn' (cf. *meminī* 'I recall'), and some denominatives from declension (2), e.g. *fatērī* 'to confess', O. *FATÍUM* from **fato-* 'spoken'. (4) has a few denominatives from (3b)-nouns, e.g. *fīnīre* from *fīnis* 'finish'. Together with (3b) it also reflects **-jo-* verbs, as in *ueniō* (4) < **gʷnjō*, *faciō* (3b, cf. O. *FAKIIAD* 3 sg. subj) < **dhə₁jō*. The distribution between the two conjugations, at first phonologically determined, had long since become more casual. A number of verbs show doublet forms in (3b) and (4), e.g. Lat. *cupiō* 'I desire', U. *HERTER* 'it is required' (<**heri-*) but *HERI* 'he wishes' (< **herī-*).

Some verbs with long-vowel presents show a different formation in the perfect, e.g. *moneō* : *monu-ī*, *ueniō* : *uēn-ī*, also *iuuō* (1) 'I help' : *iūuī*. Others generalised the long vowel, e.g. *cūrō* : *cūrāuī*, *audiō* 'I hear' : *audīuī*. This is typical of a general Latin tendency: cf. the spread of the infixed nasal from *iungō* 'I join' to *iunxī* beside the more conservative *rumpō* : *rūpī*.

The most important opposition in the Latin verb was originally between (I) imperfective and (II) perfective aspect. Within each of these two divisions there was a further opposition between (A) the unmarked base form and a pair marked for (B1) prospective and (B2) retrospective tense. The unmarked imperfective form was located in the present tense, the unmarked perfective form was temporally ambivalent between present and past. The following second singular forms of *monēre* illustrate the original distribution of the forms that they reflect:

I	A	monē-s			
		B1	monē-b-is	B2	monē-b-ās
II	A	monu-istī			
		B1	monu-er-is	B2	monu-er-ās

This system was not inherited, and the conjugation that is closest to a Proto-Indo-European type, (3), shows a different pattern in IA and B:

I   A   dīc-is   B1   dīc-ēs

                                 B2   dīcē-bās

where *dīcēs* was originally the subjunctive to *dīcis*. This pattern in fact spread via (3b) to (4): *audīs, audiēs*. It has a parallel in the relation between U. *PURTUVIS* 'you offer' and *PURTUVIES* 'you will offer'.

The Oscan and Umbrian material is very incomplete; there are no reflexes of II B2, for instance, and only one of I B2. But the following Oscan forms reveal a system, and it is different both from Proto-Indo-European and from Latin:

I   A   FAAMA-T (3 sg.)
           B1   deiua-s-t (3 sg.)
                 B2   FU-F-ANS (3 pl.)
II   A   PRÚFATT-ENS (3 pl.)
           B1   TRÍBARAKATT-U-S-ET (3 pl.)
                 B2 —

Here the I B1 form is from *-se-*, also attested in early Lat. *faxit*, an infrequent synonym of *faciet* 'he will do', while the unique I B2 form is from *-bhwā-*, attested in Lat. *bā-*.

Also exemplified in these examples is the diversity of perfective formants: Lat. /w/ in *curā-uī, mon-ŭ-ī*, O. /tt/ in *PRÚFATTENS*. There are others too; e.g. U. /l/ in *apelus* 'you will have weighed (< *anpend-luses*), O. /f/ in *SAKRAFIR* (pass. subj.) 'let there be a consecration'. Some are shared with Latin, e.g. reduplication in U. *DEDE* 'he gave', Lat. *dedit*; long root vowel in O. *hipid* 'he had' (< *hēb-* beside Lat. *habuit*), cf. Lat. *cēpi* 'I took'. The sigmatic formation, productive in Latin, e.g. *dīxī* (cf. Gk. aor. *édeixa*), has no other Italic attestation.

The six tenses had by historical times been reorganised thus:

Future (< I B1): monēbis 'you will warn', deiuast 'he will swear'.
Past-in-the-Future/Future Perfect (< II B1): monueris 'you will have warned', TRÍBARAKATTUSET 'they will have built'.
Present (< I A): monēs 'you warn', FAAMAT 'he orders'.
[Past] Imperfect (< I B2): monēbās 'you were warning', FUFANS 'they were'.
[Pres.] Perfect/Past Definite (< II A): monuistī 'you warned', PRÚFATTENS 'they approved'.
Past-in-the-Past/Past Perfect (< II B2): monuerās 'you had warned'

The original aspectual oppositions survive only in the imperfect and perfect, having become neutralised in the future and present. The temporal relationship between imperfect and past-in-the-past, *monē-b-ās: monu-er-ās*, has been replicated in *monē-b-is : monu-er-is*, with the transfer of the latter from perfective-future to future-perfect function.

The syncretic character of the Italic perfect is reflected in Latin both in its stem classes, which contain inherited perfect (reduplication) and aorist (sigmatic) formants, and in its personal inflections: sg. *uēn-ī, uēn-istī, uēn-it*; pl. *uēn-imus, uēn-istis, uēn-ēre* and *uēnĕrunt*. This contrasts sharply with the inflections of all the other five tenses, which, apart from first person singular forms in vowel + *m* in the imperfect, past perfect and all subjunctives, are very homogeneous. (In Oscan and Umbrian what can be discerned of the perfect inflections is less idiosyncratic).

The present-perfect functions of the Latin perfect are well attested, e.g. *nōuī* 'I know', perfect of *nōscō* 'I come to know', *periī* 'I am ruined', perfect of *pereo* 'I perish'. They were especially prominent in the passive, where a stative meaning is predictably more frequent anyway and the analytic exponents had a present orientation: *epistulae scrīptae sunt* like O. *scriftae set* was originally a present-perfect 'the letters are in a written state', even though it is the regular passive also to the past-definite meaning of *scrīpsī* 'I wrote'.

The ambiguities resulting from the syncretism in the perfect were resolved in the classical period of Latin by the development of two new tenses: an active present-perfect corresponding to *scrīptae sunt* 'they are written' and a passive past-definite for *scrīpsī (epistulās)*:

	Act.		Pass.
Perf.	scrīptās habeō (new)	←	scrīptae sunt
			↓
Past Def.	scrīpsī		scrīptae fuērunt (new)

The innovations never established themselves fully in the written language but became current in Post-Classical Vulgar Latin.

The Italic exponents of medio-passive voice are partly reflexes of middle forms in *-r*, which are attested in Hittite and Old Irish, partly the phrases with the *-to-* participle cited above. Thus U. *EMANTUR* 'they are to be taken', Lat. *emantur* 'they are to be bought', U. *screhto est*, Lat. *scriptum est* 'it has been written'. The relation between the medio-passive and active paradigms can be seen in:

1			*3a*	
Sg.	*Pl.*		*Sg.*	*Pl.*
1	cūr-o-r	cūr-ā-mu-r	dīc-o-r	dīc-i-mu-r
2	-ā-ris	-ā-minī	-e-ris	-i-minī
3	-ā-t-ur	-a-nt-ur	-i-t-ur	-u-nt-ur

Most transitive verbs show the live opposition of passive to active. Sometimes the verb is intransitive and the passive therefore subjectless, an impersonal equivalent to an active form, e.g. *pugnātur* 'there is fighting' = *pugnant* 'they (unspecified) are fighting'.

The old middle voice is discernible in occasional uses of these forms, e.g. *mouētur* 'it moves (itself)', *uertitur* 'he turns (himself) around' and more rarely accompanied by a direct object *indūtus tunicam* 'having put on a tunic', cf. *induit tunicam* 'he puts a tunic on (somebody else)'. Sometimes the active and middle forms are synonymous, e.g. *adsentiō/or* 'I agree', *mereō/or* 'I earn'. In a number of verbs, the so-called deponents, only the medio-passive form occurs, either with a middle meaning, e.g. *moror* 'I delay (myself)', O. *KARANTER* 'they enjoy', cf. Lat. *uescuntur*, or more often with a meaning indistinguishable from the active, e.g. *opīnor* 'I believe' beside *crēdō*, *prōgredior* 'I advance' beside *prōcēdō*.

Of the three moods the imperative has only second and third person forms; Lat. *ī* 'go!', *ītō* 'go!' or 'let him go!' < **ei+tōd*, cf. U. *ETU*: Lat. *agitō*, O. *actud*, U. *AITU* 'let him act/move' < **age+tōd*. Italic subjunctives reflect in form and function both the subjunctive and optative moods of Proto-Indo-European. Thus O. *FUSÍD* = Lat. *foret* 'it was to be' with Proto-Indo-European thematic subjunctive **-ē-*; U. *EMANTUR* 'they are to be taken', cf. Lat. *emantur*, with **-ā-*, a subjunctive formant also found in Celtic, U. *sir* = Lat. *sīs* 'may you be' with *-ī-*, originally the plural allomorph of *-iē-*, the athematic optative formant. The meanings of will (subjunctive) and wish (optative) are illustrated by these examples and by O. *NEP PÚTÍAD* 'nor may he be able', Lat. *nēue possit*, O. *ni hipid* 'let him not hold', with perfect subjunctive as in Lat. *nē habuerit*. Prospective (subjunctive) and hypothetical (optative) meanings are found in Lat. *sī id dīcās, ueniat* 'if you were to say it [in future], she would come' (pres. subj.), *sī id dīcerēs uenīret* 'if you were saying it [now], she would be coming' (imperf. subj.). The introduction into the subjunctive of temporal distinctions modelled on the indicative (*dīcat : dīceret : dīxerit* ← *dīcit : dīcēbat : dīxit*) and the decline of the purely aspectual ones (as in *nē dīxerit* 'he is not to say' vs. *nē dīcat* 'he is not to be saying') are notable innovations in Italic.

Sometimes in Latin subordinate clauses the distinction between indicative and subjunctive is neutralised; cf. *currit nē cōnspiciātur* 'he runs in order not to be seen' (volitive: purpose) with *tam celeriter currit ut nōn cōnspiciātur* 'he runs so fast that he is not seen' (for **cōnspicitur*, declarative); *haec quom dīxisset* (subj.), *ēuāsimus* with *ubi haec dīxit* (indic.), *ēuāsimus* 'when she had said this (declarative), we left'.

In indirect discourse declarative utterances were normally represented by the accusative plus infinitive. It was precisely in order to encode the necessary tense and voice distinctions that Latin developed its heterogeneous collection of infinitives, possibly under the influence of

Greek, the only other Indo-European language to employ elaborate forms of accusative plus infinitive. The tense of the direct-discourse verb was reproduced in the infinitive: *uenīs* 'you are coming', *dīcō/dīxī tē uenīre* 'I say you are/said you were coming'. The construction was very inefficient: the temporal distinctions between *ueniēbās* 'you were coming', *uēnistī* 'you came' and *uēnerās* 'you had come' were lost in *dīcō/dīxī tē uēnisse* 'I say you have/said you had come'; similarly the modal distinction between *ueniās* 'you would come' and *ueniēs* 'you will come' disappears in *tē uentūrum esse*. Eventually the accusative plus infinitive was replaced by *quod* or *quia* + finite verb constructions, perhaps partly under Greek influence, though in contrast to Greek there is a tense shift (see below). The replacement was almost total in Vulgar Latin but only partial in the written language.

In indirect commands, questions, etc. and in all subordinate clauses within indirect discourse finite verbs were used, but with transpositions of mood and tense, the indicative being replaced by subjunctive and the tense being determined not by the tense in direct discourse but by the tense of the governing verb: *imperāuī ut uenīrēs* 'I gave orders for you to come' (← imper. *uenī!*), *rogāuī quor uēnissēs* 'I asked why you had come' (← indic. *quor uēnistī?*). This was almost certainly a native Italic development within the register of laws and edicts: cf. O. *KÚMBENED THESAVRÚM PÚN PATENSÍNS MÚÍNÍKAD TANGINÚD PATENSÍNS* 'it was agreed that the treasury, when they opened it, by a joint decision they should open' with Lat. *conuēnit ut thēsaurum cum aperīrent commūnī sententiā aperīrent*; U. *EHVELKLU FEIA SVE REHTE KURATU SIT* 'a vote he is to hold (as to) whether the matter rightly has been taken care of' with Lat. *sententiam roget num rēctē cūrātum sit*.

The Italic languages had a free word order in the sense that variations from normal patterns did not affect syntactic relationships or make nonsense, but were motivated by pragmatic considerations — topicalisation, emphatic juxtaposition — or by the aesthetics of prose or verse rhythm, etc. However, the unmarked, viz. most frequent, order was SOV. Thus in Latin *informīs hiemēs redūcit Iuppiter*, from a lyric poem by Horace, contrasts with the unmarked classical prose order *Iuppiter hiemēs informīs redūcit* 'Jupiter winters ugly brings back'. The cooccurrence of SOV with noun-adjective patterns generally in Italic characterises the languages as typologically mixed or 'transitional'. Consistent with SOV are: (i) the order genitive-noun attested in O. *SENATEÍS TANGINÚD*, cf. Lat. *senatūs cōnsultō* 'by decision of the senate'; (ii) the anastrophe of prepositions, common in Umbrian but rare in Oscan and Latin, e.g. U. *ASAMAŘ* = Lat. *ad āram* 'to the altar', U. *FRATRUSPER* = *prō frātribus* 'for the brothers' (cf. O. *censtom-en* = *in cēnsum* 'for the census', Lat. *mēcum* 'with me'); (iii) the early Latin placing of relative clauses before their antecedents. However, none of these was an unmarked order in Latin of the classical period, a fact that confirms its mixed character. The order SOV is overwhelmingly the most frequent in the prose of Cicero and Caesar, and in the post-classical written registers was especially tenacious in subordinate clauses, where it provided a 'punctuating' signal, often combined with rhythmic cadences (*clausulae*). Nevertheless there are signs in the dialogue of Plautus' comedies (early second century BC) that SVO was becoming established in Vulgar Latin. The reduction of morphological distinctions between nominative and accusative in Vulgar Latin drastically limited the choice of the marked options OSV and OVS. Furthermore the replacement of certain cases by prepositional phrases favoured the fronting of head nouns: *dīmidium praedae* seems to have been replaced by *dīmidium dē praedā* more easily than the marked *praedae dīmidium* by *dē praedā dīmidium*.

A notable feature of the literary register in Classical and Post-Classical Latin was the elaboration of complex and in particular periodic sentence structure. Heavily influenced by Greek rhetoric doctrine and oratorical practice, it became a feature of both formal prose and verse. In a highly inflected language the grammatical concords facilitate the detachment of participial phrases from the nominals on which they depend and enable clausal exponents of subordinate constituents to be embedded without any loss of semantic coherence. The following is typical:

(1) posterō diē,
(2)   quom per explōrātōres cognōuisset
(3)   quō in locō hostēs
(4)   quī Brundisiō profectī erant
(3)   castra posuissent,
(1) flūmen trānsgressus est,
(5)   ut hostīs,
(6)   extrā moenia uagantēs
(7)   et
(8)   nūllis custōdibus positīs
(7)   incautōs,
(5)   ante sōlis occāsum aggrederētur.

(lit. 'on the next day, | when by reconnaissance patrols he had discovered | in what place the enemy | who from Brindisi had set out | camp had pitched, | the river he crossed | in order that the enemy, | outside the camp wandering | and [being] | with no guards posted | unwary, | before the sun's setting he should attack').

This is not strictly a period since a well-formed sentence can be concluded before the final clause, in fact at *trānsgressus est*; but it illustrates the technique very well. (4) is embedded in (3) and the group (2)–(4) in (1); similarly (8) in (7) and (6)–(8) in (5). All the modes of subordination are exemplified: adverbial and relative clauses in (2) and (4), participial and absolute phrases in (6) and (8). The deployment of information in participial exponents ((6)–(8)) dependent on the object of the volitional verb in (5) has both pragmatic significance and the aesthetic effect of contributing variety and balance to the sentence. Latin complex and periodic structure provided the model for similar developments in the formal discourse of later European vernaculars, though none of these possessed the morphological resources to emulate it fully.

4 Lexicon

With so small and specialised a body of data from Oscan and Umbrian it is hazardous to generalise, and we can do no more than note a few specific items in their basic vocabulary. For instance, U. *pir* (cf. O. *PURASÍAÍ* (adj.)) and *UTUR* have widespread Indo-European cognates outside Italic, e.g. *fire*, *water*, but not in Latin (*ignis*, *aqua*); O. *touto*, U. *totam* (acc.) 'community' have specifically West Indo-European cognates, again excluding Latin. On the other hand, some words are peculiar to Italic; e.g. Lat. *cēna*, O. *KERSNU* 'dinner' (the root is Indo-European, meaning 'cut'); *habēre* 'to have', cf. U. *HABIA* (3 sg. subj.); *ūtī* 'to use', cf. O. *ÚÍTTIUF* 'use' (nom. sg.), of no certain etymology; and *familia*, O. *famelo* 'household', probably from Etruscan. Many words attested in Italic generally have of course Indo-European cognates; e.g. *māter* 'mother', O. *MAATREÍS* (gen.); *pēs* 'foot', U. *PEŘI* (abl.); *duodecim*, U. *desenduf* (acc.) 'twelve (two + ten)'; *ferre* 'to bear', U. *FEREST* (3 sg. fut.); *sedēre* 'to sit', U. *ZEŘEF* (pres. part.). A few of these show a semantic specialisation peculiar to Italic; e.g. *dīcere*, O. *DEÍKUM* 'to say' (< 'to point, show'); *diēs*, O. *zicolom* 'day' (< 'sky'); *agere*, O. *acum* 'to do' (< 'to move along').

In addition to the items just mentioned there are a number of Latin words for which neither cognates nor synonyms happen to be recorded in Italic but which have well established Indo-European etymologies; e.g. *ego* 'I', *canis* 'dog', *nix*, 'snow', *pectus* 'breast', *rēx* 'king', *dūcere* 'to lead', *loquī* 'to speak'. Among the older Indo-European languages Latin's basic vocabulary has closest affinities with Gothic, with which it shares some 38 per cent of items, and Vedic (35 per cent); it has least in common with Old Irish (27 per cent) and Old Armenian (26 per cent). The relatively low percentages and the narrow band within which they cluster indicate a long period of separation between Latin (presumably with Italic) and the rest.

Some frequent Latin words have no etymology even in Italic; e.g. *bonus* 'good', *hīc* 'this', *mulier* 'woman', *omnis* 'all'. Loanwords can be identified at all periods, often by their phonology; e.g. *rosa* 'rose' from an unknown Mediterranean source, *bōs* 'cow' from Sabine, *taberna* 'shop' from Etruscan, *carrus* 'cart' from Celtic, *wadium* 'pledge, wage' from Gothic. By far the largest group is from Greek: not only cultural terms — *balneum* 'bath', *epistula* 'letter', *māchina* 'device', *nummus* 'coin' (all early), *architectus*, *poēta* and Christian terms like *ecclēsia* 'church' and *baptizāre* 'to baptize' — but also more basic items like *āēr* 'air', *bracchium* 'arm', *camera* 'room', *hōra* 'hour' and in Vulgar Latin *colpus* 'blow', *gamba* 'leg', *petra* 'stone', replacing the native words *ictus*, *crūs* and *lapis*. A number of Latin words, especially in the technical registers of philosophy, philology and the arts and crafts, were either created on Greek models, e.g. *quālitās* 'quality' (Gk. *poiótēs*), *indīuiduum* 'the indivisible thing' (Gk. *átomos*), *accentus* 'accent' (Gk. *prosōdía* lit. 'a singing in addition'), or semantically adjusted to them e.g. *cāsus* 'a falling' > 'noun case' (Gk. *ptōsis*) and *conclūsiō* 'an enclosing' > 'syllogism' (Gk. *sullogismós*).

The lexical stock was extended by the usual morphological processes. Complex words were created by suffixation. For instance, the diminutive *-lo-* used both literally, e.g. *puella* '(little) girl' : **puera* (cf. *puer* 'boy'), *ōsculum* 'kiss' (cf. *ōs* 'mouth'), *articulus* '(small) joint' (cf. *artus* 'joint, limb'), and affectively, e.g. *misellus* 'poor little' (cf. *miser* 'wretched'), *ocellus* 'dear little eye' (cf. *oculus*). In Vulgar Latin some words were displaced by their diminutives, e.g. *culter* 'knife' by *cultellus*, *uetus* 'old' by *uetulus*.

Among the most frequent verbal noun formants in Italic were **-ion-* and **-tion-*, which originally signalled action but were often extended by metonymy to the concrete result of action; e.g. O. *TRÍBARAKKIUF* ('act of building' >) 'a building', *legio* ('act of choosing' >) 'a legion', O. *medicatinom* (acc.) 'judgement' from **medicaum* 'to judge', U. *NATINE* (abl. 'act of birth' >) 'tribe', cf. Lat. *nātiō*. In fact *-tiōn-* was productive at all periods of Latin, e.g. *mentiō* 'an act of reminding' > 'mention' (cf. OIr. *air-mitiu* 'respect, honour') beside *mēns* (< *mentis*) 'mind'; *ōrātiō* 'act of pleading' > 'a speech, a prayer' from *ōrāre*; Medieval Lat. *wadiātiō* 'the act of *wadiāre* (to pledge, give security)'. Often associated with *-tiōn-* in Latin is the agent suffix *-tōr-*, e.g. *ōrātor*, *wadiātor*. By contrast *imperātor* (O. *EMBRATUR*) 'commander' is from *imperāre* but the action noun is *imperium*; *auctor* (U. *UHTUR*) 'initiator' from *aug-* 'to enlarge' but *auctoritās*, U. *UHTRETIE* (loc.) 'the status of initiator' with the denominative suffixes in *-tāt-* and *-tiā-* (cf. Lat. *amīc-itia* 'friendship').

Among the productive verb suffixes is *-tā-*, with intensive, in particular frequentative, meanings: *itāre* 'to go often' beside *īre* 'to go', cf. U. *ETAIANS* (3 pl. subj.) < **eitā-*; *habitāre* 'to live' beside *habēre* 'to have'; *tractāre* 'to handle' beside *trahere* 'to drag'. There was a tendency especially in Vulgar Latin for these to replace the simple verbs; e.g. *spectāre* 'to look at', *cantāre* 'to sing', *iactāre* 'to throw' for *specere* (archaic), *canere*, *iacere*. This led to greater morphological uniformity; cf. *cantō*, *cantāuī* and *iactō*, *iactāuī* with *canō*, *cecinī* and *iaciō*, *iēcī*. The intensive meanings themselves came to be hypercharacterised, as *dict-itāre* for *dic-tāre* from *dīcere* 'to say'.

Italic compound words, formed from the stems of two or more distinct

lexemes, mostly conform to the OV type. Thus O. *MEDDÍSS* 'magistrate' <
*medo-dik- 'rule-declaring', cf. Lat. *iū-dex* 'judge' < 'law-setting/giving', O.
KÚM-BENN-IEIS (gen.) 'assembly' < 'a together-coming', cf. Lat. *con-
uen-tūs*, O. *TRÍB-ARAK-AVÚM* (infin.) 'to build' < 'to house-strengthen',
cf. Lat. *aedi-fic-āre*, U. *petur-purs-us* (dat.) 'animals' < 'four-footed', cf.
Lat. *quadru-ped-ibus*. Some prefixes acquired intensive force; cf. *cōnficere*
'to complete' with *cōnferre* 'to bring together', *efficere* 'to effect' with
effluere 'to flow out'. In the literary register compounding was usually a
mark of Greek influence. It was associated particularly with high epic, e.g.
caelicola 'sky-dweller', *suāuiloquēns* 'pleasant-speaking', and parodies
thereof, e.g. *dentifrangibulus* 'teeth-breaking'; also with philosophical and
philological terminology, where, as we have seen, the precise models were
Greek. Latin was never a heavily compounding language like Ancient
Greek, Vedic or modern German, and the chief morphological expansions
of the lexicon were through the formation of compound-complex words,
e.g. **prīmo-cap-* 'first taking' in *prīnceps* 'chief', whence *prīncipium* 'a
beginning' (< *-iom*, as in O. *KÚMBENNIEÍS*), *principālis* 'primary'
(< *-āli-*, as in O. *FERTALIS* 'with sacrificial cakes, *ferta*'), *prīncipātus*
'leadership' (< *-ātu-* (4); cf. *-āto-* (2) reflected in U. *FRATRECATE* <
*fratr-ik-ātei (loc.) 'in the office of the master of the brothers, **frātrik(o)s*').
These processes and many of the actual formants continued in use for as long
as Latin survived.

Bibliography

Brief but reliable accounts of the history of Latin are Stolz et al. (1966) and Collart
(1967). More detailed, especially on the literary registers, is Palmer (1954). The most
comprehensive description of the language is Leumann et al. (1963-72); it is,
however, inadequate for Vulgar Latin, for which see Väänänen (1963), and for the
written registers of post-classical periods, for which see Löfstedt (1959) and Norberg
(1968). On particular topics, Kent (1945) on phonology and Kent (1946) on
morphology are both predominantly historical, while Woodcock (1958) on syntax is
predominantly descriptive; for word order, Adams (1976) is important.

For the other Italic languages, Buck (1928) is still the standard work on Oscan and
Umbrian, while Poultney (1959) is comprehensive on Umbrian. Pisani (1964)
includes all the Italic languages and also Venetic, Messapic and Etruscan.

References

Adams, J.N. 1976. 'A Typological Approach to Latin Word Order', *Indogermanische
Forschungen*, vol. 81, pp. 70-99
Allen, W.S. 1975. *Vox Latina: A Guide to the Pronunciation of Classical Latin*
(Cambridge University Press, Cambridge)
Bonioli, M. 1962. *La pronuncia del latino nelle scuole dall'antichità al rinascimento*,
vol. 1 (Università di Torino Pubblicazioni, Facoltà di Lettere e Filologia, Turin)
Buck, C.D. 1928. *A Grammar of Oscan and Umbrian* (Ginn, Boston)

Collart, J. 1967. *Histoire de la langue latine* (Presses Universitaires de France, Paris)
Cooper, F.C. 1895. *Word Formation in the Roman Sermo Plebeius* (Trow Directory, New York)
Grandgent, C.H. 1907. *An Introduction to Vulgar Latin* (D.C. Heath, Boston)
Kent, R.G. 1945. *The Sounds of Latin* (Linguistic Society of America, Balitmore)
—— 1946. *The Forms of Latin* (Linguistic Society of America, Baltimore)
Leumann, M., J.B. Hoffmann and A. Szantyr. 1963-72. *Lateinische Grammatik*, 2 vols. (C.H. Beck, Munich)
Löfstedt, E. 1959. *Late Latin* (Aschehoug, Oslo)
Norberg, D. 1968. *Manuel pratique de latin médiéval* (Picard, Paris)
Palmer, L.R. 1954. *The Latin Language* (Faber and Faber, London)
Pisani, V. 1964. *Le lingue dell' Italia antica oltre il latino*, 2nd ed. (Rosenberg and Fellier, Torino)
Poultney, J.W. 1959. *The Bronze Tablets of Iguvium* (American Philological Association, Baltimore)
Stolz, F., A. Debrunner and W.P. Schmid (eds.) 1966. *Geschichte der lateinischen Sprache* (Walter de Gruyter, Berlin)
Väänänen, V. 1963. *Introduction au latin vulgaire* (Klincksieck, Paris)
Woodcock, E.C. 1958. *A New Latin Syntax* (Methuen, London)

8 Romance Languages

John N. Green

The Romance languages derive, via Latin, from the Italic branch of Indo-European. Their modern distribution is the product of two major phases of conquest and colonisation. The first, between c. 240 BC and c. AD 100, brought the whole Mediterranean basin under Roman control; the second, beginning in the sixteenth century, annexed the greater part of the Americas and sub-Saharan Africa to Romance-speaking European powers. Today, some 580 million people speak, as their first or only language, one that is genetically related to Latin. Although for historical and cultural reasons preeminence is usually accorded to European Romance, it must not be forgotten that European speakers are now outnumbered by non-Europeans by a factor of more than two to one.

The principal modern varieties of European Romance are indicated on the map. No uniformly acceptable nomenclature has been devised for Romance and the choice of term to designate a particular variety can often be politically charged. The Romance area is not exceptional in according or withholding the status of 'language' (in contradistinction to 'dialect' or 'patois') on sociopolitical rather than linguistic criteria, but additional relevant factors in Romance may be cultural allegiance and length of literary tradition. Five national standard languages are recognised: Portuguese, Spanish, French, Italian and Rumanian (each treated in an individual chapter below). 'Language' status is usually also accorded on cultural/literary grounds to Catalan and Occitan, though most of their speakers are bilingual in Spanish and French respectively, and the 'literary tradition' of Occitan refers primarily to medieval Provençal, whose modern manifestation is properly considered a constituent dialect of Occitan. On linguistic grounds, Sardinian too is often described as a language, despite its internal heterogeneity. Purely linguistic criteria are difficult to apply systematically: Sicilian, which shares many features with southern Italian dialects, is not usually classed as an independent language, though its linguistic distance from standard Italian is no less than that separating Spanish from Portuguese. 'Rhaeto-Romance' is nowadays used as a cover term for a number of varieties spoken in southern Switzerland (principally Engadinish, Romansh and Surselvan) and in the Dolomites, but it is no longer taken to subsume Friulian. Romansh (local form *romontsch*) enjoys an official status for cantonal administration and so perhaps fulfils the requirements of a language. Another special case is Galician, located in Spain but genetically and typologically very close to Portuguese; in the wake of political autonomy, *galego* is now generally referred to in Spain as a language, although elsewhere it continues to be thought of (erroneously) as a regional dialect of Spanish. Corsican, which clearly belongs to the Italo-Romance group, would be in a similar position if the separatist movement gained autonomy or independence from France.

Map 8.1

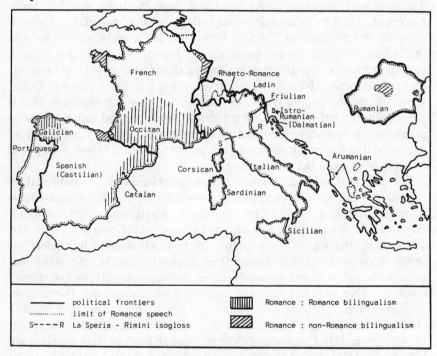

———— political frontiers	▦ Romance : Romance bilingualism
·········· limit of Romance speech	▨ Romance : non-Romance bilingualism
S————R La Spezia - Rimini isogloss	

Outside Europe, Spanish, Portuguese and French, in descending order of native speakers, have achieved widest currency, though many other varieties are represented in localised immigrant communities, such as Sicilian in New York, Rumanian in Melbourne, Sephardic Spanish in Seattle and Buenos Aires. In addition, the colonial era gave rise to a number of creoles, of which those with lexical affinities to French are now the most vigorous, claiming upward of eight million speakers.

In general, European variants are designated by their geographical location; 'Latin', as a term for the vernacular, has survived only for some subvarieties of Rhaeto-Romance (*ladin*) and for Biblical translations into

Judaeo-Spanish (*ladino*). 'Romance' derives, through Spanish and French, from *ROMĀNICĒ* 'in the Roman fashion' but also 'candidly, straightforwardly', a sense well attested in early Spanish. The terminological distinction may reflect early awareness of register differentiation within the language, with 'Latin' reserved at first for formal styles and later for written language and Christian liturgy. The idea, once widely accepted, that Latin and Romance coexisted for centuries as *spoken* languages, is now considered implausible.

Among the chief concerns of Romance linguists have always been: the unity or otherwise of the proto-language, the causes and date of dialect differentiation and the classification of the modern variants. Plainly, Romance does not derive from the polished literary models of Classical Latin. Alternative attestations are quite plentiful, but difficult to interpret. Attempts to echo popular speech in literary works may be suspected of stylistic artifice; inscriptional evidence is formulaic; the abundant Pompeian graffiti may be dialectal, and so on. Little is known of Roman linguistic policy or of the rate of assimilation of new conquests. We may however surmise that a vast territory, populated by widely differing ethnic groups, annexed over a period exceeding three centuries, conquered by legionaries and first colonised by settlers who were probably not native speakers of Latin, and never enjoying easy or mass communications, could scarcely have possessed a single homogeneous language.

The social conditions which must have accompanied latinisation — including slavery and enforced population movements — have led some linguists to postulate a stage of creolisation, from which Latin slowly decreolised towards a spoken norm in the regions most exposed to metropolitan influences. Subsequent differentiation would then be due to the loss of administrative cohesion at the break-up of the Empire and the slow emergence of local centres of prestige whose innovations, whether internal or induced by adstrate languages, were largely resisted by neighbouring territories. Awareness of the extent of differentiation seems to have come very slowly, probably stimulated in the west by Carolingian reforms of the liturgical language, which sought to achieve a uniform pronunciation of Church Latin at the cost of rendering it incomprehensible to uneducated churchgoers. Sporadic attestations of Romance, mainly glosses and interlinear translations in religious and legal documents, begin in the eighth century. The earliest continuous texts which are indisputably Romance are dated: for French, ninth century; for Spanish and Italian, tenth; for Sardinian, eleventh; for Occitan (Provençal), Portuguese and Rhaeto-Romance, twelfth; for Catalan, thirteenth; for Dalmatian (now extinct), fourteenth; and for Rumanian, well into the sixteenth century.

Most classifications of Romance give precedence, explicitly or implicitly, to historical and areal factors. The traditional 'first split' is between East and West, located on a line running across northern Italy between La Spezia and

Rimini. Varieties to the north-west are often portrayed as innovating, versus the conservative south-east. For instance, West Romance voices and weakens intervocalic plosives: *SAPŌNE* 'soap' > Ptg. *sabão*, Sp. *jabón*, Fr. *savon*, but It./Sard. *sapone*, Rum. *săpun*; *RŌTA* 'wheel' > Ptg. *roda*, Sp. *rueda*, Cat. *roda*, Fr. *roue*, but It./Sard. *rota*, Rum. *roată*; *URTĪCA* 'nettle' > Ptg./Sp./Cat. *ortiga*, Fr. *ortie*, but Sard. *urtica*, It. *ortica*, Rum. *urzică*. The West also generalises /-s/ as a plural marker, while the East uses vocalic alternations: Ptg. *as cabras* 'the goats', Cat. *les cabres*, Romansh *las chavras*, contrast with It. *le capre* and Rum. *caprele*. In vocabulary, we could cite the verb 'to weep', where the older Latin word *PLANGĚRE* survives in the East (Sard. *pranghere*, It. *piangere*, Rum. *a plînge*) but is completely replaced in the West by reflexes of *PLORĀRE* (Ptg. *chorar*, Sp. *llorar*, Cat. *plorar*, Oc. *plourà*, Fr. *pleurer*). In this classification, each major group splits into two subgroups: 'East' into Balkan-Romance and Italo-Romance, 'West' into Gallo-Romance and Ibero-Romance. The result is not entirely satisfactory. While, for example, Arumanian dialects and Istro-Rumanian group quite well with Balkan-Romance, our scant evidence of Dalmatian suggests it shared as many features with Italo-Romance as with the Balkan group. Catalan is a notorious difficulty, having been subject for centuries to alternating Occitan and Spanish influences. The unity of 'Rhaeto-Romance' also fails to survive close scrutiny: Ladin groups fairly well with Friulian as part of Italo-Romance, but southern Swiss varieties share many features with eastern French dialects.

'Family-tree' classifications, in which variants are each assigned to a single node, give only a crude indication of relationships in Romance and tend to obscure the convergence brought about by centuries of borrowing from Latin and criss-crossing patterns of contact. This is readily illustrated from the lexicon. The *PLANGĚRE/PLORĀRE* example, though supportive of the East-West split, is in fact rather atypical. More common are innovations spreading from central areas but failing to reach the periphery. 'To boil' is Ptg. *ferver*, Sp. *hervir*, Rum. *a fierbe* (< *FERVĒRE/FERVĚRE*), but Cat. *bullir*, Oc. *boulí*, Fr. *bouillir*, It. *bollire* (< *BULLĪRE*, originally 'to bubble'); 'to request' is Ptg./Sp. *rogar*, Rum. *a ruga* (< *ROGĀRE*), but Cat. *pregar*, Oc. *pregá*, Fr. *prier*, It. *pregare* (< *PRECĀRE*, originally 'to pray'); 'to find' is Ptg. *achar*, Sp. *hallar*, Rum. *a afla*, but Cat. *trobar*, Oc. *trobà*, Fr. *trouver*, It. *trovare* (both forms are metaphorical — classical *INVENĪRE* and *REPERĪRE* do not survive). Among nouns, we may cite 'bird': Ptg. *pássaro*, Sp. *pájaro*, Rum. *pasăre* (< *PASSARE*), versus Oc. *aucèu*, Fr. *oiseau*, Romansh *utschè*, It. *uccello* (< *AUCELLU*); and 'cheese': Ptg. *queijo*, Sp. *queso*, Rum. *caş* (< *CĀSEU*), versus Cat. *formatge*, Oc. *froumage*, Fr. *fromage*, It. *formaggio* (< *[CĀSEU] FORMATICU* 'moulded [cheese]'). Almost the same distribution is found in a morphosyntactic innovation: the Latin synthetic comparative in *-IŌRE* nowhere survives as a productive form, but peripheral areas have *MAGIS* as the analytic replacement ('higher' is Ptg. *mais alto*, Rum. *mai înalt*) whereas the centre prefers *PLŪS* (Fr. *plus haut*, It. *più alto*).

Despite this differential diffusion and the divergences created by localised borrowing from adstrate languages (notably from Arabic into Portuguese and Spanish, from Germanic into northern French, from Slavonic into Rumanian), the modern Romance languages have a high degree of lexical overlap. Cognacy is about 40 per cent for all major variants using the standard lexicostatistical 100-word list. For some language pairs it is much higher: 65 per cent for French-Spanish (slightly higher if suffixal derivation is disregarded), 90 per cent for Spanish-Portuguese. This is not, of course, a guarantee of mutual comprehensibility (untrained observers are unlikely to recognise the historical relationship of Sp./oxa/ 'leaf' to Fr./fœj/), but a high rate of cognacy does increase the chances of correct identification of phonological correspondences. Intercomprehensibility is also good in technical and formal registers, owing to extensive borrowing from Latin, whether of ready-made lexemes (abstract nouns are a favoured category) or of roots recombined in the naming of a new concept, like Fr. *constitutionnel*, *émetteur*, *exportation*, *ventilateur*, etc. Indirectly, coinings like these have fed the existing propensity of all Romance languages for enriching their word stock by suffixal derivation.

Turning to morphosyntax, we find that all modern Romance is VO in its basic word order, though southern varieties generally admit some flexibility of subject position. A much reduced suffixal case system survives in Rumanian, but has been eliminated everywhere else, with internominal relations now expressed exclusively by prepositions. All variants have developed articles, the definite ones deriving overwhelmingly from the demonstrative *ILLE/ILLA* (though Sardinian uses *IPSE/IPSA*), the indefinite from the numeral *ŪNU/ŪNA*. Articles, which precede their head noun everywhere except in Rumanian where they are enclitic, are often obligatory in subject position. Concord continues to operate throughout noun phrases and between subject and verb, though its range of exponents has diminished with the loss of nominal case. French is eccentric in virtually confining plural marking to the determiner, though substantives still show number in the written language. Parallel to the definite articles, most varieties have developed deictic object pronouns from demonstratives. These, like the personal pronouns, often occur in two sets, one free and capable of taking stress, the other cliticised to the verb. There is some evidence of the grammaticalisation of an animate/inanimate distinction, both in the clitic pronouns and in the prepositional marking of specific animate objects. This latter is widespread (using *a* in West Romance and *pe* in Rumanian) but not found in standard French or Italian.

Suffixal inflection remains vigorous in the common verb paradigms everywhere but in French. Compound tense forms everywhere supplement the basic set, though the auxiliaries vary: for perfectives, *HABĒRE* is most common: 'I have sung' is Fr. *j'ai chanté*, It. *ho cantato*, but Ptg. *tenho cantado* (< *TENĒRE* originally 'to hold') and Cat. *vaig cantar* (< *VĀDO CANTĀRE* 'I am going to sing'), a combination which would elsewhere be interpreted as a periphrastic future. Most Romance varieties have a basic imperfective/perfective aspectual opposition, supplemented by one or more of punctual, progressive and stative. The synthetic passive has given way to a historically-reflexive medio-passive which coexists uneasily with a reconstituted analytic passive based on the copula and past participle. The replacement of the future indicative by a periphrasis expressing volition or mild obligation (*HABĒRE* is again the most widespread auxiliary, but *deppo* 'I ought' is found in Sardinian and *voi* 'I wish' in Rumanian) provided the model for a new paradigm, the conditional, which has taken over a number of functions from the subjunctive. The subjunctive has also been affected by changes in complementation patterns, but a few new uses have evolved during the documented period of Romance, and its morphological structure, though drastically reduced in spoken French, remains largely intact.

In phonology, it is more difficult to make generalisations (see the individual language sections below and, for the development from Latin to Proto-Romance, pages 182–3). We can, however, detect some shared tendencies. The rhythmic structure is predominantly syllable-timed. Stress is on the whole rather weak — certainly more so than in Germanic — and is dynamic rather than tonal; some variants, notably Italian, use higher tones as a concomitant of intensity, but none rely on melody alone. The loss of many intertonic and post-tonic syllables suggests that stress may previously have been stronger, witness *IŪDĬCE* ['ju-di-ke] 'judge' > Ptg. *juiz*, Sp. *juez*, Cat. *jutge*, Fr. *juge*; *CUBĬTU* ['ku-bi-tu] 'elbow' > Sp. *codo*, Fr. *coude*, Rum. *cot*. The elimination of phonemic length from the Latin vowel system has been maintained with only minor exceptions. A strong tendency in early Romance towards diphthongisation of stressed mid vowels has given very varied results, depending on whether both higher and lower mid vowels were affected, in both open and closed syllables, and on whether the diphthong was later levelled. Romance now exhibits a wide range of vowel systems, but those of the south-central group are noticeably simpler than those of the periphery: phonemic nasals are found only in French and Portuguese, high central vowels only in Rumanian, and phonemic front rounded vowels only in French, some Rhaeto-Romance and north Italian varieties and São Miguel Portuguese. Among consonantal developments, we have already mentioned lenition, which led to wholesale reduction and syllable loss in northern French dialects. Latin geminates generally survive only in Italo-Romance, and many other medial clusters are simplified (though new ones are created by various vocalic changes). Although Latin is in Indo-European terms a centum language (with *k* for PIE *k̂*), one of the earliest and most far-reaching Romance changes is the palatalisation, and later affrication, of velar and dental consonants before front vowels. Only the most conservative dialect of Sardinian fails to palatalise (witness *kenapura* 'Holy supper = Friday'), and the process itself has elsewhere often proved cyclic.

Developments in phonology illustrate a more general characteristic of Romance: the tendency for a small number of identical *processes* to affect all varieties, though at slightly different rates and with slightly different exponents as the outcome. Whether this is due to directly inherited tendencies, or to analogical development of shared stock, remains a matter of debate — neither standpoint would question the fundamental unity of Romance.

Bibliography

Harris and Vincent (1988) provides detailed typological descriptions of Latin and all principal varieties of modern Romance including creoles. Agard (1984) is a compendious introduction to synchronic description and internal history; it usefully complements Elcock (1975), an excellent external history concentrating on philological aspects. Wright (1982) deals with early history and the reconceptualisation of Romance as independent of Latin. Manoliu-Manea (1985) is an authoritative discussion of comparative syntax, while Hope (1971) is a copiously illustrated study of vocabulary enrichment, with particular reference to French–Italian exchanges. Rohlfs (1971) is an approachable introduction to dialectology, with some 100 maps showing the diffusion of individual words and expressions; Rohlfs (1986) is a sequel, with a further 275 maps.

Anderson and Creore (1972) is a collection of 27 articles dealing with phonology, morphology and syntax, some pan-Romance in scope. A state-of-the-art survey of the discipline, with detailed bibliographic appraisals, is given by Posner and Green (1980–2): vol. 1 concentrates on historical linguistics, vol. 2 on synchronic perspectives, vol. 3 on philology and 'minor' languages, and vol. 4 on national and regional approaches to the subject.

References

Agard, F.B. 1984. *A Course in Romance Linguistics*, 2 vols. (Georgetown University Press, Washington D.C.)

Anderson, J.M. and J.A. Creore (eds.) 1972. *Readings in Romance Linguistics* (Mouton, The Hague)

Elcock, W.D. 1975. *The Romance Languages*, 2nd ed. (Faber and Faber, London)

Harris, M. and N. Vincent (eds.) 1988. *The Romance Languages* (Routledge, London and Oxford University Press, New York)

Hope, T.E. 1971. *Lexical Borrowing in the Romance Languages*, 2 vols. (Basil Blackwell, Oxford)

Manoliu-Manea, M. 1985. *Tipología e historia* (Gredos, Madrid)

Posner, R. and J.N. Green (eds.) 1980–2. *Trends in Romance Linguistics and Philology*, 4 vols. (Mouton, The Hague)

Rohlfs, G. 1971. *Romanische Sprachgeographie* (C.H. Beck, Munich)

—— 1986. *Panorama delle lingue neolatine* (G. Narr, Tübingen)

Wright, R. 1982. *Late Latin and Early Romance* (Francis Cairns, Liverpool)

9 French

Martin Harris

1 Introduction

French, currently by any standards one of the major languages of the world, is a Romance language, descended directly from the Latin which came to be spoken in what was then Gaul during the period of the Roman Empire. As that Empire crumbled, a number of major dialectal divisions developed, which do not necessarily correspond to present-day political or linguistic frontiers. Such a major division was to be found within medieval France (see map 9.1), with the dialects of the north and centre (and part of modern

Map 9.1: The Dialect Divisions of Medieval France

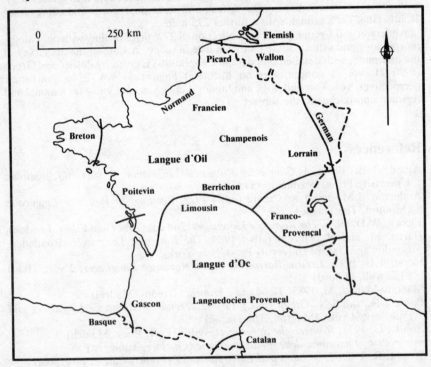

Belgium), known collectively as *langue d'oil*, being sharply distinguished
from those of the south, *langue d'oc* (*oil* and *oc* being characteristic markers
of affirmation in the relevant areas), with a third smaller area in the south-
east, known as Franco-Provençal, generally taken to include the French
dialects of Switzerland and the Val d'Aosta in Italy. The division between
north and south is so marked that it has frequently been argued that, on
purely linguistic grounds, the dialects of the south, now generally known
collectively as *occitan*, are best not regarded as Gallo-Romance at all, but
rather as closely linked with Catalan, the resultant grouping being distinct
from Hispano-Romance also.

Within these major dialectal areas, further linguistic fragmentation took
place, divergence being strongly favoured by the lack of social cohesion
during the so-called Dark Ages. One of the dialects of the *langue d'oil* which
emerged in this way was *francien*, the dialect of the Ile de France, and it is
from this dialect that, once circumstances arose which favoured the growth
of a national language, modern standard French has developed. (Another
northern dialect was Norman, which had such a profound influence on the
development of English.) The establishment of a fixed royal court in Paris,
the recrudescence of an educational and of a legal system in that same city,
and the fact that the abbey at St.-Denis, close by, was in effect the spiritual
centre of the kingdom, all of these factors tended to favour the dialect of
Paris and the surrounding area for the status of national language. Since the
twelfth and thirteenth centuries, when *francien* (a modern name) gradually
came to be accepted as a norm to aim towards, at least in writing and in
cultivated speech in northern and central France, progress has been slow but
steady. It is worth pointing out, however, that although the literary form of
occitan, Provençal, never recovered from the devastation caused by the
Albigensian crusade, and although French came to be virtually ubiquitous as
the written language after the *Ordonnances de Villers Cotterets* (1539), it
was not until the nineteenth and even the twentieth centuries, particularly in
the south, that French came to be so wholly dominant within the boundaries
of France, at first among the bourgeoisie and in the cities, and later also in
the remoter rural areas. Indeed, French's long period of predominance as
the major international language of culture and diplomacy long antedates its
general use as a spoken language within France: by the end of the
seventeenth century, French had in effect replaced Latin in the former role,
to the point that the Berlin Academy was able to ask in 1782, as a matter of
fact, 'Qu'est-ce qui a rendu la langue françoise universelle?' ('What has
made the French language universal?'). This situation persisted until the
First World War and even beyond.

Within Europe, French is now spoken by some 51 million people within
France (and Monaco), and by some 4 million Walloons in Belgium,
principally in the four francophone districts of the south, Hainaut, Namur,
Liège and Luxembourg, and in the bilingual district of Brussels the capital.

The rivalry between French and Dutch within Belgium, which extends far beyond the linguistic plane, is well known. Around half a million people live in the Grand-Duchy of Luxembourg, where the native language of most speakers is a German dialect but where French is the language of education and administration, while in Switzerland, the most recent figures suggest that approaching 20 per cent of a total population of some 6.3 million are French speakers. In northern Italy, the Val d'Aosta has a French-speaking population of around 100,000.

Outside Europe, indigenous French speakers are to be found in almost every continent. In Canada, there are some six million francophone descendants of the original colonists, three quarters of these living in the province of Quebec (where they form some 80 per cent of the total population). Strenuous efforts are made to preserve and strengthen French, particularly in Quebec, within what has been since 1867 officially a bilingual country. Descendants of another group of French colonists in Acadia (the easternmost provinces of Canada), driven out in the mid-eighteenth century, carried their language southwards down the eastern seaboard of the United States and into Louisiana. As a result, although there are relatively few French speakers in Acadia today except in New Brunswick (some 200,000), there are significant numbers — approaching one million — in New England (where there is a major admixture also directly from Quebec) and in Louisiana, French until 1803, where the immigrants were primarily from Acadia, and are indeed called 'Cajuns': their form of speech, *français acadien*, is in regular use by perhaps a further one million people, alongside a small elite speaking more or less standard French and also a French-based creole.

Elsewhere, French is generally in competition not with another European language but with indigenous non-European languages and/or with French-based creoles in former French (or Belgian) colonies. In the West Indies, French is found for instance in Haiti (where it is the official language of some five million people but where the great majority actually use creole) and in islands such as Martinique and Guadeloupe. By far the most important areas, however, are the countries of the Maghreb (Algeria, Morocco and Tunisia), where French appears to be holding its own since independence: in Algeria, for example, it is estimated that some 20 per cent of the population can read and write French, with a much higher proportion able to speak it, above all in the cities. In black Africa, there are sixteen independent francophone states comprising a great swathe across the west and the centre of the continent from Senegal to Zaire, together with Madagascar, and there is a further group of French-creole-speaking islands (e.g. Mauritius, Seychelles, Réunion) in the Indian Ocean. In most of these countries, the future of French as a second language, used for a variety of official, technical or international purposes in place of one or more indigenous languages, seems secure.

Like all languages with any significant degree of diffusion, French is of course not a single homogeneous entity. Just as in France itself there is within most regions a spectrum of variation from 'pure' patois (the original local dialect, now often moribund) through *français régional* (largely the standard grammar, with a more or less regionally-marked phonology and a greater or lesser number of non-standard lexical items) to the standard language (which itself has a wide range of styles and registers), so too one finds a similar spectrum in most if not all of the areas discussed above, often with the added dimension of a French-based creole. In Quebec, for example, one finds 'educated Quebec French' shading imperceptibly through to the fully popular variant known as *joual* (from the local pronunciation of *cheval* 'horse') associated primarily with Montreal. French-based creoles are spoken not only in Louisiana (alongside Cajun, discussed above), Haiti and various islands mentioned earlier, but arguably also in parts of black Africa, in the form of such variants as *petit-nègre* or *petit français*. As in the case of *français régional*, there is very frequently a standard-creole continuum, with more educated speakers tending perhaps increasingly towards the metropolitan norms. It is these which are described in what follows, although some attempt will be made to indicate major divergences between popular and more educated varieties of the language.

Before the internal structure of the language itself is examined, however, one should look briefly at French orthography. When the first vernacular texts came to be written down, it was natural that the scribes should turn to the Latin alphabet, despite the obvious fact that it was less than ideal to represent a language whose phonological system had, as we shall see, already evolved considerably from Latin and which was to continue to develop rapidly. Nevertheless, despite the difficulties, a relatively standardised and quasi-phonemic orthography was widely used during the eleventh, twelfth and thirteenth centuries, 'quasi-phonemic' in the sense that it relied in part on 'distributional rules' (e.g. 'c' represents [k] in certain environments but [ts] (later [s]) in others) and in part on the use of one letter to indicate that an adjacent letter had a special value ('g' before 'n' marks the palatal nasal: thus 'gn' = [ɲ]). The shortcomings of the vowel system, however, especially the need to use one symbol (e.g. 'e') with various values (e.g. [e], [ɛ], [ə]), could only be somewhat alleviated by the use of certain conventional digraphs (e.g. 'ez' for [e]).

During the following three centuries, two major developments occurred to overturn the relative stability just described. Firstly, there was a further period of very rapid and radical phonetic change (one particular consequence of which was the emergence of many monosyllabic homophones), and secondly, not unconnected, there was a marked increase in the use of quasi-etymological spellings, in which one or more letters appropriately present in a Latin etymon were reinserted in the corresponding French derivative, even though the sound they represented had been modified or lost in the interim, thus *doi(g)t* < *DIGITUM* 'finger' although the [g] had long been effaced and similarly *pie(d)* < *PEDEM* 'foot', *se(p)t* < *SEPTEM* 'seven'. (The label 'quasi-etymological' is used because recourse was not infrequently had to incorrect etyma: thus *poi(d)s* 'weight' does *not* come from *PONDUS* but from *PENSUM.) The sixteenth and seventeenth centuries saw various attempts at reform, and in particular the acceptance of distinction between 'i' and 'j' and between 'u' and 'v' and the use of the cedilla; the other three principal accents were not finally accepted by the Academy until 1740. Some of the more extraordinary 'gothic' spellings (e.g. *sçapvoir* for *savoir* 'know') have also been resimplified. The nineteenth and twentieth centuries have seen repeated attempts at reform, both unofficial and official, the best known of the latter being the reports of the two Beslais commissions, in 1952 and 1965. The second of these proposed a small number of sensible and limited reforms, such as the use of 's' as a standard plural marker (thus *bijous* for *bijoux* 'jewels'), the simplification of many unnecessary double consonants, and the rationalisation of the use of accents (e.g. *è* for *é* as the second vowel in *événement* 'event'). However, nothing has in fact happened, and the situation remains more or less as it has been since the 1740 edition of the Academy dictionary.

2 Phonology

One of the most immediately striking facts about French in comparison with its sister languages is the radical nature of the phonological changes which the language has undergone, changes which differentiate not just French from, say, Spanish or Italian but indeed the *langue d'oil*, and *francien* in particular, from the dialects of the south of the country. Four processes in particular have contributed to this global effect: the evolution of the tonic vowel system and the very significant reduction of atonic vowels; a period of nasalisation and subsequent partial denasalisation of vowels preceding nasal consonants; the widespread palatalisation of many consonants in appropriate environments (which in turn affected the vowel system); and, more recently, the effacement of most final consonants and, for most speakers, of final /ə/ also.

Consider first the effects of stress on the overall shape of French words. In the Latin of Gaul, the intensity of the stress accent grew, to the point where most tonic vowels lengthened and broke (i.e. diphthongised) and even more significantly, virtually all post-tonic vowels except /ə/ were eventually lost. The effect of this was to create a fixed-stress language, with the stress either on the final syllable or the penultimate syllable if the vowel of the final syllable was /ə/; subsequent effacement of final /ə/ in (standard) spoken French has further simplified the position, and the tendency for both verbal and nominal groups to function as ever more tightly bound units, discussed later, has meant that such units have increasingly borne only one stress. Essentially, therefore, we may say that modern French is a final-stress, phrase-stress language, with a very strong tendency, in non-learned words, towards monosyllabism. A clear example of the process can be seen by comparing the development of the trisyllabic Latin word *PÓPULUM* 'people' to a monosyllable *peuple* /pœpl/ (via /pœ-plə/) in French, compared with It. *popolo* and Sp. *pueblo*.

Of the seven tonic vowels inherited by Gallo-Romance, no fewer than five diphthongised in free syllables; only /i/ remained essentially unchanged, while /u/ fronted to /y/. The most interesting development is the passage of Latin /a/, via a diphthong, to a front mid vowel very early, a marked characteristic of *langue d'oil* (*MATREM* > *mère* /mɛʁ/ 'mother'). Of the four remaining diphthongs, two ([we] < GR /ɔ/ and [eu] < GR /o/) monophthongised and merged as /ø~œ/ (see below), i.e. as a second front rounded vowel, another distinguishing mark of northern French. A third diphthong, OFr. /oi/, passed to [wɛ] and then split in a most unusual way, passing either to ModFr. /wa/ or to /ɛ/, on no discernible phonetic or lexical basis: compare, for example, the nationality adjectives *français* 'French' and *anglais* 'English', with /ɛ/, and *danois* 'Danish' and *suédois* 'Swedish', with /wa/. The fourth diphthong /jɛ~je/ remains largely unchanged.

Various other developments of tonic vowels in specific environments ensured that both half-open and half-close back and front vowels and a back close vowel were once again present in the system by the Middle French period, and we end up with an oral vowel system in the modern language as shown in table 9.1.

Table 9.1: Oral Vowel Phonemes in Contemporary French

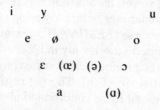

Note: There is in addition a wide range of diphthongs and triphthongs incorporating the semi-consonants /j/ /w/ and /ɥ/. In this connection, one should note in particular the passage of /ʎ/ to [j], a process which began in the seventeenth century and was fully accepted by the nineteenth, and which contributed to such forms as /vjej/ (*vieille* 'old' (f.)) in the modern language from earlier /viɛʎ/.

Two main points need to be noted about this system. Firstly, of the pairs of half-open and half-close vowels, only the opposition between /o/ and /ɔ/ is clear and stable (*saute* /sot/ 'jumps': *sotte* /sɔt/ 'foolish' (f.)); /o/ has generalised in free final position. In the case of /œ~ø/, again the close variant has generalised in free final position, but the position is less clear elsewhere, with analogical forces noticeably at work. In terms of classical minimal pairs, however, there are very few indeed (e.g. *jeune* /ʒœn/ 'young' vs. *jeûne* /ʒøn/ 'fasts'), and the distinction is certainly not made by all native speakers. It is for this reason that /œ/ as a phoneme is bracketed in the table above. In the case of /e/:/ɛ/, neutralisation would almost certainly have occurred (with [e] in free final syllables and [ɛ] elsewhere), but for a concerted attempt, dating back to the seventeenth century, to retain [ɛ] also in free final position, and thus minimal pairs of the type *piqué* 'stung':*piquait* 'was stinging' (/pike/: /pikɛ/). Again, this distinction is not by any means consistently made: however, it seems that both /e/ and /ɛ/ should be retained within the inventory of phonemes for the time being. Finally in this section we should note that the phonological opposition between /ɑ/ and /a/ has already been lost in much of France (to the profit of /a/), and is retained only by older speakers in the Parisian area: hence /ɑ/ is firmly bracketed in the table above.

The last topic we should mention briefly in this sketch of the French vowel system is the existence of a set of four nasal vowel phonemes. During the period from the tenth to the thirteenth centuries, all vowels and diphthongs occurring before any nasal consonant nasalised, the low vowels first, then the mid and finally the close vowels. This development took place regardless of whether the syllable concerned was blocked or free and in many instances the resulting nasalised vowel was lowered; diphthongs tended to monophthongise. To give just one example, *FINEM* gave [fin] then [fĩn] then /fẽn/. During the latter part of the Middle French period, syllable structure became crucial, in that where the nasal consonant was in a different syllable from the preceding vowel, nasalisation was reversed, and the vowel became once again oral, sometimes before lowering (*FINAM* > *fine* 'fine' (f.) /fi-nə/), sometimes afterwards (*FEMINAM* > *femme* 'woman' /fa-mə/, not */fɛ-mə/). This left nasalised vowels only in blocked syllables, where the nasal consonants ceased to be pronounced: contrast *inconfortable* (initial vowel /ɛ̃/) and *inévitable* (initial vowel /i/). The net result of these changes was that nasalised vowels ceased to be conditioned allophones of oral vowels before a nasal consonant, and became phonemes in their own right, the number of minimal pairs being greatly increased by the effacement of final [ə] (see above) after denasalisation. (Thus /fi-nə/ and /fa-mə/ in our examples passed to /fin/ and /fam/.) Compare the development of the masculine and feminine forms of the adjective *SANUM* 'healthy': both nasalise, but only the latter denasalises, thus: (m.) *SANUM* > sãin > sẽn > sẽ; (f.) *SANAM* > sãinə > sẽnə > sɛn.

The outcome was the addition of the following nasal phonemes to the vowel inventory of French: /ɛ̃/, (/œ̃/), /ɔ̃/, /ɑ̃/. Of these four nasal monophthongs, one, /œ̃/, has a very low functional yield, and is in the process of being absorbed by /ɛ̃/, the few distinctions such as that between *brin* 'sprig' /bʀɛ̃/ and *brun* 'brown' /bʀœ̃/ thus being lost. It is therefore bracketed. There is also a full range of nasal diphthongs, e.g. /bjɛ̃/ *bien* 'well' ([bjɛ̃]).

Various attempts to view nasal vowels as conditioned allophones of oral vowels in specifiable contexts do not appear convincing, and their status as phonemes seems secure.

The French consonant system will be dealt with even more summarily. The inventory of phonemes is given in table 9.2.

Table 9.2: French Consonant Phonemes

	Labial	Dental	Palatal	Velar	Uvular
Plosive	p b	t d		k g	
Fricative	f v	s z	ʃ ʒ		ʁ
Nasal	m	n	ɲ		
Lateral		l			

Several points are worth noting. In Old French, there were four affricates, /ts, dz, tʃ, dʒ/, all of which had resulted from palatalisation under many and varied circumstances. One particular source of /tʃ/ was from /k/ before /a/, tonic or atonic, a development highly characteristic of *francien* vis-à-vis almost every other Romance dialect, thus *CARUM* > *cher* 'dear' OFr. [tʃier], *CABALLUM cheval* 'horse' OFr. [tʃəval]. /ts, dz/, originally palatal, early dentalised and later simplified, to merge with /s, z/. /tʃ, dʒ/ simplified to the palatal fricatives shown in the table above. The palatal lateral was progressively lost, as we have seen, from the seventeenth century onwards, whereas the palatal nasal still flourishes. /h/ survived in initial position, mostly though not exclusively in words of Germanic origin, until the Middle French period, but its loss was acknowledged as irreversible by the seventeenth century: one residual effect is the absence of liaison in cases such as /la aʃ/ *la hache* 'axe'. Finally, we should note that /ʁ/ is included in the table, as a uvular fricative is the normal urban pronunciation of the 'r' phoneme, at least in northern French, although a uvular trill is not infrequent and a dental trill is still found, particularly in the south.

One aspect of the French consonant system is worthy of special note. Consonants already final in Latin were widely effaced in earliest French, only the dentals /s, n, l, r/ in general surviving. A whole range of secondary final consonants were created in Old French, however, by the loss of post-tonic syllables, already discussed: *PONT(EM)* > *pont* 'bridge' (OFr. [pɔnt]) is a case in point, as is *CAP(UT)* > *chef* 'chief' (OFr. [tʃief]). In fact, the Old

French final consonant system, which subsumed the four earlier survivors mentioned above, consisted of twelve phonemes, involving all the modes and points of articulation. Of these twelve, the fate of nasals and of /ʎ/ has already been considered, while /l/ and to some extent /ʁ/ have been maintained. The fate of final voiceless plosives and fricatives, however, has been more complex. The general tendency was for two or even three distinct pronunciations to develop, one before a pause, one before a subsequent initial consonant and one before a subsequent initial vowel, a situation which has survived in some cases to the present day: an obvious example is that of *dix* 'ten', pronounced as /dis/ in isolation, /di/ before a consonant (*dix femmes* 'ten women'), and /diz/ before a vowel (*dix élèves* 'ten pupils'). It will be noted that the final consonant has been lost completely before a following initial consonant, and it is in this environment that the effacement of many final consonants appears to have begun. By the middle of the seventeenth century, most final plosives and fricatives — including /s/, the plural marker, a point discussed later — had fallen silent, except in a number of monosyllables (where the danger of homonymic clash is greatest), and except before a word beginning with a vowel within the same sense group.

The modern phenomenon of liaison has its roots in this development. According to the traditional rules, final consonants are pronounced if the following word within the immediate sense unit begins with a vowel, a voiceless fricative (though not a plosive) being voiced. Thus we find *il faut y aller* /ifotiale/ or *les enfants* /lezɑ̃fɑ̃/. It has to be said, however, that the principle of invariability exerts a strong pressure, and that even in careful speech, let alone more casual registers, liaison is often not made: in other words, the last vestiges of the secondary final plosives and fricatives are tending to be lost, thus *pas encore* 'not yet', often /paɑ̃kɔʁ/.

It might be thought that that would be the end of the story of final consonants. Not so, however. With the effacement of final /ə/, already alluded to on several occasions, a range of tertiary final consonants has come into being, a range which includes in fact every one of the consonantal phonemes of the modern language, thus *vache* 'cow' /vaʃ/, *vigne* 'vine' /viɲ/ etc. These consonants show no sign whatever of weakening or loss: that particular stage in the language's history is over. Indeed, as will be noted in the discussion of English loanwords (page 234), blocked monosyllables are currently very much a favoured word type in French.

Finally a last word about /ə/. Its loss in word-final position is in fact part of a much more general tendency for it to be effaced in speech whenever its loss would not lead to unacceptable initial or medial consonant clusters. Given that words within a sense group function, as we have seen, very much like a single word, these rules apply across the phrase rather than to words in isolation. Thus *elle est petite* 'she is small' may well be pronounced /ɛ-lɛp-tit/, whereas *une petite femme* 'a small woman' is more likely to be /yn-pə-tit fam/ to avoid the sequence /npt/. Compare also *petite amie* 'small friend' /p(ə)-ti-ta-mi/ (initial /pt/ being acceptable only in fairly rapid speech) with *ma petite amie* 'my small friend' /map-ti-ta-mi/ where the problem does not arise. Interestingly, in speech, /ə/ may actually be introduced, for instance to avoid a three consonant cluster, thus *Arc de Triomphe* /aʁ-kə-də-tʁi-ɔ̃f/, *des contacts pénibles* '(some) uncomfortable contacts' /dekɔ̃taktəpenibl/. The question of the phonemic status of [ə] is left open here. It may well be acceptable to view schwa in contemporary French as a positional variant of /ø/, its realisation in those rare instances when it is stressed (e.g. *fais-le* do it /fɛlø/); at times, however, it is simply introduced in speech in the way just described.

3   Morphology

The verbal morphology of contemporary French is not particularly complex. Superficially at least, the four conjugation types of Latin have been retained, as *-er* (*donner* 'give'), *-oir* (*voir* 'see'), *-re* (*rompre* 'break') and *-ir* (*venir* 'come') verbs respectively. In practice, however, the *-oir* and *-re* classes are closed in contemporary French, membership of the former group in particular being heavily restricted. Almost all new verbs in French enter the *-er* class, though the *-ir* class will admit new members if there is a strong analogical reason to do so (e.g. *alunir* 'to land on the moon': cf. *atterrir* 'to land', i.e. on earth). The *-ir* class in fact comprises three subtypes, those (the vast majority) which have incorporated an infix *-iss* (originally inceptive in value, but now an empty morph) into verbal paradigms based on the present stem ((*nous*) *fin-iss-ons* 'we finish' < *fin-ir*), a much smaller group which do not ((*nous*) *ven-ons* 'we come' < *ven-ir*), and an even smaller group (essentially *ouvrir* 'open', *couvrir* 'cover' and derivatives) which form their present tense like *-er* verbs.

French inherited a set of suffixed person markers which varied according to conjugation type and paradigm. The history of the language shows a marked tendency for the generalisation of a lesser number of variants, the clearest cases being in the plural where (with the sole exception of the past simple, discussed below) the appropriate suffixes are now orthographed 1 pl.: *-ons*; 2 pl.: *-ez*; 3 pl.: *-nt*. In the singular, there are in effect three patterns in the written language, namely (i) 1 sg.: *-e*; 2 sg.: *-es*; 3 sg.: *-e*, (ii) 1 sg.: *-s*; 2 sg.: *-s*; 3 sg.: *-t* and (iii) 1 sg.: *-ai*; 2 sg.: *-as*; 3 sg.: *-a*, i.e. the present tense of *avoir* 'have' which, in the singular at least, has resisted analogical levelling. The first of these sets is associated primarily with the present indicative of *-er* verbs, and with the present (and imperfect) subjunctive of all verbs; the second set is associated with the present indicative of non-*er* verbs, and with the imperfect and conditional paradigms of all verbs (and compounds thereof), the third set with the present perfect and future paradigms of all verbs, for reasons to be discussed hereafter. A heavily simplified tabulation of French verbs as they appear in the written language is thus as shown in the chart of indicative verbal paradigms and participles.

Indicative Verbal Paradigms and Participles

(a) Conjugation type and present indicative

donner	*rompre*	*voir*	*finir*	*venir*	*ouvrir*
donn-e	romp-s	voi-s	fini-s	vien-s	ouvr-e
donn-es	romp-s	voi-s	fini-s	vien-s	ouvr-es
donn-e	romp-t	voi-t	fini-t	vien-t	ouvr-e
donn-ons	romp-ons	voy-ons	fin-iss-ons	ven-ons	ouvr-ons
donn-ez	romp-ez	voy-ez	fin-iss-ez	ven-ez	ouvr-ez
donn-ent	romp-ent	voi-ent	fin-iss-ent	vienn-ent	ouvr-ent

(b) Imperfect of all verbs
   donn-ais (cf. fin-iss-ais)
   donn-ais
   donn-ait
   donn-ions
   donn-iez
   donn-aient

(c) Present subjunctive of all verbs
   romp-e
   romp-es
   romp-e
   romp-ions
   romp-iez
   romp-ent

(d) Future of all verbs
   fini-r-ai
   fini-r-as
   fini-r-a
   fini-r-ons
   fini-r-ez
   fini-r-ont

(e) Conditional of all verbs
   fini-r-ais
   fini-r-ais
   fini-r-ait
   fini-r-ions
   fini-r-iez
   fini-r-aient

(f) Past participle
   donn-é, romp-u, v-u, fin-i, ven-u, ouv-ert

Several things need to be noted about this tabulation. Firstly, the stress pattern inherited from Latin varied through the paradigm of the present indicative, thus *DÓN-AT* 'he gives' (a 'strong' form stressed on the root) but *DON-ÁMUS* 'we give' (a 'weak' form stressed on the desinence). Given what we have already seen about the divergent development of tonic and atonic vowels in French, it is not surprising that paradigms with two stems frequently emerged, thus OFr. *aim-e < ÁMAT* 'he loves' but *am-ons < AMÁMUS* 'we love'. In general, the 'weak' form prevailed, thus for example the stem *treuv-e* 'finds' (strong) ceded to *trouv-ons* (weak) during the sixteenth century: persistence of the strong stem *aim-* is accordingly exceptional. In a small number of cases, both stems have survived: *venir* in the chart (*vient* : *venons*) is an instance of this.

The chart of verbal paradigms omits the past simple. This paradigm, and the related imperfect subjunctive paradigm, unlike those considered so far, is not morphologically based on the 'present' stem inherited from Latin, but on the so-called 'historic' stem, which in the case of irregular verbs may be significantly different. It has also resisted the analogical levelling of its personal suffixes. Both these paradigms have been ousted from normal spoken French (see below). Specimen paradigms are given in the chart of past simple paradigms.

Past Simple Paradigms

(a) Regular
   donn-ai, donn-as, donn-a, donn-âmes, donn-âtes, donn-èrent (*donner*)
   fin-is, fin-is, fin-it, fin-îmes, fin-îtes, fin-irent (*finir*)
(b) Irregular
   vins, vins, vînt, vînmes, vîntes, vinrent (*venir*)

The future tense of modern French derives from the infinitive followed by (a reduced form of) the present tense of *avoir* 'have' which has now been fully assimilated, thus *fini-r-ai* '(I) shall finish' in the chart of verbal paradigms. The conditional is formed in the same way with an even more reduced form of the imperfect of *avoir*. There is a full range of compound tenses formed with the various paradigms of *avoir* (or *être* in the case of certain intransitive verbs) and the past participle, thus *ai donné* 'have given' (cf. *suis venu* 'have come', lit. 'am come'). The uses of certain of these paradigms are discussed later, as is that of the so-called *temps surcomposés*, the 'double compound' tenses. The combination of forms of *être* with the past participle of transitive verbs as a marker of the passive should also be noted.

Two verbs only in contemporary French may be said to have a truly idiosyncratic morphology: *être* 'be' (combining forms of both Vulgar Latin *ESSERE* and *STARE* 'stand') and *aller* 'go' (combining forms of *VADERE* 'go', 'walk' (e.g. *va* '(he) goes'), *IRE* 'go' (e.g. *ira* '(he) will go') and *ALLARE*, generally thought to be a reduced form of *AMBULARE* 'to walk').

Finally, we should note that in respect of most paradigms in actual usage four of the six personal endings whose orthographic representations we have discussed are in fact silent (and hence of course homophonous) in modern French, only -*ons* ([ɔ̃]) and -*ez* ([e]) being pronounced. How the identity of the subject is in fact marked in the contemporary language is discussed below.

As far as noun morphology is concerned, French has dramatically simplified the five-declension, five-case, three-gender system it inherited.

The case system in fact survived longer in French than anywhere else except Rumanian, to the extent that, for many nouns at least (mainly those of masculine gender), a nominative:oblique distinction was maintained in Old French, being progressively lost only during the thirteenth and fourteenth centuries to the profit in all but a few cases of the oblique form, which thus underlies almost all French nouns. Thus, to take a typical case, Lat. *ÍNFANS* (nom.) gave OFr. *enfes* while *INFÁNTEM* (acc.) gave *enfant*. (Recall the earlier discussion of strong and weak verb forms.) It is *enfant* which has prevailed as the modern French form. In a handful of instances only, the nominative form prevailed, either alone (*prêtre* < *PRESBYTER* 'priest') or as well (*sire* < *SENIOR* (nom.), *seigneur* < *SENIOREM* (acc.), lit. 'elder'). One interesting such doublet is *on* 'one' < *HOMO* (nom.) and *homme* 'man' from *HOMINEM* (acc.). In synchronic terms, however, such nouns are no longer in any way distinctive.

The only survivor of Latin inflectional noun morphology lies in the almost universal use of *-s* (of which *x* is an orthographic variant) as the marker of plurality; this derives directly from the *-s* of the Latin accusative plurals *-AS*, *-OS* and *-ES*, and thus generalised as oblique forms ousted nominatives. This final *-s*, however, is now purely orthographic in all but liaison contexts: plurality, like gender, which survives in the form of a binary masculine: feminine opposition, is actually dependent for overt marking in almost all instances on the form of the associated determiner (see section 4) thus *le père* 'father' : *la mère* 'mother' : *les pères* 'fathers' : *les mères* 'mothers' (/lə pɛʁ/:/la mɛʁ/:/le pɛʁ/:/le mɛʁ/). Oppositions such as *le cheval* : *les chevaux* (/lə ʃəval/ : /le ʃəvo/), due to earlier phonetic changes (in this case the vocalisation of /l/ preconsonantally ([ls] > [us]) but not finally, i.e. in the plural but not the singular), are very much the exception in the modern language.

Adjective morphology is extremely simple. Adjectives vary according to the number and gender of the noun with which they are collocated. In respect of number, the point just made applies: the distinction is orthographic rather than phonetic in most cases. Many feminine adjectives, however, are quite distinct from their masculine counterparts, in that the presence of [ə] at the time final consonants were effaced prevented their loss in feminine adjectives. Numerous pairs of adjectives are therefore distinguished orthographically by the presence or absence of a final *-e*, but phonetically by the presence or absence of a final consonant, thus m. *grand*: f. *grande* 'big' (/gʁɑ̃/ : /gʁɑ̃d/). Current thinking is that these consonants should not be viewed as underlyingly present but deleted from the masculine forms, but that the feminine forms, seen (traditionally) as derived, should be considered to undergo rules of consonant insertion. In other cases, that same [ə] prevented devoicing at an earlier stage in the language's history (m. *vif* : f. *vive* 'lively') or provoked denasalisation (see above), thus m. *plein* /plɛ̃/ : f. *pleine* /plɛn/ 'full'. In many instances, however, there is no phonetic distinction between masculine and feminine adjectives in contemporary French (e.g. m.-f. *rapide*). Adjectives derived from the Latin third declension frequently did not distinguish between masculine and feminine forms in Old French for etymological reasons: gradually, however, these came to be assimilated to the normal pattern, with the result that forms such as *Rochefort* and *grand-mère* 'grandmother' (for *Rocheforte and *grande-mère) are isolated relics.

Among the various sets of pronouns, we shall note just two. Personal pronouns in French fall into two sets, conjunctive (i.e. those which can occur only immediately preceding a verb form) and disjunctive (i.e. those which can occur independently of a verb). (Special rules apply in relation to pronouns cooccurring with imperatives.) Conjunctive pronouns retain a nominative:oblique distinction in the first and second persons singular (*je* 'I', *me* 'me'/'to me') and a unique threefold distinction in the third person (e.g. masculine *il* 'he', *le* 'him', *lui* 'to him'): there is also a third person reflexive form *se* serving for both genders and both numbers. In the first and second persons plural, the nominative:oblique distinction is neutralised, as is indeed the conjunctive:disjunctive opposition, *nous* and *vous* serving with all values: elsewhere, the disjunctive pronoun is formally distinct, *moi* for instance in the case of the first person singular (cf. *je/me* above). We may therefore contrast singular *tu te lèves, toi?* (with three distinct forms) with plural *vous vous levez, vous?* ('are you getting up, you?').

The position in the third person is rather complex. A system in which the basic distinctions were gender and case is rivalled, at least in part, by one in which sex rather than gender is a crucially relevant parameter. Thus the conjunctive subject pronouns *il* and *elle* (and even more so the corresponding disjunctive pronouns *lui* and *elle*), ostensibly to be used for both males and masculines, females and feminines respectively, are increasingly restricted to animates, in particular to humans, to the profit of the originally 'neuter' *ce*. Thus *il est beau, lui* 'he's good-looking, him' is naturally interpreted as referring to a man, the corresponding description of a non-human masculine referent frequently being *c'est beau ça*. So far, however, *ce* has not entirely ousted *il* from another of its functions, that of 'unmarked' subject pronoun, a category necessary in French because of the absolute requirement for an overt subject even when none is semantically motivated, as for example with weather verbs, e.g. *il pleut* ('it is raining'). A further complication is that the 'non-human' conjunctive set includes a so-called 'genitive' form *en* ('of it'/'from it' etc.), which has no human counterpart, so that *je m'en souviens* (lit. 'I remind myself of it', i.e. 'I remember it') cannot, according to the rules of prescriptive grammar, have a human referent, i.e. cannot be interpreted as 'I remember him/her'. In informal registers, however, this is a possible interpretation, which in turn disrupts the long-standing parallel distribution of *en* and the 'non-human' dative *y*. To cut a long story short, *y* is now encroaching on to the 'animate' territory of *lui* and *leur*, in parallel as it were with the advance of *en*, which is simply filling a *case vide*. One final point of interest is that *ça*, which we saw earlier as the appropriate non-human disjunctive form, can also be used with a human referent, usually with a pejorative sense: *ça me dégoûte, les conservateurs* lit. 'that disgusts me, the conservatives', i.e. 'they disgust me . . .' Using only the singular forms, we may attempt to tabulate the position as in the chart of pronouns, the forms in round brackets being not as yet fully accepted, and those in square brackets being those ostensibly required for non-human referents of known gender.

French Singular Pronouns of the Third Person

| | Human | | | | Non-human | |
	Male		Female			
Nom.	il	(ça)	elle	(ça)	[il]	[elle]
					ce/ça;	il
Acc.	le		la		le/la	
Dat.	lui	(y)	lui	(y)	y	
Gen.		(en)		(en)	en	
Disj.	lui		elle		ça	

Two other points deserve brief mention. We have already seen that the Latin nominative *HOMO* 'man' gave a form *on* alongside *homme* < *HOMINEM*. This form *on* has been wholly assimilated into the personal pronoun system as a conjunctive subject form, at first with an impersonal value (*on dit* 'people say'; cf. German *man sagt*), but later as an alternative to various other subject pronouns and in particular to *nous*, which it has largely ousted in this function from the popular spoken language (*on part en voyage* 'we're off on a trip'). Note that *on* has neither an oblique nor a disjunctive form; within the immediate verb phrase, the third person reflexive form *se* is used (*on se lève de bonne heure* 'we get up early'); elsewhere, the semantically appropriate form reappears, thus *nous, on va sortir avec nos amis* (lit. 'us, one is going to go out with our friends' — note also the first person plural possessive form *nos*, to the exclusion of the third person singular form *ses*).

The relationship between *tu* and *vous* is not a straightforward singular:plural one. Since the seventeenth century, it has been normal to use *vous* in the case of singular addressees to mark 'respect', *tu* being limited to intimate contexts (e.g. within a family) or to mark a superior-inferior relationship (e.g. master to servant). *Vous* used as a 'respectful' singular shows singular concord outside the immediate verb phrase: *vous êtes content, monsieur?* (not *contents*) 'are you satisfied, sir?' As elsewhere, the 'intimate' forms are tending to gain ground in all but the most formal situations.

The demonstrative pronouns of French represent a twofold opposition of proximity, as do the corresponding determiners. In the contemporary language, this opposition is marked by the suffixes *-ci* and *-là* 'here' and 'there'), thus *celui-ci* : *celui-là* ('this' : 'that', masculine singular pronouns), *cette femme-ci* : *cette femme-là* ('this woman' : 'that woman'). There is also a genderless pair of demonstrative pronouns *ceci* and *cela*, a reduced form of the latter yielding *ça* which we have already discussed as a 'personal pronoun' and which has lost its distal value. The suffixes *-ci* and *-là* may be omitted when proximity marking is not essential, principally when the identity of the referent is immediately made clear, thus *celui que j'ai trouvé* lit. 'that that I have found' i.e. 'the one that I've found'; the omission of *-ci* and *-là* is relevant also to the discussion of determiners in French, below. It should be noted also that usage of the proximal and distal demonstratives heavily favours the latter, particularly in speech: *celui-là* may somewhat surprisingly be used both for 'this one' and 'that one' even in a context where they are juxtaposed, *celui-là-bas* 'that one over there' being used to disambiguate if absolutely necessary.

4 Syntax

The verbal system of French presents a number of interesting features. Within the indicative mood, the basic pattern is of four temporal possibilities on each of two time axes (a pattern familiar to speakers of English), with only one fully grammaticalised aspectual opposition, that between punctual and durative at the simultaneous point on the past axis. This may be represented as in figure 9.1. The reason that *a fait* appears in the table twice and that *fit* appears only in brackets is that the inherited aspectual distinction

Figure 9.1: French Verbal System

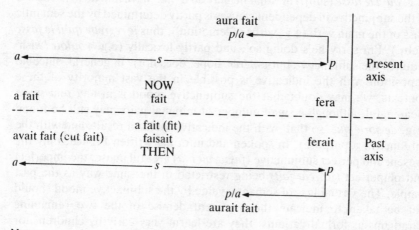

Note: *a.* anterior; *s.* simultaneous; *p.* posterior

between *faisait* 'was doing/used to do' and *fit* 'did' is now maintained in all spoken and most written registers by the use of *a fait* for *fit*, the former paradigm having taken over the functions of the latter (while retaining its own of marking a past event with present relevance) during the seventeenth and eighteenth centuries; *fit* is now restricted in effect to formal written registers. (The loss of *fit* necessarily entailed the loss of *eut fait* in the same circumstances.) The *a fait* paradigm thus corresponds both to English 'has done' and to 'did', while the original punctual:durative aspectual distinction is now maintained by *a fait:faisait*.

Synthetic forms, the 'future' (*fera*) and 'conditional' (*ferait*) paradigms, mark posterior time on each axis. However, these synthetic forms with future time reference are rivalled by analytic forms incorporating as an auxiliary the verb of motion *aller*, thus *va faire* 'is going to do' and *allait faire* 'was going to do' respectively. The present perfect *a fait* having lost its unambiguously 'present relevance' meaning, an alternative structure *vient de faire* (lit. 'comes from doing' i.e. 'has just done') is available for use, but this has not been incorporated into the system to anything like the same extent as *va faire*. Finally within the indicative mood, we should note the use of the *temps surcomposés*, ('double compound tenses') of the type *il a eu fait* (lit. 'he has had done'). These forms are used by some (but by no means all) native speakers as an optional marker of perfectivity (*quand il a eu payé...* lit. 'when he has had paid', the sense being 'as soon as he had finished paying'), thus restoring to the language the possibility of marking an aspectual distinction which had been central to the verbal system of Latin.

The subjunctive mood in contemporary French survives largely only as a conditioned variant in specifiable subordinate contexts, having been eliminated from main clauses in all but a handful of idioms (e.g. *advienne* (subj.) *que pourra* 'come what may') and the so-called 'jussive' structure (e.g. *qu'il le fasse* (subj.) lit. 'that he may do it' i.e. 'have him do it'). The use of the subjunctive in dependent clauses is partly determined by the semantic class of the main verb (e.g. verbs of 'emotion'), thus *je regrette qu'il le fasse* (subj.) 'I'm sorry he's doing so', and partly lexically (e.g. *vouloir* 'wish' requires the subjunctive but *espérer* 'hope' does not). In general, since no opposition with the indicative is possible in the vast majority of these contexts, we may doubt that the subjunctive mood is in any real sense meaningful, although a small number of minimal pairs may still be found (e.g. *de sorte que* 'so that' with the indicative marks a result, and with the subjunctive a purpose). In spoken and informal written French, only the present and perfect subjunctive (*fasse, ait fait*) are still in use, the imperfect and pluperfect (*fît, eût fait*) being restricted in the same way as the past simple. The virtual loss of semantic value by the subjunctive mood should not be taken to indicate the imminent demise of the two remaining paradigms as formal variants: they are learnt very early by children, for example, collocated with *(il) faut que* 'it is necessary that', and the present subjunctive forms of the commonest irregular verbs are very distinctive (*soit*, *ait*, *fasse*, *vienne*, *aille*, *puisse*, *sache*: 'be', 'have', 'do', 'come', 'go', 'be able', 'know').

The modal nuances previously carried by the subjunctive mood have very largely passed to the *fera* and in particular the *ferait* paradigms, noted earlier as the markers of posterior time on the two temporal axes within the indicative mood. The *ferait* paradigm can be used in main clauses (*le roi serait mort* lit. 'the king would be dead' i.e. 'the king is reputedly dead'), in apodoses (*il le ferait si . . .* 'he would do it if . . .') and in many subordinate clauses where the subjunctive is required by the rules of prescriptive grammar (*je cherche une maison qui aurait un jardin* 'I'm looking for a house that would have a garden', the precise identity or location of such a house being at present unknown). The most obvious use of the future paradigm with a modal value is in cases such as *ce sera Pierre* 'that'll (possibly) be Peter'.

One of the most interesting developments in the verbal system of at least popular spoken registers of French has been the change in status of the conjunctive subject pronouns discussed earlier. It will be recalled that four of the person-marking suffixes are homophonous in contemporary speech. Given the progressive replacement of *nous* by *on* (i.e. of *nous donnons* by *on donne* /dɔn/), only *-ez* /e/ is now distinctive, and the effective suffixal marking of the subjects of finite verbs in the case of most paradigms still in current use is a dead letter. This has not however resulted in the loss of person and number marking; rather, the appropriate conjunctive pronouns, which had become obligatory where there was no other subject by the end of the Middle French period, have become steadily more tightly bound to the verb of which they are subject, to the extent that they are found not only when a disjunctive pronoun of equivalent value is also present (*moi je pense...* lit. 'me I think...') but, in popular speech, increasingly even when there is an overt nominal subject (*mon père il dit que...* lit. 'my father he says that...'). The virtual elimination of the preverbal negative element *ne* and the widespread avoidance of inversion in interrogatives (see below) have facilitated the tendency for the sequence 'conjunctive subject pronoun + finite verb' to become indivisible, and for these pronouns to be reanalysed as bound prefixes with their semantic value unchanged. Put at its simplest, we may regard French *ils aiment* /izɛm/ 'they love' as one polymorphemic word (subject-prefix + stem) in exactly the same way as one regards Latin *AMANT* or OFr. *aiment* as one polymorphemic word (stem + subject-suffix). Parallel developments in the case of non-subject pronouns, and the interaction of all of these changes with sentential word order are discussed later.

One final word on the verb. There exists a passive structure of a familiar kind, which permits both subject deletion (*il a été écrasé* 'he has been crushed') and subject demotion (*il a été écrasé par la voiture* 'he has been crushed by the car'). When the underlying agent is human but cannot be or is not to be specified, the pronoun *on*, already discussed, is very frequently pressed into service, the voice of the verb remaining active (*on a ouvert la porte* 'someone has opened the door'/'the door has been opened'). Another strategy when the object is not human, used less than in Italian or Spanish but nevertheless not uncommon, is the pseudo-reflexive structure, that is, the use of the active forms of a verb reflexive in appearance in a 'passive' sense (*les fleurs se vendent ici le dimanche* lit. 'flowers sell themselves . . .' i.e. 'flowers are sold here on Sundays'). The original object may, as here, be promoted to subject, with appropriate verbal concord, or not, in which case an impersonal pseudo-reflexive structure is found, thus *il se pense toujours beaucoup plus de choses qu'il ne s'en dit* lit. 'it thinks itself always many more things than it says itself of them' i.e. 'many more things are thought than are said'. (Note the unmarked third person singular verb because no subject has been promoted and the empty subject pronoun *il* necessary to prevent the 'subject' slot from being left empty.)

The morphosyntax of the nominal group can be dealt with more briefly. We have seen that there are no consistent markers of gender on nouns in contemporary French (although gender is marked in the case of many adjectives) and that the sign of plurality, the suffix -*s*, is purely orthographic in the vast majority of instances. Gender and number — or, to be more accurate, gender *or* number — are nevertheless clearly phonologically indicated in the case of most noun phrases. The reason is simply that in most contexts nouns are accompanied by a determiner, and that these determiners are almost all grouped in sets of three which distinguish a masculine from a feminine in the singular and also a plural, thus *le, la, les* (the definite article), *un, une, des* (the indefinite article), *du, de la, des* (the partitive article), *ce, cette, ces* (demonstrative), *mon, ma, mes* (possessive) etc. It is true that nouns can occur without a determiner (for example in fixed phrases, e.g. *avoir faim* 'to have hunger' i.e. 'to be hungry', often after the preposition *en*, or in partitive constructions e.g. *assez de lait* 'enough (of) milk') or with a determiner that does not mark gender (*chaque* 'each', numerals) or even number (*beaucoup de fromage(s)* 'much cheese'/'many cheeses', given that final orthographic 's' is silent, reveals neither the gender nor the number of *fromage(s)*); nevertheless, the general pattern is that determiners do function in this way.

In the vast majority of cases, of course, a determiner is semantically motivated, and nothing more needs to be said. There is, however, one important consequence of the strong tendency for nouns to need an accompanying determiner. In Old French, a zero determiner was readily tolerated when the meaning of the noun in question was not to be specified in any precise way. In the contemporary language, however, this is no longer so, and the distribution of the indefinite article, and in particular the partitive article (the greatly increased use of which is a characteristic of

French) and the definite article has expanded to cover the ground where previously no determiner was required. One clear-cut consequence of this is that, out of context, *j'aime le fromage* can mean either 'I like the cheese' (the original meaning of the definite article) or 'I like cheese', a generic sense being one of those gained during the evolution of the language. As so often, however, a solution is to hand, in that whereas *ce fromage-ci* and *ce fromage-là* are utilised as demonstratives as we have seen, *ce fromage* without a suffix is often best translated as 'the (particular) cheese' rather than 'this' or 'that cheese'. Put in other words, in one, but only one, of the two senses mentioned above, that of the original definite article, *le fromage* can be and often is replaced by *ce fromage*. It may well be that, ultimately, *ce/cette/ces* will emerge as the definite article in French, leaving *le/la/les* as the unmarked or fall-back determiner used to indicate the gender and number of the relevant nominal and little else.

It is interesting to observe the striking parallelism between verb phrases and noun phrases in contemporary French, a parallelism, what is more, which reflects a complete reversal of the initial situation in Latin. In verb phrases, almost all relevant grammatical information is carried by auxiliary verbs and by clitic pronouns (bound affixes) which precede the verbal stem (and not by suffixes); in noun phrases, almost all relevant grammatical information is carried by determiners and by prepositions which precede the nominal stem (and not by suffixes). Personal pronouns and determiners are both virtually obligatory, with the result that 'unmarked' forms chosen from an identical source are needed when no pronoun or determiner is semantically motivated. The evolution and present-day structures of noun phrases and verb phrases are quite astonishingly similar.

Finally in this section, a brief glance at two other topics: sentential word order, and interrogative and negative structures. As far as the order of basic constituents is concerned, standard literary French is often said to be a canonical SVO language, that is, the subject (which is obligatory) precedes the verb which precedes the complement(s) in positive, declarative utterances. This situation has come about only since Middle French, after a period in which the language was strongly 'verb second', that is, the finite verb followed immediately after one (and only one) preceding element, whether or not this was the subject (cf. main clauses in modern German, pages 132–3). A few survivors of this verb-second structure can be found in formal styles, for instance *peut-être vient-il demain* lit. 'perhaps comes he tomorrow' i.e. 'perhaps he's coming tomorrow', but essentially SVO came to be overwhelmingly preferred, even to the extent of strongly inhibiting the use of a variant order in interrogative sentences (see below). Note that exceptionally when the complement is a conjunctive personal pronoun, it precedes the finite verb.

Alongside this SVO order, however, there is a wide variety of other possible orders, involving the dislocation of one or more of the nominal elements associated with a verb to the left and/or to the right of the core sentence. Thus alongside SVO *je déteste Marie* ('I loathe Mary'), we find, in appropriate pragmatic circumstances, *moi, je déteste Marie*; *je déteste Marie, moi*; *Marie, je la déteste*; *je la déteste, Marie*; and even double dislocations to the right, to the left or both (e.g. *je la déteste, moi, Marie*); treble dislocations of the type *je le lui ai donné, moi, le livre, à Pierre* (lit. 'I gave it to him, me, the book, to Peter') are not unknown. (The commas are conventional: the question of intonation is discussed beow.) From these examples, it will be noted that not only is the subject clitic *je* retained even if *moi* is present elsewhere in the sentence but that there is in addition a clitic coreferential with the direct object when this constituent is displaced (e.g. *je la déteste, Marie*, lit. 'I loathe her, Mary') and even with the indirect object, thus *lui = à Pierre* in the example of treble dislocation given above. In other words, the 'true' subject and/or complements can be placed, in either order relative to each other, before or after the core sentence, which remains grammatically complete because of the clitic pronouns, while the sentence as a whole normally remains unambiguous because these coreferential clitics, now effectively prefixes bound to the finite verb, make the function of each nominal clear. In this way, *je l'aime, moi, Marie* (subject before object) and *je l'aime, Marie, moi* (object before subject) both mean 'I love Mary', the 'verb' being *je l'aime*. Of course, so long as these structures remain dislocated — that is, so long as the commas correspond to a genuine intonation break — then the original word order of the core sentence is unaffected. As soon, however, as the nominal groups are felt to be reabsorbed into the core sentence, and the intonation break is lost, then we must speak of an alternative sentential word order. This is a most complex area, but in essence it seems that left-dislocated nominals generally remain outside the core sentence serving as a familiar kind of topic slot (*Marie, je la déteste*, in other words, is not (yet) an object-initial sentence), but right-dislocated nominals frequently are assimilated, so that *on y va nous à Paris* (lit. 'one there goes, us, to Paris' i.e. 'we're off to Paris') can be analysed as verb (*on-y-va*) + subject + complement. (Note the absence of commas on this occasion.) Be that as it may, we can certainly agree that popular spoken French has a highly flexible word order of the kind often called 'free', and that the device which all such languages necessarily have to avoid ambiguity is in the case of French not a set of nominal case affixes as in Latin but a complex system of preverbal affixes derived from earlier conjunctive personal pronouns.

As far as interrogative sentences are concerned, Old French made use of the fact that there were heavy restrictions on the initial placement of verbs in declarative sentences, in unmarked contexts at least, to grammaticalise subject-verb inversion as a principal mode of question forming. This structure still survives when the subject is a conjunctive pronoun (*vient-il?* 'comes he?' i.e. 'is he coming?') and in written French, in a construction known as *fausse inversion*, also when the subject is a noun, thus *le président vient-il?* lit. 'the president comes he?'. In practice, alongside the rise of SVO as the normal order in declarative sentences, interrogative inversion was progressively ousted from spoken French, questions being marked either by the use of intonation alone, or by the use of an element *est-ce que*, originally a phrase meaning 'is it (a fact) that?' but now better analysed as /ɛsk(ə)/, a question-forming particle (*est-ce que le président vient?*). When there is an interrogative word present, fronting involves inversion in the literary language (*où vas-tu?* lit. 'where go you?'): in speech, however, this can be avoided in at least four ways (*où est-ce que tu vas? où que tu vas? où tu vas? tu vas où?*). Perhaps the most interesting development in this area is that of the particle /ti/, (written *ti, ty, t'y* etc.) found in structures such as *tu viens-ti?* Still very much regarded as substandard, this particle arose through a popular reanalysis of forms such as *vient-il?* /vjɛ̃ti/ as stem (/vjɛ̃/) and interrogative marker (/ti/): thus also with *aime-t-il?* (/ɛmti/). The particle gradually detached itself from the third person, and became usable in principle with any form of the verb, thus *j'puis-t'y entrer* 'can I come in?'.

The history of negation in French shows a constant see-saw between one- and two-word patterns. The literary language currently utilises an embracing structure, requiring *ne* between subject clitic and the following constituent, and another element — pronoun, adverb or simply 'reinforcer' — after the finite verb, thus *il ne vient pas* lit. 'he not comes step', i.e. 'he isn't coming', or *il ne l'a jamais fait* 'he not it has (n)ever done', i.e. 'he has never done it'. These post-verbal elements were (with one or two exceptions) originally positive in value, thus *ne... rien* 'not... a thing', *ne ... personne* 'not... a person', *ne... pas* 'not... a step'. *Pas* has generalised in contexts where no more specific negative element was needed, though *point* is also still found in certain circumstances.

The constant collocation of words such as *rien* with *ne* has led to them becoming themselves negative in value, so that *rien, personne, jamais* and the like now carry the values 'nothing', 'nobody', 'never' (*Qui est là? Personne.* 'Who's there? Nobody'). Furthermore, the preverbal particle *ne* is now frequently omitted in spoken French, including educated speech, formal *je ne sais pas* 'I don't know' being read /ʃsepa/, i.e. *j'sais pas*. We can therefore safely argue that alongside the embracing construction, there exists an alternative structure in which the post-verbal elements, whether *pas* or a more specific item, alone carry the negative value. From this position, *pas* has become the everyday negator in virtually all other environments: thus an original *non moi* 'not me' has passed, via *non pas moi*, to *pas moi* in all but the most formal registers. Interestingly, double negation has in effect returned in the most popular registers, *je ne sais rien* passing, via *je sais rien* (see above) to *je sais pas rien*, though this is certainly regarded as non-standard. The loss of *ne* from the position between conjunctive pronoun subject and finite verb removes the only element (apart from other conjunctive pronouns) which hindered the total fusing of subject pronoun + verb as a single 'word' consisting of prefix and stem, a process discussed above in relation to the 'free' word order of contemporary spoken French.

5 Lexicon

The core vocabulary of French derives in very large measure from the Latin spoken in Gaul, the lexical items in question having in general undergone all the phonetic changes discussed briefly earlier which so often distinguish a French word so sharply from its cognates elsewhere in Romance. This Latin stock incorporated, before the linguistic fragmentation of the Romance-speaking area, a number of words from other sources, the subsequent development of which has been indistinguishable from that of their indigenous counterparts. We might mention Greek (e.g. *COLAPHUM* > *coup* 'blow', *CHORDAM* > *corde* 'rope', *PETRAM* > *pierre* 'stone'), particularly important as the source towards the end of the Empire of much specifically Christian vocabulary, some of which later greatly expanded its meaning (*ECCLESIAM* > *église* 'church', *PRESBYTER* > *prêtre* 'priest' (discussed earlier) but *PARABOLAM* 'parable', now > *parole* 'word'). Equally, among the earliest people whose territory was overrun by the Romans were the Celts, and some Celtic words — recognisable by their widespread distribution — were borrowed and assimilated into Latin very early: these included, for instance, *CAMISIAM* > *chemise* 'shirt', *CABALLUM* > *cheval* 'horse' and, more surprisingly, a very common verb *CAMBIARE* > *changer* 'to change'. The Celtic word *CARRUM* 'cart' underlies not only standard French *char* and (with a diminutive suffix) *charrette* 'cart', but also Norman French *carre*, whence English *car*, a word which has prospered not only in English but once again in French in the sense of '(motor) coach'. More specifically French, however, are the words, generally agreed to be approaching 200, which passed into the language from the local form of Celtic, Gaulish, many of them representing the names of plants, birds or other rural objects: one thinks, for instance, of *chêne* 'oak tree', *if* 'yew-tree', *alou-ette* 'lark', *soc* 'ploughshare' and *raie* 'furrow'. The word *grève*, in the sense of 'sandy river bank', is Celtic in origin: on one such bank of the Seine, unemployed workmen gathered, *en grève* thus coming to mean 'out of work' and later 'on strike'. A Celtic vigesimal counting system survives in *quatre-vingts* 'four score' i.e. 'eighty' (*huitante* and similar forms are found in many dialects: cf. *huit* 'eight').

The Roman occupation of Gaul was ended by the Germanic invasions. Although the conquerors eventually came to be French-speaking, they made a very significant impression on the language. Not only is the development of a strong stress accent, with such radical consequences on the phonological evolution of Latin words in Gaul, frequently attributed to Germanic influence, but so too are syntactic features such as the prolonged preference for a verb-second word order or the use of *on* as an alternative to the passive. While none of these claims is wholly beyond dispute, what is certain is that many words in contemporary French can be traced back either to Frankish or to less specific Germanic sources: of the 1,000 most frequently used words in contemporary French, some 35 are from this source, whether found also in other Romance languages (e.g. *guerre* 'war', *franc* 'free', *riche* 'rich', *blanc* 'white', *jardin* 'garden') or more specifically French (e.g. *bleu* 'blue', *joue* 'cheek'). The fact that so many of these words have a direct cognate in English, itself of course a Germanic language, is readily apparent.

Much the biggest influence on the French lexicon, however, is from a perhaps unexpected source, namely Latin itself (with a not insignificant admixture from Greek). This is because, from the time of the very earliest texts and even more so during and after the Renaissance, the core vocabulary inherited directly via the spoken tradition proved inadequate for the new demands made of it. This process of enrichment has yielded a very large number of 'learned' words in modern French, many of them now 'learned' only in the technical sense that they have not undergone the phonetic changes that would have affected truly 'popular' words, thus *nature*, *facile* 'easy', *imaginer*. Often indeed one finds a doublet in modern French, that is, a 'popular' and a 'learned' derivative of the same word: consider, for example, *loyal/légal* (< *LEGALEM*); *peser* 'weigh', *penser* 'weigh up mentally', i.e. 'think' (< *PENSARE*); *frêle/fragile* 'breakable'. This last pair, both derived from *FRAGILEM*, shows particularly clearly how much closer phonetically the 'learned' word will often be to its etymon.

By far the most significant present-day source of loanwords is English, reflecting at times a genuine cultural or technical innovation, but at times simply a change of fashion. During the eighteenth century, many political and legal terms (*budget*, *vote*, *jury*, *parlement*) were borrowed, reflecting admiration in France for the form of government in Britain at that time. (Note that many of these had themselves earlier been borrowed into English from (Norman) French, including all of those listed above.) During the nineteenth century, various kinds of sport were emulated, giving words such as *sport*, *golf*, *jockey*, *turf* ('racecourse', 'horseracing'), *boxe* 'boxing' etc., whereas words reflecting England's lead in the Industrial Revolution were also borrowed, particularly in the domain of the railway and textile industries. (Again, many words such as *ticket* and *tunnel* themselves had earlier passed from French to English). The twentieth century has seen many borrowings which meet a need in this way, but also many which merely reflect either the belief on the part of advertisers and others that an English name or slogan will enhance sales (*le drink pour les men* is somehow superior to *la boisson pour les hommes*) or simply the willingness of those such as pressmen constantly engaged with material in both English and French to use an English word that is readily to hand. (*Pipeline* is a much-quoted example, with the indigenous *oléoduc* now strongly favoured in its place.) Many of the borrowings take the form of blocked monosyllables, a particularly favoured phonological type in modern French as we have seen (*cross* 'cross-country race', *test*, *pull* 'pullover', *spot* 'spot-light', *star* etc.), or of polysyllables ending in *-ing* (*parking* 'car park', *dumping*) or *-man* (*rugbyman*).

Just as there has always been an exceptionally high degree of interest among educationalists and the French public more generally in the niceties of grammar, so too the present wave of Anglicisms has not passed unnoticed. Efforts have been made to staunch the inflow of such borrowings, both where they are clearly unnecessary and, more importantly, in a wide range of specialist areas where, given a little thought, a perfectly acceptable French word could become widely used and accepted. The *Office du vocabulaire français*, founded in 1957, surveys all aspects of the contemporary vocabulary, especially, but not exclusively, loanwords, and makes recommendations which, at least in written French, may at times carry the force of law.

French, then, is a language still evolving rapidly in all its aspects, particularly in respect of its grammatical system (where the gap between the classical model which is prescribed and what even educated speakers actually do is quite extraordinarily wide at times) and its lexicon. The previous very radical waves of phonetic change appear to have given way, for the time being at least, to relative stability. As a world language, French is holding its own surprisingly well in the face of constant competition from English, although only time will tell how long this can be sustained.

Bibliography

Price (1971) is an excellent survey, very readable, of the contemporary language, seen from a historical perspective. Grevisse (1980) is an outstanding descriptive/ prescriptive grammar of the modern language, with brief historical notes. A somewhat idiosyncratic but very well documented survey of certain points of interest in the modern language is given by Harmer (1954), while Frei (1929) is a fascinating analysis of how the popular language actually operates, with a wealth of illustrative material. For phonology, Fouché (1959) is a standard work on the pronunciation of contemporary French, while Tranel (1981) discusses current issues in phonological theory, clearly illustrated with French data. Von Wartburg and Zumthor (1958) is a clear and detailed survey of the syntax of the contemporary language, and Kayne (1975) is the outstanding analysis of French syntax within current grammatical theory.

Among works dealing with the history of the language, Ewert (1943) is a comprehensive but atheoretical survey, now somewhat outdated. Von Wartburg (1971) is a good general history of the language; Brunot and Bruneau (1969) is a concise and very well presented survey of the evolution of French grammar; while Pope (1952) is an exceptionally detailed historical phonology and morphology. Harris (1978) presents an analysis of French morphology and syntax within a comparative framework, diachronically with Latin and synchronically with Spanish and Italian.

Guiraud (1963) is a clear and concise survey of dialects and dialect study in France. Deniau (1983) is an excellent brief survey of the distribution and role of French in the world today, by the Président du Comité de la Francophonie; the previous standard survey, more comprehensive in its coverage, is Viatte (1969).

References

Brunot, F. and Ch. Bruneau. 1969. *Précis de grammaire historique de la langue française* (Masson, Paris)

Deniau, X. 1983. *La Francophonie* (Presses Universitaires de France, Paris)

Ewert, A. 1943. *The French Language*, 2nd ed. (Faber and Faber, London)

Fouché, P. 1959. *Traité de prononciation française*, 2nd ed. (Klincksieck, Paris)

Frei, H. 1929. *La Grammaire des fautes* (reprinted by Slatkine Reprints, Geneva, 1971)

Grevisse, M. 1980. *Le Bon usage*, 11th ed. (Duculot, Paris and Gembloux)

Guiraud, P. 1963. *Patois et dialectes français*, 3rd ed. (Presses Universitaires de France, Paris)

Harmer, L. C. 1954. *The French Language Today: Its Characteristics and Tendencies* (Hutchinson, London)

Harris, M. 1978. *The Evolution of French Syntax: A Comparative Approach* (Longman, London)

Kayne, R. 1975. *French Syntax: The Transformational Cycle* (MIT Press, Cambridge, Mass.)

Pope, M. K. 1952. *From Latin to Modern French, With Especial Consideration of Anglo-Norman*, 2nd ed. (Manchester University Press, Manchester)

Price, G. 1971. *The French Language: Present and Past* (Edward Arnold, London)

Tranel, B. 1981. *Concreteness in Generative Phonology: Evidence from French* (University of California Press, Berkeley and Los Angeles)

Viatte, A. 1969. *La Francophonie* (Larousse, Paris)

Von Wartburg, W. 1971. *Évolution et structure de la langue française*, 10th ed. (Francke, Bern)

—— and P. Zumthor. 1958. *Précis de syntaxe du français contemporain*, 2nd ed. (Francke, Bern)

10 Spanish

John N. Green

1 Introduction

Spanish is by far the most widely spoken Romance language. At a conservative estimate, there are now some 280 million native speakers, scattered through all continents, but most densely concentrated in Central and South America, where Spanish-speaking countries form a great swathe from the United States-Mexico border right to Tierra del Fuego. Spanish is the national language of 19 countries, in descending order of population: Mexico, Spain (including the Balearic and Canary Islands and the enclaves of Ceuta and Melilla on the North African coast), Argentina, Colombia, Venezuela, Peru, Chile, Cuba, Ecuador, Guatemala, Dominican Republic, Bolivia, El Salvador, Honduras, Paraguay, Uruguay, Nicaragua, Costa Rica, Panama. There are large Spanish-speaking minorities in the United States (including Puerto Rico, which is predominantly Spanish-speaking), officially estimated at 10–11 million but probably much higher. Spanish is also the official language of Equatorial Guinea, and is spoken by significant minorities in the Philippines and Australia, Morocco and Western Sahara, the Balkan countries and Israel.

Like all spatially diffused languages, Spanish is subject to regional and sociolinguistic variation (some specific features are discussed in sections 3 and 4 below). Despite some well-publicised heterogeneous characteristics, the range of variation is not very great and only rarely disrupts mutual comprehensibility. Difficulties do however arise with the Spanish-based creoles of the Philippines and Colombia, and with Judaeo-Spanish, the linguistic consequence of the expulsion of Sephardic communities from Spain in 1492. *Sefardí* is reputed to have preserved numerous features of fifteenth-century usage, but the claim is exaggerated: some phonetic traits, like the preservation of initial /f-/, are indeed archaic, but *sefardí* has evolved extensively in its morphology and has assimilated large numbers of lexical borrowings.

Natural tendencies towards linguistic divergence are combatted in the case of Spanish by powerful cultural bonds and also by well-developed normative mechanisms, whose antecedents go back several centuries. (One of the earliest and best known literary examples of linguistic prejudice is the criticism meted out by Juan de Valdés in his *Diálogo de la lengua*, of c. 1535, against Antonio de Nebrija's excellent *Gramática de la lengua castellana*, of 1492, on the grounds that Nebrija, as an Andalusian, could not be expected to know Castilian well enough for the task in hand!) In a puristic context, 'Spanish' almost invariably means 'Castilian' and for many speakers on both sides of the Atlantic the language can be indifferently designated *español* or *castellano*. Since 1714, when it received a royal charter, the *Real Academia de la Lengua* has had normative authority over the language. Unlike its French counterpart, the Spanish Academy is composed of linguists and philologists, with the result that its decisions, though invariably conservative, command some respect.

In matters of orthography, the Academy has steered a reasonably successful course by dint of approving fairly minor adjustments at regular intervals. Spanish orthography, though popularly reputed to be 'phonetic' (by which is meant 'phonemic'), is in fact quite highly conventionalised. The letter/sound correspondence is skewed. Once the conventions have been mastered, it is relatively easy to pronounce the written language; but transcribing from speech is altogether trickier, as attested by the difficulty Spanish schoolchildren experience with dictation exercises. The main cause is the preservation of etymological spellings. *C* and *g* have two pronunciations depending on the following vowel — *cerca* 'near' = /θerka/ or /serka/, *gigante* 'giant' = /xigante/; *h* is never sounded — *huérfano* 'orphan' = /werfano/; *b* and *v* correspond to only one phoneme and are not in the same distribution as its two allophones — *beber* 'to drink' = /beber/ [be'βɛr], *vivir* 'to live' = /bibir/ [bi'βir]. Words containing *b* and *v* are often misspelled, even on public notices; two recently observed in Segovia province read *se prohive aparcar* (= *prohibe*) 'no parking' and *coto pribado de caza* (= *privado*) 'private hunting'. Etymological spellings can, of course, be justified on grounds of continuity and cultural relationship, but they are not compatible with phonemic principles. If both French and Spanish were to be spelled phonemically, their visual relatedness would disappear overnight.

2   Historical Background

'Spanish' is conventionally dated to the second half of the tenth century, the date of a religious text from the monastery of San Millán in the Rioja region, whose scribe openly acknowledged the discrepancy between written Latin and spoken vernacular by including parenthetical translations of the words and phrases he knew would be unintelligible to contemporary readers. Latin had been introduced into the Iberian peninsula by Roman soldiers and colonists over a period of more than two centuries beginning during the Second Punic War (218–201 BC), when Rome was obliged to subdue the Carthaginians in Spain in order to protect its northern front, and ending in

15 BC, when a long and arduous campaign finally brought the north-west (modern Galicia and Asturias) under Roman rule. Latin took firm enough root in the regions first colonised — the Levant and the Guadalquivir valley — to produce noted centres of learning and some authors celebrated for their style, including Martial and Seneca. By the time of the first Germanic incursions in the third century AD, Latin had long supplanted the indigenous languages of Iberia, with the sole exception of Basque in the north-east. Prolonged contact with Germanic and later Arabic certainly affected its evolution, but at no time does there appear to have been a serious risk that the mass of the population would cease to be Romance-speaking.

In the tenth century there could have been little reason to suppose that Castilian, an obscure dialect of the central Cantabrian seaboard, would become a national, let alone a world, language. The history of its rise is essentially that of the Christian Reconquest, pursued with fluctuating determination and shifting alliances among the medieval kingdoms until the definitive expulsion of the Moorish rulers of Granada in 1492. Though this date is symbolic in Spanish history, the major part of the Reconquest had been achieved much earlier, the first phase culminating in the recapture of Toledo in 1085 by Alfonso VI. This was the king who banished Ruy Diaz, the Cid, and who (according to the epic) had reason to be grateful for the Cid's glorious campaigns against a new wave of Almoravid invaders who at one stage seemed likely to reverse the Christians' recent gains.

The southerly expansion of Castilian has been likened to a wedge driven between the dialects of León to the west and Aragón to the east. Castilian differed from its lateral neighbours in a number of phonological characteristics which, while not signalling any differentiation of fundamental structure, made it sound quite distinct. One of these was the loss from many words of an initial /f-/, via an intermediate stage of strong aspiration which is still preserved in the orthography; another was the tendency of the clusters /pl-/, /fl-/ and /kl-/ to palatalise; both are illustrated in the passage of *FAFLĀRE* 'to sniff out' to *hallar* /aʎar/ 'to find'. Castilian also affricated the medial cluster -*CT*-, as in *LACTE* 'milk' > *leche* /letʃe/, Aragonese *leyt*; but failed to diphthongise lower mid vowels before a palatal sound, as in *TENEO* 'I hold' > *tengo*, Aragonese *tiengo*. There has been intense linguistic debate on whether these and other features should be ascribed to the influence of Basque (the *f- > h-* change, for instance, also happens in parts of south-west France which used to be Basque-speaking). We cannot be certain. All the changes involve linguistic processes which are well attested elsewhere. The most we can safely conclude is that Basque influence would reinforce some developments which could have started independently.

Castilian, which had a flourishing tradition of oral literature culminating in the epic *Poema de Mio Cid* (variously dated between c.1140 and the early thirteenth century), consolidated its national position and its international respectability in the reign of Alfonso X 'El Sabio' 'The Wise', 1252–84. The king, himself a poet and intellectual, assembled a court of international scholars and undertook the translation into Spanish of literary, historical and scientific works written in Latin, Greek, Arabic and Hebrew. Since that time, the preeminence of Castilian has never been challenged, though there have always been local norms of pronunciation (see section 3), and relations with Catalan-speaking areas along the eastern coast have not always been easy. Both Galician and Catalan, probably in reaction to years of linguistic repression during the Franco era, have received a fillip from the regional autonomy policy espoused in the late 1970s, but the position of Spanish as the national language is enshrined in the constitution and seems unlikely to be undermined in the long term.

The purely linguistic consequences of this turbulent history are fewer than one might expect. Some phonological changes, as we have seen, may be attributable to Basque; one, the velarisation of medieval /ʃ/ to /x/ in a few nouns and southern place names (*SŪCU* 'juice' > *jugo*), can probably be traced indirectly to Arabic via a medieval pronunciation of /s/ as [ʃ] in the southern dialect of Mozarabic. Some syntactic calques from Arabic survive as fossilised expressions and, more importantly, the persistence of VSO word order (which is also common in other southern Romance languages, especially Portuguese) may have been reinforced by Arabic VSO order. No inflectional morphology has been shown to derive from any source but Latin.

This leaves the lexicon (including place and personal names) as the chief repository of historical accretions. A few pre-Roman words are still in use, including *páramo* 'moor'. *vega* 'river plain', *pizarra* 'slate', *manteca* 'lard' and perhaps the adjective *gordo* 'fat'; the most frequent is probably *izquierdo* 'left', which has a cognate in Basque, but may be a borrowing there too. Most of the words of Celtic origin, like *cerveza* 'beer', *camisa* 'shirt', *cambiar* 'to change', are widely distributed in western Romance, and it is therefore difficult to decide whether they are survivors of the Celtic substratum in north and central Iberia or were introduced via Latin. A significant number of Germanic words remain in regular use, nearly all shared with French, some of them having probably been diffused via Latin before the main period of invasions. They include military terminology — *guerra* 'war', *guardia* 'guard', *tregua* 'truce', *espuela* 'spur', *estribo* 'stirrup', *yelmo* 'helmet' — but also some everyday words, like *ropa* 'clothing', *falda* 'skirt', *jabón* 'soap', *ganso* 'goose', *ganar* 'to win', together with a set of common adjectives — *rico* 'rich', *blanco* 'white', *gris* 'grey' — and a few abstract concepts: *orgullo* 'pride', *galardón* 'reward' and Old Spanish *fonta/ honta* 'shame'. Also Germanic are numerous place and personal names; the common suffix *-ez* of Spanish family names (*López*, *Martínez*, *González*, etc.) though Latin in origin, probably owes its diffusion to the Visigoths.

Approaching 4,000 words can be traced to Arabic, almost all nouns and a high proportion beginning with *a-* or *al-*, representing the agglutination of the Arabic definite article. An important group relates to horticulture and water management: *acequia* 'irrigation channel', *noria* 'water wheel', *aljibe* 'cistern', *aceite* 'olive oil', *alcachofa* 'artichoke', *algodón* 'cotton', *arroz* 'rice', *azafrán* 'saffron', *azúcar* 'sugar', *naranja* 'orange', *zanahoria* 'carrot'. Others concern civil administration — *aduana* 'customs', *alcaide* 'governor/ gaoler', *alcalde* 'mayor', *alguacil* 'constable' — and still others have entered international scientific vocabulary: *alcohol*, *algebra*, *cifra* 'figure/cipher', *cenit* 'zenith', *nadir* etc. For the tourist, some of the most 'typical' features of southern Spain are designated by Arabic words: *azahar* 'orange blossom', *azotea* 'flat roof', *azucena* 'lily' and *azulejo* 'ceramic tile' (so called because the basic colour was a deep blue — *azul*). In categories other than nouns, Arabic has given the adjective *mezquino* 'mean', the verb *halagar* 'to flatter' (both well adapted to Romance grammatical patterns), the preposition *hasta* 'up to' and the exclamative *ojalá* 'would that...' (literally, 'May Allah grant...').

Since the Renaissance, Spanish has borrowed extensively from other Romance languages and from Latin; from Amerindian languages spoken in its overseas colonies; and most recently from English (often American rather than British). The borrowings from Latin confront the descriptive linguist with an interesting dilemma. Many of them are related to words which have had a continuous history in the language and have undergone more extensive phonological modification than the late-comers, which were generally admitted in a hispanicised pronunciation of the original spelling. The question is whether these 'doublets' should be related by productive rules to the indigenous items. Consider the twelve examples given here, where a common noun or verb is paired with an adjective of the same root meaning but more elevated register.

hierro 'iron':	férrico	heder 'to stink':	fétido
hijo 'son':	filial	hembra 'female':	femenino
hado 'fate':	fatal	hongo 'mushroom':	fungoso
hambre 'hunger':	famélico	hormiga 'ant':	fórmico
harina 'flour':	farináceo	huir 'to flee':	fugaz
hastío 'distaste':	fastidioso	hurto 'theft':	furtivo

These give an idea of the scale of the phenomenon, being only a subgroup of those involving the phonological change *f-* > *h-* > ∅. We shall not attempt an answer, but merely observe that any across-the-board solution, whether concrete or abstract, will run foul of mixed derivational sets: *humo* 'smoke' has regular derivatives *humoso* 'smoky' and *ahumar* 'to preserve food by smoking', but is also clearly related to *fumar* 'to smoke' (of fires or of people).

We end this section on a note of optimism. Although purist hackles have been raised by the recent influx of anglicisms (as in France), the productive patterns of the language remain resolutely Romance. Spanish has at all periods created new vocabulary by suffixal derivation. The following selection, all of Latin origin, remain highly productive: the diminutives *-ito*, *-illo*, *-iño*; the augmentative *-ón*; the agentive *-dor*; the adjectivals *-oso*, *-ero*; the nominals *-aje*, *-ción*, *-miento*. Nor are derivational processes respecters of alien origin: the Germanic borrowings quoted above, *guerra* and *orgullo*, form adjectives *guerrero* and *orgulloso*, and the Arabic *halagar* forms *halagueño* — a powerful means of integrating the borrowing. Purists can take heart from new coinings like *urbanización* 'housing development', currently to be seen on builders' placards all over Spain, and composed of impeccably classical roots. Many other fairly recent inventions which might have attracted foreign labels have in fact been named by compounding indigenous roots: *parachoques* 'bumper bar', *limpiaparabrisas* 'windscreen wiper', *tallalápices* 'pencil sharpener'. Through developments of this kind, Spanish is becoming more, not less, Romance in its structure.

3   Phonology

Like other world languages, Spanish shows a good deal of internal variation. This extends to all linguistic levels but is most noticeable in the phonology. For international trade and diplomacy and for pedagogical purposes, two norms are recognised: either the educated usage of Castile (traditionally identified with Burgos, but now displaced by Madrid) or that of Bogotá, Colombia (itself increasingly eclipsed, both linguistically and culturally, by Mexico City). In the Middle Spanish period a further model was provided by Seville, which remained a flourishing cultural centre throughout the first period of colonisation of Central and South America. The fact that most of the early settlers were of Andalusian origin, and the existence of the Sevillean 'norma culta', are now generally believed to explain the present-day differences between Latin American and Castilian usage, at both popular and educated levels.

The segmental inventory of Castilian is given in table 10.1. The phonemic consonant system can be presented as neatly symmetrical, with four articulatory positions and five degrees of aperture, but this disguises some interesting irregularities in distribution. While, for instance, the absence of any point-of-articulation opposition between plosives and affricates argues for their merger, they differ in that /dʒ/ is by no means securely established in the system and neither palatal enters into syllable-initial clusters, which plosives do freely. The reintroduction of [dʒ], which was present (probably as an allophone of /ʒ/) in Old Spanish, is comparatively recent and its phonemic status remains doubtful. It represents a strengthened form of certain [j] sounds, some of them apparently determined lexically (especially the personal pronoun *yo* = [dʒo]) and others arising from an earlier weakening of palatal /ʎ/ known as 'yeísmo'. Both innovations are

Table 10.1: Segmental Sounds of Castilian

Consonants

	Bilabial	Dental	Palatal	Velar
Plosives				
[−voice]	p	t		k
[+voice]	b	d		g
Affricates			tʃ	
			(dʒ)	
Fricatives				
[−voice]		f θ s		x
Nasals				
[+voice]	m	n	ɲ	
Laterals				
[+voice]		l	ʎ	
Vibrants				
[+voice]		r/r̄		

Vowels				Semi-vowels	
High	i	u		j	w
Mid		e o			
Low		a			

sociolinguistically marked: while the pronunciation of *calle* 'street' as [kaje] is now very widespread in informal speech, the intermediate variant [kaʒe] is often regarded as uneducated and the affricate realisation [kadʒe] is usually stigmatised as vulgar.

The voiceless plosives are all unaspirated. The voiced series is in complementary distribution with a corresponding set of voiced spirants which occur intervocalically, thus *boca* 'mouth' [boka] but *cabo* 'end' [kaβo], *donde* 'where' [dɔnde] but *nudo* 'knot' [nuðo], *gato* 'cat' [gato] but *lago* 'lake' [laɣo]. In indigenous words neither /b/ nor /g/ occurs word-finally; orthographic -*d* is weakened to [θ] or lost completely. It has traditionally been assumed that the spirants are the subordinate members of these pairs, since the weakening of the plosives in some environments is well attested as a historical process. Recent research on language acquisition among Mexican children, however, seems to show that the spirants are acquired first and remain dominant.

The voiceless fricatives represent the remnants of a much larger set of sibilants in Old Spanish, including a phonemic voiced series; its demise is still not wholly explained. The absence of phonemic voiced sibilants now sets Spanish apart from most other Romance varieties; [z] occurs infrequently as an allophone of /s/ before voiced obstruents, but not intervocalically, thus *desde* 'from/since' [dɛzde] but *esposa* 'wife' [ɛsposa] — compare Portuguese [ʃpozɐ], Italian [spɔːza] and French [epuz]. American Spanish and most varieties of Andalusian lack the distinctive Castilian opposition between /θ/ and /s/, as in *cima* 'summit' /θiɪna/ : *sima* 'abyss' /sima/, *caza* 'hunt' /kaθa/ : *casa* 'house' /kasa/, *haz* 'bundle' /aθ/ : *as* 'ace' /as/. Throughout South America and in most of Andalucía, only [s] is found — a feature popularly called 'seseo'. In a few parts of Andalucía, [θ] alone is used — labelled 'ceceo'. It is probably not true that American Spanish *lost* the /θ/ : /s/ opposition; more likely it was not present in the language of the first colonists. The merger, whatever its exact date, seems to have led to some vocabulary changes in order to avoid ambiguity: the Castilian minimal pair *coser* 'to sew' /koser/ : *cocer* 'to cook' /koθer/ poses no problem in America, where *coser* is maintained, but *cocinar* /kosinar/ is the verb 'to cook'.

The three nasals contrast intervocalically, where there are numerous permutations of minimal pairs and a few triads: *lama* 'slime' /lama/ : *lana* 'wool' /lana/ : *laña* 'clamp' /laɲa/. Elsewhere, the opposition is incomplete. Word-initially, /ɲ-/ is very rare, confined to a few affective coinings and Amerindian borrowings; among Latinate items, only /m-/ and /n-/ are possible. Nasals combine freely with obstruents to form heterosyllabic clusters, in which seven or more phonetic variants can be detected, always homorganic with the following consonant and therefore neutralising the opposition — *infeliz* 'unhappy' [iɱfeliθ], *incierto* 'uncertain' [in̪θjɛrto], *incapaz* 'unable' [iŋkapaθ], etc. The opposition is also neutralised in word-final position, where only /-n/ occurs. A variant pronunciation, previously common in Andalucía and parts of Latin America, is now spreading rapidly in Spain though it remains sociolinguistically marked: word-final and sometimes syllable-final /-n/ is realised as -[ŋ]. Some phoneticians believe this may be the prelude to phonemic nasalisation of the preceding vowel, a development Spanish has so far resisted.

Turning to the liquids, we find /l/ is pronounced either dental or alveolar but never dark, and /ʎ/, as we noted above, is tending to lose its lateral element. /r/ and /r̄/ are unique in contrasting at the same point of articulation, but the opposition is only intervocalic — *caro* 'expensive' /karo/ : *carro* 'cart' /kar̄o/; elsewhere the two sounds are in complementary distribution. In standard Castilian the difference seems to be one of tenseness rather than length: /-r-/ is usually a flap and /-r̄-/ a full-bodied alveolar trill. But in some dialects /-r̄-/ is realised as a weaker sound with palatal friction [ɼ]. This development suggests an intriguing historical parallel with the palatals /ʎ/ and /ɲ/ which also had a principal source in Latin intervocalic geminates and appear to have evolved via a stage of tenseness.

Before passing on to vowels, we should say a few words about prosodic features, both for their intrinsic interest and because vocalic structure cannot be examined in isolation from stress and rhythm. Spanish has often been quoted as a textbook example of a syllable-timed language, with a delivery sometimes likened to a recalcitrant machine gun. A newer proposal suggests Spanish would be more accurately described as 'segment-timed' since the delivery, though perceptually regular, does not always produce isochronous syllabification *or* isochronous stress intervals. The rhythmic pattern, naturally, has implications for intonation, which tends to avoid abrupt changes and readily accommodates melodic units of ten to fifteen syllables. Castilian, whose everyday register is confined to little more than an octave, has a basic rise-fall for simple declaratives, a sustained rise for most yes-no questions, and the characteristic western Romance level or rising tone to mark enumerations and sentence-medial clause boundaries. A prominent feature of Castilian is its 'dynamic' or intensity accent, which is noticeably free from tonal modulation. Most writers also comment on the resonant quality that Castilians and northern dialect speakers impart to their everyday speech. This has been variously ascribed to an unusual articulatory setting, to the rhythmic structure, to the predominance of low, open vowels, and to the stability of vowel sounds in both stressed and unstressed positions. Though all these factors may be contributory, the principal cause must be articulatory setting, since many other regional varieties of Spanish are produced with a less marked resonant quality despite sharing the other structural features of Castilian.

As will be apparent from table 10.1, the five simple vowels form a classic symmetrical triangle. Their frequency of occurrence in running prose also follows a regular pattern: low vowels are more frequent than high, front more so than back (hence in ascending order, /u, i, o, e, a/). All five occur as independent words, with /e/ and /a/ both representing homophones. All occur both stressed and unstressed, in open and closed syllables, though /i/ and /u/ are rare in word-final position. As we noted above, there is little tendency to weakening or centralisation in unstressed syllables, a feature which sets Spanish clearly apart from its peninsular neighbours Portuguese and Catalan. Regardless of the presence or absence of stress, however, all vowels are represented by laxer variants in closed syllables; the high and mid series are lowered slightly and /a/, which in citation has a central low articulation, may be displaced forward or backward depending on the adjacent consonant: *presté* 'I lent' /pres'te/ [prɛs'te], *cortó* 'it cut' /kor'to/ [kɔr'to], *jaulas* 'cages' /'xaulas/ ['χɑwlạs].

This unexceptional laxing has paved the way for a change in Andalusian and some Latin American varieties which may have far-reaching consequences for the vowel system and for plural marking. The great majority of Spanish nouns in the singular end in open /-a/, /-o/ or /-e/, but the addition of the plural marker /-s/ closes the syllable and produces the regular allophonic variation in the vowel:

hermano(s) 'brother(s)' /ermano/ [ɛr'mano] + /s/ = [ɛr'manɔs]
hermana(s) 'sister(s)' /ermana/ [ɛr'mana] + /s/ = [ɛr'manæs]
madre(s) 'mother(s)' /madre/ ['maðre] + /s/ = ['maðrɛs]

In Andalusian, syllable-final /-s/ often weakens to an aspiration [-h], so *los hermanos* becomes [lɔʰ ɛrmanɔʰ] etc. This substitution, though phonetically salient, does not affect the phonemic status of the vowels. In a more 'advanced' variety of Andalusian, however, the aspiration is lost altogether and with it the conditioning factor for the vowel alternation. Now [la maðre] contrasts functionally with [læ maðrɛ], and we are obliged to recognise a new system of plural marking — not too different from the vocalic alternations of Italian — and with it three new vowel phonemes.

Table 10.1 shows no diphthongs or triphthongs. On the phonetic level, combinations of vowels and vowel-like elements are common, but their phonemic status has always been among the most controversial areas of Spanish linguistics. Eighteen monosyllabic combinations can be distinguished, eight with a glide onset /ja, je, jo, ju, wa, we, wi, wo/, six with an off-glide /aj, aw, ej, ew, oj, ow/ and a further four with both on- and off-glides /waj, wej, jaw, waw/ of which the last two are very rare. The analyst's task is complicated by the existence of numerous other combinations, both within and across word boundaries, of vowels 'in hiatus' — pronounced as two syllables in careful speech but readily coalescing into monosyllables in rapid or informal delivery.

To explain the controversy, we must make a brief foray into stress assignment. Stress in Spanish is usually predictable and is not used as the sole means of differentiating lexical items. Stress position is calculated from the end of the word: those ending in a consonant other than /-n/ or /-s/ are stressed on the final syllable, almost all others are stressed on the penultimate. It follows that nearly all plural forms are stressed on the same syllable as the corresponding singular. A few words, mainly borrowings, are stressed on the antepenultimate — a feature known by the convenient mnemonic of *esdrújulo*. These are not predictable (except as plurals maintaining the pattern of paroxytone singulars, like *jóvenes* 'youths'); they all have an open penultimate syllable but this is a necessary, not sufficient, condition. Stress can only move further back than the third syllable if the word is clearly compound; *entregándomelo* 'handing it to me', *fácilmente* 'easily', though the latter has a secondary stress in the expected position. This fairly straightforward account of stress is complicated when we turn to verb inflection. Here, stress operates functionally to differentiate otherwise identical forms of the same lexeme — *hablo* 'I speak' : *habló* '(s)he spoke', *¡cante!* 'sing!' : *canté* 'I sang', *tomara* '(s)he might/would take' : *tomará* '(s)he will take'. It follows that an analysis wishing to view stress as generally predictable must make reference to morphological information. Some theories, of course, rule this out by axiom.

Returning to what we earlier labelled 'semi-vowels', we can now appreciate the problem. At first sight, [j, w] appear to be in complementary distribution with the vowels /i, u/ respectively (a pattern which holds good even for the speakers who regularly substitute [j] for /ʎ/). The economical analysis requires prior knowledge of stress position: /i/ is realised as [j] (or becomes [-syllabic] in generative terminology) if and only if it is unstressed and adjacent to some other vowel. Now, some linguists have hankered after the neatest solution, that both semi-vowels and stress assignment are predictable. Can it be done? Consider these examples:

amplio ['am-pljo]   : amplío [am-'pli-o]   : amplió [am-'pljo]
'ample'   'I broaden'   '(s)he broadened'
continuo [kɔn-'ti-nwo] : continúo [kɔn-ti-'nu-o] : continuó [kɔn-ti-'nwo]
'continuous'   'I continue'   '(s)he continued'

Here, the occurrence of the full vowel or glide is predictable, once stress is known. But the converse is not true: stress cannot be predicted using only the phonological information given here. Nor can it be made predictable by including general morphological conditions, since other verbs behave differently in the middle form of the series: *cambiar* 'to change' and *menguar* 'to lessen' give respectively ['kam-bjo] and ['mɛŋ-gwo] not *[kam-'bi-o] or *[mɛŋ-'gu-o]. For reductionists, the consequences are uncomfortable: neither semi-vowels nor stress assignment can be predicted on strictly phonological criteria.

An allied debate has raged around the predictability or otherwise of the verb stem alternations traditionally called 'radical changes'. The two most frequent ones involve semi-vowels and stress assignment. The verb *poder* 'to be able' has two stems: /pod-/ when the following vowel is stressed and /pwed-/ when the stem itself is stressed. This results in a heterogeneous paradigm, very striking in the present indicative, with 1 sg. *puedo* alongside 1 pl. *podemos*. Similarly, *helar* 'to freeze', has the stressed stem *hielo* /jelo/ alongside *helamos* /elamos/. Some 400 verbs follow these two patterns, far more than one would normally wish to describe as 'irregular'. In any event, the observable changes are perfectly regular once one knows the stress assignment. But the interesting question is whether membership of the radical changing pattern is itself predictable. It used to be. Most western Romance dialects inherited a seven-term vowel system /i, e, ɛ, a, ɔ, o, u/ in which the mid vowels /e:ɛ/ /o:ɔ/ were phonemically distinct. In northern Spain, /ɛ/ and /ɔ/ diphthongised when stressed. This was a regular phonological change, affecting all word classes equally and all types of syllable (in northern French, the same vowels diphthongised only in *open* syllables). So, Spanish verbs with /ɛ/ or /ɔ/ as their stem vowel were regularly subject to diphthongisation under stress, stress in turn being positioned according to the number of syllables in the inflection.

What has changed between early and modern Spanish is the loss of the phonemic opposition between the mid vowels in favour of an allophonic variation predictable from syllable structure (see above). It is no longer possible to tell, from an infinitive, whether a verb will be radical-changing or not: the stem vowel of *podar* 'to prune' is identical to that of *poder* but does not diphthongise; neither does the *e* of *pelar* 'to peel', although it is phonetically indistinguishable from that of *helar*. Some linguists, arguing that so common an alternation must be produced by regular rule, have postulated underlying vowels /ɛ, ɔ/ for radical-changing verbs and thus claim the synchronic process is identical to the historical change. Others reject this abstract analysis, but point out the alternation is 99 per cent predictable if a form like *puede* is taken as basic rather than the infinitive. Yet others believe that Spanish speakers cannot predict these alternations at all, and must learn them as inherent features of the individual verb (rather like learning the gender of a noun). This last group point to two pieces of evidence. Firstly, derivational processes have destroyed the earlier phonological regularity of diphthongisation: *deshuesar* 'to remove bones/pits' is a verb coined from the noun *hueso*, but the diphthong which regularly occurs under stress in the noun is irregular in the infinitive, where it is unstressed. Parallel examples are *ahuecar* 'to hollow out' from *hueco*, or *amueblado* 'furnished' from *mueble*. Secondly, speakers of some varieties stigmatised as non-standard, especially Chicano, regularly keep the diphthongised stem throughout a paradigm regardless of stress placement, saying *despiertamos*, *despiertáis* for standard *despertamos*, *despertáis* 'we/you awaken'. All told, it looks as though a process which at first was phonologically regular has passed through a stage of morphological conditioning and is now giving way to lexical marking on individual words. As often happens in linguistic change, this will preserve analogical relationships at the expense of phonological regularity.

4   Morphology

It is well known that the Romance languages have, over the centuries, eliminated much of the inflectional morphology that characterised formal Latin. Spanish is no exception to the general trend away from synthetic towards more analytic forms of expression. At the same time, historical accounts, by concentrating on what has been eliminated, tend to exaggerate the extent to which Spanish has abandoned inflection. True, the declension system for nouns and related forms has been radically simplified, and some extensive areas of verbal inflection (including the entire morphological passive) have been lost without trace. Nevertheless, the most frequently occurring forms of the verb remain highly synthetic in structure, and derivational patterning has always been a favoured and vigorous means of enriching the vocabulary. In consequence, Modern Spanish is far from being an isolating language: very few words consist of only one morph and the 'synthesis index' for running prose has been calculated at between 1:1.9 and 1:2.2 depending on the complexity of the register.

We begin with the simple tense-forms of the verb. Spanish verbs are traditionally said to belong to one of three conjugations, with infinitives in

-ar, *-er* and *-ir*. The *-ar* group, deriving from the Latin first conjugation in
-ĀRE, is by far the largest and the one which accommodates almost all new
coinings (compare *alunizar* 'to land on the moon' with French *alunir*). The
distinction between the *-er* and *-ir* patterns is more apparent than real: aside
from the future and conditional paradigms (which necessarily diverge since
they take the infinitive as their stem) their endings are identical in all but four
instances. We shall therefore distinguish only two basic conjugations for
regular verbs, as set out in the chart given here.

The Simple Tense-forms of Regular Verbs, Showing the Stress and a Possible Morphological Analysis

Conjugation I: tomar 'to take'   Conjugation II: comer 'to eat'

(a) Present

Indicative	Subjunctive	Indicative	Subjunctive
tóm-Ø-o	tóm-e-Ø	cóm-Ø-o	cóm-a-Ø
tóm-a-s	tóm-e-s	cóm-e-s	cóm-a-s
tóm-a-Ø	tóm-e-Ø	cóm-e-Ø	cóm-a-Ø
tom-á-mos	tom-é-mos	com-é-mos	com-á-mos
tom-á-is	tom-é-is	com-é-is	com-á-is
tóm-a-n	tóm-e-n	cóm-e-n	cóm-a-n

(b) Imperfect

Indicative	Subjunctive (1)	or (2)	Indicative	Subjunctive (1)	or (2)
tom-á-ba-Ø	-á-se-Ø	-á-ra-Ø	com-í-a-Ø	-ié-se-Ø	-ié-ra-Ø
tom-á-ba-s	-á-se-s	-á-ra-s	com-í-a-s	-ié-se-s	-ié-ra-s
tom-á-ba-Ø	-á-se-Ø	-á-ra-Ø	com-í-a-Ø	-ié-se-Ø	-ié-ra-Ø
tom-á-ba-mos	-á-se-mos	-á-ra-mos	com-í-a-mos	-ié-se-mos	-ié-ra-mos
tom-á-ba-is	-á-se-is	-á-ra-is	com-í-a-is	-ié-se-is	-ié-ra-is
tom-á-ba-n	-á-se-n	-á-ra-n	com-í-a-n	-ié-se-n	-ié-ra-n

(c) Preterit or simple past (indicative only)

tom-Ø-é	(? = á+i)	com-Ø-í	(? = í+i)
tom-á-ste		com-í-ste	
tom-Ø-ó	(? = á+u)	com-i-ó	
tom-á-mos		com-í-mos	
tom-á-ste-is		com-í-ste-is	
tom-á-ro-n		com-ié-ro-n	

(d) Future indicative (all verbs)   Conditional (all verbs)

tom-a-r-é	com-e-r-ía
tom-a-r-ás	com-e-r-ías
tom-a-r-á	com-e-r-ía
tom-a-r-émos	com-e-r-íamos
tom-a-r-éis	com-e-r-íais
tom-a-r-án	com-e-r-ían

As in Latin, each paradigm consists of six forms representing three
grammatical persons in both singular and plural. In general, all six forms are

distinct, though there is some syncretism in first and third persons singular (and more in dialects which have lost final /-s/). As we noted earlier, stress operates functionally to differentiate otherwise identical forms. The unmarked paradigm is the present indicative and the unmarked person the third singular, which is the morphological shape assumed by the handful of verbs that do not accept animate subjects (*nieva* 'it is snowing', *tronó* 'it thundered'). It is useful to distinguish a 'theme vowel' after the lexical stem, /-a-/ for the first conjugation and for the second /-e-/ or /-i-/, in a rather complicated phonological distribution. It can then be seen that the distinction between the present indicative and subjunctive rests on a reversal of the theme vowel.

The order of morphemes is fixed: lexical stem + theme vowel + tense marker (sometimes including an empty morph) + person marker. Some forms, however, have fused in the course of history and a neat segmentation is not always possible. The preterit is the most difficult paradigm to analyse, since the theme vowel is sometimes indistinguishable, and segmenting the second and third person plural markers in the regular way, /-is, -n/, leaves an awkward residue which occurs nowhere else in the system. (We should perhaps add that the Latin perfect, from which this paradigm is derived, is scarcely more amenable to segmentation!) The future and conditional pose a rather different problem: both have evolved during the history of Spanish (see below) from combinations of the infinitive with either the present or imperfect of the auxiliary *haber* 'to have', and despite considerable phonetic reduction the 'endings' still contain traces of this verb's lexical stem. This secondary derivation explains the identity of the conditional endings with those of the second conjugation imperfect.

Spanish is in the unusual position of having alternative forms for the imperfect subjunctive, neither of which is a reflex of the Latin. The *-se* series derives from the Latin pluperfect subjunctive, and the *-ra* from the pluperfect indicative. In northwestern dialects and parts of Latin America, *-ra* is still used as a pluperfect. In standard Spanish, the two forms are not quite interchangeable: in the 'attenuating' sense *quisiera* 'I should like' and *debiera* 'I really ought' cannot be replaced by the *-se* counterparts, and elsewhere their distribution may be determined by considerations of symmetry or by sociolinguistic factors.

By the strictest criteria, almost 900 Spanish verbs are irregular in one or more of the simple tense-forms. This disconcerting figure contains a very few with anomalies in their endings; all the others are subject to alternations in the stem, with varying degrees of predictability. (The total, incidentally, excludes numerous other verbs which, though perfectly regular in their morphology, undergo orthographic changes and which are misguidedly classified as irregular in some manuals.) Over half the total are 'radical changing', of the types discussed above or of a minor type affecting only *-ir* verbs; some others, like *huir* 'to flee', insert a glide under predictable conditions. A significant minority retain the Latin opposition between primary and historic stems; those which do, have their preterit and both imperfect subjunctives built on a different stem from all other paradigms (see the chart of irregular verbs). Some twenty verbs of conjugation II modify their infinitival stem in the future and conditional. Finally, a handful of very frequent verbs are totally eccentric and even undergo stem suppletion.

Five Irregular Verbs Used as Auxiliaries, Given in Standard Orthography

ser 'to be'	estar 'to be'	haber 'to have'	tener 'to have'	ir 'to go'

(a) Present indicative

soy	estoy	he	tengo	voy
eres	estás	has	tienes	vas
es	está	ha	tiene	va
somos	estamos	hemos	tenemos	vamos
sois	estáis	habéis	tenéis	vais
son	están	han	tienen	van

(b) Present subjunctive (endings regular, same stem throughout)

sea	esté	haya	tenga	vaya

(c) Imperfect indicative (endings regular, same stem throughout)

era	estaba	había	tenía	iba

(d) Future indicative (endings regular, same stem throughout)

seré	estaré	habré	tendré	iré

(e) Preterit indicative (endings slightly irregular, same stem throughout)

fui	estuve	hube	tuve	fui
fuiste	estuviste	hubiste	tuviste	fuiste
fue	estuvo	hubo	tuvo	fue
fuimos	estuvimos	hubimos	tuvimos	fuimos
fuisteis	estuvisteis	hubisteis	tuvisteis	fuisteis
fueron	estuvieron	hubieron	tuvieron	fueron

(f) Imperfect subjunctive (endings regular, same stem throughout)

(1) fuese	estuviese	hubiese	tuviese	fuese
(2) fuera	estuviera	hubiera	tuviera	fuera

One class, amounting to some 200 including compounds, deserves special mention. Polysyllabic verbs which end in -cer or -cir preceded by a vowel, like *conocer* 'to know' or *relucir* 'to flaunt', have an extra velar consonant before non-front vowels, *conozco* being pronounced [ko-'nɔθ-ko] in Castilian and [ko-'nɔs-ko] in 'seseo' districts of Andalucía and throughout Latin America. The intriguing question is: where does the velar come from? Is it part of the underlying stem but lost before front vowels? Or is it epenthetic, and if so under what conditions? The first answer is historically correct: all these verbs contain an originally inchoative infix -*ISC*- whose velar regularly palatalised before a front vowel and assimilated to the preceding sibilant. But it seems unlikely that contemporary speakers recapitulate this process to produce the less frequent of the two alternants. If the velar is regarded as epenthetic (though phonetically unmotivated), it remains predictable in Castilian but only by reference to the phoneme /θ/. In 'seseante' dialects which lack the /θ:s/ opposition, the alternation is unpredictable: speakers cannot know from the phonological structure that *reconocer* 'to recognise' [re-ko-no-'sɛr] requires [-k-] while *recoser* 'to sew up' [re-ko-'sɛr] does not. They must, in other words, learn the alternation as an inherent lexical feature of the verb. Castilians, too, may do this; but they appear to have a choice.

In addition to its simple paradigms, Spanish is particularly well endowed with compound or periphrastic forms, more so than any other standard Romance language. Usually, these consist of an inflected auxiliary followed by a non-finite form of the lexical verb (an infinitive or participle), but more complex combinations are also possible. Virtually all are Romance creations, though some embryonic models are attested in Latin. The most far-reaching innovation was the compounding of *HABĒRE*, originally meaning 'to possess', with a past participle. *HABEO CĒNA(M) PARĀTA(M)* first meant 'I have the supper here, already prepared', but with increased use and a change of word order, it soon came to mean simply 'I've prepared the supper'. The new construction provided a powerful model: in principle, any paradigm of *HABĒRE* could be combined with the past participle to make a new tense-form. This remains true in Modern Spanish: all eight simple paradigms of *haber*, including the rare future subjunctive, can be compounded (their meanings are discussed in section 5). Although the compounds were flourishing in Old Spanish, they could only be used with transitive verbs, a direct consequence of their etymology. Intransitives were conjugated with *ser*, rather as in Modern French. It was only at the end of the fifteenth century that *haber* ousted *ser* for all verbs, and the past participle became invariable. In Spanish, *tener* can also be used as an auxiliary: *tengo preparada la cena*, with agreement, means the same as the Latin expression from which we set out.

The chart of irregular verbs, detailing the most common auxiliaries, shows two verbs 'to be', a notorious difficulty for foreign learners of Spanish. At some risk of oversimplification we shall say that *ser* is the normal copula, denoting inherent qualities, while *estar* focuses on resultant states; compare *la pimienta es picante* 'pepper is hot' (inherently) with *la sopa está fría* 'the soup's cold' (because it's cooled down). Both verbs can be used as auxiliaries, in conjunction with a past participle, to make analytic passives. This results in a plethora of forms, since any paradigm of *ser* or *estar* can be used, including those which are already compound. Nor are the two passives synonymous: *ser* denotes the action or process, as in *el dinero ha sido robado (por un atracador)* 'the money has been stolen (by a gangster)', whereas *estar* denotes the subsequent state, as in *la tienda está abierta* 'the shop's open' (because it has been opened). *Estar* also combines with a present participle to create a range of progressive forms. In turn, these may combine with other compounds, without grammatical restriction. Nevertheless, three-term compounds like *había estado andando* 'I'd been walking' are not frequent, and monsters like *ha estado siendo construído* 'it's been being built' are usually avoided in compassion for the listener.

By comparison with the verb, the Spanish noun and its related forms have a very simple inflectional structure. This is mainly due to the complete elimination of the Latin declension system, from a very early date and well before the emergence of vernacular texts in the tenth century. Nonetheless, as we hinted earlier, the effect of vigorous derivational processes has been to create large numbers of nouns whose overall morphological structure, while reasonably transparent, can hardly be described as simple. An abstract nominal like *desaprovechamiento* 'negligence' probably consists of six synchronic morphemes, with a further historical division fossilised in the root *-pro(-vech)-*. The majority of nouns consist of at least two morphemes, a root and gender marker, to which a plural marker is affixed if need be.

The categories of number and gender inherited from Latin are for the most part overtly marked on determiners, demonstratives, pronouns and adjectives of all kinds, as well as nouns. In Castilian, all plural substantives and determiners end in /-s/, though the derivation of plurals from singulars is not quite so straightforward as this implies, since a sizable minority adds the full syllable /-es/ and a few already ending in /-s/ remain unchanged. We have already seen the drastic effect on plural marking in those dialects which have lost final /-s/. Modern Spanish has only two genders, which normally respect the sex of animate beings, but must be regarded as inherent and semantically arbitrary for inanimate nouns. The Latin neuter was eliminated from substantives, usually in favour of masculine, before the Old Spanish period, but faint traces of it persist in the pronoun system. Thanks to the frequency of the markers *-a* (overwhelmingly feminine) and *-o* (almost exclusively masculine) the gender of a high proportion of nouns is immediately apparent, though predictability for other endings is much lower. Curiously, *-a* and *-o* derive from Latin suffixes whose primary purpose was to mark not gender, but declension membership, from which gender was in turn partly predictable.

The demonstratives form a three-term system which correlates with grammatical person: *este* 'this (of mine)' : *ese* 'that (of yours)' : *aquel* 'yonder (of his/hers/theirs)'. One set of forms doubles up for adjectives and pronouns (the latter take an orthographic accent) and the system is essentially identical to its Latin forerunner, though with different exponents. In European Spanish, person is undoubtedly a three-term system if approached via verbal inflection, but there are in fact twelve pronouns to distribute among the six inflectional endings, and it is the third person that proves obligingly polysemous. Since the end of the Middle Spanish period, the physical distance encoded in the person category (and in demonstratives) has been exploited metaphorically as a marker of social distance. Thus the 'polite' address forms *usted/ustedes* colligate with third person endings, emphasising the differential status accorded by the speaker to the addressee. The minor semantic clash of second person referent with third person verb is resolved in West Andalusian and Canary Island dialects by colligating *ustedes* with second person morphology: *ustedes sois*, etc. In Latin America, the position is more complicated. *Vosotros*, the familiar plural form, has given way to *ustedes*, used with third person inflection, as a generalised plural. *Vos*, which in medieval Spanish had been used as a polite singular (just as Modern French *vous*), has taken over in many varieties as the generalised singular, colligating with inflections which are historically both singular and plural, sometimes even blends. 'Voseo' is not a recent phenomenon; its roots must be sought in the colonial period, and recent archival research has revealed that it was well established in educated Buenos Aires usage by the beginning of the last century.

5 Syntax

Spanish has sometimes been described as having free, or relatively free, word order. Without qualification, this is misleading. What is usually meant is that subject noun phrases are not fixed by grammatical requirements at a particular point in the sentence. This is a salient characteristic, one which differentiates Spanish from French (in its formal registers) and more so from the major Germanic languages, but which is less unusual among the southern Romance group. At the same time, Spanish has strong constraints on word order *within* the main syntactic constituents and even the theoretical freedom available elsewhere is subject to pragmatic conventions. As a general rule, themes precede rhemes and new information is located towards the end of the utterance.

To characterise the purely syntactic constraints, we must recognise the categories of subject, verbal unit, object and complement (abbreviated as S, V, O, C). Within the simple declarative sentence, object and complement phrases follow the verb: *Elena compró un coche* 'Helen bought a car', *el libro parecía interesante* 'the book seemed interesting'. In everyday language, the VO/VC order is fixed; objects cannot precede their verbs — **Elena un coche compró*. It is certainly possible to topicalise an object consisting of a definite noun phrase or proper noun by moving it to the front of the sentence, but when this happens there is an intonation break after the topic, and an object clitic is obligatorily inserted before the verb: *el coche, lo compró Elena* '(as for) the car, Helen bought it'. The result is no longer a simple sentence; *lo compró Elena* is a complete structure in its own right.

Subject phrases are harder to pin down. Because of the marked tendency for the topic to coincide with the grammatical subject in spoken language, SVO/SVC order is very frequent, especially where the subject consists of a single proper noun or very short phrase. So ?*compró Elena el coche* would sound very odd, and *compró el coche Elena* would tend to be reserved for contradiction or contrast — 'it was Helen (not Jane) who bought the car'. Nevertheless, in more formal registers VSO order is common, and in all registers unusually long or 'heavy' subject phrases appear to the right of the verb: *han llegado todos los transeuntes de la Compañía X* 'all passengers travelling with Company X have now arrived'. VS order is the norm in many types of subordinate clause even when the subject consists of a single word: *no vi lo que leía Juana* 'I didn't see what Jane was reading'. VS is also obligatory in existentials, *viven gitanos en las cuevas* 'there are gypsies living in the caves', and in questions beginning with an interrogative word: *¿qué quieren ustedes?* 'what would you (pl.) like?', but not *¿qué ustedes quieren?* Interrogatives of this kind should not be assumed to entail syntactic inversion since VS, as we have seen, frequently occurs in statements and conversely yes-no questions may show either VS or SV order, relying entirely on the intonation to differentiate questions from corresponding statements.

On most of the criteria favoured by typological theory, Modern Spanish is a consistent VO language. Briefly: in simplex sentences VO/VC order is obligatory; noun phrase relationships are expressed exclusively by prepositions; genitives follow their head noun; the standard follows the comparative; most adjectives and all attributive phrases and relative clauses follow their head noun; most adverbs follow the verb they modify; auxiliaries are frequent and always precede the lexical stem; quantifiers and negatives precede the item they qualify and have only forward scope; interrogative words are always phrase-initial. Needless to add, there are some complications. Among the adjectives, some of the most common always precede their noun, most others may precede if used figuratively, and a few are polysemous according to position: *un pobre pueblecillo* 'a miserable little town', *un aristócrata pobre* 'an impoverished aristocrat'. Adverbs acting as sentential modifiers are usually the first word, *desgraciadamente*, ...'unfortunately, ...'; adverbs modifying adjectives almost always precede whereas those modifying verbs just as regularly follow, so that scope (for manner adverbials at least) is pivotal.

The most serious discrepancy for VO typology, however, is the vigour of suffixal inflection in the verb system, a feature little modified by the development of auxiliaries, since auxiliaries themselves are both frequent and highly inflected. Verbal inflection has two important syntactic functions. In conjunction with the concord system (see below) it guarantees the freedom of movement of subject phrases. It also tends to preserve the optionality of subject pronouns, permitting many grammatical sentences of V(S)O form with no overt subject nominal. Spanish, as we have seen, shows little syncretism in its inflections and, unlike French, rarely needs subject pronouns to avoid syntactic ambiguity, though they are regularly used for emphasis and contrast. At the same time, any move to increase the use of personal pronouns (and there is some evidence this is happening in colloquial registers) would undermine the necessity to preserve verbal inflection.

Spanish has a fully explicit concord system which marks number and gender on all modifiers within the noun phrase, and number and person (and occasionally gender too) between the subject and verb. There is no concord between verb and object. In most cases, concord unambiguously assigns a subject to a verb, and any ambiguity arising in this relationship (if, for instance, both subject and object are third person singular) is usually resolved by syntactic differences between subjects and objects. They differ in two important ways, both connected with specificity. The first is illustrated in *el hombre compra huevos* 'the man is buying (some) eggs'. The subject phrase in Spanish — whether definite, indefinite or generic — requires a determiner, but the object does not. In this respect Spanish differs considerably from Latin, which had no articles and did not require determination of either subjects or objects, but has evolved less far than French, which requires both. The second distinction is illustrated in *vi a tu hermana* 'I saw your sister', where the specific, animate object is introduced by the preposition *a* (popularly known as 'personal *a*'). At first sight, this looks like a nominative:accusative opposition, and it may indeed represent a remnant of the defunct case system. In fact, the opposition is between particularised animate beings and all other object phrases (with a little latitude for metaphorical extension). Moreover, this distinction is preserved at the expense of another: since *a* is also the preposition used to introduce datives, there is no overt difference between the majority of direct and indirect objects. Whether the categories have genuinely fused or are merely obscured by surface syncretism is hard to say. Most Latin American varieties preserve a distinction between third person direct and indirect pronominal objects, but this too has been lost in much of Spain.

Curiously, voice is the verbal category with which pronominals have been most closely linked during the history of Spanish. The connection, brought about by cliticisation of part of the pronoun system, seems likely to result in the evolution of a new set of medio-passive paradigms. Whereas Latin pronouns were free forms not necessarily positioned adjacent to the verb, in most Romance varieties they have become clitic, sometimes resulting in differentiated sets of free and bound forms. In Spanish, clitics may appear alone or supported by a corresponding free form, but the converse is not true: *te vi* 'I saw you', *te vi a ti* 'I saw **you**', but not **vi a ti*. Enclisis, which was frequent in older stages of the language, has been virtually eliminated from contemporary spoken Spanish, where clitics 'climb' from a lower clause to the front of the main verb — compare formal *tiene que traérmelo* 'he must bring it for me' with colloquial *me lo tiene que traer*. As we noted earlier, clitics show a direct:indirect opposition only in the third person, and not always there. Reflexivity is distinguished, if at all, only in third person *se*, which neutralises not only direct:indirect, but also number and gender.

Recently, *se* and its congeners in other Romance languages have been the focus of intense linguistic debate. The problem is whether *se* should be treated as one single morpheme or a set of homophonous forms. Traditional accounts distinguish three or four functions: a true reflexive pronoun — *se lavó* 'he washed himself'; a passive marker — *el congreso se inauguró* 'the congress was opened'; an impersonal marker — *se habla inglés* 'English spoken'; and a substitute form of *le/les* when used with another deictic pronoun — *se lo dio* 'she gave it to him', not * *le lo dio*. (The latter usage is peculiar to Spanish and is known to have a different historical origin from the others.) These four functions, however, seem to be semantically compatible, yet Spanish never permits more than one *se* per verb phrase. Combinations of, for instance, an 'impersonal' *se* with a 'reflexive' verb are ungrammatical — * *se se esfuerza por ...*'one struggles to ...' — as are many other apparently reasonable pairs. If *se* were only one morpheme, the problem would not arise; but can such disparate meanings be reconciled? Two accounts are now available which solve most of the problems. In one, *se* is viewed as a pronoun with very little inherent meaning ('third person, low deixis'), which acquires significance from contextual inferences. In the other, *se* is seen as part of a new medio-passive paradigm, its third person impersonal use paralleling that of Latin: *VĪVITUR* = *se vive* = 'one lives'. In neither treatment is *se* a reflexive pronoun!

If Spanish is indeed creating new inflectional morphology, it would not be the first time. The clearest example is the new future paradigm we mentioned above, a compound of the lexical verb plus *HABĒRE* (/kantar + 'abjo/ > /kanta're/ etc.), which originally expressed mild obligation 'I have to sing' and whose component parts were still separable in Old Spanish. Another example would be the adverbials in *-mente*, compounded from the ablative of the feminine noun *MĒNS* 'mind/manner' with a feminine adjective, thus *STRICTĀ MĒNTE* > *estrechamente* 'narrowly' (notice the Latin adjective position); here the two components remain separable. But is Spanish really in need of a new passive when it already has a plethora of compound forms with *ser* and *estar*? All we can reply is that they have discrete functions: only the 'reflexive' passive is used in an inchoative sense — *se vio obligado a ...*'he became compelled to ...'; only the *ser* passive is acceptable to most speakers with an explicit agentive phrase. But the major difference is one of register: *ser* passives, though common in journalistic and technical writing, have been virtually ousted from speech and from literary styles to the advantage of the clitic forms, which may eventually generalise to all contexts.

We have so far said little on the verbal categories of tense, aspect and mood, and will devote our remaining space to them. The first two are inextricably bound up with the evolution of auxiliaries, in which Spanish is particularly prolific. Auxiliaries usually derive from full lexical verbs whose semantic content is progressively weakened as they become 'grammaticalised'. By the strictest definition — a verb with no independent lexical meaning — Spanish has only one auxiliary: *soler* as in *Juan suele madrugarse* 'John habitually gets up at dawn'. *Haber*, *ser* and *estar* come close behind, having only remnants of lexical meaning: *yo soy* 'I exist', *Ana no está* 'Anne's not at home'. After that comes a continuum of more than fifty verbs, ranging from *tener* and *ir* which have important auxiliary functions, to those like *caminar* 'to walk/journey' which in expressions like *camina enlutada* 'she goes about in mourning' contrive to support the past participle while preserving most of their lexical content. True auxiliaries carry tense and aspect information for the main verb and this is clearly one reason for the grammaticalisation of *HABĒRE*. The Latin system opposed three time values to two aspects, imperfective and perfective, giving a six-cell structure; but one paradigm, usually called 'perfect', was bivalent between present perfective and past punctual meaning. The development of *HABĒRE* compounds not only preserved the morphological marking of aspect (previously perfective was signalled by a stem alternation) but also resolved this bivalency, *VĪDĪ* in the sense of 'I have seen' being replaced by *HABEO VĪSU(M) > he visto*, leaving the original to mean 'I caught sight of'. In the 'core' system of Modern Spanish this opposition is maintained, though in Castilian the perfect *he visto* is beginning to encroach on contexts previously reserved for the preterit *vi*. It is not yet clear whether Spanish is moving towards the pattern of Modern French (see pages 225–6, for details), but certainly the elimination of the preterit paradigm would provoke a major realignment of functions.

All varieties of Spanish preserve a vigorous subjunctive mood (see the charts of regular and irregular verbs for the morphology). Opinion is divided, however, on whether the subjunctive — which does not occur in declarative main clauses — should be viewed as a 'mere' marker of subordination or as a meaningful category. In many contexts, its use seems to be grammatically determined; *querer* 'to want', for instance, when followed by a clause always takes a subjunctive — *quiero que lo hagas/ *haces* 'I want you to do it'. In others, the conditioning is more subtle: *busco a un amigo que puede ayudarme* 'I'm looking for a (particular) friend to help me' alternates with *busco un amigo que pueda ayudarme* 'I'm looking for a (=any) friend to help me', but the subjunctive may still be grammatically conditioned by the indeterminacy of the object noun phrase. There are a few instances, however, where a genuine alternation is possible: *¿crees que vendrá?* and *¿crees que venga?* can both be translated as 'do you think he'll come?', but the first is neutral in implicature while the second conveys the speaker's belief that he won't. If such examples are taken as criterial, the 'grammatical marker' hypothesis cannot be maintained. In any event, the complementiser *que* is a much more efficient marker of subordination, and most complement clauses dependent on verbs of saying, thinking or believing require an indicative rather than a subjunctive. Nevertheless, it remains very difficult to find a single, uniform meaning for the subjunctive, the traditional suggestions of 'doubt' or 'uncertainty' being only partially accurate. The most we can say is that the 'meaningful' uses of the subjunctive, though rather few, are Romance creations and appear to be increasing rather than decreasing.

Bibliography

The best reference grammar of (American) Spanish is Bello (1981), while Real Academia Española (1973) is the draft version of the new normative grammar, completely revising the unsatisfactory edition of 1931. Modern descriptions include: Marcos Marín (1980), an introduction to linguistic analysis very fully exemplified from Spanish, with an excellent bibliography; and Whitley (1986), a comprehensive contrastive grammar of Spanish and English. Harris (1983) is an application of metrical theory to Spanish phonology, superseding the author's earlier classic on the subject; it can usefully be supplemented by the five articles on the interface of phonology and morphology in Nuessel (1985). The most reliable dictionary of modern Spanish usage is Moliner (1982).

For the history of the language, Lapesa (1980) is the classical external account paying special attention to literary sources; a reliable, if rather technical, treatment of internal changes in phonology and morphology can be found in Lloyd (1987). An excellent etymological dictionary is Corominas and Pascual (1980–8). For regional variants, Zamora Vicente (1967) is a historical description of peninsular dialects with shorter sections on Spanish outside Spain. For Latin America, Sala (1982) is a useful general survey of vocabulary, while Canfield (1982) is a brief but authoritative guide to pronunciation arranged by country. Amastae and Elías-Olivares (1982) is a collection of 18 articles on sociolinguistic variation, Chicano, and aspects of language policy in the USA. For Judaeo-Spanish, Sala (1976) provides a good survey and bibliography.

References

Amastae, J. and L. Elías-Olivares (eds.) 1982. *Spanish in the United States* (Cambridge University Press, Cambridge)

Bello, A. 1981. *Gramática de la lengua castellana*, critical edition by R. Trujillo. (Instituto Universitario de Lingüística, Tenerife)

Canfield, D.L. 1981. *Spanish Pronunciation in the Americas*, 2nd ed. (University of Chicago Press, Chicago)

Corominas, J. and J.A. Pascual 1980–8. *Diccionario crítico etimológico castellano e hispánico*, 6 vols. (Gredos, Madrid)

Harris, J.W. 1983. *Syllable Structure and Stress in Spanish* (MIT Press, Cambridge, Mass.)

Lapesa, R. 1980. *Historia de la lengua española*, 8th ed. (Gredos, Madrid)

Lloyd, P.M. 1987. *From Latin to Spanish* (American Philosophical Society, Philadelphia)

Marcos Marín, F. 1980. *Curso de gramática española* (Cincel-Kapelusz, Madrid)

Moliner, M. 1982. *Diccionario de uso del español*, 2 vols. (Gredos, Madrid)

Nuessel, F.H. (ed.) 1985. *Current Issues in Hispanic Phonology and Morphology* (Indiana University Linguistics Club, Bloomington)

Real Academia Española. 1973. *Esbozo de una nueva gramática de la lengua española* (Espasa-Calpe, Madrid)

Sala, M. 1976. *Le judéo-espagnol* (Mouton, The Hague)

—— 1982. *El español de América, 1: Léxico* (Instituto Caro y Cuervo, Bogotá)

Whitley, M.S. 1986. *Spanish/English Contrasts* (Georgetown University Press, Washington D.C.)

Zamora Vicente, A. 1967. *Dialectología española*, 2nd ed. (Gredos, Madrid)

11 Portuguese

Stephen Parkinson

1 Introduction

Portuguese, the national language of Portugal and Brazil, belongs to the Romance language group. It is descended from the Vulgar Latin of the western Iberian Peninsula (the regions of Gallaecia and Lusitania of the Roman Empire), as is Galician, often wrongly considered a dialect of Spanish.

Portugal originated as a county of the Kingdom of Galicia, the westernmost area of the Christian north of the peninsula, the south having been under Moorish rule since the eighth century. Its name derived from the towns of Porto (Oporto) and Gaia (< *CALE*) at the mouth of the Douro river. As Galicia fell under Castilian rule, Portugal achieved independence under the Burgundian nobility to whom the county was granted in the eleventh century. Alfonso Henriques, victor of the battle of São Mamede (1128), was the first to take the title of King of Portugal. Apart from a short period of Castilian rule (1580–1640), Portugal was to remain an independent state.

The speed of the Portuguese reconquest of the Moorish areas played an important part in the development of the language. The centre of the kingdom was already in Christian hands, after the fall of Coimbra (1064), and many previously depopulated areas had been repopulated by settlers from the north. The capture of Lisbon in 1147 and Faro in 1249 completed the expulsion of the Moors, nearly 250 years before the end of the Spanish reconquest, bringing northern and central settlers into the Mozarabic (arabised Romance) areas. The political centre of the kingdom also moved south, Guimarães being supplanted first by Coimbra, and subsequently by Lisbon as capital and seat of the court. The establishment of the university in Lisbon and Coimbra in 1288, to move between the two cities until its eventual establishment in Coimbra in 1537, made the centre and south the intellectual centre (although Braga in the north remained the religious capital). The form of Portuguese which eventually emerged as standard was the result of the interaction of northern and southern varieties, which gives Portuguese dialects their relative homogeneity.

For several centuries after the independence of Portugal, the divergence of Portuguese and Galician was slight enough for them to be considered variants of the same language. Galician-Portuguese was generally preferred to Castilian as a medium for lyric poetry until the middle of the fourteenth century. Portuguese first appears as the language of legal documents at the beginning of the thirteenth century, coexisting with Latin throughout that century and finally replacing it during the reign of D. Dinis (1279–1325).

In the fifteenth and sixteenth centuries the spread of the Portuguese Empire established Portuguese as the language of colonies in Africa, India and South America. A Portuguese-based pidgin was widely used as a reconnaissance language for explorers and later as a lingua franca for slaves shipped from Africa to America and the Caribbean. Some Portuguese lexical items, e.g. *pikinini* 'child' (*pequeninho*, diminutive of *pequeno* 'small'), *save* 'know' (*saber*), are common to almost all creoles. Caribbean creoles have a larger Portuguese element, whose origin is controversial — the Spanish-based Papiamentu of Curaçao is the only clear case of large-scale relexification of an originally Portuguese-based creole. Brazilian Portuguese (BP), phonologically conservative, and lexically affected by the indigenous Tupi languages and the African languages of the slave population, was clearly distinct from European Portuguese (EP) by the eighteenth century. Continued emigration from Portugal perpetuated the European norm beside Brazilian Portuguese, especially in Rio de Janeiro, where D. João and his court took refuge in 1808. After Brazil gained its independence in 1822, there was great pressure from literary and political circles to establish independent Brazilian norms, in the face of a conservative prescriptive grammatical tradition based on European Portuguese.

With over 160 million speakers, Portuguese is reckoned to be the fifth most widely spoken language in the world. It is spoken by 10 million people in Portugal and approaching 150 million in Brazil; it remains the language of administration of the former colonies of Angola, Mozambique, Guiné-Bissau, S. Tomé-Principe and the Cape Verde Islands (where it exists beside Portuguese-based creoles) and is spoken in isolated pockets in Goa, Timor, Malaysia, Macao and in emigré communities in North America.

The standard form of European Portuguese is traditionally defined as the speech of Lisbon and Coimbra. The distinctive traits of Lisbon phonology (centralisation of /e/ to /ɐ/ in palatal contexts; uvular /ʀ/ in place of alveolar /r/) have more recently become dominant as a result of diffusion by the mass media. Unless otherwise stated, all phonetic citation forms are of European Portuguese.

Of the two main urban accents of Brazilian Portuguese, Carioca (Rio de Janeiro) shows a greater approximation towards European norms than Paulista (São Paulo). While the extreme north and south show considerable conservatism, regional differences in Brazilian Portuguese are still less marked than class-based differences; non-standard, basilectal varieties show considerable effects of creolisation, with drastic simplifications of inflectional morphology and concord.

2 Phonology

Portuguese orthography (summarised in table 11.1) is phonological rather than narrowly phonemic or phonetic, assuming knowledge of the main phonological and morphophonemic processes of the language. It also uses a variety of devices to indicate word stress. Final stress is regular (i.e. orthographically unmarked) in words whose final syllable either (a) contains an oral diphthong, one of the nasal vowels /ã õ ĩ ũ õĩ/ or orthographic *ão*, *i*, *u*, *ãe* (as opposed to *am*, *e*, *o*, *em* (*en*), which indicate unstressed final syllables); or (b) ends in *r*, *l* or *z* (but not *s*, which generally indicates

Table 11.1: Portuguese Orthography

a	/a ɐ/*	lh	/ʎ/
á	/a/ (stressed)*	m (final)	nasality of preceding vowel*
ã	/ẽ/	(elsewhere)	/m/
â	/ɐ/ (stressed)*	n (final)	nasality of preceding vowel*
ãe	/ẽĩ/	(elsewhere)	/n/
ão	/ẽũ/	nh	/ɲ/
b	/b/	ó	/ɔ/ (stressed)*
c (+a, o, u)	/k/	ô	/o/ (stressed)*
(+i, e)	/s/	o	/o ɔ u/*
ç	/s/	ou	/o/
ch	/ʃ/	õe	/õĩ/
d	/d/	p	/p/
e	/e,(ɐ),ɛ,ə, i/*	qu (+a, o)	/kw/
é	/ɛ/ (stressed)*	(+i, e)	/k/
ê	/e/ (stressed)*	r	/r, ʀ/*
f	/f/	rr	/ʀ/
g (+a, o)	/g/	s (final)	/z ʃ ʒ/*
(+i, e)	/ʒ/	(intervocalic)	/z/
gu (+a, o)	/gw/	(elsewhere)	/s/
(+i, e)	/g/	t	/t/
h	silent (but cf. ch,lh,nh)	u	/u/
		v	/v/
i	/i,j/*	x	/ʃ (ks,gz,z)/
j	/ʒ/	z (final)	/z ʃ ʒ/*
l	/l/	(elsewhere)	/z/

Note: This table represents European Portuguese pronunciation. * marks points (including Brazilian Portuguese variants) explained in the text. ai, au, ei, éi, eu, éu, iu, oi, ói, ui represent falling diphthongs. k,w are only found in foreign words. final = word- and syllable-final.

inflectional endings). Otherwise, penultimate stress is regular. Any irregular stress pattern, including all cases of antepenultimate stress, is marked by a written accent. These accents also indicate vowel quality (often redundantly). The circumflex accent ˆ indicates closed vowels [ɐ e o], while the acute accent ´ indicates open vowel qualities [a ɛ ɔ] and is also used to mark stress on *i*, *u*, which are deemed to have no 'closed' phonetic values. In a few cases these two accents are still used to indicate vowel quality in regularly stressed words (e.g. *três* 'three', *pôde* '(s)he could' vs. *pode* '(s)he can', *pó* 'dust') and to distinguish stressed monosyllables from clitics, e.g. *dê* [de] 'give (3 sg. pres. subj.)' – *de* [də] 'of'. The grave accent has a very limited use to indicate unreduced atonic vowels (usually /a/). Nasality is indicated either by the til ˜ or by a nasal consonant following the vowel.

Brazilian and Portuguese orthographies have been progressively harmonised by agreements between the respective governments and academies, latterly in 1971 decrees in both countries, in which the distinctively Brazilian convention of marking unpredictable closed mid vowels with the circumflex was abandoned, as part of a rationalisation of the use of accents. The orthographic differences that remain reflect phonological differences between European and Brazilian Portuguese.

The vowel system of Portuguese (tables 11.2 and 11.3) is one of the most complex of the Romance family. Portuguese is rich in monophthongs and (falling) diphthongs, as a result of two developments which set it off from Castilian. There was no diphthongisation of Vulgar Latin /ɛ ɔ/, (compare Cast. *nueve*, Ptg. *nove* < *NOVEM* 'nine', Cast. *diez*, Ptg. *dez* < *DECEM* 'ten') with the result that the seven-vowel system inherited from Vulgar Latin remains complete. Intervocalic /l/ was effaced, and /n/ fell after nasalising the preceding vowel: these two processes, in addition to the deletion of intervocalic /d g/, resulted in Old Portuguese being characterised by large numbers of sequences of vowels in hiatus: e.g. *BONUM* > *bõo* 'good', *MALUM* > *mao* 'bad', *MOLINUM* > *moĩo* 'mill', *PEDEM* > *pee* 'foot'. Many of these hiatuses were resolved as monophthongs or falling diphthongs: *pee* > *pé*; *bõo* > *bõ*; *mao* > *mau*. Nasal vowels in unresolved hiatuses were denasalised (*BONAM* > *bõa* > *boa* 'good (f.)'; **PANATARIUM* > *pãadeiro* > *paadeiro* > *padeiro* 'baker') except for the sequences [ĩo], [ĩa] where the hiatus was broken by a palatal nasal glide [j̃] which subsequently developed into the nasal [ɲ], e.g. *moinho* [mu'iɲu] < *moĩo*. The effacement of intervocalic /l n/ has been morphologised, in the inflection of nouns and adjectives with root-final /l/ e.g. *azul* 'blue', plural *azuis*, and in derivational morphology, partly as the result of the introduction of unevolved forms: *céu* 'heaven, sky' (< *CAELUM*) corresponds to *celeste* 'heavenly'; *fim* [fĩ] 'end' (< *FINEM*) to *final* 'final'; beside *irmão* 'brother' there is a familiar form *mano* (borrowed from Castilian *hermano*).

The phoneme /ɐ/ is only found in the European Portuguese system, and

Table 11.2: Portuguese Vowels

Monophthongs

i	ī		u	ū	High
		(ə)			
e	ē		o	ō	High mid
ɛ		(ɐ)ẽ	ɔ		Low mid
		a			Low

Diphthongs	*Front*		*Central*	*Back*	
	iu			ui	ūī
	eu	ei	ēī	(ou)oi	õī
	ɛu	ɛi	(ɐi)	ɔi	
		ai	ēī au	ẽū	

Note: sounds enclosed in brackets are distinct phonemes in only some varieties.

there in a marginal role. In Brazilian Portuguese, [ɐ] is an allophone of /a/, in post-tonic position and in nasal contexts; in European Portuguese, [ɐ] is likewise tied to atonic and nasal contexts, but the exclusion of [a] from the same contexts is not absolute, leading to occasional contrasts not found in Brazilian Portuguese, e.g. *nação* [nɐ'sẽu] 'nation' – *acção* [a'sẽu] 'action'; *a* (preposition, f. sg. def. art.) [ɐ] vs. *à* (*a + a*) [a]; *-amos* (1 pl. pres. indic., 1st conjug.) -['ɐmuʃ] vs. *-ámos* (ibid., pret.) -['amuʃ]; *casa suja* ['kazɐ'suʒɐ] 'dirty house' – *casa azul* ['kaza'zul] 'blue house'. In Lisbon, /ɐ/ is found preceding the palatal consonants [ʃ ʒ ʎ ɲ], where other accents have /e/, and the diphthongs /ɐi/ and /ɐ̃ī/ correspond to /ei/ and /ēī/ in other accents.

Of the large inventory of phonemic diphthongs (ignoring those phonetic diphthongs arising by vowel contraction) most have a limited distribution. /ūī/ is found only in *muito* 'much, many' (and is often realised as [wī]); /iu/ is only found in preterit forms of third conjugation verbs; /ɛu/, /ɛi/, ēī/, /ẽū/, /ēī/, /ui/, /õī/ and /ɔi/ are found almost exclusively in stem-final position, and are closely associated with inflectional patterns. /ēī/ (Lisbon /ẽī/) is a word-final variant of /ē/, as can be seen from the doublet *cento* 'hundred' [sētu], *cem* 'hundred' [sēī], and also occurs preceding inflectional *-s*: *nuvem* 'cloud' [nuvēī] plural *nuvens* ['nuvēīʃ]. (The orthographic change of *m* to *n* is without phonetic significance.) In most dialects there is a distinction between /ēī/ and the relatively uncommon /ēī/: *quem* 'who' /kēī/ vs. *cães* 'dogs' /kēīʃ/. In Lisbon the centralisation of /ē/ eliminates the distinction by realising all cases of /ēī/ as /ēī/. Some dialects retain the diphthong /ou/ distinct from /o/ (European Portuguese has evidence for a morphophonemic /ou/, in cases of unreduced atonic /o/). In Brazilian Portuguese, the vocalisation of postvocalic /l/ creates a new series of falling diphthongs, e.g. *sol* 'sun' [sɔu] (BP), [sɔl] (EP).

The vowel system is further complicated by a regular alternation of high vowels (/i u/), low mid vowels (/ɛ ɔ/) and high mid vowels (/e o/) inside verbal paradigms. The alternation is found in the second and third conjugations, where root-final mid vowels are realised as /e o/ (2nd conjug.) or /i u/ (3rd conjug.) in the first person singular present indicative, and the whole of the present subjunctive (which always takes its stem form from the first person singular present indicative) but as /ɛ ɔ/ in the remaining root-stressed forms of the indicative (2 sg., 3 sg., 3 pl.). Thus *meter* 'put' (see the chart of verb forms) has present indicative forms ['metu] (1 sg.), ['mɛtə] (3 sg.), and *fugir* 'flee' ['fuʒu] (1 sg.), ['fɔʒa] (3 sg.). This alternation is known as 'metaphony' in token of its origin in an assimilation of the open root vowel to the theme vowel in the first person singular, where the theme vowel was semi-vocalised and lost, e.g. *FUGIO* > **fogjo* > *fujo*. The process has long been morphologised, but can still be analysed as an assimilation in a relatively abstract morphophonemics. It was extended by analogy to some third conjugation verbs where the root vowel was originally a high /i u/ e.g. *fugir* 'to flee'. Vowel alternation is found in a more restricted domain in adjectives and nouns, where it is less easily explicable as assimilation. Adjectives with stem-final /o/, particularly those ending in *-oso* (f. *-osa*) have a closed /o/ in the masculine singular form and open /ɔ/ elsewhere, e.g. *formoso* 'beautiful' [fur'mozu], f. sg. *formosa* [fur'mɔzɐ], pl. [fur'mozuʃ], [fur'mɔzɐʃ]. A similar alternation is found in a restricted set of nouns such as *ovo* 'egg', sg. ['ovu], pl. ['ɔvuʃ].

Nasal vowels are in contrast with the corresponding oral vowels in open syllables (medial and final): e.g. *mudo* ['mudu] 'dumb' – *mundo* ['mũdu] 'world'; *ri* [ʀi] 'laugh' – *rim* [ʀĩ] 'kidney'. There is no contrast between nasal vowels and sequences of vowel + nasal consonant in this position, nasal vowels being very frequently followed by a more or less consonantal nasal off-glide, e.g. ['mũdu] = ['mũndu], so that it is frequently argued that nasal vowels can be analysed phonologically as vowel + nasal consonant sequences. (This analysis is problematic because it cannot easily accommodate nasal diphthongs, and is not easily reconciled with morphophonemic rules relating nasal vowels and nasal consonants.) There is a general phonetic tendency for nasal consonants to cause nasalisation of preceding and following vowels; in Brazilian Portuguese the resulting nasality can be as strong as phonemic nasality. (Historical progressive nasalisation accounts for the nasal vowels of *mãe* 'mother' (< *MATREM*); *muito* (< *MULTUM*); *mim* 'me' (< *MIHI*), *nem* 'nor' (< *NEC*) and for the palatal nasals of *ninho* 'nest' ['niɲu] < *nĩo* < **nio* < *NIDUM* and *nenhum* 'no, not any' < *nẽ ũu* < *NEC UNUM*.)

The open vowels /a ɛ ɔ/, absent from the nasal series, are also excluded from contexts where a nasal consonant follows. This restriction is absolute in Brazilian Portuguese; in European Portuguese it is overridden by morphophonemic processes leading to open vowels (notably metaphony) and by antepenultimate stress. A verb such as *comer* 'eat' shows metaphonic alternations in European but not in Brazilian Portuguese; BP *tônico* 'tonic' corresponds to EP *tónico*.

The morphophonemics of nasal vowels were complicated by a series of changes resulting in the syncretism of the word-final nasal vowels -[ã], -[õ], with -[ãũ] (>[ẽũ]), leading to alternations such as *cão* (sg.) 'dog' (< *cã*) – *cães* (pl.); *razão* (sg.) 'reason' (< *razõ*) – *razões* (pl.); *fala* (3 sg. 'speak') – *falam* ['falẽũ] (3 pl.). This phonological change was effectively morphologised when it was obscured by the subsequent reintroduction of final -*õ* and -*ã* by the contraction of -*õo* and -*ãa*: *bom* < *bõo*, *irmã* < *irmãa* in the fifteenth century.

Stress, (or more precisely, lack of stress) is a major conditioning factor in vowel quality, the range of atonic vowel contrasts being systematically limited, as shown in table 11.3. There is large-scale neutralisation of vowel

Table 11.3: Atonic Vowel Systems

	EP			BP		
Final (including clitics)		ə	u	i		u
		ɐ			a (=[ɐ])	
Non-final	i	ə	u	i		u
			(o)	e		o
	(ɛ)	ɐ	(ɔ)			
		(a)			a	

quality contrasts in the front and back vowel series, most of all in final syllables, where each series is represented by a single vowel: the front vowels by EP [ə], BP [i], the back vowels by /u/. (In European Portuguese atonic final [i] is very rare, and can usually be replaced by [ə]: *táxi* 'taxi' ['taksi], ['taks(ə)].) As in English, EP [ə] is a 'neutralisation vowel' rather than an independent phoneme. In European Portuguese (and to a lesser extent in Brazilian Portuguese) the rules relating tonic and atonic systems are the source of widespread allomorphic variation in inflectional and derivational morphology: e.g. *casa* ['kazɐ] 'house', *casinha* [kɐ'ziɲɐ] 'little house', *mora* ['mɔrɐ] '(s)he lives', *morara* [mu'rarɐ] (BP [mo'rarɐ]) '(s)he had lived', *bate* ['batə] '(s)he hits', *bater* [bɐ'ter] 'to hit', *peso* ['pezu] 'weight', *pesar* [pə'zar] (BP [pe'zax]) 'to weigh'. In some accents of Brazilian Portuguese similar effects result from a rule of vowel harmony by which pretonic /e o/ are raised to /i u/ when a high vowel (usually /i/) follows, e.g. *dormir* [dux'mix] 'to sleep', *medir* [mi'dix] 'to measure'. In European Portuguese there are many 'irregular' forms in which pretonic /a o ɛ ɔ/ appear (hence their appearance in parentheses in table 11.3). Most are explicable as originating in vowel sequences or diphthongs which were not subject to atonic vowel reduction (as diphthongs and nasals are still exempt): e.g. *pregar* 'preach' [prɛ'gar] < *preegar* < *PREDICARE*; *corado* 'red, blushing' [kɔ'radu] < *coorado* < *COLORATUM*; *roubar* 'steal' [ʀo'bar] (EP), [xou'bax] (BP) < OPtg. *roubar*. Other cases of pretonic /ɛ ɔ a/ occur in syllables closed by plosives e.g. *secção* [sɛk'sẽũ], *optar* [ɔp'tar] 'to choose', where Brazilian Portuguese has open syllables.

Atonic vowels are also involved in a major feature of phrasal phonetics, the contraction of vowels across word boundaries. This most typically takes the form of the fusion of word-final atonic vowels or clitic articles with word-initial vowels or clitics, and results in a wide range of diphthongs and monophthongs: *o uso* 'the custom' /u uzu/, [u:zu]; *uma amiga* 'a friend' /umɐ ɐ'migɐ/, [uma'migɐ]; *é o Pedro* 'it's Pedro' /ɛ u 'pedru/ [ɛu'pedru].

Like English, Portuguese is nominally a free-stress language, with stress being nonetheless predictable in the majority of words, by a complex of grammatical and morphophonological factors. Stress generally falls on the penultimate syllable (or the final syllable, if it is strong, that is, closed by any consonant except inflectional /z/ or containing as its nucleus a diphthong or nasal vowel); in verbs (simple forms) stress falls on the final vowel of the stem, unless this vowel is word-final, when penultimate stress is the rule. It should be noted that the (morpho)phonological regularities of stress placement do not always agree with the orthographic rules previously given. European Portuguese is a clear case of a stress-timed language. Atonic syllables are considerably shorter than tonic ones, the vowels being centralised and raised; [ə] and [u] are frequently effaced or reduced to secondary articulation of preceding consonants. Brazilian Portuguese has considerable reduction of atonic final vowels, but otherwise is mainly syllable-timed. This difference in timing is related to syllable structure. Brazilian Portuguese tends towards a simple consonant-vowel structure, allowing few syllable-final consonants, weakening syllable-final /l r/, and breaking medial clusters by vowel epenthesis, e.g. *advogado* 'lawyer' EP [ɐdvu'gadu], BP [adivo'gadu]. The epenthetic vowels are often counted as full syllables for metrical purposes. European Portuguese allows more syllable-final consonants (compare EP *facto* 'fact' ['faktu], BP ['fatu]; EP *secção* [sɛk'sẽũ], BP *seção* [se'sẽũ]) and freely uses them in acronyms (e.g. *CUF* [kuf] *Companhia União Fabril* compared to BP *PUC* ['puki] *Pontifícia Universidade Católica*); large numbers of clusters and syllable-final consonants result from the effacement of European Portuguese atonic [ə].

The consonant system, displayed in table 11.4, is less complex. As in Spanish the contrast between the two 'r' phonemes is neutralised in all except intervocalic position. Elsewhere, /ʀ/ is always found in syllable-initial position; in many Brazilian Portuguese accents /ʀ/ also fills syllable-final positions, invariably filled by /r/ in European Portuguese. This is closely connected to the phonetic realisations of /ʀ/. In European Portuguese /ʀ/ is a strong uvular or postalveolar trill, its distribution following a well known

Table 11.4: Portuguese Consonants

	Bilabial (and Labio-dental)	Dental	Palatal (Palato-alveolar)	Velar	Uvular
Plosives	p	t		k	
	b	d		g	
Fricatives	f	s	ʃ		
	v	z	ʒ		
Nasals	m	n	ɲ		
Laterals		l	ʎ		
Vibrants		r [ɾ]			ʀ
Semi-vowels	(w)		(j)		

Hispanic pattern of strengthening of sonorants in 'strong' syllabic contexts; in Brazilian Portuguese /ʀ/ is realised as a fricative or frictionless continuant, the range of phonetic variants including [h x χ ʁ], and thus occupies the 'weak' syllable-final contexts originally filled by /r/. In both languages syllable-final r is subject to further weakening; EP /r/ may be an approximant [ɹ], while BP /ʀ/ is frequently effaced.

The sibilants /s z ʃ ʒ/ are only in contrast intervocalically (inside the word) and word-initially (where /ʃ/ derives mainly from palatalised plosive + lateral clusters, e.g. chama 'flame' < FLAMMA, chuva 'rain' < PLUVIA); elsewhere they are subject to complex distributional (or morphophonemic) rules. Before a voiceless consonant or pause, only /ʃ/ (EP) or /s/ (BP) is found; before a voiced consonant only /ʒ/ (EP) or /z/ (BP); before a word-initial vowel only /z/ (EP and BP). Northern dialects of European Portuguese retain an apico-alveolar series of fricatives (the 's beirão') which was originally distinct from the dental and palato-alveolar series. In all except the most northerly dialects this three-way contrast has been reduced to a binary contrast, between dentals and palato-alveolars in the south and between apico-alveolars and palato-alveolars in the centre, together with the loss of the contrast between palato-alveolar affricate [tʃ] and the corresponding fricative [ʃ]. Northern dialects show their affinity to Galician by having no contrast between /b/ and /v/.

In many Brazilian Portuguese accents the dental plosives /t d/ are realised as palato-alveolar affricates [tʃ dʒ] when followed by /i/: o tio Dino vende um lote 'Uncle Dino sells a piece of land' [u tʃiu dʒinu vẽdʒi ũ lɔtʃi].

The semi-vowels /j w/ are marginal phonemes. In most cases [j w] result from the semi-vocalisation of atonic /i u/ in hiatus: diário ['djarju] (=[di'ariu]) 'daily', suar 'to sweat' [swar] (=[su'ar]), except for a few borrowings (e.g. iate 'yacht' ['jatə]) and /kw gw/ (in quando 'when' ['kwẽdu], guarda 'policeman' ['gwardɐ]) which are perhaps best analysed as labialised velars /kʷ gʷ/.

3   Morphology

The basic morphological structure of Portuguese simple verb forms is stem + tense/aspect/mood + person/number. For the present, imperfect and pluperfect indicatives, and the future subjunctive and (regular) imperfect subjunctive, the stem is made up of the root and the theme (conjugation class) vowel (first conjugation /a/; second /e/; third /i/ subject to some morphophonemic variation); the present subjunctive has the same structure with mood indicated by reversed theme vowels (first conjugation /e/, second/ third /a/); the remaining tenses employ special stem forms (basic stem + r for the future group; suppletive stem forms for irregular preterits) and idiosyncratic person-number morphs. (It is possible, but not always plausible, to devise abstract underlying forms of a uniform morphological structure for all synthetic forms). There is a nucleus of irregular verbs resisting easy incorporation in any conjugation; ser 'to be', ir 'to go', which incorporate forms from more than one Vulgar Latin verb, and ter 'to have', vir 'to come', pôr 'to put', (OPtg. têer < TENERE, vĩir < VENIRE, põer, poer < PONERE) which incorporate nasal root vowels with a variety of realisations. Regular and irregular paradigms of the types described are displayed in the chart of verb forms, tentatively segmented.

Alongside the synthetic past tenses (imperfect, preterit, pluperfect) there exists a series of analytic forms, made up of the auxiliary ter and the past participle: perfect, pluperfect and future perfect tenses (indicative and subjunctive) are formed using the present, imperfect and future tense forms of ter. (Ter has replaced haver (< HABERE) not only as auxiliary but also as the verb of possession; in Brazilian Portuguese even the existential há 'there is', havia 'there was', etc. has been taken over by forms of ter: tem (present), tinha (imperfect).) Only in the pluperfect are the synthetic and analytic forms equivalent (though the former is rarely used in colloquial registers). The (synthetic) preterit is aspectually complex. It is a non-durative past tense, in opposition to the durative imperfect; it can also have the value of a present perfect (o que se passa? — perdi a caneta 'what's the matter? — I've lost my pen') because the (analytic) perfect tense represents only continued or repeated action in the near past (tenho tomado banho todos os dias 'I've been bathing every day'). The perfect subjunctive, however, is a genuine present perfect: não é possível que ele tenha feito isso, 'he cannot have done that' (lit. 'it is not possible that he has done that'). The perfect and pluperfect subjunctives have no synthetic form. There is a wide range of periphrastic verbal expressions (which traditional grammar does not clearly distinguish from verb complementation structures) expressing temporal, modal and aspectual values: estar + -ndo (present participle) (progressive); ir + infinitive (future); haver de + infinitive (predictive/ obligative); ter que + infinitive (obligative); ficar + present participle (resultative). In European Portuguese the constructions with the present

Portuguese Verb Forms

Regular verbs

	falar 'speak'		*meter 'put'*		*partir 'depart'*	
Present indicative	fal-o (a+u)	fala-mos	met-o (e+u)	mete-mos	part-o (i+u)	parti-mos
	fala-s	(fala-is)	mete-s	(mete-is)	parte-s	(partís (i+i))
	fala	fala-m	mete	mete-m	parte	parte-m
Imperfect indicative	fala-va	falá-vamos	meti-a	metí-amos	parti-a	partí-amos
	fala-vas	etc.	meti-as	etc.	parti-as	etc.
Pluperfect indicative	fala-ra	falá-ramos	mete-ra	meté-ramos	parti-ra	partí-ramos
	fala-ras	etc.	mete-ras	etc.	parti-ras	etc.
Imperfect subjunctive	fala-sse etc.	falá-ssemos	mete-sse etc.	metê-ssemos	parti-sse etc.	partí-ssemos
Present subjunctive	fal-e (a+e)	fal-emos	met-a (e+a)	met-amos	part-a (i+a)	part-amos
	fal-es	(fal-eis)	met-as	(met-ais)	part-as	(part-ais)
	fal-e	fal-em	met-a	met-am	part-a	part-am
Future subjunctive	fala-r	fala-rmos	mete-r	mete-rmos	parti-r	parti-rmos
	fala-res	(fala-rdes)	mete-res	(mete-rdes)	parti-res	(parti-rdes)
	fala-r	fala-rem	mete-r	mete-rem	parti-r	parti-rem
Infinitive	falar	falar-mos	meter	meter-mos	partir	partir-mos
	falar-es	(falar-des)	meter-es	(meter-des)	partir-es	(partir-des)
	falar	falar-em	meter	meter-em	partir	partir-em
Future	falar-ei	falar-emos	meter-ei	meter-emos	partir-ei	partir-emos
	falar-ás	(falar-ais)	etc.	etc.	etc.	
	falar-á	falar-ão	etc.	etc.	etc.	
Conditional	falar-ia	falar-íamos	etc.	etc.	etc.	
Present participle	fala-ndo		mete-ndo		parti-ndo	
Past participle	fala-do		meti-do		parti-do	
Preterit (regular)	falei (a+i)	fala-mos	meti (e+i)	mete-mos	parti (i+i)	parti-mos
	fala-ste	(fala-stes)	mete-ste	(mete-stes)	parti-ste	(parti-stes)
	falou (a+u)	fala-ram	mete-u	mete-ram	parti-u	parti-ram

Irregular verbs

	estar 'be'		*dizer 'say'*		*poder 'be able'*	
Preterit	estive	estive-mos	disse	disse-mos	pude	pude-mos
	estive-ste	(estive-stes)	disse-ste	(disse-stes)	pude-ste	(pude-stes)
	esteve	estive-ram	disse	disse-ram	pôde	pude-ram
Pluperfect	estive-ra	estivé-ramos	disse-ra	dissé-ramos	pude-ra	pudé-ramos
Future subjunctive	estive-r etc.	estive-rmos	disse-r etc.	disse-rmos	pude-r etc.	pude-rmos
Imperfect subjunctive	estive-sse etc.	estivé-ssemos	disse-sse etc.	dissé-ssemos	pude-sse etc.	pudé-ssemos

participle are interchangeable with constructions with *a* + infinitive.

The future and conditional still retain a mark of their origin in analytic forms incorporating the auxiliary *(h)aver*; clitic pronouns are mesoclitic — affixed between stem and ending — e.g. *amar-me-á* '(s)he will love me'. (This feature is not found in Brazilian Portuguese, where either the pronoun is proclitic to the whole verb form or an alternative verb form is used.)

Two noteworthy morphological peculiarities of Portuguese are the retention of a future subjunctive form and the appearance of an infinitive inflected for person/number. (In neither is it unique in the Romance sphere: Old Castilian had the former, and Sardinian is reported to have the latter. Only in Portuguese do both appear, with a close link between them.) In regular verbs the forms are identical (though possibly of different structure, cf. the chart of verb forms). In irregular verbs the future subjunctive uses the strong preterit stem, instead of the infinitive stem, betraying its origin in the Latin future perfect indicative (*FABULARINT* > *falarem*: *DIXERINT* > *disserem*). The origin of the personal infinitive is less clear: its form derives from the Latin imperfect subjunctive (*FABULARENT* > *falarem*, *DICERENT* > *dizerem*), but its use (see section 4) is a Galician-Portuguese innovation.

Gender and number are the only two grammatical categories relevant to noun and adjective inflection. Singular number is unmarked; plural is marked by *-s* (morphophonemic /z/ realised as /s z ʃ ʒ/ according to the sibilant system) with a number of consequent stem alternations in roots with final consonants (e.g. *flor – flores* 'flower(s)'; *raiz – raizes* 'root(s)'; *sol – sóis* 'sun(s)'; *pão – pães* 'loaf, loaves'). Nouns are classified by gender as masculine or feminine, grammatical gender usually correlating with natural gender, with a few exceptions, e.g. *cônjuge* (m.) 'spouse'; *criança* (f.) 'child'. Stem-final /u/ usually corresponds to masculine gender, stem-final /a/ to feminine; other endings can correspond to either gender, e.g. *amor* (m.) 'love', *cor* (f.) 'colour'; *rapaz* (m.) 'lad', *paz* (f.) 'peace'; *estudante* (m. and f.) 'student'. Similar patterning is found in adjectives, except that the lack of a gender suffix is more frequently a mark of masculine gender, in opposition to the regular feminine suffix /a/: e.g. *inglês – inglesa* 'English', as it is in animate nouns, e.g. *professor – professora* 'teacher'. (There is a tendency to extend this pattern to nouns ending in *-e*: in popular speech the feminine counterpart of *estudante* is *estudanta*, following the pattern of *monge* (m.) 'monk' – *monja* (f.) 'nun'.)

The determiner system includes definite and indefinite articles (the former identical to weak direct object pronouns (see the chart of pronouns), the latter, *um*, f. *uma* identical in the singular to the numeral *um* '1') and a three-term demonstrative system, *este* 'this' (first person) *esse* 'that' (second person) *aquele* 'that' (third person) parallel to the adverbs *aqui*, 'here', *aí*, 'there', *ali* 'over there'. The indefinite inanimate demonstrative pronouns (*isto, isso, aquilo*) are the nearest thing to a morphological neuter.

The Portuguese pronoun systems are displayed in the chart given here. Modern Portuguese distinguishes weak (clitic) pronouns from strong pronouns: the former are used as verbal objects, the latter as subjects or prepositional objects. The pronoun system has been radically affected by the development of the address system.

Portuguese Pronouns

	Strong Pronouns		Weak Pronouns	
	Subject	Object	Dir. Obj.	Indir. Obj.
1 sg.	eu	mim (OPtg. mi)	me	me
2 sg.	tu	ti	te	te
3 sg.	ele (m.), ela (f.)	ele, ela	o (m.), a (f.)	lhe
(address)	você	você, si		
	o senhor (etc.)	o senhor		
1 pl.	nós	nós	nos	nos
(2 pl.	vós	vós	vos	vos)
3 pl.	eles, elas	eles, elas	os, as	lhes
(address)	vocês	vocês, si		
	os senhores	os senhores		

Portuguese maintains a highly structured system of address forms which has been compared to the honorific systems of oriental languages. Second person plural forms are no longer used except in a religious or highly formal ceremonial context (and accordingly appear in parentheses in the charts of verb forms and pronouns). Second person singular forms are used for familiar address in European Portuguese (and conservative Brazilian Portuguese dialects); otherwise, third person verb forms are used for all address in Brazilian Portuguese, and formal (and plural) address in European Portuguese, with the pronoun *você* or (in EP) the partly pronominal *o senhor* (m.), *a senhora* (f.). In addition, a wide range of titles can be used as address forms e.g. *o pai* 'father', *o senhor doutor* 'Doctor', *a avó* 'grandmother' etc., with third person verb forms. Accordingly, third person object pronouns *o(s)*, *a(s)*, have also acquired second person reference. Brazilian Portuguese has been resistant to this: there is a tendency for *lhe*, exclusively used as an indirect object in European Portuguese, to be used for second person functions. Alternatively, the second person object pronoun *te* is used even where the corresponding subject pronoun and verb forms are missing, or else weak forms are avoided altogether: *eu vi ele* 'I saw him', *eu vi você* 'I saw you'.

4 Syntax

The basic word order of Portuguese simplex sentences is subject–verb–object (SVO): *o gato comeu a galinha* 'the cat ate the hen'.

(All of the features of VO typology identified in the chapter on Spanish — page 254 — are equally applicable to Portuguese.) In the absence of any morphological case marking, word order indicates grammatical subjects and objects, and is little varied. The order VS is very common with intransitive verbs, especially those of temporal or locative content: *chegou o domingo* 'Sunday came'; *apareceu um homem no jardim* 'a man appeared in the garden', reflexives, *libertaram-se os escravos* 'the slaves freed themselves' (or 'the slaves were freed'), and in sentences with heavy subject clauses, *entraram dois homens gordos e um rapaz loiro* 'two fat men and a fair-haired boy came in'. This is closely related to the principle of thematic organisation which specifies that new information is placed at the end of sentences for maximum prominence. Noun phrases may be dislocated for the purposes of topicalisation: *comeu a galinha, o gato* (VOS), though objects cannot be preposed without a pronoun copy (cf. the discussion in the chapters on French and Rumanian, pages 229–30 and 315): *a galinha, o gato comeu-a* (OSVPron), *a galinha, comeu-a o gato* (OVPronS). Topicalisation is more usually by varieties of cleft or pseudo-cleft constructions: *foi a galinha que o gato comeu, foi o gato que comeu a galinha* (clefting); *o que comeu a galinha foi o gato*; *o que o gato comeu foi a galinha* (normal pseudo-cleft); *o gato comeu foi a galinha* (elliptical pseudo-cleft) including the emphatic use of *é que: o gato é que comeu a galinha*.

Word order changes are not greatly used for other grammatical functions. Interrogation is by intonation (*o seu pai está aqui?* lit. 'your father is here?'), by tag question (*o seu pai está aqui, não é?* 'your father is here isn't he?'), or by means of *é que: é que o seu pai está aqui?* lit. 'is it (true) that your father is here?'. In non-polar questions inversion is the rule after non-pronominal interrogatives: *quando morreu o seu pai?* lit. 'when died your father', *onde mora você?* 'where live you?' (the same order being possible in non-interrogative subordinate clauses: *quando morreu o seu pai, o que é que você fez?* 'when your father died, what did you do?'); normal SVO order can still be preserved by use of the *é que* periphrasis: *quando é que o seu pai morreu?* As the interrogative pronouns *quem* 'who(m)', *o que* 'what' have no case marking, inversion is avoided and the *é que* form used in object interrogation: *o que (é que) matou a galinha?* 'what killed the hen?', *o que é que o gato matou?* 'what did the cat kill?'. Replies to yes-no questions take the form of an echo of the main verb: *(você) tem lume? — tenho (sim) / não tenho*, 'do you have a light?' – '(yes) I have' / no I have not' (the appropriate response to an *é que* question being *é* or *não é*.)

The principal means of negation is the negative particle *não* inserted before the verb (or the auxiliary, in the case of an analytic form). Multiple negation occurs with additional negative elements following the verb: when they precede it, *não* is not inserted: *não veio ninguem = ninguem veio* 'nobody came'; *não fiz nada = nada fiz* 'I did nothing'. The indefinite *algum* 'some' may be used as an emphatic negative; *não vi nenhum homem* 'I didn't see any man', *não vi homem algum* 'I didn't see any man whatsoever'. (*Nada* is rarely used as a subject, and may be used as an adverb *não gostei nada da comida* 'I didn't like the meal at all'.)

Aspectual contrasts are behind the distinction between the copular and auxiliary verbs *ser* and *estar* (see the chapter on Spanish, pages 251–2). *Ser* (< *ESSERE/SEDERE*) is used in non-progressive (stative) expressions and *estar* (< *STARE*) in progressive expressions (including its use as the auxiliary for progressive verb forms). In the majority of cases the aspectual value is expressed by (or inherent in) the context, so that the choice of verb is conditioned rather than contrastive: *o João é bombeiro* 'João is (**ser**) a fireman', *o Pedro está zangado* 'Pedro is (**estar**) angry'; *o João é um desempregado* 'João is (permanently) unemployed', *o Pedro está desempregado* 'Pedro is unemployed'; *o João é esquisito* 'João is an awkward person', *o Pedro está (sendo) esquisito (hoje)* 'Pedro is (being) awkward (today)'. For expressing location, the aspectually neutral verb *ficar* is more often used: *onde fica o Turismo?* 'where is the Tourist Office?'.

Ser functions as auxiliary for the passive construction: *a casa foi construída por J. Pimenta*, 'the house was built by J. Pimenta'. There is a good case for analysing the passive as a copula + adjective (passive participle) construction. The alternative copula can be used to form passives, *a casa está cercada por soldados* 'the house is surrounded by soldiers'. Where verbs have two forms of the past participle, e.g. *prendido*, *preso* from the verb *prender* 'to arrest', the strong form is usually used as passive participle and the weak form as an active participle. Frequently used alternatives to the passive are the reflexive passive (common in the Romance languages), *aqui alugam-se quartos* 'rooms are let here', and the impersonal construction using *se* as marker of an indefinite subject, with third person singular verb forms, *aluga-se quartos aqui* (cf. the discussion in the chapter on Spanish, page 256).

The extensive set of verb forms outlined in section 3 is rarely utilised in spoken forms of Portuguese. The present indicative is used in place of the future (*se tiver tempo, falo com você* 'if I have time I (will) talk with you'). The imperfect indicative replaces the conditional both in temporal and modal functions: *eu disse que vinha* ...'I said I would come', *eu queria perguntar*...'I would like (lit. 'wanted') to ask...'.

As in Spanish, the subjunctive mood occupies a less central position, especially in spoken registers. Its use is determined by a complex of grammatical and semantic factors, so that any attempt to define its 'meaning' must come to terms with the fact that it is rarely independently meaningful. The subjunctive is used to the exclusion of the indicative in a wide range of subordinate clauses: *se ele viesse, não o cumprimentaria* 'if he came, I would not greet him', *que os meninos bebam vodka não me aflige* 'I'm not worried about the children drinking vodka', *chamei para que ela me ajudasse* 'I called for her to help me', *grito sem que me ouçam* 'I shout without them hearing me'. The indicative only appears in subordinate clauses expressing real events: the subjunctive has thus been characterised negatively as the mood of suspension of reality. Only in a few rather recondite cases, however, does the context permit a contrast of indicative and subjunctive, so that the subjunctive form can carry all the connotations of irreality. Contrasts like *gritei de maneira que me ouviram* 'I shouted so that they heard me' vs. *gritei de maneira que me ouvissem* 'I shouted so that they should hear me' are not the stuff of normal colloquial speech. In spoken Portuguese the present subjunctive is frequently replaced by the indicative.

The most vital subjunctive form is the one whose use is most restricted, namely the future subjunctive. It is used in temporal or conditional clauses with future reference (not necessarily expressed by a main verb in the future tense): *quando vier o pai, teremos comida* (future)/ *avisa-me* (imperative)/ *vou-me embora* (present), 'when Father comes we will have some food/tell me/I'll go away'. In some registers it is the only non-past verb form used with *se* and *quando*.

One of the main functions of the personal infinitive is to circumvent problems of mood. Being a verb form marked only for person/number it is used where contrasts of tense and mood are (or can be) neutralised, but where the non-identity of the subjects of the main and subordinate clauses would otherwise require a finite verb form (and the selection of an appropriate tense/mood). Many of the preceding examples can be recast using the personal infinitive: *não me aflige os meninos beberem vodka*; *chamei para vires*; *grito sem me ouvirem*; *gritei de maneira de eles me ouvirem*. The usage of the personal infinitive (vis-à-vis the plain infinitive) cannot be precisely defined because of a tendency to use personal and impersonal infinitives indiscriminately with overt subjects, following the widespread belief that extensive use of the personal infinitive is a mark of good style. (The fact that in the first and third persons singular the forms are identical is an additional problem for description.)

Subject pronouns are duplicated by verb inflection (except in basilectal Brazilian Portuguese where there is a tendency for verbs to be invariable) and are frequently omitted, especially in the unambiguous first and second person forms. Third person forms are more ambiguous. The use of third person grammatical forms as the main form of address restricts the omission of pronouns to clear cases of anaphora or address. Otherwise, subjectless third person verbs are interpeted as having indefinite subjects *é horrível* 'it is terrible', *dizem que é proibido* 'they (people) say that it is forbidden'.

Weak object pronouns are usually enclitic to the verb in European Portuguese and proclitic in Brazilian Portuguese: *o pai deu-me um bolo* (EP), *o pai me deu um bolo* (BP) 'Father gave me a cake'. In written Brazilian Portuguese, as in European Portuguese, sentence-initial clitics are excluded, but this does not hold for spoken Brazilian Portuguese. In both varieties the clitic will invariably precede the verb if any item except a lexical subject noun phrase precedes; negatives, subordinating conjunctions, notably *que*, relative pronouns, interrogative pronouns and (in literary language) preposed adverbs all trigger clitic attraction, e.g. *não me deu o bolo* 'he did not give me the cake', *se me der o bolo* 'if he gives (fut. subj.) me the cake', *quero que me dê o bolo* 'I want him to give me the cake'.

5 Lexicon

The main body of the Portuguese lexicon is predictably of Latin origin, either by direct transmission through Vulgar Latin or as a result of borrowing at some stage of the language's history. The same Latin etymon can thus surface in several different phonetic and semantic guises: *ARTICULUM* was the source for OPtg. *artelho* 'ankle', modern *artigo* (< *artigoo*) 'article' and *artículo* 'joint'; in the fifteenth century *flor* 'flower' was reborrowed to replace the older *frol* and *chor* (< *FLOREM*).

Portuguese shows a typical Iberian conservatism of vocabulary, preserving Latin terms which French and Italian replaced: *queijo* 'cheese' < *CASEUM* (cf. Castilian *queso*, Rumanian *caş*); *uva* 'grape' (cf. Fr. *fromage*, *raisin*). Portuguese is alone in maintaining unchanged the old Christian denominations of days of the week: after *domingo* 'Sunday', first day of the week, come the weekdays numbered two to six: *segunda-feira* (< *FERIAM SECUNDAM*), *terça-feira*, *quarta-feira*, *quinta-feira*, *sexta-feira* until *sábado* ushers in the weekend. (The weekdays are often reduced to their number, *chegará na quinta* 'he will arrive on Thursday'.)

Portuguese shares the common Romance and Ibero-Romance heritage of pre-Roman Celtic and post-Roman Germanic vocabulary: *barro* 'mud', *veiga* 'plain', *manteiga* 'butter' are Celtic terms shared with Castilian; *guerra* 'war', *guardar* 'guard', *roubar* 'steal', *branco* 'white' are common Germanic items. The Arabic adstrate of the South contributed some 1,000 words to Portuguese, such as *alface* 'lettuce', *arroz* 'rice', *armazém* 'store', *azulejo* 'glazed tile', and many placenames, e.g. *Alfama*, *Algarve*.

The African element is fairly strong in Brazilian Portuguese, particularly in those areas of popular culture and belief with strong African roots: *macumba* 'voodoo ritual', *samba*, *marimba*; *cachimbo* 'pipe' has passed into common European Portuguese usage. Tupi contributes a large vocabulary of Brazilian Portuguese flora and fauna: *maracujá* 'passion-fruit', *piranha* 'piranha fish'. Contacts with the Far East contributed *chá* 'tea' (borrowed from Mandarin: English *tea* is the Min form); *mandarim* 'mandarin' from Malay *mantri* contaminated by Ptg. *mandar* 'to order'.

Portuguese makes extensive use of derivational suffixes. As well as the common stock of noun- and verb-forming suffixes derived and borrowed from Latin (e.g. *-izar* (verb-forming), *-ismo*, *-ista* (noun-forming), *-ção* (< *-TIONEM*) (nominalising)) there is a large stock of productive and semi-productive suffixes with semantic (rather than grammatical) content, frequently involving emotive as well as referential meaning. Prominent among these are diminutive and augmentative suffixes. The most productive diminutives are -*(z)inho* (feminine -*(z)inha*) and -*(z)ito* (-*(z)ita*): *pedra* 'stone', *pedrinha* 'pebble', *pedrazinha* 'small stone'; *casa* 'house', *casita* 'little house'. These diminutives have connotations of endearment or disparagement (according to situational context) which become prominent when they are applied to humans: *mulher* 'woman', *mulherinha* 'scheming woman'; *avó* 'grandmother', *avozinha* '(dear old) granny', and especially when used to modify adverbs or interjections: *adeus* 'goodbye', *adeusinho* 'bye-bye' (familiar), *devagar* 'slowly', *devagarinho* 'little by little'. Augmentative suffixes have strong pejorative overtones: *mulher* 'woman', *mulherona* 'stout woman'.

A further set of suffixes has a very wide range of meanings (including augmentatives, collectives and instrumentals) such that the suffix can only be taken as signalling the morphological link between the derived form and the base, while the precise meaning of the word is an independent lexical unit: the suffix -*ada* is identifiable in *palmada* 'slap' (*palma* 'palm of hand'); *colherada* 'spoonful' (*colher* 'spoon'); *rapaziada* '(gang of) kids' (*rapaz* 'boy'); *marmelada* 'quince conserve' (source of Eng. *marmelade*) from *marmelo* 'quince'; *noitada* 'night out' (*noite* 'night').

In those suffixes with alternative forms incorporating the augment -*z*- (e.g. -*(z)inho*), the unaugmented variant functions as an internal suffix, forming a complex stem which is stressed like simple forms, while the augmented suffix functions as an external suffix, forming compounds in which the base and the suffix both have gender and number markers (the latter being overt only when plural number is realised by stem mutations as well as suffixes, e.g. *pãozinho* 'bread roll', plural *pãezinhos*) and are both stressed. (Similar structure is found in the adverbs formed with -*mente* e.g. *novamente* [nɔvɐ'mẽtə] 'recently, newly' where the suffix is affixed to the feminine form of the adjective *novo* 'new' and the base vowel quality is preserved.) The augmented suffixes thus give a morphological transparency, which is matched by a semantic transparency: forms incorporating internal suffixes are more likely to have unpredictably restricted meanings, e.g. *folha* 'leaf, sheet of paper', *folhazinha* 'small leaf', *folhinha* 'calendar'.

Bibliography

Cámara (1972) is a synchronic and diachronic description by the principal Brazilian linguist. Among reference grammars, Cuesta and Luz (1971) Cunha and Cintra (1984) and Teyssier (1984) are reliable, the latter two with greater coverage of Brazilian Portuguese, while Mateus et al. (1983) is a modern linguistic account, mainly concerned with syntax. For phonology, Viana (1973) contains the collected articles of the great nineteenth-century phonetician, including the standard descriptions of European Portuguese; Mateus (1982) is the first and most complete generative phonological study of European Portuguese, though needing some revision to modify the excesses of abstract morphophonemics. Thomas (1969) is a thorough study of differences between written and spoken varieties of Brazilian Portuguese.

Teyssier (1982) is a concise history of the language.

References

Câmara, J. Mattoso. 1972. *The Portuguese Language*, translated by A.J. Naro. (University of Chicago Press, Chicago)

Cuesta, P. Vázquez and M. Luz. 1971. *Gramática portuguesa*, 3rd ed., 2 vols. (Gredos, Madrid)

Cunha, C.F. and Cintra L.F.L. 1984. *Nova gramática do português contemporâneo* (João Sá da Costa, Lisbon)

Mateus, M.H.M. 1982. *Aspectos da fonologia portuguesa*, 2nd ed. (INIC, Lisbon)

—— et al. 1983. *Gramática da língua portuguesa* (Almedina, Coimbra)

Teyssier, P. 1984. *Manuel de langue portugaise (Portugal-Brésil)*, 2nd ed. (Klincksieck, Paris)

—— 1982. *História da língua portuguesa* (Sá da Costa, Lisbon)

Thomas, E.W. 1969. *The Syntax of Spoken Brazilian Portuguese* (Vanderbilt University Press, Nashville)

Viana, A.R. Gonçalves. 1973. *Estudos de fonética portuguesa* (Imprensa Nacional, Lisbon)

12 Italian

Nigel Vincent

1 Introduction

'Italy', in the words of Count Metternich, 'is a geographical expression'. He might with equal truth have added that Italian is a linguistic expression. While there is now, almost a century and a quarter after political unification, a fair measure of agreement on the grammar and the morphology and, to a lesser extent, on the phonology and lexis of the standard language as used in the written and spoken media and as taught in schools and to foreigners, it is still far from being the case that Italians speak only, or in many instances even principally, Italian. It is appropriate, therefore, to begin this chapter with a general survey in two dimensions, historical and geographical.

Historically, Italian is clearly one of the modern-day descendants of Latin, but the line of descent is not altogether direct. With the dismemberment of the Roman Empire, the spoken Latin of everyday usage — what has come to be called Vulgar Latin — gradually split into a series of regional vernaculars, whose boundaries are identifiable by bundles of isoglosses in a linguistic atlas. The most important of these, which separates Western (French, Spanish, Portuguese etc.) from Eastern (Italian, Rumanian etc.) Romance, cuts right across peninsular Italy to form the so-called La Spezia-Rimini line. Dialects to the north of the line are divisible in turn into Gallo-Italian (Piedmontese, Ligurian, Lombard and Emilian) and Venetian, with the latter sharing some of the properties of other northern dialects and some of the properties of Tuscan. Typical northern traits include the loss of final vowels (*pan* vs. st. It. *pane* < Lat. *PANEM* 'bread'), often with devoicing of the resultant final obstruents and velarisation of a nasal; lenition or even loss of intervocalic stops (*-ado* or *-ao* vs. *-ato* < *-ATUM* 'past participle suffix'); palatalisation of *-kt-* clusters (*lač* vs. *latte* < *LACTEM* 'milk'), and of *Cl*-clusters (*čatsa* vs. *piazza* < *PLATEAM* 'square'); development of front rounded vowels (*čöf* vs. *piove* < *PLUIT* 'it rains'), frequent use of subject pronouns, usually derived from the Latin accusative; loss of the synthetic preterit in favour of the present perfect periphrasis; a two-term deictic system; etc. These dialects, then, are often structurally closer to French and Occitan than to the dialects south of the line. The latter may in turn be further subdivided into Tuscan, Central (Umbrian and the dialects of northern Lazio and the Marches) and Southern dialects (Abruzzese, Neapolitan, Pugliese, Calabrese, Sicilian). Relevant Southern features here are NC > NN (*monno* vs. *mondo* < *MUNDUM* 'world', *piommo* vs. *piombo* < *PLUMBUM* 'lead'); characteristic patterns of both tonic and atonic vowel development; use of postposed possessives (*figliomo* vs. *mio figlio* 'my son'); extensive use of the preterit; etc. A number of features mark off Tuscan from its neighbours: absence of metaphony (umlaut); -V*ri*V- > -V*i*V- (*IANUARIUM* > *gennaio*, cf. *Gennaro*, patron saint of Naples); fricativisation of intervocalic voiceless stops — the so-called *gorgia toscana* 'Tuscan throat' — which yields pronunciations such as [la harta] *la carta* 'the paper', [kaɸo] *kapo* 'head', [lo θiro] *lo tiro* 'I pull it'; etc.

Such divisions reflect both geographical and administrative boundaries. The La Spezia-Rimini line corresponds very closely both to the Appennine mountains and to the southern limit of the Archbishopric of Milan. The line between Central and Southern dialects approximates to the boundary between the Lombard Kingdom of Italy and the Norman Kingdom of Sicily, and to a point where the Appennines broaden out to form a kind of mountain barrier between the two parts of the peninsula. The earliest texts are similarly regional in nature. The first in which undisputed vernacular material occurs is the Placito Capuano of 960, a Latin document reporting the legal proceedings relating to the ownership of a piece of land, in the middle of which an oath sworn by the witnesses is recorded verbatim: *sao ko kelle terre, per kelle fini que ki contene, trenta anni le possette parte Sancti Benedicti* 'I know that those lands, within those boundaries which are here stated, thirty years the party of Saint Benedict owned them'. The textual evidence gradually increases, and by the thirteenth century it is clear that there are well-rooted literary traditions in a number of centres up and down the land. These are touched on briefly by the Florentine Dante (1265–1321) in a celebrated section of this treatise *De Vulgari Eloquentia*, but it is the poetic supremacy of his Divine Comedy, rapidly followed in the same city by the achievements of Petrarch (1304–74) and Boccaccio (1313–75), which ensured that literary, and thus linguistic, pre-eminence should go to Tuscan.

There ensued a centuries-long debate about the language of literature — *la questione della lingua* 'the language question', with Tuscan being kept in the forefront as a result of the theoretical writings of the influential Venetian (!) Pietro Bembo (1470–1547), especially his *Prose della volgar lingua* (1525). His ideas were adopted by the members of the Accademia della Crusca, founded in Florence in 1582–3, which produced its first dictionary in 1612 and which still survives as a centre for research into the Italian language. Meanwhile, although the affairs of day-to-day existence were largely conducted in dialect, the sociopolitical dimension of the question increased in importance in the eighteenth and nineteenth centuries, assuming a particular urgency after unification in 1861. The new government appointed the author Alessandro Manzoni (1785–1873) — himself born in Milan but yet another enthusiastic non-native advocate of Florentine usage — to head a commission, which in due course recommended Florentine as the linguistic standard to be adopted in the new national school system. This suggestion was not without its critics, notably the great Italian comparative philologist, Graziadio Ascoli (1829–1907), and a number of the specific recommendations were hopelessly impractical, but in any case the core of literary usage was so thoroughly Tuscan that the language taught in schools was bound to be similar. Education was, of course, crucial since the history of standardisation is essentially the history of increased literacy. On the most conservative estimate only 2½ per cent of the population would have been literate in any meaningful sense of the word in 1861, although a more recent and more generous estimate would go as high as 12½ per cent. The figure had increased to about 91½ per cent by 1961, the centenary of unification and the thousandth anniversary of the first text. Even so, there is no guarantee that those who can use Italian do so as their normal daily means of communication, and it was only in 1982 that opinion polls recorded a figure of more than 50 per cent of those interviewed claiming that their first language was the standard rather than a dialect. Yet the opposition language/dialect greatly oversimplifies matters. For most speakers it is a question of ranging themselves at some point of a continuum from standard Italian through regional Italian and regional dialect to the local dialect, as circumstances and other participants seem to warrant. Note too that the term dialect means something rather different when used of the more or less homogeneous means of spoken communication in an isolated rural community and when used to refer to something such as Milanese or Venetian, both of which have fully-fledged literary and administrative traditions of their own, and hence a good deal of internal social stratification.

Another significant factor in promoting a national language was conscription, first because it brought together people from different regions, and second because the army is statutorily required to provide education equivalent to three years of primary school to anyone who enters the service illiterate. Indeed, it is out of the analysis of letters written by soldiers in the First World War that some scholars have been led to recognise *italiano popolare* 'popular Italian' as a kind of national substandard, a language which is neither the literary norm nor yet a dialect tied to a particular town or region. Among the features which characterise it are: the extension of *gli* 'to him' to replace *le* 'to her' and *loro* 'to them', and, relatedly, of *suo* 'his/her' to include 'their'; a reduction in the use of the subjunctive in complement clauses, where it is replaced by the indicative, and in conditional apodoses, where the imperfect subjunctive is replaced by the conditional, and the pluperfect subjunctive is replaced by either the conditional perfect or the imperfect indicative (thus standard *se fosse venuto, mi avrebbe aiutato* ('if he had come he would have helped me') becomes either *se sarebbe venuto, mi avrebbe aiutato* or *se veniva, mi aiutava*, the latter having an imperfect indicative in the protasis too; the use of *che* 'that' as a general marker of subordination; plural instead of singular verbs after nouns like *la gente* 'people'. Some of these uses — e.g. *gli* for *loro*, the reduction in the use of the subjunctive and the use of the imperfect in irrealis conditionals — have also begun to penetrate upwards into educated colloquial usage, and it is likely that the media, another powerful force for linguistic unification, will spread other emergent patterns in due course. Industrialisation, too, has had its effect in redrawing the linguistic boundaries, both social and geographical.

In addition to the standard language, the dialects and the claimed existence of *italiano popolare*, there are no less than eleven other languages spoken within the peninsula and having, according to one recent but probably rather high estimate, a total of nearly 2¾ million speakers. Of these, more than two million represent speakers of other Romance languages: Catalan, French, Friulian, Ladin, Occitan and Sardinian. The remaining languages are: Albanian, German, Greek, Serbo-Croat and Slovene. Amidst this heterogeneity, the Italian national and regional constitutions recognise the rights of four linguistic minorities: French speakers in the autonomous region of the Valle d'Aosta (approx. 75,000), German speakers in the province of Bolzano (approx. 225,000), Slovenian speakers in the provinces of Trieste and Gorizia (approx. 100,000), Ladin speakers in the province of Bolzano (approx. 30,000). Yet French (and Occitan — approx. 200,000) and German speakers outside the stated areas are not protected in the same way. Nor paradoxically are the ½ million speakers of Friulian, very closely related to Ladin, the two in turn being sub-branches of the Rhaeto-Romance group. The recognised linguistic minorities are, not surprisingly, in areas where the borders of the Italian state(s) have oscillated historically. In contrast, the southern part of the peninsula is peppered with individual villages which preserve linguistically the traces of that region's turbulent past. It is here that we find Italy's 100,000 Albanian, 20,000 Greek and 3,500 Serbo-Croat speakers, as well as a number of communities whose northern dialects reflect the presence of mediaeval settlers and mercenaries.

Sardinia too contains a few Ligurian-speaking villages and 15,000 Catalan speakers in the port of Alghero as evidence of former colonisation. More importantly, the island has almost 1,000,000 speakers of Sardinian, a separate Romance language which has suffered undue neglect ever since Dante said of the inhabitants that they imitated Latin *tanquam simie homines* 'as monkeys do men'. What he was referring to was the way in which Sardinian, both in structure and vocabulary, reveals itself to be the most conservative of the Romance vernaculars. Thus, we find a vowel system with no mergers apart from the loss of Latin phonemic vowel length;

an absence of palatalisation of *k* and *g*; preservation of final *s* (with important morphological consequences); a definite article *su*, *sa*, etc. which derives from Latin IPSE rather than ILLE. Old Sardinian also maintained direct reflexes of the Latin pluperfect indicative and imperfect subjunctive, and the language is one of the few not to retain a future periphrasis from Latin infinitive + *HABEO*, using instead of reflex of Latin *DEBERE* 'to have to', e.g. *des essere* 'you will be'. On the lexical side we have *petere* 'to ask', *imbennere* 'to find' (cf. Lat. *INVENIRE*), *domo/domu* 'house', *albu* 'white', etc. (contrast It. *chiedere*, *trovare*, *casa*, *bianco*).

The presence of Italian outside the boundaries of the modern Italian state is due to two rather different types of circumstance. First, it may be spoken in areas either geographically continuous with or at some time part of Italy, as in the independent Republic of San Marino (population 13,000), enclosed within the region of Emilia-Romagna, and in Canton Ticino (population approx. 250,000), the entirely italophone part of Switzerland. Both have local dialects, Romagnolo in San Marino and Lombard in Ticino, as well as the standard language of education and administration. Elsewhere, the historical continuity is reflected at the level of dialect, but with the superimposition of a different standard language. Thus, in Corsica (population approx. 200,000) the dialects are either Tuscan (following partial colonisation from Pisa in the eleventh century) or Sardinian in type, but the official language has since 1769 been French. The same situation obtains for those Italian dialects spoken in the areas of Istria and Dalmatia now part of the state of Yugoslavia.

The second circumstance arises when Italian, or more often Italian dialects, has been carried overseas, mainly to the New World. In the USA the 3.9 million Italian speakers constitute the second largest linguistic minority (after Hispano-Americans). They are concentrated for the most part either in New York, where they are mainly of southern origin and where a kind of southern Italian dialectal koine has emerged, and in the San Francisco Bay area, where northern and central Italians predominate, and where the peninsular standard has had more influence. Italian language media include a number of newspapers, radio stations and television programmes. The current signs of a reawakening of interest in their linguistic heritage amongst Italo-Americans are paralleled in Canada and Australia, each with about half a million Italian speakers according to official figures. There were also in excess of three million emigrés to South America, mostly to Argentina, and this has led, on the River Plate, to the development of a contact language with Spanish known as 'cocoliche'. If Italian in the Americas and Australia had its origins in the language of an underprivileged and often uneducated immigrant class, in Africa — specifically Ethiopia and Somalia and until recently Libya — Italian survives as a typical relic of a colonial situation. Ethiopia also has the only documented instance of an Italian-based pidgin, used not only between

Europeans and local inhabitants but also between speakers of mutually unintelligible indigenous languages. The position of Italian in Malta is similarly due to penetration at a higher rather than a lower social level. Research is only now beginning into the linguistic consequences of the post-war migration of, again mainly southern, Italian labour as 'Gastarbeiter' in Switzerland and West Germany. Finally, two curiosities are the discovery by a group of Italian ethnomusicologists in 1973 in the village of Štivor in northern Bosnia of a community of 470 speakers of a dialect from the northern Italian province of Trento, and the case of a group of emigrés from two coastal villages near Bari in Puglia, who settled in Kerch in the Crimea in the 1860s and whose dialectophone descendants have only died out in the last decade.

2 Phonology

One of the consequences of the chequered and fragmented linguistic and political history outlined in the previous section is that at the phonetic and phonological level there has been even less uniformity of usage than at other levels. The conventional starting point for any treatment of Italian phonology is the speech of educated Florentines. Incidentally, most of the letters of the Italian alphabet correspond closely to the IPA value of that symbol, but the following exceptions should be noted: -gl- = /ʎ/, -gn- = /ɲ/, sc(i) = /ʃ/, s = /s/ or /z/ (see below on the status of /z/), z = /ts/ or /dz/, c, g = /k, g/ before a, o and u, and /tʃ, dʒ/ before i and e. The digraphs ch, gh represent /k, g/ before i, e, and ci, gi represent /tʃ, dʒ/ before a, o and u. No orthographic distinction is made between /e/ and /ɛ/ or between /o/ and /ɔ/, although in stressed final position /e/ is represented normally by é and /ɛ/ by è. Stress is marked only when final, usually by a grave accent (except on /e/); other accent marks used in this chapter are for linguistic explicitness and are not part of the orthography.

Table 12.1 sets out the consonant phonemes usually recognised in the Florentine system. Some comments on points of detail are in order. First, note that for the vast majority of speakers [s] and [z] do not contrast: in initial position before a vowel all speakers have [s], including after an internal boundary as in ri[s]aputo 'well known' — cf. [s]aputo 'known'; [s]taccato[s]i 'having detached oneself' — cf. [s]taccare 'to detach' and [s]i '3rd pers. refl. pron.'. Preconsonantally the sibilant takes on the value for voicing of the following segment. Intervocalically, when no boundary is present, northern speakers have only [z] and southern speakers only [s]. However, in parts of Tuscany, including Florence, it is possible to find minimal pairs: chie[s]e 'he asked' vs. chie[z]e 'churches'; fu[s]o 'spindle' vs. fu[z]o 'melted'. The opposition between /ts/ and /dz/ is also somewhat shaky. In initial position, although both are found in standard pronunciation — /ts/ in zio 'uncle', zucchero 'sugar', and /dz/ in zona 'zone', zero 'zero', there is

Table 12.1: Italian Consonant Phonemes

	Bilabial	Labio-dental	Dental	Alveolar	Palato-alveolar	Palatal	Velar
Stop	p b		t d				k g
Affricate				ts dz	tʃ dʒ		
Fricative		f v		s (z)	ʃ		
Nasal	m			n		ɲ	
Lateral				l		ʎ	
Trill				r			

an increasing tendency due to northern influence for /dz/ to be used in all words. Medially, the two sounds continue to exist side by side, and a few genuine minimal pairs can be found, e.g. *ra*[tts]*a* 'race' vs. *ra*[ddz]*a* 'ray fish'. /ts, dz/ share with /ʃ, ʎ, ɲ/ the property of always occurring long intervocalically, an environment in which for all other consonants there is an opposition between short and long (or single and double): e.g. *copia* 'copy' vs. *coppia* 'couple'; *beve* 'he drinks' vs. *bevve* 'he drank'; *grato* 'grateful' vs. *gratto* 'I scratch'; *vano* 'vain' vs. *vanno* 'they go'; *serata* 'evening' vs. *serrata* 'lock-out'; etc.

The vowel system is displayed in table 12.2. /i, u/ have allophones [j, w] in non-nuclear position in the syllable: *più* ['pju] 'more', *può* ['pwɔ] 'he can'.

Table 12.2: The Vowels of Italian

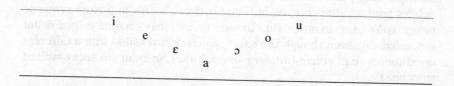

The oppositions /e~ɛ/ and /o~ɔ/ are neutralised outside stress, but even allowing for this their status is problematic, since, although most speakers have the four sounds, the lexical classes and phonological rules which govern their distribution vary widely.

Another important type of neutralisation in Italian phonology is that which affects nasals before consonants and ensures that the whole cluster is homorganic. This is only reflected orthographically in the case of bilabials — hence *campo* 'field', *impossibile* 'impossible' etc., but labio-dentals, dentals etc. are always spelt *n*C: *inferno* [iɱfɛrno] 'hell', *indocile* [iɳdɔtʃile] 'unmanageable', *incauto* [iŋkauto] 'incautious'. The same process also operates across word boundaries in a fully productive manner: *con Paolo* 'with Paul' [..mp..] vs. *con Carlo* 'with Charles' [. .ŋk. .], etc. A morphophonemic process of more limited applicability is the synchronic residue of Romance palatalisation, which is revealed in alternations such as *amico* 'friend (m. sg.)' with $c = [k]$ and *amici* 'friends (m. pl.)' with $c = [tʃ]$, and *vin*[k]*o* 'I win' but *vin*[tʃ]*i* 'you win'. Note that the *e* which marks feminine plural (< Latin *AE*) does not trigger this process nor does plural -*i* in most nouns, and hence the spellings *amiche* 'friends (f.)', *buchi* 'holes'. *e* as a thematic vowel (see p. 289), a direct reflex of the Latin thematic *e*, does; thus *vincere* 'to win', *vince* 'he wins', *vinceva* 'he was winning', all with [tʃ]. The same patterning is also found with the voiced congeners of [k, tʃ], namely [g, dʒ], in the paradigm of a verb such as *volgere* 'to turn'. A further synchronic residue is observable in what are traditionally called *dittonghi mobili* 'mobile diphthongs', as in *buono* 'good' but *bontà* 'goodness', *viene* 'he comes' but *venire* 'to come'. They are the result of a historical process causing the diphthongisation of Latin *Ĕ, Ŏ* in stressed, open syllables. The pattern is, however, being gradually eroded away by analogical generalisations in both directions, e.g. *suono* 'I play' had a past participle *sonato* but one now more commonly finds *suonato*, whereas *provo* 'I try' has replaced an earlier *pruovo*.

Italian words may consist of one or more syllables and are subject to a general constraint that they be vowel-final. Exceptions to this are certain loanwords (*sport, boom, slip, camion* etc.), a handful of Latinisms (*lapis* 'pencil', *ribes* 'blackcurrant') and an increasing number of acronyms (*Agip, Fiat*). Some grammatical words — e.g. the masculine singular of the definite article *il*, the prepositions *in, con, per*, the negative particle *non* — have final consonants, but the rules of the syntax will never allow them to appear in sentence-final position. Similarly, there is a vowel truncation rule which deletes final /e/ after /l, r, n/, but only between words in a close syntactic nexus: *volere dire* 'to mean' (lit. 'to want to say') may become *voler dire* but not *volere dir*, even though the latter sequence is possible with a different constituency, e.g. *volere (dir bene di qualcuno)* 'to want (to speak well of someone)'.

Words may begin with either a consonant or a vowel. A word-initial single consonant may be any of those given in table 12.1, though initial /ɲ/ is rare (*gnomo* 'gnome', *gnocco* 'a kind of dumpling' and a few others) and initial /ʎ/ non-existent in lexical words. However, since the form *gli* /ʎi/ occurs both as the masculine plural of the definite article before vowel-initial nouns (*gli amici* 'the friends') and as the masculine singular dative unstressed pronoun (*gli dissi* 'I said to him'), /ʎ/ in utterance-initial position is very common.

Apart from in borrowings and in technical terms, two-member initial clusters are limited to the following types:

(i) /p b t d k g f/ + r
(ii) /p b k g f/ + l
(iii) s + /p b t d k g tʃ dʒ f v l r m n/

(Note that /s/ is realised as [z] before voiced consonants — hence not just [zb] in *sbagliare* 'to make a mistake' or [zdʒ] in *sgelo* 'thaw', but also [zl] in *slitta* 'sledge', [zn] in *snello* 'slim', etc. It should also be noted that purists do not admit [stʃ], but it is regularly heard in words where there is a clear morphemic boundary, e.g. *scentrato* 'off centre'.)

Three-member clusters can only consist of /s/ plus any of the possible two-member clusters under (i) or (ii). A non-final syllable may end in /l, r, s/ or a nasal. Examples of such clusters can be created productively by juxtaposing forms such as *il*, *per*, *bis*, and *in* with a noun or an adjective, although only a subset of the possible clusters generated in this fashion are attested internally in existing lexical items. An intervocalic cluster may also consist of a geminate consonant, with a syllable boundary between the two: *piop-po* 'poplar', *gof-fo* 'clumsy', *cad-de* 'he fell', *bel-lo* 'beautiful'. Indeed, the evidence of syllable division is one of the principal reasons for treating them as geminates rather than long consonants. Note that in such groups, if the first member is a stop or affricate, it is unreleased, hence such transcriptions as [pat-tso] for *pazzo* 'mad', [fat-tʃa] for *faccia* 'face'.

Tautosyllabic vowel sequences all conform to the pattern of a nuclear vowel followed or preceded, or both, by [j] or [w]: *piano* 'flat' [pjano], *sai* [saj] 'you know'. Otherwise, vowel sequences involve a hiatus between two syllables: *teatro* 'theatre', *poeta* 'poet'. We have both in *laurea* 'university degree' ['law-re-a].

Primary or lexical stress is not predictable on phonological grounds alone, hence such minimal pairs as *princìpi* (plural of *princìpio* 'principle') and *prìncipi* (plural of *prìncipe* 'prince'), or *càpito* 'I turn up', *capìto* 'understood', *capitò* 'he turned up'. There are, however, a number of morphological cues to stress. A third person singular preterit verb form is always final-stressed, while all second person plural forms are penultimately stressed. Such patterns are best described by distinguishing in the morphology between stress-neutral and stress-attracting suffixes. The lexical bases which receive these suffixes may be either penultimately or antepenultimately stressed: *cànta* 'sing' vs. *fàbbrica* 'make'. A stress-neutral suffix attached to the latter produces stress four syllables from the end: *fàbbricano* 'they make'. If clitics are attached post-verbally, stress may be made to appear even farther from the end of the word: *fàbbricalo* 'make it', *fàbbricamelo* 'make it for me', *fàbbricamicelo* 'make it for me there'. Underived words, however, can only have stress on one of the last three syllables: *ànima* 'soul', *lèttera* 'letter', *perìodo* 'period'; *radìce* 'root', *divìno* 'divine', *profòndo* 'deep'; *virtù* 'virtue', *caffè* 'coffee', *velleità* 'wish'. Final-stressed words are either loanwords, often from French, or the results of a diachronic truncation: *virtù* < Old Italian *virtude* < Lat. *VIRTUTEM*. Secondary stress is not in general contrastive, but is assigned rhythmically in such a way as to ensure that (a) the first syllable, if possible, is stressed; (b) there are never more than two unstressed syllables in sequence; (c) there are never two adjacent stressed syllables. Apparent minimal pairs have, nonetheless, been adduced such as: ‚auto-reattòre 'auto-reactor' vs. au‚tore-attòre 'author-actor' (contrasting position of secondary stress); procùra 'he procures' vs. ‚pró-cùra 'for-care' (two stresses vs. one).

Stress interacts with vowel length and the distribution of geminate consonants. Vowels are always short if not primarily stressed, or if followed by a consonant in the same syllable. They are long, therefore, in stressed, open syllables: ànima ['aː-ni-ma], lèttera ['lɛt-te-ra], divino [di-'viː-no], profondo [pro-'fon-do]. Final vowels are always short, so that if stressed and in close nexus with a following word, they ought to create a violation of our previously stated principle. Such a situation, however, is avoided by so-called raddoppiamento sintattico 'syntactic doubling', whereby the initial consonant of the following word is geminated: parlò chiaro 'he spoke clearly' [par-'lɔk-'kjaː-ro]. The double consonant here also seems to act as sufficient barrier to permit two adjacent main stresses. It has recently been pointed out that in the north, where the doubling effect is not found, the first of the two stresses is retracted instead. This doubling also takes place after a number of words which have lost the final consonant they had in Latin: tre 'three' < Lat. TRES, a 'to' < Lat. AD, though again this effect is only found south of the La Spezia-Rimini line. Raddoppiamento, then, is typical of central and southern speech, and the failure of northern speakers to adopt it mirrors its absence from their own dialects, and explains their tendency to produce only those geminates which the orthography indicates. Indeed, it can be argued more generally that there is emerging in Italy a kind of standardised spelling pronunciation based on the interaction of northern phonetic habits and an orthography which reflects the Florentine origin of the standard language.

3   Morphology

In morphology Italian exhibits a typically Indo-European separation of verbal and nominal inflection, the latter also encompassing pronouns, articles and adjectives.

3.1   The Noun

Nouns inflect for gender — masculine and feminine — and number — singular and plural — according to the following patterns:

Singular	Plural	Gender	
-o	-i	m.	libro 'book'; exception mano f. 'hand' (< Lat. MANUS f.)
-a	-e	f.	casa 'house', donna 'woman'
-e	-i	m. or f.	monte m. 'mountain', mente f. 'mind'
-a	-i	m.	problema 'problem' and other words of Greek (sistema, programma, etc.) or Latin (artista, poeta, etc.) origin.

Such a system of plural by vowel alternation rather than by suffixing of -s is one of the features which marks Italian off from Western Romance languages such as French, Spanish and Portuguese. Nouns which in the singular end in -i, e.g. *crisi* 'crisis', in stressed vowels, e.g. *città* 'town', *tribù*, 'tribe' and in consonants, e.g. *sport*, *camion* 'lorry', are unchanged in the plural. A small class of nouns — e.g. *dito* 'finger', *uovo* 'egg', *lenzuolo* 'sheet' — distinguish between a collective and a non-collective plural: *osso* 'bone', *le ossa* 'bones (together, as in a skeleton)', *gli ossi* 'bones (scattered)'. The synchronically unusual -a in the collective plural is a residue of the Latin neuter plural. Note that articles and adjectives going with such nouns are masculine in the singular and feminine in the plural.

Adjectives fall into two principal classes, having either four forms: *buono*, -i, -a, -e 'good' or two: *felice*, -i 'happy' (with a few like *rosa* 'pink' that are uninflected). The four-form pattern also shows up in the unstressed pronoun system: *lo/la/li/le*. In Old Italian these were also the forms of the definite article, but the modern language has a more irregular pattern: m. sg. *lo* only before /ʃ/, s + consonant, and certain other groups, *il* elsewhere; m. pl. *gli* corresponding to *lo* and *i* to *il*; f. sg. *la*; f. pl. *le*. In the case of both articles and pronouns the vowels of the singular forms commonly delete before an initial vowel in the following word.

3.2   The Verb

The chart of verb forms represents the paradigmatic structure of three typical regular verbs exemplifying the three traditional conjugations, each of which is marked by a characteristic thematic vowel, *a*, *e* or *i*. The chart is organised in such a way as to bring out the four classes of elements in the verbal structure — stem, thematic vowel, tense/aspect/mood markers and person/number markers — whose linear relations are schematically displayed as: STEM + TV + (T/A/M) + P/N. The use of curly brackets seeks to highlight some of the patterns of overlap between the traditional conjugations (at the expense of some non-traditional segmentations), and the numbers here and throughout this section refer to the six grammatical persons, three singular and three plural.

However, a classification of this kind is inadequate in two apparently contradictory respects. On the one hand, it does not allow for a number of further classes which seem to be necessary, for instance to distinguish between two types of *e*-verb according to whether they have stem or ending stress in the infinitive: *crèdere* 'to believe' and *vedère* 'to see' do not rhyme. Historically, in fact, the stem-stressed verbs have in some cases even undergone loss of the theme vowel in the infinitive with attendant consonant deletion or assimilation: Lat. *PONERE*, *DICERE*, *BIBERE* > It. *porre*, *dire*, *bere*. We also need to recognise two types of *i*-verb, one with the stem augment -isc- in persons 1/2/3/6 of the present and one without: *capisco* 'I understand' but *servo* 'I serve', and *partisco* 'I divide' as against *parto* 'I

Finite Forms of Italian Regular Verbs

	1	*2*	*3*	*4*	*5*	*6*
Present indicative	cant / tem / sent } -o	-i	canta / tem } / sent } -e	cant / tem / sent } -iamo	canta / teme / senti } -te	canta-no / tem } / sent } -ono
Imperfect	{{ canta / teme / senti } -v }-o	-i	{{ canta / teme / senti } -va }-∅ -mo		-te	-no
Present subjunctive	cant -i / tem } -a / sent }	-i / -a	-i / -a	cant / tem } / sent } -iamo	-iate	cant -i / tem } -a }-no / sent }
Preterit	canta / teme } -i / senti }	-sti	cantò / temè / sentì	canta / teme } -mmo / senti }	-ste	-rono
Past subjunctive	{{ canta / teme }-ss }-i / senti }	-i	-e	-imo	canta / teme } -ste / senti }	-ss -ero
Future	canter / temer } -ò / sentir }	-ai	-à	-emo	-ete	-anno
Conditional	-ei	-esti	-ebbe	-emmo	-este	-ebbero

leave'. These latter two verbs have a number of homophonous forms elsewhere in the paradigm: *partiamo, partire, partivo*, etc. On the other hand, a basically tripartite classification fails to capture the generalisation that *e-* and *i*-verbs are a good deal more similar to each other morphologically than either is to *a*-verbs (which constitutes the main open class for new coinings and borrowings). This relationship is particularly noticeable in forms 3/6 of the present indicative, and in the reversal effect whereby the present subjunctive vowel is *-i-* for *a*-verbs and *-a-* for *i/e*-verbs. Hence a better representation of Italian conjugational structure might be as in figure 12.1.

Figure 12.1: A Model of Italian Conjugation Structure

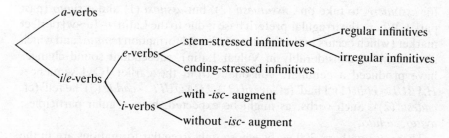

In addition to these finite forms, each verb has a past participle (*cant-a-to, tem-u-to, sent-i-to*) and a gerund (*cant-a-ndo, tem/sent-e-ndo*), which are used both independently and in a number of verbal periphrases (see section 4 for details of these and of the grammar and meaning of the various finite forms). The present participle formation (*-a/e/ie-nte*) is of more equivocal status since the possibilities for its use are grammatically very circumscribed.

As in any language, there are a number of verbs which fail to conform to the schemata established above, but it would be neither possible nor helpful in the present context to list all such idiosyncrasies. It is, however, of interest to note the ways in which patterns of irregularity intersect with the regular verb paradigms. For example, no verb has any irregularity in the imperfect (except *essere* 'to be', which seems to stand outside all such generalisations), and, again excluding *essere*, only *dare* 'to give' and *stare* 'to be, stand' have irregular past subjunctives (*dessi, stessi* for the expected **dassi, *stassi*). Discrepancies in the future and the conditional (and no verb is irregular in one without having the same irregularity in the other) are due either to the verb already having an exceptional infinitive — *porrò, dirò, farò* — or to the historical effects of syncope on the periphrases from which they derive: *VENIRE + HABEO > verrò, VOLERE + HABUIT > vorrebbe* etc.

By far the largest number of exceptions, however, are to be found in three parts of the paradigm: the present (indicative and subjunctive), the preterit and the past participle. Of these, the latter two are closely related: very few verbs have an irregular preterit and a regular past participle, and even fewer have an irregular past participle and a regular preterit. The characteristic perturbation in both cases is a reduced stem, which appears in persons 1/3/6 and the participle: e.g. for *prendere* 'to take', we have *preso* (past part.) and *presi* (1), *prese* (3), *presero* (6) vs. *prendesti* (2), *prendemmo* (4), *prendeste* (5). The patterns are best accounted for by assuming a base form with no theme vowel (hence no stress on the ending) but in its place a sigmatic preterit marker (ultimately of Indo-European origin but considerably generalised in its applicability in Vulgar Latin). This form, *prend-s-i* etc., can then be converted into the surface forms by a set of phonotactically motivated rules of consonant cluster reduction and assimilation. The sigmatic form in the participle (e.g. *preso*) is less common, but the regular suffix *-to* will trigger the same effects if not preceded by a theme vowel: e.g. for *assumere* 'to take on', *assumesti* (2), but *assunsi* (1) and *assunto* (past part.). Where the irregular preterit base is due to the Latin *-u-* [u~w] perfect marker (which occurs in the regular participial formation *temuto*, and which also extended considerably in Vulgar Latin), subsequent sound changes have produced a geminate consonant from the earlier [Cw] sequence: *HABUI* > *ebbi* (1) 'I had' (cf. *avesti* (2)), *CADUIT > *cadde* (3) 'he fell' (cf. *cadesti* (2)). Such verbs, as might be expected, have regular participles: *avuto*, *caduto*.

There are perhaps 200 verbs whose only irregular formations are in the preterit and the past participle, almost without exception members of the class of *e*-verbs. On the other hand, there are less than 50 which are irregular in the present, and they are spread throughout the conjugation classes. We cannot characterise all the patterns here, but once again it is worth noting how the incidence of stress was one of the principal determining factors for these alternations in the diachronic perspective (we have added the accent marks for clarity here, although the normal orthography does not use them). Thus, we find *uscìre* 'to go out' has *èsco* (1), *èsci* (2), *èsce* (3), *èscono* (6), and *èsca(no)* (subj.), but *usciàmo* (4), *uscìte* (5) and *uscìvo* (imperf.), *uscìi* (pret.) etc. For *avère* 'to have', we find (and the *h* here is purely orthographic) *hò* (1), *hài* (2), *hà* (3), *hànno* (6), but *àbbia(no)* (subj.), *abbiàmo* (4) and *avète* (5) *avèvo* (imperf.). Notice too how a verb like *andàre* 'to go' may be suppletive in the stem-stressed forms: *vàdo* (1), *vài* (2), *và* (3), *vànno* (6), *vàda(no)* (subj.), but almost entirely regular elsewhere: *andiàmo* (4), *andàte* (5), *andàvo* (imper.), *andài* (pret.) *andàto* (past part.) — but note the minor irregularity in the future and conditional: *andrò*, *andrei* etc. This is also a good example of the way in which a verb may be irregular to the point of suppletion in the present and show few or no ill effects elsewhere in its paradigm.

A number of other exceptional formations involve the morphophonemic processes of diphthongisation and palatalisation discussed in section 2.

Thus, *sedère* 'to sit': *sièdo* (1), *sièdi* (2), *sième* (3), *sièdono* (6) vs. *sediàmo* (4), *sedète* (5); *morìre* 'to die': *muòio* (1), *muòri* (2), *muòre* (3) *muòiono* (6) vs. *moriàmo* (4), *morìte* (5) exhibit clearly the effects of the so-called *dittonghi mobili*. Palatalisation is to be seen in *dico* 'I say' where c = [k] vs. *dici* 'you say' where c = [tʃ].

The conjugation of *essere* is as follows: Present 1 *sono*, 2 *sei*, 3 *è*, 4 *siamo*, 5 *siete*, 6 *sono*. Imperfect 1 *ero*, 2 *eri*, 3 *era*, 4 *eravamo*, 5 *eravate*, 6 *erano*. Present subjunctive 1, 2, 3 *sia*, 4 *siamo*, 5 *siate*, 6 *siano*. Preterite 1 *fui*, 2 *fosti*, 3 *fu*, 4 *fummo*, 5 *foste*, 6 *furono*. Past subjunctive 1, 2 *fossi*, 3 *fosse*, 4 *fossimo*, 5 *foste*, 6 *fossero*. Future 1 *sarò*, etc. Conditional 1 *sarei*, etc. Present participle *essendo*. Past participle *stato*.

Finally with regard to the verb, mention must be made of the system of address. Like many languages, Standard Italian distinguishes between a familiar and a polite style. The former is expressed through the use of the second person singular forms *tu, ti, tuo* and the imperatives *canta, temi, senti* (note again the formal overlap of the *i/e*-verbs). The latter requires the deferential pronoun *Lei*, which is grammatically third person singular and is therefore accompanied by clitic *si* and possessive *Suo*. In lieu of the imperative the present subjunctives *canti, tema, senta* are used. The use of *Lei* goes back to Late Latin, and became widespread due to Spanish influence in the Renaissance. Until quite recently the same distinction could be regularly maintained in the plural with *voi, vi, vostro* for familiar usage and *Loro* (lit. 'they') as the polite form. The latter is becoming increasingly rare and is now only used in the most formal circumstances — otherwise *voi* serves both functions. *Voi* as a polite singular, on the other hand, is still common in parts of southern Italy, particularly amongst older speakers.

3.3 Suffixes

Italian has an unusually rich range of affective suffixes relating to the size and the speaker's (dis)approval of the object in question. Thus, from *ragazzo* 'boy', we have *ragazzino, ragazzetto, ragazzuccio* 'little boy', *ragazzone* 'big lad', *ragazzaccio* 'nasty boy, lout', *ragazzotto* 'sturdy lad'. The chief analytical problem is that not all suffixes combine with all nouns, yet no clear rules are discernible for predicting the possible combinations: *-ello* is a diminutive but **ragazzello* cannot be used for 'little boy'. Sometimes too a noun plus suffix has acquired independent status as a lexical item: *pane* 'bread', *panetto* 'small loaf', *panino* 'bread roll' and *panettone* (etymologically containing two contradictory suffixes *-ett-* 'small' and *-one* 'large') refers to a special kind of fruit cake eaten at Christmas. This process is reminiscent of the way certain items of Italian vocabulary are derived from Latin diminutives — e.g. Lat. *AURIS* 'ear', but It. *orecchio* < *AURICU-LUM*. These suffixes are most commonly attached to nouns, but can also be used with other categories: adjectives — *facile* 'easy', *facilino* 'quite easy', *caro* 'dear', *caruccio* 'quite expensive' (but note *carino* 'pretty'); adverbs —

bene 'well', *benone* 'very well', *benino* 'quite well'; verbs — *dormire* 'to sleep', *dormicchiare* 'to snooze', *sputare* 'to spit', *sputacchiare* 'to splutter'.

4   Syntax

We shall concentrate here on aspects which either seem to typify Italian as opposed to other languages, or which have aroused interest amongst syntactic theorists, the two naturally not being unconnected.

4.1   The Nominal Group

Nouns in Italian may be accompanied by articles, definite or indefinite, numerals and quantifiers, demonstratives, possessives and adjectives. Of these, demonstratives and articles have parallel distribution and may be united in a single class of determiners. It is worth noting that only a two-term deictic opposition survives in modern usage, *questo* 'this' vs. *quello* 'that'. The often cited third term, *codesto* 'that by you' (cf. Spanish *ese*), is now limited to Tuscany, and is archaic even there. Possessives behave distributionally more like adjectives than determiners and, except in the case of nouns for close members of the family, never occur unaccompanied by an article or demonstrative: *mio zio* 'my uncle', *la mia macchina* 'my car', *un tuo cugino* 'one of your cousins' (lit. 'one your cousin'), *questi suoi libri* 'these books of his' (lit. 'these his books'). Quantifiers such as *alcuni* 'some', *parecchi* 'several', *pochi* 'few' may also precede the possessive: *parecchi nostri amici* 'several (of) our friends'. This class includes some words which in a different sense follow the noun as independent adjectives: *certe persone* 'a certain number of people' and *certi miei colleghi* 'some of my colleagues', but *persone certe* 'people who are certain', *diversi tuoi professori* 'several (of) your teachers' but *due caratteri diversi* 'two different characters'.

Examples such as these in turn raise one of the central issues of the syntax of the noun phrase in Italian: the function and position of the adjective. It is clear that there are independent pre- and post-nominal positions: *una breve visita* 'a short visit', *una visita turistica* 'a sightseeing visit', *una breve visita turistica* 'a short sightseeing visit'. Three questions arise: are there any constraints on how the two positions may be filled? Can a systematic meaning be attached to each position? Is one position dominant, such that it would make sense to say that Italian had noun-adjective order, say, in the way that typological cataloguing seems to require? Note first that although there is a small class of adjectives where a change of position corresponds to a quite discernible change of meaning, cf. the above examples and others: *un semplice soldato* 'a mere soldier' vs. *un soldato semplice* 'a private soldier', *numerose famiglie* 'many families' vs. *famiglie numerose* 'large families', most adjectives can occur in either position. Nor is length a decisive factor: the heptasyllabic *interessantissimo* 'very interesting' frequently precedes the noun in the speech of the more gushing interviewers and journalists! What distinguishes the two positions rather is the function of the adjective: if it is used in a distinguishing or restrictive sense, it follows; if the use is descriptive, rhetorical, emphatic or metaphorical, it precedes. *Pietre preziose* are 'precious stones' as opposed to ordinary ones, but one would refer to *i preziosi gioielli della contessa* 'the countess's precious jewels', where the value is taken for granted. Similarly, courtesy would require one to thank a friend for *il suo prezioso aiuto* 'his valuable help'. Hence, whether an adjective precedes or follows will depend on how easily its inherent meaning lends itself to one or other or both types of use. Adjectives of place and nationality are normally contrastive and therefore tend to follow: *i turisti inglesi* 'English tourists', *l'industria settentrionale* 'northern industry'. To distinguish Florentine literature from that of Rome or Venice one would talk of *la letteratura fiorentina*, but since everybody knows that 'The Divine Comedy' is by a Florentine, the adjective has a more rhetorical function and precedes in *la fiorentina Divina Commedia*. A postposed adjective would suggest Dante had a rival elsewhere!

We are, then, required to say that Italian has two equal but different adjective positions. The opposition having thus been grammaticalised, the typological parameter of adjective-noun order in such a language is rendered irrelevant.

4.2   The Verbal Group

We begin with some remarks on the meaning and use of the verbal forms set out in section 3, paying particular attention to mood, aspect, valency and voice.

The subjunctive mood is clearly identifiable both in terms of its morphological marking and its grammatical and semantic role. The latter emerges perhaps most evidently in pairs of the following kind: *Pietro vuole sposare una ragazza che ha* (indic.)/*abbia* (subj.) *studiato l'astrofisica* 'Peter wants to marry a girl who has (indic./subj.) studied astrophysics'. The indicative verb tells us there is a particular girl, one of whose attributes is that she has studied astrophysics; with the subjunctive we know only what Peter considers to be the desirable quality in a future wife, but not whether such a person exists. The function of the subjunctive, then, is to deny, put in doubt or suspend judgement on the question of the independent existence of the state of affairs referred to in the relevant proposition. Hence it is mandatory in the complement clauses of verbs which express attitudes towards possible, desired, feared etc. situations rather than assert that such situations actually obtain: *voglio/temo/spero che il treno sia* (subj.) *in ritardo* 'I want/fear/hope that the train is late'. With other verbs a contrast emerges: *se pensi che ha* (indic.) *soltanto dodici anni* 'if you think (= bear in mind) that he is only twelve' vs. *se pensi che abbia* (subj.) *soltanto dodici anni* 'if you think (= believe) that he is only twelve'. Likewise, the subjunctive is also appropriate after a negated verb: *capisco perché l'ha* (indic.) *fatto* 'I understand why he did it' but *non capisco perché l'abbia* (subj.) *fatto* 'I don't understand why he did it'; and after conjunctions that introduce an element of doubt or futurity: *prima che il gallo canti* (subj.) 'before the cock crows', *benché Giorgio sia* (subj.) *partito* 'although George has left', *lavora sodo perché lo si paga* (indic.) *bene* 'he works hard because they pay him well' vs. *lavora sodo perché lo si paghi* (subj.) *bene* 'he works so that they will pay him well'. Similar factors are involved in the use of the subjunctive with *se* in conditionals, but space prohibits even a cursory treatment of this complex area. Nor indeed has it been possible to survey all other uses of the subjunctive, but the foregoing should suffice to demonstrate that the category is semantically productive in the modern language. We may note finally that the subjunctive is less widely used in some colloquial registers, including so-called *italiano popolare*, and in some regions. On the other hand, in Sicilian and some other southern dialects where a conditional verb form has not emerged historically, the subjunctive has an even wider range of functions.

The central issue regarding aspect is the relation between the imperfect (*cantava*), the preterit (*cantò*), and the present perfect (*ha cantato*) (see section 3 for a full list of forms). The conventional view is that the first of these expresses an incomplete or a habitual action — 'he was singing' or 'he used to sing' — while the latter two refer instead to single completed actions. The difference between them in turn involves the recentness and the relevance of the events described to the current situation. Hence, in native grammatical terminology, *ha cantato* is dubbed the *passato prossimo* 'near past' and *cantò* the *passato remoto* 'distant past'. However, the imperfect is often found, particularly with verbs of mental state — *non sapeva cosa dirmi ieri* 'he didn't know what to say to me yesterday' — and in journalism and less formal writing where traditional usage might require one of the other two forms. Hence it has recently been argued that the imperfect is the unmarked past tense, deriving its precise value from the context, whereas both the perfect and the preterit have an inbuilt aspectual value. One advantage of this view is that it more easily accommodates the common, though by no means obligatory, progressive periphrasis *stava cantando* (cf. the present *sta cantando* 'he is singing'). In the case of the preterit and the present perfect, the issue is further complicated by the fact that spoken usage varies considerably up and down the peninsula. Northern speakers rarely utter the preterit, so the perfect subsumes both functions (cf. the discussion of French on pp. 225–6), while southern speakers often use only the preterit, reserving the reflex of the Latin HABEO + past participle periphrasis for a sense more like that in English 'I have the letter written'. The traditional distinction lives on in Central Italian (including Florentine and Roman) speech, but northern influence is strong even here and may eventually come to predominate.

One question not treated in the preceding discussion concerns the choice of auxiliary verb in constructing the perfect periphrasis. There are four possibilities: (a) some verbs always take *avere* 'to have' — *ho pensato* 'I have thought', *ha viaggiato* 'he has travelled', *abbiamo letto il libro* 'we have read the book'; (b) others always take *essere* 'to be' — *è uscita* 'she has (lit. is) gone out', *è morto* 'he has died'; (c) some take either auxiliary, but with more or less discernible differences of sense — *hanno aumentato il prezzo* 'they have increased the price', but *è aumentato il prezzo* 'the price has gone up'; *ha corso* 'he has run (= done some running)' vs. *è corso* 'he has run (= gone by running)'; (d) a very small number of verbs, particularly weather verbs, take either auxiliary with no difference of meaning — *è/ha piovuto* 'it has rained'. Crucial to an understanding of the process of auxiliary selection is an appreciation of the semantic relation between the subject and the verb. If the subject is the agent or experiencer (for a verb of mental state), then the auxiliary is *avere*; hence type (a) regardless of whether the verb is transitive or intransitive. If the subject is more neutrally involved in the activity or state defined by the verb — in traditional terms a patient, then the auxiliary is *essere*. Such verbs will by definition be intransitive — *andare* 'to go', *salire* 'to go up' (contrast *arrampicare* 'to climb' with *avere*), *morire* 'to die', *ingiallire* 'to turn yellow, wither'. If a verb can take two different types of subject — *aumentare* 'to increase', *correre* 'to run', *crescere* 'to grow', *procedere* 'to proceed' (with patient subject and *essere*) vs. *procedere* 'to behave' (with agent subject and *avere*), then it can take both auxiliaries. If the distinction between agent and patient is not valid for certain types of activity/state, then either auxiliary may be chosen indifferently — *piovere* 'to rain', *vivere* 'to live'. A final point to note here is that if the infinitive following a modal verb would independently take *essere*, then by a process of auxiliary attraction the modal itself, which would normally take *avere*, may take *essere*: either *ho dovuto uscire* or *sono dovuto uscire* 'I had to go out'.

Patient as subject not only identifies *essere*-taking verbs but is of course the time-honoured way of characterising the passive voice, and it is not coincidental that *essere* is also the auxiliary in passive constructions — *gli svedesi vinceranno la battaglia* 'the Swedes will win the battle', *la battaglia sarà vinta dagli svedesi* 'the battle will be won by the Swedes'. In fact, if we regard the subject of *essere* as itself being a patient (i.e. having a neutral role as the person/thing/etc. about which predications are made), then we can achieve a unified explanation of why (a) it takes *essere* as its own auxiliary; (b) it is the active auxiliary of the appropriate subclass of intransitives and the passive auxiliary of all transitives; (c) the other two verbs which enter into passive periphrases are also patient subject verbs. The first of these is *venire* 'to come', which may be regularly substituted for *essere* to distinguish an 'action' from a 'state' passive. Thus, *la bandiera veniva/era issata all'alba* 'the flag was hoisted at dawn', but only *essere* in *in quel periodo la bandiera era issata per tutta la giornata* 'at that time the flag was hoisted (i.e. remained aloft) all day'. The second is *andare* 'to go', which combines with the past participle to express the meaning 'must be V-ed', e.g. *questo problema va risolto subito* 'this problem must be solved at once'. One interesting morphosyntactic restriction is that neither *andare* nor *venire* can occur in these functions in their compound forms, whereas *essere* of course can. Curiously, *andare* does occur as a compound auxiliary in *la casa è andata distrutta* 'the house was (lit. is gone) destroyed', but then there is no sense of obligation and the construction is limited to verbs of loss and destruction.

Essere is also the auxiliary for all reflexives: *Maria si è criticata* 'Mary criticised herself'. Since a reflexive is only a transitive verb where agent and patient happen to be identical, one might expect to find *avere*, as indeed one sometimes does in Old Italian and in some, notably southern, dialects. However, another very frequent use of the reflexive construction is as a kind of passive. Thus, in *le finestre si sono rotte* 'the windows got broken' (lit. 'broke themselves') the sentence is formally reflexive but the subject is patient rather than agent (contrast the non-reflexive in *Giorgio ha rotto le finestre* 'George has broken the windows'). Furthermore, since patient-subject verbs and constructions in Italian frequently have post-verbal subjects (see below), we also have the possibility of *si sono rotte le finestre*, a structure which is susceptible to an alternative analysis, viz.: *si* (su.) V *le finestre* (obj.). Evidence that such a reanalysis has taken place comes from the fact that, colloquially at least, such sentences often have a singular verb: *si parla diverse lingue in quel negozio* 'several languages are spoken in that shop', and from the extension of the construction to intransitive verbs of all kinds: *si parte domani* 'one is leaving tomorrow', *si dorme bene in campagna* 'one sleeps well in the country'. Indeed, it is even possible to have the so-called impersonal *si* in combination with a reflexive verb: *ci si lava(no) le mani prima di mangiare* 'one washes one's hands before eating' (where *ci* is a morphophonemic variant of *si* before *si*).

These two *si*s (impersonal and reflexive) take different positions in clitic sequences: *lo si dice* 'one says it', *se lo dice* 'he says it to himself' (*se* for *si* before *lo* is a consequence of a regular morphophonemic adjustment), and hence with both present we find *ce lo si dice* 'one says it to oneself'. Notice too that if *si* in impersonal constructions is taken as subject, then examples like *si rilegano libri* 'one binds books' have to be construed as involving object agreement on the verb. Subject *si* is also unusual in that in predicative constructions while the verb is singular, following adjectives, participles and predicate nominals are plural: *si è ricchi* (m. pl.) 'one is rich', *si è usciti* 'one has gone out', *quando si è attrici* (f. pl.) 'when one is an actress'. Compare in this regard the plural with other impersonal verbs; *bisogna essere sicuri* 'it is necessary to be safe'. On the other hand if impersonal *si* is found with a verb which normally requires *avere*, the auxiliary becomes *essere*, as with reflexive *si*, but the past participle does not agree; *si è partiti* 'one has left' vs. *si è detto* 'one has said'.

As the preceding examples have shown, one feature of the Italian verbal group is the possible presence of clitic pronouns, whose categories and basic order are set out in the following table:

1st sg.	3rd sg. dative	2nd pl.	2nd sg.	1st pl.	Refl.	3rd sg./pl. accusative	Imp.	Partitive
mi	gli (m.) le (f.)	vi	ti	ci	si	lo (m. sg.) la (f. sg.) li (m. pl.) le (f. pl.)	si	ne

Note, however, that combinations of *ne* and the third person accusative forms are rare, but when they do occur, *ne* precedes: *ne la ringrazierò* 'I'll thank her for it'. In clitic clusters there is a morphophonemic adjustment of /i/ to /e/ before sonorants. Hence *me lo*, *te ne*, etc. Standard too in such clusters is the replacement of *le* 'to her' by its masculine congener *gli*, so that *gliene* translates as 'of it to him/her'. *Gli* for *le* in isolation is becoming increasingly common, but is still regarded as non-standard. Much more acceptable is *gli* for *loro*, the latter being anomalous in occurring post-verbally: *ho detto loro* 'I said to them'. Likewise, *suo* 'his/her' is extending ground to replace *loro* 'their' in the possessive. In *italiano popolare* and in many dialects the whole system *gli/le/loro* merges with the neuter *ci*, which thus becomes an omni-purpose indirect object clitic. Note that, whereas in modern Italian, unlike in earlier stages of the language, the past participle in the perfect does not normally agree with its object, clitic objects do trigger agreement: *ho trovato Maria* 'I found Mary' vs. *l'ho trovata* 'I found her'. *Ne* also causes agreement (contrast French *en*): *ne hanno mangiati tre* 'they have eaten three of them'.

A further complication arises in the rules for placement of the clitics or clitic clusters. The general principle is that they precede finite verb forms but follow non-finite ones: *me lo darà* 'he will give it to me', *deve darmelo* 'he must give it to me', *avendomelo dato* 'having given it to me'. Certain verbs, however, which take a dependent infinitive allow the latter's clitics to 'climb' and attach to the governing verb: *vuole parlarti* or *ti vuole parlare* 'he wants to speak to you', *volendo parlarti* or *volendoti parlare* 'wanting to speak to you'. Such clitic-climbing is obligatory with the causative *fare*: *me lo farà dare* 'he will have it given to me', even if this formally converts the causative into a reflexive and provokes an attendant auxiliary change: *si è fatto dare un aumento di stipendio* 'he got himself given a rise'. Furthermore, if the clitics climb (and in a cluster they must all move or none), then the phenomenon of auxiliary attraction mentioned earlier becomes obligatory: *non ho/sono potuto andarci* 'I couldn't go there' but only *non ci sono potuto andare*.

4.3 The Sentence
We conclude with some brief remarks relating to overall sentence structure,

beginning with the question of word order. Assuming a traditional division of the sentence, we find both the orders subject-predicate and predicate-subject attested: *Pietro fumava una sigaretta* 'Peter was smoking a cigarette', *è arrivato il treno* 'the train has arrived'. To understand what distinguishes the two orders we need to add the concepts of theme (= what is being talked about) and rheme (= what is said about the theme), and the ordering principle 'theme precedes rheme'. In the unmarked case, a subject which identifies the agent-experiencer of the activity/state expressed by the verb will constitute the theme, and will accordingly come first. The rheme will consist of the verb plus, where appropriate, an object whose interpretation follows directly from the meaning of the verb, what we have earlier called a patient. Thus, S V (O) is a natural order for sentences with any transitive and some intransitive verbs in Italian. If we extend the notion object to include the sentential complements of verbs of saying, thinking etc. and also allow for indirect objects and prepositional objects, we can say that the rheme consists of the verb followed by its complement(s). If, however, the subject is rhematic with respect to its verb, as it will be if its semantic role is patient, then it will normally follow. Hence the characteristic post-verbal subjects in the *essere*-taking constructions discussed above: *verrà Giorgio* 'George will come' (taking the 'mover' as patient with a verb of motion), *domani saranno riaperti il porto e l'aeroporto* 'tomorrow the docks and the airport will be reopened', *si svolgeva il dibattito* 'the debate took place'. In appropriate circumstances and with suitable intonation the basic patterns can be reversed, but that does not alter the fact that the position of the subject in Italian is not fixed but depends on its semantic relation to the verb. Moving the object from its post-verbal position is, by contrast, less easy and normally requires a pronominal copy: *quel libro, non lo legge nessuno* 'that book nobody reads'. Similarly, it is rare and decidedly rhetorical for the subject to be interposed between verb and object. Adverbs and subcategorised adjectives on the other hand regularly separate verb and noun: *parla bene l'italiano* 'he speaks Italian well', *il professore ha fatto felici gli studenti* 'the teacher made the students happy'.

The possibility of post-verbal subjects with *essere*-taking verbs and the general optionality of pronominal subjects have been linked in the recent generative literature with another detail of Italian syntax, namely the fact that sentences such as *chi credi che verrà?* 'who do you think will come?' are grammatical (contrast the ungrammaticality of the literal English rendering **who do you think that will come?*). If such an example was derived from an intermediate structure like *credi che verrà chi*, then Italian and English both agree in being able to extract from a post-verbal position (cf. English *who do you think that Fred saw?*), but differ in what may occupy such a position. The preverbal subject is treated throughout as a dummy category licensed by the putatively universal Empty Category Principle (ECP), and languages like Italian have thus become known as pro-drop or null-subject languages. In addition to the properties already mentioned, such languages are claimed to have rightward agreement of the copula (*sono io* 'it's me'), so-called 'long' *wh*-movement of the subject (*l'uomo che mi domando chi abbia visto* 'the man that I wonder who he saw' cf. the ungrammaticality of the English translation) and the possibility of an empty resumptive pronoun in embedded clauses (*ecco la ragazza che mi domando chi crede che vincerà* vs. English '*there's the girl that I wonder who believes that she will win'). Unfortunately, there is not room here to examine in more detail these fascinating insights into Italian syntax.

Bibliography

Lepschy and Lepschy (1988) is an excellent general manual which is refreshingly up-to-date and unprescriptive in its approach to points of grammar. Muljačić (1982) is a very handy one-volume bibliographical guide.

Among descriptive grammars, Fogarasi (1983) is a comprehensive, if rather conservative, reference grammar; nine of a projected twelve volumes of Brunet (1978–) have so far appeared, an exhaustive compilation of modern usage with relatively little grammatical analysis or commentary; Schwarze (1983–) — projected to be in three volumes, of which two have appeared — provides a series of excellent and detailed studies of modern usage. Chapallaz (1979) is a good traditional account of the phonetics of the standard language; Muljačić (1972) is a useful survey of work done on Italian phonology from a variety of theoretical viewpoints; Bertinetto (1981) is an excellent study of the suprasegmental phonology of Italian. Rizzi (1982) is a collection of articles by one of the leading figures in the investigation of Italian in the light of recent generative theory.

Rohlfs (1966–9) is a classic historical grammar with very generous attention to the dialects; Tekavčić (1980) is an indispensable manual combining factual detail on the history of the language and largely structuralist methods of analysis and interpretation. Migliorini and Griffith (1984) is the best external history of the language.

De Mauro (1983) is the standard account of the changes in the linguistic situation in the peninsula since unification in 1861. Two volumes out of four have so far appeared of Cortelazzo (1969–), one of Italy's leading dialectologists; unfortunately, we still await the main descriptive volume. Albano Leoni (1979) is a wide-ranging set of conference proceedings which give a clear picture of the current linguistic complexity of the peninsula.

Acknowledgement

I am grateful to Joe Cremona, Martin Harris, Giulio Lepschy, Žarko Muljačić and Donna Jo Napoli for their comments on an earlier version of this chapter.

References

Albano Leoni, F. (ed.) 1979. *I dialetti e le lingue delle minoranze di fronte all'italiano*, 2 vols. (Bulzoni, Rome)

Bertinetto, P. M. 1981. *Strutture prosodiche dell'italiano* (Accademia della Crusca, Florence)

—— 1986. *Tempo aspetto e azione nel verbo italiano*: il sistema dell'indicativo (Accademia della Crusca, Florence)

Berruto, G. 1987. *Sociolinguistica dell'italiano contemporaneo* (La Nuova Italia Scientifica, Rome)

Brunet, J. 1978–. *Grammaire critique de l'italien*, 9 vols. (Université de Paris VII, Vincennes)

Burzio, L. 1986. *Italian Syntax* (Reidel, Dordrecht)

Chapallaz, M. 1979. *The Pronunciation of Italian* (Bell and Hyman, London)

Cortelazzo, M. 1969–. *Avviamento alla dialettologia italiana*, 4 vols. (Pacini, Pisa)

De Mauro, T. 1983. *Storia linguistica dell'Italia unita*, 8th ed. (Laterza, Bari)

Fogarasi, M. 1983. *Grammatica italiana del Novecento*, 2nd ed. (Bulzoni, Rome)

Lepschy, A. L. and G. C. 1988. *The Italian Language Today*, 2nd ed. (Hutchinson, London; Italian edition: *La lingua italiana*, Bompiani, Milan, 1981)

Migliorini, B. and T. G. Griffith. 1984. *The Italian Language*, 2nd ed. (Faber and Faber, London; translation and adaptation of B. Migliorini, *Storia della lingua italiana*, 5th ed., Sansoni, Florence, 1978)

Muljačić, Ž. 1972. *Fonologia della lingua italiana* (Il Mulino, Bologna)

—— 1982. *Introduzione allo studio della lingua italiana*, 2nd ed. (Einaudi, Turin)

Rizzi, L. 1982. *Issues in Italian Syntax* (Foris Publications, Dordrecht)

Rohlfs, G. 1966–9. *Grammatica storica della lingua italiana e dei suoi dialetti*, 3 vols. (Einaudi, Turin; translation and revision of *Historische Grammatik der italienischen Sprache und ihrer Mundarten*, 3 vols., Francke, Bern, 1949–54)

Schwarze, C. (ed.) 1983–. *Bausteine für eine italienische Grammatik*, 2 vols. (Gunter Narr, Tübingen)

Tekavčić, P. 1980. *Grammatica storica della lingua italiana*, 2nd ed., 3 vols (il Mulino, Bologna)

13 *Rumanian*

Graham Mallinson

1 Introduction

The relative neglect of Balkan Romance by linguists in favour of the Western Romance languages is attributable in part to the geographical isolation of the country where most Rumanian speakers live. The Socialist Republic of Rumania has a population of well over 20 million, of which some 90 per cent have Rumanian as their first language. There are some speakers of Rumanian in the border areas of neighbouring countries, including over 2½ million speakers of the Moldavian dialect in the Moldavian Soviet Socialist Republic (formed from areas annexed by the Soviet Union during the course of the twentieth century). This failure of linguistic and national borders to coincide reflects the fluid political history of the Balkans. Rumania itself is host to several minority language groups, including German-speaking Saxons (over half a million) and Hungarians (at least one million and perhaps over two million). Both these minorities are concentrated in Transylvania, the presence of so many Hungarian speakers resulting from the acquisition by Rumania of the province from Hungary at the end of the First World War.

A number of features at all linguistic levels serve to highlight the differences between Rumanian and the Western Romance languages, many being attributable to its membership of the Balkan Sprachbund. In each of the four main sections which follow, reference will be made to such features in describing the divergence of Rumanian from mainstream Romance evolution.

The form of Balkan Romance to be discussed is Daco-Rumanian, so named because it is associated with the Roman province of Dacia, on the north bank of the lower Danube (part of the Empire for a relatively short period from the first decade of the second century to AD 271). The wider term Balkan Romance includes three other varieties: Arumanian, spoken in northern Greece, Albania and southern Yugoslavia; Megleno-Rumanian, spoken in a small area to the north of Salonika; Istro-Rumanian, spoken in the Istrian peninsula of western Yugoslavia. All four varieties are deemed to have a common origin, with the initial split dating from the second half of the first millennium. Because the earliest extant Rumanian texts date from as late as the beginning of the sixteenth century, the history of Balkan Romance involves a great deal of speculation (compare the dates of early extant texts for Old French).

Besides the question of dating the breakup of Common Rumanian, other controversies include the problem of whether the original centre of dispersion was north of the Danube in Dacia, or south of the Danube in Moesia; also, whether Arumanian, Megleno- and Istro-Rumanian are dialects of Rumanian or constitute separate languages. In the latter case, one can say that the four varieties are very closely related but that the three minor varieties have each been heavily influenced by the national languages of the countries in which they are spoken. Mutual intelligibility between Daco-Rumanian and Arumanian would be at a very low level on first contact but would increase dramatically in a very short period. However, in this area of Europe it is extra-linguistic factors such as nationalism that are more pertinent to the perception of linguistic identity (compare the discussion in the chapter on Serbo-Croat about the relations between Serbian and Croatian). In the case of Balkan Romance I will leave this sensitive question open, since I will be concentrating on Daco-Rumanian (henceforth simply 'Rumanian'), the national language of Rumania.

Map 13.1

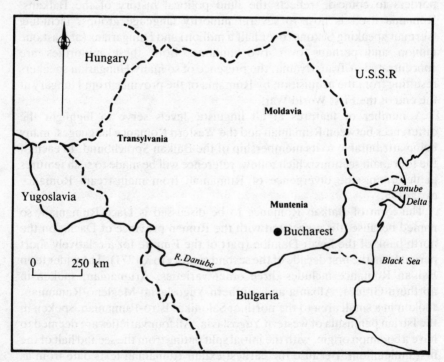

Finally, Rumanian is also spoken by a considerable number of immigrants to the New World. Even in Australia there are enough Rumanian speakers to warrant a weekly one-hour programme in both Sydney and Melbourne on ethnic radio, though not enough to have given rise to discernible, institutionalised features of Antipodean Rumanian such as one finds in the larger Italian and Greek communities.

Rumanian proper can be divided into several (sub)dialects. The major forms are Moldavian and Muntenian, spoken in the former principalities of Moldavia (northeast) and Muntenia, or Wallachia (southeast), though several other minor dialects can be discerned within present-day Rumania. These are spoken in the north and west of the country, including much of Transylvania. Despite its political history in relative isolation from the two principalities, it is, however, inaccurate to speak of a Transylvanian dialect as such. Both Moldavian and Muntenian cover parts of Transylvania, and there is, as one would expect, overlap between dialects spoken in adjoining regions.

During the course of the nineteenth century, Muntenian was gradually adopted as the national and literary standard, the final step in this process being the union of the principalities in 1859 as an independent state with Bucharest as the capital. The use of Muntenian as the point of entry into Rumanian of Western Romance vocabulary and morphosyntactic innovations over the last 150 years (a period marked at times by what has been described as 'Gallomania') has served to set this dialect off from the others. However, communication and education in modern society have allowed many innovations to filter through and dilute other dialects, including the original spoken Muntenian on which the national standard is based and which was itself left behind by the developing literary language.

Even so, spoken Muntenian was already somewhat more innovative than the other spoken dialects. For example, it showed a greater tendency to fricativise voiced dental plosives before front vowels: Lat. *DĪCO* > *zic* /zik/ 'say', compared with Moldavian affrication in /dzik/. Muntenian has also gone further towards complete elimination of the high, back vowel /u/ from Latin words ending in -*o*(+C) and -*u*(+C): *AMĀRU-* > *amar* /amar/ 'bitter', compared with Moldavian /amar^u/. Both /dz/ for /z/, and final /u/ are also typical of Arumanian.

The 'reromancing' tendency of the last two centuries has gone some way towards countering the specifically Balkan character of earlier Rumanian development. Such Western Romance influence was by no means accidental, however, and groups of writers during the late eighteenth and early to mid-nineteenth centuries made positive efforts to import French- and Italian-based vocabulary to fill gaps in the native lexical stock. The Transylvanian School made the first real attempt to replace the Cyrillic orthography with a Roman one, as well as engineering Rumanian vocabulary to substitute Romance for Slavonic. However, they had only limited success in each case, their main fault being an overzealous desire to hark back to the Latin origins of the language. Their etymological spelling system (that rendered /tʃintʃ/ 'five' by *quinqui* — compare the modern spelling *cinci*) could serve only to confuse the populace whom they wished to educate.

It was the mid-nineteenth-century writers of Muntenia, with their less extreme attitude towards renewing the language, who had the greatest influence in resurrecting its Romance character. Yet one should point out also that political developments helped to bring to prominence the dialect in which they wrote. One can only speculate on the likelihood of some Transylvanian-based form of Rumanian having come to the fore had that province not been isolated from the two principalities. And if some other dialect had been adopted as the national standard, one might also ask how great a difference there would have been today between the other three varieties of Balkan Romance and a national language of Rumania based on a more conservative form.

2 Orthography and Phonology

The Cyrillic writing system was introduced into the area occupied by the modern language when Old Church Slavonic (see pages 322–3) became the medium for religious texts. Given the absence of contact between Rumanian and Latin in medieval times (compare the situation in the west of Romania), it was inevitable that when Rumanian words and names of places and people began to appear sporadically in Old Church Slavonic texts from the thirteenth century, they too should be written in Cyrillic script. The first extant texts wholly in Rumanian merely followed this tradition so that a non-Roman alphabet was dominant for the greater part of the four and a half centuries since then.

Two clear factors led to dissatisfaction with this system and thus to the eventual adoption of a Roman script: the practical problem of adapting the Cyrillic system to match phonemes found in Rumanian and those introduced with Romance loans from the west; and the growing feelings of national awareness that increased as contact with the Western Romance languages grew and brought widespread recognition of linguistic ties with Latin, Italian and French. Nevertheless, it was not until the union of the principalities in the late nineteenth century that the Cyrillic system was finally replaced by a Roman one. During the last century, various attempts were made to adapt the Roman alphabet to Rumanian, including systems of a transitional nature with a largely Roman alphabet but with Cyrillic symbols for those sounds not represented orthographically in Western Romance — for example, the middle vowel /ə/ was represented by ъ and the post-alveolar fricative /ʃ/ by ш.

Today Rumanian is written and printed in a wholly Romanised alphabet with three diacritics, though the Moldavian spoken in the Moldavian SSR is represented by an adaptation of the Russian Cyrillic alphabet. Because it is a relatively short time since the current Rumanian alphabet was instituted, there has been little opportunity for the spoken and written languages to diverge. For this reason, Rumanian examples will normally be given in their orthographic form. The phonemic values of the letters are shown in table 13.1, with some oddities discussed in the remarks which follow it. One value of using the orthography is that, as with French, it provides some insight into the history of the language, because of the method used for representing final palatalised consonants.

Among the vowel symbols, *â* is an archaic form of *î* and is normally reserved for words representing the name of the country and its people and language: *România* 'Rumania', *românesc/român* 'Rumanian', *românește* 'Rumanian language'. A limited number of words beginning with *e-* are pronounced /je-/, this ioticisation apparently a Slavonic inheritance. More recent loans from Western Romance are unaffected, giving rise to the occasional doublet: *era* /éra/ 'the era' but *era* /jerá/ 'was'. Initial *i-* before another vowel is also pronounced /j-/: *iute* /jute/ 'quick'; *iar* /jar/ 'again'. Final *-i* normally represents palatalisation of the preceding consonant: *lup* /lup/ 'wolf' but *lupi* /lupʲ/ 'wolves'. However, this does not apply when the preceding consonant cluster is consonant+liquid: *tigri* /tigri/ 'tigers'. Final *-ii* represents a full /i/ and so the system allows for the differentiation of some masculine nouns into three forms. Thus, the singular *lup* /lup/ 'wolf' is made plural by the palatalisation of the final plosive: *lupi* /lupʲ/ 'wolves', and

Table 13.1: Orthographic System of Modern Rumanian

a	/a/		m	/m/
ă	/ə/		n	/n/
b	/b/		o	/o/
c (+h)	/k/		p	/p/
c (+i/e)	/tʃ/		r	/r/
d	/d/		s	/s/
e	/e/		ş	/ʃ/
f	/f/		t	/t/
g (+h)	/g/		ţ	/ts/
g (+i/e)	/dʒ/		u	/u/
h	/h/		v	/v/
i	/i/**		# w	/v/ or /w/
î/â	/ɨ/		x	/ks/
j	/ʒ/		y	/j/
k	/k/		z	/z/
l	/l/			

Note: *******i* is the most troublesome orthographic symbol in Rumanian. The phoneme equivalent given here relates to full vowels. See the text for comments on other values. # Used for common international terms only, e.g. *weekend, watt.*

definite plural by addition of a full /i/: *lupii* /lupi/ 'the wolves'. This can be alarming when the stem of the noun ends in *-il*. The noun *copil* 'child' has a plural *copii* /kopi/ 'children' (the final /l/ is palatalised out of existence) and a definite plural *copiii* /kopiʲi/ 'the children'. The three major diphthongs /ea/, /oa/ and /eo/ are represented by their starting and finishing points — *ea*, *oa* and *eo*. The sequence *au* is pronounced as two separate vowels, as normally is *ău* too.

Among the consonant symbols, *k* is a comparative rarity (being reserved for international terms such as *kilogram*, *kilometru*) and the voiceless velar plosive is represented by *c* (*ch* before front vowels). Similarly, the voiced velar plosive is represented by *g* (*gh* before front vowels). The post-alveolar affricates /tʃ/ and /dʒ/ are also represented by *c* and *g*, but by the digraphs *ci* and *gi* (sometimes *ce* and *ge*) before back and middle vowels (see Italian, page 284). The fronting of velar plosives before front vowels is a characteristic Rumanian shares with Western Romance, and is discussed later in this section.

Standard Rumanian has 32 phonemes (or more, depending on the method of phonological analysis employed — the series of palatalised consonants being treated either as a distinct set or as the non-palatal series plus a recurring palatal off-glide). The neatest system identifies 7 simple vowels, 3 diphthongs and 22 consonants, which include two semi-vowels. The number of diphthongs is increased substantially if the semi-vowel /j/ is treated as a vowel unit rather than as a consonant (thus /je/ would be a diphthong, but is treated here as a consonant-vowel sequence). The phoneme inventory is set out in figures 13.1 and 13.2, and table 13.2.

Figure 13.1: Vowels	**Figure 13.2: Diphthongs**

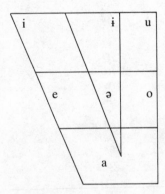

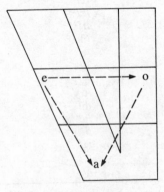

The two back vowels are rounded, the remainder are unrounded.

All three diphthongs are rising, with stress on the second element.

Table 13.2: Consonants

	Bilabial	Labio-dental	Dental	Post-alveolar	Palatal	Velar	Glottal
Stops	p b		t d			k g	
Affricates			ts	tʃ dʒ			
Fricatives		f v	s z	ʃ ʒ			h
Nasals	m		n				
Liquids			l r				
Semi-vowels	w				j		

There is some symmetry within the consonant system, most obstruents being in voiced/voiceless pairs. Voiced and voiceless plosives alike are unaspirated. Unpaired are the glottal fricative /h/ (often pronounced with audible friction) and the dental affricate /ts/ — though in more conservative dialects this too is matched with the voiced equivalent /dz/. There are only two nasals, the gap in the system being the velar nasal, which occurs only as an allophone of /n/ before velar plosives. There are two liquids, /r/ being a lingual flap or light roll, and the dental lateral /l/ being consistently clear.

As mentioned earlier, Rumanian has followed the normal Romance path of fronting velar plosives before front vowels, giving rise to the post-alveolar affricates. However, /k/ and /g/ also occur slightly fronted as an allophonic variation before front vowels: *chema* 'call' and *ghetou* 'ghetto'. The failure of the velar plosives to front all the way to post-alveolar affricates in many words reflects the distinct treatment of words inherited directly from Latin and those borrowed from other languages at later dates, e.g. from Slavonic: *chilie* '(monk's) cell' (from *kelija*) or from Hungarian: *chip* 'face, facial expression' (from *kép*).

Among consonants also attributable to contact with other languages is /ʒ/. This derives from Latin *-di-* sequences: *DEORSUM > jos* 'down'; *ADJŪTO > ajut* 'help'; but also from Latin *j* + back vowels: *JUGUM > jug* 'yoke'; *JOCUM > joc* 'game'. Its presence in Slavonic-based words (*grajd* 'stable'; *jar* 'live coals') testifies to its reinforcement through contact with Southern Slavonic if it is not actually a Slavonic-induced development.

The glottal fricative /h/ has an uncertain history, some linguists claiming it was reintroduced after its loss in Vulgar Latin in order to bring symmetry back to the plosive/fricative system (thus: p~f; t~s; k~h). Again this development was reintroduced, if not necessarily induced, by languages Rumanian came into contact with: from Slavonic, *duh* 'soul' and *hrană* 'food, fodder'; from Hungarian, *hotar* 'border' and *hîrdău* 'bucket'; from Turkish, *hamal* 'porter' and *huzur* 'leisure'.

A substratum influence from Dacian/Thracian has been suggested for some distinctive phonological developments in Balkan Romance, though this is highly speculative, given the dearth of extant material from such a substratum. Comparison with Albanian shows some parallels: /ə/ from unstressed /a/ is found in both Rumanian and Albanian, as well as Bulgarian; Rumanian /ɨ/ from /a/ before nasals in closed syllables: Latin *CAMPUM* > *cîmp* 'plain', but not in open syllables: Latin *ANNUM* > *an* 'year' (-*nn*- appears to have become a long, rather than geminate, consonant and was grouped with the following vowel); labialisation of velars in velar+dental clusters: Latin *COXAM* > *coapsă* 'thigh' (Albanian *kofshë*). Treatments like this last one also provide useful patterns for comparison between Balkan and Western Romance:

Latin	Rumanian	French	Italian	Spanish
FACTUM	fapt	fait	fatto	hecho
LACTEM	lapte	lait	latte	leche

Like Italian, however, Rumanian inherits vowel-final plurals from Latin, with loss of final -*s*: *FLŌRES* > *flori* 'flowers' (though, of course, final -*i* now represents palatalisation of the final consonant).

In some instances there was substitution of one liquid for the other: *CAELUM* > *cer* 'sky'; *MELLEM* > *miere* 'honey'; *SALEM* > *sare* 'salt'. Later loans from Western Romance thus gave rise to doublets: *ceresc~celest* 'celestial/of the sky'. Sixteenth-century texts of the north Transylvania area of Maramureş also show evidence of rhotacism, with intervocalic /n/ becoming /r/: *lumiră* for *lumină* 'light'; *tire* for *tine* 'you'. This is a feature also of Istro-Rumanian: *pliră* for *plină* 'full'; *lîră* for *lînă* 'wool'.

Consonant clusters also show differences between Rumanian and Western Romance. Matching the voiceless /str/ and /skl/ are the voiced /zdr/ and /zgl/; /zb/ and /zg/ match /sp/ and /sk/; /zv/ matches /sf/; /zm/ and /zl/ also occur; while the presence of post-alveolar /ʃ/ leads to the existence of clusters such as /ʃt(r)/ and /ʃp (l~r)/. While all these clusters fill natural gaps in the Romance system, phonotactically much more unexpected are: /hl/, /hr/, /ml/ and /mr/ as well as word-initial /kt/.

Finally, stress is free and variable, giving rise to doublets: *módele* 'the fashions' but *modéle* 'models'; *cíntă* 'sings, sing!' but *cîntắ* 'sang'. Rumanian orthography does not regularly mark stress but it will be marked here whenever it is relevant to the discussion.

3 Morphology

As in Western Romance, the Latin declension system for nouns and adjectives was reduced in Balkan Romance through phonetic attrition. However, Rumanian is more conservative to the extent that it retains three distinct case forms: nominative/accusative, genitive/dative, vocative. It has also reintroduced what has been described as a neuter gender. This diversity of case forms is most evident among feminines, but also with masculines

Nouns

(a) some typical masculine nouns

(i) lup 'wolf'

	Sg.	Pl.
Nom./acc. -def	lup	lupi
+def	lupul	lupii
Gen./dat. -def	lup	lupi
+def	lupului	lupilor

Some further sg./pl. alternations: *om-oameni* 'man'; *împărat-împăraţi* 'emperor'; *băiat-băieţi* 'boy'; *cal-cai* 'horse'; *fiu-fii* 'son'; *brad-brazi* 'fir tree'.

(ii) arbore 'tree'

	Sg.	Pl.
Nom./acc. -def	arbore	arbori
+def	arborele	arborii
Gen./dat. -def	arbore	arbori
+def	arborelui	arborilor

(iii) codru 'forest'

	Sg.	Pl.
Nom./acc. -def	codru	codri
+def	codrul	codrii
Gen./dat. -def	codru	codri
+def	codrului	codrilor

(b) some typical feminine nouns

(i) casă 'house'

	Sg.	Pl.
Nom./acc. -def	casă	case
+def	casa	casele
Gen./dat. -def	case	case
+def	casei	caselor

Some further sg./pl. alternations: *basma-basmale* 'kerchief'; *viaţă-vieţi* 'life'; *carte-cărţi* 'book'; *fată-fete* 'girl'; *dovadă-dovezi* 'proof'; *bară-bări* (metal) bar'.

(ii) stea 'star'

	Sg.	Pl.
Nom./acc. -def	stea	stele
+def	steaua	stelele
Gen./dat. -def	stele	stele
+def	stelei	stelelor

(iii) cîmpie 'plain'

	Sg.	Pl.
Nom./acc. -def	cîmpie	cîmpii
+def	cîmpia	cîmpiile
Gen./dat. -def	cîmpii	cîmpii
+def	cîmpiei	cîmpiilor

(c) some typical 'neuter' nouns

(i) studiu 'study(ing)'

	Sg.	Pl.
Nom./acc. -def.	studiu	studii
+def	studiul	studiile
Gen./dat. -def	studiu	studii
+def	studiului	studiilor

Some further sg./pl. alternations: *tablou-tablouri* 'picture'; *nume-nume* 'name'; *templu-temple* 'temple'.

(ii) oraş 'town'

	Sg.	Pl.
Nom./acc. -def.	oraş	oraşe
+def	oraşul	oraşele
Gen./dat. -def	oraş	oraşe
+def	oraşului	oraşelor

(iii) deal 'hill'

	Sg.	Pl.
Nom./acc. -def.	deal	dealuri
+def	dealul	dealurile
Gen./dat. -def	deal	dealuri
+def	dealului	dealurilor

when the noun is definite. A characteristic that Rumanian shares with Bulgarian and Albanian is the use of suffixes to mark definiteness: Latin *HOMO ILLE* > *omul* 'the man', with fusion of the demonstrative (compare the normal pattern in the West from *ILLE HOMO*). Indefinites follow the normal Romance pattern: *un om* 'a man'.

The representative sample in the chart of nouns demonstrates the greater variation in form within the feminines in the non-definite paradigms. Vocatives are discussed separately, as they are irregular and relatively infrequent. It will be seen that morphologically the neuters are masculine in the singuar and feminine in the plural. They have also been described as *ambigeneric* for this reason. Syntactically, it is difficult to choose between the two labels, the only relevant data, involving the agreement between adjectives and conjoined nouns of different genders, being highly unreliable.

The examples in the chart of nominal paradigms show that masculines and neuters are invariable without the definite suffix, in both singular and plural paradigms. In the indefinite system it is only feminines that show a distinction between nominative/accusative and genitive/dative, the feminine genitive/dative singulars normally coinciding in form with the plural. It is the suffixal nature of the definite marker that has contributed most to the apparent conservative nature of the Rumanian case system.

The vocative case is defective, being reserved mainly for animates, especially humans. It also usually occurs in the definite form: *om* 'man' → *omule* 'o man'; *cumătru* 'godfather' → *cumătrule* 'o godfather' (but also *cumetre* — the use of kin terms without possessives or definite determiners being common in Rumanian, as in other languages).

Proper names also occur as vocatives, the use of the definite suffix depending on the stem termination: *Radu* → *Radule* but *Gheorghe* → *Gheorghe* (not *Gheorghele*); *Ana* → *Ana, Ană* or *Ano*.

The vocative is under very heavy pressure and is likely to disappear. Its occurrence in the modern language, as limited as it is, is felt to be a Slavonic legacy — in particular, feminines in -*o* (*Ano; vulpe* 'vixen' → *vulpeo* 'o vixen' — though this latter is admittedly rare). This directly reflects a Slavonic termination and cannot readily be accounted for by normal evolution from the Latin vocatives.

Adjectives follow the same morphological pattern as nouns, with which they agree in gender, number and case. There are some less variable adjectives which do not distinguish masculine and feminine in the indefinite form of the nominative/accusative: *mare* 'big' (m./f. sg.) ~ *mari* 'big' (m./f. pl.), but genitive/dative feminine singular follows the same pattern as the nouns in matching the plural forms: *unui om mare* 'of/to a big man', *unei fete mari* 'of/to a big girl'. Normal adjectives inflect like the noun they agree with: *om bun* 'good man', *fată bună* 'good girl'; feminine/neuter plural adjectives take the -*e* form, not -*uri*. Finally, it is also possible for adjectives to take definite suffixes: *omul bun* 'the good man' and *bunul om* 'the *good* man'.

The personal pronoun system derives directly from Latin. The chart of personal pronouns shows cliticised and free forms for nominative, accusative and dative.

Personal Pronouns

		1st sg.	2nd sg.	3rd sg. (m.)	3rd sg. (f.)	1st pl.	2nd pl.	3rd pl. (m.)	3rd pl. (f.)
Nominative	Cliticised	eu	tu	el	ea	noi	voi	ei	ele
	Free								
Accusative	Cliticised	mă	te	îl	o	ne	vă	îi	le
	Free *pe* +	mine	tine	el	ea	noi	voi	ei	ele
Dative	Cliticised	îmi	îţi	îi	îi	ni	vi	le	le
	Free	mie	ţie	lui	ei	nouă	vouă	lor	lor

Note: The cliticised forms are the full forms. Syncope takes place depending on environment: for example, *îmi dau cadoul* 'they give the present to me' but *mi-l dau* 'they give it to me'.

The preposition *pe* is an accusative marker — its distribution is dealt with in section 4.

There are from three to five verb conjugations, depending on how strong is the linguist's desire to relate them to the classical Latin system. The infinitive and present indicative and subjunctive of the different types, together with *have* and *be*, are given in the chart of verb forms. The greatest controversy is whether verbs like *vedea* 'see' (from Latin second conjugation verbs like *VIDĒRE* and *MONĒRE*) are in the process of being absorbed into the larger pattern represented by *face* 'do, make'. Following the chart there is some discussion of the forms of the various tenses, moods and voices, with comments on their origins.

The future in Rumanian is periphrastic, and appears to have been so throughout its history. The more literary form is *voi cînta*, deriving from Vulgar Latin forms of *VOLEO* 'wish' (*voi, vei, va, vom, veţi, vor*) + infinitive. The selection of 'wish' as the auxiliary is characteristic of Balkan languages. Periphrastic too is the spoken future: *am să cînt* (lit.) 'have to sing' — formed from the auxiliary 'have' from *HABEO* + subjunctive; the invariable particle *o* also occurs in a similar structure: *o să cînt* 'I will sing', *o să cînţi* 'you will sing'.

The imperfect is a direct development from Latin -*BAM* forms: *cîntam, cîntai, cînta, cîntam, cîntaţi, cîntau* 'I etc. was singing/used to sing'. The perfect derives from the Latin perfect: *CANTĀVĪ > cîntai, cîntaşi, cîntă,*

Present Indicative and Subjunctive

	Type I (a) cîntá 'sing'	Type II vedeá 'see'	Type IV (a) **dormí 'sleep'	Type V (a) omorí 'kill'	Irregulars aveá 'have'	
1 sg.	cínt	vắd	dórm	omór	ám	
2 sg.	cínţi	vézi	dórmi	omóri	ái	
3 sg.	cíntă	véde	dóarme	omoáră	áre	
1 pl.	cîntắm	vedém	dormím	omorím	avém	
2 pl.	cîntáţi	vedéţi	dormíţi	omoríţi	avéţi	
3 pl.	cíntă	vắd	dórm	omoáră	áu	
3 subj.	să cínte	să vádă	să doármă	să omoáre	să aíbă	

	Type I (b) lucrá 'work'	Type III fáce 'make/do'	Type IV (b) **zidí 'build'	Type V (b) urí 'hate'	fi 'be' Indicative	Subjunctive
1 sg.	lucréz	fác	zidésc	urắsc	sínt	să fíu
2 sg.	lucrézi	fáci	zidéşti	urắşti	éşti	să fíi
3 sg.	lucreáză	fáce	zidéşte	urắşte	é(ste)	să fíe
1 pl.	lucrắm	fácem	zidím	urím	síntem	să fím
2 pl.	lucráţi	fáceţi	zidíţi	uríţi	sínteţi	să fíţi
3 pl.	lucreáză	fác	zidésc	urắsc	sínt	să fíe
3 subj.	să lucréze	să fácă	să zideáscă	să urắscă		

Note: Stress is shown on all forms, though it is normally unmarked in written Rumanian. Comparison between types II and III shows that type II has stress on the termination in 1 and 2 plural; in type III, stress is consistently on the stem.
** Orthography is irregular here — consistent system would show full vowel value of -i by -ii.

cîntárăm, cîntáráţi, cîntáră 'I etc. sang'. However, this is normal only in Oltenia, the western region of Muntenia (as well as in Arumanian, where its use matches that of the Greek aorist). Normally in Rumanian the compound perfect is used: *am, ai, a, am, aţi, au cîntat* 'I etc. sang/have sung' (based on *HABEO* + past participle). Conversely, in Rumanian the compound pluperfect does not exist, the synthetic forms deriving from Latin pluperfect subjunctives: *cîntásem, cîntáseşi, cîntáse, cîntáserăm, cîntáseráţi, cîntásera* 'I etc. had sung' (while in Arumanian, Greek contact is again reflected in the use of a compound pluperfect).

Morphologically, the present subjunctive has been all but neutralised with the indicative being differentiated from the present indicative only in the third person, except for the irregular *fi*. The remaining forms of the verb paradigm are periphrastic, with combinations of *voi* (future marker), *să* (subordinating particle) or *aş* (conditional particle) followed by the BE infinitive *fi* and then either the past participle (*chemat*) or the gerundive (*chemînd*). That is:

$$\left\{\begin{array}{l} \text{voi} \\ \text{să} \\ \text{aş} \end{array}\right\} \qquad \text{fi} \qquad \left\{\begin{array}{l} \text{chemat} \\ \text{chemînd} \end{array}\right\}$$

for example: *să fi chemat* (perfect subjunctive); *aş fi chemînd* (conditional presumptive).

Most notable of the periphrastic forms is the conditional: *aş, ai, ar, am, aţi, ar cînta* 'I etc. would sing'. This seems to represent the unusual process of a synthetic form being reinterpreted diachronically as an analytic construction, i.e. from original *cîntareaş*, the *-re* termination having been lost after the periphrastic form came about, in line with the general loss of the *-re* termination on all infinitives.

The morphological material on which the numeral system is based is predominantly Latin (with the exception of *sută* 'hundred', from Old Slavonic *sŭto*). There has, however, been a calquing on the Slavonic pattern for the teens and multiples of ten: *QUATTUOR SUPER DECEM* > *patrusprezece* 'fourteen'; *QUATTUOR + DECEM* > *patruzeci* 'forty'. Arumanian is more conservative in retaining the Latin 'twenty' (/jingits/, from *VĪGINTI*), but less conservative in following the Slavonic pattern for 'twenty-one' to 'twenty-nine' as well as for 'eleven' to 'nineteen' (/patrusprejingits/ 'twenty-four').

4 Syntax

The basic order of major constituents is: subject–verb–object (SVO), though variations occur under a variety of circumstances. Yes-no questions are normally represented by a change in intonation but inversion of subject and (part of the) verbal complex is an option, and normal with *wh*-questions: *cînd a venit Ion?* 'when did Ion come?'. Heavy constituents also may result in a change of word order, with long noun phrases containing embedded clauses being extraposed: *Merită să fie notate în această ordine încercările scriitorului de a găsi un echivalent sunetelor ă şi î* lit. 'deserve to be noted in this respect the attempts of the writer to find an equivalent for the sounds *ă* and *î*'. Pronouns also complicate discussion of word order. They can occur in different positions as clitics from their full noun phrase equivalents: *bărbatul a dat carnetul copilului* 'the man gave the notebook to the child', but *(el) i l-a dat* lit. '(he) to him it gave'. Along with most other Romance languages Rumanian subject personal pronouns can be dispensed with, there being sufficient morphological differences between the personal verb forms to make them redundant, except for emphasis or contrast.

OVS is also a common alternative to SVO, as in other Balkan languages such as Greek. The ability to distinguish subject from object morphologically increases the incidence of this reversed order. The preposition *pe* (normally 'on') acts as an accusative marker for all pronouns but also for full noun phrases high in animacy (and thus to some extent corresponds to Spanish *a* — see page 255). It can thus decode noun phrase–verb–noun phrase structures and is assisted in this by the use of reduplicative pronouns. *Ion a văzut-o pe Maria* lit. 'Ion saw her Maria' occurs as an alternative to *Ion a văzut Maria* 'Ion saw Maria', but both *pe* and the clitic must appear when the order is OVS: *pe Maria a văzut-o Ion* lit. 'Maria saw her Ion'. Resumptive pronouns also occur as a cross-reference for lower items on the animacy hierarchy when these occur as initial objects (though *pe* is not obligatory under these circumstances): *singura menţiune a acestei părţi de cuvînt o găsim în...* lit. 'the only mention of this word part (we) it find in...'; and in relative clauses, a relativised object must be represented by both decoding methods: *acesta e carnetul pe care l-am furat* lit. 'this is the notebook which (I) it stole'.

Variability in the use of *pe* as an object marker (it is a feature more of formal than of informal language) leads to hypercorrection. The Rumanian linguist Graur notes examples such as: *îmi trebuie pe cineva care...* lit. 'to me is necessary someone who...', where speakers have treated the grammatical subject *cineva* as an object.

Within noun phrases the normal order is:

(a)	Determiner	–	Noun	–	Adjective
	Un/acest		copil		bun
	'A/this good child'				
(b)	Noun+def	–	Demonstrative+def	–	Adjective
	Copilul		acesta		bun
	'This good child'				
(c)	Adjective+def	–	Noun		
	Bunul		copil		
	'The good child'				

Thus, indefinite determiners precede the noun, while adjectives (and relative clauses) follow it, except for contrastive use, as in (c); when demonstratives follow the noun (as in (b)), both are marked for definiteness.

Definiteness on nouns is unmarked when the noun is part of a prepositional phrase (*cu* 'with' is an exception), unless the noun is further modified: *masă* 'table'; *masa* 'the table'; *sub masă* 'under the table'; *sub masa pe care ai construit-o* 'under the table that you constructed (it)'. This phenomenon provides a useful method of distinguishing restrictive and non-restrictive relative clauses. Compare the following *non*-restrictive example, where the head noun is *not* marked for definiteness: *sub masă, pe care ai construit-o* 'under the table, which you constructed (it)'.

Rumanian retains the reflexive *se*, but with an increase in its use. In addition to its true reflexive sense (*se bate* 'beat oneself'), it has semi-fossilised to form verbs without a reflexive interpretation (*se duce* '(he) goes, to go'); it is used as an impersonal (*se spune* 'it is said') and as a passive (*aici se vînd cărţile* 'here are sold books').

Features shared with other Balkan languages include the periphrastic future, with 'wish' as the auxiliary; the use of a suffixal definite marker (found not only in Rumanian and Albanian, but also in Bulgarian/ Macedonian, unusual among the Slavonic languages in having the equivalent of the definite article in English); the use of cliticised resumptive pronouns (these occur in Western Romance but are usually part of a dislocated structure); and a severe decline in the use of the infinitive.

Like Western Romance, Rumanian inherited an infinitival complement clause structure in addition to indicative and subjunctive structures. However, where French and Italian would now use an infinitive Rumanian is more likely to use a subjunctive: Fr. *je veux chanter*; It. *volo cantare*; Rum. *vreau să cînt* 'I want to sing'. Within the auxiliary system one can see retention of the short infinitive: *voi cînta* 'I will sing'; *aş cînta* 'I would sing'. Many speakers also use *pot cînta* for *pot să cînt* 'I am able to sing'. Given the modal value of verbs representing ability or possibility, such an option is not surprising — the short infinitive can be seen as a stem form of the verbal complex and *pot* straddles the boundary between main verb and auxiliary verb.

The decline of the infinitive appears to be relatively recent. It is used as a complement clause marker in regular alternation with the subjunctive in a mid-eighteenth century grammar: *se cuvine a păzi/se cuvine să păzească* 'it is proper to be on guard'. Hand in hand with the reduction in use of the infinitive went its truncation (by loss of its Latin *-re* termination). In the modern language, *-re* forms are now clearly established as nominals and correspond closely to gerunds or derived nominals in English: *se întoarce* 'to return, he returns' → *întoarcerea lui neaşteptată* 'his unexpected return'.

Despite these Balkan characteristics, there has been some tendency during the last 150 years for the language to move towards the mainstream Romance pattern in syntax. The infinitive has begun to appear more regularly as a complement clause marker, and the periphrastic passive has made great inroads into the area occupied by the reflexive passive: *a fost furat* lit. 'was stolen' is more common than *s-a furat* lit. 'stole itself'. The regional use of a preposition to mark possession or indirect objects has found some currency in the spoken standard language, rather than the genitive/dative case marking. A much-cited example of a prepositional indirect object marking is : *dă apă la vite* instead of *dă apă vitelor* 'give water to the cattle'; and street vendors in Bucharest were noted between the wars as using the prepositional *planul de Bucureşti* in place of *planul Bucureştiului* 'plan of Bucharest'. In Arumanian it is normal to find the *la* 'to' + nominative/accusative structure with full noun phrases instead of the dative case, since Greek also has a prepositional construction: *ðíno ta práɣmata stin yinéka* 'I give the things to the woman'.

It is, of course, impossible to predict how far this reromancing tendency will go in morphosyntax but it is certainly the case that in some areas of structure change is unlikely. Thus, while there has been a resurgence in the use of the infinitival future (*voi cînta*) rather than the subjunctive alternative (*o să cînt*) in literary texts, it is hard to imagine Rumanian adopting a future based on infinitive + 'have' in line with Western Romance. Indeed, it would appear that in Western Romance a periphrastic future is also on the increase.

5   Vocabulary

Since vocabulary is more readily borrowed than other linguistic features, it is in its lexical stock that Rumanian has shown the greatest tendency to reromance during the last 150 years. For the same reason, however, the language had also had its original Latin lexical base diluted by contact with other languages in the Balkans, not least Slavonic. The total Slavonic element in Rumanian has been put as high as 40 per cent, though recent borrowings of international vocabulary have reduced this overall proportion considerably. It is in any case misleading to give a single figure for the language as a whole, since no speaker will use, or even know, all the words in the language. In everyday conversation the proportion of words from one source may well differ from the overall proportion in the language of material from that source. Using a basic 100- or 200-item word list relating to everyday life, it can be shown that Rumanian has a Latin lexical base of well over 90 per cent.

Nevertheless, the overall Slavonic element in Rumanian cannot be ignored, even if the Romance structure of the language has been left relatively unaffected. For the remainder of this section I give a brief résumé of the various lexical influences Rumanian has undergone, with examples from the major sources.

There is little evidence of substratum influence in Balkan Romance. Latin appears to have replaced the local Thracian language to such an extent that only a few words can even be considered Thracian in origin. Some of these are cognate with Albanian words and it is possible that they represent the remains of some Thraco-Illyrian language base. The following words are possible candidates, though it cannot be ruled out that they are indigenous Albanian words borrowed from Albanian by Rumanian: Rum. *abure* 'steam' (Alb. *avull*); Rum. *brad* 'fir' (Alb. *bredhi*); Rum. *mal* '(river) bank' (Alb. *mal*); Rum. *vatră* 'hearth' (Alb. *vatrë*).

Slavonic vocabulary in Rumanian can be divided into two main groups: popular, borrowed from the time of earliest contact between Balkan Romance and South Slavonic (approximately from the sixth century onwards); and technical or literary borrowings, from the thirteenth century onwards. This gave rise to doublets: from Old Slavonic *săvărșiti* came popular *sfîrşi* and literary *săvîrşi* 'finish, complete'. Borrowing was not always direct and calques can be found. One much-cited example: on the basis of the two meanings of the South Slavonic *svĕtŭ* 'light' and 'world', Latin *LŪMEN – LŪMINIS* 'light' had two derivations in Rumanian — *lume* 'world' and *lumină* 'light'.

Much religious vocabulary in Rumanian has a Slavonic character — as pointed out in section 2, Old Church Slavonic was the official language of the Orthodox church in what is now Rumania. When the vernacular became the norm, much of the Old Church Slavonic terminology was taken over. At the same time, it should be appreciated that an original source of much of this vocabulary was Greek, Old Church Slavonic merely being the vehicle for its transfer to Rumanian. The word *chilie* 'cell' attributed in section 2 to Slavonic was in fact borrowed originally by Old Church Slavonic from Greek *kéllion*. It is partly for this reason that Greek influence on Balkan Romance was much greater than on Western Romance. Greek words also found their way into Rumanian via popular Slavonic language: *broatec* 'toad' derives via Slavonic from Greek *brotachos*, with cognate forms in Albanian and Arumanian. However, the early borrowing *drum* 'way, road' via Bulgarian from Greek *ðrómos* is not found in the Arumanian of present-day Greece, where a derivative of Latin *CALLEM* 'track' is used instead (Arumanian /kale/; Rum. *cale* does exist but has a more restricted sense than the general word *drum*).

During the Phanariot period (1711–1821), when the principalities of Moldavia and Wallachia were administered for the Turks by Greek princes, many words were borrowed from Greek by Rumanian, though it has been calculated that of the more than 1,200 words borrowed in this period only 250 are left in the modern language (e.g. *stridie* 'oyster' from *stríði*; *aerisi* 'air, ventilate, fan' from the aorist of *aerízo*). During this period too, Turkish words found their way into Rumanian but many of these have also disappeared from use. Perhaps three per cent of Rumanian vocabulary is Turkish in origin, and relatively common words include: *duşman* 'enemy' (Tk. *duşman*) and *chior* 'one-eyed' (Tk. *kör*).

Over the last 200 years the influence of Western Romance and Latin on Rumanian has been substantial. The Transylvanian School began importing Western Romance loans from the late eighteenth century, but interest was more in the Latin origins of the language than in Romance relationships. Consequently, not only did they etymologise their writing system (see section 1), but they also set about purging the language of Slavonic loans and creating new Latin-based vocabulary. Some portmanteau words were created: from Slavonic-based *război* 'war' and Latin *BELLUM* was created *război*, which has not survived into the modern language; on the other hand, the combination of Slavonic-based *năravuri* 'customs' and Latin *MŌRES* gave *moravuri* 'customs, morals', which is in common use today. The desire to 'improve' and 'purify' Rumanian on the part of the Transylvanian School has complicated considerably the already difficult task of carrying out research on the origins of Rumanian vocabulary.

It was the rise of France and French as cultural models during the nineteenth century that did most to change the overall pattern of the Rumanian word stock. French became the source of much new vocabulary but also the vehicle for the entry of words from other languages. For example, a modern dictionary attributes *miting* '(political) meeting' and *dumping* '(trade) dumping' to 'French (from English)'. On the other hand, some French vocabulary entered Rumanian via Russian. As Russian influence increased during the second half of the nineteenth century, military and administrative terms were introduced: *infanterie* 'infantry', *cavalerie* 'cavalry', *parlament* 'parliament' and *administraţie* 'administration' all appear to have followed this route.

There were two distinct attitudes among writers of the Muntenian school towards the treatment of Romance loans. There were those who, like the Transylvanian School, wanted to modify considerably in line with what were felt to be normal Rumanian developments. This gave rise to linguistic terms such as *obiept* and *subiept* in place of *obiect* and *subiect* (though the *-pt-* form reflects the $CT > pt$ pattern discussed in section 2, it was the *-ct-* form that survived). Other writers took a more realistic approach and, while only using words for which there was not already an adequate native Rumanian equivalent, embraced the imported vocabulary without amendment. Nevertheless, the lack of a clear relationship between French spelling and pronunciation has meant that, for example, Fr. *réveillon* is rendered in Rumanian today as both *reveion* and *revelion* 'New Year celebration'. Finally, French loans also gave rise to doublets as Latin-based words came face to face again. In addition to the example in section 2, *sentiment* was imported alongside the more native *simţămînt* 'feeling, sentiment'.

Today, the effect of American economic power and technological growth can be felt in the importing of many English technical and commercial terms into Rumanian, their fate regulated to some extent by the Rumanian Academy, which began to unify the treatment of neologisms (choosing, for example, the appropriate gender and plural forms) from 1940 onwards. The irony is of course that much of this new vocabulary from English has itself Latin and Romance origins, thus adding yet another layer onto what was already a very complex foundation.

Bibliography

Much of the material produced on the language is inaccessible, being either published in Rumania or written in Rumanian. A thorough reference grammar in English does not exist, though one is in preparation by this author for the Croom Helm Descriptive Grammars series.

Agard (1958) is a short volume in structuralist mould, concentrating on phonology and morphology, while Lombard (1974) is a detailed structural description, fuller than Agard but more difficult to find one's way around. Deletant (1983) is a very good introduction to the language for those wishing to speak it. The Academy grammar, Graur et al. (1963), is very thorough and better than many academy grammars, though it has the usual slightly prescriptive bias. Sandfeld and Olsen (1936–62) is a full description of the syntax of the written language, with many examples, in the style of Lombard; a transformational description of the major syntactic structures, in the framework of Chomsky's Standard Theory, is provided by Vasiliu and Golopenția-Eretescu (1969).

For the history of the language, Rosetti (1968) gives a wealth of detail on the development of the language from Latin and its contact with other languages, and is well worth the effort for those with an interest in Romance languages; Rosetti (1973) is a brief summary of this magnum opus. Close (1974) is an excellent discussion of the rise of the Muntenian dialect as the standard language, with great detail on the nineteenth-century vogue for Romance and particularly French linguistic culture.

References

Agard, F.B. 1958. *Structural Sketch of Rumanian* (Linguistic Society of America, Baltimore)

Close, E. 1974. *The Development of Modern Rumanian — Linguistic Theory and Practice in Muntenia 1821–1838* (Oxford University Press, Oxford)

Deletant, D. 1983. *Colloquial Romanian* (Routledge and Kegan Paul, London)

Graur, Al. et al. 1963. *Gramatica limbii romîne*, 2 vols. (Academy of Sciences, Bucharest)

Lombard, A. 1974. *La Langue roumaine — une présentation* (Klincksieck, Paris)

Rosetti, Al. 1968. *Istoria limbii române de la origini pînă în secolul al XVII-lea* (Bucharest)

—— 1973. *Brève histoire de la langue roumaine des origines à nos jours* (Mouton, The Hague)

Sandfeld, Kr. and H. Olsen. 1936–62. *Syntaxe roumaine*, 3 vols. (Droz, Paris)

Vasiliu, E. and S. Golopenția-Eretescu. 1969. *Sintaxa transformațională a limbii române* (Bucharest; also available in an irritatingly poor English translation, *The Transformational Syntax of Romanian*, Mouton, The Hague, 1972)

14 Slavonic Languages

Bernard Comrie

The approximate present distribution of the Slavonic languages can be seen from the attached sketch-map. The languages currently spoken, according to their genetic relations within Slavonic (see below) are: South Slavonic: Bulgarian, Macedonian, Serbo-Croat, Slovene; West Slavonic: Czech, Slovak, Polish, Upper and Lower Sorbian (Lusatian); East Slavonic: Russian, Ukrainian, Belorussian (White Russian). In addition, two extinct Slavonic languages are known from texts: Polabian (a West Slavonic language spoken in northern Germany until around 1700) and Old Church Slavonic (Old Bulgarian) (a South Slavonic language attested by a huge volume of texts starting in the ninth century). In phonological and morphological structure the Slavonic languages are very close to one another, more so than the Romance languages. The same applies to their basic lexicon; for more abstract and technical vocabulary, however, there is considerable language diversity, reflecting different national policies towards loanwords and use of native word-forming techniques: thus Russian and Polish use the international word *teatr* 'theatre', while Czech uses *divadlo* (from a root meaning 'look') and Serbo-Croat has two words, the western variety preferring *kazalište* (from a root meaning 'show'), the eastern variety *pozorište* (from a root meaning 'see').

The earliest Slavonic texts are from the ninth century (though extant copies are later), in Old Church Slavonic. Since the final break-up of Common Slavonic unity is dated towards the beginning of our millennium, Old Church Slavonic is very close to Late Common Slavonic, although Old Church Slavonic does have distinctive South Slavonic (more specifically, Bulgarian-Macedonian) features. Two alphabets were in use in the early period, both providing a good fit to the phonemic system of Old Church Slavonic: Glagolitic and Cyrillic. Glagolitic is usually considered the older; the forms of its letters are quite distinctive, although similarities to the alphabets of other important Christian languages of the period are detectable. The Cyrillic alphabet is more closely modelled on Greek (see the chapters on Russian and Serbo-Croat for two modern Cyrillic alphabets). The Cyrillic alphabet continues in use among Slavonic peoples of traditional

Map 14.1: Approximate Distribution of Slavonic Languages in Europe

(adapted from Jakobson 1955)

Orthodox religion (i.e. for the East Slavonic languages, Bulgarian, Macedonian and the eastern variety of Serbo-Croat), while the others use the Roman alphabet.

Within the Indo-European family, the Slavonic languages are satem languages, with sibilant reflexes of PIE $\hat{k}$, e.g. PIE *$dek\hat{m}$ 'ten', OCS $dese\iota\iota$. An interesting development in the vowel system, of major importance for the later development of Slavonic, is the shift of PIE *i, *u to reduced vowels (jers), symbolised ι, ι, e.g. OCS $m\iota gla$ 'mist' (cf. Lith. $migl\grave{a}$), OCS $sn\iota xa$

'daughter-in-law' (cf. Skt. *snuṣā́*). Two main sets of sound changes separate Proto-Indo-European from Common Slavonic. One is a tendency for sounds within the syllable to be arranged in order of increasing sonority (i.e. obstruents, then liquids and semi-vowels, then vowels). Particular changes instantiating this tendency are: (a) loss of syllable-final consonants, e.g. OCS *synъ* 'son' (cf. Lith. *sūnùs*); (b) the development of certain sequences of vowel plus nasal within the syllable to nasalised vowels, of which Common Slavonic has back *$*ǫ$ and front *$*ę$, e.g. OCS *svętъ* 'holy' (cf. Lith. *šveñtas*), OCS *pǫtь* 'way' (cf. Lat. *pons*, gen. *pontis* 'bridge'); (c) the monophthongisation of diphthongs, e.g. OCS *iti* 'to go' (cf. Lith. *eīti*), OCS *suxъ* 'dry' (cf. Lith. *saūsas*); (d) the development of sequences of *$*o$ or *$*e$ plus a liquid within the syllable (symbolised *$*tort$) either by metathesis (South and West Slavonic) or by insertion of a vowel after the liquid (East Slavonic), e.g. OCS *glava*, Cz. *hláva*, Po. *głowa*, Rus. *golova* 'head' (cf. Lith. *galvà*).

The second major set of sound changes is a series of palatalisations. By the first palatalisation, *$*g$, *$*k$, *$*x$ become, respectively, *ž, č, š* before original front vowels, e.g. OCS *živъ* (cf. Lith. *gývas*). By the second palatalisation, the same three consonants become, respectively, ʒ (a voiced dental affricate, subsequently de-affricated to *z* in most languages), *c* (voiceless dental affricate) and *s* (but *š* in West Slavonic) before front vowels newly arisen from monophthongisation, e.g. OCS *cěna* 'price' (cf. Lith. *káina*). Thus the first palatalisation took place before monophthongisation had occurred, the second palatalisation after. The third palatalisation has the same effect as the second, but occurs after front vowels, e.g. OCS *kъnęʒь* 'prince', a loan from Common Gmc. *$*kuningaz$ 'king'. Since a given morpheme can occur sometimes before a back vowel, sometimes before a front vowel, the palatalisations give rise to synchronic morphophonemic alternations, e.g. OCS *mǫka* 'torment', *mǫčiti* 'to torture'; *noga* 'leg', locative singular *noʒě* (where *ě* is from *$*āi$). In addition to the three palatalisations, Common Slavonic also developed palatal consonants *nj, lj, rj* from sequences of sonorant plus semi-vowel; despite the usual transcription, these are unit phonemes. Finally, sequences of dentals plus *$*j$ also gave rise to palatal consonants, e.g. OCS *šyti* 'to sew' (cf. Lith. *siūti*).

In terms of nominal declension, the oldest Slavonic languages are conservative Indo-European languages. Three numbers are distinguished (singular, dual, plural), as are three genders (masculine, feminine, neuter) and seven cases (nominative, vocative, accusative, genitive, dative, instrumental, locative). The distinct declension classes and the distinction between substantival and pronominal declension are retained, though there are many analogies leading to the combination of similar declension classes (for instance, of masculine *o*-stems and *u*-stems, see below). An important innovation of the Common Slavonic period is the relevance of animacy to declension, whereby certain animate nouns (originally only some masculine singulars) replace the accusative by the genitive, e.g. OCS *bogъ* 'God', accusative *boga*, but *gradъ* 'city', accusative *gradъ*. An innovation within the morphology of adjectives is the development of pronominal adjectives, initially used only attributively and indicating a definite noun phrase, e.g. OCS *dobryjь člověkъ* 'the good man', cf. *dobrъ člověkъ* 'a good man'; Common Slavonic, like most of the modern languages (except Bulgarian and Macedonian), has no articles.

The verbal morphology of Common Slavonic represents a more radical departure from Proto-Indo-European. The morphological encoding of person and number in finite verbs is retained, as is the present/imperfect/aorist opposition. Morphologically expressed voice and mood distinctions are lost, except for that between indicative and imperative. There is no morphologically expressed future. The aspectual opposition between imperfective and perfective, so characteristic of the modern Slavonic languages (see further the chapter on Russian, pages 340–1), is already present, at least in embryonic form, from the earliest Slavonic texts. Various periphrastic verb constructions are found: the perfect, formed with the auxiliary 'be' and the past participle, occurs in all the languages, while the auxiliaries used for the future vary considerably from language to language.

Within the Indo-European family, the Slavonic languages are particularly close to the Baltic languages (Lithuanian, Latvian, Old Prussian), whence the frequent use of Lithuanian in this section for comparison with Slavonic. One particularly striking parallelism is the above-mentioned development of pronominal adjectives, cf. Lith. *geràsis žmogùs* 'the good man', *gēras žmogùs* 'a good man'. At one time these similarities were considered evidence for a single Balto-Slavonic branch of Indo-European, but now most scholars adhere rather to the view that such similarities, to the extent that they are not independent parallel developments, represent close contact between the two branches, rather than a period of common development.

As indicated above, the Slavonic languages subdivide into three groups, which can be identified on the basis of phonological criteria. The most salient characteristic of East Slavonic is the already cited insertion of an extra vowel in **tort* sequences (*polnoglasie*), as in Rus. *golova* 'head'. One salient characteristic of West Slavonic is the development of **tj* to *c* and of **dj* to *ʒ* (later de-affricated in most languages to *z*), e.g. PIE **medhjos*, Po. *miedza*, Cz. *meze*, cf. Rus. *meža*, OCS *mežda*, SCr. *mèđa*, Slovene *méja* 'boundary'; another is the development of **x* to *š*, rather than *s*, under the second and third palatalisations, e.g. Po. *szary*, Old Cz. *šěrý*, cf. Old Rus. *sěrъ*, Slovene *sęr* 'grey'. South Slavonic is a much less homogeneous grouping, and the only clear common phonological innovation is the development of Early Common Slavonic **jōns* (which occurs in a few morphological forms) to *ę* rather than to *ě*; indeed, the apparent unity of South Slavonic may well be in large measure an artefact of its physical separation from the other Slavonic languages, in particular Slovak, by the incursion of Hungarian and the expansion of Rumanian.

It is more difficult to say much that is interesting and reliable about Common Slavonic syntax. Most of the earliest texts are rather literal translations, especially from Greek, and it is therefore difficult to know to what extent word order, for instance, follows native Slavonic preferences or is calqued directly from the original. On the basis of the early textual evidence and comparison with later stages of the Slavonic languages, one can however state two generalisations that tie in intimately with the rich morphological system. Word order is grammatically free, i.e. there is no fixed order among subject, predicate, objects, adverbial modifiers etc.; the case inflections are usually sufficient to retrieve these grammatical relations, and variation in word order correlates primarily with pragmatic distinctions such as that between topic and comment (see further the chapter on Russian, pages 344–6). The rich morphological system also provides rich possibilities for agreement: thus, the verb agrees in person and number with its subject, and adjectives agree in gender, number and case with their head noun.

Later phonological, morphological and syntactic developments belong properly to the histories of the individual Slavonic languages, but the seeds of some of these later developments can already be seen in the Late Common Slavonic period, representing changes that had already begun in the Common Slavonic period but then took somewhat different paths in the different languages. Above, we have already discussed the different details of palatalisation and of *tort sequences in different branches of Slavonic. One major innovation of the early literary period that unites the Slavonic languages in type but divides them in detail is the subsequent development of the jers. In all Slavonic languages, a distinction is made between strong and weak jers, where in general a weak jer is one in word-final position or in a syllable preceding a full vowel, while a strong jer is one in a syllable preceding a weak jer. Weak jers are lost, while strong jers are strengthened to full vowels, but the precise full vowel to which each of the two jers is strengthened varies from language to language. In Common Slavonic *sъnъ 'sleep', the first jer is strong, the second weak. In Russian, strong ъ gives o, i.e. son; in Polish it gives e, i.e. sen. The loss of the jers has a major effect on the phonological structure of words in Slavonic languages, since it leads to consonant clusters that were previously impossible: thus Common Slavonic *gъdanьskъ is contracted from four syllables to one in Polish Gdańsk.

Another phonological development that characterises much of the Slavonic domain, especially East Slavonic and Polish, is the further development of a systematic opposition between plain and palatalised consonants. Weak ь, though lost as a segment, palatalises a preceding consonant, e.g. Rus. pjat´ 'five', cf. OCS pętь. In Common Slavonic, there is no possible palatalisation opposition before o, whereas language-particular developments in Russian and Polish give rise to just this contrast: from the Common Slavonic stem *nes- 'carry' Russian has /ńos/ '(he) carried' (cf. *nos* 'nose'), while Polish has *niosę* (phonemically /ńosē/) 'I carry'.

The rich nominal morphology of Common Slavonic is remarkably stable over most of the Slavonic territory. Only Bulgarian and Macedonian have completely lost morphological case. The dual has been lost in all Slavonic languages except Slovene and Sorbian. Most languages have undergone some simplification of the remaining distinctions, the main line of innovation being the loss of minor declension types in favour of the three main declension classes (*o*-stems, *a*-stems, *i*-stems), though in some instances the actual surviving inflection is taken from the minor class (e.g. the most common Polish suffixes for genitive and dative of masculine *o*-stems are *-u* and *-owi*, originally from the *u*-stems).

The morphology of the verb has undergone more radical shifts. Here, Bulgarian and Macedonian prove to be most conservative in retaining the rich Common Slavonic system, although both have also innovated in the development of special periphrastic verb constructions to indicate events not directly witnessed by the speaker (*preizkazvane*), e.g. Bulgarian *toj bil peel* 'he was (they say) singing', cf. *toj peeše* 'he was singing'. The aorist and imperfect have been ousted by the originally compound perfect in most Slavonic languages: apart from Bulgarian and Macedonian, these verb forms survive only in Sorbian and in literary Serbo-Croat. The aspectual opposition between imperfective and perfective has developed in all Slavonic languages (including Bulgarian and Macedonian) into a fully-fledged morphological opposition.

Bibliography

Jakobson (1955) is an introductory survey of the family and the individual languages, including comparative grammar. De Bray (1980) gives a concise grammar of each of the modern literary languages and Old Church Slavonic, with comparative and historical commentary and a good, up-to-date bibliography. Though rather dated, Entwistle and Morison (1964) is the only comprehensive comparative grammar available in English. Bräuer (1961-) is an excellent condensation of traditional Slavonic comparative grammar lore, but the morphology volumes to date unfortunately cover only noun declension. Vaillant (1950–77) is a solid comparative grammar. Schenker and Stankiewicz (1980) deals with each of the literary languages, including Old Church Slavonic and Cassubian, and is useful equally for the languages not given separate sections in this volume.

References

Bräuer, H. 1961–. *Slavische Sprachwissenschaft* (Walter de Gruyter, Berlin)
De Bray, R.G.A. 1980. *Guide to the South Slavonic Languages*; *Guide to the West Slavonic Languages*; *Guide to the East Slavonic Languages*, 3 vols. (Slavica, Columbus, Oh.) (= *Guide to the Slavonic Languages*, 3rd ed.)

Entwistle, W.J. and W.A. Morison. 1964. *Russian and the Slavonic Languages* (Faber and Faber, London)

Jakobson, R. 1955. *Slavic Languages: A Condensed Survey* (King's Crown Press, New York)

Schenker, A.M. and E. Stankiewicz (eds.) 1980. *The Slavic Literary Languages: Formation and Development* (Yale Concilium on International and Area Studies, New Haven, Conn.)

Vaillant, A. 1950–77. *Grammaire comparée des langues slaves*, 5 vols. (vols. 1–2, IAC, Paris; vols. 3–5, Klincksieck, Paris)

15 Russian

Bernard Comrie

1 Historical Background

Russian, together with Ukrainian and Belorussian, is a member of the East Slavonic group within the Slavonic branch of Indo-European. Although the three languages are now considered distinct literary languages, they are very close to one another, with a high degree of mutual intelligibility. At the time of the emergence of writing in East Slavonic, around the year 1000, there was just a single language, conventionally called Old Russian. In terms of the development of Russian as a modern literary language and of the separation of Ukrainian and Belorussian, there are two strands that must continually be borne in mind: the relation between native East Slavonic forms and forms borrowed from South Slavonic, and the relations among regional variations within East Slavonic.

Although there is some controversy concerning the possible independent, native development of writing in Russian, it is generally agreed that writing was introduced to Russia together with Christianity towards the end of the tenth century. The liturgical language that was introduced in this process was Old Church Slavonic, a South Slavonic language. At this period Old Church Slavonic and Old Russian were presumably easily mutually intelligible, yet still there were clear differences between them, namely the criterial differences between East and South Slavonic (see page 325). At this early period, much of the writing was of religious content (biblical and liturgical translations, saints' lives) or was written by monks (for instance, historical chronicles), and in such writing the attempt was made to write Church Slavonic, avoiding local East Slavonic dialect peculiarities. In practice, the Russian monks writing these manuscripts often erred by allowing East Slavonic forms to creep into their texts, but many of the religious texts of this time are very close to canonical Old Church Slavonic. Parallel to this writing in Church Slavonic, secular writing also developed, in particular for legal purposes (law codes, contracts, wills, treaties), later also personal messages. The language of these secular documents is much closer to the East Slavonic of the time, although inevitably, since any scribe was trained in Church Slavonic, numerous Church Slavonic forms crept into secular texts. Thus

Old Russian of this early period was characterised by diglossia between native East Slavonic (the low variety) and Church Slavonic (the high variety).

With the passage of time, the divergence between the two varieties became gradually less, in particular with many Church Slavonic forms gaining acceptance into even the lowest forms of language. A break in this process was marked by the second South Slavonic influence. A number of South Slavonic clerics were appointed to important ecclesiastical offices in Russia in the late fourteenth and early fifteenth centuries, and one effect of their influence was a return, in religious writing, to a more correct imitation of canonical Old Church Slavonic. While South Slavonic forms already accepted into lower styles remained, the higher styles now followed an archaic Church Slavonic language far removed from the spoken language of the period.

By the eighteenth century, in particular through the modernisation and secularisation efforts of Peter the Great, need was felt for a written language that would be closer to the educated spoken norm. The brilliant polymath M.V. Lomonosov, in his *Russian Grammar* (1755), set out a theory of three styles. According to this theory, there should be a high style, i.e. Church Slavonic, which would be used (in addition to religious purposes) for high poetic genres; a low style, almost purely East Slavonic (except for fully assimilated Church Slavonic features), to be used for personal correspondence and low comedy; and a middle style, to be used for lyric poetry, literary prose and scientific treatises. The modern standard language is closest to the middle style, though recent suggestions assign a much greater role to the spoken language of the aristocracy in its development. In any event, the modern standard language is already established by the time of A.S. Pushkin (1799–1837), the first of the great writers of Russia's nineteenth century. Although the language has continued to develop during the intervening two centuries, which have included the major social upheaval of the October Revolution (1917), the modern Russian literary language is still defined chronologically as the language from Pushkin to the present day.

The coexistence of East Slavonic and South Slavonic forms from the earliest Old Russian to the present day is one of the salient characteristics of the language. It may be compared with the coexistence of Anglo-Saxon and Norman French elements in English, with the exception that East and South Slavonic are much closer to one another genetically than are English and French. In modern Russian, it is common to find doublets, i.e. derivatives of the same Common Slavonic root in both East Slavonic and Church Slavonic forms, the Church Slavonic form usually having a more abstract or learned connotation. One of the main differences between East Slavonic and South Slavonic is the treatment of Common Slavonic sequences of *o/e* followed by a liquid between consonants, symbolised **tort*. In East Slavonic, this sequence yields *torot*, while in South Slavonic it yields *trat*. In modern

Russian, alongside East Slavonic *golová* 'head', there is also South Slavonic *glavá* 'chief; chapter'. (Note that in English *head* is of Anglo-Saxon origin, whereas *chief* and *chapter* are of Romance origin.) Another distinction between the two groups of Slavonic languages is the treatment of Common Slavonic **tj*, **dj*, which give East Slavonic *č*, *ž*, but South Slavonic *šč* (more accurately: *št*, but pronounced *šč* in Russian Church Slavonic), *žd*: contrast the East Slavonic form *gorjáčij* 'hot' with the present participle *gorjáščij* 'burning', which, like all modern Russian present participles, is of Church Slavonic origin. Since Common Slavonic had, within the paradigm of the same verb, some forms with just **t* and others with **t* followed by **j*, this gives rise to morphophonemic alternations in modern Russian, either between *t* and *č* (East Slavonic forms, e.g. *platít'* 'to pay', *plačú* 'I pay') or between *t* and *šč* (Church Slavonic forms, e.g. *sokratít'* 'to abbreviate', *sokraščú* 'I shall abbreviate'). In addition to East Slavonic and Church Slavonic doublets of the above kinds, there are also some instances where the Church Slavonic form has completely supplanted the native form, e.g. *sládkij* 'sweet', cf. Old Russian *solodъkъjь*.

At the time of the oldest Russian texts, the main dialect division was between Northern and Southern Russian, the dividing line running approximately along the latitude of present-day Moscow. The cultural centre of the south was Kiev; the north had several centres, the most important being Novgorod. In texts from the northern area, a number of regional features occur, one of the most salient being the neutralisation of *c* and *č* into a single affricate, usually *c*. It is probable that at this early period north and south were already divided by what is still one of the major dialect divisions in Russian, namely the pronunciation of Common Slavonic **g*, the north having a plosive [g], the south a fricative [ɣ]; the age of this feature is suggested, among other things, by the fact that modern Ukrainian and Belorussian share this feature with Southern Russian dialects. Unfortunately, the Cyrillic alphabet has no way of distinguishing between the plosive and fricative sounds, so textual evidence is inconclusive.

The linguistic separation of Ukrainian and Belorussian runs parallel to their political separation. In the mid-thirteenth century, Russia proper fell under Tatar domination, and subsequently what are now the Ukraine and Belorussia fell under Lithuanian, subsequently Polish hegemony. The distinctive features of Ukrainian are most marked, with Belorussian often occupying an intermediate position between the other East Slavonic languages. During the period of political separation, innovations that began in the Ukraine were in general unable to penetrate to Russian, and vice versa. One of the main characteristics of Ukrainian is the development of Common Slavonic **ě*, which in standard Russian ultimately merged with *e*, to *i*, e.g. Old Russian *lěto*, Russian *léto*, Ukrainian *líto* 'summer'. Another characteristic of Ukrainian is that consonants lose their palatalisation before reflexes of Old Russian *e* (Ukrainian *e*) and *i* (Ukrainian *y*). Belorussian has fewer unique characteristics, one being the affrication of palatalised *t*, *d* to *ć*, *ʒ́*, just as in Polish.

Meanwhile, in Russian proper, another phonological development of major importance for the dialectal composition of the language was taking place, namely *ákan'e*. This refers to the pronunciation of Old Russian unstressed *o* as *a*, e.g. of *vodá* 'water' as [vadá]. This change probably started somewhere in the south of Russia, but spread rapidly to cover the whole of the south, some central areas, and also Belorussia (but not the Ukraine, further evidence of its greater separateness). Lack of *ákan'e* is referred to as *ókan'e*. This phonological development ties in with a crucial political development. In the struggle against the Tatars, a key role came to be played by Muscovy, the area around Moscow, leading to the independence and unification of Russia (minus the Ukraine and Belorussia) under Moscow by the late fifteenth century. Although Moscow seems originally to have been part of the *ókan'e* dialect area, the city and surrounding area succumbed to the spread of *ákan'e*. Moscow's central position, coupled with the fact that it combined features of Northern dialects (in particular, the plosive pronunciation of *g*) and of Southern dialects (in particular, *ákan'e*), led to the formation of a new intermediate dialect grouping, the Central dialects, which lie at the basis of the modern standard language. Although the orthography still fails to record *ákan'e* (thus the word for 'water' is spelled *voda*), *ákan'e* was admitted as the norm in the middle style by Lomonosov and has since then been required in the standard language. The main dialect areas in Russian are thus: Northern (*ókan'e*, plosive *g*), Central (*ákan'e*, plosive *g*) and Southern (*ákan'e*, fricative *g*), with the standard language following the compromise Central dialect distribution of these features. Despite the huge area over which Russian is spoken, dialect differences, whether regional or social, are remarkably small and are, as in many other countries, becoming ever smaller with the spread of education.

In addition to examining Russian relative to its own internal divisions, it is also important to recognise that it is the major language of a multi-national state, the USSR (until 1917: the Russian Empire), and that it therefore interacts with over a hundred other languages, many of them genetically totally unrelated to Russian. In the USSR, Russian serves as the effective official language for all purposes other than local affairs in non-Russian-speaking areas. According to the 1979 census, Russian is spoken natively by 153.5 million people in the USSR, or 58.6% of the total population. It is dominant in European Russia and also in large parts of Siberia and the Far East, where Russian immigration over the last few centuries has resulted in the original inhabitants becoming often a small minority in their homeland. Of those Soviet citizens who are not native speakers of Russian, 61.3 million claimed fluent command of Russian as a second language, giving a total of 214.8 million first- and second-language speakers. (The number of Russian speakers outside the USSR is minimal in comparison with this total.)

2 Phonology

The segmental phonemes of Russian (stressed vowels, consonants) are set out in table 15.1; certain minor phonemes, which occur only in the speech of some speakers of the standard language, have been omitted. One striking feature of this phoneme inventory is the richness of the consonant system, in large measure due to the almost completely systematic opposition of palatalised and non-palatalised consonants, as in *brat'* 'to take' [brat´] versus *brat* 'brother' [brat]. The only non-palatalised consonants to lack palatalised counterparts are [c], [š], [ž]. Conversely, a few consonants are always palatalised with no non-palatalised counterpart: [č], [š:], [j]. (The functional yield of palatalisation with the velars is, incidentally, minimal.)

Table 15.1: Segmental Phonemes of Russian

Vowels

i	ɨ	u
e		o
	a	

Consonants

	Plain stop		Affricate	Fricative		Nasal	Lateral	Trill	Semi-vowel
Bilabial	p	b				m			
	ṕ	b́				ḿ			
Labio-dental				f	v				
				f́	v́				
Dental	t	d	c			n	l		
	t́	d́				ń	ĺ		
Alveolar				s	z			r	
				ś	ź			ŕ	
Palato-alveolar			č	š	ž				
				š:					j
Velar	k	g		x					
	ḱ	ǵ		x́					

The vowels represented in table 15.1 are those found in stressed syllables. In Russian, stress is free (can occur in principle on any syllable of a word) and mobile (different forms of the same word can have different stresses). Thus lexical items can be distinguished solely by stress, e.g. *muká* 'flour', *múka* 'torment', as can morphological forms of the same lexical item, e.g. genitive singular *rukí*, nominative plural *rúki*, from *ruká* 'hand'. Although there are some principles of accentuation (e.g. perfective verbs with the prefix *vy-* always stress this prefix), there is much that is purely conventional, and even within the standard language there are many instances of alternative stresses. Within the stressed vowel system, the phonemic status of the *i/i* opposition is debatable: in general, *i* occurs only after non-palatalised consonants, *i* only after palatalised consonants and word-initially. One of the main characteristics of Russian phonology is that the vowel system of unstressed syllables is radically different, because of a number of vowel neutralisations affecting, for many speakers, all vowels except *u*. By the phenomenon of *ákan'e*, the *o/a* opposition is neutralised in unstressed syllables (for the position after a palatalised consonant, see below): word-initially and in the immediately pretonic syllable, both vowels appear phonetically as [ʌ], elsewhere as [ə], e.g. *golová* 'head' [gəlʌvá], *magazín* 'shop' [məgʌzín]. After palatalised consonants, all of *a/e/o*, for some speakers also *i*, are neutralised to give [ɪ], e.g. *mestá* 'places' [mʲɪstá], *časý* 'clock' [čɪsí] (this phenomenon is referred to as *íkan'e*; the precise

Table 15.2: Russian Alphabet

Printed		Handwritten		Transliteration
А	а			a
Б	б			b
В	в			v
Г	г			g
Д	д			d
Е	е			e
Ё	ё			ë
Ж	ж			ž
З	з			z
И	и			i
Й	й			j
К	к			k
Л	л			l
М	м			m
Н	н			n
О	о			o
П	п			p
Р	р			r
С	с			s
Т	т			t
У	у			u
Ф	ф			f
Х	х			x
Ц	ц			c
Ч	ч			č
Ш	ш			š
Щ	щ			šč
	ъ			"
	ы			y
	ь			'
Э	э			e
Ю	ю			ju
Я	я			ja

nature of *íkan'e* is subject to a number of more specific constraints and also to some variation, even within the standard language).

The Russian writing system uses the Cyrillic alphabet (table 15.2). The writing system is based, like the Greek and Roman alphabets, on the alphabetic system, with as a basic principle one letter per phoneme. To assist the reader in converting the transliterations used in this section to a reasonably accurate phonetic representation, some details of divergences between phoneme and letter sequences will be noted. Although stress is phonemic in Russian, it is not usual to mark stress in writing; in this chapter, however, stress is always marked by an acute accent. Likewise, the diacritic on *ë*, which is always stressed, is usually omitted in writing Russian, but is systematically included here. Otherwise, for vowels, it should be noted that Russian orthography does not represent the effects of *ákan'e* and similar phenomena: thus the unstressed vowels of голова (*golová*) 'head' and магазин (*magazín*) 'shop' are distinguished orthographically, but not phonetically.

In pronunciation, Russian word-final obstruents are always voiceless, but orthographically voiced and voiceless obstruents are distinguished: thus рот (*rot*) 'mouth' and род (*rod*) 'birth' are both pronounced [rot]. Similarly, in Russian, sequences of obstruents assimilate in voicing to the last obstruent, but this is not shown in the orthography, e.g. гибкий (*gíbkij*) 'flexible' [ǵípkij]. The main complication in relating spelling to pronunciation, however, is the representation of palatalisation. It will be seen from comparison of tables 15.1 and 15.2 that Russian has no special letters for palatalised consonants. Rather, palatalisation is indicated by modifying the non-palatalised consonant letter as follows. Word-finally or before a consonant, palatalisation is indicated by adding the letter ь after the non-palatalised consonant, as in брать (*brat'*) 'to take' [braf], тьма (*t'ma*) 'mist' [t́ma]. Before a vowel, different vowel symbols are used to distinguish palatalised and non-palatalised consonants. After a non-palatalised consonant, the vowel letters а, э, ы, о, у (*a, è, i, o, u*) are used; after a palatalised consonant я, е, и, ё, ю (*ja, e, i, ë, ju*) are used; e.g. мать (*mat'*) 'mother' [maf], мять (*mjat'*) 'to crumple' [ḿat]. The unpaired consonants ц, ч, ш, щ, ж, (*c, č, š, šč, ž*) are treated differently: after them one always writes а, е, и, у (*a, e, i, u*), which thus have no effect on the palatalisation status of the preceding consonant (both *o* and *ë* are used; after *c, y* is written in native words). Thus: шить (*šit'*) 'to sew' [šít], час (*čas*) 'hour' [čas]. The representation of the phoneme /j/ is also complex and intertwined with the representation of palatalisation. In syllable-final position, the special letter й (*j*) is used, e.g. мой (*moj*) 'my' [moj], война (*vojná*) 'war' [vʌjná]. Word-initially and after a vowel, the special letters я, е, ё, ю (*ja, e, ë, ju*) represent the sequence of /j/ plus vowel, e.g. яма (*jáma*) 'pit' [jámə], союз (*sojúz*) 'union' [sʌjús]. After a consonant, /j/ is represented by using the letter ь (') (across prefix-stem boundaries, ъ (")) followed by я, е, и, ё, ю (*ja, e, i, ë, ju*), e.g. пьяный (*p'jányj*) 'drunk' [pjáṅij], муравьи (*murav'í*) 'ants' [murʌvʹjí]. Although the representation of palatalisation in Russian may seem complex, it does, given the richness of the consonant system and the relative poverty of the vowel system, enable the full range of phonemic oppositions to be maintained orthographically with a restricted set of distinct letters.

It will now be useful to consider some of the main historical phonological processes that have affected Russian in its development from Common Slavonic, in particular in that these relate to the morphophonemic alternations to be discussed below. The Common Slavonic nasal vowels, as in most Slavonic languages except Polish, were lost in Russian (before the earliest written texts), *o becoming *u* and *e becoming *a* with palatalisation of the preceding consonant, e.g. Common Slavonic *$poto$ 'way', *$peto$ 'five', Russian *put'*, *pjat'*. The Common Slavonic (and Old Russian) reduced vowels (jers) are lost in Russian as in the other Slavonic languages. In Russian, strong ъ and ь give *o* and *e* respectively; the weak jers are lost, but ь causes palatalisation of the preceding consonant, e.g. Old Russian *sъnъ*, genitive *sъna* 'sleep', modern *son*, *sna*; Old Russian *dьnь* 'day', genitive *dьnja*, modern *den'*, genitive *dnja*.

Another innovation in Russian is the shift of Old Russian *e* to *o* before non-palatalised consonants, but with retention of palatalisation in the preceding consonant. Thus Old Russian *nesъ* 'carried' gives modern *nës*. The effect of this change, like some of those already discussed (loss of *e, loss of ь) is to increase the domain of the palatalisation opposition, since *nës* contrasts with *nos* 'nose'. One of the latest changes in the vowel system, and one not shared by all dialects of Russian, is the merger of Old Russian *ĕ* and *e* (of which the former probably had a closer pronunciation in Old Russian, as still in those dialects that retain it) to *e*. (Distinct orthographic symbols were retained until 1918.) This shift of *ĕ* to *e* post-dates the shift of *e* to *o* noted above and is thus not subject to it, thus further reinforcing the phonemic distinctiveness of the palatalisation opposition: Modern Russian has the triple *voz* (Old Russian *vozъ*) 'cart', *vëz* (Old Russian *vezъ*) 'transported', *ves* (Old Russian *vĕsъ*) 'weight'.

Other changes in the vowel system already referred to are *ákan'e* and related phenomena (e.g. *íkan'e*), leading to neutralisation of unstressed vowels. In the obstruent system, the voice opposition was neutralised word-finally by the devoicing of voiced obstruents, leading to the merger of Old Russian *rъtъ* 'mouth' and *rodъ* 'birth' in modern pronunciation as [rot], and by assimilation of obstruents to the voice of a following obstruent, so that Old Russian *gibъkъjь* 'flexible' gives the modern pronunciation [ǵípḱij].

One of the main characteristics of modern Russian is the large number of morphophonemic alternations. Indeed, it is perhaps not accidental how much of modern morphophonemic theory has been developed by Russian phonologists and by phonologists working on Russian: Trubetskoy, Jakobson, Halle; since Polish shares this typological feature with Russian one can enlarge the list to include Baudouin de Courtenay. Some of the alternations are inherited from Indo-European, in particular ablaut (see pages 49–50), as in the alternation between the stem vowels of *tekú* 'I flow' and *tok* 'current' (Indo-European *e/o* ablaut). The more systematic alternations, however, are those that have arisen through innovatory sound changes in Common Slavonic or Russian. The main Common Slavonic innovations relevant here are the palatalisations and other processes leading to the development of palatal consonants. Thus the first palatalisation gives rise to the modern Russian *k/č* alternation in *pekú* 'I bake', *pečёš'* 'you bake': the original segment is **k*, retained before the back vowel (Common Slavonic **ǫ*) in the first member of the pair, but palatalised before the front vowel (Common Slavonic **e*) in the second item. The shift of **sj* to **š* in Common Slavonic turns up in modern Russian in the alternation found in *pisát'* 'to write', *pišú* 'I write', where the second item in early Common Slavonic was, with morpheme breaks, **pis-j-ǫ*.

Post-Common Slavonic innovations that have given rise to morphophonemic alternations include the loss of the jers. Since strong jers develop to full vowels while weak jers are lost, and since a given Old Russian jer might be strong in some morphological forms of a word but weak in others, the Old Russian predictable alternation of strong and weak jers gives rise in the modern language to alternation between a full vowel and zero, as in *son* 'sleep', genitive *sna*, *den'* 'day', genitive *dnja*.

Ákan'e and related phenomena give rise to vowel alternations, given the mobile stress. Thus we find nominative singular *golová* 'head' [gəlʌvá], nominative plural *gólovy* [góləvɨ], genitive plural *golóv* [gʌlóf], with alternation of the vowels in the first two syllables, and alternation of the first vowel in nominative singular *seló* 'hamlet' [śɪló], nominative plural *sёla* [śólə]. In morphophonemic transcription, the stems of these two words would be {golov-} and {śol-}. Lastly, final devoicing and consonant voice assimilation give rise to morphophonemic alternations. Final devoicing gives rise to alternations because in different morphological forms of the same word a consonant can appear now word-finally, now followed by a vowel, as in *rod* 'birth' [rot], genitive *róda* [ródə]. Voicing assimilation gives rise to alternations because of the alternation between vowel and zero resulting from the loss of the jers, as in *pryžók* 'jump' [prižók], genitive *pryžká* [priška].

3 Morphology

Russian nominal morphology is illustrated in the chart of declension types, with examples of the four major types of noun declension and of adjective declension. The nominal morphology turns out to be typologically very close to that of the oldest Indo-European languages. In particular, the morphology is fusional: thus, in the declension of nouns, it is not possible to

Russian Declension Types

Singular:	a-*stem*	Masculine o-*stem*	Neuter o-*stem*	i-*stem*
Nominative	straná	stol	mésto	brov'
Accusative	stranú	stol	mésto	brov'
Genitive	straný	stolá	mésta	bróvi
Dative	strané	stolú	méstu	bróvi
Instrumental	stranój	stolóm	méstom	bróv'ju
Locative	strané	stolé	méste	bróvi
Plural:				
Nominative	strány	stolý	mestá	bróvi
Accusative	strány	stolý	mestá	bróvi
Genitive	stran	stolóv	mest	brovéj
Dative	stránam	stolám	mestám	brovJám
Instrumental	stránami	stolámi	mestámi	brovjámi
Locative	stránax	stoláx	mestáx	brovjáx

Adjective Singular:	Masculine	Neuter	Feminine
Nominative	stáryj	stároe	stáraja
Accusative	stáryj	stároe	stáruju
Genitive		stárogo	stároj
Dative		stáromu	stároj
Instrumental		stárym	stároj
Locative		stárom	stároj
Plural:			
Nominative		stárye	
Accusative		stárye	
Genitive		stáryx	
Dative		stárym	
Instrumental		stárymi	
Locative		stáryx	

segment one inflection encoding number and another encoding case, rather these two categories are encoded by a single formative, so that the final -*u* of dative singular *stolú* represents 'dative singular', rather than part of it representing 'dative' and some other part 'singular'. In the adjective declension, the inflections are fusional for gender as well as for number and case, so that the inflection of *stár-uju* encodes the complex 'feminine singular accusative'. In fact, with nouns, there is fusion of yet another category, namely that of declension type: thus in the *a*-stems -*u* indicates 'accusative singular', whereas in the *o*-stems it indicates 'dative singular'. Although there is a high correlation between gender and declension type, it is not absolute: most *a*-stem nouns are feminine, but those with clear male reference are masculine; nearly all *i*-stem nouns are feminine, but *put'* 'way' is an isolated exception, being masculine; a masculine noun with male reference might be either an *o*-stem or an *a*-stem, while a feminine noun might be either an *a*-stem or an *i*-stem. In addition to the major declension types, there are also minor types represented by just a handful of nouns (e.g. ten neuter nouns follow the pattern of *ímja* 'name', genitive *ímeni*), in addition to idiosyncratic irregularities, including in particular the personal pronouns (e.g. *ja* 'I', genitive *menjá*).

One important parameter in Russian nominal declension not revealed by the table is animacy. In Russian, animate nouns (i.e. nouns referring to humans or other animals), and also their attributes, have the accusative case like the genitive rather than the form given in table 15.3 if they are either masculine *o*-stems or plural (of any gender or declension type). Thus *stáryj stol* 'old table' has accusative *stáryj stol*, but *stáryj slon* 'old elephant' has *stárogo sloná*; likewise nominative-accusative plural *stárye stolý*, but nominative plural *stárye sloný* and accusative-genitive *stáryx slonóv*. An animate noun not belonging to the *o*-stems, such as *žába* 'toad', has accusative singular *žábu*, nominative plural *žáby*, accusative plural *žab*.

Although Russian nominal morphology may look complex in comparison with, say, English, it reflects a number of significant simplifications relative to Old Russian or Common Slavonic. Few categories have been lost altogether, these being the dual number and the vocative case. However, several Common Slavonic declension types have been lost through merger with the more common types, such as *u*-stems with *o*-stems, most consonant stems with one of the other declension types. In addition, there has been some neutralisation (syncretism) leading to simplification, the most noticeable such effect being the loss of gender distinctions in the plural: thus the modern nominative plural *stárye* represents the merger of three distinct Old Russian forms: masculine *starii*, feminine *staryě*, neuter *staraja*. In addition to the overall pattern of simplification, there has also been some complication. For instance, some masculine *o*-stems have a partitive genitive in -*u* distinct from the regular genitive in -*a*; some masculine *o*-stems form the nominative (and inanimate accusative) plural in -*á* rather than -*y*, e.g. *gorodá*, plural of *górod* 'city'. In addition, some forms continuing Old Russian types have been retained as idiosyncratic irregularities (e.g. the endingless genitive plural of masculine *o*-stems in *glaz* 'eye', genitive plural also *glaz*).

In Common Slavonic, there were two declensions of adjectives, the so-called simple declension (identical to noun declension) and the pronominal declension. In attributive usage, they were distinguished in terms of definiteness, e.g. Old Russian *starъ gorodъ* 'an old town', *starъjь gorodъ* 'the old town'. In modern Russian, only the pronominal adjective survives in attributive usage, as in *stáryj górod* '(the/an) old town', and it is this form, conventionally termed the long form, that is given in the table of declensions. In predicative usage, either the long form or the so-called short form, continuing the Old Russian simple declension of adjectives, may be used, i.e. *górod stáryj/star* 'the town is old', *straná krasívaja/krasíva* 'the country is beautiful'. Since the short form is only used predicatively, it does not decline, but does distinguish gender and number (singular masculine *star*, feminine *stará*, neuter *stáro*, plural for all genders *stáry* or *starý*).

Russian verbal morphology is rather less like that of the older Indo-European languages. Inflectionally, only a small number of categories are distinguished, as represented in the chart of conjugation types. Among the finite forms, the only mood distinct from the indicative is the imperative. Within the indicative, there is a binary morphological opposition between non-past (i.e. present-future) and past. In the non-past, verbs agree with their subject in person and number; in the past, they agree in gender and number. Of the non-finite forms, the infinitive is in common use, in particular after certain finite verbs, e.g. *ja xočú čitát'* 'I want to read'. Modern Russian also has participles (verbal adjectives) and gerunds (verbal adverbs), but use of these is primarily restricted to literary and scientific writing.

Russian Conjugation Types

	I Conjugation	*II Conjugation*
Infinitive	čitát' 'to read'	govorít' 'to speak'
Non-past:		
Singular 1	čitáju	govorjú
2	čitáeš'	govoríš'
3	čitáet	govorít
Plural 1	čitáem	govorím
2	čitáete	govoríte
3	čitájut	govorját
Past:		
Singular masculine	čitál	govoríl
feminine	čitála	govoríla
neuter	čitálo	govorílo
Plural	čitáli	govoríli
Imperative:		
Singular 2	čitáj	govorí
Plural 2	čitájte	govoríte

In addition to the categories represented in the chart, Russian has a further category, that of aspect, with an opposition between imperfective and perfective. The general morphological principle is as follows. Simple verbs without a prefix are usually imperfective, e.g. *pisát'* 'to write'. Attachment of a prefix to such a verb makes it perfective, e.g. *na-pisát'* 'to write', *o-pisát'* 'to describe'. Usually, for a given simple verb there is one (unpredictable) prefix which adds no semantic component other than that of perfectivity, so that *pisát'–napisát'* (likewise *čitát'–pročitát'* 'to read') can be considered an imperfective-perfective pair. Other prefixes do make other semantic modifications, e.g. *opisát'* means 'to describe', not just 'to write', but such verbs can be given imperfective counterparts by suffixation, thus giving a pair *opísyvat'–opisát'*. In addition, there are less common ways of forming aspectual pairs, such as suffixation of non-prefixed verbs, e.g. perfective *rešít'*, imperfective *rešát'* 'to decide'. In general, then, Russian verbs come in imperfective-perfective pairs, but it is often impossible to predict what the perfective counterpart of a given imperfective verb will be or vice versa.

While the meaning of tense is to locate a situation (action, event, state) in a certain time (for instance, past tense in the time before the present moment), the meaning of aspect is concerned rather with the subjective way of viewing the internal temporal constituency of the situation. More particularly, the perfective views a situation as a single whole, effectively as a point, while the imperfective views a situation as having internal constituency. This distinction can be clarified by some actual examples. In a narrative, one normally presents a series of events each of which is viewed as complete in itself, and here the perfective is appropriate, as in *ja vošël v kómnatu, sel i vzjal knígu* 'I entered the room, sat down and took a book'. In background description, however, one presents situations that are on-going throughout the whole of a narrative sequence, and here the imperfective is appropriate, as in *pápa sidél v zelënom kreslé i spal* 'Father was sitting in the green arm-chair and was sleeping' (sc. when I entered the room etc.). The imperfective is thus also ideal for habitual situations, which serve as a potential background to individual events, as in *kogdá ja byl mál'čikom, ja sobirál počtóvye márki* 'when I was a boy I used to collect postage stamps'. Although there are differences of detail, the distinction between imperfective and perfective in Russian can be compared to that between the imperfect and preterit in Romance languages; in non-habitual, non-stative meaning, the opposition can be compared to that between progressive and non-progressive in English — all of these are aspectual oppositions.

In Russian, this aspectual opposition applies throughout the verb system, in particular in the infinitive (e.g. *čitát'–pročitát'*), in the non-past (e.g. *čitáju–pročitáju*; here the imperfective has present meaning, the perfective future meaning), in the past (*čitál–pročitál*) and in the imperative (*čitáj–pročitáj*).

In addition to morphological forms, Russian also has a small number of periphrastic verb forms. The conditional is formed by adding the invariable clitic *by* to the past tense, e.g. *ja čitál by* (perfective: *ja pročitál by*) 'I would read'. The imperfective future uses the auxiliary *búdu* 'I will be' in the appropriate person and number with the imperfective infinitive, e.g. *on búdet čitát'* 'he will read, be reading'. (Only the verb *byt'* 'to be' has a morphological future, namely *búdu* itself.) There is thus a certain discrepancy between the tense-aspect correlation in form and in meaning in the non-past. In form, *čitáju* and *pročitáju* go together in contrast to the periphrastic *búdu čitát'*, which has no perfective counterpart; in meaning, however, *čitáju* is the isolated form — Russian has no perfective present — while *búdu čitát'* and *pročitáju* form an aspectual pair.

Historically, this represents a considerable simplification of the Old Russian verb system, virtually the only complication being the fully-fledged development of the aspectual opposition. Gone completely are, in addition to the dual number, the Old Russian simple past forms (imperfect and aorist) inherited from Common Slavonic. The modern Russian past tense derives from an Old Russian perfect, somewhat similar to English *I have read*, except that the auxiliary 'be' rather than 'have' is used with the past participle. Thus Old Russian has a present perfect *jazъ esmь čitalъ* 'I have read', and also equivalent forms in other tenses, e.g. pluperfect *jazъ běxъ čitalъ* 'I had read'. Of these, only the present perfect survives to modern Russian; as elsewhere in Russian, the copula is lost in the present tense, giving modern Russian *ja čitál*, which, with the loss of all the other past tenses, now survives as the basic and only past tense. The fact that the form *čitál* is etymologically a participle (i.e. a verbal adjective) accounts for why it agrees in gender and number rather than in person and number with its subject.

4   Syntax

In this brief discussion of Russian syntax, attention will be focused on two features: agreement and word order. In order to follow the example sentences, two particular features of Russian syntax should be noted in advance. Russian lacks equivalents to the English definite and indefinite articles, so that a noun phrase like *sobáka* will sometimes be glossed as 'a dog', sometimes as 'the dog'. In copular constructions in the present tense, there is usually a zero copula, so that corresponding to English 'Viktor is a student' we have *Víktor studént*. In other tenses, however, there is an overt copula, as in *Víktor byl studéntom* 'Viktor was a student'; this overt copula usually governs the instrumental case of a predicate noun, although the nominative is also possible.

In Russian, most predicates must agree, in some combination of person, gender and number, with their subject; the only exceptions are adverbial predicates and predicate nouns (or noun phrases) with the zero copula, as in *Víktor/Léna zdes'* 'Viktor/Lena is here'. Finite verbs in the non-past tense agree with their subject in person and number, e.g. *ja čitáju* 'I read', *on/oná čitáet* 'he/she reads', *oní čitájut* 'they read', *mál'čiki čitájut* 'the boys read'; despite the rich agreement morphology on the verb, it is not usual in Russian to omit unstressed subject pronouns (in this respect Russian differs from many other Slavonic languages, including Polish, Czech and Serbo-Croat). Finite verbs in the past tense agree with their subject in gender and number, e.g. *ja/on čitál* 'I (male referent)/he read', *ja/ona čitála* 'I (female referent)/ she read', *oní čitáli* 'they read'. Predicate adjectives agree in gender and number with their subject, whether there is an overt or a zero copula, e.g. *Víktor glup* 'Viktor is stupid', *Léna glupá* 'Lena is stupid', *Víktor i Léna glúpy* 'Viktor and Lena are stupid', *Víktor byl glúpym* 'Viktor was stupid', *Léna bylá glúpoj* 'Lena was stupid', *Víktor i Léna býli glúpymi* 'Viktor and Lena were stupid' (the adjectives in the past-tense sentences are in the instrumental case, although the nominative or the short form would also be possible).

Attributive adjectives (including possessive and demonstrative adjectives) agree in number, gender and case with their head noun. Thus from nominative singular *bédnyj mál'čik* 'poor boy' we can form genitive *bédnogo mál'čika*, nominative plural *bédnye mál'čiki*, dative plural *bédnym mál'čikam*; taking a feminine noun, we have nominative singular *bédnaja dévuška* 'poor girl', genitive *bédnoj dévuški*, nominative plural *bédnye dévuški*; taking a neuter noun, we have *bédnoe seló* 'poor hamlet', genitive *bédnogo selá*. Agreement of possessive and demonstrative adjectives can be illustrated by: *étot mál'čik* 'this boy', genitive *étogo mál'čika*; *éta dévuška* 'this girl', genitive *étoj dévuški*; *náše seló* 'our hamlet', genitive *nášego selá*.

One particularly complex area of Russian syntax, reflecting an unusual interplay of agreement and government, is the syntax of noun phrases involving numerals. In Russian, the numeral 'one' is an adjective, agreeing in case, gender and number with its head noun, e.g. *odín mál'čik* 'one boy', genitive *odnogó mál'čika*; *odná bédnaja dévuška* 'one poor girl'; the plural form is used with nouns that occur only in the plural but refer to a single object, e.g. *odní nóžnicy* 'one (pair of) scissors'. The numerals 'two', 'three', 'four' in the nominative-accusative govern a noun in the genitive singular, while an accompanying adjective may stand in either the nominative plural or the genitive plural (usually the latter), e.g. *dva mál'čika* 'two boys', *dve bédnye/bédnyx straný* 'two poor countries', *tri/četýre mál'čika/straný/selá* 'three/four boys/countries/hamlets'; note that of these numerals, 'two' distinguishes masculine-neuter *dva* from feminine *dve*. In the other cases, these numerals agree in case with their head noun (and show no gender distinction, as is usual in Russian in the plural), e.g. dative *dvum/trëm/četyrëm bédnym mál'čikam/stránam/sëlam*. Numerals from 'five' up to 'nine hundred' in the nominative-accusative govern a following noun (with attributes) in the genitive plural, e.g. *pjat' bédnyx mál'čikov/dévušek/sël* 'five poor boys/girls/hamlets'; in other cases, they agree with the head noun, e.g. dative *pjatí bédnym mál'čikam/dévuškam/sëlam*. The numeral 'thousand' may either follow this pattern or govern the genitive plural in all cases: *týsjača bédnyx mál'čikov* 'a thousand poor boys', dative *týsjače bédnyx mál'cikov/bédnym mál'čikam*. The numeral 'million' and higher numerals take a following genitive plural irrespective of case, e.g. *millión bédnyx dévušek* 'a million poor girls', dative *milliónu bédnyx dévušek*.

Apart from the idiosyncrasy of the genitive singular after the numerals 'two' to 'four' (with nominative or genitive plural attributes), the other patterns can all be described in terms of the interaction of attributive adjective syntax (attributive adjectives agree with their head) and measure-noun syntax (nouns of measure govern a following count noun in the genitive plural, e.g. *vedró červéj* 'a bucket of worms'): thus, the numeral 'one' behaves consistently as an adjective, while the numerals from 'million' on behave consistently as measure nouns, the numerals from 'five' to 'thousand' combining aspects of adjective and measure-noun syntax. The synchronically unusual system can best be understood in terms of its historical origin. In Old Russian, 'one' is an adjective, while all numerals from 'five' on are measure nouns; diachronically, adjective properties have been creeping up the number scale. In Old Russian, the numeral 'two' is followed by the dual; although the dual as a separate category has been lost in modern Russian, the synchronic genitive singular found after 'two' derives etymologically from a nominative dual, i.e. originally this was an instance of agreement; for a few nouns, the genitive singular and the form used after 'two' still differ in stress, e.g. *čas* 'hour', genitive *čása*, but *dva časá* 'two hours'. The use of the erstwhile dual, now genitive singular, after 'three' and 'four' is a later analogical development.

Turning now to word order, we may distinguish between word order within the noun phrase and word order within the clause (i.e. the order of major constituents within each clause). Within the noun phrase, word order is fairly rigid in Russian, in particular in the written language, especially in scientific writing. Adjectives, including demonstrative and possessive adjectives, precede the head noun, as in *stáraja sobáka* 'old dog', *mojá sobáka* 'my dog', *éta sobáka* 'this dog'. Genitives, on the other hand, follow the head noun, as in *sobáka Víktora* 'Viktor's dog'. Relative clauses follow the head noun, e.g. *sobáka, kotóruju ja vídel, ukusíla tebjá* 'the dog that I saw has bitten you'; this reflects the general tendency in Russian for non-adverbial subordinate clauses to follow main clauses (i.e. Russian, like English, is a right-branching language). We may also note at this point that Russian has prepositions rather than postpositions, e.g. *v dóme* 'in the house', *péred dómom* 'in front of the house'; prepositions govern various cases, other than the nominative.

With respect to the order of major constituents within the clause, Russian is often referred to as a free word order language. This means that, in general, any permutation of the major constituents of the clause produces a grammatical sentence with essentially the same meaning as the original order (in particular, with the same truth conditions). Thus alongside *Víktor celúet Lénu* 'Viktor kisses Lena', one can also say: *Víktor Lénu celúet*; *Lénu Víktor celúet*; *Lénu celúet Víktor*; *celúet Víktor Lénu*; *celúet Lénu Víktor*. In Russian, the morphology is nearly always sufficient to provide unique recovery of the grammatical relations of the various major constituents: in these examples, the nominative *Víktor* is unambiguously subject, while the accusative *Lénu* is unequivocally direct object. To say 'Lena kissed Viktor', one would have to change the cases to give *Léna celúet Víktora* (or any permutation of these three words). In some instances, agreement may reveal the grammatical relations, as in *mat' zaščiščáet snarjády* 'the mother defends the missiles', where the singular verb *zaščiščáet* allows *mat'* 'mother', but disqualifies *snarjády* 'missiles' as subject. It is actually quite difficult to construct sensible sentences where the morphology is insufficient to disambiguate, e.g. *mat' celúet doč'*, literally 'mother kisses daughter', where both nouns happen to have the same form for nominative and accusative and are of the same person and number. In such sentences, the most salient interpretation is 'the mother kisses the daughter', one of the pieces of evidence suggesting that the basic word order in Russian, as in English, is subject–object–verb. But whereas in English departures from this order produce either nonsense or sentences with different meanings (*Viktor Lena kisses*; *Lena kisses Viktor*), in Russian the main clue to grammatical relations is the morphology, thus giving rise to the phenomenon of free word order.

This does not mean, however, that there are no principles of word order in Russian. Word order of major constituents within the clause is governed by two main principles. The first is that the topic of the sentence, i.e. what the sentence is about, comes initially. The second is that the focus of the sentence, i.e. the essential new information communicated by the sentence, comes last. Thus word order in Russian is largely pragmatically determined. (A further pragmatic principle, this time shared with English, is that interrogative pronouns and relative pronouns occur clause-initially, as in *kogó ty vídel?* 'whom did you see?'; *mál'čik, kotórogo ja vídel* 'the boy that I saw'.) One way of illustrating these principles is to produce miniature dialogues where the choice of topic and focus in the final sentence is forced by the context. Imagine that we have a discourse about kissing. If we ask *who kissed X?*, then in the answer *X kissed Y*, *Y* must be the focus, since it is the new information communicated. Conversely, given the question *what about Y?*, in the answer the topic must be *Y*, since any reasonable answer to a question about Y must have Y as its topic. The following miniature dialogues illustrate pragmatic word order in Russian, in each case the relevant sentence being the last one of the discourse:

(a)	-Víktor pocelovál Lénu.	-Viktor kissed Lena.
	-A Róbert, kogó on pocelovál?	-And what about Robert, whom did he kiss?
	-*Róbert* pocelovál Mǎšu.	-*Robert* kissed Masha.
(b)	-Víktor pocelovál Lénu.	-Viktor kissed Lena.
	-A Mášu, kto pocelovál eë?	-And as for Masha, who kissed her?
	-*Mášu* pocelovál Rŏbert.	-Rŏbert kissed *Masha*.

In each example, the topic is italicised and the focus marked with the diacritic ". In English, the final turns in (a) and (b) are distinguished by sentence stress, this stress falling in each case on the focus. In Russian, too, the sentence stress falls on the focus, but there is the added differentiation brought about by the word order, which can thus be used to indicate topic and focus even in writing, where sentence stress is not indicated. (In the spoken language, for emotive effect, departures from the 'focus-last' principle are possible, but such deviations would be quite out of place in a scientific treatise.)

Freedom of word order in Russian applies primarily to major constituents of the clause. Under certain circumstances it is, however, possible to extract constituents of major constituents for purposes of topic or focus, as in *knígi u menjá xoróšie*, literally 'books at me good', i.e. 'I have good *books*'.

In English, the variation in word order that is possible directly in Russian can sometimes be achieved by less direct means. Thus one of the differences in English between the active voice, as in *Viktor kissed Lena*, and the passive voice, as in *Lena was kissed by Viktor*, is topicalisation of the patient in the passive. In English the order subject–verb–object is fairly rigid, but since the passive voice presents the direct object of the active sentence as subject of the passive sentence, this change in voice effectively allows one to prepose the patient to give a close equivalent to Russian *Lénu poceloválu Víktor*. Russian does have a passive similar in form to that of English, e.g. *Léna bylá pocelóvana Víktorom*, but this construction is much less frequently used in Russian than in English — it serves primarily as an indicator of literary style — and, moreover, given the free word order of Russian it is possible to invert the order of the noun phrases to have the agent, though not subject, as topic, i.e. *Víktorom bylá pocelóvana Léna*!

This infrequent use of the passive in Russian as compared to English is a particular case of a general phenomenon distinguishing the two languages. English has a wide range of possibilities for the link between the grammatical relations of a sentence and its semantic roles. Thus the subject is agent in *Viktor kissed Lena*, but patient in *Lena was kissed by Viktor*; in *lightning killed the soldier*, the subject is a natural force. In Russian, the fit between semantic roles and grammatical relations is much closer. As already indicated, avoidance of the passive is one instance of this. The most natural Russian translation of *lightning killed the soldier* (and equally of *the soldier was killed by lightning*) is impersonal (subjectless), with neither 'lightning' nor 'soldier' as subject: *soldáta* (accusative) *ubílo mólniej* (instrumental), literally (apart from word order) 'it killed the soldier by lightning'. In yet further instances where English allows a given predicate to take grammatical relations with different semantic roles, Russian allows this only if the predicate is marked overtly to indicate the difference in semantic roles. Thus, in English the verb *close* can take an agentive subject transitively in *Lena closed the door* and a patient subject intransitively as in *the door closed*; in Russian, the second usage must be overtly distinguished by the reflexive clitic *-sja/-s'*: *Léna zakrýla dver'*; *dver' zakrýlas'*. In English, the same verb can be used in *the collective farmer sowed maize in the field* and in *the collective farmer sowed the field with maize*, while Russian requires different prefixes on the verbs: *kolxóznik poséjal kukurúzu v póle*; *kolxóznik zaséjal póle kukurúzoj*. The interaction among morphology, word order, grammatical relations, semantic roles and pragmatic roles is one of the major typological differences between the grammars of Russian and English.

Bibliography

Ward (1955) is a useful introduction to the structure of Russian and its historical and social setting. The selection of reference grammars available in English is rather poor, one of the best being Pulkina (n.d.); for those who read German, Isačenko (1968) is an excellent descriptive morphology, including the meanings of the morphological categories. Švedova et al. (1980) is the latest Academy grammar, a major improvement over previous Academy grammars, in particular in syntax, semantics and pragmatics. For individual topics, Halle (1959) is a pioneering work on the synchronic analysis of Russian morphophonemics; Forsyth (1970) is an excellent account of aspect in Russian; Krylova and Khavronina (1976) is an account of Russian word order intended primarily for advanced students of Russian.

For the history of the language, Vinokur (1971) is a concise account of the historical and sociological development, while Comrie and Stone (1978) deals with post-Revolutionary developments in the language, including those subject to current variation, against a background of social factors. A standard handbook for the internal history is Borkovskij and Kuznecov (1965), as is Avanesov and Orlova (1965) for dialectology.

References

Avanesov, R.I. and V.G. Orlova (eds.) 1965. *Russkaja dialektologija*, 2nd ed. (Nauka, Moscow)

Borkovskij, V.I. and P.S. Kuznecov. 1965. *Istoričeskaja grammatika russkogo jazyka*, 2nd ed. (Nauka, Moscow)

Comrie, B. and G. Stone. 1978. *The Russian Language Since the Revolution* (Clarendon Press, Oxford)

Forsyth, J. 1970. *A Grammar of Aspect: Usage and Meaning in the Russian Verb* (Cambridge University Press, London)

Halle, M. 1959. *The Sound Pattern of Russian* (Mouton, The Hague)

Isačenko, A.V. 1968. *Die russische Sprache der Gegenwart, Teil 1: Formenlehre* (Max Niemeyer, Halle (Saale))

Krylova, A. and S. Khavronina. 1976. *Word Order in Russian Sentences* (Russian Language Publishers, Moscow; translated from the simultaneously published Russian edition)

Pulkina, I.M. n.d. *A Short Russian Reference Grammar* (Moscow)

Švedova, N.Ju. et al. (eds.) 1980. *Russkaja grammatika*, 2 vols. (Nauka, Moscow)

Vinokur, G.O. 1971. *The Russian Language: A Brief History* (Cambridge University Press, London; translated from the Russian edition of 1959)

Ward, D. 1955. *The Russian Language Today* (Hutchinson University Library, London)

16 Polish

Gerald Stone

1 Historical Background

The West Slavonic languages include a subgroup, known as 'Lechitic', comprising Polish (its easternmost variety) and the other Slavonic languages once spoken throughout what is now north Germany as far west as the Lüneburg Heath. Most of the dialects of Lechitic were extinct by the late Middle Ages and are attested only by fragmentary evidence, principally in the form of place names; but its westernmost variety, which has been given the name 'Polabian' by philologists, survived until the eighteenth century and is recorded in a number of substantial texts. Unless we bestow separate status on Cassubian, a variety of Lechitic still spoken by perhaps as many as 150,000 people near the Baltic coast to the west of the Bay of Gdańsk, Polish is the only Lechitic language which survives to the present day. Cassubian, despite features testifying to its former independence, is now generally regarded as a dialect of Polish. Within West Slavonic the Lechitic subgroup on the one hand and the Czecho-Slovak on the other constitute the two extremities. A link between them is provided by Sorbian.

Our earliest evidence of the Polish language comes in the form of place names, tribal names, and personal names recorded in medieval Latin documents going back to the ninth century AD. Among the most useful records of this kind are the Papal Bull of Gniezno (1136) which contains 410 names and the Bull of Wrocław (Breslau) (1155) containing about 50 more. The same kind of evidence becomes even more plentiful in the thirteenth century, by which time we also find isolated words other than proper nouns imbedded in Latin texts and accompanied by Latin explanations. In about 1270 the Cistercian monks of Henryków, near Wrocław, wrote a history of their monastery (in Latin) and included several Polish words. Their history also contains the first known Polish sentence: 'daj ać ja pobruczę a ty poczywaj' ('Let me grind and you rest'), which is quoted to explain the etymology of the place name Brukalice.

It is only in the fourteenth century that we find entire Polish texts consisting of many sentences. The earliest of these are the undated *Kazania Świętokrzyskie* ('Holy Cross Sermons'), which are attributed to the middle of the century or a little later. A translation of the Book of Psalms into Polish, known as the *Psałterz Floriański* ('St. Florian Psalter'), is reckoned to date from the end of the century, as are the *Kazania Gnieźnieńskie* 'Gniezno Sermons'. There are also court records, dating from 1386 onwards, in which the main account is written in Latin, but the actual words of depositions sworn by witnesses and litigants are in the original Polish. The number of such depositions dating from before 1500 exceeds 8,000 and collectively they constitute one of our main sources for the state of medieval Polish. There are, however, many other sources, mostly of a devotional and literary kind, dating from this period. They include a manuscript of the greater part of the Old Testament, known as *Biblia królowej Zofii* ('Queen Sophia's Bible'), dating from around 1455.

The spelling in these early texts is far from systematic and it is consequently, in particular, almost impossible to distinguish between the three series of sibilants: /tɕ/, /ɕ/, /ʑ/ : /tʃ/, /ʃ/, /ʒ/ : /ts/, /s/, /z/, which in modern Polish are written respectively: *ć, ś, ż : cz, sz, ż : c, s, z* (see section 2). However, the local features in most of these texts are far less prominent than one might expect them to have been in the speech of the areas they came from. Clearly, certain standardising processes had been at work. Nevertheless, some local features may be detected in almost any medieval text of reasonable size. To a large extent the medieval dialectal features can be correlated with those observed in modern dialects. For example, the feature *chw → f* (e.g. *chwała* 'glory' pronounced as *fała*) is known to most modern dialects with the exception of that of Great Poland (Wielkopolska). Therefore, medieval spellings with *f* (such as *fala* 'glory') indicate that the text in question could not have originated in Great Poland. The reconstruction of medieval dialectal divisions is greatly helped by the forensic records owing to the fact that they almost always include the exact date and place of origin. Most of the devotional texts can be assigned either to Little Poland (Małopolska) (e.g. The St. Florian Psalter) or to Great Poland (e.g. The Gniezno Sermons). The centre of gravity of the Polish state is known to have been in Great Poland until the reign of Kazimierz the Restorer (reigned 1034–1058), but in 1037 the capital was moved to Cracow, and the position of importance consequently acquired by Little Poland was maintained until, and even after, the further transfer of the capital to Warsaw in 1596.

The modicum of standardisation exhibited by our fourteenth- and fifteenth-century manuscripts attracted a lot of interest among Polish scholars in the first half of the twentieth century. It was asserted by one faction that the standard must have been based on the dialect of Great Poland, which even after 1037 retained the seat of the archbishop (at Gniezno) and exerted great authority. Others claimed that the new capital Cracow must have provided the variety on which the standard was based. (No one doubted that Mazovia, which with its capital, Warsaw, was united to Poland only in the sixteenth century, could have had no influence in the

Map 16.1: Traditional Regions of Poland

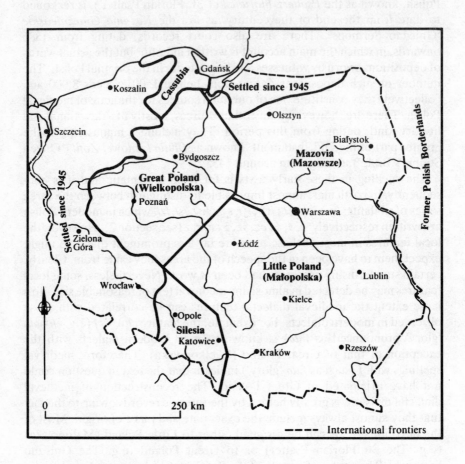

matter.) One of the crucial features in this argument was that known as
mazurzenie, i.e. the neutralisation of the distinction between *c*, *s*, *z* and *cz*,
sz, *ż* respectively. It was held that deliberate avoidance of this feature in the
language of many scribes and later in printed books meant that the standard
was based on a variety unaffected by *mazurzenie*. Dialectologists were able
to show that Great Poland did not have *mazurzenie*, whereas (by the time
dialectologists enquired, at least) Little Poland did. The question now
turned on dating the arrival of *mazurzenie* in Little Poland. But the
controversy was never settled.

The arrival of printing in Poland (the first book in Polish was printed in
1513) put an end to the untidy spelling system used by the scribes. The
printers aimed for less ambiguity and more standardisation. The sixteenth

century, known as the Golden Age of Polish literature, was also the age in which the first dictionaries and grammars appeared. The most important of these are Jan Mączyński's *Lexicon latinopolonicum* (Königsberg 1564), which contains 20,700 Polish words, and the *Polonicae grammatices institutio* (Cracow 1568) of Piotr Statorius (Stojeński). Also, at least five different treatises on spelling were published.

Towards the end of the fifteenth century the Polish vocalic system underwent a great change. It had hitherto involved the opposition of long and short vowels, but now vocalic quantity ceased to be a relevant phonemic distinction. The long vowels, in losing their length, acquired a new quality. At the beginning of the fifteenth century only the vowels /i/ and /u/ were unaffected by a quantitative distinction. Short /ɑ/, /ɛ/, /ɔ/, and /ā/ were distinguished from long /ɑː/, /ɛː/, /ɔː/, and /āː/. But by the sixteenth century there were ten qualitatively distinguished vowel phonemes: /a/, /ɑ/, /ɔ/, /o/, /u/, /i/, /e/, /ɛ/, /ē/, and /ɔ̃/. Books printed in the sixteenth century and later frequently made use of the acute accent to distinguish between /a/, and /ɑ/, /ɔ/ and /o/, /e/ and /ɛ/. In standard pronunciation, however, the ten-vowel system was eventually reduced to seven vowels, as the distinction between /a/ and /ɑ/, /o/ and /u/, and /e/ and /ɛ/ was neutralised. The last relic of the ten-vowel system is in the modern spelling system, which still uses *ó* for reasons of tradition (as in *wóz* 'cart, car', *gród* 'castle', etc.), though this letter now represents the same sound as the letter *u*.

With the First Partition of Poland in 1772 the Polish language entered a period of trial that was to last until the restoration of independence after the First World War. After 1795, when Poland disappeared from the map altogether, there were attempts by all the partitioning powers (Prussia, Austria and Russia) at one time or another to reduce the social functions of Polish and replace it with German or Russian. After 1848, however, language policy in the Austrian partition was modified to the advantage of the Poles and their language was henceforth able to thrive here. In the other two partitions users of Polish suffered numerous indignities. As a result of its prohibition from the schools a clandestine system of Polish instruction grew up to ensure the language's survival. Matters came to a head in May 1901 in a school in Września (Posnania), where the compulsory use of German during religious instruction led to a riot which attracted the attention of world public opinion.

By this time, owing to the practical advantages of knowing German or Russian and the influence of military service on the male population, a large proportion of educated Poles were bilingual. Bilingualism was most common in the Prussian partition, where educational standards were higher than in Russia or Austria. The existence of three separate administrations fostered the Polish language's existing tendency to regional variation. Some of the regional features first observed then have survived until recent times even in educated usage: e.g. *kurczak* 'chicken' (Warsaw) corresponding to *kurczę* elsewhere; *na polu* 'outside' (Cracow) corresponding to *na dworze* (Poznań) and *na dworze* or *na dworzu* (Warsaw); *listonosz* 'postman' (Cracow) corresponding to *listowy* (Poznań) and *listonosz* or *bryftrygier* (Warsaw).

After the First World War Polish was restored to its position as the language of the Polish state, but there were also many speakers of other languages living in Poland. At the 1931 census a population of 32,107,000 was recorded, of whom only 21,993,000 gave Polish as their native language. This situation was completely changed in the upheaval brought about by the Second World War. The population according to the first census held within the post-war frontiers (1946) was 23,930,000. Since then it has expanded to over 35 million, of whom almost all have Polish as their native language. The national minorities total about one per cent of the population. At the same time, there are millions of Polish speakers living outside Poland, including over 300,000 in the USSR and perhaps as many as six million in the USA.

2 Phonology

The segmental phonemes of Polish are set out in table 16.1.

Table 16.1: Segmental Phonemes of Polish

Vowels		Oral		Nasal	
	i		u		
	ɛ		ɔ	ɛ̃	ɔ̃
		a			

Consonants	Plain stop		Affricate		Fricative		Nasal	Lateral	Trill	Semi-vowel
Bilabial	p	b					m			w
	p̡	b̡					m̡			
Labio-dental					f	v				
					f̡	ɣ				
Dental	t	d	ts	dz	s	z	n	l		
Alveolar			tʃ	dʒ	ʃ	ʒ			r	
Pre-palatal			tɕ	dʑ	ɕ	ʑ	ɲ			
Post-palatal	k̡	g̡								j
Velar	k	g			x					

As in the case of Russian, the richness of the consonant system is striking. However, certain Russian oppositions between palatalised dentals (t:t̡; d:d̡; r:r̡) have no counterpart in Polish. On the other hand, Polish has an additional type of opposition, viz. that between tʃ and tɕ, dʒ and dʑ, ʃ and ɕ, ʒ and ʑ. This distinction depends less on the precise portion of the roof of the mouth involved in the articulation than on the fact that tʃ, dʒ, ʃ and ʒ are articulated with the tip of the tongue, whereas tɕ, dʑ, ɕ and ʑ are produced with the middle of the tongue.

The functional load of dʒ is very light, since it is largely restricted to loanwords, but the rest of these oppositions have a substantial yield. Some have a role in the morphological system, e.g. *duży* /duʒi/ 'big' (masculine nominative singular) : *duzi* /duʑi/ 'big' (masculine personal nominative plural); *lepszy* /lɛpʃi/ 'better' (masculine nominative singular) : *lepsi* /lɛpɕi/ 'better' (masculine personal nominative plural).

Double consonants are not uncommon in Polish and their phonological function is well attested, e.g. *lekki* /lɛkki/ 'light' (masculine nominative singular) : *leki* /lɛki/ 'medicines'. Phonetically they may be double or long, but there are no cases of the opposition of morphologically indivisible long and short consonants. The example given breaks down into *lek-* (stem) and *-ki* (ending). Loss of this distinction (e.g. the pronunciation of *lekki* as /lɛki/) is a regional feature of Great Poland (Wielkopolska) and Silesia.

The distribution of the nasal vowels in restricted. They may only occur at the end of a word or before fricatives, e.g. *chodzę* /xɔdzɛ̃/ 'I walk', *gęś* /gɛ̃ɕ/ 'goose', *mąż* /mɔ̃ʃ/ 'husband'. (The nasal vowel *letters*, however, appear before consonants of all kinds and are therefore phonetically misleading.) In addition to /ɛ̃/ and /ɔ̃/ other nasal vowels may occur, but only before fricatives, e.g. *tramwaj* [trãvaj] 'tram', *inspektor* [ĩspɛktɔr] 'inspector', *triumf* [triũf] 'triumph'. Before fricatives the vowels /ɛ̃/ and /ɔ̃/ may be spelled *en*, *em*, *on* or *om*, e.g. *sens* /sɛ̃s/ 'sense', *konferencja* /kɔ̃fɛrɛntsja/ 'conference'. Before plosives and affricates, however, only the sequence oral vowel (abbreviated as V) plus nasal consonant (phonemes /n/, /ɲ/ and /m/) (abbreviated as N) may occur. Therefore, with the exception of /ɛ̃/ and /ɔ̃/ at the end of a word, nasal vowels are positional variants of VN. Clearly, [ĩ], [ã], [ũ] are not phonemes, and even the phonemic status of /ɛ̃/ and /ɔ̃/ depends solely on their occurrence at the end of a word before a pause, e.g. *tą* /tɔ̃/ 'that' (instrumental feminine singular) is distinct from *to* /tɔ/ 'that' (nominative neuter singular), *ton* /tɔn/ 'tone' and *tom* /tɔm/ 'volume'; *listę* /listɛ̃/ 'list' (accusative singular) is distinct from *listem* /listɛm/ 'letter' (instrumental singular); *piszę* /piʃɛ̃/ 'I write' is distinct from *pisze* /piʃɛ/ 'he writes'. However, no one, not even actors, consistently pronounces /ɛ̃/ at the end of words. *Piszę* 'I write', for example, may be realised as /piʃɛ/, in which case it becomes indistinguishable from *pisze* 'he writes'. On the other hand, no speaker of the standard language consistently denasalises final /ɛ̃/ and the possibility of making the distinction always exists. Therefore /ɛ̃/ is a phoneme. There is even less doubt in the case of /ɔ̃/, since denasalisation of final /ɔ̃/ is less common.

The distinction between voiced and voiceless paired consonants (i.e. between /b/ and /p/, /d/ and /t/, /v/ and /f/, /dz/ and /ts/, /z/ and /s/, /dʒ/ and /tʃ/, /ʒ/ and /ʃ/, /dʑ/ and /tɕ/, /ʑ/ and /ɕ/, /g/ and /k/) is neutralised at the end of a word. Thus, for example, *Bóg* /buk/ 'God' and *buk* /buk/ 'beech' are homophones. At the end of a word only the voiceless member of the pair can occur, but this feature is not reflected in the spelling, as we may see from such examples as *ząb* /zɔmp/ 'tooth', *nóg* /nuk/ 'feet' (genitive plural), *mosiądz* /mɔçɔnts/ 'brass', *mąż* /mɔ͡ʃ/ 'husband', *ród* /rut/ 'breed'.

With few exceptions, Polish words are stressed on the penultimate syllable. Thus, for example, *ziemia* 'earth' is pronounced as ['ʑɛmˌa], *sprawiedliwość* 'justice' as [spraʐɛ'dlivɔçtɕ] and *sprawiedliwości* 'justice' (genitive, dative or locative singular) as [spraʐɛdli'vɔçtɕi]. The exceptions are mainly words of Greek origin, such as *muzyka* ['muzika] 'music', or of Latin origin, such as *uniwersytet* [unˌi'vɛrsitɛt] 'university', but even a few Slavonic words are irregular, such as *rzeczpospolita* [ʒɛtʃpɔ'spɔlita] 'commonwealth'. In addition, the first and second persons plural of the past tense of verbs have antepenultimate stress, e.g. *byliśmy* ['biliçmi] 'we were', *wiedzieliście* [ʐɛ'dʑɛliçtɕɛ] 'you knew' (masculine personal plural).

The Polish writing system uses an alphabet based on Latin, making liberal use of digraphs and diacritics. The Latin language and its alphabet were introduced to Poland simultaneously with Christianity in the tenth century AD. Gradually the alphabet was adapted to make it fit Polish.

Table 16.2: The Polish Alphabet

A	a	M	m
Ą	ą	N	n
B	b	Ń	ń
C	c	O	o
Ć	ć	Ó	ó
D	d	P	p
E	e	R	r
Ę	ę	S	s
F	f	Ś	ś
G	g	T	t
H	h	U	u
I	i	W	w
J	j	Y	y
K	k	Z	z
L	l	Ź	ź
Ł	ł	Ż	ż

Note: In addition to the 32 letters shown above, Q q, V v and X x may occasionally be found in foreign words, e.g. *Quebec*, *vademecum*, *Pax*. The digraphs *ch*, *cz*, *rz*, *sz*, *dz*, *dź*, *dż*, for the purpose of alphabetic order, are treated as sequences of separate letters.

The vowel letters *i* and *y* do not represent separate phonemes. They both stand for the phoneme /i/, but have separate functions in reflecting the quality of the consonant immediately preceding. Thus, for example, the written sequences *ci, dzi, si, zi, pi, bi, mi, fi, wi, ni* correspond respectively to /tɕi/, /dʑi/, /ɕi/, /ʑi/, /pʲi/, /bʲi/, /mʲi/, /fʲi/, /vʲi/, /ɲi/, whereas *cy, dzy, sy, zy, py, by, my, fy, wy, ny* represent /tsi/, /dzi/, /si/, /zi/, /pi/, /bi/, /mi/, /fi/, /vi/, /ni/. Except in words of foreign origin or in onomatopoeic words, the letter *i* is rarely or never written after the letters *d, t, cz, dz, sz, ż, ch, ł, r.* Subject to exceptions of the same kind, the letter *y* does not occur after *k, g,* or *l.*

The phoneme /tɕ/ is represented by *ć* or *ci,* the phoneme /dʑ/ by *dź* or *dzi,* the phoneme /ɕ/ by *ś* or *si,* the phoneme /ʑ/ by *ź* or *zi,* and the phoneme /ɲ/ by *ń* or *ni.* There is an orthographical convention whereby *ć, dź, ś, ź* and *ń* are written only at the end of a word (as in *być* /bitɕ/ 'to be') or immediately before another consonant (as in *ćma* /tɕma/ 'moth'). Elsewhere (i.e. before a vowel), *ci, dzi, si, zi* and *ni* are used (as in *ciemny* /tɕɛmni/ 'dark', *siano* /ɕano/ 'hay', and *ziarno* /ʑarnɔ/ 'grain'). If the vowel following is /i/, it is not shown separately in the spelling. For example, *ci* /tɕi/ 'to you', *nikt* /ɲikt/ 'nobody', *musi* /muɕi/ 'he must', *zima* /ʑima/ 'winter'. In such cases the letter *i* has a double function: it participates with the consonant letter in the representation of the consonant and also stands for the vowel /i/. Any other vowel, however, is shown separately in the spelling. In our examples *ciemny, siano* and *ziarno* (see above) the letter *i* is relevant only to the representation of the consonant.

The bilabial and labio-dental consonants /pʲ/, /bʲ/, /mʲ/, /fʲ/ and /ɣ/ can only occur immediately before a vowel, e.g. *biały* /bʲawi/ 'white'. In the sixteenth century they could occur at the end of a word and their palatalised quality was then sometimes indicated by means of a diacritic. The gradual process whereby they were replaced in this position by their non-palatalised counterparts was complete by the nineteenth century. As a result, we sometimes find palatalised and non-palatalised labials alternating in the stems of certain nouns, e.g. *gołąb* (nom. sg.) 'dove': *gołębia* (gen. sg.); *Wrocław* (nom. sg.): *Wrocławia* (gen. sg.). This tendency has gone even further in the north-east, including Warsaw, where even before vowels the palatalised labials are often replaced by the sequence non-palatalised labial + /j/, e.g. not /bʲawi/ but /bjawi/.

The following are some of the less obvious graphemic-phonemic correspondences:

Grapheme	Phoneme
ą	finally and before fricatives: /ɔ̃/ e.g. *mąż* /mɔ̃ʃ/ 'husband', *idą* /idɔ̃/ 'they go'
	before dental plosives and affricates: /ɔn/ e.g. *kąt* /kɔnt/ 'angle', *zając* /zajɔnts/ 'hare'
	before /k/ and /g/: /ɔn/ (phonetically [ɔŋ]) e.g. *łąka* [wɔŋka] 'meadow'
	before /p/ and /b/: /ɔm/ e.g. *dąb* /dɔmp/ 'oak'
	before /w/: /ɔ/ e.g. *wziął* /vʑɔw/ 'took'
ę	(i) finally and before fricatives: /ɛ̃/ e.g. *chcę* /xtsɛ̃/ 'I want', *często* /tʃɛ̃stɔ/ 'often'
	(ii) finally (colloquially): /ɛ/ e.g. *chcę* /xtsɛ/ 'I want'

	(iii)	before dental plosives and before dental and alveolar affricates: /ɛn/ e.g. *okręt* /ɔkrɛnt/ 'ship', *nędza* /nɛndza/ 'poverty', *tęcza* /tɛntʃa/ 'rainbow'
	(iv)	before pre-palatal affricates: /ɛɲ/ e.g. *pięć* /pɛɲ͜tɕ/ 'five'
	(v)	before /k/ and /g/: /ɛn/ (phonetically [ɛŋ]) e.g. *ręka* [rɛŋka] 'hand'
	(vi)	before bilabial plosives: /ɛm/ e.g. *postęp* /pɔstɛmp/ 'progress'
	(vii)	before /w/ and /l/: /ɛ/ e.g. *wzięli* /vʑɛli/ 'they took'

c	/ts/ e.g. *noc* /nɔts/ 'night'
ch h }	/x/ e.g. *suchy* /suxi/ 'dry', *błahy* /bwaxi/ 'trivial'
ć ci }	/tɕ/ e.g. *być* /bitɕ/ 'to be', *ciemny* /tɕɛmni/ 'dark'
cz	/tʃ/ e.g. *czas* /tʃas/ 'time'
ł	/w/ e.g. *łapać* /wapatɕ/ 'to catch'
rz ż }	/ʒ/ e.g. *rzeka* /ʒɛka/ 'river', *żagiel* /ʒagɛl/ 'sail'
ś si }	/ɕ/ e.g. *oś* /ɔɕ/ 'axis', *siano* /ɕanɔ/ 'hay'
sz	/ʃ/ e.g. *szok* /ʃɔk/ 'shock'
ó u }	/u/ e.g. *róg* /ruk/ 'corner', *mur* /mur/ 'wall'
w	/v/ or /ɣ/ e.g. *kawa* /kava/ 'coffee', *wiara* /ɣara/ 'faith'
ź zi }	/ʑ/ e.g. *luźny* /luʑni/ 'loose', *zima* /ʑima/ 'winter'

In the speech of a rapidly diminishing minority of Poles the archaic variant [ɫ] in place of normal [w] may be heard. The articulation of this dental lateral involves raising the back of the tongue. It is similar to the Russian non-palatalised /l/. Until recently Polish [ɫ] was obligatory in stage-pronunciation and it is still used by many actors. Regionally, it is mainly associated with the speech of Poles from the eastern areas now in the USSR, but it may also be encountered as a dialectal feature in the Tatra Mountains. The change [ɫ] > [w] began several centuries ago, but is still not complete.

Another feature characteristic of speakers from the eastern parts of the Polish speech area is the distinction of two separate phonemes /h/ and /x/, whereas most speakers have only one, viz. /x/. The phoneme /h/, which is a voiced laryngeal fricative, usually corresponds to the letter *h*. It is consequently possible in this type of pronunciation to make distinctions such as that between *hełm* [hɛɫm] 'helmet' and *Chełm* [xɛɫm] (a town in eastern Poland). For the vast majority of Poles these two words are homophones, both being pronounced [xɛwm].

The distinction between voiced and voiceless consonants is often neutralised as a result of assimilation, but the effects of assimilation are not always shown in the orthography. The orthography reveals that there was a time in the past when assimilation could operate progressively (i.e. towards the end of the word), e.g. *przy* /pʃi/ 'near'; but the active processes of assimilation are now only regressive (i.e. towards the beginning of the word), e.g. *prośba* /prɔʑba/ 'request'. Regressive assimilation may take place not only within the body of a word but also at the boundary between words. For example, *jak dobrze* 'how good' is pronounced /jag dɔbʒɛ/, *naród polski* 'the Polish nation' is pronounced /narut pɔlski/. This kind of assimilation is found on all social levels in all parts of Poland. However, if the second word begins with a vowel or a sonant (/m/, /n/, /r/, /l/, /w/), the presence or absence of assimilation by voicing is a regional feature distinguishing the north-east (including Warsaw) from the south and west (including Cracow and Poznań). In the north-east voicing is absent, e.g. *tak mało* 'so little' is pronounced /tak mawɔ/, *róg ulicy* 'the corner of the street' is pronounced /ruk ulitsi/. The corresponding variants in the south and west are /tag mawɔ/ and /rug ulitsi/. This variable is unaffected by social level. (Prepositions ending in a voiced consonant, however, are not affected by this type of variation. Their final consonants remain voiced before vowels and sonants in all parts of Poland.)

The results of the historical progressive assimilation of /v/ within the body of the word also varies regionally regardless of social factors. The pronunciation of such words as *twój* 'your', *kwiat* 'flower' with /f/ or /f̦/ (/tfuj/, /kf̦at/) is found in all parts of Poland except the eastern borderlands, Great Poland and Pomerania, where we hear /tvuj/, /kɣat/, etc.

We now come to consider some of the sound changes which have taken place in Polish and which distinguish it from the other Slavonic languages:

(i) The Common Slavonic nasal vowels were inherited by Polish and wherever the letters *ę* and *ą* are written today we may conclude that there was once a nasal vowel. However, as we have seen, these letters nowadays represent phonetically nasal vowels only in certain positions. The earliest records indicate that the Common Slavonic nasal vowels *ę* and *ǫ* were still distinguished in Polish until the beginning of the fourteenth century. During the course of this century, however, they appear to have coalesced as a single nasal vowel, written with the letter *ǿ*. Depending on prosodic factors, however, this single nasal underwent new changes, so that by the beginning of the sixteenth century (or perhaps even earlier) there were again two nasals (now written *ę* and *ą*). The present-day spelling system still reflects the state of the nasals in the sixteenth century. Of course, there is no correlation between the Polish letter *ę* and Common Slavonic *ę*, nor between Polish *ą* and Common Slavonic *ǫ*. For example, Polish *ręka* 'hand', *zięć* 'son-in-law', *rząd* 'row', *ząb* 'tooth' correspond to Common Slavonic *rǫka, *zętь, *rędъ, *zǫbъ, respectively.

(ii) The Common Slavonic reduced vowels or *jers* (ъ and ь) in strong positions give Polish *e*. In weak positions they are lost. The distinction between ъ and ь, whether strong or weak, survives in the quality of the preceding consonant. For example, *pьsъ > pies 'dog', but *vьsь > wieś 'village'; *sъnъ > sen 'sleep', but *dьnь > dzień 'day'.

(iii) In early Polish consonants located immediately before the front vowels (*e*, *i*, *ě*, *ь*, *ę*) were palatalised. In the case of the labials and labio-dentals this has resulted in the existence of pairs of consonants distinguished from each other solely by the feature 'palatalised' (i.e. the raising of the middle of the tongue to the hard palate). This is the only feature distinguishing /ḅ/ from /b/, /ṗ/ from /p/, /ɣ/ from /v/, /f̦/ from /f/ and /m̦/ from /m/. In the case of the dentals *s*, *z*, *t*, *d* and *n*, however, the change eventually involved more than the addition of the feature 'palatalised': /s/ > /ç/, /z/ > /ʐ/, /t/ > /tç/, /d/ > /dʐ/, /n/ > /ŋ/. For example, **osь* > *oś* 'axis', **zemja* > *ziemia* 'earth', **tęžьkъjь* > *ciężki* 'heavy', **kъdě* > *gdzie* 'where', **dьnь* > *dzień* 'day'. In each case the place of articulation of the resultant sound is entirely different from that of its origin (see table 16.1). Nevertheless, the native speaker, owing mainly to morphological alternations, feels that the relationship between the members of these pairs is the same as that between the non-palatalised and palatalised members of the labial and labio-dental pairs. The same is true of the pairs /w/ : /l/ and /r/ : /ʒ/, in each of which the phonological distinction also originally stems from the palatalisation of the second member before front vowels. Nowadays, however, neither member of either pair is palatalised.

(iv) Polish, in common with the other Lechitic languages, is affected by changes in certain Common Slavonic vowels if they were followed by the dental consonants *s*, *z*, *t*, *d*, *r* or *l*, and these consonants were themselves not followed by a front vowel. Thus, in this position, *e* > *'o* (i.e. *o* with palatalisation of the preceding consonant), e.g. **sestra* > *siostra* 'sister', **berǫ* > *biorę* 'I take'. In the same conditions, *ě* > *'a* (i.e. *a* with palatalisation of the preceding consonant), e.g. **lěsъ* > *las* 'forest', **větrъ* > *wiatr* 'wind'. In all other positions *e* and *ě* coalesced as *e*, e.g. **večerъ* > *wieczór* 'evening', **běgati* > *biegać* 'to run'. This is one of several sound changes that have led to morphophonemic vowel alternations.

3 Morphology

Polish nominal morphology is illustrated in the chart of declension types, with examples of the four main types of noun declension and of adjective declension. Although there is a high correlation between gender and declension type, it is not absolute: most *a*-stems are feminine, but those with clear male reference are masculine, e.g. *mężczyzna* 'man'. There are, in addition, subsidiary types such as that exemplified by *źrebię* 'foal', which has genitive singular *źrebięcia* and nominative plural *źrebięta*. The only noun belonging to this declension which is not neuter is *książę* 'prince'.

Two important interrelated distinctions in Polish nominal declension not revealed by the table are animate/non-animate and masculine personal/non-masculine personal. Masculine *o*-stem nouns and adjectives referring to human beings and other animals (and their attributes) in the singular have

Polish Declension Types

Singular:	a-*stem*	Masculine o-*stem*	Neuter o-*stem*	i-*stem*
Nominative	głowa	ptak	słowo	noc
Vocative	głowo	ptaku	słowo	nocy
Accusative	głowę	ptaka	słowo	noc
Genitive	głowy	ptaka	słowa	nocy
Dative	głowie	ptakowi	słowu	nocy
Instrumental	głową	ptakiem	słowem	nocą
Locative	głowie	ptaku	słowie	nocy

Plural:				
Nominative	głowy	ptaki	słowa	noce
Vocative	głowy	ptaki	słowa	noce
Accusative	głowy	ptaki	słowa	noce
Genitive	głów	ptaków	słów	nocy
Dative	głowom	ptakom	słowom	nocom
Instrumental	głowami	ptakami	słowami	nocami
Locative	głowach	ptakach	słowach	nocach

Adjective

Singular:	Masculine		Neuter	Feminine
Nominative	stary		stare	stara
Vocative	stary		stare	stara
Accusative	stary		stare	starą
Genitive		starego		starej
Dative		staremu		starej
Instrumental		starym		starą
Locative		starym		starej

Plural:	
Nominative	stare
Vocative	stare
Accusative	stare
Genitive	starych
Dative	starym
Instrumental	starymi
Locative	starych

an accusative case coinciding in form with the genitive singular. This is demonstrated by the example *ptak* 'bird' in the chart of declension types. In all other cases, the accusative singular of masculine *o*-stems coincides with the nominative singular. Thus, for example, *stary dom* 'an old house' has accusative singular *stary dom*, but *stary Polak* 'an old Pole' has *starego Polaka*. Masculine *a*-stems, such as *kolega* 'friend', like all other *a*-stems, have an accusative singular ending in -*ę*, e.g. *kolegę*. But adjectives agreeing with such nouns have an accusative singular coinciding with the genitive, e.g. *starego kolegę*. The masculine adjectival forms shown in the chart of declension types are those appropriate to a non-animate noun.

In the plural, however, the criterion is not whether the noun is animate, but whether it refers to a group embodying the two features 'masculine' and 'human'. If it does, the accusative plural has the same form as the genitive plural. If not, the accusative plural is the same as the nominative plural. Thus, for example, the accusative plural of *stary Polak* is *starych Polaków*, whereas the accusative plural of *stara Polka* 'an old Polish woman' is *stare Polki*, coinciding with the nominative plural. The masculine personal subgender is also manifested in the endings of the nominative plural. Some masculine personal nouns have the nominative plural ending *-owie*, e.g. *synowie* (nom. pl. of *syn* 'son'). Others have an ending which has evolved from the Common Slavonic nominative plural ending *-i*, but which in Polish is written *-i* or *-y*, depending on the nature of the preceding consonant, e.g. *chłopi* (nom. pl. of *chłop* 'peasant'), *Polacy* (nom. pl. of *Polak* 'Pole'). Masculine personal adjectives in the nominative plural can have only the *-i/-y* ending, e.g. *słabi* (from *słaby* 'weak'). This ending, whether used with nouns or adjectives, involves stem-consonant alternations, most of which result from the Common Slavonic second palatalisation of velars (see page 324) or from the Polish palatalisation of consonants before front vowels, but some of which are the result of analogy. Thus, for example, *k* alternates with *c* (e.g. *Polak:Polacy*), *g* with *dz* (e.g. *szpieg* 'spy' : *szpiedzy*), *s* with *ś* (e.g. *prezes* 'chairman' : *prezesi*), and (in adjectives only) *ż* with *ź* (e.g. *duży* 'big' : *duzi*), *sz* with *ś* (e.g. *lepszy* 'better' : *lepsi*).

Polish Conjugation Types

	Conjugation 1	Conjugation 2	Conjugation 3	Conjugation 4
Infin.	pisać 'to write'	lubić 'to like'	padać 'to fall'	jeść 'to eat'

Non-past:

Sg.		Conjugation 1	Conjugation 2	Conjugation 3	Conjugation 4
Sg.	1	piszę	lubię	padam	jem
	2	piszesz	lubisz	padasz	jesz
	2 or 3	pisze	lubi	pada	je
Pl.	1	piszemy	lubimy	padamy	jemy
	2	piszecie	lubicie	padacie	jecie
	2 or 3	piszą	lubią	padają	jedzą

Imperative:

Sg.	2	pisz	lub	padaj	jedz
Pl.	2	piszcie	lubcie	padajcie	jedzcie

Past:

		Masculine	Neuter	Feminine
Sg.	1	pisałem	–	pisałam
	2	pisałeś	pisałoś	pisałaś
	2 or 3	pisał	pisało	pisała

		Masculine personal	Non-masculine personal
Pl.	1	pisaliśmy	pisałyśmy
	2	pisaliście	pisałyście
	2 or 3	pisali	pisały

However, the masculine personal/non-masculine personal distinction is not shown in the ending of most nouns whose stem ends in *c, ć, dź, j, ń, ś, ź, l, cz, dż, dz, rz, sz,* or *ż*. Thus, for example, the nominative plural *żołnierze* 'soldiers' is not morphologically distinct from *kołnierze* 'collars'. Masculine personal nouns ending in the nominative singular in *-ec* have nominative plural *-cy*, e.g. *chłopiec* 'boy' : *chłopcy*. They are thus morphologically distinguished from non-masculine personal nouns like *dworzec* 'station' : *dworce*. But other nouns ending in *-c* are not distinguished, e.g. *szlachcic* 'nobleman' : *szlachcice*, cf. *szkic* 'sketch' : *szkice*.

Polish verbal morphology is in many ways similar to that of Russian, but conventionally four conjugational types are distinguished (as opposed to two in Russian), principally on the basis of the vowel occurring in the endings of the middle four members of the paradigm (*-e-, -i-,* or *-a-*) of the present tense. Conjugation 4 scarcely deserves separate status, as it includes only four verbs (viz. *umieć* 'to be able', *śmieć* 'to dare', *wiedzieć* 'to know', and *jeść* 'to eat') and their derivatives. Even these four differ in the third person plural (*umieją, śmieją, wiedzą, jedzą*). The paradigm of *być* 'to be' in

The Verb 'to be' in Polish

Infinitive   *być* 'to be'

Present:

Sg.	1	jestem
	2	jesteś
2 or 3		jest
Pl.	1	jesteśmy
	2	jesteście
2 or 3		są

Imperative:

Sg.	2	bądź
Pl.	2	bądźcie

Past:

		Masculine	*Neuter*	*Feminine*
Sg.	1	byłem	–	byłam
	2	byłeś	byłoś	byłaś
2 or 3		był	było	była

		Masculine personal	*Non-masculine personal*
Pl.	1	byliśmy	byłyśmy
	2	byliście	byłyście
2 or 3		byli	były

Future:

Sg.	1	będę	Pl.	1	będziemy
	2	będziesz		2	będziecie
2 or 3		będzie		2 or 3	będą

the present tense is unique.

Most finite verbal forms are unambiguously first, second or third person, singular or plural, and it is consequently not usual for them to be accompanied by personal pronouns, except for the purpose of emphasis. Exceptions to this rule, however, are the honorific second person pronouns *pan* (masculine singular), *pani* (feminine singular), *panowie* (masculine plural), *panie* (feminine plural), *państwo* (mixed gender plural). They are used with forms of the verb which are identical with those used in the third person. Therefore, unless the pronouns are expressed, the meaning is unambiguously third person. For example, *panowie piszą* 'you (m. pl.) are writing', but *piszą* 'they are writing'. These non-familiar address pronouns are all gender-specific and thus inevitably involve sexual discrimination.

The Polish personal pronouns (apart from the second person honorifics *pan* etc., already mentioned) are: *ja* 'I', *ty* 'you' (singular familiar), *on* 'he, it' (m.), *ona* 'she, it' (f.), *ono* 'it' (nt.), *my* 'we', *wy* 'you' (plural, familiar; or singular, honorific), *oni* 'they' (masculine personal), *one* 'they' (non-masculine personal). The most widespread type of non-familiar address is with one of the pronouns, *pan*, *pani* etc. (see above) in conjunction with a verb in the same form as for the third person, e.g. *pan pisze* 'you are writing', but *wy* with forms of the second person plural is used to address one person by peasants and members of the Polish United Workers' Party. Most Poles address older kin with *ty* and the corresponding verbal forms, but in the country *wy* often has this function, e.g. *coście powiedzieli, matko?* 'what did you say, mother?'. In this type of address masculine personal forms are used, even if the addressee is a female. In some families kinship terms are used as second person pronouns to address older kin in conjunction with verbs in the same form as the third person, e.g. *co mama powiedziała?* 'what did you say?' (lit. 'what did mummy say?').

The past tense (as may be seen from the chart of conjugation types) is derived from the same stem as the infinitive, e.g. *pisa-*, to which are added *-ł-* or *-l-* (denoting 'past'), a vowel (including zero) denoting gender and number and an ending (including a zero ending) denoting person. Historically, the form ending in *l*/*l* is a participle; the ending is part of the present tense of the auxiliary *być* 'to be'. The erstwhile independence of the ending is demonstrated by the fact that it need not follow the *l*/*l* participle, but may appear elsewhere in the sentence, e.g. *gdzieście byli?* or *gdzie byliście?* 'where have you been?'.

The aspectual system is similar to that of Russian (see pages 340–1). Non-past imperfective verbs (e.g. those in the chart of conjugation types) have present meaning. Non-past perfective verbs have future meaning, e.g. *napiszę* 'I shall write'. The imperfective future is expressed periphrastically using the auxiliary *będę* 'I shall be' in the appropriate person and number with the imperfective infinitive, as in Russian, e.g. *będzie pisać* 'he will write, be writing', or with the *l*/*l* participle, e.g. *będzie pisał*. The participle agrees in number and gender with the subject.

The conditional is formed by the addition of the invariable clitic *by* to the past tense. Most commonly it is inserted between the *ł/l* participle and the personal ending, e.g. *pisałbym* 'I should write', *panowie pisaliby* 'you would write' (m. plural). There is also a past conditional formed by the addition of the present conditional of the verb *być* 'to be' to the *ł/l* participle, e.g. *byłbym pisał* 'I should have written', *byłabyś pisała* 'you would have written' (familiar, feminine singular).

The pluperfect also exists, though it is extremely rare and is found only in a formal literary style. The *ł/l* participle of the auxiliary *być* is added to the past tense, e.g. *pisałem był* 'I had written, been writing'.

There are two declined participles (one active, one passive). The active declined participle is derived from the present stem of imperfective verbs by means of the morpheme *-ąc-* to which the adjectival endings are added, e.g. *piszący* 'writing' (masculine nominative singular). The passive declined participle, which may be formed from both imperfective and perfective verbs, is derived from the past (or infinitive) stem by means of the morpheme *-t-* or *-n-* followed by the adjectival endings, e.g. *kryty* 'hidden', *pisany* or *napisany* 'written'. The present undeclined (adverbial) participle is identical with the active declined participle minus the adjectival endings, e.g. *pisząc* 'writing'. There is also a past undeclined (adverbial) participle, which is derived from the past stem by the addition of *-wszy*, e.g. *napisawszy* 'having written'. It may be formed only from perfective verbs.

The passive need not involve the use of the passive participle. It may also be expressed by means of a finite form of the verb accompanied by the reflexive particle *się*, e.g. *książka się drukuje* 'the book is being printed' (lit. 'the book prints itself'). Such expressions may also be impersonal, e.g. *mówi się* 'it is said', *drukuje się książkę* (accusative). There are, in addition, impersonal constructions involving the use of special forms of the passive participle ending in *-no* or *-to*, e.g. *zaczęto taniec* 'the dance has been begun', *zamknięto okno* 'the window has been shut', *podano herbatę* 'tea is served'. As in the personal counterparts of these constructions (*podali herbatę* 'they served tea' etc.) the object is in the accusative.

The morphology of numerals in Polish is complicated by the fact that their gender system is different from that of nouns. In particular, the numeral 'two' manifests a fourfold distinction between *dwa* (masculine non-personal and neuter), *dwie* (feminine), *dwaj* (or *dwóch* or *dwu*) (group consisting exclusively of male persons), and *dwoje* (one man and one woman). (However, *dwoje* is also used with nouns which exist only in the plural or denote young creatures, including children.) Although this degree of subtlety is restricted to this numeral and words for 'both', the morphological specification of groups consisting exclusively of male persons is characteristic of numerals generally and in contradistinction to nominal gender, which only specifies groups containing at least one male person.

4 Syntax

Main verbs agree in number and person with their subjects. For example, *urzędnik pisze* 'the official is writing' (3 singular), *urzędnicy piszą* 'the officials are writing' (3 plural). Past tense verbs, in addition, agree in gender with their subject. For example, *urzędnicy pisali* 'the officials were writing' (3 plural, masculine personal), *nauczycielki pisały* 'the teachers (feminine) were writing' (3 plural, non-masculine personal), *koty siedziały* 'the cats were sitting' (3 plural, non-masculine personal). In the case of composite subjects the two features 'masculine' and 'personal' may be supplied separately by two nouns one of which is masculine (but not human) and the other of which is human (but not masculine). Thus: *nauczycielka i kot siedzieli* 'the teacher (feminine) and the cat (masculine) were sitting'.

Adjectives agree in number, case and gender with the nouns they modify, e.g. *Jadwiga jest chora* 'Jadwiga is ill' (feminine nominative singular), *mam młodą córkę* 'I have a young daughter' (feminine accusative singular). Nouns which refer to male human beings may, for expressive purposes (positive or negative), be used in the non-masculine personal form, e.g. *morowe chłopy* 'fine lads' (instead of masculine personal *morowi chłopi*). In such cases, both adjectives and past tense verbs may agree with the expressive form, e.g. *jakieś idioty to wymyśliły* 'some idiots have dreamed that up' (rather than *jacyś idioci to wymyślili*). Certain essentially expressive words hardly ever or never appear in the masculine personal form, e.g. *Szwab* 'German' (derogatory) always has plural *Szwaby*. (*Szwabi* or *Szwabowie* means 'Swabians' i.e. 'inhabitants of Swabia').

From some masculine nouns referring to professional posts and titles it is possible to derive feminine counterparts, e.g. from *nauczyciel* 'teacher' (masculine) we derive *nauczycielka* 'teacher' (feminine). Words like *nauczycielka* are straightforward feminine nouns and take normal feminine agreement. In some other cases, however, particularly those of professions which until recently were mainly the preserve of men, there is no feminine form. Therefore, the originally masculine noun is now usually of common gender, i.e. it is masculine when referring to a man and feminine when referring to a woman. This is so, for example, in the case of *doktor* 'doctor', *inżynier* 'engineer', *ambasador* 'ambassador', *architekt* 'architect'. It is possible, when referring to a woman, to retain masculine agreement, e.g. *nasz doktor wyjechał* 'our doctor has gone away' *may* refer to a woman. But in practice the predominant tendency is to avoid ambiguity by using feminine agreement, e.g. *nasza doktor wyjechała*. Similarly, when the syntax demands an oblique case, it is permissible to decline such nouns according to the masculine paradigm, but a sentence such as *oddałem książkę redaktorowi* 'I returned the book to the editor' will normally be taken to imply that the editor is a man. Therefore, the usual practice, if one of these nouns refers to a woman, is to leave it undeclined, e.g. *oddałem książkę redaktor*, thereby leaving no room for doubt as to the editor's sex.

Some collective nouns ending in *-stwo*, e.g. *państwo* 'ladies and gentlemen', *wujostwo* 'uncle and aunt', decline as singular nouns, but take plural, masculine personal agreement. For example, *Doktorostwo Kowalscy byli u nas wczoraj* 'Doctor and Mrs Kowalski were visiting us yesterday', *ci państwo przyszli* 'that lady and gentleman have arrived'. This syntactic property is one of the features distinguishing *państwo* 'ladies and gentlemen, Mr and Mrs etc.' from *państwo* 'state', which takes neuter singular agreement.

The numeral 'one' takes agreement in the singular, e.g. *jeden dzień* 'one day', *jedna kobieta* 'one woman', and itself agrees in gender and case with the noun it modifies. It also has a plural form *jedne/jedni* meaning 'some' or 'certain'. In compound numerals ending in 'one' *jeden* is invariable, e.g. *kupiliśmy dwadzieścia jeden książek* 'we bought twenty-one books'. The numerals 'two', 'three' and 'four' take the plural and agree in gender and case with the noun they modify, e.g. *dwa konie* 'two horses' (masculine non-personal nominative and accusative), *dwie książki* 'two books' (feminine nominative and accusative). The masculine personal category (i.e. *exclusively* masculine) is expressed by means of the forms *dwaj* 'two', *trzej* 'three', *czterej* 'four', e.g. *czterej urzędnicy pisali* 'four officials were writing', or by means of a genitive subject, e.g. *czterech urzędników pisało* 'four officials were writing'. The current tendency is for the latter type to become increasingly common at the expense of the former type. In the case of numerals from 'five' upwards, if the subject is masculine personal (exclusively) it *must* be in the genitive, e.g. *osiemdziesięciu czterech robotników pracowało* 'eighty-four workmen were working'. If the subject is not exclusively masculine personal, numerals from 'five' upwards are followed by the genitive plural e.g. *dwadzieścia ptaków odleciało* 'twenty birds flew away', unless they are composite and end in one of the numerals 'two' to 'four', in which case the form of the noun is determined by the last component, e.g. *dwadzieścia trzy ptaki odleciały* 'twenty-three birds flew away'.

The collective numerals *dwoje, troje, czworo, pięcioro* etc. have among their functions the possibility of referring to groups containing, but not consisting exclusively of, male persons. Thus, for example, the phrase *ich czworo* '(there are) four of them' (if it refers to adult human beings), reveals that there is at least one man and at least one woman in the group. When in the subject, the collective numerals are always followed by the genitive plural of the noun they modify.

One of the striking features of the Polish system of gender and agreement is the high degree of redundancy. The same information on gender and number may be repeated several times in the sentence. Even more striking, however, is the lack of non-specific forms. It is difficult to make any observation about any plural entity without sizing up its human or non-human and sexual properties. The word *osoba* 'person', which is always feminine, is a boon to those wishing to be non-specific about human groups. But from the problem of deciding whether one's interlocutor (even on the telephone) is male (requiring the address pronoun *pan* + masculine agreement) or female (requiring the address pronoun *pani* + feminine agreement) there is no escape.

Bibliography

Szober (1968) is a standard reference grammar in Polish, while Brooks (1975) is the best reference grammar available in English; Urbańczyk et al. (1978) is an encyclopedia covering all aspects of Polish. For pronunciation, Karaś and Madejowa is a dictionary of Polish pronunciation using the International Phonetic Alphabet, with an introduction in English; Puppel et al. (1977) is the only book of its kind presenting Polish pronunciation in English.

The standard history of the Polish language is Klemensiewicz (1974), while Klemensiewicz et al. (1965) is the standard historical grammar. For historical phonology, Stieber (1973) is a classic work, better than anything in Polish on this subject (including Stieber's own work). Westfal (1985) is a useful account of the language with historical explanations.

References

Brooks, M.Z. 1975. *Polish Reference Grammar* (Mouton, The Hague)

Karaś, M. and M. Madejowa. 1977. *Słownik wymowy polskiej PWN* (Państwowe Wydawnictwo Naukowe, Warsaw and Cracow)

Klemensiewicz, Z. 1974. *Historia języka polskiego* (Państwowe Wydawnictwo Naukowe, Warsaw)

——, T. Lehr-Spławiński and S. Urbańczyk. 1965. *Gramatyka historyczna języka polskiego*, 3rd ed. (Państwowe Wydawnictwo Naukowe, Warsaw)

Puppel, S., J. Nawrocka-Fisiak and H. Krassowska. 1977. *A Handbook of Polish Pronunciation for English Learners* (Państwowe Wydawnictwo Naukowe, Warsaw)

Stieber, Z. 1973. *A Historical Phonology of the Polish Language* (Carl Winter Universitätsverlag, Heidelberg)

Szober, S. 1968. *Gramatyka języka polskiego*, 10th ed. (Państwowe Wydawnictwo Naukowe, Warsaw)

Urbańczyk, S. et al. (eds.) 1978. *Encyklopedia wiedzy o języku polskim* (Ossolineum, Wrocław, Warsaw, Cracow and Gdańsk)

Westfal, S. 1985. *The Polish Language*, 2nd ed. (Veritas Foundation Publication Centre, London)

17   Czech and Slovak

David Short

1   Introduction

Czech and Slovak are by no means major languages on purely statistical
grounds, with around 9.5 million and 4.5 million speakers respectively in
Czechoslovakia itself, whereas Ukrainian, for example, has around
40 million speakers in the Soviet Union. Czechs and Slovaks are, however,
to be found scattered worldwide, either diffused or in close-knit villages and
some larger communities in Rumania, Yugoslavia, Hungary and Poland,
due to local small-scale migrations or the vagaries of political frontiers, or
Canada, the USA and South America, due to the modern tradition of
economic or political emigration. These pockets add several hundred
thousand to the total numbers of speakers; their languages, however,
necessarily differ, through physical separation and the external influence of
dominant languages in the alien environment, from the Czech and Slovak to
be described in the following pages.

If not on statistical grounds, then historically Czech at least does have a
claim as a major language: the Kingdom of Bohemia controlled, in the
Middle Ages, a much vaster area than just the Lands of the Bohemian
Crown (Bohemia and Moravia); Bohemian kings have been Holy Roman
Emperors; and twice there have been Anglo-Bohemian dynastic links
through marriage. More recently Czechoslovakia has been, between the
wars, a major economic force in Europe. By contrast Slovakia has rarely
enjoyed independence, coming closest to it briefly during the last war as a
client state of Germany, and since 1968 when it became one of the two
federated republics that now constitute Czechoslovakia.

The two languages are taken together in this volume because, despite the
natural processes of divergence brought about by geography, geopolitical
separation and exposure to different influences of neighbouring languages
(Czech is heavily influenced by German, Slovak by Hungarian), the two
languages share a great deal and are on average 90 per cent mutually
intelligible. Now sharing a common state, Czechs and Slovaks are
constantly exposed each to the other's language and mutual intelligibility is
reinforced by, for example, labour mobility, military service and the media.

The similarities are highest, and increasing, at the lexical level (where there are also some of the most striking individual differences), while phonologically and morphologically the differences affect most words, though not enough to inhibit comprehension. The overall distinctiveness is, however, great enough for translations between the literatures to be a meaningful exercise.

2 The Historical Background

The written tradition in what is now Czechoslovakia goes back to the ninth century, with the Christian mission of Saints Cyril (Constantine) and Methodius to Great Moravia, where they prepared Slavonic translations of the central religious texts. At the time the Macedonian dialect of Slavonic which they used was readily comprehensible to all other Slavs. Although used for centuries afterwards in Eastern Orthodox Christianity, in the west it fell into disuse after the Slavonic monks were driven from the Sázava monastery in Bohemia in 1097. The existence of this early standardised literary language contributed to the general stability of the early literary tradition in Bohemia, but the Slavonic alphabets used in it, the Glagolitic created by St Cyril and the Cyrillic still used by Bulgarian, Macedonian and Serbian and the East Slavonic languages, were not widely employed. Czech and Slovak used a modified Latin alphabet, possibly because Cyril and Methodius were actually preceded by western missionaries from Italy, Bavaria and Ireland. The earliest texts show developing refinements of the Latin alphabet as it was adapted to express the non-Latin sounds of Czech, and the first attempt to systematise the orthography is generally attributed to the religious reformer Jan Hus (1373–1415). Amongst many other linguistic guidelines, Hus introduced systematically diacritics to replace the many cumbersome digraphs in use until then. His system was not adopted universally or immediately, but a version of it became generalised when adopted by the Czech Brethren, whose authority and literary output guaranteed its ultimate acceptance. This sixteenth-century 'Brethren' orthography differed from the modern in the use of g, ǧ, j, w, v and au for j, g, í, v, u and ou respectively, and critically in the distribution of i and y. The modern values of the letters were established fairly painlessly in a sequence of nineteenth-century reforms, except in the case of i/y, which was a major controversy. The distinction between i and y as accepted in the modern orthographies is on etymological or morphological grounds and represents the victory of the 'iotist' camp in the nineteenth-century debate. The 'ypsilonists' gave precedence to phonetic considerations in certain critical environments. The iotist victory was assured once Josef Jungmann (1773–1847) and Josef Dobrovský (1753–1829) firmly adopted the new conventions, the matter being essentially settled about 1817–19. It was not laid to rest completely, however, until the death of the chief ypsilonist Jan

Nejedlý in 1834, though Jiří (Juraj) Palkovič (1769–1850) continued with the *y*-convention in Slovakia until his death.

Since the nineteenth century there have been further minor reforms, notably in the distribution of *s* and *z* medially and as prefixes, the two languages being not quite in step here. And recently the old *i/y* problem has resurfaced. Early in 1984 it seemed quite likely that *y* would be eliminated altogether in favour of *i* in Czech, except after *d*, *t* and *n*, which as hitherto would represent palatal stops before *i* and alveolar before *y*, and that *ů* would be replaced by *ú*. However, the public outcry over the consequences for language study and language learning, not to mention the continuing need to be able to read with ease texts in the prereform orthography which would be unlikely to be reprinted, has meant that the proposal has now been dropped.

The father of Slavonic studies, Josef Dobrovský, produced the first scientifically based modern grammar of Czech, at a time when the French Enlightenment and Austrian responses to it (the reforms of Josef II) had spurred on the National Revival and a new interest in the Czech nation and language. As his sources Dobrovský took both the best of the Humanist tradition, associated with the name of Jan Blahoslav (1523–71), the Kralice Bible (1579–93) and the printer Daniel Adam z Veleslavína (1546–99), and the living language of the rural Czech populace. The resultant grammar, still the basis of modern Czech, contained perforce many archaic features, and Dobrovský himself was not convinced that the language could be fully revived. It fell largely to Josef Jungmann to demonstrate, through translations of, amongst others, Milton's *Paradise Lost* and Goethe's *Herrmann und Dorothea*, that Czech was capable of high-style verse, and to provide Czech with a complete lexicon, his Czech-German dictionary of 1834–9. Czech was no longer a vehicle with limited capacity for expressing the full breadth of human communicational needs. Jungmann himself, and those who followed in the provision of technical terminologies, drew on some of the earlier vocabularies and on knowledge of other Slavonic languages as a source for rationally based loan-neologisms.

Meanwhile in Slovakia the language situation was also evolving. As part of Hungary, its official language had been Latin or Hungarian, while the Protestant liturgy continued to use Czech, the Czech of the Kralice Bible. The first attempted codification of Slovak was by Anton Bernolák (1762–1813), a Catholic priest, who produced a grammar based on a Western Slovak dialect, and a six-volume dictionary published posthumously in 1825–7. Bernolák's version of literary Slovak failed to gain wide approval, unlike the second attempt, by Ľudovít Štúr (1815–56), whose 1846 work, based on Central Slovak, found immediate favour. There have been changes since, in both the morphology and the lexicon of the standard, but the modern language still owes most to Štúr. Before Štúr and Bernolák there had been writing in 'Slovak' — various hybrids of Czech and local dialects written according to a variety of spelling conventions. It has recently become the practice to refer to these prestandardisation versions of the language as 'cultured (*kultúrna*) western/central/eastern Slovak'. Throughout the gestation and parturition of Slovak as an independent literary language there was also a continuous current which favoured the use of Czech, either as such, or in a mutation of a common Czechoslovak; the latter survived as a linguistic myth right through the First Republic.

In many ways Slovak is more modern than Czech, especially morphologically, for it has far fewer surviving redundant distinctions. Czech has more later phonological innovations, and even more still in its most progressive form, Common Czech, based on the Central Bohemian dialect. This has evolved into a remarkably distinct version of the national language.

Although there has been a strong tendency in the past to keep Slovak maximally distinct from Czech and free of Bohemicisms, there are some signs of a reverse tendency, due in part to the shift of the languages' centres of gravity away from the high literary towards the technical. Both languages resort to neologisms, and standardisation to international norms often means coincidence rather than further division. Added to that, Slovak, despite the opposition of purists, remains open to influences from Czech; Slovak influence on Czech is much slighter, though not yet fully appreciated.

3   The Alphabets, Orthography and Phonology of Czech and Slovak

Table 17.1: The Alphabets of Czech and Slovak

Czech	Slovak	Czech	Slovak
a, á	a, á	n, ň	n, ň
	ä	o, ó	o, ó
b	b		ô
c	c	p	p
č			
d, ď	d, ď	q	q
	dz	r	r, ŕ
		ř	
	dž	s	s
e, é, ě	e, é	š	š
f	f	t, ť	t, ť
g	g	u, ú, ů	u, ú
h	h	v	v
ch	ch	w	w
i, í	i, í	x	x
j	j	y, ý	y, ý
k	k	z	z
l	l, ľ, ĺ	ž	ž
m	m		

Typographically similar letters given on the same line, e.g. *a*, *á*, have no effect on ordering in the dictionary, those on separate lines, e.g. Slovak *a*, *ä*, are ordered separately. The three digraphs *ch*, *dz*, *dž* are treated in every respect as single letters. Although *d/d'*, *t/t'*, *n/ň* and *l/l'* are ordered indiscriminately in accordance with the following letter, i.e. *t'uh ̌ýk* will always precede *tuk*, the sounds represented by each member of the pairs are phonetically and phonologically distinct, as alveolar and palatal respectively. But because of certain spelling conventions a *d*, *t*, *n* or *l* may have the palatal values of *d'*, *t'*, *ň* and *l'*, notably before *ě* and *i* in Czech and (in most cases) *e* and *i* in Slovak. Note also the conventions whereby *d'* and *t'* use the hook ˇ instead of the apostrophe on capitals, in handwriting and on the Czech typewriter keyboard. Of the other consonants, *h* is a voiced glottal fricative, *c* and *dz* represent alveolar affricates, *č* and *dž* palato-alveolar affricates, *š* and *ž* palato-alveolar fricatives, and *ř* a rolled post-alveolar fricative (never the sequence of [r] + [ʒ] commonly attempted by non-Czechs in the name *Dvořák*). The letters *q*, *w* and *x* are confined to loanwords, though for perhaps obvious reasons only *x* is particularly common. In Slovak *g* is marginally more common than in Czech, thanks to a number of words containing /g/ that are not merely loans or onomatopoeic. By contrast *f* is more domesticated in Czech, having evolved as the voiceless counterpart of /v/, though it too is most frequent in loanwords. In circumstances parallel to the Czech devoicing of /v/ to /f/, Slovak has the bilabial /w/, not represented orthographically other than as *v* after any vowel or *u* after *o* in set morphological circumstances. The remaining consonant symbols have values similar to English, but the voiceless plosives represented by *p*, *t* and *k* are never aspirated.

Of the vowel symbols *ě* signals that a preceding *d*, *t* or *n* is to be pronounced as the appropriate palatal counterpart, or that a preceding *b*, *p*, *f*, *v* or *m* is to be pronounced [bj], [pj], [fj], [vj] or [mɲ]. Slovak *ä* represents a sound between /a/ and /e/, but is often indistinguishable from the latter, which the orthoepic norm allows. Slovak *ô* represents the diphthongal phoneme /uo/, and the circle on Czech *ů* is a historical convention appearing in circumstances where a long /u/ has evolved from a long /o/. Length in a vowel and Slovak syllabic /l/ and /r/ is otherwise marked by the 'acute accent'. Long *ó* occurs only in loanwords.

In addition to /uo/ (*ô*) Slovak has three other diphthongs represented by *ia*, *ie* and *iu*. Czech has one diphthong /ou/, spelled *ou* (contrast the Slovak *ou* sequence as [ow]).

Voice assimilation in clusters of consonants is important in Czech and Slovak, but is only sporadically reflected in the spelling. Voice assimilation in consonant clusters works right through both languages where paired consonants are involved, e.g. *bt* and *tb* will be pronounced /pt/ and /db/ respectively, and in Slovak also before *r*, *l*, *l'*, *m*, *n*, *ň* and *j* at word or morpheme boundaries. Czech and Slovak spelling is thus morphophonemic rather than phonetic.

One phonetic difference, not reflected in the orthography, is the presence and absence of the glottal stop in Czech and Slovak respectively; it appears in Czech between vowels and before words beginning with a vowel.

Both languages have fixed stress, on the first syllable, and this usually passes forward onto a preceding monosyllabic preposition.

4   The Evolution of Czech and Slovak

Among the early dialect divisions of Slavonic are the different resolutions of the *tort formula, as indicated on page 325. Importantly, Czech and Slovak here share the South Slavonic resolution, namely *trat, unlike Polish *trot; the only Czech/Slovak inconsistencies here are in variations of vowel length, brought about by different patterns of accent-shifting or the workings of analogy. Where they are distinct is in the related word-initial *ort formula: Central Slovak (the basis of the standard language) has fairly consistently *rat, while Czech has *rat or *rot according to whether the original tone had been rising or falling. Slovak is thus united to South Slavonic by an extra isogloss, cf. Cz. role 'field', rádlo 'plough', Slk. raľa, radlo, Serbo-Croat ral, ralo.

The palatalisations (see page 324) produced two Czech/Slovak distinctions. Under the second palatalisation of velars ch yielded š in Czech as in West Slavonic generally, but s in Slovak (another feature shared with South Slavonic), hence Češi/Česi 'Czechs'. The affricate dz had two origins: from g by the second and third palatalisations, and from d + j. Whereas in Czech dz of either origin de-affricated to z (see page 324), suggesting near simultaneity of the two processes, in Slovak they must have been separated in time, since de-affrication only affected dz < g. The change of d + j to dz came about only after de-affrication was completed, leaving this second appearance of dz unchanged as the source of this Slovak-only phoneme.

To the Slavist knowing, say, Russian or Polish, a striking feature of Czech and Slovak is the absence of g from the native word stock and its replacement by h. This is a consequence of the realignment of consonantal parallelisms after the de-affrication of dž to ž. Prior to that there was symmetry between k:g (voiceless and voiced velar plosives) and č:dž (their post-palatalisation corresponding palatal affricates), with ch and its counterpart š standing to one side. Subsequently a voiced/voiceless relationship emerged between ž and š, not matched by g:ch. This led to the change g > h, leaving h:ch as a nearly matching pair of fricatives, differing slightly in the place of articulation (glottal and velar respectively). Before and after de-affrication the picture was thus:

Before: k:g   ch   After: k   h:ch
        č:dž š   č   ž:š

The resolution of the jers (see page 326) is another area in which Czech and Slovak differ. Czech has all strong jers vocalised to *e*, while Slovak has essentially followed the Russian pattern, i.e. *e* for ь, *o* for ъ. Slovak also uses *a*, for which many conflicting theories have been advanced, as also for the explanation of the not infrequent cases of *o* for ь and *e* for ъ.

One of the more striking differences between Czech and Slovak (and also the easternmost dialects of Czech itself) is the outcome of the processes known in Czech as *přehláska* (approximately 'umlaut') whereby the back vowels *a/á*, *u/ú* and *o/ó* underwent a forward shift to *ě/ie*, *i/í* and *ě/ie*. The three sets of changes were not quite simultaneous, nor did they happen under exactly the same circumstances. The common factor was basically the influence of a preceding soft (palatalised) consonant, and although later developments, especially the effect of analogy, have 'undone' some of the effects, the consequences have been far-reaching phonologically (in the range of new syllable types), morphemically (in the increased incidence of root-vowel alternation, as in *pět/pátý* 'five/fifth' or *přítel/přátel* 'friend (nom. sg./gen. pl.)', cases where for *a* > *ě*, *á* > *ie* > *í* the nature of a following consonant was also relevant) and morphologically. Here it led on the one hand to a proliferation of hard/soft oppositions in the declensional paradigms: *žena:duše* 'wife:soul', acc. sg., *ženu:duši*, *oknům:mořím* 'window:sea' dat. pl., (*ů* < *ó*, *í* < *ie* < *ó*); and on the other hand it led, after the change of *ie* > *í*, to the obliteration of case-distinct forms in one particular large neuter paradigm (the contemporary *í*-declension, in which the only distinctively marked cases are those commonly associated with a consonant). Slovak was quite untouched by *přehláska*.

Czech and Slovak both possess syllabic liquids. The original **trt*, **tlt* have survived with fewer innovations in Slovak, while Czech has, in different circumstances, supporting vowels after *č* and *ž* with *r*, hence *čerpat* 'draw (water)', *žerd'* 'pole' to Slovak *črpat'*, *žrd'*, and after all consonants with *l*, except after labials where the *l* was of the soft variety, hence *žlutý* 'yellow', *dlouhý* 'long' to Slovak *žltý*, *dlhý*, but *vlk* 'wolf' and *plný* 'full' in both languages. As a consequence of the loss of the weak jers, many new consonantal clusters arose, often containing liquids. The picture is a complex one, with up to five different solutions to the problem, varying with position in the word and geographical distribution. Of most significance here are the initial and final positions, since this time it is Slovak which evolves supporting vowels, hence *luhat'* 'lie, fib', *l'ahostajný* 'indifferent', *ruvat'* 'tear', *ruman* 'camomile', *eržat'* 'neigh' correspond to the Czech *lhát*, *lhostejný*, *rvát*, *rmen*, *ržát* (where the initial liquids are only semi-syllabic, i.e. they do not attract the stress), and *niesol* 'he carried', *mysel'* 'mind', *vietor* 'wind' to the Czech *nesl*, *mysl*, *vítr* (where the liquids are syllabic and indistinguishable from original syllabic *l* and *r*). The failure of Slovak to evolve secondary final syllabic liquids underlies one of the contrasts in the absorption of loanwords in the two languages (there are of course others).

Where Czech spelling and pronunciation have here too a syllabic *l* or *r*, as in *menšestr* or *manšestr* 'corduroy', *metr* 'metre' or *triangl* 'triangle' — the instrument, Slovak has *menčester*, *meter* and *triangel*, and the orthoepic pronunciation of foreign toponyms etc. is analogously distinct (/menčestr/ vs./menčester/).

In the consonant systems mention must be made of the almost uniquely Czech phoneme represented by *ř*, a fully palatalised historically soft *r*.

This background account of the history of distinctive phonological features is by no means exhaustive, but there remains one more which cannot be overlooked, namely the so-called rhythmical law of Slovak. In essence this states that where two (historically) long syllables appear in succession, the second one shortens. This is most conspicuous in adjectival endings, which by the process of contraction were long. Contraction operated in most cases where there were two vowels in sequence separated by jot, hence in the adjectives **krásnъjь*, **krásnaja*, **krásnoje* 'beautiful (nom. sg. m., f., nt.)' gave *krásný, krásná, krásné*. By the rhythmical law the second long vowels shortened, hence modern Slovak *krásny, krásna, krásne*, which does not apply if the preceding syllable is short, as in *pekný* 'nice' (Cz. *pěkný*). Forms such as *krásne* are ambiguous in Slovak (on paper) as between some cases of the adjective (e.g. neuter singular nominative) and the adverb (equivalent to Czech *krásně*), but there is a pronunciation difference, the *n* of the adverb being palatal, that of the adjectival forms being alveolar. No Slovak *e* that has shortened in this manner causes prepalatalisation. The rhythmical law can be seen operating on various suffixes, such as *-ník*, as in *strážnik* 'policeman', cf. Czech *strážník*, as opposed to Slovak/Czech *hutník* 'smelter', or in diminutive formation, as in *národík, králiček*, from *národ* 'nation', *králik* 'rabbit' respectively, cf. Czech *nárůdek, králíček*. The Slovak rhythmical law is consistent throughout the word, i.e. it is not confined to shortening of final syllables, but there are some half-dozen morphologically governed circumstances when it is not observed. These include the third person plural of *i*-conjugation verbs, e.g. *chvália* 'praise' (*ia* is a diphthong and therefore long; diphthongs are generally covered by the rhythmical law otherwise), the genitive plural of some noun types, e.g. *piesní* 'songs', and adjectives formed from the names of animals, e.g. *vtáčí* 'birds'.

Both languages have evolved fixed stress, on the first syllable; this contrasts with Polish, where it is fixed on the penultimate, and Russian or Serbo-Croat, where it is mobile.

5 Morphology

Czech and Slovak have, like most of the Slavonic languages, been fairly conservative in their morphology, although they are by no means identical.

They both have three genders and a fully developed case system. There is one difference here, however, in that Slovak has lost the vocative (though remnants survive). The number system has become bipartite, singular and plural, with just a few remnants in Czech of the old dual declension surviving as anomalous plurals, chiefly associated with parts of the body. Standard literary Czech is the most conservative, Slovak and Common Colloquial Czech having proceeded further in the direction of eliminating redundant distinctions, notably in having a near-universal instrumental plural ending in -*mi* and -*ma* respectively (with an appropriate linking vowel where relevant). The latter -*ma* ending is a curiosity in that it comes from the instrumental dual, although the dual survives 'legitimately' only in the remnants mentioned.

The main distinctions between the two languages in noun morphology have come about because of the *přehláska* changes which affected Czech, while a not unimportant difference comes in the feminine hard *a*-declension where the more conservative Czech retains the products of palatalisation in the dative and locative singular, Slovak having evolved, like Russian, with forms which eliminate stem alternation; thus to the words *matka* 'mother', *kniha* 'book', *socha* 'statue' the dative/locative singular forms are *matce*, *knize*, *soše* and *matke*, *knihe* and *soche* in Czech and Slovak respectively.

Czech and Slovak Noun Declensions Compared

		Czech	*Slovak*
Masculine hard declension — animate			
Sg.	Nom.	chlap 'fellow'	chlap
	Voc.	chlape, synu 'son', bože 'god'[1]	
	Acc.	chlapa	chlapa
	Gen.	chlapa	chlapa
	Dat.	chlapovi, -u[2]	chlapovi
	Inst.	chlapem	chlapom
	Loc.	chlapovi	chlapovi
Pl.	Nom.	chlapi, sousedé 'neighbour', filologové 'philologist'	chlapi, občania 'citizen', filológovia
	Acc.	chlapy	chlapov
	Gen.	chlapů	chlapov
	Dat.	chlapům	chlapom
	Inst.	chlapy	chlapmi
	Loc.	chlapech, soudruzích 'comrade'	chlapoch
Masculine soft declension — animate			
Sg.	Nom.	muž 'man'	muž (declined as chlap)
	Voc.	muži, otče 'father'	
	Acc.	muže	muža
	Gen.	muže	muža
	Dat.	muži, mužovi	mužovi
	Inst.	mužem	mužom
	Loc.	muži, mužovi	mužovi

		Czech	Slovak
Pl.	Nom.	muži, otcové, učitelé 'teacher'	muži, otcovia, učitelia
	Acc.	muže	mužov
	Gen.	mužů	mužov
	Dat.	mužům	mužom
	Inst.	muži	mužmi
	Loc.	mužích	mužoch

Notes: [1] Subclasses of each paradigm may vary in one or more case. [2] Alternative forms exist, but may vary functionally.

Masculine hard declension — inanimate

		Czech	Slovak
Sg.	Nom.	hrad 'castle'	hrad
	Voc.	hrade	
	Acc.	hrad	hrad
	Gen.	hradu, lesa 'forest'	hradu, duba 'oak'
	Dat.	hradu	hradu
	Inst.	hradem	hradom
	Loc.	hradě, rohu 'horn, corner'	hrade, rohu, mieri 'peace'
Pl.	Nom.	hrady	hrady
	Voc.	hrady	
	Acc.	hrady	hrady
	Gen.	hradů	hradov
	Dat.	hradům	hradom
	Inst.	hrady	hradmi, listami 'leaf'
	Loc.	hradech	hradoch

Note: The ending -a in the gen. sing. is confined in Czech to a fairly small number of nouns; in Slovak it is the preferred ending for concreta.

Masculine soft declension — inanimate

		Czech	Slovak
Sg.	Nom.	stroj 'machine'	stroj
	Voc.	stroji	
	Acc.	stroj	stroj
	Gen.	stroje	stroja, čaju 'tea'
	Dat.	stroji	stroju
	Inst.	strojem	strojom
	Loc.	stroji	stroji
Pl.	Nom.	stroje	stroje
	Voc.	stroje	
	Acc.	stroje	stroje
	Gen.	strojů	strojov
	Dat.	strojům	strojom
	Inst.	stroji	strojmi
	Loc.	strojích	strojoch

Feminine hard declension

		Czech	Slovak
Sg.	Nom.	žena 'woman', hradba 'rampart'	žena, hradba
	Voc.	ženo	
	Acc.	ženu	ženu
	Gen.	ženy	ženy
	Dat.	ženě	žene
	Inst.	ženou	ženou
	Loc.	ženě	žene

		Czech	*Slovak*
Pl.	Nom.	ženy	ženy
	Voc.	ženy	
	Acc.	ženy	ženy
	Gen.	žen, hradeb	žien, budov 'building', záhrad 'garden', hradieb
	Dat.	ženám	ženám
	Inst.	ženami	ženami
	Loc.	ženách	ženách

Feminine soft declension — basic type

Sg.	Nom.	duše 'soul', ulice 'street', chvíle 'moment'	duša
	Voc.	duše	
	Acc.	duši	dušu
	Gen.	duše	duše
	Dat.	duši	duši
	Inst.	duší	dušou
	Loc.	duši	duši
Pl.	Nom.	duše	duše
	Voc.	duše	
	Acc.	duše	duše
	Gen.	duší, ulic, chvil	dúš, dielní 'workshop'
	Dat.	duším	dušiam
	Inst.	dušemi	dušami
	Loc.	duších	dušiach

Note: The fill vowel in the genitive plural is in Czech always -*e*-, whereas in Slovak there are several possibilities: *hradieb*, *vojen* 'war', *kvapôk* 'drop', *sestár* 'sister', *látok* 'material'.

Feminine soft declension — mixed type

Sg.	Nom.	dlaň 'palm (of hand)'	dlaň
	Voc.	dlani	
	Acc.	dlaň	dlaň
	Gen.	dlaně	dlane
	Dat.	dlani	dlani
	Inst.	dlaní	dlaňou
	Loc.	dlani	dlani
Pl.	Nom.	dlaně	dlane
	Voc.	dlaně	
	Acc.	dlaně	dlane
	Gen.	dlaní	dlaní
	Dat.	dlaním	dlaniam
	Inst.	dlaněmi	dlaňami
	Loc.	dlaních	dlaniach

Feminine i-declension

Sg.	Nom.	kost 'bone'	kosť'
	Voc.	kosti	
	Acc.	kost	kosť'
	Gen.	kosti	kosti
	Dat.	kosti	kosti
	Inst.	kostí	kosť'ou

		Czech	*Slovak*
	Loc.	kosti	kosti
Pl.	Nom.	kosti	kosti
	Voc.	kosti	
	Acc.	kosti	kosti
	Gen.	kostí	kostí
	Dat.	kostem	kostiam
	Inst.	kostmi	kost'ami
	Loc.	kostech	kostiach

Neuter hard declension

Sg.	Nom./		
	Voc./		
	Acc.	město 'town'	mesto
	Gen.	města	mesta
	Dat.	městu	mestu
	Inst.	městem	mestom
	Loc.	městě, suchu 'drought', dobru 'good'	meste, suchu, dobre, vnutri 'interior', nebi 'sky'
Pl.	Nom./		
	Voc./		
	Acc.	města	mestá
	Gen.	měst	miest
	Dat.	městům	mestám
	Inst.	městy	mestami
	Loc.	městech, ložiskách 'deposit, bearing'	mestách

Neuter soft declension, equivalent to above

Sg.	Nom./		
	Voc./		
	Acc.	srdce 'heart'	srdce
	Gen.	srdce	srdca
	Dat.	srdci	srdcu
	Inst.	srdcem	srdcom
	Loc.	srdci	srdci
Pl.	Nom./		
	Voc./		
	Acc.	srdce	srdcia
	Gen.	srdcí, letišt' 'airport'	sŕdc, polí 'field'
	Dat.	srdcím	srdciam
	Inst.	srdci	srdcami
	Loc.	srdcích	srdciach

Neuter 'long' soft declension

Sg.	Nom./		
	Voc./		
	Acc.	vysvědčení 'certificate'	vysvedčenie
	Gen.	vysvědčení	vysvedčenia
	Dat.	vysvědčení	vysvedčeniu
	Inst.	vysvědčením	vysvedčením
	Loc.	vysvědčení	vysvedčení
Pl.	Nom./		
	Voc./		
	Acc.	vysvědčení	vysvedčenia

CZECH AND SLOVAK   379

	Czech	*Slovak*
Gen.	vysvědčení	vysvedčení
Dat.	vysvědčením	vysvedčeniam
Inst.	vysvědčeními	vysvedčeniami
Loc.	vysvědčeních	vysvedčeniach

Neuter '-nt-' declension

Sg.	Nom./		
	Voc.	děvče 'girl', kníže (m.) 'prince'	dievča, holúbä 'young pigeon'
	Acc.	děvče, knížete	dievča
	Gen.	děvčete	dievčat'a
	Dat.	děvčeti	dievčat'u
	Inst.	děvčetem	dievčat'om
	Loc.	děvčeti	dievčati
Pl.	Nom./		
	Voc./		
	Acc.	děvčata, knížata (nt.)	dievčatá	dievčence, holúbätá
	Gen.	děvčat	dievčat	dievčeniec, holúbät
	Dat.	děvčatům	dievčatám	dievčencom
	Inst.	děvčaty	dievčatami	dievčencami
	Loc.	děvčatech	dievčatách	dievčencoch

alternative plurals

Animacy, as a subcategory of the masculine gender (only) in Czech and Slovak, shows some further important differences. The singular of the masculine nouns central to the inanimate-animate distinction is fairly similar, in having -a for the animate genitive singular and -ovi for the animate dative/locative singular, compare, e.g. *pána, pánovi, pánovi* 'mister' to *hradu* (gen.), *hradu (dat.)* and *hradě* (loc.) (In Czech alone the soft animate genitive, dative and locative forms coincide with those of the inanimate declension.) In common with general practice in the Slavonic languages, the animate genitive form is also used in the animate accusative. In the plural, however, the two languages differ in their expression of animacy: in Slovak it operates in a manner similar to the singular, i.e. the genitive form in the accusative, but in Czech it is expressed through the survival of the ancient nominative-accusative opposition, lost in the singular, cf. Czech *páni* (nom. pl.), *pány* (acc.), *pánů* (gen.) and Slovak *páni, pánov, pánov*. Another difference between Czech and Slovak is that while all nouns denoting living creatures that are grammatically masculine are 'animate' in both languages in the singular, the same applies in the plural only to Czech. In the Slovak plural it is confined to human males (cf. Polish). Another uniquely Slovak feature is the treatment of animacy in the peripheral masculine *a*-declension, which, other differences apart, has produced syncretism between the accusative and genitive singular, as one expects, but based on the accusative form. In Czech this declension retains most of the case distinctions of the central feminine *a*-declension.

	Masc. animate Czech/Slovak	Feminine a-decl. Czech/Slovak	Masculine a-decl. Czech	Slovak
Nom.	pán	žena	hrdina 'hero'	hrdina
Acc.	pána	ženu	hrdinu	hrdinu
Gen.	pána	ženy	hrdiny	hrdinu

This same distribution of endings in Slovak also applies to most native names ending in -o, e.g. *Botto, Bottu, Bottu*.

The basic neuter declensions in both languages are very conservative. On the Slovak side, however, there are three innovations worthy of mention: lengthening of the ending of the nominative/accusative plural, unless inhibited by the rhythmical law, e.g. *mesto* (nom./acc. sg.) but *mestá*, cf. Czech *město*, *města*; the extending of the feminine *a*-declension locative ending -*ách*/-*iach* to the neuters, e.g. *zenách*/*dušiach* (f.) and *mestách*/*poliach*, in contrast to Czech *městech*/*polích* which retain their affinity with the masculine (there is some penetration of *a*-declension endings into the neuter in Czech in the case of velar stems, e.g. *kolečkách* 'wheel' (diminutive), which avoids stem alternation of the type *kolečcích*); and vowel lengthening before the zero ending of the genitive plural if not inhibited by the rhythmical law, e.g. *mesto* (nom. sg.), *miest*. This last is another feature shared with the *a*-declension, cf. *žena*/*žien*, and an interesting aspect of it is that it applies equally to a true stem vowel and any fill vowel which might appear, e.g. *okno*/*okien* 'window'. (Note that vowel lengthening often, as in these examples, means diphthongisation.)

Apart from the above, Czech noun morphology is generally more conservative than Slovak in the greater degree of preservation of the effects of the second palatalisation of velars, in the locative plural masculine (*jazycích* 'tongue', Slovak *jazykoch*) and the nominative plural animate, where it affects all three velar consonants: *žák*/*žáci* 'student', *Čech*/*Češi*, *vrah*/*vrazi* 'murderer'; in Slovak this only applies to the first two, hence: *žiak*/*žiaci*, *Čech*/*Česi*, but *vrah*/*vrahovia* (-*ovia*, Czech -*ové* is an alternative nominative plural masculine animate ending used with specific subclasses of nouns; a third is -*ia*, Czech -*é*).

Adjective declension is typified by the presence of long vowels in the ending (unless inhibited by the rhythmical law in Slovak as in the example following) as a result of contraction, cf. the disyllabic endings, in the nominative at least, in Russian, where contraction did not occur: Czech *krásný* 'beautiful' (m. sg.), *krásná* (f. sg.), *krásné* (n. sg.), *krásní* (m. anim. pl.), *krásné* (m. inanim. and f. pl.) and *krásná* (nt. pl.), Slovak *krásny* (m. sg.), *krásna* (f. sg.), *kraśne* (nt. sg.), *krásni* (m. hum. pl.), *krásne* (all other plurals), Russian *krasnyj* (m. sg.), *krasnaja* (f. sg.), *krasnoje* (nt. sg.) and *krasnyje* (all plurals).

Apart from the operation of the rhythmical law in Slovak the other main differences between the Czech and Slovak adjectival declension can be

Adjective Declension

	Czech			**Slovak**		
Adjectival declension — hard						
Sg. Nom.	dobrý 'good'	-á	-é	dobrý	-á	-é
Voc.	dobrý	-á	-é			
Acc.	{dobrý / dobrého}	-ou	-é	{dobrý / dobrého}	-ú	-é
Gen.	dobrého	-é	-ého	dobrého	-ej	-ého
Dat.	dobrému	-é	-ému	dobrému	-ej	-ému
Inst.	dobrým	-ou	-ým	dobrým	-ou	-ým
Loc.	dobrém	-é	-ém	dobrom	-ej	-om
Pl. Nom.	{dobré / dobří}	-é	-á	{dobré / dobrí}	-é	-é
Voc.	{dobré / dobří}	-é	-á			
Acc.	dobré	-é	-á	{dobré / dobrých}	-é	-é
Gen.	dobrých			dobrých		
Dat.	dobrým			dobrým		
Ins.	dobrými			dobrými		
Loc.	dobrých			dobrých		
Adjectival declension — soft						
Sg. Nom.	cizí 'alien'	-í	-í	cudzí	-ia	-ie
Voc.	cizí	-í	-í			
Acc.	{cizí / cizího}	-í	-í	{cudzí / cudzieho}	-ej	-ie
Gen.	cizího	-í	-ího	cudzieho	-ej	-ieho
Dat.	cizímu	-í	-ímu	cudziemu	-ej	-iemu
Inst.	cizím	-í	-ím	cudzím	-ou	-ím
Loc.	cizím	-í	-ím	cudzom	-ej	om
Pl. Nom.	cizí			{cudzie / cudzí}	-ie	-ie
Voc.	cizí					
Acc.	cizí			{cudzie / cudzích}	-ie	-ie
Gen.	cizích			cudzích		
Dat.	cizím			cudzím		
Inst.	cizími			cudzími		
Loc.	cizích			cudzích		

Note: Pairs of forms joined by braces indicate variation by animacy, inanimate above, animate below. The masculine plural animate ending -í causes palatalisation of dental and velar stems in Czech, but not in Slovak.

explained by the relative conservatism of Slovak phonology, notably the absence of *přehláska* and the non-monophthongisation of *ie*, both affecting the soft adjectives and illustrated in, for example, the feminine and neuter singular forms *cudzia*, *cudzie*, Czech *cizí* 'alien, someone else's'.

It is worth noting that Czech retains a number of so-called short adjectives, e.g. *zdráv* 'healthy', *živ* 'alive', *jist* 'sure', *zvědav* 'curious', *vědom* 'aware', *bos* 'barefoot', which only occur in the predicate and in a narrow range of essentially idiomatic usages. Both Czech and Slovak have the short adjective *rád/-a/-o* which has no long counterpart and serves in conjunction with any verb to express the meaning 'like -ing'. Both languages show full adjective-noun agreement in case, number and gender including animacy. A curiosity on the Czech side is the special form of the instrumental plural in -*ýma*, used in agreement with the handful of nouns which retain -*ma* in that case — one of the dual remnants referred to earlier, occurring in *ruce–rukama* 'hands, arms', *nohy–nohama* 'feet, legs', *uši–ušima* 'ears', *oči–očima* 'eyes'.

An interesting morphological innovation is to be found in the declension of numerals in Slovak. The core system is as in Czech: *jeden* 'one' varies by gender and has case (and number) agreement (it actually declines in Czech like the demonstrative pronoun *ten*); *dva* 'two' has a special form *dve* (*dvě* in Czech) for feminine and neuter (contrast Russian, where *dve* is feminine only, with *dva* for masculine and neuter); *dva/dve*, *tri* 'three', *štyri* 'four' (*tři*, *čtyři* in Czech) 'three', 'four' all agree with their noun; *päť* (*pět*) 'five' and higher numerals take the genitive plural of the counted noun when the entire phrase is in any nominative or accusative slot in the sentence, otherwise there is case agreement (marked only rudimentarily in Czech) except after prepositions, when *päť* etc. do not decline. Slovak's innovation is in the possession of forms *dvaja*, *traja*, *štyria*, *piati* and onwards for use with animates; all such forms show agreement with the counted noun. The genderless *päť* and above may be used instead of *piati* etc., but the survival of the latter is ensured through the Slovak mutation of the expression of animacy, which has consistently distinctive forms in the nominative and the genitive-accusative. Hence not only *krásni muži–krásnych mužov*, but also *dvaja–dvoch*, *traja–troch*, *štyria–štyroch* and *piati–piatich*.

Verbal morphology in Czech and Slovak differs basically in consequence, again, of *přehláska* in Czech and the rhythmical law in Slovak. Slovak has, however, gone further than Czech in having consistent person markers, notably in having -*m* as the universal marker of first person singular. In both languages this has spread from a minor conjugation, the so-called athematic verbs (with the meanings 'be', 'have', 'know', 'eat' and 'give'), which formed a distinctive group in Proto-Slavonic and continue to exhibit various anomalous features, especially in Czech. Where Czech has not evolved the -*m* first person marker is in the conjugations here described as *e*-, *ne*-, *uje*- (the same endings also shared by the *je*-type): *e*-: *nést–nesu* 'carry', *brát–beru* 'take', *mazat–mažu/-i* 'smear', *péci–peču* 'bake', *umřít–umřu* 'die'; *ne*-: *tisknout–tisknu* 'print', *minout–minu* 'pass', *začít–začnu* 'begin'; *je*-: *krýt–kryji/-u* 'cover'; *uje*-: *kupovat–kupuji/-u* 'buy'. The original ending in these classes was -*u* (from the nasal *ǫ*), which has since given -*i* in cases where *přehláska* operated. The tolerance which the standard language has shown for a reversal of this *i*-ending to -*u*, by analogy with the majority, has

varied from type to type, coming latest with those classes containing a final
-*j*- in the present tense stem.

Slovak has long had -*t'* as the sole infinitive marker, whatever the shape of
the remainder of the infinitive stem: *niest'*, *brat'*, but also *piect'*, while in the
latter type Czech has had an anomaly in -*ci* (*péci*, *říci*, *moci* etc.), with forms
in -*t* only in Common Czech. By a recent reform, however, the compelling
force of analogy has led to a degree of upward mobility of the forms in -*t*
(*péct*, *říct*, *moct*) towards their acceptance in the more colloquial version of
the standard literary language.

Czech and Slovak, like Russian, but unlike Serbo-Croat, have moved
right away from a complex tense system, still alive in Old Czech, to an
aspect-based system, with pairs of verbs for all meanings that are acts, and
single verbs for activities and states. The two members of the aspect category
(perfective and imperfective) are much the same as for the other Slavonic
languages: perfective for a single action seen as a whole, completed and
potentially having consequences for subsequent actions, imperfective for an
action in progress, repetition or the action *per se*, which may be completed
but where consequence is immaterial. Differences of detail between Czech/
Slovak and Russian relate in particular to the aspect form used in certain
cases with explicitly expressed repetition; in Czech/Slovak the choice often
hinges on the semantics of specific conjunctions and adverbs. The specific
consequence for Czech/Slovak is the use of the perfective present (formally
the same as the perfective future) in certain general or non-actual present
time contexts, whereas it is normally the case that the only aspect in the
present is the imperfective.

Having an aspect-based system, Czech and Slovak overcome the
impoverishment of the tense system and the general Slavonic lack of
sequence-of-tense rules by expressing anteriority, posteriority and
simultaneity, in certain important subordinate clause types, e.g. after *verba
dicendi*, by past, future and present tense forms, whatever the tense of the
main clause: Czech *řekl/říká/řekne, že přijde* 'he said/is saying/ will say that
he would/will come', *řekl/říká/řekne, že tam byl* 'he said/is saying/will say
that he had/has been there', *řekl/říká/řekne, že nekouří* 'he said/is saying/
will say that he did/does not smoke'.

Both Czech and Slovak, unlike Russian, use auxiliary verbs in the past
tense (omitted in the third persons), while in the conditional the auxiliary
(evolved out of the aorist of *být* 'be') conjugates. A difference between
Czech and Slovak is that the plural forms of the past *l*-participle do not mark
gender in Slovak (cf. Russian), a simplification present only in colloquial
Czech. Another difference of detail is in the greater refinement of the
expression of the second person in the past tense in Czech, which can
discriminate between not only the sex (gender) of the addressee, but also
number and degree of familiarity, hence *byl jsi* 'you were' is singular familiar
masculine, *byla jsi* singular familiar feminine, *byl jste* singular formal

Conjugation[1]

	Czech	*Slovak*
e-conjugation		
Infin.	nést 'carry'	niest'
Pres. sg.	nesu neseš nese	nesiem nesieš nesie
pl.	neseme nesete nesou	nesieme nesiete nesú
Imperative	nes nesme neste	nes nesme neste
Past	nesl	niesol
Transgressive	nesa nesouc nesouce[2]	nesúc
Past transg.	-nes -nesši -nesše[2]	
Pass. part.	nesen/-ý	nesený
ne-conjugation		
Infin.	vadnout 'fade'	vädnút'
Pres. sg.	vadnu vadneš vadne	vädnem vädneš vädne
pl.	vadneme vadnete vadnou	vädneme vädnete vädnú
Imperative	vadni vadněme vadněte	vädni vädnime vädnite
Past	vadl	vädol
Transgressive	vadna vadnouc vadnouce	vädnúc
Past transg.	vadnuv vadnuvši vadnuvše	
Pass. part.	tištěn/tisknut/-ý[3]	-tisnutý
uje-conjugation		
Infin.	kupovat 'buy'	kupovat'
Pres. sg.	kupuji kupuješ kupuje	kupujem kupuješ kupuje
pl.	kupujeme kupujete kupují	kupujeme kupujete kupujú
Imper.	kupuj kupujme kupujte	kupuj kupujme kupujte
Past	kupoval	kupoval
Transg.	kupuje kupujíc kupujíce	kupujúc
Past transg.	na-kupovav -ši -še	
Pass. part.	kupován/-aný	kupovaný
i-conjugation		
Infin.	prosit 'ask for'	prosit'
Pres. sg.	prosím prosíš prosí	prosím prosíš prosí
pl.	prosíme prosíte prosí	prosíme prosíte prosia
Imper.	pros prosme proste	pros prosme proste
Past	prosil	prosil
Transg.	prose prosíc prosíce	prosiac
Past transg.	poprosiv -ivši -ivše	
Pass. part.	prošen/-ý	prosený
a-conjugation		
Infin.	volat 'call'	volat'
Pres. sg.	volám voláš volá	volám voláš volá
pl.	voláme voláte volají	voláme voláte volajú
Imper.	volej volejme volejte	volaj volajme volajte
Past	volal	volal
Transg.	volaje volajíc volajíce	volajúc
Past transg.	zavolav -avši -avše	
Pass. part.	volán/-aný	volaný

Notes: [1] This summary of the basic conjugational types cannot show the imbalance brought about by *přehláska*, particularly in the distribution of verbs among the *a*- and *i*-conjugations. Each class in both languages has various subtypes. [2] The present and past transgressives (the traditional term in Czech and Slovak grammars) are the gerunds of other Slavonic languages. The three forms in Czech are for masculine, feminine/neuter and plural, agreement being governed by the subject of the main clause. [3] Forms from the transitive verb *tisknout* 'print'; *vadnout* 'fade' is intransitive and therefore has no passive participle.

masculine, *byla jste* singular formal feminine, *byli jste* plural masculine or mixed, *byly jste* plural feminine (in speech the last distinction is not heard, thanks to the phonetic equivalence of *i* and *y*). Slovak distinguishes gender in the familiar singular: *bol/bola si*, but all other forms are *boli ste*.

6 Syntax

A complete description of Czech and Slovak syntax is beyond the scope of the present outline, but some features are worthy of special mention. These include the use and position of enclitics (mostly the auxiliary verbs and pronouns) and the expression of the passive. Both have a bearing on word order, on which more will be said in the concluding sentences.

Czech, and to a lesser degree Slovak, has quite strict rules on word order with enclitics. In a nutshell, these say that any enclitic will appear in the second grammatical slot (not merely second word) in the sentence, i.e. there must be at least one stressed word at the beginning of a sentence on which the stressless enclitics can lean. The critical first slot may be occupied by the subject, object, an adverb or conjunction (but not the weak coordinating conjunctions *a* 'and', *i* 'and even', *ale* 'but', *nebo* 'or'; this last constraint applies much less in Slovak). It may also be occupied by a subject pronoun, which will be there for emphasis, since subject pronouns are not normally required, person being adequately expressed in the verb, even in the past tense, thanks to the use of auxiliaries (unlike in Russian). Within the second, enclitic slot the ordering is also fixed: an auxiliary verb in the past tense or conditional (but not the imperfective future auxiliary) will always take precedence, followed by dative, then accusative (occasionally genitive) object pronouns, and finally certain enclitic adverbs or particles. Hence, in Czech, for example:

| Včera | jste | | mi | ji | však | nedal. |
| Yesterday | 2nd pers. aux. | me (dat.) | it (f.) | though | not gave |
| 'But yesterday you did not give it to me.' |

The only refinements to this rule in Czech relate to the use of the reflexive pronouns *se/si* (accusative and dative respectively) either of which takes precedence over all other pronoun objects, and to the referentially vague *to* which, whether subject or object, i.e. nominative or accusative, stands in the accusative/genitive enclitic slot: *včera jste mi to neřekl* 'you did not tell me (it) yesterday', *Petrovi by se to* (subject) *nelíbilo* 'Peter would not like it/ that' (*líbit se* 'be pleasing'). The situation as described is beginning to break down, the enclitics, especially *se*, showing a tendency to be more closely associated with the verb phrase wherever it may stand. In Slovak the process has gone slightly further.

The passive in Czech and Slovak is only rarely expressed by the periphrastic form analogous to the English passive, although it is quite common in technical and some journalistic texts. Instead the shift of emphasis, or perspective, from 'Peter killed Paul' to 'Paul was killed by Peter' is carried by simple inversion of subject and object: *Petr zabil Pavla*, *Pavla zabil Petr*, an obvious possibility in a language where syntactic relations are explicit in the morphology and where there are relatively few constraints on word order. Very widespread in both languages are passive, quasi-passive and impersonal constructions, comparable to many passive-like constructions in English, based on verb phrases with *se*, here best interpreted as a passivising or intransitivising particle. They are used typically where no agent is (or can be) named (*talíř se rozbil* 'the plate broke/ got broken'), in the language of instructions (*cibule se tam dá nejdřív* 'the onion is put in first', *tato samohláska se vyslovuje dlouze* 'this vowel is pronounced long'), and in depersonalised accounts of events (*pivo se pilo, písničky se zpívaly a okna se rozbíjela* 'beer was drunk, songs were sung and windows were broken'); in this last type the same construction is available with intransitive verbs, always in the third person singular neuter (*nepracovalo se a šlo se domů brzy* 'no work was done and people went home early' lit. 'it was not being worked and it was gone home early')

Word order in Czech and Slovak, as was hinted above, is governed primarily by functional sentence perspective. That element which carries most emphasis, or most new information, is reserved to the end of the sentence. In general terms, the 'communicative dynamism' of an utterance builds up from low to high as the sentence unfolds. This allows maximum exploitation of 'free word order', which of course does not mean random word order. A great deal of work has been done on the subtleties of word order, ever since Vilém Mathesius and the Prague Linguistic Circle, and new theories and descriptions continue to appear. It has also been an area of study in contrastive, comparative and confrontational linguistics. It is perhaps worth noting that a major impulse here has undoubtedly been the very strong tradition of translating into Czech and Slovak: Czechoslovakia translates an average of 650 non-dramatic works of literature, 150 plays and 200 films (dubbed or subtitled) annually, and about 28 per cent of television time is spent on translated material. These are figures which can be matched by few other countries.

7 The Contemporary Language Situation

As with any modern language, Czech and Slovak show much variation in regional and social dialects. Czech divides into four main regional dialect groupings, Slovak into three.

The Czech macrodialects are: Bohemian, Central Moravian (Haná), Eastern Moravian or Moravian Slovak, and Silesian (Lach). The dialect differences have evolved in fairly recent times, mostly since the twelfth century, but particularly during the fourteenth to sixteenth centuries. Some prehistoric differences are also present, in the distribution of some lexical items, suffixes and vowel quantity in certain prosodically distinct word types: long in Bohemian *práh* 'threshold', *bláto* 'mud', *žába* 'frog', *bříza* 'birch', *moucha* 'fly', *vítr* 'wind', short in Central Moravian *prah*, *blato*, *žaba*, *březa*, *mucha*, *vjetr*.

One of the most important sound changes in the history of Czech was, as mentioned earlier, *přehláska*. That of *a* to *ě* was carried through in a decreasing number of environments the further east one goes through Moravia, while *u* > *i* is practically unknown anywhere in Moravia. One consequence of this is the much greater degree of similarity between 'soft' and 'hard' declensional paradigms than in standard Czech and a measure of interchange between them, words in *-sa*, *-za* and *-la* with originally hard *s*, *z*, and *l* tending to shift to the equivalent soft paradigm.

The Lach dialects separated from the rest of Czech by the retention of softness in the syllables *d'e*, *t'e*, *n'e*, the loss of distinctions of vowel quantity, and the development, as in Polish, of fixed stress on the penultimate.

Typical of the Bohemian dialects are the changes of *ý* into *ej* and *ú* into *ou*, which took over two centuries to complete, peaking in the sixteenth century. Eastern Moravian and the Lach dialects show no sign of this shift, cf. for *strýc* 'uncle' Cent. Boh. *strejc*, E. Mor. *strýc*, Lach *stryc*, and for *múka* 'fly' Cent. Boh. *mouka*, E. Mor. *múka*, Lach *muka*. (Note that the forms used in standard Czech are *strýc* and *mouka* respectively, though *strejc* is colloquial; few words with *ej* < *ý* have passed into the standard language whereas *ou* < *ú* is the norm except initially.) The same dialects were also unaffected by the Central Bohemian change of *aj* to *ej* in closed syllables and *é* to *í*, hence *daj* 'give (sg. imper.)' for Central Bohemian and standard Czech *dej* and *dobré mléko* 'good milk' for Central Bohemian *dobrí mlíko*. (Here standard Czech has *dobré mléko*, one of the reasons why Moravians are often heard to assert that they speak a 'better' Czech than the Bohemians.)

Eastern Bohemian was once distinguished by the loss of softness from labials before *e*, giving rise to syllables *pe*, *be*, *me*, *ve* where elsewhere Czech has /pje/, /bje/, /mně/ and /vje/, though this feature has largely yielded to the more universal version of these syllables. By contrast, one of the features marking out the south-west group of Bohemian dialects is the survival of softness, again expanded to a *j*, even before *i*, as in *pjivo* 'beer'.

These days the most typical features of north-east Bohemian are the bilabial pronunciation of *v* in closed syllables, much as in Slovak, and, in morphology, the spread of the ending *-ej* in the instrumental singular of soft feminine nouns. The Giant Mountains area is renowned for the appearance of *e* before syllabic *r*: *perší* '(it) rains', *perkno* 'board' for standard *prší*, *prkno*.

The last major contributor to the distinctness of the Moravian centre, the Haná and related dialects, is a change of *ej* to *é* and *ou* to *ó*. The former is very widespread, since it affects *ej* from *ý*, *ej* from *aj* and cases where the *e* and the *j* straddle a morpheme boundary, hence Central Bohemian *dobrej strejc* 'good uncle' (from *dobrý strýc*), *dej* (from *daj*) and *nejsem* '(I) am not' (from *ne* + *jsem*) correspond to Haná *dobré stréc*, *dé* and *nésem*. Related changes in the short vowels produce so many local variants that the Moravian dialect area is fragmented on this basis alone into dialects with five-, six- or seven-member vowel systems in various combinations.

From all the foregoing it follows that the Eastern Moravian dialects have been the most conservative, untouched by many of the sound changes mentioned. In this, and in certain other respects, they represent a transition to Slovak.

The dialect situation in Slovakia is even more complex than in the Czech-speaking areas. Three macrodialects are usually pinpointed, but each has numerous subdivisions, partly understandable from a glance at the country's physical geography.

Since Central Slovak became the basis for the Slovak literary language, it is usually taken as the reference point against which to describe the other main dialect groupings. Not all of the features typical of the central dialects have been adopted by the standard language. Some of the distinctive Central Slovak features are as follows:

The reflexes of the jers and the so-called fill vowels vary more than in any other Slavonic language or dialect, with *e*, *o* or *a* in short syllables and *ie*, *uo* (orthographically *ô*) or *á* in long syllables; in Western Slovak, as in Czech, it is always *e*, and in Eastern Slovak predominantly so, with sporadic instances of *o*. The *ä* of the standard language (where /e/ is a tolerated alternative pronunciation) is replaced after labials by *e*, alternating with *ia* in cognate long syllables; in Western Slovak the alternation is between *a* and *á*, and in Eastern between *e* and *ia*. There are the four diphthongs of the standard language, with none in Western Slovak, and local survivals of *ie* and *uo* in Eastern dialects. The syllabic liquids occur in long and short syllables, but in Western Slovak they are only short as in Czech. In Eastern Slovak they have not even survived as syllabic and are always accompanied by a vowel, with considerable local variation. The standard language owes its rhythmical law to Central Slovak, since Western Slovak reveals no such vowel shortening, and phonological quantity has totally disappeared from Eastern Slovak. Central Slovak morphological features include the long *á* or *ia* ending in the neuter plural of nouns, the *e*-ending of soft neuter nouns in the nominative singular (*o* in Western and Eastern Slovak, hence *vreco* 'sack', *ojo* 'shaft' to Central and standard Slovak *vrece*, *oje*), the instrumental singular feminine ending *-ou* (*-ú* in the west, *-u* in the east), and two very distinctive adjectival endings: nominative neuter singular in *-uo*, contrasting with *-é* in the west and *-e* in the east, and the locative singular masculine and neuter ending *-om* as against *-ém* in most of the west and *-im* in the east. The third person plural of the verb 'to be' is generally *sa*, which also occurs in parts of the west, but the standard form has adopted *sú*, the Western Slovak form, comparable also with *su* in the east.

Two important Western Slovak features not mentioned (and there are others of course) are the absence of the soft /l'/ phoneme, and the curious extension of the third person singular of the verb *byt'* 'to be' in the negative (*neni*) into the function of simple negator, hence *neni som* 'am not', originally 'isn't am'.

Additional distinctive Eastern Slovak features include: stress on the penultimate, as in Polish, complete absence of phonological quantity, a change of *ch* [x] into *h*, and the adoption of a universal genitive and locative plural ending for all genders, usually *-och* (*bratoch* 'brother', *ženoch* 'woman', *mestoch* 'town' etc.) and locally *-of*.

The foregoing are only a sample of the most striking features and those which cover most of the respective macrodialect areas. What they do not reveal immediately is something which has provided material for numerous books and papers, namely that there are a number of similarities between Western and Eastern Slovak which make them jointly distinct from the Central macrodialect. It is now generally accepted that this is a consequence of the different route and chronology in the arrival of the Slavonic-speaking population of the area. A number of features which Central Slovak shares with South Slavonic suggests a period of contiguity with the South Slavs and that colonisation of Central Slovakia proceeded from the south. The full details of this prehistory are still the subject of debate.

In addition to the horizontal (geographical) division of Czech and Slovak into dialects, there is a vertical division into the more or less conventional range of styles, registers, social dialects, slangs and so forth. On the whole it is probably safe to say that Slovak is the less interesting of the two, though not for any lack of richness or variety. There is indeed a full range of linguistic variation, much of it still being described for the first time. The slightly greater interest of Czech stems from the fact, already mentioned, of a literary standard language rich in essentially archaic features, some of which are jettisoned in the colloquial (*hovorový*) versions of it, and the parallel existence of Common Czech, or Common Colloquial Czech (*obecná čeština*). This is phonologically and morphologically closely related to the Central Bohemian dialect, syntactically to the less strict versions of Colloquial Czech, with some other features often ascribed to the influence of

German, and lexically often quite distinct, i.e. there are many lexical items peculiar to Common Czech which have to be 'translated' into standard Czech, e.g. *táta* = *otec* 'father'. Although rooted in Central Bohemia, Common Czech has spread well beyond the frontiers of that dialect area, especially to the major urban centres and then outward from them. However, with this spread it is also ceasing to be a universal koine and other versions are being observed to arise, especially in Moravia. Here the influence of the distinctive local dialects proper has given rise to the fairly recent conception of a Common Moravian Czech. A great deal of work has been conducted in recent decades on analyses of urban speech (*městská mluva*) in a number of large towns, and this has shown how Common Czech is contributing to the disappearance of local dialects while taking on specific local variations of detail from them.

Czech and Slovak are also both very rich in slangs, and although there are large areas of difference, it is interesting to note that here, as with the standard languages, there is a degree of convergence. This is understandable when one appreciates the cross-mobility, within a unitary state, of such groups as students, members of the armed forces or those involved in the pop-music and other subcultures. This is not to suggest that here, or at any other level, the process of convergence will ever be more than partial.

Bibliography

The standard reference grammar of Czech is Havránek and Jedlička (1981), although this is soon to be superseded by an entirely new work from the Academy of Sciences. Mazon (1952) is a classic but dated reference work. Kučera (1961) is a structuralist phonology of literary and colloquial Czech.

For Slovak, there is a new descriptive grammar by Pauliny (1981), in addition to the classical reference grammar by Bartoš and Gagnaire (1972); Mistrík (1983) is a descriptive reference grammar, marred by quirky English.

Millet (1983) is an excellent external history of Czech since the National Revival, including a section on the emergence of Slovak.

References

Bartoš, J. and J. Gagnaire. 1972. *Grammaire de la langue slovaque* (Institut d'Études Slaves, Paris and Matica Slovenská, Bratislava)

Havránek, B. and A. Jedlička. 1981. *Česká mluvnice*, 4th ed. (Státní Pedagogické Nakladatelství, Prague)

Kučera, H. 1961. *The Phonology of Czech* (Mouton, The Hague)

Mazon, A. 1952. *Grammaire de la langue tchèque*, 3rd ed. (Institut d'Études Slaves, Paris)

Millet, Y. 1983. 'Continuité et discontinuité: cas du tchèque', in I. Fodor and C. Hagège (eds.), *Language Reform: History and Future*, vol. 2 (Helmut Buske, Hamburg), pp. 479–504.

Mistrík, J. 1983. *A Grammar of Contemporary Slovak* (SPN, Bratislava)

Pauliny, E. 1981. *Slovenská gramatika* (Slovenské Pedagogické Nakladatel'stvo, Bratislava)

18 Serbo-Croat

Greville Corbett

1 Historical Background

The line which divided Europe into east and west, Orthodox and Catholic, runs right through the part of the Balkans where Serbo-Croat (or Serbo-Croatian) is spoken. Various states have prospered at different times in this region, such as the Serbian medieval kingdom under rulers like Stefan Nemanja and Stefan Dušan and the unique city state of Dubrovnik (Ragusa). Parts of the territory have been under Venice, Austro-Hungary and the Turks. We can only hope to hint at the complex and turbulent history of the area.

The ancestors of the South Slavs arrived in the Balkans during the sixth and seventh centuries and within the next two centuries the first Slav states of the area sprang up. By this time too the main linguistic divisions were evident. There were two main sets of dialects: East South Slavonic would later develop into Bulgarian and the closely related Macedonian, while West South Slavonic was the basis for Slovene and Serbo-Croat. From the ninth century the Slovenes in the north-west were ruled by Bavarian and Austrian princes and so were separated from their Slavonic neighbours. In the remaining area, roughly equivalent to modern Yugoslavia excepting Slovenia and Macedonia, a range of dialects was spoken, which would give rise to modern Serbo-Croat.

Christianity was accepted in the ninth century, with certain political repercussions. The tenth-century Croatian kingdom looked to Rome in matters of religion. Serbia's adoption of Orthodoxy meant that it looked first to Constantinople and later, after the fall of Constantinople, to Moscow for support. Montenegro was also Orthodox. The picture was complicated by the invasion of the Turks, who defeated the Serbs at Kosovo in 1389, and by the resulting migrations of population. In the next century the Turks occupied Bosnia and Hercegovina, where a large proportion of the population adopted Islam, and Montenegro. By the time the Turks were finally removed (1878), Croatia was part of the Austro-Hungarian Empire, which took over Bosnia and Hercegovina. It was not until 1918 that the different groups were united into one state.

Three main dialect groups had emerged, which take their names from the interrogative pronoun 'what?': Čakavian (*ča?* 'what?'), Kajkavian (*kaj?*) and Štokavian (*što?*). Kajkavian was spoken in the north, Čakavian in the west and Štokavian in the east, centre and south-west. However, the dialectal, political and religious boundaries did not match in a straightforward way. Despite this troubled history there have been some remarkable flowerings of literature. When the Serbian Kingdom was at its height during the twelfth to fourteenth centuries, literature flourished, written not in the vernacular but in the Serbian version of Church Slavonic. In the west too, Church Slavonic was used at first, but by the sixteenth century major writers like Marulić, Hektorović, Zoranić and Lucić were using Čakavian. The rise of Dubrovnik brought Štokavian to the fore also in the sixteenth century. And in the eighteenth century, Kajkavian was widely used in Croatia around Zagreb.

This diversity of literary tradition, mirroring the dialectal fragmentation of the area, naturally impeded the development of a common literary language in the west. In the east, Turkish domination had severely hampered the development of the Serbian Church Slavonic tradition. Russian Church Slavonic was adopted in the eighteenth century and a hybrid language (Slavenoserbian) evolved, with elements of Russian Church Slavonic and vernacular Serbian. Its artificiality, contrary both to the aspirations of intellectuals influenced by the Enlightenment and to the needs of modern society, led to a movement towards a more popular language, which was brought to fruition by Vuk Karadžić (1787–1864). Karadžić rejected Slavenoserbian, insisting that the new literary language must be based on the vernacular and on a single dialect, the Štokavian dialect of East Hercegovina. He made his revolutionary proposals in his dictionary (1818), which also contained a grammar of the language. There had already been some movement in the west towards basing the literary language on Štokavian. The Zagreb editor Ljudevit Gaj (1809–72) and other intellectuals helped accelerate this trend. In 1850 the Literary Accord between Croats and Serbs was signed in Vienna. It justified the use of Štokavian (Hercegovinian dialect) as the literary language and gave rules for writing it. Reactions to the Accord varied; not surprisingly it aroused a great deal of hostility, but gradually it gained support. Yet the centuries of division between different dialects, religions, cultures and political groups could not be removed by such an agreement. In any case, the major task of adapting the chosen variant to all the functions of a modern literary language had still to be faced. Nevertheless the Accord crystallised a unifying trend. A major success associated with this trend was the reform of the writing system.

2   Writing System

The original alphabet was Glagolitic. In the eastern, Orthodox area this was replaced from the twelfth century on by Cyrillic. In the west, the Latin alphabet was introduced in the fourteenth century, under Catholic influence. However, Glagolitic remained in use in the west, particularly among priests on the Dalmatian coast and islands, even into this century. From the sixteenth century until the Second World War, some Moslem writers in Bosnia used the Arabic script.

Neither in the east nor in the west was the writing system satisfactory. The version of the Cyrillic alphabet employed was appropriate for Church Slavonic but not for the contemporary language, while the use of the Latin alphabet in the west was influenced by Italian or Hungarian practice (depending on the area), neither of which was a suitable model for a Slavonic language. In his dictionary of 1818, Vuk Karadžić justified and used a new version of Cyrillic. This was a major reform involving simplifying the alphabet, using a single letter per sound and adopting a phonemically based orthography. He eliminated several unnecessary letters and introduced six new ones. Despite initial angry opposition, his alphabet was adopted and, with one minor modification, is in use today.

The equivalent reform for the Latin alphabet was carried out a little later by Ljudevit Gaj, using diacritic symbols on the Czech model. With minor modifications, Gaj's alphabet is the present one. Unlike the Cyrillic alphabet it includes digraphs: *lj*, *nj* and *dž* (also *dj* though this latter is usually written *đ*). Single symbols exist for these but their use is restricted to certain academic publications. The digraphs cause little problem; the combination *l* + *j* does not occur, while *n* + *j* and *d* + *ž* are rare; an example is *nadživeti* 'to outlive', where *d* + *ž* represent separate sounds. The two modern alphabets are given in table 18.1.

Table 18.1: The Alphabets of Serbo-Croat

Latin		Cyrillic		Latin		Cyrillic	
A	a	А	а	L	l	Л	л
B	b	Б	б	Lj	lj	Љ	љ
C	c	Ц	ц	M	m	М	м
Č	č	Ч	ч	N	n	Н	н
Ć	ć	Ћ	ћ	Nj	nj	Њ	њ
D	d	Д	д	O	o	О	о
Dž	dž	Џ	џ	P	p	П	п
Đ	đ	Ђ	ђ	R	r	Р	р
E	e	Е	е	S	s	С	с
F	f	Ф	ф	Š	š	Ш	ш
G	g	Г	г	T	t	Т	т
H	h	Х	х	U	u	У	у
I	i	И	и	V	v	В	в
J	j	Ј	ј	Z	z	З	з
K	k	К	к	Ž	ž	Ж	ж

The characters are arranged in the Latin order; the Cyrillic order is: А, Б, В, Г, Д, Ђ, Е, Ж, З, И, Ј, К, Л, Љ, М, Н, Њ, О, П, Р, С, Т, Ћ, У, Ф, Х, Ц, Ч, Џ, Ш. This Cyrillic list includes six characters not found in Russian Cyrillic; conversely, Russian has nine characters not used in Serbo-Croat. Note from the table that there is an exact correspondence, letter for letter, between the two alphabets of Serbo-Croat. The digraphs in the Latin version function as autonomous letters. This means that in a dictionary, all words beginning with *lj* are grouped together after all those with initial *l* (unlike English, where *thin* comes before *tin*); in a crossword, *lj* occupies a single square. The exact correspondence between the two alphabets means that transliteration is automatic; a typescript may be submitted in the Latin alphabet though it is to be printed in Cyrillic. This parallel use of the alphabets is found in the east, while in the west the Latin alphabet is found almost exclusively. There appears to be a trend in the east towards greater use of the Latin alphabet. In present-day Belgrade the two coexist with no apparent confusion: one sees shop windows with notices in both alphabets side by side, or a lecturer may begin labelling a diagram in one alphabet and then continue in the other.

The orthography of Serbo-Croat is based on the phonemic principle. Assimilations are indicated in spelling, for example, *redak* (masculine singular) 'rare' but *retka* (feminine singular); *top* 'gun' but *tobdžija* 'gunner'. If a consonant is dropped it is omitted in spelling, for example, *radostan* (masculine singular) 'joyful' but *radosna* (feminine singular). Though there are rare exceptions, this phonemic principle is applied (at the expense of the morphological principle) with unusual consistency.

3   The Contemporary Situation: Dialects and Varieties

Serbo-Croat is the major language of Yugoslavia; it is spoken in the Yugoslav republics of Bosnia and Hercegovina, Croatia, Montenegro and Serbia, by a total of over 17 million according to the 1981 census. Slovenia and Macedonia have their own languages but many Slovenes and Macedonians know Serbo-Croat (as do large numbers of the sizable populations of Albanians and Hungarians living in Yugoslavia and of the smaller groups of Bulgarians and Rumanians). Many hundreds of thousands of Serbo-Croat speakers now live abroad, notably in the United States and Australasia, and in West Germany and Sweden.

As stated earlier, there are three main dialects: Čakavian, Kajkavian and Štokavian. Each of these is in fact a set of related dialects. In contrast to their earlier importance, Čakavian and Kajkavian are spoken in relatively small areas, so we shall discuss them briefly. Čakavian survives along the Dalmatian coastal fringe, on the Adriatic islands, in Istria and in a small part of northern Croatia. As we shall see in the next section, it preserves an interesting accentual system; in morphology too it is more conservative than

Štokavian. Kajkavian is spoken around Zagreb in the north of Croatia, bordering on Slovenia. It shares several features with Slovene. Like Čakavian, it retains distinct dative, instrumental and locative plural endings, which are merged in Štokavian; another interesting archaic feature is the preservation of the supine to express purpose.

The main dialect, Štokavian, is spoken over the remainder of the Serbo-Croat area. It is divided first into New Štokavian (the innovating dialects, typically those which underwent the stress shift described in the next section) and Old Štokavian (those which did not). The most important of the Old Štokavian dialects are the Prizren-Timok dialects, which are spoken in the south-east of Serbia, bordering on Bulgaria and Macedonia. They have lost the infinitive and reduced the case system to three cases only and are therefore clearly transitional to Bulgarian and Macedonian. The Kosovo-Resava dialects run in a band from south-west to north-east, between the Prizren-Timok dialects and the rest of the Štokavian dialects, and share features with both.

Within New Štokavian, the traditional feature for distinguishing between dialects is the reflex of Common Slavonic *ě* (*jat´*), which may be *i*, *e* or *ije*/*je*. This gives three dialect groups: Ikavian, Ekavian and Ijekavian, in which the word, say, for 'child' is *dite*, *dete* and *dijete* respectively. The Ikavian dialect is found in Dalmatia, the west of Bosnia and Hercegovina and parts of Lika and Slavonia. It is no longer used as a literary language (though certain Ikavian features are established in the literary language). This leaves the two major dialects of New Štokavian: Ekavian is spoken in most of Serbia; Ijekavian is found in the western part of Serbia, Montenegro, the east of Bosnia and Hercegovina and in those parts of Croatia not previously mentioned. Ekavian is the basis of the eastern variety of the literary language, which has Belgrade as its centre; Ijekavian is the foundation of the western variety, whose focal point is Zagreb, even though Zagreb is in a traditionally Kajkavian area. The Ijekavian of Bosnia and Hercegovina, the starting point of the new literary language, is transitional between the two varieties. Montenegro is particularly interesting in that it is Ijekavian, but in terms of lexis belongs to the eastern variety of the literary language.

It is worth looking in a little more detail at the differences between the two main varieties of Serbo-Croat. As previously mentioned, the western variety is predominantly Ijekavian. This means that Common Slavonic *ě* is represented as *ije*, in long syllables, e.g. *snijeg* 'snow', and as *je* in short syllables: *snjegovit* 'snowy'. In Ekavian, *e* is found in both cases: *sneg*, *snegovit*. The western variety is written in the Latin alphabet, the eastern traditionally in Cyrillic, but now also in the Latin alphabet. The other most obvious area of difference is in lexis. Several very common objects are referred to by different words in the two varieties: 'bread' is *kruh* in the west, but *hleb* in the east; a 'train' is *vlak* in the west, but *voz* in the east. There are fewer borrowings in the west and correspondingly more calques and neologisms; we find, for example, *sveučilište* 'university' (based on *sve* 'all' and the root *uč-* 'teach, learn') whereas the east has *univerzitet*. Those words which have been borrowed into the western variety come predominantly from German, Latin and also Czech, while borrowings from Turkish, Greek and Russian are more common in the east. Words borrowed into both varieties may show differences in derivational morphology. Thus *student* 'male student' is found in both; 'female student' is *studentica* in the west, *studentkinja* in the east. Salient differences in inflectional morphology and in syntax will be pointed out in the appropriate sections.

While considerable differences exist, most of them are not absolute but are a matter of frequency of usage. Many features often quoted as characteristic of one variety actually occur in the other, though they are less common there. The whole question of the status of the two varieties is very sensitive, because of the cultural and political implications. To the outside linguist, the numerous shared features between the varieties added to the ease of mutual comprehension suggest one language with two varieties, and many Yugoslavs concur. But we must accept that some Yugoslavs feel it important, often for non-linguistic reasons, to recognise Croatian and Serbian as distinct languages. In what follows we will use Ekavian forms, but in the Latin alphabet.

4   Phonology

Serbo-Croat's inventory of segmental phonemes is one of the smallest in the Slavonic family, since it does not have the range of palatalised consonants found, say, in Russian. Generally 25 consonants are recognised. Of these *r*,

Table 18.2: Segmental Phonemes of Serbo-Croat

Vowels

	i	r	u
	e		o
		a	

Consonants

	Plain stop	Affricate	Fricative	Nasal	Lateral	Trill	Semi-vowel
Bilabial	p b			m			
Labio-dental			f v				
Dental	t d	c		n	l		
Alveolar			s z			r	
Palato-alveolar		č dž	š ž				
Palatal		ć đ		nj	lj		j
Velar	k g		h				

which is trilled, can be syllabic, as in *trg* 'square'. In addition there is a straightforward five-vowel system. The phonemes are presented in table 18.2, using the normal orthography, which does not distinguish syllabic *r* and which includes digraphs for single sounds.

The vowel system provides the most interesting feature of Serbo-Croat phonology, namely accentuation. The classical account goes back to Karadžić and his follower Daničić and is that found still in most modern descriptions. In this analysis, vowels (including syllabic *r*) vary according to length and pitch. Vowels may be long or short, both in stressed position and in positions after the stress. Pitch is differentiated only in initial stressed position, where there is an opposition between rising and falling tone. These possibilities are indicated using the symbols given in table 18.3. The top four

Table 18.3: Serbo-Croat Accentuation

		long	*short*
stressed syllables	falling tone	ˆ	˵
	rising tone	´	ˋ
unstressed syllables		–	

symbols indicate the position of the stress, tone and length. Thus *govòriti* 'to talk' is stressed on the second syllable, where there is a short vowel with rising tone. On unstressed syllables length is indicated; the absence of a marker, as on the other three vowels of this example, indicates an unstressed short vowel. Long vowels are indicated as follows: *glèdalācā* (genitive plural) 'of the spectators'. The first vowel is stressed and has falling tone and is short; the second is unstressed and short; the other two are unstressed and long.

These symbols are used in dictionaries and grammars but are not printed in ordinary texts. We shall include them when discussing phonology and morphology but not in the syntax section. An indication is given in texts to avoid confusion, notably for the genitive plural, which in many nouns is identical to the singular, apart from vowel length. For example, *rȉbāra* (genitive singular) 'fisherman', *rȉbārā* (genitive plural). The first would be printed without accent, the second as *ribarâ*, using the circumflex. (This actually retains Karadžić's usage; the macron ¯, given in our table, is a twentieth-century innovation in linguistic usage.) While the opposition of genitive singular to genitive plural is the most crucial distinction which depends on the accentual system, other morphological distinctions rest on it in some words. Furthermore, there is a small number of frequently quoted minimal pairs: *grâd* 'city', *grȁd* 'hail'; *pâs* 'belt', *pȁs* 'dog'; *kúpiti* 'to buy', *kȕpiti* 'to collect'; *pàra* 'para' (unit of currency), *pȁra* 'steam'.

There are severe restrictions on the distribution of tone and length, which are best understood in terms of historical development. Falling tone is found only on initial syllables and monosyllables always have falling tone. Apart from monosyllables, and a few recent borrowings, stress is never on the final syllable of a word. Long vowels occur in stressed position or after the stress. When we compare the position of the stress in Serbo-Croat with that of the other Slavonic languages which have free stress and which, in the main, preserve the Common Slavonic stress position (the East Slavonic languages and Bulgarian) then we find that normally the Serbo-Croat stress is one syllable nearer the beginning of the word, for example *sèstra* 'sister', as compared to the Russian *sestrá*.

Serbo-Croat had inherited quantitative opposition in vowels; of the other Slavonic languages only Slovene, Czech and Slovak preserve this opposition. There was also an opposition, for long vowels, between acute (′) and circumflex (ˆ) intonations; the origin of this opposition is open to debate, many claiming it is of Indo-European origin, others believing it dates only from Common Slavonic times. In very broad outline the development was as follows. The acute was replaced by a short vowel with falling pitch. A special rising tone, however, had arisen when the ultra-short vowels (jers) could no longer carry stress: *krāljь̆* > *krāljь* 'king'. This long rising accent, denoted ˜, and called the 'neo-acute', is preserved in Čakavian and Kajkavian dialects. In Štokavian, with the exception of some dialects in Slavonia, the neo-acute became identical with the long falling accent. At this stage, then, vowels were opposed in length (long or short only, after the loss of the jers). As a result of various changes, this opposition occurred in stressed position, immediately before the stress and in all post-tonic positions.

The crucial development took place around the fourteenth century in the central Štokavian dialects. The stress moved one syllable towards the beginning of the word, creating new rising tones. If the stress moved onto a long vowel, long rising tone resulted (′), and short rising (ˋ) if the vowel was short. The modern restrictions on tone and length are explicable in terms of this change. Falling tone is found only on initial syllables since stress moved from all other syllables to produce rising tone. Monosyllables have falling tone because they were not involved in stress shifts. Stress is not found on final syllables because, of course, it has moved forward. Finally, length is found in stressed and post-tonic positions only, because the earlier additional position (immediate pretonic) was covered by the accentual shift.

This, then, is the classical account of Serbo-Croat accentuation and its development. However, an extensive survey by Magner and Matejka revealed that the Karadžić-Daničić system is not so well preserved in towns as in rural areas. The influx of population to urban centres with the resultant mixing of dialects has led to a less clear situation. In particular, many speakers do not distinguish length on unstressed (post-tonic) vowels.

5 Morphology

Serbo-Croat has been generally conservative, maintaining most of the categories of Common Slavonic and changing some of the actual forms remarkably little. However, there have also been some surprising innovations. Seven cases have been preserved, together with three genders, which are distinguished in the plural as well as the singular (unlike Russian). The dual number has been lost, but it has left its mark on the plural oblique case forms (a Serbo-Croat innovation). The chart given here shows the main types of noun declension, corresponding to those given for Russian.

Serbo-Croat Nominal Declension

	a-*stem*	Masculine o-*stem*	Neuter o-*stem*	i-*stem*
Singular:				
Nom.	žèna 'woman'	zákon 'law'	sèlo 'village'	stvâr 'thing'
Voc.	žèno	zákone	sèlo	stvâri
Acc.	žènu	zákon	sèlo	stvâr
Gen.	žènē	zákona	sèla	stvâri
Dat.	žèni	zákonu	sèlu	stvâri
Inst.	žènōm	zákonom	sèlom	stvârju/stvâri
Loc.	žèni	zákonu	sèlu	stvári
Plural:				
Nom.	žène	zákoni	sèla	stvâri
Voc.	žène	zákoni	sèla	stvâri
Acc.	žène	zákone	sèla	stvâri
Gen.	žénā	zákōnā	sêlā	stvárī
Dat.	žènama	zákonima	sèlima	stvárima
Inst.	žènama	zákonima	sèlima	stvárima
Loc.	žènama	zákonima	sèlima	stvárima

In broad typological terms, the picture is similar to that of Russian: the morphology is fusional, and there is a high, but not absolute, correlation of gender with declensional class. When we look in more detail, however, we find interesting differences as compared to Russian. The vocative case is preserved, requiring a mutation of consonants for many masculine nouns. Thus *drûg* 'comrade', vocative singular *drûže*, *prèdsednîk* 'chairman', vocative singular *prèdsednîče*. These mutations go back to the first palatalisation (see page 324). The second palatalisation is well preserved too. It is found in the singular of feminine a-stems: *knjîga* 'book', dative and locative singular *knjîzi*; *réka* 'river', dative and locative singular *réci*. In addition, it occurs in the plural of masculine nouns: *ìzlog* 'shop window', nominative plural *ìzlozi*, dative, instrumental and locative plural *ìzlozima*; *tèpih* 'carpet', nominative plural *tèpisi*, dative, instrumental and locative plural *tèpisima*. The innovatory mutation *l/o* also affects nominal paradigms: *pèpeo* 'ash', genitive singular *pèpela*. When combined with a fleeting *a*, the reflex of both jers in 'strong' position, it can make forms from a single paradigm sound very different: *čìtalac* 'reader', vocative singular *čìtaoče*, accusative singular *čìtaoca*, genitive singular *čìtaoca*. These last examples illustrate the genitive-accusative syncretism found with animate nouns. In Serbo-Croat this is much more restricted than in Russian, being limited to masculine singular nouns. Note, however, that masculine plurals have an accusative form distinct from both and nominative and genitive. While Serbo-Croat preserves the vocative, it has all but lost the distinction between dative and locative. Probably the major innovation in the nominal paradigms is the genitive plural -*ā*, for most nouns except *i*-stems. The origin of this form is still subject to debate. An *ā* may also be inserted to avoid consonant clusters before this ending, for example, *stùdent* 'student', genitive plural *stùdenātā*.

There are various smaller declensional classes which complicate the picture: some consonant stems are preserved, though with regularised endings, and certain suffixes may be added or lost in the declension of masculine nouns. And as the first noun in our chart shows, the length and tone of the stressed syllable may change within a paradigm; furthermore, as in Russian, the position of the stress may move as well. Before leaving the declension of nouns, it is interesting to note that, with a very few exceptions, all Serbo-Croat nouns are declinable. Even borrowings ending in a vowel decline: *bìrō* 'office', genitive singular *biròa*, unless they are feminine. This contrasts with Russian, where nouns whose stem ends in a vowel (a considerable number) are normally indeclinable. On the other hand, most of the numerals in Serbo-Croat no longer decline, while in Russian they decline fully.

Many of the adjectival endings (as shown in the chart of adjectival declension) are similar to those of Russian, though contraction has applied to a greater extent. The accusative singular masculine form depends on the animacy of the noun. The forms given in brackets are optional additions; thus the genitive singular masculine and neuter is *mlâdōg* or, less usually, *mlâdōga*. Note that the three genders are distinguished in the direct cases of the plural. The forms given in the chart are the definite (pronominal, long) forms. Serbo-Croat retains indefinite forms, though these are distinguished by inflection in the masculine singular only; elsewhere the difference is normally one of length, the definite endings including a long vowel and the indefinite endings typically a short one. The distinction is best preserved in the nominative singular masculine: *dòbrī čòvek* 'the good man' contrasts with *dòbar čòvek* 'a good man'. Thus noun phrases are clearly marked for definiteness providing they include an attributive adjective and a masculine singular noun in the nominative case (or accusative-nominative). As in other Slavonic languages, though later than in most, the indefinite forms are being lost. The main reason why they are best preserved in the nominative, is that when the adjective is used predicatively it stands in the nominative and the

Serbo-Croat Adjectival Declension (Definite)

	Masculine	Neuter	Feminine
Singular:			
Nom.-Voc.	mlâdī 'young'	mlâdō	mlâdā
Acc.	as nom. or gen.	mlâdō	mlâdū
Gen.	mlâdōg(a)		mlâdē
Dat.	mlâdōm(e)		mlâdōj
Inst.	mlâdīm		mlâdōm
Loc.	mlâdōm(e)		mlâdōj
Plural:			
Nom.-Voc.	mlâdī	mlâdā	mlâdē
Acc.	mlâdē	mlâdā	mlâdē
Gen.		mlâdīh	
Dat.		mlâdīm(a)	
Inst.		mlâdīm(a)	
Loc.		mlâdīm(a)	

indefinite form is used. Definite forms are therefore attributive, indefinites could be attributive or predicative and are increasingly a sign of predicative usage. A secondary reason for the retention of the opposition in the masculine concerns case marking. Subjects and direct objects are clearly distinguished for animate nouns since, as mentioned earlier, animates have accusative forms identical to the genitive. For inanimates, however, nominative and accusative are identical. In actual text, a high proportion of subjects is definite, while most direct objects are indefinite. Therefore, for inanimate masculine nouns, the opposition of definite and indefinite forms helps to mark case.

When we move to verbal morphology, we find a plethora of forms. Serbo-Croat is moving from a system based on tense to one in which aspect has a

Serbo-Croat Conjugation Types

	I Conjugation	II Conjugation	III Conjugation
Infinitive	pèvati 'to sing'	nòsiti 'to carry'	trésti 'to shake'
Present:			
Singular 1	pèvām	nòsīm	trésēm
2	pèvāš	nòsīš	trésēš
3	pèvā	nòsī	trésē
Plural 1	pèvāmo	nòsīmo	trésēmo
2	pèvāte	nòsīte	trésēte
3	pèvajū	nòsē	trésū
Imperative:			
Singular 2	pèvāj	nòsi	trési
Plural 1	pèvājmo	nòsimo	trésimo
Plural 2	pèvājte	nòsite	trésite

central role, but it has not lost the redundant tense forms as most other Slavonic languages have. A concomitant change involves greater use of compound tenses. We start, however, with simple forms. The main conjugations are given in the chart of conjugation types (there are several variations on these forms which will be omitted).

Similarities with the present tense forms in the other Slavonic languages already given are evident. The main innovation is in the first person singular. The -m has spread from the very small group of athematic verbs to all the verbs in the language (with two exceptions: *mòći* 'to be able', first person singular *mògu*, and *htèti* 'to want', first person singular *hòću* or *ću*). As stated earlier, long vowels after the stress, which occur in all persons in the present tense, are shortened by many speakers. Serbo-Croat preserves two more simple tenses, the imperfect and the aorist, illustrated in the charts displaying these forms. Note that in the imperfect the stem may show a

The Imperfect Tense in Serbo-Croat

	I Conjugation	II Conjugation	III Conjugation
Infinitive	pèvati 'to sing'	nòsiti 'to carry'	trésti 'to shake'
Imperfect			
Singular 1	pèvāh	nòšāh	trésijāh/trésāh
2	pèvāše	nòšāše	trésijāše/trésāše
3	pèvāše	nòšāše	trésijāše/trésāše
Plural 1	pèvāsmo	nòšāsmo	trésijāsmo/trésāsmo
2	pèvāste	nòsāste	trésijāste/trésāste
3	pèvāhu	nòšāhu	trésujāhu/trésāhu

consonant mutation, as in the case of *nòšāh* from *nòsiti*; several verbs have two possible forms, while *ìmati* 'to have' has three: *ìmāh*, *ìmàdijāh* and *ìmađāh*. The imperfect indicates action in process in the past. It contrasts with the aorist, which is normally used for a completed single action in the past. Both tenses are particularly used for events witnessed by the speaker.

The Aorist Tense in Serbo-Croat

	I Conjugation	II Conjugation	III Conjugation
Infinitive	sàznati 'to find out'	kúpiti 'to buy'	istrésti 'to shake out'
Aorist			
Singular 1	sàznah	kúpih	istrésoh
2	sàzna	kûpī	ìstrēse
3	sàzna	kûpī	ìstrēse
Plural 1	sàznasmo	kúpismo	istrésosmo
2	sàznaste	kúpiste	istrésoste
3	sàznaše	kúpiše	istrésoše

In the aorist of third conjugation verbs, a mutation of velar consonants may occur in the second and third persons singular (first palatalisation), for example, *rèći* 'to say', first singular aorist *rèkoh*, second and third singular aorist *rèče*. In the first conjugation, some forms coincide with the imperfect — apart from post-accentual length. There is, however, little possibility of confusion, since the imperfect is formed only from imperfective verbs and the aorist usually, but not exclusively, from perfectives (hence the different illustrative verbs given in the chart of aorist tense forms). The notion of aspect is discussed in the chapter on Russian (page 340–1). In broad outline, the aspectual system is similar in Serbo-Croat both in morphology (perfectives are typically derived from imperfectives by prefixation, and imperfectives from perfectives by suffixation) and semantics (the perfective views a situation as a single whole, the imperfective views a situation as having internal constituency). Given the basic aspectual meanings, it is not surprising that the imperfect is found with imperfective verbs and the aorist typically with perfectives. However, the increasing importance of the aspectual opposition imperfective-perfective, which duplicates the imperfect-aorist opposition, is leading to the supplanting of both tenses by a compound past tense, which can be formed from verbs of either aspect. We shall refer to it simply as the 'past tense'; it is sometimes referred to as the 'perfect'. For some speakers, particularly in Croatia, the past tense is replacing both the imperfect and aorist, the aorist being the better preserved.

Before going on to the past and other compound tenses, we should return for a moment to the present tense. Whereas in Russian, only imperfectives have a present tense (forms with the morphological appearance of the present formed from perfective verbs are future perfective), in Serbo-Croat there is a present perfective, distinct from the future. It is formed identically to the examples given in the chart of conjugation types, but from perfective verbs. Thus *istrésti* 'to shake out', first person singular present *istrésēm*. The perfective present has a range of uses, but is not used for events occurring at the moment of speech. In the example: *stò ne sèdnēš?* (perfective present) 'why don't you sit down?', the addressee is evidently not actually doing so. This tense is frequently used in subordinate clauses; examples will be given in the syntax section.

Of the compound tenses, the past is easily the most important. It is formed using the past participle of the verb. This participle agrees in gender and number, as is illustrated using the verb *znàti* 'to know'.

Forms of the Past Participle

	Masculine	*Feminine*	*Neuter*
Singular	znȁo (<znal)	znȁla	znȁlo
Plural	znȁli	znȁle	znȁla

The other component of the past tense consists of the present tense forms of the auxiliary verb *bìti* 'to be'. These agree in person and number, and they are enclitic (see section 6), though there are also long forms used for emphasis and in questions. Subject personal pronouns are normally omitted in Serbo-Croat unless they are under contrastive or emphatic stress. If there is no nominal subject or other preceding word in the sentence, the participle precedes the enclitic, which cannot of course stand in first position. The past tense paradigm is therefore as that given for *znàti* 'to know'. The past tense

The Past Tense in Serbo-Croat

Infinitive   znàti 'to know'

Past Tense
Singular 1   znào/znàla sam
         2   znào/znàla si
         3   znào/znàla/znàlo je
Plural 1   znàli/znàle smo
       2   znàli/znàle ste
       3   znàli/znàle/znàla su

can be formed from imperfective verbs, like *znàti*, and such forms have largely supplanted the imperfective tense. The past tense can also be formed from perfectives in just the same way: *sàznati* 'to find out', *sàznao sam* 'I found out', (such forms replace the aorist). Compare *písala je písmo* (imperfective) 'she was writing a letter', *napísala je písmo* 'she wrote a letter'.

While the past is easily the most common tense for reference to past events, there is in addition a pluperfect tense. This can be formed from the imperfect of *bìti* plus the past participle, for example *bèjāh pèvao* 'I had been singing'. As elsewhere, the past can replace the imperfect, so an alternative formation with the past tense of *bìti* is *bìo sam pèvao*. The pluperfect occurs infrequently. If the aorist of *bìti* is combined with the past participle, then the conditional results: *pèvao bih* 'I would sing'. These auxiliary forms are again enclitics. The inflections of the aorist are being lost in this usage and the uninflected form *bi* is taking over (as has happened in Russian, see page 341). There is also a past conditional: *bìo bi rèkao* 'he would have said'. This tense is found in the western variety but has practically died out in the east.

All the compound tenses discussed so far use the auxiliary *bìti*. In contrast, the future tense is formed with the verb *htèti* 'to want' together with the infinitive. Normally the short forms of *htèti* are used (singular *cú*, *ćeš*, *će*, plural *ćemo*, *ćete*, *ćē*), for example, *žèna će znàti* 'the woman will know'. These short forms are enclitic, so that if no subject is expressed the infinitive is likely to precede: *dóći ću* 'I will come'. If an infinitive in *-ti* precedes the auxiliary, the *-ti* is not pronounced. This is reflected in the spelling in the east: *znàću* 'I will know'; the pronunciation is the same in the west, but only the *i* is dropped in the spelling: *znàt ću*. The long forms of *htèti* can be used for emphasis: *hòću dóći* '**I will** come', and in questions: *hòću li dóći?* 'shall I come?'. As our examples show, the future is formed with verbs of both aspects: *znàti* is imperfective and *dóći* is perfective. Particularly in the east, the infinitive is frequently replaced by *da* plus verb in the present tense; we return to this topic in the next section.

There are two other future tenses. The first, sometimes called the 'future exact', is formed from a second set of present tense forms of *bìti* 'to be' (singular: *bùdēm, bùdēš, bùdē*; plural: *bùdēmo, bùdēte, bùdū*) plus the past participle. It is used only in subordinate clauses, especially those introduced by *àko* 'if' and temporal conjunctions such as *kàd* 'when': *àko bùdeš dòšao* 'if you come'. In the case of perfective verbs, the present perfective can be used instead; this normally happens in the western variety. The future exact is much more common in the east. The other future tense, which is very rare, is formed from the future of *bìti* 'to be' and the past participle. It indicates supposition: *bìćete čùli* 'you will have heard' ('I suppose you have heard').

Of all the tenses described, the ones which form the backbone of the system in the modern language are the present, the past (*znào sam* 'I knew') and the future (*znàću* 'I will know'). Each of these can be formed from perfective and imperfective verbs, giving six possibilities, which cover most situations. As aspect has gained in significance, tenses other than the main ones have been reduced to marginal status. It will be interesting to observe how many of them survive and for how long.

In contrast to the wealth of tense forms, the inventory of non-finite verbal forms is limited. There are two indeclinable adverbs, termed 'gerunds'. The present gerund is formed from imperfective verbs (*pèvati* 'to sing' gives *pèvajūći* 'singing') and denotes action contemporaneous with that of the main verb. The past gerund, normally formed from perfective verbs (*sàznati* 'to find out': *sàznāvši* 'having found out'), is for an action prior to that of the main verb. There is also the past passive participle, formed more frequently from perfective verbs than imperfectives, for example, *kúpiti* 'to buy', *kûpljen* 'bought'. The past passive participle takes adjectival endings and, with *bìti* 'to be' as auxiliary, forms the passive voice.

6 Syntax

Two particularly interesting aspects of Serbo-Croat syntax (enclitics and the replacement of the infinitive by a subordinate clause) have already been mentioned and will be described in more detail. In addition, we shall give brief consideration to agreement.

Serbo-Croat enclitics are already familiar to many non-Slavists through the work of Wayles Browne, who showed the problems they posed for transformational theory. Enclitics must come in second position in a clause.

There are six 'slots', each of which may be filled by one enclitic, in the strict order given in table 18.4. As examples, consider the following: *gde ste me videli?* (enclitics II, V) 'where did you see me?'; *želim mu ih dati* (III, V) 'I wish to give them to him'; *našao ga je* (V, VI) 'he found it'; *sećate li me se?* (I, IV, V) (*sećati se* is a reflexive verb which governs the genitive) 'do you remember me?'

Table 18.4: Serbo-Croat Enclitics

I	Interrogative particle: li
II	Verbal auxiliaries: sam, si, smo, ste, su (not *je*)
	ću, ćeš, cé, ćemo, ćete, će
	bih, bi, bi, bismo, biste, bi
III	Dative pronouns: singular: mi, ti, mu, joj (reflexive *si* in west only)
	plural: nam, vam, im
IV	Genitive pronouns: singular: me, te, ga, je
	plural: nas, vas, ih
V	Accusative pronouns: identical to the genitive pronouns with the addition of the reflexive *se*
VI	Third singular form of *biti*: je

There are two special rules concerning *je*, the third person singular of *biti*. If the combination *se je* is expected, then *je* is dropped. *Vratiti se* 'to return' is a reflexive verb; the expected third singular masculine of the past tense would be *vratio se je*, but we find *vratio se* 'he returned'. This is now an absolute rule in the east but occasional forms with *se je* still occur in the west. The other special rule prohibits the combination **je je*, where the first is the accusative case of the personal pronoun (third singular feminine) and the second is the third singular of *biti*. Instead, the first is replaced by the form *ju*, for example, *video ju je* 'he saw her'.

Earlier it was stated that enclitics stand in 'second' position. The expected interpretation of this statement might be after the first accented constituent. This interpretation would fit the examples given so far, as well as sentences like: *taj pesnik mi je napisao pesmu* 'that poet wrote me a poem'. If an initial constituent is separated by a pause, enclitics will then occur in second position counting from the pause: *ove godine, taj pesnik mi je napisao pesmu* 'this year, that poet wrote me a poem'. In some cases an initial long constituent is disregarded though there is no pause. More surprisingly, the enclitics may stand after the first accented word, even though by doing so they split a constituent: *taj mi je pesnik napisao pesmu* (lit. 'that to me is poet written poem') 'that poet wrote me a poem'; similarly: *jedan je hodža imao kuću...* ('one is priest had house') 'one (Muslim) priest had a house...'.

Enclitics are found in the other Slavonic languages, though Serbo-Croat has preserved them particularly well and has created new ones, such as the clitic forms of *hteti*. Our next point of interest, however, is unusual in Slavonic (being found only in Bulgarian and Macedonian in addition to Serbo-Croat) but shared with other language of the Balkans (e.g. Rumanian and Greek — see pages 316–7 and 433–4). Mainly in the eastern variety, Serbo-Croat tends to replace the infinitive by a construction consisting of the conjunction *da* plus a verb in the present tense. The infinitive with purposive meaning is most likely to be replaced, so that examples like: *Jovan je došao da kupi knjigu* (lit. 'Jovan came that he buys a book') 'Jovan came to buy a book', occur freely in the western variety as well as in the east. With verbs like *želeti* 'to wish', both constructions occur: *Jovan želi da kupi knjigu/ Jovan želi kupiti knjigu* 'Jovan wishes to buy a book', but the first is more likely in the east and the second in the west. The construction with *da* has spread into the ordinary future: *Jovan će da kupi knjigu* 'Jovan will buy a book'. This is common in the east, much less so in the west, where one would expect the infinitive: *Jovan će kupiti knjigu*. Broadly speaking, as one moves eastwards, so the infinitive becomes rarer, though there is considerable variation even among individuals. In eastern dialects transitional to Bulgarian and Macedonian the infinitive is effectively excluded.

The last area to consider is agreement. Like the other Slavonic languages described, Serbo-Croat shows agreement of attributive modifiers with their head nouns in gender, number, case and, to a limited extent, in animacy. Main verbs agree in person and number with their subjects, participles in gender and number. There are various complications. For example, a few nouns are of different gender in the singular and the plural: *to* (nt. sg.) *oko* 'that eye'; *te* (f. pl.) *oči* 'those eyes'. Then there is a class of nouns ending in -*a*, which have the appearance of feminines but refer to males. In the singular, these are masculine: *naš gazda* 'our master'. In the plural, both masculine and feminine agreements are found: *naši/naše gazde* 'our masters'. Furthermore, a small group of nouns, instead of having a normal plural paradigm, takes another singular. Thus *dete* (nt. sg.) 'child' has the form *deca* 'children', which declines like the feminine singular noun *žena* in the chart of nominal declension. Agreement with *deca* is singular or plural, depending on the construction: *majka ove* (gen. sg. f.) *dece* 'the mother of these children'; *deca spavaju* (pl.) 'the children are sleeping'.

Since Serbo-Croat retains the original gender distinctions in the plural, there are rules for agreement with conjoined noun phrases, which may be of different genders. If all conjuncts are feminine, then feminine agreements are found (all these examples are from works by the Nobel prize-winning novelist, Ivo Andrić): *nad njim su stajale* (f. pl.) *Jelenka* (f.) *i Saveta* (f.) 'over him were standing Jelenka and Saveta'. In all other cases, the masculine plural is used even if no masculine is present: *znanje* (nt. sg.) *i intuicija* (f. sg.) *su kod njega sarađivali* (m. pl.)... 'knowledge and intuition worked together in him...'. Conjoined neuter singulars similarly require a masculine plural predicate. Similar rules are found in Slovene.

However, Serbo-Croat has made an interesting innovation. If the conjuncts are all of feminine gender, but at least one is of the *-i* declension (like *stvar* in the chart of nominal declension), then masculine agreements may be found: *službena revnost* (f. sg., *-i* declension) *i lična sujeta* (f. sg.) *zanosili* (m. pl.) *su ih*... 'professional zeal and personal vanity carried them away...'. The *i*-stem declension includes a large proportion of abstract nouns and few animates. It appears, therefore, that Serbo-Croat is moving towards a position in which the feminine plural will be required for agreement with conjoined nouns referring to females, the feminine will be optional for other feminine nouns and the masculine will be used under all other circumstances.

This last construction typifies the particular interest of Serbo-Croat for the linguist. The preservation of the original gender distinctions in the plural is an example of its conservatism; there are, as we have seen, various forms still found in Serbo-Croat which have been lost in most of the other Slavonic languages. On the other hand, the innovation permitting masculine agreement with feminine nouns (depending on their type) is, like other innovations we have noted, a surprise and a challenge for the linguist.

Bibliography

Partridge (1972) is a solid grammar in textbook form, with brief but helpful background notes. Descriptive grammars include Meillet and Vaillant (1969), with thorough coverage of morphology but somewhat dated, and Leskien (1914), a landmark in its time. The following deal with accent: Lehiste and Ivić (1963), an extensive acoustical study; Magner and Matejka (1971), a challenge to traditional accounts, perhaps overstated, though a good entry point to the extensive literature on the subject; Gvozdanović (1980), an acoustical study, with a useful introduction to the phonology of Serbo-Croat. The *Publications of the Yugoslav Serbo-Croatian-English Contrastive Project* (1968–) contain papers covering a range of topics, especially in syntax and lexicon; for instance, *Contrastive Analysis of English and Serbo-Croatian*, vol. 1 (1975) includes a paper by W. Browne giving a detailed account of clitics.

For the history of the language, Naylor (1980) provides a clear account of the external history of Serbo-Croat; Popović (1960) lays particular emphasis on the early period and on contacts with other languages; while Vaillant (1928–79) is a historical grammar of wider scope than its title suggests. Ivić (1958) provides a survey of Serbo-Croatian dialects by one of Yugoslavia's foremost linguists.

Acknowledgement

I am very grateful to all of the following for helpful comments on an earlier draft of this chapter: W. Browne, P.V. Cubberley, P. Herrity, Milka and Pavle Ivić, D.J.L. Johnson, Lj. Popović and R.D. Sussex.

References

Gvozdanović, J. 1980. *Tone and Accent in Standard Serbo-Croatian (With a Synopsis of Serbo-Croatian Phonology)* (Österreichische Akademie der Wissenschaften, Vienna)

Ivić, P. 1958. *Die serbokroatischen Dialekte: ihre Struktur und Entwicklung, I: Allgemeines und die štokavische Dialektgruppe* (Mouton, The Hague)

—— 1986. *Word and Sentence Prosody in Serbocroatian* (MIT Press, Cambridge, Mass.)

Lehiste, I. and P. Ivić. 1963. *Accent in Serbocroatian: An Experimental Study* (University of Michigan, Ann Arbor)

Leskien, A. 1914. *Grammatik der serbokroatischen Sprache, I: Lautlehre, Stammbildung, Formenlehre* (Carl Winter, Heidelberg)

Magner, T.F. and L. Matejka. 1971. *Word Accent in Modern Serbo-Croatian* (Pennsylvania State University Press, University Park and London)

Meillet, A. and A. Vaillant. 1969. *Grammaire de la langue serbo-croate*, 2nd ed. (Champion, Paris)

Naylor, K.E. 1980. 'Serbo-Croatian', in A.M. Schenker and E. Stankiewicz (eds.), *The Slavic Literary Languages: Formation and Development* (Yale Concilium on International and Area Studies, New Haven, Conn.), pp. 65–83

Partridge, M. 1972. *Serbo-Croat: Practical Grammar and Reader*, 2nd ed. (Izdavački zavod Jugoslavia, Belgrade)

Popović, I. 1960. *Geschichte der serbokroatischen Sprache* (Otto Harrassowitz, Wiesbaden)

Publications of the Yugoslav Serbo-Croatian-English Contrastive Project (1968–) (Institute of Linguistics, University of Zagreb, Zagreb)

Vaillant, A. (1928–79), *La Langue de Dominko Zlatarić, poète ragusain de la fin du XVIe siècle*, 3 vols. (Institut d'Études Slaves, Paris and Serbian Academy of Sciences, Belgrade)

19 Greek

Brian D. Joseph

1 Historical Background

The Greek language forms, by itself, a separate branch of the Indo-European family. It is one of the oldest attested Indo-European languages, being attested from c. 1400 BC in the Mycenaean Greek documents found on Crete (and from somewhat later, on the Greek mainland) written in the Linear B syllabary. Except for a break in attestation between the end of the Mycenaean empire (c. 1150 BC) and roughly 800 BC, a period sometimes referred to as the 'Dark Ages' of Greek culture, Greek presents a continuous record of attestation for the linguist, right up to the present day.

Commonly called *Greek* in English, based on the term *Graeci* used by the Romans to label all the Greeks (though originally the name may have properly applied only to a tribe in the north-west of Greece), the language is also referred to as *Hellenic*, from the Greek stem Ἑλλην-*, used in the *Iliad* to refer to a Thessalian tribe but in Herodotus (and elsewhere) to designate the Greeks as a whole as opposed to barbarians; indeed, the Greeks themselves have generally referred to their language as ἑλληνική, though contemporary Greeks also use the designation ῥωμαίικα, an outgrowth of their connection historically with the Eastern Roman Empire based in Constantinople.

Within Indo-European, Greek can be classified as a 'centum' language, for it shows a distinct set of reflexes for the Indo-European labio-velars, opposed to a single set of reflexes for the Indo-European palatals and velars combined; thus, Greek shows a root πρια- 'buy' (cf. also Mycenaean *qi-ri-ja-to* 'bought' showing the labio-velar preserved as ⟨q⟩) from Proto-Indo-European *$k^w riH_2$- (cf. Sanskrit root *krī-* 'buy'), a noun κρέας 'meat' from Proto-Indo-European *$krewH_2s$ (cf. Sanskrit *kravis-* 'raw flesh'), and a root κει- 'lie (down)' from Proto-Indo-European *$\hat{k}ei$- (cf. Sanskrit root *śī:-* 'lie'), in which the plain *k of the proto-language and the palatal *$\hat{k}$ show a merger while the labio-velar *k^w is kept distinct. Greek also shows some particular

*Greek forms are cited throughout in the Greek alphabet. See table 19.1 for the pronunciation of the letters.

410

affinities with Armenian and Indo-Iranian, sharing with these branches, for example, the past-tense morpheme *e- (the 'augment'), and the use of the negator *$mē$: (Greek μή), and with Armenian alone the vocalisation of the Indo-European 'laryngeal' consonants in initial position, and some notable parallels in vocabulary (e.g. ἀλώπηξ 'fox' = Arm. *aluēs*, where no other Indo-European language has precisely this form, or πρωκτός 'anus' = *erastank'* 'buttocks'). Moreover, Greek preserves the Indo-European vowel system (with long and short *a *e *i *o *u) more faithfully than any other language in the family.

Differentiating Greek from the other members of the Indo-European family, though, are several particular features. In morphology, Greek innovated a (past and future) passive marker -θη- and elaborated the infinitival system. With regard to phonology, Greek alone in Indo-European shows voiceless aspirates (in the ancient language) as the continuation of the Indo-European voiced aspirate consonants (e.g. φερ- 'carry' from *$bher$-, cf. Sanskrit *bhar*-); in addition, Greek lenited Indo-European *s to h in many environments, ultimately losing it intervocalically (e.g. ἑπτά 'seven' from *$septm̥$, cf. Latin *septem*, or γένε-ι 'in, at, to a race, kind (dat. sg.)' from *$genes$-i, cf. Sanskrit *janas-i* 'in the people (loc. sg.)'). Also, Greek deleted original word-final stops (e.g. μέλι 'honey' from *$melit$, cf. Hittite *milit* 'honey').

Moreover, although Common Greek preserved the Indo-European labiovelars as such, to judge in part from their preservation in Mycenaean (cf. *qi-ri-ja-to* above), the ancient language is characterised by a number of complex dialectal developments with *k^w, *g^w and *g^wh. Labial reflexes occur in some environments and in some dialects (e.g. pan-Greek interrogative stem πο- from *k^wo-, Aeolic (Boeotian) πέτταρες 'four' from *$k^wetwr̥$-), dental reflexes in other environments, also dialectally conditioned (e.g. τίς 'who' from *k^wis, and non-Aeolic (Attic) τέτταρες 'four'), and even velar reflexes in some dialects when adjacent to *u or *w (e.g. εὐχ- 'wish' from *ewg^wh-). Further Greek-particular developments setting the language off from other Indo-European languages include a number of complex treatments of clusters of obstruent + *y and of clusters of resonant (*r *l *m *n *y *w) + *s (examples below in section 4.1). A final diagnostic feature for Greek within Indo-European is a three-way distinction in reflexes of the laryngeal consonants, represented by ε, α, and ο in Greek; this feature is likely to represent the continuation of a three-way Proto-Indo-European contrast in the laryngeals, but by some accounts, it is a significant Greek innovation (perhaps morphologically induced).

The early attestation of Greek and the archaic nature of the Homeric epic corpus together serve to make Greek extremely important for the understanding and reconstruction of all aspects of Proto-Indo-European language and culture. In addition, the literary output of writers of Greek has throughout the ages been of utmost importance to Western culture so that

Greek has a special place in a variety of humanistic pursuits, including the history of linguistics because of the native Greek grammatical tradition developed by the Alexandrians in the Hellenistic era. Finally, the long and relatively continuous attestation of the Greek language gives it a significance for general historical linguistics, as it offers a 'window' on the nature of language change which few other languages can provide.

With such a long historical record for the language, it is convenient, as well as conventional, to break the span up into several major periods of development. These periods are defined in part by external, especially political and historical, factors, but also reflect real linguistic developments. These periods are:

(a) Mycenaean Greek (c. 1500–1150 BC)
(b) Classical Greek, including Homeric Greek (c. 800–300 BC)
(c) Hellenistic Greek, including New Testament Greek (c. 300 BC–AD 300)
(d) Middle Greek, comprising Byzantine Greek (c. AD 300–1100) and Medieval Greek (c. AD 1100–1600)
(e) Modern Greek (c. AD 1600 to the present).

With such a long period of attestation for Greek, it is of course natural to find that there are some significant differences between Greek of the fourteenth century BC and Greek of the twentieth century AD, and these differences are chronicled in the sections to follow. At the same time, though, there are some aspects of the language, occasionally isolated ones though some fit into a system, which show remarkable continuity and stability over some 3,500 years. Among these are the past tense augment ε-, still found in stressed positions in the modern language, the personal endings in the present active and medio-passive present and past (excepting the third person plural), the general structure of the nominal and verbal systems and numerous lexical items, including some which have changed neither phonetic form (excepting the realisation of accent) nor meaning, e.g. ἄνεμος 'wind'.

2 Greek in its Geographic and Social Context

Greek has been spoken in the southern Balkans since early in the second millennium BC, according to conventional accounts of the coming of the Greeks to the area. Arriving most likely in waves of different tribes over a period of several centuries, the Greeks absorbed some autochthonous groups, traces of whose language(s) can probably be seen in numerous place names and terms for native flora and fauna containing the sequences -νθ- and -σσ-, among others (e.g. Κόρινθος, μίνθη 'mint', Παρνασσός etc.), and possibly also in Indo-European-like words with a somewhat aberrant phonology for Greek (e.g. ἀλείφ-ω 'I anoint' with a prefixed ἀ- and a voiceless aspirate consonant, both unexpected if the word were inherited directly from Proto-Indo-European into Greek, versus inherited Greek λίπος 'fat', from an Indo-European root *leip-). Greek has remained in the Balkans since that early period, although it has spread to other areas as well.

In ancient times, Greek colonies were established in Cyprus (perhaps as early as the twelfth century BC) and southern Italy (c. eighth century BC), and there have been Greek speakers continuously in these places up to the present day. Similarly, colonies established in western Asia Minor were continuously peopled by Greek speakers up to the beginning of the twentieth century, when population exchanges in the 1920s between Greece and Turkey led to the relocation of most of the Greeks back to Greece. All of these settlements were renewed with further Greek speakers throughout the Hellenistic period, when Greek spread as the lingua franca for all of the eastern Mediterranean, the Middle East and into Central Asia as far east as Persia and India. Some of the pockets of Greek speakers established in that period remain to this day, for example in Alexandria (Egypt).

In the Middle Greek period, the geographic domain of Greek became somewhat more restricted, with important centres still in Constantinople, Asia Minor in general, Alexandria, Cyprus, and elsewhere in the general eastern Mediterranean area, including the Ukraine. The modern era has seen the reduction in the number of Greek speakers in all these areas except Cyprus, but also the expansion of Greek into the 'New World'. There are now significant Greek-speaking communities in America (especially the urban centres of the East), in Canada, in Britain and in Australia. The speakers in Greece, Cyprus and elsewhere in the Mediterranean together with those in the 'Hellenic diaspora' number some 12 million today (c. nine million in Greece).

Despite the rather widespread geographic distribution of Greek throughout its history, it is Balkan Greek, i.e. Greek of the southern Balkans including the Greek islands and Crete, that is of primary importance here. The dialect diversity in ancient times, with four main dialect groups (Attic-Ionic, Aeolic, Arcado-Cyprian, and West Greek (comprising Northwest Greek and Doric)) as well as the earlier Mycenaean Greek (problematic in terms of its connections with these dialect groups), centred more on matters of detail in phonological and morphological development rather than on broad structural aspects. Thus, Attic, the dialect of Athens and the preeminent dialect from a cultural and political standpoint, and more generally the Attic-Ionic branch of Greek, constitute the primary representative of Ancient Greek. Moreover, Attic-Ionic provided the basis for the Hellenistic koine (ἡ κοινὴ διάλεκτος 'the common dialect'), which showed considerable uniformity across the whole area of its use. This koine, in turn, provided the basis for the Middle and Modern Greek dialects, with the exception of Tsakonian, spoken in the eastern part of the Peloponnesus, which derives from the ancient Doric dialect. Finally, the language of the modern Hellenic diaspora, while incorporating features, mainly lexical items, from the local dominant languages, has nonetheless remained true to its Attic-Ionic origin in terms of general structural characteristics.

Focusing on Balkan Greek is important for another reason. This particular geographic setting is crucial for understanding the development of the language in the late Middle Greek and early Modern Greek periods, and especially for understanding many of the differences, to be discussed in more detail below, between these later stages of the language and its earlier stages. Greek in these later stages shows numerous linguistic features that are found as well in other languages of the Balkans, such as Albanian, Rumanian, Macedonian, Bulgarian and to a somewhat lesser extent, Serbo-Croat. These features include various mergers of nominal case functions, especially possessive and indirect object functions in a single form, the formation of a future tense with a form of the verb 'want' (e.g. Modern Greek θά from earlier impersonal θέλει 'wants' + verbal particle νά), the widespread use of finite complement clauses where many other languages (and indeed, earlier stages of the languages in question, for the most part) would use non-finite forms and others of a more particular nature.

The exact nature of the relation between developments of this sort in Greek and parallel developments in the other Balkan languages is not clear; some scholars argue that Greek underwent the changes as part of its natural development and that (many of) these changes spread to the other languages from Greek, while others argue that their appearance in Greek is the result of the importation of foreign features into the language through contact with the other Balkan languages. It is more likely, though, that no single explanation can be found to be valid for all of these common features, and that some may have begun in Greek and spread from there, others may have made their way into Greek from elsewhere, and others may even be the result of a combination of Greek-internal developments enhanced or guided along a particular path through language contact.

One final aspect of the social setting of Greek that is vital to an understanding of the language concerns the extent to which a high- versus low-style distinction, inherent, probably, in all languages, has come to pervade Greek language use. In Ancient Greek, there is evidence for a distinction at least between the literary language in which most of the classical works (drama, poetry, philosophy etc.) were written and the colloquial language as evidenced in numerous inscriptions; recent investigations into the inscriptions of the Athenian ἀγορά ('marketplace') have indicated that colloquial usage was marked by pronunciations which came to be more current in later stages of the language, e.g. [iː] for [eː] and a spirantal pronunciation of the voiced stops, and observations contained in Plato's dialogue *Cratylus* provide confirmation of this point. Similarly, the

Greek of the non-literary papyri of Hellenistic Egypt gives a good indication of what must have been true colloquial usage through numerous hypercorrections and mistakes in approximating 'correct', i.e. high-style, Attic Greek.

In later stages of Greek, though, a consciously archaising tendency on the part of many Middle Greek writers to 'Atticise', i.e. emulate Classical Attic Greek spelling, morphology, syntax and usage, served to create a large stylistic rift in the language. Consequently, there were writers in the Middle Greek era who wrote in a language not unlike Classical Attic Greek (though it must be noted that mistakes abound!), while others wrote in a form more in line with colloquial usage of the day, the result of several centuries of natural linguistic development from the Hellenistic koine. Even in such a speech form, though, numerous learned borrowings occur, owing to the prestige enjoyed by the archaising style. Accordingly, even 'pure' colloquial Greek, what has come to be called Demotic (Greek: δημοτική), at all times in the post-classical period has incorporated many historically anomalous and anachronistic elements; this is, of course, an expected development in a language with a long literary history available to speakers and writers at all times (compare the situation in India with regard to Sanskrit and the modern Indic languages, the Romance languages and Latin, and the Slavonic languages and Old Church Slavonic).

In the case of Greek, though, with the founding of the Greek national state in the 1820s and the desire at the time for a unified form of a national language, this stylistic rift has become institutionalised and politicised. The debate over which form of Greek to use in this context, the consciously archaising so-called 'puristic' Greek (Greek: καθαρεύουσα 'purifying') or the form more based in the colloquial developments from the koine, the Demotic Greek, has occupied much of the linguistic and political energy of the Greeks since the 1820s; the current official position on the 'language question' (Greek: τὸ γλωσσικὸ ζήτημα) is in favour of the Demotic, with the now-standard language being based generally on the southern (i.e. Peloponnesian) dialect.

3 Writing Systems for Greek

Greek has been written in a variety of writing systems throughout its history. The earliest written Greek is found in the syllabic system known as Linear B, in which Mycenaean Greek documents were written, generally on clay tablets. A syllabic system, related in some way to that of Linear B (though the exact details of the relationship are controversial) was also used in Cyprus in ancient times to write many of the ancient Cyprian dialect inscriptions. In addition, Greeks in Asia Minor in medieval times occasionally used the Arabic alphabet and even the Hebrew alphabet to write Greek.

The most enduring writing system for Greek, though, is the Greek alphabet. Adapted from the old North Semitic alphabet (traditionally, according to the Greeks themselves, transmitted through the Phoenicians) and embellished with separate signs for vowel sounds, the Greek alphabet has served the Greek language well for some 2,800 years since its introduction into Greece in the tenth or ninth century BC.

The system is basically a one-letter-to-one-phoneme system, though there are some 'double letters' representing clusters and at all stages some distinctive oppositions are either not represented at all (e.g. [a] versus [aː] in Ancient Greek) or represented only secondarily via clusters of letters (as with [d] versus [ð], spelled ⟨ντ⟩ and ⟨δ⟩, respectively, in Modern Greek). Also, diacritics to represent pitch accent in Ancient Greek were not introduced until Hellenistic times (c. 200 BC) by the Alexandrian grammarians, and changes in the accentual system, from a pitch accent to a stress accent, left the writing system with more diacritics than needed for Middle and Modern Greek (though a recent official orthography has been adopted with but a single accentual diacritic). Moreover, the phonetic values of the letters have changed over time, so the current orthography is not as well matched with the phonological system as in earlier stages. Table 19.1 gives the information about the former and current phonetic values and transcriptions of the letters of the Greek alphabet.

Table 19.1: The Greek Alphabet, with Transliteration and Pronunciation for Ancient (Attic) Greek and (Standard) Modern Greek, plus Diphthongs and Clusters

Capital letter	Small Letter	Ancient phonetics	Usual transliteration	Modern pronunciation	Usual transliteration
Α	α	[a]	a	[a]	a
Β	β	[b]	b	[v]	v
Γ	γ	[g]	g	[j] (/__ i, e) [γ] (elsewhere)	y g(h)
Δ	δ	[d]	d	[ð]	d(h)
Ε	ε	[ɛ]	e	[ɛ]	e
Ζ	ζ	[zd]	z	[z]	z
Η	η	[ɛː]	eː, ē	[i]	i
Θ	θ	[tʰ]	th	[θ]	th
Ι	ι	[i]	i	[i]	i
Κ	κ	[k]	k	[k]	k
Λ	λ	[l]	l	[l]	l
Μ	μ	[m]	m	[m]	m
Ν	ν	[n]	n	[n]	n
Ξ	ξ	[ks]	x	[ks]	ks, x (as in box)
Ο	ο	[o]	o	[o]	o
Π	π	[p]	p	[p]	p

Capital letter	Small Letter	Ancient phonetics	Usual transliteration	Modern pronunciation	Usual transliteration
Ρ	ϱ	[r]	r	[ɾ]	r
Σ	σ (ς ##)	[s]	s	[s]	s
Τ	τ	[t]	t	[t]	t
Υ	υ	[y]	y, u	[i]	i
Φ	φ	[pʰ]	ph	[f]	f
Χ	χ	[kʰ]	ch, kh	[χ]	h, x (IPA value)
Ψ	ψ	[ps]	ps	[ps]	ps
Ω	ω	[ɔ:]	o:, ō	[o]	o
	αι	[ai̯]	ai	[ɛ]	e
	αυ	[au̯]	au	[av] (/__ +voice) / [af] (/__ −voice)	av / af
	ει	[e:]	ei	[i]	i
	ευ	[ɛu̯]	eu	[ev] (/__ +voice] / [ef] (/__ −voice)	ev / ef
	οι	[oi̯]	oi	[i]	i
	ου	[o:]	ou	[u]	u
	υι	[yi̯]	yi, ui	[i]	i
	γ before γ χ ξ	[ŋ]	n(g, kh, ks)	[ŋ]	n(g, h, ks)
	γκ	[ŋk]	nk	[(ŋ)g] (medially) / [g] (initially)	(n)g / g
	μπ/μβ	[mp/mb]	mp/mb	[(m)b] (medially) / [b] (initially)	(m)b / b
	ντ/νδ	[nt/nd]	nt/nd	[(n)d] (medially) / [d] (initially)	(n)d / d
	τζ	------	------	[dz]	dz
(##)ʽ		[h]	h	Ø	Ø
(##)ʼ		Ø (absence of #h)		Ø	Ø

4 Structural Features of Greek

Although five different periods were distinguished for the purposes of outlining the internal and external history of the Greek language over the approximately 3,500 years of its attestation, for the purpose of giving the major structural features of the language, it is more useful to examine the ancient language in contrast with the modern language. In general, then, the relevant distinction is between Classical Greek and Post-Classical Greek, for most of the changes which characterise the difference between these two stages of the language are already under way and evident in the koine of the

Hellenistic period. Similarly, the differences between Middle Greek and Modern Greek are not great, and some scholars even date the beginning of the modern era to around the tenth or eleventh centuries AD. Accordingly, the whole post-classical period can be treated in a unified fashion, with the understanding that what is described in the modern language is the end-point of a long period of development from the classical language, and the stages of Hellenistic and Middle Greek defined earlier represent way stations on the road to Modern Greek; references to individual stages in particular developments, though, are made whenever necessary or appropriate.

4.1 Phonology

The consonant inventory of Ancient Greek included three distinctive points of articulation — labial, dental and velar — and three distinctive manners of articulation among the stops — voiced, voiceless unaspirated and voiceless aspirated. As noted above, in Common Greek (c. 1800 BC) and in Mycenaean Greek, there were also labio-velar consonants, which later merged with the labial, dental and velar stops under the conditions alluded to earlier. In addition, Greek had a single sibilant [s] (with [z] as an allophone before voiced consonants), the resonants [r] (with a voiceless allophone [ɹ̥] in initial position) and [l], the nasals [m] and [n] (with [ŋ] as an allophone before velar consonants) and the glottal fricative [h]. There may have been an affricate [dᶻ], though most of the evidence concerning the pronunciation of the letter ⟨ζ⟩ suggests it represented a true cluster of [z + d] not a unitary affricated segment (cf. spellings such as Διόζοτος for *Διὸς δοτός, literally 'given by Zeus'). The Common Greek [j] and [w] had been eliminated in many positions by Classical Greek, though they did remain as the second element of several diphthongs in the classical language; moreover, [j] is found in Mycenaean in several positions (e.g. *jo-i-je-si* 'so they send', interpretable 'alphabetically' as ὡς ἱενσι), and [w] occurs in many of the dialects (e.g. Mycenaean *wo-i-ko*, Doric, Thessalian and Arcadian ϝοῖκος, where the letter ⟨ϝ⟩ ('digamma') represents [w], to be compared with Attic οἶκος 'the house').

By contrast to this relatively straightforward and simple consonant inventory, the vowel system of Ancient Greek was most complex. Length was distinctive and several degrees of height were distinguished as well; moreover, there were numerous diphthongs. The system of monophthongs is summarised in table 19.2 and the diphthongal system is given in table 19.3. It should be noted that the front rounded vowels ([y] and [yː] of table 19.2) are characteristic of the Attic-Ionic dialect only; the other dialects had back [u] and [uː] corresponding to these Attic-Ionic vowels. Furthermore, the gaps in the short diphthongs (absence of [ei̯] and [ou̯]) are the result of early sound changes by which *ei̯ became [eː] and *ou̯ became [oː]. Finally, the long diphthongs were somewhat rare and had a very low functional load; in

Table 19.2 Ancient (Attic) Greek Monophthongs (IPA Symbols)

i iː y yː				
e eː			o oː	
ɛː				ɔː
		a aː		

Table 19.3: Ancient (Attic) Greek Diphthongs (IPA Symbols)

	eu̯	yi̯	eːi̯	eːu̯
ai̯	au̯		aːi̯	aːu̯
oi̯			oːi̯	

fact, early on in the classical period, [eːi̯], [aːi̯], and [oːi̯] lost their off-glide and merged with the corresponding long pure vowels.

Although there are dialectal differences in the consonants, these tend not to be in the consonantal inventory but rather have to do more with the outcome of the Common Greek labio-velars (e.g. labials generally in Aeolic versus conditioned (before front vowels) dental reflexes or (elsewhere) labial reflexes in other dialects, as in πέτταρες/τέτταρες 'four' cited above), and the outcome of complex cluster developments involving obstruent plus glide combinations and resonant or nasal plus s. For example, generally speaking — there are several exceptional cases — t + y yielded a geminate -ss- (graphic ⟨σσ⟩) in Ionic, Doric in general, Arcadian and part of Aeolic, a geminate -tt- (graphic ⟨ττ⟩) in Attic and part of Aeolic (Boeotian), and various spellings (⟨ζ⟩, ⟨ττ⟩, ⟨θθ⟩, which may represent developments of something like [ts]) in Central Cretan (Doric), as in the feminine adjectival ending (from *-e(n)t-ya) (χαρί-)εσσα (Ionic), (Παδο-)εσσα (Arcadian), (οἰνοῦ-)ττα (Attic), (χαριϝ-)ετταν (Boeotian), (ἑα-)σσα (Doric), (ια-)τταν (Central Cretan). Similarly, for certain classes of words and with some obscuring of dialect distribution due to analogies and some borrowings, there is a major split in the Greek dialects concerning the outcome of t before the vowel i, with West Greek and part of Aeolic (Thessalian and Boeotian) preserving t in this context and the other dialects assibilating it to s, as in Doric εἶτι '(s)he goes' versus Attic-Ionic εἶσι.

The vowel systems of the ancient dialects, however, show considerable variation, with alternations of length and quality and in the outcome of contractions serving to distinguish the dialects from one another. Particularly notable is the raising and fronting of Common Greek *a: to [æː] and ultimately [ɛː] in the Attic-Ionic dialect; thus one finds Attic-Ionic μήτηρ 'mother' versus Doric (for example) μάτηρ from Common Greek *ma:te:r. The fronting of [u] to [y] in Attic-Ionic has already been noted. Lengthening (often due to the loss of *s or *y in a cluster with a resonant) and contraction (of combinations of e and o) gave rise in Attic-Ionic to the long closed ([eː] and [oː]) vowels and likewise in parts of Doric (e.g. Corinthian and Delphian) and Thessalian and Boeotian (both Aeolic), while in Lesbian (Aeolic) and Arcadian and the rest of Doric (e.g. Cretan, Laconian) long open vowels ([ɛː] and [ɔː]) are found as the corresponding elements. For example, Attic-Ionic has εἰμί [eːmi] 'I am' from Common Greek *esmi, while Doric has ἠμί [ɛːmi]; similarly, Attic-Ionic has τρεῖς [treːs] 'three' from Common Greek *treyes, while Doric has τρης.

Among the peculiarities of Ancient Greek phonotactics, the following are to be noted: [r] could not occur in initial position; one finds instead the unvoiced allophone [r̥] (which has sometimes been described as an aspirated r). In final position, only [r], [s], [n] and vowels were permitted. Geminate consonants were permitted, though geminate labial and velar stops occur most often in onomatopoeic, nursery and expressive words. Lastly, Ancient Greek tolerated numerous consonant clusters, including a variety of initial clusters: any stop plus r or l is permitted (including #τλ-); all but *βν-, *βμ-, *γμ-, *θμ-, *πμ-, *τν-, *φμ- and *χμ- are found for stop plus nasal clusters, though φν- occurs only in a single onomatopoeic form, and τμ-, δν- and κμ- are quite rare; two stops are permitted initially if they differ in point of articulation but agree in manner and the second stop is a dental, though the voiced such clusters (βδ- and γδ-) were found in only a small number of words; and clusters of s plus as many as two consonants occur (e.g. σχίζω 'cut', σπλάγχνα 'innards', σκνίπτω 'pinch, nip', etc.).

The Ancient Greek accentual system was based on a pitch accent. There were a high pitch (the acute, Greek ὀξύς, marked with the diacritic ⟨´⟩), a low pitch (the grave, Greek βαρύς, marked with the diacritic ⟨`⟩), and a contour pitch (the circumflex, Greek περισπομένος, marked with the diacritic ⟨˜⟩) which consisted of an acute plus a grave on the same syllable and occurred only on long vowels or diphthongs. At most, one high pitch, either an acute or circumflex, occurred per word (except for some special developments with enclitics), and all non-high syllables were considered grave.

Accent placement was predictable (for the most part — some exceptions exist) only in finite verb forms and in declined forms of certain nouns, e.g. those with antepenultimate accent in their lexical form; for such forms, the accent is said to be 'recessive', i.e. as far from the end of the word as permitted. Also, the placement of accent was predictable in certain morphologically definable formations, e.g. compounds with εὐ- 'well, easy' had recessive accent, verbal adjectives in -τος were accented on the final syllable, etc. In other contexts, accent placement was unpredictable and was therefore an element of the underlying (lexical) form of the word in question, though there were some regularities in the realisation of the accent (e.g. circumflex if the accent fell on a long penultimate syllable when the ultima was short). Thus, accent was distinctive in the Ancient Greek phonological system, for some words were distinguished only by the type of accent on a given syllable (e.g. locative adverbial οἴκοι 'at home' versus nominative plural οἶκοι 'houses') and others only by the placement of the accent (e.g. τιμά 'two honours' versus τίμα '(you) honour!').

An overriding principle in the placement of the pitch accent in Ancient Greek is the so-called 'Dreimorengesetz' (Law of Three Morae), by which the accent could only occur on the antepenultimate, penultimate or ultima syllable and never earlier in the word than that. With a few exceptions, this restriction can be stated in terms of morae (hence the name 'Dreimorengesetz'), so that Ancient Greek was probably a mora-timed language (note also that syllable quantity mattered for purposes of the ancient poetic metres). This restriction gave rise to certain of the predictable aspects of the placement of accent, especially in those forms which had recessive accent. For example, a noun such as θάλαττα 'sea' was lexically accented on the antepenultimate syllable, as indicated by the citation form (nominative singular); in the genitive singular, though, the final syllable is long (θαλάττης) and as a result, the accent cannot stand on the antepenultimate syllable. Instead, it predictably is pulled forward to the penultimate, so that it does not stand more than three morae from the end. Similarly, a finite verb form such as κελεύω 'I order' was predictably accented on the penultimate syllable because the ultima is long and finite forms have recessive accent; the first person plural present form κελεύομεν and the first person singular past form ἐκέλευσα, however, are both accented on the antepenultimate syllable because the ultima is short. By contrast, the perfect middle participle of this verb, a non-finite form, had penultimate accent (e.g. in the nominative singular masculine form) even though the ultima was short, i.e. κεκελευμένος. In this way, therefore, accent placement in the verb serves also as a correlate of the morphosyntactic category of finiteness; recessive accent correlates with the presence of person and number markings on the verb, but not with the absence of such markings, in general.

With regard to the morphophonemics of Ancient Greek, three types of alternations must be distinguished: vowel alternations that represent a remnant — by then fully morphologically conditioned — of the Indo-European ablaut patterns (see pages 49–50), alternations caused by the sound changes that separate Greek from Proto-Indo-European and that distinguish the individual dialects of Greek itself, and alternations due to natural processes such as assimilation.

Within paradigms, except for a few irregular verbs (e.g. εἶ-μι 'I go' versus ἴ-μεν 'we go') with alternations between e-grade and zero-grade retained from the proto-language, the vowel alternations one finds in Greek are those of length. This situation occurs in a few verbs (e.g. δί-δω-μι 'I give' versus δί-δο-μεν 'we give', actually a remnant of Proto-Indo-European full-grade/zero-grade ablaut transformed in Greek into simply a length distinction) and in a large number of nominal forms of the consonant stem declension (e.g. nominative singular τέκτων 'carpenter' versus genitive singular τέκτον-ος, nominative singular ποιμήν 'shepherd' versus genitive singular ποιμέν-ος, masculine adjective ἀληθής 'true' versus neuter ἀληθές, etc.).

Across paradigms, between derivationally related forms of the same root, one finds alternations in vowel quality as well as quantity. For example, the inherited *e/o*-ablaut is found in numerous Greek pairs of related forms, such as λέγ-ω 'I say' versus λόγ-ος 'word', φέρ-ω 'I bear' versus φόρ-ος 'tribute, (tax) burden' (and compare also the related form φώρ 'thief (i.e. one who bears off something)' for a length alternation); moreover, it has a grammatical function still in forms such as present tense λείπ-ω 'I leave' versus perfect λέ-λοιπ-α 'I have left' (and note the zero-grade reflex in past ἔ-λιπ-ον 'I did leave'). This *e/o*-ablaut interacts with the development of the labio-velars to give etymologically related (but probably synchronically unrelated) pairs such as θείνω 'I strike' from *g^when-yo*: versus φόνος 'murder' from *g^whon-os*. Transformations of the Indo-European ablaut due to sound changes are also to be found, such as in the masculine stem τέκτον- 'carpenter' versus the feminine τέκταινα 'carpentress', where the -o-/-αι- alternation results from an alternation which in pre-Greek terms would have been *-on-Ø* versus *-n̥-ya* (with -αιν- from *-n̥y-*).

Among the sound changes that left traces in morphophonemic alternations, one noteworthy one that operates in noun paradigms is the loss of final stops. Thus one finds such alternations as γάλα 'milk' (nominative singular) versus γάλακτ-ος (genitive singular), or λέων 'lion' (nominative singular) versus λέοντ-ος (genitive). Similarly, the loss of medial *s* created paradigmatic alternations such as γένος-Ø 'race, kind' (nominative singular) versus γένε-α (nominative plural), from *genes-a*. Across paradigms, the developments of clusters with *y* gave rise to derivational alternations, since *-ye/o-* was an especially common present tense formative — compare ταραχ-ή 'trouble, disorder' with the related verb ταράττ-ω (Ionic ταράσσ-ω) 'disturb, trouble' from *tarak^h-yo:*, for example — and since *-y-* figured in other derivational processes, as with the formation of certain comparative adjectives (e.g. μέγ-ας 'big' versus μείζων 'bigger' from *meg-yo:n*). Furthermore, in dialects with the assibilation of *t* to *s* before *i*, one finds such alternations as πλοῦτ-ος 'wealth' versus πλούσ-ιος 'wealthy'. In addition, the *-s-* formative, which appeared in some past tense forms, created alternations in vowel quality with the dialectal resolution of resonant plus *s* clusters, e.g. νέμ-ω 'I distribute' versis ἔ-νειμ-α 'I distributed' (Doric ἔ-νημ-α, both from *e-nem-s-a*).

Finally, many morphophonemic alternations are the result of more or less natural processes that take effect when certain segments come together as the result of word formation processes. For example, assimilation in voicing is common, as seen in the pair ἄγ-ω 'I lead' versus ἄξ-ω (i.e. *ak-s-o:*) 'I will lead' where *-s-* is the marker for future tense, or in the pair κρύπ-τω 'I hide' versus κρύβ-δην 'secretly'. Similarly, deaspiration before -s- occurs, as in γράφ-ω 'I write' versus γράψ-ω (i.e. *grap-s-o:*) 'I will write', and assimilation in aspiration to a following aspirate is found as in τρίβ-ω 'I rub' versus ἐ-τρίφ-θην 'I was rubbed' (cf. also τρίψ-ω 'I will rub').

The phonology of Ancient Greek has been described in such detail here because it provides the appropriate starting point for a discussion of Post-Classical Greek phonology. The relation is not merely chronological here, for in Post-Classical Greek and on into Modern Greek, one finds that many of the same general phonological characteristics occur in the language, but with different realisations. For example, by the Hellenistic period, systematic shifts in the consonant inventory were under way — to be completed later in Post-Classical Greek — which nonetheless preserved the earlier three-way contrast but with new distinctive oppositions established. The voiced stops became voiced spirants and the voiceless aspirates became voiceless spirants, while the voiceless plain stops remained the same (in general). Thus one finds in Post-Classical Greek the system:

v	p	f
ð	t	θ
γ	k	χ

replacing the earlier *b p p^h/d t t^h/g k k^h* system. In addition, *z* became a distinctive sound (with phonemic status) and *h* was lost.

A [j] reentered the language, originally as an allophone of [γ] before front vowels and of unstressed [i] before vowels, but now it (probably) has phonemic status in the modern language. Similarly, throughout the post-classical period, new voiced stops (*b*, *d*, *g*) arose, first as allophones of voiceless (and original voiced) stops after homorganic nasals, and later as distinctive segments (although their synchronic status is still somewhat controversial) through further sound changes that obscured the original conditioning factors. Thus the verb ἐντρέπομαι 'I feel misgivings about' has yielded Modern Greek ντρέπομαι [drεpomε] 'I feel ashamed' through the stages *endrep-* > *edrep-* (with reduction of nasal plus stop clusters, a process still present but now sociolinguistically and stylistically conditioned, and still found in many of the regional dialects) > *drep-* (with loss of unstressed initial vowels, a sound change of Middle Greek). In addition, borrowings have provided new instances of voiced stops in the language (e.g. more recently μπάρ 'bar', ντάμα 'queen (in cards)', γκαράζ 'garage' etc., but some even as early as Hellenistic times).

Finally, in Middle Greek a *ts* and a *dz* were added to the language, partly through dialectal affrications and borrowings from other languages. These sounds probably represent unitary sounds (affricates) in the modern language, but a cluster analysis cannot be ruled out entirely for them.

The major changes in the vowel system were also beginning in the Hellenistic period, though, as noted above, some of the innovative pronunciations may have been associated with an originally non-standard sociolect of Attic Greek in the late classical period. The principal changes are as follows: length became non-distinctive; the diphthongs monophthongised, with [ai̯] becoming [ɛ], [yi̯] and [oi̯] becoming [i] (presumably through a stage of [y], still present probably as late as the tenth century AD), and the off-glide in [e(ː)u̯] and [au̯] becoming fully consonantal, realised as [f] before voiceless sounds and as [v] before voiced ones, and several of the height distinctions were neutralised with a tendency for vowels to move to [i]. The result is that the Modern Greek vowel system (and that of late Middle Greek as well) consists of five short 'pure' vowels: *i e a o u*. Sequences which are diphthong-like, though perhaps still to be analysed as true sequences of vowels, have arisen through the loss of intervening consonants, as with λέει ([leï]) '(s)he says' from Ancient Greek λέγει through the Middle (and careful Modern) Greek pronunciation [léyi], and through borrowings (e.g. τσάï 'tea', λαοῦτο 'lute', etc.). Nonetheless, there are some words that are probably best analysed as having underlying diphthongs, e.g. γάïδαρος 'donkey', which would violate the modern equivalent of the 'Dreimorengesetz' if it were /γáiðaros/.

Since the vowel length came to be non-distinctive in the later stages of Greek, it is not surprising that the principles upon which accent placement was based would change, inasmuch as vowel quantity mattered for Ancient Greek accent placement. Modern Greek generally has accent placed in the same positions in words as Ancient Greek, and the 'Dreimorengesetz' still holds now though as a 'three syllable rule'. The realisation of accent has changed, though, and Modern Greek now has a stress accent, not a pitch accent, with prominent stress corresponding to the earlier high (acute or circumflex) pitch (and note that by Middle Greek, the basis for poetic metre was syllable counting, with a 15-syllable line being the preferred metrical unit). Modern Greek thus has some of the same accent shifts as Ancient Greek, as for example in ἄνθρωπος 'man' (nominative singular) versus ἀνθρώπου (genitive), but because of the absence of a phonological motivation for them, numerous levellings have occurred, resulting in stable stress throughout a paradigm (as in πράσινος 'green' (nominative singular masculine) versus πράσινου (genitive) from Ancient Greek πράσινος/πρασίνου, and in dialectal forms such as ἄνθρωπου for standard ἀνθρώπου). The recessive accent rule for finite verb forms no longer holds in general, but is valid for the simple past and imperfect tenses of verbs which are stem-stressed (as opposed to end-stressed) in the present (e.g. νομίζω 'I think' versus νόμιζα 'I was thinking', νομίζαμε 'we were thinking', νόμισα 'I thought', νομίσαμε 'we thought'). Stress placement, though, is distinctive, as shown by pairs such as κοπή 'cutting' – κόποι 'troubles, reward', κύριος 'master' – κυρίως 'above all, chiefly', among others.

The major change in phonotactics concerns new final sequences which have entered the language through borrowings (e.g. final [l] in γκόλ 'goal' from English, final [z] in γκαράζ 'garage' from French, final [p] in the current slang expression εἶμαι ἄπ 'I am up (in spirits)' from English, etc.). One noteworthy change in allowable clusters, though, affected combinations of voiceless stops and combinations of Ancient Greek voiceless aspirated stops. Both types of clusters, e.g. πτ- and φθ-, have converged, through what has been described as a manner dissimilation, on the combination of voiceless fricative plus voiceless (unaspirated) stop. Thus earlier πτ has yielded φτ [ft], as in πτέρον 'feather' > φτέρο (with regular loss of final *n* as well), and earlier φθ has also yielded φτ, through a stage of [fθ], as in φθάνω > φτάνω 'I arrive'. The effects of the diglossia alluded to earlier can be seen especially clearly in this aspect of the phonology, for in many words of learned origin, the non-dissimilated clusters remain and both cluster types occur as stylistic variants within one and the same speaker's idiolect even, because of the stylistic mixing induced by the diglossic situation.

For the most part, the later stages of Greek preserved the same types of morphophonemic alternations as Ancient Greek, though again with different phonetic realisations. Thus one now finds alternations such as γράφ-ομε 'we write' versus γράψ-αμε 'we wrote' with an *f*/*p* alternation (Ancient Greek p^h/*p* alternation), ἀνοίγ-ω 'I open' versus ἄνοιξ-α 'I opened' with a *γ*/*k* alternation (Ancient Greek *g*/*k* alternation), where the structure of the alternations is the same but the segments involved have changed in part. Various morphological changes in the noun in particular have undone many of the Ancient Greek nominal alternations, as with Ancient Greek φλέψ (i.e. [p^{h}lep-s]) 'vein' (nominative singular) versus φλέβ-α (accusative) being remade to a paradigm with φλέβα [fleva], the continuation of the old accusative form, serving as the nominative and accusative form. One can still find the Ancient Greek alternations preserved relatively intact, though, in the archaising linguistic forms of early Post-Classical Greek on through Middle Greek and into Modern Greek; such forms are not — and probably never were — in current colloquial usage, however.

A final point about Post-Classical Greek phonology concerns some of the major differences that characterise the Modern, and to a large extent the Middle, Greek dialects. Characteristic of the northern dialect zone (north of Attica on the mainland, though excluding the urban Thessaloniki dialect, and the islands of the northern Aegean including Thasos, Samothraki, Lemnos and Lesbos, and also the more southerly Samos) is the raising of unstressed mid vowels and the deletion of unstressed high vowels. Thus one finds paradigms such as present [pirmén] '(s)he waits' (cf. standard περιμένει), imperfect [pirímini] '(s)he was waiting' (cf. standard περίμενε). This syncope has also given rise in these dialects to consonant clusters not found in the standard language and the more southerly and eastern dialects (e.g. [éstla] 'I sent' for standard ἔστειλα). Another isogloss distinguishing the regional dialects is the presence of palatalisations (especially [č] for [k] before front vowels) in the southeastern dialects (of Chios, the Dodekanese islands including Rhodes, and Cyprus), in Cretan and in Old Athenian (the dialect of Attica before the establishment of the standard language in the 1820s, which still survives in a few isolated pockets), but not in the northern dialects (in general, though [š] for [s] before front vowels is common) nor in the standard language, based as it is on the Peloponnesian-Ionian (Island) dialect.

4.2 Morphology

It is safe to say that the general character of Greek morphological structure has remained fairly stable over the 3,500 years of our knowledge of the language, though, of course, there have been numerous significant changes as well. Greek has been a fusional language throughout all stages in its development; in Middle and Modern Greek, though, there is a distinct tendency in the direction of analytic expressions, examples of which are given below *passim*. To illustrate the fusional character of the language, one need only consider the nominal ending -ους (Ancient Greek [-oːs], Modern Greek [-us]), for it marks accusative case, plural number and masculine gender, all in a single unanalysable unit, for the so-called *o*-stem nouns. Moreover, even though there is a nominal ending -ου and another nominal ending -*s*, so that one might attempt to analyse -ους as -ου plus -*s*, such an analysis cannot work: -ου marks genitive singular for masculine *o*-stem nouns and -*s* marks nominative singular for certain masculine and feminine consonant stem nouns in Ancient Greek and for masculine nouns in general in Modern Greek.

The relevant morphological categories for the Greek nominal system, comprising nouns, adjectives and pronouns, are as follows. In Ancient Greek, there were five cases (nominative, accusative, genitive, dative and vocative), three numbers (singular, dual and plural), and three genders (masculine, feminine and neuter). In Modern Greek, by contrast, there are four cases (nominative, accusative, genitive and vocative), two numbers (singular and plural), and the same three genders. The loss of the dative is under way as early as Hellenistic Greek, though this change was not completed until well into the Middle Greek era (in part because of the pressure from the learned language in which the dative was retained). In Modern Greek, the genitive case has assumed some of the typical functions of the earlier dative case, e.g. the expression of indirect objects, but one also finds, in keeping with the analytic tendency noted above, indirect objects expressed in a prepositional phrase (σ(έ) 'in, at, to', from Ancient Greek εἰς 'in, into', plus accusative). It is worth noting as well that the genitive plural is obsolescent in Modern Greek for many nouns and for many speakers, with periphrases of the preposition ἀπό 'from' plus accusative being used instead.

In both Ancient and Modern Greek, these nominal morphological categories were realised in different ways depending on the class of noun involved. In Ancient Greek, the assignment to inflectional class was based on phonological characteristics of the nominal stem, so that one finds *o*-stem nouns, *a:*-stem nouns and consonant stem nouns (including *i*- and *u*-stems as consonantal); within these stem classes, all three genders were represented, though feminine *o*-stems were rare as were masculine *a:*-stems (neuter *a:*-stems being non-existent). In Modern Greek, the assignment to inflectional class is by and large based on gender, not phonological stem shape, so that in general, the masculine nouns are inflected alike, especially in the singular, with -*s* in the nominative singular versus -Ø in the accusative singular and -Ø

Nominal Inflection in Ancient and Modern Greek

	Feminine a:-stem	Masculine o-stem	Neuter o-stem	Feminine Consonant stem	Masculine	Neuter
	γνώμα:- 'opinion'	λόγο- 'word'	δῶρο- 'gift'	φλέβ- 'vein'	φύλακ- 'watchman'	σῶματ- 'body'
Ancient Greek						
Nom. sg.	γνώμη	λόγος	δῶρον	φλέψ	φύλαξ	σῶμα
Acc. sg.	γνώμην	λόγον	δῶρον	φλέβα	φύλακα	σῶμα
Gen. sg.	γνώμης	λόγου	δώρου	φλεβός	φύλακος	σώματος
Dat. sg.	γνώμηι	λόγωι	δώρωι	φλεβί	φύλακι	σώματι
Voc. sg.	γνώμη	λόγε	δῶρον	φλέψ	φύλαξ	σῶμα
Nom. du.	γνώμα:	λόγω	δώρω	φλέβε	φύλακε	σώματε
Acc. du.	γνώμα:	λόγω	δώρω	φλέβε	φύλακε	σώματε
Gen. du.	γνώμαιν	λόγοιν	δώροιν	φλεβοῖν	φυλάκοιν	σωμάτοιν
Dat. du.	γνώμαιν	λόγοιν	δώροιν	φλεβοῖν	φυλάκοιν	σωμάτοιν
Voc. du.	γνώμα:	λόγω	δώρω	φλέβε	φύλακε	σώματε
Nom. pl.	γνώμαι	λόγοι	δῶρα	φλέβες	φύλακες	σώματα
Acc. pl.	γνώμα:ς	λόγους	δῶρα	φλέβας	φύλακας	σώματα
Gen. pl.	γνωμῶν	λόγων	δώρων	φλεβῶν	φυλάκων	σωμάτων
Dat. pl.	γνώμαις	λόγοις	δώροις	φλεψί	φύλαξι	σώμασι
Voc. pl.	γνώμαι	λόγοι	δῶρα	φλέβες	φύλακες	σώματα
Modern Greek						
Nom. sg.	γνώμη	λόγος	δώρο	φλέβα	φύλακας	σώμα
Acc. sg.	γνώμη	λόγο	δώρο	φλέβα	φύλακα	σώμα
Gen. sg.	γνώμης	λόγου	δώρου	φλέβας	φύλακα	σώματος
Voc. sg.	γνώμη	λόγε	δώρο	φλέβα	φύλακα	σώμα
Nom. pl.	γνώμες	λόγοι	δώρα	φλέβες	φύλακες	σώματα
Acc. pl.	γνώμες	λόγους	δώρα	φλέβες	φύλακες	σώματα
Gen. pl.	γνωμών	λόγων	δώρων	φλεβών	φυλάκων	σωμάτων
Voc. pl.	γνώμες	λόγοι	δώρα	φλέβες	φύλακες	σώματα

Note: Accentuation in Modern Greek forms follows current official monotonic orthography, with a single accentual diacritic. The colon (:) for length in the Ancient Greek forms is given here only to indicate pronunciation; it was not a part of the Ancient Greek orthography.

in the genitive singular, and the feminines are inflected alike, again especially in the singular, with a -Ø ending in the nominative and accusative singular versus -*s* in the genitive singular. As with most changes between Ancient and Modern Greek, the beginnings of this shift in inflectional class assignment can be seen early in the post-classical period. In the chart given here the inflection of six nouns is given for Ancient and Modern Greek by way of illustrating the basic patterns for these stages and of highlighting the differences between the two. Although the nominal system of Greek, especially the ancient language, shows a goodly number of inflectional categories and markers, it is the verbal system that presents the greatest morphological complexity in the language. Moreover, despite a number of reductions in this complexity between Ancient and Modern Greek, especially in the realm of non-finite verbal forms, Modern Greek still has a verbal system that is, in basic character, very like its ancient source.

Ancient Greek, for instance, distinguished three persons in verbal inflection, and three numbers (singular, dual and plural), although the combination of first person with dual number was not realised inflectionally in the language at all. A significant distinction was made in the verbal system between finite and non-finite forms, with the relevant morphological distinction for finiteness being the presence of person and number markings; as noted above in the section on accentuation, though, recessive accent placement also served to distinguish finite from non-finite forms. Among the non-finite forms were several different infinitives and several different participles, as enumerated below, differing in voice, aspect and tense, and two verbal adjectives (denoting capability and obligation, respectively).

As indicated, there were inflectional categories for voice, with active, passive and middle voice being distinguished. The middle voice indicated reflexive action (though there were also available in the language overt reflexive pronominal forms), or more generally, action one undertook on one's own behalf or to one's own benefit. For example, the active βουλεύω means 'to take counsel' while the middle βουλεύομαι means 'to take counsel with oneself, to deliberate', and the active λούω means 'to wash' while the middle λούομαι means 'to wash oneself, to bathe'. The passive was formally distinct from the middle only for future tense and simple past (aorist) forms. In addition, there were four moods, an indicative, a subjunctive, an optative (used in the expression of potentiality and for past time in indirect discourse, for example) and an imperative, all fully inflected for all the voice, number and person categories, as well as most of the temporal/aspectual categories described below.

Finally, Ancient Greek is usually described as having seven 'tenses', a present, a future, a (present) perfect, a pluperfect, a future perfect (which is usually passive), an imperfect past and a simple past (known as the aorist). In actuality, these 'tense' forms encoded two different types of distinctions — a purely temporal one of present time versus future time versus past time, and an aspectual one of action that is continuous (imperfective) versus action that is completed (perfective) versus action that is simply taking place (aoristic). The three-way distinction is realised fully in past time forms only, incompletely in the present, and via a formal merger of two categories in the future. These relations are summarised in table 19.4 below (adapted from Goodwin and Gulick 1958):

Table 19.4 Ancient Greek Tense-Aspect Relations

Tense Aspect	*Present*	*Past*	*Future*
Continuous	present	imperfect	future
Simple			
occurrence	(no realisation)	aorist	future
Completed	perfect	pluperfect	future perfect

Illustrative examples are: present γράφω 'I am writing', perfect γέγραφα 'I have written', imperfect ἔγραφον 'I was writing', aorist ἔγραψα 'I did write, I wrote', pluperfect ἐγεγράφη 'I had written', future γράψω 'I will be writing (continuous aspect), I will write (simple occurrence)', and future perfect γεγράψεται 'it will have been written'.

The non-finite forms show the aspectual nature of the category oppositions especially clearly, for one finds a present infinitive and participle, an aorist infinitive and participle, and a perfect infinitive and participle, corresponding to the continuous, simple and completed aspectual distinctions in the finite verbal system. In addition, though, there is a future infinitive and participle, so that the non-finite system too shows some purely temporal as well as aspectual distinctions. As with the different moods, the non-finite forms occur in all voices, so that there are 11 different infinitival types and a like number of participles.

Many of the complexities of this system are retained in Post-Classical Greek and on into Modern Greek, though in some instances, there is only apparent, and not actual, continuity. Some of the differences are the result of responses to system-internal pressures, as for example, with the changes in the voice and aspect categories, while others may have been, at least in part, induced by external factors, as with the changes in the non-finite system and the future tense. Many, however, are in keeping with a tendency toward analytic expressions where Ancient Greek had synthetic ones.

The only difference in person and number categories is that, as in nominal inflection, the dual number category has been eliminated, its demise evident as early as Hellenistic Greek. The moods too have been altered. The optative began to fall into disuse in the Koine period, partly as a result, no doubt, of sound changes leading to partial homophony (in four of eight forms) with the subjunctive and (less so) with the indicative. Similarly, it is a matter of some debate even today as to whether Greek now has a distinct subjunctive mood, for there is no formal difference between the continuation of the old present indicative and present subjunctive due to various sound changes, and virtually all 'subjunctive' uses are marked with a verbal particle νά, giving an analytic counterpart to the Ancient Greek synthetic subjunctive (e.g. νὰ γράψεις versus ancient γράψηις 'that you (might) write'). Finally, where Ancient Greek had synthetic forms for non-second person imperatives, Modern Greek has, again, analytic forms, marked by the particle ἄς, though distinct (synthetic) second person imperative forms remain.

Greek maintains an opposition among active, middle and passive voices, though from a formal standpoint, the middle voice and passive voice are never distinct; the cover term medio-passive is thus perhaps more appropriate. This development seems to be a natural outgrowth of the Ancient Greek system in which the distinction was realised formally only in the aorist and future tenses but in no others. Thus in Modern Greek, and earlier stages of Post-Classical Greek as well, a form such as πλύθηκα, a medio-passive aorist of the verb πλύνω 'wash', can mean 'I was washed (by someone)' or 'I washed myself', with the context of the utterance generally being the only determinant of which of these interpretations is preferred.

The Ancient Greek tenses all remain in Modern Greek, but here the continuity is apparent only. In the Koine period, the perfect tense system was eliminated, with the simple past (aorist) taking over some of the old perfect functions and various periphrastic (i.e. analytic) constructions (e.g. εἰμί 'be' plus the perfect participle) taking over other of its functions. Thus there was a period in the post-classical language in which there was no formal perfect tense system. By the middle of the Middle Greek period, approximately the tenth century, though, a pluperfect arose, formed with the aorist of 'have' plus one continuation of the Ancient Greek infinitive (e.g. εἶχα γράψαι 'I had written', later εἶχα γράψει); this construction was originally used, in late Hellenistic and early Middle Greek, as a conditional but later passed over into a true pluperfect meaning. The relation between it and the *habeō* + infinitive/participle formations found in Vulgar Latin and Romance (see page 208–9) is uncertain, but some influence through Balkan Romance cannot be discounted. From that pluperfect, a new perfect system, with the full range of inflectional categories, was spawned; a present perfect was created consisting of the present of 'have' plus this continuation of the old infinitive, and later a future perfect was formed with the Middle and Modern Greek future formants, an imperative perfect arose, etc. The Modern Greek perfect system, therefore, represents a considerable elaboration within the Post-Classical Greek verbal system, and though only indirectly connected with them, parallels the Ancient Greek perfect system forms.

Similarly, Modern Greek has a future tense, just as Ancient Greek had, but again one finds an analytic expression in place of the earlier synthetic one, with only an indirect connection between the two forms. In the case of the future, though, as opposed to the perfect, there seems never to have been a period in which the future tense failed to exist as a formal category in the language. Within the Hellenistic period, the use of the older synthetic future, e.g. γράψω 'I will write', became obsolescent, with various periphrases arising to compete with it, including the present of 'have' plus a continuation of the infinitive and other quasi-modal constructions (e.g. μέλλω 'be about to' plus infinitive). With the passage of the 'have' forms into the incipient perfect system, as just described, a new future periphrasis arose, by the tenth century, completely ousting the earlier synthetic form. This was a future based on the verb 'want' (θέλω); as with the perfect, the relation between this form and similar ones found in virtually all the Balkan languages is controversial. In the medieval period, an unusual variety of future formations with this verb can be found, consisting of combinations of inflected forms of θέλω plus uninflected (infinitival) main verbs, uninflected (i.e. invariant third person singular) forms of θέλω plus inflected forms of main verbs, inflected forms of θέλω plus inflected forms of a main verb, the optional use of the verbal particle νά and so forth; representative examples of these patterns would be θέλω γράψει(ν) (infinitive), θέλει (invariant) (νὰ) γράψω, θέλω (νὰ) γράψω, all meaning 'I will write'. Ultimately, the formation of the type θέλει νὰ γράψω won out, and through various reductions, the modern standard and widespread dialectal future particle θά (e.g. θά γράψω 'I will write') was created.

Going along with these future formations were parallel conditional formations consisting of a past tense of the auxiliary-like verb plus a form of the main verb (compare the ἔχω 'have' plus infinitive future and εἶχα plus infinitive conditional of early Post-Classical Greek). These conditional formations have no formal category correspondent in Ancient Greek (the modal particle ἄν with the optative mood is the Ancient Greek potential/conditional expression), so that here too one finds an elaboration within the earlier tense/mood system.

The aspectual system too has undergone various rearrangements from the Ancient Greek system. In this case, the internal pressures within the system, partly as a result of the incomplete realisation of the aspect system within the tense system (see table 19.4) were a major factor in the developments. The basic opposition of continuous versus punctual aspect has been maintained throughout the development of Post-Classical Greek and, with the new periphrastic formations, has been extended to the future tense as well (e.g. θά γράφω 'I will be writing' versus θά γράψω 'I will write', in Modern Greek, or θέλω γράφει(ν) versus θέλω γράψει(ν) in Middle Greek). The completed aspect category now finds expression in the new perfect system, though one can still find uses of the simple past (aorist) which signal completed action as opposed to simply past action, as with the 'pro futuro' use of the aorist (e.g. ἔφυγα 'I'm about to leave' lit. 'I (have) left; my leaving is over and done with').

Finally, Modern Greek, as well as Post-Classical Greek in general, maintains the Ancient Greek distinction of finite versus non-finite forms, though this opposition has undergone perhaps the greatest series of restructurings of any part of the verbal system. In particular, the realisation of the opposition has changed considerably. In Ancient Greek the imperative patterned with the finite forms in terms of accent placement and person/number markings, while in Modern Greek it patterns instead with the non-finite forms; like the participles (and unlike, for example, the indicative), the imperative allows only enclitic pronoun objects and not proclitic ones, and like the participles (and again unlike the indicative), it is arguably marked only for number and not for person (cf. singular δές '(you) see!' versus plural δέσ-τε '(you) see!' where the only formal difference is -∅ versus -τε and the only semantic difference singular versus plural) — recall that non-second person imperative forms of Ancient Greek gave way to analytic expressions with the particle ἄς in later Greek. Moreover, the number of participles has been reduced, so that Modern Greek has only a present (continuous aspect) medio-passive participle (e.g γραφόμενος 'being written') and a present (continuous aspect) active participle, also called a gerundive, which generally serves only as an adverbial adjunct modifying the surface subject of a sentence (e.g. γράφοντας '(while) writing').

Similarly, the category of *infinitive* has been eliminated entirely from the language, although the indications are that it was maintained until approximately the sixteenth century as at least a marginal category. The details of this development are discussed more in the following section on syntax. The only remnant of the earlier infinitive is in the new perfect system, for the second part of the perfect periphrasis (γράψει in ἔχω γράψει 'I have written') continues a Middle Greek analogical replacement for the Ancient Greek aorist infinitive (so also in the medio-passive, e.g. ἔχει γραφθεῖ 'it has been written' from Middle Greek ἔχει γραφθῆν(αι)). There is no synchronic justification, though, for treating these remnants as categorically distinct within the morphology, and they perhaps are to be considered now as the punctual aspect counterparts to the continuous aspect participles (thus γράψει versus γραφθεῖ as γράφοντας versus γραφόμενος). In both the case of the reduction of the participle and the case of the demise of the infinitive, the Modern Greek situation represents the end-point of a long and gradual process whose roots are to be found in Hellenistic Greek usage of the non-finite forms.

4.3 Syntax

A considerable amount of space has been spent on the phonology and morphology of Greek, both from a synchronic standpoint for relevant periods and from a diachronic standpoint, in part because it is possible to give a fairly complete picture of these components of a language in a relatively short space. With regard to the syntax, it is of course impossible to do justice to any stage of the language in anything less than a full-sized monograph (and it is worth noting that there are numerous lengthy works dealing with individual constructions in single periods of the language). Nonetheless, a few of the especially noteworthy aspects of the syntactic combinations of the language can be mentioned, along with a sketch of their development over the centuries.

Perhaps one of the most elaborate parts of the Ancient Greek syntactic system was the system of verbal complementation. Not only were there so many non-finite forms — infinitives and participles — available which were utilised in forming complements to main verbs, but there were also a good number of finite forms, differing, as has been described, in aspect and mood, which could combine with a variety of subordinating conjunctions to form verbal complements. Thus a major part of the description of Ancient Greek syntax must deal with the question of how the moods, aspects and non-finite forms were actually used. Not surprisingly, there is a fairly complex set of sequence of tense conditions governing allowable combinations of main verb and dependent verb, especially in indirect discourse and in conditional sentences.

One significant development in the verbal complementation system in later stages of Greek is the demise of the infinitive, mentioned above in its purely morphological context. From as early as Hellenistic Greek, finite clause complements are found in places in which Classical Greek had used an infinitive (or even participle). For example, in the New Testament, a finite clause complement is found in competition with an infinitive with the adjective ἄξιος 'worthy, deserving', a context in which only an infinitival complement could appear in Classical Greek:

(a) οὗ   οὐκ εἰμὶ   ἄξιος τὸ ὑπόδημα τῶν ποδῶν   λῦσαι
                                                         (Acts 13.25)
    whose not am/1 sg. worthy the-sandal   the-feet/gen. loosen/infin.
    '(One) of whom I am not worthy to loosen the sandal from his feet.'
(b) οὗ οὐκ εἰμὶ ἐγὼ ἄξιος ἵνα λύσω   αὐτοῦ τὸν ἱμάντα τοῦ
                                          ὑποδήματος   (Jo. 1.27)
    I/nom.   that loosen/1 sg. subj. his   the-thong/acc.
                                          of-the-sandal

The spread of finite complementation, most usually introduced by the particle ἵνα (later Greek νά through an irregular stress shift and regular sound changes) but also with the true complementisers such as the neutral ὅτι (comparable to English *that*), at the expense of infinitival complements continued throughout the post-classical era, working its way through syntactically defined classes of construction type (e.g. like-subject complements versus unlike-subject complements) and within each such class diffusing across the range of governing lexical items. By Middle Greek, the only productive uses of the infinitive were with the verbs ἔχω and θέλω in the perfect and future periphrases, respectively, though a few sporadic uses of the infinitive with other verbs (e.g. (ἠ)μπορῶ 'can') and as an adverbial adjunct are to be found as well.

The spread of finite complementation is complete, though, in Modern Greek, and there are no instances of non-finite complementation remaining. Thus from the standpoint of typology, Modern Greek, unlike its predecessors, is a language in which all complement verbs are fully finite, marked for person, number and tense/aspect. Greek thus now diverges considerably from the Indo-European 'norm', but interestingly, as noted earlier, converges on this point with the other languages of the Balkans; in fact, Greek, along with Macedonian, shows the greatest degree of infinitive loss among all the Balkan languages. As with the other Balkan areal features, the extent to which the developments with the infinitive represent an internal development in Greek (and the other languages) or a contact-induced one is debated; in this case, a combination of internal and external factors seems to provide the best account for this phenomenon within each language, Greek included, and within the Balkans as a whole.

It is to be noted, moreover, that the replacement of the infinitive by finite expressions with a verbal particle ties in with the general trend towards analytic constructions seen in the morphology. Other syntactic reflexes of this move towards analysis include comparison productively via the particle πιό with an adjective in Modern Greek versus a bound suffix -τερος in Ancient Greek (e.g. ἀξιώτερος 'more worthy' > πιό ἄξιος), and the expression of indirect objects with a prepositional phrase (σ(έ) plus accusative) versus the Ancient Greek dative case alone.

The developments with the moods and the tenses and the infinitive between Ancient and Modern Greek show also a trend towards the development of a system of preverbal particles, for example the future particle θά, the subjunctive and infinitival replacement particle νά, the non-second person imperatival ἄς (from earlier ἄφησε 'let', itself an imperative). A further reflection of this development is to be seen in the pronominal system of Modern Greek as compared with that of Ancient Greek. While Ancient Greek had both strong forms of the personal pronouns and weak (clitic) forms, the weak forms were restricted to the oblique (non-nominative) cases only, and use of the clitic genitive forms in the expression of possession was somewhat limited; true possessive adjectives were substitutable for the clitic forms in all persons and numbers and were the preferred variant in the first and second person plural. In Modern Greek, by contrast, there is now a set of nominative clitic pronominal forms (though they are restricted to use just with the deictic particle νά 'here (is)!' and the interrogative particle ποῦ(ν) 'where (is)?') and the primary means of expressing possession is with clitic genitive forms of the personal pronouns for all persons and numbers. Thus in Ancient Greek one finds both ὁ σὸς ἀδελφός (lit. 'the your brother') and ὁ ἀδελφός σου (lit. 'the brother of you') for 'your brother', while Modern Greek has only the latter type.

Similarly, the clitic object pronouns (both accusative and genitive) of Ancient Greek have been expanded in use in Modern Greek. In particular, they are now quite commonly used to cross-index definite and specific objects, as in:

(a) τόν   εἶδα   τόν Γιάννη
    him/acc. clit. saw/1 sg. the-John/acc.
    'I see John.'
(b) τοῦ   (τό)   ἔδωσα   τοῦ Γιάννη   τό βιβλίο
    him/gen. clit. it/acc. clit. gave/1 sg. the-John/gen. the-book/acc.
    'I gave the book to John.'

This feature represents another way in which Modern Greek diverges from Ancient Greek in the direction of the other Balkan languages (though again the causes for the divergence and convergence are subject to debate). For some speakers of Greek, this clitic doubling is obligatory at least for indirect objects, while for others it is an optional process with an emphatic function.

Two relatively stable elements of the syntax of Greek over the centuries are to be found in the syntax of the nominal system — the use of the definite article and adjectival position. The development of a definite article took place within the history of Greek, for in Homeric Greek, the form which became the Classical definite article is generally used as a demonstrative pronoun, and a few traces of this usage survive in the classical language. The definite article in classical times came to be used also as a means of substantivising virtually any part of speech or phrasal category, including adverbs (e.g. τοῖς τότε 'to the (men) of that time' (lit. 'the (dat. pl. masc.) then')), infinitives, whether alone or in a verb phrase (e.g. τὸ δρᾶν 'the acting, action', τὸ βίαι πολίτων δρᾶν 'acting in defiance of citizens'), and so on. Moreover, virtually any type of modifier, whether adverb, prepositional phrase, noun phrase or adjective, could be placed between the article and a modified noun. This construction with the definite article and modified nominals is to be found throughout the history of Greek, so that in Modern Greek in place of the 'articular infinitive' one finds nominalised finite clauses (e.g. τό νά εἶναι ῞Ελληνας 'the (fact of) being a Greek'), extended prenominal modifiers (though these can have a bookish feel, e.g. ὁ μορφομένος στό Παρίσι γειτονάς μου 'my educated-in-Paris neighbour'), etc.

As just noted, adjectives could in Ancient Greek, and still can in Modern Greek, appear prenominally. Throughout the history of Greek, there has been an important contrast in the position of an adjective based on its function. An adjective standing outside the article had, and still has, a predicative function, defining a clause without the necessity for an overt copular verb, e.g.:

(a) καλός   ὁ ἀδελφός   (b) ὁ ἀδελφὸς καλός
good (nom. sg. m.)   the-brother (nom. sg.)
'The brother is good.'

When the adjective occurs between the article and the noun or if no article is present, then the adjective has attributive function, and a noun phrase is defined:

(a) ὁ καλὸς ἀδελφός   (b) καλὸς ἀδελφός
    'the good brother'   'a good brother'

Other aspects of Greek word order have remained more or less stable throughout its development. In particular Greek has always enjoyed a relatively free ordering of the major constituents of a sentence, with grammatical relations and relations among constituents being encoded in the inflectional morphology, although certain patterns seem to be preferred in particular contexts (e.g. verb–subject–object order in the modern language in sentences presenting wholly new information).

4.4 Lexicon

At all points in its history, the Greek lexicon has incorporated a large number of native (inherited) lexical roots and stems. As noted earlier, some of these have remained more or less intact over the years, e.g. ἄνεμος 'wind', ἄλλος 'other'; more usually, though, words in Modern Greek show the effects of regular sound changes, e.g. γράφω 'I write' (with [γ] and [f] for earlier [g] and [pʰ]), μέρα 'day' (Ancient Greek ἡμέρα), changes in form and meaning, e.g. χῶμα 'bank, mound (Ancient Greek); soil (Modern)' and morphological reshapings (e.g. φύλακας versus φύλαξ — see the chart of nominal inflection). Finally, many words in the later language are built up out of native elements but with no direct ancestor in the ancient language, e.g. πιστοποίηση 'guarantee', and the many modern scientific terms built out of Greek morphemes by non-Greek speakers and reborrowed back into Greek, e.g. ἀτμοσφαῖρα 'atmosphere'.

At the same time, though, there has always been also in Greek a significant number of foreign elements. Ancient loans from Semitic (e.g. χιτών 'tunic', σαγήνη 'large drag-net'), Anatolian (e.g. κύανος 'dark blue enamel', κύμβαχος 'crown of a helmet'), and other languages of the ancient Near East can be identified, and as noted in section 2 above, there may be numerous words in Ancient Greek taken over from the languages indigenous to Greece before the arrival of the Greeks proper. During the

Hellenistic period, a major source of loanwords into Greek was Latin. During the later periods, one finds first an influx of Venetian (Italian) words and somewhat later an admixture of some Slavonic and Albanian words but mainly Turkish lexical items and phrases. More recently, loans from French and especially English have entered the language in great numbers. One final important source of borrowings in Greek has always been Greek itself; due to the long literary record of the language and the importance placed from a sociolinguistic standpoint on the literary language (recall the discussion of Greek diglossia in section 2), there has always been pressure to borrow from the literary language into the colloquial language, so that Modern Greek now has an internal lexical stratification parallel to what is found in Slavonic or Romance.

Bibliography

With the possible exception of English, there has probably been more written on the Greek language than on any other language. Consequently, giving references for information on Greek in its various aspects is difficult. None the less, it is possible to identify a number of basic and representative works on the language.

Grammars of the Ancient language abound, and the most detailed available, though a bit difficult to use because of a somewhat odd arrangement of facts, is Schwyzer (1939) and Schwyzer and Debrunner (1950). This work, moreover, contains much information on the historical development of the language and on the ancient dialects. For practical purposes, the more pedagogically oriented grammars of Smyth (1920) or Goodwin and Gulick (1958) contain sufficient information for the understanding of the structure of the language. Vilborg (1960) offers a grammatical sketch of Mycenaean Greek, as does Ventris and Chadwick (1973). More specialised works include Lejeune (1972) (on the historical phonology in general, including Mycenaean), Sommerstein (1973) (a generative treatment of Attic phonology), Teodorsson (1974) (also on Attic phonology) and Chantraine (1973) (on the morphology, especially diachronically). The basic treatment in English of the dialects is Buck (1955).

For the Hellenistic period, the best grammars available are Moulton (1908) and Blass and Debrunner (1961), both of which deal primarily with New Testament Greek.

For Greek of the Byzantine and Medieval periods, unfortunately no standard grammar is available. Perhaps the best general statement on Greek of that period is the (relatively brief) description found in Browning (1982). More is available on the modern language, and many of the historically oriented works fill in some of the gaps in the literature on Middle Greek, Mirambel (1939; 1959) are standard structuralist treatments of Modern Greek, and Householder et al. (1964) provides a useful account in English. Though now a bit outdated, however, Thumb (1964) is the best general work available in English, providing much on the dialects and general historical development of Modern Greek as well as numerous sample texts. Newton (1972) is a study within the generative framework of Greek dialect phonology, including, to a certain extent, the dialect bases of the standard language. Warburton (1970) and Sotiropoulos (1972) provide a modern treatment of the verb and noun respectively. As yet there is no full-length generative study of Greek syntax, though there is a growing body of such literature (see Kalmoukos and Phillipaki-Warburton (1982) for some references, many in English).

Finally, there are several general surveys of the Greek language, covering all or most of the stages in its development. Meillet (1920) and Palmer (1980) focus more on the earlier stages, though both treat Middle and Modern Greek as well. Browning (1982) focuses primarily on the later stages, but gives the necessary background on the early stages too. Mention can also be made of Costas (1936), Atkinson (1933), Thomson (1966), and Householder and Nagy (1972).

References

Atkinson, B.F.C. 1933. *The Greek Language* (Faber and Faber, London)

Blass, F. and A. Debrunner. 1961. *A Greek Grammar of the New Testament and Other Early Christian Literature* (Cambridge University Press, Cambridge; translated and revised by R. Funk from the 9th-10th ed. of *Grammatik des neutestamentlichen Griechisch*, Vandenhoeck and Ruprecht, Göttingen)

Browning, R. 1982 *Medieval and Modern Greek* (Cambridge University Press, Cambridge)

Buck, C.D. 1955. *The Greek Dialects*, revised ed. (University of Chicago Press, Chicago, reprinted 1973)

Chantraine, P. 1973. *Morphologie historique du grec*, 2nd ed. (Klincksieck, Paris)

Costas, P. 1936. *An Outline of the History of the Greek Language with Particular Emphasis on the Koine and the Subsequent Periods* (reprinted by Ares Publishers, Chicago, 1979)

Goodwin, W. and C. Gulick. 1958. *Greek Grammar* (Blaisdell, Waltham, Mass.)

Householder, F., K. Kazazis and A. Koutsoudas. 1964. *Reference Grammar of Literary Dhimotiki* (Mouton, The Hague)

Householder, F. and G. Nagy. 1972. *Greek. A Survey of Recent Work* (Mouton, The Hague)

Kalmoukos, X. and I. Philippaki-Warburton. 1982. 'Βιβλιογραφικό σημείωμα των εργασιών σχετικά με την σύνταξη και την μορφολογία της Νέας Ελληνικής που έχουν εκπονηθεί κατά το πρότυπο της γενετικής μετασχηματιστικής γραμματικής' ('Bibliographic Notice of Works Concerning the Syntax and Morphology of Modern Greek which have been Produced According to the Model of Generative-Transformational Grammar'), *Mantatoforos*, vol. 20, pp. 8–17

Lejeune, M. 1972. *Phonétique historique du mycénien et du grec ancien* (Klincksieck, Paris)

Meillet, A. 1920. *Aperçu d'une histoire de la langue grecque*, 2nd ed. (Hachette, Paris)

Mirambel, A. 1939. *Précis de grammaire élémentaire du grec moderne* (Société d'Édition 'Les Belles Lettres', Paris)

—— 1959. *La langue grecque moderne: description et analyse* (Paris)

Moulton, J. 1908. *A Grammar of N.T. Greek* (T. and T. Clark, Edinburgh)

Newton, B. 1972. *(The Generative Interpretation of Dialect: A Study of Modern Greek Phonology* (Cambridge University Press, Cambridge)

Palmer, L. 1980. *The Greek Language* (Humanities Press, Atlantic Heights, NJ)

Schwyzer, E. 1939. *Griechische Grammatik, I: Lautlehre, Wortbildung, Flexion* (C.H. Beck, Munich)

—— and A. Debrunner, 1950. *Griechische Grammatik, 2: Syntax und syntaktische Stilistik* (C.H. Beck, Munich)

Smyth, H. 1920. *A Greek Grammar for Colleges* (American Book Co., New York)

Sommerstein, A. 1973. *The Sound Pattern of Ancient Greek* (Basil Blackwell, Oxford)

Sotiropoulos, D. 1972. *Noun Morphology of Modern Demotic Greek* (Mouton, The Hague)

Teodorsson, S.-T. 1974. *The Phonemic System of the Attic Dialect, 400–340* BC (= Studia Graeca et Latina Gothoburgensia XXXVI, Göteborg)

Thomson, G. 1966. *The Greek Language*, 2nd ed. (Heffer, Cambridge)

Thumb, A. 1964. *A Handbook of the Modern Greek Language: Grammar, Texts, Glossary* (Argonaut Inc., Chicago; translated from the 2nd ed. of *Handbuch der neugriechischen Volkssprache. Grammatik. Texte. Glossar*, Karl I. Trübner, Strassburg)

Ventris, M. and J. Chadwick. 1973. *Documents in Mycenaean Greek*, 2nd ed. (Cambridge University Press, Cambridge)

Vilborg, E. 1960. *A Tentative Grammar of Mycenaean Greek* (= Studia Graeca et Latina Gothoburgensia IX, Göteborg)

Warburton, I. 1970. *On the Verb in Modern Greek* (Mouton, The Hague)

20 Indo-Aryan Languages

George Cardona

1 Introduction

Indo-Aryan languages, the easternmost group within Indo-European, are spoken by approximately five hundred million persons in India, Pakistan, Bangladesh, Nepal and other parts of the Himalayan region, as well as in Sri Lanka. Gypsy (Romany) dialects of the USSR, the Middle East and North America are also of Indo-Aryan origin. Indo-Aryan is most closely related to Iranian, with which it forms the Indo-Iranian subgroup, speakers of which shared linguistic and cultural features, including a name they called themselves (Sanskrit *ārya-*, Avestan *airya-*). Among the innovations that characterise Indo-Iranian is the merger of Proto-Indo-European *ĕ*, *ŏ*, *ă* into *ă*: Skt. *asti* 'is', *pati-* 'master, husband', *ajati* 'leads', *dadhāti* 'puts, makes', *dadāti* 'gives', *mātr̥-* 'mother': Av. *asti*, *paiti-*, *azaiti*, *dadāiti* ('puts, makes, gives'), *mātar-*: Gk. *estì*, *pósis*, *ágei*, *títhēsi*, *dídōsi*, *mā́tēr* (Dor.). Two major phonological features distinguish Indo-Aryan from the rest of Indo-European, including Iranian. One of these is an inherited property: Indo-Aryan retains voiced aspirated stops, as in Skt. *gharma-* 'warmth', *dadhāti*, *bharati* 'carries'. The other is an innovation: Indo-Aryan languages distinguish dental and retroflex stops. Originally, retroflex *-ḍ-*, *-ḍh-* arose through sound changes, as in Skt. *nīḍa-* 'resting place, nest', *mīḍha-* 'reward', with *-īḍ-*, *-īḍh-* from *-iẓḍ-*, *-iẓḍh-* (< *-izd-*, *-izdh-*). Such developments resulted in contrastive retroflex stops, albeit restricted, and the compass of such consonants was extended through borrowings from Dravidian languages. Most Indo-Aryan languages still have voiced aspirates and retroflex stops, although in certain ones, abutting on non-Indo-Aryan languages, these contrasts have been reduced: Sinhalese (Sinhala) has no aspirated stops, Kashmiri lacks voiced aspirates and Assamese (Asamiya) has no retroflex stops.

Old Indo-Aryan is represented in numerous sources (see the chapter on Sanskrit). The earliest preserved Middle Indo-Aryan documents are Aśoka's edicts (third century BC), in various dialects. Middle Indo-Aryan languages were also used for other literary, philosophical and religious works. The Buddhist canon and later treatises of Theravada Buddhism are

440

in Pāli, the Jaina canon in Ardhamāgadhī; Jainas also used Jaina Māhārāṣṭrī and Śaurasenī in works. The literary exemplar of Middle Indo-Aryan, however, is Māhārāṣṭrī, and the most advanced stages of Middle Indo-Aryan developments are found in Apabhraṁśa dialects, used as literary vehicles from before the sixth century. All Middle Indo-Aryan varieties can be subsumed under the label Prakrit (Skt. *prākṛta-*, Pkt. *pāia-* 'stemming from the original, natural'), referring to vernaculars in contrast to the polished language called *saṁskṛta*. Traditionally, most Indian commentators and grammarians of Prakrits derive these from Sanskrit, but there are formations in Prakrits found in Vedic sources but not in Classical Sanskrit. Thus, as Classical Sanskrit is not derivable from a single attested Vedic dialect, so the Prakrits cannot be derived from Classical Sanskrit. In the present sketch, I use *Prakrit* in a narrow sense, of Middle Indo-Aryan languages other than Aśokan dialects, Pāli or Apabhraṁśa. There are abundant literary sources for New Indo-Aryan languages from the twelfth century on, some materials from earlier times.

Several scripts have been and currently are used for Indo-Aryan languages. In ancient times, two major scripts were used on the subcontinent: Kharoṣṭhī, written from right to left, was predominantly used in the north-west, Brāhmī, written from left to right, elsewhere. Most scripts used for Indo-Aryan languages stem from Brāhmī, including Devanāgarī (see section 2 of the chapter on Sanskrit), widely employed for Sanskrit and now the official script for Hindi, Marathi, Nepali. The Arabic script, with modifications, is used for some Indo-Aryan languages, including Urdu.

2   Phonological and Grammatical Developments

In the following, I sketch major phonological and grammatical developments that characterise Middle and New Indo-Aryan, using Old Indo-Aryan as a point of reference (see sections 1.2, 2 of the chapter on Sanskrit).

2.1   Phonology

In Middle Indo-Aryan, word-final consonants other than *-m*, which developed to *-ṁ* with shortening of a preceding vowel, were lost: Skt. *putrāt* (abl. sg.) 'son', *putrās* (nom. pl.), *putram* (acc. sg.): Pāli *puttā*, *puttaṁ*. Interior clusters of dissimilar consonants were generally eliminated through assimilation (as in *puttā*) or epenthesis: Skt. *sakthi-* 'thigh', *varga-* 'group', *agni-* 'fire', *śukla-* 'white', *pakva-* 'cooked, ripe', *satya-* 'true', *adya* 'today': Pāli *satthi-*, *vagga-*, with assimilation of the first consonant to the second, *aggi-*, *sukka-*, *pakka-*, with the second consonant assimilated to the first, and *sacca-*, *ajja-*, with palatalisation; similarly, Skt. *rājñā* (inst. sg.) 'king', *rājñas* (gen. sg.): *rāññā*, *rāñño* in the Girnār version of Aśoka's first rock edict, but *lājinā*, *lājine*, with epenthesis, in the Jaugaḍa version. Generally, a nasal remains unassimilated before an obstruent: Skt. Pāli *danta-* 'tooth'. Metathesis applies in clusters of *h* with nasals or *y*, *v*: Skt. *cihna-* 'mark', *sahya-* 'to be endured', *jihvā-* 'tongue': Pāli *cinha-*, *sayha-*, *jivhā-*. Clusters of voiceless spirants with obstruents develop to obstruent sequences with aspiration: Skt. *paścāt* 'afterwards', *hasta-* 'hand': Pāli *pacchā*, *hattha-*. Further, clusters with voiceless spirants and nasals show voice assimilation and metathesis, resulting in nasals followed by *h*: Skt. *tṛṣṇā-* 'thirst, longing': Pāli *taṇhā-*. Initial clusters changed in the same ways, with subsequent simplification: Skt. *prathama-* 'first', *tyajati* 'abandons', *skandha-* 'shoulder', *snāti* 'bathes': Pāli *paṭhama-*, *cajati*, *khandha-*, *nhāyati*. In compounds and preverb-verb combinations where the assimilated cluster was intervocalic, it was retained, resulting in alternations such as Pāli *pamāṇa-* 'measure': *appamāṇa-* 'without measure, endless' (Skt. *pramāṇa-*, *apramāṇa-*). In early Middle Indo-Aryan, word-internal single consonants were retained, as shown in examples cited. Later, as exemplified in Māhārāṣṭrī, non-labial non-retroflex unaspirated obstruents were generally deleted, and *p*, *b* changed to *v*: *loa-* 'world, people', *naa-* 'mountain', *paura-* 'ample', *gaa-* 'elephant', *viāṇa-* 'awning', *savaha-* 'oath': Skt. *loka-*, *naga-*, *pracura-*, *gaja-*, *vitāna-*, *śapatha-*. Presumably, an intermediate step prior to loss involved the voicing of consonants, and some dialects reflect this; for example, in Śaurasenī intervocalic dentals were voiced (*ido* 'hence', *tadhā* 'thus': Skt. *itas*, *tathā*), and *thūbe* 'stupa' (Skt. *stūpas*) occurs in Aśokan. The loss of consonants resulted in word-internal sequences of vowels that were not found in Old Indo-Aryan, though such vowels were separated by *y*, *v* in some dialects. Intervocalic non-retroflex aspirates generally changed to *h*, but *-ṭ-*, *-ṭh-* were voiced, and *-ḍ-* developed to *-ḷ-*, whence *-l-*: Pkt. *sāhā-* 'branch', *meha-* 'cloud', *naḍa-* 'actor', *maḍha-* 'cloister' (Skt. *śākhā-*, *megha-*, *naṭa-*, *maṭha-*), Skt. *krīḍati* 'plays': Pāli *kīḷati*, Pkt. *kīlai*. The spirantal system of Old Indo-Aryan was also generally simplified. On the evidence of Aśokan documents, dialects of the extreme north-west retained *ś ṣ s*, as in Shāhbāzgaṛhī *paśucikisa* 'medical treatment for cattle', *vaṣeṣu* (loc. pl.) 'years'. But elsewhere the sibilants merged to *s*, and later in the east, as represented by Māgadhī, one has *ś* (e.g. *keśeśu* (loc. pl.) 'hair', *śahaśśa-* 'thousand': Skt. *keśeṣu*, *sahasra-*). In Apabhraṁśa, *-s(s)-* developed to *-h-*, as in *taho* 'of that' (Pāli *tassa*, Skt. *tasya*), and intervocalic nasals lost their occlusion, resulting in nasalisation, as in *gāū* 'village' (Pkt. *gāmo*, Skt. *grāmas*), *pasāē* 'through the grace of' (Pkt. *pasāeṇa*, Skt. *prasādena*).

The Middle Indo-Aryan vowel system also shows major developments. As shown, word-internal vowel sequences not permitted earlier now occurred. Conversely, overheavy syllables — with long vowels followed by consonant clusters — permissible in Old Indo-Aryan, were eliminated, through shortening of vowels or reduction of clusters. Moreover, as -V̄C- and -V̄CC- were prosodically equivalent, one has either as reflex of earlier -V̄C-, -V̆CC-. For example: Skt. *lākṣā-* 'lac', *dīrgha-* 'long', *śvaśrū-* 'mother-in-law', *sarṣapa-* 'mustard seed': Pāli *lākha-, dīgha-, sassū-, sāsapa-*: Pkt. *lakkhā-, diggha-/digha-, sāsū-, sāsava-*. In addition, vocalic *ṛ* is replaced by various vowels, *ai, au*, were monophthongised to *e, o*; *-aya-, -ava-* developed to *-e-, -o-*; and short *ĕ, ŏ* arose through shortening before clusters: Skt. *ṛkṣa-* 'bear', *vṛścika-* 'scorpion', *pṛcchati* 'asks', *taila-* 'oil', *jayati* 'is victorious', *prekṣate* 'looks', *aurasa-* 'legitimate', *bhavati* 'is', *maulya-* 'price': Pāli *accha-, vicchika-, pucchati, tela, jeti, pekkhati, orasa-, hoti, molla-*. Moreover, many of the complex morphophonemic alternations that applied in Old Indo-Aryan across word boundaries (see section 1.2 of the chapter on Sanskrit) were eliminated. Certain phonological developments also characterised major dialect areas. As noted, the extreme north-west retained different sibilants. In addition, at Aśoka's time the extreme west and east respectively were characterised by having *r*, consonant assimilation and *-o* for earlier *-as* and its variants as opposed to *l*, a tendency to epenthesis and *-e*: *rāñño* versus *lājine*.

Some of the tendencies observed earlier continue in evidence into New Indo-Aryan. Thus, the resolution of -V̄CC- to -V̄C- takes place in some areas: Gujarati *pākū* 'ripe', *lāḍu* 'a sweet': Hindi *pakkā, laḍḍu*. Though *ai, au* are retained well into the modern period and still found, they are also monophthongised, as in Hindi *hɛ* 'is', *cɔthā* 'fourth' (spelled *hai, cauthā*). Middle Indo-Aryan *ḍ, ḍh* develop to flaps (but the etymological spellings are retained) except in initial position and after nasals; e.g., Hindi *sāḍī* 'sari' (Pkt. *sāḍiā-*). In the north-west, assimilation affects a sequence of a nasal with an obstruent: Panjabi *dand* 'tooth' versus Hindi *dãt*. On the other hand, the widespread loss of earlier final vowels results in word-final consonants, although in certain areas the final vowels are retained; e.g. Panjabi *dand*, Hindi *dãt*, but Sindhi *Ḍandu*. The last has an initial imploded stop, characteristic of Sindhi and some adjacent languages. Dialectal developments have resulted in other phonological features not found in Middle Indo-Aryan. For example, Panjabi developed a tonal system; Kashmiri has developed pharyngealised consonants; in languages of the south-west there are two sets of affricates, as in Marathi *c* (= *ts*) versus *č*; and languages of the extreme east have rounded the vowel *a*, as in Bengali (Bangla), where one also finds limited vowel harmony.

2.2 Morphology and Syntax

The grammatical system of Middle Indo-Aryan is characterised by a general reduction of complexities in comparison with Old Indo-Aryan. The dual is eliminated as a category distinct from the plural. The trend to replace variable consonant stems with single stems ending in vowels, already evident in Old Indo-Aryan (e.g. Skt. *danta-* 'tooth', earlier *dant-/dat-*), continues: Pāli *gacchanta-* 'going' (masc. nom. sg. *gacchanto*, gen. pl. *gacchantānaṁ*) as against Skt. *gacchant-/gacchat-* (see section 2.2.2 of the chapter on Sanskrit). The loss of final consonants also contributed to the steady elimination of consonant stems, e.g. Pāli *āpā-* 'emergency', *sappi-* 'butter': Skt. *āpad-*, *sarpis-*. The nominal case system too is reduced. At an early stage, the dative is replaced by the genitive except in expressing a goal or purpose: Pāli *etesaṁ pi abhayam dammi* 'I grant (*dammi*) them too (*etesaṁ pi*) security' has a genitive *etesaṁ* construed with *dammi*, and Jaina Māhārāṣṭrī *namo tāṇaṁ purisaṇaṁ* 'homage to those men' has a genitive in construction with *namo*. Formal datives occur in examples like Aśokan *etāya atthāya idaṁ lekhāpitaṁ* 'this (*idaṁ*) has been caused to be written (*lekhapitaṁ*) for this purpose (*etāya atthāya*)', Pāli *jhassu rūpaṁ apunabbhavanāya* 'give up (*jhassu*) your body (*rūpaṁ*) so as not to be born again (*apunabbhavanāya*)'. In addition, nominal and pronominal types are less strictly segregated, as can be seen from *etāya, tāṇaṁ* (Skt. *etasmai, teṣām*) in examples cited.

Although early Middle Indo-Aryan retains middle forms, the contrast between active and medio-passive in the verb system is generally obliterated. Thus, Pāli has *maññati* 'thinks', *jāyati* 'is born' and passives of the type *vuccati* 'is said', with etymologically active endings; contrast Skt. *manyate, jāyate, ucyate*. The contrast between two kinds of future formations is absent in Middle Indo-Aryan, which has the type Pāli *hossati* 'will be'. Further, the distinction among aorist, imperfect and perfect is obliterated. With few exceptions, the sigmatic aorist supplies the productive preterit. Thus, Pāli has several preterital formations, but the productive one is sigmatic and based on the present stem, not on the root as in Old Indo-Aryan: *ahosi* 'was' (3 sg.), *ahosuṁ* 'were' (pres. *hoti honti*), *agacchi, agacchisuṁ* (*gacchati, gacchanti*). In later Middle Indo-Aryan, verbally inflected preterits are generally given up in favour of participial forms, as in Śaurasenī *mahārāo vi āado* 'the king (*mahārāo*) also (*vi*) has arrived (*āado*)', where *āado* agrees in case, number and gender with *mahārāo*. The participle of a verb that takes a direct object shows object agreement: in Jaina Māhārāṣṭrī *teṇa vi savvaṁ siṭṭhaṁ* 'he too has told everything', *teṇa* (inst. sg.) refers to the agent, and *siṭṭhaṁ* 'told' agrees with *savvaṁ* (nom. sg. nt.) 'everything'. If no object is explicitly referred to, the neuter nominative singular of a participle is used; e.g., Jaina Māhārāṣṭrī *pacchā raṇṇā cintiyaṁ* 'afterwards, the king (inst. sg. *raṇṇā*) thought (*cintiyaṁ*)'.

Alternations of the type Skt. *asti–santi* (see section 2.2.3 of the chapter on Sanskrit) are eliminated in Middle Indo-Aryan, where the predominant present formation involves a single stem: Pāli *eti* 'goes' *enti* 'go', *sakkoti–sakkonti* (*sak* 'be able'), *chindati–chindanti* (*chid* 'cut'). Stems like *chinda-* reflect a generalisation, based on a reanalysis of third plural forms, of stems with -*a*. The elimination of strictly athematic presents with variable stems allowed the use of the second singular imperative -*hi* in a domain wider than this had in Old Indo-Aryan; e.g., Pāli *jīvāhi* 'live' (Skt. *jīva*). Similarly, optatives with -*e*- and -*yā*- are not sharply segregated; a form like Pāli *bhaveyya* (3 sg.) shows a blend of the two. Middle Indo-Aryan continues to use morphological causatives with -i-/-e- (Pāli 3 sg. pres. *kāreti*), but the type in -*āpe*- (Pkt. -*āve*-) is extended beyond its earlier domain, as in Pāli *vasāpeti* 'has ... stay'.

Nominal forms of the Middle Indo-Aryan verb system are of the same types as in Old Indo-Aryan: present and past participles (see above), gerundives (Pāli *kātabba*- 'to be done', *dassanīya*- 'worthy of being seen'), gerunds, infinitives, with some innovations. For example, Pāli *nikkhamitvā* 'after leaving' has -*tva*- after a compound, and *pappotuṁ* has -*tuṁ* added to the present stem, not the root. Contrast Skt. *niṣkramya, prāptum*.

The late Middle Indo-Aryan stage represented in Apabhraṁśa foreshadows New Indo-Aryan in several ways. Forms of the nominal system with -*au*, -*aū*, -*ī* presage the modern oppositions among masculine, neuter and feminine types such as Gujarati *navo, navū, navī* 'new', Hindi *nayā, naī* (m., f.). The case system of Apabhraṁśa is at a more advanced stage of disintegration than found earlier. For example, instrumental and locative plurals are now formally identical, and etymologically instrumental singular forms like *dāhiṇabhāē* are used in locatival function: *dāhiṇabhāē bharahu thakku* 'Bharata is located (*thakku*) in the southern division'. The paucity of distinct forms is evident in personal pronouns, where, for example, *maī, paī* (1st, 2nd person sg.) have functions equivalent to older accusative, instrumental and locative forms. Although Apabhraṁśa has some presents like *hoi* 'is', stems in -*a* of the type *kara*- 'do, make' (3 sg. *karai*) predominate. The Apabhraṁśa causative type *karāva*- (*karāvai*) is comparable to New Indo-Aryan formations (e.g. Gujarati *karāve chε* 'has... do'). Moreover, Apabhraṁśa has causative formations found in modern languages but not attested earlier in Middle Indo-Aryan; e.g. *bhamāḍ-a*- 'cause to turn' (Gujarati *bhamāḍ*-).

The gender system of earlier Indo-Aryan is retained in some modern languages (e.g. Gujarati, see above), but is reduced in others (e.g. Hindi, with masculine and feminine only); some languages (e.g. Bengali) have eliminated systematic gender distinctions. Various inflectional forms are retained (e.g. Gujarati agentive *mē* 'I'), but the prevalent modern nominal system involves stems and postpositions or, much less commonly, prepositions. Over a large area of New Indo-Aryan, one finds variable nominals with direct and oblique forms, the former used independently, the latter with postpositions and other clitic elements. For example, Gujarati has singular direct forms in -*o* (m.), -*ū* (nt.), -*ī* (f.), oblique forms in -*ā* (m.-nt.), -*ī*. Some languages (e.g. Hindi) distinguish direct and oblique in the plural, others (e.g. Gujarati) do not. There are also nominals without these variations. Combinations of stems and postpositions serve the functions of inflected forms in earlier Indo-Aryan. Different languages have different postpositions for the same functions; e.g. Hindi -*ko*, Gujarati -*ne* mark definite direct objects, regularly animate, and indirect objects. Adjectives in general are formally like nouns, which they regularly precede in attributive constructions, and, with few exceptions, postpositions follow such phrases, not individual components; e.g. Gujarati *mɛ̃ tamārā dikrā-ne joyo* 'I saw your son'. Second person pronouns in New Indo-Aryan are differentiated essentially according to distinctions of deference, distance and familiarity, not according to number; e.g. Hindi *āp* has plural agreement but can refer to one person. Languages of the south-west also distinguish between first person inclusive and exclusive forms; e.g. Gujarati *ame* (exclusive), *āpṇe*. In demonstrative and relative pronouns, languages differ with regard to gender distinctions made; e.g. Marathi relative singular *jo* (m.), *je* (nt.), *ji* (f.), Gujarati *je* for all genders. They also differ in the deictic distinctions made.

The tendency to incorporate nominal forms in the verb system, evident in earlier times, continues into New Indo-Aryan. For example, Hindi has a contrast comparable to that of Bengali *korchi* 'am doing', *kori* 'do', both verbally inflected, but instead uses nominally inflected forms: *kar rahā/rahī hū̃* 'am doing', *kartā/kartī hū̃* 'do'. Gujarati lacks the contrast, but has verbally inflected presents (*karū chū* 'do, am doing') and nominally inflected preterits (*karto hato, kartī hatī*). Temporal auxiliaries like Hindi *hū̃*, Gujarati *chū* show verbal inflection, as do imperatives and some other forms. Person-number distinctions accord with the use of pronouns, but some languages (e.g. Bengali) have given up number distinctions in the verb. Future formations also show areal differences. Some languages have futures with -*š*- or -*h*- (e.g. Gujarati *kariš* 'I will do'), but -*b*- is characteristic of the east (e.g. Bengali *jabe* 'will go') and there are future formations that include gender distinctions, as in Hindi *jāegā* 'he will go', *jāegī* 'she will go'. The perfective of many New Indo-Aryan languages is semi-ergative, reflecting earlier participial constructions. For example, Gujarati *gher gayo/gaī* 'he/she went home' has masculine *gayo*, feminine *gaī*, depending on whether the agent is a man or a woman, but in *mɛ̃ tamārā dīkrā-ne joyo* 'I saw your son' agreement (m. sg. *joyo*) is determined by the object (*dīkrā-ne* 'son'). Some languages (e.g. Hindi) suspend agreement if an object nominal takes a postposition, so that the construction is no longer strictly passive. A formal passive such as *nahī bulāyā jāegā* (m. sg.) 'will not be invited' in an example like Hindi *baccõ-ko nahī bulāyā jāegā* 'children will not be invited' is also construed with a noun phrase containing an object marker (*baccõ-ko*), so that this construction too is different from the passive of earlier Indo-Aryan. Moreover, formal passives normally are used in sentences without agent expressions except under particular semantic conditions; e.g. Gujarati *mārā-thī nahi jawāy* 'I (agentive *mārā-thī*) won't be able to go', with the passive *jaw-ā-y* (3 sg. pres.). As shown, formal passives are also not restricted to transitive verbs, and in some languages they are formed with a suffix, in others they are periphrastic formations.

Examples cited illustrate the usual unmarked word order of most New Indo-Aryan languages: subject (including agentive forms), object (with attributive adjectives, including number words, before this and preceded by possessives), verb (with auxiliaries). Adverbials can precede sentences or the verb. Relative clauses generally precede correlative clauses. A notable exception to the above, at least in its superficial order, is Kashmiri, where the verb occurs in second position.

Bibliography

Cardona and Emmerick (1974) contains a survey of Indo-Aryan on pages 439b–457a, including a table of languages and a map. Bloch (1965) is a general and masterful survey of the historical developments, while Varma (1972–6) is a handy summary of Grierson's survey of the modern languages, still valuable, though in serious need of updating. Turner (1966–9) is an indispensable reference work for lexicon, and includes an index by D.R. Turner.

References

Bloch, J. 1965. *Indo-Aryan from the Vedas to Modern Times* (Adrien-Maisonneuve, Paris; translation by A. Master, with revisions, additions and an index, of *L'Indo-Aryen du véda aux temps modernes*, Adrien-Maisonneuve, Paris, 1934)

Cardona, G. and R.E. Emmerick. 1974. 'Indo-Aryan Languages', in *The New Encyclopaedia Britannica: Macropaedia*, 15th ed., pp. 439b–457a (Encyclopaedia Britannica, Chicago)

Turner, R.L. 1966–9. *A Comparative Dictionary of the Indo-Aryan Languages*, 2 vols. (Oxford University Press, London)

Varma, S. 1972–6. *G.A. Grierson's Linguistic Survey of India, a Summary*, 3 vols. (Vishveshvaranand Institute, Panjab University, Hoshiarpur)

21 Sanskrit

George Cardona

1 Background

1.1 Introduction

Sanskrit (*saṃskṛta-* 'adorned, purified') refers to several varieties of Old Indo-Aryan, whose most archaic forms are found in Vedic texts: the *Rigveda* (*Ṛgveda*), *Sāmaveda*, *Atharvaveda*, *Yajurveda*, with various branches. Associated with these are groupings of explicatory and speculative works (called *brāhmaṇas*, *āraṇyakas*, *upaniṣads*) as well as texts concerning the performance of rites (*kalpa-* or *śrauta-sūtras*), treatises on phonetics, grammar proper, etymological explanations of particular words, metrics and astrology. Early Vedic texts are pre-Buddhistic — the composition of the *Rigveda* is plausibly dated in the mid-second millennium BC — although their exact chronology is difficult to establish. Brāhmaṇas and early sūtra works can properly be called late Vedic. Also of the late Vedic period is the grammarian Pāṇini (not later than early fourth century BC), author of the *Aṣṭādhyāyī*, who distinguishes between the language of sacred texts (*chandas*) and a more usual language of communication (*bhāṣā*, from *bhāṣ* 'speak'), tantamount to Classical Sanskrit. Epic Sanskrit is so called because it is represented principally in the two epics, *Mahābhārata* and *Rāmāyaṇa*. The date of composition for the core of early epic is considered to be in the first centuries BC. It is in the *Rāmāyaṇa* that the term *saṃskṛta-* is encountered probably for the first time with reference to the language. Classical Sanskrit is the language of major poetical works, dramas, tales and technical treatises on grammar, philosophy and ritual. It was not only used by Kalidasa and his predecessors but continued in use after Sanskrit had ceased to be a commonly used mother tongue. Sanskrit is a language of learned treatises and commentaries to this day. It has also undergone a literary revival, and original works are still being composed in this language. Indeed, Sanskrit is used as a lingua franca by paṇḍitas from different parts of India, and several thousand people claim it as their mother tongue.

1.2 Diachronic Changes Within Sanskrit

Linguistic changes are discernible in Sanskrit from earliest Vedic down to the language Pāṇini describes. The nominative plural masculine in *-āsas* (*devāsas* 'gods'), which has a counterpart in Iranian, is already less frequent in the *Rigveda* than the type in *-ās* (*devās*), and continues to lose ground; in Brāhmaṇas, *-ās* is the norm. The *Rigveda* has examples of an archaic genitive plural in *-ām* to *a*-stems, but the form in *-ānām* prevails here and is the only one used later. The instrumental singular of *a*-stems has both *-ā* and *-ena* (originally a pronominal type) in the *Rigveda* (*vīryā/vīryeṇa* 'heroic might, act'), but the latter is already prevalent and becomes the norm later. The Rigvedic nominative-accusative dual masculine of *a*-stems ends in *-ā* or *-au* (*mitrāvaruṇā/-varuṇau* 'Mitra and Varuṇa'), distributed according to phonological environments in early parts of the *Rigveda*, but *-au* steadily gains the upper hand and finally ousts *-ā* completely. For the nominative-accusative plural of neuter *a*-stems, the *Rigveda* has forms in *-ā* and *-āni:* *bhīmāni āyudhā* 'fearful weapons'. The former predominates in the *Rigveda*, but the situation is reversed in the *Atharvaveda*; later, *-āni* is the norm. Early Vedic had derivate *ī*-stems of two types, as in *vṛkīs* 'she wolf', *devī* 'goddess' (nom. sg.), *vṛkyas*, *devīs* (nom. pl.). The type *vṛkī-* is gradually eliminated as an independent formation, but leaves traces incorporated into the *devī* type (e.g. nom. pl. *devyas*). Rigvedic feminine *i*- and *u*-stems have instrumental singular forms of the type *ūtī* 'with, for help', *jātū* 'by nature' in addition to forms with *-ā* (*ūtyā*, *dhenvā* 'cow'). Even in the *Rigveda*, *u*-stems usually have forms of the type *dhenvā*, and the type *ūtyā* also becomes the norm later. Masculine and neuter stems in *-i*, *-u* have Rigvedic instrumental singulars with *-ā* (*pavyā*, *paśvā* to *pavi-* 'felly', *paśu-* 'animal') and *-nā* (*agninā* 'fire, Agni', *paśunā*). The latter predominate in the *Atharvaveda* and ultimately take over except for a few nouns (*patyā* 'husband', *sakhyā* 'friend'). The *Rigveda* has *avyas*, *madhvas*, genitive singulars of *avi-* 'sheep', *madhu-* 'honey'; the regular later forms are *aves*, *madhunas* (also *madhos* in Vedic). Endingless locatives like *ahan* (*ahan-* 'day') are also gradually eliminated in favour of forms with the ending *-i*: *ahani/ahni*. Early Vedic has pronominal forms not found in Classical Sanskrit: *asme*, *yuṣme* (loc. pl.) from the first and second person pronouns, replaced by *asmāsu*, *yuṣmāsu*; *āvos* (1st person gen.-loc. du.), *mahya* (1st person dat. sg.), replaced by *āvayos*, *mahyam*. Pāṇini expressly classes such earlier Vedic forms as belonging to the language of sacred texts.

The verbal system shows comparable differences. Early Vedic had modal forms from several stems: present, aorist, perfect. For example, the Rigvedic imperatives *śṛṇudhi*, *śṛṇuhi*, *śṛṇu* (2 sg.) and the Atharvavedic optative *śṛṇuyāt* (3 sg.) are formed to the present stem *śṛṇu-* of *śru* 'hear, listen', but the Rigvedic imperative *śrudhi* (2 sg.) and optative *śruyās* (3 sg.) are formed to the aorist stem. In later Sanskrit, imperatives and optatives regularly are formed from present stems. The first plural primary active ending -*masi* (*bharāmasi* 'we carry'), which has an equivalent in Iranian, predominates over -*mas* in the *Rigveda*, but not in the *Atharvaveda*, and later -*mas* is the rule. Early Vedic forms like *ās* 'was' (3 sg. imperfect of *as*) and *avāṭ* (3 sg. aorist of *vah* 'transport') show the effects of the simplification of word-final clusters. Such forms are replaced by the types *āsīt*, *avākṣīt*, with -*īt* (2 sg. -*īs*), in which endings are clearly shown. Aorist forms made directly from verb roots are also replaced by forms from stems in -*a* or sigmatic stems, the latter especially in the medio-passive. Thus, the *Rigveda* has 1 sg. *akaram*, 2 sg. *akar* (< *akar-s*), 3 sg. *akar* (< *akar-t*), but the *Atharvaveda* has 2 sg. *akaras*, 3 sg. *akarat*, from *kṛ* 'make, do', and the *Rigveda* has not only a root aorist third plural middle *ayujran* but also a sigmatic form *ayukṣata* 'they yoked'. Commentators like Patañjali (mid-second century BC) and the etymologist Yāska before him used the sigmatic form *akṛṣata* (3 pl. middle) in paraphrasing a Vedic verse with the root aorist form *akrata*. Early Vedic forms of the type *śaye* 'is lying' are gradually replaced by the type *śete*, with *te*, which is explicitly marked for person.

Early Vedic distinguishes among the aorist, imperfect and perfect. The aorist is commonly used to refer to something that has recently taken place, and the imperfect is a narrative tense form used of acts accomplished or states prevailing at a past time not close at hand. For example, *úd u jyótir ... savitā́ aśret* 'Savitṛ has set up (*úd ... aśret*) the light (*jyótis*)', spoken at dawn, has the aorist *úd ... aśret*, but *ná mṛtyúr āsīd amṛ́taṁ ná tárhi ná rā́tryā áhna āsīt praketáḥ* 'then (*tárhi*) was there (*āsīt*) not (*ná*) death (*mṛtyús*) or deathlessness (*amṛ́tam*), nor was there the mark (*praketás*) of night (*rā́tryās*) or day (*áhnas*)' has the imperfect *āsīt*. The perfect originally signified, as in early Greek, a state of being; e.g. *bibhā́ya* '... is afraid'. From the earliest Vedic texts, however, this is not always the use of the perfect, which came to be used as a narrative tense. For example, the following Brāhmaṇa passage has both perfect and imperfects: *yajño vai devebhya ud akrāman na vo'ham annaṁ bhaviṣyāmīti/ neti devā abruvan annam eva no bhaviṣyasīti/ taṁ devā vimethire ... te hocur devā na vai na itthaṁ vihṛto'laṁ bhaviṣyati hantemaṁ yajñaṁ saṁ bharāmeti/ tatheti taṁ saṁ jabhruḥ* 'the sacrifice (*yajñas*) fled (*ud akrāmat*) from the gods (*devebhyas*), saying (citation particle *iti*), "I will not be (*na bhaviṣyāmi*) food (*annam*) for you (*vas*)"; the gods (*devās*) said (*abruvan*), "No, you will be (*bhaviṣyasi*) food for us (*nas*)"; the gods tore it apart (*taṁ vi methire*) ... the gods said (*ūcus*), "Truly (*vai*), it will not be sufficient (*na ... alaṁ bhaviṣyati*) for us thus (*ittham*) torn apart (*vihṛtas*), so let us put this sacrifice together (*imaṁ yajñaṁ saṁ bharāma*)"; they agreed (*tatheti* 'yes') and put it together (*taṁ saṁ jabhrus*)'. The imperfect *ud akrāmat*, *abruvan* and the perfect *vi methire*, *saṁ jabhrus* occur in similar contexts. This passage also illustrates the normal later combination of preverbs and verbs: preverbs immediately precede the verb stems with which they are connected; in earlier Vedic, tmesis was common — as in *úd ... aśret* of the Rigvedic passage cited earlier.

In addition, the augment became obligatory, as it had not been before, in imperfect and aorist forms.

The Brāhmaṇa passage just quoted also contains the future forms *bhaviṣyāmi, bhaviṣyasi, bhaviṣyati*, from the verb *bhū*, with the augmented suffix *-iṣya*. This and the unaugmented suffix *-sya* (*dāsya-* 'will give') are used from earliest Vedic on, but there is also a composite type, originally formed from an agent noun of the type *kartṛ-* (nom.sg. *kartā́*) followed, except in the third person, by forms of the verb 'be': *kartāsmi* 'I will do', *kartāsi* 'you will do', *kartā* 'he will do'. This formation, which was in common use at Pāṇini's time, was rare in early Vedic. The perfect also has a periphrastic formation, for derived verbs such as causatives; e.g. *gamayāñ cakāra* (3 sg.) 'made to go' (3 sg. present *gamayati*), formed with the accusative singular of an action noun (*gamayā-*) and the perfect of *kṛ* 'do'. This type first appears in the *Atharvaveda* (form cited), and gains currency; Pāṇini recognises it not only as the regular perfect for derived verbs but also for some primitive verbs. Corresponding to future forms such as *bhariṣyati* 'will carry', there were, from earliest Vedic, secondary augmented forms like *abhariṣyat* 'was going to carry', and these are later to become the regular verbal constituents in contrary-to-fact conditional sentences.

Early Vedic has a category that goes out of use later: the injunctive, formally an unaugmented secondary form; for example, *bhūt, carat* are third person singular injunctives corresponding to the aorist *abhūt* and the imperfect *acarat*. In a *Rigveda* passage such as *agníḥ sáptiṁ vājambharáṁ dadāti ... agnī́ ródasī ví carat* 'Agni (*agnís*) gives (*dadāti*) a horse (*sáptim*) that carries away prizes (*vājambharám*) ... Agni wanders through (*ví carat*) the two worlds (*ródasī*)', the injunctive *ví carat* and the present *dadāti* are juxtaposed, both used of general truths. In such statements, Vedic also uses subjunctives, characterised by the vowel *-a-* affixed to a present, aorist or perfect stem, as in Rigvedic *ná duṣṭutī́ mártyò vindate vásu ná śrédhantaṁ rayír naśat* 'a mortal (*mártyas*) does not find (*ná vindate*) treasure (*vásu*) through bad praise (*duṣṭutī́*), nor does wealth (*rayís*) come to (*naśat*) one who faulters in the performance of rites (*śrédhantam*)', where the present *vindate* is juxtaposed with the aorist subjunctive *naśat* 'reach'. In addition, subordinate clauses such as *pūṣā́ no yáthā ... ásad vṛdhé rakṣitā́* 'so that (*yáthā*) Pūṣan be (*ásat*) our protector in order that we might grow (*vṛdhé*)' use the subjunctive, which also occurs in requests; e.g. *devó devébhir ā́ gamat* 'may the god come (*ā́ gamat*) with the gods (*devébhis*)'. In negative commands, the injunctive is used with the particle *mā*, as in *mā́ no vadhīḥ ... mā́ párā dāḥ* 'do not kill (*mā́ vadhīs*) us (*nas*), do not forsake (*mā́ párā dās*) us', with the second person singular aorist injunctives *vadhīs, parā dās*. The regular negative particle used with a subjunctive, however, is *na*: e.g. *sá jáno ná reṣan máno yó asya ... ā vívāsāt* 'that person (*sá jánas*) does not suffer ill (*ná reṣat*), who seeks to win (*yás ā vívāsāt*) his (*asya*) spirit (*mánas*)' has the aorist subjunctive *reṣat* and the subjunctive of the present desiderative stem *ā vivāsa-* (*-sāt* < *-sa-a-t*). Later, the injunctive is retained only in negative commands of the type *mā vadhīs*, 3 sg. *mā vadhīt*. The subjunctive also steadily loses ground until it is no longer current; for Pāṇini, subjunctive forms belong to the language of sacred texts. Only the first person type *karavāṇi* 'I may do, let me do', incorporated into the imperative system, is retained. The functions of the subjunctive are taken over by the optative and the future. For example, in Vedic a subordinate clause introduced by *yathā* may have a subjunctive or an optative, but *yadi* 'if' is regularly used with a subjunctive in early Vedic. Thus, a passage cited above has *yathā ... asat*, and *yáthā bhávema mīḷhúṣe ánāgāḥ* 'that we may be (*yáthā bhavema*) sinless (*ánāgās*) towards the gracious one (*mīḷhúṣe*)' has the optative *bhavema*, but *ā́ gha gamad yádi śrávat* 'let him come (*ā́ ... gamat*) if he hear (*yádi śrávat*)' has the aorist subjunctive *śravat*. In later Vedic, however, *yadi* is used with an optative, as in *yádi bibhīyā́d duścármā bhaviṣyāmíti somapauṣṇáṁ śyāmám ā́ labheta* 'if he fear (*yádi bibhīyā́t*) that he might be (*bhaviṣyāmíti* 'I will become') stricken by a skin disease (*duścármā* 'bad-skinned'), let him immolate (*ā́ labheta*) a black goat (*śyāmám* 'black') dedicated to Soma and Pūṣan'.

Nominal forms within the verbal system of early Vedic are numerous. The Rigveda has derivatives with *-ya*, *-tva* that function as gerundives: *vācya-* 'to be said' (root *vac*), *kartva-* 'to be done' (*kṛ*). In addition, the *Atharvaveda* has forms with *-(i)tavya*, *-anīya*: *hiṁsitavya-* 'to be harmed', *upajīvanīya-* 'to be subsisted upon'. By late Vedic, the type with *-tva* has lost currency, and for Pāṇini the regular formations are of the types *kārya-*, *kartavya-*, *karaṇīya-*. In Indo-Aryan from Vedic down to modern times, gerunds are used with reference to the earlier of actions performed in succession, usually by the same agent ('after doing A, ... does B', '... does A before doing B'); e.g. *yuktvá háribhyāṁ úpa yāsad arvā́k* 'let him yoke his bay horses to his chariot (*yuktvā* 'after yoking') and come hither (*upa yāsad arvāk*) with them (*haribhyām* 'with two bay horses')', *gūḍhvī́ támo ... abodhi* '(dawn) has awakened (*abodhi*) after hiding away (*gūḍhvī*) the darkness (*támas*)', *piba niṣadya* 'sit down (*niṣadya* 'after sitting down') and drink (*piba*)'. The *Rigveda* has gerunds with *-tvā*, *-tvāya* *-tvī*, *-(t)ya*, but these are ultimately reduced to two main types: *-tvā* after simple verbs or verbs with the negative prefix *a(n)-*, *-ya* after compounds with preverbs. Early Vedic uses a variety of case forms of action nouns, including root nouns, as what western grammarians traditionally call infinitives; e.g. dat. sg. *vṛdhe* (root noun *vṛdh-* 'growing'), *-tave* (*dātave* 'to give'), gen. sg. *-tos* (*dātos*), the last two from a derivative in *-tu* which also supplies the accusative *-tum* (*dātum*). There are other Vedic types, but nouns in *-tu* are noteworthy in that for later Vedic the accusative with *-tum* and the genitive in *-tos*, the latter construed with *īś* or *śak* 'be able', become the norm. According to Pāṇini, forms in *-tum* and datives of action nouns are equivalent in sentences like *bhoktum/ bhojanāya gacchati* '...is going (*gacchati*) in order to eat'.

1.3   Sanskrit Dialects

That some formations fell into disuse in the course of Old Indo-Aryan is no surprise: the developments sketched above represent chronological and dialectal changes. Such changes were recognised by grammarians who spoke the language. Patañjali notes that second plural perfect forms like *cakra* or *ūṣa* (*vas* 'dwell) were not used in his time; instead, one used participial forms such as *kṛtavantas, ūṣitās* (nom. pl. m.). Grammarians also recognised that various dialects existed. Pāṇini takes note of forms used by northerners, easterners and various dialectal usages described by other grammarians. The etymologist Yāska notes, as does Patañjali, that finite forms of the verb *dā* 'cut' were used in the east, while in the north the verb occurred in the derivative *dātra-* 'sickle'. Earlier documents also afford evidence of dialect differences. The major dialect of the *Rigveda* is one in which Proto-Indo-European *l* merged with *r* (e.g., *pūrṇa-* 'full'), but other dialects developed *l*, and one finds doublets such as *rohita-/lohita-* 'red'. The development of retroflex liquids *-ḷ-, -ḷh-* from intervocalic *-ḍ- -ḍh-* is another characteristic of some areas, among them the major dialect of the *Rigveda*.

1.4   Sanskrit and Other Languages

Classical Sanskrit represents a development of one or more such Old Indo-Aryan dialects, accepted as standard, at a stage when archaisms such as those noted (section 1.2) had largely been eliminated. It is plausible to accept that both Classical Sanskrit and earlier dialects of Indo-Aryan coexisted with vernaculars that were removed from these by changes which characterise Middle Indo-Aryan, just as in later times Sanskrit and vernaculars were used side by side under particular circumstances. There is evidence to support this view, particularly in Patañjali's *Mahābhāṣya*, where he discusses the use of 'correct speech forms' (*śabda*) and 'incorrect speech forms' (*apaśabda*), considered corruptions (*apabhraṁśa*) of the former. Patañjali speaks of *śiṣṭas*, model speakers, who are characterised as much by moral qualities as by their speech. They are Brāhmaṇas who reside in Āryāvartta, the land of the Āryas in north-central India, who at any time have only as much grain as will fit in a small pot, who are not greedy, who behave morally without ulterior motives and who attain full knowledge of traditional learning with consummate ease, not having to be taught. These model speakers are those one should imitate and, it is assumed, the models Pāṇini followed in composing his grammatical rules. However, even learned men did not avoid vernaculars, as Patañjali also points out. He remarks that a restriction such that correct speech forms should be used to the exclusion of others is absolute only in respect of rituals. To illustrate, Patañjali speaks of sages who said *yar vā ṇaḥ* 'what is ours', *tar vā ṇaḥ* 'that is ours' instead of *yad vā naḥ, tad vā naḥ* but did not use such forms in the course of ritual acts. Now, forms like *yar* instead of *yad* reflect an Indo-Aryan tendency to eliminate obstruence for non-initial retroflex and dental stops; the particular change in question is seen also in Prakrit *bāraha* as opposed to Sanskrit *dvādaśa* 'twelve'. Moreover, Patañjali must have been, if not a native speaker of Sanskrit in the strictest sense, at least one fully fluent in the language, with authority concerning its usage. For he explicitly distinguishes between what is desirable — that is, what is required by accepted usage — and what obtains by grammatical rules. At Patañjali's time, then, Sanskrit must have been a current vehicle of communication in certain circles and under particular social and religious conditions, used concurrently with vernaculars. Much the same picture is painted for later periods, when Sanskrit was doubtless revived. Thus, in his *Kāmasūtra*, Vātsyāyana notes that to be held in high esteem a man-about-town should use neither Sanskrit nor a local language exclusively. Indeed, the coexistence of Middle Indo-Aryan and Sanskrit speech is to be envisaged even for the time when very early texts were given their final redactions. The *Rigveda* has forms like *vikaṭa-* 'deformed' and *jyotis-* 'light'. The former is a Middle Indo-Aryan form of *vikṛta-*, with *-aṭ-* for *-ṛt-*, comparable to Aśokan *kaṭa-* 'made' (Skt. *kṛta*), and the latter had *jy-* for *dy-*. It has been suggested, plausibly in my estimation, that there was an archaic Middle Indo-Aryan contemporaneous with early Vedic.

Sanskrit was also subject to non-Aryan influence from early on. In the sixth century BC Darius counted Gandhara as a province of his kingdom, and Alexander the Great penetrated into the north of the subcontinent in the fourth century. From Iranian come terms such as *lipi-* 'writing, script', *kṣatrapa-* 'satrap', and Greek is the source of such words as *kendra-* 'centre', *jāmitra-* 'diameter', *horā-* 'hour'. At a later time borrowings entered from Arabic and other sources. But long before this Sanskrit was influenced by Dravidian, from which it borrowed terms such as *kāla-* 'black', *kuṭī-* 'hut' (cf. Tamil *kaṟ* 'blackness', *kuṭi*) and the influence of which contributed to the spread of retroflex consonants (see section 1 of the chapter on Indo-Aryan). It is not certain in every instance, however, that borrowing proceeded from Dravidian to Indo-Aryan, since Dravidian languages also freely borrowed from Indo-Aryan. For example, some scholars maintain that Skt. *kaṭu-* 'sharp, pungent' is a Dravidian borrowing, but others treat it as a Middle Indo-Aryan development of **kṛtu-* 'cutting' (root **kṛt* 'cut'). Whatever be the judgement on any individual word, nevertheless, it is clear that Sanskrit and other Indo-Aryan dialects borrowed from Dravidian sources.

2 Brief Description of Classical Sanskrit

2.1 Sound System and Script

The sounds of Sanskrit are shown in table 21.1. In the present context, it is not necessary to take a particular stand about which sounds should be considered 'basic', 'underlying' or 'phonemic'. Suffice it to note that sounds

Table 21.1 The Sounds of Sanskrit

Vowels									
i ī				u ū					
		e			o				
			a						
			ā						
ṛ [r̄] [ḷ]				ai au					

Consonants								
	Obstruents		Nasals	Semi-	Liquid	Tap	*Spirants*	
	Voiceless	Voiced		*vowels*			Voiceless	Voiced
Pharyngeal							[ḥ]	h
Velar	k	kh	g	gh	[ṅ]			[χ]
Palatal	c	ch	j	jh	[ñ]	y		ś
Retroflex	ṭ	ṭh	ḍ	ḍh	ṇ		r*	ṣ
Alveolar							r*	
Dental	t	th	d	dh	n	l		s
Labio-dental						v		
Labial	p	ph	b	bh	m			[φ]
					[ṁ]			

Note: *Some ancient authorities say *r* is retroflex, others say it is alveolar.

of table 21.1 within square brackets have restricted distributions. r̄ occurs only in accusative or genitive plurals of *r*-stems (*pitr̄n* 'fathers', *mātr̄s* 'mothers', gen. pl. *pitr̄ṇām*, *mātr̄ṇām*, rare nom.-acc. pl. nt. *kartr̄ṇi* 'which do'); *ḷ* is found only in forms of *kḷp* 'be fit, arrange, imagine' (past participle *kḷpta-*). Due to the reduction of word-final clusters, -*ṇ* occurs in words such as *prāṇ* (nom. sg.) 'directed forward, toward the east', but otherwise *ṇ* and *ñ* are found before velar and palatal stops, respectively, though not necessarily as replacements of *n* or *m* at morph boundaries. The nasal off-glide *ṁ* occurs word-internally before spirants at morph boundaries as the final segment of items that have -*n* or -*m* before vowels and in word-final position before spirants and semi-vowels or stops, where it varies with nasalised semi-vowels and nasal stops homorganic with following stops. *ḥ* is a word-final segment in prepause position or before voiceless spirants, velars and labials. *χ φ* are alternants to -*ḥ* before velars and labials. Like *ṅ* and *ñ*, *ṇ* is not the initial sound of lexical items. It occurs in word-final position, though rarely except before nasals as the final sound of a morph that has a non-nasal retroflex stop before vowels, but intervocalic -*ṇ*- is found in words like *kaṇa-* 'grain, atom', that do not contain sounds which condition retroflexion.

The vowels *i*, *u* and *ī*, *ū* differ essentially in duration: short vowels last one mora (*mātrā*), long vowels two morae; however, in accepted modern pronunciations, *i* and *u* can be lower than their long counterparts. *e*, *o* are monophthongs of two morae, though they derive historically from diphthongs and alternate with *ay*, *av* before vowels. *ai*, *au* are diphthongs for which ancient phoneticians and grammarians recognised dialect variants: for example, the first segment of each was a closer vowel in some dialects than in others. Prosodically, however, *ai, au* behave in the manner of simple long vowels, and there are good reasons for not treating them as combinations of *ā* with *i, u. ṛ* is also a complex sound, consisting of *r* surrounded by vowel segments, according to a fairly old description, but this also behaves prosodically as a single vowel. In north-central India, *ṛ* is pronounced as *r* followed by short *i. a, ā* behave as a pair of short and long vowels, but they are also qualitatively different, as shown. Vowels can be unnasalised or nasalised. They also have pitch differences such that they are called *anudātta, udātta* and *svarita*. Pāṇini's statements concerning these are best understood as reflecting a system in which an anudātta vowel is low-pitched, an udātta vowel is high-pitched, and a svarita vowel has a combination of both pitches: *a, á, à*. According to Pāṇini, a svarita vowel is high-pitched for the duration of half a mora from its beginning, low-pitched for its remainder, but there were dialectical variations, as can be seen from other ancient descriptions. There are also differences in Vedic traditions of recitation concerning the relative pitches of the vowels in question.

Sanskrit generally does not allow word-final clusters, although *-rC* is permitted if both consonants belong to the same element; e.g. *ūrk* (nom. sg.) 'strength' (acc. sg. *ūrj-am*). Sanskrit also has a fairly complex system of morphophonemic adjustments (*sandhi*) across grammatical boundaries, at word boundaries if the items in question are pronounced in close juncture (*saṃhitāyām*). Some of these adjustments are illustrated in examples given; e.g. in the Brāhmaṇa passage cited in section 1.2: *yajño vai* ← *yajnas vai, devebhya ud* ← *devebhyas ud, akrāman na* ← *akrāmat na, voham* ← *vas aham, annaṃ bhaviṣyāmīti* ← *annam bhaviṣyāmi iti, neti* ← *na iti, devā abruvan* ← *devās abruvan, no bhaviṣyasi* ← *nas bhaviṣyasi, taṃ devā vi methire* ← *tam devās vi methire, hocur devā na* ← *ha ūcus devās na, tatheti* ← *tathā iti, taṃ saṃ jabhruḥ* ← *tam sam jabhrus*, the last with *-ḥ* instead of *-s* in pausa. These adjustments also affect vowel pitches. The particular place of a high-pitched vowel in an underived base is not predictable. In general, a syntactic word has one high-pitched vowel only — but may have none — and a finite verb form following a term that is not a finite verb has no high-pitched vowel except in particular collocations. Further, a low-pitched vowel following a high-pitched one shifts to a svarita vowel, as in *á gàmat* ← *á gamat*. There are other accentual adjustments that involve considerable complexity and dialectal variation.

Sanskrit was and continues to be written in various scripts in different areas, but the most widely recognised is the Devanāgarī script, the symbols of which are shown in table 21.2. These are traditionally arranged as follows: symbols for vowels, then for consonants; the latter are subdivided into: stops (five groups of five), semi-vowels, voiceless spirants, *h*. In addition, there are symbols for *ḷ* and *ḥ. ṃ* is designated by a dot (*bindu*) over a consonant or a

Table 21.2 Devanāgarī Symbols and their Transliterations

Vowels (*svarāḥ*)

अ	आ	इ	ई	उ	ऊ	ऋ	ॠ	लृ	ए	ऐ	ओ	औ
a	ā	i	ī	u	ū	r̥	r̥̄	l̥	e	ai	o	au

Consonants (*vyañjanāni*)

Stops (*sparśāḥ*)					Semi-vowels (*antaḥsthāḥ*)	Spirants (*ūṣmāṇaḥ*)	Others
क	ख	ग	घ	ङ		ह	ः
k	kh	g	gh	ṅ		h	ḥ
च	छ	ज	झ	ञ	य	श	
c	ch	j	jh	ñ	y	ś	
ट	ठ	ड	ढ	ण	र	ष	ळ
ṭ	ṭh	ḍ	ḍh	ṇ	r	ṣ	ḷ
त	थ	द	ध	न	ल	स	
t	th	d	dh	n	l	s	
प	फ	ब	भ	म	व		
p	ph	b	bh	m	v		

Examples of combinations

का	काँ	कि	की	कु	कू	कृ	कॄ	कॢ	क्त	क्र	क्ष	ज्ञ	त्र	त्व	द्य
kā	kāṁ	ki	kī	ku	kū	kr̥	kr̥̄	kl̥	kta	kra	kṣa	jña	tra	tva	dya

द्र	द्व	प्त	ब्द	र्क	र्कं	श्च	श्र	श्व	स्त	स्य	स्र	स्व	ह्म
dra	dva	pta	bda	rka	rkaṁ	śca	śra	śva	sta	sya	sra	sva	hma

ह्य	ह्र	ह्ल	ह्व	त्स्न्य
hya	hra	hla	hva	rtsnya

Numerals

१	२	३	४	५	६	७	८	९	०
1	2	3	4	5	6	7	8	9	0

Note: I have adopted the most generally accepted order of symbols and the subgroupings most widely accepted traditionally; the usual Sanskrit terms for sound classes are given in parentheses.

vowel symbol, nasalisation by a dot within a half-moon (*ardhacandra*) over a symbol; χ φ are designated by ⵗ before symbols for voiceless velars and labials.

In referring to vowels, one pronounces the sounds in question; e.g. '*a*' denotes the vowel *a*. Consonants in general are referred to by a combination of the sounds and a following *a*: e.g., '*ka*' denotes *k*. In addition, a sound name is formed with suffixed *-kāra*; e.g., '*akāra*', '*kakāra*' refer to *a*, *k*.

Certain sounds, however, have particular names: *r ḥ ṁ χ φ*, respectively, are called *repha*, *visarjanīya* (or *visarga*), *anusvāra*, *jihvāmūlīya*, *upadhmānīya*.

Consonant symbols, except those for *ḥ ṁ χ φ*, without any appended element, denote consonants followed by *a*. Other consonant-vowel combinations are designated by consonant symbols with appended vowel symbols, which may precede, follow, or come under the former, as illustrated in table 21.2. There are also ligatures for consonant combinations, some of which are illustrated in table 21.2. Finally, there is a set of Devanāgarī numerals. Variants of symbols are found in different areas.

2.2 Grammar

2.2.1 Introduction
Although many archaic features of earlier Vedic dialects have been eliminated in Sanskrit, the grammatical system nevertheless remains quite rich. Singular, dual and plural forms are distinguished in both the nominal and the verbal systems, and ablaut variations are maintained in many types of formations.

2.2.2 Nominal system
Eight cases can be distinguished, although the vocative does not have a syntactic status comparable to the others: nominative (nom.), vocative (voc.), accusative (acc.), instrumental (inst.), dative (dat.), ablative (abl.), genitive (gen.), locative (loc.), according to traditional western terminology. All eight are formally distinguished in the singular of masculine *a*-stems; e.g. *deva-* 'god': nom. *devas*, voc. *deva*, acc. *devam*, inst. *devena*, dat. *devāya*, abl. *devāt*, gen. *devasya*, loc. *deve*. Otherwise, there are homophonous forms as follows. All stems: dual nom.-voc.-acc., inst.-dat.-abl., gen.-loc.: *deva-*: *devau, devābhyām, devayos*; *phala-* (nt.) 'fruit': *phale, phalābhyām, phalayos*; *senā-* (f.) 'army': *sene, senābhyām, senayos*; *agni-* (m.) 'fire': *agnī, agnibhyām, agnyos* (similarly *kṛti-* (f.) 'deed'); *vāri-* (nt.) 'water': *vāriṇī, vāribhyām, vāriṇos*; *vāyu-* (m.) 'wind': *vāyū, vāyubhyām, vāyvos* (similarly *dhenu-* (f.) 'cow'); *madhu-* (nt.) 'honey': *madhunī, madhubhyām, madhvos*; *devī-* 'goddess': *devyau, devībhyām, devyos*; *vadhū-* 'bride': *vadhvau, vadhūbhyām, vadhvos*; *sakhi-* (m.) 'friend': *sakhāyau, sakhibhyām, sakhyos*; *pitṛ-* 'father': *pitarau, pitṛbhyām, pitros* (similarly *mātṛ-* 'mother'); *kartṛ-* 'doer, maker': *kartārau* (m.) *kartṛṇī* (nt.), *kartṛbhyām, kartros*; *go-* 'ox, cow': *gāvau, gobhyām, gavos*; *rājan-* 'king': *rājānau, rājabhyām, rājños*; *vāc-* (f.) 'voice, speech': *vācau, vāgbhyām, vācos*; *sraj-* (f.) 'garland': *srajau, sragbhyām, srajos*; nom.-voc. pl.: *devās, phalāni, senās, agnayas, kṛtayas, vārīṇi, vāyavas, dhenavas, madhūni, devyas, vadhvas, sakhāyas, pitaras, mātaras, kartāras kartṝṇi, gāvas, rājānas, vācas, srajas*. All stems except personal pronouns:

dat.-abl. pl.: *devebhyas, phalebhyas, senābhyas* etc. (with *agni-* etc. and *-bhyas*), *rājabhyas, vāgbhyas, sragbhyas,* but dat. *asmabhyam* 'us', *yuṣmabhyam* 'you', abl. *asmat, yuṣmat.* Nom.-acc. of all numbers for neuter stems: sg. *phalam, vāri, madhu, kartṛ;* for dual and plural see above. Abl.-gen. sg. except for masculine and neuter *a*-stems and personal pronouns: *senāyās, agnes, kṛtes/kṛtyās, vāriṇas, dhenos/dhenvās, madhunas, devyās, vadhvās, sakhyus, pitus, mātus, kartus, gos, rājñas, vācas, srajas,* but *devāt devasya* (similarly for *phala-*), *mat mama, tvat tava.* The accusative plural of feminine *ā*-stems and consonant stems is homophonous with the nominative and vocative plural (see above), but other stems make a distinction: *devān, agnīn, kṛtīs, vāyūn, dhenūs, devīs, vadhūs, sakhīn, pitṝn, mātṝs, kartṝn, rājñas.* In the singular, a few stems make no distinction between nominative and vocative (e.g. *gaus, vāk, śrīs* 'splendour, wealth'), but the two are usually distinguished: *devas, deva; senā, sene; agnis, agne; kṛtis, kṛte; vāri, vāre/vāri; vāyus, vāyo; dhenus, dheno; madhu, madho/madhu; devī, devi; vadhūs, vadhu; sakhā, sakhe; pitā, pitar* (similarly *mātṛ-, kartṛ-*); *rājā, rājan.* As can be seen, certain endings have variants according to stems, and this is true of the genitive plural, which has *-ām* after consonant stems (*rājñām, vācām, srajām*) and some vowel stems (e.g. *śriyām, gavām*) but *-nām* after most vowel stems, with lengthening of short vowels before this ending: *devānām, phalānām, senānām, agnīnam* etc.; however, personal pronouns have *-kam* (*asmākam, yuṣmākam*), and other pronominals have *-sām* (e.g. *teṣām* 'of them').

Endings are divisible into two groups with respect to phonological and grammatical alternations; nominative, vocative, accusative singular and dual and nominative plural for non-neuter stems as well as the nominative and accusative plural for neuter stems are strong endings, others are weak endings. Consonant-initial weak endings behave phonologically as though they were separated from stems by a word boundary; for example, *as*-stems have variants with *-o* before *-bhyām* (inst.-dat.-abl. du.), *-bhis* (inst. pl.), *-bhyas* (dat.-abl. pl.), *-aḥ* before *-su* (loc. pl.): *manas-* 'mind, spirit': nom.-acc. sg. *manas,* inst. sg. *manasā* but *manobhyām, manobhis, manaḥsu.*

Stems show variation that in part reflects Proto-Indo-European ablaut alternation. For example: *agni/agne-* (*agnay-* before vowels), *vāyu-/vāyo-* (*vāyav-*), *sakhi-/sakhe-/sakhāy/sakhā-, pitṛ-/pitar-/pitā-, kartṛ-/kartar-/kartār-/kartā-, rājan-/rājān-/rājā-/rājñ-* (before vocalic weak endings)/*rājā-* (before consonantal weak endings). There are also heteroclitic stems such as *asthi-/asthan-* (nt.) 'bone': nom.-acc. sg. *asthi,* du. *asthinī,* pl. *asthīni,* inst.-dat.-abl. du. *asthibhyām,* etc., with *asthi-* before consonantal weak endings, but inst. sg. *asthnā* etc., with *asthn-* before vocalic weak endings, and loc. sg. *asthani/asthni.* Due to the palatalisation of *k, g* to *c, j* before front vowels prior to the merger of *ĕ* with *ă* and to analogic realignments, there are stems with palatals before vocalic endings and velars elsewhere; e.g. *vāc-, sraj-* (see above).

Adjectives generally pattern in the manner of comparable nouns. For example, *śukla-*, *śuklā-* 'white', *śuci-* 'bright', *guru-* 'weighty, heavy', *paṅgū-* 'lame' inflect in the same way as noun stems in *-a, -ā, -i, -u, -ū*. There are also consonant stem adjectives with ablaut alternation; e.g. *sant-/sat-* 'being' (m. nom. sg. *san*, nom.-acc. du. *santau*, nom. pl. *santas*, acc. sg. *santam*, acc. pl. *satas*, inst. sg. *satā*, inst.-dat.-abl. du. *sadbhyām*, etc.), *gacchant-/gacchat-* 'going' (*gacchan, gacchantau, gacchantas, gacchantam, gacchatas, gacchatā, gacchadbhyām*, etc.), *vidvans-/vidvāns-/viduṣ-/vidvad-* 'one who knows' (*vidvān, vidvan* (voc. sg.), *vidvāṃsau, vidvāṃsas, vidvāṃsam, viduṣā, vidvadbhyām*, etc.). In addition, there are adjectives that inflect pronominally. For example, nom. pl. *sarve*, dat. sg. *sarvasmai* (m.-nt.), *sarvasyai* (f.), gen. pl. *sarveṣām, sarvāsām*, from *sarvă-* 'whole, all', are comparable to *te, tasmai, tasyai, teṣām, tāsām* from *tă-* 'this, that'.

Personal pronouns not only have variants but also distinguish between independently accented and enclitic forms: acc. sg. *mā tvā*, dat. sg. *me te*, acc.-dat.-gen. du. *nau vām*, acc.-dat.-gen. pl. *nas vas* are enclitics corresponding to sg. acc. *mām tvām*, dat. *mahyam tubhyam*, gen. *mama tava*, du. acc. *āvām yuvām*, dat. *āvābhyām yuvābhyām*, gen. *āvayos yuvayos*, pl. acc. *asmān yuṣmān*, dat. *asmabhyam yuṣmabhyam*, gen. *asmākam yuṣmākam*. Demonstrative pronouns distinguish various degrees of proximity and distance: *etad* 'this here', *idam* 'this', *tad* 'this, that', *adas* 'that yonder' (all nom.-acc. sg. nt.). Interrogative and relative pronouns respectively have *kă-*, *yă-*, which inflect like pronominal *a*-stems except in the nominative and accusative singular neuter of the former (*kim yad*).

The Sanskrit system of number words is a familiar Indo-European one in that terms for 'one' to 'four' show inflectional and gender variation, but it also differs from the system of other ancient Indo-European languages in that higher number words also inflect; e.g. inst. pl. *pañcabhis* 'five', *ṣaḍbhis* 'six', *saptabhis* 'seven', *aṣṭābhis* 'eight', *navabhis* 'nine', *daśabhis* 'ten'.

Sanskrit is also like other older Indo-European languages in using suffixes for deriving what are traditionally called comparatives and superlatives, with two kinds of suffixes. For example, *garīyas-* 'quite heavy', *gariṣṭha-* 'exceedingly heavy' have *-īyas* and *-iṣṭha* following *gar-*, a form of the base that appears in the adjectival derivative *guru-*, but *-tara* and *-tama* follow adjectival stems, as in *madhumattara-* 'quite sweet', *madhumattama-* 'exceedingly sweet', from the stem *madhumat-*. It is noteworthy that *-tara*, *-tama* are used not only in derivates like *uttara-* 'upper, superior', *uttama-* 'highest', from *ud* 'up', but also in derivates from terms like *na* 'not' and finite verb forms: *natarām* 'the more not so (in view of an additional argument)', *natamām* 'all the more not so', *pacatitarām* 'cooks quite well', *pacatitamām* 'cooks exceedingly well'.

Derived nominal bases formed directly from verb roots include action nouns like *gati-* 'going', *pāka-* 'cooking', agent nouns such as *kartṛ-*, *kāraka-* 'doer, maker', object nouns like *karman-* 'deed, object', instrument nouns such as *karaṇa-* 'means', participles like *gata-* 'gone', *kṛta-* 'done, made', gerunds, gerundives and abstract nouns that function as infinitives (see section 1.2). Bases with secondary derivate affixes (*taddhita* affixes) are of several types. There is a large group of derivates that correspond to phrases of the type *X-E Y-*, with which they alternate, where the values of *X-E* are case forms of particular nominals and *Y* stands for a nominal whose meaning is attributable to the derivational affix. For example, there are patronymics such as *dākṣi-* 'son of Dakṣa': any case form of *dākṣi-* corresponds to and alternates with a phrase containing the genitive *dakṣasya* 'of Dakṣa' and a form of *putra-* 'son' or a synonym. Other derivatives are formed from a more restricted set of nominals — predominantly pronominals — and correspond to particular case forms; e.g. *tatas* 'from that, thence', *tatra* 'in that, there' correspond respectively to ablative and locative forms of *tad-* 'this, that', with which they alternate. There are also redundant affixes. For example, *aśvaka-* 'nag' differs in meaning from *aśva-* 'horse', but *avika-* and *avi-* 'sheep' show no such semantic difference. Moreover, some taddhita affixes form derivates which do not alternate with forms or phrases containing items to which they are added. Thus, *kṛtrima-* 'artificial' has a suffix -*ma*, but *kṛtrima-* does not alternate with a phrase containing a form of *kṛtri-*, since there is no such action noun: once -*tri* is affixed to *kṛ*, then, -*ma* is obligatory.

Compounds are of four general types: tatpuruṣa (determinative), dvandva (copulative), bahuvrīhi (exocentric), and a type that is usually invariant (avyayībhava). The first member of a tatpuruṣa compound is generally equivalent to a case form other than a nominative. For example, *tatpuruṣas* (nom. sg. m.) 'his man, servant' is equivalent to *tasya puruṣas*, with which it can alternate. Similarly, *grāmagatas* 'gone to the village' is equivalent to *grāmaṁ gatas*, with the accusative *grāmam* 'village'. There is a subtype of tatpuruṣa compounds in which the first member is coreferential with the second, which it modifies, as in *nīlotpalam* 'blue (*nīla-*) lotus', equivalent to *nīlam utpalam*, with two nominatives. Copulative compounds are equivalent to phrases with *ca* 'and'; e.g. *mātāpitarau* 'mother and father' alternates with *mātā pitā ca*. The term *bahuvrīhi* is an example of a bahuvrīhi compound: *bahuvrīhis* is equivalent to *bahur vrīhir asya*, used with reference to someone who has (*asya* 'of this') much (*bahus*) rice (*vrīhis*); similarly: *prāptodaka-* '(somewhere) that water (*udaka-*) has reached (*prāpta-*)', *ūḍharatha-* '(an animal) by which a chariot (*ratha-*) has been drawn (*ūḍha-*)'. There are also exocentric compounds which, for technical reasons, belong to the tatpuruṣa group; e.g. *pañcagava-* 'a group of five cows', a member of the subgroup of tatpuruṣas called *dvigu*. Avyayībhava compounds are generally, though not always, invariant; e.g. *upāgni* 'near the fire', *anujyeṣṭham* 'according to (*anu*) seniority (*jyeṣṭha-* 'oldest')'. Compounds like *upāgni* do not have alternative phrases containing the members of the derivate.

2.2.3 Verbal System

The basic elements on which the Sanskrit verbal system is built are the verb base or root, either primary or derived, and the present-imperfect stem. The root is the base for the present-imperfect stem, for various aorist stems and future formations, the perfect, the conditional and the precative. The present-imperfect stem is the basis not only for present and imperfect forms but also for imperative and optative forms. Although Sanskrit has eliminated quite a few complexities found in Vedic, its verbal system is still varied.

There is a systematic contrast between active and medio-passive. Some verbs take only active endings in agentive forms, others only middle endings. For example, the present *asmi, asi, asti* (1, 2, 3 sg.), *svas, sthas, stas* (1, 2, 3 du.), *smas, stha, santi* (1, 2, 3 pl.) and the imperfect *āsam āsīs āsīt, āsva āstam āstām, āsma āsta āsan* have only active endings with *as* 'be', and *āse āsse āste, āsvahe āsāthe āsāte, āsmahe ādhve āsate, āsi āsthās āsta, āsvahi āsāthām āsātām, āsmahi ādhvam āsata* have middle endings with *ās* 'be seated'. Other verbs take either active or middle endings in agentive forms, depending on a semantic contrast: if the result of the act in question is intended for the agent, middle endings are used, if not, active endings occur. For example, *kurute* is used with reference to someone making something for himself, *karoti* of one making something for another. Medio-passive endings alone are used in passives; e.g. *kaṭaḥ kriyate* 'a mat (*kaṭas*) is being made', with *-te* after the passive stem *kriya-*. Sanskrit also has formally passive forms comparable to the impersonal middle found in other Indo-European languages (the type Latin *itur* 'it is gone' i.e. 'one goes'), but it allows an agent to be signified with an instrumental in construction with such forms; e.g. *devadattena supyate* 'Devadatta is sleeping', with the formally passive *supyate* (act. *svapiti*) and the agentive instrumental *devadattena*. In both active and middle sets, three groups of endings are distinguished, which, following usual western terminology, I shall call primary, secondary and perfect endings. Although comparative evidence shows that certain primary endings were originally complexes with a particle, analogic developments have obscured this relation in some instances. The contrast between primary and secondary endings has been illustrated above: primary active; *-mi, -si (asi < as-si), -ti; -vas, -thas, -tas; -mas, -tha, -anti/ati* (e.g. *juhvati* 'they offer oblations'); secondary active: *-am, -s, -t* (augmented *-īs -īt); -va, -tam, tām; -ma, -ta, -ant/us* (e.g. *ajuhavus* 'they offered oblations', *adus* 'they have given', *akārṣus* 'they have made'); primary medio-passive: *-e, -se, -te; -vahe, -āthe, -āte; -mahe, -dhve (ādhve < ās-dhve), -ate/ante* (e.g. *edhante* 'they thrive'); secondary medio-passive: *-i, -thās, -ta; -vahi, -āthām, -ātām; -mahi, -dhvam, -ata/anta*. Certain endings are particular to the perfect, as can be seen from the following (*kṛ*): active: *cakăr-a, cakar-tha, cakār-a; cakṛ-va, cakr-athus, cakr-atus; cakṛ-ma, cakr-a, cakṛ-us;* medio-passive: *cakr-e, cakṛ-ṣe, cakr-e; cakṛ-vahe, cakr-āthe, cakr-āte; cakṛ-*

mahe, cakṛḍhve, cakr-ire.

There is also a contrast between augmented and unaugmented stems. Indicative imperfect and aorist forms, as well as those of the conditional, have augmented stems. The augment is *a* for consonant-initial bases, *ā* for vowel-initial bases; e.g. imperfect *akarot*, aorist *akārṣīt*, conditional *akariṣyat* from *kṛ*, imperfect *āsit* (3 pl. *āsan*) from *as*.

Present-imperfect stems may be considered according to two major criteria. Some stems consist simply of verb roots, others have affixes; some stems exhibit grammatical alternation (ablaut), others do not. Stems that do not show grammatical alternation regularly have suffixes with *-a*: root-accented *bhav-a-* 'be, become' (*bhavāmi, bhavasi, bhavati; bhavāvas, bhavathas, bhavatas; bhavāmas, bhavatha, bhavanti*); *edh-a-* 'thrive' (*edhe, edhase, edhate; edhāvahe, edhethe, edhete; edhāmahe, edhadve, edhante*); *dīv-ya-* 'gamble' (*dīvyāmi* etc.); suffix-accented *tud-a-* 'goad, wound' (*tudāmi* etc.), passive *kri-ya-*. Such stems have *-ā* (< **o* by 'Brugmann's Law') before *-v-, -m-* of endings and *-e-* in second and third dual medio-passive forms. Root presents generally exhibit ablaut variation: full-grade in the singular active indicative, zero-grade elsewhere. For example: *as-ti, s-tas, s-anti; han-ti, ha-tas, ghn-anti* (*han* 'kill'); *dveṣ-ṭi, dviṣ-ṭas, dviṣ-anti; dviṣ-ṭe, dviṣ-āte, dviṣ-ate* (*dviṣ* 'hate'); *dog-dhi, dug-dhas, duh-anti; dug-dhe, duh-āte, duh-ate* (*duh* 'milk'). On the other hand, *ad* 'eat' has an invariant root stem (*at-ti at-tas ad-anti*) due in the first instance to phonologic developments (e.g. 3 du. **tas < ttas < d-tas*) that led to remodelling, and bases in *-ā* generalised this vowel in root presents, as in *yāti, yātas, yānti* (*yā* 'go, travel'). Moreover, there are some verbs with inherited invariant root presents, such as *ās, vas* 'have on, wear' (*vas-te, vas-āte, vas-ate*), *śī* 'lie, recline' (*śe-te, śay-āte, śe-rate*). Further, root presents of verbs in *-u* have *-au* instead of *-o* in alternation with *-u*; e.g. *stau-ti, stu-tas, stuv-anti* (*stu* 'praise'). There are also reduplicated stems, as in *juho-ti, juhu-tas, juhv-ati* (*hu* 'offer oblations'). In addition, ablauting present-imperfect stems are formed with suffixes and an infix. Thus, *śakno-/śaknu-* (*śak* 'be able'), *cino-/cinu-* (*ci* 'gather, heap'), *suno-/sunu-* (*su* 'press juice out of something') have a suffix *-no-/-nu-* (*-nv-* before vowels, *-nuv-* if the root ends in a consonant): *śaknoti, śaknutas, śaknuvanti; cinoti, cinutas, cinvanti, cinute, cinvāte, cinvate; sunoti, sunute*, etc. But *chi-na-d-/chi-n-d-* (*chinatti, chinttas, chindanti; chintte, chindāte, chindate*) shows an infix *-na-/-n-* added to *chid* 'cut'. Stems such as *pu-nā-/pu-nī-/pu-n-* 'purify' (*punāti, punītas, punanti, punīte, punāte, punate*), with short root vowels (contrast *pū-ta-* 'purified'), reflect an inherited formation with an infix added to a laryngeal base (Proto-Indo-European **-ne-H-/-n-H-*), but the types *krī-ṇā-...* 'buy' (*krīṇāti krīṇite* etc.), *badh-nā-...* 'tie up' (*badhnāti* etc.), with *-nā* etc. after a long vowel (cf. *krī-ta-* 'bought') or a consonant, show that this has been reanalysed as a suffix comparable to *-no-/-nu-*. Historical developments led to the creation of a stem *karo-/kuru-* (*karoti, kurutas, kurvanti, kurute, kurvāte, kurvate*) from *kr̥*, in addition to the earlier *kr̥n̥o-/kr̥n̥u-*, which allowed the abstraction of a suffix *-o/-u-*, as in *tano-/tanu-* (*tanoti, tanute* etc.), comparable to *śakno-/ śaknu-*, from *tan* 'stretch', although originally this was the same suffix as in the type *śakno-/śaknu-*, only with bases in *-n* (*tano-/tanu-* < **tn̥-neu-/tn̥-nu-*).

Third person active and medio-passive imperative forms respectively have *-u*, *ām* instead of *-i*, *-e* of present indicatives; e.g. *as-tu, s-antu; ās-tām, ās-ātām, ās-atām*. However, second singular active imperatives of stems in *-a* have no overt ending: *bhav-a, dīv-ya, tud-a*. The same is true of the type *ci-nu*. However, if *-u* of the suffix *-nu-* follows a cluster, the imperative retains the ending *-hi*: *śaknuhi*; and this ending has a variant *-dhi* after *juhu-* and consonant-final stems: *juhudhi, chindhi* (< *chinddhi*). In addition, following consonant-final stems one has *-āna-* for presents with *-nā-*: *punīhi, krīṇīhi*, but *badhāna*. Second singular middle imperatives have a suffix *-sva*: *āssva, edhasva, cinuṣva*. First person imperative forms are historically subjunctives (see section 1.2): *bhavāni, bhavāva, bhavāma; edhai, edhāvahai, edhāmahai*. Other forms simply have secondary endings. In addition, there is an imperative with *-tāt* for both second and third singular, which, according to Pāṇini's description, was used in wishing someone well, as in *jīvatāt* 'may you/he live long'.

Stems in *-a* form optatives with *-ī-/-īy-*; other stems have optatives with *-yā-/-y-* in active forms and *-ī-/-īy-* in medio-passive forms. Optatives have the usual secondary endings except for active third plural *-us*, middle first singular *-a*, third plural *-ran*. For example: *bhaveyam, bhaves, bhavet, bhaveva, bhavetam, bhavetām, bhavema, bhaveta, bhaveyus; edheya, edhethās, edheta, edhevahi, edheyāthām, edheyātām, edhemahi, edhedhvam, edheran; syām, syās, syāt, syāva, syātam, syātām, syāma, syāta, syus* (*as* 'be'); *āsīya, āsīthās, āsīta, āsīvahi, āsīyāthām, asīyātām, āsimahi, āsīdhvam, āsīran*. Although synchronically the types *bhavet, edheta* are analysable as containing *-īy-/-ī-* (*-ey-* < *-a-īy-*, *-e-* < *-a-ī-*), these correspond to optatives elsewhere in Indo-European that point to **-oi-*. In addition, the use of *-yā-* in active and *-ī-* in medio-passive forms represents a redistribution of ablaut variants of an original single affix.

Aorists are either radical or formed with suffixes. Unreduplicated root aorists are rare in Classical Sanskrit as compared with earlier Vedic. Except for the third person singular passive aorist type *akāri* 'has been made' — which is freely formed to any verb, but is not necessarily to be analysed as a root aorist — only active forms of bases in *-ā* (e.g. *dā* 'give': *adāt, adātām, adus*) and of *bhū* 'be, become' (*abhūt, abhūtām, abhūvan*) regularly belong to this type, although some middle forms of root aorists have been incorporated into the sigmatic system. There are also stems in *-a*, such as *agama-* (*agamat, agamatām, agaman: gam* 'go'), *aghasa-* (*ghas* 'eat'), *aśaka-* (*śak* 'be able'). In addition, a reduplicated stem in *-a* regularly corresponds to a causative (see below) and supplies aorist forms to a few other verbs; e.g. *adudruva-* (*dru* 'run'). However, the productive Sanskrit aorist formation is sigmatic, of four subtypes: -s-, -iṣ, -siṣ-, -sa-. The last developed from the middle of the s-aorist of duh (e.g. 1 sg. adhukṣi, 3 sg. du. pl. adugdha, adhukṣātām, adhukṣata), as can be seen from the earliest usage in Vedic, from the fact that s-forms are indeed incorporated into the sa-paradigm (e.g. mid. 1 sg. adhukṣi, 3 sg. adugdha/adhukṣata), and from the fact that this aorist is formed only with verbs that have penultimate i, u, ṛ and final consonants which give -kṣ- in combination with the -s- of the suffix. The s-aorist itself is characterised by particular variants of roots preceding the suffix. Verbs with -ĭ, -ŭ, -ṛ have alternants with -ai, -au, -ār before -s- in active forms, and verbs with -ĭ, -ŭ have variants with -e, -o in medio-passive forms; e.g. ci: acaiṣīt, acaiṣṭām, acaiṣus, aceṣṭa, aceṣātām, aceṣata; hu: ahauṣīt, kṛ: akārṣīt (but middle akṛta akṛṣātām akṛṣata). Verbs with medial vowels also have alternants with vṛddhi vowels in active forms, but they have medio-passives with -a-, -i-, -u-, -ṛ-; e.g. pac 'cook': apākṣīt, chid: achaitsit, rudh 'obstruct': arautsit, mṛṣ 'suffer, allow': amārṣīt versus apakta, achitta, aruddha, amṛṣṭa. Forms such as akṛta, adita (dā 'give') beside akṛṣātām, adiṣātām etc. and active adāt etc. reflect the incorporation of root aorist forms into the productive sigmatic system. The iṣ-aorist is probably best considered originally an s-formation to verbs with -i from a laryngeal, then spread well beyond these limits. This also has vṛddhi vowels in forms such as apāvīt, apāviṣṭām, apāviṣus (pū), but in general not for consonant-final bases; e.g. div 'gamble': adevīt. The siṣ-aorist, obviously a combination of -s- and -iṣ-, is of very limited compass, predominantly from verbs in -ā; e.g. ayāsīt (yā).

Although scholars disagree concerning the historical origins of the precative, the place of the forms in question within the Sanskrit system viewed synchronically is fairly clear. The active precative type bhuyāt, bhuyāstām, bhuyāsus 'may... be, prosper' is radical, and the middle type edhiṣīṣṭa, edhiṣīyāstām, edhiṣīran 'may... thrive' is sigmatic.

The semantically unmarked future of Sanskrit has a suffix -(i)ṣya after a root. In addition, there is a future used with reference to a time beyond the day of reference. In origin, this is a periphrastic formation (see section 1.2), but synchronically it cannot be treated as such in view of forms like edhitāhe, edhitāsve, edhitāsmahe (1 sg. du. pl. mid.), since as does not regularly have middle inflection. The future in -(i)ṣya (e.g., bhaviṣyati, edhiṣyate) is the basis for the Sanskrit conditional, of the type abhaviṣyat, aidhiṣyata — with augment and secondary endings — used in both the protasis and the apodosis of contrary-to-fact conditional sentences.

The Sanskrit perfect is generally characterised not only by particular endings but also by reduplication (see above). Yet one inherited perfect, which in Sanskrit functions as a present, lacks reduplication: veda, vidatus, vidus 'know(s)'. As can be seen, perfect stems show the same kind of grammatical alternation as found in present and aorist stems. However, for verbs of the structure CaC, in which -a- is flanked by single consonants the first of which is not subject to modification in a reduplicated syllable, instead of -CC- preceded by a reduplicated syllable, one has C*e*C alone; e.g. *tan*: *tatāna*, *tenatus*, *tenus*; *śak*: *śaśāka*, *śekatus*, *śekus* (contrast *gam*: *jagāma*, *jagmatus*, *jagmus*). This represents the spread of a particular form from verbs like *yam* 'extend' (*yayāma*, *yematus* (< *ya-ym-*) ...), *sad* 'sit' (*sasāda*, *sedatus* (< *sa-zd-*) ...). There is also a periphrastic perfect, which in Sanskrit has been extended to some primary verbs; e.g. *hu*: *juhavāñ cakāra* beside *juhāva*.

As can be seen from what has been said, it is not possible in Sanskrit to predict an aorist formation from the present-imperfect stem of a verb. There are instances where totally separate roots are used suppletively in different formations. Thus, *as* supplies only a present-imperfect stem; other forms are from *bhū* 'be, become': aorist *abhūt*, future *bhaviṣyati*, perfect *babhūva*, infinitive *bhavitum*, past participle *bhūta-* etc. Similarly: *han* 'strike, kill': aorist *avadhīt*, precative *vadhyāt*, *ad* 'eat': aorist *aghasat*, *i*: aorist *agāt*.

Derived verbs are deverbative or denominative. Causatives are formed with *-i-/-e-*; e.g. *kṛ*: *kār-i* 'have ... do, make' (*kār-ay-a-ti*, *kār-ay-ate*), *pac*: *pāc-i*, *chid*: *ched-i*, *yuj-* 'connect, yoke': *yoj-i*. Certain verbs have augmented variants before the causative suffix. For example, many verbs with *-ā* take the augment *-p*, as in *dāp-i* 'have ... give' (*dā*). The causative is also connected with a particular active aorist formation, a reduplicated *a*-aorist; e.g. *kār-i*: *acīkarat* etc. (but medio-passive *akārayita*, *akārayiṣātām*, etc.). Desideratives are formed with *-sa-*, which conditions reduplication; e.g. *kṛ*: *cikīrṣa-* (*cikīrṣati*, etc.). Desiderative forms alternate with phrases consisting of a verb meaning 'wish' and infinitives; e.g. *cikīrṣati* = *kartum icchati* '... wishes to do, make'. Intensives are formed with *-ya-*, which also conditions a particular type of reduplication; further, intensives have middle inflection; e.g. *kṛ*: *cekrīya-* (*cekrīyate*) 'do intensely, repeatedly', *chid*: *cechidya-*, *yuj*: *yoyujya-*, *pac*: *pāpacya-*. Derived verbs form periphrastic perfects, as in *gamayāñ cakāra*, *cekrīyāñ cakre*. Moreover, such deverbative formations can involve suppletion; e.g. *ad*: desiderative *jighatsa-*, *i*: *jigamiṣa-*. Denominatives are formed with several suffixes, principal among which is *-ya-*, and have a broad range of meanings. For example, *putrīyati* (*putrīya-*) corresponds to *putram icchati* '... desires a son', *putram ivācarati* '... behaves (*ācarati*) towards ... as though he were his son (*putram iva*)'; *śyenāyate* corresponds to *śyena ivācarati* 'behaves like a falcon (*śyena iva*)', *tapasyati* is equivalent to *tapaś carati* 'carries out (*carati*) ascetic acts (*tapas*).' Especially noteworthy in view of the later Indo-Aryan causative type in *-āv-e-* (see section 2.2 of the chapter on Indo-Aryan) is the denominative type *satyāpi-* (*satyāpayati*) 'say something is true (*satya*)', known already to Pāṇini, which involves *-āp-* and the suffix *-i-/-e-*.

2.2.4 Syntax

In major aspects of syntax Sanskrit is a fairly conservative Indo-European language, although it exhibits specifically Indic features. Examples given in the following sketch are based on Pāṇinian sources, reflecting usage that antedates classical literary works, but every construction illustrated has a counterpart in Vedic (see section 1.2) and literary texts of later times.

The seven cases of the nominal system excluding the vocative (section 2.2.2) are used with reference to various roles participants play in respect of what is signified by verbs in general or by particular verbs. Typical roles and case forms linked with them are illustrated by the following. In *devadattaḥ kaṭaṁ karoti* 'Devadatta is making (*karoti*) a mat (*kaṭam*)', *devadatto grāmaṁ gacchati* 'Devadatta is going (*gacchati*) to the village (*grāmam*)', the accusatives *kaṭam, grāmam* refer to objects, the latter specifically to a goal of movement. Such a goal is alternatively signified by a dative: *devadatto grāmāya gacchati*. In addition, an object can be designated by a genitive in construction with an agent noun; e.g. *sa kumbhānāṁ kartā* 'he (*sa*) (is) a maker (*kartā*) of pots (*kumbhānām*)'. In the passive sentence *devadattena kaṭaḥ kriyate* 'a mat is being made (*kriyate*) by Devadatta', the instrumental *devadattena* refers to an agent, as does the same form in *devadattena supyate* (section 2.2.3). The instrumental *dātreṇa* 'sickle' of *dātreṇa lunāti* '...cuts (*lunāti*) with a sickle', on the other hand, refers to a means of cutting. A dative can be used with references not only to a goal of movement but also to a desired object, in construction with *spṛh* 'yearn for': *puṣpebhyaḥ spṛhayati* '... yearns for flowers (*puṣbebhyas*)'. More generally, dative forms designate indirect objects, as in *māṇavakāya bhikṣāṁ dadāti* '... gives (*dadāti*) alms (*bhikṣām*) to the lad (*māṇavakāya*)'. Ablatives can be used to signify points of departure, as in *grāmād ā gacchati* '...is coming (*ā gacchati*) from the village', but they have other functions as well; for example, in *vṛkebhyo bibheti* '... is afraid (*bibheti*) of wolves', *vṛkebhyas* refers to wolves as sources of fear. Locative forms are used of loci where agents and objects are while they are involved in whatever a verb signifies; e.g. *devadattaḥ sthālyāṁ gṛha odanaṁ pacati* 'Devadatta is cooking (*pacati*) rice (*odanam*) in a pot (*sthālyām*) in the house (*gṛhe*)'.

There are also relations that do not directly involve verb meanings, so that syntactically one has nominals directly linked with each other. The typical case form for such relations is the genitive; e.g. *vṛkṣasya śākhā-* 'branch (*śākhā-*) of a/the tree (*vṛkṣasya*)' in *vṛkṣasya śākhāṁ paraśunā chinatti* '... is cutting a branch (*śākhām*) of the tree with an axe (*paraśunā*)'. Particular nominals, however, co-occur with other case forms. For example, *namo devebhyaḥ* '(let there be) homage (*namas*) to the gods' has the dative *devebhyas* in construction with *namas*. Moreover, pre- and postposed particles take part in such constructions: *sādhur devadatto mātaraṁ prati* 'Devadatta (is) good (*sadhus*) towards his mother (*mātaraṁ prati*)', *putreṇa sahāgataḥ* 'he came (*āgatas*) with his son (*putreṇa saha*)', *māṣān asmai tilebhyaḥ prati dadāti* '... gives (*dadāti*) this man (*asmai*) māṣa-beans (*māṣān*) in exchange for sesame seeds (*tilebhyaḥ prati*)', *ā pāṭaliputrād varṣati* 'it is raining (*varṣati*) up to Pāṭaliputra (*ā pāṭaliputrāt*)', have the accusative *mātaram* linked to *prati*, the instrumental *putreṇa* connected to *saha*, and the ablatives *tilebhyas*, *pāṭaliputrāt* construed with *prati* and *ā*.

There are different kinds of complex sentences. Some involve related finite verb forms, others finite forms connected with particular nominal derivates, infinitival and participial. For example, optatives are used in conditional sentences such as *mriyeya ... na syās tvaṁ yadi me gatiḥ* 'I would die (*mriyeya*) if (*yadi*) you (*tvam*) were (*syās*) not (*na*) my (*me*) refuge (*gatis*)', but *edhān āhartum gacchati* '... is going (*gacchati*) in order to fetch (*āhartum*) firewood (*edhān*)' has *gacchati* linked to the infinitive *āhartum*, itself connected with the accusative *edhān*. There is an elliptical version of the second sentence type, with a dative referring to the direct object in question: *edhebhyo gacchati* '... is going for firewood'. Present participle forms occur in complex sentences such as *pacantaṁ devadattam paśyati* '... is watching (*paśyati*) Devadatta cook', in which *pacantam* 'cooking' agrees with *devadattam*, or *grāmaṁ gacchatā devadattena bhuktam* 'Devadatta ate on his way to the village', where the participial form *gacchatā* 'going' agrees with the agentive instrumental *devadattena*, both construed with *bhuktam* 'eaten'. In addition, Sanskrit has absolute constructions, the prevalent one being a locative absolute, as in *goṣu duhyamānāsu gataḥ* 'he left (*gatas*) while the cows were being milked': the present participle *duhyamānāsu* (loc. pl. f.) agrees with *goṣu* 'cows', both used absolutely. Where two or more verbs signify sequentially related acts or states, Sanskrit subordinates by using gerunds; e.g. *bhuktvā vrajati* '... eats before going out', with the gerund *bhuktvā* 'after eating', *piba niṣadya* (see section 1.2).

Examples cited illustrate the agreement features of Sanskrit. Finite verb forms — which themselves signal person and number differences — agree in person and number with nominals that function as grammatical subjects used in referring to agents or objects. Participial forms and other adjectivals, whether attributive or predicative, agree in gender and number with the nominals to which they are complements. The examples also illustrate the most common aspects of Sanskrit word order. What may be called the neutral word order in prose, where metrical constraints are not at play, generally has the verb in last position. However, a sentence does not necessarily have an overt verb: Sanskrit has nominal sentences, in which a third person present form of a verb meaning 'be' is not overtly expressed. There are few restrictions on word order that are strictly formal, but the position of certain particles is fixed: particles like *vai* 'as is known, truly', *ced* 'if ' occupy second position, as does *ca* 'and' used as a sentence connective. Similarly, the enclitic pronouns *mā*, *tvā* etc. (section 2.2.2) are excluded from sentence-initial position.

An aspect of overall sentence prosody is worth noting in this context. A sentence-internal vocative generally has no high-pitched vowel. Under certain conditions, however, the vowels of an utterance are all pronounced monotone, except for the last vowel, which is then not only high-pitched but also prolated. For example, in *ā gaccha bho māṇavaka devadatta* 'come along (*ā gaccha*), Devadatta my boy (*bho māṇavaka devadatta*)', used in calling Devadatta from afar, all the vowels up to the -*a* of the vocative *devadatta* are uttered without pitch variations, but this last vowel is prolated and udātta.

Bibliography

Burrow (1965) is a summary of the prehistory and history of Sanskrit, including Vedic, with references to Middle Indo-Aryan; somewhat personal views are given in places, but the work remains valuable. For a good summary of views on the dialects of Old Indo-Aryan, with discussion of theories proposed and references, see Emeneau (1966).

The standard reference grammar is Whitney (1889). Renou (1956) is an insightful summary of the grammar, vocabulary and style of different stages of Sanskrit, including Vedic, with text selections and translations. Wackernagel (1896–) is the most thorough reference grammar of Sanskrit, but remains incomplete: the published volumes are: I (*Lautlehre*), reissued with a new 'Introduction générale' by L. Renou and 'Nachträge' by A. Debrunner (1957); II, 1 (*Einleitung zur Wortlehre, Nominalkomposition*), 2nd ed. with 'Nachträge' by A. Debrunner (1957); II, 2 (*Die Nominalsuffixe*), by A. Debrunner (1954); III (*Nominalflexion – Zahlwort – Pronomen*) (1930); there is also a *Register zur altindischen Grammatik von J. Wackernagel und A. Debrunner* by R. Hauschild (1964).

References

Burrow, T. 1965. *The Sanskrit Language*, 2nd ed. (Faber and Faber, London)
Emeneau, M.B. 1966. 'The Dialects of Old Indo-Aryan', in H. Birnbaum and J. Puhvel (eds.), *Ancient Indo-European Dialects* (University of California Press, Berkeley and Los Angeles), pp. 123–38.
Renou, L. 1956. *Histoire de la langue sanskrite* (IAC, Paris)
Wackernagel, J. 1896–. *Altindische Grammatik* (Vandenhoek and Ruprecht, Göttingen)
Whitney, W.D. 1889. *Sanskrit Grammar, Including Both the Classical Language and the Older Dialects, of Veda and Brahmana*, 2nd ed. (Harvard University Press, Cambridge, Mass.)

22 Hindi-Urdu

Yamuna Kachru

1. Introduction

Hindi is a New Indo-Aryan language spoken in the north of India. It belongs to the Indo-Iranian branch of the Indo-European family of languages. It is spoken by more than two hundred million people either as a first or second language in India, and by peoples of Indian origin in Trinidad, Guyana, Fiji, Mauritius, South Africa and other countries. Along with English, it is the official language of India. In addition, it is the state language of Bihar, Haryana, Himachal Pradesh, Madhya Pradesh, Rajasthan and Uttar Pradesh.

Urdu, a language closely related to Hindi, is spoken by twenty-three million people in India and approximately eight million people in Pakistan as a mother tongue. It is the official language of Pakistan and the state language of the state of Jammu and Kashmir in India.

It is difficult to date the beginnings of the New Indo-Aryan languages of India. Scholars generally agree that the development of Indo-Aryan languages of India took place in three stages. The Old Indo-Aryan stage is said to extend from 1500 BC to approximately 600 BC. The Middle Indo-Aryan stage spans the centuries between 600 BC and AD 1000. The Middle Indo-Aryan stage is further subdivided into an early Middle Indo-Aryan stage (600–200 BC), a transitional stage (200 BC–AD 200), a second Middle Indo-Aryan stage (AD 200–600), and a late Middle Indo-Aryan stage (AD 600–1000). The period between AD 1000–1200/1300 is designated the Old New Indo-Aryan stage because it is at this stage that the changes that began at the Middle Indo-Aryan stage became established and the New Indo-Aryan languages such as Hindi, Bengali, Marathi etc. assumed distinct identities.

Before proceeding with a description of Hindi-Urdu, it may be useful to sketch briefly the sociolinguistic situation of Hindi-Urdu in the Indian subcontinent (Rai 1984).

The name Hindi is not Indian in origin; it is believed to have been used by the Persians to denote the peoples and languages of India (Verma 1933). Hindi as a language is said to have emerged from the patois of the market

470

place and army camps during the period of repeated Islamic invasions and establishment of Muslim rule in the north of India between the eighth and tenth centuries AD. The speech of the areas around Delhi, known as *kharī bolī*, was adopted by the Afghans, Persians and Turks as a common language of interaction with the local population. In time, it developed a variety called *urdū* (from Turkish *ordu* 'camp'). This variety, naturally, had a preponderance of borrowings from Arabic and Persian. Consequently, it was also known as *rextā* 'mixed language'. The speech of the indigenous population, though influenced by Arabic and Persian, remained relatively free from large-scale borrowings from these foreign languages. In time, as Urdu gained some patronage at Muslim courts and developed into a literary language, the variety used by the general population gradually replaced Sanskrit, literary Prakrits and Apabhraṁśas as the literary language of the midlands (*madhyadeśa*). This latter variety looked to Sanskrit for linguistic borrowings and Sanskrit, Prakrits and Apabhraṁśas for literary conventions. It is this variety that became known as Hindi. Thus, both Hindi and Urdu have their origins in the *kharī bolī* speech of Delhi and its environs although they are written in two different scripts (Urdu in Perso-Arabic and Hindi in Devanāgarī). The two languages differ in minor ways in their sound system, morphology and syntax. These differences are pointed out at appropriate places below.

Hindi and Urdu have a common form known as Hindustani which is essentially a colloquial language (Verma 1933). This was the variety that was adopted by Mahatma Gandhi and the Indian National Congress as a symbol of national identity during the struggle for freedom. It, however, never became a language of literature and high culture (see Bhatia 1987 for an account of the Hindi-Urdu-Hindustani controversy in the late nineteenth and early twentieth centuries).

Both Urdu and Hindi have been in use as literary languages since the twelfth century. The development of prose, however, begins only in the eighteenth century under the influence of English, which marks the emergence of Hindi and Urdu as fully-fledged literary languages.

2 Phonology

The segmental phonemes of Hindi-Urdu are listed in table 22.1. The phonemes that occur only in the highly Sanskritised or highly Persianised varieties are given in parentheses. The two noteworthy features of the inventory of consonant phonemes are the following: Hindi-Urdu still retains the original Indo-European distinction between aspirated and unaspirated voiced plosives (cf. Indo-European *ghṛdho* and Hindi *ghər* 'house'). It retains the distinction between aspirated and unaspirated voiceless plosives that emerged in Indo-Aryan, i.e. the distinction between *kal* 'time' and *khal* 'skin'. Another Indo-Aryan feature, that of retroflexion, is also retained in Hindi-Urdu, cf. *tota* 'parrot' and *ṭoṭa* 'lack'. These two features, i.e. those of aspiration and retroflexion, are mainly responsible for why Hindi-Urdu sounds so different from its European cousins.

Table 22.1: Phonemes of Hindi-Urdu

Vowels

	Front	Centre	Back
High	i		u
	ɪ		ʊ
Mid High	e		o
Mid Low	ɛ	ə	ɔ
Low		a	

Consonants

			Labial	Dental	Retro-flex	Alveo-Palatal	Velar	Back Velar
Stop	vls.	unasp.	p	t	ṭ	č	k	(q)
		asp.	ph	th	ṭh	čh	kh	
	vd.	unasp.	b	d	ḍ	j	g	
		asp.	bh	dh	ḍh	jh	gh	
Nasal			m	n	(ṇ)	(ñ)	(ŋ)	
Flap	vd.	unasp.			ṛ	r		
		asp.			ṛh			
Lateral						l		
Fricative	vls.		(f)	s	(ṣ)	š	(x)	
	vd.			(z)		(ž)	(ɣ)	
Semi-vowels			w (v)			y		

Note: Oral and nasal vowels contrast, e.g. *ak* 'a plant' and *āk* 'draw, sketch'; hence, nasalisation is distinctive. Short and long consonants contrast, e.g. *pəta* 'address', *pətta* 'leaf'; hence, length is distinctive.

The contrast between aspirated and unaspirated consonants is maintained in all positions, initial, medial and final. The distinction between tense *i* and lax *ɪ* and tense *u* and lax *ʊ*, however, is lost in the final position except in very careful and formal speech in the highly Sanskritised variety.

Stress is not distinctive in Hindi-Urdu; words are not distinguished on the basis of stress alone. For instance, a word such as *kəla* 'art', whether stressed as 'kəla or kə'la, means the same. The tense vowels are phonetically long and in pronunciation the vowel quality as well as length is maintained irrespective of the position of the vowel or stress in the word. For instance, the word *muskərahəṭ* 'smile' can either be stressed as 'muskərahəṭ or muskə'rahəṭ, in either case, the vowel quality and length in the syllable -ra-remains unaffected. Words such as *jamata* 'son-in-law' are pronounced with three successive long vowels although only the first or the second syllable is stressed. Stressing and destressing of syllables is tied to syllable weight in Hindi-Urdu. Syllables are classified as one of the three measures of weight: light (syllables ending in a lax, short vowel), medium (syllables ending in a tense, long vowel or in a lax, short vowel followed by a consonant) and heavy (others). Where one syllable in a word is of greater weight than others, the tendency is to place the word stress on it. Where more than one syllable is of maximum weight in the word (i.e. there is a succession of medium or heavy syllables), usually the last but one bears the word stress. This stress pattern creates the impression of the staccato rhythm that speakers of English notice about Hindi-Urdu.

The predominant pattern of penultimate stress in Hindi-Urdu is inherited from an earlier stage of Indo-Aryan, i.e. the Middle Indo-Aryan stage. Old Indo-Aryan had phonemic accent of the pitch variety and there is evidence for three pitches in Vedic: *udātta* 'high, raised', *anudātta* 'low, unraised' and *svarita* 'high falling, falling' (see section 2.1 of the chapter on Sanskrit). At a later stage of Old Indo-Aryan, Classical Sanskrit does not record accent. By late Old Indo-Aryan, pitch accent seems to have given way to stress accent. There are different opinions about stress accent in Middle Indo-Aryan. It is generally believed that stress occurred on the penultimate syllable of the word, if long, or on the nearest preceding syllable if the penultimate was not long; in words with all short syllables, stress occured on the initial syllable.

Syllable boundaries in Hindi-Urdu words fall as follows: between successive vowels, e.g. *pa-e* 'legs', *a-ɪ-e* 'come' (hon.), *nə-i* 'new' (f.), *so-ɪ-e* 'sleep' (hon.); between vowels and following consonants, e.g. *ro-na* 'to cry', *pə-ta* 'address', *ū-ča* 'tall, high'; between consonants, e.g. *sər-kē* 'roads', *pət-la* 'thin', *hɪn-di* 'Hindi language'.

As has already been said, Hindi is written in the Devanāgarī script, which is the script used by Sanskrit, Marathi and Nepali also. On the basis of the evidence obtained from the ancient inscriptions, it is clear that Devanāgarī is a descendant of the Brāhmī script. Brāhmī was well established in India some time before 500 BC. Despite some controversy regarding the origin of the Brāhmī script, it is generally believed that its sources lie in the same Semitic script which later developed into the Arabic, Hebrew, Greek, Latin scripts etc. The scripts used for the New Indo-Aryan and the Dravidian languages of India are believed to have developed from the northern and southern varieties of Brāhmī.

There are minor differences between the scripts used for Hindi, Sanskrit, Marathi and Nepali. For instance, Hindi does not have the retroflex lateral ळ or the retroflex vowels ऋ, ॠ and ॡ. It uses the retroflex vowel symbol ऋ and the symbol for weak aspiration : only in words borrowed from Sanskrit. Although written as ऋ, the vowel is pronounced as a combination of *r* and *ɪ*.

In general, there is a fairly regular correspondence between the script and the pronunciation. The one notable exception is the pronunciation of the inherent vowel *ə*. The Devanāgarī script is syllabic in that every consonant symbol represents the consonant plus the inherent vowel *ə*, thus, the symbol क represents the sound *k* plus *ə*, or *kə*. Vowels are represented differently according to whether they comprise entire syllables or are parts of syllables, i.e. are immediately preceded by a consonant: thus, the symbol ई represents the syllable *i*, but in the syllable *ki*, it has the shape ी which is adjoined to the symbol for *k*, resulting in की . Even though each consonant symbol represents a consonant plus the inherent vowel, a word written as कल , i.e. *kələ*, is not pronounced as *kələ*, it is pronounced as *kəl* 'yesterday, tomorrow'. That is, all the final inherent vowels are dropped in pronunciation. The rules regarding the realisation of the inherent vowel in pronunciation are as follows; in two or three syllable words, the penultimate inherent vowel is pronounced when the final one is dropped, and in words of four syllables, both the final and the antepenultimate inherent vowels are dropped while the others are pronounced. Thus, *səməjhə* is pronounced as *səməjh* 'understanding', *mehənətə* is pronounced as *mehnət* 'hard work'. These general principles, however, do not apply to words containing medial *h*, loanwords, compounds and words formed with derivational suffixes. For instance, *səməjh* with the inflectional suffix of perfective -*a* is pronounced as *səmjha* 'understood', but with the derivational agentive suffix -*dar* is pronounced *səməjhdar* 'sensible' (see Ohala (1983) for details of *ə*-deletion).

Although most derivational and inflectional morphology of Hindi is affixal in nature (i.e. Hindi mostly utilises prefixes and suffixes), there are remnants of the morphophonemic ablaut alternation of vowels of the *guṇa* and *vṛddhi* type (see pages 43–4) in a substantial number of verbal roots and nominal compounds in Hindi. These are the most frequent and regular of vowel changes for derivation as well as inflection in Sanskrit. A *guṇa* vowel differs from a simple vowel by a prefixed *a*-element which is combined with the other according to the usual rules; a *vṛddhi* vowel, by the further prefixation to a *guṇa* vowel. *a* is its own *guṇa* and *ā* remains unchanged for both *guṇa* and *vṛddhi*. The series of corresponding degrees is as follows (Kellogg 1875):

Simple vowels:	a	ā	i	ī	u	ū	ṛ	ḷ
guṇa vowels:	a	ā		e		o	ar	al
vṛddhi vowels:		ā		ai		au	ār	

The *guṇa* increment is an Indo-European phenomenon, the *vṛddhi* increment is specifically Indian in origin. These processes are still utilised to some extent in coining new compounds of borrowings from Sanskrit for modernising Hindi. Some examples of the verbal roots that exemplify these processes are pairs such as *khul* 'open' (intr.) and *khol* 'open' (tr.); *kəṭ* 'cut' (intr.) and *kaṭ* 'cut' (tr.), *dɪkh* 'be visible' and *dekh* 'see'; and some examples of nominal compounds are *pərəmə + išvərə = pərəmešvər* 'Supreme God'; *məha + išə = məheš* 'Great God' (a name of Šiva); *səda + evə = sədɛv* 'always'. Some examples of modern vocabulary coined on the same principles are *sərvə + udəyə = sərvodəy* 'universal welfare', *mətə + ɛkyə = mətɛky* 'unanimity of opinion', *šubhə + ɪččhʋ = šubhɛččhʋ* 'well wisher'.

Table 22.2 gives the Devanāgarī script as used for Hindi:

Table 22.2: Chart of Devanāgarī Alphabet

Vowels
Independent

अ	आ	इ	ई	उ	ऊ	ऋ
ə	a	ɪ	i	ʋ	u	rɪ
ए	ऐ	ओ	औ	अं	अ:	
e	ɛ	o	ɔ	əm	əh	

Following Consonant

ा	ि	ी	ु	ू	े	ै	ो	ौ	ं	:
a	ɪ	i	ʋ	u	e	ɛ	o	ɔ	əm	əh

Consonants

क	ख	ग	घ	ङ			
kə	khə	gə	ghə	ŋə			
च	छ	ज	झ	ञ			
čə	čhə	jə	jhə	ñə			
ट	ठ	ड	ढ	ण			
ṭə	ṭhə	ḍə	ḍhə	ṇə			
त	थ	द	ध	न			
tə	thə	də	dhə	nə			
प	फ	ब	भ	म			
pə	phə	bə	bhə	mə			
य	र	ल	व	श	ष	स	ह
yə	rə	lə	və	šə	ṣə	sə	hə
क़	ख़	ग़	ज़	फ़			
qə	xə	γə	zə	fə			

To the extent that it shares a basic vocabulary with Hindi, the *guṇa* and *vṛddhi* phenomena are applicable to Urdu as well. The Urdu writing system, however, is based on the Perso-Arabic script. As is clear from table 22.3, the script lacks adequate vowel symbols but has an overabundance of consonant symbols for the language. Table 22.3 lists the independent forms only (see also the discussion of script in the chapters on Arabic and Persian).

Table 22.3: The Urdu Alphabet

Letter	Pronunciation	Urdu Name
ا	a*	əlyf
ب	b	be
پ	p	pe
ت	t	te
ٹ	ṭ	ṭe
ث	s	se
ج	ǰ	ǰim
چ	č	če
ح	h	he [/bəṛi he/]
خ	x	xe
د	d	dal
ڈ	ḍ	ḍal
ذ	z	zal
ر	r	re
ڑ	ṛ	ṛe
ز	z	ze
ژ	ž	že
س	s	sin
ش	š	šin
ص	s	swad
ض	z	zwad
ط	t	to, toe
ظ	z	zo, zoe
ع	*	əyn
غ	γ	γəyn
ف	f	fe
ق	q	qaf
ک	k	kaf
گ	g	gaf
ل	l	lam
م	m	mim
ن	n	nun
و	v	vao
ہ	h	he [/choṭi he/]
ی	y	ye

Note: əlyf is pronounced as *ā* following a consonant; əyn is either not pronounced at all or given the value of *a* or *ā* following a consonant. It is pronounced as a glottal stop only in High Urdu.

3 Morphology

A brief description of Hindi-Urdu nominal and verbal morphology follows (for a detailed discussion of derivational and inflectional morphology, see McGregor (1972), Sharma (1958) and Bailey (1956)).

3.1 Nominal

Forms of Hindi-Urdu nouns undergo changes in order to indicate number, gender and case. There are two numbers, singular and plural; two genders, masculine and feminine; and three cases, direct, oblique and vocative. Nouns are declined differently according to the gender class and the phonological property of the final segment in the word. Given here are paradigms of the major classes of masculine and feminine nouns.

Paradigm of Masculine Nouns Ending in -*a*

	Sg.	*Pl.*
Dir.	lərka 'boy'	lərke
Obl.	lərke	lərkõ
Voc.	lərke	lərko

Ending in -*i*

Dir.	mali 'gardener'	mali
Obl.	mali	malıyõ
Voc.	mali	malıyo

Ending in -*u*

Dir.	sarhu 'wife's sister's husband'	sarhu
Obl.	sarhu	sarhʊõ
Voc.	sarhu	sarhʊo

Ending in a consonant

Dir.	nɔkər 'servant'	nɔkər
Obl.	nɔkər	nɔkərõ
Voc.	nɔkər	nɔkəro

Certain masculine nouns ending in -*a* such as *raja* 'king' and kinship terms such as *pıta* 'father', *čača* 'father's younger brother', *mama* 'mother's brother' are exceptions in that they do not change for direct plural and oblique singular in modern standard Hindi.

Paradigm of Feminine Nouns Ending in -*i*

	Sg.	*Pl.*
Dir.	lərki 'girl'	lərkıyã
Obl.	lərki	lərkıyõ
Voc.	lərki	lərkıyo

Ending in -*a*

Dir.	mata 'mother'	matae
Obl.	mata	matao
Voc.	mata	matao

Ending in -*u*

Dir.	bəhu 'daughter-in-law'	bəhʊẽ
Obl.	bəhu	bəhʊõ
Voc.	bəhu	bəhʊo

Ending in a consonant

Dir.	bəhən 'sister'	bəhnē
Obl.	bəhən	bəhnõ
Voc.	bəhən	bəhno

In Perso-Arabic borrowings, High Urdu keeps the Perso-Arabic plural markers, e.g. *kaɣəz* 'paper': *kaɣzat* 'papers'.

The oblique case forms are used whenever a noun is followed by a postposition, e.g. *lərke ko* 'to the boy', *ghərõ mē* 'in the houses', *lərkɪyõ ke sath* 'with the girls' etc.

The adjectives occur before the noun and agree with their head noun in number, gender and case. They do not, however, exhibit the full range of forms. This can be seen in the paradigm of *əččhA* 'good' (*A* is a cover symbol for the various inflections).

əččhA 'good'

	Masculine		Feminine	
	Sg.	Pl.	Sg.	Pl.
Dir.	əččha	əččhe	əččhi	əččhi
Obl.	əččhe	əččhe	əččhi	əččhi
Voc.	əččhe	əččhe	əččhi	əččhi

The adjectives that end in a consonant, e.g. *sʊndər* 'beautiful', and in a vowel other than *-a*, e.g. *nəkli* 'false, artificial', are invariant, e.g. *sʊndər lərka/lərki* 'handsome boy/beautiful girl', *nəkli dāt* (m.)/*bāh* (f.) 'artificial teeth/arm'.

The main postpositions that indicate case relations such as accusative, dative, instrumental etc. are the following: *ne* 'agentive, marker of a transitive subject in the perfective', *ko* 'accusative/dative', *se* 'instrumental/ablative/comitative', *mē, pər* 'locative', *kA* 'possessive/genitive', and *ke lɪye* 'benefactive'. There are several other postpositions that indicate location, direction, etc. such as *ke pas* 'near', *ki or* 'toward', *ke samne* 'in front of', *ke pĩche* 'behind', *ke bahər* 'out (of)', *ke əndər* 'inside', *ke par* 'across', *ke bɪna* 'without', *ke sath* 'with' and *ke hath/dvara* 'through'.

The pronouns have more case forms than the nouns, as is clear from the following paradigm:

	1st		2nd		3rd	
	Sg.	Pl.	Sg.	Pl.	Sg.	Pl.
Dir.	mẽ	həm	tu	tʊm	yəh/vəh	ye/ve
Obl.	mʊjh	həm	tʊjh	tʊm	ɪs/ʊs	ɪn/ʊn
Poss.	merA	həmarA	terA	tʊmharA	ɪs/ʊs kA	ɪn/ʊn kA

The third person pronominal forms are the same as the proximate and remote demonstratives, *yəh* 'this' and *vəh* 'that', and their inflected forms.

The possessive form of the pronouns behaves like an adjective and agrees with the possessed noun in number, gender and case, e.g. *mere beṭe ko* 'to my son', *tʊmhari kɪtabō mē* 'in your books', *ʊnki bəhnō ke sath* 'with their sisters' etc. The oblique forms are used with the postpositions except that the first and second person pronouns are used in their direct case forms with the agentive postposition *ne*. The third person plural pronouns have special combined forms when they are followed by the agentive postposition, e.g. *ɪn + ne = ɪnhōne* and *ʊn + ne = ʊnhōne*. All the pronouns listed above have special contracted forms when followed by the accusative/dative postposition, e.g. *mʊjh + ko = mʊjhe*, *tʊjh + ko = tʊjhe*, *ɪs/ʊs + ko = ɪse/ʊse*, *həm + ko = həmē*, *tʊm + ko = tʊmhē*, *ɪn/ʊn + ko = ɪnhē/ʊnhē*.

In addition to the pronouns listed above, Hindi-Urdu has a second person honorific pronoun *ap* which is used with both singular and plural reference for both male and female addressees. The honorific pronoun has the same form in all numbers and cases, i.e. it is invariant. The possessive is formed by adding the postposition *kA* to *ap*. To make the plural reference clear, the item *səb* 'all' or *log* 'people' may be added to the form *ap*, e.g. *ap səb/log*.

Hindi-Urdu also has a reflexive pronoun *ap* 'self ' which has an oblique form *əpne* and a possessive form *əpnA*. The form *ap* is used for all persons. There is a reduplicated form of *ap*, i.e. *əpne ap*, which is also used as the reflexive pronoun in Hindi-Urdu, e.g. *ram ne əpne ko/əpne ap ko šiše mē dekha* 'Ram looked at himself in the mirror'.

The two interrogative pronouns, *kɔn* and *kya* are used for human and non-human respectively. The oblique forms of these pronouns are *kɪs* in the singular and *kɪn* in the plural. The possessive is formed by adding the possessive postposition *kA* to the oblique. Similar to the third person pronouns, these pronouns also have combined forms such as *kɪnhōne*, *kɪse* and *kɪnhē*.

The devices of reduplication and partial reduplication or echo-compounding are used for expressing various meanings. For instance, reduplication of adjectives has either an intensive or a distributive meaning, e.g. *lal-lal saṛi* 'very red saree', *taza-taza dudh* 'very fresh milk', *kale-kale bal* 'jet-black hair', *ūče-ūče pəhaṛ* 'tall mountains', etc. Echo-compounding of adjectives, nouns and verbs has the meaning 'and the like', e.g. *sʊndər-vʊndər* 'pretty and such', *čay-vay* 'tea and other such things', *mɪlna-vɪlna* 'meeting and other such things' etc. The echo-compounding usually tones down the meaning of the adjective; it, however, adds to the meaning of other word classes. For instance, *čay-vay* means not only tea but snacks that go with tea, *pəṛhna-vəṛhna* means not only reading but other activities that go with studying.

In addition to reduplication and echo-compounding, another device used extensively is that of compounding two words with related meanings, e.g. *hōsi-xuši* 'laughter and happiness' (pleasant state or occasion), *dʊkh-taklif* 'sorrow and pain' (state full of sorrow), *šadi-byah* 'wedding' etc. Note that in all these examples, one item is from Indic sources, the other from Perso-Arabic sources. This is extremely common, though not absolutely obligatory.

In Hindi-Urdu, the possessor normally precedes the possessed and the possessive postposition *kA* agrees with the possessed in number, gender and case, e.g. *lərke ki kıtab* 'the boy's book', *lərke ke sır pər* 'on the boy's head' etc. High-Urdu has an alternative construction where the possessed precedes the possessor following the convention of the ezafe-construction in Persian (see page 532), e.g. *šer-e-kəšmir* 'the lion of Kashmir', *qəvaɪd-e-urdu* 'grammar of Urdu', etc.

3.2   Verbal

Two most noticeable things about Hindi-Urdu verbs are their occurrence in morphologically related sets and in series. The first phenomenon is known as causal verbs and the second as compound verbs. Whereas the causative is inherited from Old Indo-Aryan, the development of compound verbs in New Indo-Aryan is recent — it became frequent only in the period between AD 600 and 1000.

Some examples of causal verbs can be seen in the chart given here.

Causal Verbs

Intr.	Tr.	Dbl. tr.	Caus.
uth 'rise'	utha 'raise'	–	uthva 'cause to rise/raise'
kət 'be cut'	kat 'cut'	–	kətva 'cause to (be) cut'
–	sun 'hear'	suna 'recite/narrate'	sunva 'cause to hear/narrate'
–	kha 'eat'	khıla 'feed'	khılva 'cause to eat/feed'

Examples of compound verbs are *gır ǰana* 'fall go = fall down', *kha lena* 'eat take = eat up', *pərh lena* 'read take = read to oneself ', *pərh dena* 'read give = read out loud to someone'.

Hindi-Urdu verbs occur in the following forms: root, e.g. *kha* 'eat', *a* 'come', imperfect stem, e.g. *khatA*, *atA*, perfect stem, e.g. *khayA*, *ayA*, and infinitive, *khanA*, *anA*. The stems behave like adjectives in that they agree with some noun in the sentence in number and gender. The imperfect and perfect participles, which are made up of the imperfect and perfect stems followed by the perfect stem of the verb *ho* 'be', i.e. *huA*, agree in case also. This means that the stem final -*A* changes to -*e* or -*i* for agreement. Whereas the imperfect and perfect aspectual distinction is expressed by suffixation, the continuous aspect is indicated by an independent lexical item, *rəhA*. This marker follows the root and behaves like the imperfect and perfect stems with regard to gender and number agreement.

The tense distinction of present versus past is expressed with the forms of the auxiliary verb, the present auxiliary *hE* and the past auxiliary *thA*. These are the present and past forms of the stative verb *honA* 'be'. As in all Indo-

European languages, the verb 'be' is irregular in Hindi. It has the following forms: root *ho*, imperfect stem *hotA*, perfect stem *huA*, infinitive *honA*, stative present *hE*, stative past *thA*. The stem-final -*A* changes to -*e*, -*i* or -*ī* for number and gender agreement and the final -*E* changes to various vowels to indicate person, number and gender agreement. The forms of the verb *honA* in stative present are as follows: 1st person sg. *hū*, 2nd and 3rd person sg. *hɛ*, 2nd person pl. *ho*, and 1st and 3rd person pl. and 2nd hon. *hɛ̃*.

In addition to tense and aspect distinctions, the verbal forms express mood distinctions as well. There is no distinction made between indicative and interrogative, i.e. in assertions as well as questions, the verbal forms are made up of the stems and auxiliaries described above. Historically, Old Indo-Aryan did not make a distinction between these two moods either. The moods in Old Indo-Aryan were indicative, imperative, optative and subjunctive. In Hindi-Urdu, the optative forms are made up of the root and the following suffixes: 1st person sg. -*ū*, 2nd and 3rd person sg. -*e*, 1st and 3rd pl. and 2nd honorific -*ē*, and 2nd pl. -*o*. The future tense is formed by adding the suffix -*gA* to the optative forms, e.g. *ja-ū-ga* 'I (m.) will go', *jaogi* 'you (f.) will go' etc. The following are the imperative forms: root form of the verb (intimate or rude), 2nd pl. optative (familiar), root with the suffix -*ɪye* (honorific, polite), root with the suffix -*ɪye* followed by the suffix -*ga* (remote, therefore, extra polite) and the infinitive form of the verb (remote imperative, therefore even when used with second plural, polite). Thus, the imperative forms of the verb *kha* are *(tu) kha* 'you (intimate) eat', *tum khao* 'you (familiar) eat', *(ap) khaɪye* 'you (honorific) eat', *(ap) khaɪyega* 'you (honorific) please eat (perhaps later?)', *(tum) khana* 'you (familiar, polite) eat' or 'you (familiar) eat (perhaps later?)'.

The paradigm of the verb *ghumna* 'to take a walk' illustrates the full range of the forms discussed above.

Paradigm of Verb Forms

Root: ghum 'take a walk'
Imperfect stem: ghumtA
Perfect stem: ghumA
Infinitive: ghumnA
Optative: ghumū (1st sg.), ghumo (2nd pl.), ghume (2nd and 3rd sg.), ghumē (1st and 3rd pl., 2nd honorific)
Imperative: ghum (2nd sg., intimate/rude), ghumo (2nd pl., familiar), ghumɪye (2nd honorific, polite), ghumɪyega (2nd honorific, extra polite)

Future

	1st		2nd		3rd	
	M.	F.	M.	F.	M.	F.
Sg.	ghumunga	ghumungi	ghumega	ghumegi	ghumega	ghumegi
Pl.	ghumenge	ghumengi	ghumoge	ghumogi	ghumenge	ghumengi
Hon.	–	–	ghumenge	ghumengi	ghumenge	ghumengi

Present imperfect

		Sg.	Pl.	Hon.
1st	M.	ghumta hũ	ghumte hẽ	–
	F.	ghumti hũ	ghumti hẽ	–
2nd	M.	ghumta hɛ	ghumte ho	ghumte hẽ
	F.	ghumti hɛ	ghumti ho	ghumti hẽ
3rd	M.	ghumta hɛ	ghumte hẽ	ghumte hẽ
	F.	ghumti hɛ	ghumti hẽ	ghumti hẽ

Past imperfect: ghumta tha, ghumte the, ghumti thi, ghumti thī, etc.
Present perfect: ghuma hũ, ghumi hũ, etc.
Past perfect: ghuma tha, ghumi thi, etc.
Present continuous: ghum rəha hũ, ghum rəhi hũ, etc.
Past continuous: ghum rəha tha, ghum rəhi thi, etc.

In general, Urdu speakers use the masculine plural form as undifferentiated for gender in the first person, e.g. *həm kəl kəlkətte ǰa rəhe hẽ* 'We (m./f.) are going to Calcutta tomorrow.'

The contingent, past contingent and presumptive tenses are formed with the imperfect and perfect stems and the continuous form followed by the auxiliaries *ho* 'contingent', *hotA* 'past contingent', and *hogA* 'presumptive'. Roughly, these three are translatable into English as follows: *ata ho* '(he) may be coming', *aya ho* '(he) may have come', *ata hota* 'had (he) been coming', *aya hota* 'had (he) come', *ata hoga* '(he) must be coming', *aya hoga* '(he) must have come'.

Hindi-Urdu verbs are very regular, which means that once we know the infinitive form of the verb, we can isolate the root and derive the imperfect and perfect stems by suffixing *-tA* and *-A* respectively. Thus, from *hõsna* 'laugh', we get the imperfect stem *hõstA* and perfect stem *hõsA*. Note that when the root ends in a vowel and the perfect stem-forming suffix *-A* is added to it, a semi-vowel is inserted to separate the two vowels. If the root ends in *-i*, *-a* or *-o*, a *-y-* is inserted, if the root ends in *-u*, a *-v-* is inserted, e.g. *kha + -A = khaya* 'ate (m.)', *ro + -A = roya* 'cried (m.)', *pi + -A = pɪya* 'drank (m.)', *čhu + -A = čhʊva* 'touched (m.)'.

One verb, *čahɪye*, is completely irregular in that it has only this form. It takes a dative subject and means 'to need' or 'want'. The following have irregular perfect stems: *kər* 'do' – *kɪya*, *le* 'take' – *lɪya*, *de* 'give' – *dɪya*, *ǰa* 'go' – *gəya*. The following have irregular polite imperative forms: *kər* 'do' = *kiǰɪye*, *le* 'take' = *liǰɪye*, *de* 'give' = *diǰɪye*, *pi* 'drink' = *piǰɪye*.

Hindi-Urdu has two types of compound verbs: those that involve verbs in a series and those that involve a nominal and a verbal. Some examples of the former have already been given (see page 480), a few examples of the latter follow: *svikar kərna* 'acceptance do' or 'to accept', *pəsənd hona* 'liking be' or 'to like' (non-volitional), *pəsənd kərna* 'liking do' or 'to like' (volitional), *təng ana* 'torment come' or 'to be fed up'.

In the verbs-in-series type of compound verbs, usually the meaning of the whole is derived from the meaning of the first, or main, verb; the second, or explicator, verb performs the function of either restricting, or adding some specific shade of meaning to, the meaning of the main verb. Also, the explicator verb necessarily expresses the meaning 'a one-shot action or process'. For instance, *marna* can mean either 'hit' or 'kill', *mar ḍalna* 'hit/ kill pour' means only 'kill'; *lɪkhna* means 'write', *lɪkh marna* 'write hit' means 'to dash off a few lines in a hurry/thoughtlessly'; *rəkhna* means 'keep, put', *rəkh čhoṛna'*, 'keep leave' means 'save'. The main explicator verbs are the following and they roughly signify the meanings described below:

ana 'come' occurs with intransitive verbs of motion and indicates that the action of the main verb is oriented towards a focal point which may be a person or which may be set in time or space; e.g. *vəh sɪṛhɪyā čəṛh ai* 'she came up the steps' and *vəh sɪṛhɪyõ se utər ai* 'she came down the steps'.

jana 'go' occurs with intransitive verbs of motion and other change-of-state verbs and indicates motion away from the focal point; with dative subject verbs, it indicates definitive meaning; and with transitive verbs, it indicates hurried, compulsive action; e.g. *vəh sɪṛhɪyā čəṛh gəi* 'she went up the steps', *raju ko kɪtab mɪl gəi* 'Raju got the book', *vəh gusse mẽ jane kya-kya lɪkh gəya* 'who knows what he dashed off in his anger!'

lena 'take' occurs with affective (see page 485) (transitive) verbs and indicates completive meaning; with other transitive verbs, it indicates a self-benefactive meaning; and with certain intransitive verbs, it indicates internal expression; e.g. *usne kam kər lɪya* '(s)he completed (his/her) job', *mẽ ne thik soč lɪya hɛ* 'I have made a decision'.

dena 'give' occurs with transitive verbs other than affective verbs and indicates that the action is directed towards a beneficiary other than the agent of the action denoted by the main verb; and with intransitive verbs of expression, it indicates external expression; e.g. *usne sara rəhəsy bəta dɪya* 'he divulged the whole secret', *sima zorõ se hãs di* 'Sima laughed loudly'.

uṭhna 'rise' occurs with intransitive and transitive verbs of punctual action and indicates suddenness; e.g. *vəh mujhe dekhte hi ro uṭhi* 'she suddenly began to cry when she saw me'.

bɛṭhna 'sit' occurs with certain transitive verbs and indicates impudence; e.g. *vəh əpne 'bas' se ləṛ bɛtha* 'he fought with his boss'.

pəṛna 'fall' occurs with intransitive change-of-state verbs, and certain verbs of expression, and indicates suddenness; e.g. *ləɽki bərf pər phɪsəl kər gɪr pəri* 'the girl slipped and fell on the ice'.

ḍalna 'pour' occurs with transitive verbs that express violent action and certain transitive verbs (*kər* 'do', *pəɽh* 'read', *lɪkh* 'write') and indicates violence; e.g. *jəldi se pətr lɪkh dalo!* 'write the letter quickly (get it over with)!'

rəkhna 'keep' occurs with certain transitive verbs and indicates a temporary state resulting from the action of the main verb; e.g. *mɛ̃ ne khana pəka rəkha hɛ* 'I have cooked (and saved) the food'.

čhoɽna 'leave' occurs with certain transitive verbs and indicates dissociation of the agent with the result of the action; e.g. *pɪtaji ne meri pəɽhai ke lɪye pɛse rəkh čhoɽe hɛ̃* 'father has put aside money for my education'.

marna 'hit' occurs with very few verbs and indicates rash action; e.g. *kuč bhi lɪkh maro!* 'just write something!'

dhəməkna 'thump' occurs with *ana* 'come' and *jana* 'go' and indicates unwelcome arrival; e.g. *vəh subəh-subəh a dhəmka, mujhe nəhane tək ka mɔka nəhi mɪla* 'he showed up very early, I did not even have time to shower'.

pəhũčna 'arrive' occurs with *ana* 'come' and *jana* 'go' and indicates arrival rather than motion; e.g. *šyam dɪlli ja pəhũča* 'Shyam arrived in Delhi'.

nikəlna 'emerge' indicates sudden emergence from some enclosed space — real or imaginary; e.g. *uski ãkhõ se ãsu bəh nɪkle* 'tears began to flow from her eyes'.

4   Syntax

In this brief section on syntax, I will discuss mainly the verbal syntax of Hindi-Urdu after a few remarks on word order. The reason for this will become clearer as the discussion progresses.

Hindi-Urdu is a verb final language, i.e. the order of words in a sentence is subject, object and verb. Actually, the position of the verb is relatively more fixed than the position of any other constituent. Since most grammatical functions of nouns are indicated by the postpositions following them, the nominal constituents can be moved around freely for thematic purposes. The position of the verb is changed only in poetic or extremely affective style. Historically, word order was relatively free in Old Indo-Aryan, but became more fixed in Middle Indo-Aryan between AD 200 and 600.

In existential sentences, the locational/temporal adverbial comes first: *mez pər kɪtab hɛ* 'there is a book on the table', *kəl bəri ʈhəṇḍ thi* 'it was very cold yesterday'. The verb agrees with the unmarked noun in the sentence. In intransitive and non-perfective transitive sentences, where the subject is unmarked, the verb agrees with the subject, e.g. *lərke bɛʈhe* 'the boys sat', *lərki səmačar sʊn rəhi hɛ* 'the girl is listening (f.) to the news (m.)', *raǰu čay pita hoga* 'Raju (m.) must be drinking (m.) tea (f.)'. In transitive sentences in the perfective, where the subject is followed by the postposition *ne*, the verb does not agree with the subject. It agrees with the object if it is unmarked; if the object is followed by the postposition *ko*, the verb remains in its neutral form, i.e. third person singular masculine: cf. *raǰu ne kɪtab pərhi* 'Raju (m.) read (f.) the book (f.)', *əfsərō ne əpni pətnɪyō ko bʊlaya* 'the officers called (3rd sg. m.) their wives'. Not all transitive verbs require that their subjects be marked with the agentive postposition *ne*: e.g. *bolna* 'speak', *lana* 'bring' do not take *ne, səmə jhna* 'understand' can occur either with or without *ne*: *mɛ apki bat nəhī səmǰha* 'I do not understand you', *ap ne kya səmǰha?* 'what did you understand?' In the case of compound verbs, only if both the main and the explicator verbs require *ne* does the compound verb require *ne*: *šila ne dudh pɪya* 'Sheila drank the milk', *šila ne dudh lɪya* 'Sheila took the milk', *šila ne dudh pi lɪya* 'Sheila drank up the milk', but *šila dudh pi gəi* 'Sheila drank up the milk' since the intransitive verb *ǰa* 'go' is not a *ne* verb.

Semantically, Hindi-Urdu makes a distinction between volitional versus non-volitional verbs and affective versus non-affective verbs. A verb is volitional if it expresses an act that is performed by an actor/agent. A verb is affective if the act expressed by the verb is directed towards the actor/agent, i.e. it is self-benefactive. Ingestive verbs such as *khana* 'eat', *pina* 'drink' etc. are good examples of affective verbs in that it is the actor/agent of eating, drinking etc. who benefits from these acts. Verbs such as 'work', 'write' etc., on the other hand may be either self-benefactive or directed toward some other beneficiary. Typically, the explicator verb *lena* 'take' occurs with an affective verb, the explicator *dena* 'give' does not, i.e. sentences such as the following are ungrammatical in Hindi-Urdu: *ʊsne khana kha dɪya* 'he/she ate for someone else' because *khana* 'eat' is an ingestive verb whereas the explicator *dena* 'give' indicates that the beneficiary is someone other than the actor/agent of the main verb. Verbs such as *girna* 'fall', *ǰana* 'go' etc. express self-directed actions, hence are affective.

These distinctions are important for the verbal syntax of Hindi-Urdu. Transitivity, volitionality and affectiveness do not necessarily coincide. For instance, *sona* 'sleep' is intransitive, volitional and affective, *sikhna* 'learn' is transitive, volitional and affective, *gɪrna* 'fall' is intransitive, non-volitional and affective, *ǰana* 'go' is intransitive, volitional and affective. Only the affective verbs participate in the compound verbal construction with *lena* 'take' as the explicator, only volitional verbs occur in the passive construction (Kachru 1980; 1981).

In many cases, verbs in Hindi-Urdu come in related forms so that the stative versus active and volitional versus non-volitional meanings can be expressed by varying the syntactic constructions. For instance, the verb *mɪlna* can mean both 'to run into someone' (accidental meeting) or 'to go see someone' (deliberate meeting). In the first case, the verb is used with a dative subject and the object of meeting is unmarked, in the second case, the subject is unmarked and the object is marked with a comitative postposition *se*, e.g. *kəl bazar ǰate hʋe muǰhe ram mɪla tha* 'yesterday while going to the market I ran into Ram', *kəl mẽ ram se ʋske dəftər mẽ mɪla tha* 'yesterday I met Ram in his office'. In a large number of cases, the intransitive verb denotes non-volitional action and if the actor is to be expressed, it is expressed with the instrumental postposition *se*, e.g. *apka šiša muǰhse ṭuṭ gəya* 'your mirror got broken by me'. The deliberate action is expressed with the related transitive verb in the agentive construction, e.g. *ɪs šərarti bəčče ne apka šiša toṛ ḍala* 'this naughty child broke your mirror'. Most intransitive and all dative subject verbs are either stative or change-of-state verbs and are non-volitional. Hindi-Urdu has sets of stative, change-of-state and active verbs of the following types:

Stative	Change-of-state	Active
khʋla hona 'be open'	khʋlna	kholna
krʋddh hona 'be angry'	krodh ana	krodh kərna
yad hona 'remember'	yad ana	yad kərna
pəsənd hona 'like'	pəsənd ana	pəsənd kərna

Note that the stative verbs are usually made up of an adjective or past participle and the verb 'be', the change-of-state verbs are either lexical verbs or compounds made up of a nominal and the verb 'become' or 'come', and the active is either a causal verb morphologically derived from the intransitive or a compound made up of a nominal and the verb 'do' (or a small set of other active transitive verbs).

This, however, does not mean that all intransitive verbs in Hindi are of the above types. There are active intransitive verbs such as the verbs of motion (*ǰa* 'go', *čəl* 'move' etc.), verbs of expression (*hə̃s* 'laugh', *ro* 'cry' etc.) and others. Note that verbal compounding is also exploited to reduce volitionality of verbs, e.g. *ro pəṛna* 'cry + fall = to burst out crying', *bol ʋṭhna* 'speak + rise = to blurt out' etc.

The non-volitional intransitive sentence above (*apka šiša muǰhse ṭuṭ gəya* 'your mirror got broken by me') has been translated into English with the passive; it is, however, not a passive construction in Hindi-Urdu. The passive in Hindi-Urdu is formed by marking the agent of the active sentence, if retained, with the instrumental postposition *se* and using the perfect stem of the verb and the auxiliary *ǰa* 'go' which takes all the tense-aspect endings: e.g. *ram ne khana nəhī khaya* 'Ram did not eat' vs. *ram se khana nəhī khaya gəya* 'Ram was not able to eat'. The translation equivalent of the Hindi-Urdu passive in English points to an interesting fact about this construction. If the agent is retained and marked with the instrumental postposition, the passive sentence is usually interpreted as a statement about the capability of the agent; if, however, the agent is deleted, the passive sentence has a meaning similar to that of English. That is, the sentence is interpreted as being about the object in the active sentence and the agent is either unknown or not important enough to be mentioned (Guru 1920; Kachru 1980).

In addition to the present and past participles, there are two other participles in Hindi which are used a great deal: the conjunctive participle which is formed by adding the form *kər* to the root of the verb and the agentive participle which is formed by adding the suffix *-vala* to the oblique form of the verbal noun, e.g. *lıkhnevala* 'writer', *ǰanevala* 'one who goes', *sonevala* 'one who sleeps', *ʋgnevala* 'that which rises or grows', etc. This suffix has become a part of the English lexicon in the form *wallah* and is used extensively in Indian English and the native varieties of English, especially in the context of topics related to India. Forms such as *Congresswallah* ('one belonging to the Indian National Congress'), *Bombaywallah* ('one from Bombay') are common in literature dealing with India.

The syntax of Hindi-Urdu differs from that of English most noticeably in the use of the participles. For instance, the preferred constructions for modifying nouns or conjoining clauses are the participles: the present, past and agentive for modifying nouns and the conjunctive participle for conjoining clauses. Compare the following Hindi sentences with their English translations: *vəh gēd khelte hue bəččõ ko dekh rəha tha* 'he was observing the children (who were) playing ball'; *tumhē mohən ki likhi hui kəvıtaē pəsənd hē?* 'do you like the poems written by Mohan?'; *mujhe ʔat bat pər ronewale bəčče bılkʋl pəsənd nəhī* 'I do not like children who cry at every thing'; *vəh ghər a kər so gə ya* 'he came home and went to sleep'. Both the present and the past participles are used adjectivally as well as adverbially, cf. *mā ne rote hue bəčče ko god mē uṭha lıya* 'Mother picked up the child who was crying' vs. *vəh rote hue bhag gəya* 'he ran away, crying' and *mē vəhā beṭhi hu ləṛki ko nəhī ǰanti* 'I don't know the girl seated over there' vs. *ləṛki vəhā beṭhi (hui) pətr lıkh rəhi hɛ* 'the girl is writing a letter sitting there'. The agentive participle is used both as an agentive noun, e.g. *(gaṛi) cəlanevala* 'driver (of a vehicle)' and as an adjective, e.g. *bhərət se anevale čhatr* 'the students who come from India'. The conjunctive participle is used to express the meanings of sequential action, related action, cause-effect relationship and purpose adverbial, e.g. *vəh hındi pəṛh kər khelne ǰaega* 'he will go to play after studying Hindi', *vəh kʋd kər upər a gəi* 'she jumped and came up', *həm ne use pese de kər xuš kər lıya* 'we pleased him by giving him money', *jəldi se bazar jakər dudh le ao* 'go quickly to the market and bring some milk' (Kachru 1980).

Although the participial constructions are preferred in Hindi-Urdu, there are linguistically determined environments where full relative and other types of subordinate and conjoined clauses are used. The relative clause, unlike in English, is not a constituent of the noun phrase. It may either precede or follow the main clause as in the following: *jo lərka vəhā beṭha hε vəh mera bhai hε* or *vəh lərka mera bhai hε jo vəhā beṭha hε* 'the boy who is seated there is my brother'. Note that, depending upon the order of the relative and the main clause, either the noun in the subordinate or the main clause is deleted, i.e. the above are the results of deleting the noun in parentheses in the following: *jo lərka vəhā beṭha he vəh (lərka) mera bhai hε* or *vəh lərka mera bhai hε jo (lərka) vəhā beṭha hε*. The relative marker *jo* (obl. sg. *jɪs*, obl. pl. *jɪn*, special forms with *ne* and *ko*, *jɪnhõne* and *jɪnhẽ*) and the correlative marker *vəh*, which is identical to the remote demonstrative/third person pronoun, function like a determiner to their respective head nouns. Both the head nouns may be retained in the case of an emphatic construction; in normal speech/writing, however, the second instance is deleted. Under the influence of Persian and later, English, the relative clause is sometimes positioned following the head noun, e.g. *vəh lərka jo vəhā beṭha hε mera bhai hε*; in this case, the second instance of the noun (following *jo*) must be deleted.

Earlier, it has been said that the nominal constituents of a sentence in Hindi-Urdu can be moved around freely for thematic purposes. Usually, the initial element in a sentence in Hindi coincides with the theme. The focus position in Hindi is identified with the position just before the main verb. In addition to manipulating the word order, heavy sentence stress and certain particles are used to indicate focus, e.g. *'ram' ne mohən ko piṭa* 'it was Ram who hit Mohan', *šila hi ne yəh bat kəhi thi* 'it was Sheila who had said this', *sima to čali gəi*, 'as for Sima, she has left', where the item in quotes in the first sentence and the items followed by the particles *hi* and *to* in the second and the third sentence respectively are under focus. As the initial position is not the favoured device for indicating focus, the interrogative pronouns in Hindi-Urdu do not necessarily occur sentence-initially; compare the Hindi-Urdu sentences with their English equivalents, *ap kya pəṛh rəhe hẽ?* 'what are you reading?', *vəh kəl kəhā gəya tha?* 'where did he go yesterday?', *ɪn mẽ se ap ko kɔn si kɪtab pəsənd hε?* 'which of these books do you like?'.

To sum up, Hindi-Urdu differs from its European cousins typologically in several respects. Phonologically, aspiration, retroflexion, nasal vowels and lack of distinctive stress mark Hindi-Urdu as very different from English. Morphologically, the gender and case distinctions and the devices of reduplication and echo-compounding exemplify the major differences between the two languages. Syntactically, the word order differences are striking. So is the fact that Hindi-Urdu makes certain semantic distinctions which are not made as clearly in English, viz. volitionality and affectiveness. These distinctions result in a closer correspondence between semantic and syntactic grammatical roles that nominal constituents have in a sentence, e.g. all agentive (-ne-marked) subjects are agents, all dative (ko-marked) subjects are experiencers, and so on. Many of these characteristics of Hindi-Urdu are shared by not only the other Indo-Aryan but also the Dravidian and other languages of India.

Bibliography

The standard reference grammar for modern standard Hindi is Guru (1920). Other reference grammars are Sharma (1958) and McGregor (1972), the latter directed to the needs of learners of Hindi. Kellogg (1875) describes Hindi and the major dialects of the Hindi area, and contains a good introduction to Hindi prosody; data are drawn mostly from literary texts of the period and the work is hence dated. For Urdu, see Bailey (1956). For an account of the parallel development of Hindi-Urdu see Rai (1984).

Ohala (1983) is a phonological description of Hindi, while Kachru (1980) describes syntactic constructions of Hindi in non-technical language. Verma (1933) is a brief sketch of the history of the Hindi language. Kachru (1981) contains a supplement on transplanted varieties of Hindi-Urdu and one on transitivity in Hindi-Urdu. Bhatia (1987) discusses the native and non-native grammatical tradition.

References

Bailey, T.G. 1956. *Teach Yourself Urdu* (English Universities Press, London)
Bhatia, T.K. 1987. *A History of Hindi (Hindustani) Grammatical Tradition* (E.J. Brill, Leiden)
Guru, K.P. 1920. *Hindi vyākaraṇ* (Kashi Nagri Pracharini Sabha, Banaras)
Kachru, Y. 1980. *Aspects of Hindi Grammar* (Manohar Publications, New Delhi)
—— 1981. 'Dimensions of South Asian Linguistics', *Studies in the Linguistic Sciences*, vol. 11, no. 2
Kellogg, S.H. 1875. *A Grammar of the Hindi Language* (Routledge and Kegan Paul, London)
McGregor, R.S. 1972. *Outline of Hindi Grammar* (Oxford University Press, London)
Ohala, M. 1983. *Aspects of Hindi Phonology* (Motilal Banarsidass, Delhi)
Rai, A. 1984. *A House Divided* (Oxford University Press, Delhi)
Sharma, A. 1958. *A Basic Grammar of Modern Hindi* (Government of India, Ministry of Education and Scientific Research, Delhi)
Verma, Dh. 1933. *Hindi bhaṣa ka itihas* (Hindustani Academy, Allahabad)

23 Bengali

M. H. Klaiman

1 Historical and Genetic Setting

Bengali, together with Assamese and Oriya, belongs to the eastern group within the Magadhan subfamily of Indo-Aryan. In reconstructing the development of Indo-Aryan, scholars hypothetically posit a common parent language from which the modern Magadhan languages are said to have sprung. The unattested parent of the Magadhan languages is designated as Eastern or Magadhi Apabhraṁśa, and is assigned to Middle Indo-Aryan. Apart from the eastern languages, other modern representatives of the Magadhan subfamily are Magahi, Maithili and Bhojpuri.

Within the eastern group of Magadhan languages, the closest relative of Bengali is Assamese. The two share not only many coincidences of form and structure, but also have in common one system of written expression, on which more details will be given later.

Historically, the entire Magadhan group is distinguished from the remaining Indo-Aryan languages by a sound change involving sibilant coalescence. Specifically, there occurred in Magadhan a falling together of three sibilant elements inherited from common Indo-Aryan, dental /s/, palatal /š/ and retroflex /ṣ/. Among modern Magadhan languages, the coalescence of these three sounds is manifested in different ways; e.g. the modern Assamese reflex is the velar fricative /x/, as contrasted with the palatal /š/ of Modern Bengali.

The majority of Magadhan languages also show evidence of historical regression in the articulation of what was a central vowel /ă/ in common Indo-Aryan; the Modern Bengali reflex is /ɔ/.

Although the Magadhan subfamily is defined through a commonality of sound shifts separating it from the rest of Indo-Aryan, the three eastern languages of the subfamily share one phonological peculiarity distinguishing them from all other modern Indo-Aryan languages, both Magadhan and non-Magadhan. This feature is due to a historical coalescence of the long and short variants of the high vowels, which were distinguished in common Indo-Aryan. As a result, the vowel inventories of Modern Bengali, Assamese and Oriya show no phonemic distinction of /ĭ/ and /ī/, /ŭ/ and /ū/.

490

Moreover, Assamese and Bengali are distinguished from Oriya by the innovation of a high/low distinction in the mid vowels. Thus Bengali has /æ/ as well as /e/, and /ɔ/ as well as /o/. Bengali differs phonologically from Assamese principally in that the latter lacks a retroflex consonant series, a fact which distinguishes Assamese not just from Bengali, but from the majority of modern Indo-Aryan languages.

Besides various phonological characteristics, there are certain grammatical features peculiar to Bengali and the other Magadhan languages. The most noteworthy of these features is the absence of gender, a grammatical category found in most other modern Indo-Aryan languages. Bengali and its close relative Assamese also lack number as a verbal category. More will be said on these topics in the section on morphology, below.

Writing and literature have played no small role in the evolution of Bengali linguistic identity. A common script was in use throughout eastern India centuries before the emergence of the separate Magadhan vernaculars. The Oriya version of this script underwent special development in the medieval period, while the characters of the Bengali and Assamese scripts coincide with but a couple of exceptions.

Undoubtedly the availability of a written form of expression was essential to the development of the rich literary traditions associated not just with Bengali, but also with other Magadhan languages such as Maithili. However, even after the separation of the modern Magadhan languages from one another, literary composition in eastern India seems to have reflected a common milieu scarcely compromised by linguistic boundaries. Although vernacular literature appears in eastern India by AD 1200, vernacular writings for several centuries thereafter tend to be perceived as the common inheritance of the whole eastern area, more so than as the output of individual languages.

This is clearly evident, for instance, in the case of the celebrated Buddhist hymns called the *Caryāpada*, composed in eastern India roughly between AD 1000 and 1200. Though the language of these hymns is Old Bengali, there are reference works on Assamese, Oriya and even Maithili that treat the same hymns as the earliest specimens of each of these languages and their literatures.

Bengali linguistic identity is not wholly a function of the language's genetic affiliation in the Indo-Aryan family. Eastern India was subjected to Aryanisation before the onset of the Christian era, and therefore well before the evolution of Bengali and the other Magadhan languages. Certain events of the medieval era have had a greater significance than Aryanisation in the shaping of Bengali linguistic identity, since they furnished the prerequisites of Bengali regional and national identity.

Among these events, one of the most crucial was the establishment of Islamic rule in the early thirteenth century. Islamisation led to six hundred years of political unity in Bengal, under which it was possible for a distinctly national style of literary and cultural expression to evolve, more or less unaffected by religious distinctions. To be sure, much if not all early popular literature in Bengali had a sacred basis; the early compositions were largely translations and reworkings of Hindu legends, like the Krishna myth cycle and the *Rāmāyaṇa* religious epic. However, this material seems to have always been looked upon more as a product of local than of sectarian tradition. From the outset of their rule, the Muslim aristocracy did little to discourage the composition of literature on such popular themes; on the contrary, they often lent their patronage to the authors of these works, who were both Muslim and Hindu. Further, when in the sixteenth and seventeenth centuries Islamic writers ultimately did set about creating a body of sectarian, didactic vernacular literature in Bengali, they readily adapted the originally Hindu motifs, themes and stories that had become part of the local cultural tradition.

The relative weakness of religious identity in Bengali cultural institutions is perhaps best interpreted in light of a major event which occurred concomitant to the rise of Islamic rule. This event was a massive shift in the course of the Ganges River between the twelfth and sixteenth centuries AD. Whereas it had earlier emptied into the Bay of Bengal nearly due south of the site of present-day Calcutta, the river gradually approached and eventually became linked with the Padma River system in the territory today called Bangladesh. The shift in the Ganges has been one of the greatest influences upon material history and human geography in eastern India; for, prior to the completion of the river's change of course, the inhabitants of the eastern tracts had been virtually untouched by civilisation and sociocultural influences from without, whether Islamic or Hindu. Over the past four centuries, it is the descendants of the same people who have come to make up the majority of speakers of the Bengali language; so that the basis of their Bengali identity is not genetic and not religious, but linguistic. That the bulk of the population perceives commonality of language as the principal basis of its social unity is clear from the name taken by the new nation-state of eastern Bengal following the 1971 war of liberation. In the proper noun *Bangladesh* (composed of *bāṅglā* plus *deśa*, the latter meaning 'country'), the first part of the compound does not mean the Bengali people or the territory of Bengal; the term *bāṅglā* specifically refers, rather, to the Bengali language.

The Muslim aristocracy that ruled Bengal for some six centuries was supplanted in the eighteenth century by new invaders, the British. Since the latter's withdrawal from the subcontinent in 1947, the community which identifies itself as Bengali has been divided between two sovereign political entities. However, the Bengali language continues to be spoken throughout Bengal's traditional domains, and on both sides of the newly-imposed international boundary. Today, Bengali is one of the official regional speeches of the Indian Union, a status which is also enjoyed by the other eastern Magadhan languages, Oriya and Assamese. Among the three languages, the one which is currently in the strongest position is Bengali, since it alone also has the status of a national language outside India's present borders. In India, about eight per cent of the overall population, or some 55 million people per 1981 census figures, speak Bengali. The great bulk of these speakers reside in West Bengal, the Indian state contiguous to Bangladesh. At the same time, in Bangladesh, 1980 census figures report a population of nearly ninety million, of whom over 95 per cent are Bengali speakers. Thus the combined community of Bengali speakers in India and Bangladesh approaches 145 million, a larger body of native speakers than currently exists for French.

2   Orthography and Sound System

The writing system of Modern Bengali is derived from Brāhmī, an ancient Indian syllabary. Brāhmī is also the source of all the other native Indian scripts (including those of the modern South Indian languages) as well as of Devanāgarī, a script associated with classical Sanskrit and with a number of the modern Indo-Aryan languages.

The scripts of the modern eastern Magadhan languages (Oriya, Assamese and Bengali) are based on a system of characters historically related to, but distinct from, Devanāgarī. The Bengali script is identical to that of Assamese except for two characters; while the Oriya script, though closely related historically to the Bengali-Assamese script, is quite distinctive in its appearance.

Like all Brāhmī-derived scripts, Bengali orthography reads from left to right, and is organised according to syllabic rather than segmental units.

Table 23.1: Bengali Script

Vowel Segments

Special name of character, if any	Independent form	Combining form (shown with the sign kɔ)	Transliteration
	অ	ক	ɔ
	আ	কা	a
hrɔsso i	ই	কি	i
dirgho i	ঈ	কী	ī
hrɔsso u	উ	কু	u
dirgho u	ঊ	কূ	ū
ri	ঋ	কৃ	ri
	এ	কে	e
	ঐ	কৈ	oy
	ও	কো	o
	ঔ	কৌ	ow

Consonant Segments

	Ordinary form	Special form(s)	Transliteration (so-called 'inherent vowel' not represented)
	ক		k
	খ		kh
	গ		g
	ঘ		gh
	ঙ	ং	ṅ
	চ		c
	ছ		ch
	জ		j
	ঝ		jh
	ঞ		ñ
	ট		ṭ
	ঠ		ṭh
	ড		ḍ
	ঢ		ḍh
	ড়		ṛ
	ঢ়		ṛh
	ণ		ṇ
	ত	ৎ	t
	থ		th
	দ		d
	ধ		dh
	ন		n
	প		p
	ফ		ph
	ব		b
	ভ		bh
	ম		m
ontostho jɔ	য	য়	j
ontostho ɔ	য়		y, w
	র	◌ৰ	r
	ল	◌ৢ	l
talobbo sɔ	শ		ś
murdhonno sɔ	ষ		ṣ
donto sɔ	স		s
	হ	ঃ	h
Special diacritics cɔndrobindu hɔsonto	ঁ ্		~

Accordingly, a special diacritic or character is employed to represent a single consonant segment in isolation from any following vowel, or a single vowel in isolation from any preceding consonant. Furthermore, the writing system of Bengali, like Devanāgarī, represents characters as hanging from a superimposed horizontal line and has no distinction of upper and lower cases.

Table 23.1 sets out the Bengali script according to the traditional ordering of characters, with two special diacritics listed at the end. Most Bengali characters are designated according to the pronunciation of their independent or ordinary form. Thus the first vowel character is called ɔ, while the first consonant character is called kɔ. The designation of the latter is such, because the corresponding sign in isolation is read not as a single segment, but as a syllable terminating in /ɔ/, the so-called 'inherent vowel'. Several Bengali characters are not designated by the pronunciation of their independent or ordinary forms; their special names are listed in the leftmost column of table 23.1. Among the terms used in the special designations of vowel characters, *hrɔsso* literally means 'short' and *dirgho* 'long'. Among the terms used in the special designations of consonant characters, *talobbo* literally means 'palatal', *murdhonno* 'retroflex', and *donto* 'dental'. These terms are used, for historical reasons, to distinguish the names for the three sibilant characters. The three characters (transliterated *ś*, *ṣ* and *s*) are used to represent a single non-obstruent sibilant phoneme in Modern Bengali. This phoneme is a palatal with a conditioned dental allophone; further discussion will be given below. It might be pointed out that another Bengali phoneme, the dental nasal /n/, is likewise represented in orthography by three different characters, which are transliterated *ñ*, *ṇ*, and *n*.

In Bengali orthography, a vowel sign normally occurs in its independent form only when it is the first segment of a syllable. Otherwise, the combining form of the vowel sign is written together with the ordinary form of a consonant character, as illustrated in table 23.1 for the character kɔ. There are a few exceptional cases: for instance, the character hɔ when written with the combining form of the sign *ri* appears not as হৃ , but as হৃ (pronounced [hri]). The character rɔ combined with *dirgho u* is written not as রূ , but as রু [ru]. The combination of *talobbo sɔ* with *hrɔsso u* is optionally represented either as শু or as শু (both are pronounced [šu]), while gɔ, rɔ and hɔ in combination with *hrɔsso u* yield the respective representations গু [gu], রু [ru], and হু [hu].

Several of the consonant characters in Bengali have special forms designated in table 23.1; their distribution is as follows. The characters ŋɔ and tɔ occur in their special forms when the consonants they represent are the final segments of phonological syllables. Thus /baṅla/ 'Bengali language' is written বাংলা , while /šɔt/ 'true' is written সৎ .

The character *ɔntostho ɔ* has a special form listed in table 23.1; the name of this special form is *jɔ phɔla*. Generally, *jɔ phɔla* is the form in which *ɔntostho ɔ* occurs when combined with a preceding ordinary consonant sign, as in ত্যাগ [tæg] 'renunciation'. When combined with an ordinary consonant sign in non-initial syllables, *jɔ phɔla* tends to be realised as gemination of the consonant segment, as in গ্রাম্য [grammo] 'rural'. The sign *ɔntostho ɔ* in its ordinary form is usually represented intervocalically, and generally realised phonetically as a front or back high or mid semi-vowel. Incidentally, the character *ɔntostho ɔ* in its ordinary form is not to be confused with the similar looking character that precedes it in table 23.1, the *ɔntostho jɔ* character. This character has the same phonemic realisation as the consonant sign *jɔ* (listed much earlier in table 23.1), and is transliterated in the same way. While *jɔ* and *ɔntostho jɔ* have the same phonemic realisation, they have separate historical sources; and the sign *ɔntostho jɔ* occurs today in the spelling of a limited number of Bengali lexemes, largely direct borrowings from Sanskrit.

The sign *rɔ* exhibits one of two special forms when written in combination with an ordinary consonant sign. In cases where the ordinary consonant sign represents a segment which is pronounced before /r/, then *rɔ* appears in the combining form *rɔ phɔla*; to illustrate: প্রেত [pret] 'ghost, evil spirit'. In cases where the sound represented by the ordinary consonant sign is realised after /r/, *rɔ* appears in the second of its combining forms, which is called *reph*; as in অর্থ [ɔrtho] 'value'.

The sign *hɔ* has a special form, listed in table 23.1, which is written word-finally or before a succeeding consonant in the same syllable. In neither case, however, is the special form of *hɔ* very commonly observed in Bengali writing.

Two special diacritics are listed at the end of table 23.1. The first of these, *cɔndrobindu*, represents the supersegmental for nasalisation, and is written over the ordinary or combining form of any vowel character. The other special diacritic, called *hɔsonto*, is used to represent two ordinary consonant signs as being realised one after another, without an intervening syllabic, in the same phonological syllable; or to show that an ordinary consonant sign written in isolation is to be realised phonologically without the customary 'inherent vowel'. Thus: বাক্ [bak] 'speech', বাক্শক্তি [bakšokti] 'power of speech'. In practice, the use of this diacritic is uncommon, except where spelling is offered as a guide to pronunciation; or where the spelling of a word takes account of internal morpheme boundaries, as in the last example.

Table 23.1 does not show the representation of consonant clusters in Bengali orthography. Bengali has about two dozen or so special *sɔñjukto* (literally 'conjunct') characters, used to designate the combination of two, or sometimes three, ordinary consonant signs. In learning to write Bengali, a person must learn the *sɔñjukto* signs more or less by rote.

Before considering the sound system of Bengali, it should be mentioned that the spelling of Bengali words is well standardised, though not in all cases a strict guide to pronunciation. There are two especially common areas of inconsistency. One involves the representation of the sound [æ]. Compare the phonetic realisations of the following words with their spellings and transliterations: [æto] এত (transliterated *etɔ*) 'so much, so many'; [bæsto] ব্যস্ত (transliterated *byɔstɔ*) 'busy'; and [læj] ন্যাজ (transliterated *lyajɔ*) 'tail'. The sound [æ] can be orthographically represented in any of the three ways illustrated, and the precise spelling of any word containing this sound must accordingly be memorised.

Another area of inconsistency involves the realisation of the 'inherent vowel'. Since, as mentioned above, the diacritic *hɔsonto* (used to indicate the absence of the inherent vowel) is rarely used in practice, it is not always clear whether an unmodified ordinary consonant character is to be read with or without the inherent vowel. Compare, for example, [kɔto] কত (transliterated *kɔtɔ*) 'how much/how many' with [mɔt] মত (transliterated *mɔtɔ*) 'opinion'. This example makes it especially clear that Bengali spelling is not an infallible guide to pronunciation.

The segmental phonemes (oral vowels and consonants) of the standard dialect of Bengali are set forth in table 23.2. As table 23.2 makes clear, the feature of aspiration is significant for obstruents and defines two phonemically distinct series, the unaspirates and the aspirates. Though not represented in the table since it is non-segmental, the feature of nasalisation is nonetheless significant for vowels and similarly defines two phonemically distinct series. Thus in addition to the oral vowels as listed in table 23.2, Bengali has the corresponding nasalised vowel phonemes /ɔ̃/, /ã/, /æ̃/, /õ/, /ẽ/, /ũ/ and /ĩ/.

Table 23.2: Segmental Phonemes of Bengali

Consonants

	Labial	Dental	Retroflex	Palatal	Velar	Post-velar
Obstruents						
voiceless:						
unaspirated	p	t	ṭ	c	k	
aspirated	ph	th	ṭh	ch	kh	
voiced:						
unaspirated	b	d	ḍ	j	g	
aspirated	bh	dh	ḍh	jh	gh	
Nasals	m	n			ṅ	
Flaps		r	ṛ			
Lateral		l				
Spirants				s		h

Vowels

	Front		Back			
High	i		u			
High mid	e		o			
Low mid	æ		ɔ			
Low			a			

The phonemic inventory of modern standard Bengali marks it as a fairly typical Indo-Aryan language. The organisation of the consonant system in terms of five basic points of articulation (velar, palatal, retroflex, dental and labial) is characteristic, as is the stop/flap distinction in the retroflex series.

(Hindi-Urdu, for instance, likewise has several retroflex stop phonemes and retroflex flaps.) Also typically Indo-Aryan is the distinctive character of voicing in the Bengali obstruent inventory, along with the distinctive character of aspiration. The latter feature tends, however, to be suppressed preconsonantally, especially in rapid speech. Moreover, the voiced labial aspirate /bh/ tends to be unstable in the pronunciation of many Bengali speakers, often approximating to a voiced labial continuant [v].

In the consonant inventory, Bengali can be regarded as unusual only in having a palatal sibilant phoneme in the absence of a dental sibilant. The historical background of this has been discussed in the preceding section. The phoneme in question is realised as a palatal [š] in all environments, except before the segments /t/, /th/, /n/, /r/, and /l/, where it is realised as a dental, i.e. as [s]. For simplicity, this Bengali sibilant is represented as *s* in the remainder of this chapter.

Nasalisation as a distinctive non-segmental feature of the vowel system is typical not only of Bengali but of modern Indo-Aryan languages generally. In actual articulation, the nasality of the Bengali nasalised vowel segments tends to be fairly weak, and is certainly not as strong as the nasality of vowels in standard French.

The most interesting Modern Bengali phonological processes involve the vowel segments to the relative exclusion of the consonants. One process, Vowel Raising, produces a neutralisation of the high/low distinction in the mid vowels, generally in unstressed syllables. Given the stress pattern of the present standard dialect, which will be discussed later, Vowel Raising generally applies in non-word-initial syllables. Evidence for the process is found in the following alternations:

mɔl	'dirt'	ɔmol	'pure'
sɔ	'hundred'	ækso	'one hundred'
æk	'one'	ɔnek	'many'

A second phonological process affecting vowel height is very significant because of its relationship to morphophonemic alternations in the Bengali verbal base. This process may be called Vowel Height Assimilation, since it involves the assimilation of a non-high vowel (other than /a/) to the nearest succeeding vowel segment within the phonological word, provided the latter has the specification [+high]. Outside the area of verbal morphophonemics, the evidence for this process principally comes from the neutralisation of the high/low distinction in the mid vowels before /i/ or /u/ in a following contiguous syllable. Some alternations which illustrate this process are:

æk	'one'	ekṭi	'one' (plus classifier -ṭi)
lɔjja	'shame'	lojjito	'ashamed'
nɔṭ	'actor'	noṭi	'actress'
æk	'one'	ekṭu	'a little, a bit'
tɔbe	'then'	tobu	'but (then)'

At this point it will be useful to qualify the observation drawn earlier that Bengali is — phonologically speaking — a fairly typical Indo-Aryan language. It is true that most of the segments in the Modern Bengali sound system can be traced more or less directly to Old Indo-Aryan. However, the retroflex flap /ṛ/ of the former has no counterpart in the latter, and its presence in modern standard Bengali (and in some of its sisters) is due to a phonological innovation of Middle Indo-Aryan. Furthermore, while the other retroflex segments of Modern Bengali (/ṭ/, /ṭh/, /ḍ/, /ḍh/) have counterparts in the Old Indo-Aryan sound system, their overall frequency (phonetic load) in Old Indo-Aryan was low. On the other hand, among the modern Indo-Aryan languages, it is Bengali (along with the other Magadhan languages, especially the eastern Magadhan languages) which demonstrates a comparatively high frequency of retroflex sounds. Some external, i.e. non-Aryan influence on the diachronic development of the Bengali sound system is suggested. Such a hypothesis ought logically to be tied in with the observation in the earlier section of this essay that the numerical majority of Bengali speakers represents what were, until recent centuries, culturally unassimilated tribals of eastern Bengal, about whose prior linguistic and social history not much is known.

Further evidence of probable non-Aryan influence in the phonology is to be found in the peculiar word stress pattern of Modern Bengali. Accent was phonemic only in very early Old Indo-Aryan, i.e. Vedic (see page 456). Subsequently, however, predictable word stress has typified the Indo-Aryan languages; the characteristic pattern, moreover, has been for the stress to fall so many morae from the end of the phonological word. Bengali word stress, though, is exceptional. It is non-phonemic and, in the standard dialect, there is a strong tendency for it to be associated with word-*initial* syllables. This pattern evidently became dominant after AD 1400, or well after Bengali acquired a linguistic identity separate from that of its Indo-Aryan sisters. What this and other evidence may imply about the place of Bengali within the general South Asian language area is an issue to be further pursued toward the end of this essay.

3 Morphology

Morphology in Modern Bengali is non-existent for adjectives, minimal for nouns and very productive for verbs. Loss or reduction of the earlier Indo-Aryan adjective declensional parameters (gender, case, number) is fairly typical of the modern Indo-Aryan languages; hence the absence of adjectival morphology in Modern Bengali is not surprising. Bengali differs from many of its sisters, however, in lacking certain characteristic nominal categories. The early Indo-Aryan category of gender persists in most of the modern languages, with the richest (three-gender) systems still to be found in some of the western languages, such as Marathi. Early stages of the

Magadhan languages (e.g. Oriya, Assamese and Bengali) also show evidence of a gender system. However, the category is no longer productive in any of the modern Magadhan languages. In Modern Bengali, it is only in a few relic alternations (e.g. the earlier cited pair *nɔṭ* 'actor'/*noṭi* 'actress') that one observes any evidence today for the system of nominal gender which once existed in the language.

The early Indo-Aryan system of three number categories has been reduced in Modern Bengali to a singular/plural distinction which is marked on nouns and pronouns. The elaborate case system of early Indo-Aryan has also been reduced in Modern Bengali as it has in most modern Indo-Aryan languages. Table 23.3 summarises the standard Bengali declension for full nouns (pronouns are not given). Pertinent parameters not, however, revealed in this table are animacy, definiteness and determinacy. Generally, the plural markers are added only to count nouns having animate or definite referents; otherwise plurality tends to be unmarked. Compare, e.g. *jutogulo dɔrkar* 'the (specified) shoes are necessary' versus *juto dɔrkar* '(unspecified) shoes are necessary'. Further, among the plurality markers listed in table 23.3, *-gulo* (nominative), *-guloke* (objective), *-gulor* (genitive) and *-gulote* (locative-instrumental) are applicable to nouns with both animate and inanimate referents, while the other markers cooccur only with animate nouns. Hence: *chelera* '(the) boys', *chelegulo* '(the) boys', *jutogulo* 'the shoes', but **jutora* 'the shoes'.

Table 23.3: Bengali Nominal Declension

	Singular	Plural
Nominative	Ø	-ra/-era; -gulo
Objective	-ke	-der(ke)/-eder(ke); -guloke
Genitive	-r/-er	-der/-eder; -gulor
Locative-Instrumental	-te/-e *or* -ete	-gulote

The Bengali case markers in table 23.3 which show an alternation of form (e.g. *-r/-er*, *-te/-e* or *-ete*, *-der(ke)/-eder(ke)*, etc.) are phonologically conditioned according to whether the forms to which they are appended terminate in a syllabic or non-syllabic segment respectively. Both *-eder(ke)* and *-ete* are, however, currently rare. The usage of the objective singular marker *-ke*, listed in table 23.3, tends to be confined to inanimate noun phrases having definite referents and to definite or determinate animate noun phrases. Thus compare *kichu (*kichuke) caichen* 'do you want something?' with *kauke (*kau) caichen* 'do you want someone?'; but: *pulis caichen* 'are you seeking a policeman/some policemen?' versus *puliske caichen* 'are you seeking the police?'.

Bengali subject-predicate agreement will be covered in the following section on syntax. It bears mentioning at present, however, that the sole parameters for subject-verb agreement in Modern Bengali are person (three are distinguished) and status. Inflectionally, the Bengali verb is marked for three status categories (despective/ordinary/honorific) in the second person and two categories (ordinary/honorific) in the third. It is notable that the shapes of the honorific inflectional endings are modelled on earlier Indo-Aryan plural inflectional markers. Table 23.4 lists the verbal inflection of modern standard Bengali.

Table 23.4: Bengali Verbal Inflection

	1st person	2nd person despective	2nd person ordinary	3rd person ordinary	Honorific (2nd, 3rd persons)
Present imperative	–	Ø	-o	-uk	-un
Unmarked indicative					
and -(c)ch- stems	-i	-is	-o	-e	-en
-b- stems	-o	-i	-e	-e	-en
-t- and -l- stems	-am	-i	-e	-o	-en

The most interesting area of Bengali morphology is the derivation of inflecting stems from verbal bases. Properly speaking, a formal analysis of Bengali verbal stem derivation presupposes the statement of various morphophonological rules. However, for the sake of brevity and clarity, the phenomena will be outlined below more or less informally.

But before the system of verbal stem derivational marking can be discussed, two facts must be presented concerning the shapes of Bengali verbal bases, i.e. the bases to which the stem markers are added.

First, Bengali verbal bases are all either monosyllabic (such as *jan-* 'know') or disyllabic (such as *kamṛa-* 'bite'). The first syllabic in the verbal base may be called the root vowel. There is a productive process for deriving disyllabic bases from monosyllabics by the addition of a stem vowel. This stem vowel is *-a-* (post-vocalically *-oa-*) as in *jana-* 'inform'; although, for many speakers, the stem vowel may be *-o-* if the root vowel (i.e. of the monosyllabic base) is [+high]; e.g. *jiro-*, for some speakers *jira-* 'rest'. Derived disyllabics usually serve as the formal causatives of their monosyllabic counterparts. Compare: *jan-* 'know', *jana-* 'inform'; *oth-* 'rise', *otha-* 'raise'; *dækh-* 'see', *dækha-* 'show'.

Second, monosyllabic bases with non-high root vowels have two alternate forms, respectively called low and high. Examples are:

	Low alternate base	High alternate base
'know'	jan-	jen-
'see'	dækh-	dekh-
'sit'	bɔs-	bos-
'buy'	ken-	kin-
'rise'	oth-	uth-

When the root vowel is /a/, /e/ is substituted to derive the high alternate base; for bases with front or back non-high root vowels, the high alternate base is formed by assimilating the original root vowel to the next higher vowel in the vowel inventory (see again table 23.2). The latter behaviour suggests an extended application of the Vowel Height Assimilation process discussed in the preceding section. It is, in fact, feasible to state the rules of verb stem derivation so that the low/high alternation is phonologically motivated; i.e. by positing a high vowel (specifically, /i/) in the underlying shapes of the stem-deriving markers. In some verbal forms there is concrete evidence for the /i/ element, as will be observed below. Also, Vowel Height Assimilation must be invoked in any case to account for the fact that, in the derivation of verbal forms which have zero marking of the stem (that is, the present imperative and unmarked (present) indicative), the high alternate base occurs before any inflection containing a high vowel. Thus *dækh-* 'see', *dækho* 'you (ordinary) see', but *dekhi* 'I see', *dekhis* 'you (despective) see', *dekhun* (honorific) 'see!', etc. That there is no high-low alternation in these inflections for disyllabic bases is consistent with the fact that Vowel Height Assimilation only applies when a high syllabic occurs in the immediately succeeding syllable. Thus *otha-* 'raise (cause to rise)', *othae* 'he/she raises', *othai* (**uthai*) 'I/we raise', etc.

The left-hand column of table 23.4 lists the various Bengali verbal stem types. Two of the verbal forms with Ø stem marking, the present imperative and present indicative, were just discussed. It may be pointed out that, in this stem type, the vowel element /u/ of the third person ordinary inflection *-uk* and of the second/third person honorific inflection *-un*, as well as the /i/ of the second person despective inflection *-is*, all disappear post-vocalically (after Vowel Height Assimilation applies); thus (as above) *dekhis* 'you (despective) see' but (from *hɔ-* 'become') *hok* 'let him/her/it/them become!'; *hon* 'he/she/you/they (honorific) become!'; *hos* 'you (despective) become'.

A verbal form with Ø stem marking not so far discussed is the denominative verbal form or verbal noun. The verbal noun is a non-inflecting form and is therefore not listed in table 23.4. In monosyllabic bases, the marker of this form is suffixed *-a* (*-oa* post-vocalically); for most standard dialect speakers, the marker in disyllabics is *-no*. Thus *oth-* 'rise', *otha* 'rising', *otha-* 'raise', *othano* 'raising'; *jan-* 'know', *jana* 'knowing', *jana-* 'inform', *janano* 'informing'; *ga-* 'sing', *gaoa* 'singing', *gaoa-* 'cause to sing', *gaoano* 'causing to sing'.

Continuing in the leftmost column of table 23.4, the stem-deriving marker *-(c)ch-* signals continuative aspect and is used, independent of any other derivational marker, to derive the present continuous verbal form. The element (*c*) of the marker *-(c)ch-* deletes post-consonantally; compare *khacche* 'is eating' (from *kha-*) with *anche* 'is bringing' (from *an-*). In forming the verbal stem with *-(c)ch-* the high alternate base is selected, unless the base is disyllabic or is a monosyllabic base having the root vowel

/a/. Compare the last examples with *uṭhche* 'is rising' (from *oṭh-*), *oṭhacche* 'is raising' (from *oṭha-*). In a formal treatment of Bengali morphophonemics, the basic or underlying form of the stem marker could be given as *-i(c)ch-*; in this event, one would posit a rule to delete the element /i/ after Vowel Height Assimilation applies, except in a very limited class of verbs including *ga-* 'sing', *sɔ-* 'bear' and *ca-* 'want'. In forming the present continuous forms of these verbs, the element /i/ surfaces, although the element (*c*) of the stem marker tends to be deleted. The resulting shapes are, respectively: *gaiche* 'is singing' (*gacche* is at best non-standard); *soiche* (**socche*) 'is bearing'; *caiche* 'is wanting' (*cacche* does, however, occur as a variant).

The stem-deriving marker *-b-* (see table 23.4) signals irrealis aspect and is used to derive future verbal forms, both indicative and imperative (except for the imperative of the second person ordinary, which will be treated after the next paragraph). In Bengali, the future imperative, as well as the present imperative, may occur in affirmative commands; however, the future imperative, never the present imperative, occurs in negative commands.

In forming the verbal stem with *-b-*, the high alternate base is selected except in three cases: where the base is disyllabic, where the monosyllabic base has the root vowel /a/ and where the monosyllabic base is vowel-final. Thus: *uṭhbo* 'I/we will rise' (from *oṭh-*), but *oṭhabo* 'I/we will raise' (from *oṭha-*); *janbo* 'I/we will know' (from *jan-*), *debo* 'I/we will give' (from *de-*). Compare, however, *dibi* 'you (despective) will give', where Vowel Height Assimilation raises the root vowel. It is possible, again, to posit an underlying /i/ in the irrealis stem marker's underlying shape (i.e. *-ib-*), with deletion of the element /i/ applying except for the small class of verbs noted earlier; thus *gaibo* (**gabo*) 'I/we will sing', *soibo* (**sobo*) 'I/we will bear', *caibo* (**cabo*) 'I/we will want'.

The future imperative of the second person ordinary takes the termination *-io*, which can be analysed as a stem formant *-i-* followed by the second person ordinary inflection *-o* (which is also added to unmarked stems, as table 23.4 shows). When combining with this marker *-i-*, all monosyllabic bases occur in their high alternate shapes; e.g. *hoio* 'become!' (from *hɔ-*). The *-i-* marker is deleted post-consonantally, hence *uṭho* 'rise!' (from *oṭh-*); it also deletes when added to most monosyllabic bases terminating in final /a/, for instance: *peo* 'get!' (**peio*) (from *pa-* 'receive'); *geo* 'sing!' (from *ga-* 'sing'). Bengali disyllabic bases drop their final element /a/ or /o/ before the future imperative stem marker *-i-*. Vowel Height Assimilation applies, hence *uṭhio* 'you must raise!' (from *oṭha-*), *dekhio* 'you must show!' (from *dækha-*), *kamṛio* 'you must bite!' (from *kamṛa-*).

Continuing in the left-hand column of table 23.4, the stem-deriving marker *-t-* signals non-punctual aspect and appears in several forms of the Bengali verb. The Bengali infinitive termination is invariant *-te*, e.g. *jante* 'to know' (from *jan-*) (as in *jante cai* 'I want to know'). The marker *-t-* also occurs in the finite verbal form used to express the past habitual and perfect conditional, e.g. *jantam* 'I/we used to know' or 'if I/we had known'. The high alternate of monosyllabic bases cooccurs with this marker except in those bases containing a root vowel /a/ followed by a consonant. To illustrate, the infinitive of *oṭh-* 'rise' is *uṭhte*; of *oṭha-* 'raise', *oṭhate*; of *de-* 'give', *dite*; of *hɔ-* 'become', *hote*; of *kha-* 'eat', *khete*; of *an-* 'bring', *ante* (**ente*). Similarly, *uṭhtam* 'I/we used to rise' or 'if I/we had risen'; *oṭhatam* 'I/we used to raise' or 'if I/we had raised', etc. As before, evidence for an /i/ element in the underlying form of the marker *-t-* (i.e. *-it-*) comes from the earlier noted class of verbs 'sing', etc.; for example, *gaite* (**gate*) 'to sing', *gaitam* (**gatam*) 'I/we used to sing' or 'if I/we had sung'; *soite* (**sote*) 'to bear', *soitam* (**sotam*) 'I/we used to bear' or 'if I/we had borne'; *caite* (**cate*) 'to want', *caitam* (**catam*) 'I/we used to want' or 'if I/we had wanted', etc.

The stem-deriving marker *-l-* signals anterior aspect and appears in two verbal forms. The termination of the imperfect conditional is invariant *-le*, e.g. *janle* 'if one knows' (from *jan-*). The marker *-l-* also occurs in the ordinary past tense verbal form, e.g. *janlam* 'I/we knew'. The behaviour of monosyllabic verbal bases in coocurrence with this marker is the same as their behaviour in cooccurrence with the marker *-t-* discussed above. Thus *uṭhle* 'if one rises', *oṭhale* 'if one raises', *dile* 'if one gives', *hole* 'if one becomes', *khele* 'if one eats', *anle* 'if one brings'; *uṭhlam* 'I/we rose', *oṭhalam* 'I/we raised'; and, again, *gaile* (**gale*) 'if one sings', *soile* (**sole*) 'if one bears', *caile* (**cale*) 'if one wants'; *gailam* 'I/we sang', and so on.

To complete the account of the conjugation of the Bengali verb it is only necessary to mention that certain stem-deriving markers can be combined on a single verbal base. For instance, the marker *-l-* combined with the uninflected stem in *-(c)ch-* yields a verbal form called the past continuous. Illustrations are: *uṭhchilam* 'I was/we were rising' (from *oṭh-*), *oṭhacchilam* 'I was/we were raising' (from *oṭha-*), *khacchilam* 'I was/we were eating' (from *kha-*).

It is also possible to combine stem-deriving markers on the Bengali verbal base in the completive aspect. The marker of this aspect is *-(i)e-*, not listed in table 23.4 because it is not used in isolation from other stem-forming markers to form inflecting verbal stems. Independently of any other stem-forming marker it may, however, be added to a verbal base to derive a non-finite verbal form known as the conjunctive participle (or gerund). An example is: *bujhe* 'having understood' from *bujh-* 'understand' (note that the element (*i*) of *-(i)e-* deletes post-consonantally). When attached to the completive aspect marker *-(i)e-*, all monosyllabic bases occur in their high alternate shapes; disyllabic bases drop their final element /a/ or /o/; and in the latter case, Vowel Height Assimilation applies. Thus: *uṭhe* 'having risen' (from *oṭh-*); *jene* 'having known' (from *jan-*); *diye* 'having given' (from *de-*); *uṭhie* 'having raised' (from *oṭha-*), *janie* 'having informed' (from *jana-*). Now the stem-deriving marker *-(c)ch-* may combine with the verbal stem in *-(i)e-*, yielding a verbal form called the present perfect; the combining shape of the

Bengali Verbal Conjugation Types

	pa- 'receive'		an- 'bring'		bɔs- 'sit'		bɔsa- 'seat'	
Verbal noun	paoa	'receiving'	ana	'bringing'	bɔsa	'sitting'	bɔsano	'seating'
Present indicative	pae	'receives'	ane	'brings'	bɔse	'sits'	bɔsae	'seats'
Present imperative	pak	'let him/her/them receive!'	anuk	'let him/her/them bring!'	bosuk	'let him/her/them sit!'	bɔsak	'let him/her/them seat!'
Present continuous	pacche	'is receiving'	anche	'is bringing'	bosche	'is sitting'	bɔsacche	'is seating'
Future indicative/ future imperative	pabe	'will receive'/ 'must receive!'	anbe	'will bring'/ 'must bring!'	bosbe	'will sit'/ 'must sit!'	bɔsabe	'will seat'/ 'must seat!'
Infinitive	pete	'to receive'	ante	'to bring'	boste	'to sit'	bɔsate	'to seat'
Perfect conditional/ past habitual	peto	'would receive'	anto	'would bring'	bosto	'would sit'	bɔsato	'would seat'
Imperfect conditional	pele	'if one receives'	anle	'if one brings'	bosle	'if one sits'	bɔsale	'if one seats'
Ordinary past	pelo	'received'	anlo	'brought'	boslo	'sat'	bɔsalo	'seated'
Past continuous	pacchilo	'was receiving'	anchilo	'was bringing'	boschilo	'was sitting'	bɔsacchilo	'was seating'
Conjunctive participle	peye	'having received'	ene	'having brought'	bose	'having sat'	bosie	'having seated'
Present perfect	peyeche	'has received'	eneche	'has brought'	boseche	'has sat'	bosieche	'has seated'
Past perfect	peyechilo	'had received'	enechilo	'had brought'	bosechilo	'had sat'	bosiechilo	'had seated'

former marker in such cases is invariably *-ch-*. This is to say that the element *(c)* of the marker *-(c)ch-* not only deletes post-consonantally (see the earlier discussion of continuous aspect marking), but also following the stem-deriving marker *-(i)e-*. Some examples are: *dekheche* 'has seen' (from monosyllabic *dækh-*), *dekhieche* 'has shown' (from disyllabic *dækha-*), *diyeche* 'has given' (from *de-* 'give'). The verbal stem in *-(i)e-* followed by *-(c)ch-* may further combine with the anterior aspect marker *-l-* to yield a verbal form called the past perfect; e.g. *dekhechilam* 'I/we had seen', *dekhiechilam* 'I/we had shown'.

Examples of conjugation for four Bengali verbal bases are given in the chart of verbal conjugation types. The inflection illustrated in the chart is the third person ordinary.

4 Syntax

The preceding discussion of declensional parameters (case and number for nouns, person and status for verbs) ties in naturally with the topic of agreement in Bengali syntax. A number of modern Indo-Aryan languages (see, for example, the chapter on Hindi-Urdu) demonstrate a degree of ergative patterning in predicate-noun phrase agreement; and Bengali, in its early historical stages, likewise showed some ergative patterning (i.e. sentential verb agreeing with subject of an intransitive sentence but with object, not subject, of a transitive sentence). However, this behaviour is not characteristic today of any of the eastern Magadhan languages.

Thus in Modern Bengali, sentences normally have subjects in the nominative or unmarked case, and the finite predicates of sentences normally agree with their subjects for the parameters of person and status. There are, however, two broad classes of exceptions to this generalisation. The passive constructions exemplify one class. Passive in Modern Bengali is a special variety of sentence nominalisation. When a sentence is nominalised, the predicate takes the verbal noun form (discussed in the preceding section) and the subject is marked with the genitive case. Under passivisation, a sentence is nominalised and then assigned to one of a small set of matrix predicates, the most common being *hɔ-* 'become' and *ja-* 'go'; and when the latter is selected, the subject of the nominalised sentence is obligatorily deleted. Examples are: *tomar jɔthesṭo khaoa hoyeche?* (your enough eating has-become) 'have you eaten enough?' (i.e. has it been sufficiently eaten by you?) and *oke paoa gælo* (to-him getting it-went) 'he was found' (i.e. him was found). In a passive sentence, the matrix verb (*hɔ-* or *ja-*) lacks agreement with any noun phrase. In particular, it cannot agree with the original subject of the active sentence — this noun phrase has become marked with the genitive case under nominalisation, or deleted altogether. This is to say that the Modern Bengali passive construction lacks a formal subject; it is of a type referred to in some grammatical literature as the 'impersonal passive'. These constructions form one class of exceptions to the characteristic pattern of Bengali subject-verb agreement.

The other class of exceptions comprises certain expressions having subjects which occur in a marked or oblique case. In Bengali there are a few complex constructions of this type. Bengali also has several dozen predicates which regularly occur in non-complex constructions with marked subjects. These constructions can be called indirect subject constructions, and indirect subjects in Modern Bengali are invariably marked with the genitive case. (At an earlier historical stage of the language, any of the oblique cases could be used for the marking of the subject in this sort of construction.) In the Modern Bengali indirect subject construction, the finite predicate normally demonstrates no agreement. An example is: *maer tomake pɔchondo hɔy* (of-mother to-you likes) 'Mother likes you'. Bengali indirect subject predicates typically express sensory, mental, emotional, corporal and other characteristically human experiences. These predicates constitute a significant class of exceptions to the generalised pattern of subject-finite predicate agreement in Modern Bengali.

The remainder of this overview of Bengali syntax will be devoted to the topic of word order, or the relative ordering of major constituents in sentences. In some literature on word order types, Bengali has been characterised as a rigidly verb-final language, wherein nominal modifiers precede their heads; verbal modifiers follow verbal bases; the verbal complex is placed sentence-finally; and the subject noun phrase occupies the initial position in a sentence. In these respects Bengali is said to contrast with earlier Indo-Aryan, in which the relative ordering of sentential constituents was freer, notwithstanding a statistical tendency for verbs to stand at the ends of their clauses.

It is true that the ordering of sentential elements is more rigid in Modern Bengali than in Classical Sanskrit. However, the view that Bengali represents a 'rigid' verb-final language does not adequately describe its differences from earlier Indo-Aryan word order patterning.

Word order within the Modern Bengali noun phrase is, to be sure, strict. An adjective or genitive expression is always placed before the noun it modifies. By contrast, in earlier Indo-Aryan, adjectives showed inflectional concord with their modified nouns and consequently were freer in their positioning; more or less the same applied to the positioning of genitive expressions with respect to nominal heads. Not only is the ordering of elements within the noun phrase more rigid in Modern Bengali, but the mutual ordering of noun phrases within the sentence is strict as well, much more so than in earlier Indo-Aryan. The subject noun phrase generally comes first in a Modern Bengali sentence, followed by an indirect object if one occurs; next comes the direct object if one occurs; after which an oblique object noun phrase may be positioned. This strictness of linear ordering can be ascribed to the relative impoverishment of the Modern Bengali case system in comparison with earlier Indo-Aryan. Bengali case markers are, nonetheless, supplemented by a number of postpositions, each of which may govern nouns declined in one of two cases, the objective or genitive.

We will now consider word order within the verb phrase. At the Old Indo-Aryan stage exemplified by Classical Sanskrit, markers representing certain verbal qualifiers (causal, desiderative, potential and conditional) could be affixed to verbal bases, as stem-forming markers and/or as inflectional endings. Another verbal qualifier, the marker of sentential negation, tended to be placed just before the sentential verb. The sentential interrogative particle, on the other hand, was often placed at a distance from the verbal complex.

In Modern Bengali, the only verbal qualifier which is regularly affixed to verbal bases is the causal. (See the discussion of derived disyllabic verbal bases in section 3 above.) The following pair of Bengali sentences illustrates the formal relationship between non-causative and causative constructions: *cheleṭi ciṭhiṭa poṛlo* (the-boy the-letter read) 'the boy read the letter'; *ma cheleṭi-ke diye ciṭhiṭa pɔṛalen* (mother to-the-boy by the-letter caused-to-read) 'the mother had the boy read the letter'. It will be noted that in the second example the non-causal agent is marked with the postposition *diye* 'by' placed after its governed noun, which appears in the objective case. Usually, when the verbal base from which the causative is formed is transitive, the non-causal agent is marked in just this way. The objective case alone is used to mark the non-causal agent when the causative is derived either from an intransitive base, or from any of several semantically 'affective' verbs — transitive verbs expressing actions whose principal effect accrues to their agents and not their undergoers. Examples are: 'eat', 'smell', 'hear', 'see', 'read' (in the sense of 'study'), 'understand' and several others.

It was mentioned above that the modalities of desiderative and potential action could be marked on the verbal form itself in Old Indo-Aryan. In Modern Bengali, these modalities are usually expressed periphrastically; i.e. by suffixing the infinitive marker to the verbal stem, which is then followed by a modal verb. To illustrate: *uṭhte cae* 'wants to rise', *uṭhte pare* 'can rise'.

Conditional expressions occur in two forms in Modern Bengali. The conditional clause may be finite, in which case there appears the particle *jodi*, which is a direct borrowing from a functionally similar Sanskrit particle *yadi*. To illustrate: *jodi tumi kajṭa sarbe (tɔbe) eso* (if you the-work will-finish (then) come) 'if/when you finish the work, (then) come over!'. An alternate way of framing a conditional is by means of the non-finite conditional verbal form (imperfect conditional), which was mentioned in section 3. In this case no conditional particle is used; e.g. *tumi kajṭa sarle (tɔbe) eso* (you the-work if-finish (then) come) 'if/when you finish the work, come over!'.

The particle of sentential negation in Bengali is *na*. In independent clauses it generally follows the sentential verb; in subjoined clauses (both finite and non-finite), it precedes. Thus: *boslam na* (I-sat not) 'I did not sit'; *jodi tumi na bɔso* (if you not sit) 'if you don't sit'; *tumi na bosle* (you not if-sit) 'if you don't sit'. Bengali has, it should be mentioned, two negative verbs. Each of them is a counterpart to one of the verbs 'to be'; and in this connection it needs to be stated that Bengali has three verbs 'to be'. These are respectively the predicative *hɔ-* 'become'; the existential verb 'exist', having independent/subjoined clause allomorphs *ach-/thak-*; and the equational verb or copula, which is normally Ø but in emphatic contexts is represented by *hɔ-* placed between two arguments (compare, for example, non-emphatic *ini jodu* (this-person Ø Jodu) 'this is Jodu' versus emphatic *ini hocchen jodu* (this-person is Jodu) 'this (one) is Jodu'). While the predicative verb 'to be' has no special negative counterpart (it is negated like any other Bengali verb), the other two verbs 'to be' each have a negative counterpart. Moreover, for each of these negative verbs, there are separate allomorphs which occur in independent and subjoined clauses. The respective independent/subjoined shapes of the negative verbs are existential *nei/na thak-* (note that the verb *nei* is invariant) and equational *nɔ-/na hɔ-*. It bears mentioning, incidentally, that negative verbs are neither characteristic of modern nor of earlier Indo-Aryan. They are, if anything, reminiscent of negative copulas and other negative verbs in languages of the Dravidian (South Indian) family, such as Modern Tamil.

The Modern Bengali sentential interrogative particle *ki* is inherited from an earlier Indo-Aryan particle of similar function. The sentential interrogative *ki* may appear in almost any position in a Bengali sentence other than absolute initial; however, sentences vary in their presuppositional nuances according to the placement of this particle, which seems to give the most neutral reading when placed in the second position (i.e. after the first sentential constituent). To illustrate, compare: *tumi ki ekhane chatro?* (you interrogative here student) 'are you a student here?'; *tumi ekhane ki chatro?* (you here interrogative student) 'is it here that you are a student?'; *tumi ekhane chatro (na) ki?* (you here student (negative) interrogative) 'oh, is it that you are a student here?'.

To complete this treatment of word order, we may discuss the relative ordering of marked and unmarked clauses in Bengali complex sentences. By 'marked clause' is meant either a non-finite subordinate clause or a clause whose function within the sentential frame is signalled by some distinctive marker; an instance of such a marker being *jodi*, the particle of the finite conditional clause. As a rule, in a Bengali sentence containing two or more clauses, marked clauses tend to precede unmarked. This is, for instance, true of conjunctive participle constructions; e.g. *bari giye kapor chere ami can korlam* (home having-gone clothes having-removed I bath did) 'going home and removing my clothes, I had a bath'. Relative clauses in Bengali likewise generally precede main clauses, since they are marked (that is, with relative pronouns); Bengali, then, exhibits the correlative sentential type which is well attested throughout the history of Indo-Aryan. An illustration of this construction is: *je boiṭa enecho ami seṭa kichu din rakhbo* (which book you-brought I it some days will-keep) 'I shall keep the book you have brought for a few days'. Finite complement sentences marked with the complementiser *bole* (derived from the conjunctive participle of the verb *bɔl-* 'say') likewise precede unmarked clauses; e.g. *apni jacchen bole ami jani* (you are-going complementiser I know) 'I know that you are going'.

An exception to the usual order of marked before unmarked clauses is exemplified by an alternative finite complement construction. Instead of clause-final marking (with *bole*), the complement clause type in question has an initial marker, a particle *je* (derived historically from a complementiser particle of earlier Indo-Aryan). A complement clause marked initially with *je* is ordered invariably after, not before, the unmarked clause; e.g. *ami jani je apni jacchen* (I know complementiser you are-going) 'I know that you are going'.

5 Concluding Points

In this final section the intention is to relate the foregoing discussion to the question of Bengali's historical development and present standing, both within the Indo-Aryan family and within the general South Asian language area. To accomplish this, it is useful to consider the fact of lectal differentiation in the present community of Bengali speakers. Both vertical and horizontal varieties are observed.

Vertical differentiation, or diglossia, is a feature of the current standard language. This is to say that the language has two styles used more or less for complementary purposes. Of the two styles, the literary or 'pundit language' (*sadhu bhasa*) shows greater conservatism in word morphology (i.e. in regard to verbal morphophonemics and the shapes of case endings) as well as in lexis (it is characterised by a high frequency of words whose forms are directly borrowed from Sanskrit). The less conservative style identified with the spoken or 'current language' (*colti bhasa*) is the everyday medium of informal discourse. Lately it is also gaining currency in more formal discourse situations and, in written expression, has been encroaching on the literary style for some decades.

The institutionalisation of the *sadhu-colti* distinction occurred in Bengali in the nineteenth century, and (as suggested in the last paragraph) shows signs of weakening today. Given (1) that the majority of Bengali speakers today are not Hindu and cannot be expected to maintain an emotional affinity to Sanskritic norms, plus (2) the Bangladesh government's recent moves to enhance the Islamic character of eastern Bengali society and culture and (3) the fact that the colloquial style is overtaking the literary even in western Bengal (both in speech and writing), it remains to be seen over the coming years whether a formal differentiation of everyday versus 'pundit' style language will be maintained.

It should be added that, although throughout the Bengali-speaking area a single, more or less uniform variety of the language is regarded as the standard dialect, the bulk of speakers have at best a passing acquaintance with it. That is, horizontal differentiation of Bengali lects is very extensive (if poorly researched), both in terms of the number of regional dialects that occur and in terms of their mutual divergence. (The extreme eastern dialect of Chittagong, for instance, is unintelligible even to many speakers of other eastern Bengali dialects.) The degree of horizontal differentiation that occurs in the present Bengali-speaking region is related to the ambiguity of Bengali's linguistic affiliation, i.e. areal as contrasted with genetic. It is to be noted that the Bengali-speaking region of the Indian subcontinent to this day borders on or subsumes the domains of a number of non-Indo-Aryan languages. Among them are Malto (a Dravidian language of eastern Bihar); Ahom (a Tai language of neighbouring Assam); Garo (a Tibeto-Burman language spoken in the northern districts of Bengal itself); as well as several languages affiliated with Munda (a subfamily of Austro-Asiatic), such as Santali and Mundari (both of these languages are spoken within as well as outside the Bengali-speaking area).

It has been pointed out earlier that modern standard Bengali has several features suggestive of extra-Aryan influence. These features are: the frequency of retroflex consonants; initial-syllable word stress; absence of grammatical gender; negative verbs. Though not specifically pointed out as such previously, Bengali has several other formal features, discussed above, which represent divergences from the norms of Indo-Aryan and suggest convergence with the areal norms of greater South Asia. These features are: post-verbal negative particle placement; clause-final complement sentence marking; relative rigidity of word order patterning in general, and sentence-final verb positioning in particular; proliferation of the indirect subject construction (which was only occasionally manifested in early Indo-Aryan).

In addition to the above, it may be mentioned that Bengali has two lexical features of a type foreign to Indo-Aryan. These features are, however, not atypical of languages of the general South Asian language area (and are even more typical of South-East Asian languages). One of these is a class of reduplicative expressives, words such as: *kickic* (suggesting grittiness), *miṭmiṭ* (suggesting flickering), *ṭɔlmɔl* (suggesting an overflowing or fluid state). There are dozens of such lexemes in current standard Bengali. The other un-Aryan lexical class consists of around a dozen classifier words, principally numeral classifiers. Examples are: *du jon chatro* (two human-classifier student) 'two students'; *tin khana boi* (three flat-thing-classifier book) 'three books'.

It is probable that the features discussed above were absorbed from other languages into Bengali after the thirteenth century, as the language came to be increasingly used east of the traditional sociocultural centre of Bengal. That centre, located along the former main course of the Ganges (the present-day Bhagirathi-Hooghley River) in western Bengal, still sets the standard for spoken and written expression in the language. Thus standard Bengali is defined even today as the dialect spoken in Calcutta and its environs. It is a reasonable hypothesis nevertheless, as suggested above in section 1, that descendants of non-Bengali tribals of a few centuries past now comprise the bulk of Bengali speakers. In other words, the vast majority of the Bengali linguistic community today represents present or former inhabitants of the previously uncultivated and culturally unassimilated tracts of eastern Bengal. Over the past several centuries, these newcomers to the Bengali-speaking community are the ones responsible for the language's having acquired a definite affiliation within the South Asian linguistic area, above and beyond the predetermined and less interesting fact of its genetic affiliation in Indo-Aryan.

Bibliography

Chatterji (1926) is the classic, and indispensable, treatment of historical phonology and morphology in Bengali and the other Indo-Aryan languages. A good bibliographical source is Čižikova and Ferguson (1969). For the relation between literary and colloquial Bengali, see Dimock (1960).

The absence of a comprehensive reference grammar of Bengali in English is noticeable. Ray et al. (1966) is one of the better concise reference grammars. Chatterji (1939) is a comprehensive grammar in Bengali, while Chatterji (1972) is a concise but thorough treatment of Bengali grammar following the traditional scheme of Indian grammars. Two pedagogical works are also useful: Dimock et al. (1965), a first-year textbook containing very lucid descriptions of the basic structural categories of the language, and Bender and Riccardi (1978), an advanced Bengali textbook containing much useful information on Bengali literature and on the modern literary language. For individual topics, the following can be recommended: on phonetics-phonology, Chatterji (1921) and Ferguson and Chowdhury (1960); on the morphology of the verb, Dimock (1957), Ferguson (1945) and Sarkar (1976); on syntax, Klaiman (1981), which discusses the syntax and semantics of the indirect subject construction, passives and the conjunctive participle construction in modern and earlier stages of Bengali.

References

Bender, E. and T. Riccardi, Jr. 1978. *An Advanced Course in Bengali* (South Asia Regional Studies, University of Pennsylvania, Philadephia)

Chatterji, S.K. 1921. 'Bengali Phonetics', in *Bulletin of the School of Oriental and African Studies*, vol. 2, pp. 1–25

—— 1926. *The Origin and Development of the Bengali Language*, 3 vols. (Allen and Unwin, London)

—— 1939. *Bhāṣāprakāśa bāṅgālā byākaraṇa* (Calcutta University, Calcutta)

—— 1972. *Sarala bhāṣāprakāśa bāṅgālā byākaraṇa*, revised ed. (Bāk-sāhitya, Calcutta)

Čižikova, K.L. and C.A. Ferguson. 1969. 'Bibliographical Review of Bengali Studies', in T. Sebeok (ed.), *Current Trends in Linguistics*, vol. 5: *Linguistics in South Asia* (Mouton, The Hague), pp. 85–98

Dimock, E.C., Jr. 1957. 'Notes on Stem-vowel Alternation in the Bengali Verb', *Indian Linguistics*, vol. 17, pp. 173–7

——— 1960. 'Literary and Colloquial Bengali in Modern Bengali Prose', *International Journal of American Linguistics*, vol. 26, no. 3, pp. 43–63

——— et al. 1965. *Introduction to Bengali*, part 1 (East-West Center, Honolulu; reprinted South Asia Books, Columbia, Mo., 1976)

Ferguson, C.A. 1945. 'A Chart of the Bengali Verb', *Journal of the American Oriental Society*, vol. 65, pp. 54–5

——— and M. Chowdhury. 1960. 'The Phonemes of Bengali', *Language*, vol. 36, pp. 22–59

Klaiman, M.H. 1981. *Volitionality and Subject in Bengali: A Study of Semantic Parameters in Grammatical Processes* (Indiana University Linguistics Club, Bloomington)

Ray, P.S., et al. 1966. *Bengali Language Handbook* (Center for Applied Linguistics, Washington, DC)

Sarkar, P. 1976. 'The Bengali Verb', *International Journal of Dravidian Linguistics*, vol. 5, pp. 274–97

24 Iranian Languages

J.R. Payne

The approximate present distribution of the Iranian languages is illustrated in the attached sketch-map. The languages currently spoken, according to their genetic relations within Iranian (see below) are:

South-West Iranian: Persian (Iran, Persian Gulf); Dari (Afghanistan); Tajiki (USSR); Luri and Bakhtiari (nomadic, Iran); Kumzari (Persian Gulf); non-Persian dialects of Fars province, centred on Shiraz, Kazerun, Sivand and Lar (Iran); Tati (USSR).

North-West Iranian: Kurdish (Turkey, Iran, Iraq, Syria, USSR); Talishi (USSR, Iran); Balochi (Pakistan, Iran, Afghanistan, USSR, Persian Gulf); Gilaki (Iran); Mazandarani (Iran); Zaza (Turkey); Gurani (Iran, Iraq); Bashkardi (Iran); Parachi (Afghanistan); Ormuri (Afghanistan, Pakistan); Semnani and related dialects (Iran); 'Tat' dialects, centred on Tabriz, Zanjan, Qazvin and Saveh (Iran); Vafsi and Ashtiyani (Iran); dialects of central Iran, centred on Kashan, Esfahan, Yazd, Kerman and the Dashte-Kavir (Iran).

South-East Iranian: Pashto (Afghanistan, Pakistan); Yazgulami (USSR); Shughni (USSR, Afghanistan); Roshani (USSR, Afghanistan); Bartangi (USSR); Oroshori (USSR); Sarikoli (China); Ishkashmi (Afghanistan, USSR); Sanglechi (Afghanistan); Zebaki (Afghanistan); Wakhi (Afghanistan, USSR, Pakistan, China); Munji (Afghanistan); Yidgha (Pakistan).

North-East Iranian: Ossete (USSR), Yaghnobi (USSR).

It will be noted that the names of the genetic groups do not always accurately reflect the geographic location of the modern languages. In particular, Ossete, which belongs to the North-East group, is spoken in the Caucasus, which represents the north-west of the present Iranian language area, and Balochi, which belongs to the North-West group, is located in the extreme south-east on either side of the Iran-Pakistan border. In fact, the geographic nomenclature is more closely tied to the distribution of extinct Iranian languages from the Old Iranian (up to the fourth/third centuries BC) and Middle Iranian (from the fourth/third centuries BC to the eighth/ninth centuries AD) periods.

The oldest attested forms of Iranian are Old Persian, known from the cuneiform inscriptions of the Achaemenid emperors, in particular Darius the Great (521–486 BC) and Xerxes (486–465 BC), and Avestan, the language of the Avesta, a collection of sacred Zoroastrian texts. The oldest parts of the Avesta, the Gathas or songs attributed to the prophet Zoroaster himself, reflect a slightly more archaic stage of development than the Old Persian inscriptions, and must therefore be dated to the sixth century BC or earlier, although the first manuscripts are from the thirteenth and fourteenth centuries AD. Genetically, Old Persian can be clearly associated with the South-West Iranian group, the Achaemenid empire being centred on the province of Persis in the south-west of modern Iran, and must be considered a direct precursor of forms of Middle and Modern Persian. The position of Avestan is, however, complex and disputed, as might be expected of an orally transmitted religious text. The focus of Zoroastrian conversion is held to be Bactria, south of the Oxus river in the east, and the Gathas do indeed show some east Iranian characteristics, notably a tendency to voice clusters which appear as -ft- and -xt- in West Iranian (see below). A possible explanation for the occurrence of some West Iranian forms is the subsequent spread of Zoroastrianism towards Media in the north-west. It is clear, nevertheless, that Avestan shows none of the features characteristic of South-West Iranian.

From archaeological and textual evidence, it can be deduced that Iranian languages at the time of the Achaemenid empire had a wider geographical distribution than at present, extending from the steppes of southern Russia in the west to areas of Chinese Turkestan (Sinkiang) in the east. Old Persian and Avestan are the main linguistic sources from this period; however, proper names and toponyms provide some information about Median, the language of the province of Media centred on Ecbatana (modern Hamadan in north-west Iran), and about the language of the Scythian and Sarmatian tribes of the south Russian steppes. The Median dialect, which belongs genetically to the North-West group, was originally the language of the Median empire (eighth to sixth centuries BC), and some of its influence can be seen in the Old Persian inscriptions. Knowledge of the Scythian and Sarmatian dialects is based on the analysis of proper names and toponyms in inscriptions from the Greek colonies of the period and by comparison with forms of Ossete, the only modern descendant.

By comparison, the Middle Iranian period provides a wealth of materials.

Map 24.1: Approximate Distribution of Iranian Languages

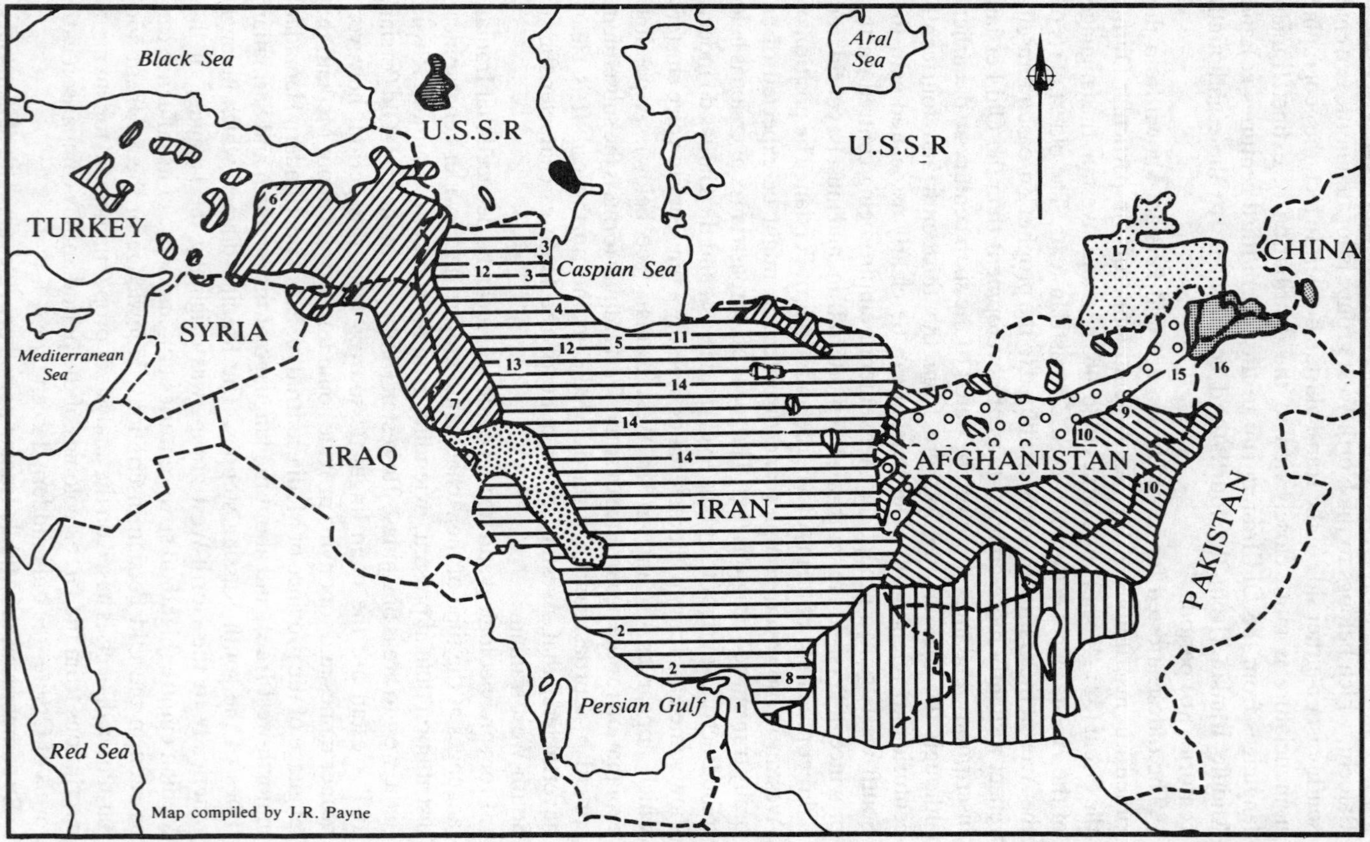

Map compiled by J.R. Payne

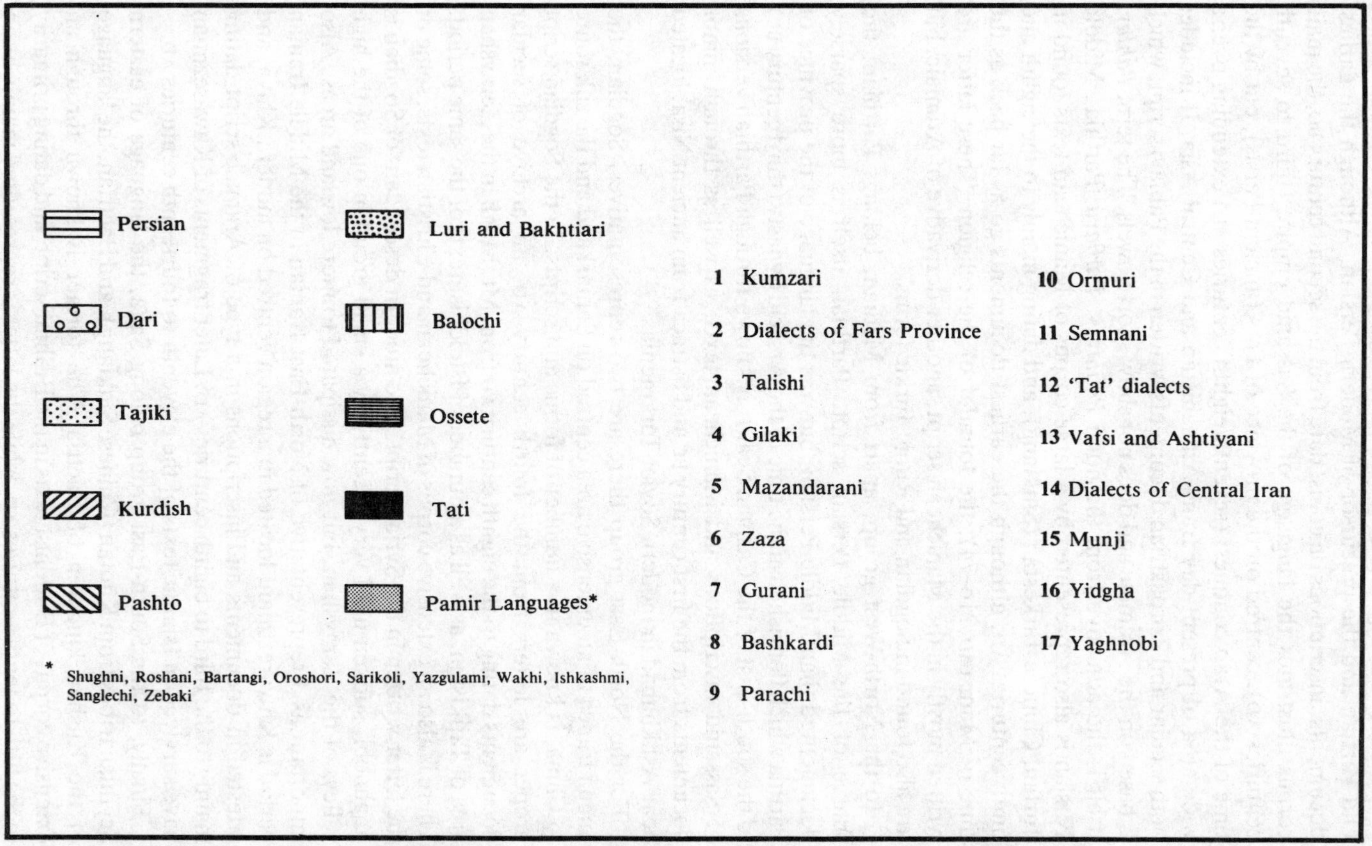

Persian

Dari

Tajiki

Kurdish

Pashto

Luri and Bakhtiari

Balochi

Ossete

Tati

Pamir Languages*

1 Kumzari
2 Dialects of Fars Province
3 Talishi
4 Gilaki
5 Mazandarani
6 Zaza
7 Gurani
8 Bashkardi
9 Parachi
10 Ormuri
11 Semnani
12 'Tat' dialects
13 Vafsi and Ashtiyani
14 Dialects of Central Iran
15 Munji
16 Yidgha
17 Yaghnobi

* Shughni, Roshani, Bartangi, Oroshori, Sarikoli, Yazgulami, Wakhi, Ishkashmi, Sanglechi, Zebaki

To the South-West group belongs Middle Persian, the direct descendant of Old Persian and the precursor of Modern Persian. Although the earliest documents, inscriptions on coins, date from the second century BC, the main corpus illustrates the language of the Sassanid empire (third to seventh centuries AD), centred on the province of Fars (ancient Persis), but by the time of the Arab conquest (seventh/eighth centuries AD) extending over a wide area of present-day Iran, Afghanistan and Central Asia. It includes both secular and Zoroastrian documents written in the Pahlavi script, which is based on the Aramaic and does not show short vowels. The term *Pahlavi* itself is the adjective from the noun *Pahlav* < *Parθava* 'Parthia'. Middle Persian is also represented by a large corpus of Manichean texts found in Turfan, Chinese Turkestan (Sinkiang), and dating mainly to the eighth and ninth centuries AD, although the earliest documents go as far back as the time of Mani (AD 216–74), the founder of the religion. These latter are written mostly in the Manichean script, another derivative of Aramaic, but are also found in Sogdian and Runic Turkic forms.

To the North-West group, apart from Median, belongs Parthian, the source of the Middle Persian script. Parthian itself is more sparsely documented than Middle Persian, but was the language of the province of Parthia which flourished at the time of the Arsacid dynasty (third century BC) to the south-east of the Caspian Sea. It is known through Parthian versions of Sassanid inscriptions and Manichean texts, as well as through minor documents from the first century BC and ostraca from ancient Nisa, located near Ashkhabad in modern Soviet Turkmenia.

For the North-East group there are two representatives. Sogdian, the lingua franca of an extensive area centred on Samarkand and the silk route to China, is known in a number of forms and scripts. In the Sogdian script proper are letters from the fourth century AD, an archive of secular documents dating to the eighth century AD from Mt. Mugh in the Zeravshan area of Tajikistan, as well as a number of Buddhist texts of the same period. There is also an extensive corpus of Manichean and Christian texts, some of the latter written in the Syriac script. The modern descendant of Sogdian is Yaghnobi, spoken until very recently by a small group in one of the high valleys of the Zeravshan, but now dissipated to more lowland areas. Also important as a representative of North-East Iranian in the Middle Iranian period is Khwarezmian, located in a region centred on modern Khiva, and attested in documents and inscriptions in a type of Aramaic script dating mainly to the third to eighth centuries AD. Later fragments of Khwarezmian have survived in Islamic texts of the eleventh to fourteenth centuries AD.

Finally, to the South-East group belong Saka, the language of eastern Scythian tribes from Khotan (Chinese Sinkiang), and Bactrian, the language of the Kushan kingdom of Bactria. The former is known through an extensive corpus of Buddhist texts in the Brahmi script, and dating primarily to the fifth to tenth centuries AD, while the latter is represented mainly by an inscription of twenty-five lines in a variant of the Greek script, found at the temple of Surkh Kotal in northern Afghanistan.

Within the Indo-European family, the Iranian languages are satem languages, e.g. Proto-Indo-European *k̂m̥tom 'hundred', Avestan satəm, and show a very close relationship to the Indo-Aryan (and Dardic) branches. Three common phonological developments separate Iranian and Indo-Aryan from the rest of Indo-European: (1) the collapse of Proto-Indo-European *a, *e, *o, *n̥, *m̥ into a, and correspondingly of *ā, *ē, *ō, *n̥̄, *m̥̄ into ā, e.g. Proto-Indo-European *dek̂m̥ 'ten' > Avestan dasa, Sanskrit dáśa, but Old Church Slavonic desętъ, Latin decem; (2) the development of Proto-Indo-European *ə into i, e.g. Proto-Indo-European *pətē(r) 'father' > Old Persian pitā, Sanskrit pitắ, but Latin pater; (3) the development of Proto-Indo-European *s into š or ṣ after *i, *u, *r, *k, e.g. Proto-Indo-European *u̯eks- 'grow' > Old Persian and Avestan vaxš-, Sanskrit vakṣ-, but German wachs-, English wax; Proto-Indo-European *sed- 'sit' > Old Persian ni-šad-, Sanskrit ni-ṣīd- (with additional prefix), but Latin sed-, English sit. In addition, Iranian and Indo-Aryan inherit from Proto-Indo-European strikingly similar verbal conjugations and nominal declensions. Compare for example the following forms of the first person singular pronoun 'I': (a) nominative: Old Persian adam, Avestan azəm, Sanskrit ahám; (b) accusative: Old Persian mām, Avestan mām, Sanskrit mắm; (c) genitive: Old Persian manā, Avestan mana, Sanskrit máma; (d) enclitic accusative: Old Persian -mā, Avestan -mā, Sanskrit -mā; (e) enclitic genitive: Old Persian -maiy, Avestan -mōi, Sanskrit -mē; (f) enclitic ablative: Old Persian -ma, Avestan -maṯ, Sanskrit -mát.

In total, according to a recent count, the number of isoglosses linking Iranian with Indo-Aryan is 57, compared with 27 between Indo-Aryan and Greek, 24 between Indo-Aryan and Slavonic and 22 between Indo-Aryan and Baltic. These linguistic facts, in conjunction with shared cultural features such as the name arya- 'Aryan', suggest that the Iranian and Indo-Aryan tribes represent a single ethnic and linguistic group within the Indo-European family. Opinions differ, however, as to the dates and routes of migration which led both Iranians and Indo-Aryans away from the Indo-European homeland into the Iranian plateau, Central Asia and India. Since the Rigveda, composed no earlier than the middle of the second millennium BC, already places the Indo-Aryans in India, this date sets a terminus ante quem for the loss of Indo-Iranian unity. According to the traditional view, the Aryans must have been in close contact for some time after the break-up of Indo-European, migrating together during the third millennium BC towards Central Asia and the Hindukush. Central Asia then became the focus for the later expansion of Indo-Aryans into India (middle of second millennium BC) and eventually of Iranians into Iran and further west (beginning of first millennium BC). An alternative view, based primarily on archaeological evidence and inscriptions from Mesopotamia, suggests that the Indo-Aryans split from the Iranians by migrating through the Caucasus at the beginning of the second millennium BC, at a time when both groups were still in contact with other Indo-European groups in southern Russia. Iranian tribes would have maintained this contact, in particular with Greek and Armenian, until they too (at least the western Iranian precursors of the Medes and Persians) entered Iran from the north through the Caucasus at the turn of the first millennium BC.

The main linguistic features characterising the split of Iranian and Indo-Aryan are: (1) Indo-Iranian voiced aspirates *bh, *dh, *gh (< Proto-Indo-European *bh, *dh, *gh) are preserved in Indo-Aryan but converted to b, d, g in Iranian, e.g. Sanskrit bhrātar, Old Persian and Avestan brātar; (2) Indo-Iranian voiceless aspirates *ph, *th, *kh (< Proto-Indo-European *ph, *th, *kh primarily) are preserved in Indo-Aryan but converted to voiceless fricatives f, θ, x in Iranian, or unaspirated stops p, t, k after s, e.g. Sanskrit path- 'path', Old Persian and Avestan paθ-, Sanskrit sthā- 'stand', Old Persian and Avestan stā-; (3) Indo-Iranian voiceless *p, *t, *k (< Proto-Indo-European *p, *t, *k) become f, θ, x in Iranian when initial in a consonant cluster, e.g. Sanskrit putrá- 'son', Avestan puθra-, Old Persian puça- (with subsequent θr > ç), but Wakhi, one of the most archaic languages phonologically, preserves the cluster -tr-, e.g. pətr 'son'; (4) Indo-Iranian palatals *ć, *ǰ, *ǰh (< Proto-Indo-European *k̂, *ĝ, *ĝh) are realised as s, z, z or θ, d, d in Iranian, but ś, j, h in Indo-Aryan, e.g. Sanskrit hasta- 'hand', Avestan zasta-, Old Persian dasta-; (5) Indo-Iranian *s is preserved in Indo-Aryan, but converted in Iranian, except before *p, *t, *k, into h, e.g. Sanskrit ásmi '(I) am', Avestan ahmi, Old Persian amiy (where the h is not written). This isogloss s > h, shared by Greek and Armenian, is used in support of the hypothesis that Iranian tribes entered Iran via the Caucasus rather than from the east.

By the time of the Achaemenids in the middle of the first millenium BC, it is clear that the dialectal divisions are already established which give rise to the modern genetic groupings within Iranian. The basic division between East and West Iranian is characterised by the following correspondences: (1) West Iranian preserves b, d, g, but these are mainly converted in East Iranian into the corresponding voiced fricatives β (v, w), δ, γ, e.g. Old Persian brātar 'brother', Modern Persian berādar, Balochi brās, but Sogdian βr't, Yaghnobi virōt; Avestan dasa 'ten', Modern Persian dah, Bakhtiari deh, Zaza däs, but Sogdian δs', Shughni δīs; Old Persian gauša 'ear', Modern Persian gōš, Gurani goš, Kurdish goh, but Sogdian γwš, Ossete γos, Bartangi γu; (2) West Iranian preserves č, but this is mainly converted into c in East Iranian, e.g. Middle Persian čahār 'four', Balochi čār, but Khwarezmian cf'r/cβ'r, Shughni cavōr; (3) the consonantal clusters -ft- and -xt- are preserved in West Iranian, but converted into the voiced counterparts -vd- and -γd- in East Iranian, equally originally voiced clusters of this type tend to be preserved in East Iranian but devoiced in West

Iranian, e.g. *hafta 'seven' > Middle Persian *haft*, Kurdish *häft*, but Khwarezmian '*βd*, Ossete *avd*, Yazgulami *uvd*; *duγdar 'daughter' > Modern Persian *doxtar*, Gilaki *duxtər*, but Avestan *dugədā*, Khwarezmian δγd, Wakhi δəγ́d.

Further phonological characteristics separate the South-West and North-West groups. The South-West Iranian languages, in particular, represent a close-knit group sharing a number of features which distinguish them not only from North-West Iranian but also from East Iranian. The earliest of these, characteristic of the Old Iranian period, is the correspondence North-West, East *s*, *z* = South-West *θ*, *d*, both deriving from the original palatal series (see above), e.g. Avestan *masišta* 'longest', Parthian *msyšt*, but Old Persian *maθišta* 'biggest', Middle Persian *mahist* (with subsequent *θ* > *h*); Avestan *zān-* 'know', Parthian *z'n-*, Gurani *zān-*, Kurdish *zan-*, but Old Persian *dān-*, Modern Persian *dān-*, Tati *dan-*. Later changes *j* > North-West *ǰ-/ž-*, South-West *z-*, and *dv-* > North-West *b-*, South-West *d-*, also clearly differentiate the groups, e.g. Parthian *ǰn* 'woman', Zaza *ǰan*, but Middle Persian *zan*, Modern Persian *zan*; Parthian *br* 'door', Zaza *bär*, but Middle Persian *dar*, Modern Persian *dar*. Further subclassification within the North-West group is complicated by the fragmented nature of much of the material and the influence of Persian on many of the dialects, but Gurani and Balochi both preserve archaic characteristics.

Within the East Iranian group, subdivision into South-East and North-East Iranian is based on both phonological and morphological features. The morphological feature characterising the North-East group is the development of a plural marker in *-t* from a suffix originally deriving abstract nouns. Examples of this marker are Sogdian *'wt'k* 'place', plural *'wt'kt*, Yaghnobi *pōda* 'foot', plural *pōdō-t*, and Ossete *sər* 'head', plural *sər-tə*. The South-East group, on the other hand, shows a variety of voiced continuants in place of invervocalic *-š-*, e.g. Yaghnobi *γuš* 'ear', but Shughni *γůγ̌*, Munji *γūy*, as well as a tendency to develop retroflex consonants (though these are lacking in the Shughni-Roshani subgroup of Pamir languages). Within the South-East group, Shughni, Roshani, Bartangi, Oroshori and Sarikoli (and more distantly Yazgulami) form a genetic subgroup, as do Ishkashmi, Zebaki and Sanglechi, and Munji and Yidgha. Munji and Yidgha share with Pashto the development of *d* > *l* (see the chapter on Pashto).

All Iranian languages of the Middle and Modern periods exhibit some common characteristics. The unmarked word order is typically verb-final, and the tense system is invariably based on two verb stems, present and past. Whereas the present stem continues the Old Iranian present, inherited directly from Indo-European, the past stem is based on a participial form of the verb ending in *-ta*. This participle had an active orientation for intransitive verbs, but was originally passive in the transitive paradigm, as in Old Persian *hamiçiyā hagmatā* (rebels (nom.) assembled (nom. m. pl.)) 'the rebels assembled', *ima tya manā kartam* (this what me (gen.) done (nom. nt.

sg.)) 'this is what was done by me'. The subsequent reanalysis of the passive participle as an active verb leads to ergative past tenses, preserved in a number of languages including Kurdish and Pashto, e.g. Kurdish (Kurmanji dialect) *ez ket-im* (I (abs.) fell (1 sg.)) 'I fell', but *min çîrok xwend* (I (obl.) story (abs.) read (3 sg.)) 'I read a story'. The majority of the modern Iranian languages exhibit various stages in the decay of the past tense ergative system into a nominative one, as preserved in the tenses based on the present stem. Modern Persian is typical here of the final stage, with no traces of ergativity except the form of the first person singular pronoun *man* 'I' (< Old Persian genitive *manā*).

Bibliography

The fullest and most detailed general survey available is Rastorgueva (1979–); planned in five volumes, four have appeared so far: 1 (*Drevneiranskie jazyki*) on Old Iranian (1979), 2 (*Sredneiranskie jazyki*) on Middle Iranian (1981), 3 (*Novoiranskie jazyki: zapadnaja gruppa, prikaspijskie jazyki*) on the South-West Iranian and Caspian languages (1982), 4 (*Novoiranskie jazyki; vostočnaja gruppa*) on the East Iranian languages (1987). Spuler (1958) is the only comprehensive handbook in a language other than Russian, although Payne (1981) gives a short survey of linguistic properties of Iranian languages of the USSR. Oranskij (1963) includes annotated specimens of many of the languages and a useful map. Among bibliographical resources, MacKenzie (1969) is a short survey of Iranian studies and full basic bibliography; Oranskij (1975) is a very thorough bibliographical guide to the Iranian languages of the USSR; Redard (1970) is a comprehensive survey of the study of minor Iranian languages, with full bibliography.

References

MacKenzie, D.N. 1969. 'Iranian Languages', in T.A. Sebeok (ed.), *Current Trends in Linguistics*, vol. 5 *Linguistics in South Asia* (Mouton, The Hague), pp. 450–77.
Oranskij, I.M. 1963. *Iranskie jazyki* (Izd-vo Vostočnoj Literatury, Moscow)
—— 1975. *Die neuiranischen Sprachen der Sowjetunion*, 2 vols. (Mouton, The Hague)
Payne, J.R. 1981. 'Iranian languages', in B. Comrie, *The Languages of the Soviet Union* (Cambridge University Press, Cambridge), pp. 158–79
Rastorgueva, V.S. (ed.) 1979–. *Osnovy iranskogo jazykoznanija* (Nauka, Moscow)
Redard, G. 1970. 'Other Iranian Languages', in T.A. Sebeok (ed.), *Current Trends in Linguistics*, vol. 6 *Linguistics in Southwest Asia and North Africa* (Mouton, The Hague), pp. 97–135
Spuler, B. (ed.) 1958. *Handbuch der Orientalistik. Abt. I, Bd. IV, 1, Iranistik* (Brill, Leiden)

25 Persian

Gernot L. Windfuhr

1 Historical Background

1.1 Dialectology

Within the Iranian branch of Indo-European, Persian is a member of the West Iranian group, together with the Iranian languages and dialects spoken in Iran and others spoken also outside of Iran, such as Kurdish and Balochi. Within West Iranian, Persian is a member of the South-Western branch, together with other dialects spoken mainly in the southwestern province of Fars, such as Luri and Bakhtiari.

Persian has various dialects. The three major representatives of these are the Persian of Iran in the west, the Persian of Afghanistan now called Dari in the east and the Persian spoken in Soviet Tajikistan in Central Asia in the north-east. Each again has its own dialectal divisions. The number of speakers in each country is approximately: Iran 30 million, Afghanistan five million, USSR 2.2 million.

Iran is a multi-lingual country. While Persian is the official language of Iran, it is the mother tongue of only about 50 per cent of the population. Speakers of non-Persian Iranian dialects constitute some 25 per cent. The remainder speak non-Iranian languages. Besides Arabic, New Aramaic, Armenian, Georgian and Gypsy, Turkic dialects are the most widely spoken, such as Azerbaidjani in the north-west, the archaic Khalaj in the centre of Iran, Turkmenian in the north-east and Qashqa'i in the south-west. Turkic dialects have virtually erased Iranian in northern Afghanistan and Central Asia except for the Tajiki enclave. The Turkisation of much of these areas began before the end of the first millennium AD and does not seem to have halted yet. (Incidentally, those are the same areas where Iranians first took hold on the plateau some 2,000 years earlier.)

1.2 Origins

The evolution of Persian as the culturally dominant language of the eastern Near East, from Iran to Central Asia to northwestern India until recent centuries, began with the political domination of these areas by dynasties

523

originating in the southwestern province of Iran, Parsa, later Arabicised to Fars: first the Achaemenids (559–331 BC) whose official language was Old Persian; then the Sassanids (c. AD 225–651) whose official language was Middle Persian. Hence, the entire country used to be called '*persē*' by the Ancient Greeks, a practice continued to this day. The more general designation 'Iran(-shahr)' derives from Old Iranian *aryānām* (*khshathra*) '(the realm) of the Aryans'.

The dominance of these two dynasties resulted in Old and Middle Persian-speaking colonies throughout the empire, most importantly for the course of the development of Persian, in the north-east, i.e. what is now Khorasan, northern Afghanistan and Central Asia, as documented by the Middle Persian texts of the Manicheans found in the oasis city of Turfan in Chinese Turkestan (Sinkiang). This led to a certain degree of regionalisation.

1.3   The Formative Period

None of the known Middle Persian dialects is the direct predecessor of New Persian. There are indications that New Persian developed between the seventh to ninth centuries, the period of the Muslim conquest of Iran and later of the high culture of the Arabic-speaking Abbasid court in Baghdad (c. 750–850), to which Iranians contributed so decisively. The first preserved documents come from the eastern regions: three brief inscriptions dating from the middle of the eighth century found in eastern Afghanistan. They were written in Hebrew characters, indicating the early use of the new vernacular by minorities less dominated by the written standards of the time, i.e. Arabic, Middle Persian or local languages such as East Iranian Sogdian.

It was in the north-east, more distant from the caliphate in Baghdad, where Iranian nationalism reasserted itself by the eleventh century. Persian became the universally accepted language first in poetic diction. The major document of this period is the *Shāh-nāmah* 'The Book of Kings', the monumental epic by Firdausi of Tus in Khorasan about the Iranian glory from creation to the Muslim conquest, written in the early eleventh century in an archaising language which used comparatively few Arabic words. It soon became also accepted as the language of official communication and of prose writing vis-à-vis Arabic, the sacred language of the Qur'an and the 'Latin' of the Muslim Near East. For example, the philosopher Ibn-e Sina, Latinised Avicenna, d. 1047, while mostly writing in Arabic, chose to write his *Metaphysics* in Persian for which he created his own Persian terminology.

The 'Persianists' won over the 'Arabists'. Muslim religious propaganda began to contribute considerably to the ever-extending use of Persian through popularising texts such as commentaries on the Qur'an, lives of saints, edificational and moral and religious treatises.

Until the Mongol conquests in the middle of the thirteenth century, the north-east, with cultural centres such as Samarkand, Bukhara, Balkh, Merv, Herat and Nishapur, continued to be the major area of New Persian and its literature. Thereafter, the focus shifted to the west, a major centre being the city of Shiraz in Fars with its most famous poets Sa'di (d. 1292) and Hafiz (d. 1390), from where it shifted to the north, first to Isfahan, the splendid capital of the Safavids (1501–1731), then, from the first half of the nineteenth century, to Tehran, the new capital of the Qajars (1779–1924).

1.4   Standardisation

Persian appears fairly standardised first in early poetic diction, which shows few dialectal variations by the tenth century. (This may be partially due to standardisation by copyists.) Nevertheless, the peculiarities of the eastern poets, especially in their lexicon, led to the compilation of dictionaries explaining those in 'common' Persian, such as the dictionary by Asadi from the middle of the eleventh century.

The formative period for prose writing lasted until the end of the twelfth century. The utilitarian religious texts, just as scientific, historical, geographic, philosophical and mystical writings, naturally paid less attention to high style than to reaching the local public. They retained a considerable degree of local features (in spite of the hands of copyists). Most of the preserved texts originate in the eastern regions, and as such exhibit a fair degree of linguistic homogeneity.

By the thirteenth century, the beginning of Classical Persian, the regionally marked features had largely disappeared in both poetry and prose. This process is concomitant not only with the expansion of Persian, but also with the shift of cultural centres to the west, specifically to Fars. The literary standard was achieved not only through the efforts of poets and writers but, perhaps most importantly, through the efforts of the court chanceries where guides and textbooks on style and rhetoric were compiled from the tenth century.

The dominance of Classical Persian continued to a considerable degree until the beginning of the nineteenth century. At that time new political, economic and cultural conditions, not least under influence from Europe, sponsored gradual simplifications of style. With it came the acceptance in writing of features of the educated spoken language that had developed in the capital Tehran, at first in journalism, then in prose and finally in poetry. Thus emerged contemporary standard Persian. At the same time, Tajikistan under Russian and Soviet rule developed its own literary language which is based on local dialects and written in the Russian alphabet. Iranian Persian ceased to be the accepted standard. It is still the norm in Afghanistan, but decreasingly so as the official language beside East Iranian Pashto.

1.5   Colonial Persian

Persian was cultivated at the courts of the Ottoman rulers, several of whom are known for composing Persian poetry. Literary Ottoman Turkish is a virtual amalgam of Turkish and Persian (with all of the latter's Arabic loan elements). Similarly, Urdu, '(the language of the) military camp', developed under heavy Persian influence. Persian first entered India with the conquest of north-west India by Ghaznavid armies in the eleventh century. Four centuries later, Persian in its classical form was chosen as the court language of the Mogul kings (1530–1857), who were major patrons of Persian literature and poets from Iran, unlike the contemporary Safavids in Iran. It was at the courts of India and Turkey where many of the major traditional dictionaries of Persian were compiled from the fifteenth to the eighteenth centuries, many with grammatical treatises. Simultaneously, there developed in India a Persian vernacular, and it was from the Indian scribes and secretaries that the English officers of the East India Company, many of whom wrote grammars of Persian, learned their Persian, with all its local idiosyncrasies. Persian was abolished in its last official bastion — the courts of law — in 1837 by the authorities of the East India Company.

2   Phonology

2.1   Sound System
The sound system of contemporary standard Persian is quite symmetric. Its 29 segmental phonemes consist of four pairs of stops and four pairs of fricatives, two nasals and two liquids, three glides, and three pairs of vowels.

Table 25.1: The Persian Phoneme System

Stops	tense/voiceless	p	t	č	k
	lax/voiced	b	d	ǰ	g
Fricatives	tense/voiceless	f	s	š	x
	lax/voiced	v	z	ž	q
Nasals		m	n		
Liquids		l	r		
Glides		y	h	'	
Vowels	tense/long	i	ā	u	
	lax/short	e	a	o	

2.2   Writing System
The Persian writing system uses the Arabic alphabet, which is a consonantal system (see the chapter on Arabic). Vowels are written as follows: long vowels are represented by the letter of the consonant nearest in pronunciation. Thus, the letter ⟨y⟩ represents both /y/ and /i/, ⟨w⟩ both /v/ and /u/, and ⟨alef⟩ both the glottal stop /'/ and /ā/. Short vowels may be, but are usually not, represented by diacritics which ultimately derive from the same letters ⟨w⟩, ⟨y⟩, and ⟨alef⟩. The main innovations in Persian are two: unlike Arabic, short vowels are always represented by consonantal letters in final position, final /o/ by ⟨w⟩, and final /e/ and /a/ by ⟨h⟩. Also, 'Persian'

letters were created for the four Persian consonants /p/, /č/, /g/, /ž/ by adding three dots to the 'Arabic' letters <b>, <j>, <k>, <z> (the dots merged into an oblique stroke in the case of <g>). The Persian alphabet is given in table 25.2.

Table 25.2: The Persian Alphabet

Alone	End	Middle	Initial			Name
ا	ا	ا	ا	'		alef
ب	ب	ـبـ	بـ	b		be
پ	پ	ـپـ	پـ	p	P	pe
ت	ت	ـتـ	تـ	t		te
ث	ث	ـثـ	ثـ	s	A	se-ye senokte
ج	ج	ـجـ	جـ	j		jim
چ	چ	ـچـ	چـ	c	P	če
ح	ح	ـحـ	حـ	h	A	he-ye jimi
خ	خ	ـخـ	خـ	x		xe
د	د	د	د	d		dāl
ذ	ذ	ذ	ذ	z	A	zāl
ر	ر	ر	ر	r		re
ز	ز	ز	ز	z		ze
ژ	ژ	ژ	ژ	ž	P	že
س	س	ـسـ	سـ	s		sin
ش	ش	ـشـ	شـ	š		šin
ص	ص	ـصـ	صـ	s	A	sād
ض	ض	ـضـ	ضـ	z	A	zād
ط	ط	ط	ط	t	A	tā
ظ	ظ	ظ	ظ	z	A	zā
ع	ـع	ـعـ	عـ	'	A	'eyn
غ	ـغ	ـغـ	غـ	q		qeyn
ف	ف	ـفـ	فـ	f		fe
ق	ق	ـقـ	قـ	q		qāf
ک	ک	ـکـ	کـ	k		kāf
گ	گ	ـگـ	گـ	g	P	gāf
ل	ل	ـلـ	لـ	l		lām
م	م	ـمـ	مـ	m		min
ن	ن	ـنـ	نـ	n		nun
و	و	و	و	v		vāv
ه	ـه	ـهـ	هـ	h		he-ye dočašm
ی	ی	ـیـ	یـ	y		yā
ء	أ	ء	أ	'		hamze

A=letters occurring mostly in Arabic loanwords; P=letters found in Persian only.

The Arabic orthography, the pharyngeal consonants of which are not phonemically distinct in Persian, is retained in all Arabic loans. Other than in Arabic loans, the orthography of Persian is basically phonemic, except for the writing of short vowels discussed above, only rarely using a pharyngeal letter such as ⟨ṣ⟩ in ⟨ṣad⟩ /sad/ 'hundred'.

2.3 Features

In spite of systemic simplicity, there remains considerable debate about the features distinguishing both individual phonemes and sets of phonemes, and about their development. A particularly interesting point is the degree of integration of the foreign loan component, most importantly Arabic, into the system inherited from Middle Persian.

Consonant gemination is a distinctive characteristic of Arabic, whereas in Persian it is a marginal feature. While probably retained in Classical Persian, and still in poetry, it is eliminated in the standard pronunciation of today; for example, Persian *matté* 'drill', Arabic *talaffóz* 'pronunciation' today are pronounced /mate/, /talafoz/.

The highly developed consonantal system of Arabic is considerably reduced in Persian. The non-strident interdental fricatives θ and $\eth$ merged with the respective strident fricatives *s* and *z*. Similarly, the distinctively Arabic pharyngeals merged with non-pharyngeals. Two of the more complex mergers are the following.

The phoneme *q* is intriguing because of its diverse origins and its present articulation and conditioned variation. On the one hand, it originates in an indigenous Persian/Iranian voiced velar fricative with limited functional load. On the other hand, it originates in loans. It represents the merger of the Arabic uvular voiceless stop *q* with the uvular voiced fricative (represented by the respective Arabic letters *qaf* and *γeyn*), as well as the voice-neutral back velar stop before back vowels in Turkish (represented by *either* of the Arabic letters). Its peculiar Persian articulation appears like a virtual compromise of its origins: intervocalically it is a voiced fricative; in initial and final position it is partially or fully devoiced, following the devoicing rule, and may have an affricate-like voiced release before vowels (varying with the speaker).

In Persian, glottalic vocalic onset is an automatic feature before initial vowels and in hiatus and as such was originally not phonemic. Arabic, however, has a phonemic voiced pharyngeal ʿ (represented by the letter *ʿeyn*) and a glottal stop ʾ (represented by ⟨alef⟩ or the diacritic ⟨hamze⟩), which may occur in any position. It is the latter which represents the Persian glottal stop and hiatus in writing, e.g. onset *ʾin* /ʾin/ 'this', hiatus *pāʾíz* /pāʾiz/ 'autumn', affixal hiatus *xāné-i* /xāne-ʾi/ 'a house', *qahve-í* /qahve-ʾi/ 'brown (coffee-ish)'. Phonemically, in Persian the pharyngeal merged with the glottal and with vocalic onset.

2.4 Syllable Structure

The syllable structure of Middle Persian generally reflected that of Old Iranian. This included initial consonantal clusters, which were broken up in Early New Persian by the insertion of a vowel, e.g. MP *brādar* > NP *barādár* 'brother', or by initial vowel, e.g. MP *brū-g* > NP *abrú* 'brow' (so mostly if initial sibilant; note modern loans like *estudiyó* 'studio'). This structure thus agrees with that of the Arabic loan component which has only initial CVC. Since the automatic onset before initial vowel has become phonemic, all Persian syllables now have initial CV, e.g. *in* → /'in/ 'this'.

Vowels may be followed by none, one or two consonants, i.e. CV, CVC, CVCC. This makes syllabic boundaries predictable: in any sequence, the consonant immediately preceding a vowel begins a new syllable. This structure has also implications for the status of the two diphthongs of Persian, formerly *ai*, *au*, today assimilated to *ey*, *ow*. Since these are never followed by two consonants like the other vowels, they must be interpreted as a sequence of short vowel + glide, e.g. *dowr* 'turn' as CVCC. They have thus no independent phonemic status, just as in Arabic.

2.5 Stress

The basic stress pattern of Persian is predictable and non-phonemic. Word stress is progressive, i.e. on the last non-enclitic syllable. Phrase stress is regressive. This is evident in pseudo-pairs like *bāz-kón* 'opener' : *báz kon* 'open!' (*kon* 'to make, do'), where the compound noun has final stress and the verb phrase has stress on the initial member. The third rule, continued from Indo-European, is that stress is on the initial syllable of the vocative noun or phrase, e.g. *xànandé-y-e azìz* → *xánandè-y-e azìz* 'Dear reader!'

2.6 Morphophonemic Alternation

Unlike Eastern Iranian languages such as Pashto, the rules of morphophonemic alternation of Old Iranian had already ceased to be productive in Persian by the end of the Achaemenid period (c. fourth century BC). This alternation is fossilised in the present and past stems of the so-called irregular verbs and in root nouns. Of course, other changes have long since distorted the regular alternation. Moreover, many such verbs have become regularised and their old past stems lost, a process which has been especially observable in recent centuries.

A considerable portion of the morphophonology of Arabic has been borrowed together with the lexicon. Most complex is that of the verbal system as reflected in verbal nouns and participles borrowed into Persian; to cite only a few frequent forms of the root *n-z-r* 'see, watch': *nazár* 'view', *nazír* 'similar, like', the passive participle *manzúr* 'considered, intended', also 'viewpoint, opinion', the verbal noun of the Arabic eighth formation *èntezár* 'expectation' with the participle *mòntazér* 'expecting, waiting'.

Probably the most conspicuous part of borrowing is the Arabic plural. Its complex morphophonology has generally been accepted as an integral part of Persian. The many classes of broken plurals are retained to a considerable degree, varying with the word, certainly with style and possibly with semantic field. The extent of such borrowing has induced the authors of many grammars of Persian to include a considerable section on Arabic morphophonology. However, unlike English which has reanalysed Romance to a certain degree (e.g. 'to **re**-do'), in Persian Arabic morphophonology only applies to Arabic loans and it is not productive, certainly not with the uneducated speaker, rarely affecting Persian words, other than those borrowed early into Arabic and then borrowed back, e.g. *gauhár* > Ar. *ǰauhár* 'essence, jewel', pl. *ǰàvāhír*, and was then borrowed back into Persian.

3 Morphology and Syntax

In terms of morphology Persian with its dialects may be called the most atypical Iranian language. It is to Iranian what English is to Germanic. Unlike East Iranian Pashto and many smaller dialects, it has almost completely lost the inherited synthetic nominal and verbal inflection and their inflectional classes, and thus the *inflectional* distinction of case, number and gender as well as of tense, mood, aspect and verbal gender. This process began already in late Old Persian times. Person and number are, however, distinguished, so is human and non-human gender. The pronouns and endings are shown in the chart given here.

	Singular			*Plural*		
	1	2	3	1	2	3
Pronouns						
Independent	man	to	u	mā	šomá	išán/ān-há
Suffixed	-am	-at	-aš	-emān	-etān	-ešan
Endings						
Present stem	-am	-i	-ad	-im	-id	-and
Past stem	-am	-i	-Ø	-im	-id	-and
Perfect stem/'to be'	-am	-i	-ast	-im	-id	-and

The second person singular imperative ending is zero, the second person plural ending is *-id*.

The independent and suffixed pronouns alternate in dependent noun constructions, e.g. *ketáb-e man*/*ketáb-am* 'my book'. The three sets of personal endings differ only in the third person singular. The third set is in fact the substantive verb 'to be', which is always enclitic, as opposed to the existential *hast-* 'to be (there)', which takes the endings of the past stem.

Pronouns and endings distinguish between human and non-human. All independent pronouns refer to humans only. Thus *u* only means 'he/she', *išán* has become almost exclusively used for third person singular in polite phraseology and has been replaced as a plural by the unmarked *ān-há*. Non-human items are referred to by the use of the demonstratives *in/ān* 'this/ that'. There is no equivalent of 'it' in Persian. This distinction is also found in the interrogative and indefinite pronouns, *ki* 'who' : *če* 'what', *hár-ki* 'whoever' : *hár-če* 'whatever'. Moreover, non-human plurals do not require plural pronouns or endings; their plural marking seems to imply individuation.

3.1 Nouns and Noun Phrases

3.1.1 Nominals

Nouns are simple or compound, based on nominal or verbal stems, e.g. *sāhéb* 'owner', *xāné* 'house', *sāhèb-xāné* 'landlord', *hāvắ* 'air' -*peymắ* 'to transverse', -*bar* 'to carry', [*havà-peymà*]-*bár* '[aircraft] carrier'; or are nominalised noun and verb phrases, e.g. *ràft-o-āmád* 'traffic', past stems of *raft-án* 'to go' and *āmad-án* 'to come', *bād be-zán* 'fan' lit. 'hit wind'.

There are numerous derivational suffixes. The two semantically least restricted ones, which can be freely added even to phrases are: the abstract suffix -*í*, e.g. *mard-í* 'man-liness', *bozorg-í* 'great-ness', *malèk-o-š-šo'arā-í* 'the status of being poet laureate', and the homophonous denominal relational suffix -*í*, e.g. *ìrān-í* 'Iran-ian', [*zèdd-e irān*]-*í* '[anti-Iran]-ian'.

The comparative suffix is -*tár*, e.g. *bozorg-tár* 'great-er'; the ordinal suffix is -*óm*, e.g. [*pajằh-o yek*]-*óm* 'fifty-first' (except for Arabic *avvál* 'first' and *āxár* 'last').

3.1.2 Noun Phrases

The basic structure of the noun-adjective phrase and the noun-noun phrase is as follows (N = noun, A = Adjective):

NA: *in* – Measure, Number, Kind–Noun–*hắ–e–*Adjective–*i*
    ān
NN: NA^1–*e*–NA^2
    NA–Personal Suffixes

The general plural marker is -*hắ*, and -*ân* for adjectival and indefinite pronominal human plurals, e.g. *bozorg-ắn* 'the elder (people), leaders', *digar-ắn* 'the others'. The latter is also used for human and human-related plural in literary registers. In addition, there are the plurals of the Arabic loan component which tend to function as a marker of a complex unit. Thus, the plural of *taráf* 'side, direction', *atrắf*, has developed the connotation 'surroundings, about', the plural of *vaqt* 'time', *owqắt*, generally means 'humour, mood', the loaned feminine-abstract plural -*āt* generalises, e.g. *deh-ất* 'the rural area' vis-à-vis the Persian plural *deh-hắ* 'villages'.

The indefinite marker for both singular and plural is -*i*, e.g. *ketắb-i/ketāb-*

há-i 'a book/(certain) books'. It follows the adjective, but often the noun in the presence of more than two adjectives.

Measure, numbers and kind precede the noun and in turn are preceded by the demonstratives *in/ān* 'this/that', e.g. *sé (tā) ketàb* 'three (items) of books', *ín do now' qālì* 'these two kinds of carpet'.

Dependent nominals follow the head noun and are connected by *-e*, e.g. *ketáb-e bozorg-tàr* 'a larger book'. The general function of this construction with dependent nouns and noun phrases, traditionally called *ezāfe* 'addition', is the identification of class and item, the latter ranging from persons, to names and names of species, to numbers, e.g. *ketàb-e mán* 'the book of me/my book'; *xānòm-e Ǎavādí* 'Mrs Javadi', *hasàn-e mokrí* 'Hassan Mokri', *gòl-e róz* 'the rose(-flower)', *sǎ'àt-e sé* 'three o'clock', *dàrs-e haftóm* 'the seventh lesson'.

3.1.3 Topicalisation

The unmarked sequence head–*e*–dependent is inverted to dependent–Ø–head by topicalisation, most prominently with noun–adjective, noun–comparative, and noun–ordinal, e.g. *kàr [-e xúb]-i →* *[xúb] kàr-i* 'good work', *fìlm [-e beh-tár] → [beh-tar-ín] fìlm* 'the best film' (the so-called superlative), *sāl-gàrd [-e sad-óm] → [sad-om-ín] sāl-gàrd* 'the hundredth anniversary'.

3.2 Single Clauses

Subjects are formally unmarked, indirect objects are in general marked by the preposition *be*, direct objects are marked by the postposition *rā* if specific, adverbial phrases are marked by the prepositions *az* 'from, by, than', *bā* 'with', *tā* 'till, than (comparing clauses)', *dar* 'in/into', *be* 'to' and other functions. The latter two may be elided. These combine with nouns to give numerous adverbial phrases such as *ba-rǎ-y-e* 'for the reason of, for', *(be/dar) rú-y-e* '(to/on) the face of, on, onto' largely supplanting *bar* 'on'.

Persian is an SOV language. The unmarked sequence of the parts of speech in all clauses is subject–adverb–object–verb. Interrogatives do not change this sequence, but occur where the respective answer would be, e.g. *(to) ketàb-rā be kí dād-i* lit. 'you the book to whom gave?'. Inversions only occur through topicalisation. In general, sentence-initial and preverbal positions are topical, e.g. *be ù ǰaváb dād-am/ǰavàb be ú dād-am* 'I gave him an answer/I gave an answer to him'.

3.3 Categories

In spite of the relative simplicity of the formal aspects of the noun phrase, the syntactic-semantic aspects present problems many of which have not yet been solved. The major ones involved are genericity, definiteness, specificity and reference.

3.3.1 Genericity and Plural

Any unmodified noun in Persian may be generic and imply single or more items, whether subject, predicative complement, direct object or other, e.g. *man ketáb lāzèm dār-am* 'I need a book/books', *ketàb mofíd ast* 'a book is/ books are useful', *àn ketáb ast* 'that is a book/those are books' (note the singular pronoun *ān*). This function is exploited in compound verbs (see discussion below), where the verbal content is expressed by a noun followed by a small set of function verbs, e.g. *kàr kard-án* 'work-doing/working', *tarǰomè kard-án* 'translation-making/translating'.

Accordingly, plural is not obligatory when more than one item is implied, unlike English, and plurals in Persian have a more restricted function. The condition for plural marking is restriction of genericity, by reference to specific items or simply by qualifying attributes, as in *u mehmán dār-ad* 'he has a guest/guests' vs. *u mehmān-hà-y-e āmrikā-í dār-ad* 'he has American guests'. This applies, of course, to covert reference as well, as is seen in the pair *ān-hà mo'allém–Ø hast-and* 'they are teachers' vs. *ān-hà mo'allem-hǎ hast-and* 'they are **the** teachers'. This distinction is, however, neutralised after numbers, where plural is never marked.

The basic function of *hā* is not plural, but 'amplification'. While this is interpreted as plural with count nouns, it expresses increase or extent with mass mouns, e.g. *āb-hǎ* 'waters, all kinds of waters, plenty of water', and generalisation with adverbs, e.g. *bālā-hǎ-y-aš* 'somewhere up there'. This function is most conspicuous with generic objects which remain unmarked, as mentioned. In that case, the presence of *hā* does not express plural, even with count nouns (for specific objects see discussion below), but amplification, e.g. *mà mehmán–Ø dār-im* 'we have guests' vs. *mà mehmān-hǎ dār-im* 'we have lots of, all kinds of guests'.

3.3.2 Genericity and Indefiniteness

Persian distinguishes between genericity and indefiniteness, which latter is marked by the clitic *i*. It occurs with count and mass nouns as well as with singular and plural. As such, it marks restrictive selection out of a generic unit or out of a plurality, e.g. *ketáb-i* 'some/a book' and *ketāb-hǎ-i* 'some books', *āb-ǰów-i* 'some, a beer' and *āb-ǰow-hǎ-i* 'some kinds of beer'. This function is clearly evident in compound verbs where the presence of *i* eliminates genericity, as in the pair *kǎr mi-kon-am* 'I am working' vs. *kǎr-i mi-kon-am* 'I am doing something/some work, I am working some/a little'. The restrictive-selective function of *i* is distinct from that of *yek* 'a, one', which counts an item or a group of items. Unlike English 'a' and 'one', both are compatible in Persian, e.g. *yek ketáb-i be-deh* 'give me a (one, some) book'.

There is, however, the similarity between the two languages in that indefiniteness may refer either to specific items known to the speaker or to non-specific items, e.g. *dombàl-e apārtemán-i mi-gard-am* 'I am looking for an apartment' may either imply a specific apartment (which I read about in the papers), or any apartment (that will do). In either case indefiniteness is opposed to genericity, as in *dombāl-e apārtemǎn mi-gard-am* 'I am apartment-hunting'.

3.3.3 *Rā*

Unlike indefiniteness, definiteness is not formally marked in Persian and is only evident in the presence of inherent definites such as demonstratives, personal pronouns, superlatives and ordinal numbers, proper names etc. Thus, the sentence just cited as generic may likewise be interpreted as definite in another context: 'I am looking for **the** apartment'. Until recently it was assumed that there is at least one marker of definiteness, if only with definite direct objects, viz. the postposition *rā*, which was said to be obligatory with such objects. However, not only are there definite direct objects without *rā*, but *rā* is also compatible with indefinite *i*. What is marked by *rā* is not definiteness, but topicalisation or specificity. Thus, since all definite direct objects are normally, but not necessarily specific-referential, they are normally marked by *rā*. It also follows that *rā* is compatible with the indefinite marker *i*, if the latter is specific and implies a unique referent 'a certain, some'. For example, one of the environments where an indefinite is likely to refer to specifics is in sentences with past verbs, as in *xāné-i-rā ātèš zad-and* 'they burned a (certain) house' as opposed to *xāné-i ātèš zad-and* 'they burned a house'. (The sequence indefinite *i* – topicalising *rā* may be roughly compared to the indefinite-specific use of 'this' in colloquial English as in 'they burned **this** house, you know', which refers to a house only known to, or seen by, the speaker.)

While *rā* overwhelmingly topicalises direct objects, it is not confined to them. Thus, it occurs with adverbial phrases of temporal and spatial extension, e.g. *em-šáb-rā in-jǎ bāš* 'be/stay here (for) tonight', *hamé-y-e šàhr-rā gàšt* 'he walked all around the city'. Neither with such adverbial phrases nor with direct objects is *rā* obligatory unless topicalisation is involved. This explains why *rā* may be absent in spite of definiteness in sentences like *pà tu káfš kard o ràft* 'she put (her) feet ('foot') in her shoes ('shoe') and left' vs. topicalised *pa-hǎ-aš-rā tu kàfš kard o ràft* 'she put **her** feet in her shoes and left' and *èšq né-mi-fahm-ad* 'he does not understand love' vs. *éšq-rā né-mi-fahm-ad* 'he does not understand the notion of love/ what love is'.

The topicalising function is also found in highly literary registers, where *rā* may occur in initial phrases, such as [*došmán-rā*] ... *hamé darb-hà-rā be ru-ye ù mí-band-im* 'as to the enemy, we will close all doors except ...' (note the direct object *darb-hā-rā*). The initial phrase *došman-rā* here may well be interpreted as indirect object 'for the enemy'. In fact, there is a small number of verbs where the indirect object is marked by *rā*, such as *má-rā dād* 'he gave (it to) me' side by side *be mán dād. Rā* as opposed to *be* appears thus to topicalise these indirect objects as well.

3.3.4 Personal Suffixes

The personal suffixes express not only the experiencing indirect object, but also any direct object: in opposition to topicalised definite direct objects marked by *rā* they express definite non-topical direct objects, e.g. *man ù-rā díd-am* → *díd-am-aš* 'I saw him'. In fact, the independent personal pronouns are always topical. Thus, it follows that independent possession always requires the independent pronoun, e.g. *màl-e mán* 'mine' lit. 'possession of mine'. By contrast, the corresponding suffixes are always non-topical. In addition to the cases mentioned, they function as non-topical objects of prepositions, e.g. *az ù porsíd-am* → *àz-aš porsíd-am* 'I asked (of) him', and as possessors in noun phrases, e.g. *ketàb-e ú* → *ketáb-aš* 'his book'.

In the latter function, they also participate in a remarkable noun phrase inversion, possessor topicalisation: the dependent noun, i.e. the possessor of the subject phrase, is replaced by the respective unstressed suffix, and is itself placed in clause-initial position assuming primary stress so that both bracket the head noun, e.g. *èsm[-e ín āqā] číst* → *[ín āqā] èsm[-aš] číst* 'what is the name of this gentleman'. With pronouns, there is a threefold gradation: *pedàr[-am] ostàd ast* → *pedàr[-e mán] ostàd ast* → *[mán] pedàr[-àm] ostàd ast* 'my father/mý father/me, my father is a professor'.

The [non-topical:topical] function of the pronouns is most widely utilised in the colloquial language where, for example, the indirect construction is expanding. More widely than in the standard language, it functions as the non-topical correlate of direct active constructions, e.g. *gárm [hast-]am* 'I am warm' → *gárm-am ast* 'I feel warm' lit. 'to me it is warm'. Pragmatically this gives the speaker the option to describe himself as the 'object' of such mental and bodily sensations which are 'coming or happening to him' without his doing, or as the 'subject' with his active involvement.

Similarly, the possessive construction with *dāšt-án* 'to have' may alternate in colloquial speech with the suffixal construction, as long as no true possession is implied, e.g. 'he is two years old' may be expressed as *ù dó sāl dār-ad* 'he has two years' or as *dó sāl-eš e* (← *ast*) 'two years are to him'.

It is evident, then, that the personal suffixes have the general function of what may be called non-topical 'oblique case'.

3.4 The Verb Phrase

The basic verb system of contemporary Persian may be as given in the chart using the verb *rav/raft* 'go' in the third person singular with negation. As is evident, several of these verb forms have double function.

	Indicative	*Non-Indicative*	
Imperfective:			
Present	né-mi-rav-ad	bé-rav-ad/ná-rav-ad	Subjunctive
Past	né-mi-raft	né-mi-raft	Counterfactual
Inferential Past	né-mi-raft-e ast	né-mi-raft-e ast	Counterfactual
Aorist:	ná-raft	ná-raft	Subjunctive

Perfective:

Present	ná-raft-e ast	ná-raft-e bắš-ad	Subjunctive
Past	ná-raft-e bud	ná-raft-e bud	Counterfactual
Inferential Past	ná-raft-e bud-e ast	ná-raft-e bud-e ast	Counterfactual

The stative verb *bud-án* 'to be' has only an imperfective subjunctive without *be-*, *bắš-ad*, and no past perfect, but a literary present *mi-bắš-ad*. *Dāšt-án* 'to hold, keep, have' has only a perfective subjunctive, *dāšt-é bāš-ad*. Neither has *mi-* when used as imperfective past and counterfactual. This restriction does not apply to the use of *dāšt-án* in compound verbs.

The verb forms are based on three stems: present, aorist and perfect, the last regularly derived from the aorist stem by *-e*. All perfect forms are periphrastic with forms of the verb 'to be'. The imperfective prefix *mi-* occurs with all three stems, while the subjunctive prefix *be-* occurs only with the present stem and is mutually exclusive with negation.

The nominal forms are the three stems and the verbal noun, called 'infinitive', marked by *-an* as in *raft-án* 'to go, going'.

3.4.1 Categories
This verb system used to present considerable problems. Until very recently a good many grammars and textbooks omitted some of the more complex forms, while others postulated non-existing, usually obsolete, forms. And if the complex forms were mentioned, their function was mostly only circumscribed.

3.4.2 Aspect and Tense
The key to the understanding of the system is the recognition of the functions of the forms marked by *mi-*, of the forms marked by the perfect stem in *-e* and, most importantly, of the aorist *raft* which used to be identified as (simple) past or preterit for the obvious reason that this is the general form used in simple past narrative. With the 'past' *raft* opposed to the present *mí-rav-ad*, there appeared to be a system based on tense distinction, quite similar to Western European systems, notably the French system as traditionally understood. This was reinforced by the pair of the present and past perfects *raft-é ast* and *raft-é bud* and the imperfect *mí-raft*.

However, aspect is as basic a categorical vector of the system as is tense. *Mi-* is the marker of imperfectivity. As such it may express habitual action, progressive-ingressive action, as well as future action in the present and past, e.g. present *hamišè/al'àn/fardà kár mi-kon-am* 'I always work/I am working (right) now/I will work, will be working tomorrow', past *hamišè/dirùz/fārdà kár mi-kard* 'he was always working, would always work/he was working yesterday (when I came)/(he thought:) he would work, would be working the next day', the latter in contexts such as anticipation in an interior monologue.

The perfect forms are not simply perfective, but resultative-stative. This is most evident with change-of-state verbs, e.g. *hasán ān-ǰà nešast-è ast/bud* 'Hasan has/had sat down there' = 'Hasan is/was sitting there', *Maryàm lebàs-e qašáng-i pušid-è ast/bud* 'Maryam has/had put on a nice dress' = 'Maryam is/was wearing a nice dress'. Both occur also in a future context, e.g. *fardà sā'at-e sè raft-é am/raft-é bud-am* 'by three o'clock tomorrow I will be gone/by three o'clock the next day I would be gone', the latter again in anticipation in the past.

Most instructively, the aorist is not confined to past contexts, but occurs in present and future contexts as well, most evident with verbs implying motion, e.g. in a past context *hasán diruz be bāzár raft va ín-rā xarid* 'Hasan went to the market yesterday and bought this', in a present context *to bàš-i, man ráft-am* 'you stay here, I am on my way/am going now', which may be said when still seated, or in a future context *šàyad mà ham raft-im* 'we will most likely go, too', said after hearing that someone will go to see an exhibition. The future use of this form is largely confined to the colloquial language. In educated registers a formation with *xāh*, the unmarked present stem of *xašt-án* 'to want, will', is used followed by the uninflected form, *ná-xāh-ad raft* 'he will not go'.

The aorist does thus certainly not indicate past tense; rather, it is tense-neutral and it is the context which identifies time. It is a member of both the present and past subsystems, and therefore is called here 'aorist'.

3.4.3   Inferential Past

The complex forms *mí-raft-e ast*, which combines imperfective *mi-* with the perfect *-e*, and *raft-é bud-e ast*, a double perfect, express remote past in the literary register. However, they are not confined to literary style, but are as frequent in the colloquial language without referring to remote past. What they express is the category of inference, that is mainly second-hand knowledge, conclusion and reminiscence. In this they are joined by the perfect form *raft-é ast* which also functions as the inferential aorist. All three forms of the inferential past are thus derived from the perfect as is the case in a good number of other languages which have that category. To give one example: *zāher-án nevisandé, vàqt-i ān nāmè-rā mi-nevešt-é (ast), xód-aš-rā bā ín āmpúl-i, ke ruz-e qàbl xarid-è bud-é (ast), košt-é (ast)* 'apparently, the writer killed (*košt-e ast*) himself with this injection, which he had bought (*xarid-é bud-e ast*) the day before, while he was writing (*mí-nevešt-e ast*) that letter'. The non-inferential past forms in this context would imply a fact or be at least uncommitted.

The tense opposition [present:[past:inferential past]] is therefore likewise a fundamental vector of the system. Future, however, is not a tense, but at best a modality. As is evident in the examples above, all present and past forms may be used in a future context.

3.4.4 Mood

The basic function of the subjunctive is to express potential action. As such it functions as adhortative, e.g. *bé-rav-ad* 'he should go/let him go'. It is obligatory after verbs with potential connotations such as modal verbs and expressions and verbs like 'to fear/be afraid to', 'to hope to' etc., e.g. *bà-y-ad bé-rav-ad* 'he must go', *mì-tars-ad bé-rav-ad* 'he is afraid to go'. (The infinitive-verbal noun is strictly nominal and expresses 'the going' rather than 'to go'.)

The basic function of the counterfactual is to express actions or states which are unlikely to, or did not, come about. As such it functions in wishes and hypothetical statements. It is thus tense-neutral, and the distinction is strictly one of aspect, e.g. *kàš mí-raft* may be interpreted as 'if he would only go' or 'if he had only gone'. Similarly, the perfective, e.g. *kàš raft-é bud* is either 'if he were only gone' or 'if he had only left'.

In connection with necessity, it also expresses an action which should have, but did not, happen, as well as an action which had to be done instead of another, e.g. *bà-y-ad fardá mi-resid* 'he should arrive, have arrived tomorrow (but now they say...)', *tāzè qàbl-aš ham bà-y-ad mí-raft-im qazá be-xor-im* 'we first had to go to have some food (and thus did not come)'.

3.4.5 Causation

The causal suffix is *ān*, e.g. *xor* 'to eat' vs. *xor-án* 'to make eat, feed', *rav* 'to go, leave' vs. *rān* 'to drive' (< *rav-ān*). Today, this suffix appears to be increasing in productivity, perhaps due to increased linguistic consciousness of writers. But it had been on the decline along with the general tendency, beginning in Early New Persian, to replace simple verbs by compound verb constructions consisting of a nominal followed by a relatively small set of verbs, the most frequent of which are *kard-án* 'to do, make' and *šod-án* 'to become' (originally 'to go'). These two function as markers of causality. Three stages of causation are distinguished: in simple inherently causative verbs, agent mentioned is expressed actively, agent implied by the third person plural ending, agent not implied by the perfect participle + *šod-án*, e.g. *dár-rā bàst* 'he closed the door', *dár-rā bàst-and* 'they/someone closed the door', *dàr bast-é šod* 'the door closed/was closed'. In compound verbs, *kard-án* assumes the causative function, e.g. *ù-rā bidár kard* 'he woke him up', *ù-rā bidár kard-and* 'they/someone woke him up', *bidár šod* 'he woke up'.

The non-agentive construction with *šod-án* has generally been identified as passive, since with inherently causative verbs it appears like a Western European passive, e.g. *košt-é šod* 'he got killed' is assumed to be a equivalent to 'he was killed'. The Persian passive, however, is strictly agentless: unlike English (*he was killed by X*), it excludes the expression of a known agent. Moreover, it is confined to causal verbs, which may imply a change of state, such as *košt-án* 'to kill', creation, such as *nevešt-án* 'to write', *sāxt-án* 'to build', movement of an object, such as *āvard-án* 'to bring', and observation, such as *nešān dād-án* 'to show'. Its function as a non-agentive construction is utilised pragmatically whenever the speaker wishes not to mention the agent, as is often the case in bureaucratic jargon and in polite phraseology so typical for Persian.

3.5 Subordinate Clauses

3.5.1 Relative Clauses
Relative clauses are introduced by the general relative pronoun *ke* 'that'. The head noun is taken up again in the relative clause by the respective independent or suffixed pronoun, e.g. *àn márd ke māšín-rā [az u] xaríd-i* 'that man, from whom you bought the car'. This pronoun is optional if *ke* functions as the subject or direct object of the relative clause.

Restrictive relative clauses are marked by *-i*, e.g. *àn márd-i ke māšín-rā az-aš xarid-í* 'that man from whom you bought the car' (not the other one etc.). This *-i* merges with the homophonous indefinite *-i*, e.g. *márd-i ke zan ná-dār-ad tanhá ast* 'a man who has no wife is lonely'.

3.5.2 Sequence of Clauses
The basic rule for the sequence of main and subordinate clauses in contemporary Persian may be stated as follows: subordinate clauses with actions or states which logically or temporally precede others, i.e. cause, time and condition, precede the main clause; those whose actions and states logically or temporally follow others, i.e. explanation, sudden interruption, time of potential or factual completion and exception, follow the main clause.

This basic rule is seen in the pattern of the most frequent adverbial clauses.

Preceding			Following		
Cause	čun	'because'	Explanation	zí-rā	'(that is) because'
Time	váqt-i	'when'	Interruption	ke	'when (suddenly)'
Point/	tā	'as soon as'	End point	tā	'until, so that'
Stretch		'as long as'			
Condition	ág'ᵃr	'if'	Exception	mág'ᵃr	'unless, if not'

The semantically neutral enclitic conjunction *ke* may be substituted for the conjunctions of preceding clauses, e.g. *čun/váxt-i/tā/ág'ᵃr pul nà-dār-ám, né-mi-rav-am* 'because/when/as long as/if I have no money I will not go', all → *púl-ke nà-dār-am, né-mi-rav-am*. In addition to these, there are numerous adverbial conjunctival phrases either with nouns, such as *(dar) mowqé-i ke āmád* '(at) the moment (that) he came', or with adverbs, such as *piš az ín ke be-rav-ád* 'before (this that) he left'. Their general structure shows that syntactically they are relative clauses, restrictive relative clauses with nouns, [N-*i ke*], and non-restrictive with adverbs, [- *in ke*]. Since adverbs are strictly prenominal they require a 'dummy' noun to introduce the dependent clause, either *in* 'this' or less frequently *ān* 'that'.

Object, subject and complement clauses, which express facts or possibilities depending on the main clause, follow the main clause, e.g. object *díd-am* (*ke*) *ān-jã níst* 'I saw that he is not there', subject *ma'lúm ast ke u níst* 'it is obvious that he is not here', complement *hàqq-aš ín ast ke pùl ná-dār-am* 'the truth of it is (this) that I have no money'. As is evident, the conjunction *ke* is optional with object clauses, but obligatory with subject and complement clauses.

Syntactically, these clauses are relative clauses as well, as seen most clearly by topicalising inversion: *ín ke u níst ma'lúm ast* '(this) that he is not here is obvious', *ín ke u ān-jã níst díd-am* '(this) that he was not there I noticed'.

3.5.3 Verbal Categories

The 'logic' of the sequence of clauses is paralleled by the 'logic' of the verbal categories. All subordinate clauses, including relative clauses, strictly follow the semantics of tense, aspect and mood.

Factual actions and states are in the indicative, even in conditional clauses, e.g. [*àgar mí-xāh-i*], *mí-rav-im* 'if you (really) want to, we will go'. Potential actions and states are in the subjunctive in clauses with potential connotation such as final, concessive and conditional clauses, as well as in temporal and relative clauses with implicit condition, therefore also including those with conjunctions like 'before', 'without', e.g. *ráft* [*tā az ù bé-pors-ad*] 'he went in order to ask him', [*àgar/vàqt-i be-rav-ád*] *kàs-i digàr níst* 'if/when he goes there will be no one left', *fárš-i* [*ke gere-hã-y-aš riz-tàr bãš-ád*] *beh-tár ast* 'a carpet the knots of which are finer is better', [*pìš az ín ke bè-rav-í*] *telefón kon* 'before you go, call'. Unlikely or impossible actions or states are in the counterfactual.

Similarly, aspect. Incomplete actions are expressed by the imperfective, resulting states by the stative and completed perfective actions by the aoᵣist. This is true for both the indicative and the non-indicative. Most instructive in this context is the use of the aorist in explicitly or implicitly conditional contexts. There it expresses the potential completion as a condition for another action, in contrast with the imperfective subjunctive, e.g. subjunctive [*àgar hasàn be-rav-ád*] *be màn telefón kon* 'if Hassan leaves/should he leave, give me a call', aorist: [*àgar hasàn-rā did-í*] *be màn telefón kon*, [*àgar na-búd*] *yād-dãšt-i bè-nevis* 'if/as soon as you find Hassan, give me a call; if he is not there, write a note'.

Finally, tense. Most instructive in this context are object clauses expressing observed facts, including reported speech. Not only do these require the indicative, but also the imperfective or stative present if the action or state is simultaneous with the time of the main verb (whereas in

English the tense of the main verb has to be 'mapped' onto the dependent verb), e.g. *vàqt-i resid-ím šeníd-im* [*ān-jà čand ruz-è bārán mi-ā-y-ad*] 'when we arrived we heard that it had been raining there for several days', *gòft* [*ke né-mi-ā-y-ad*] 'he said he would not come'. On the other hand, completed past action is obligatorily expressed by the past perfective, e.g. *fàsl-i* [*ke ferestād-è bud-íd*] *resíd* 'the chapter you sent has just arrived' (note the simple past in English).

3.6 Continuity and Innovation
The following is a brief summary of the diachronic development of the forms and categories of Persian and of the main divergences between the three main dialects of Persian. Both reflect the continuity of earlier categorical distinctions as well as the process of ever-increasing differentiation after the collapse of the Old Iranian inflectional system.

3.6.1 Gender
The Old Iranian distinction between masculine, feminine and neuter gender had been lost in late Old Persian. Subsequent stages developed various means of distinguishing between animate and inanimate, as in the case of contemporary Persian, described above.

3.6.2 Noun Phrase

Categories. The history of noun phrase morphosyntax is the history of the foregrounding of genericity, indefiniteness and specificity. Already in Old Persian, the singular could be used generically. However, it was restricted to non-human. This still held in Early New Persian where human plural was marked in predicative position, e.g. *havā-šenās*[-*ān*] *bud-and* 'they were meteorologists'. In contemporary Persian, genericity is generalised.

The indefinite marker -*i* originates in the Old Iranian prenominal number *aiwa* 'one'. In Middle Persian it developed the secondary function of indefiniteness if following the noun. In Early New Persian this use was generalised to singular and plural nouns, but it was still immediately attached to the noun. Today, it generally follows the adjective with a few marked exceptions.

The history of *rā* and of the pronominal suffixes is the coming into syntactic-semantic prominence of the direct object and specificity. *Rā* originates in the Old Persian postposition *rādi* 'by reason of, concerning', cf. Latin *ratiōne*. Thus in Middle Persian *rā* expressed cause, purpose and reference (partially like English '(as) for'). By extension of the implicit directional meaning its range began to include occasional use with indirect and direct objects in Late Middle Persian, a range continued in Early New Persian.

In Early New Persian, *rā* had a similar range, but was not obligatory with either direct or indirect objects. The reduction of its range towards specificity may be shown with the following examples. *rā* marked indirect objects which could be: (a) the beneficiary of an action, alternating with the preposition *ba* 'to'; (b) the possessor, alternating with the verb *dāšt-an* 'to have'; and (c) the experiencer in indirect constructions expressing mental and bodily sensations such as hunger and liking, alternating with the personal suffixes. In contemporary Persian, a virtual semantic-syntactic split has occurred. The three indirect objects are now distinctively marked by the alternates, e.g. *man ō-rā mē-gōy-am* > *man be u mi-gu-y-am* 'I am telling him', *ō-rā du pisar bud-and* 'to him were two sons' > *u do pesar dār-ad* 'he had two sons', *az an ma-rā xwaš āmad* > *az ān xoš-am āmad* 'I liked it'. In the Persian of today, for most other uses *rā* has been preserved in, and was replaced by, the prepositional phrase *ba-rā-y-e X* 'for X'.

Nominal Subordination. The function of nominal subordination to express class-item, among which possession is only one, continues an Old Iranian formation, verbless appositional phrases introduced by the generalised relative pronoun Old Persian *haya*/Avestan *yat* > *-e*. This progressive subordination, NN^1-*e* NN^2, is typically South-Western Iranian in terms of dialectology. The marked topical inversions in Persian are the unmarked ones in North-Western Iranian, and can in part be understood as originally marked borrowed features.

The range of the general conjunction *ke* is the result of the merger in New Persian of three Middle Persian conjunctions, *kē* 'who, which', *kā* 'when' and *kū* 'where'. The use of *-i* to introduce restrictive relative clauses, and thus the marking of restrictiveness of relative clauses in contemporary Persian, is the result of a similar generalisation. It originates in the indefinite marker *-ē*, and was exclusively used in Early New Persian with indefinite head nouns.

3.6.3   Verb Phrase

The endings of the aorist continue the Middle Persian substantive verb 'to be', thus MP *h-am* > NP *-am*. The infinitive-verbal noun continues the Old Iranian verbal noun marked by *-tan-*. The endings of the present continue Old Iranian, and ultimately Indo-European endings, as is evident in the endings of the third persons *-ad* < *-a-t-i*, *-and* < *-a-nt-i*, as is the case with the endingless imperative of the second person singular and the initial stress in the imperative and the vocative.

Aspect. The functions of the three stems of the verb reflect their history. Present stems originate in the Old Persian 'present', i.e. imperfective, stems (e.g. OP *bar-a-* > NP *bar-* 'to carry, bear', *da-dā* > NP *dah-* 'to give', *kr-nu-* > NP *kon* 'to do, make'). 'Past', i.e. aorist, stems originate in the Old

Persian perfect participle in *-ta* (e.g. OP *br̥-tá* > NP *bord*, *dā-tá* > NP *dād*, *kr̥-tá* > NP *kard*). Functionally, constructions with this participle and the copula served as the successor of the older inflectional forms of the Old Iranian 'perfect' and 'aorist' systems, a process that had begun already in Old Iranian. This construction lost its 'perfect' function in Middle Iranian, and a new perfect stem developed in New Persian and a regionally confined number of other dialects, which is derived from the aorist stem by the substantive suffix *-e* (< *-ag* < *-ak-a*).

Similarly, the history of *mi-* reflects the evolution of aspect. *Mi-* originates in the Old Iranian adverb *hama-aiwa-da* 'at the same time, place'. Middle Persian *hamē(w)* 'always, continuously', besides its adverbial function, was also used to express durative action or state, which was extended to iterative and distributive function in Early New Persian.

At that stage, habitual action in past and present, as well as counterfactual action, were expressed by *-ē(d)*, which originates in the generalised third person singular optative *hait* 'may it be' in Old Iranian, where optatives had already a secondary habitual past function. This clitic was virtually lost in Classical Persian, and both habitual and counterfactual functions were taken over by *mē-*, by then strictly an aspectual prefix, with the secondary function of counterfactuality together with the past perfect, as is the case in contemporary Persian.

4   Dialectology

The three main dialects of Persian in Iran, Afghanistan and Tajikistan have diverged in their phonology, most prominently in their vocalic systems. The developments in their morphosyntax is the history of the increasing differentiation prominently in their verb systems by the development of new formations expressing aktionsarten, mood and causation, partially under the influence of Turkic.

The development of the vowels is shown in the diagram given here.

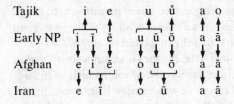

Compared with Early New Persian, Afghan Persian is the least changed, lowering the short high vowels as in Iran to mid vowels, which are now opposed to the retained long mid vowels, while the old long high vowels lose their length distinction. Tajiki is the most changed, losing the length distinction, most likely under the influence of Turkic, by the merger of the short and long high vowels and the rounding of long *a*.

In terms of nominal syntax, the marked inversion of possessor head noun, *pedar-e man* > [*man*] *pedar* [*-am*] 'my father', has become the unmarked construction in Tajiki, again under the influence of Turkic. The colloquial language in Iran has developed a focalising suffix *-é*, e.g. *sag-é* 'the dog mentioned'.

Inference is found in both Afghan and Tajik Persian. Similar forms are found in Early New Persian prose texts, most of which originate in the east, as mentioned, but they disappeared as regionally marked features in Classical Persian. Their appearance in early texts, as well as their reappearance in contemporary standard Persian of Iran, can again be explained by interference from Turkic where inference is marked by *emiš* (see the discussion of Turkish *-mǐş*, page 632). Unlike Turkic, inference is not tense-neutral in Persian, but confined to the past. In Tajiki, however, *mi-raft-e ast* has already become tense-neutral.

The verb forms of Turkic are mostly based on participles. In Tajiki, this has resulted in the development of participial formations with so-called con-verbs, where the participial main verb is followed by a varied set of verbs whose meaning is generalised to express various aktionsarten. For example, *šud-an* 'to become' expresses completion, *bar-omad-an* 'to come out of' thorough completion, and *guzašt-an* 'to pass through, by' completion after a prolonged action, as in [*kitob-ro xond-a*] *šud/bar-omad/guzašt* 'he completed reading the book/he completed reading through the book/he completed the book after prolonged reading'.

Similarly, in Tajiki the progressive is a participial formation with *istod-an* 'to stand', as in [*kitob-ro xond-a*] *istod-a ast* 'he is reading the book'. This development has progressed less in Afghan Persian, which has developed two participial formations, the progressive marked by the con-verb *raft-an* 'to go', as in [*ketāb-ra xānd-a*] *mē-rav-ad* 'he is reading the book', and the dubitative based on the particle *xāt* < *xāh-ad* 'it will/may (be)', as in [*zad-a*] *xat bud-om* 'I might hit'.

In contrast, in the formations developing in Iranian colloquial Persian both verbs are inflected as seen in the progressive based on *dāšt-an* 'to keep, hold, have', as in *dār-ad* [*ketāb-rā mi-xān-ad*] 'he is reading/is about to read the book', in the potential progressive in Tehrani based on *raft-an* 'to go' + subjunctive, as in *mi-rav-ad* [*be-suz-ad*] '(the motor) is about to burn', or in the formation expressing sudden action based on *zad-an* 'to hit', as in *zad-and* [*raft-and*] 'off they went'. Similarly, a new causative formation, 'have-other-do', based on *dād-an* 'to give', inflects both causer and caused, as in *raft va dād* [*šāx-hā-y-aš-rā tiz kard-and*] '(the goat) went and had her horns sharpened' lit. 'she gave, they sharpened'.

Participial formations are already found in the early prose texts, most of which originate in the east. For example, continuity was expressed by *dāšt-*

an 'to keep, hold, behold' with transitives and by *mānd-an* 'to remain, stay' with intransitives, as in [*girift-a*] *dār-ad* 'he keeps [holding]' and [*halāk šud-a*] *bi-mān-and* 'they will keep [perishing]'. Again, in Classical Persian these eastern features were eliminated.

However, the 'passive' in contemporary Persian does originate in such a formation. In Early New Persian there existed a participial formation based on either *āmad-an* 'to come' or *šud-an* 'to become', earlier 'to go', which occurred with both transitives and intransitives, e.g. [(*ān-rā*) *yād kard-a*] *āmad-a/šud-a ast* 'it has been recalled', and [*būd-a*] *šud/āmad* 'it came into [being]'. In Classical Persian, the use with intransitives and 'come' is lost, and the active participle eliminated: (*ān*) *yād šod-a ast*.

Bibliography

Windfuhr (1979) is the 'state-of-the-art' concise survey of the study of Persian grammar, theoretical approaches and analyses, including new insights into syntax-semantics and phonology with extensive references, together with the most comprehensive alphabetical and topical bibliographies to date. Lazard (1957) is an excellent detailed descriptive-structuralist grammar of contemporary Persian. Phillott (1919) is the most extensively documented grammar of Persian to date, with notes on dialectal variations and many illuminating insights into the pragmatic use of the language. Lumsden (1810) is still the only grammar to make thorough use of the indigenous Muslim grammatical theory and insights, many of which were only rediscovered more recently. Jensen (1931) is a comprehensive descriptive and comparative grammar of Classical Persian with notes on contemporary Persian. For the earlier history, Lazard (1963) provides an abundantly documented analytic description of the Persian of prose texts of the eleventh and twelfth centuries, with historical and dialectal annotation.

Acknowledgement

Work on this chapter was supported by a generous grant from the National Endowment for the Humanities for the comprehensive study of the languages and dialects of Iran.

References

Jensen, H. 1931. *Neupersische Grammatik, mit Berücksichtigung der historischen Entwicklung* (Carl Winter Universitätsverlag, Heidelberg)
Lazard, G. 1957. *Grammaire du persan contemporain* (Klincksieck, Paris)
——— 1963. *La langue des plus anciens monuments de la prose persane* (Klincksieck, Paris)
Lumsden, M. 1810. *A Grammar of the Persian Language; Comprising a Portion of the Elements of Arabic Inflection, Together with Some Observations on the Structure of Either Language Considered with Reference to the Principles of General Grammar*, 2 vols. (Calcutta)

Phillott, D.C. 1919. *Higher Persian Grammar for the Use of the Calcutta University, Showing Differences Between Afghan and Modern Persian with Notes on Rhetoric* (The University Press, Calcutta)

Windfuhr, G.L. 1979. *Persian Grammar. History and State of its Study* (Mouton, The Hague, Paris and New York)

26   Pashto

D.N. MacKenzie

1   Introduction

Long recognised as the most important language of the North-West Frontier Province of British India, now Pakistan, where it is spoken by 90 per cent of the population, Pashto was by royal decree of 1936 also declared to be the national language of Afghanistan in place of 'Dari' Persian. This official preeminence was artificial, however, and it now shares the honour with Persian. The areas of Afghanistan to which Pashto is native are those in the east, south and south-west, bordering on Pakistan, but in recent years Pashto speakers have also settled in parts of the northern and eastern provinces of the country. Reliable census figures of the number of speakers are only available from Pakistan. There, in the fifties, the total number of Pashto speakers was stated to be nearly 5.35 million, of whom 4.84 million (4.47 million of them in the North-West Frontier Province and 270,000 in Baluchistan) claimed it as their mother tongue. In Afghanistan in the same period semi-official estimates gave the number of speakers (presumably including those for whom it was a second language) as between 50 and 60 per cent of the total population of 13 million, i.e. between 6.5 and 7.8 million. Even allowing for some nationalistically inspired exaggeration in these figures, it seems permissible to assume that today at the very least 10 million people in Afghanistan and Pakistan are native speakers of Pashto. In terms of numbers it is, therefore, the second most important of modern Iranian languages.

The name of the language, properly *Paxto*, also denotes the strong code of customs, morals and manners of the Pashtun (*Paxtun*, Indianised as *Paṭhān*) nation, also called *Paxtunwālay* — whence the saying *Paxtun haya nə day če Paxto wāyi lekin haya če Paxto lari* 'A Pashtun is not he who speaks Pashto, but he who **has** Pashto.'

2   History

Pashto belongs to the North-Eastern group within the Iranian branch of Indo-European. The relationship can best be demonstrated by two phonological features characteristic of most members of this branch, viz. the

547

development of the Old Iranian initial voiced plosives *b*, *d*, *g* and of the dental groups -*ft*-, -*xt*-. Initial *b*, *d*, *g*, preserved in Western Iranian, regularly became the voiced fricatives β, γ, δ in Khwarezmian and Sogdian. For example, Old Iranian *brātar*- 'brother', **buza*- 'goat', **duγdar*- 'daughter', *dasa*- 'ten', *gauša*- 'ear', **gari*- 'mountain' yield Sogdian β*r't*, *'βz*-, δ*wγt'*, δ*s'*, γ*wš*, γ*r*-, Khwarezmian β*r'd*, *'βz*, δγ*d*, δ*s*, γ*wx*, γ*ryck*. Pashto shows the same development of *g*-, in γ*waǧ* 'ear', γ*ar* 'mountain'; *b*-, however, has passed through β- to the labial continuant *w*-, *wror* 'brother', *wəz* 'goat', and *d*-through δ- to *l*-, *lur* 'daughter', *las* 'ten'.

The dental group -*ft*-, also preserved in Western Iranian, becomes voiced in Eastern Iranian to [-βd-]: e.g. Old Iranian **hafta*- 'seven', **tafta*- 'heated', **xšwifta*- 'milk' give Sogdian *'βt*, *tβt*, *xšyβt*, Khwarezmian *'βd*, —, *xwβcy* [**xuβji*]. In Pashto the group has been simplified either to -*(w)d*- (cf. Khotanese Saka: *hauda*, *ttauda*, *svīda*), as in *tod*, feminine *tawda* 'hot', *šodə/e* 'milk', or to -*w*-, as in *owə́* 'seven'. -*xt*- coincides with -γ*d*- in Eastern Iranian, e.g. *suxta*- 'burnt', *baxta*- 'shared', *duγdar*- 'daughter' give Sogdian *swγt*, β*γt*-, δ*wγt'*, Khwarezmian —, β*γd*, δγ*d*. Just as -γ*d*- was reduced in Khotanese, via [-d-], to a hiatus-filling [-w-] (*sūta* [**sūda*-] > -*suva*, *būta* [**būda*] > *būva*, *dūta* [**dūda*] > *dūva*), so in Pashto it has either become *w* or, finally, dropped without trace: *sə́way* 'burnt', *su*, feminine *swa* 'it burnt', *tə* 'went' < **taxta*-, *tar-lə́* 'father's brother's daughter' < **-duγda*-.

The change of *d* to *l*, already mentioned, is found in other neighbouring languages: there is evidence for it having occurred in at least some Sogdian dialects and in Bactrian (e.g. Βαγολαγγο < **bagadānaka*-, the modern Baghlan), and it is normal in modern Munji (where *luγda* 'daughter', *pāla* 'foot' < **pādā*-). Pashto goes further, however, in that all dentals, *t*, θ, *d*, become -*l*- post- or intervocalically; e.g. OIran. *pitar*- 'father', *sata*- 'hundred', *paθana*- 'broad', **čaθwar*- 'four', **gada*- 'robber', **wadi*- 'stream', yield Pashto *plār*, *səl*, *plən*, *calor*, γ*al*, *wāla*. In other contexts though the dentals were often preserved, e.g. *tə* 'thou' < *tú*, *dre* 'three' < **θrayah*, *atə́* 'eight' < *ašta*, (*yaw*-, etc.)*wišt* 'twenty(-one, etc.)' < **wísati* (contrast *šəl* 'twenty' alone < **wīsáti*).

Only a few other sound changes can be mentioned. Perhaps the most striking in Pashto, as in the Pamir languages, are those undergone by some *r*-groups. Both -*rt*- and -*rd*- changed into the retroflex -*r̂*-, and -*rn*- into its nasalised counterpart -*n̂*-: e.g. **ārta*- 'milled' > *or̂ə́* 'flour', *mr̥ta*- 'dead' > *mər̂*, **zr̥dya*- 'heart' > *zr̂ə*, **amarnā*- > *man̂á* 'apple', **karna*- 'deaf' > *kun̂*. The presence of a sibilant complicated matters. *sr* and *rš* became *x̌* and *ǧ* respectively (on the phonemes written *x̌*, *ǧ*, see below), e.g. **hwasrū*- 'mother-in-law' > *xwáx̌e*, **r̥ša*- 'bear' > *yaǧ*, and in -*str*-, -*štr*-, -*ršt*- the -*t*- was lost, leaving -*x̌*-, e.g. *uštra*- 'camel' > *ux̌*, *wāstra*- 'grass' > *wāx̌ə́*, **hr̥štaka*- 'left' > *íx̌ay*. -*rs*-, on the other hand, coincided with -*rst*- to yield -*x̌t*-, and -*rz*- similarly gave -*ǧd*-, e.g. **uz-kr̥staka*- 'cut out' > *skə́x̌tay*, *pr̥sa*- 'ask' > *pux̌t*-, **warsya*- 'hair' > *wex̌tə́*, **br̥z*- > *uǧd* 'long', **arzana*- 'millet' > *ǧdən*. It is an example of this development of -rs- that has given *Pašto* its name, from an original **Parsawā-* closely akin to the old names of the Persians and Parthians, respectively *Pársa-* (< **Parswa-* ?) and *Parθawa-*. *Paštun* probably continues an old **Parswāna-*.

The Pashto lexicon is as fascinating as an archaeological museum. It contains side-by-side words going back to the dawn of Iranian, neologisms of all ages and loanwords from half a dozen languages acquired over a couple of millennia. The oldest of these loans date from the Greek occupation of Bactria in the third century BC, e.g. *mečón* (feminine) 'hand-mill, quern' taken over from *mēkhanḗ* at a time when *kh* was still an aspirated *k*, or *mačóγna*, *mačnóγza*, *mačlóγza* 'sling', which may be evidence for a weapon called *manganiká* (cf. Arabic *manjanīq* 'mangonel') already at the same period. No special trace of a Zoroastrian or a Buddhist past remains, but the Islamic period has brought a great number of Arabic and Persian cultural words. Throughout the centuries everyday words also have been borrowed from Persian in the west and from Indo-Aryan neighbours in the east. Usually it is difficult to establish when: *maryalára* 'pearl', for example, could be from Greek *margarítēs*, or like it from an Old Persian **margāritā-*, or later from a Parthian or Sogdian form. Irregular assimilation makes it hard to decide when, say, *blárba* 'pregnant', *cerá* 'face, picture', *jalá* 'separate', *peš* 'happening' were acquired from Persian *bārbar*, *čihra*, *judā*, *peš*, but it was long ago. The different stages of assimilation show that *žranda* 'water-mill' and *jandra* 'padlock' have been borrowed at different times from Lahnda (Western Panjabi) *jandar* 'mill' and *jandrā* 'padlock'. The sources of the many such Indian loanwords are particularly hard to distinguish. It is only when we come to *jarnáyl* 'general', *lāṭ* 'lord', *palṭón* 'platoon, regiment', *ṭikós* 'ticket, stamp' and *ṭwal* 'towel' that we are on firm ground again. The greater part of the basic vocabulary is nevertheless inherited Eastern Iranian. Still it is noteworthy how many original words have given way to neologisms. Most striking among these are some words for parts of the body: *γāx̌* 'tooth' (< **gaštra-* *'biter'), *stórga* 'eye' (< **stṛkā-* *'little star'), *təndáy* or *wəčwúlay* 'forehead' (the *tónda* 'thirsty' or *wəč* 'dry' part), *tóray* 'spleen' (the *tor* 'dark, black' organ), and several of unknown origin, such as *šā* 'back', *xwla* 'mouth'.

3   Phonology

The maximum inventory of segmental phonemes in Pashto is set out in table 26.1. Besides the common consonant stock of most modern Iranian languages, it comprises the dental affricates *c*, *j* [ts dz] and, thanks to its neighbourhood to Indo-Aryan languages, a set of retroflex, or cerebral, sounds. While the retroflex stops *ṭ*, *ḍ* occur only in loanwords, the *ṛ* has, as we have seen, also developed within Pashto. In distinction from the alveolar trill *r* and from the dental (or alveolar) lateral *l*, it is basically a retroflexed lateral flap. Its nasal counterpart *ṅ*, which does not occur word-initially, is a nasalised *r̂* — the nasalisation often extending to the preceding vowel — and not simply a retroflex nasal (which latter only occurs as an allophone of dental *n* before *ṭ, ḍ*).

Table 26.1: The Segmental Phonemes of Pashto

Vowels

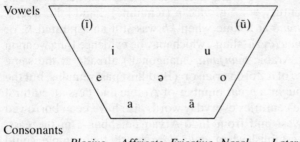

Consonants

	Plosive	Affricate	Fricative	Nasal	Lateral	Trill	Semi-vowel
Bilabial	p b			m			w
Labio-dental			(f)				
Dental	t d	c j		n	l		
Alveolar			s z			r	
Retroflex	ṭ ḍ		(x̌ ǧ)	ṅ r̂			
Post-alveolar		č ǰ	š ž				y
Velar	k g		x γ				
Uvular	(q)						
Glottal	(')		h				

The bracketed *f*, *q* and ' occur only in the elegant pronunciation of unassimilated loanwords from Persian and Arabic. Generally *f* is replaced by *p* (occasionally by *w*), e.g. *fatīla* > *palitá* 'wick', *tafaḥḥuṣ* > *tapós* 'enquiry', *lafz* > *lawz* 'word, promise', *qiṣṣa* > *kisá* 'story', *qawm* > *kām* 'tribe'. The glottal stop (representing both Arabic *hamza* ' and *'ayn* ') is usually dropped, either without trace, e.g. *mas'ala* > *masalá* 'question, matter', or having widened the adjacent vowel, as in *šar'* > *šára* 'holy law', *ma'mūr* > *māmúr* 'official', *šurū'* > *šuró* 'beginning', *mawẓi'* > *mawzé* 'place'. This resembles the treatment of word- and syllable-final *h*, *ḥ* in loanwords, e.g. *ṣaḥīḥ* > *sahí* 'correct', *fatḥ* > *fáta* 'victory', *iḥtirām* > *etərám* 'respect', *makrūh* > *makró* 'abominable'.

Characteristic of Pashto are the two phonemes written *x̌*, *ǧ*. These developed originally as retroflex spirants [ŝ ẑ] and continue generally as such in the southwestern dialects, particularly the prestigious one of Qandahar, where they contrast with the post-alveolar *š*, *ž*. In the southeastern dialects this contrast has been lost. In most central dialects these phonemes are still realised distinctly, but as palatal spirants [x̌ ɣ̌]. In the north-east, however, they have coincided entirely with velar *x* and *g* (not *γ*!). The non-phonetic symbols *x̌*, *ǧ* thus represent a compromise between [ś/š/x̌/x] and [ẑ/ž/ɣ̌/g] respectively. This wide and striking variation between southwestern [pašto] and north eastern [paxto] accounts for the description of the different dialects as 'soft' and 'hard' Pashto. It is noteworthy that the hard dialects, most directly exposed to Indo-Aryan influence, have also abandoned the dental affricates *c*, *j* (which lose their plosive element, to coalesce with *s*, *z*) and *ž* (which joins the affricate *ǰ*): in other words, with the exception of *x*, *γ* and *z*, their phonemic system has largely been Indo-Aryanised.

A notable feature of Pashto phonology, in which it differs from most other modern Iranian languages, is its toleration of groups of two or (including *w*) three consonants in word-initial position. Some hundred such groups occur, e.g. eleven with *š*- alone: *šp-*, *št-*, *šk-*, *šx-*, *šxw-*, *šm-*, *šn-*, *šl-*, *šr-*, *šr̂-*, *šw-*. Such initial groups are particularly unstable, being subject to various metatheses, assimilations and dissimilations. Thus *pža* 'foot', *kžəl* 'pull' and *psarláy* 'spring' become hard *xpa*, *xkəl*, and *sparláy* respectively; *nwar* 'sun' occurs in different dialects as *nmar* and *lmar*, *rwaj* 'day' as *wraj*, *ǧmənj* 'comb' as *g(u)manj*, *mangáz*, and so on.

The vowel phonemes in table 26.1 are the stressed ones of standard Pashto, stress also being phonemic. The following diphthongs also occur: *ay*, *əy*, *āy*, *oy*, *uy*; *aw*, *āw*. The phonemic status of the historically long vowels *ī*, *ū* is questionable. In most dialects they have been reduced to coincide with *i*, *u*; i.e. length is here, as in the case of *e*, *o*, no longer significant but depends on position and stress. Stressed *a*, *ə*, are entirely distinct, e.g. *bal* 'alight': *bəl* 'other', *γla* 'female thief': *γlə* 'male thieves'. In unstressed position, however, they are usually in free variation. It is convenient to regard unstressed [a ə] both as allophones of *a*, i.e. to regard *ə* only as a strong- or weak-stressed phoneme. Otherwise (as is unfortunately the case in some modern works on Pashto, both Afghan and foreign) there are some dangers of confusion, for example in writing the diphthongs unstressed *ay* [~ əy] and stressed *óy*. In fact there is an important morphophonemic distinction between final *-áy*, *´-ay* and *-óy*. In the hard dialects *-ay* is generally monophthongised to an open [ɛ(:)], allowing *-əy* to shift and take its place at [ɛi]. In all dialects, but especially those of the south-west, there is a tendency towards regressive vowel harmony, in that the middle vowels *e*, *o* in syllables preceding high vowels *i*, *u* are themselves raised. Also in the south-west unstressed final *e*, *o* often coalesce with *i*, *u*, but not to the extent that morphological distinctions are lost. Thus *óse* 'you dwell' remains, in contrast to *ósi* 'he dwells'. *mor*, oblique *móre* 'mother', however, becomes *móri* [mu:ri], though still without rhyming with *lur*, obl. *lúre* 'daughter' > *lúri*. In some non-standard mountain dialects of the Afghan-Pakistan borderland, particularly of the Afridi and Wazir tribes, there is a vowel shift of *ā* to [ɔ:], *o* to [œ: > ɛ:], and *ū* to [i:] (but not *u > i*); e.g. Waziri [plɔ:r] 'father', [mɛ:r] 'mother', [li:r] 'daughter'.

Three degrees of stress can be recognised: strong, medium and weak. Strong stress is comparatively free, in that it can occur on any syllable of a word, but it is mainly restricted to the first, last or penultimate syllables. It can also, particularly in verbal inflection, be mobile, though the shifts involved follow regular patterns, e.g. from *prewatə́l* 'to fall', also 'they (masculine) were falling', *préwatəl* 'they fell' and *prewátay* 'fallen (masculine singular)'. Occasionally lexical items may be distinguished solely by stress, e.g. *áspa* 'mare' : *aspá* 'spotted fever', *gorá* 'fair-skinned, European' : *góra* 'look!', *palitá* 'wick' : *palíta* 'indecent woman', *wā̂rə́* 'small (masculine plural)' : *wā̂ra* [-ə] 'all'.

4 Script

The earliest authenticated records of Pashto as a literary language date from the late sixteenth century, at a time when the whole area was, if turbulently, a part of the Mogul empire. The language has always been written in the

Table 26.2: Pashto Alphabet, with Transliteration

*	ا	ā medial	س	ـس	s
	آ	ā initial	ش	ـش	š
	ب	b	ښ	ـښ	x̌
	پ	p	[ص	ـص	ş]
	ت	t	[ض	ـض	z̧]
	ټ	ṭ (P also Urdu ٹ)	[ط		ṭ, occasionally for ṭ]
[	ث	s̱]	[ظ		z̧]
	ج	j	[ع	ـع	ʿ]
	چ	č	غ	ـغ	γ
	څ	{j (A خ)	ف	ـف	f
		{c	[ق	ـق	q]
[	ح	ḥ]	ک	ـک	k
	خ	x	ګ	ـګ	g
	د	d	ل	ـل	l
	ډ	ḍ (P also Urdu ڈ)	م	ـم	m
[	ذ	z]	ن	ـن	n
	ر	r		نـ	n̂ (A ڼ ڼ)
	ړ	r̂ (P also Urdu ڑ)	*	و	w
	ز	z	*	ه	h
	ژ	ž	*	ی	y
	ږ	ǧ			

Note: *On the function as vowel carrier of ا and ه in word-initial and final position respectively, and of و and ی medially and finally, see the discussion in the chapters on Arabic and Persian and table 26.3.

Perso-Arabic script (see the discussion of script in the chapters on Arabic and Persian), with the addition of certain modified letters to represent the peculiar consonant phonemes of Pashto. In the earliest manuscripts, from the late seventeenth to early eighteenth century, there is considerable variety in the representation of these consonants, but later a standard system emerged which persisted until recently. Since the adoption of Pashto as a national language in Afghanistan a number of innovations have been introduced into the script, which in the main make for more clarity. In Pakistan, on the other hand, there have been some tendencies, e.g. the occasional use of Urdu forms of letters and the phonetic representation of hard dialect forms (ğ as g, x̌ as x, j as z etc.), causing a departure from the classical standard. In table 26.2 the standard alphabet is given, with the modern Afghan (A) and Pakistani (P) forms as variants. The letters in square brackets occur only in unassimilated Arabic loanwords and the diacritics used in the transliteration are merely for mnemonic purposes, and have no phonetic significance. Thus ذ z̲, ض z̤, ظ z̧ are all pronounced [z], i.e. are all allographs of the phoneme z, usually written ز .

The Perso-Arabic script is by nature a consonantal one. The means by which the relatively simple vowel systems of Arabic and Persian are represented in it are inadequate for Pashto, where vowel representation is thus somewhat complicated: see table 26.3. The short vowels a, ə are not normally written, but are represented notionally by the superscript signs ´ zwar for a, ¯ zwar-akay for ə. In standard script the latter is sometimes represented by the sign ٔ hamza, e.g. زۀ zə 'I'. The signs ِ zer and ُ peš can represent i or e and u respectively, though all these vowels may also (particularly in Afghan practice) be written plene with the appropriate semi-vowel letters ی and و respectively; e.g. injár انجر or اينجر 'fig', kisá قصه or کيسه 'story', de دِ or دی 'your', gul ګل or ګول 'flower'.

Table 26.3: Vowel Representation

	Initially	*Medially*	*Finally*
a	ا	ـَ	ـه
ā	آ	ا	ـا
ə	-	ـَ	ـه (P ـٔ)
e	اِﺑ	؟	ي (P ـ) (P in particles)
ay	اَي	ٔ	ي (P ـ)
əy	-	ـ	ﯼ (A ﯼ nominal, ـٔ verbal)
i	اِ	ِ (A ـ)	-
ī	اِﺑ	ِ	ي
o	او	و	و
aw	او	و	و
u	اُ	ُ (A و)	و (P ٔ)
ū	او	و	و

5   Morphology

Although it has departed considerably from the morphological patterns of Old and even Eastern Middle Iranian (as evidenced, for example, by Sogdian and Khotanese Saka) Pashto has nevertheless a remarkably complex nominal and verbal morphology. Two grammatical genders (masculine and feminine) and two numbers (singular and plural) are distinguished in both noun and, in part, verb. Although the nominal case system has essentially been reduced to a contrast between direct and oblique, there is in the singular also a vocative and a second oblique case used in conjunction with certain prepositions. Moreover the formatives used are not, as in practically all other still inflectional Iranian languages, restricted to suffixes. Alterations of stem vowels and stress and the substitution of endings also come into play.

Old Iranian masculine stems in -*a*, -*i*, (-*u*) have generally lost their final vowel, to appear in Pashto as consonant stems: *kāra-* > *kor* 'house, family', *gauša-* > *ɣwağ* 'ear', **gari-* > *ɣar* 'mountain'. The old feminine stems in -*ā* alone have survived practically unscathed as -*a* stems: *aspā-* > *áspa* 'mare', *uštrā-* > *úxa* 'she-camel', *wanā-* > *wóna* 'tree', *xšapā-* > *špa* 'night'. Old -*an*-stems similarly preserved their nominative singular -*ā* to emerge as masculine nouns in -*a*: **maiθman-* > *melmá* 'guest'. Feminine stems in -*ī*, (-*ū*) also lost their final vowel, e.g. *hapaθnī-* > *bən* 'co-wife', **raθī-* > *lār* 'way, road', **witasti-* > *wlešt* 'span', but generally they adopt an -*a* from the general feminine form: **sraunī-* > *xn-a* 'buttock, leg', **strī-čī-* > *xój-a* 'woman', **wahunī-* > **wēn* > *wín-a* 'blood', **zanu-* > *zón-a* 'chin'. Neuter stems joined either masculine or feminine, in the latter case also generally adopting a final -*a*: *raučah-* > *rwaj* f. 'day', **asru-* > *óx-a* 'tear', **gauna-* > *ɣún-a* 'colour', **parna-* > *páń-a* 'leaf'. Only rarely do old masculines become feminine, e.g. *angušta-* > *gút-a* 'finger', *safa-* > *sw-a* 'hoof'. Several forms in -*ya*-, nominal or adjectival (including the comparative in -*yah*-) yield Pashto -*ə*: **(p)tṛwya-* > *trə* 'paternal uncle', **t(a)igriya-* > *terə́* 'sharp', *srayah-* 'better' > *xə* 'good', **abrya-* > *orə́* 'cloud'. A more common formative, however, as in Sogdian and Khotanese Saka, was the suffix -*ka*-. The resulting stems in -*aka*-, -*ika*-, -*uka*- became, via nominative or genitive **-ai* (as in Khotanese), either stressed or unstressed -*ay*. The feminine equivalent, originally **-akī-*, became -*ə́y* when stressed but -*e* when not: **daru-ka-ka-* > *largáy* 'wood', **sarda-ka-* > *saráy* 'man', **spaka-* > *spay* 'dog': **spakī-* > *spəy* 'bitch', **āsu-kī-* > *(h)osə́y* 'deer', **náwa-ka-* > *nə́way* m. 'new' : **náwa-kī-* > *nə́we* f. 'new'. The result of these far-reaching changes was three main masculine stem-types, ending in a consonant, stressed -*áy* or unstressed -*ay* respectively, and three corresponding feminine stem-types, ending in (generally unstressed) -*a*, stressed -*ə́y* or unstressed -*e*. There are also several exceptions which fit into this scheme as best they can, e.g. masculines ending in -*ə*, -*ā*, -*ū* and feminines in a consonant, -ā, -e, -o, all unchanged in the singular but approximating to the masculine consonant or feminine -a declension in the plural, or again masculines (professions) and feminines (abstracts) in -i joining the -áy and -śy stems respectively. The stem-types pair up in the case of adjectives to form the three declensions numbered 1, 4, 5 in the chart of adjectival declension. In all adjectival declensions the oblique singular forms are identical with the direct plural. Only nouns generally distinguish plural forms by plural markers, of bewildering variety. The 'prepositional' case is marked in the masculine by an unstressed -a, which probably represents an old ablative ending -āt, added to the direct case stem. In the feminine it coincides with the direct case. The vocative coincides in most, but not all, masculine singulars with the prepositional form and in most feminines with the oblique. The oblique, and also vocative and prepositional, plural marker -o (in soft dialects, stressed -ó, unstressed -u) is common to all declensions.

Adjectival Declension

	1 'other'	2 'ripe, cooked'	3 'bitter'	4 'thin, narrow'	5 'new'
Masculine					
Singular					
Direct	bəl	pox	trix	naráy	nə́way
Vocative	bə́la	póxa	tríxa	naráya	nə́we
Prepositional	bə́la	póxa	tríxa	naráya	nə́wi
Oblique	bəl	pāxə́	tarxə́	narí	nə́wi
Plural					
Direct	bəl	pāxə́	tarxə́	narí	nə́wi
Oblique					
(Voc., Prepl.)	bə́lo[2]	paxó	tarxó	narío[2]/naró	nə́wyo[2]/nə́wo[2]
Feminine					
Singular					
Direct	bə́la	paxá	tarxá	naráy	nə́we
Vocative	bə́le[1]	paxé	tarxé	naráy	nə́we[1]
Prepositional	bə́la	paxá	tarxá	naráy	nə́we[1]
Oblique	bə́le[1]	paxé	tarxé	naráy	nə́we[1]
Plural					
Direct	bə́le[1]	paxé	tarxé	naráy	nə́we[1]
Oblique					
(Voc., Prepl.)	bə́lo[2]	paxó	tarxó	narə́yo[2]/naró	nə́wyo[2]/nə́wo[2]

Note: Qandahari: [1]bə́li, nə́wi. [2]bə́lu, naríu, nə́w(y)u.

There are also two further types of consonant stem (declensions 2, 3), represented among both nouns and adjectives, in which stress and vowel changes occur which may go back to a very early stage of the language. In the first type, comprising some (but not all) monosyllabic nouns and adjectives with the stem vowel *o* or *u* and some nouns with final *-un*, the oblique singular and direct plural masculine substitute the vowel *-ā-*, and the oblique plural and entire feminine the vowel *-a-*, all with additional stressed endings. In the other type the same stressed endings occur with a stem either unchanged or with the stem vowel reduced to an *-a-* or nil. Thus *kuñ* 'deaf' has the plural *kāñə́* and feminine *kañá*, but *ruñ* 'light' plural *ruñə́*, feminine *ruñá*; *soŕ* 'cold', plural *sāŕə́*, but *sur* 'red' plural *srə*. Similarly declined are a few words ending in stressed *-ə*: *x̌ə* 'good', singular and plural masculine, *x̌a* feminine singular, *x̌e* plural. A last set of adjectives comprises all those which end in any other vowel — *a, ā, e, i, o, u*. These are indeclinable for number, gender or case, except that they may take the universal oblique plural *-o*.

The plural of masculine nouns of the first declension, which also includes those ending in *-ə, -a, -u*, is generally *-úna*, oblique *-úno*, e.g. *lās* 'hand', *lāsúna*, *zṛə* 'heart', *zṛúna*. Animate nouns take the suffix *-ā́n*, borrowed from Persian, oblique *-ā́no*, e.g. *ux̌* 'camel', *ux̌ā́n*, *lewə́* 'wolf', *lewā́n*; before this suffix a *-y-* is inserted after *-ā*, e.g. *mullāyā́n* 'mullahs', or a *-g-* after other vowels, e.g. *nikəgā́n* 'ancestors'. Inanimate nouns in *-u* take the same ending: *bāñugā́n* 'eye-lashes'. Feminine nouns of this declension ending in a consonant or *-a* behave like adjectives even in the plural, e.g. *lār* 'road', plural *lā́re*, *xwla* 'mouth', *xwle*. Animate ones ending in *-o*, however, take the mixed Persian and Pashto suffix *-gā́ne*, e.g. *pišogā́ne* 'cats', and those in *-e* change this to *-yā́ne*, e.g. *xwā́x̌e* 'mother-in-law', *xwāx̌yā́ne*. Inanimate feminine nouns in *-ā, -o* on the other hand take an unstressed plural ending *-we*, e.g. *mlā́we* 'waists'. Nouns of declension 2 generally follow the adjectival pattern, e.g. *sor* 'rider', direct plural *swārə́*, oblique *swaró*, *paxtún* 'Pashtun', plural *paxtānə́*, feminine *paxtaná* 'Pashtun woman', etc. Some such nouns, however, follow declension 1 in the plural, e.g. *žwandún* 'life, livelihood', oblique singular *žwandānə́*, plural *zwandunúna*. This is also the case with declension 3: *γar* 'mountain', plural *γrə* or *γrúna*, *trə* 'paternal uncle', *trə* or *trúna*. A number of nouns which only modify the vowel of their final syllable can also be classed here: *melmá* 'guest', plural *melmə́* (or *melmānə́*), *dux̌mán* 'enemy', *dux̌mən*. A few nouns ending in *-ba* (sometimes alternating with *-bun*) follow declension 3 in the singular and 2 in the plural, e.g. *γobá* (or *γobún*) 'cowherd', oblique singular *γobə́* (*γobānə́*), plural *γobānə́*, *γobanó*. Nouns of declensions 4 and 5 also follow the adjectival pattern, except that animates may also take the appropriate *-ān* ending, e.g. *spay* 'dog', plural *spi* or *spiā́n*, *spəy* 'bitch', *spəy* or *spiā́ne*, *buḍəy* 'old woman', *buḍəygā́ne* or *buḍyā́ne*. Even this catalogue does not exhaust the full variety of plural forms. The class of nouns of relationship is particularly rich in irregularities, as the following list will show: *plār* 'father', plural *plắrúna*; *mor* 'mother', *máynde* (*mándi*); *xor* 'sister', *xwáynde* (*xwándi*); *tror* 'aunt', *tráynde* (*trándi*), *troryā́ne*; *yor* 'husband's brother's wife', *yúñe*; *lur* 'daughter', *lúñe*; *wror* 'brother', *wrúña*; *wrārə* 'brother's son', *wrerúna*; *zoy* (*zuy*) 'son', *zāmə́n*.

Several nouns, particularly those denoting substances, occur only in the plural, whether masculine, e.g. *čars* 'hashish', *γanə́m* 'wheat', *γwařî* 'cooking oil', *māγzə́* 'brain', *ořə́* 'flour', *tambākú* 'tobacco', *wāx̌ə́* 'grass', or feminine, e.g. *čāy* 'tea', *obə́* 'water', *orbə́še* 'barley', *šomlé* 'buttermilk'. To these may be added words with a collective meaning, such as *xalk* 'people', onomatopoeics ending in *-ahár* denoting noises, e.g. *šrapahár* 'splashing' and all verbal infinitives used as nouns. A last quirk of nominal declension concerns masculine consonant stems, mostly inanimate, when qualified by and directly following a cardinal number higher than 'one', or a similar adjective such as *co* 'several, how many?'. Instead of appearing in the plural, as all other nouns then do, they take a 'numerative' ending *-a* in the direct case. This also affects the higher numbers (*š̌əl* 'score', *səl* 'hundred', which then takes the form *saw*, *zər* 'thousand') and the enumerative words which frequently appear between number and noun: *co jə́la* 'how many times?', *dre kə́la* 'three years', *calór sáwa saří* 'four hundred men', *pinjə́ zə́ra míla* 'five thousand miles', *atə́ kitába* or *atə ťuka kitābúna* 'eight (volumes) books'. This numerative ending may well be a last relic of the ancient dual.

The direct case of nouns serves both for the grammatical subject and direct object of verbs. Case relationships are all expressed by pre- and postpositions or a combination of both, used with one of the oblique cases: an oblique form alone may have adverbial sense, e.g. *yáwa wráje* 'one day'. The simple prepositions are *da* 'of', which provides the only means of expressing a genitive or possessive relationship, *la* 'from', *pa* 'in, at etc.', *tar* 'to, from': postpositions, appearing independently or in combination with prepositions, are *na* 'from', *ta* 'to', *bánde* 'on', *cə́xa* and *jə́ne* 'from', *kx̌e* (generally reduced to *ke*, *ki*) 'in', *lánde* 'under', *lará* 'for', *pās* 'above', *pasé* 'after', *póre* (*púri*) 'up to', *sará* 'with'. Combinations of pre- and postpositions vary somewhat from dialect to dialect: common examples are *da... na* 'from', *la... sará* 'with', *pa... kx̌e* 'in', *pa... bánde* 'on', *tar... póre* 'up to, till'. Most pre- and all postpositions take the main oblique case. The second oblique case, which as it serves no other function can for convenience be called the 'prepositional' case, is as a rule taken only by the simple prepositions *be* 'without', *la* and *tar* and by *pa* (*...kx̌e*), but this last, remarkably, with feminine nouns only.

With pronouns things are somewhat different. Pashto has, in fact, comparatively few independent pronouns. Besides those for the first and second persons, singular and plural, there are proximate and remote demonstrative pronouns, which double for the third persons, and a few indefinite and interrogative forms. For the rest paraphrase is used, much as in English. e.g. *jan* 'body, self' for 'my-, your-, himself etc.', *yaw... bəl* 'one... other' for 'each other'. The place of a relative pronoun is taken by the conjunctive particle *če* 'that', '(the man) who came' being expressed as 'that he came', and 'whose house...' as 'that his house...' and so on.

Pronouns

	Singular		Plural			'who?, somebody'	'what?, something'
	1	2	1	2			
Direct	zə	tə	muǧ¹	tåso	(tåsi)	cok	cə
Oblique	mā	tā	muǧ	tåso	(tåsi)	čā	cə
Possessive	jmā	stā	jmuǧ¹	ståso	(ståsi)	da čā	

	'this'			'that'
Masculine				
Direct	day	dáɣa		háɣa
Oblique	də	dáɣə		háɣə
Feminine				
Direct	dā	dáɣa		háɣa
Oblique	de	dáɣe		háɣe
Plural				
Direct	duy	dáɣa		háɣa
(Personal)		dáɣuy		háɣuy
Oblique	duy, dío	dáɣo		háɣo

Note: ¹ Hard dialects, mung, zmung.

Of those pronouns which show a difference, the first and second person singular ones are unique in that the direct forms act only as subject, the oblique case forms (distinct only in the singular) being used both for the direct and a prepositional object. The personal pronouns also have distinct possessive forms, combining the old preposition *hača* 'from' in the form *j-*, (*z-*), *s-*, which may also occur with postpositions usually combined with *da*, e.g. *jmā na* 'from me'. There are also two kinds of pronominal particle, one independent and one enclitic. The enclitics are only incompletely distinguished for person and number: 1st singular *me*, 2nd singular *de*, 3rd singular and plural *(y)e*, 1st and 2nd plural *mo*. They fulfil all the oblique functions of the pronouns except that of prepositional object, though even in this case there are traces of the third person form to be seen in combinations of the sort of English 'therefrom, -on, -in', Pashto *tre* < **tar-e*, *pre* < **par-e*, *pakše* < **pa kšé-ye*. The independent forms, *rā*, *dar*, *war*, are by origin local adverbs 'hither, thither' and 'yonder' and still act as such when no person is involved. They come to act as pseudo-pronouns, however, distinguishing only person, neither number nor gender. Thus they may be governed by post- but not prepositions, e.g. *dar sara* 'with you', or serve as a prepositional object with certain verbs: *war ba nənawózəm* 'I shall enter therein' or 'go in to him', according to context.

The verbal morphology of Pashto, as with all other modern Iranian languages, is based on the opposition between two stems, one present and one past. Present stems are either simple (inherited or borrowed ones) or secondary (made with the formatives *-eǧ-* intransitive or *-aw-* transitive and causative). These latter both generally form denominatives (*num-eǧ-* 'be named') or serve to assimilate loan-words (*bah-eǧ-* 'flow', from Hindi *bah-nā*), but in some cases *-eǧ-* also distinguishes a continuous sense from a timeless or habitual one: *dəlta ḍera wāwra óri* 'here much snow falls (lit. rains)' : *oréǧi* 'it is raining'. The past stems are essentially old perfect passive participles in *-ta-*, though more often than in any other Iranian language phonetic developments have disguised the characteristic dental ending. In contrast, for example, to Persian *sūz-ad*, *sūxt* 'it burns, burnt', Pashto has *swaj-i, su*. A dental may even arise in the present and disappear from the past, e.g. *təšt-* 'flee' < **tṛsa-*, against *təš* 'fled' < **tṛšta-*, or the two stems may coincide, as in *ačaw-* 'throw' < **ā-škaba-* and *-škafta-*. As a result a new past marker has emerged, a stressed *-ə́l-*, identical with the infinitive ending *-ə́l* (<**-ati-*), which is added to the past stem whenever the need is felt to arise. Corresponding to the intransitive present formative *-eǧ-*, and generally but not always paired with it, there is a past formative *-ed-*.

On the basis of these two stems simple tenses are formed by the addition of personal endings, stressed or not according to the stem, which distinguish first and second persons singular and plural, but third person only, without difference of number. Thus, from *lwedə́l* 'fall' and *ačawə́l* 'throw' are formed the present and past paradigms shown here.

		Present		Past	
Singular	1	lwéǧ-əm	acaw-ə́m	lwéd-əm	ačaw-ə́l-əm
	2	lwéǧ-e	acaw-é	lwéd-e	ačaw-ə́l-e
	3 m.	lwéǧ-i	acaw-í	lwéd(-ə́)	ačāwə́
	3 f.			lwed-ə́la	ačaw-ə́la
Plural	1	lwéǧ-u	acaw-ú	lwéd-u	ačaw-ə́l-u
	2	lwéǧ-əy[1]	acaw-ə́y[1]	lwéd-əy[1]	ačaw-ə́l-əy[1]
	3 m.	lwéǧ-i	acaw-í	lwéd-ə́l	ačaw-ə́l
	3 f.			lwed-ə́le	ačaw-ə́le

Note: [1] Qandahari, 2nd plural *-āst*, thus *lwéǧ-āst* etc.

The original composition of the past tense, from a passive participle and the copula, is still clear in the third person, where the copula is lacking and the forms are declined like adjectives, though frequently with an irregular masculine singular form in which a stem vowel *-a-* is lengthened to *-ā-* or changed to *-o-* (*xatə́l* 'rise', *xot* 'rose'). Moreover the old participle of transitive verbs, as past stem, retains its passive meaning throughout: *ačawə́m* 'I throw', but *ačawə́ləm* 'I was being thrown'. This is also true of the modern past participle, a regular adjective of declension 5, e.g. *lwedə́lay* 'fallen', *ačawə́lay* '(having been) thrown', which with the auxiliary verb 'be' forms periphrastic tenses. The modern copula similarly betrays the probable pronominal origin of its third person forms. The simple perfect, for example, is formed as in the chart given here.

	Masculine	Feminine	M./F.
Singular 1	lwedálay yəm	lwedále yəm	ačawəlay/e yəm
2	lwedálay ye	lwedále ye	ačawəlay/e ye
3	lwedálay day	lwedále da	ačawəlay/e day/da
Plural 1	lwedáli yu	lwedále yu	ačawəli/e yu
2	lwedáli yəy	lwedále yəy	ačawəli/e yəy
3	lwedáli di	lwedále di	ačawəli/e di

'I have fallen' etc., but 'I have been thrown', etc. In contrast to the present tenses, 'I throw it' etc., there is thus no means of expressing the active non-present tenses of the transitive verbs by forms in concord with a logical subject or agent in the direct case. Instead of 'I threw it', therefore, an ergative construction is obligatory, which — to avoid the passive 'it was thrown by me' — can only be expressed in English as 'me thrown it'. In Pashto the logical object but grammatical subject, inherent in the verb, may of course be expressed by an independent form, but if it is pronominal it need not be. The agent, however, must appear, in the oblique case. A personal pronoun may then be represented either by an independent form (mā etc.), which then generally precedes the grammatical subject, or by an enclitic (me, etc.). Various different possible paradigms thus arise (a matter to which we shall return), e.g.:

mā káñay...	or kắñay me ačawálay day	'I have thrown a stone',
tā zə...	or zə de ačawálay yəm	'you have thrown me',
hayə ačawálay day	or ačawálay ye day	'he has thrown it'.

In contrast to this a real passive usually only occurs when the agent is unknown or at least not expressed. Such a passive is formed by the past participle, or in soft dialects the 'old past participle', i.e. the third person past forms, with the auxiliary verb kedəl/šwəl 'become': ačāwá/ačawálay keǧəm 'I am being thrown', ačawála/ačawále šwa 'she was thrown', ačawál/ačawəli šáwi di 'they have been thrown'. A full passive, with the agent expressed by a prepositional phrase like 'by means of', as in kāle če da nāwe la xwā roy šəwe wi 'clothes which will have been made by (lit. from the side of) the bride', is a rarity.

Pashto employs two further means, besides the different temporal stems, for distinguishing a series of forms which intricately mark differences of mood and aspect. The one means is to provide each verb with secondary stems, present and past II. This is mostly done by means of a stressed separable prefix wə́ (eastern (w)u), e.g. wə́lweǧ-, wə́lwed-. With an initial a- the prefix forms wā-, which then makes itself independent of the verb as a pseudo-preverb, e.g. wắčaw-, wắčawəl-. True preverbs, like kše and nə́na 'in', póre 'to, across', pre 'off, from', exclude the prefix wə́. Instead they attract the stress to themselves, e.g. from kšewatál 'enter', present stem I kšewáz-, II kšéwəz-, past II kšéwat-. Half a dozen of the commonest verbs combine stems of widely different origins, so that the I and II stems are sufficiently distinct to dispense with the help of *wə*. Among these are *kedə́l* 'become', present I *kéǧ-*, II *š-*, past II *šw-*; *kawə́l* 'do, make', present I *kaw-´*, II *k(ŕ)-´*, past II *kŕ-*; and the particularly complicated *tləl* 'go', present I *j-*, II *wlāŕ š-*, past II *wlāŕ-*, but *rā-tlə́l* 'come (hither)', present I *rā-j-´*, II *rá̄-š-*, past II *rá̄-γl-*, which follows the same pattern with alternative prefixes in *dar-tlə́l* 'come, go to you', *war-tlə́l* 'go to him'. Denominative verbs distinguish their I and II stems in yet another way. Here the composite primary stems are opposed to secondary stems in which the independent inflected nominal form is compounded with the secondary stems of *kedəl* or *kawəl*: thus from *joŕ* 'well, ready, agreeable', *joŕedə́l* 'get well, be made, made ready, agree', present I *joŕéǧ-*, II *jóŕ š-*, past II *jóŕ šw-*. The contrast is even more marked with words of declension 2 or 3, since they form denominatives from the 'weak' feminine stem, e.g. from *pox* 'cooked, ripe', *paxawə́l* 'cook', present I *paxaw-´*, II *póx k(ŕ)-*, past II *póx kŕ-*.

The other means is a movable enclitic particle *ba*. Its movements call to be described below, but for the moment we shall consider it in relation to the finite verb alone. It remains only to mention the distinctive endings of the imperative (singular *-a*, plural *-ay*) and of the conditional mood (*-āy*, eastern *-ay*, for all persons) and we have all the ingredients for the first part of the verbal system sketched in table 26.4. The lower part comprises both the periphrastic tenses, formed from the past participle, and the forms expressing the potential mood, which are compounded of the simple conditional form and the auxiliary verb *šwəl* (Qandahari *swəl*) 'be able', the forms of which chance to be identical with the secondary ones of *kedəl* 'become'. Here the prefix *wə* seems to have lost its significance, to become facultative.

Between the present I and II there is a difference of mood, I being indicative, 'falls, is falling', II subjunctive, '(that, if) it fall'. In the corresponding future forms, however, with the addition of the particle *ba*, there is a distinction of aspect, I being durative, 'will be falling', II perfective, 'will fall'. This holds good also in part for the imperative, I 'keep on falling', II 'fall'. But the prohibitive, with the particle *ma* 'not', cuts across this. It is normally only formed from stem I, regardless of aspect: *má lweǧa* 'do not fall'. The past II is again perfective, 'fell', in contrast to the past I with durative sense, 'was falling', or occasionally inchoative, 'was about to fall'. The addition of *ba* in this case, although giving a sense of customariness, does not entirely remove the aspectual distinction: III 'used to fall, be falling, continuously' : IV 'used to fall repeatedly'. With the conditional forms I and II no aspectual difference can be seen: both can express present or future conditions, '(if) it were falling' or 'were to fall', the possible consequences '(then) it would fall' being expressed either by the past III or IV, or the conditional III (IV being unusual). The periphrastic tenses are by nature all perfective. With the perfect forms the sense follows that of the

Table 26.4: The Verbal System

Present I	Present II	Future I	Future II
lwéǧi	wə́lweǧi	lwéǧi ba	wə́-ba-lweǧi
Imperative I	Imperative II		
lwéǧa	wə́lweǧa		
Past I	Past II	Past III	Past IV
lwedə́	wə́lwed	lwedə́ ba	wə́-ba-lwed
Conditional I	Conditional II	Conditional III	
lwedǎy	wə́lwedǎy	lwedǎy ba	
Perfect I	Perfect II		Future Perfect
lwedə́lay day	lwedə́lay wi		lwedə́lay ba wi
Past Perfect I		Past Perfect III	
lwedə́lay wə		lwedə́lay ba wə	
Perfect Conditional I		Perfect Conditional III	
lwedə́lay wǎy		lwedə́lay ba wǎy	
Potential Present		Future	
(wə́)lwedǎy ši		(wə́)lwedǎy ba ši	
Past		Past III	
(wə́)lwedǎy šu		(wə́)lwedǎy ba šu	
Conditional			
(wə́)lwedǎy šwǎy			

auxiliary verb, i.e. between perfect I and II there is a difference of indicative, 'has fallen', and subjunctive, '(if) it (should) have fallen', in the third person only, as the other persons of the copula have common forms for both I and II. The future perfect only occurs in the II form, there being no durative future form of the copula. It has both senses of the corresponding English tense, 'it will (i.e. must) have fallen (by now, or some past time')', or 'it will have fallen (by some future time)'. The perfect conditional I expresses no longer possible conditions, '(if) it had fallen', and the past perfect III or the perfect conditional III the consequence, '(then) it would have fallen'.

6   Syntax

The first important syntactic feature to be considered is word order, which, starting from the noun phrase, is fairly inflexible in Pashto. All qualifiers precede the head of a noun phrase. The English freedom to say 'that man's hand' or 'the hand of that man' is denied a Pashto-speaker, who has only *da hayə saɽi lās* 'of that man hand'. Missing is an article in Pashto, though this lack may occasionally be made up by the use of a demonstrative or the word *yaw* 'one'. Combining *yaw zoɽ kálay* 'an old village' and *tange kucé* 'narrow streets' yields *da yawə zāɽə káli tange kucé* 'an old village's narrow streets'. Only the personal possessive forms can precede the *da* group: *stáso da kálo kucé* 'your villages' streets'. The apparent parallelism breaks down, however, when the noun phrase is governed by a pre- or postposition. The postposition appears at the end of the entire phrase, but a lone or accompanying preposition must be placed immediately before the head and its attributes. Thus 'from the very narrow streets of your old villages' can only be *stáso da zaɽo kálo la ɖero tango kucó na* 'your of-old-villages from very-narrow-streets-from'.

Since both subject and direct object of a non-past transitive verb appear in the direct case, only a fixed word order can disambiguate them. Pashto has therefore become an inflexible subject–object–verb language: *saɽáy xája wíni* 'man woman sees' can only mean 'the (a) man sees the (a) woman'. The positioning of adverbial phrases is freer. The order of the following sentence seems to be the most natural one: *(A:hara wraj) (B:pa kum waxt če kəli ta ji) yaw saɽay (C: pa ɖer tājub) yawa barbanɖa xəja (D: pa lāra kže) wini* '(every day) (at what time he goes to the village) a certain man (to his great surprise) sees a naked woman (on the road)'. But an alternative arrangement *(A) (C) yaw saɽay (B) (D) yawa barbanɖa xəja wini* is just as thinkable as the English '(A), (C), a certain man, (B), sees (D) a naked woman'. Given the inflexibility of the SOV order in the non-past, it is not surprising that the ergative construction of the past parallels it. With independent forms the necessary word order is agent–patient–verb or, translated into terms of grammatical concord, agent (oblique)–subject (direct)–verb (concord): *mā saɽáy wálid* 'I saw the man', *saɽí xája wálidəla* 'the man saw the woman', *zaɽo kálo ba tange kucé larále* 'old villages used to have narrow streets'. This simple rule is disturbed, however, by the fact already noted that a pronominal agent may be expressed by an enclitic form, and enclitics are a law unto themselves in Pashto.

Besides those already met, pronominal *me, de, (y)e, mo* and verbal *ba*, Pashto has a few more enclitics. *de (di)* may lose its original pronominal force and, as an ethic dative, simply give the present II (subjunctive) form a jussive sense: *kitābúna de ráwɽi* 'let him bring the books'. Then there are the conjunction *xo* 'but' and the adverb *no* 'so, then, still, yet', which can be used enclitically. Two or three of these may occur together, when they have the following fixed pecking order:

xo / ba / me, de, ye, mo / no

pré-xo-ba-ye-ná-ğdəm 'but I shall not leave it', *dá-xo-ba-me ná kāwə* 'but this I used not to do'. As a group they always seek the earliest possible support in a clause, namely the first syntagm, be it word, phrase or more, bearing at least one main stress. In short, when the agent is expressed by an enclitic pronoun its position is not relative to the grammatical subject at all, but is governed by the word order of the clause as a whole: *šikāyát-ye wɔ́kəî* 'complaint him made', i.e. 'he complained', *(da xéîe la xwɔ́ǧ cəxa)-ye šikāyát wɔ́kəî* '(of stomach from pain-from) him complaint made', i.e. 'he complained of stomach ache', *hálta-ye (da... cəxa) šikāyát wɔ́kəî* 'there he complained (of stomach-ache)'. Conversely as the content of a sentence is reduced an enclitic agent is forced back until it may be supported by parts of the verb, including a preverb, alone: *paroskál-ba-mo xar râwost/xár-ba-mo râwost/rá-ba-mo-wost* '(last year) we used to bring (the donkey) it'. All this is equally true of the enclitic pronouns in their other functions, as direct object or possessive: *nɔ́-ye wažni* 'he does not kill it', *magar wažnɔ́y-ba-ye nɔ́* 'but kill them you shall not'; *(stā da xeîe ilɔ́j kawa* or) *da xeîe ilɔ́j-de kawa* 'have your stomach treated', *xayrāt pradáy wə, no xéîa-xo-de xpɔ́la wa* 'the free food was provided by somebody else, but the stomach was your own'. Even poetic licence and transpositions *metri causa* cannot affect the rule. Instead of prosaic **mine-ba-me laryun da tan kor səway wə, ka-me žaîâ pa himāyat nə rātlay* 'love would long since have burnt the house of my body, if weeping had not come to my support (in dousing it)', the poet 'Abdul Hamid Mohmand has:

> da tan kór-ba-me laryún wə mine sɔ́way
> ka-me nɔ́ rātlay žaîâ pa himāyát.

The only constituent that can hold an enclitic back from its natural support is a relative clause immediately following it. A clause is clearly felt to be too diffuse to support enclitics, which are forced to attach themselves to the next best, i.e. following, syntagm: *haya nǰəlɔ́y-me māšâm sinemâ ta byāyi* 'that girl is taking me to the cinema this evening', *haya nǰəlɔ́y, če os-mo wɔ́lidəla, māšâm-me sinemâ ta byāyi* 'that girl we just saw is taking me to the cinema this evening'. Sometimes, however, an enclitic may burst the bounds of its own subordinate clause to move to the front of the main clause, e.g. instead of *har sabā če yrə-ta-ba tə,* 'every morning, when he would go to the mountain', we find *har sabā-ba če yrə-ta tə*; instead of *pa har jāy-kše če mumí-ye,* 'in whatever place he finds it' — *pa har jāy-kše-ye če mumi.*

Of agreement in Pashto there is little to be said except that, where the forms permit it, it is all-pervading. Adjectives, whether attributive or predicative, agree in number, gender and case with their head nouns or subjects respectively: *zmā grâna aw mehrabâna plâra* 'my dear and kind father!' (masculine singular vocative), *klâka zmɔ́ka* 'firm earth', *zmɔ́ka klâka da* 'the earth is hard' (feminine singular direct), *če stā mlā sáma ši yā da nóro xálko mlāgâne kubɔ́y ši* (they asked a hunchback whether he wanted) 'that your back should become straight (feminine singular direct) or other people's (masculine plural oblique) backs should become hunched (feminine plural direct)'. This agreement extends to adjectives used adverbially, e.g. *đer* 'much, many' but also 'very', *hawá đéra tawdá wi* 'the climate is (always) very hot' (feminine singular direct), *kištə́y-e kláka wə́niwəla* 'he siezed hold of the boat firmly' (feminine singular direct). While the agreement of subject and verb is normally restricted to person and number (note *Tor zə aw tə botlu* 'Tor took (1st plural) me and you'), with the third person singular copula gender also comes into play: *ás day* 'it is a horse', *áspa da* 'it is a mare'. In the ergative construction, with all third person forms both gender and number are marked throughout: *x̌ə́je ās wə́wāhə* 'the woman struck the horse', *áspa-ye wə́wahəla* 'he/she/they struck the mare', *āsúna-ye wə́wahəl* '...struck the horses', *áspe-ye wə́wahəle* '...struck the mares'. In the perfective forms of denominative verbs, in which the nominal element is free, agreement is naturally to be expected: *zə bāyad γwáx̌e paxé kəm* 'I must cook some meat (feminine plural direct of *pox*)'. More unexpectedly, even nouns forming denominatives become adjectivised in this context: thus from the Persian loanword *yād* 'memory', forming *yādedə́l* 'be remembered', we find *haγa x̌ə́ja-me yáda šwa* 'I remembered that woman'.

If we compare the archaic structure of Pashto with the much simplified morphology of Persian, the leading modern Iranian language, we see that it stands to its 'second cousin' and neighbour in something like the same relationship as Icelandic does to English.

Bibliography

The best modern study in English is Penzl (1955), despite minor errors; it is based on the work of Afghan grammarians. Trumpp (1873) remains, despite its age, the best grammar based on classical Pashto literature. For syntax, Lorimer (1915) is an amateur study, but a mine of information. Morgenstierne (1942) is a unique historical study, by the leading specialist.

References

Grjunberg, A.L. 1987. *Očerk grammatiki afganskogo jazyka (Pašto)* (Nauka, Leningrad)

Lorimer, D.L.R. 1915. *(A) Syntax of Colloquial Pashtu* (Oxford University Press, Oxford)

Morgenstierne, G. 1942. 'Archaisms and Innovations in Pashto Morphology', *Norsk Tidskrift for Sprogvidenskap*, vol. XII, p. 87–114

Penzl, H. 1955. *A Grammar of Pashto* (American Council of Learned Societies, Washington, DC)

Trumpp, Ernest. 1873. *Grammar of the Paštō or Language of the Afghans* (Trübner, London)

27 URALIC LANGUAGES

Robert Austerlitz

The term 'Uralic' refers to a language family with one large branch, Finno-Ugric, and one smaller one, Samoyedic. Each branch is further subdivided into sub-branches and these into individual languages. *Finno-Ugric* is often used in its wider meaning of Uralic. Though this is sanctioned by usage, it will be avoided here. Equally inaccurate is a vague association of Uralic with Turkic languages. (See page 620.) Ural-Altaic is a superstructure, a unit larger than a family (also called stock or phylum).

The best known Uralic languages are Hungarian, with some fourteen million speakers, Finnish with some five million, and Estonian with about one and a half million. These are also the populations which are most thoroughly integrated into the European cultural and economic community.

Hungarian and Finnish are related only remotely, while Finnish and Estonian are related much more intimately. The network which unites the entire family genetically can be seen in figure 27.1.

In terms of numbers of speakers of the remaining Uralic languages, Mordva is the largest, followed by Mari and Udmurt.

In terms of positions on today's political map, only Finnish and Hungarian are spoken completely outside the confines of the USSR. The bulk of the speakers of Lapp live in Norway and Sweden; about 1,500 live in Finland and another 1,500 in the Soviet Union. All of the other Uralic languages are spoken in the Soviet Union. For general geographical locations, see the accompanying map.

In terms of very broad cultural features, the Hungarians are Central Europeans, the Finns, and to some extent, the Lapps are Fenno-Scandians, the Estonians and the other Baltic-Finnic speakers are Balts. The Mari, Mordva and Udmurt are agrarian populations. Komi culture occupies an intermediate position between that of the central-Russian agrarians and a sub-Arctic form of living. The Ob-Ugrians and the Samoyeds were, until this century, sub-Arctic peoples, as were the northernmost Lapp.

The family tree of the Uralic languages (figure 27.1) shows that this is a closely-knit family in the accepted sense. Only two questions are still awaiting resolution: (1) The precise position of Lapp within the family. This

Figure 27.1: The Uralic Language Family

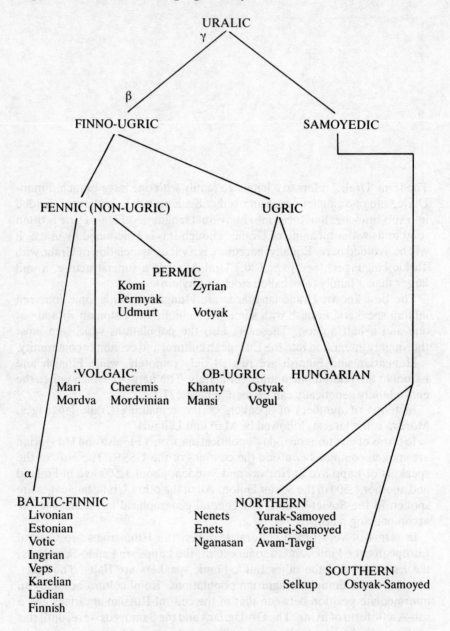

URALIC
γ

β

FINNO-UGRIC   SAMOYEDIC

FENNIC (NON-UGRIC)   UGRIC

PERMIC
Komi   Zyrian
Permyak
Udmurt   Votyak

'VOLGAIC'   OB-UGRIC   HUNGARIAN
Mari   Cheremis   Khanty Ostyak
Mordva Mordvinian Mansi   Vogul

α

BALTIC-FINNIC   NORTHERN
Livonian   Nenets   Yurak-Samoyed
Estonian   Enets   Yenisei-Samoyed
Votic   Nganasan Avam-Tavgi
Ingrian
Veps
Karelian   SOUTHERN
Lüdian   Selkup   Ostyak-Samoyed
Finnish

LAPPIC
Saam   Lapp
(Various languages considered
dialects)

Map 27.1: Location of Uralic Languages

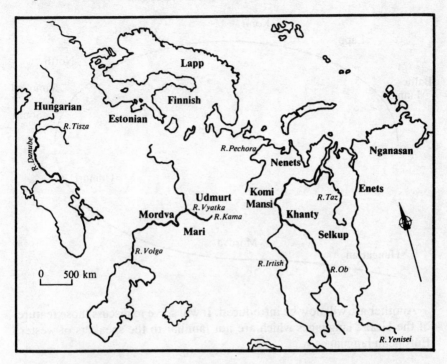

group of languages has been considered Baltic-Finnic (node α), Finno-Ugric (node β), a separate branch of Uralic (node γ) and a 'mixed language', a vague term which generates further questions. (2) The precise relationship between Mordva and Mari.

The Uralic languages can also be plotted along an ear-shaped geographical arc extending from Fenno-Scandia and the Baltic in the West, extending eastward over the Kola peninsula into the basins of the Pechora, Ob and Yenisey rivers. At that point the arc is broken. It begins again in the Volga-Kama basin and ends, after another break, into the Carpathian basin (see figure 27.2). The model of this arc can also serve as a device for visualising the order in which the forebears of the speakers of today's Uralic languages separated out of early family groupings and ultimately out of the original proto-language. The generally accepted order is: Samoyed (estimates of the date of separation range from the fourth to the second millennium BC); Ugric, which split into an early form of Hungarian on the one hand and the language which later developed into Khanty and Mansi on the other. The last group to split up was Permic, around the seventh or eighth century AD. Hypothetical dates for the formation of the individual Baltic-Finnic languages as well as the proto-history of the Mari and the Mordva remain in dispute.

Figure 27.2: Schematic Location of Uralic Languages

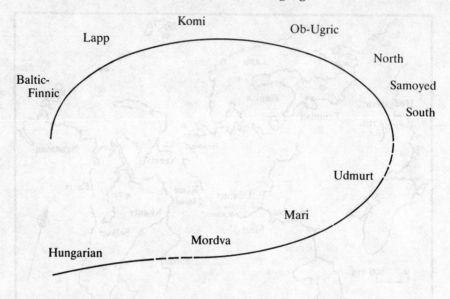

Another arc will now be introduced. It will serve to discuss those features of the Uralic languages which are not familiar to the speakers of western European languages.

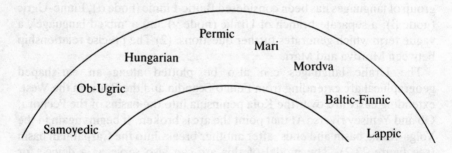

Consonant gradation is a prominent phenomenon in Baltic-Finnic and Lapp. Thus, *-nt-* (strong grade) in Finnish *anta-vat* 'they give' alternates with *-nn-* (weak grade) in *anna-n* 'I give'. Originally, the strong-weak opposition correlated with open versus closed syllable, as in this Finnish example. Traces of this phenomenon can be found in Mordva and Mari. It is absent from the other languages.

The only typically Uralic grammatical feature found in the Permic languages is the so-called negative conjugation: Komi *o-g mun* 'I do not go', *o-z mun* 'you (sg.) do not go', *e-g mun* 'I did not go'. In this construction it is not the main verb (*mun* 'to go'), but the auxiliary negative verb (present *o-*, past *e-*) which is conjugated (*-g* 'I', *-z* 'you (sg.)'). Mari, Mordva, some of the Baltic-Finnic languages, and the Samoyedic languages (except Selkup) also have such a device for negating the verb.

Vowel harmony occurs in Hungarian, in some of the Baltic-Finnic languages and in various degrees of development elsewhere (Mordva, Mari, Khanty, Samoyedic). It is absent from Permic and Lapp. The rules of vowel-harmony require that only specific subclasses of vowels coexist in a non-compounded word. Thus, in Finnish, the sign of the third person plural is *-vat* and *-vät* as in *anta-vat* 'they give' and *kyntä-vät* 'they plough' (read *y* as *ü*); cf. Hungarian *lop-nak* 'they steal' vs. *tör-nek* 'they break'. The vowel of the suffix adjusts to the vowels contained in the stem. The specific subclasses of vowels are determined by physiological factors, basically the position of the tongue (front/back) and of the lips (rounded/unrounded).

The grammatical category of the dual ('two of a kind') plays an important role in Ob-Ugric, in Samoyedic and in Lapp. The following Mansi example will also illustrate the possessive suffix of the third person singular, *-et-* 'his/her', and the instrumental case, *-l* 'with': *aamp-aγ-et-l* 'with his two dogs' (*-aγ-* is the dual, 'two'). In Lappic, the dual occurs only in pronouns and in the verb. The dual, then, is found only in the languages at the two extremes of the arc and can be thought of as closing the circle.

Another typological feature, reference to a specific object within the verbal complex (also called the objective conjugation), is more difficult to place on the arc: it predominates on the left (Ugric, Samoyedic) but is also found in Mordva. The details of this feature differ strongly from one subgroup to another. Essentially, it signals the presence of a specific object, e.g. Hungarian *lop-j-uk* 'we steal it' as against *lop-unk* 'we steal' (without reference to a specific third-person object in the latter).

Mordva and Hungarian also have a definite article. In Hungarian *a ház* 'the house' the article *a* precedes the noun and is separable from it (*a kék ház* 'the blue house'), as in English. In Mordva *kudo-ś* 'house-the' the article is suffixed, as in the Scandinavian languages and some Balkan languages (e.g. Rumanian, see page 310).

The basic and still prevalent rule of word order in the Uralic languages is subject–object–verb (SOV). However, this rule is rigid only in Ob-Ugric and in Samoyedic — on the left side of the arc — while Baltic-Finnic languages are basically SVO. The other languages have so-called free word order. Thus, in Hungarian, all permutations are possible: *A fiúk krumplit lopnak* 'the boys are stealing potatoes' (lit. 'the boys potato[-object] steal'), *krumplit lopnak a fiúk*, *lopnak a fiúk krumplit*, *lopnak krumplit a fiúk*, *a fiúk lopnak krumplit* and *krumplit a fiúk lopnak* can all occur under specific circumstances. The nuances of meaning expressed are in the areas of emphasis and focus. Those languages which lack this sort of syntactic elasticity have other ways of expressing emphasis and focus, generally particles which attach to specific parts of the sentence.

All of the Uralic languages have a set of spatial cases which convey such meanings as 'in', 'from', 'to' etc. The languages richest in this respect are Hungarian and Permic. In Baltic-Finnic and Lapp one such local case, the partitive, which originally meant 'from' has acquired the additional function of partitive object, as in French, e.g. Finnish *juo-n maito-a* 'I am drinking milk' (lit. in French, *bois-je lait-du*)' as against *juo-n maido-n* 'I am drinking (the) (entire quantity of) milk (which has already been specified in the discourse)'. The *-n* in *maido-n* is the accusative case marker. The more archaic function of the partitive (*-a*) can be seen in *taka-a* '(movement) from behind (something)'; contrast *taka-na* '(which is) behind'. Also in Finnish, all negative objects must be in the partitive, e.g. *e-n juo maito-a* 'I do not drink milk'; a sentence such as **e-n juo maido-n* (with the object in the accusative) is impossible.

Some of the salient features of the sound systems of the Uralic languages are: (1) word stress on the first vowel of the word, with the notable exception of Udmurt, where it falls on the last (and less striking exceptions in Mordva, Mari, Komi and Permyak); (2) vowel systems with reduced vowels: Mari, Ob-Ugric, Northern Samoyedic; (3) vowel systems with front rounded vowels (*ü, ö*): Baltic-Finnic, Mari, Hungarian (and, in a less developed form, in Khanty). Vowel systems with back unrounded vowels: Estonian (and some other Baltic-Finnic languages), Permic. A vowel system with both front rounded and back unrounded vowels is found in Selkup. (4) A correlation of palatalisation: Mordva, Permic, Samoyedic. (5) Rich systems of affricates: Hungarian, Permic, Selkup. (6) A correlation of voice in the obstruents: Hungarian, Permic, Lapp (rudimentary in Mordva).

Each Uralic language has a constellation of typological features of the kind discussed above which is unique unto itself and which lends it its own particular profile. The features themselves evolved and crystallised during the historical development of each individual language for a variety of reasons — the economy of the phonology and grammar of each language, stimuli from other, related or unrelated, languages or combinations of the two. One task of the specialist is to peel off the layers of each Uralic language and to find correspondences among subsets of related languages. Such correspondences eventually permit the reconstruction of a parent language. By the same token, it is the task of the specialist to identify innovations in each language.

One tractable approach to the history of each of the Uralic languages is the study of loanwords — vocabulary items which entered each individual language in the course of its history as a result of contact with other languages and cultures. All of the Uralic languages have loanwords from Slavonic, acquired relatively recently. All of the Finno-Ugric languages have loans from Iranian or perhaps even Indo-Iranian, acquired so long ago that it is thought that they entered the proto-language and were passed on to its descendants along with the native vocabulary. One such item is Finnish *sata*, Hungarian *száz* 'hundred', an item which has implications for early commercial contacts between the two parties.

Table 27.1 gives a synoptic view of the lending and the borrowing parties.

Table 27.1: Loanwords in Uralic Languages

	Later Iranian	East Turkic	West Turkic	Baltic	Germanic Older	Germanic 1200–	Slavonic
Samoyedic	+	+					+
Ob-Ugric	+	+					+
Hungarian	+	+	+			+	+
Permic	+	+	+				+
Mari	+	+	+				+
Mordva	+	+	+	+			+
Baltic-Finnic			+	+	+	+	+
Lapp			+	+	+	+	+

The systematic comparison of the Finno-Ugric languages amongst themselves has provided a glimpse into both the structure of an earlier, hypothetical Proto-Finno-Ugric language and, through it, of some aspects of the culture of the population which spoke this language. Analogously, the same has been done for the Samoyedic languages. The comparison of Proto-Finno-Ugric with Proto-Samoyedic, then, affords an insight into the still earlier Proto-Uralic hypothetical language. Table 27.2 displays the data on

Table 27.2: A Proto-Uralic Reconstruction

URALIC	SAMOYEDIC		South	Kamassian Selkup	t'en čɔt, tən	Proto-Samoyedic: *cən	Proto-Uralic: *səne
			North	Nganasan Enets Nenets	taŋ ti/tino- teʔ/ten-		
	FINNO-UGRIC	UGRIC	Ob-Ugric	Khanty Mansi Hungarian	ton, lan, jan taan, tən ín/ina-	Proto-Finno-Ugric: *sone, *soone, *səne	
			Permic	Udmurt Komi	sən sən		
		FENNIC	(Volgaic)	Mari Mordva	šün, śün san		
			Balto-Finnic	Livonian Estonian Finnish	suón/suonə- soon/soone- suoni/suone-		
	LAPP			Lapp	suodnâ/suonâ-		

which such a step-by-step comparison is carried out. The word in question is thought to have meant 'vein' but may also have meant something like 'sinew' and thus carries suggestions about the use of the objects denoted — archery, fishing equipment and the like. What can be reconstructed in the area of vocabulary has analogues in grammar. Proto-Uralic probably had a nominative (or absolute case, with no overt marker), an accusative, a genitive, at least three local cases (locative, allative, ablative), adverbial cases (with such meanings as 'with'), aspect (or tense) in the verb, an imperative and possibly an impersonal form of the verb.

Bibliography

Harms (1974) is a careful, comprehensive survey of the family. Among more extensive surveys, Hajdú (1975) provides a historically orientated introduction; Comrie (1981) discusses the phonology, grammar, typology and sociolinguistics of the Uralic languages of the USSR; Collinder et al. (1957) provides descriptive sketches and texts from thirteen languages — to be used with caution. Décsy (1965) is the basic text, on historical and comparative principles and rich in detail; the comparative grammar by Collinder (1960) is idiosyncratic but comprehensive.

References

Collinder, B. 1960, *Comparative Grammar of the Uralic Languages* (Almqvist & Wiksell, Stockholm)
—— et al. 1957. *Survey of the Uralic Languages* (Almqvist and Wiksell, Stockholm)
Comrie, B. 1981. 'Uralic Languages', in B. Comrie, *Languages of the Soviet Union* (Cambridge University Press, Cambridge, pp. 92–141
Décsy, Gy. 1965. *Einführung in die finnisch-ugrische Sprachwissenschaft* (Otto Harrassowitz, Wiesbaden)
Hajdú, P. 1975. *Finno-Ugrian Languages and Peoples*, translated and adapted by G.F. Cushing (André Deutsch, London)
Harms, R.T. 1974. 'Uralic Languages', in *The New Encyclopaedia Britannica: Macropaedia*, vol. 18 (Encyclopaedia Britannica, Chicago), pp. 1022–32

28   Hungarian

Daniel Abondolo

1 Introduction

Hungarian (native name *magyar*) is the only Uralic language spoken in central Europe. In terms of number of speakers, Hungarian ranks twelfth among the languages of Europe: c. 10 million in Hungary and c. three million elsewhere in Europe, mostly in Rumania, Czechoslovakia and Yugoslavia. There are also about one million Hungarian speakers elsewhere, mostly in the United States and Canada.

Because it is a Uralic language, Hungarian is typologically unlike the majority of European languages. But paradoxically, Hungarian is also atypical among the Uralic family. It is by far the largest, disproportionately so, in the sense that more than half of all speakers of Uralic languages speak Hungarian. It has both a rich vocalism (14–15 vowels) and a rich inventory of voiced/voiceless oppositions in its consonantism (which includes four affricates). Most of its inflectional morphemes are innovations. Its syntax boasts an impressive set of coordinating conjunctions. The array of foreign elements in its lexicon rivals that of Gypsy (Romany). Unlike Finnish, Hungarian has no close relatives; the Ob-Ugric languages, traditionally bundled together with Hungarian into the Ugric subgroup of the Uralic family, are radically different from Hungarian in their phonology, syntax and vocabulary.

This singular character is due to one decisive difference: migration by the Proto-Hungarians, first southward from the Uralic Urheimat into the maelstrom of cultures in the South Russian steppe, then westward into the heart of Roman Christian Europe.

This rudimentary sketch outlines only a few of the more salient features of Hungarian grammar and lexicon. In order to compress the presentation without sacrificing accuracy of detail, the following typographic conventions have been observed: suffixes are written to the right of a hyphen (-) if inflectional, of an equals sign (=) if derivational. A double equals sign (==) marks a coverb to its left.

2 Sounds and Orthography

2.1 Vowels

The short vowels are *i*, *e*, *a*, *o*, *u* and the front rounded *ü*, *ö*, marked with umlaut as in German. These seven vowels are sounded much as in German, with two important exceptions: *e*, which is an open vowel resembling the *a* of English *mat*; and *a*, which is pronounced with a slight rounding of the lips, as in English *chalk*.

Nearly one half of Hungarian speakers distinguish an eighth, short *e*-type vowel like that of English *met*; this sound is written throughout this chapter (and in Hungarian dialectology) as *ë*, for example: *szëg* 'carpenter's nail' (rhymes with English *beg*). For speakers who distinguish this sound, this word differs in pronunciation from the verb *szeg-* 'break' somewhat as English *set* differs from *sat* (in the Hungarian words, however, both vowels are equally short).

The long vowels are indicated in the orthography with an acute accent (*í*, *é*, *á*, *ó*, *ú*) or, if marked with umlaut when short, with a double acute accent, a diacritic unique to Hungarian (*ű*, *ő*). Phonetically, these seven long vowels are simply longer versions of their short counterparts, again with two important exceptions: (1) *é* is *not* a long version of *e* (which would be the *ä* of literary German *gäbe*), but rather a long high *e*-sound similar to the first *e* of German *gebe*; and (2) *á* is not a long version of *a*, which would have lip-rounding as in English *caught*, but rather is a long open unrounded *a*-sound as in German *Gabe*. The vowel system of Hungarian is set out in table 28.1.

Table 28.1: Hungarian Vowel Phonemes

i	ü	u		í	ű	ú
(ë)	ö	o		é	ő	ó
e		a				á

The salient assimilatory phenomenon associated with the Hungarian vowels is called vowel harmony. This is a mechanism which, at one time, regulated the quality (front vs. back) of vowels within the word, but which today affects only suffixal vowels. Over-simplifying, we may state that stems containing only front vowels select front-vowel variants of suffixes (e.g. *szűr-tök* 'you (pl.) strain'), while other stems select back vowel variants (e.g. *szúr-tok* 'you (pl.) pierce'). An important exception is the class of verb roots whose sole vowel is *i* or *í*, most of which take back vowel suffix forms (e.g. *ír-tok* 'you (pl.) write'). Note also that oblique stem vowels of nouns (see section 3.2) play a decisive role in suffix vowel selection, e.g. *híd-ról* 'off (the) bridge' (and not *híd-ről: this noun has an oblique stem hida- with back vowel a).

Vowel harmony also affects the roundedness of vowels in certain suffixes. For example, the second person plural suffix (-tök/-tok above) is -tëk after unrounded front vowels: ér-tëk 'you (pl.) arrive'.

Another prevalent vowel alternation is that of the short mid vowels (o, ö, ë) with zero. This alternation is evident in allomorphy such as that of the accusative suffix, which is -ot/-öt/-ët (according to vowel harmony, cf. above) after labials, velars, apical stops and affricates and consonant-final oblique stems, but -t after vowels and apical continuants (r, l, ly/j, n, ny, sz, s, z, zs). Sample accusative forms:

ostrom-ot	'siege'
hercëg-ët	'duke'
ökr-öt	'ox' (citation form ökör)
korbács-ot	'scourge'
lakat-ot	'(pad)lock'
ládá-t	'crate'
hajó-t	'ship'
jege-t	'ice' (citation form jég)
mája-t	'liver' (citation form máj)
lakáj-t	'lackey'
gúny-t	'mockery'

2.2 Consonants

The consonant system and its regular orthographic representations are given in table 28.2.

Table 28.2: Hungarian Consonantism

phonemes				orthography			
	r				r		
	l	j			l	j,ly	
m	n	ń		m	n	ny	
p	t	t́	k	p	t	ty	k
b	d	d́	g	b	d	gy	g
f	s	š	h	f	sz	s	h
v	z	ž		v	z	zs	
	c	č			c	cs	
	3	ǯ			dz	dzs	

In modern Hungarian, j and ly (originally a palatal lateral) are pronounced alike. Noteworthy are the oppositions palatal vs. non-palatal among the oral and nasal stops (t vs. t́, d vs. d́, n vs. ń) and sibilant vs. shibilant among the apical fricatives and affricates (s vs. š, z vs. ž, c vs. č, 3 vs. ǯ). From the historical point of view, the development of the opposition of voice (p vs. b, f vs. v etc.) is particularly striking (within Uralic, it is developed fully only in the rather distantly related Permic languages — see the chapter on Uralic languages).

The most conspicuous assimilatory phenomena affecting the consonants centre on the above outlined three oppositions. Thus: (1) unpalatalised /t/ followed by palatal /ń/ yields the palatal sequence /t́ń/, e.g. *cipő-t nyer* /cipőt́ńer/ 'wins (a pair of) shoes'; (2) sibilant /z/ followed by shibilant /ž/ yields the shibilant sequence /žž/, e.g. *tíz zsaru* /tīžžaru/ 'ten cops'; (3) distinctively voiced /z/ followed by distinctively voiceless /s/ yields the voiceless sequence /ss/, e.g. *tíz szarka* /tīssarka/ 'ten magpies'.

Other assimilatory phenomena include (a) combinations of the above three types; thus (1+3) /t/ + /d́/ yields /d́d́/, e.g. *cipő-t gyárt* /cipőd́d́ārt/ 'manufactures shoes', (2+3) /z/ + /š/ yields /šš/, e.g. *tíz saru* /tīššaru/ 'ten (pairs of) sandals'; and (b) adaffrication, e.g. /t/ + /š/ yields /čč/, e.g. *rét=ség* /rēččēg/ 'meadow +(collective/abstract suffix)' = 'meadowlands'.

3   Inflection

3.1   Conjugation

Every Hungarian conjugated verb form may be analysed as consisting of three parts: (1) a stem, followed by (2) a tense/mood suffix, followed by (3) a person-and-number suffix. The four forms of the verb *mën-* 'go' listed below, all with second person plural subject, illustrate the four tenses/moods occurring in the present-day language:

present	mën-Ø-tëk	'you (pl.) go'
past	mën-te-tëk	'you (pl.) went'
conditional	mën-né-tëk	'you (pl.) would go'
subjunctive	mën-je-tëk	'you (pl.) should go; go!'

The suffix of the present tense is zero (-Ø-). The suffixes of the past, conditional and subjunctive are subject to considerable formal variation, conditioned by the phonological and grammatical make-up of the morphemes which flank them. Compare the various shapes of the subjunctive suffix (-*ja*-, -*je*-, -*já*-, -*j*-, -*zé*-, -*s*-, -*Ø*-) in the following forms (the list is not exhaustive):

vár-ja-tok	'you (pl.) should wait'
mér-je-tëk	'you (pl.) should measure'
vár-já-l	'you (sg.) should wait'
vár-j-on	'(s)he/it should wait'
néz-zé-l	'you (sg.) should watch'
mos-s-on	'(s)he/it should wash'
mos-Ø-d	'you (sg.) should wash it'

The person suffixes present a complex and intriguing picture. Each person suffix refers not only to the person and number of the subject (as, for example, in Latin, Russian or Finnish), but also to the person — but not the number — of the object. Certain suffixes are explicit and unambiguous with regard to the person of the object; for example, the first person singular suffix $-l_ak^e$ refers explicitly, and exclusively, to a second person object: *lát-lak* 'I see you' (more precisely, *lát-Ø-lak* 'see-present-I/you'). On the other hand, certain other suffixes are ambiguous with regard to object person and indeed need not refer to any object whatsoever. For example, the form *lát-Ø-nak*, built with the third person plural suffix $-n_ak^e$, may be translated as 'they see me', 'they see you', 'they see us', or simply 'they (can) see (i.e. are not blind)'. The form *lát-Ø-nak* is explicit with regard to object person only in a negative sense: the object cannot be a specific third person object known from the context, that is, this form cannot mean 'they see him/her/it/them'.

One way to think about object-person marking in Hungarian is to arrange the persons (first, second, and third) on a concentric model with first person (the speaker) at the centre (figure 28.1). A form such as *lát-Ø-lak* 'I see you'

Figure 28.1

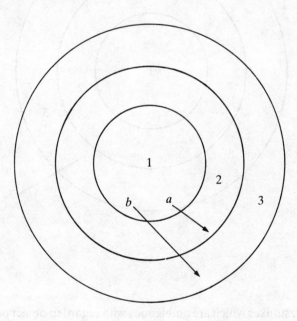

may then be plotted on the model as an arrow which starts at the centre (subject = first person) and points outward (object = second person); see arrow *a* in figure 28.1. All forms having such centrifugal orientation on the model are unambiguous with regard to object person. It follows, therefore, that there is a separate form meaning 'I see him/her/it/them', namely *lát-Ø-om*, symbolised by arrow *b* in figure 28.1.

Similarly, the form *lát-Ø-ja* '(s)he/it sees him/her/it/them' is also unambiguous with regard to object person, since the object is invariably third person. Such a form is also centrifugal in orientation, since there is an unlimited supply of potential third person subjects. The arrow representing this form points outward into the realm of other third person objects, schematically 3*a* in figure 28.2:

Figure 28.2

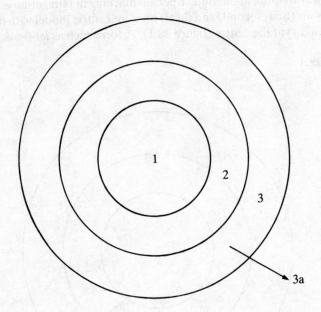

Conversely, suffixes which are ambiguous with regard to object person show only inward-pointing arrows on the concentric model and may therefore be termed centripetal. For example, the form *lát-Ø-nak* cited above may refer to a first or a second person object (arrows *a* and *b* in figure 28.3) or to no object at all (point *c* in figure 28.3).

Figure 28.3

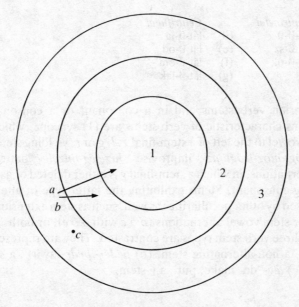

The seven singular forms of the present tense of the verb *lát-* 'see' may therefore be presented synoptically as in figure 28.4.

Figure 28.4

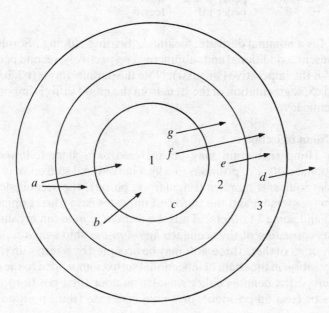

These forms (*a* to *g* in figure 28.4) are:

	Centripetal		Centrifugal
(a)	lát-Ø-Ø	(d)	lát-Ø-ja
(b)	lát-Ø-sz	(e)	lát-Ø-od
(c)	lát-Ø-ok	(f)	lát-Ø-om
		(g)	lát-Ø-lak

All Hungarian verb stems end in a consonant or a consonant cluster. Alternations characteristic of verb stems are (1) syncope, which deletes a short mid vowel to the left of a stem-final *z*, *l*, *g* or *r*, yielding stem alternates such as *rögtönöz-/rögtönz-* 'improvise', *hízelëg-/hízelg-* 'flatter'; and (2) *v*-stem alternations, in which a stem-final *v* is either deleted or assimilates to a following consonant. Stems exhibiting the latter type of alternation are characterised by other peculiarities as well, such as stem extension (with =*sz* or =V*d*) or stem vowel alternations (*o ö ë* with *ó ő é*), or both.

Below, three verb stem types are contrasted. They are represented by (a) *ver-* 'beat', a non-alternating stem, (b) *pëdër-/pëdr-* 'twirl', a syncopating stem and (c) *tëv-* 'do, make, put', a *v*-stem.

	a	b	c
1	ver=és	pëdr=és	tëv=és
2	ver-Ø-tëk	{ pëdr-Ø-ëtëk / pëdër-Ø-tëk }	të=sz-Ø-tëk
3	ver-né-tëk	{ pëdr-ené-tëk / pëdër-né-tëk }	tën-né-tëk
4	ver-je-tëk	pëdër-je-tëk	tëgye-tëk
5	ver-j-Ø	pëdër-j-Ø	tégy-Ø

Form 1 is a nominal derivate: 'beating', 'twirling', 'doing'. Forms 2, 3 and 4 are present, conditional and subjunctive, respectively, second person plural; form 5 is the imperative (singular). Note the parallel forms (b2, b3). In forms c4 and c5, segmentation of the stem from the mood suffix is impossible at the phonemic level.

3.2 Noun inflection

Every Hungarian noun may be analysed as a stem followed by three inflectional slots, i.e. positions in which inflectional suffixes may occur. The first slot indicates number (singular vs. plural), the second slot indicates person (possessor) and the third slot indicates case (direct object, indirect object and some 14 others). Thus the form *hajóimon* 'on my ships' may be seen as consisting of the sequence *hajó-i-m-on* 'ship-s-my-on'.

Any or all of these three slots may be occupied by a zero suffix. According to its position in the chain of inflectional suffixes appended to the noun stem, this zero suffix denotes either singular number (first position), absence of possessor (second position), or nominative case (third position). Thus we have: *hajó-Ø-m-on* 'ship-Ø-my-on' = 'on my ship', *hajó-k-Ø-on* 'ship-s-Ø-on' = 'on ships', *hajó-i-m-Ø* 'ship-s-my-Ø' = 'my ships'. Notice that the plural suffix is *-i-* when second position is occupied by a person/possessive suffix but *-k-* when second position is occupied by zero (i.e. no possessor).

The case suffixes may be classified into two basic groups, local and non-local. The local cases form a neat system defined by concrete spatial and kinetic oppositions such as interior vs. exterior, stationary vs. moving etc., shown schematically in table 28.3.

Table 28.3: Locative Cases

		Stationary	Moving Approach	Depart
Interior		1 $-b^e_a n$	2 $-b^e_a$	3 $-b^{ő}_{ó}l$
Exterior	Surface	4 $-n$	5 $-r^e_a$	6 $-r^{ő}_{ó}l$
	Proximity	7 $-n^é_á l$	8 $-h^{ö}_{o}z$	9 $-t^{ő}_{ó}l$
	Terminus		10 $-ig$	

A few concrete examples will illustrate the meanings of these cases. Within the category 'moving/approaching' (the middle column in table 28.3) four degrees of intimacy are distinguished: suffix 2 (illative) indicates movement into an interior, e.g. *fal-ba* 'into (the) wall'; suffix 5 (sublative) indicates movement onto a surface, e.g. *fal-ra* 'onto (the) wall'; suffix 8 (allative) indicates movement into an immediate proximity, e.g. *fal-hoz* '(moving) over to the space immediately next to (the) wall'; and suffix 10 (terminative) indicates movement as far as, but no farther than, a point in space, e.g. *fal-ig* 'as far as (the) wall but no farther'.

The non-local cases normally express primary syntactic or adverbial functions, e.g. subject, direct and indirect object, possessor or instrument. The traditional names of these cases can be quite misleading; the so-called dative ($-n_a^e k$), for example, may mark not only the indirect object, but also the possessor or a predicate construed with an infinitive. Note the dative form of the noun *katona* 'soldier' in the sentences:

(1) Odaadta a katonának. 'He gave it *to the soldier*.'
(2) A katonának nehéz az élete. '*A soldier's* life is difficult.'
(3) Katonának lenni nehéz. 'To be *a soldier* is difficult.'

The other non-local cases are: nominative (-Ø); accusative (-*t*); essive (-$^{ü}_{u}l$, e.g. *cél-ul* '(considered) as a goal'); causal/final (-*ért*, indicating the efficient or final cause, e.g. *hazá-ért* '(sacrificed his life) for (the) fatherland'); instrumental (-$v_a^e l$, e.g. *olló-val* 'with (a pair of) scissors'); and translative

(-vá, indicating transformation into another state, e.g. *só-vá* '(turned) into salt'). The *v* initial in the last two suffixes assimilates to a preceding consonant, e.g. *olló-m-mal* '(pair of) scissor(s)-my-with' = 'with my scissors', *kenyér-ré* '(turned) into bread'.

In contrast to verb stems, noun stems may end in either a consonant or a vowel. The vowel may be any save *o, ö, ë* or *á*; the consonant may be any save *dz*, but *dzs, zs, ty, f* and *h* are rare.

All stems with final *a* or *e* exhibit lengthening of this vowel before most suffixes, whether declensional or derivational. Examples: *alma/körte* 'apple'/'pear', *almá-m/körté-m* 'my apple'/ 'my pear', *almá=s/körté=s* 'containing apples'/'containing pears'. This is by far the largest class of vowel-final noun stems. It contains more than 1,200 underived stems (like *alma* and *körte* above) and thousands of derivates such as *jár=da* 'sidewalk' (from the verb *jár-* 'be in motion, walk'), *cukor=ka* 'bonbon' (from *cukor* 'sugar'), *pëng=e* 'blade' (from the verb *pëng-* 'ring, clang').

There is also a closed set of nearly 500 stems which exhibit a special stem form only when followed by certain suffixes. This special stem form, termed here for convenience the 'oblique stem', differs from the nominative singular (citation form) by the presence of a stem-final *a* or *e*, the absence of a stem-penultimate *o, ö* or *ë* or both. For example: from their nominative singular forms, it would appear that the nouns *dal* 'song' and *fal* 'wall' are parallel in shape and, presumably, inflectional pattern. This is not so, however, because *fal*, unlike *dal*, has an oblique stem with final *a*, namely *fala-*; compare the accusative forms *dal-t, fala-t*. Similarly, *nyomor* 'misery' and *gyomor* 'stomach' display different inflectional patterns because the latter noun has an oblique stem which lacks the penultimate *o*, namely *gyomr-*; compare the accusative forms *nyomor-t, gyomr-ot*. Finally, some noun stems (about 115) exhibit both types of alternation simultaneously, e.g. *sátor* 'tent', in the oblique stem of which we find at once the absence of the penultimate *o* and the presence of final *a*; contrast *sátra-m* 'my tent' with *mámor-om* 'my rapture'.

Nouns whose oblique stems have final *a* or *e* may be subclassified according to additional alternations. For example, it was noted above that the oblique stem of the noun *fal* 'wall' differs from its nominative singular only by virtue of a stem-final *a*; this is not the case with the noun *falu* 'village', whose oblique stem has not only a final *a* but also *v* instead of *u*, namely *falva-*, as in the form *falva-k* 'villages'. Contrast a stem such as *kapu* 'gate', which has no oblique stem and therefore forms its plural simply as *kapu-k* 'gates'. Another characteristic subtype of oblique-stem alternation involves the long vowels *á* and *é*, which when penultimate in the oblique stem occur as short *a* and *e*, e.g. *madár* 'bird', oblique stem *madara-*, thus: *madara-k* 'birds'.

Broadly speaking, the oblique stem of a noun occurs only to the left of derivational suffixes and older declensional suffixes. This distribution in the present-day language reflects the historical fact that most nouns which now exhibit oblique stems date from at least Ugric and often Finno-Ugric or even Uralic times. An important exception to this distribution is the derivational suffix $=i$, which normally requires the nominative singular form of the stem, e.g. *madár=i* 'avian', *fal=i* 'wall-' as in *fal=i óra* 'wall-clock'.

4   Derivation

Both the verb and the nominal are capable of extensive derivation. Examples of nominal derivation: *ház* (oblique stem *háza-*) 'house'; *ház=i* 'domestic'; *háza=s* 'married'; *ház=i=as* 'homely'; *háza=tlan* 'houseless', especially in the construction *háza=tlan csiga* 'houseless snail' = 'slug'; *háza=cska* 'cottage'; *ház=beli* 'tenant'. Examples of verbal derivation: *fog-* 'seize, grasp'; *fog=ad-* 'accept'; *fog=an-* 'become pregnant, conceive'; *fog=dos-* 'handle, paw at'; *fog=lal-* 'occupy'; *fog=lal=koz-* 'occupy oneself'.

Combined verbal and nominal derivatives are extremely common, e.g. *öle=l=és* 'embrace (noun)', cf. *öle=l-* 'embrace (verb)' and *öl/öle-* 'lap, space between shoulders and knees'; *ad=ag=ol-* 'measure out', cf. *ad=ag* 'portion' and *ad-* 'give'.

Verbal derivation is especially enriched by the coverbs, which are a special class of adverb-like forms. Like preverbs in Slavonic languages, Hungarian coverbs are connected with aspect; like verbal prefixes in German, they are not always to be found in preverbal position (see section 6). The change in meaning effected by the addition of a coverb may be obvious (e.g. *jön* 'comes': *vissza==jön* 'comes back') or less than obvious (e.g. *meg==jön* 'comes (back) to one's proper place (as was hoped/expected)'). Often, the role played by a coverb (or by its absence) is entirely outside the limits of the sentence in which it occurs/is lacking; for example, in the sentence pair

(1) Mikor vetted meg azt a cipőt?
(2) Mikor vetted Ø   azt a cipőt?

both translatable as 'when did you buy those shoes?', sentence (1) is a sincere request for information, while sentence (2) may veil criticism of the shoes' appearance.

5   Lexicon, History

The existence of Hungarian independent of its closest congeners Mansi and Khanty is reckoned to be some 2,500 to 3,000 years old. Evidence of early forms of Hungarian may be found in documents only for the last millennium of this period. The earliest such documents are Arab, Persian and Byzantine political and geographical tracts in which Hungarian personal and tribal names are cited in isolation. While extremely useful as historic and linguistic sources, such documents contain no connected passages of Hungarian. The oldest source to contain a running text in Hungarian is the *Halotti Beszéd* (Funeral Oration), c. 1200, a free — and elegant — translation of a Latin text contained in the same codex.

The first 1,500 to 2,000 years of the Hungarian language can be studied only indirectly, through the historiography of neighbouring peoples and with the aid of the tools of archaeology, philology, and linguistics. For example, the frequent denomination of the Hungarians as 'Turks' in various early sources (e.g. *toúrkoi* in the mid-tenth century *De Administrando Imperio* of Constantinos Porphyrogennetos) suggests that from the seventh to the ninth centuries at least a part of the Hungarians were under Turkic dominance.

It is the evidence of loanwords, however, which paints the most vivid picture of this long period in Hungarian chronology and culture. The trajectory of migration, first southward, then westward, from the Urals to the Carpathian basin, can be traced in reverse by unpeeling, one by one, the layers of foreign elements in the Hungarian lexicon.

Immediately beneath the rich top layer of pan-Europeanisms such as *atléta* 'athlete', *pësszimista* 'pessimist' are hundreds of loans originating in or mediated through German. Thus, from the eighteenth and nineteenth centuries: *copf* 'braid; pigtail', *púdër* '(cosmetic) powder', *fasírt* 'ground meat' (*falschiert(es Fleisch)*), *vigéc* 'commercial traveller (slang)' (*wie geht's*), *priccs* 'cot'; from the sixteenth and seventeenth centuries: *lakáj* 'lackey', *prés* 'wine-press', *tucat* 'dozen', *pisztoly* 'pistol'. Older still (twelfth to fifteenth centuries) are such loans as *hercëg* 'duke', *kastély* 'castle', *tánc* 'dance', *céh* 'guild', *polgár* 'Bürger', *ostrom* 'siege, attack' (*Sturm*).

Of loanwords from the Romance languages, the most recent (and thinnest) layer is borrowed from Rumanian. Although the oldest known Rumanian loanword in Hungarian, *ficsúr* 'dandy, fop', dates from the fourteenth century, most are from the sixteenth to the eighteenth centuries: *cimbora* 'pal, crony', *poronty* 'brat', *málé* 'polenta, corn-cake', *tokány* 'a kind of ragoût', *cujka* 'a kind of fruit brandy'.

The richest stock of Romance vocabulary is from Italian. Hungarian-Italian contacts grew in breadth and intensity from military, then trade contacts with Venice in thirteenth-century Dalmatia through the Angevin dynasty (1308–86), culminating in the decidedly Tuscan-oriented rule of Mathias I, 'Corvinus' (ruled 1458–90). Examples: *dús* 'luxurious' (from Venetian *dóse* 'doge', probably by way of Croatian), *paszomány* 'braiding, piping', *piac* 'market-place', *lándzsa* 'lance', *pálya* 'course, track'.

There is also a small set of loanwords from Old French and Provençal dating from the twelfth and thirteenth centuries (later French influence, in the eighteenth and nineteenth centuries, was filtered through Vienna and therefore through German; cf. *púdër* above). Although the earliest French contacts were monastic (Benedictines, Cistercians, Premonstratensians), the earliest Old French loanwords are secular in meaning, e.g. *lakat* '(pad)lock' (*loquet*), *mécs* 'wick' (*mèche*), *kilincs* 'latch' (*clinche*).

Religious vocabulary, not surprisingly, is overwhelmingly Latin in origin, e.g. *templom* 'house of worship', *mise* 'mass', *ostya* 'Host', *angyal* 'angel'. The list extends even to terms exclusively Protestant in implementation, e.g. *ëklézsia* 'congregation', *kollégium* 'dormitory' (originally 'seminary'). Although Latin loanwords belong primarily to the area of Christian terminology, numerous other semantic areas may also be cited, e.g. schooling (*tinta* 'ink', *tábla* 'blackboard', *lénia* 'ruler'), medicine and horticulture (*kúra* 'course of treatment', *petrezselyëm* 'parsley') or jurisprudence (*juss* 'patrimony' from Latin *ius*). Even a few Latin adverbs survive in present-day colloquial Hungarian: *persze* 'of course' (*per sē*), *plánë* 'especially' (*plānē* 'smoothly; really'); note also *ipse* 'fellow, chap' (*ipse* 'he himself'). The time-frame for Latin influence on the Hungarian lexicon is extremely broad: Latin was (at least nominally) the official language of the Kingdom of Hungary from its inception (1001) until the mid-nineteenth century. On the other hand, direct ties to the Christian East were tenuous and short-lived, a fact reflected in the very small number of words borrowed directly from the Byzantine Greek: *paplan* 'quilt', *iszák* 'knapsack', *katona* 'soldier' and perhaps a few others.

The two largest and most important sets of loanwords are those from Slavonic and Turkic languages. It is not surprising, given the geographical location of Hungary, that loans from the Slavonic languages are both numerous (c. 500) and central to basic vocabulary. Examples drawn only from the Hungarian word stock beginning with *p-* are *pad* 'bench', *palack* 'bottle', *pálinka* 'distilled spirits', *pap* 'clergyman', *pëcsënye* 'roast', *patak* 'brook', *pëlënka* 'diaper', *poloska* 'bedbug', *pók* 'spider', *puszta* 'bare, deserted'. Slavonic languages served as mediators for terminology of both Byzantine(-Christian) and Roman Christian culture. Examples of the former: *terëm* '(large public) room', *pitvar* 'porch', *palota* 'palace', *kërëszt* 'cross'; of the latter: *malaszt* 'grace', *apáca* 'nun'. The intensity and variety of contact with different forms of Slavonic may be inferred from doublets internal to Hungarian such as *vacsora* 'evening meal', *vëcsërnye* 'Vespers'; *rozsda* 'rust', *ragya* 'mildew; rust (on plant)'; *mëgye* 'county', *mezsgye* 'boundary-mark between ploughed fields'; *család* 'family', *cseléd* 'servant'.

The Turkic component of the Hungarian lexicon is a unique amalgam of elements borrowed from several different Turkic peoples over a span of some 1,500 years. The most recent layer dates from the Ottoman (Osmanli) occupation (sixteenth and seventeenth centuries); this layer is quite thin (about 30 words), e.g. *zseb* 'pocket', *findzsa* 'demi-tasse', *korbács* 'scourge', *kávé* 'coffee'. An earlier layer, also quite thin, of Turkic loanwords dates from the two or three centuries following the arrival of the Hungarians in Europe (tenth to thirteenth centuries). The words of this layer are borrowed from the languages of the Pechenegs and the Cumans, e.g. *csősz* 'field-guard', *koboz* 'a type of lute', *orosz* 'Russian'.

By far the most numerous and culturally significant, however, are the loanwords taken from Turkic languages during the Hungarian migration westward across southern Russia. Some 300 such loanwords entered during this period (roughly fifth to ninth centuries). A small sampling reveals the cultural breadth and depth of this Old Turkic component of the Hungarian lexicon: *dél/dele-* 'south, noon', *idő* 'time', *szél/szele-* 'wind', *szám* 'number', *ok* 'cause', *tanú* 'witness', *ír-* 'write', *bocsát-* 'forgive', *sátor/sátra-* 'tent', *sëprő* 'broom', *szék* 'chair', *gyümölcs* 'fruit', *szőlő* 'grape', *bor* 'wine', *bika* 'bull', *ökör/ökr-* 'ox', *borjú/borja-* 'calf', *ünő* 'heifer', *disznó* 'pig', *gödény* 'pelican', *kar* 'arm', *boka* 'ankle', *gyomor/gyomr-* 'stomach', *köldök* 'navel', *szakáll/szakálla-* 'beard', *szeplő* 'freckle'.

Older still are three thin layers of Iranian loanwords acquired at the earliest stages of the Hungarian migration. To the most recent of these three layers belong *vám* 'tithe, toll, customs-station' and *vásár* 'bazaar' from Persian; older are *híd/hida-* 'bridge' and *asszony* 'woman (as opposed to girl)', from Alanic (= Old Ossete); and oldest are *tehén/tehene-* 'cow', *tej/teje-* 'milk', *nemez* 'felt', and perhaps *vászon/vászna-* 'linen', from an Iranian language which cannot be precisely identified.

But the oldest layers of the Hungarian vocabulary are of course not borrowed at all; rather, they are descended from the common Ugric, Finno-Ugric or Uralic lexical stock. To these layers belong hundreds of basic vocabulary items from such semantic domains as kinship (*fiú/fia-* 'son', *mëny/mënye-* 'daughter-in-law', *vő/veje-* 'son-in-law', *öcs/öccs(é)-* 'younger brother'); parts of the body (*fej/feje-* 'head', *szëm* 'eye', *nyelv/nyelve-* 'tongue', *ín/ina-* 'tendon', *epe* 'gall', *máj/mája-* 'liver'); natural phenomena (*ég/ege-* 'sky', *hajnal* 'dawn', *tél/tele-* 'winter', *jég/jege-* 'ice', *tó/tava-* 'lake'); animals, hunting and fishing (*fogoly/fogly-* 'partridge', *fajd* 'grouse', *íj/íja-* 'bow', *nyíl/nyila-* 'arrow', *hal/hala-* 'fish', *háló* 'net'); and primary functions and activities expressed by monomorphemic verbs (*lësz/lëv-* 'become', *él-* 'live', *hal-* 'die', *öl-* 'kill', *mëgy/mën-* 'go', *jön/jöv-* 'come', *ëszik/ëv-* 'eat', *iszik/iv-* 'drink').

The statistically preponderant component of the Hungarian lexicon is neither borrowed nor inherited. These words are constructions built from mostly native elements during the independent existence of Hungarian; they range in age and type from unconscious and doubtless quite old onomatopoeic and affective vocabulary (e.g. *rëcs=ëg* 'creak, squeak', *krák=og* 'caw', *mëk=ëg* 'bleat', *hömpöly=ög* 'billow, surge') to conscious creations which often can be attributed to a particular language reformer who either sired or fostered them, for example *vissz+hang* 'back+sound' = 'echo' (Dávid Baróti Szabó, 1739–1819), *könny+elmű* 'light+minded' = 'heedless' (Ferenc Kazinczy, 1759–1831). Thousands of such new terms survived but briefly, e.g. *ibl=any* 'violet+(suffix)' = 'iodine' (Pál Bugát, 1793–1845); in this and countless similar instances, the Hungarian term which prevailed is the Europeanism (*jód* 'iodine').

The creation of new vocabulary of this sort, termed language renewal (*nyelvújítás*), was practised even by its harshest critics, e.g. Ferenc Verseghy (1757–1822) who, on the analogy of verb/noun pairs such as *tag=ol-/tag* 'dismember/member', introduced such new coinages as *gúny* 'mockery', *pazar* 'spendthrift', by subtracting the final *ol*-sequence from the verbs *gúnyol* 'mock' and *pazarol* 'squander'.

6 Syntax

In the noun phrase, demonstratives alone agree in number and case with their head, e.g. *ez-ëk-ben a nagy görög ládá-k-ban* 'in these large Greek crates', where *nagy* 'large' and *görög* 'Greek' lack the plural and inessive suffixes *-(ë)k* and *-bạn*. Cumulative plural subjects are usually construed with a singular predicate, especially if they are members of a coherent semantic set, e.g. *a só mëg a bors itt van a ládá-ban* 'the salt and pepper are (lit: is) here in the crate'.

The elements of a Hungarian sentence are ordered according to the textually and contextually determined factors of topic (what is assumed) and focus (the central component of the comment about the topic). Focus position is immediately to the left of the finite verb; topic position is normally sentence-initial. Thus in the sentence *a pék elfutott* 'the baker ran away', the baker (*a pék*) is the topic and 'away' (*el*) is the focus of the comment about him. By relocating the coverb *el*, the baker can be made into the focus: *a pék futott el* 'it is the baker who ran away'. The coverb can also be placed in sentence-initial position and thus be topicalised: *el a pék futott* 'as for (running) away, it is the baker (who did that)'.

The situation is much more complex, however, since certain grammatical and semantic categories are inherently associated with focus, for example negation in the examples *a pék nem futott el* 'the baker did not run away', *nem a pék futott el* 'it is not the baker who ran away', *el nem a pék futott* 'as for (running) away, it is not the baker (who did that)'. Different stress patterns produce different types of contrastive focus, e.g. *a pék nem 'elfutott, hanem 'befutott* 'the baker didn't run *away*, he ran *in*', or *a pék nem el'futott, hanem el'sétált* 'the baker didn't *run* away, he *sauntered* away'. For many speakers, stress also plays a role in the rendering of aspect. Thus if both verb and coverb receive stress in the sequence *a pék futott el* cited above, the meaning is something like 'the baker was (in the act of) running away'.

Bibliography

Three general works on Hungarian can be recommended: Simonyi (1907) is still the best introduction, encyclopaedic and circumstantial; Sauvageot (1971) is an insightful overview, primarily historical; Benkő and Imre (1972) is a general work, whose best chapters are those by Hajdú and Imre. Lotz (1939) is an unsurpassed reference grammar. Given the importance of derivation in Hungarian, the reverse-alphabetised dictionary by Papp (1969) is indispensable.

References

Benkő, L. and S. Imre (eds.) 1972. *The Hungarian Language* (Mouton, The Hague and Paris)

Lotz, J. 1939. *Das ungarische Sprachsystem* (Ungarisches Institut, Stockholm)

Papp, F. 1969. *A magyar nyelv szóvégmutató szótára/Reverse-Alphabetized Dictionary of the Hungarian Language* (Akadémiai Kiadó, Budapest)

Sauvageot, A. 1971. *L'Édification de la langue hongroise* (Klincksieck, Paris)

Simonyi, S. 1907. *Die ungarische Sprache* (Karl J. Trübner, Strassburg)

29 Finnish

Michael Branch

1 Introduction

Finnish (native name *suomi*) is one of a group of closely related and to some
extent mutually intelligible languages, known collectively as Baltic-Finnic.
They are spoken mainly in the Republic of Finland, the Karelian ASSR
(USSR), the Estonian Soviet Socialist Republic, and adjacent areas of the
Russian and Latvian Soviet Socialist Republics. The other languages in the
group and the numbers of peoples speaking them (according to the 1979
Soviet census figures) are: Karelian, 138,400; Vepsian, 8,100; Ingrian, 700;
Estonian, 1,019,900. Of historical interest, but almost extinct are Votic
(c. 30) and Livonian (c. 500). Finnish and Estonian are also spoken by
migrants and descendants of migrants in Sweden and North America. Of the
present-day population of Finland, c. 4,900,000, the vast majority, speak
Finnish as their first language. Of the total population of Finland
approximately 300,000 Finnish citizens speak Finland-Swedish as their first
language and, depending on the statistical source, between 1,500 and 5,000
speak Lapp (*sami*); most speakers of Finland-Swedish and the Lapp dialects
of Finland are also competent in Finnish.

The relationship of Finnish to the other major Finno-Ugric language,
Hungarian, is described elsewhere in this book (see pages 569–70).
Attempts to reconstruct anything more than a relative chronology of the two
languages' separate development from ancient Finno-Ugric origins are
inevitably speculative, and indeed there remain many uncertainties even
about the historical development of the Baltic-Finnic languages. Until
recently, scholars had assumed that speakers of a language of Finno-Ugric
origin, 'Pre-Finnic', had migrated from regions to the east and southeast,
reaching the area of present-day Estonia about 500 BC. There they were
thought to have lived for several centuries in close contact first with Ancient
Balts and then with groups of East Germanic peoples. According to this
theory, about two thousand years ago a group of people speaking 'Proto-
Finnic' — a development of 'Pre-Finnic' — was thought to have divided into
smaller units which slowly migrated in various directions: south and south-
east, north across the Gulf of Finland into Finland proper, and north-east

around the Gulf into Ladoga Karelia and thence into eastern Finland or further north and north-east into Olonets and Archangel Karelia. It was further thought that the northern lands into which these groups had migrated were largely empty of population apart from groups of Lapps, who had moved north ahead of the Baltic-Finnic newcomers and who spoke a language that derived, probably through borrowing, from 'Pre-Finnic'.

In recent years, comparative multidisciplinary research has led to substantial revision of this theory. Archaeologists have shown that Finland has been continuously inhabited for at least 8,000 years; comparative linguists and ethnographers now believe that speakers of Germanic and Baltic languages have inhabited various parts of the lands now occupied by speakers of the Baltic-Finnic languages for at least the last 3,500 years. Thus the early theory of a clearly stratified hierarchy of language contact and development has given way to one of a mosaic of sporadic contacts over a far longer time and probably of greater influence in shaping the grammar, syntax and lexicon of the Baltic-Finnic languages than had earlier been thought possible.

A number of dialects, from which present-day Finnish took shape, were probably being spoken in southern and western Finland in the early centuries AD. The available evidence indicates an area of small, isolated settlements, inhabited by hunters and fishermen; wandering northwards they began to combine pastoralism with food gathering and then slowly adapted to a primitive agricultural way of life, largely dependent on burn-beat cultivation. In the southern coastal regions contacts were formed with traders coming from the east and Vikings from the west. Although fragments of Christianity began to penetrate from the east during the late dark ages, the inhabitants' religious world-view appears to have been shamanistic, and it was not until the twelfth century, with the Swedish Crusades, that efforts were made to replace this ancient world-view with that of Roman Catholic Christianity. At the same time a centrally based system of government was instituted which demanded faith in the Christian deity, loyalty to a ruler, service to those in authority and the payment of taxes. The confluence in Finland of influences from various directions and their impact on Arctic and sub-Arctic cultures account for the present-day east-west distribution of linguistic, anthropological and ethnographical distinctive features along an axis running north-west from the region of Viipuri in the south to Oulu in the north; historically and politically this division was fixed by the Treaty of Schlüsselburg signed between Sweden and Novgorod in 1323. Although there have been various changes in the frontier since then (notably in 1595, 1617, 1721, 1743, 1809 and 1944), none of these has altered in any significant way the east-west linguistic, anthropological and ethnographical division.

Since the late middle ages the dominant political and cultural influences that have shaped — and preserved — Finnish were religion and nationalism.

The earliest written record known to survive in a Baltic-Finnic language is a spell written in a Karelian dialect, and dated to the thirteenth century. Although there is sufficient evidence from secular and non-secular sources to show that Finnish was in use as a written language during the late middle ages, when the Church of Rome was still dominant, the earliest surviving specimens of continuous passages in Finnish date from the 1540s with the publication in 1542 of Bishop Mikael Agricola's *Abckiria* ('ABC book'), the first known printed book to appear after the declaration of the Reformation in Finland in 1527. This was followed by various liturgical and biblical works written or translated in a 'literary' language which was codified from dialects spoken in south-west Finland and which was to remain the canonical form of Finnish until the early nineteenth century.

The growth of a national consciousness that began at the end of the eighteenth century awoke among a small but influential number of intellectuals a desire to cultivate a distinctive Finnish national identity rooted in the Finnish language. This ideal gained powerful momentum early in the nineteenth century when Finland became a Grand Duchy in the Russian Empire, and the following generation of nationalists took as their aim the elevation of Finnish to equal standing with Swedish as a language of government, trade, commerce, education and culture. This aim was achieved in 1863 with the issue of the Language Edict. A literary language, codified in the course of the nineteenth century, retained much of the old canon, although its structure and lexicon were revised and standardised to take account of the dialects of Eastern Finland that had acquired prominence through the publication in 1835 and 1849 of Elias Lönnrot's compilation of oral epic poems, *Kalevala*.

Finnish shares with Hungarian a rich vocalism, but unlike Hungarian it has relatively few consonant phonemes. It is an agglutinative language with a complex but consistent regularity in its morphophonology; inflectional suffixes, of which a large number have cognates in most other Finnic-Ugric languages, account for a wide range of grammatical functions, while a large stock of derivational suffixes provides a productive source of word creation. Of particular interest in the structure of Finnish is the case system and the variety of finite and non-finite verbal categories. (In the present description of the characteristic features of Finnish, the typographic conventions used in the chapter on Hungarian have been observed (i.e. suffixes are written to the right of a hyphen (-) if they are inflectional, or to the right of an equals sign (=) if they are derivational.))

2 Phonology and Orthography

The orthography of standard Finnish is for the most part phonetic. With three exceptions each letter represents a single phoneme; with two exceptions all sounds are marked orthographically. If a letter is written twice, it indicates that quantity is double the length of a single sound.

2.1 Vowels

Finnish has eight monophthong phonemes and sixteen diphthong phonemes. The short front vowels are *ü* (*y* in orthography), *ö* and *ä*; *i* and *e* are regarded as 'neutral' vowels in respect of vowel harmony; the back vowels are *u*, *o* and *a*. The front vowel *ä* is pronounced as in English *bad*; the other two front vowels are pronounced as in German. The back vowels are pronounced as in English *pull*, *hot* and *father*. The neutral vowels *i* and *e* are as in English *hit* and *pet*. Each of these sounds can be pronounced long, doubling the quantity but not changing the quality.

Table 29.1: Finnish Vowel Phonemes

Monophthongs	i		y		u		ii		yy		uu
	e		ö		o		ee		öö		oo
		ä		a				ää		aa	
Diphthongs	ei		äy		eu						
	äi										
	ui										
	ai				au						
	oi				ou						
	öi		öy								
	yi										
	ie										
			yö		uo						
					iu						

With the exception of certain recent loanwords, the vowels in a Finnish word are subject to partial assimilation. This phenomenon, known as *vowel harmony*, requires that all the vowels of a word are front or back depending on the category of the vowel in the first syllable of the word. In compound words vowel harmony affects each lexical component separately, e.g. *työaika*: *työ* 'work' + *aika* 'time'. This assimilatory phenomenon determines suffix-vowel selection in those inflectional and derivational suffixes which allow front/back vowel opposition: e.g. *pöydä-llä* 'on the table' but *tuoli-lla* 'on the chair'. In compound words vowel harmony in suffixes is determined by the vowel category of the final lexical component. Each neutral vowel word has a fixed requirement for front or back suffixal forms determined on historical grounds: e.g. *silmä-llä* 'with an eye' but *silla-lla* 'on the bridge'; *elä-mä-llä-än* 'by his/her life' but *ehdo-i-lla-an* 'on his/her conditions'. On the basis of such oppositions some scholars classify the neutral vowels as each having front and back allophones: the /e/ opposition has a cognate in

Estonian front -*e*- and back -*õ*-, while the /i/ variation can be compared with a similar phenomenon in Hungarian (see pages 578–9).

2.2 Consonants

The consonant system has 15 phonemes and 13 letters. Letters preceded by an asterisk (*) occur only in foreign toponyms and commercial brand names or in very recent loans; for many speakers the pronunciation of these sounds will vary between the non-Finnish sound and an assumed Finnish correspondent. A hyphen to the right of a consonant (e.g. h-) indicates that it occurs only in syllable-initial position, to the left (-h) only in syllabic-final positions; hyphens on either side (-d-) indicate that the sound can occur only in a word-medial position. Underlining indicates that the item also occurs as a long sound and in orthography is written twice.

Table 29.2: Finnish Consonant Phonemes

Phonemes			Orthography			Recent loans		
r			r					
l	j		l	j				
m n	-ŋ-/-ŋŋ-		m	n	nk/ng			
p t	k -ʔ		p	t	k ∅	*b	*d- *g-	
-d-			d					
s	h- -h		s	h	h	*f	*š	
v			v(w)					*z
						*ts/*c *tš		

The pronunciation of the consonant phonemes is close to that of English. The lack of voiced/unvoiced opposition among the stops, of an apical sibilant *s* (Finnish *s* is more palatalised than general European *s*) and of an unvoiced labio-dental *f*, however, results in less marked opposition between the distinctive categories. Thus Finnish *v* is more labialised than in English. The final-position glottal stop /ʔ/ represents a former /k/ that occurred word-finally after /e/ and as a component of suffixes marking the final sound of the short infinitive (e.g. *haluta* 'to want') and certain negative and imperative forms. In spoken Finnish the glottal can be heard if followed by a vowel sound; otherwise it assimilates with a following consonant to form a long sound: e.g. *perhe saapuu* pronounced /perhessaapuu/ 'the family arrives'; *en käytä maitoa* /enkäytämmaitoa/ 'I don't take milk'. Partial assimilation occurs at word juncture where a final dental nasal is followed by a bilabial stop, e.g. *talonpoika* /talompoika/ 'farmer'.

2.3 Quantity and Syllable Structure

Opposition between a long and short sound is an important distinctive feature (e.g. *tapan* 'I kill', but *tapaan* 'I meet'; *tuli palaa* 'the fire burns' but *tuuli palaa* 'the wind returns'). A syllable may have only one vowel sound. The minimum component of a syllable is a vowel (i.e. a short or long monophthong or a diphthong). A syllable ending in a vowel is classified as 'open': e.g. *vai/ke/a* 'difficult', *sa/no/a* 'to say', both of which have three syllables. The second syllable type, classified 'closed', comprises [vowel +consonant] or [consonant+vowel+consonant]: e.g. *Hel/sin/ki/in* 'to Helsinki', which has four syllables. Variation in the 'open' or 'closed' status of a syllable is determined by the addition of inflectional and derivational suffixes and frequently causes a phonological change at the word stem (see sections 3.1.1 and 3.1.2).

2.4 Stress

The main stress falls on the first syllable of a word, with decreasing secondary stress on the third and fifth syllables; similarly sentence intonation is generally falling, although there may be a small rise at the beginning of the final word or constituent.

3 Inflection

3.1 The Word Stem

Morphophonemic alternation at the juncture of the word stem is a characteristic feature of Finnish. It is determined by the phonology and environment of derivational and inflectional suffixes and accounts for the 85 declension classes and 45 conjugation classes identified in the definitive dictionary of Finnish, *Nykysuomen sanakirja*. In respect of morphophonemic alternation this classification into nominal and verbal categories is functional, serving the purpose of convenient grammatical description. In effect, the 130 classes listed in the *Nykysuomen sanakirja* represent the narrow realisation of regular phonemic change conditioned by specific morphological and phonemic environments.

The phonemic features underlying this complex set of realisations at the end of the word stem are consonant gradation, total or partial consonant assimilation, vowel mutation, and vowel loss (Holman's terminology). They can operate either singly or in various combinations. The environment in which they operate is determined by stress, which varies according to the syllable in which the stem juncture is located (see section 2.4), and by the phonology of the set of suffixes added to the word. In distinguishing between various forms of the narrow realisation account must also be taken of the historical development of Finnish and in certain cases of the irregular selection of alternative forms to avoid ambiguity. An example of this is the change, or lack of change, in situations where the sounds /t/+/i/ combine, yielding either *-si-* at a very early period (e.g. *ves-i-llä* 'on the waters', *halus-i* 'wanted') but *-ti-* at a later period (e.g. *tina* 'tin', *vuot-i* 'leaked'). The difference between the noun forms is explained by historical period (i.e. the change *ti* > *si* had ceased to be effective by the time the Germanic **tina-* had entered Finnish), but it is the need to avoid homonymic clash that accounts for the variation in the verbal forms (**vuosi* would conflict with the noun *vuosi* 'year').

Suffixes are added to an oblique stem. Every Finnish word has an oblique stem ending in a vowel. In many words this is the only stem and for nominals it is often identical with the nominative case which is also the dictionary referent (e.g. *yö* 'night', *talo* 'house', *asema* 'station', *ruskea* 'brown'). For those verbs which have only one oblique stem the stem is identified by removing the infinitive marker from the dictionary referent, i.e. the short 1st infinitive (e.g. *syödä* → *syö-* 'eat', *sanoa* → *sano-* 'say', *lähteä* → *lähte-* 'depart'). In certain nominals, however, the vowel of the oblique stem differs from that of the nominative: e.g. *järve-* 'lake' but nominative *järvi*, *suure-* 'large' but nominative *suuri*. In such cases the stem vowel should be considered primary and the vowel of the nominative stem as the result of sound change in final, unmarked positions. As with the /t/+/i/ feature discussed above, such change is historically determined, as can be seen from comparison of *risti* 'cross', which has the oblique stem *risti-* (a Slavonic loan adapted to the prevailing phonological system of early Finnish by simplification of the initial consonant cluster through consonant loss and of the final cluster through the addition of *-i*). Since *risti* entered Finnish at a time when the *-e* > *-i* change in final unmarked position was no longer operative on new items, the nominative form also functions as the oblique stem.

Several classes of Finnish nominals have, in addition to an oblique stem ending in a vowel, a second oblique stem that ends in a consonant; the stem to which suffixes are added is determined by the morphophonemic environment. Nominals of this type fall into two main categories: those in which the nominative ends in a vowel and those in which it ends in a consonant; in each sub-category the stem to be used is environmentally determined. Examples of the first category are: *tuli* 'fire', vowel stem *tule-* (e.g. genitive *tule-n*), consonant stem *tul-* (e.g. partitive *tul-ta*); *pieni* 'small', (*piene-*, gen. *piene-n*, partitive *pien-tä*); *lumi* 'snow', vowel stem *lume-* (e.g. gen. *lume-n*), consonant stem *lun-* (e.g. partitive *lun-ta*). Examples of consonant-ending nominatives are *sydän* 'heart', vowel stem *sydäme-* (e.g. gen. *sydäme-n*), consonant-stem *sydän-* (partitive *sydän-tä*); *punainen* 'red', vowel stem *punaise-*, consonant stem *punais-* (e.g. *punaise-n*, *punais-ta*).

Reference has already been made to verbs that have only one oblique stem. Similarly, however, there are categories of verbs which also have vowel and consonant stems, whose selection is determined by comparable morphophonemic environmental features. An example of the verb type with a single oblique stem is *puhua* 'to speak' (e.g. *puhu-n* 'I speak', *puhu-kaamme!* 'let us speak'). Sub-categories of the two-stem type are illustrated by *ansaita* 'to earn' and *levätä* 'to rest': vowel stems *ansaitse-* (e.g. *ansaitse-n* 'I earn'), *lepää-* (e.g. *lepää-t* 'you. (sg.) rest'); consonant stems *ansait-* (e.g. *ansait-kaa!* '(you pl.) earn!'), *levät-* (e.g. *levät-kööt!* 'let them rest').

3.1.1 Consonant Gradation

Alternation caused by consonant gradation affects the stops /k/, /p/ and /t/. The type of alternation depends on the length of the stop and on whether it occurs alone and intervocalically or as the first or second component of an intervocalic cluster of which the other consonant is /m/, /n/, /ŋ/, /l/, /r/, or /h/. Alternation is classed as qualitative or quantitative; a qualitative alternation changes the sound, whereas in a quantitative alternation it is the length of the stop that changes. The operation of alternation is dependent on the status of the stem syllable as determined by the morphophonemic environment: an open syllable requires the strong grade of the alternation, a closed syllable the weak grade, though subsequent changes have sometimes obscured the original environment. Thus there is in Finnish a strong/weak gradation correlation with open/closed syllable form (see page 598). The most common examples of gradation are illustrated in table 29.3.

Table 29.3: Finnish Consonant Gradation

			Strong		*Weak*	
Quantitative						
kk	~	k	akka-	~	akassa	(inessive 'old woman')
pp	~	p	piippu-	~	piipusta	(elative 'pipe')
tt	~	t	matto-	~	maton	(genitive 'mat')
Qualitative						
t	~	d	vete-	~	vedestä	(elative 'water')
k	~	Ø	ruoka-	~	ruoan	(genitive 'food')
k	~	v	suku-	~	suvulla	(adessive 'family')
p	~	v	lupa-	~	luvatta	(abessive 'promise')
mp	~	mm	kampa-	~	kamman	(genitive 'comb')
nt	~	nn	tunte-	~	tunnen	('I feel')
nk	~	nŋ	hanke-	~	hangella	(adessive 'snow crust')
lt	~	ll	multa-	~	mullassa	(inessive 'soil')
rt	~	rr	saarta-	~	saarramme	('we surround')

Less frequent forms of gradation in standard Finnish are *ht ~ hd*, *lke ~ lje*, *rke ~ rje*, *hke ~ hje*; further variations occur in dialects.

3.1.2 Other Changes at the Stem

Partial consonant assimilation affects intervocalic *-t-* and causes the change *-t- → -s-* in an environment in which it is followed by *-i-* (allowing for the variation described in section 3.1). In nominals this environment arises most commonly from the change of final *-e* → *-i* and from the suffixing of the oblique plural marker, e.g. stem *käte-* 'hand', nominative singular *käsi*, adessive plural *käs-i-llä* 'with the hands'. In verbal forms the environment usually arises from the suffixing of the imperfect *-i-* marker to those categories of verbs that have a consonant stem (see section 3.1), e.g. consonant stem *levät-* 'rest', imperfect *lepäs-i* 'rested'.

Total consonant assimilation at the stem occurs only in verbal morphology and affects the consonant stems ending in *-t-*, *-n-*, *-l-* and *-r-* when suffixes are added to mark the active indicative past participle (*-nut/-nyt*), the active potential mood suffix (*-ne-*), the 1st short infinitive *-ta/-tä* suffix type, and the passive-impersonal present voice of verbs of the same category. In the case of past participles and the potential, total assimilation also occurs in *-s-* consonant stems. The influence of total assimilation in these occurrences is either regressive or progressive. In the case of *-t-* stems, assimilation is regressive after suffixing of the past participle and potential markers (e.g. *levät-* → *levän-nyt, levän-ne-*) but is progressive in its influence on the infinitive and passive-impersonal forms (e.g. *levät-ä, levät-ään*). Total assimilation is progressive in all four verbal forms where the stem consonant is *-n-*, *-r-* or *-l-* (e.g. *pan-* 'put, place' → *pan-nut, pan-ne-, pan-na, pan-naan*; *kuul-* 'hear' → *kuul-lut, kuul-le-, kuul-la, kuul-laan*; *sur-* 'grieve' → *sur-rut, sur-re-, sur-ra, sur-raan*) and in the two forms affecting consonant stems in *-s-* (e.g. *pes-* 'wash' → *pes-syt, pes-se-*).

Vowel mutation or vowel loss at the word stem is caused by the suffixing of *-i-*; in nominals this arises most commonly from the oblique plural suffix, in verbs the *-i-* sound functions as the imperfect tense suffix and as a component of the conditional mood suffix (*-isi-*). In most instances the result of this suffixing is phonemically determined irrespective of nominal or verbal categories. The short stem vowels subject to loss or mutation are *-a-*, *-ä-*, *-e-* and *-i-*. In two-syllable words stem *-a-* labialises if the vowel of the first syllable is *-a-*, *-e-* or *-i-* (e.g. *kirja-* 'book', inessive plural *kirjo-i-ssa; maksa-* 'pay', 3rd person singular imperfect *makso-i*); if the vowel of the first syllable is labial (*-o-* or *-u-*), the stem vowel is lost (e.g. *kunta-* 'group(ing), region', inessive plural *kunn-i-ssa; osta-* 'buy', imperfect *ost-i*). Where the stem vowel of a two-syllable word is *-e-* or *-ä-*, the vowel is always lost (e.g. *isä-* 'father', adessive plural *is-i-llä; kiittä-* 'thank, praise', imperfect *kiitt-i, saare-* 'island', adessive plural *saar-i-lla; näke-* 'see', imperfect *näk-i*).

In nominals only a stem *-i-* mutates to *-e-* (e.g. *viini-* 'wine', inessive plural *viine-i-ssä*). In verb forms only, stem vowels *-a-* and *-ä-* mutate to *-e-* in the formation of the stem form of the passive-impersonal voice (e.g. *hoita-* 'care for', passive-impersonal present *hoide-taan; estä-* 'prevent', passive-impersonal *este-tään*). Both these features also occur in all other syllables of nominals and verbs respectively in the specific categories described. Apart from these specific categories, the short stem vowels discussed above are normally lost in words of more than two syllables when an *-i-* is added; the only exception is -a- which in certain vowel and consonant environments may labialise (e.g. *asia*- 'thing', adessive plural *asio-i-lla*).

The result of suffixing -*i*- markers to a long monophthong or diphthong is shortening of the monophthong or mutation of the diphthong. In the case of all long monophthongs, irrespective of the syllable in which the stem is located, the -*i*- sound becomes the second component of the resulting diphthong (e.g. *maa*- 'land', inessive plural *ma-i-ssa*; *saa*- 'obtain', imperfect 3rd person singular *sa-i*; *saappaa*- 'boot', inessive plural *saappa-i-ssa*; *pelkää*- 'fear', conditional present 3rd person singular *pelkä-isi*; *venee*- 'boat', inessive plural *vene-i-ssä*; *kaunii*- 'beautiful', adessive plural *kauni-i-lla*; *talkoo*- 'group work', adessive plural *talko-i-lla*). A diphthong can occur as a stem vowel in monosyllabic words only. From a synchronic point of view the effect of an -*i*- marker on such stems (unless the second component of the diphthong is also -*i*-) appears to work differently, causing loss of the first component of the diphthong (e.g. *yö*- 'night', inessive plural *ö-i-ssä*; *luo*- 'create', imperfect 3rd person singular *lo-i*; *tie*- 'road, way', adessive plural *te-i-llä*). As each of these diphthongs has evolved from a long monophthong, however (i.e. *öö, *oo, *ee respectively, cf. Estonian cognates *öö*, *loo*-, *tee*), the effect of suffixing the -*i*- sound is historically consistent with the long-monophthong examples. Where diphthong stems end in -*i*-, the stem -*i* can be assumed to have been lost (e.g. *voi*- 'be able', imperfect 3rd person singular *vo-i*). In dialects, alternative realisations of these sound changes are common. A rare example of an alternative realisation becoming established as the canonical form is the imperfect and conditional present of *käy*- 'go, visit' (e.g. 3rd person singular *kävi*, *kävisi*). More common is the destabilising influence of alternative realisations on the standard language, illustrated by the variants *myi*- and *möi*- as acceptable forms for many speakers of the imperfect of *myy*- 'sell'.

3.2 Verbal Morphology and Usage

The finite forms of the Finnish verb comprise two voices, active and passive-impersonal. Each voice has four moods: indicative, potential, conditional and imperative. The indicative mood has four tenses, two primary and two secondary. The primary tenses are the present-future (non-preterite in Holman's classification) and the imperfect; the secondary tenses, formed with the auxiliary *olla* 'to be' and a past participle, are the perfect and pluperfect. The potential, which conveys the possibility of something happening, and the conditional each have one secondary form based on the auxiliary *olla* and a past participle. Apart from certain fixed forms of expression, the potential mood has fallen out of common use in the modern spoken language and occurs with decreasing frequency in modern written usage. Various secondary forms of the imperative can also be construed but their realisation in normal usage is very rare; the use of the imperative in certain specific situations is also decreasing (see section 3.2.2).

3.2.1 Active Voice
In the active voice an inflected verb form can comprise up to four components in fixed sequence. Slot 1: *stem* (including any embedded derivational suffix). Slot 2: *tense/mood suffix*. Slot 3: *number-and-person suffix* (historically both items are present but have undergone partial fusion in the 1st and 2nd persons). Slot 4: *enclitic suffixes*. Back/front variation occurs in vowel components as a result of vowel harmony. Depending on the particular emphasis of a statement and the syntactic environment, the 1st or 2nd personal pronoun can also be used as a separate item in other parts of the sentence either before or after the verb, depending on the nature of the emphasis required. When the subject of the 3rd person is the personal pronoun *hän* 'he, she' or *he* 'they (animate)', the pronoun must be used (except in the imperative mood). The variation in the use of the personal pronouns is probably explained by the fact that the suffixes of the 1st and 2nd persons evolved from suffixing pronominal items to the verb, whereas 3rd-person forms of the active voice appear to derive from an active present participle suffix. Some scholars argue that the [verb + personal suffix] structure of the 1st and 2nd person markers has its realisation in the 3rd person in the passive-impersonal voice, and would prefer to classify the latter as the 4th person of the active voice (see section 3.2.2).

The basic verbal morphological structure, excluding Slot 4, is illustrated in the chart given here, in which the present-future tense of the verb *puhua* 'to speak' is conjugated.

The Present-future Tense of *puhua*

	Slot 1	*Slot 2*	*Slot 3*	
Personal pronoun	Stem	Tense/mood suffix	Number/person suffix	Example
[minä]	puhu-	-Ø-	-n	puhun
[sinä]			-t	puhut
hän			stem vowel lengthens	puhuu
[me]			-mme	puhumme
[te]			-tte	puhutte
he			-vat/-vät	puhuvat

This paradigm structure applies to all verb types in the present-future tense with variation only in the formation of the 3rd person singular. Instead of lengthening the stem vowel, verbs with long-vowel or diphthong stems mark the 3rd person singular by -Ø (e.g. stems *jää-* 'remain', *syö-* 'eat', *luetteloi-* 'classify' → 3 sg. *jää*, *syö*, *luetteloi*).

In the imperfect, the tense suffix (Slot 2) is *-i-*, in the potential present the mood suffix (Slot 2) is *-ne-*, and in the present conditional it is *-isi-*, e.g.

imperfect: *puhu-i-n, puhu-i-t, hän puhu-i* etc. ('I spoke' etc.). In all forms of the imperfect the 3rd p. singular marker is -∅- (see section 3.1.2).

potential: *puhu-ne-n, puhu-ne-t, hän puhu-ne-e*, etc. ('I might speak' etc.). As discussed above (see section 3.1.2), a morphophonemic feature of the potential in certain verb types is the use of a consonant stem with regressive or progressive assimilation at the stem juncture (e.g. *tule-* 'come' → potential *tullen; nouse-* 'rise' → *nousset*).

conditional: *puhu-isi-n, puhu-isi-t, hän puhu-isi*, etc. ('I should speak' etc.).

The secondary forms of the active indicative, potential and conditional are formed with the appropriate tenses or moods of the auxiliary *olla* and an active past participle formed from [verb stem + suffix *-nut/-nyt*, plural *-neet*]. Where the participle is formed from a consonant stem, regressive or progressive assimilation at the stem juncture occurs in specific morphophonemic environments (e.g. *ole-* 'be' → *ollut*, plural *olleet* 'been', see section 3.1.2). The conjugation of the auxiliary *olla* follows the above pattern but with two differences: the 3rd person forms of the present-future tense are *on* and *ovat* respectively, and in the potential mood the auxiliary is the cognate *liene-* 'might be', e.g.

perfect: *olen, olet, hän on puhu-nut, olemme, olette, he ovat puhu-neet*; pluperfect: *olin puhunut*, etc.; potential perfect: *lienen puhunut*, etc.; conditional perfect: *olisin puhunut*, etc.

Negation in all the above forms is based on a negative auxiliary: [*e-* + person marker] (i.e. *en, et, hän ei, emme, ette, he eivät*). Tense or mood is indicated by the form of the principal verb. In the present tense this is [verb stem + orthographically unmarked glottal] (e.g. *en puhu*). The imperfect negative is indicated by [negative verb + past participle of the principal verb] (e.g. *en puhunut, emme puhuneet*). In the potential and the conditional it is the mood stem that follows the negative auxiliary verb (e.g. potential *hän ei puhune, he eivät puhune*; conditional *en puhuisi, emme puhuisi, he eivät puhuisi*).

Structurally the fourth mood, the imperative, comprises similar components although they have a different morphophonemic realisation. Thus *sano-* 'say' has the forms: 2nd person singular [*sano-* + orthographically unmarked glottal]; 3rd person singular *sano-koon*; plural *sano-kaamme, sano-kaa, sano-koot* (front vowel variants: *-köön, -käämme, -kää, -kööt*). Similarly, the negative employs an auxiliary *äl-* (thus *äl-ä, äl-köön*, etc.) followed by a form of the principal verb, e.g. [*sano-* + orthographically unmarked glottal], in the 2nd person singular, and by the form [principal verb + *-ko/-kö*] (e.g. *sanoko*) in all other forms, e.g. *älä sano* but *älkäämme sanoko*). The function of the imperative tends to be instructional in the 1st person plural and in the second persons, but exhortative in the third persons. In normal modern speech the use of the passive-impersonal voice is more common for the persuasive or exhortative imperative in the 1st person plural. Thus the grammatical imperative *menkäämme!* 'let's go!' is likely to be used in situations where orders are expected to be given and obeyed, whereas in ordinary social situations the passive-impersonal *mennään!* is preferred.

3.2.2 Passive-impersonal

The morphological structure of the passive-impersonal voice has the same pattern as the active voice forms; morphological differences concern the stem (Slot 1) and the number-person suffix (Slot 3). Historically the stem appears to have embedded in it a derivational suffix which once generated a reflexive or medio-passive function. The mood and tense markers are identical with those of the active voice. According to some scholars the person component of the number-person suffix consists of items cognate with the historical form of the 3rd person singular pronoun *hän*. The passive-impersonal verb paradigm is illustrated by *sanoa* 'to say' and *lähteä* 'to depart'.

The Passive-impersonal Voice of *sanoa* and *lähteä*

Present/future	sano-taan	lähde-tään
Imperfect	sano-ttiin	lähde-ttiin
Potential	sano-tta-neen	lähde-ttä-neen
Conditional	sano-tta-isiin	lähde-ttä-isiin
Past participle	sano-tt-u	lähde-tt-y

The negative auxiliary is the 3rd person singular *ei*, while the mood and tense are marked by the appropriate passive-impersonal stem (e.g. present-future *ei sanota*, conditional *ei lähdettäisi*). Regular variation in stem forms and in the length and form of vowels and consonants is explained by the working of consonant gradation, various forms of assimilation, mutation and loss of vowels and consonants (see sections 3.1.1, 3.1.2).

All verbs can occur in the passive-impersonal voice irrespective of their transitivity or intransitivity. In modern literary Finnish a very common function of this voice is to express impersonal general statements of the kind introduced in German by *man* or in French by *on* (e.g. *täällä puhutaan suomea* 'Finnish spoken here'). In modern colloquial language, the use of the passive-impersonal in sentence-initial position is the usual way of expressing the 1st person plural imperative (e.g. *syödään!* 'let's eat!'). When preceded by the personal pronoun *me* 'we', a passive-impersonal form commonly — and in some social groups, always — replaces the active first person plural forms (e.g. *me lähdetään kotiin junalla* 'we shall go home by train', *me oltiin siellä kaksi viikkoa* 'we were there for two weeks'). In active functions of this kind the object of a transitive verb is also marked (e.g. *me nähtiin sinut koulussa* 'we saw you in school', *me ei osteta omenia* 'we shall not buy any apples').

There is a restricted use of the passive-impersonal voice that corresponds to English passive usage. This is found in statements about an action which is performed intentionally by an inferred but unspecified human agent, e.g. *mies pelastettiin merestä* 'the man was rescued from the sea', i.e. the man was saved by some human intervention. If there had been no information about how the man survived or if his escape had been by his own efforts, Finnish would require the use of an appropriately derived verb in the active voice, e.g. *mies pelastui merestä* 'the man saved himself from the sea'.

3.3 Nominal Morphology and Usage

The morphology of the Finnish noun and adjective provides for the expression of five functions. The noun has five slots in fixed sequence. Slot 1: *stem* (including any embedded derivational suffix). Slot 2: *number* (singular vs. plural). Slot 3: *case suffix*. Slot 4: *personal possessor suffix*. Slot 5: *enclitic suffixes*. Demonstratives and adjectives used attributively precede the noun and there is concord in Slots 2 and 3, but they have no marking in Slot 4. Demonstratives and adjectives may have enclitic suffixes independently of the head word.

In Slots 2, 3, 4 and 5, function is indicated by the opposition zero vs. suffix. In Slot 2 zero marks singular. Grammatical plurality is marked by -*t* in the nominative and accusative cases, by -*t*-, -*i*-, or by both in the genitive case, and by -*i*- in all other cases. If a personal possessor suffix is added to the nominative or accusative plural, the -*t* suffix is not used and plurality is indicated by context or syntax, or both, e.g. *poikani on täällä* 'son-my is here', but *poikani ovat täällä*, where the plural verb *ovat* signifies the plural number of homonymic *poikani*.

3.3.1 The Case System

In Slot 3 a zero suffix indicates nominative singular. All other cases are marked. Back/front variation occurs in the vowel component of certain case suffixes as a result of vowel harmony. In the chart showing the case system the front vowel form follows the stroke in the suffix column; in the partitive, genitive and illative cases, variation in the phonemic structure of the suffix is dependent on the class of word stem (see sections 3.1, 3.1.2). The two examples in the chart, *mies* 'man' and *kirja* 'book' illustrate, in addition to vowel harmony and phonemic structure variation, two stem types: *mies* represents one of the types of word that has a consonant and a vowel stem (e.g. *mies*-, *miehe*-), while *kirja* is typical of words that have only a vowel stem (*kirja*-). Where more than one realisation of a suffix occurs, the form most common in standard usage is given. The accusative case has two suffixes in the singular; *-n* marks the accusative of all nouns and adjectives, *-t* that of the personal pronouns (i.e. *minu-t* 'me', *sinu-t* 'you (familiar)', *häne-t* 'him/her') and the interrogative pronoun *kuka* (accusative *kene-t*) 'who'. In the illative case *-V-* is identical with the stem vowel subsequent to the marking of number; the bracketed form in the translative is used when a personal possessor suffix follows in Slot 4; the bracketed form in the comitative marks attributive adjectives.

The Case System of *mies* and *kirja*

Case	Suffix	Singular	Plural
Nominative	-Ø; -t	mies; kirja	miehet; kirjat
Accusative	-n (-t); -t	miehen; kirjan	miehet; kirjat
Genitive	-n	miehen; kirjan	miesten; kirjojen
General local cases			
Essive	-na/ä	miehenä; kirjana	miehinä; kirjoina
Partitive	-a/ä; -t/ä; -tta/ä	miestä; kirjaa	miehiä; kirjoja
Translative	-ksi (→-kse-)	mieheksi; kirjaksi	miehiksi; kirjoiksi
Interior local cases			
Inessive	-ssa/ä	miehessä; kirjassa	miehissä, kirjoissa
Elative	-sta/ä	miehestä; kirjasta	miehistä; kirjoista
Illative	-Vn; -hVn;		
	-sVVn	mieheen; kirjaan	miehiin; kirjoihin
Exterior local cases			
Adessive	-lla/ä	miehellä; kirjalla	miehillä; kirjoilla
Ablative	-lta/ä	mieheltä; kirjalta	miehiltä; kirjoilta
Allative	-lle	miehelle; kirjalle	miehille; kirjoille
Instructive	-in	miehin; kirjoin	miehin; kirjoin
Comitative	-ineen (-ine)	miehineen; kirjoineen	miehineen; kirjoineen
Abessive	-tta/ä	miehettä; kirjatta	miehittä; kirjoitta

There are marked differences in the productivity of the various cases. Apart from the nominative, the cases in most common use are the accusative, genitive, the three so-called general 'local' cases (essive, partitive, translative) and the six specific 'local' cases, which are subdivided into interior (inessive 'in', elative 'from (outside)', illative 'into') and exterior (adessive 'at or near', ablative 'from (outside)', allative 'to, towards'). Certain cases, such as the instructive (e.g. *hampa-in kyns-in* 'with tooth and nail', *kaik-in voim-in* 'with all one's might') and comitative (e.g. *äiti perhe-ineen* 'the mother accompanied by her family'), are only productive nowadays in very restricted areas of usage. The abessive (e.g. *raha-tta* 'moneyless'), for example, occurs productively mainly in non-finite verbal constructions (see section 5.3); used with nominals it has largely given way to prepositional *ilman* (e.g. *ilman rahaa* 'without money'). In addition to its function as the subject of a sentence the nominative singular stands in certain specific environments as object. The most common of these environments is in marking nouns and adjectives which are the direct object in affirmative sentences of monopersonal (i.e. 3rd person singular) verbs of obligation (e.g. *meidän täytyy ostaa kirja* lit. 'us-to it is necessary buy-to the book'), the 2nd persons and the 1st person plural of the imperative mood (e.g. *osta kirja!* 'buy the book!'), and verbs in the passive-impersonal voice (e.g. *me ostetaan kirja* 'we buy the book'). If the object is a personal pronoun or the interrogative pronoun *kuka*, however, it is marked in all these forms by the *-t* accusative suffix.

In modern Finnish the accusative of nouns and adjectives is marked in the singular by the same suffix as the genitive singular. Historically, however, they are of different origin (acc. *-n* < *-*m*). In affirmative sentences the accusative denotes the object of a resultative action (e.g. *hän osti kirjan* 'he/she bought the book') and an object that is in itself definite and total (e.g. *hän joi maidon* 'he/she drank (all) the milk', cf. partitive object *maitoa* denoting that only some of the milk was drunk). In normal usage the difference in accusative and genitive function of the *-n* suffix is made clear by the contextual and syntactic environment. In the genitive case nominal items precede the constituent they govern (e.g. *nuoren tytön musta koira* 'the young girl's black dog'). The second major area of usage of the genitive case is in the headwords of postpositions (e.g. *talon takana* 'behind the house', *mäen päällä* 'on top of the hill'). In certain constructions the genitive has a dative function. This is most apparent in fixed expressions such as *Jumalan kiitos* 'God-to thanks', i.e. 'thanks be to God', and in statements of state or condition of the kind *minun on jano* 'me-to is thirst', i.e. 'I am thirsty'. The dative function in the expression of obligation occurs with monopersonal verbs (e.g. *minun pitää äänestää* 'I must vote') and in various constructions based on the verb *olla* (e.g. *minun on mentävä* 'I have an obligation to go').

Comparison with other Finno-Ugric languages and the evidence of certain historically fixed forms indicate that the components of the general local case suffixes once denoted various perceptions of location and movement. The essive case appears to have indicated a stationary location (cf. fixed forms *kaukana* 'far away', *ulkona* 'outside'). The partitive marked separation, movement away from the main body or substance (cf. *kaukaa* 'from afar', *ulkoa* 'from outside'). The translative, which historically is much younger than the essive or partitive, appears to have indicated movement towards an object, a function still found in such forms as *lähemmäksi* 'coming closer', *rannemmaksi* 'moving closer to the shore' (e.g. a boat). While comparable spatial and kinetic features underlie certain of the present-day functions of these cases, the specific oppositions of location and movement are expressed with greater precision by the six interior and exterior local cases, in which some features of the morphology of the general local cases are embedded. Adessive *-ssa/-ssä*, for example, is thought to derive from internal location marker *-s* + *n*V, elative *-sta/-stä* from *-s-* + separation marker *-t*V. Similarly the *-n*V and *-t*V components have been identified in the adessive *-lla/-llä* and ablative -*lta*/-*ltä* with the initial -*l*- thought to derive from an exterior locative.

While retaining certain features of their original spatial and kinetic functions all the general local cases have developed additional temporal, syntactic and adverbial functions. The essive denotes various static positional and temporal states, e.g. *hän on opettajana siellä* 'he/she is (in employment as) a teacher there', cf. *hän on opettaja* 'he/she is a teacher (but may not be employed as such)'; *pidän häntä hyvänä opettajana* 'I consider him/her a good teacher', *hän opetti siellä kolmena vuotena* 'he/she taught there for three years'.

In modern Finnish the main function of the partitive case is the marking of various categories of the direct object. The object of any verb in the negative is always in the partitive. In affirmative statements several categories of verbs govern a partitive object (e.g. those expressing emotional values). In opposition with the accusative object, the partitive denotes an incomplete or continuing action (e.g. *Mikko söi kanaa* (partitive object) 'Mikko ate some chicken' but *Mikko söi kanan* (accusative object) 'Mikko ate all the chicken'). Other functions of the partitive include that of subject and predicative, where an indefinite divisible quantity is denoted (e.g. *maitoa* 'some milk', *tulta* 'some fire'). Of the secondary functions performed by the translative, the three most productive are those denoting change of form (e.g. *poika kasvoi mieheksi* 'the boy grew into a man'), time (e.g. *menin sinne kolmeksi kuukaudeksi* 'I went there for three months'), and the expression of purpose or intention (e.g. *poika aikoo lääkäriksi* 'the boy intends to become a doctor').

Schematically the oppositions of exterior and interior space and direction of movement can be represented in part by the same model as for the corresponding cases in Hungarian (see page 585, table 28.3).

Table 29.4: The Finnish Interior and Exterior Local Cases

	Stationary	*Moving* Approaching	Departing
Interior		-Vn	
	-ssa/ä	-hVn	-sta/ä
		-sVVn	
Exterior	-lla/ä	-lle	-lta/ä

Lacking from the Finnish scheme, compared to that of Hungarian, is the closer definition of exterior location and movement in terms of the oppositions of surface, proximity and terminus. In Finnish such distinctions are either contextually determined or require the use of specific postpositions or, less commonly, prepositions.

The range of spatial, temporal and syntactic functions performed by the interior and exterior local cases can be illustrated by the example of the adessive. Spatially it refers to static position on the surface of an object, e.g. *pöydällä* 'on the table', *seinällä* 'on the wall'. In denoting geographic location it functions often in opposition with the static interior case, the inessive, e.g. *maa* 'earth; land; countryside': inessive *maassa* 'in the earth' but *maalla* 'out in the country'; *koulu* 'school': *koulussa* 'in school' but *koululla* 'somewhere on the school premises (inside or outside)'. In temporal expression the adessive denotes time when or during which an action takes place, e.g. *kesällä voimme uida meressä* 'in summer we can swim in the sea', *ensi viikolla olen ulkomailla* 'next week I shall be abroad'. A third area of function is instrumental, denoting the means of performing an action, e.g. *kaadoin koivun kirveellä* 'I felled the tree with an axe', *kuljen Helsinkiin autolla* 'I shall go to Helsinki by car'. A major area of usage is the expression of ownership corresponding to that of English 'have', e.g. *isällä on suuri saari* 'father has a large island', *lehmällä on vasikka* 'the cow has a calf ').

3.3.2 Personal Possessor Suffixes

The fourth slot in the morphology of the noun is occupied by the suffix of personal possessor. The item possessed and its attributes can be preceded by the genitive of the personal pronoun in the 1st and 2nd persons if particular emphasis is required; in the 3rd person the preceding pronoun in the genitive is necessary (cf. use of personal pronouns in the verbal system, section 3.2.1):

Personal Possessor Suffixes

Personal pronoun	Possession suffix	Example		
[minun]	-ni	inessive	veneessäni	'in my boat'
[sinun]	-si	elative	kirjoistasi	'about your books'
hänen	-nsa/ä	nominative	talonsa	'his/her house(s)'
	-Vn	ablative	ystäviltään	'from his/her friends'
		allative	sisarelleen	'to his/her sister'
[meidän]	-mme	adessive	kirkollamme	'at our church'
[teidän]	-nne	elative	kirjeestänne	'from your letter'
heidän	-nsa/ä	illative	kotiinsa	'to their home(s)'
	-Vn	adessive	saarellaan	'on their island'

In modern Finnish the use of the 3rd person suffix *-nsa/ä* is mainly used to mark the singular and plural of the nominative and accusative, when it is added to the vowel stem, and of oblique cases which end in a consonant. The *vowel* + *n* suffix marks possession in oblique cases ending in a vowel; the vowel component is the same as that of the case suffix vowel, thus generating a long vowel. Possession in the oblique cases ending in a vowel may also be marked by the *-nsa/ä* suffix, although this is becoming less frequent.

Where a case suffix ends in a consonant, that consonant is totally assimilated regressively by the adjacent consonant of the person suffix (e.g. *talo* 'house', illative *taloon* → *taloosi* 'into your house', *taloomme* 'into our house'. Assimilation of this kind leads to homonymic conflict: *taloni* can be the singular or plural of the nominative or accusative, or it can be the singular genitive of *talo*; function is defined by context and syntax. This same assimilation process also produces forms in which consonant gradation is expected but does not occur (e.g. *puku* 'suit', nom. plural *puvut*, gen. singular *puvun* produce, for example, *hänen pukunsa* 'his/her suit', *pukumme* 'our suits', *pukunne* 'your suits'). The explanation for this homonymic clash and the absence of consonant gradation rests on a theory of the historical fusion of embedded case and plural markers. Comparison with other Baltic-Finnic languages in which the same feature occurs suggests that, at an ancient period before the fusion of the markers was complete, the strong grade in the personal possessor forms occurred as part of the language's normal morphophonemic variation. As the fusion process produced various realisations, analogy and levelling focused on the present strong grade forms which have remained fixed.

4 Lexicon

The vocabulary of modern Finnish has several sources. A large stock of words for which no loan source can be identified dates from an ancient Finno-Ugric phase and from the subsequent era lasting until the division of the Baltic-Finnic languages into their present groups. For the sake of reference this part of the lexicon may conveniently be called 'indigenous'. Throughout this era and subsequently the vocabulary has been extended both by loans and by the spontaneous and conscious operation of the language's derivation mechanisms on indigenous and loan materials alike. In particular, conscious derivation, compounding and calquing have played an important role in the generation of Finnish since the Reformation; and in the past one hundred and fifty years, with the planned cultivation of Finnish, these mechanisms have enabled the language to handle change and innovation in the modern world.

Examples of words belonging to the oldest Finno-Ugric layers of indigenous vocabulary refer to such categories as parts of the body (*käsi* 'arm, hand', *pää* 'head', *silmä* 'eye'), gender differentiation and kinship (*uros* 'male animal', *naaras* 'female animal', *isä* 'father', *emo* 'mother', *miniä* 'daughter-in-law'), environment and survival (*vesi* 'water', *joki* 'river', *kala* 'fish', *kuu* 'moon', *kota* 'shelter, house', *talvi* 'winter', *jää* 'ice', *lumi* 'snow'), and verbs denoting numerous basic activities (*elä-* 'live', *kuole-* 'die', *kaata-* 'fell', *mene-* 'go', *otta-* 'take', *teke-* 'do, make', *näke-* 'see', *tietä-* 'know').

The oldest layer of loanwords shows the influence of Indo-European languages during the Finno-Ugric period (*mesi* 'honey', *sata* 'hundred') and intermittently thereafter. Vocabulary sheds very little light on the nature of the contacts between the ancestors of the speakers of Finnish during the thousands of years separating the Finno-Ugric period and the earliest documentation of their location in the Baltic-Finnic region in the last centuries BC. Loans dating from the so-called Pre-Finnic and Proto-Finnic periods suggest the existence of contacts concurrently with speakers of Ancient Baltic and Germanic over at least one millennium in various areas north, east and south of the Gulf of Finland. Lexical materials from this phase indicate development in social organisation with some evidence of pastoralism and simple agriculture in addition to improved techniques of food gathering. In each set of examples, words of Ancient Baltic origin are given first, with examples of East or North Germanic origin following the semicolon. The main areas of borrowing represent experience and perception of nature (*meri* 'sea', *routa* 'permafrost'; *aalto* 'wave', *kallio* 'rock, cliff', *turska* 'cod'), parts of the body (*hammas* 'tooth'; *maha* 'stomach', *kalvo* 'membrane'), technology (*aisa* 'harness shaft', *kirves* 'axe', *tuhat* 'thousand'; *airo* 'oar', *satula* 'saddle', *keihäs* 'spear', *rauta* 'iron'), dwellings (*lauta* 'plank', *tarha* 'enclosure'; *ahjo* 'forge', *porras* 'step', *tupa* 'hut, room'), livelihood (*ansa* 'trap', *lohi* 'salmon', *herne* 'pea'; *leipä* 'bread', *sima* 'mead', *seula* 'sieve'), social organisation (*heimo* 'tribe', *seura* 'group', *talkoot* 'group labour'; *kuningas* 'king', *kauppa* 'trade', *hallitse-* 'rule, govern'), belief (*virsi* 'sacred song', *perkele* 'devil'; *pyhä* 'sacred', *runo* 'poem', *vihki-* 'make sacred').

As the ancestors of the Finns became established in the area of present-day Finland and the neighbouring regions, new vocabulary was borrowed from both western and eastern sources. Early Slavonic materials entered by various routes. Certain Slavonic loans appear to have been borrowed by Finnish as early as the fifth or sixth century to denote early Christian concepts (e.g. *pappi* 'priest', *pakana* 'pagan') and various features of domestic life (e.g. *palttina* 'linen', *saapas* 'boot'). During the middle ages and later the largest number of Slavonic and, more specifically, Russian loans was borrowed by Karelians who lived under Russian rule and belonged to the Russian Orthodox Church. Some of these loans entered Finnish much later in the eighteenth and nineteenth centuries as a result of closer contacts between Karelians and speakers of the eastern Finnish dialects, and in the late nineteenth and twentieth centuries as Finnish language reformers combined features of western and eastern dialects in their shaping of Finnish into a language of culture, business, government and administration.

For almost a thousand years, from the early middle ages until the present century, Swedish was the largest source of loans. As Finland evolved into a modern European society, Swedish loans were adapted to the phonological system of Finnish to convey new and more precise concepts of religion, government, domestic and economic life, and culture. Much of the vocabulary acquired in this way was not in itself native Swedish but was transmitted in its Swedish form from other languages, most importantly from Latin, Greek, German and French, but also from Italian, Arabic, Spanish and English. It is only in the present century that English and German on any significant scale began to reach Finnish directly, and it was not until after the Second World War that English rivalled Swedish as an intermediate source of new loans.

A complex system of derivational suffixes has always provided a very productive source of new vocabulary. Nominal and verbal forms are generated from either nominal or verbal base forms: 85 suffixes create nominals from nominal forms, and 21 create verbs from nominals; from verbs, 44 suffixes generate nominals and 34 generate verbs. An example of how nouns and adjectives are generated can be seen in the following illustration: noun *usko* 'belief' → adj. *usko=ll=inen* (stem: *uskollis-*) 'faithful, loyal' → noun *usko=ll=is=uus* 'fidelity, loyalty'; verb *syö-* 'eat' → noun *syö=minen* 'eating'. The great flexibility that exists between the verb and nominal categories in derivation is apparent from the analysis of the Finnish word for 'invincibility', *voi=tta=ma=ttom=uus*, which comprises five components: (1) verb stem *voi-* 'to be able'; (2) causative suffix *-tta-* → 'to beat, conquer'; (3) *-ma-* noun formative → 'beating, conquering'; (4) *-ttom-* negating adjectival suffix → 'non-beaten, non-conquered'; (5) *-uus* abstract noun suffix.

A distinctive feature of Finnish is the productivity of the language's stock of verbal derivational suffixes. With these the main verb can be adapted to perform several specific verbal functions. Although the examples given below are all well established in the language, the pattern of derivation illustrated is commonly used by native speakers to produce new and immediately intelligible items: *seiso-* 'stand' → momentaneous *seis=ahta-* 'halt'; *pure-* 'bite' → momentaneous *pur=aise-* 'take a bite'; *sylke-* 'spit' → frequentative *sylje=ksi-* 'spit habitually'; *ui-* 'swim' → frequentative *ui=skentele-* 'float'; *hake-* 'fetch' → causative *ha=etta-* 'have fetched'; *siirtä-* 'move, shift (causative)' → intransitive *siirt=y* 'move, shift'; *maista-* 'taste' (transitive) → *maist=u-* 'taste of'.

During the past 150 years all the above methods of vocabulary generation have been cultivated by linguists in their development of Finnish as a national language. Nowadays the government funds a language office to advise on the generation of new items and to monitor linguistic usage generally. Yet despite the numerous layers of loans and later creations that make up the lexicon of Finnish, frequency analyses show that some 60–70 per cent of any modern Finnish text is likely to consist of words belonging to the indigenous lexicon or generated from lexical, morphological and derivational items within that lexicon.

5 Syntax

In view of the morphosyntactic character of Finnish, various features of syntax have already been touched upon in the sections on verbal and nominal morphology. The present section will concern itself with four features of Finnish syntax: concord, numerals, non-finite verbal forms and word order.

5.1 Concord

There are no lexical items in Finnish equivalent in function to the English definite or indefinite article, but various degrees of definiteness can be denoted, where this is not already contextually defined, by the use of three degrees of demonstratives (*tämä* 'this', *tuo* 'that', *se* 'further away (either spatially or figuratively)'); similarly, indefiniteness can be marked by two degrees (*eräs* 'a certain', *yksi* 'one').

In noun phrases, there is concord in number and case of demonstratives and adjectives with their head noun. In the standard literary language there will also be concord in number between a nominative subject and the verb (except where the subject is an accumulation of singular items). In normal spoken language, however, the singular form of the 3rd person usually occurs; in sentences where the use of the singular creates ambiguity (e.g. *poikani on täällä* 'my son is here' or 'my sons are here') the speaker will frequently seek periphrastic ways of conveying plurality rather than use the verb in the plural.

5.2 Numerals

In noun phrases containing numerals and certain measure words, concord and government work differently. The numeral *yksi* 'one' functions as an adjective in concord with the head word (e.g. *yksi kirja jäi pöydälle* 'one book remained on the table', *yhdestä kirjasta en pidä* '(there is) one book I do not like', *hän näki yhden kirjan pöydällä* 'he/she saw one book on the table'). All other numerals and most measure words in the nominative and accusative cases (the Ø-marked accusative is used in such occurrences) govern a noun and its attributes in the partitive singular; in all other cases the numeral governs singular number, but there is concord of case between the numeral and head word (e.g. *kaksi nuorta miestä istui huoneessa* 'two young men were sitting in the room', *huomasin kaksi nuorta miestä huoneessa* 'I noticed two young men in the room', but *kahden nuoren miehen avulla maalasin huoneen* 'with the help of two young men I painted the room').

5.3 Non-finite Verbal Forms

Finnish grammarians have traditionally described as infinitives and participles a complex system of forms that 'function as nouns and noun-like words, adjectives, and adverbs with various shades of verbal meaning'

(Holman page 27). Attention will be drawn here to several of these forms that are productive and determine a range of syntactic relations. The first infinitive has a short and long category. The short category, which serves as the verb referent in dictionaries, functions in much the same way as the English verb infinitive as the complement of an auxiliary (e.g. *haluan laula-a* 'I want to sing'); in certain environments the infinitive can also function as a coverb (e.g. *tyttö juosta viipotti* 'the girl ran daintily').

The long form of the first infinitive and the two forms of the second infinitive are close in structure to the short first infinitive but carry case suffixes and in certain circumstances personal possessor suffixes. The long infinitive is in the translative case and person is marked by the nominal personal possessor markers (e.g. short infinitive *tul-la* 'to come', long form *tulla-kse-ni*, *tullaksesi* etc.), and expresses purpose (e.g. *ostin karttakirjan suunnitellakseni automatkan* 'I bought an atlas in order to plan a car journey'). The second infinitive is marked by the inessive and a historically fixed singular form of the instructive (*-en*). The function of the second infinitive is adverbial, indicating simultaneity (inessive) or manner of action (instructive) (e.g. *auringon paistaessa söimme ulkona* 'while the sun was shining we ate outside'; *hän löi lasta kaikkien nähden* 'he/she beat the child as all were watching'). From the examples cited here, it can also be seen that these infinitives govern the object in the same way as finite verb forms.

The most complex of the infinitives is the third. Its base form is marked by *-ma/mä* and the lexicon includes a stock of nouns formed in this way which are no longer perceived by speakers as non-finite verbal forms (e.g. *kuolema* 'death' ← *kuolla* 'to die', *sanoma* 'message' ← *sanoa* 'to say'). An important function of the third infinitive is as 'agential participle' (Holman) (e.g. *isän rakentama talo* lit. 'father's the building house', i.e. 'the house built by father'); where the agent is a personal pronoun, there is suffix concord with the participle (e.g. *minun rakentamani talo* 'the house built by me'). Concord also exists between the categories of singular and plural and case (e.g. *paljon ihmisiä asui isän rakentamissa taloissa* 'many people lived in the houses built by father').

The second area of usage is after a coverb when the third infinitive occurs in the singular illative, inessive, elative, adessive, or abessive cases. In the inessive case the infinitive functions with the coverb *olla* 'to be' to express continuity of action (e.g. *äiti oli lukemassa sanomalehtiä kun saavuin* 'mother was reading the newspapers when I arrived'; *sunnuntaina olen hoitamassa pihaani* 'on Sunday I shall be tending my garden'; *koko perhe oli keittiössä juomassa kahvia* 'the whole family was in the kitchen drinking coffee'). The illative usage, which is also very common, denotes that an action is about to take place (e.g. *hän tuli syömään lounasta* 'he/she came to eat lunch'; *lähdemme nyt juoksemaan* 'we are going to (start) run(ning) now'). The frequency of usage is also to some extent explained by the fact that a large number of verbs, and also adjectives taking a complement, govern this non-finite form of the verb (e.g. *ruveta* 'to begin', *pyytää* 'to ask, request', *oppia* 'to learn'; *halukas* 'keen, willing', *valmis* 'ready'). A similar pattern of development characterises the elative case, which as part of the third infinitive usually conveys separation (e.g. *tulin taloon sisään hoitamasta pihaani* 'I came into the house after tending my garden'; *perhe tuli juomasta kahvia* 'the family came (once they had finished) from drinking coffee'), but is governed as complement by specific verbs (e.g. *lakata* 'to stop, cease', *kieltää* 'to forbid'). In adessive usage it is the instrumental function of the case which is represented, indicating how the action of the finite verb is accomplished (e.g. *lukemalla kirjallisuutta oppisit maailman menosta* 'by reading literature you would learn about the ways of the world'; *maalaamalla talomme itse säästimme paljon rahaa* 'by painting our house ourselves we saved a lot of money'). As mentioned in section 3.3.1 the use of the abessive third infinitive accounts largely for the productive use of this case in the modern language. Its function is to show that an action does not take place (e.g. *työt jäivät tekemättä* 'the jobs remained undone'; *hän asui Helsingissä kaksi vuotta oppimatta suomea* 'he/she lived in Helsinki for two years without learning Finnish').

5.4 Word Order
Word order in a noun phrase constituent is fixed: demonstrative–numeral–adjective(s)–noun. Within the clause the normal order of constituents is subject–verb–object. This order remains in the type of questions that require the addition of a question word at the beginning of the clause (e.g. *sinä odotat meitä kotona* 'you will wait for us at home', but *missä sinä odotat meitä?* 'where will you wait for us?' or *miksi sinä odotat meitä kotona?* 'why are you waiting for us at home?'). Where a question word is not used, as in the clause 'are you waiting for us at home?', Finnish preposes the focus of the question to which the particle *ko/kö* is suffixed: *odotatko sinä meitä kotona?* 'will you wait for us at home?'.

Since the morphosyntactic system usually makes the grammatical, syntactic and semantic functions of each constituent in the clause unambiguous, considerable flexibility is possible within the general SVO framework, allowing shifts of emphasis and focus to be marked by word order variation. When special emphasis or change of focus is required, word order is usually pragmatically determined in order to place the focus as the first constituent of the clause, e.g. *kotona sinä odotat meitä* 'it is at home that you will wait for us (and nowhere else)'; *meitä sinä odotat kotona* 'you will wait for us (and no one else) at home', *kotona sinä meitä odotat* 'it is at home (and nowhere else) that you will wait for us (and no one else)'.

Bibliography

L. Hakulinen (1979) is an extensive survey of the development of Finnish in the context of the other Baltic-Finnic languages and the Finnish dialects; particular attention is paid to derivation and loanwords.

Among grammars of Finnish in English, Atkinson (1977) is a succinct introductory sketch of Finnish morphology and syntax, while Karlsson (1983) is an intelligent presentation of the morphology of Finnish for the adult student, including useful sections on pronunciation and intonation and on the differences between the colloquial and literary languages. Holman (1984) is a concise linguistic analysis of the finite and non-finite categories of the Finnish verb. Denison (1957) is a pioneering work on the form and numerous functions of the partitive case in all the Baltic-Finnic languages. A. Hakulinen and Karlsson (1979) is the best work on Finnish syntax in recent years; the authors rationalise many of the complications of Finnish by the application of modern linguistic methodology.

Tuomi (1972) is an indispensable tool in studying derivation; Saukkonen *et al.* (1979), a frequency dictionary based on the language of the 1960s, is an invaluable analysis of frequency of vocabulary and parts of speech in various registers.

References

Atkinson, J. 1977. *A Finnish Grammar* (Suomalaisen Kirjallisuuden Seura, Helsinki)

Denison, N. 1957. *The Partitive in Finnish* (Finnish Academy of Sciences, Helsinki)

Hakulinen, A. and F. Karlsson. 1979. *Nykysuomen lauseoppia* (Suomalaisen Kirjallisuuden Seura, Jyväskylä)

Hakulinen, L. 1979. *Suomen kielen rakenne ja kehitys* (4th ed.) (Otava, Helsinki). An abridged English version, *The Structure and Development of the Finnish Language* (trans. J. Atkinson), of the 1st edition (1941, 1946) was published in 1961 (Indiana University Press, Bloomington)

Holman, E. 1984. *Handbook of Finnish verbs* (Suomalaisen Kirjallisuuden Seura, Vaasa)

Karlsson, F. 1983. *Finnish Grammar* (Werner Söderström, Juva)

Saukkonen, P., M. Haipus, A. Niemikorpi, H. Sulkala, 1979. *Suomen kielen taajuussanasto* (Werner Söderström, Porvoo)

Tuomi, T. (ed.) 1972. *Suomen kielen käänteissanakirja. Reverse Dictionary of Modern Standard Finnish* (Suomalaisen Kirjallisuuden Seura, Hämeenlinna)

30 TURKISH AND THE TURKIC LANGUAGES

Jaklin Kornfilt

1 General and Historical Background

A strict terminological distinction should be drawn between Turkic, the name of a language family, and Turkish, the name of a language. Although Turkish is by far the largest language (in terms of number of speakers) in the Turkic family, it accounts for only some 40 per cent of the total number of speakers of Turkic languages. The main geographic locations of Turkic languages are: (1) Turkey (Turkish), (2) the USSR and Iran: the Caucasus and northwestern Iran (e.g. Azerbaidjani), Soviet Central Asia, Kazakhstan and southern Siberia (e.g. Uzbek, Kazakh, Turkmenian, Kirghiz) and on the Volga (e.g. Tatar). One Turkic language (Yakut) is spoken in northern Siberia. (More than one Soviet citizen in ten is a native speaker of a Turkic language). In addition, there are substantial Turkic-speaking communities in northwestern China (Uighur and Kazakh).

In terms of linguistic structure, the Turkic languages are very close to one another, and most of the salient features of Turkish described below (e.g. vowel harmony, agglutinative morphology, verb-final word order, nominalised subordinate clauses) are true of nearly all Turkic languages, with only minor modifications. This similarity of structure makes it difficult to determine the precise number of Turkic languages and their boundaries and to sub-classify them, since one typically finds chains of dialects, with adjacent dialects in essence mutually intelligible and mutual intelligibility

619

decreasing as a function of distance, rather than clear language boundaries. Only one Turkic language, Chuvash, spoken on the middle Volga, is radically different from all its relatives.

The external genetic relationships of the Turkic family remain controversial. The most widely accepted affiliation is with the Mongolian languages (in Mongolia, northern China and parts of the USSR) and the Tungusic languages (Siberia and northeastern China), to form the Altaic phylum; the typological similarities among these three families, though striking (e.g. vowel harmony, SOV word order typology) are not proof of genetic relationship, while even the shared vocabulary has been argued to be the result of intensive contact rather than common ancestry. Bolder hypotheses would extend the Altaic phylum eastwards to include Korean, perhaps even Japanese; or northwards to include the Uralic family (to give a Ural-Altaic phylum).

Turkish is the official and dominant language of Turkey (Turkish Republic), where it is the native language of over 90 per cent of the population, i.e. some 45 million people. (The largest linguistic minority in the Turkish Republic is formed by Kurdish speakers, mainly in southeastern Turkey.) Turkish is also a coofficial language (with Greek) in Cyprus, where it is spoken by 19 per cent of the population, or about 120,000 people. But the largest number of Turkish speakers outside Turkey, perhaps one million, is to be found in the Balkans, especially Bulgaria, but also Yugoslavia (especially Macedonia) and Greece.

Although there is no general agreement in Turkological literature on the most adequate geographic grouping of the Turkic languages, we shall go along with those sources that classify the contemporary language spoken in the Turkish Republic within a South-West (or Oγuz) group, together with Gagauz, Azerbaidjani and Turkmenian, the latter forming the eastern component of the group. Within this group, some sources differentiate a subgroup called *Osman* (i.e. Ottoman), which would consist of the following dialects: Rumelian, Anatolian and South Crimean. Modern standard Turkish represents a standardisation of the Istanbul dialect of Anatolian.

The question of the ancestor language of this group is not settled, either. It seems established, however, that the language of the oldest documents (i.e. the Orkhun inscriptions and the Old Uighur manuscripts) is the ancestor of another group, namely of the Central Asiatic Turkic languages; the South-West languages are presumably descendants of the language of the 'Western Türküt' mentioned in the Chinese Annals.

The ancient languages of this group would be Old Anatolian (Seljuq) and Old Osman. These labels themselves are misleading, however, and have more political and historical justification than linguistic motivation, since there are no clear-cut criteria to distinguish the languages they represent from one another — while there might be more reason to distinguish Old Osman (which is usually claimed to extend until the fifteenth century, ending with the conquest of Constantinople) from Ottoman proper; but, even there, no justification exists for a strict cut-off point.

The first Anatolian Turkish documents date from the thirteenth century and show that the literary tradition of Central Asia was only very tenuously carried over by the Turkish people (who had been converted to Islam earlier) after invading Anatolia from the east in the late eleventh century. It is clear that these tribes were influenced heavily by both Persian and Arabic from the very beginnings of their settling down in Anatolia, given the higher prestige and development of the culture and literature of these neighbouring Muslim nations. The number of works in Turkish written by the Turks of Anatolia (as opposed to those written by them in Arabic and Persian and even Greek) greatly increased in the fourteenth century, together with the Selǰuqi period of feudalism in Anatolia. The gap between the eleventh and thirteenth centuries with respect to the lack of written documents can probably be explained by assuming that the Turkish leaders used Arabic and Persian, not finding a local Turkic language in their new surroundings and not having a strong literary tradition to fall back on — given that these Turkish tribes (to a large part belonging to the Oγuz) were not among the culturally more advanced Turkic groups and, moreover, were geographically separated at that time from the Central Asian centres of Turkic literature.

From the very beginning of its Anatolian period, Turkish was written in the Arabic script, until the Latin script was adopted in the course of the so-called 'writing reform' of 1928 (put into force in 1929), one of the various reforms introduced after the founding of the Turkish Republic with the aim of westernising the country. However, the Uighur script was also employed by the Anatolian Turks up to the fifteenth century, which might explain some features of the Arabic script as used by the Turks of that period and which differ from standard Arabic usage, e.g. vowels are written out in Turkish words. This point, incidentally, has often been brought up to motivate the so-called 'writing reform', arguing that the multiple ambiguities that arise in Turkish within a non-vocalised orthography made the Arabic system highly inadequate for Turkish.

The dialect of the earliest Anatolian texts has various features in common with the Oγuz dialect as documented for the eleventh century, before the migration to Anatolia, and with Qïpchaq (an ancient language of the North-western group) and Turkmenian. Some of these are listed below:

(1) *d* for *t* in Old Turkic. (A number of these *d*s became devoiced again through assimilation in the fifteenth century.)
(2) Initial *b* changes to *v*: *bar-* > *var-* 'to go; to arrive'; *ber-* > *ver-* 'to give'
(3) Suffix-initial γ, g disappears.
(4) Word-final γ, g disappears in polysyllabic words.

(5) Instead of the second person plural imperative ending -*ler*, -*lar* in Old Turkic, -*nüz*, -*nuz* is found (and remains until today).

Forms which are limited to Anatolian Turkish are the following:

(1) The suffix -*ecek*, -*acaq* appears for the first time in the thirteenth century (but is used as a participle and not yet as a finite verb, as is also possible in Modern Turkish).

(2) The suffix -*iser*, -*ïsar* is the most widely used suffix for the future tense in Anatolian Turkish between the thirteenth and fifteenth centuries and is seen only very infrequently in some Turkmenian and Qïpchaq works.

However, the differences between Old Turkic and early Anatolian Turkish must not have been great and their phonology essentially identical. The vocabulary is also similar to a large extent, although obviously many borrowings from Islamic sources are seen in the realm of religious-mystical concepts.

In the works of the fourteenth century and afterwards, peculiarities of Eastern Turkic, which had crept into Anatolian Turkish because of the Eastern origins of some authors, disappear almost completely, while the component of Arabic and Persian words and forms increases; such Eastern Turkic features include: initial *m* instead of *b* in words containing a nasal: *men* instead of *ben* 'I'; *min*- instead of *bin*- 'to ride'; initial *b*, which, as mentioned above, changed to *v* in Anatolia and neighbouring areas, remained unchanged in Eastern Turkic and is also sporadically found in early Anatolian works: *ber*- instead of *ver*- 'to give'; and, as another example for a different feature, *bol* instead of *ol* 'to be'.

In the literature written for scholarly, administrative and literary purposes, the Persian and Arabic components became so prevalent that 'Ottoman' became a mixed language, having lost some of its characteristic Turkic properties to the point of not being usable as a medium of communication common to all social classes. During the same time, however, there also was a considerable production of mystical literature and folk poetry which was written for the less educated classes, in the language used by those segments of the population, namely Anatolian Turkish as influenced very little by Persian and Arabic. These works are very close to the 'Republican Turkish' of today and can essentially be understood without too much difficulty. Among the authors of the 'court literature' there were, time and again, also some who called for a purification of the language and ultimately, starting in the eighteenth century, there was a general movement towards a language with local (rather than foreign) features.

The culmination of such movements was reached after the turn of the century. In 1909, a 'Turkish Club' (*Türk Derneği*) was founded in Istanbul and started publishing a journal, proclaiming its aims for a simpler Turkish.

Similar movements and journals followed soon and literary works written in a 'purified' Turkish were produced (see, for instance, the works of Ömer Seyfettin and Ziya Gökalp). Conscious and systematic efforts to establish criteria for maintaining the vocabulary as well as the structural properties of Turkish were continued through the 'War of Liberation' (after World War I) into the founding of the Republic and the reform movements. The language reform, which can be said to have started with the 'writing reform', should therefore be viewed within a tradition of a search for a national identity, combined with a general campaign for westernisation. A Turkish Language Academy was founded in Ankara, with the tasks of etymological research and creation of new words, the latter in accordance with the Turkish rules of word formation and using Turkic roots, where the 'purification' of the language from Arabic and Persian vocabulary had created gaps which could not be filled with current synonyms. Although some of these new creations were judged to be just as foreign to the current colloquial language as the borrowed vocabulary and dropped out of usage almost as soon as they were introduced, the work of the Academy can be judged to have been essentially successful in creating a widely understood language with a transparent morphological component and its own, typologically consistent syntax.

2 Phonology and Orthography

The vowel inventory of Turkish is very symmetric. The eight phonemic vowels are grouped into foursomes with respect to the features of height, backness and rounding, as in table 30.1.

Table 30.1: Turkish Vowels

	[−back] [−round]	[+round]	[+back] [−round]	[+round]
[+high]	i	ü	ɨ	u
[−high]	e	ö	a	o

All vowels of the native vocabulary are underlyingly (or, say, phonemically) short. There is, however, vocalic length on the surface, having various sources: (1) borrowings with unpredictably long vowels; e.g. *ha:dise* 'event, happening'; *ma:zi:* 'past'; (2) compensatory lengthening of words of Turkic origin, where an original voiced velar fricative (which is no longer part of the *surface* inventory of segments in modern standard Turkish) used to follow a vowel. There are some arguments that show this segment to be part of the *phonemic* inventory, since it behaves like a consonant in stem-final position with respect to allomorphy choice of following suffixes. For example, the accusative and dative suffixes are: *-I* and *-A* after a consonant, but *-yI* and

-*yA* after a vowel, respectively. (For the notation with capital letters, see page 627.) After a stem-final phonetically long vowel due to 'compensatory lengthening' (but not after an *inherently* long vowel), the allomorph regularly chosen by consonant-final stems appears; e.g. orthographic *dağ* 'mountain', pronounced *da:*, accusative *daɨ*, dative *daa*. Compare these forms with: *araba* 'car', accusative *arabayɨ*, dative *arabaya*, and *bina:* 'building', accusative *bina:yɨ*, dative *bina:ya*. Where that segment (which is, as shown in the examples above, rendered by the sign *ğ* in Turkish orthography and can never occur word-initially — see also the section on the historical background of Turkish) is in either word-final or pre-consonantal (i.e. in syllable-final) position, the preceding vowel is lengthened; e.g. orthographic *çağ* 'era', pronounced *ča:*, locative *çağda*, pronounced *ča:da*.

Another peculiarity of Turkish vowels is that non-high vowels cannot be round, unless they are in a word-initial syllable. While many borrowed stems are exceptional in this respect (e.g. *dekor* 'stage design'; *pilot* 'pilot'), there is only one affix that is exceptional: the progressive suffix -*(I)yor*.

Perhaps the most prominent property of the Turkish vowels is the fact that they undergo vowel harmony with respect to backness and rounding. We shall discuss this issue in more detail later on, when the phonological rule system of the language is investigated.

The consonant inventory of Turkish is given in table 30.2. The consonants *k*, *g* and *l* have two forms: palatal and velar. Their distribution is, in general,

Table 30.2: Turkish Consonants

	Bilabial	Labio-dental	Dental, Alveolar	Palato-alveolar	Palatal	Velar	Glottal
Stop voiceless	p		t	č		k	
voiced	b		d	ǰ		g	
Fricative							
voiceless		f	s	š			
voiced		v	z	ž			
Nasal	m		n				
Lateral							
approximant			l				
Central							
approximant			r		y		h

determined by the backness versus frontness of the tautosyllabic vowel, e.g. *čök* 'collapse' versus *čok* 'many; very'; *bel* 'waist' versus *bal* 'honey'; *kör* 'blind' versus *kor* 'ember'; *ilik* 'marrow' versus *ilik* 'luke-warm'. (*x* denotes a palatal consonant.) These assimilative changes are not always predictable, however; there are some borrowings where the palatal variant precedes or follows a tautosyllabic back vowel; e.g. *kalp* 'heart'; *kar* 'profit'.

The Latin alphabet used for modern standard Turkish is, both in its printed and handwritten versions, the familiar system used in more familiar European languages — as, for example, in English. The diacritics used for less common sounds make some of the signs very similar to some versions of the phonetic script; for instance, the phonetic symbols for vowels given in table 30.1 are also the ones used in Turkish orthography, with one exception: Instead of *i*, the sign used for the high back non-round vowel, we find *ı*, i.e. a dotless *i*. The difference between the two non-round high vowels is signalled in the same way for capital letters: *İ* for the front, *I* for the back, high non-round vowel. As for the consonants, we have commented on the 'silent' *ğ* earlier. Other letters that don't correspond to the familiar phonetic symbols are the following: *c* for [ǰ], *ç* for [č], *ş* for [š], *j* for [ž].

The orthographic conventions correspond roughly to those of a broad phonetic transcription. Predictable alternations (e.g. those due to syllable-final oral stop devoicing, to voicing assimilation or to vowel harmony) are written out, differing in this respect from, say, the German orthography. Other predictable alternations are not signalled, however: since there are no special signs for the palatal versus velar *k*, *g* and *l*, the alternations that these segments undergo remain unexpressed by the orthography. Unpredictable occurrences of the palatal variants of these consonants with back vowels *is* sometimes shown, however, by placing a circumflex on the vowel: *kâr* [kyar]. (A front glide is inserted when the consonant in question is a *ḵ*.) Inherent vowel length is not shown by the writing, although it is unpredictable.

With the exception of some learned words and the borrowed vocabulary of native speakers who either have some knowledge of European languages or live in big cities with extensive western influence, Turkish does not allow consonant clusters in initial position. In standard pronunciation (and increasingly also in the orthography) such clusters that enter the language via borrowings are broken up by an epenthesised high vowel, which — in general — harmonises with the following vowel(s) in backness and rounding, e.g. learned *ḵlüp* 'club', colloquial *kulüp*; learned *kral* 'king', colloquial *kiral*.

Turkish is somewhat more tolerant of syllable-final consonant clusters. Three types of clusters are allowed as a coda: (a) sonorant + obstruent: *ḵent* 'city', *harf* 'letter'; (b) voiceless fricative + oral stop: *çift* 'couple', *şevḵ* (pronounced [šefk]) 'fervour'; (c) *k* + *s*: *raks* 'dance', *boks* 'boxing'. Where a stem has a consonant cluster in syllable-final position that does not fall under any of the permissible sets, again a high vowel is epenthesised which undergoes harmony, e.g. 'forehead' accusative *aln+ı*, nominative *alın*; 'nose' accusative *burn+u*, nominative *burun*; 'city' accusative *şehr+i*, nominative *şehir*; 'time' accusative *vakt+i*, nominative *vakit*.

A subcase of underlying syllable-final consonant clusters are geminate consonants. While Turkish does tolerate geminate consonant sequences when their members are heterosyllabic (e.g. *et+te* 'meat+loc.'), it does not allow them to occupy syllable-final position. Rather than breaking up such clusters by epenthesis, however, the language has a rule of degemination, e.g. 'feeling' accusative *hiss+i*, nominative *his*; 'line' accusative *hatt+ı*, nominative *hat*.

In addition to some rules discussed above (i.e. vowel epenthesis, consonant degemination), there are a few other important phonological rules that were mentioned in passing and which will receive further attention below.

Syllable-final oral stop devoicing: similar to the more general obstruent devoicing rule in languages like German and Russian, Turkish has a rule that devoices oral non-continuants (i.e. regular stops as well as affricates) in syllable-final position, e.g. *kitap* 'book', accusative *kitab+ı*, locative *kitap+ta*; *kireç* 'lime', accusative *kirec+i*, locative *kireç+te*.

The k/Ø alternation: The final *k* of a polysyllabic word is deleted phonetically in intervocalic position, where the preceding vowel is short. This k/Ø alternation is orthographically rendered as a k/ğ alternation, e.g. *kabak* 'pumpkin', accusative *kabağı* [kabai]; *kabuk* 'crust', accusative *kabuğu* [kabuu]. It is possible to view this phenomenon as a subcase of the voiced/voiceless alternation discussed in the previous section. If it is assumed that the alternating *k*s are derived from underlying *g*s as a result of syllable-final stop devoicing and if a rule of intervocalic fricativisation is posited for the voiced velar stop, the data are essentially covered.

Word-final liquid devoicing: another striking phenomenon somewhat related to stop devoicing is the word-final devoicing of liquids, especially common in the Istanbul dialect and in the speech of educated speakers in the other big cities: *ka̲r* 'snow', *bakı̲r* 'copper', *ḵe̲l* 'bald'. It should be noted, however, that this is not a completely unified phenomenon; some speakers devoice only the palatal *l*, while other speakers do not make a distinction between the two variants of the lateral. (The *r* is devoiced by all speakers who observe the liquid devoicing rule.) It should also be pointed out that liquid devoicing differs from oral stop devoicing in applying at word boundary rather than at syllable boundary; e.g. while the underlying stem-final *b* devoices in: *kitap + lık* 'object designated for books; bookshelf', the stem-final *r* remains voiced in a similar environment: *kar + lı* 'with snow; snowy' (and not: *ka̲rlı*).

Morpheme-initial voicing assimilation: a morpheme-initial obstruent assimilates in voicing to the preceding segment within the word. This rule has to apply after syllable-final stop devoicing has taken place, e.g. (a) *gemi + ci* 'sailor' (cf. *gemi* 'ship'), *iz + ci* 'boy-scout' (cf. *iz* 'track, trace'), *bakır + cı* 'coppersmith' (cf. *bakır* 'copper'); (b) *kitap + çı* (cf. *kitap* 'book', underlying /kitab/), *şarap+çı* 'wine maker, wine seller' (cf. *şarap* 'wine', underlyingly /şarab/).

Vowel harmony: perhaps the most striking property of Turkish phonology is the fact that the distribution of vowels within a word is governed by vowel harmony, i.e. vowels share the specification for the feature [back] and, if they are high, they also share the specification for [round]: *bülbül + ümüz + ün* 'nightingale + 1 pl. + gen.', 'belonging to our nightingale'; *bülbül + ler + imiz + in* 'nightingale + pl. + 1 pl. + gen.', 'belonging to our nightingales'; *kol + umuz + un* 'arm + 1 pl. + gen.', 'belonging to our arm'; *kol + lar + ımız + ın* 'arm + pl. + 1 pl. + gen.', 'belonging to our arms'. Note that the [−high] vowel of the plural morpheme, while undergoing vowel harmony for backness, does not undergo rounding harmony. Moreover, since there is a condition (mentioned earlier in this section) on [−high] vowels to the effect that they have to be [−round] if they are in a non-initial syllable, the negative specification of this vowel for rounding is fully determined. Note also that once a non-round vowel follows a round vowel (as in the second and fourth examples above) all vowels to the right of that non-round vowel will be non-round as well, irrespective of their height.

This situation can be characterised in more general terms: where a vowel does not share the specification for a harmony feature with preceding vowels, it will create its own harmony domain, in the sense that it will determine the specification with respect to that particular feature for the following vowels. This description also characterises the application of vowel harmony where an exceptional vowel occurs. As mentioned before, many stems have exceptional vowels that violate either backness or rounding harmony or both at once; the second vowel of the progressive marker *-(I)yor* is also exceptional in this respect and never alternates. (Capital letters denote archiphonemes whose missing feature values are predictable by rule. In the case of vowels, *I* stands for a [+high], *A* for a [−high] vowel before application of vowel harmony. In the case of consonants, a capital letter stands for a segment which will undergo syllable-final stop devoicing, morpheme-initial voicing assimilation or intervocalic *k*-deletion. Symbols in parentheses denote affix allomorphy in those instances where the segment in question deletes after a 'like' segment (i.e. a vowel after a vowel, a consonant after a consonant).) In such cases, it is the exceptional vowel (or, if there is more than one, the last exceptional vowel) that determines what kind of vowel harmony the following vowels will undergo. Observe the following examples: *dekor + un + u* 'stage design + 3 sg. + acc.', 'his stage design, acc.', *otobüs + ün + ü* 'bus + 3 sg. + acc.', 'his bus, acc.'; *buket + in + i* 'bouquet + 3 sg. + acc.', 'his bouquet, acc.'; *ermeni + stan + ın + ı* 'Armenian + 'country' + 3 sg. + acc.', 'his Armenia, acc.'.

Sometimes, however, a consonant rather than a vowel can determine (backness) harmony. This happens when a palatal consonant unpredictably follows a back vowel in the same syllable and where that consonant is in stem-final position (or a member of a stem-final consonant cluster). In such cases the following vowels will exhibit *front* harmony; i.e. the 'trigger' of vowel harmony will be the exceptional consonant rather than the regular vowel, e.g. *petrol* 'petrol, gasoline', accusative *petrol + ü*; *kalp* 'heart', accusative *kalb+i*; *vals* 'waltz', accusative *vals + i*.

Labial Attraction: there are a number of stems with a vowel sequence of *a...u* and an intervening labial consonant (the latter can also be part of a consonant cluster). Since the second vowel, being high, should undergo rounding harmony, it should surface as an *ı*. Its rounding has traditionally been ascribed to the preceding labial consonant. Some examples are *karpuz* 'watermelon', *kavun* 'melon'. The status of this observation in terms of a rule (of assimilation) in modern standard Turkish has been challenged more recently. While such an assimilatory process might have been productive in Early Anatolian Turkish (and could even have been a feature common to the Southwestern Turkic group), it seems that it is less general in the contemporary language; there are a number of examples where the sequence *a...ı* shows up in spite of an intervening labial consonant, e.g. *çarmıh* 'cross', *sabır* 'patience', *kapı* 'door'. Furthermore, an even larger number of stems exhibit *a...u* sequences without any intervening labial consonant; e.g. *ka:nun* 'law', *arzu* 'desire', *fasulya* 'bean'.

Turkish has in general word-final stress: *kitáp* 'book'; *gör + ebil + ecek + lerin + í* 'see + abilit. + fut. + 3 pl. + acc.' 'that they will be able to see'. Some suffixes are exceptional, however, in: (a) rejecting stress when in word-final position: *gör + ecék + ti* 'see + fut. + past' 'he was going to see'; (b) dividing the word into stress domains where not word-final: *gör + é + me + yecek + lerin + ì* 'see + abilit. + neg. + fut. + 3 pl. + acc.' 'that they will not be able to see'. Under both circumstances, the vowel preceding the exceptional morpheme (or, rather, the exceptional vowel) receives primary stress.

A rule that applies within a phrase to reduce stresses left-to-right is needed independently: *dérs kitab + ì* 'course book + compound marker', 'textbook'. This rule can be used to account for the stress in words like *görémeyeceklerinì* which consist of more than one stress domain and exhibit word-final non-primary stress.

Exceptionality with respect to stress is also exhibited by some unsuffixed stems. Such items do not fall into one clearly and independently defined set. Many (but not all) borrowed stems and almost all place names fall under this group, within which there are subregularities: they are stressed on the antepenultimate syllable, if it is the first non-final closed syllable; otherwise, the penultimate syllable is stressed. Some illustrative examples follow: *İstánbul*, *Ánkara*, *İzmir*, *fasúlya* 'bean', *lokánta* 'restaurant'.

3 Morphology

Turkish morphology is agglutinative and suffixing; there are only very few exceptions to the one-to-one relationship between morpheme and function and only one process that is prefixing rather than suffixing, namely reduplication of the first syllable (with an inserted consonant) in intensifying adjectives and adverbs; e.g. *beyaz* 'white', *bembeyaz* 'completely white'; *çabuk* 'fast', *çarçabuk* 'very fast'.

In the following, a brief survey will be given of the most productive suffixes and some restrictions will be stated that govern their occurrence and the ordering among those morphemes that can cooccur; later on, specific categories of special interest will be discussed. Inflectional suffixes will be referred to as 'verbal' or 'nominal' according to the category of the stem they attach to. By 'nominal stems' are meant nouns, adjectives and adverbs. (Participials and gerundives will fall under the 'nominal' group in this respect.)

As to be expected, derivational suffixes precede inflectional ones. Not surprisingly, among those morphemes that derive nominals, those that attach to verbal stems precede those that attach to nominal ones, where the two types cooccur: *ver + im* 'give + abstr. n.', 'profit'; *ver + im + li* 'give + abstr. n. + *with* (*adj.*)', 'profitable'; *ver + im + li + lik* 'give + abstr. n. + with (adj.) + abstr. n.', 'profitability'. The suffixes exemplified in the last two examples can attach to underived nominals, as well: *balkon + lu* 'with a balcony; balconied'; *dürüst + lük* 'honest + abstr. n.', 'honesty'. Both groups are productive; two other productive members of the first group are the action/manner suffix *-(y)Iş*, the result/action morpheme *-mA* and the infinitive marker *-mAK*. In the second group, we find *-CI*, deriving nouns meaning 'professional', and *-sIz*, deriving adjectives meaning 'without'.

The first member of a sequence of nominal inflectional suffixes and hence immediately following derivational morphemes, if present, is the plural marker *-lAr*: *gül + üş + ler* 'laugh + act. n + pl.', 'laughters; manners of laughing'; *at + lar* 'horse + pl.', 'horses'.

Next come nominal agreement suffixes. These are often referred to as 'possessive suffixes' in traditional literature, the reason being that the nominal stem they attach to is often, if not always, interpreted as possessed by a noun phrase within the clause or phrase. The reason they are referred to as 'agreement suffixes' here is that they express the person and number features of their 'possessors'. A more detailed account of these suffixes will be offered in the next part of this section which will be devoted to issues of special interest.

Case morphemes occur last, e.g. *üstün + lüğ + ümüz + ü* 'superior + abstr. n. + 1 pl. + acc.' 'our supremacy (accusative)'. The group of agreement morphemes will be discussed in more detail in the second part of this section. It should be mentioned here, however, that not more than one case morpheme can occur within an immediate sequence of suffixes.

There is only one completely productive morpheme that derives verbs from nominals: *-lA*, which has a meaning related to the causative; e.g. *karşı + la + mak* 'opposite + deriv. morph. + infin.', 'to go to meet; to oppose; reply to'; *kara + la + mak* 'black + deriv. morph. + infin.', 'to blacken'. This morpheme can then be followed by the various verbal suffixes which we shall briefly discuss according to the sequential order in which they occur within the word.

The leftmost productive class in the string of verbal suffixes is the category often called 'voice' by traditional grammars. This group consists of the middle/reflexive (-(I)n), the reciprocal (-(I)ş), the passive (-Il/n) and the causative (-DIr/t). (The -IL allomorph of the passive follows consonants, the -n allomorph vowels. -DIr is the basic allomorph of the causative; -t occurs after polysyllabic stems which end in a vowel or in the oral sonorants r and l.) The middle/reflexive and the reciprocal cannot cooccur; where the passive cooccurs with either one, it has to follow them. In the very few examples where the causative can cooccur with the middle/reflexive and the reciprocal it has to follow them, and, while it can cooccur with the passive, it has to precede it; e.g. tanı + ş + tır + ıl + dı + lar 'know + recip. + caus. + pass. + past + 3 pl.' 'they were caused to know each other; they were introduced to each other'.

Suffixes of this group can be followed by the verbal negation marker -mA, which is one of the suffixes that are exceptional from the point of view of word stress in rejecting word-final stress and causing the preceding vowel to be stressed. This suffix, in turn, is followed either by one of the various mood markers or by purely verbal or gerundive/participial forms, the latter expressing tense in varying degrees of differentiation. The mood markers are: the desiderative -sA, the necessitative -mAlI and the optative -(y)a; e.g. gör + üş + me + meli + yiz 'see + recip. + neg. + necess. + 1 pl.', 'we shouldn't/mustn't see each other'. The suffixes of the mood category are mutually exclusive.

The tenses are: definite past: -DI; reported past: -mIş; aorist: -(A)r; future: -(y)AcAK; present progressive: -(I)yor. These forms have also aspectual connotations: the past tenses denote accomplished actions and the aorist actions that are either extended or repeated over a period of time. The present progressive is similar to its English equivalent in denoting an action that, roughly speaking, takes place at the time of the utterance. One difference is that stative verbs, unlike those in English, can take the progressive in Turkish:

ev   + e   git + mek isti +   yor   + um
home + dat. go + infin. want + pres. prog. + 1 sg.
'I want (*am wanting) to go home'

The main participial forms are those used in relative clauses: -(y)An and -DIK, and they will be discussed in section 4. Also in this group (from the point of view of positional slots within the morphological word) are so-called verbal nouns and converbs (these are terms often used in traditional literature). The verbal nouns consist mainly of the infinitive suffix -mAK and the result/action noun marker -mA and were also listed among the derivational morphemes that convert verbs into nominals. Converbs (or gerundives, as they are also called) are suffixes that yield adverbial forms. Some examples are the manner suffix *-(y)ArAk*, the conjunction adverbial *-(y)Ip* which denotes close successions of actions and the time adverb suffix *-(y)IncA*. In general, only one of the suffixes in this group can occur at a time. In other words, within the morphological sequence, the various gerundive, participial and nominal markers take the place of the tense or mood markers, whether they have tense connotations themselves or not.

However, two tense markers (as well as a tense and a mood marker) *can* cooccur in immediate succession to form complex tenses; in such examples, it might be appropriate to view the second marker as a copula carrying the main tense or mood and the preceding sequence as a participial:

imtihan +   ım   +   a   başlı +   *yor*   +   *du*   +   m
exam   +   1 sg. +   dat.   start +   prog.   +   past +   1 sg.
'I was starting my exam (when...)'

Note that in such sequences, the present progressive marker *-(I)yor* retains its aspectual meaning.

The reported past marker *-mIş* is used as a perfective aspect marker in such sequences (i.e. when it is the first member of the sequence):

imtihan +   ım   +   a   başla +   *mış*   +   *tı*   +   m
exam   +   1 sg +   dat.   start +   perf.   +   past +   1 sg.
'I had started my exam (when...)'

All tense and some mood markers can occur as the first members in these sequences; however, only the two past tense markers and the mood marker for the desiderative (the latter as a conditional) can occur as the second member, i.e. as the main tense or modality marker. However, all the tenses can be used as a main tense or modality within a periphrastic construction with an auxiliary verb. The most widely used auxiliary is the verb *ol-* 'be, become'; e.g.

imtihan + ım + a   başlı +   *yor*   ol +   *acağ* +   ım
                    +   prog.   be +   fut.   +   1 sg.
'I shall be starting my exam...'
imtihan + ım + a   başla +   *mış*   ol +   *acağ* +   ım
                    +   perf.
'I shall have started my exam'

This mixed positional group is followed by agreement markers, wherever such markers are possible. (Among the suffixes that cannot be followed by agreement markers are the infinitive marker *mAK*, the participial marker *-An* (unless it functions as a verbal noun) and the gerundive marker *-(y)Ip*.)

Now that we have looked at the most productive morphemes and some regularities of their distribution, let us discuss some typological characteristics of the morphological system.

Gender is neither overtly expressed in nouns (or pronouns), nor does it affect agreement. Agreement itself (by which term we shall mean agreement of the verbal or nominal head of a construction with its subject in terms of the features of person and number) can be either verbal or nominal; in other words, there are two slightly different paradigms, given in table 30.3.

Table 30.3: Agreement Markers

	Verbal	Nominal
1 sg.	-Im	-(I)m
2 sg.	-sIn	-(I)n
3 sg.	-∅	-(s)I(n)
1 pl.	-Iz	-(I)mIz
2 pl.	-sInIz	(I)nIz
3 pl.	-lAr	-lArI(n)

Note: As before, the suffix-initial vowels in parentheses are deleted after a stem-final vowel; the suffix-initial consonant in parentheses is deleted after a stem-final consonant. The suffix-final consonant in parentheses is deleted in word-final position.

The verbal paradigm appears with the predicates of main clauses and of 'direct complements' (for discussion of the latter, see section 4); the nominal paradigm is used on the head nouns of possessive noun phrases as well as on the nominalised verbs of gerundive and participial complements. Some illustrative examples follow:

Verbal agreement used with a main clause predicate verb:

(Ben) bu   makale + yi   yarın   bitir + eceğ + *im*
I   this article + acc. tomorrow   finish + fut. + 1 sg.
'I shall finish this article tomorrow'
(Biz) her   akşam   çok   çalış +   ır   + *ız*
we   every evening a lot work +   aor. + 1 pl.
'We work a lot every evening'

Verbal agreement used with a main clause predicate adjective:

(Ben) bugün   çok   yorgun + *um*
I   today   very   tired + 1 sg.
'I am very tired today'
(Siz) çok   güzel + *siniz*
you   very   pretty + 2 pl.
'You are very pretty'

Nominal agreement in a possessive noun phrase:

(Biz-im)   heykel + *imiz*
we-gen.   statue + 1 pl.
'our statue'
Ayşe-nin   araba + *sı*
Ayşe-gen.   car   + 3 sg.
'Ayşe's car'

Nominal agreement used in a gerundive complement:

Herkes   [(biz + im) heykel + i   kır   + dığ + *ımız*] + ı
everybody we + gen. statue + acc. break + ger. + 1 pl. + acc.
                                             bil   + iyor
                                             know   + 3 sg.
'Everybody knows that we broke the statue'
Herkes   [Ayşe + nin heykel + i kır + ma + sın] + ı   isti + yor
                                           + ger. + 3 sg.   want + 3 sg.
'Everybody wants Ayşe to break the statue'

Another property of Turkish agreement worth remarking on is the lack of it
where modifiers are concerned. This means that neither singular/plural
properties of a noun nor its case marking will 'spread' onto its adjective
modifier(s) or any of its determiners. As a matter of fact, another striking
property of Turkish in this respect is the lack of overt plural marking on a
noun where its quantifier clearly expresses plurality; this generalisation
holds irrespective of the grammatical relation of the noun phrase involved.
The following examples will illustrate this point:

Subject noun phrase:

Beş   adam   (*adam + *lar*)   heykel + i   kır + dı
five man   (man + pl.)   statue + acc. break + past
'Five men broke the statue'

Indirect object noun phrase:

Beş   adam + a   (*adam + *lar* + a) yardım et + ti + m
five man + dat. (man + pl. + dat.)   help   do + past + 1 sg.
'I helped five men'

Let us now return to subject-head agreement. The two paradigms in table
30.3 might be slightly misleading in that the suffixes for plural subjects are
presented as unanalysed morphemes. However, especially the nominal
paradigm in table 30.3 can substantiate a possible claim that, at least for the
first and second person plural forms, those suffixes consist of two
morphemes: 1 sg. -*(I)m*, 2 sg. -*(I)n*, 1 pl. -*(I)m* + *Iz*, 2 pl. -*(I)n* + *Iz*. Hence,

it would make sense to view the suffix -*Iz* as a plural marker. (This plurality would have to be confined to subject agreement, however, since the general plurality morpheme, *lAr*, is different.)

The same analysis carries over to the verbal paradigm, if it is assumed that the suffix for person is, idiosyncratically, unrealised in the first person plural agreement form: 1 sg. -*Im*, 2 sg. -*sIn*, 1 pl. -∅ + *Iz*, 2 pl. -*sIn* + *Iz*. The agreement suffixes for third person plural subjects do not seem to fall under this generalisation, simply because their shape is rather different from those of the first and second person plural agreement morphemes. However, we would like to claim that there, too, a further analysis into a person morpheme, distinct from a number morpheme, is possible. Once again, we shall start with the nominal paradigm, which is more perspicuous than the verbal paradigm, since all morphemes are overtly realised: 3 sg. -*(s)I(n)*, 3 pl. -*lAr* + *I(n)*. Two factors are worth noticing: in comparison with the agreement forms for first and second person plural subjects, the order between the person and number suffixes is switched around, i.e. the number morpheme precedes the person morpheme. In addition, the number morpheme itself is suppletive. Instead of the form -*Iz*, the agreement morpheme for (plural) number exhibited elsewhere in both paradigms, we see here the general plurality morpheme -*lAr*. (Note, incidentally, that the suffix for third person appears in a perfectly regular shape: we know that the parenthesised initial *s* of that morpheme is deleted after a consonant. Since, within the third person plural agreement form, the third person suffix always follows the plural number suffix — and hence an *r* — that suffix will always surface without that *s*.)

Once again, the analysis carries over to the verbal paradigm. The agreement form for third person plural exhibits the suppletive morpheme -*lAr* for plural number. Since the third person morpheme remains unexpressed in the verbal paradigm, nothing else but the plural -*lAr* is included in the total form of the third person plural morpheme, as the last line of table 30.3 shows.

Yet another peculiarity of the third person plural morpheme is that, under some circumstances, it can be omitted. Essentially, when the subject noun phrase is overtly present (as we shall see in section 4, subjects can be omitted), the plural 'submorpheme' is optional (and, as a matter of fact, its omission is stylistically preferred):

```
Adam + lar    heykel + i    kır + dı (+lar)
man + pl.     statue + acc.  break + past (+3 pl.)
'The men broke the statue'
Hasan [adam + lar + ın    heykel + i              kır + dık + [lar + ın]] -ı /
                + gen. statue + acc.       break + dık + pl. + 3 pers.-acc./
                       kır + dığ + [ın] + ı    bil + iyor
                                + 3 pers.    know + pres. prog.
'Hasan knows that the men broke the statue'
```

None of the other agreement morphemes exhibits this freedom of partial occurrence.

Yet another property that determines the occurrence of the plural 'submorpheme' of third person plural agreement is the animacy of the subject noun phrase. The stylistic preference we mentioned in favour of omitting the morpheme in question strengthens to the point of almost a grammatical prohibition against its occurrence when the subject is inanimate:

Kitap + lar   masa + dan   yer + e   düş + tü   (??/*+ler)
book + pl.   table + abl.   floor + dat.   fall + past   (3 pl.)
'The books fell from the table to the floor'

Let us now turn to the case system in Turkish. It is a matter of some controversy how many cases Turkish has. Traditional Turkish grammars usually assume five cases: nominative: not marked overtly; accusative: *-(y)I*; dative: *-(y)A*; locative: *-DA*; ablative: *-DAn*. Turkish has also a genitive: *-(n)I(n)*, and an instrumental: *-(y)lA*. It is probably because the genitive is not 'governed' by verbs, but is rather a structural property of the subjects of nominal phrases or clauses, that many grammarians were reluctant to recognise it as a regular case. As for the instrumental, it is a cliticised form of a formerly unbound morpheme; from the synchronic point of view, there are two criteria that could argue against viewing it as a case morpheme: (a) it is exceptional from the point of view of stress (as are all other cliticised morphemes), while all other case morphemes (including the genitive) are regular; (b) it follows the genitive when it is suffixed to a personal pronoun and hence behaves like a postposition that governs a case — namely the genitive in this instance — and not like a regular case morpheme, which can never immediately follow another case suffix, as was mentioned earlier. We shall not take a stand here on this issue.

In conjunction with the discussion about the status of the instrumental, it should be mentioned that various postpositions 'govern' certain cases, similarly to verbs. The point of interest within the context of morphology is that regular nouns are treated differently from pronouns in this respect by those postpositions that take objects in the nominative. Specifically, while full nouns appear in the nominative in those contexts, pronouns have to be marked with the genitive: *kadın gibi* 'like a woman', *Ahmet kadar* 'as much as Ahmet'; but: *ben + im gibi* 'like me', *ben + im kadar* 'as much as I'.

4   Syntax

Turkish is a perfect example of a left-branching type of language where governed elements precede their governors, i.e. objects precede the verb, the postpositional object precedes the postposition and the (adjective, genitive) modifier precedes the modified head.

The unmarked word order in sentences is SOV; if there is more than one object, and if one of them is a direct object, the order with the direct object closer to the verb seems less marked than others:

Hasan çocuğ + a   elma + yı   ver + di
       child + dat.   apple + acc. give + past
'Hasan gave the apple to the child'

However, other orders are possible, as well. As a matter of fact, Turkish is rather free in its word order. Often (but not always), the divergences from the unmarked order have a pragmatic, discourse-oriented function, in that the position immediately preceding the verb is the focus position and the sentence-initial position is topic position. New information and material stressed for emphasis appear in focus position and, in addition to being syntactically marked in this way, also receive intonational stress. The topic, i.e. the material that the sentence is about, is placed at the beginning of the sentence and is often separated from it — orthographically by a comma and by a slight pause in speech.

Differently from other SOV languages (e.g. Japanese), Turkish is so lenient about non-canonical word orders that it even permits non-verb-final constructions. Such sentences arise when material is added as an afterthought or when the speaker assumes the hearer to know about it: *Hasan çocuğ + a ver + di elma + yı*. For this example to be felicitous, it must be clear within the discourse that something happened to the apple or even that Hasan gave the apple to somebody.

An embedded sentence takes up the same position that the corresponding noun phrase with the same grammatical relation would and can move around within the main clause with the same ease as a regular noun phrase:

Hasan ban + a   [*imtihan + ı   geç + tiğ + in*] + i   anlat + tı
      I + dat. exam + acc.   pass + fact. n. + 2 sg. + acc.   tell + past
'Hasan told me that you passed the exam'
Hasan ban + a   anlat + tı   [*imtihan + ı geç + tiğ + in*] + i

The constituents of the embedded sentence are somewhat less free in their word order. While they can still successfully violate the canonical SOV order within their own clause, they have to move to the right of the highest sentence when they cross the boundary of their own clause and cannot 'scramble into' higher material; thus, compare the following examples with the last set of examples above:

Ahmet ban + a   [___ geç + tiğ + in] + i anlat + tı *imtihan + ı*
*Ahmet ban + a   [___ geç + tiğ + in] + i *imtihan + ı* anlat + tı
(The original site of the 'scrambled' constituent is marked with a ___)

In possessive noun phrases, the possessor precedes the head noun; in 'regular' noun phrases, modifiers precede the head. Where there is both an adjectival modifier and an article (only the indefinite article is overtly expressed in Turkish), the adjective precedes the article; where there is both a numeral and an adjective, the unmarked order is for the numeral to precede the adjective:

Ahmed	+ in	kitab + ı		
	+ gen.	book + 3 sg.	'Ahmet's book'	
ilgi	+ nç	bir kitap		
interest	+ ing	a book	'an interesting book'	
üç	ilginç	kitap		
three			'three interesting books'	

The genitive-marked possessor can 'scramble' in either direction, while the article and numerals cannot. The adjective is not free to move, either, as far as spoken language and written prose are concerned. In poetry, however, an adjective can occur to the right of its head. Let us also mention, without going into details, that parts of nominal compounds cannot scramble and that postpositions cannot be stranded.

One striking characteristic of Turkish is that a subject can be left unexpressed in finite clauses (i.e. those exhibiting some type of subject-predicate agreement) as well as in possessive noun phrases:

___okul + a	gid +	eceğ + im	
school + dat	go +	fut. + 1 sg.	
'I shall go to school'			
Ahmet	[___kitab + ım] + ı	kayb + et + miş	
	book + 1 sg. + acc.	loss + do + rep. past	
'It is said that Ahmet lost my book'			

(The sites of the missing constituents are underlined.) This possibility has been traditionally linked to the rich agreement morphology of Turkish, i.e. to the fact that agreement suffixes will uniquely 'identify' the person and number of the subject which is unexpressed.

Although Turkish has no agreement markers for non-subjects, it is also possible to 'drop' such constituents; e.g. *bul + du + m* 'find + past + 1 sg.' 'I found (it)'. Such examples are more restricted, however, than 'subject-drop' examples. They can never start a discourse, while 'subjectless' finite sentences can. Such constructions are felicitous only if the antecedent of the 'dropped' constituent has been mentioned in the discourse or has somehow been made clear by a pragmatic act.

As we saw before, passive is marked by the morpheme *-Il* (with a morphophonemic alternant *-n*) on the verbal stem. From the syntactic point of view, there are two types of passive constructions; they will be referred to as 'transitive passive' and 'intransitive passive'; the former type is derived from transitive verbs, the latter from intransitive ones. By 'transitive verb' we mean verbs that take direct objects (noun phrases that are marked accusative when they are specific), and by 'intransitive' verbs that do not take such objects (i.e. that either lack objects altogether or take only indirect or oblique objects). The two constructions exhibit the following surface differences: the patient of the action (or, in other words, the direct object of the corresponding active sentence) is the subject of the transitive passive construction. This claim is substantiated by the fact that these subjects exhibit syntactic properties typical of subjects in general: they appear in the nominative case, and in an unmarked word order, in sentence-initial position; the verb agrees with them; they can be the accusative-marked subjects of clauses that act as complements to 'believe-type' verbs (see page 641); they can correspond to the understood subjects of infinitivals; and the agent of the action can appear in an agentive phrase. However, the non-accusative objects that an intransitive verb might cooccur with are not surface subjects in an intransitive passive construction (in the sense that they do not exhibit the criteria just enumerated), and agentive phrases are judged to be awkward at best, if not completely ungrammatical. Some illustrative examples for these differences follow:

(*Biz*)   döv + *ül* + dü + *k*
we   hit + pass. + past + 1 pl.
'We were hit'
Biz + *e*   yardım ed + *il* + di
we + dat. help   do + pass. + past
'We were helped'
*biz(+e)   yardım ed + *il* + di + *k*

(Biz$_i$) [PRO$_i$ döv + *ül* + *mek*]   iste + mi + yor + uz
we   hit + pass. + infin.   want + neg. + pres. prog. + 1 pl.
'We don't want to be hit'
*(biz$_i$) [PRO$_i$ yardım ed + *il* + *mek*] iste + mi + yor + uz
                help   do
'We don't want to be helped'

Obviously, verbs that do not take any objects at all can also appear in impersonal passive constructions:

Koş + *ul*   + du
run +   pass. + past
'It was run (i.e. running took place)'
Eğlen + *il*   + di
amuse + pass. + past
'Fun was had'

Agentive phrases are completely ungrammatical in such objectless constructions.

It has been claimed in some relevant literature that only verbs with agentive semantics can enter the intransitive passive construction, but that stative verbs cannot. While this generalisation does hold for most cases in Turkish, it is possible to find examples where non-agentive verbs can successfully enter the construction. Such examples are best when combined with a 'tense' that has an aspectual connotation of duration (rather than, say, momentary or completed action):

Böyle   bir   hava + da   iyi   uyu + n + ur
such   a   weather + loc. good   sleep + pass. + aor.
'One sleeps well in such a weather'

Compare this quite acceptable sentence with the following ungrammatical ones:

*Şimdi   iyi   uyu + n + uyor
now   good   sleep + pass. + pres. prog.
'Now it is being slept well (i.e. one is sleeping well now)'
*Dün   bütün   gün   uyu + n + du
yesterday   whole   day   sleep + pass. + past
'Yesterday it was slept the whole day (i.e. one slept the whole day yesterday)'.

Turkish has various *wh*-question particles most of which are morphologically derived from the particle *ne* 'what': *ne* 'what', *neden* 'why', *niçin* 'why', *niye* 'why', *hangi* 'which', *kim* 'who'. These elements are found in two positions in the sentence: In pre-verbal position (which is, as we saw, the focus position) and in sentence-initial position. The first one of the two is strongly preferred:

Çocuğ + a   kitab + ı   *kim*   ver + di
child + dat.   book + acc.   who   give + past
'Who gave the book to the child?'

Yes-no questions are formed by suffixing the particle *-mI* to the constituent questioned; if the whole sentence is questioned, the particle is attached to the verb, preceding the subject agreement markers in simple tense/aspect forms and preceding the copula and its tense and agreement markers in complex forms:

(Sen)   çocuğ + a   kitab + ı   ver + di + n + *mi*
you   child + dat.   book + acc.   give + past + 2 sg. + *mI*
'Did you give the book to the child?
(Sen) çocuğ + a   kitab + ı   ver + ecek + *mi* + y + di +n
                                        +fut. +   *mI* + cop. + past + 2 sg.
'Were you going to give the book to the child?'

It should be noted that the particle *-mI* exhibits dual behaviour with respect to the phonology of the language: it is exceptional from the point of view of word stress (rejects domain-final stress), but regular with respect to vowel harmony.

A few examples follow where -*mI* takes a constituent into its scope:

Çocuğ + a   kitab + ı   sen + *mi*   ver + di + n
                                you + *mI*   give + past + 2 sg.
'Was it you who gave the book to the child?'
(Sen)   kitab + ı   çocuğa + a + *mı*   ver + di + n
'Was it the child that you gave the book to?'
(Sen)   çocuğ + a   kitab + ı + *mı*   ver + di + n
'Was it the book that you gave to the child?'

The translations show that such constituent questions correspond to clefted questions in English. (Turkish has also a cleft construction which can enter yes-no questions; formally, the construction consists of a relative clause lacking a head noun.) Note that the questioned constituent is located in the focus position.

One general property of embedded sentences in Turkish is that they lack complementisers that introduce (or terminate) clauses, as say the complementisers *that* or *for...to* in English. But a perhaps even more striking characteristic feature of such clauses is exhibited by their predicates: rather than being fully finite in exhibiting the various tense and aspect markers and their combinations as is the case with verbs of main clauses, the predicates of embedded clauses are 'nominalised' with the help of various morphemes (as we saw in the section on morphology). We also saw that the subject agreement markers on these 'nominalised' predicates come from the nominal rather than the verbal paradigm; one additional criterion for calling these clauses 'nominalised' is that their predicates carry overt case markers:

[Ahmed + in ben + i sev + *diğ* + *in*] + i
    + gen.   I + acc. love + fact. n. + 3 sg. (nom.) + acc.
bil + iyor + um
know + pres. prog. + 1 sg.
'I know that Ahmet loves me'
[Ahmed + in ben + i sev + *me* + *sin*] +i   isti + yor + um
                                + act./res. n. + 3 sg. (nom.) + acc. want +
'I want Ahmet to love me'

The two 'nominalisation' morphemes exhibited above are the forms exhibited by embedded clauses that function as arguments of the verbs of the higher clause. The semantics of that higher verb and the propositional properties of the clause determine which one of the two morphemes will be chosen, as illustrated by the examples above and their translations.

A subset of the verbs that take clauses with the 'action nominal' marker also take clauses that are marked with the infinitive suffix -*mAK*. These are comparable to English infinitivals in that they necessarily lack overt subjects; note also that they do not carry agreement morphology:

Ben   [sev + il + *mek*]   isti + yor + um
      love + pass. + infin.   want + pres. prog. + 1 sg.
'I want to be loved'

Infinitivals can take case markers, too, and are thus shown to be genuine nominalised clauses, as well:

Ahmet [ben + i   sev + *meğ*] + e   başla + dı
       I + acc.   love + infin. + dat.   start + past
'Ahmet has started loving me'

Clauses which are postpositional objects and adverbial clauses are also nominalised; in part, their morphology and syntax are similar to those of argument clauses as illustrated above and in part somewhat different. But to discuss these details would go beyond the scope of this chapter.

A very small subset of embedded clauses exhibits verbal morphology and syntax identical to that of main sentences. Such clauses occur with verbs of belief and are, essentially, interchangeable with corresponding -*DIK* clauses (i.e. factive nominals) which can also be taken by verbs of belief. In some of the few instances where these constructions have been noted, they have been called 'direct complements'. They are of two types: (a) the embedded subject is marked nominative; the embedded verb exhibits regular verbal subject agreement marking:

Herkes   [(ben) üniversite + ye   başla + *yacağ + ım*] san + ıyor
everybody I   university + dat. start + fut. + 1 sg.   believe + pres. prog.
'Everybody believes that I shall start university'

(b) the embedded subject is marked accusative; the embedded verb exhibits only tense/aspect marking, but no agreement marking:

Herkes [ben + *i* üniversite + ye   başla   + *yacak*] san + ıyor
             + acc.   + fut.
(Same gloss as for the previous example.)

In addition, there are speakers who also accept a hybrid form where the embedded subject is accusative, but where the embedded verb exhibits regular verbal agreement markers:

Herkes [ben   + *i* üniversite + ye   başla   + *yacağ*   + *ım*]   san + ıyor
             + acc.   + fut.   + 1 sg.

Like all modifiers in the language, relative clauses in Turkish precede their heads. The verbs of such clauses are nominalised, and just as is the case with all regular embedded clauses, they lack complementisers. There is a gap in the position of the constituent within the clause that corresponds to the head.

The factive nominal marker -*DIK* is the basic type of morphology in these constructions; -*mA*, the 'result action' nominal, never occurs, and neither does the infinitive. -*DIK* is replaced by the morpheme -*An* where the 'relativised' constituent is a subject, part of a subject or a non-subject of a clause that lacks a subject (e.g. of an intransitive passive construction as in the last example below); yet another difference between the two constructions follows from this last property: -*DIK* is, as usual, followed by nominal agreement morphology; -*An* never is:

[Ahmed   + *in*   git + *tiğ* + *i*]   okul
              + gen.   go + *DIK* + 3 sg.   school
'the school that Ahmet goes to'
[okul + a   gid + *en*]   çocuk
school + dat.   go + *An*   child
'the child that goes to school'
[[oğl + u]   okul + a   gid +*en*]   adam
son + 3 sg.   school + dat.   go + *An*   man
'the man whose son goes to school'
[gid + *il* + *en*]   okul
go + pass. + *An*   school
'the school that is gone to'

Embedded questions have essentially the shape of regular embedded clauses: they are nominalised. Only -*DIK*-clauses can be embedded questions; -*mA*-clauses cannot. (This probably goes together with the fact that -*DIK*-clauses are independent from the main clause with respect to tense and aspect, since they are overtly marked for at least the future/non-future distinction; -*mA*-clauses lack tense completely and are dependent on the main clause for tense and aspect.) This does not mean that *wh*-elements cannot occur within -*mA*-clauses; when they do, however, the main clause is interpreted as a question rather than the embedded clause, while with -*DIK*-clauses either interpretation is possible:

Ahmet   [okul + a   *kim* + *in*   git + *tiğ* + in] + i   duy + du
              school + dat.   who + gen.   go + *DIK* + 3 sg. + acc.   hear + past

This has the embedded question reading: 'Ahmet heard who went to school' and the main clause question reading: 'Who did Ahmet hear goes to school?' (i.e. about whom did Ahmet hear whether he goes to school?'). (These two interpretations are distinguished intonationally, with falling intonation on the main clause verb for the former and slightly rising intonation for the

latter.) This ambiguity disappears when the question element occurs with a
-*mA*-clause:

Ahmet   [okul + a   *kim + in*   git   + *me* + sin] + i   isti + yor
                who + gen.   + *mA* +   want + pres. prog.
'Who does Ahmet want to go to school?'

The embedded question reading is not possible: '*Ahmet wants whom to go
to school?'.

Yes-no questions are also basically similar to regular embedded clauses,
particularly where constituents of the embedded clause are questioned;
however, where the whole embedded clause is questioned, and where
attachment of the question particle -*mI* is expected on the embedded verb, a
periphrastic construction in the shape of a participial coordinate structure is
found instead (sometimes referred to as an 'A-not-A construction'):

Ahmet   [(ben + im) okul + a   gid + *ip*   git + *me* + *diğ* + im] + i
        I + gen.   go + and   go + neg. + *DIK* + 1 sg. + acc.
                                              sor + du
                                              ask + past
'Ahmet asked whether I go/went to school (or not)'

One cannot say, in this meaning,

*Ahmet [(ben + im) okul + a git + tiğ + im + i + mi] sor + du,

although this is grammatical with the interpretation 'is it about my going to
school that Ahmet asked?'.

One more construction with a main/embedded clause asymmetry in the
sense that a given constraint holding of the embedded structure does not
hold of the main clause is verb-gapping in coordinate structures. In main
clause coordinate structures with identical verbs, either the first or the
second conjunct can lack its verb:

Ahmet   balığ + ı   *pişir + di*,   Mehmet   + *te*   ıstakoz + u
        fish + acc.   cook + past   + and lobster + acc.
'Ahmet cooked the fish and Mehmet (cooked) the lobster'
Ahmet balığ + ı, Mehmet + *te* ıstakoz + u *pişir + di*
'Ahmet (cooked) the fish, and Mehmet cooked the lobster'

Most SOV languages (e.g. Japanese) do not allow 'forward gapped'
structures like the first one above. Interestingly enough, Turkish itself does
not allow such structures when they are embedded:

(Ben) [Ahmed + in   balığ + ı,   Mehmed + in + *de*   ıstakoz + u
                    pişir + diğ + in] + i   bil + iyor + um
'I know that Ahmet (cooked) the fish and Mehmet cooked the lobster'
*(Ben) [Ahmed + in balığ + ı   *pişir + diğ + in + i*,   Mehmed + in + *de*
                              ıstakoz + u]   bil + iyor + um
'I know that Ahmet cooked the fish and Mehmet (cooked) the lobster'

This concludes our overview of the syntax of Turkish.

Bibliography

For the classification of the Turkic languages, reference may be made to the contributions in Deny et al. (1959). The following works are useful for the historical background to Turkish: Karamanlıoğlu (1972) — an overview of some historical literature, offering the author's own views on the development and geographical typology of the Turkic languages, especially those closely related to Turkish, and a discussion of the language reform — Von Gabain (1963) and Mansuroğlu (1954).

Lewis (1967) is a comprehensive and detailed treatment of the grammar with useful quotations from contemporary literature and the press; Underhill (1976) is a semi-pedagogical grammar, written in an informal generative framework.

Turkish phonology (and not only vowel harmony) has proved of continual interest to generative phonologists, starting with Lees' (1961) pioneering treatment, and new solutions to various problems continue to appear regularly in the generative phonological literature.

The fullest account of the pragmatic functions of Turkish word order is Erguvanlı (1984).

References

Deny, J., K. Grønbech, H. Scheel and Z.V. Togan (eds.) 1959. *Philologiae Turcicae Fundamenta*, vol. 1 (Steiner, Munich)

Erguvanlı, E.E. 1984. *The Function of Word Order in Turkish Grammar* (University of California Press, Berkeley, Los Angeles and London)

Karamanlıoğlu, A. 1972. *Türk Dili — Nereden Geliyor, Nereye Gidiyor* (= Hareket Yayınları, no. 46, Istanbul)

Lees, R.B. 1961. *The Phonology of Modern Standard Turkish* (Indiana University Press, Bloomington)

Lewis, G.L. 1967. *Turkish Grammar* (Oxford University Press, Oxford)

Mansuroğlu, M. 1954. 'The Rise and Development of Written Turkish in Anatolia', in *Oriens*, vol. 7, pp. 250–64.

Menges, K.H. 1959. 'Classification of the Turkic Languages, II', in Deny et al. (1959), pp. 5–10.

Underhill, R. 1976. *Turkish Grammar* (MIT Press, Cambridge, Mass.)

Von Gabain, A. 1963. 'Die Südwest-Dialekte des Türkischen', in *Handbuch der Orientalistik*, I. Abt., 5. Band, 1. Abschn. (E.J. Brill, Leiden), pp. 174–80.

31 AFROASIATIC LANGUAGES

Robert Hetzron

1   Introduction

The approximately 250 Afroasiatic languages, spoken by about 175 million ethnically and racially different people, occupy today the major part of the Middle East, all of North Africa, much of North-East Africa and a considerable area in what may roughly be defined as the northwestern corner of Central Africa. Though the distribution and spread of the specific languages was substantially different, about the same area was covered by Afroasiatic languages in antiquity. In the Middle Ages, the southern half of Spain and Sicily were also conquered by those who were to become the largest Afroasiatic-speaking people, the Arabs. Today, only Maltese represents this family as a native language in Europe.

The term 'Semitic' was proposed in 1781 for a group of related tongues, taken from the Bible (Genesis 10–11) where Noah's son Shem is said to be the ancestor of the speakers of these languages — showing, incidentally, awareness of linguistic relationships at this time. When it was realised that some other languages were further related to this group, the term 'Hamitic', based on the name of Shem's younger brother Ham (Cham), the biblical ancestor of Egypt and Kush, was coined for the entire family. Later the composite term Hamito-Semitic (sometimes Semito-Hamitic) was introduced. However, this created the wrong impression that there exists a 'Hamitic' branch opposed to Semitic. Of all the other terms proposed (Erythraic, Lisramic, Lamekhite), 'Afroasiatic' has been gaining ground. Even this name has the inconvenience of being misinterpreted as a group including all the languages of Africa and Asia. To dispel this, a further contraction, Afrasian, has also been used.

2   Division

Afroasiatic is composed of several branches. Various proposals have been made concerning the internal relationship between the branches, but none of these subdivisions are convincing enough to be adopted. The main branches are the following.

(a) **Egyptian** is the extinct language of one of the major civilisations of antiquity, that of Pharaonic Egypt (in today's Egypt, Arabic is spoken). This language can boast the longest continuous history. Its earliest documentations are from 3000 BC. From AD 300 on, the term 'Coptic' is used for the Egyptian idiom of monophysite Christians. It was spoken till the sixteenth century, perhaps even later; it is still used as a liturgical language.

(b) **Semitic** (see separate chapter).

(c) **Cushitic** consists of about 40 languages, spoken by 15 million people in Ethiopia, Somalia, northwestern Kenya and adjacent areas. Beja (of eastern Sudan and northern Ethiopia), with about 200,000 Muslim speakers, has been classified as North Cushitic, but there is some likelihood that it constitutes a separate branch of Afroasiatic. Central Cushitic or Agaw used to be the major language of Ethiopia before the Semitic conquest. It has split into a number of languages and is still spoken, by few, in scattered enclaves. Rift Valley (or Highland East) Cushitic is spoken by nearly two million people around the Ethiopian Great Rift Valley. Its best known representative is Sidamo. Lowland (East) Cushitic is numerically the most important group. Among others, it comprises Afar-Saho (Dankali) along the Red Sea, Oromo (formerly Galla), spoken by 8–10 million people, Somali, the official language of the Republic of Somalia and the vehicle of about 4 million Muslims, the Dullay languages etc. The status of South Cushitic is debated; many consider it a separate main branch, but it may also be a southern offshoot of Lowland Cushitic.

The oldest Cushitic texts are from the eighteenth century. Note that the term 'Cush' was originally applied to an unrelated country and civilisation: Meroë.

(d) **Omotic** is the name of a group of about 40 languages in the Omo Valley of southern Ethiopia, with about 1,300,000 speakers. It used to be classified as West Cushitic. Yet the great divergences led scholars to list it as a separate branch. On the other hand, since the divergences mainly consist of absence of some typical Cushitic features, Omotic may also be a simplified, pidginised offshoot of some branch of Cushitic.

(e) **Berber** is a cluster of closely related yet not always mutually intelligible dialects. Once the major language of all of North Africa west of Egypt, it still has some 10 million speakers, with the heaviest concentration in Morocco. The earliest documentation is provided by the Lybian inscriptions (the only one dated is from 139 BC). The major dialects are Tuareg, Tamazight, Tshalhit, Tirifie, Kabyle, Chawiya and Zenaga. An old consonantal alphabet, the *tifinagh*, has survived among the Tuareg. The extinct language of the Canary Islands, Guanche, may have also been a Berber tongue.

(f) **Chadic** (see separate chapter).

3   Problems of Relationship

The assertion that certain languages are related means that it is assumed that they are descended from a single common ancestor. Naturally, this is not necessarily true of the speakers themselves. It often happens that the same sedentary population switches language, adopting, with a certain degree of modification, the type of speech that has been imported by a relatively small, yet dominant group of newcomers. Thus, it could be just the language that wanders, whereas the people remain stationary and only change linguistic allegiance. This explains why so many anthropological types are found in this family: the brown-skinned Mediterranean Semites, the white-skinned Berber, the black-skinned, yet in many ways still different, Cushites and Chadic speakers.

Since Semitic, a linguistically fairly homogeneous group, seems to have had its major branches already established at least 5,000 years ago, and further, taking into consideration the great internal heterogeneity of Cushitic and Chadic, the period when the putative ancestral common Afroasiatic language was spoken must be placed at a much earlier period than the usually assumed sixth millennium BC. The location of this hypothetical tongue has been assumed to have been in North Africa, perhaps in the area which is now the Sahara desert, and the various branches must have diffused from there.

Theories have been advanced about further relationships of Afroasiatic with other languages, especially with Indo-European within a wide superfamily, Nostratic, also including Uralic, Altaic, Kartvelian, Dravidian etc. In view of the enormous time-depth that has to be accounted for, it is extremely hard to form any critical opinion of the reconstructions proposed to support this or other such proposals.

4   On Afroasiatic Comparison

In view of the great diversity among the branches of Afroasiatic, one should not expect many features in common that are to be found everywhere. Some such features do exist, such as gender distinction with t as a mark of the feminine, an element k as a mark of the second person, some vocabulary items such as the root *mut 'die'. Otherwise, we have to content ourselves with features that are found in several, but not all, branches, yielding an intertwined system that ultimately makes the unity of the family quite obvious. Thus, the root *šim 'name' is found everywhere but in Egyptian, the prefix conjugation is attested in Semitic, Cushitic and Berber, the stative suffix conjugation in Semitic, Egyptian, Berber and possibly Cushitic, etc. Naturally, for comparative purposes, it is sufficient for an item to be attested in at least one language of a branch to be used as an isogloss, e.g. the suffix conjugation only in Kabyle within Berber, the root *mut clearly only in Rendille within Cushitic.

Because of the fact that Semitic exhibits such a great deal of regularity and also because of its being the best known branch, some of the reconstructions have been strongly inspired by phenomena of Semitic. The opposite attitude, rejecting Semitic phenomena in reconstruction in order to avoid bias, has also been seen. Other disturbing factors are: lack of knowledge of Egyptian vowels (only Coptic provides clues about them), quite recent attestation and no ancient documents of most Cushitic, Omotic and Chadic languages, contrasting with millennia-old Semitic and Egyptian data. Nevertheless, one should not dogmatically believe that older data necessarily reflect a more archaic situation. Some phenomena found in recently discovered languages may be direct survivals from the oldest times.

5   Some Afroasiatic Features

The following is a brief listing of linguistic features that may be original Afroasiatic.

5.1   Phonetics

All branches except Egyptian exhibit a special set of consonants, besides voiced and voiceless pairs, the 'emphatic' series, realised as pharyngealised (velarised) in Arabic and Berber, glottalised (ejective, explosive) in South Arabian, Ethiopian and Cushitic and glottalised (explosive or implosive) in Chadic; Egyptian, incidentally, also lacked voiced consonants (*d* stands for /t/, *t* for /t^h/, in the standard transliteration). There is evidence for several lateral consonants in Proto-Semitic; they are still used in modern South Arabian, South Cushitic and some Chadic languages (e.g. *balsam* ultimately comes from the Semitic root *bs̍m* where *s̍* must have been a lateral fricative). Laryngeal sounds ʿ, *ḥ* and *x* are found in Egyptian, Cushitic, Berber and Semitic. A prenasalised phoneme *^{m}b has also been reconstructed.

The original vowel system is assumed to be long and short *a, i, u*, as still in Classical Semitic. Cushitic, Omotic and Chadic have tonal systems, e.g. Awngi (Cushitic, Agaw) *aqá* '(turn) into a man', *aqâ* 'I have been' and *áqâ* 'I have known'; *a* represents mid tone, *á* high tone, *à* low tone and *â* falling tone.

5.2   Morphology

In the pronominal system, **an* for 'I' in Semitic and Cushitic vs. **ana:ku* 'I' with a further velar in Egyptian and marginally in Semitic (perhaps also in the Berber suffix -γ), or *ka* for masculine 'thee, thy' in Semitic and Chadic vs. *ku* in Cushitic and marginally in Semitic (unclear for Egyptian) with different vowels, may represent original dialectal variations in Afroasiatic. The opposition *u/i* for masculine/feminine, especially in third person singular pronouns, seems to be original as well: Akkadian (Semitic) *šu:/ši:*, Somali (Cushitic) *-uu/-ay* 'he/she', Omotic: *-o/-e* gender markers in Kafa, parts of the third person singular masculine/feminine verb endings in Dizi, noun gender markers in Mubi (Chadic) (e.g. *mùndúrò*/*mìndíré* 'boy/girl') and perhaps Egyptian *-f/-s* 'his/her' (from *h^w/h^y*?).

In the demonstrative system the following gender-and-number markers are found: m. sg./f. sg./pl. *n/t/n* (Semitic, Chadic, traces in Berber), *ku/ti/hu* (Cushitic, also Chadic: Mubi *g-/d-/h-*), *p/t/n* (Egyptian) and for m./f. *w/θ* (in Berber). It is possible that both *p* and *w* come from *ku*.

Two verbal conjugation systems are found in more than one branch. One, found in Semitic, Cushitic and Berber, operates with the prefixes: *ʔ-* or *a-* for first person singular, *n-* for first person plural, *t-* for second person and for third person singular feminine and *y-* for the other third persons. Further suffixes added to the second and third person plurals and, in Semitic and Beja, to the second person singular feminine make up the full conjugations. Note the homonymy of second person singular masculine and third person singular feminine. The Cushitic languages have all switched to suffix conjugations by means of prefix-conjugated postposed auxiliaries, though a few of them have maintained the original conjugation for a limited number of verbs. This suffix conjugation is not to be confused with the original Afroasiatic suffix conjugation which can be reconstructed for predicates expressing a state, rather than an action, and is attested in Semitic (with the original value in Akkadian), Egyptian, Kabyle (Berber, for predicative adjectives) and probably in Cushitic.

In spite of its absence from Egyptian, Omotic and Chadic, it is likely that the prefix conjugation harks back to Proto-Afroasiatic.

Internal inflection, i.e. internal vocalic changes within a consonantal root to express tense, mood and other categories (the *root-and-pattern* system) is an operative principle in Semitic (Akkadian *i-prus* 'he divided', *i-parras* 'he divides', root *p-r-s*), less systematically in Berber (*-θ-lal* 'she (will) be born', *θ-lula* 'she was born'), in traces in Cushitic (Beja *ʔadanbíil* 'I collect', *ʔadbìl* 'I collected', root *d-b-l*). In Chadic, where the person of the subject is expressed by means of preposed particles which are very similar in shape to the oblique pronouns of other branches and where other categories like tense, mood etc. are either expressed by elements attached to these particles or, in part at least, by the stem form of the verb, alternations like Mubi *ní-túwà* 'I (will) eat'/*nɔ́-tî* 'I ate' have been considered traces of the Afroasiatic internal inflection by some scholars, while others have attributed them to independent developments. It is likely that an internal *a* is to be posited to mark the non-past in Afroasiatic. Internal *a/u* for non-past/past is attested in Semitic, Berber and Cushitic.

The verbal derivation system plays an important part in Afroasiatic vocabulary. Verbal roots are subject to modification; new verbs are created by the addition of derivative affixes. The element *s* produces a causative, the addition of *t* or *n* makes the verb intransitive (passive or reflexive). Repetition of the root or part of it or mere consonantal gemination expresses repeated action. Berber: *aɣəm* 'to get water', *ss-iɣəm* 'cause to get water', *ttuy-uɣəm* '(water) be drawn'; Beja *tam* 'eat', *tamtam* 'gobble'.

Classical Semitic and Egyptian used to have a dual in their nominal system, e.g. Egyptian *sn* 'brother', *sn.wy* 'two brothers', *sn.w* 'brothers'. For plural marking, several devices are found. The endings *-u:/-w* and *-n* seem to be attested all over. Repetition of the last consonant is found in Cushitic (Somali *miis/miisas* 'table/tables') and Chadic (Mubi *lísí/lésas* 'tongue'). In Cushitic and Chadic, one finds singulative systems where the basic form is a collective and the addition of a suffix makes it singular, e.g. Mubi (Chadic) *mándàr* 'boy(s) (in general)'/*mùndúrò* 'boy'. Yet the most interesting plural formation is what has been called the broken plural, based on internal inflection, *sinn-/asna:n-* in Arabic (Semitic), *sini/san* in Logone (Chadic) for 'tooth/teeth', Xamta (Agaw, Cushitic) *gezéŋ/agzéŋ* 'dog/dogs', Berber *ikərri/akrarən* (with a further *-n*) 'ram/rams'. Though the basic principle seems to be the infixation of an *a*, the broken plural forms cannot be predicted automatically from the singular. This is also an argument in favour of their archaic character. Thus, some form of internal inflection *must* have existed indeed in Afroasiatic. The Afroasiatic noun also distinguished between the genders masculine and feminine. The latter is used not only for female animates, but often also for derivatives such as diminutives, e.g. Berber *axam* 'tent' – *θaxamθ* 'small tent'. Furthermore, Semitic and Cushitic have traces of polarity whereby a noun changing number may also change its gender, e.g. Sidamo (Cushitic) *ko beetti* 'this boy'/*te ooso* 'these boys' vs. *te seemo* 'this girl'/*ko seenne* 'these girls' (m. *ko*, f. *te*).

In nominal derivation, the prefix *ma-* plays an important role to form agent, locative or instrumental nouns.

5.3 Word Order
Classical Semitic, Egyptian and Berber are VSO languages, Cushitic is almost all SOV, while Chadic is mainly SVO. The reconstruction of Proto-Afroasiatic word order is open to speculation.

Bibliography

Diakonoff (1965) is a short yet highly informative comparative presentation, the best so far in the field. Hodge (1971) is a collection of chapters from the *Current Trends in Linguistics* series, somewhat uneven, partly inevitably obsolete, but still an important research tool. Cohen (1947) is a pioneering work in comparative Afroasiatic, but restricted to vocabulary and with only few references to Chadic. Bender (1976) provides concise yet comprehensive sketches of the structure of the major Cushitic languages, with state-of-the-art introductions, and is a ground-breaking publication. Valuable discussions of Afroasiatic are also included in two more general Africanist publications: Greenberg (1963) and Heine et al. (1981).

References

Bender, M.L. (ed.) 1976. *The Non-Semitic Languages of Ethiopia* (Michigan State University, East Lansing)

Cohen, M. 1947. *Essai comparatif sur le vocabulaire et la phonétique du chamito-sémitique* (Champion, Paris)

Diakonoff, I.M. 1965. *Semito-Hamitic Languages* (Nauka, Moscow)

Greenberg, J.H. 1963. *The Languages of Africa* (Indiana University, Bloomington and Mouton, The Hague)

Heine, B. et al. (eds.) 1981. *Die Sprachen Afrikas* (H. Buske, Hamburg)

Hodge, C.T. (ed.) 1971. *Afroasiatic: A Survey* (Mouton, The Hague)

32 Semitic Languages

Robert Hetzron

1 Introduction

Originally limited to the area east of the Mediterranean Sea, the Semitic languages and civilisations spread into North Africa, southern Europe and the Horn of Africa. In antiquity, the Assyrian and Babylonian Empires were major centres of civilisation. Phoenician traders were roaming and establishing colonies all over the Mediterranean basin. Hebrew culture, through its monotheistic religion, Judaism, has exerted an exceptional influence, directly or indirectly (through the two great religions inspired by it: Christianity and Islam), on all of mankind. Arabic, in addition to being the carrier of an important medieval civilisation, has become one of the major languages of the world today.

While the ancestor of Semitic, Proto-Afroasiatic, is assumed to have originated in Africa, the homeland of Semitic itself, i.e. the area where, having arrived from Africa, the different branches started to split off, may have been approximately the region where the Arabian peninsula reaches the continental bulk of the Near East.

2 Division

The following is a listing of the Semitic languages according to the latest classification, with summary information on the speakers.

(A) East Semitic: Akkadian was the language of ancient Mesopotamia (approximately today's Iraq), the carrier of a grandiose civilisation from c. 3000 BC to the beginnings of the Christian era. Akkadian gradually replaced the unrelated Sumerian which had greatly influenced it. It was soon divided into Assyrian (northern) and Babylonian (southern) branches, corresponding to a political division. The last written documents date from the first century AD. Afterwards, Akkadian was completely forgotten and had to be rediscovered, with its writing system deciphered, in the nineteenth century. The Akkadian script, usually written from left to right, is called cuneiform, i.e. 'wedge-shaped', because of the graphic components of the symbols.

(B) West Semitic, the other major branch of Semitic, is divided into two sub-branches.

(a) South Semitic is composed of three groups, the exact relationship of which has not yet been determined.

(i) Epigraphic South Arabian (attested from the ninth century BC to the sixth century AD) is known only from short inscriptions written in a consonantal script. Its dialects were Sabaean (of Sheba), Minean, Awsani, Qatabani and Hadramauti. Once spoken in the southern half of the Arabian peninsula, they were completely replaced by Arabic.

(ii) Modern South Arabian, a group of non-Arabic languages (that are apparently not the descendants of Epigraphic South Arabian), is still spoken by some 25,000 people in the Dhofar (Oman): Shahri, Mahri and Harsusi, and on the island of Socotra off the Arabian coast: Soqotri. Serious investigation of them has started only recently.

(iii) Ethiopian. Speakers of South Arabian crossed the Red Sea millennia ago — much earlier than the usually given date of the fourth century BC — into the highlands of Ethiopia and mixed with the local Cushitic population, who gradually adopted their language and modified it to a significant extent. The Ethiopian Semitic (Ethio-Semitic) languages are to be divided into two main branches.

(α) North Ethiopic comprises the following: the now extinct Ge'ez, attested between the fourth and ninth centuries AD, was the language of the Axumite Empire. It is still used as the liturgical language of the Ethiopian Coptic Church, occasionally also for literature. Almost all of the Ge'ez material comes from a period when it was no more in everyday use, which makes the data less reliable. Tigrinya has nearly four million speakers in Eritrea and in the Tigre Governorate-General. Tigré is spoken by about 350,000 Muslims.

(β) South Ethiopic has two branches: (I) Transversal South Ethiopic which comprises Amharic, the official language of modern Ethiopia, the native language of about eight million Coptic Christians and the secondary language of about as many more; the almost extinct Argobba; Harari (Adare), the language of the Muslim city of Harar, and East Gurage (Zway, the Selti-Wolane-Ulbarag cluster), a practically undescribed unit. (II) Within Outer South Ethiopic, the very recently extinct Gafat, Soddo (the language of about 100,000 Christians) and Goggot constitute the n-group; Muher and Western Gurage (Masqan, the 'Central' Ezha-Gumer-Chaha-

Gura cluster and the 'Peripheral' Gyeto-Ennemor-Endegeñ-Ener cluster) make up the *tt*-group. As can be deduced, Gurage is not a valid linguistic term, it designates a number of Semitic languages belonging to different branches, spoken in one specific area.

(b) Central Semitic has fared relatively the best in this family.

(i) Aramaic is the label for a group of related dialects, originally spoken in what is Syria today. It is attested since the beginning of the first millennium BC. It later spread to all of the Near East, replacing Akkadian, Hebrew and other languages, only to be replaced, in turn, by Arabic after the rise of Islam in the seventh century AD. Major parts of the biblical books of Ezra and Daniel are in Aramaic. Jesus' native tongue was Palestinian Aramaic. Nabatean was spoken by ethnic Arabs around the beginning of the Christian era. The Babylonian Talmud was written in Eastern Aramaic, a language close to Syriac, the language of the Christian city of Edessa (till the thirteenth century AD), still the liturgical language of the Nestorian and Jacobite Christian Churches. Classical and Modern Mandaic are associated with a Gnostic sect. Today, a variety of Western Aramaic is spoken in three villages near Damascus, Syria. Dialects of Eastern Neo-Aramaic (Modern Syriac) are still vigorous in Christian communities in north-western Iran and adjacent areas in Iraq, in Soviet Georgia and in scattered communities around the world. The speakers (at least 300,000) are sometimes inappropriately called Chaldean, (Neo-)Assyrian. Eastern Neo-Aramaic is further maintained by Jews coming from the same region in Israel and elsewhere. The consonantal Aramaic square script is used for Hebrew today (see the chapter on Hebrew).

(ii) South-Central Semitic

(α) Arabic (see separate chapter; the traditional assignment of Arabic to South Semitic is, incidentally, untenable).

(β) Canaanite. Ancient Canaanite inscriptions of Byblos are from the sixteenth and fifteenth centuries BC. Moabite (ninth century BC) is known from one inscription only. Three ancient, long-extinct languages may also be Canaanite, though further study is needed: Ugaritic, the language of the city-state of Ugarit (now Ras Shamra, Syria, on the Mediterranean) around the fourteenth/thirteenth centuries BC, with an impressive literature written in a cuneiform consonantal script; the poorly attested Amorite (the first half of the second millennium BC) and the recently discovered language of Ebla (the third millennium BC).

Phoenician was originally spoken on the coastal areas of today's Lebanon and is attested through inscriptions (from the twelfth century BC to AD 196). Phoenician merchants, however, established settlements all over the Mediterranean area: Cyprus, Greece, Malta, Sicily, Sardinia, southern France, southern Spain and, above all, North Africa. In the latter area, the city of *Qart Ḥadašt* 'New City', known in Europe as Carthage, founded in 814 BC, developed into a large empire after the fifth century BC. It was destroyed, under the rule of Hannibal, in 146 BC by the Romans. Their variety of late Phoenician is called Punic, attested till the fifth century AD.

The Phoenician consonantal script of 22 letters, written from right to left, practically identical with the old Hebrew script, is probably of Egyptian origin. It is the direct ancestor of the Greek and Latin alphabets. The Arabic, South Semitic (including Ethiopian) and Syriac scripts also come from the Canaanite writing system. Furthermore, the writing systems of Central Asia (e.g. Mongolian writing) and India (the Devanāgarī script) are also descended from the Syriac one.

For the historically most important Canaanite language, Hebrew, see the separate chapter.

3 The Structure of Semitic

3.1 Phonology

The original vowel system consisted of long and short *a*, *i* and *u*. Consonants occurred simple or doubled (geminated). A typical feature of the consonantal system is the existence of 'triads', groups of three consonants with the same point of articulation: voiced (e.g. *d*), voiceless (*t*) and 'emphatic' (*ṭ*). The latter are pronounced pharyngealised ('dark') in Arabic, as glottalised ejectives (where the glottal closure is maintained till high pressure is achieved, then the closure is released with an explosion) in Ethiopian and Modern South Arabian (though the two do not sound the same) and dropped in Modern Hebrew (where they are pronounced voiceless, except *ṣ* > *ts*). The nature of the articulation is unknown in the extinct languages. The original set of laryngeals, *ʔ*, *ʕ* (a voiced pharyngeal constriction), *ḥ* (voiceless pharyngeal constriction) and *x* (voiceless uvular constriction) has been maintained in full in Arabic only. Ethiopian script still marks them, but of all the living languages, only Tigrinya and Tigré kept all but *x* (but a *x* was secondarily developed). Akkadian had lost all of them (lost *ḥ* and *ʕ* left their trace in changing a neighbouring *a* into *e*).

In the causative prefix, in the third person independent pronouns, in the archaic dative endings and in some other cases, one finds an inter-lingual alternation *š* (e.g. Akkadian) ~ *h* (Hebrew), etc. This may go back to an old phoneme **š* which merged with other phonemes in different ways, possibly an original voiceless lateral or palatal fricative. There is strong evidence for Arabic *ḍ* and Hebrew *ś* once having been lateral; Modern South Arabian still has the laterals *ś* and *ż*.

In Arabic and South Semitic, old *p* became *f*, and in most of Arabic, *g* became *ǰ*. In Aramaic, Hebrew and several Ethiopian languages, a morphophonemic process of spirantisation took place, leading to alternations in different forms of the same root. Post-vocalic non-geminate stops of Hebrew (see page 694): *p, t, k, b, d, g* became *f, θ, x, β, ð, γ* respectively. In modern North Ethiopic, only *k* and *q* were spirantised (the latter yielding a curious spirant ejective sound). In Outer South Ethiopic *tt*-languages, complicated spirantisation processes, also depending on position in the root, took place, *k~h* being the most basic. In some of these, all geminate consonants became voiceless and simple. Thus, there is Ezha *bäkkʸä-*, Chaha *bäkʸä-* 'he cried', but *yəβähʸ* 'he cries' for both (note the spirantisation *b~β* as well, root *b-k-y*). For 'he broke/breaks', Ezha has *säbbärä-/yəsäbər,* Chaha *säpärä-/yəsäβər* (root *s-b-r*).

3.2 Morphology

In the noun, there was a distinction between masculine and feminine genders (the latter marked by -(*a*)*t*), e.g. Ge'ez *nəgus* 'king'/*nəgəst* 'queen'; for number: a singular, a dual (for two units; alive in Arabic, Epigraphic and Modern South Arabian, only in traces in Akkadian and Hebrew, lost in Ethiopian; marked by -*a:/-ay*) and a plural. For plural marking, the suffixal (sound) plural had, as its markers: lengthening of the last vowel most often followed by -*n*(*a*) in the masculine and -*t* (i.e. -*a:t*) in the feminine, but most frequently internal vocalic changes formed it (the so-called 'broken plural'). Examples (sg./pl.): Akkadian *šarr-/šarr*+long vowel or *šarra:n-* 'king', Ge'ez *nəgəst/nəgəstat* 'queen' (sound), *ləbs/albas* 'clothing', *nəgus/nägäst* 'king' (broken). The -*t* of the latter is the trace of an interesting old phenomenon, polarity, whereby in changing number nouns also change gender. Hence the feminine ending after the plural of a masculine. For the opposite direction, much rarer, see Ge'ez *tə ʔmərt/tə ʔamər* 'miracle', where the plural loses its feminine ending. Polarity is never a truly consistent principle in any Semitic language, but it left traces in plural formation, in the Arabic agreement rules (see page 678) and in the numeral system (see below).

The type of vocalisation assumed by the broken plural form is predictable from the singular in a minority of cases only. Usually, it has to be memorised separately. One noun may have several broken plural forms, e.g. Ge'ez *kälb* 'dog', pl. *käläbat, akləbt* or *aklab* (cf. *kalb/kila:b* in Arabic), sometimes with differences of meaning. Broken plurals are widely used in Arabic, Modern South Arabian, North Ethiopic, with some traces in South Ethiopic and Hebrew (e.g. *kɛlɛb/klåbīm* 'dog/dogs', with a further sound plural ending), no traces in Akkadian.

A further morphological category applying to nouns is 'state': the construct state (a phonetically shortened form in Hebrew, with an ending -*ä* in Ge'ez) is for the noun attached to a genitival noun; the pronominal state is used before possessive suffixes; the predicative state in Akkadian is the shape of a predicative noun, containing also subject endings; in Aramaic, the emphatic state (suffix -*å*) refers to a definite noun; otherwise the noun is in the absolute state (with an ending -*m* in the singular in Akkadian).

The basic case system consists of a nominative case and an oblique one. In the singular, the latter is subdivided into an accusative and a genitive. Construct state nouns have only a 'genitive/all the rest' opposition in Akkadian and no case in Ge'ez. In the singular, the endings are nom. -u, acc. -a, gen. -i; in the dual nom. -a:, obl. -ay; in the plural nom. -u:, obl. -i:. Prepositions combine with the genitive/oblique case. Proto-Semitic probably had a richer case system, as suggested by the evidence of some traces. The above system is found in Akkadian and Classical Arabic only, Ge'ez has acc. -ä vs. -Ø in the singular only (East Gurage has -ä for a definite accusative). The prepositional system that had been the mainstay of case marking since Proto-Semitic has completely taken over everywhere else (for dual and plural marking, the oblique forms were generalised), with further postpositions (forming circumpositions) developing in modern Ethiopian, and with postpositions only (some of them used to be prepositions) in Harari (e.g. Proto-Semitic *bi-bayt-i 'in-house-gen.', Ge'ez bä-bet, East Gurage bä-gar wəsṭ (='inside'), Harari gar-be for 'in (a/the) house').

In the pronominal and verbal system, no distinction of gender is made in the first persons, but the second and third persons have both a masculine and a feminine, in the singular everywhere, but no more in the plural in modern East Aramaic, Transversal South Ethiopic and Gafat (and some modern Arabic dialects).

There are three basic sets of personal pronouns: independent ones for subject and predicate functions, possessive pronouns suffixed to nouns (Amharic bet-e 'house-my') or to prepositions (Hebrew b-ī 'in-my' for 'in me') and object pronouns attached to verbs.

Beside basic adjectives, nouns may be adjectivised by means of the suffix -i:/-iyy (the so-called nisbe), e.g. Arabic bayt-iyy- 'domestic, home-made'.

Numerals from 'three' to 'ten' (with some complications, from 'eleven' to 'nineteen' as well in South-Central Semitic) show clear traces of polarity. Numerals with a feminine ending precede masculine nouns and those without such an ending occur with feminine nouns. This harks back to the prehistoric period when the plural of a masculine was indeed a feminine and vice versa.

The centrality of the verb has always been pointed out in the description of Semitic. Verbal morphology is an essential part of grammar. Most nouns are derived from verbs and, conversely, most nouns that seem to be basic may be the sources of verbal roots (e.g. Arabic ba:ta 'spend the night' from bayt- 'house'). And it is here that the most important feature of Semitic morphology, the root-and-pattern system (see broken plurals above) ought to be properly introduced.

The Semitic root consists of a set of consonants, ideally three, but sometimes four, e.g. Akkadian p-r-s 'divide, decide, etc.'. There is strong evidence that pre-Semitic may have had also biconsonantal roots which were later made triconsonantal by the addition of another consonant; cf. the

Hebrew roots *p-r-d* 'divide', *p-r-m* 'open, seam', *p-r-s* 'break up, divide up', suggesting an old root *p-r. Roots that behave regularly are called 'sound roots', as opposed to 'weak roots' which have a weak root consonant, such as a semi-vowel *y* or *w* which may be reduced to a vowel (*i/u* respectively) or disappear, for Akkadian and Hebrew also *n* which may assimilate to the subsequent consonant; or else, to be 'weak', the last two consonants may be identical, like *p-r-r* 'annul', which may be subject to contractions through the conjugation. Such roots are combined with patterns made up of vowels and often also consonants in a prefixal, suffixal or, more rarely, infixal position. Thus, in Akkadian, the pattern CCuC yields *-prus*, the past tense 'divided', whereas the present has CaC:aC, leading to *-parras* (where the gemination is part of the pattern); Ca:CiC is the active participle: *pa:ris-* 'divider'; CtaCaC is the perfect theme *-ptaras* 'has divided'; šaCCVC is the causative stem, where the value of V depends on tense: *-šapras* for the present and *-šapris* for the past; with a further *mu-*, we obtain an active participle: *mušapris-* 'the one who makes divide'; some nominal patterns: CiCiCt- (*t* for feminine) *pirist-* 'decision', CaCC for *pars-* 'part' etc.

There are two sets of basic conjugations in Semitic, one called 'prefixal', in reality a combination of four prefixes and, in seven cases out of twelve, further suffixes, and one purely 'suffixal'. In table 32.1 are the forms that may be reconstructed for Proto-Semitic. (There are uncertainties about the first person dual. In the prefix conjugation, note the identity of second person singular masculine and third person singular feminine and, more puzzling, of the dual and the feminine plural. The first person plural typically has no suffix.)

Table 32.1: Person-markers of the Verb

	Prefix M.	Common	F.	Suffix M.	Common F.
Singular					
1st		a-...			...-ku
2nd	ta-...		ta-...-i:	...-ta	...-ti
3rd	ya-...		ta-...	...Ø	...-at
Dual					
2nd		ta-...-a:			...-tuma:
3rd		ya-...-a:			...-a:
Plural					
1st		ni-...			...-nu/-na:
2nd	ta-...-u:		ta-...-a:	...-tumu:	...-tinna(:)
3rd	ya-...-u:		ya-...-a:	...-u:	...-a:

These affixes are attached to various stem forms to create verbal words. Stem forms (as the term is used here) consist of the verbal root and the pattern expressing tense, mood and type of derivation (see below). In the following, the root *p~f-r-s* (Akkadian 'divide', Arabic 'make a kill (of a predatory animal)', Ge'ez 'destroy') is used to illustrate the forms. For Proto-Semitic we reconstruct:

Non-past (= present or future) *-parrVs   Prefix
Past *-prVs ~ jussive (imperative-like) *-prVs   Prefix
Stative (see below) *parVs-   Suffix

The stative originally referred to the state in which the object, or sometimes the subject, finds itself as a lasting result of a previous action (e.g. Akkadian *parsa:ku* 'I have been cut away'). The past and the jussive were almost homophonous but, most probably, distinguished by the stress: on the prefix for the past and on the stem for the jussive (*y'iprus* 'he divided', *yipr'us* 'let him divide!'). 'V' above refers to the 'thematic vowel', *a, i* or *u*, specified for each verb in the lexicon, but not necessarily the same in the three basic forms of the same verb. It is most probably the remnant of an old semantic distinction between active and stative (transitive and intransitive?) verbs. *a* is still often associated with passive-intransitive.

The above system is more or less valid for Akkadian, which, however, had in addition a resultative-perfect (with an infix *-ta-* after the first root consonant: *-ptaras*). West Semitic dropped the old prefix-conjugated past (which, however, left some traces) and promoted the original stative into a past tense. Furthermore, South Semitic replaced the *-t-* of the second person suffixes by *-k-*, whereas Central Semitic changed the first person singular to *-tu*, Central Semitic underwent a radical change. It dropped the original non-past forms (*-parras*) and adopted the jussive forms followed by indicative endings as a new non-past. The vocalisation of the prefixes was also reorganised. Some examples of non-past/past (2 sg. f.): Akkadian *taparrasi:/taprusi:*, Ge'ez *təfärrəsi/färäski*, Arabic *tafrisi:-na/farasti*.

The verbal derivational system is of great importance in Semitic. The above samples represent the 'basic' form ('stem' in the traditional terminology). Derivation is made through root-internal and prefixal modification. A gemination of the middle radical throughout creates an 'intensive' form, mainly for repeated action. A long vowel after the first radical produces the 'conative' form, comparable to what is called 'applicative' in other language families (e.g. Bantu), i.e. with the function of making an indirect object into a direct one. This system of three units, basic-intensive-conative, is but one axis of the derivation. Prefixed *ni-* or *ta-* (the latter sometimes infixed) forms an intransitive — passive or reflexive. The prefix *ša-/ha-/ʔa-* produces a causative. A compound *a/ista-* is a causative or reciprocal or has other values. Originally, all of these prefixes (questionable for *ni-*, which may have been reserved to the basic form) could be combined with any of the root-internally distinguished forms (Ge'ez is still the closest to this), but now combinations are strictly limited according to the language.

Moreover, the meanings attributed to them above is actually true in part only. Only some of the derivations are free, only some of the meaning modifications may be predicted. The actual occurrences of a verb in various forms is defined by the lexicon. Thus, 'causative' is to be understood more as a morphological label than a semantic one, though many causative-prefixed verbs are indeed the causatives of the corresponding basic forms. Derived forms have no special thematic vowels and the internal and prefix vocalisation is also different.

In the South Central Semitic languages 'internal passives' are also found. The introduction of an *u* after the first consonant makes a form a passive: Arabic *tufrasi:-na/furisti* 'you (f. sg.) were killed (as prey by an animal)'. Modern South Arabian (Shahri) has *yə'rɔfəs/rə'fɔs* 'he kicks/kicked' and an internal passive *yər'fɔs/rə'fis* 'he is/was kicked', but the latter may be the remnant of the old thematic vowel change making a verb stative-intransitive.

3.3 Notes on Syntax
Proto-Semitic word order is assumed to have been VSO, still so in Classical Arabic, to a decreasing extent in Biblical Hebrew and, less clearly, in Ge'ez. Akkadian was SOV under the influence of the Sumerian substratum, as is modern Ethiopian, copying the Cushitic system. Later Hebrew and Arabic are basically SVO. The adjectives, however, always follow the noun, except in modern Ethiopian (and partly in Ge'ez). Numerals most often precede the noun. Demonstratives follow, except in Arabic and part of modern Ethiopian. Residual case endings aside, case marking is predominantly prepositional (see above). Subordinate clauses follow the head, except in modern Ethiopian.

Adjectives agree with the noun they qualify in gender and number and, when used attributively, also in suffixal case and definiteness/state (e.g. Akkadian *umm-a-m damiq-t-a-m* 'the good mother' lit. 'mother-acc.-abs. good-f.-acc.-abs.', Aramaic *yamm-å rabb-å* 'sea-the big-the'). For numeral agreement, see 'polarity' above. For Arabic subject-verb agreement, see page 683.

There are usually two genitive constructions, one using the construct state, one with a genitive particle, e.g. Ge'ez *betä nəguš* or *bet zä-nəguš* 'the king's house' (*bet* 'house', *zä-* 'of'). Except in modern Ethiopian, the order is always possessed-possessor (cf. Amharic *yä-nəgus bet* for the opposite order).

In Akkadian and Ethiopian (and originally in Aramaic), the 'of' particle also serves as a relative particle. The function of the head noun is marked by a pronoun next to the verb, as a suffix: Akkadian *awi:l-a-m ša šarr-u-m bi:t-a-m iddin-u-šu amur* 'man₍-acc.-abs. that king-nom.-abs. house-acc.-abs. he+gave-subordinate suffix him₍ I+saw', Amharic *nəgus bet-u-n yä-sättu-t-ən säw ayyähu-t* 'king house-the-acc. that-he+gave-him₍-acc. man₍ I+saw-him' for 'I saw the man to whom the king gave the house'; with an independent prepositional pronoun: Akkadian *ša ittišu tuššabu*, Amharic *kəssu gar yämməttənor*, 'that with him you live', i.e. 'with whom you live' etc. As can be seen, the Akkadian verb has a special suffix for the subordinate verb (here *-u*).

Subordinating particles are clause-initial, except in modern Ethiopian where they are affixed to the clause-final verb. Another example of the latter in Tigré: *dərho ʔət bet kəm ʔatrafawo* 'chicken in house as they+left+him' for 'as they left the chicken at home'.

4 Closing Words

For the comparative linguist, the Semitic languages exhibit a great deal of similarity. The family is much more uniform than, say, Indo-European. Yet, from a practical point of view, these languages are very different, there being no mutual comprehensibility even between the close relatives. On the other hand, however compact the family, scholars do not always agree on matters of reconstruction. Semitic scholarship is a very active field, further enlivened by the recent involvement of other branches of Afroasiatic.

Bibliography

There is a serious need for an up-to-date manual on comparative Semitic. Brockelmann (1908–13) is the classical work in the field. Gray (1934) is a useful, but outdated, introduction. Moscati et al. (1964) is the result of the cooperation between specialists of the main branches; it is conservative in approach and to be used with caution. Bergsträsser (1983) is a collection of sample texts preceded by sketch grammars; while still valuable in many details, it is now altogether obsolete, in spite of attempts at updating by the translator.

References

Bergsträsser, G. 1983. *Introduction to the Semitic Languages* (Eisenbrauns, Winona Lake, Ind.; translated by P.T. Daniels from the German original, *Einführung in die semitischen Sprachen*, Max Hueber, Munich, 1928, 2nd ed. 1963)

Brockelmann, C. 1908–13. *Grundriß der vergleichenden Grammatik der semitischen Sprachen* (Reuther und Reichard, Berlin; reprinted G. Olms, Hildesheim, 1961)

Gray, L.H. 1934. *Introduction to Semitic Comparative Linguistics* (Columbia University, New York)

Moscati, S. et al. 1964. *An Introduction to the Comparative Grammar of the Semitic Languages, Phonology and Morphology* (O. Harrassowitz, Wiesbaden)

33 Arabic

Alan S. Kaye

1 Arabic and the Semitic Languages

Arabic is by far *the* Semitic (or indeed Afroasiatic) language with the greatest number of speakers, probably now in excess of 150 million, although a completely satisfying and accurate estimate is lacking. It is *the* major language throughout the Arab world, i.e. Egypt, Sudan, Libya, the North African countries usually referred to as the Maghrib (such as Tunisia, Morocco and Algeria), Saudi Arabia, Iraq, Jordan, the Gulf countries etc., and it is even the major language of non-Arab countries such as the Republic of Chad in central Africa (i.e. more Chadians speak Arabic as their mother tongue than any other language).

Arabic is also a minority language in other countries such as Nigeria, Iran and the Soviet Union (the speakers — some 4,000 — of Soviet Central Asian Arabic have probably all assimilated to another language). Furthermore, Arabic is in wide use throughout the Muslim world as a second language and as a learned, liturgical language (e.g. in Pakistan, India, Indonesia). Indeed among orthodox Muslims Arabic is *luɣat almalāʔikah* 'the language of the angels', and the language *par excellence* in the world since Allāh himself speaks Arabic and has revealed his Holy Book, the Qurʔān, in the Arabic language. One can also easily comprehend that the Arabs are very proud of their (most beautiful) language since there is even a verb *ʔaʕraba* 'to speak clearly and eloquently' from the root *ʕRB*, also occurring in the word *alʕarabiyyah* 'the Arabic language' or *lisān ʕarabī* 'the Arabic language' in the Qurʔān.

There is even a historical dialect of Arabic, Maltese, sometimes, although erroneously, called Maltese Arabic, which, due to its isolation from the rest of the so-called Arab world, developed into a new Semitic language in its own right (a similar, but weaker, argument could be made also for Cypriot Maronite Arabic). The two major reasons for my claiming that Maltese is not to be regarded synchronically as a dialect of Arabic are: (1) Maltese, if an Arabic dialect today, would be one without diglossia, i.e. it does not have Classical Arabic as a high level of language (more on this important topic later); and (2) it would be the *only* Arabic dialect normally written in the Latin script.

2 Arabic as Central Semitic

According to the new classification of the Semitic languages proposed by R. Hetzron (see the chapter on Semitic languages), there is evidence that Arabic shares traits of both South Semitic and North-West Semitic. Arabic preserves Proto-Semitic phonology almost perfectly (Epigraphic South Arabian is even more conservative), except for Proto-Semitic *$p > f$ and Proto-Semitic *$\acute{s} > s$. But Arabic also shares features with Hebrew, Ugaritic and Aramaic such as the masculine plural suffix -*īna*/*īma* and the internal passive, e.g. Arabic *qatala* 'he killed' vs. *qutila* 'he was killed' and Hebrew *hilbīš* 'he dressed someone' vs. *hulbaš* 'he was dressed (by someone)'.

The morphology of the definite article in Hebrew (*ha*- + gemination of the following consonant if that consonant is capable of gemination) and Arabic (*?al*-, which assimilates before dentals or sibilants, producing a geminate) also points to a common origin and so on. The Hebrew *ha*-, in fact, also shows up in the Arabic demonstratives, *hāδā* 'this, m. sg.' *hāδihi* 'f.' and *hā?ulā?i* 'pl.'. Even the broken plurals of Arabic may be compared with Hebrew *segholate* plurals such as *kəlāvīm* 'dogs' (cf. sg. *kɛlɛv* + -*īm* 'm. pl.'), where one can easily see the vocalic change in the stem (cf. Arabic *kilāb*).

There are some other very striking morphological affinities of Arabic with Hebrew such as the ancient dialectal Arabic relative particle *δū*, cf. Biblical Hebrew *zū*, while the Western form *δī* occurred in Arabic *?allaδī* 'who, m. sg.' and Aramaic *dī*. Some Eastern dialects also reflected Barth's Law, i.e. they had *i* as the imperfect preformative vowel with *a* of the imperfect system like the Canaanite dialects.

3 Some Characteristics of Arabic and the Designation 'Arabic'

Arabic sticks out like a sore thumb in comparative Semitic linguistics because of its almost (too perfect) algebraic-looking grammar, i.e. root and pattern morphology. It is so algebraic that some scholars have accused the medieval Arab grammarians of contriving some artificiality about it in its classical form. For instance, the root *KTB* has to do with 'writing'. In Form I (the simple form of the verb corresponding to the Hebrew *qal* stem), *kataba* means 'he wrote', imperfect *yaktubu* 'he writes', with three verbal nouns all translatable as 'writing' — *katb*, *kitāba* and *kitba*. In Form II (the exact nuances of the forms will be discussed in section 9), *kattaba*, imperfect *yukattibu* means 'to make write'; Form III *kātaba*, imperfect *yukātibu* means 'to correspond'; Form IV *?aktaba*, imperfect *yuktibu* 'to dictate'; Form VI *takātaba*, imperfect *yatakātabu* 'to keep up a correspondence'; Form VII *?inkataba*, imperfect *yankatibu* 'to subscribe'; Form VIII *?iktataba*, imperfect *yaktatibu* 'to copy'; Form X *?istaktaba*, imperfect *yastaktibu* 'to ask to write'. There are ten commonly used forms of the verb (five others occur but are very uncommon); the root *KTB* does not occur in Form V, which is often a passive of Form II ('to be made to write'?), or Form IX, which is a very special form reserved only for the semantic sphere of colours and defects (so we would not expect it to occur in this form). The linguists who have seen a much too regular *Systemzwang* in this particular case have doubted the authenticity of some of the forms with this root and have asked about an automatic plugging in of the root into the form to obtain a rather forced (artificially created) meaning.

There are also many other words derivable from this triconsonantal root by using different vocalic patterns. For instance, *kitāb* 'book' (vowel pattern = $C_1iC_2āC_3$) with its pl. *kutub* ($C_1uC_2uC_3$), *kutubī* 'bookseller', *kuttāb* 'Koran school', *kutayyib* 'booklet', *kitābī* 'written', *katība* 'squadron', *maktab* 'office', *maktaba* 'library', *miktāb* 'typewriter', *mukātaba* 'correspondence', *ʔiktitāb* 'registration', *ʔistiktāb* 'dictation', *kātib* 'writer', *maktūb* 'letter, note' etc.

The Arabic dictionary lists words under their respective roots, thus all of the above are found under the root *KTB*. However, in most native but older dictionaries, a word is listed by what it ends with, so that all of the above words would be listed under /b/. The reason that this was done was to make life very easy for the poets (who were the real inventors of the classical language), since the usual state of a traditional Arabic poem was that it would have only one general rhyming pattern (Arabic poetry is also metrical).

It is very important to keep in mind that one must sharply distinguish what is meant by the term 'Arabic' language. Our preceding examples have all come from modern standard Arabic, sometimes called modern literary Arabic or modern written Arabic, which is essentially a modernised form of Classical Arabic. All of these three designations just mentioned are known as *ʔalʕarabiyya alfuṣħā* or *ʔalʕarabiyya alfaṣīħa* (the 'pure' or 'clear' language). On the other side of the coin is a language which many Arabs think is devoid of grammar, the colloquial language, *luɣat alʕāmma* or *ʔalluɣa alʕāmmiyya* or *addāriǰa* or *lahaǰāt* ('dialects').

ʔalʕarabiyya alfuṣħā originated from the ancient poetic language of the Arabs in pre-Islamic Arabia, which was a period of idol worship (known in Arabic as *ʔaljāhiliyya* 'the period of ignorance'). The linguistic situation in ancient Arabia was such that every tribe had its own dialect, but there evolved a common koine used by the *rāwīs* (the ancient poets), which helped the preservation of the language and assisted in its conservatism. The Holy Qurʔān, written in this dialect (of course it was at first oral) but with linguistic features of Muħammad's speech (the Meccan dialect), eventually became *the* model for the classical language. Surprisingly enough, due principally to Islam, the classical language has changed in grammar very little since the seventh century AD. In fact, most students are amazed at the easy transition between reading a modern novel and a *sūra* of the Qurʔān (vocabulary and stylistics are other matters, however).

The colloquial dialects number in the thousands. The number reported on in an ever-growing literature runs in the hundreds. There are many remarkable parallels in the development of the modern Arabic dialects and the development of the Romance languages from a Latin prototype, the most notable of which is a general grammatical simplification in structure (i.e. fewer grammatical categories). Three such simplifications are: (1) loss of the dual in the verb, adjective and pronoun; (2) loss of case endings for nouns and adjectives; and (3) loss of mood distinctions in the verb. In addition to a demarcation of the colloquial dialects of various countries, cities, towns and villages, there are many sociolects which can be observed. Educated speech is, of course, quite distinct from that of the *fallāhīn* (peasants). In terms of comparative Arabic dialectology, more is known about urban dialects than rural (Bedouin) counterparts.

One should also keep in mind that the differences between many colloquials and the classical language are so great that a *fallāh* who had never been to school could hardly understand more than a few scattered words and expressions in it without great difficulty. One could assemble dozens of so-called Arabs (*fallāhīn*) in a room, who have never been exposed to the classical language, so that not one could properly understand the other. One should also bear in mind that educated Arabs use their native dialect in daily living and have all learned their colloquial dialects first. Indeed all colloquial Arabic dialects are acquired systems but the classical language is always formally learned. This has probably held true from the beginning.

4   The Influence of Arabic on Other Languages

As Islam expanded from Arabia, the Arabic language exerted much influence on the native languages with which it came in contact. Persians and speakers of other Iranian languages such as Kurdish and Pashto, Turkic-speaking peoples, Indians, Pakistanis, Bangladeshians and many speakers of African languages such as Hausa and Swahili (this list is by no means exhaustive) used the Arabic script to write their own native languages and assimilated a tremendous number of Arabic loanwords. One did not have to become a Muslim to embrace Arabic as Judeo-Arabic proves (Jews in Arabic-speaking countries, who spoke Arabic natively, wrote it in Hebrew characters with a few diacritical innovations). Words of ultimate Arabic origin have penetrated internationally and interlingually. A recent study turned up 400 'common' Arabic loanwords in English based on the *Random House Dictionary of the English Language, Webster's Third New International Dictionary* and the *Shorter Oxford English Dictionary*. A few examples will illustrate: the *al-* definite article words such as *algebra, alkali, alcohol, alcove* and many other famous ones such as *Allah, artichoke, assassin, Bedouin, cadi, cipher, emir, gazelle, giraffe, harem, hashish, imam*, *Islam*, *lute*, *mosque*, *mullah*, *Muslim*, *nadir*, *saffron*, *sheikh*, *sherbert*, *syrup*, *talc* and *vizier*.

It is important to point out that some of the loanwords mentioned earlier have as many as five alternate spellings in English due to transliteration differences and preferences so that a word such as *cadi* (< Arabic *qāḍin* 'judge', *ʔalqāḍī* 'the judge' — there is no Classical Arab word *qāḍī) can also be spelt *kadhi*, *kadi*, *qadi* and *qazi* (this latter pronunciation reflects a Perso-Indian influence since in those languages /ḍ/ > /z/); *emir* can also be spelt as *ameer*, *amir* or *emeer*.

5 Phonology

The consonantal segments of a fairly typical educated pronunciation of modern standard Arabic can be seen in table 33.1 (of course, there can always be a debate about the exact meaning of 'fairly typical').

Table 33.1: Arabic Consonant Phonemes

	Bilabial	Labio-dental	Inter-dental	Dental	Emphatic	Palatal	Velar	Uvular	Pharyngeal	Laryngeal
Stops	b			t d	ṭ ḍ		k	q		ʔ
Affricates						ǰ				
Fricatives		f	θ ð	s z	ṣ ẓ (z̧)	š		x ɣ	ħ ʕ	h
Nasals	m			n						
Liquids (lateral and trill)				l r	ḷ					
Approximants	w					y					

The symbols are IPA or quasi-IPA symbols (as used by linguists who specialise in Arabic and the other Semitic languages). The Arabic alphabet is a very accurate depiction of the phonological facts of the language, however it should be noted that there are some pronunciations different from the ones presented in table 33.1. For instance, /q/ is voiced in many dialects, both ancient and modern, i.e. [G], especially the Bedouin ones, which probably reflects its original pronunciation; the *ǰīm* (the name of the letter represented by the grapheme ⟨ǰ⟩) corresponds to many pronunciations such as [dʸ], [gʸ], [g] or [ž], stemming from a Proto-Semitic */g/.

Every consonant may be geminated, in contradistinction to Hebrew, for example, which can not geminate the so-called 'gutturals' (ʔ, ʕ, h, ħ and r).

Classical Arabic does not have a /p/, but standard pronunciations tend to devoice a /b/ before a voiceless consonant, e.g. /ħabs/ → [ħaps] 'imprisonment' or /ħibs/ → [ħips] 'dam'. Some modern Arabic dialects, notably those in Iraq, have both /p/ and /p̣/ (emphatic); however, the great majority of Arabic speakers will produce English /p/s as /b/ due to interference modification (one Arab asks another, 'Which Bombay are you flying to? Bombay, India or Bombay (Pompei), Italy?'). Incidentally, Persian, Urdu and other languages which have /p/ have taken the grapheme for /b/ = ﺑ and made ﭖ by placing three dots underneath its basic configuration of ﺑ = ⟨p⟩. This grapheme, in turn, has been reborrowed by some Iraqi Arabs.

Classical Arabic does not have a /v/, but phonetically, due to regressive assimilation, a [v] might occur as in /ħifð/ → [ħivð] 'memory'. /n/ also assimilates regressively, i.e. *nb* → *mb*, and *nk* → *ŋk* as in /bank/ → [baŋk] 'bank'.

The 'emphatic' consonants, often misleadingly called velarised-pharyngealised, are depicted with a dot underneath the particular consonant. Perhaps nowhere else in Arabic linguistic literature is there more controversy and more debate than in this area of the emphatics and how they are to be described and how they function. The vowels around an emphatic consonant tend to become lower, retracted or more centralised than around corresponding non-emphatics (the very back consonants /x, ɣ, q, ħ, ʕ/ have a similar effect on vowels), which is why the vowel allophonics of Arabic are much more cumbersome and intricate than the consonantal allophonics.

In Old Arabic, the primary emphatics were, in all likelihood, voiced, i.e. /ḍ/ < [ẓ^λ] (lateralised), /ṭ/ < /ḍ/, /ð̣/ or /ẓ/ < /ð̣/ and /ṣ/ < /ẓ/.

W. Lehn reviewed much of the previous literature including Arab grammatical thought and concluded, at least for Cairo Arabic, that the minimum domain of emphasis is the syllable and the maximum domain is the utterance. Lehn has suggested that emphasis not be treated as a distinctive system of the consonant or vocalic system but as a redundant feature of both. In later works, Lehn underscores all emphatic syllables.

The /ḷ/, which occurs only in the name of God, /ʔaḷḷāh/ (but not after /i/ as in /bismillāh/ 'in the name of Allah') was shown to be a phoneme in Classical Arabic by C.A. Ferguson. Some modern Arabic dialects have many more examples of /ḷ/, especially those spoken in the Gulf countries.

Arabic is perhaps the best known of the world's languages to linguists for its vowel system. It has the classical triangular system, which preserves Proto-Semitic vocalism:

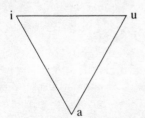

For Classical and modern standard Arabic, these may be short or long (geminated). Many modern Arabic dialects have, however, developed other vowels such as /ə/, /e/, /o/ etc., just as the other Semitic languages had done centuries earlier through the general process of 'drift' (i.e. parallel development).

The vowel allophonics are much richer than the consonantal allophonics chiefly because vowels take on the colouring of the adjacent emphatic and emphatic-like consonants (including /r/), while the non-emphatic consonants push the vowels to higher and less centralised qualities. What is important to keep in mind is that the pronunciation of the standard language or any oral interpretation of the classical language is all directly dependent on the nature of one's native colloquial dialect.

The vowel allophonics have been accurately described on the basis of detailed spectrographic analysis for the modern standard Arabic as used in Iraq. The rules may be stated as follows:

(1) /ī/ → [ɨ]/ – [+emphatic] – (except /l/)

          → [Ī]/ – $\left\{ \begin{matrix} ʕ \\ ɣ \end{matrix} \right\}$ –

          → [ī]/ ...

(2) /i/ → [ɨ]/ – [+emphatic] –

          → [I]/ – $\left\{ \begin{matrix} ʕ \\ ɣ \end{matrix} \right\}$ –

          → [i]/ ...

(3) /ū/ → [Ū]/ – [+emphatic] – (except /l/)

          → [ū]/ ...

(4) /u/ → [U]/ – [+emphatic] –

          → [u]/ ...

(5) /ā/ → [ā]/ – $\left[- \left\{ \begin{matrix} \text{+emphatic} \\ \left\{ \begin{matrix} q \\ r \end{matrix} \right\} \end{matrix} \right\} - \right]$

          → [ᴧ]/ $\left[- \left\{ \begin{matrix} ʕ \\ ɣ \end{matrix} \right\} - \right]$

          → [æ]/ ...

(6) /a/ → [ə]/ ____# (but not next to /q/, /ʕ/, /r/ and /ɣ/)

          → [a]/ $\left[- \left\{ \begin{matrix} \text{+ emphatic} \\ \left\{ \begin{matrix} q \\ r \end{matrix} \right\} \end{matrix} \right\} - \right]$

          → [ᴧ]/ $\left[- \left\{ \begin{matrix} ʕ \\ ɣ \end{matrix} \right\} - \right]$

          → [æ]/ ...

What tends to happen in modern Arabic dialects is that the short vowels are more susceptible to change than the long ones. Thus Classical /i/ and /u/ in

Damascus Arabic, for instance, both merge into /ə/. Indeed /a/ can usually be regarded as the most stable and conservative of the three short vowels, yet it too is now becoming subject to change or deletion as in many dialects; /yā/ + /maḥammad/ → /ya mḥammad/ 'Oh Muhammad!'. Classical Arabic knows many doublets in its short vowel configuration such as /ḥubs/ ~ /ḥibs/ 'inalienable property, the yield of which is devoted to pious purposes' or /laṣṣ/ ~ /liṣṣ/ ~ /luṣṣ/ 'thief' (a triplet!).

Diphthongs are two in number: /aw/ and /ay/ as in /θawr/ 'bull' and /bayt/ 'house', respectively. In most of the colloquial dialects, diphthongs have monophthongised into /ē/ and /ō/, respectively (and /ī/ and /ū/ in Moroccan dialects, which occurred in Akkadian centuries before and is another good attestation of 'drift' in the Semitic languages).

There are two well-known phonological processes which deserve mention. The first is called ʔimāla (lit. 'inclination'), which refers to /ā/-raising, usually due to the umlauting influence of /i/, which means that words such as ʕibād 'slaves' could have had a dialectal (peculiar, at first, perhaps) pronunciation ʕibēd or ʕibīd. ʔimāla has produced the very distinctive high vowel pronunciations of /ā/ in many Syro-Lebanese dialects giving for /bāb/: [bēb] or [bīb] 'door' or phonetic qualities in between those or adjacent to them, which may be compared with Maltese bieb 'door' (Maltese has for Arabic kalimāt 'words' kelmiet and for Arabic kitāb 'book' ktieb).

The second process is known as ʔišmām ('delabialisation'), which explains /ū/ → /ī/ (through an intermediate stage of [ü]) as in rūm ~ rīm 'Rome' or some dialectal pronunciations of /rudda/ as /rüdda/ 'it was returned' or /qũla/ for /qīla/ 'it was said', which derives from /quwila/, the passive form I of the root QWL. This phonological process may also explain why ū rhymes with ī in Koranic Arabic.

Stress is one of the most involved topics in Arabic phonology (even for the Nigerian dialect of Arabic I researched at first hand, stress was the most intricate part of the entire phonology). The Arab grammarians never mentioned it, and therefore the modern-day pronunciation of the standard (classical) language is directly dependent on the stress rules of the native colloquial dialect counterpart. Thus for the word 'both of them (f.) wrote', segmentally /katabatā/, graphemically <ktbt?>, which of the four possible syllables receives the main stress? Indeed some native Arabic speakers say: (1) /kátabatā/ (Iraqis); others (2), /katabátā/ (Egyptians); still others (3), /katabatá/ (many Syrians and Lebanese); and others (4), may say /katábatā/. Thus it is possible to stress any of the four syllables and still be correct. This is one of the reasons why I consider modern standard Arabic an ill defined system of language, whereas I deem all colloquials well defined.

There are, however, rules of syllabicity which can be described with a greater degree of accuracy. Long vowels are shortened in closed syllables, which explains why one says /yákun/ 'let him be' (jussive of /yakūnu/ 'he will be') instead of the expected (apocopated imperfect) */yakūn/. The only exception is that /ā/ may occur in a closed syllable, but it is not necessary to enter into the details of this here. Also, syllable-initially and finally, only single consonants occur. Thus a borrowing like Latin *strāta* 'path' > /ṣirāṭ/ (the *str-* consonant cluster was, at first, simplified to *sr-* and then an anaptyctic vowel /i/ was inserted between the /ṣ/ and the /r/; further the emphatic /ṣ/ and /ṭ/ are typical of what Arabic does in its loanword phonology).

Rules for the assignment of lexical stress are:

(1) When a word is made up of CV syllables, the first syllable receives the primary stress, e.g. /kátaba/.

(2) When a word contains only one long syllable, the long syllable receives the primary stress, e.g. /kātib/.

(3) When a word contains two or more long syllables, the long syllable nearest to the end of the word receives the primary stress, e.g. /raʔīsuhúnna/ 'their (f. pl.) chief'.

The normal use of modern standard Arabic requires an understanding of pausal forms. When a pause occurs in speech (reflected in reading as well), speakers drop final short vowels (case and mood markers) and drop or shorten case endings. For example, Arabic marks indefiniteness by what is called nūnation (named after the Arabic letter *nūn*): *-un* for nominative, *-in* for genitive and *-an* for accusative (there are only three cases). At the end of an utterance (i.e. sentence, breath group), a word such as /mudarrisun/ 'a teacher' → /mudarris/, /mudarrisin/ → /mudarris/ but /mudarrisan/ → /mudarrisā/ (note that Arabic words are usually cited with nūnation, called in Arabic, *tanwīn*), and /mudarrisatun/ → /mudarrisah/ 'a teacher' (f. sg.).

6   Morphophonemic Changes

We shall not list all occurrences because that would require more space than allotted to us. We will rather present a few of the most common changes occurring in Classical Arabic.

(1) $awa \rightarrow \bar{a}$ — $qawama \rightarrow q\bar{a}ma$ 'he stood up'

(2) $C_1aC_2aC_2a \rightarrow C_1aC_2C_2a$ — $radada \rightarrow radda$ 'he returned'

(3) $? \left\{ \begin{matrix} a \\ i \\ u \end{matrix} \right\} ? \rightarrow ? \left\{ \begin{matrix} \bar{a} \\ \bar{i} \\ \bar{u} \end{matrix} \right\}$ – $?a?l\bar{a}m \rightarrow ?\bar{a}l\bar{a}m$ 'pains'

(4) $uw \rightarrow \bar{u}$ — $suwdun \rightarrow s\bar{u}dun$ 'black' (m. pl.)

(5) $\bar{u}y \rightarrow \bar{i}$ — $b\bar{u}ydun \rightarrow b\bar{i}dun$ 'white' (m. pl.); $mudarris\bar{u}ya \rightarrow$ $mudarris\bar{i}ya$ 'my teachers' (m., all cases)

(6) $yw \rightarrow yy$ — $?ayw\bar{a}mun \rightarrow ?ayy\bar{a}mun$ 'days'

(7) Haplology: $tataq\bar{a}tal\bar{u}na \rightarrow taq\bar{a}tal\bar{u}na$ 'you are fighting each other'

(8) Dissimilation: *madīnīyun* → *madanīyun* 'urban'
(9) *āw* → *ā?* — *qāwilun* → *qā?ilun* 'speaker'

7 The Arabic Alphabet

The Latin script is used by more languages than any other script ever invented (and it is used for languages as diversified in structure as Polish, English and Vietnamese). After Latin, the Arabic alphabet is number two because it was or is used to write a vast number of different languages such as Persian, Urdu, Pashto (all Indo-Iranian), Hausa (the Chadic sub-branch of Afroasiatic), Swahili (Bantu), Turkish (Altaic), Malay (Austronesian) and over a hundred others. The reason for this diversity is undoubtedly due to the spread of Islam.

The earliest Arabic inscription is dated AD 512. According to an early Arab scholar, Ibn Khaldūn, the Arabic alphabet had evolved from the Epigraphic South Arabian script; however, we know that it was borrowed from the Nabatean alphabet (which was, in turn, borrowed from Aramaic), which consisted of twenty-two consonantal graphemes. The Nabateans added six more graphemes representing phonemes which did not occur in Aramaic (the oldest Nabatean inscription dates from AD 250, found at Umm al-Jimāl): ت, ذ, ض, ظ, خ, and غ. The oldest Arabic inscription written in the Nabatean script is the Namāra inscription, a grave inscription of seventy-one lines found in southeastern Syria, which dates from AD 328 (the inscription was discovered in 1902).

Like Phoenician, Hebrew, Ugaritic and other Semitic alphabets (or syllabaries), the adapted Nabatean system used by the pre-Islamic Arabs represents only consonants, which is appropriate to the root structure of Semitic.

The invention of diacritical marks to indicate vowels was borrowed from Syriac in the eighth century AD. In fact, the invention is attributed to Al-Khalil ibn Ahmad. Arabic's written development can be explained as follows. The Arabs grew tired with fifteen basic letter shapes for twenty-eight phonemes (the confusion must have been overwhelming), so dots were invented above and below the letters in groups of one to three to distinguish the underlying grapheme. The process of using the dots (inserting the diacritics) is called *?iʕjām* and although it is used for Aramaic, the Arabs began to use it very systematically.

Arabic calligraphy is truly an art. There are many styles of the script, and table 33.2 presents the *nasxī* one, commonly used for print. Column 5 presents the final unconnected allograph of the grapheme. The script is written, like Hebrew, from right to left, and tends to be very cursive (although the Persians have gone even further), especially in handwritten forms. All the graphemes can be attached to preceding ones, but six never connect to what follows: *?alif*, *dāl*, *ðāl*, *rā?*, *zāy* and *wāw*. There are no

Table 33.2: The Arabic Alphabet

Transliteration	Final	Medial	Initial	Alone	Name	Numerical value
ā	ا			ا	ʔalif	1
b	ب	ﺒ	ﺑ	ب	bāʔ	2
t	ت	ﺘ	ﺗ	ت	tāʔ	400
θ	ﺚ	ﺜ	ﺛ	ث	θaʔ	500
ǰ	ﺞ	ﺠ	ﺟ	ج	ǰīm	3
ħ	ﺢ	ﺤ	ﺣ	ح	ħāʔ	8
x	ﺦ	ﺨ	ﺧ	خ	xāʔ	600
d	ﺪ			د	dāl	4
ð	ﺬ			ذ	ðāl	700
r	ﺮ			ر	rāʔ	200
z	ﺰ			ز	zāy	7
s	ﺲ	ﺴ	ﺳ	س	sīn	60
š	ﺶ	ﺸ	ﺷ	ش	šīn	300
ṣ	ﺺ	ﺼ	ﺻ	ص	ṣād	90
ḍ	ﺾ	ﻀ	ﺿ	ض	ḍād	800
ṭ	ﻂ	ﻄ	ﻃ	ط	ṭāʔ	9
ẓ	ﻆ	ﻈ	ﻇ	ظ	ẓaʔ	900
ʕ	ﻊ	ﻌ	ﻋ	ع	ʕayn	70
ɣ	ﻎ	ﻐ	ﻏ	غ	ɣayn	1000
f	ﻒ	ﻔ	ﻓ	ف	fāʔ	80
q	ﻖ	ﻘ	ﻗ	ق	qāf	100
k	ﻚ	ﻜ	ﻛ	ك	kāf	20
l	ﻞ	ﻠ	ﻟ	ل	lām	30
m	ﻢ	ﻤ	ﻣ	م	mīm	40
n	ﻦ	ﻨ	ﻧ	ن	nūn	50
h	ﻪ	ﻬ	ﻫ	ه	hāʔ	5
w	ﻮ			و	wāw	6
y	ﻲ	ﻴ	ﻳ	ى	yāʔ	10

capital letters and table 33.2 presents the graphemes and their allographs as well as their older Semitic numerical values (the so-called ʔabǰad).

Handwriting generally shortens the strokes and replaces the three dots with ˆ and two dots with ¯, allowing it to be written very quickly in comparison to the painstaking effort required for the printed forms.

The vowel diacritics are: fatħa ˊ /a/; ḍamma ˋ /u/; kasra ˎ /i/; and sukūn ˚ for zero (no vowel). Long vowels are represented thus: /ā/ by ʔalif or ʔalif madda (initially), آ; /ī/ by yāʔ; and /ū/ by wāw.

There are other details such as ligatures, nūnation, stylistic variations etc., for which the reader should refer to Mitchell (1953).

8 Diglossia

A very interesting and relatively rare linguistic phenomenon has developed in Arabic, called diglossia, which is often confused with bilingualism. There can be no doubt that it is an old phenomenon going back, in all likelihood, to the pre-Islamic period, although J. Blau states it arose as late as the first Islamic century in the towns of the Arab empire as a result of the great Arab conquests (I do not agree with Blau that there was no intermediary of the Arabic koine). Diglossia involves a situation in which two varieties of the same language live side by side, each performing a different function. It involves the use of two different variations of a single language whereas bilingualism definitely involves two different languages. The two variations are: (1) a 'high' one used in relatively formal situations; and (2) a 'low' one used colloquially and usually informally. Although the term was coined by the Arabist W. Marçais in 1930 (*diglossie*), it was C.A. Ferguson who brought it to the attention of general linguistics and ethnology.

'High' Arabic, which we have been calling modern standard Arabic, and 'Low' Arabic, a colloquial dialect which native speakers acquire as a mother tongue, have specialised functions in Arab culture. The former is learned through formal education in school like Latin, Sanskrit and Biblical Hebrew and would be used in a sermon, university lecture, news broadcast and for mass media purposes, letter, political speech (except, perhaps, after an informal greeting or the first few sentences, as was typical in the speeches of Gamal Abdul Nasser), while the latter is always an acquired system (no formal learning ever takes place to learn anyone's native tongue) and is the native language used at home conversing with family or friends or in a radio or television soap opera. It is important to realise that a small elite has developed in the Arab countries very proud of their linguistic skills in the standard language (Modern Classical Arabic). There have even been reports that certain individuals have adapted the standard language as their exclusive means of oral communication, yet I have reservations about this.

Many native speakers, regardless of the level of education, maintain a set of myths about the 'high' language: that it is far more beautiful than any dialect (colloquial), far more logical, more elegant and eloquent, has much more vocabulary available to it, especially for the expression of philosophical ideas, and is far better able to express all the complex nuances of one's thoughts. Arabs also believe (and other Muslims too) that Arabic is the most perfect of all languages since God speaks it and has revealed his message in the Holy Qurʔān in it. If asked which dialect is closest to the classical, many Arabs will respond that their own dialect is! Of course, this may be a relative answer depending upon who else is present and where the question is asked — another common answer is that the Bedouin on the desert speaks a dialect nearest to the classical. In fact, the Bedouin has often been called upon to settle linguistic arguments of all kinds.

Classical Arabic has always had situations where its use was required and it was never acquired by all members of the particular society in question. Modern standard Arabic continues the tradition and unifies the Arab world linguistically as it is the official language of Iraq, Jordan, Egypt, Sudan,

Tunisia, Algeria, Morocco, Kuwait, Saudi Arabia, Lebanon, Libya, both Yemens, Oman, the Gulf countries etc. It is the mark of ʕurūba or Arabism (pan-Arabism), since there can be a high degree of mutual unintelligibility among the various colloquial dialects, where a Syrian Arabic-speaking friend of mine once heard a tape of a Nigerian speaking Nigerian Arabic and confessed he understood almost nothing in it.

There is also a tremendous amount of sociological concern about language, dialect and variety in the Arab world. Let me illustrate what I mean by relating a true story. I once participated in a long conversation one entire afternoon in a Beirut coffee house with two other gentlemen. One fellow was Lebanese, but he did not want to appear uneducated, so he spoke French, a language he knew quite well and which he had studied for years formally. The other gentleman was French, but he did not want to come off as any sort of colonialist, so he was speaking colloquial Lebanese Arabic, which he knew beautifully, and I, an American-trained linguist who had studied a variety of modern dialects, spoke modern standard Arabic, since I knew that language better than the other two choices represented. And the conversation was delightful, each of us taking turns in this trialogue about all sorts of subjects.

It is important to realise that there are a few Arabic speech communities where diglossia is unknown. Cypriot Maronite Arabic spoken in Kormakiti, Cyprus, by about 1,200 (as of two decades ago) is one such example as are most dialects of Nigerian and Chadian Arabic.

Perhaps the most striking feature of diglossia is the existence of many paired vocabulary items (the examples are from C.A. Ferguson).

Classical Arabic	Gloss	Egyptian colloquial Arabic
raʔā	'he saw'	šāf
ħiðāʔun	'shoe'	gazma
ʔanfun	'nose'	manaxīr
ðahaba	'went'	rāħ
mā	'what'	ʔē(h)
ʔalʔāna	'now'	dilwaʔti

To demonstrate how different the modern dialects can be, consider 'now'. In addition to the words cited, Moroccan has dába, Algerian delwóq or druk, Tunisian tawwa, Saudi Arabian daħħīn(a), Hassaniyya dark, Syrian hallaʔ, Nigerian hatta or hassa or dātēn; consider also 'good, well': Moroccan mizyán or wáxxa, Algerian mlīeħ, Syrian-Lebanese mnīħ, Libyan bāhi, Tunisian ṭayyab, Nigerian zēn or ṭayyib, Egyptian kuwayyis. Finally, consider 'nothing': Moroccan wálu, Algerian ši, Libyan kān lbarka, Tunisian šay, Saudi Arabian walašay, Nigerian še. Indeed sometimes it is in the basic everyday vocabulary that one can most easily spot such major distinctions.

To give the linguist somewhat of a feel for this, Ferguson cites the nearest English parallel such as illumination vs. light, purchase vs. buy, and children vs. *kids*. I should also mention the elegance one can immediately feel when one is invited to *dine* vs. plain 'ole *eat*. The verb *dine* certainly involves higher cost as well as getting dressed up and lovely and expensive surroundings (tablecloth, utensils, décor etc.). 'High' Arabic gives one the feeling of dining at a fine restaurant, whereas 'Low' Arabic is eating the same old thing day in and day out. In addition to the lexical distinctions, there are also different grammatical systems involved in diglossia.

In support of the hypothesis that modern standard Arabic is ill-defined is the so-called 'mixed' language or 'Inter-Arabic' being used in the speeches of, say, President Bourgiba of Tunisia, noting that very few native speakers of Arabic from any Arab country can really ever master the intricacies of Classical Arabic grammar in such a way as to extemporaneously give a formal speech in it. This may perhaps best be illustrated in the use of the Arabic numerals, in which the cardinal numbers from 'three' to 'ten' govern the indefinite genitive plural, but from 'eleven' to 'nineteen' govern the indefinite singular accusative (in addition to being indeclinable, with the exception of 'twelve'), whereas cardinal numbers such as 'one thousand', 'two thousand', 'three thousand', 'million' etc. take the indefinite genitive singular.

9   Nominal Morphology

Modern standard Arabic nouns are inflected for case, determination, gender and number. The function of the noun is usually indicated by short vowel suffixes — /u/ marking nominative, /i/ genitive and /a/ accusative (with added nūnation marking indefiniteness). Thus /kitābun/ 'a book' (nom.), gen. /kitābin/ and acc. /kitāban/ (this is an example of a triptote since it takes all three case endings). Determination is normally handled by the definite article which is /ʔal-/, but it assimilates before the so-called 'sun' letters (*t, d, θ, ð, s, z, ṭ, ḍ, ṣ, ẓ, n, l, r, š*) (they are called this because the word /šams/ 'sun' begins with one; all the others are called 'moon' letters because the word /qamar/ 'moon' begins with one). When /ʔal-/ prefixes a noun, there is no longer any reason to have the nūnation since it marks the indefinite, thus /ʔalkitābu/ 'the book' (nom.), with /ʔalkitābi/ (gen.) and /ʔalkitāba/ (acc.) (the /ʔ/ and initial vowel are subject to the rules of elision after vowels).

The diptote noun, which is in the minority when one compares to triptotes, does not take nūnation and merges the accusative -*a* with the genitive, e.g. /ʔaħmadu/ 'Ahmad' (nom.), with gen.-acc. /ʔaħmada/. Many broken (internal) plural patterns are diptotic, as are many proper names, elatives (i.e. comparatives and superlatives), colours and other forms.

Dual and so-called 'sound' (i.e. no morphophonemic alternation) plural suffixes also do not differentiate the genitive and accusative (called 'oblique'). 'Teachers' (m.) is /mudarrisūna/, obl. /mudarrisīna/, f. /mudarrisātun/, obl. /mudarrisātin/. The masculine forms remain the same with the article, but lose the nūnation with the feminine. The dual is marked by /-āni/, obl. /-ayni/; thus 'two teachers' (m.) is /mudarrisāni/, obl. /mudarrisayni/; feminine counterparts are /mudarrisatāni/ and /mudarrisatayni/, respectively.

Gender and number are obligatory grammatical categories. Feminine nouns take feminine concord and government and tend to be overtly marked with /-at/ followed by the case marker, e.g. /mudarrisatun/, pausal form /mudarrisah/ 'teacher'. Very few feminine-marked nouns are masculine, e.g. /xalīfatun/ 'caliph'. Many nouns which are not overtly marked feminine are so, e.g. body parts which occur in pairs (this is common Semitic) such as /riǰlun/ 'foot, leg' and the names of countries and cities; in addition, plurals of irrational beings are treated as feminine singulars.

Mention has already been made of the dual number and the 'sound' masculine and feminine endings. All lose nūnation in a construct state (*status constructus*), which is the normal means of expressing the possessive (genitive) relationship (/kitābu lmaliki/ 'the book of the king' or 'the king's book' — the first member of a construct (called in Arabic /ʔiḍāfa/) has neither the article nor nūnation), e.g. 'the teachers of the school' can be /mudarrisā lmadrasati/ (the second member of a construct state is always in the genitive), obl. /mudarrisay lmadrasati/, f. /mudarrisatā lmadrasati/, obl. /mudarrisatay lmadrasati/, m. pl. /mudarrisū lmadrasati/, obl. /mudarrisī lmadrasati/, f. /mudarrisātu lmadrasati/, obl. /mudarrisāti lmadrasati/.

Most Arabic nouns do not take the sound plurals but have a broken (ablaut) plural, which can involve the addition of prefixes and/or suffixes. There are several dozen possible patterns in common usage and very few are predictable. The three most common broken (sometimes also called 'inner') plural patterns, based on data in the Lane Lexicon, are: (1) $ʔaC_1C_2āC_3$, e.g. /lawħun/ 'blackboard', pl. /ʔalwāħun/; (2) $C_1iC_2āC_3$, e.g. /raǰulun/ 'man', pl. /riǰālun/; (3) $C_1uC_2ūC_3$, e.g. /baytun/ 'house', pl. /buyūtun/.

There are many prefixes and suffixes in derivational morphology such as the *nisba* (this is a well-known international linguistic term) /-īyun/, colloquial /-i/, which forms relative adjectives (which is well known since so many different languages have borrowed it, e.g. *Kuwait, Kuwaiti*), such as /lubnānīyun/ '(a) Lebanese', colloquial /lubnāni/, f. /lubnānīyatun/, m. pl. /lubnānīyūna/, obl. /lubnānīyīna/, f. pl. /lubnānīyātun/, obl. /lubnānīyātin/. Among the most common (and recognisable, due to loanwords such as 'Muslim') is /m-/, marking nouns of time or place, instruments, active and passive participles and verbal nouns (*maṣdar*), e.g. /maktabun/ 'office', /maktabatun/ 'library', related to /kataba/ 'he wrote', /maktūbun/ 'written', coming to mean 'anything written' or 'letter' (passive participle of Form I), /miftāħun/ 'key', related to /fataħa/ 'he opened'. (Incidentally, since a language like Persian, of the Indo-Iranian family, has borrowed so many Arabic loanwords and since a Persian dictionary is arranged alphabetically and not on the basis of a triconsonantal root, it is safe to say that, due to the statistically high occurrence of /m-/ from Arabic loanwords, /m-/-initial words make up the largest section in a Persian dictionary; thus in F. Steingass, *A Comprehensive Persian-English Dictionary* (Routledge and Kegan Paul Limited, London, 1863) the letter *mīm* (i.e. <m>) runs from pp. 1136 to 1365 — the entire dictionary has 1539 pages.)

10   Verbal Morphology

Some preliminary information on the algebraically predictable verbal system has been mentioned in section 3. Person, mood and aspect are marked by prefixes and suffixes. There are nine derived themes (forms) or stems of the verb plus a basic one, i.e. Form I, yielding a total of ten verbal forms (and five more that are archaic or very rare), each with a 'normal' range of semantic value, e.g. intensivity, causativity, reflexivity etc. Each form has its own set of active and passive particles and verbal nouns (sometimes called 'verbal abstracts'). Further, there is an internal passive for each one of the forms, formed by vocalic change from its corresponding active, in form but often not in meaning (i.e. the forms are therefore hypothetical).

Form I verbs are of three types dependent on the second vowel of the perfect: /qatala/ 'he killed', /ʕalima/ 'he knew', and /ħasuna/ 'he was good'. /i/ in the perfect usually marks an intransitive verb, denoting often a temporary state; /u/ in the perfect usually marks an intransitive verb expressing a permanent state.

Form II is formed by geminating the second radical of the root so that the verb functions like a quadriradical (statistically these are in the very small minority of roots, e.g. /tarjama/ 'he translated'), e.g. /ʕallama/ 'he taught'. Among the meanings of Form II are: (1) intensiveness, /kasara/ 'he broke' vs. /kassara/ 'he smashed'; (2) iterative, /qataʕa/ 'he cut' vs. /qattaʕa/ 'he cut up'; (3) causativity, /ʕallama/ 'he taught' is the causative of /ʕalima/ 'he knew', i.e. 'to cause to know'; (4) estimation, /kaðaba/ 'he lied' vs. /kaððaba/ 'he considered someone a liar'; (5) denominative function, /xaymatun/ 'a tent' yields /xayyama/ 'he pitched a tent'; and (6) transitivity, /nāma/ 'he slept' produces /nawwama/ 'he put to sleep'.

Form III is formed by lengthening the first /a/. The meanings are; (1) reciprocity (directing an action towards somebody), e.g. /kātaba/ 'he corresponded with', /qātala/ 'he fought with and tried to kill'; and (2) the attempt to do something, e.g. from /sabaqa/ 'he preceded' one forms /sābaqa/ 'he competed with' (i.e. 'he attempted to precede').

Form IV is formed by prefixing a glottal stop (= Hebrew /h-/ and Ancient Egyptian /s-/) followed by /a/ and making the first radical vowel-less, e.g. /ǰalasa/ 'he sat (down)' has /ʔaǰlasa/ 'he seated' as its causative. In addition to the (primary) causative meaning, one encounters: (1) a declaration, e.g. /ʔakðaba/ 'he called a liar', related to /kaðaba/ 'he lied'; and (2) a characteristic (used with /mā/ 'how; what' in the third person perfect only), e.g. /mā ʔaħsanahu/ 'how handsome he is!' There are often Form IV verbs with the meaning 'became', e.g. /ʔaṣbaħa/ 'he became' (also /ʔamsā/ and /ʔaḍħā/. Also one finds denominatives of place names, e.g. from /naǰdun/ 'Najd' (north-central Saudi Arabia) one obtains /ʔanǰada/ 'to go to Najd'.

Forms V and VI are passives and reflexives of Forms II and III, respectively, and are both formed by prefixing /ta-/ to those forms. From /ʕallama/ 'he taught' one obtains /taʕallama/ 'he taught himself', i.e. 'he learned' or 'he was taught' (one can understand the verb both ways in terms of English). From /qātala/ and /kātaba/ one obtains /taqātala/ 'to fight each other' and /takātaba/ 'to correspond with each other', respectively. Form VI also denotes a pretence, e.g. from /mariḍa/ 'he was sick' one obtains /tamāraḍa/ 'he pretended to be sick', or from /nāma/ 'he slept' one obtains /tanāwama/ 'he pretended to be asleep' (this is a good example of what is called a 'hollow' verb because a morphophonemic //w// occurs in the root, which manifests itself in Form VI but not in Form I).

Form VII is formed by prefixing a vowel-less /n-/ to Form I. As no morpheme can begin with a vowel-less consonant, an anaptyctic vowel /i/ is inserted and, initially, a prothetic /ʔ/ precedes the /i/ since no morpheme can begin with a vowel. (This is true of Hebrew too, with only one exception.) It is usually the passive or reflexive of Form I, e.g. Form I /kasara/ 'he broke' (transitive) forms Form VII as /ʔinkasara/ 'it broke' (intransitive).

Form VIII, the only infixing form, infixes /-ta-/ between the first and second radicals. As the first radical is vowel-less, it uses the anaptyctic /i/ rule and glottal stop insertion, as did Form VII (see above). It is usually the reflexive of Form I, but contrary to Form VII, it may take a direct object. As examples, one notes: /ʔiktataba/ 'he was registered' and /ʔiqtatala/ 'to fight with one another'. Occasionally, there is no difference in meaning between Forms I and VIII, e.g. /šarā/, imperfect /yašrī/ 'he bought' (Form I) = /ʔištarā/, imperfect /yaštarī/.

Form IX is very restricted semantically, i.e. the meaning revolves around a colour or a physical defect, e.g. /ʔiswadda/ 'he became black' or /ʔiʕwaǰǰa/ 'he became bent'. It is made by geminating the third radical of the root and deleting the vowel of the first radical with the appropriate anaptyctic /i/ and glottal stop insertion (see the remarks for Form VII).

Form X is formed by making the first radical of the root vowel-less and prefixing /sta-/. Like the preceding forms, there is anaptyxis and glottal stop insertion (see the remarks for Form VII). It is the reflexive of Form IV or has to do with asking someone for something (for oneself) in terms of the basic sememe of the root. Also, there is a meaning of consideration. From /ʔaʕlama/ 'he informed' one obtains /ʔistaʕlama/ 'he inquires' (i.e. 'he asks for information for himself'); from /kataba/ 'he wrote' one obtains /ʔistaktaba/ 'he asked someone to write'; from /ħasuna/ 'he was good' one obtains /ʔistaħsana/ 'he considered (as) good'.

The conjugation of a regular verb in the perfect and imperfect (Form I) is shown in the chart given here.

Perfect

1	qataltu 'I killed or have killed'	qatalnā 'we killed'
2	qatalta 'you (m.) killed'	qataltum 'you (m. pl.) killed'
2	qatalti 'you (f.) killed'	qataltunna 'you (f. pl.) killed'
2	qataltumā 'you (m. and f. du.) killed'	
3	qatala 'he killed'	qatalū 'they (m.) killed'
3	qatalat 'she killed'	qatalna 'they (f.) killed'
3	qatalā 'they (m. du.) killed'	qatalatā 'they (f. du.) killed'

Imperfect

1	ʔaqtulu 'I kill, am killing, shall kill'	naqtulu 'we kill'
2	taqtulu 'you (m.) kill'	taqtulūna 'you (m. pl.) kill'
2	taqtulīna 'you (f.) kill'	taqtulna 'you (f. pl.) kill'
2	taqtulāni 'you (du.) kill'	
3	yaqtulu 'he kills'	yaqtulūna 'they (m.) kill'
3	taqtulu 'she kills'	yaqtulna 'they (f.) kill'
3	yaqtulāni 'they (m. du.) kill'	taqtulāni 'they (f. du.) kill'

There are five forms of the imperative of the regular verb: *ʔuqtul* 'kill!'. *ʔuqtulī* 'f. sg.', *ʔuqtulū* 'm. pl.', *ʔuqtulna* 'f. pl.', and *ʔuqtulā* 'du.'.

There are three moods of the imperfect: the indicative (given in the chart of regular verb forms), the subjunctive and the jussive. To form the subjunctive, the basic change is from the -*u* ending to -*a*. Those persons which end with -*na/i* preceded by a long vowel lose that ending after the last radical of the root. The second and third person feminine plural forms are the same in all three moods.

The jussive is formed by apocopating the imperfect indicative, i.e. those persons which end with the last radical of the root lose their final vowel. The other persons are the same as the subjunctive.

Perfect

1	qultu 'I said'	qulnā 'we said'
2	qulta 'you (m.) said'	qultum 'you (m. pl.) said'
2	qulti 'you (f.) said'	qultunna 'you (f. pl.) said'
2	qultumā 'you (m. and f. du.) said'	
3	qāla 'he said'	qālū 'they (m.) said'
3	qālat 'she said'	qulnā 'they (f.) said'
3	qālā 'they (m. du.) said'	qālatā 'they (f. du.) said'

Imperfect

1	ʔaqūlu 'I say'	naqūlu 'we say'
2	taqūlu 'you (m.) say'	taqūlūna 'you (m. pl.) say'
2	taqūlīna 'you (f.) say'	taqulna 'you (f. pl.) say'
2	taqūlāni 'you (du.) say'	
3	yaqūlu 'he says'	yaqūlūna 'they (m.) say'
3	taqūlu 'she says'	yaqulna 'they (f.) say'
3	yaqūlāni 'they (m. du.) say'	taqūlāni 'they (f. du.) say'

The conjugation of a Hollow verb (i.e. one with *w* or *y* as middle radical) is as shown above in the perfect and imperfect (Form I). The forms of the imperative are: *qul, qūlī, qūlū, qulna* and *qūlā*.

11 Verbal Aspect

Many Semitists agree that the semantic system of the Arabic verb is very difficult to examine from an Indo-European perspective. Arabic has a *māḍī* ('past' or generally-called 'perfect' or 'perfective') or suffixed conjugation and a *muḍāriʕ* ('similar to the triptote noun in taking three case endings'; 'imperfect' or 'imperfective' or 'non-past') or prefixed conjugation. The imperfect can refer to present, future and past; the perfect can refer to pluperfect, future or present. The fact that the perfect can refer to the present is illustrated by the following. In a buying-selling transaction, once the event is regarded (in the mind of the speaker) as completed (or 'manifest', to use a Whorfian term), one may say *biʕtuka hāðā* lit. 'I sold (perfect) you this', which means 'I sell you this' or 'I am (now) selling you this'. No money has yet exchanged hands, though. That the imperfect can express a past action is illustrated by the following: *ǰāʔū ʔabāhum yabkūna* lit. 'they came to their father — they will cry', which means 'they came to their father crying' or *ʔatā lʕayna yašrabu* lit. 'he came to the well — he will drink', which means 'he came to the well to drink'.

Few Arabic verbs embody unambiguous time. The great majority of Arabic verbs are either static or dynamic. In English this will often be reflected in a different verb. From the verbal nouns *rukūbun*, the static value is 'ride' — dynamic 'mount'; *ʔiḥmirārun*, static 'be red' — dynamic 'turn red'; *ʔiqāmatun* 'reside' and 'settle', respectively; *ḥukmun* 'govern' and 'decree', respectively; *ʕilmun* 'know' and 'get to know', respectively.

The colloquial Arabic dialects have felt the need for finer tense distinctions, in addition to the opposition perfect/imperfect, and have developed overt tense markers such as /ḥa-/ marking future in Egyptian and other colloquial dialects.

The problem of aspect and tense in Arabic (and in Semitic in general) is one on which much has already been written, but much more research needs to be accomplished before the final answer is in. It remains one of the most debated and hotly-contested aspects of Semitic linguistics. Surely both aspect and (relative) tense are involved.

12 Syntax

Arabic uses a non-verbal construction for some verbs in English, the most notable of which is 'have'. Arabic uses the preposition /li-/ 'to, for' or /ʕinda/ 'with (Fr. *chez*)' for 'have', e.g. /lī kitābun/ or /ʕindī kitābun/ 'I have a book'.

English is more analytical than is Arabic. Thus in English one needs three words to say 'I killed him'. In Arabic, one word renders this sentence, *qataltuhu*. English again needs three words to say 'he is sad'; Arabic /ħazina/, or 'he makes (someone) sad', /ħazana/.

The basic word order for Classical Arabic is VSO, e.g. 'Muħammad went to school' is rendered *ðahaba* ('he went') *muħammadun* ('Muħammad', nom. sg.) *ʔilā* ('to') *lmadrasati* ('the school', gen. sg.). It is possible to begin the sentence with the subject for stylistic reasons; however, if that is done, it is usual to precede the subject with *ʔinna* 'indeed', which then forces the subject to be in the accusative, i.e. *ʔinna muħammadan*. This has been described by what has been called a focus transformation.

Colloquial Arabic dialects are basically SVO (although I think most are, I refrain from saying 'all') and there is now convincing evidence that modern standard Arabic has become SVO as well. D.B. Parkinson has investigated this by examining newspapers such as *Al-Ahrām* and *Al-Akhbār* from 1970–8 and the conclusion is that this change is still in progress. There is evidence too that SVO is the more archaic word order since proverbs may still preserve this Proto-Arabic stage, e.g. *ʔaljāhilu yaṭlubu lmāla walʕāqilu yaṭlubu lkamāla*, 'the fool seeks wealth, the wise man seeks perfection'.

If the verb precedes its subject, usually it is in the singular (Classical Arabic is more rigid than modern standard Arabic), but if it follows the subject there must be agreement in gender and number, e.g. 'the two men bought a book' *ʔištarā rrajulāni kitāban* lit. 'he-bought the-two-men (nom. du.) book (acc. sg.)' but *ʔinna rrajulayni štarayā kitāban* 'indeed the-two-men (obl. du.) they-bought (du. m.) book (acc. sg.)'.

Interrogatives are placed at the beginning of the sentence, e.g. 'where did the teacher study?' *ʔayna* ('where') *darasa* ('he studied') *lmuʕallimu* ('the teacher', nom. sg.).

Two types of clauses have been studied in detail and the first is a hallmark of Arabic. The *ħāl* or circumstantial clause is usually introduced by /wa-/ 'and', which translates into English as 'while' or 'when', e.g. 'he wrote a letter while he was sick' — *kataba* ('he wrote') *maktūban* ('a letter', acc. sg.) *wahuwa* ('and he') *marīḍun* ('sick', nom. sg.) or 'he killed him while/when she was pregnant' — *qatalahu* ('he killed him') *wahiya* ('and she') *ħāmilun* ('pregnant', fem. sg. (but m. in form)). The second is the relative clause, which contains a pronominal reference to the modified noun but no relative pronoun occurs if the modified noun is indefinite, e.g. 'he wrote a book which I read' — *kataba* ('he wrote') *kitāban* ('a book', acc. sg.) *qaraʔtuhu* ('I read it', m. sg.) vs. 'he wrote the book which I read' — *kataba* ('he wrote') *lkitāba* ('the book', acc. sg.) *llaðī* ('which', m. sg.) *qaraʔtuhu* ('I read it').

Arabic sentence structures may be divided into the nominal sentence (usually also referred to as the equational sentence or Ø copula or *ʔaljumlatu lismiyya* in Arabic) and the verbal sentence. The equational sentence is a favourite sentence type of Arabic. It consists of two parts: a topic or subject

(Arabic *mubtada?*) and a comment or predicate (Arabic *xabar*). The topic is usually a noun or pronoun (or a phrase derived thereof) and the comment is a nominal, pronominal, adjectival, adverbial or prepositional phrase. Consider 'the university library is a beautiful building' — *maktabatu* ('library' in the construct state, nom. indefinite) *lǧāmiʕati* ('the university', gen. sg. definite) *binā?un* ('building', nom. sg. indefinite) *ǧamīlun* ('beautiful', m. sg. nom. indefinite). Negation of the equational sentence is formed by the irregular verb *laysa* 'not to be', which governs a predicate in the accusative (as any other verb does). The negative of the above illustrative sentence is *laysat maktabatu lǧāmiʕati binā?an ǧadīdan*.

When the comment of an equational sentence is an adverb or a prepositional phrase and there is an indefinite subject, the normal word order is comment–topic, e.g. '(there is) a book on the table' = *ʕalā* ('on') *lmā?idati* ('the table', definite gen.) *kitābun* ('a book', indefinite nom.).

With non-present time reference, one finds verbal sentences. The verb 'to be', *kāna* in the perfect, *yakūnu* in the imperfect, occurs in the past and future and governs, like any other verb, the accusative case. The Arab grammarians also put the verb *laysa* 'not to be' into this same verbal category (called 'the sisters' of *kāna*) along with *mā zāla* 'continue to be', *mā ʕāda* 'no longer to be', *kāda* 'be on the verge of'. The following verbs all mean 'to become': *ṣāra*, *?aṣbaḥa*, *bāta*, *?amsā* and *?aḍḥā* and verbs meaning 'remain' such as *baqiya* also belong to this verbal category.

To illustrate, consider that *kāna tāǧiran* 'he was a merchant' has *tāǧiran* in the indefinite accusative singular, the plural of which is *kānū tuǰǰāran* (*tuǰǰār* is the broken plural of *tāǧir*). *Kāna tāǧirun* means 'there was a merchant'.

A major characteristic of *kāna*-type verbs is that they can govern a following imperfect instead of a noun in the accusative. Thus one can say *lā ?adrī* 'I do not know' or *lastu* (< *laysa*) *?adrī* (lit. 'I am not-I know').

Bibliography

For classical Arabic, Fleisch (1956) is a solid overview, while Wright (1955), though originally published more than a century ago, remains a superbly documented grammar. Bravmann (1953) is one of the best syntaxes available, while for phonetics, Gairdner (1925) is probably one of the finest works ever written on the subject, dealing primarily with Koranic Arabic. Fück (1955) is a most important treatise on the history and development of Classical Arabic.

Pellat (1956) is a very good learner's manual for modern standard Arabic, while Stetkevych (1970) is a solid and thorough investigation of lexical and stylistic developments.

For the modern vernaculars, there are three superb grammars in the same series: Cowell (1964) on Syrian Arabic, Erwin (1963) on Iraqi Arabic and Harrell (1962) on Moroccan Arabic. Mitchell (1956), on Egyptian Arabic, is one of the finest pedagogical grammars ever written. Qafisheh (1977), on Gulf Arabic, is a very fine grammar, based on fieldwork in the Gulf countries, and deals with the vernacular dialects of important emerging countries. For Nigerian Arabic, references may be made to Kaye (1982), a dictionary of 6,000 lexemes with illustrative sentences and a linguistic introduction.

Mitchell (1953) is a very fine treatise on the writing system.

References

Bravmann, M.M. 1953. *Studies in Arabic and General Syntax* (Imprimerie de l'Institut Français d'Archéologie Orientale, Cairo)

Cowell, M.W. 1964. *A Short Reference Grammar of Syrian Arabic* (Georgetown University Press, Washington, DC)

Erwin, W.M. 1963. *A Short Reference Grammar of Iraqi Arabic* (Georgetown University Press, Washington, DC)

Fleisch, H. 1956. *L'Arabe classique: esquisse d'une structure linguistique* (Imprimerie Catholique, Beirut)

Fück, J. 1955. *'Arabīya: Recherches sur l'histoire de la langue et du style arabe* (Marcel Didier, Paris; translated by C. Denizeau, with an introduction by J. Cantineau, from the German original, *Arabīyya: Untersuchungen zur arabischen Sprach- und Stilgeschichte*, Akademie-Verlag, Berlin, 1950)

Gairdner, W.H.T. 1925. *The Phonetics of Arabic* (Oxford University Press, London)

Harrell, R.S. 1962. *A Short Reference Grammar of Moroccan Arabic* (Georgetown University Press, Washington, DC)

Kaye, A.S. 1982. *A Dictionary of Nigerian Arabic* (Undena, Malibu, Calif.)

Mitchell, T.F. 1953. *Writing Arabic: A Practical Introduction to the Ruq'ah Script* (Oxford University Press, London)

——— 1956. *An Introduction to Colloquial Egyptian Arabic* (Oxford University Press, London)

Pellat, C. 1956. *Introduction à l'arabe moderne* (Adrien-Maisonneuve, Paris)

Qafisheh, H.A. 1977. *A Short Reference Grammar of Gulf Arabic* (University of Arizona Press, Tucson)

Stetkevych, J. 1970. *The Modern Arabic Literary Language: Lexical and Stylistic Developments* (University of Chicago Press, Chicago)

Wright, W. 1955. *A Grammar of the Arabic Language*, 3rd ed., 2 vols. (Cambridge University Press, Cambridge)

34 *Hebrew*

Robert Hetzron

1 Introduction

The importance of the Hebrew language is not to be measured by the number of its speakers at any time of its history. It is the language of the Jewish Bible, the Old Testament of Christians. It also has a very long continuous history. Kept in constant use by Jews from antiquity to modern times, its reformed version, in an unprecedented process of revival, became the official language of a recently created state, the State of Israel.

It is futile to ask whether Modern Hebrew is the same language as the idiom of the Hebrew Bible. Clearly, the difference between them is great enough to make it impossible for the person who knows one to understand the other without effort. Biblical scholars have to study the modern language if they want to benefit from studies written in Hebrew today and Israelis cannot properly follow Biblical passages without having studied them at school. Yet a partial understanding is indeed possible and the similarities are so obvious that calling them separate languages or two versions of the same tongue would be an arbitrary, only terminological decision.

Impressive as the revival of Hebrew as a modern language may be, one ought not to have an exaggerated impression of its circumstances. Since Biblical times, Hebrew has never been a dead language. True, it ceased to be a spoken language used for the 'pass me the salt' type of everyday communication, but it has been cultivated — applied not only to liturgy and passive reading of old texts, but also to correspondence, creative writing and, occasionally, conversation. Actually, it was so extensively used for writing that the language, through this medium, underwent all the changes and developments which are characteristic of a living language. The revival in Israel made it again an everyday colloquial tongue, also for all lay purposes.

2 The Script

Hebrew is written from right to left. This is essentially a consonantal script.

(In the following, capital letters will be used for the transliteration of Hebrew letters). A word like *šibbōlɛ*ŧ (*shibboleth*) 'ear of corn' is written in four letters *ŠBLT*. Yet, long *ū* and *ī* (but not long *ā* > *ō*) are indicated by the letters otherwise marking semi-vowels: *W* and *Y* respectively. Moreover, the original diphthongs **aw* and **ay*, which were legitimately represented by *W* and *Y* in the consonantal transcription, were mostly reduced to *ō* and *ē*, yet they kept their *W* and *Y* symbols, making these trivalent symbols for semi-vowels and both closed and mid labial and palatal vowels respectively. Thus, the word which was originally **hawbi:lu:* 'they carried', Biblical *hō*ʷ*bī*ʸ*lū*ʷ, modern /hov'ilu/, is written *HWBYLW*. Two more facts need to be added. The *aleph*, originally a symbol for the glottal stop *ʔ*, has been maintained in the orthography even after the *ʔ* ceased to be pronounced. Word-final *-H* was pronounced in a few cases only, otherwise the letter stands as a dummy symbol after a final vowel *-ɛ/-ē* or, more frequently, after final *-ā̊*. This latter is most often a feminine ending. The use of *-H* here preserves the second stage of the phonetic development of this ending: **-at → -āh → ā̊*.

These originally consonantal letters used for partial vowel marking are traditionally called *mātrēs lectiōnis* 'mothers (= helping devices) of reading'. I transcribe them with raised letters.

The old Hebrew consonantal script, practically identical with the Phoenician one, was gradually replaced, beginning at the end of the sixth century BC, by an Aramaic script which, through the centuries to come, evolved into what is known today as the Jewish 'square' script, the standard print. From the second century BC on, graphically more or less different cursive systems further developed for casual handwriting. Two of these are still in use today: the modern cursive and a calligraphic development of the so-called Mashait cursive, the latter used today chiefly for printing the commentaries on the Bible and the Talmud of the eleventh-century Jewish scholar, Rashi (hence the name 'Rashi script').

Table 34.1 presents the consonantal letters of the major alternative scripts. Note that the letters *K*, *M*, *N*, *P* and *Ṣ* have special 'final' versions when they occur at the end of the word. These are parenthesised in the table. The names represent the Modern Hebrew pronunciation, as they are currently used. In the transcription column, the capital letter stands for the transliteration of the script, the letters after '~' show the Modern Hebrew pronunciation. These letters may serve as number symbols up to four hundred. They may be combined — thus *KZ* stands for 'twenty-seven', *RMḤ* for 'two hundred and forty-eight' etc.

Writing systems that transcribe words incompletely or inconsistently (English is an example of the latter) may be viewed as basically mnemonic devices rather than truly efficient scripts. With the decline of Hebrew as a spoken tongue, the introduction of vowel symbols and other diacritics became necessary. In order not to alter the original sacred, consonantal texts, this was done by means of added symbols, dots or other reduced-size

Table 34.1: The Consonantal Letters

Phoenician (=Old Hebrew)	Jewish Square (modern print)	Rashi	Cursive (modern)	Name	Transcription	Numerical Value
₭	א	ƌ	k	alef	$ʔ$	1
ᐈ	ב	ჳ	ꬳ	bet	$B; b, b{\sim}v$	2
ᐱ	ג	ꬳ	₫	g'imel	$G; g, g$	3
△	ד	ヮ	?	d'alet	$D; d, d$	4
ᗐ	ה	ꬲ	ꞃ	he	$H; h$	5
Y	ו	ו	ⅼ	vav	$W; w{\sim}v, u, o$	6
ᒄ	ז	ſ	Ƅ	z'ayin	$Z; z$	7
ᘋ	ח	ח	ᴨ	xet	$H; h{\sim}x$	8
⊕	ט	ῦ	𝒢	tet	$T; t{\sim}t$	9
ᔭ	י	′	′	yod	$Y; y, i, e$	10
ᒻ	כ (ך)	כ (ך)	ꝛ(ƥ)	kaf	$K; k, k{\sim}x$	20
ᒐ	ל	₰	ſ	l'amed	$L; l$	30
Ⴑ	מ (ם)	מ (ם)	N(P)	mem	$M; m$	40
ᒀ	נ (ן)	ꬴ (ן)	J(I)	nun	$N; n$	50
₮	ס	₷	ₒ	s'amex	$S; s$	60
O	ע	ע	ᴕ	'ayin	$ʕ$	70
ᒋ	פ (ף)	ꬴ(ף)	₯(ƀ)	pe	$P; p, p{\sim}f$	80
ᖁ	צ (ץ)	₷(ץ)	ꝛ(ꝙ)	tsade	$S; s{\sim}c(=ts)$	90
φ	ק	ꝗ	ꝗ	qof	$Q; q{\sim}k$	100
ᖾ	ר	ꝛ	₹	resh	$R; r$	200
W	ש	₷	ₑ	shin	$Š; š$	300
X	ת	℔	₥	tav	$T; t, t{\sim}t$	400

designs placed under, above and in some cases in the centre of the consonantal letters. These were always considered optional supplements, omissible at will. There were several such systems, chiefly the Babylonian and the Tiberian vocalisations; the latter alone is now used. The introducers of these systems are called Masoretes, the 'carriers of tradition', who carried out their work between AD 600 and 1000.

In the Tiberian Masoretic system, for example, a dot over the top left corner of a letter indicates $ō$, and if a W had traditionally been used for the same sound, the dot is placed over the W, to distinguish it from $ū$, which has the dot in the middle. Dots in the middle of consonantal letters other than those marking laryngeals and, with some exceptions, r may mark gemination, doubling of the consonant. Yet, in the beginning of syllables, a dot in B, G, D, K, P, T (this is the traditional order of listing) means that they are to be pronounced as stops; absence of dot points at the spirantised articulation, β or v, etc. (see below). A dot in a final h indicates that it is to be pronounced and is not a mere dummy symbol, a tradition that has usually not been observed.

One diacritic symbol is used for a true phonemic distinction. Hebrew has separate letters for $Š$ and S, but in some cases, the former is read [s] as well.

To mark this, the *Š* symbol was supplemented with a dot in the right top corner for [š] and on the left for [s]. This latter is usually transcribed *ś* and represents an original separate phoneme, a lateral fricative.

The vocalic notation was brilliantly constructed, yet it is not always perfectly adequate for all traditional pronunciations. A small T-shaped symbol underneath a consonant usually stands for a long *å̄* but in some cases, in syllables that were originally closed, it may be a short *å* (< **u*), see the beginning of section 4.1. Two vertically aligned dots underneath a letter, called 'shwa', may indicate lack of vowel or, at the beginning of the word or after another shwa (and in some other cases), an ultrashort sound [ə]. After laryngeals, there are 'tainted shwas', ultrashort *ă*, *ĕ* and *å̆* (*ŏ*). At the end of the word, lack of vowel is indicated by lack of any vowel symbol, though final shwa is written in some grammatical endings under -*T* (with a dot in the middle) and always in a final -*K*.

The vowel symbol is supposed to be read after the consonantal letter to which it is attached, except in word-final *Ḥ*, *ʿ* and dotted *H* with an *A* underneath, where the vowel sounds first. This is called a 'furtive *a*', a euphonic development.

Table 34.2 illustrates the use of vowels and other diacritic symbols, traditionally called 'pointing'.

As we have seen, the Biblical Hebrew script was not exclusively

Table 34.2: The Pointing

A.   The dot in the consonant (*dagesh*)
   a.   Spirantisation.
    בּ , *b* ב , *b̠* ; גּ , *g* ג , *g̠* ; דּ , *d* ד , *d̠* ; כּ(ךּ) , *k* כ(ך) ; פּ(ףּ) , *p* פ(ף) ; תּ , *t* ת , *t̠*
   b.   Gemination.
              ...*bb* בּ   ...*ww* וּ   ...*mm* מּ   ...*qq* קּ

B.   The letter *Š*.
                שׂ , *ś*   , שׁ *š*

C.   The vowels (combined with various consonants).

	Long		Short		Ultrashort
	ṭå̄ טָ		*ṭa* טַ		*ʿă* עֲ
lēʸ לֵי	*lē* לֵ		*lɛ* לֶ		*ʔĕ* אֱ
mōʷ מוֹ	*rō* רֹ		*ṣå* צָ		*ḥå̆* חֳ
tīʸ תִי			*si* סִ		*zə, z* זְ
	nūʷ נוּ		*nu* נֻ		

consonantal. The *mātrēs lectiōnis* indicated some of the vowels. The use of these was later extended. Already in Late Biblical Hebrew, we find *W* also for *ō* that does not come from *aw. In Modern Hebrew, except for some very frequent words and common patterns (where a certain degree of convention has still been maintained), *W* may be used for any /u/ or /o/, and *Y* for any /i/.

In modern practice, consistent vowel marking is restricted to Biblical texts, poetry, dictionaries and children's books. Otherwise, only the consonantal script is used, with fuller application of *mātrēs lectiōnis* and with occasional strategically placed vowel symbols to avoid potential ambiguities. It should be noted that the duality of 'obligatory' *W*'s and *Y*'s sanctified by tradition and 'optional' ones which may appear in unvocalised texts only is very confusing to the student of Modern Hebrew. Another serious problem, for native Israelis too, is that no consistent system has been worked out for the transcription of foreign words and names. Some conventions do exist, such as *G* with an apostrophe marking [ǰ], non-final *P* in word-final positions for final *-p*; yet this is insufficient, and many such words are often mispronounced.

It should be added that the texts of the Old Testament print cantillation marks (some above, some beneath the word) which note the melodic pattern to be used in chanting the texts in the synagogue service. Their exact position provides a clue to stress in Biblical Hebrew.

Table 34.3 reproduces part of verse 24 in chapter 13 of the book of Nehemiah. First the consonantal text is presented, then the same with full pointing.

Table 34.3: Part of Nehemiah 13.24

ואינם מכירים לדבר יהודית

Transliteration: WʔYNM MKYRYM LDBR YHWDYT

וְאֵינָם מַכִּירִים לְדַבֵּר יְהוּדִית

Transliteration: wəʔē^{y}n'ā̊m makkī^{y}r'ī^{y}m lədabb'er yəhū^{w}d'ī^{y}ŧ

Translation: 'and-they-do-not know [how]-/to/speak Judean'

---

3 The Periods of Hebrew

Hebrew may be historically divided into distinct periods on the basis of grammar and vocabulary.

3.1   Pre-Biblical Hebrew

Hebrew is a Canaanite language, closely related to Phoenician. It is even likely that its northern dialect barely differed from Phoenician. There exist Canaanite documents from the mid-twentieth century to the twelfth century BC, transcribed in Akkadian and Egyptian documents. It is hard to assess their exact relationship to the contemporary ancestor of Hebrew, but the two may be assumed to be identical in essence. Case endings and other archaic elements in phonology and morphology are found here. The most important source of these data are fourteenth-century BC letters found in Tell el-Amarna, Egypt.

3.2   Biblical Hebrew

This is the most important period, documented through the Old Testament (note that substantial portions of the books of Daniel and Ezra are in Aramaic). This collection of texts spans over a millennium-long period (1200–200 BC). The literary dialect was based on southern (Judean) Hebrew, though the northern dialect of some authors does show through. It is wrong to think of Biblical Hebrew as a homogeneous dialect. It covers different places and periods.

This heterogeneity, in particular the coexistence of doublets (e.g. a dual tense system for the verb, see below), led some scholars to declare that Biblical Hebrew was a *Mischsprache*, a mixed language, representing the coalescence of the speech of Israelites arriving from Egypt and of the local Canaanites. Yet the doublets attested do not seem to be particularly exceptional in the history of standard dialects.

It is customary to speak of Early Biblical Hebrew (the Pentateuch, Joshua, Judges, Samuel, Kings, the prophetic books) and Late Biblical Hebrew (Chronicles, Song of Songs, Esther etc.) but this is a simplification. The Song of Deborah (Judges 5) is considered to be the oldest text. In several books one finds traces of their having been compiled from different sources. Poetic texts such as the Psalms, the Song of Songs and poetic inserts elsewhere have their own lexical and grammatical features.

It should also be remembered that no matter how rich the material contained in the Hebrew Bible may be, no document of even that length may represent the full riches of a living language. We shall never know the true dimensions of Biblical Hebrew as spoken at that time.

Biblical Hebrew ceased to be spoken at some unspecified time (the destruction of the First Temple of Jerusalem in 586 BC may have been a major factor), yielding to Mishnaic Hebrew (see below) and Aramaic. The very last period of written Late Biblical Hebrew extends, however, into the Christian era, as represented by texts found in Qumran, known as the Dead Sea Scrolls.

One should thus keep in mind that what is described under the label 'Biblical Hebrew' is basically hybrid material: text in a consonantal script from between 1200–200 BC, while the pointing (vowels, indication of stress, gemination, spirantisation) comes from a much later date (after AD 600), when even the next stage of Hebrew, Mishnaic, had long ceased to be spoken. True, the pointing is based on authentic tradition, but certain distortions through the centuries were unavoidable.

3.3 Mishnaic Hebrew

This dialect represents the promotion into a written idiom of what was probably the spoken language of Judea during the period of Late Biblical Hebrew (sixth century BC) and on. It ceased to be spoken around AD 200, but survived as a literary language till about the fifth century AD. It is the language of the Mishnah, the central book of the Talmud (an encyclopedic collection of religious, legal and other texts), of some of the older portions of other Talmudic books and of parts of the Midrashim (legal and literary commentaries on the Bible).

3.4 Medieval Hebrew

This was never a spoken language, yet it is the carrier of a rich literary tradition. It was used by Jews scattered by now around the Mediterranean world, for poetry (both religious and secular), religious discussions, philosophy, correspondence etc. The main spoken languages of Jews from that time on were varieties of Arabic, Spanish (later Judaeo-Spanish, Ladino) and Judaeo-German (Yiddish). The earliest layer of Medieval Hebrew is the language of the *Piyyuṭ*, poetry written for liturgical use from the fifth to sixth centuries. After a period of laxity, the great religious leader of Babylon, Saadiah Gaon (892–942), heralded a new epoch in the use of Hebrew. This reached its culmination in the Hebrew poetry in Spain (1085–1145). The eleventh to fifteenth centuries saw a richness of translations into Hebrew, mainly from Arabic. The style developed by Jews of eastern France and western Germany, who later moved to eastern Europe, is known as Ashkenazic Hebrew, the written vehicle of speakers of Yiddish. The origin of the Ashkenazic pronunciation as known today is unclear; the earliest Ashkenazim did not have it.

The Medieval Hebrew period ended along with the Middle Ages, with the cessation of writing Hebrew poetry in Italy. In the interim period that followed, Hebrew writing was confined to religious documents.

3.5 Modern Hebrew

Even though Spanish and Italian Hebrew poetry did treat non-religious topics, it was the period of Enlightenment (Hebrew *Haskalah*, from 1781 on) that restored the use of Hebrew as a secular language. This led to important changes in style and vocabulary. Words denoting objects, persons, happenings of modern life were developed. Hebrew was becoming a European language. This development was concentrated in eastern

Europe, with Warsaw and Odessa as the most important centres. The great writer Mendele Moikher Sforim (Sh. J. Abramowitz, 1835–1917) was perhaps the most important and most brilliant innovator. Hebrew began to be spoken regularly only with the establishment of Jewish settlements in Palestine, mainly from Russia. In this revolutionary development, Eliezer Ben-Yehuda (1858–1922) played the most important role as the initiator and leader of the movement. His first son, Itamar Ben-Avi, was the first native speaker of Modern Hebrew. Ben-Yehuda brought many innovations to the Hebrew language. The type of Hebrew developed for speech adopted the Sephardic pronunciation as uttered by an Ashkenazi. In 1922, Hebrew became one of the official languages of Palestine under the British Mandate. Hebrew literature, now transplanted to the Holy Land, experienced an impressive upsurge. With the creation of the State of Israel (1948), the status of Modern Hebrew as the national language was firmly established. Modern Hebrew has been to a great extent regulated by the Academy of the Hebrew Language. On the other hand, native speakers have become a majority in Israel, many of them children of native speakers themselves. In order to express themselves, they do not consult grammars and official decisions, but create their own style, their own language, based on the acquired material modified according to the universal laws of linguistic evolution. This dialect, Spoken Israeli Hebrew, itself a multi-layered complex entity, has not yet been systematically described, but its existence has been noted and its importance acknowledged. Israeli Hebrew has about four million speakers.

4   The Structure of Hebrew

In the following, emphasis will be placed on the culturally most important dialect, Biblical Hebrew. When warranted, indications will be given of parallel phenomena in later periods. Modern Hebrew data will be quoted below in phonemic transcription, between /oblique strokes/.

4.1   Phonology

There are many traditional schools of pronunciation for Hebrew. That of Biblical Hebrew is only a reconstruction. It is customary to divide the numerous traditions into two major trends: Sephardi(c) (Mediterranean), and Ashkenazi(c) (Central and Eastern European). The most striking differences between these are the pronunciation of $\bar{\mathring{a}}$ as Seph. *a* vs. Ashk. *o* (but short *å* is realised as *o* even in the Sephardic tradition) and θ as Seph. *t* vs. Ashk. *s*. To a declining extent *ḥ* and *ʿ* have been preserved in Sephardic only, vs. Ashk. *x* and zero respectively.

For consonants, in the laryngeal domain, the Semitic sounds γ and *ʿ* are represented by the single letter *ʿ*, and *x* and *ḥ* also by a single *Ḥ* in the Biblical Hebrew consonantal script. The emphatic consonants of Biblical Hebrew: *ṭ*, *ṣ*, *q* (or *ḳ*) may have been pronounced glottalised (though there is no explicit proof of this). Today, there is no feature 'emphasis' and the three consonants are realised respectively /t/, /c/ (=ts) and /k/. Thus, only the middle one remained a separate entity, the other two are pronounced the same way as original *t* and *k*.

Except for the laryngeals ʔ, ʕ, *h*, *ḥ* and *r* (this one may have been at some time a uvular, since it belongs to this class), all consonants may be single or double (geminate) in Biblical Hebrew. Gemination disappeared from Modern Hebrew. Moreover, in the Masoretic tradition, the stops *b*, *d*, *g*, *p*, *t*, *k* were spirantised respectively into *β*, *ð*, *γ*, *f*, *θ*, *x* in a post-vocalic, non-geminate position, e.g. *bayiθ* 'house', *bəβayiθ* 'in a house', vs. *babbayiθ* 'in the house', *båttīʸm* 'houses'. As can be seen, alternations within the root have resulted from this conditioned spirantisation. Some incongruities in the system (such as 'houses' with a geminate after an apparently long vowel, *habbayθåh* '(to) home' with *θ* after a diphthong) make the phonemic status of both vocalic length and spirantisation rather unclear. Therefore, a non-committal transcription *b*, *d* etc., rather than the independent symbols *β*, *γ*, etc., will be used below. Modern Hebrew has only the alternations /b/~/v/, /p/~/f/ and /k/~/x/.

The vowel system, as noted by the Masoretes, does have its problems. As just mentioned, the phonemicity of vowel length is debatable. This is why it is advisable to use the macron and not the modern symbol 'ː' to mark this questionable length. Yet it is clear that vocalic length was once indeed present in the Biblical Hebrew system and played an important role in it.

It seems that at some point of its history, Hebrew equalised the length of all full-vowelled syllables (other than *ə*). Already in Proto-Semitic, long vowels could occur in open syllables only. Now, all vowels in an open syllable became either long: $*a > \mathring{\bar{a}}$, $*i > \bar{e}$, $*u > \bar{o}$, or *ə*. Short vowels were confined to closed syllables. However, word-final short vowels with grammatical functions survived for a while. The subsequent loss of these, which made a CV̄CV# sequence into CV̄C#, did not occasion the shortening of V̄, even though the syllable became closed. This produced minimal pairs such as *zåkar* 'he remembered' (from **zakar*) vs. *zåkår* 'male' (from **zakar* + case ending).

The ultrashort vowel *ə* caused spirantisation of a subsequent non-emphatic stop. After laryngeals, it has the allophones: ultrashort *ă*, *ĕ* and *ŏ*, selected according to the context, mainly on a harmony principle. The vowel [ə] is called *shwa mobile* in contrast with *shwa quiescens*, i.e. lack of vowel, which is marked by the same diacritic symbol. From the written sign's point of view, the shwa is supposed to be pronounced (mobile) after the first consonant of a word, after a consonant cluster or a geminate and, in principle, after a long vowel; the shwa symbol stands for zero (quiescent) elsewhere. However, in some cases, a traditionally quiescent shwa does spirantise the subsequent stop (as it comes from an original short vowel). This is called *shwa medium*.

Vocalic reductions producing shwas would occur when suffixes were added: *då̄ḇår* 'thing, word', pl. *dəḇårī̄ʸm*; *dibbɛr* 'he spoke', pl. *dibbərū̄ʷ*.

Modern Hebrew gave up all length distinction and simplified the system. Shwa is pronounced (as /e/) only when otherwise an unpronounceable cluster would result.

Because of the tightly regulated syllable structure (only aggravated by some loop-holes), it is impossible to decide which one(s) of the following features: spirantisation, vocalic length, gemination and shwa were phonemically relevant in Biblical Hebrew. By dropping length, Modern Hebrew unequivocally phonemicised spirantisation: BH *så̄ḇar* 'he counted' and MH *sappå̄r* 'barber' respectively became Modern Hebrew /safar/ and /sapar/.

Biblical Hebrew stress fell on one of the last two syllables of the word. In many cases it can be shown that final stress occurs when a word-final short open vowel had disappeared. Hence it was assumed that Proto-Hebrew had uniform penultimate stress. Yet, in other cases of final stress no such development may be posited, e.g. *ʔatt'å̄ʰ* 'thou (m.)', *dibbər'ū̄ʷ* 'they (m.) spoke'. It is then possible that originally the placement of the stress was not conditioned, but may have been functionally relevant (see the discussion of the tense system below). In transcription, only penultimate stress is traditionally marked, not the final one.

A remarkable feature of Biblical Hebrew is the existence of 'pausal' forms. At the end of sentences, many words have special shapes, e.g. contextual/pausal: (a) *šå̄mərū̄ʷ/šå̄m'å̄rū̄ʷ* 'they guarded'; (b) *k'ēlɛḇ/k'å̄lɛḇ* 'dog', *b'ēgɛd/b'å̄gɛd* 'clothing'; (c) *m'ayim/m'å̄yim* 'water', *bå̄ṭ'aḥtå̄/bå̄ṭ'å̄ḥtå̄* 'you (m. sg.) trusted'; (d) *yiṭhall'ēk/yiṭhall'å̄k* 'he walks about'; (e) *wa-y-y'å̄måṭ/wa-y-yå̄m'ōṭ* 'he died'. Though the pausal form of (a) and (d) have archaic vowels, it would be wrong to view the pausal shapes as simple survivals, especially in the domain of stress. They contain melodic signals of terminality, an artistic-expressive procedure. The basic principle was that stress, or rather the melismatic tune, fell on the last vowel of the word that was followed by a consonant. This refers to the period when pausal chanting was adopted. Thus, the penultimate vowel of (a) was saved from later reduction. The penultimate stress in (e) was brought to the end. In 'water' in (c), the *i* was not syllabic (**maym*). In (b), an epenthetic *ɛ* was added. With few exceptions, the melismatic syllable had to be long, thus original short vowels were lengthened. The retention of the original vowel in (d) needs clarification. Example (b) shows that we do not have here mere archaisms: 'dog' used to be **kalb-* indeed, and the *å̄* may be viewed as a survival; yet 'clothing' was **bigd-*, and the pausal *å̄* is only the result of a secondary lengthening of the *ɛ*.

4.2 Grammar

The Semitic root-and-pattern system (see the chapter on Semitic languages, pages 659–60) was complicated in Hebrew by the alternations introduced by spirantisation as imposed on root consonants according to position. Thus, the root *K-P-R* has, among others, the following manifestations: *kāpar* (MoH /kafar/) 'he denied', *yikpōr* (MoH /yixpor/) 'he will deny'; *kippɛr* (MoH /kiper/) 'he atoned', *yəkappēr* (MoH /yexaper/) 'he will atone'.

Inspired by their Arab colleagues, Hebrew grammarians adopted the practice of marking patterns by means of the 'dummy' root *P-ʿ-L* ('do, act' in real usage), e.g. *puʿʿal* means a form where the first root consonant is followed by an *u*, the second one is doubled and is followed by an *a*.

In the verbal system, seven derivational classes (*binyanim* 'structures') are to be distinguished: (I) *pāʿal* or *qal*, the basic form (with a special subclass where the non-past has the thematic vowel *a* instead of the usual *ō*); (II) *nipʿal* (marked by a prefix *n-*, assimilated to the first radical after a prefix), a passive of I if transitive, always an intransitive verb itself, occasionally inchoative; (III) *piʿʿēl* (with gemination of the middle radical), originally an iterative (for repeated actions), denominative and some other functions (often vaguely labelled 'intensive'); (IV) *puʿʿal*, the passive of III; (V) *hip̄ʿîʾl*, originally a causative; (VI) *hāp̄ʿal*, later *hupʿal*, the passive of V and (VII) *hitpaʿʿēl*, a reflexive or reciprocal, from Medieval Hebrew on, also a passive of III and with some more functions. Note that the derivational 'meanings' are not always to be taken literally. From the transitive *binyanim* I, III and V, passive II, IV and VI may be freely formed, but a II verb does not necessarily come from I. V may be the causative of I only when sanctioned by attestation in the sources; it is thus not productive. IV and VI have only restricted, mainly participial uses from Medieval Hebrew on. Some other derivational forms are occasionally found as archaisms or innovations.

In Biblical Hebrew the passive may have the syntax of an impersonal: *lōʾ yēʔākēl ʔɛθ bəśārōʷ* (Exodus 21.28) 'not will-be-eaten acc. its-flesh' = 'its flesh will not be eaten', where an object prefix precedes what should be the subject of the passive (or the object of the corresponding active).

The weak-root classes are designated by means of two letters, first which radical is weak (using the *P-ʿ-L* system) and then specifying the weak consonant which might disappear or be transformed in the conjugation. Thus *P:y* means that the *first* radical is a *y*. The main classes, beside regular (strong) roots, are: *P:y* (with two subgroups), *P:n*, *P:ʔ*, *ʿ:w*, *ʿ:y*, *L:y* (often named *L:h* because the grapheme *H* is used here when there is no suffix), *L:ʔ*, and *ʿ:ʿ* (verbs where the last two radicals are identical). For all these roots, the conjugation presents some special features in the various tenses and *binyanim*. When *ʿ* or *ḥ* is one of the radicals, changes occur in the vocalisation.

The tense system is among the most controversial and the most variable through the periods of Hebrew. The heterogeneity of Biblical Hebrew manifests itself the most strikingly precisely here.

It seems that the archaic system may be reduced to a dual opposition of two tenses (the traditional label 'aspect' for these is unjustified and rests on indefensible arguments): past and non-past (present and future in one, though the beginnings of a separate present already show), appearing in different guises in two main contexts: sentence-initial and non-initial. The jussive (the volitive mood, order, imperative, subjunctive) is homonymous with the non-past in most, but not all verb classes.

Like Semitic in general, Hebrew has a prefix conjugation and a suffix conjugation. In non-initial contexts (when a noun, a conjunction or an adverb opens the clause, in negation etc.), the former is a non-past (present-future) and a jussive (imperative) and the latter a past. Note that occasionally, and almost always cooccurring with a coordinated suffix form, the prefix form may stand for repeated, habitual actions in the past. This is a deviation from a straightforward pattern, yet it does not qualify for analysis as aspect. Sentence-initially, on the other hand, a prefix form preceded by *wa* + gemination of the next consonant (except when there is *yə-*) expresses the past and the suffix form preceded by *wə-*, with final stress in the first person singular and second person singular masculine (instead of a penultimate one) is non-past, actually very often a jussive because of the nature of the text. The following is a tabular representation of the four basic tense forms and the jussive, using two roots: *Q-W-M*, a *ˁ:w* root used here in the *paˁal* for 'get up', and *D-B-R* in the *piˁˁēl* 'speak, talk', in the second person singular masculine, with the prefix *t-* or suffix *-tå̄*.

	Sentence-initial	Non-initial
Past	wa-t-t'å̄qå̄m, wa-t-tədabb'ēr	q'amtå̄, dibb'artå̄
Non-past	wə-qamt'å̄, wə-dibbart'å̄	tå̄q'ū^{w}m, tədabb'ēr
Jussive	tå̄q'ōm, tədabb'ēr	

For *D-B-R* there is syncretism, only one type of prefix form, but the stress difference is found in the suffix forms. For *Q-W-M*, the non-initial non-past has a long *ū^w* (from an older **taqu:m-u* with an indicative ending), whereas the initial past and the jussive have a vowel with no *māter lectiōnis* in the same position (the differentiation *å̄/ō* is secondary). It is important to notice that this verb class exhibits a stress difference between the otherwise homonymous prefix past and the jussive. This suggests that the position of the stress must have been relevant in Proto-Hebrew (and in Proto-Semitic): **y'aqum* 'he got up'/**yaq'um* 'let him get up' (cf. **yaq'u:m-u* 'he gets up'), a distinction that must have disappeared in the other verb classes.

This dual system may be explained by the assumption that in the literary dialect an archaic system became amalgamated with an innovative one. Then, the latter 'non-initial' system prevailed and became the only one in later periods of Hebrew (complemented by a new present tense). The 'initial' system had preserved the original decadent prefix-conjugated past, reinforcing it with an auxiliary of the new type: **haway(a)* 'was', later reduced to *wa-:-*, to avoid confusion with the new non-past that had become completely homophonous with it in most verb classes. As for the *wə-*+suffix form for non-past and jussive, this may have been more or less artificially created to make the system symmetrical. The fact that the two systems were distributed according to position in the sentence is not hard to explain. Proto-Hebrew must have had a stricter VSO order, whereas Biblical Hebrew shows gradual relaxation of this and the slow emergence of SVO. Thus, the old morphology was associated with the old word order and the new morphology with the new word order.

The opposite roles of prefix and suffix conjugations in the two contexts inspired the term 'converted tenses' for those preceded by *w-*, itself called 'waw conversive'. The term 'waw consecutive' is still very common, based on the contestable assumption that for its origin it is to be identified with the conjunction *wə* 'and' used as a link with what precedes, in a system where the verb is claimed to express aspect with relation to the preceding sentence, rather than tense. This is untenable. Secondarily, however, and independently of tense use, the conversive *waw* came indeed to be identified by the speakers of Biblical Hebrew as a conjunction, an understandable case of popular etymology, hence the creation of the *wə-*+suffix forms, and, more importantly, the use of the true conjunction *wə-* 'and' in the beginning of sentences, even texts (e.g. the beginning of Exodus vs. the beginning of Deuteronomy), as a stylistic convention, before nouns, demonstratives etc. as well.

After late Biblical Hebrew, the converted (*w*-marked) forms disappeared. Beginning already in Biblical Hebrew, the active participle gradually took over the expression of the present. The prefix forms were restricted to the function of jussive in Medieval Hebrew (which used a periphrastic expression for the future), but were revived also as a future in subsequent periods. 'Was' plus the active participle has been used as a habitual past from Medieval Hebrew on.

Since conjugation fully specifies the subject in the prefix and suffix conjugations, no subject pronoun is required in the first and second persons. On the other hand, the active participle as a present form expresses in itself gender and number only, so that the cooccurrence of an explicit subject, noun or pronoun, is necessary. In Modern Hebrew, a third person pronoun is required in all tenses in the absence of a nominal subject. A third person plural masculine form without any pronoun or nominal subject is used as an impersonal: /hem amru/ 'they said', but /amru/ 'one said, it was said'. The first person distinguishes no gender.

Shown in the chart is the conjugation of the root *K-T-B* 'write' (*paʿal*) in Modern Hebrew. Note the alternation due to spirantisation /k/ ~ /x/. In verb-final position, only /v/ may represent *B*. In literary usage, past pl. 2 m./ f. /ktavt'em/ktavt'en/ and pl. 2 = 3 f. /tixt'ovna/ are also attested. These continue the classical forms.

	Past		Future	
	Masculine	Feminine	Masculine	Feminine
Sg. 1.	kat'avti		ext'ov	
2.	kat'avta	kat'avt	tixt'ov	tixtev'i
3.	kat'av	katv'a	yixt'ov	tixt'ov
Pl. 1.	kat'avnu		nixt'ov	
2.	kat'avtem	kat'avten	tixtev'u	
3.	katv'u		yixtev'u	

	Present = Active Participle		Passive Participle ('written')	
	Masculine	Feminine	Masculine	Feminine
Sg.	kot'ev	kot'evet	kat'uv	ktuv'a
Pl.	kotv'im	kotv'ot	ktuv'im	ktuv'ot

Infinitive lixt'ov   Verbal Noun ktiv'a ('(the) writing')

In the nominal system, a distinction is made between a masculine and a feminine gender. The gender of objects is arbitrarily assigned. In the singular, feminine is most frequently marked by the ending $-\bar{a}^h$ ($<*-at$), but also by $-Vt$. Some nouns are feminine without an external mark: most paired parts of the body (e.g. *'ayin* 'eye') and a few more (*kikkår* 'loaf'). Some nouns may have either gender (e.g. *š'ɛmɛš* 'sun', only feminine in Modern Hebrew). Beside the singular, there is a restricted dual and a plural. The dual ending *-'ayim* is used to express two units in a few nouns, mainly relating to time units (*šənå͑t'ayim* 'two years'); it marks the plural for paired elements, such as some body parts (*'e͡yn'ayim* 'two eyes' = 'eyes') and others (e.g. *mɛlqå͑ḥ'ayim* 'tongs'). It cannot be freely used, most nouns accept the numeral 'two' only for the expression of double occurrence.

The masculine plural ending is $-\bar{\imath}^y m$ and feminine plural is $-\bar{o}^{(w)}t$. Yet a restricted number of feminine nouns may have the apparently masculine plural ending (e.g. *šå͑nå^h* 'year', pl. *šå͑nī^y m*) and, more frequently, some masculine nouns may have the feminine plural ending (e.g. *lū^{wa}ḥ* 'tablet', pl. *lū^w ḥōt*). Syntactically, however, the gender of a plural noun is always the same as in the singular (e.g. *šå͑nī^y m rabbō^w t* 'many years', where the quantifying adjective does carry the feminine plural ending). This morphologically incongruent plural marking may be a remnant of the old polarity system (see numerals below).

Nouns may change their internal vocalisation when they adopt the plural ending. An extreme and mysterious case is *b'ayit/båttī^y m* 'house/houses'. The most systematic such change takes place in the case of the bisyllabic so-called 'segholate' nouns. These are characterised by a penultimate stress and a vowel *ɛ* (a *seghol*) in their last syllable, e.g. *m'ēlɛk* 'king', *s'ēpɛr* 'book'. These originate in an old CVCC pattern **malk-* and **sipr-*, cf. still *malkå^h* for 'queen', *sifr'å^h* 'book(?)' in the feminine. The plural pattern of the segholates is CəCå͑C- — *məlå͑kī^y m* 'kings', *məlå͑kō^w t* 'queens', *səpårī^y m* 'books'. Though many scholars prefer to explain it as a phonetic reduction, this could very well be the survival of the old broken plural (see the chapter on Semitic languages, page 658).

Nouns may also appear in the construct state, which means that they precede a genitival noun. Here the feminine ending -$\bar{a}^h$ becomes -at, penultimate $\bar{a}$ becomes $ə$, -ayi- is reduced to -$\bar{e}^y$-, the masculine plural has the ending -$\bar{e}^y$ (borrowed from the dual) and some nouns do not change at all. Examples: $šənat$ 'year of', $šənō^wt$ 'years of', $\dot{e}^yn$ 'eye of', $\dot{e}^yn\bar{e}^y$ 'eyes of', $b\bar{e}^yt$ 'house of'; plurals of segholates: $mal(ə)k\bar{e}^y$ 'kings of', $sipr\bar{e}^y$ 'books of', with the archaic singular vocalisation.

Hebrew has altogether three genitival constructions. The only one occurring in Biblical Hebrew consists of a possessum in the construct state followed by the possessor: $b\bar{e}^yt$ $h\bar{a}$-$7\tilde{\imath}^yš$ 'house+of the-man' ('the man's house'). Here the possessum is always understood to be definite and never takes a definite article, but adjectives referring to it do. Moreover, this construction is not to be broken up by qualifiers. Adjectives follow the whole group, no matter which noun they refer to (only one of the nouns may be so qualified). Thus, $b\bar{e}^yt$ $h\bar{a}$-$7\tilde{\imath}^yš$ ha-g-$g\mathring{a}d\bar{o}^wl$ 'house+of the-man the-big (m. sg.)' is ambiguously 'the great man's house' or 'the man's big house'. When the two nouns govern different agreements, ambiguity is dispelled: $mišp'aḥat$ $h\bar{a}$-$7\tilde{\imath}^yš$ ha-g-$gədō^wl\mathring{a}^h$ is only 'the man's big family', for feminine 'big' agrees with the feminine 'family', whereas $mišp'aḥat$ $h\bar{a}$-$7\tilde{\imath}^yš$ ha-g-$g\mathring{a}d\bar{o}^wl$ is clearly 'the great man's family'. There is no simple expression for 'the great man's big family' in Biblical Hebrew.

In the later stages of Hebrew the role of the above construction was reduced. In Modern Hebrew, it is basically a compounding device only, e.g. /bet xolim/ 'house+of sick+pl.' for 'hospital'. Here an article before the second noun definitises the whole expression: /bet ha-xolim/ 'the hospital'. Plurality is expressed on the first noun: /bate xolim/ 'hospitals' and /bate ha-xolim/ 'the hospitals'.

The other genitival constructions, introduced in Medieval Hebrew, use the genitive particle $šel$ 'of', still in a possessum-possessor order, and no construct state: MoH /ha-b'ayit šel ha-iš/ 'the-house of the-man'. Here, an indefinite possessum may also occur. Alternatively, one may say /bet-o šel ha-iš/ 'house-his of the-man', where the possessum is always definite and its third person possessive pronominal ending agrees in number and gender with the possessor.

In Biblical Hebrew, pronominal possession is expressed by possessive endings. These are attached to a construct state-like form of the nouns, with archaic vocalisation for the segholates: $malk$-$\tilde{\imath}^y$ 'my king', $sipr$-$\tilde{\imath}^y$ 'my book', $b\bar{e}^yt$-$\tilde{\imath}^y$ 'my house', $šən\mathring{a}t$-$\tilde{\imath}^y$ 'my year' etc. The plurality of the noun is expressed by a palatal element between the noun and the ending (which may be somewhat modified thereby): $\dot{e}^yn$-$\tilde{\imath}^y$ 'my eye', but $\dot{e}^yn$-ay 'my eyes'; $\dot{e}^yn$-$\bar{e}k$/$\dot{e}^yn$-$'ayik$ 'your (f. sg.) eye-eyes'; $\dot{e}n$-$\bar{o}^w$/$\dot{e}^yn$-$\mathring{a}^yw$ 'his eye/eyes' (the last ^{y} is traditionally silent) etc. In the feminine plural, the ending -$\bar{o}^wt$ is retained:

šən-ō^wt̸-ay 'my years'. In Modern Hebrew, a periphrastic construction is used for this with a conjugated form of *šɛl* /šel/ 'of', e.g. /ha-s'efer šeli/ 'my book' ('the-book of+me'). Possessive endings are regularly used in a third kind of genitival construction (see above), occasionally in some kinship terms and other inalienable possessions (/šmi/ beside /ha-šem šeli/ for 'my name') and regularly, again, in idioms (/ma šlomxa/ 'how are you (m. sg.)?' lit. 'what (is) your+peace?'). Contrast /be-libi/ 'in my heart' used for 'inside me', 'in my thought' and /ba-lev šeli/ 'in my heart' in a physical sense.

Qualifying adjectives follow the noun and agree with it in gender, number and definiteness: *ha-m-məlǎk-ō^wt̸ ha-ṭ-ṭō^wb-ō^wt̸* 'the good queens' ('the-king-f.pl. the-good-f.pl.'), in contradistinction to the predicative construction where no definiteness agreement is enforced: *ha-m-məlǎk-ō^wt̸ ṭō^wb-ō^wt̸* 'the queens (are) good'.

Adjectives may be derived from nouns by means of the ending *-ī^y*, a device very productive in Modern Hebrew: /sifruti/ 'literary' from /sifrut/ 'literature'. Adjectives may act as nouns as well.

Demonstratives follow the noun-adjective group: *ha-m-malk-ǎ^h ha-ṭ-ṭō^wb-ǎ^h ha-z-zō ʔt̸* 'this good queen'. Note the definite articles before all three words, omissible en bloc for stylistic variation. In predicative constructions the demonstrative is initial: *zō ʔt̸ malkǎ^h ṭō^wb-ǎ^h* 'this (is a) good queen'.

As examples have already shown, the definite article is a prefix *ha+* gemination of the next consonant.

The numeral 'one' is a regular adjective. From 'two' up, cardinal numerals precede the noun (in Biblical Hebrew they may occasionally follow as well). 'Two' appears in the construct state. From 'three' to 'ten' (and with some complications from 'eleven' to 'nineteen') the external gender mark of the numerals (the 'teen' part for the latter group) is the opposite of what one would expect: *ʔarbǎ-ǎ^h bǎn-ī^ym* 'four sons', where the numeral has the ending *-ǎ^h*, elsewhere a feminine, before a masculine noun, vs. *ʔarbaʕ bǎn-ō^wt̸* 'four daughters', where the feminine numeral carries no ending. Traditional grammars sometimes adopt the misleading practice of labelling numerals with *-ǎ^h* 'feminine' and stating that they cooccur with masculine nouns. This 'incongruence' is a residue of the old polarity system (see the chapter on Afroasiatic languages, page 652). Nouns appear in the plural after numerals, with few exceptions: 'year', 'day' and a few more have the singular after the round numerals 'twenty'... *ʔarbǎʕī^ym šǎnǎ^h* 'forty years'.

Ordinal numerals, formed by means of the *-ī^y* ending for 'second' to 'tenth', are adjectives: *ha-y-yō^wm hǎ-rəbī^yʕī^y* 'the fourth day'. From 'eleven' they are homonymous with the cardinal numbers, but exhibit the syntax of adjectives: *ha-y-yō^wm hǎ-ʕarbǎʕī^ym* 'the fortieth day'.

The syntactic function of nouns in the sentence is expressed by means of prepositions. The subject carries no mark. The direct object has the preposition *ʔɛt̸* when the object is definite. Contrast: *rǎʔīʕtī^y ʔī^yš* 'I+saw (a) man/someone' and *rǎʔīʕtī^y ʔɛt̸ hǎʔī^yš* 'I+saw acc. the+man'. Proper names as objects have *ʔet* even without the article. On the other hand, nouns with possessive endings, though otherwise definite, receive no *ʔet* in most cases in Biblical Hebrew. Three prepositions are written joined to the subsequent word: *lə-* 'to', *bə-* 'in, with (instrumental)' and *miC-* (with gemination of the next consonant, an alternative to *min*) 'from'. The rest (*ʿal* 'on' etc.) are separate words. They are conjugated by means of possessive endings of the singular type *l-īʸ* 'to-me' or the plural type *ʿā̆l-ay* 'on-me'. For pronominal object (accusative), the separate word *ʔō⁽ʷ⁾t-īʸ* etc. for 'me' and so on had been available since the beginnings of Biblical Hebrew, but alternatively in Biblical Hebrew and in archaising style later, object suffix pronouns attached to the verb were also used e.g. *rå̄ʔ'ī̆ʸtī̆ʸ ʔō⁽ʷ⁾tō⁽ʷ⁾* 'I+saw him' or *rə 7ī̆ʸtī̆ʸw* with the suffix.

In the pronominal domain, three sets of pronouns are to be listed: Independent subject or predicate pronouns, object pronoun suffixes and possessive pronoun suffixes. The latter are subdivided according to whether the preceding noun is a singular or a plural (see above). The object pronoun suffixes are homonymous with the singular possessive set, except in the first person singular, not considering the connective vowels (which are not specified in table 34.4). No gender distinction exists for the first person.

Table 34.4: Personal Pronouns

	Independent		Object ~ Sg. Poss.		Pl. Poss.	
	Masculine	Feminine	Masculine	Feminine	Masculine	Feminine
Sg. 1.	ʔănīʸ = ʔā̊nōkīʸ		-nīʸ (obj.)/-īʸ(poss.)		-ay	
2.	ʔattå̄ʰ	ʔattᵊ	-kå̄	-ēk	-ˈɛʸkå̄	-ˈayik
3.	hūʷʔ	hīʸʔ	-ō⁽ʷ⁾/-w/-hūʷ	-å̄ʰ/-hå̄	-å̄ʸw	-ˈɛʸhå̄
Pl. 1.	ʔănˈaḥnūʷ		ˈ-nūʷ (unstressed)		-ˈēʸnūʷ	
2.	ʔattɛm	ʔattˈen(å̄ʰ)	-kɛm	-kɛn	-ēʸkɛm	-ēʸkɛn
3.	hˈem(må̄ʰ)	hˈennå̄ʰ	-m	-n	-ēʸhɛm	-ēʸhɛn

For the indicative prefix-conjugated non-past, in those persons where no further suffix is used, the third person singular masculine/feminine object suffixes are *-nnūʷ/-nnå̄ʰ*. Thus, *yišmōr* 'he guards/will guard' (indic.) or 'let him guard' (jussive) is disambiguated: *yišmər'ɛnnūʷ* 'he will guard/guards him' vs. *yišmər'ehūʷ* 'let him guard him'. These *-nn*-marked suffixes are not to be confused with the distributionally unlimited use of *-n-* between prefix-conjugated verbs and object suffixes, which are traces of the old 'energic' mood of the verb (for 'he *did* do; he did indeed'), the type *yišmər'ɛnhūʷ* 'he will indeed guard/guardeth him'.

The basic Biblical Hebrew word order is VSO with the converted forms of the verb and 'verb-second' with a simple tense verb, where the first word is a topic. Medieval Hebrew is still basically VSO, but no more converted tenses are used. Yet, from late Biblical Hebrew on, SVO has been becoming more and more common, and it is the basic order in Modern Hebrew. Especially the adoption of the original active participle as a present tense encouraged the adoption of SVO.

Interrogative pronouns and the yes-no interrogative particle (Biblical Hebrew *hă-*, later *ha?im*) or the introduction of a question with an obvious answer ('isn't it the case that...?') *hălō*$^?$ or *hărē*^{y} are always sentence-initial. The negative particle *lō*$^?$ 'not' precedes the predicate. The rule that required that negation in the present tense should be effected by a pre-subject *?ē*^{y}*n* (originally the negation of *yeš* 'there is') is widely disregarded in spoken Modern Hebrew. Contrast normative /eyn-i/ or /eyn'eni roce/ 'not-I want' and colloquial /ani lo roce/ 'I not want' for 'I don't want'.

Biblical Hebrew has no copula in the present. In later stages, a third person pronoun in agreement with the subject may stand for a present tense copula, obligatorily in Modern Hebrew if the predication is of some complexity: /g'ila hi ha-mora/ 'Gila is (=she) the-teacher' (definite predicate). Hebrew has no verb 'to have'. Possessive predication is expressed by means of constructions like 'there is to': *yeš l-*. An interesting development of colloquial Modern Hebrew is that when the element possessed (the grammatical subject) is definite, it receives the accusative preposition *et*, as if it were the object of a transitive verb 'have': /yeš li et ha-b'ayit/ 'I have the house'.

Relative constructions follow the Semitic pattern (see pages 662–3): *ha-m-mắqō*^{w}*m ?ăšer ?attắ*^{h} *ʿō*^{w}*mēₔ ʿălắ*^{y}*w* 'the-place that you (m. sg.) standing on+it' for 'the spot on which you are standing'. The invariable relative particle is *?ăšer* in Biblical Hebrew, originally a noun meaning 'place' with a functional change 'where' → 'that'. Medieval Hebrew uses the archaic particle *še-*, with the function also extended to many other subordinating functions. In Modern Hebrew /še-/ is the relative particle and the complementiser (Biblical Hebrew *kī*^{y}, cf. Biblical Hebrew *?ăm'artī*^{y} *kī*^{y}..., Modern Hebrew /am'arti še-... / 'I said that...'). In Modern Hebrew there is a tendency to bring forward the referential pronoun of the relative construction right after the relative pronoun: /ha-makom še-alav ata omed/ (see above).

Bibliography

Chomsky (1957) is a vividly written, scholarly, but no longer up-to-date history of the Hebrew language, with special emphasis on its role among the Jews. Kutscher (1982), a posthumous publication, shows some unfortunate traces of being unfinished, yet is extremely rich in information on the history of the language and is characterised by depth of scholarship.

For Biblical Hebrew, Gesenius (1910) is an indispensable classic; Blau (1976) is a rigorously scientific descriptive grammar, recommended to the student; Lambert (1972) is perhaps the linguistically most solid grammar. Segal (1927) is a clear descriptive grammar for all students of post-Biblical Hebrew. For Modern Hebrew, Berman (1978) is a generative account, also useful as a descriptive grammar.

Further recommended are the articles on 'Hebrew Language' and 'Pronunciations of Hebrew' in the *Encyclopaedia Judaica* (1972, vol. 13, pp. 1120–45 and vol. 16, pp. 1560–1662); these are up-to-date presentations by C. Brovender, J. Blau, E. Y. Kutscher, E. Goldenberg, E. Eytan and S. Morag.

References

Berman, R. 1978. *Modern Hebrew Structure* (University Publishing Projects, Tel-Aviv)

Blau, J. 1976. *A Grammar of Biblical Hebrew* (Otto Harrassowitz, Wiesbaden)

Chomsky, W. 1957. *Hebrew, The Eternal Language* (The Jewish Publication Society of America, Philadelphia)

Gesenius, W. 1910. *Gesenius' Hebrew Grammar*, as edited and enlarged by the late E. Kautzsch, 2nd English ed. by A.E. Cowley (Clarendon Press, Oxford)

Encyclopaedia Judaica. 1972 (Keter, Jerusalem)

Kutscher, E.Y. 1982. *A History of the Hebrew Language* (The Magnes Press, Jerusalem and E.J. Brill, Leiden)

Lambert, M. 1972. *Traité de grammaire hébraïque*, reprinted with additions (Gerstenberg, Hildesheim)

Segal, M.H. 1927. *A Grammar of Mishnaic Hebrew* (Clarendon Press, Oxford)

35 Hausa and the Chadic Languages

Paul Newman

1 Chadic

The Chadic language family, which is a constituent part of the Afroasiatic phylum, contains some 135 languages spoken in the sub-Saharan region west, south and east of Lake Chad. The exact number of languages is not known since new languages continue to be discovered while other supposedly independent languages turn out to be mere dialects or terminological variants. The most important Chadic language is Hausa, with some 25 million native speakers and perhaps half again that number using it as a second language. Other Chadic languages range from close to half a million to less than a thousand speakers.

The family can be subclassified into three major branches plus a fourth independent branch. The West Chadic Branch, which includes Hausa, contains about 60 languages which fall into seven groups. All of the languages, with the exception of Hausa, which extends into Niger, are spoken in northern Nigeria. The Biu-Mandara Branch contains about 45 languages, assigned to eleven groups, extending from the Gongola and Benue River basins in Nigeria to the Mandara mountains in Cameroon. The smaller East Chadic Branch contains about 25 languages belonging to six groups. These are scattered across central Chad in a southwest-northeast direction from the Cameroon border to the Sudan border. The Masa Branch consists of a single group of five closely related languages spoken between the most southeasterly Biu-Mandara languages and the most southwesterly East Chadic languages. A comprehensive list of Chadic languages organised by branch and group is given in table 35.1. Within each group, the languages are listed alphabetically rather than according to closeness of relationship. Names in parentheses indicate alternative nomenclature or dialect variants.

Although the relationship of Chadic (specifically Hausa) to other Afroasiatic languages was proposed a century and a half ago, it has only recently gained general acceptance. The inclusion of Chadic within Afroasiatic is based on the presence of features such as the following: (a) a formative *t* indicating feminine/diminutive/singulative; (b) an *n/t/n* 'masculine/feminine/plural' agreement marking pattern in the deictic

705

Table 35.1 The Chadic Language Family (Inventory and Classification)

I.   West Chadic Branch
    1.   Hausa group: Gwandara, Hausa.
    2.   Bole group: Bele, Bole (Bolanci), Deno (Kubi), Galambu, Gera, Geruma, Kanakuru (Dera), Karekare, Kirfi, Kupto, Maha, Ngamo, Pero, Piya (Wurkum), Tangale.
    3.   Angas group: Angas, Chip, Gerka (Yiwom), Goemai (Ankwe), Koenoem, Kofyar (Mernyang), Mapun, Montol (Teel), Pyapun, Sura (Mwaghavul), Tal.
    4.   Ron group: Fyer, Karfa, Kulere, Mundat, Ron (Bokkos, Daffo), Sha, Shagawu, Tambas.
    5.   Bade group: Bade, Duwai, Ngizim.
    6.   Warji group: Diri, Jimbin, Kariya, Mburku, Miya, Pa'a (Afa), Tsagu, Warji.
    7.   Zaar group: Barawa, Boghom, Dass, Geji, Guruntum, Jimi, Ju, Mangas, Polchi, Zaar (Sayanci), Zari (Zakshi), Zeem.
II.   Biu-Mandara Branch
    1.   Tera group: Ga'anda (Gabin), Hona, Jara, Tera (Pidlimdi, Yamaltu).
    2.   Bura group: Bura (Pabir), Chibak, Kilba, Margi, Putai (West Margi).
    3.   Higi group: Bana, Higi (Kapsiki).
    4.   Mandara group: Dghwede, Glavda, Guduf, Gvoko, Lamang (Hitkala), Mandara (Wandala), Podoko.
    5.   Matakam group: Gisiga, Hurza-Vame, Mada, Matakam (Mafa), Mofu-Duvangar, Mofu-Gudur, Moloko, Muktele, Muyang, Uldeme, Zulgo.
    6.   Sukur group: Sukur.
    7.   Daba group: Daba (Kola, Musgoi), Gawar, Hina.
    8.   Bata group: Bachama, Bata, Gude, Nzangi (Jeng).
    9.   Kotoko group: Buduma (Yedina), Kotoko, Logone.
    10. Musgu group: Mbara, Musgu (Munjuk, Mulwi).
    11. Gidar group: Gidar.
III. East Chadic Branch
    1.   Somrai group: Gadang, Miltu, Mod, Ndam, Somrai (Sibine), Tumak.
    2.   Nancere group: Gabri (Tobanga), Kabalai, Lele, Nancere.
    3.   Kera group: Kera, Kwang (Modgel).
    4.   Dangla group: Bidiyo, Birgit, Dangla (Dangaléat), Jegu, Kujarke, Mawa, Migama (Jonkor of Abu Telfan), Mogum, Mubi, Toram.
    5.   Mokulu group: Mokulu (Jonkor of Guera).
    6.   Sokoro group: Barain, Saba, Sokoro.
IV.   Masa Branch
    1.   Masa group: Marba, Masa, Mesme, Musey, Zime (Lame, Peve).

system; (c) an *m*- prefix forming agential, instrumental and locational nouns; (d) formation of noun plurals *inter alia* by a suffix *-n* and an infix *-a-*; (e) a common pronominal paradigm; (f) a pattern of suppletive imperatives with the verbs 'come' and 'go'; (g) shared gender specification of individual words; and (h) cognate items for basic vocabulary including 'body', 'die', 'drink', 'fire', 'know', 'name', 'water' and 'what'. Some scholars have suggested that Chadic is the most distant Afroasiatic family member (apart from Omotic), while others have suggested a specially close tie with Berber; but so far, such proposals have been made essentially on impressionistic grounds.

In generalising about common Chadic characteristics, it should be understood that these features are neither present nor found identically in all Chadic languages, nor are they necessarily reconstructable for Proto-Chadic.

All Chadic languages, as far as we are aware, are tonal. One finds simple two-tone systems (e.g. Margi), two tones plus downstep (e.g. Kanakuru), three tones (e.g. Tera) and three tones plus downstep (e.g. Ga'anda). Vowel systems range from two vowels, /ə/ and /a/ (as in Mandara), to seven vowels, /i e ɛ a ɔ o u/ plus distinctive vowel length (as in Dangaléat). Vowel harmony of the common West African type is rare in Chadic but it does occur (e.g. Dangaléat and Tangale). A common Chadic feature is to have a different number of vowel contrasts depending on position. Thus, a language (such as Old Hausa) might have two vowels initially, three plus vowel length medially and five vowels without a length contrast finally. Most Chadic languages have a set of glottalised consonants (usually implosives) in addition to the voiced and voiceless ones. Goemai and some other languages in the Angas group have the unusual feature of contrasting ejective and implosive consonants at the same position of articulation, e.g. /p'/ vs. /ɓ/, /t'/ vs. /ɗ/. While the glottal stop /ʔ/ occurs as a phoneme in many languages, it invariably represents a secondary historical development: it is not reconstructable for Proto-Chadic. Finally one should note the widespread presence of lateral fricatives (/ɬ/ and /ɮ/) throughout the Chadic family. They have been lost in the East Chadic Branch and in the sub-branch of West Chadic to which Hausa belongs, but elsewhere they are extremely common.

In the realm of morphosyntax, Chadic languages typically have verb stems (inaccurately called 'intensives') that indicate the plurality of action: action done a number of times, by a number of subjects or affecting a number of objects. These 'pluractional' stems are formed by reduplication, gemination and/or by insertion of an internal -a-, e.g. Ga'anda ɓəl- 'kill', ɓəɓal- 'kill many'. In a few languages, the use of pluractional stems has become grammaticalised, resulting in ergative-type number agreement, i.e. obligatory use of pluractional stems with plural subjects of intransitive verbs and plural objects of transitive verbs, e.g. Kanakuru nà ɗòpè gámínîi 'I tied the rams' (ɗope < *ɗoppe); gámínîi wù ɗòpò-wú 'the rams are tied'; cf. wù ɗòwè gámîi 'they tied the ram'; gámîi à ɗòwè-ní 'the ram is tied'. The Kanakuru examples illustrate another distinctive Chadic feature (but with a very scattered distribution), namely the so-called ICP ('Intransitive Copy Pronoun') construction. In various languages all or some intransitive verbs optionally or obligatorily suffix a pronoun that copies the person and number of the subject. In Ngizim, for example, the use of the ICP is optional and adds an extra meaning of completeness to the verb phrase. In

Kanakuru, on the other hand, the use of the ICP is obligatory with all intransitive verbs (but limited to certain tenses), whether simple intransitives or medio-passives, e.g. *kà pòrò-kó* 'you went out', not **ka poro; kíléì à tàɗè-ní* 'the pot broke', cf. *à tàɗè kíléì* 'he broke the pot'. Note that ICPs in Chadic do not have the same form as reflexive pronouns (usually made up of the noun 'head' or 'body' plus a possessive pronoun) which occur as direct objects of transitive verbs.

A common Chadic feature is for verbs to take derivational extensions generally indicating action in, towards, down, up, away or totally or partially done. Sometimes the extensions are more grammatical in nature, indicating benefactive, perfective or transitivisation or intransitivisation. In some languages, such as Tera, the extensions are separate particles; in some, such as Margi, they are semi-bound suffixes; in others, such as Hausa, they have become integrated into the verb stem. In a number of languages, former extensions have lost their meaning and have become frozen to individual verb stems, thus complicating the problem of identifying roots for comparative purposes. For example, Hausa *rúushèe* 'destroy, raze', which comes from **rib-* plus a frozen suffix *-sa*, and Ngizim *ràbgú* (same meaning), which comes from **rəb-* plus a frozen suffix *-gu*, are cognate although this is not evident on surface inspection.

Grammatical gender in Chadic is a fairly straightforward phenomenon that goes back to Proto-Chadic (and beyond). The many Chadic languages that do not now have gender have all lost it, this having happened independently a number of times at the level of language group, subgroup and cluster. Languages with gender distinguish two genders (masculine and feminine) in the singular only. Gender distinctions are absent in the plural. In the pronominal system, gender is typically marked in the second as well as the third person.

Finally, regarding word order, Chadic languages are generally prepositional and place the possessor following the thing possessed. The most common order for verbal sentences is S(ubject)–V(erb)–O(bject); but VSO does also occur, primarily in Biu-Mandara languages spoken in the Cameroon border area. SOV in Chadic is unattested. Although SVO is by far the most common order in Chadic, being found in all four branches of the family, there is evidence to suggest that the basic order in Proto-Chadic was VSO (also the most likely order for Proto-Afroasiatic).

2   Hausa

2.1   Introduction

The Hausa language is spoken as a mother tongue by the original Hausas as well as by people of Fulani ancestry who established political control over

Hausaland at the beginning of the nineteenth century and who have continued to settle among and assimilate with the Hausas. Hausa is the majority language of much of northern Nigeria and the neighbouring Republic of Niger and is spoken in small colonies of settlers and traders in many large towns in West Africa. In addition, there is a sizable Hausa-speaking community in Sudan, dating from the British take-over of northern Nigeria at the turn of this century.

Hausa is also widely spoken as a second (or third) language in northern Nigeria and Niger, functioning as a lingua franca for commercial, informational and governmental purposes. (Hausa is one of the three indigenous national languages recognised in the Nigerian constitution.) While higher education in northern Nigeria is generally in English, Hausa is commonly the language of instruction in the primary schools. Hausa is now offered as a major degree subject in a number of Nigerian universities. There are several Hausa language newspapers, a thriving literature and extensive use of the language in radio and television. Broadcasting in Hausa is done not only within Nigeria and Niger, but also by 'international' stations such as the BBC, Voice of America, Deutsche Welle and Radio Moscow. With upwards of 25 million speakers, Hausa ranks with Swahili as one of the most important languages in sub-Saharan Africa.

Within the Chadic family, Hausa constitutes a group by itself. (Gwandara, the only other member of the group, is a historically recent creolised offshoot of Hausa.) The groups most closely related to it, with which Hausa shares many features of phonology and grammar, are the Bole group and the Angas group. What sets Hausa apart from its sister (or cousin) languages is the richness of its vocabulary, due in large part to the enormous number of loanwords from other languages. Mande, Tuareg and Kanuri, for example, have all contributed to Hausa vocabulary; but the major influence by far has been from Arabic (sometimes by way of one of the just-mentioned languages). In certain semantic spheres, e.g. religion (particularly Islam), government, law, warfare, horsemanship, literature and mathematics, Hausa is literally swamped with words of Arabic origin. Interestingly, Hausa has had no difficulty in integrating these Arabic words into its own morphological system of noun plurals or verbal inflection. In this century, Hausa has had a new wave of loanwords from English (in Nigeria) and French (in Niger). This influence continues unabated. For a while it seemed that borrowings from Arabic had ceased; but recently there has been a move among Hausa intellectuals to turn to Arabic for the technical vocabulary required for modern scientific and educational purposes.

Compared with other African languages, Hausa exhibits remarkably little dialect variation. Nevertheless, on the basis of systematic differences in pronunciation and grammar, it is possible to distinguish a Western dialect (or dialects) (e.g. Sokoto and Gobir) from an Eastern dialect (Kano and Zaria). The dialect described here, which has become established as

'standard Hausa', is that of greater Kano, the largest and most important
Hausa city.

2.2 Phonology

The phonemes of the standard dialect of Hausa are presented in table 35.2.
There are thirty-two consonants, twelve vowels (five basic vowels with
corresponding long and short variants plus two diphthongs) and three tones
(two basic tones plus a compound tone). The richness in the consonantal
inventory is due to the presence of: (a) a set of glottalised consonants
alongside the voiced and voiceless ones, e.g. /ɗ/ vs. /t/ and /d/; and (b)
palatalised and labialised consonants alongside simple ones, e.g. /kʸ/ and
/kʷ/ vs. /k/. In table 35.2 (and in all examples given), the symbols c and j
represent the affricates [č] and [ǰ] respectively. The 'hooked' letters ɓ, ɗ,
and 'y represent laryngealised (sometimes implosive) stops and semi-vowel,
while ƙ, ƙy, ƙw and ts are ejectives. The standard pronunciation for the
consonant written with the digraph ts is [s'] (an ejective sibilant), but there is
individual and dialectal variation, including [č'] and [ts']. The apostrophe /'/
is used in Hausa to represent the glottal stop phoneme /ʔ/. In standard
orthography, it is not written in word-initial position.

Table 35.2: Phonemes of Hausa

Consonants

f	fy	t	c	k	ky	kw	
b		d	j	g	gy	gw	
ɓ		ɗ	'y	ƙ	ƙy	ƙw	ʔ
		s	sh				
		z					
		ts					
m		n					
		l					
		r					
		ɽ					
		y				w	h

Vowels

Short			*Long*		
i		u	ii		uu
e		o	ee		oo
	a		ai	aa	au

Tones

High: á(a);	Low: à(a);	Fall (H + L):	âa

The Hausa /f/ phoneme is variably pronounced as [f], [ɸ] or [p]. It fills the p-
slot in the consonantal inventory. Before back vowels it is pronounced (and
written) as /h/, cf. *jèefí* 'throw' with *jéehóo* 'throw in this direction'. The

nasals /n/ and /m/ are generally pronounced [ŋ] in final position, e.g. /nân/ 'here' [nâŋ]; /máalàm/ 'teacher' [máalàm] or [máalàŋ]. When immediately followed by a consonant, in the same word or across a word boundary, /n/ (always) and /m/ (usually) assimilate to the position of the abutting consonant, e.g. *sún bí* 'they followed' [súmbí]; *fàhímtàa* 'understand' [fàhíntàa]. Hausa has two distinct rhotics: a retroflex flap [ɽ] and an apical tap or roll [r]. The two sounds are not distinguished in Hausa orthography. In linguistic works on the language, the tap/roll is commonly indicated /r/ (as here) or /r̃/ to set it apart from the flap, which is written /r/, e.g. *ráanáa* 'sun', *fàrkáa* 'paramour', cf. *r̥íibàa* 'profit', *fár̥kàa* 'wake up'. All Hausa consonants can occur as geminates as well as singly, e.g. *cíllàa* 'shoot far', cf. *cílàa* 'pigeon'; *díddígèe* 'heel' (< *dígdígèe*), cf. plural *dìgàadìgái*. Although from a technical perspective the geminates need to be analysed at some level as unitary segments, for most purposes they can be viewed simply as two identical abutting consonants, i.e. *cíllàa* = /C_1íC_2.C_3àa/.

The five long vowels in Hausa have typical IPA 'Italian' values. (Though written here with double letters, they are better thought of as single vowels with an attached phoneme of length.) In non-final position, short /i/, /a/ and /u/ are more lax and centralised. (Non-final short /e/ and /o/ have a questionable status in Hausa.) The contrast between long and short vowels is extremely important, both lexically and grammatically, e.g. *ɓáacèe* 'spoil', *ɓácèe* 'vanish'; *jíimàa* 'tanning', *jímàa* 'pass time'; *'ídòo* 'eye', *'ídó* 'in the eye'; *shàafée* 'wiping', *shàafé* 'wiped (past participle)'; *táa* 'she (perfective₁)', *tá* 'she (perfective₂)'. The two diphthongs /ai/ and /au/ are best treated as complex vocalic nuclei, although many Hausaists prefer to analyse them as /ay/ and /aw/. The former is generally pronounced [ei] or even [ee], tending to merge with /ee/; the latter varies in the [ao], [au], [ou] range, normally remaining distinct from /oo/.

Hausa has two basic tones: high, indicated *á(a)*, and low, indicated *à(a)*, e.g. *góoràa* 'bamboo', *gòoráa* 'large gourd', *màatáa* 'wife', *máatàa* 'wives', *kíráa* 'call', *kíràa* 'calling', *tá* 'she (perfective₂)', *tà* 'she (subjunctive)'. A sequence of high plus low on a single syllable is realised as a falling tone, e.g. *yâaráa* 'children' (= /yáàráa/), *mântáa* 'forget' (= /má̀ntáa/). In many cases falling tones are the result of the grounding of a low tone belonging to a following morpheme, e.g. *kóomôowáa* 'returning' (= /kóomóòwaa) comes from *kóomóo* 'return' plus `-wáa '-ing'. Falling tones, being tone sequences, only occur on heavy syllables, both CVC and CVV types. Hausa does not have a rising tone corresponding to the fall. A low-high sequence on a single syllable is simplified to high, e.g. *tàusái* 'pity' < *tàusàí (= *tàusàyíi*); *ɗáukàa* 'take' < *ɗàúkàa*.

Hausa has only three syllable types: CV, CVV (where VV can be a long vowel or a diphthong) and CVC, e.g. *súu.nán.sà* 'his name', *kú.jèe.râr̥* 'the chair', *'à.kwàa.tì* 'box'. While consonants may abut across syllable boundaries, e.g. *kás.kàa* 'tick', there are no consonant clusters within a syllable. Syllable weight is an extremely important variable in Hausa. It is crucial for metrical and tonal rules and plays a major role in morphological processes. CV syllables are light; CVV and CVC syllables are heavy. Given the restriction on allowable syllable types, it follows that long vowels cannot occur in closed syllables. Such overheavy syllables, which are created in intermediate structure by morphological formations, are eliminated by automatic reduction of the nucleus, e.g. *'aíkìi-n-sà* → *'áikìnsà* 'his work' (lit. 'work-of-his'); *mâi-n gyàɗáa* → *mân gyàɗáa* 'groundnut oil'; **búuɗ-bùuɗée* → *búbbùuɗée* 'open many/often'; **fáaɗ mínì* → *fár̃ mínì* 'attacked me' (contracted form of *fáaɗàa mínì*).

2.2.1 Orthography

Hausa makes use of two writing systems, one, called *bóokòo*, based on the Roman alphabet, the other, called *'àjàmí*, based on the Arabic writing system. The Roman system was introduced by the British in Nigeria at the beginning of the twentieth century. The system as now established makes use of the symbols in table 35.2 with the following differences. Glottal stop (') is not written in word-initial position. For alphabetisation purposes, such words are treated as if they began with the following vowel. The phonemic distinction between the two *r*s is ignored. Vowel length is not marked, nor is tone. An earlier attempt in Niger to mark vowel length by double letters has been dropped, so that there is now a uniform Romanised orthography in the former French and former British countries. On the whole the writing system is phonemic (even subphonemic in places) although some assimilatory changes are not noted in order to preserve morphological regularity. Thus one writes *sun bi* 'they followed', not *súm bí*, and *ribar nan* 'this profit', not *r̃iibàn nán*. The standard Roman orthography is used in the schools, in the major Hausa newspapers and in most other modern books and magazines.

The writing of Hausa in Arabic script (*'àjàmí*) dates from the beginning of the nineteenth century, possibly a little earlier. Although government policy since the beginning of this century has been to replace *'àjàmí* by *bóokòo*, it is still widely known and used. The *'àjàmí* script is learned in Koranic schools and is preferred over *bóokòo* not only by religious writers but also by many of the more popular traditional poets. After a long period of purposeful neglect, *'àjàmí* has begun to be used again in newspapers in northern Nigeria.

2.2.2 Morphophonemic processes

Hausa exhibits a tremendous amount of morphophonemic alternation, sometimes due to active phonological rules, sometimes reflecting earlier historical changes. Depending on the phonological environment, the 'altered' segment may appear either in the basic form of a word or in a derived form. I shall here describe only some of the more general processes producing alternations. (a) When followed by a front vowel, *t*, *s* and *z* palatalise to *c*, *sh* and *j*, respectively, e.g. *sáatàa* 'stealing', *sàacé* 'stolen'; *dùkúshíi* 'colt', pl. *dùkùsái*; *míjìi* 'husband/male', pl. *mázáa* or *mázàajée*. The palatalisation rule does not apply automatically to recent loanwords, e.g. *tíitìi* 'street' (from English via Yoruba); *láfàzíi* 'proɪ ɹnciation' (from Arabic). The voiced stop *d* also changes to *j* (with resulting neutralisation of the *d*/*z* contrast), but this change is not as regular as with the other alveolars, even in native words and constructions, e.g. *gídáa* 'house', pl. *gídàajée*; cf. *kádàa* 'crocodile', pl. *kádóodíi*; *kúdù* 'south', *bàkúdèe* 'southerner'. Palatalisation also affects velars, but it is not reflected in the orthography except in the case of the *w*/*y* alternation, e.g. *ɓàráawòo* 'thief', pl. *ɓàràayíi*. (b) As indicated above, long vowels are automatically shortened in closed syllables. At normal speech tempos, resultant short *e* and *o* merge with short *a*. The original quality of the vowel often shows up as palatalisation or labialisation of the preceding consonant, e.g. *dárée-n-nàn* → *dáránnàn* 'this night'; *dàshée-n-sù* → *dàshánsù* 'their seedlings' (cf. *dásàa* 'to transplant seedlings'); *gêeffáa* → *gyâffáa* 'sides' (pl. of *géefèe*); *kánóo-ncíi* → *kánáncíi* 'Kano dialect'; *kóon-kòonáa* → *kwánkòonáa* 'keep on burning'. (c) Velar and bilabial stops (the latter in the Eastern dialects only) historically weakened to *u* in syllable-final position (with subsequent simplification of *iu* diphthongs to *uu*), e.g. *tálàkà* 'commoner', *táláucìi* 'poverty'; *búuzúu* 'Tuareg serf', pl. *búgàajée*; *júujíi* 'rubbish heap', pl. *jíbàajée*. (Note that some of these 'irregular' plurals are nowadays being replaced by more transparent forms such as *búuzàayée* and *júujàayée*.) The bilabial change also applied to *m*, but only wheɪ the abutting consonant was an alveolar sonorant, e.g. *'áurée* 'marriage', *'ámáryáa* 'bride'. (d) In syllable-final position, alveolar stops (and sometimes sibilants) change to the tap/roll *ɾ*, e.g. *mútù* 'die'; *múɾmútù* 'die one after the other'; *ɓátà* 'spoil', *ɓàɾnáa* 'destruction'; *kádà* = *kâɾ* 'negative subjunctive marker'; *fáadíi* 'breadth', *fàɾfáadáa* 'broad'; *mázámázá* = *máɾmázá* 'quickly'. When more than one process applies, related forms can differ considerably on the surface, e.g. *fáɾkée* 'trader', *fátáucìi* 'trading'. (e) Abutting sequences of C_a-C_b, where C_a is an obstruent, commonly simplify to a geminate $\widehat{CC_b}$. For alveolars, gemination is usually an alternative to rhotacisation, e.g. *kád-kàdáa* → *kákkàdáa* or *káɾkàdáa* 'keep beating'; *rìigáa-t-sà* → *rìigássà* or *rìigáɾsà* 'his gown'; *zàaf-záafáa* → *zàzzáafáa* 'hot' (not *zàuzáafáa).

2.3 Morphology
The Hausa pronominal system distinguishes five categories in the singular (1, 2-masculine, 2-feminine, 3-masculine, 3-feminine) and four in the plural (1-pl., 2-pl., 3-pl., and '4-pl', an impersonal subject). There is no gender distinction in the plural. Variant pronoun sets, differing primarily in tone and vowel length, are shown in the chart of independent, object and possessive pronouns. Their use is determined by surface syntactic position

Hausa Independent, Object and Possessive Pronouns

	a	b	c	d	e
1	níi	ní	-nì	-nì	-(w)á
2 m.	kái	ká	-kà	-kà	-kà
2 f.	kée	kí	-kì	-kì	-kì
3 m.	shíi	shí	-shì	-sà	-sà
3 f.	'ítá	tá	-tà	-tà	-tà
1 pl.	múu	mú	-mù	-nà	-mù
2 pl.	kúu	kú	-kù	-kù	-kù
3 pl.	súu	sú	-sù	-sù	-sù

Note: a = independent; b = object-pronoun; c = object-clitic; d = indirect object; e = possessive

and function. The independent pronouns (set (a)) are used as absolute pronouns, e.g. *níi nèe* 'it's me'; as subjects of equational sentences, e.g. *kái yáaròo née* 'you're a boy'; as objects of the particle *dà* 'and/with', e.g. *sún zóo dà 'ítá* 'they came with her', *níi dà kée mún yàṛdá* 'I and you (we) agree'; as direct objects when not immediately following the verb, e.g. *kàawóo míní shíi* 'bring me it'; and as fronted, focused forms, e.g. *kée cèe múkà gáníi* 'you were the one we saw', *súu nèe súkà tàfí* 'they were the ones who went'. The object pronouns (set (b)) are used as direct objects of certain 'grades' of verbs (see pages 715–6), e.g. *náa káṛàntáa sú* 'I read them'. Pronouns of the same form are also used as subjects of the verboid *zâa* 'be going', e.g. *zâa tá kàasúwáa* 'she's going to market', and of the negative *bâa*, e.g. *bâa shí dà táawùl* 'he doesn't have a towel'. The object clitics (set (c)) are used as direct object of other 'grades' of verbs, e.g. *náa tàmbàyée sù* 'I asked them', and as object of the common word *'àkwái* 'there is/are', e.g. *'àkwái sù dà yáwàa* 'there are many of them' (lit. 'there-are them with many'). The forms in set (d) are bound to the indirect object marker *má-* (with an assimilatory vowel), e.g. *másà, míní, múkù* 'to him, me, you-pl.'. The forms in set (e) are used with the gender-sensitive linkers **na* (masculine and plural),**ta* (feminine), e.g. *náakà* 'yours', *líttáafìnkà* 'your book', *táasù* 'theirs (feminine referent)', *móotàṛsù* 'their car' (*ṛ < *t*). The first person is slightly irregular, e.g. *nàawá/tàawá* 'mine', *líttáafìináa* (*-náa = ná + á*) 'my book', *móotàatáa* (*-táa = tá + á*) 'my car'. In set (e) as well as (d), the third person singular masculine pronoun *-sà* is replaced in colloquial speech by *-shì*.

Hausa 'tenses' (which reflect tense, mood, aspect and aktionsart or a combination thereof) are indicated by a marker attached to a preverbal pronoun. Some of the markers are clearly segmentable while others consist only of tone or vowel length modifications of the basic pronoun. (In the case of the subjunctive, the marker is Ø.) Thus it has become the convention in Hausa studies to treat the pronoun plus marker as a fused tense/aspect pronoun, see the chart of tense/aspect pronouns. Negative tense/aspect pronouns which differ from the corresponding affirmative ones are listed separately. Apart from the continuous, which uses a single negative marker *báa*, and the subjunctive, which uses a negative particle *kádà*, verbal sentences are negated by means of a discontinuous morpheme *bà... bá*. The meanings of the tenses are roughly deducible from their labels and will not be discussed. The syntactic opposition between the two perfective and two continuous categories is described in section 2.4.

Hausa Tense/Aspect Pronouns

	a	b	c	d	e	f	g	h	i	j
1	náa	ná	bàn...bá	zân	nâa	nákàn	'ǹ	'ńnàa	nákè(e)	báanàa
2 m.	káa	ká	bàkà...bá	záakà	kâa	kákàn	kà	kánàa	kákè(e)	báakàa
2 f.	kín	kíkà	bàkì...bá	záakì	kyâa	kíkàn	kì	kínàa	kíkè(e)	báakyàa
3 m.	yáa	yá	bài...bá	zâi	yâa	yákàn	yà	yánàa	yákè(e)	báayàa
3 f.	táa	tá	bàtà...bá	záatà	tâa	tákàn	tà	tánàa	tákè(e)	báatàa
1 pl.	mún	múkà	bàmù...bá	záamù	mâa	múkàn	mù	múnàa	múkè(e)	báamàa
2 pl.	kún	kúkà	bàkù...bá	záakù	kwâa	kúkàn	kù	kúnàa	kúkè(e)	báakwàa
3 pl.	sún	súkà	bàsù...bá	záasù	sâa	súkàn	sù	súnàa	súkè(e)	báasàa
4 pl.	'án	'ákà	bà'à...bá	záa'à	'âa	'ákàn	'à	'ánàa	'ákè(e)	báa'àa

Note: a = perfective₁; b = perfective ₂; c = neg-perfective; d = future; e = predictive; f = habitual; g = subjunctive; h = continuous₁; i = continuous₂; j = neg.-continuous.

Except for the imperative, which is marked by low-high tone (sometimes plus a final vowel change), the verb itself is not conjugated, tense, person and number being shown by the tense/aspect pronoun, e.g. *náa záunàa* 'I sat'; *bà nâa záunàa bá* 'I don't intend to sit'; *záamù záunàa* 'we will sit'; *mù záunàa* 'let's sit'; *tákàn káamàa sú* 'she catches them'; *tánàa káamàa sú* 'she is catching them'; cf. *zàunáa* 'sit!'; *kàamáa sú* 'catch them!'. Verbal morphology in Hausa reflects the verb's 'grade' and its syntactic environment. The morphological distinctiveness in each category is defined in terms of the verb's final vowel (or -VC) and overall tone. The pattern for each grade, indicated for di- and tri-syllabic verbs, is presented in table 35.3.

Grade 7 ('sustentative') indicates an agentless passive (or sometimes middle voice), action well done or potentiality of sustaining action, e.g. *náamàa yáa gàsú* 'the meat has been roasted'; *'àgóogó báayàa gyàarú-wáa* 'the watch is not repairable'. Grade 6 ('ventive') indicates movement in the direction of or for the benefit of the speaker, e.g. *kún sáyóo gíyàa?* 'did you buy (and bring) beer?'; *záatà fítóo* 'she will come out'. Grade 5 ('efferential'), traditionally termed 'causative', indicates action effected away from the speaker. It also serves to transitivise inherently intransitive verbs, e.g. *yáa 'áuráṛ dà 'yáṛsà* 'he married off his daughter'; *táa fítáṛ* 'she took (it) out'; *dón mè kíkà sáishée tà* 'why did you sell it?'. Grade 4 ('totality') indicates an action totally done or affecting all the objects, e.g. *rúwáa yáa zúbèe* 'the water all spilled out';

Table 35.3: The Hausa Grade System

	Form A			Form B			Form C	
Grade 1	-aa	H L (H)	-aa		H L (H)	-a		H L (L)
Grade 2	-aa	L H (L)	-ee		(L) L H	-i		(L) L H
Grade 3	-a	L H (L)						
Grade 4	-ee	H L (H)	-ee		H L (H)	{ -e	H L (L) }
						{ -ee	H L (H) }
Grade 5	-aṛ (< *as)	H H (H)	-shee		H H (H)			
Grade 6	-oo	H H (H)	-oo		H H (H)	-oo		H H (H)
Grade 7	-u	(L) L H						

Note: grade 1 = basic-*a* and applicative; grade 2 = basic-*i* and partitive; grade 3 = basic-*a* intransitive; grade 4 = totality; grade 5 = efferential; grade 6 = ventive; grade 7 = sustentative.

záamù sáyè shìnkáafáa 'we will buy up the rice'. With many verbs, especially when used intransitively, Grade 4 is becoming a basic, semantically neutral form. Grade 3 is an exclusively intransitive grade containing verbs with lexically underlying final -*a*, e.g. *fìtá* 'go out'; *cìká* 'be filled'. Grade 2 contains basic transitive verbs with underlying final -*i* as well as derived verbs with a partitive sense, e.g. *bàkà fàɗí gàskíyáa bá* 'you didn't tell the truth' (basic); *mù yànkí náamàa* 'let's cut off some meat' (partitive). Grade 1 contains basic transitive verbs with underlying final -*a* as well as derived 'applicatives' (often required with indirect objects). Like the efferential, grade 1 applicatives serve to transitivise intransitive verbs, e.g. *sún hákà ráamìi* 'they dug a hole' (basic); *kà fáɗàa mánà gàskíyáa* 'you should tell us the truth' (applicative); *táa fásà tùulúu* 'she smashed the pot' (applicative). Hausa has a small number of high-frequency monosyllabic verbs, e.g. *cí* 'eat', *sháa* 'drink', *bí* 'follow', *jáa* 'pull'. These do not fit into grades 1, 2 or 3, but they do appear in the other grades (with slightly variant forms), e.g. *yáa shânyè rúwáa* 'he drank up the water' (gr. 4); *múkàn cíishée sù* 'we feed them' (gr. 5); *jàawóo nân* 'pull (it) here' (gr. 6); *hányàa tâa bìyú* 'the road will be followable' (gr.7).

Independent of grade, verbs have three syntactically determined forms (omitting the pre-indirect object position, which poses special problems). Form B is used when the verb is immediately followed by a direct object personal pronoun (Grades 1 and 4 take the high tone object pronouns; all other verbs take the low tone clitics.) Form C is used when the verb is followed by any other direct object. Form A is used elsewhere, e.g.

táa tàimàkí Múusáa	'she helped Musa'	(gr. 2, C)
táa tàimàkée shì	'she helped him'	(gr. 2, B)
Múusáa nèe tá tàimákàa	'it was Musa she helped'	(gr. 2, A)
mún káṛàntà jàṛíidàa	'we read the paper'	(gr. 1, C)
mún káṛàntáa tá	'we read it'	(gr. 1, B)
wàccée kúkà káṛàntáa?	'which did you read?'	(gr. 1, A)

Grade 5 ('efferential') verbs do not have a C form since the semantic objects are expressed as oblique objects introduced by the preposition *dà* 'with', e.g. *yánàa kóoyáṛ dà Háusá* 'he is teaching Hausa'. With pronominal objects, one may use either the B form or the A form with the oblique object, e.g. *yáa cíishée tà = yáa cíyáṛ dà 'ítá* 'he fed her/it'. Some verbs allow a short form (without the suffix *-aṛ*) before *dà*, e.g. *táa zúb dà rúwáa = táa zúbáṛ dà rúwáa* 'she poured out the water'. Historically it seems that the *-dà* in the short form was a verbal extension attached to the verb (as it still is in some Western dialects) which was reanalysed as the homophonous preposition.

2.3.1 Verbal nouns

While verbs as such are not inflected for tense, in the continuous tenses they are subject to replacement by verbal-nominal forms, of which there are three general classes. (1) *-wáa* forms. When no object is expressed, verbs of grades 1, 4, 5 and 6 use a present participial-like stem formed with the suffix *-wáa*, e.g. *báasàa kóomôowáa* 'they are not returning', cf. *bàsù kóomóo bá* 'they didn't return'; *tánàa rúfèewáa* 'she is closing (it)', cf. *tánàa rúfè táagàa* 'she is closing the window'. (2) Primary verbal nouns. Grades 2, 3 and 7 form verbal nouns with a suffix *-áa*. Monosyllabic verbs add ꞉ (vowel length plus low tone). If the primary verbal noun is followed by an object, it takes a connecting linker (*-n* or *-ṛ*). The 'object' pronoun is represented by a possessive form, e.g. *tánàa tàmbáyàṛsà* 'she is asking him', cf. *táa tàmbàyée shì* 'she asked him'; *múnàa cîn* (< *cîi + n*) *náamàa* 'we are eating meat', cf. *mún cí náamàa* 'we ate meat'; *Múusáa nèe yákèe fìtáa* (< *fìtá + áa*) 'Musa is going out'; *báasàa gyàarúwáa* (< *gyàarú + áa*) 'they are not repairable'. (3) Secondary verbal nouns. Many verbs have lexically related verbal nouns that are used instead of or sometimes as an alternative to verbs or primary verbal nouns. Like primary verbal nouns, these forms require a linker before expressed objects. The shape of secondary verbal nouns is lexically specific and cannot be predicted from the form of the related verb. The following are the more common secondary verbal noun patterns:

(a) -ii H L: *gínìi* 'building'; *ɗínkìi* 'sewing'
(b) -ee L H: *sàyée* 'buying'; *bìncìkée* 'investigating'
(c) -aa H H: *gyáaráa* 'repairing'; *néemáa* 'seeking'
(d) -oo (variable): *cíizòo* 'biting'; *kòoyóo* 'learning'
(e) Ablaut H L: *jíimàa* 'tanning' (< *jéemàa*); *súukàa* 'piercing' (< *sòokáa*).

Finally, before leaving verbal morphology, two regular deverbal constructions should be mentioned. Adverbs of state are formed from verb stems by means of a suffix *-e* (with short vowel) and a L H tone pattern, e.g. *zàuné* 'seated', *dàfé* 'cooked', *wàṛwàatsé* 'scattered'. Past participial adjectives are formed from verbs by reduplicating the stem-final consonant in geminate form and adding a suffix *-ee* (masculine) or *-iyaa* (feminine) and L H H tone in the singular or a suffix *-uu* and L L H tone in the plural, e.g.

dàfáffée (m.), *dàfáffíyáa* (f.), *dàfàffúu* (pl.) 'cooked', *gàagàrárrée*, *gàagàrárríyáa*, *gàagàràrrúu* 'obstinate, rebellious'.

The major parameters in nominal morphology are gender and number. Hausa has two genders, masculine and feminine, morphologically and grammatically distinguished in the singular only. Masculine words are generally unmarked, exhibiting all possible phonological shapes. With a few exceptions, feminine words end in *-aa*, *-(i)yaa*, or *-(u)waa*, e.g. masculine: *kíifíi* 'fish', *zóobèe* 'ring', *bàkáa* 'bow', *nóonòo* 'breast', *tùulúu* 'pot'; feminine: *kúuráa* 'hyena', *múndúwáa* 'anklet', *kíbíyàa* 'arrow', *kàazáa* 'hen', *tábáryáa* 'pestle'. Adjectives, which constitute a class of 'dependent nominals', are inflected for gender and number, the feminine being formed from the masculine by the addition of *-aa* (with automatic glide insertion where required), e.g. *fáríi* (m.), *fáráa* (f.), *fáràarée* (pl.) 'white'; *shúuɗìi*, *shúuɗìyáa*, *shûɗɗáa* 'blue'; *dóogóo*, *dóogúwáa*, *dóogwàayée* 'tall'; *sàatáccée*, *sàatácciyáa*, *sàatàttúu* 'stolen'.

At the derivational level, many feminine counterparts to masculine humans and animals make use of a suffix *-n(i)yaa*, e.g. *yáaròo*, *yáarínyàa* 'boy, girl'; *màkáahòo*, *màkáunìyáa* (< *màkáafnìyáa*) 'blind man, woman', *bírìi*, *bírínyàa* 'monkey m./f.'. Other male/female pairs use the inflectional *-aa* suffix, e.g. *jàakíi*, *jàakáa* 'donkey m./f.'; *kàrée*, *kàryáa* 'dog, bitch'.

Nominal plurals represent one of the most complex areas of Hausa morphology. On the surface there are some forty different plural formations making use of infixes, suffixes, reduplication etc. If, however, one focuses on tone and final vowel, the various plurals can be grouped into a manageable number of basic patterns, see table 35.4.

Although the plural of any given word is not totally predictable, there are correlations and restrictions that hold. For example, almost all singular words that have type (2) plurals have H H tone — but not all H H singulars have type (2) plurals — while type (3) plurals are limited to H L singulars. Within type (2), the variant manifestations of the plural are determined by canonical syllabic structure. If the singular has a light first syllable, it takes a reduplicated plural; if it has an initial open heavy syllable, it takes a glide suffixing plural; if it has an initial closed syllable, it takes an infixing plural. Since there is no one-to-one fit between singulars and plurals, it is not surprising that many words allow more than one plural, e.g. *léeɓèe* 'lip', pl. *lâɓɓáa* or *léeɓúnàa*; *ɓéeɽáa* 'rat', pl. *ɓéɽàayée* or *ɓeéɽàɽɽákíi*. An ongoing process in Hausa is the treatment of historically original plurals as singulars, with the subsequent formation of new plurals. In some cases the original singular form has to be postulated; in others, it still exists as a dialectal variant, e.g. *dúmáa* 'gourd' (orig. pl. of *dúmèe*), pl. *dúmàamée*; *háƙóoríi* 'tooth' (orig. pl. of *háƙrèe*, still found as *háurèe*), pl. *háƙòoráa*; *gídáa* 'home' (orig. pl. of *gíjìi*), pl. *gídàajée*.

Hausa has a number of productive and semi-productive nominal derivational constructions, in some cases using prefixes, in others suffixes.

Table 35.4: Hausa Common Plural Patterns

Type		Plural (Singular) 'Gloss'
(1)	-ooCii	gúnóoníi (gúnàa) 'melon'
	All H	tsáróokíi (tsárkìyáa) 'bowstring'
		túmáakíi (túmkìyáa) 'sheep'
(2)	aa...ee	fágàagée (fágée) 'field'
	H L H	zóomàayée (zóomóo) 'hare'
		kásàakée (káskóo) 'bowl'
(3)	aa...aa	sír̃àadáa (sír̃ɗìi) 'saddle'
	H L H	sâssáa (sáashèe) 'section'
		yâaráa (yáaròo) 'boy'
(4)	-uKaa	ríigúnàa (rìigáa) 'gown'
	H H L	cíkúnkúnàa (cíkìi) 'belly'
	[K = n, k, w,	gár̃úkàa (gàar̃úu) 'wall'
	or C final]	yáazúuzúkàa (yáajìi) 'spice'
		gárúurúwàa (gàríi) 'town'
		cóokúlàa (cóokàlíi) 'spoon'
(5)	-Kii/-Kuu	wàtànníi (wátàa) 'moon, month'
	L L H	gòonàkíi (góonáa) 'farm'
		ràanàikúu (ráanáa) 'sun, day'
(6)	ee...aKii	gárèemáníi (gàr̃máa) 'plough'
	H L H H	gáawàwwákíi (gáawáa) 'corpse'
		márèemáríi (mármáráa) 'laterite'
(7)	-ii/-uu	bàrèeyíi (bàréewáa) 'gazelle'
	L L H	jèemàagúu (jéemáagèe) 'bat'
		màgàngànúu (màgánàa) 'speech'
(8)	-ai	kùnkùrái (kùnkúrúu) 'tortoise'
	L L H	dùbbái (dúbúu) 'thousand'
		fìkàafìkái (fíffíkèe) 'wing'
(9)	Final vowel	yáatsúu (yáatsàa) 'finger'
	change	máasúu (máashìi) 'spear'
	...H	'ár̃náa ('ár̃nèe) 'pagan'
		mázáa (míjìi) 'husband, male'
		bírái (bírìi) 'monkey'
		cínái (cínyàa) 'thigh'
		kàajíi (kàazáa) 'hen'
		bàakíi (bàakóo) 'stranger'

The following are some of the more common. (a) Ethnonymics, indicating a person's geographical or ethnic origin, social position or, less often, occupation are formed with a prefix *ba-* in the singular and a suppletive suffix *-aawaa* in the plural, e.g. *bàháushèe*, *bàháushìyáa*, *hàusàawáa* 'Hausa man, woman, people'. (b) Agentials are formed from verbs using a prefix *ma-*, a widespread Afroasiatic formative, e.g. *mánòomíi*, *mánóomìyáa*, *mánòomáa* 'farmer (m./f./pl.)'. (c) Instrumentals use the same *ma-* prefix as agentials, but with a different tone pattern and different plural formation, e.g. *mábúuɗíi*, *màbùuɗái* 'opener m./pl.'. (d) Locatives use the same *ma-* prefix, but are usually feminine and end in *-aa*, e.g. *mǎ́áikátáa*, *mà̀àikàtái* 'work-place f./pl.'. (e) Language names take a suffix -*(n)cii* and an all H tone pattern, e.g. *láṛábcíi* 'Arabic', *kánáncíi* 'Kano dialect' (but not **háusáncíi* — *háusá* being the language name). (f) Abstract nouns make use of an array of related -*(n)taa* and -*(n)cii* suffixes with varying tones, e.g. *bàu-táa* 'slavery', *gájár-tàa* 'shortness', *gùrgù-ntàa* 'lameness', *gwàní-ntàa* 'expertness', *fátáu-cìi* 'commerce', *súusá-ncìi* 'foolishness'. Another suffix -*(n)tákàa* is sometimes used instead of or in addition to the above, e.g. *shèegà-ntákàa* 'rascality', *jàaṛùn-tákàa = jáaṛúntàa* 'bravery', but *mùtùn-tákàa* 'human nature' ≠ *mútún-cìi* 'humaneness, decency'. (g) Mutuality or reciprocity is indicated by a suffix -*áyyàa* and/or -*éenìyáa*, e.g. *'àuràtáyyàa* 'intermarriage', *bùgáyyàa = bùgággéenìyáa* 'hitting one another', *yàṛjéejéenìyáa* 'mutual consent'.

2.4 Syntax

In this sketch of Hausa syntax we shall limit ourselves to a description of the internal structure of the simple noun phrase and of word order at the sentence level.

The key to the Hausa noun phrase is the 'noun phrase-of noun phrase' construction, e.g. *kàaká-n yáaròo* 'the boy's grandfather' (lit. 'grandfather-of boy'); *móotà-ṛ-kù* 'your car' (lit. 'car-of you (pl.)'); *móotóocí-n sárkíi* 'the chief's cars' (lit. 'cars-of chief'). The 'linker', as it is called by Hausaists, has two forms: -*n* (a contraction of *na*) and *ṛ* (a contraction of *ta*). The former is used if the first noun is masculine or plural, the latter if the first noun is feminine singular; the gender of the second nominal is irrelevant. Constructions with the linker have a wide variety of uses in Hausa, as can be seen from the following typical examples: *bángón ɗáakìi* 'wall of the room', *gàbán mákáṛántáa* 'in front of the school', *ɗáyáṛsù* 'one of them', *'yáa'yán 'ítàacée* 'fruit' (lit. 'offspring of tree'), *jírgín sámà* 'aeroplane' (lit. 'vehicle of sky'), *'úwáṛ rìigáa* 'body (lit. 'mother') of a gown'. The linker also serves to connect a noun and a following demonstrative, e.g. *jàakín nàn* 'this (here) donkey', *túnkìyâṛ nán* 'this (previously referred to) sheep', *dàwàakán càn* 'those horses'.

Hausa has a number of ways of expressing what in English are translated as adjectival modifiers. One means is to use 'true adjectives' (i.e. dependent nominals) before the modified noun in a linking construction, e.g. *fárí-n zánèe* 'white cloth', *fárá-ṛ rìigáa* 'white gown', *fàsàssú-n kwálàabée* 'broken bottles'. Alternatively (under poorly understood conditions) the adjective can occur to the right of the noun without the use of the linker, e.g. *zánèe fáríi*, *rìigáa fáráa*, *kwálàabée fàsàssúu*. Attributive cardinal numerals only occur in this post-nominal position, e.g. *jàakíi ɗáyá* 'one donkey', *máatáa 'úkù* 'three women', *máyàakáa dúbúu* 'a thousand warriors' (cf. *dúbú-n máyàakáa* 'thousands of warriors'). Ordinals also occur to the right of the noun, but make use of a linker (usually non-contracted), e.g. *káṛnìi ná 'àshìṛín* 'twentieth century', *'àláamàa tá bíyú* 'the second sign'. Modifiers are also commonly expressed by use of *mài/màasú* 'owner, possessor of (sg./pl)' plus an abstract qualitative nominal, e.g. *ríijìyáa mài zúrfíi* 'a deep well' (cf. *zúrfíntà* 'its depth'), *léebúṛóoṛii màasú ƙárfíi* 'strong labourers'. This construction has a negative counterpart using *máràṛ/máràsáa*, e.g. *ríijìyáa máràṛ zúrfíi* 'a not deep well', *léebúṛóoṛii máràsáa ƙárfíi* 'not strong labourers'.

Hausa lacks an exact equivalent of the English definite and indefinite articles. The bare word *yáaròo* could mean 'a boy' or 'the boy' depending on the context. To specifically indicate that a word has been previously referred to or is the thing in question, there is a suffix identical in segmental shape to the linker but with inherent low tone: *ːn* (m./pl.), *ːṛ* (f.), e.g. *yáaròn* 'the boy in question', *túnkìyâṛ* 'the sheep in question', *mútàanên* 'the men referred to'. To indicate particularised indefiniteness, Hausa uses the words *wání*, *wátá*, *wású* (= *wáɗánsú*) 'some (m./f./pl.)', e.g. *wání yáaròo yánàa kúukáa* 'a/some boy is crying'; *wású bàaƙíi súnàa jírànkà* 'some strangers are waiting for you'.

Hausa has four sentence types, which can be labelled existential, equational, verbal and statival. Existential sentences are formed with the word *'àkwái* 'there is' and the negative counterpart *bâa* (or *báabù*) 'there is not', e.g. *'àkwái 'àbíncí mài dáaɗíi* 'there is delicious food'; *bâa 'isásshén kúɗíi* 'there is not enough money'. Equational sentences have the structure (noun phrase) noun phrase *nee/cee*, where *nee* has masculine and plural agreement and *cee* (< *tee*) has feminine agreement, e.g. *shíi sóojà née* 'he is a soldier', *móotàṛ nân sáabúwáa cèe* 'this car is new'. These sentences are negated by sandwiching the second noun phrase between *bàa . . . bá*, e.g. *shíi bàa sóojà bá nèe* 'he is not a soldier', *móotàṛ nân bàa sáabúwáa bá cèe* 'this car is not new'. If the first noun phrase is missing, one has an identificational sentence comparable to the English 'it's a . . .', e.g. *kàrée nèe* 'it's a dog'; *bàa tàawá bá cèe* 'it's not mine'. Equational sentences are not marked for tense; thus the preceding sentence could equally mean 'it wasn't mine'.

Verbal sentences have the core structure subject, tense/aspect pronoun, verb, indirect object, direct object or locative goal, instrumental, e.g. *yáròo yánàa gáyàa másà làabáaṛìi* 'the boy (he) is telling him the news'; *máháukácìyáa táa káshèe shí dà wúƙáa* 'the crazy woman (she) killed him with a knife', *wàkìilái záasù kóomàa ƙásáṛsù* 'the representatives will return to their countries'. Conditionals, temporals and other complement phrases and clauses occur both before and after the core, e.g. *'ín káa yàṛdá záamù záunàa nân sái táa zóo* 'if you agree we will sit here until she comes'. In sentences without overt subjects, the tense/aspect pronoun translates as the subject, but syntactically it should not be thought of as such. Thus the sentence *yáa húutàa* 'he rested' has the structure $\emptyset_{subj.}$ *yáa*$_{tap}$ *húutàa*$_{verb}$ parallel to the sentence *yáaròo yáa húutàa* 'the boy rested'. The tenses with the segmentally full markers *nàa*, *kèe* and *kàn* do not require the third person pronominal element if an overt subject is present, e.g. *mútàanée (sú)nàa bînsà* 'the men are following him', *dóm mèe yáarínyàa (tá)kèe kúukáa?* 'why is the girl crying?'.

The normal position for the indirect object is immediately following the verb and before the direct object. Indirect object pronouns are formed with *má-*; nouns make use of a prepositional element *wà* or *mà*, e.g. *kàakáa táa mácèe mánà* 'grandmother died on us', *kádà kà káawóo wà ɗáanáa bíndígàa* 'don't bring my son a gun'. A long and complex indirect object is likely to be expressed as a prepositional phrase occurring after the direct object. The preposition used in this case is *gà*, etymologically probably the same word as *wà*, e.g. *náa núunà tákàṛdáa gà mùtúmìn dà ná gàmú dà shíi 'à ƙóofàa* 'I showed the letter to the man I met (lit. 'man that I met with him') at the door'. Compare the normal *náa núunàa wà mùtúmìn tákàṛdáa* 'I showed the man the letter'.

Question words and focused elements are fronted. One consequence (shared with relativisation) is the obligatory substitution of perfective$_2$ and continuous$_2$ for the corresponding perfective$_1$ and continuous$_1$ tense forms, e.g. *mèe súkà sàyáa?* 'what did they buy?', cf. *sún sàyí kíifíi* 'they bought fish'; *wàa yákèe kíɗàa?* 'who is drumming?' cf. *Múusáa yánàa kíɗàa* 'Muusaa is drumming'; *'ítá cèe ná gáyàa wà* 'it was she I told', cf. *náa gáyàa mátà* 'I told her'. Another consequence is the use of resumptive pronouns to fill the place of fronted instrumentals and (optionally) indirect objects, e.g. *mèe záamù ɗáurè ɓàráawòo dà shíi?* 'what will we tie up the thief with (it)?'; *Hàdíizà múkèe kóoyàa mátà (= kóoyàa wà) túuṛáncíi* 'it's Hadiza we're teaching (to her) English'.

Stative sentences make use of the continuous tense/aspect pronouns and a non-verbal predicate, of which there are three major types: locative, 'have' and stative, e.g. *múnàa nân* 'we're here'; *Wùdíl báatàa néesà dà Kánòo* 'Wudil is not far from Kano'; *súnàa dà móotàa mài kyâu* 'they have (are with) a good car', *kwáalín nàn yánàa dà náuyíi* 'this carton is heavy' (lit. 'is with heaviness'); *'àbíncí yánàa dàfé* 'the food is cooked' (< *dáfàa* 'to cook'); *tún jíyà súnàa zàuné 'à ƙóofàṛ gídánkà* 'since yesterday they have been sitting at the door of your house' (< *záunàa* 'to sit'); *múnàa sàné dà shíi* 'we are aware of it' (< *sánìi* 'to know'). As in the case of verbal sentences, fronting of a questioned or focused element triggers the use of continuous$_2$ tense/aspect pronouns. (The form differs slightly here in having a short final vowel.) For example, *'ìnáa súkè yànzú?* 'where are they now?'; *mèe kákè dà shíi?* 'what do you have?' (lit. 'what are you with it'); *tùulúu 'à cìké yákè* 'the pot is *filled*' (lit. 'the pot filled it is').

In summary, one can say that Hausa is a language with fairly fixed word order. Where changes from normal order occur, for example for questioned or focused objects, they are for specific grammatical or pragmatic purposes. Interestingly, Hausa does not deviate from normal word order for yes-no questions. These are indicated simply by a question tag (such as *kóo* 'or', or *fà* 'what about') or by question intonation (consisting in part of an old question morpheme, now reflected only as vowel length often with low tone), e.g. *Múusáa zâi yàṛdá kóo?* 'Muusaa will agree, right?'; *bàaƙíi sún fìtâa?* 'did the guests go out?' (*fìtâa* = *fìtá* + *ː*), cf. *bàaƙíi sún fìtá* 'the guests went out'.

Bibliography

Newman (1977) is the standard work on Chadic classification and the reconstruction of Proto-Chadic. Jungraithmayr and Shimizu (1981) also treat Chadic vocabulary from a comparative perspective. Newman (1980) is an attempt to establish definitively the membership of Chadic within Afroasiatic. Abraham (1959), while terribly out of date — it dates from 1940 — is the only reliable reference grammar of Hausa available. Gouffé (1981) is the best concise sketch of Hausa available. Cowan and Schuh (1976) is a widely used pedagogical course, while Kraft and Kirk-Greene (1973) is an excellent introduction to the language in the familiar *Teach Yourself* format. Parsons (1981) is an invaluable collection of papers, lecture notes etc. by the leading Hausaist of our day. A comprehensive bibliography of works on Hausa language and literature is provided by Baldi (1977), supplemented by Adwe (1988).

References

Abraham, R.C. 1959. *The Language of the Hausa People* (University of London Press, London)

Adwe, Nicholas. 1988. 'A Hausa language and linguistics bibliography 1976–86 (including supplementary material for other years)', in G. Furniss and P.J. Jagger (eds.) *Studies in Hausa Language and Linguistics in Honour of F.W. Parsons* (Kegan Paul International, London), pp. 253–78

Baldi, S. 1977. *Systematic Hausa Bibliography* (Istituto Italo-Africano, Rome)

Cowan, J.R. and R.G. Schuh. 1976. *Spoken Hausa* (Spoken Language Services, Ithaca, NY)

Gouffé, C. 1981. 'La Langue haoussa', in G. Manessy (ed.) *Les Langues de l'Afrique Subsaharienne* (CNRS, Paris), pp. 415–28

Jungraithmayr, Hermann and Kiyoshi Shimizu. 1981. *Chadic Lexical Roots. II. Tentative Reconstruction, Grading and Distribution* (Marburger Studien zur Afrika- und Asienkunde, A-26, Dietrich Reimer, Berlin)

Kraft, C. H. and A.H.M. Kirk-Greene. 1973. *Hausa* (Teach Yourself Books, London)

Newman, P. 1977. *Chadic Classification and Reconstructions* (Undena, Malibu, Calif.)

—— 1980. *The Classification of Chadic Within Afroasiatic* (Universitaire Pers, Leiden)

Parsons, F.W. 1981. *Writings on Hausa Grammar*, ed. by G. Furniss, 2 vols. (School of Oriental and African Studies, London and University Microfilms International, Books on Demand, Ann Arbor)

36 TAMIL AND THE DRAVIDIAN LANGUAGES

Sanford B. Steever

1 The Dravidian Languages

The Dravidian language family, the world's fourth largest, consists of twenty-five languages spread over the South Asian subcontinent. It has four branches: South Dravidian with Tamil, Malayāḷam, Iruḷa, Koḍagu, Kota, Toda, Badaga, Kannaḍa and Tulu; South-Central Dravidian with Telugu, Savara, Goṇḍi, Koṇḍa, Pengo, Manḍa, Kūi and Kūvi; Central Dravidian with Kolami, Naiki, Parji, Ollari and Gadaba; and North Dravidian with Kūṛux, Malto and Brahui. Over the past fifteen years reports of other languages have appeared, but without adequate grammars we cannot determine whether these are new, independent languages or simply dialects of ones already known. Indu and Āwē have been reported in South-Central Dravidian; Kuruba, Yerava, Yerukula, Kaikuḍi, Korava, Koraga, Bellari and Burgundi in South Dravidian. Certain dialects of Goṇḍi and Kūṛux may prove under closer inspection to be independent languages. The Dravidian languages are spoken by approximately 175,000,000 people.

Though concentrated in South India (see map 36.1), the Dravidian languages are also found in Maharashtra, Madhya Pradesh, Orissa, West Bengal and Bihar; and, outside India, in Sri Lanka, Pakistan, Nepal and the Maldives. The Dravidian languages share the South Asian subcontinent with three other language families: the Indo-Aryan branch of Indo-European, the Munda branch of Austro-Asiatic and Sino-Tibetan. Commerce and colonisation have carried some Dravidian languages, par-

Map 36.1: The Dravidian Languages

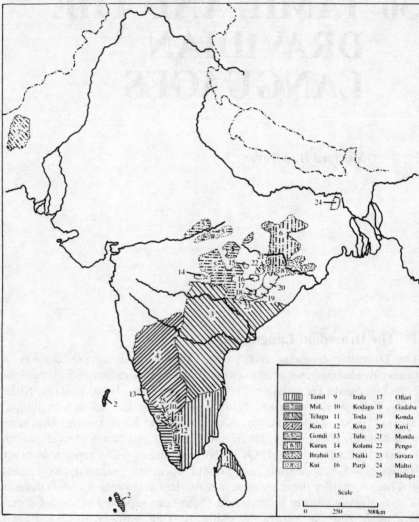

Map adapted from Bloch (1946)

ticularly Tamil, beyond South Asia to Burma, Indonesia, Malaysia, Fiji, Madagascar, Mauritius, Guyana, Martinique and Trinidad.

The Eighth Schedule of the Indian Constitution (1951) mandates the creation of states along linguistic lines, and accords official status to four Dravidian languages: Tamil in Tamil Nadu, Malayāḷam in Kerala, Kannaḍa in Karnataka and Telugu in Andhra Pradesh. These four have long histories, recorded in epigraphy and native literatures: Tamil dates from the second century BC; Kannaḍa from the fourth century AD; Telugu from the seventh century AD; and Malayāḷam from the tenth century AD.

Starting with Caldwell's (1875) *Comparative Grammar of the Dravidian Languages*, linguists have reconstructed a fragment of Proto-Dravidian. This fragment incorporates those features the Dravidian languages have in common and may be said to typify what is 'Dravidian' in a language. Proto-Dravidian has ten vowels, five short and five long: $a, \bar{a}, i, \bar{\imath}, u, \bar{u}, e, \bar{e}, o, \bar{o}$. It has sixteen consonants, including an unusual system of stops contrasting in six points of articulation: labial, dental, alveolar, retroflex, palatal and velar, viz. $p, t, R, \underline{t}, c, k$. Four nasals, $m, n, \underline{n}, \tilde{n}$; four resonants, $l, \underline{l}, r, \underline{z}$; and two glides, v, y, complete the inventory of consonants. Alveolars, retroflexes and resonants do not occur word-initially. Caldwell's Law describes the allophony of stops: they are voiceless when they occur initially or geminated, but voiced when they occur intervocalically or after nasals. Several metrical rules govern the composition of syllables, e.g. $(C_1)\bar{V}C_2$ alternates with $(C_1)\breve{V}C_2C_3$ as in the two stems of the verb 'see', $*k\bar{a}n$- vs. $*ka\underline{n}\underline{t}$-. Though bisyllabic roots are occasionally indicated, reconstructed lexical roots are by and large monosyllabic. While any of the five vowel qualities may appear in a root, only a, i, u, may appear in a derivative suffix.

Dravidian morphology is transparent, agglutinating and exclusively suffixal. The order of elements in a word is: lexical root, derivational suffix, inflectional suffix. Proto-Dravidian has two parts of speech: noun and verb, both of which appear in simple and compound forms. Nouns inflect for case, person, number and gender. Proto-Dravidian has eight cases: nominative, accusative, sociative, dative, genitive, instrumental, locative and ablative. These eight are supplemented by postpositions, derived from independent nouns or non-finite verbs. Predicate nominals can be inflected to agree with their subjects, e.g. in Ancient Tamil -$\bar{o}m$ marks the first person plural in $n\bar{a}m$ $n\bar{a}\underline{t}\underline{t}$-$\bar{o}m$ 'we$_1$ (are) countrymen$_2$'. Proto-Dravidian has two numbers: singular and plural. Proto-Dravidian gender distinguishes animate and inanimate nouns on the basis of the natural gender of the referent, not 'grammatical' or conventional gender. Animate nouns may further be classified as honorific, masculine or feminine. A noun's animacy helps determine other of its grammatical features: animates take the locative case marker *-$i\underline{t}am$, inanimates *-il; most animates have the plural marker *-ir, inanimates *-$ka\underline{l}$; the accusative case marker *-ay is obligatory for animates, but optional for inanimates. The very extensive system of compound nouns can be illustrated by the set of deictic pronouns, which contrast in four degrees: *$ivan$ 'this man', *$uvan$ 'that man nearby', *$avan$ 'that man yonder', *$evan$ 'which, any man'. These are compound nouns, e.g. *$avan$ 'that man yonder' consists of the nouns *a- 'that (one) yonder' and *-$(v)an$ 'man'. Complex compound nouns are often translated into English as a sequence of numeral, adjective and noun; but the internal structure of these Dravidian expressions is that of a compound noun.

Proto-Dravidian verbs are those forms that inflect for verbal categories such as tense and mood. There are two tenses, past and non-past, and two moods, modal and indicative. From a formal viewpoint verbs are finite or non-finite. Finite verbs inflect for tense and subject-verb agreement. These inflections are overt, or, in the imperative and optative, covert. Proto-Dravidian has a constraint that limits the number of finite verbs in a sentence to a maximum of one: that lone verb stands at the extreme end of the sentence and commands all other verbs within. In effect, it brings the sentence to a close. All remaining verbs in the sentence must be non-finite. The first major set of non-finite verbs is defined as those which combine with a following verb, with or without other grammatical material coming between the two. In this set we find the infinitive, conjunctive participle and conditional. The second major set comprises all those non-finite verbs that combine with a following noun to form relative clauses and similar structures. Dravidian languages rely on a rich system of compound verbs to extend the somewhat limited set of simple verb forms. Lexical compound verbs supplement the lexicon by providing a complex morphosyntactic vehicle for combinations of lexical meanings which are not encoded in any single lexeme of the language. For example, the Tamil lexical compound *koṇṭu vara* 'bring' consists of the conjunctive participle of *koḷḷa* 'hold' and an inflected form of *vara* 'come'. Auxiliary compound verbs, on the other hand, provide morphosyntactic vehicles for those verbal categories which are not encoded in any simple verb form of the language, e.g. perfect tense, benefactive voice. In this colloquial Kannaḍa example the auxiliary verb *iru* 'be' conveys the perfect tense: *nān band(u) iddīni* 'I₁ have₃ come₂'.

The basic word order in the Proto-Dravidian sentence is subject–object–verb (SOV). In Dravidian, as in other rigid SOV languages, genitives precede the nouns they modify, main verbs precede auxiliaries and complements precede their matrix clauses. Though explicit nominal morphology allows some freedom of variation in word order, verbs stay at the end of their clauses. Simple sentences consist of a subject and predicate. The subject is a noun phrase inflected for the nominative or, in certain predictable cases, the dative case; the predicate may be a verb or predicate nominal. Section 2.4 on Tamil syntax below addresses the issue of complex sentences in Dravidian, in particular how finite verbs and predicate nominals can be embedded.

Subsequent developments have naturally altered this picture. For example, metathesis in South-Central Dravidian permits alveolars, retroflexes and resonants to appear initially, e.g. Telugu *lē-* 'young (one)' from **iḷay* 'id.'. The influx of Indo-Aryan loanwords has introduced both initial voiced stops and the distinction between aspirated and non-aspirated stops in some languages, e.g. Malayāḷam, Kūṟux. The contrast between the dative and accusative cases has been neutralised in Pengo animate nouns in favour of what historically was the dative. When the joints of auxiliary compound verbs fuse, new conjugations arise, e.g. the Medieval Tamil present tense, the Kūi objective conjugation, the Pengo present perfect tense. The syntactic influence of neighbouring Indo-Aryan languages has reversed the order of complement and matrix in North Dravidian. Thus, Malto *ā loker ṭunḍnar tan laboh ote* 'those$_1$ people$_2$ saw$_3$ that$_4$ (it) was$_6$ heavy$_5$' contrasts with the common Dravidian order in Tamil *kaNamāka irukkiRatu eNRu avarkaḷ pārttārkaḷ* 'they$_4$ saw$_5$ that$_3$ (it) is$_2$ heavy$_1$'. Despite a certain measure of change in phonology and lexicon, Proto-Dravidian morphology and syntax has persisted remarkably well in South, South-Central and Central Dravidian.

2 Tamil

2.1 Historical Background

Tamil (*tamiẓ*) belongs to the South Dravidian branch of the Dravidian family: like other members of this branch it lost Proto-Dravidian **c-*, e.g. *il* 'not be' from **cil-*, *īy-* 'give' from **cīy-*, *āRu* 'six' from **cāRu*; and it replaced the Proto-Dravidian copula **maN* 'be located' with *iru* 'be located'. It has been spoken in southern India and northeastern Sri Lanka from prehistoric times. The earliest records of Tamil, lithic inscriptions in a variety of Aśōkan Brāhmī script, date from 200 BC. Alongside these inscriptions stands a vast and varied literature, preserved on palm-leaf manuscripts and by rote memory, covering two thousand years. Within this literary corpus is an indigenous grammatical tradition, separate from the Sanskrit grammarians: its two outstanding texts are *tolkāppiyam* (c. 200 BC) and *naNNūl* (c. AD 1000). There are three distinct stages of Tamil revealed in these records: Ancient Tamil, 200 BC to AD 700; Medieval Tamil, AD 700 to 1500; and Modern Tamil, AD 1500 to the present.

Ancient Tamil has just two tenses, past and non-past; Medieval and Modern Tamil have three, past, present and future. Ancient Tamil has many subject-verb agreement markers for each member of the paradigm, e.g. the first person singular is signalled by *-ēN*, *-eN*, *-aN*, *-al*, *-ku*, *-ṭu*, *-tu*. But Medieval Tamil retains only the first three, while Modern Tamil keeps only the first. In Ancient and Medieval Tamil, as opposed to their modern successor, predicate nominals can be inflected for subject-verb agreement, so that *-ai* marks the second person singular in *nī nāṭṭ-ai* 'you$_1$ (are a) countryman$_2$' while *-ēN* marks the first person singular in *nāN pāvi-(y)ēN* 'I$_1$ (am a) sinner$_2$'. In Medieval Tamil the set of verbal bases was open and accommodated many Sanskritic loanwords, e.g. Tamil *aNupavikka* 'to experience', derived from Sanskrit *anubhava* 'experience', but it is closed in Modern Tamil.

Between AD 800 and 1000 the western dialects of Tamil, geographically separated from the eastern by the Western Ghats, broke off and developed into Malayāḷam. Malayāḷam lost its rules of subject-verb agreement while Tamil maintained them, and it welcomed into its lexicon a great number of

Sanskrit loanwords. The Iruḷa language, spoken in the hilly spurs of the Nilgiris between Kerala and Tamil Nadu, is also closely related to Tamil.

During the past two thousand years, Tamil dialects have evolved along three dimensions: geography, caste-based society and diglossia. Today there are six regional dialects: (1) Sri Lanka; (2) Northern, spoken in the Chingleput, North Arcot and South Arcot districts; (3) Western, spoken in the Coimbatore, Salem and Dharmapuri districts; (4) Central, spoken in the Tirichirapalli, Tanjore and Madurai districts; (5) Eastern, spoken in the Putukottai and Ramanathapuram districts; and (6) Southern, spoken in the Nagercoil and Tirunelveli districts. Sri Lankan Tamil seems to be the most conservative: it preserves the four-way deictic contrast lost in the continental dialects during the Medieval period, e.g. *ivaN* 'this man', *uvaN* 'that man nearby', *avaN* 'that man yonder', *evaN* 'which, any man'. It still resists the use of initial voiced stops so that continental Tamil *dōcai* 'rice pancake' becomes *tōcai* 'id.' in Sri Lankan Tamil. Throughout its history, but most notably during the Chola Empire, AD 850 to 1250, Tamil travelled beyond South Asia to kingdoms in Burma, Cambodia, Sri Vijāya and Indonesia. During the British Raj of the nineteenth century, it was carried to South Africa, British Guiana and other parts of the British Empire.

The social dialects of Tamil particularly accentuate the distinction between brahmin and non-brahmin castes. Among brahmins the word for 'house' is *'ām*, among non-brahmins *vīṭu*; among brahmins the polite imperative of *vara* 'come' is *vāṅkō*, among non-brahmins *vāṅka*. For 'drinking water' Vaisnavite brahmins say *tīrttam*, Saivite brahmins *jalam* and non-brahmins *taṇṇīr*. Even finer gradations of caste dialects can be found in kinship terminology and proper names.

Finally, Tamil dialects show diglossic variation in which a 'high' formal variety (*centamiẓ*) contrasts with a 'low' informal variety (*koṭuntamiẓ*). The difference between these two corresponds only roughly to the difference between written and spoken Tamil. The high variety is used in most writing, radio and television broadcasts, political oratory and public lectures. While the low variety is used in virtually all face-to-face communication, it also appears in the cinema, some political oratory and some modern fiction. In Akilan's novel *ciNēkiti* 'The Girl-Friend' (1951) both dialogue and narration are in the high variety; in Janakiraman's *ammā vantāḷ* 'Here Comes Mother' (1966) the former is in low, the latter in high Tamil; and in Jeyakantan's *cila nēraṅkaḷil cila maNitarkaḷ* 'Certain Men at Certain Moments' (1970) both are in low Tamil. In high Tamil the animate and inanimate locative case markers are -*iṭam* and -*il*, respectively; but in low Tamil they are -*kiṭṭa* and -*le*. The polite imperative of *vara* 'come' is *vāruṅkaḷ* in high Tamil, but *vāṅka* or *vāṅkō* in low. The word for 'much' or 'very' is *mika* in high Tamil, but *rompa* in low (both come from the infinitives of verbs that mean 'exceed' or 'fill'). Palatalisation of -*nt*- and -*tt*- following *i*, *ī*, or *ai* is common in low Tamil, but not in high, e.g. low *aṭiccu* 'beating' corresponds to high *aṭittu* 'id.'

All speakers of Tamil, even illiterates, have recourse to both varieties and, according to the situation, must navigate between the phonological, lexical and grammatical differences that distinguish them.

The Pure Tamil Movement (*taNit tamiẓ iyakkam*) of the 1900s, a cultural branch of the politically oriented Dravidian Movement, attempted to purge Tamil of its foreign elements, especially its Sanskritic vocabulary. The first part of the legacy of this movement is the intense loyalty that Tamils feel for their language; the second is that the scientific and bureaucratic gobbledygook is ultra-Tamil, not Sanskrit as in other Indic languages. At the turn of the century, the brahmin dialect of Madras City seemed destined to become the standard dialect of Modern Tamil. Today, however, it is the high non-brahmin dialect of the Central dialect, including the cities of Tanjore, Tirichirapalli and Madurai, that is emerging as the standard dialect. This chapter describes modern standard Tamil, which is based upon and shares features of both the written language and the standard spoken Central dialect.

Tamil is recognised as one of India's fourteen national languages in the Eighth Schedule of the Indian Constitution (1951). The Tamil Nadu Official Language Act of 1956 establishes Tamil as the first official language of Tamil Nadu and English as the second. In Sri Lanka, Tamil shares with Sinhalese the title of national language. Today, Tamil is spoken by approximately 45,000,000 in India, 2½ million in Sri Lanka, and one million elsewhere.

2.2 Phonology and Orthography

The lack of an adequate phonology of modern standard Tamil has led linguists to adopt the following strategy. A transcription of written Tamil is taken as the underlying phonological representation, which is simultaneously the output of the syntactic rules and the input to the phonological rules. The corresponding spoken form is taken as the surface representation, the output of the phonological rules. Hence, the rules that convert the one into the other are held to constitute the substance of Tamil phonology. In effect, these rules enable one to read a passage of written Tamil and pronounce it in spoken Tamil. While this strategy undoubtedly fails to address some facets of modern standard Tamil phonology, it does in the long run provide a good, general picture of the phonological structure. The reason for this success can be traced directly to the transparent, agglutinating morphology of modern standard Tamil, which inhibits the growth of complicated phonological alternations.

The inventory of systematic phonemes in modern standard Tamil has a 'low' native core and a 'high' borrowed periphery. Though both are used by educated speakers, the periphery is often assimilated to the core in informal settings and in rapid, unguarded speech. Both appear in table 36.1, where parentheses enclose the sounds of the periphery. The two nasals enclosed in square brackets are graphemically but not phonemically distinct from /n/.

Table 36.1: The Sounds of Modern Standard Tamil

	Stop vls.	vd.	Fricative	Sibilant	Nasal	Lateral	Tap	Approximant	Glide
Labial	p	(b)	(f)		m				v
Dental	t	(d)			n	l	r		
Alveolar	R				[N]				
Retroflex	ṭ	(d)		(ṣ)	ṇ	ḷ		ẓ	
Palatal	c	(j)		(ś)	ñ				y
Velar	k	(g)			[ṅ]				(h)

		Front	Central	Back
High	long	ī		ū
	short	i		u
Mid	long	ē		ō
	short	e	(ə)	o
Low	long	(æ)	ā	(ɔ)
	short		a	
Diphthong		ai		au

Key: (X), X is part of the peripheral phonology of Tamil. [X], X is graphemically, but not phonemically distinct.

The core contains twelve vowels and sixteen consonants. It has five short vowels, *a, i, u, e, o*; five long vowels, *ā, ī, ū, ē, ō*; and two diphthongs, *ai, au*, each with the length of a short vowel. Included among the consonants are six stops, *p, t, R, ṭ, c, k*; four nasals, *m, n, ṇ, ñ*; two laterals, *l, ḷ*; two glides, *v, y*; one tap, *r*; and one approximant, *ẓ*. Subscript dots indicate retroflection, one of the more salient features of Tamil phonology. The sounds that appear word-initially are: all vowels, *p, t, ṭ, c, k, m, n, ṇ, ñ, l, r, y, v* (*ṭ* and *ṇ* occur in onomatopoeia, *l* and *r* often take a prosthetic *i*). The sounds that appear word-finally are all vowels except *e*, and *m, n, ṇ, l, ḷ, r, ẓ, y* (a half-short, high, back unrounded enunciative vowel often follows the consonants). In the following, words in italics represent a transliteration of the orthography; slashes enclose the phonemic analysis and square brackets the modern standard Tamil pronunciation.

Stops are voiced intervocalically and following nasals, e.g. /atu/ 'it' [aðu]; /aṅkē/ 'there' [aṅgē], but voiceless elsewhere, viz. initially, doubled or in other clusters. Intervocalic stops also undergo spirantisation so that /VkV/ becomes [VɣV], /VtV/ becomes [VðV] and /VcV/ becomes [VdʒV]. Moreover, the ɣ-allophone of /k/ becomes [h]; the dʒ-allophone of /c/, [s]. Initial /c/ is often pronounced as *s* in the speech of many educated speakers. Nasalisation converts a sequence of vowel and word-final nasal into a nasalised vowel, e.g. /maram/ 'tree' becomes [marã], but when the interrogative clitic is added to form *maram-ā* 'a tree?', nasalisation is blocked. Glide insertion transforms initial ĕ- and ŏ- into yĕ- and vŏ-, respectively. Palatalisation converts -tt- and -nt- into -cc- and -ñc-, respectively, when they follow i, ī or ai, e.g. /cirittēN/ 'I smiled' becomes [siriccē]. Cluster simplification eliminates triliteral consonant clusters either by the epenthesis of a vowel, e.g. Sanskrit tattva 'truth, reality' becomes Tamil tattuvam, or by the deletion of a consonant, e.g. /tīrttēN/ 'I finished' becomes [tīttē] (palatalisation precedes cluster simplification so [tīccē] does not occur).

Vowel lowering lowers the high vowels i and u to e and o, respectively, when followed by no more than one consonant and the vowel ă or ai, e.g. /vilai/ 'price' becomes [velai]; /utavi/ 'help', [oðavi]. The diphthongs ai and au undergo a number of changes. Non-initial ai becomes e so that /vilai/ 'price' becomes [velai], then [vele]; initial ai may be preserved, e.g. vaikai 'Vaigai River'; or become a, e.g. /aintu/ 'five' becomes [aiñcu] by palatalization, then [añcu]. ai and au are often reanalysed as a+y and a+v, respectively, so that /paiyaN/ 'boy' becomes [payyā], while English 'town' becomes [ṭavuṇ]. Occasionally, the front high and mid vowels, ĭ and ĕ, are transformed into their back counterparts, ŭ and ŏ, when they appear between a labial and a retroflex consonant, e.g. /vīṭu/ 'house' becomes [vūḍu]. While some brahmin dialects of Tanjore still pronounce ẓ as a voiced retroflex approximant, most dialects merge it with ḷ, e.g. /maẓai/ 'rain' becomes [maḷe]. N is pronounced as n; R as r, except in the Southern dialect where it is a trill as opposed to the flap r. The cluster NR is pronounced as ndr and, ultimately, nn, e.g., /eNRu/ 'saying' becomes [endru], then [ennu]; the cluster RR is pronounced as ttr, then tt, e.g., /viRRēN/ 'I sold' becomes [vittrē], then [vittē].

The peripheral sounds of modern standard Tamil include nine consonants, b, d, ḍ, j, g, f, ṣ, s, h, and three vowels, ə, æ, ɔ. In pronunciation, these sounds undergo rules that assimilate them to the nearest corresponding sounds of the phonological core. /f/ in /faiyal/ 'file' becomes p in paiyal. Voiced stops contrast with voiceless stops only in initial position because in non-initial position they are interpreted as the voiced allophones of the core's voiceless stop phonemes, so that Sanskrit agrahāra 'brahmin settlement' is phonemicised in modern standard Tamil as /akkirakāram/, where both Sanskrit g and h are treated as allophones of /k/. Initial voiced stops are usually devoiced in rapid speech so that both /bāvam/ 'facial expression' and /pāvam/ 'sin' are pronounced as [pāvā]. Sibilants tend to assimilate to /c/. The vowels ə, æ and ɔ assimilate to a, ē and ā, respectively. English loanwords have complicated the set of consonant clusters in modern standard Tamil: 'agent' is borrowed as ēyjeṇṭṭu with a cluster of nasal and voiceless stops, one which Tamil grammar traditionally prohibits.

Stress in modern standard Tamil is not distinctive and is fixed on the first syllable of every word. The syllabic structure of words is based on quantitative units known as *morae* (*acai* in traditional Tamil grammar). Handbooks of Tamil discuss other issues of segmental and suprasegmental phonology in greater detail.

Tamil is written in a syllabic script which historically derives from a version of Aśōkan Brāhmī script (see table 36.2). Each vowel has two forms in this syllabary: an independent symbol to represent it at the beginning of a word and an auxiliary symbol, which combines with consonant symbols, to represent it elsewhere. In initial position, *ā* is represented by ஆ ; but elsewhere by ா, as in கா *kā*, தா *tā*, and பா *pā*. In initial position, *i* is represented by இ ; but by ி elsewhere, as in கி *ki*, தி *ti*, and பி *pi*. Each consonant is represented by a basic symbol which has the inherent vowel *a* in the order C*a*, so that க is read as *ka*; த as *ta*; and ப as *pa*. When any auxiliary symbol is added to the consonant symbol, the inherent vowel *a* is suppressed, e.g. the symbols க *ka* and இ *i* combine to form the symbol கி , which is read as *ki*, not **kai*. The addition of a dot, called *puḷḷi*, above the consonant symbol removes the inherent vowel altogether, so that க் represents *k*; த், *t*; and ப் , *p*. The use of *puḷḷi* is instrumental in the correct representation of consonant clusters: இப்ப represents *ippa* 'now', not **ipapa*. The top row in table 36.2 presents the independent vowel symbols; the leftmost column, the basic consonant symbols modified by *puḷḷi*; and the column second from the left, the basic consonant symbol with the inherent vowel *a*. The remaining cells present the graphemic representation of the combination of basic consonant symbol and auxiliary vowel symbol.

Modern standard Tamil has a graphemic convention whereby initial stop consonants are doubled when preceded by certain forms such as the dative case marker, the accusative case marker and the demonstrative adjectives, e.g. /inta pāvam/ 'this sin' is written as *intap pāvam*. Doubling does not take place when the initial stop is voiced, e.g. /inta bāvam/ 'this facial expression' is written as *inta pāvam* (since *inta pāvam* is treated as a compound, *p* is treated as intervocalic and, therefore, voiced). The Tamil alphabetic order is *a, ā, i, ī, u, ū, e, ē, ai, o, ō, au, k, ṅ, c, ñ, ṭ, ṇ, t, n, p, m, y, r, l, v, ẓ, ḷ, R, N*. Six additional symbols may be used to represent letters in Sanskrit loans: *j, ś, ṣ, s, h, kṣ*. But these symbols may be replaced by others, e.g. *kṣ* by *ṭc*. The Tamil syllabary is adequate to represent the core phonology of modern standard Tamil.

2.3 Morphology and Parts of Speech
Although some grammars of Tamil list as many as ten parts of speech, all of them can be resolved into one of two formal categories: noun and verb. These two are distinguished by the grammatical categories for which they are inflected. (The so-called indeclinables, including interjections, seem to be variously nouns or verbs.) The morphology is agglutinating and exclusively suffixal: the inflections are marked by suffixes joined to the lexical base, which may or may not be extended by a derivational suffix.

Table 36.2: The Tamil Syllabary (Adapted from Pope 1979)

	a	ā	i	ī	u	ū	e	ē	ai	o	ō	au
—	அ a	ஆ ā	இ i	ஈ ī	உ u	ஊ ū	எ e	ஏ ē	ஐ ai	ஒ o	ஓ ō	ஔ au
க் k	க ka	கா kā	கி ki	கீ kī	கு ku	கூ kū	கெ ke	கே kē	கை kai	கொ ko	கோ kō	கௌ kau
ங் ṅ	ங ṅa	ஙா ṅā	ஙி ṅi	ஙீ ṅī	ஙு ṅu	ஙூ ṅū	ஙெ ṅe	ஙே ṅē	ஙை ṅai	ஙொ ṅo	ஙோ ṅō	ஙௌ ṅau
ச் c	ச ça	சா çā	சி çi	சீ çī	சு çu	சூ çū	செ çe	சே çē	சை çai	சொ ço	சோ çō	சௌ çau
ஞ் ñ	ஞ ña	ஞா ñā	ஞி ñi	ஞீ ñī	ஞு ñu	ஞூ ñū	ஞெ ñe	ஞே ñē	ஞை ñai	ஞொ ño	ஞோ ñō	ஞௌ ñau
ட் ḍ	ட ḍa	டா ḍā	டி ḍi	டீ ḍī	டு ḍu	டூ ḍū	டெ ḍe	டே ḍē	டை ḍai	டொ ḍo	டோ ḍō	டௌ ḍau
ண் ṇ	ண ṇa	ணா ṇā	ணி ṇi	ணீ ṇī	ணு ṇu	ணூ ṇū	ணெ ṇe	ணே ṇē	ணை ṇai	ணொ ṇo	ணோ ṇō	ணௌ ṇau
த் t	த ta	தா tā	தி ti	தீ tī	து tu	தூ tū	தெ te	தே tē	தை tai	தொ to	தோ tō	தௌ tau
ந் n	ந na	நா nā	நி ni	நீ nī	நு nu	நூ nū	நெ ne	நே nē	நை nai	நொ no	நோ nō	நௌ nau
ப் p	ப pa	பா pā	பி pi	பீ pī	பு pu	பூ pū	பெ pe	பே pē	பை pai	பொ po	போ pō	பௌ pau
ம் m	ம ma	மா mā	மி mi	மீ mī	மு mu	மூ mū	மெ me	மே mē	மை mai	மொ mo	மோ mō	மௌ mau
ய் y	ய ya	யா yā	யி yi	யீ yī	யு yu	யூ yū	யெ ye	யே yē	யை yai	யொ yo	யோ yō	யௌ yau
ர் r	ர ra	ரா rā	ரி ri	ரீ rī	ரு ru	ரூ rū	ரெ re	ரே rē	ரை rai	ரொ ro	ரோ rō	ரௌ rau
ல் l	ல la	லா lā	லி li	லீ lī	லு lu	லூ lū	லெ le	லே lē	லை lai	லொ lo	லோ lō	லௌ lau
வ் v	வ va	வா vā	வி vi	வீ vī	வு vu	வூ vū	வெ ve	வே vē	வை vai	வொ vo	வோ vō	வௌ vau
ழ் ẓ	ழ ẓa	ழா ẓā	ழி ẓi	ழீ ẓī	ழு ẓu	ழூ ẓū	ழெ ẓe	ழே ẓē	ழை ẓai	ழொ ẓo	ழோ ẓō	ழௌ ẓau
ள் ḷ	ள ḷa	ளா ḷā	ளி ḷi	ளீ ḷī	ளு ḷu	ளூ ḷū	ளெ ḷe	ளே ḷē	ளை ḷai	ளொ ḷo	ளோ ḷō	ளௌ ḷau
ற் R	ற Ra	றா Rā	றி Ri	றீ Rī	று Ru	றூ Rū	றெ Re	றே Rē	றை Rai	றொ Ro	றோ Rō	றௌ Rau
ன் N	ன Na	னா Nā	னி Ni	னீ Nī	னு Nu	னூ Nū	னெ Ne	னே Nē	னை Nai	னொ No	னோ Nō	னௌ Nau

Nouns and verbs both appear in simple and compound forms.

Nouns are inflected for person, case, number and gender. This class includes common nouns, proper names, numerals, pronouns and some so-called adjectives. There are two numbers: singular and plural. Tamil gender is based on the natural gender of a noun's referent, not on conventionally ascribed grammatical gender. There are two basic genders: 'rational' (*uyartiṇai*) and 'irrational' (*ahRiṇai*), corresponding roughly to human and non-human. Rational nouns are further classified as honorific, masculine and feminine. Nouns referring to deities and men are classified as rational; in some dialects women are classified as rational, in others as irrational. (Children and animals are normally classified as irrational.) In some cases, conventionally rational nouns are treated as irrational, e.g. when a proper name is given to an animal. By the same token, conventionally irrational nouns are treated as rational when used as epithets for men. In *ramu eṅkē? antak kaẓutai eṅkēyō pōy irukkiRāN* 'where₂ (is) Ramu₁? That₃ ass₄ has₇ gone₆ (off) somewhere₅' *kaẓutai* 'ass' is treated as a rational noun for the purposes of subject-verb agreement. A noun's gender determines other of its grammatical properties such as the choice between the animate locative case marker *-iṭam* and the inanimate *-il*.

Modern standard Tamil has eight cases: nominative, accusative, dative, sociative, genitive, instrumental, locative, ablative. There is just one declension: once the nominative singular, nominative plural and oblique stem are known, all the other forms can be predicted. Moreover, the nominative plural and oblique stem can generally be predicted from the gender and phonological shape of the nominative singular. The chart given here presents the declension of four nouns: *maNitaN* 'man', *maram* 'tree', *āRu* 'river' and *pū* 'flower'. In addition to eight cases, modern standard Tamil has postpositions, derived from independent nouns or non-finite verbs. The postposition *pārttu* 'towards', which governs the accusative case, e.g. *avaNaip pārttu* 'towards him', comes from the adverbial participle *pārttu* 'looking at'.

The Declension of Four Selected Tamil Nouns

Singular	maNitaN 'man'	maram 'tree'	āRu 'river'	pū 'flower'
Oblique Stem	maNitaN-	maratt-	āRR-	pū(v)-
Nominative	maNitaN	maram	āRu	pū
Accusative	maNitaN-ai	maratt-ai	āRR-ai	pūv-ai
Dative	maNitaN-ukku	maratt-ukku	āRR-ukku	pūv-ukku
Sociative	maNitaN-ōṭu	maratt-ōṭu	āRR-ōṭu	pūv-ōṭu
Genitive	maNitaN-uṭaiya	maratt-uṭaiya	āRR-uṭaiya	pūv-uṭaiya
Instrumental	maNitaN-āl	maratt-āl	aRR-āl	pūv-āl
Locative	maNitaN-iṭam	maratt-il	āRR-il	pūv-il
Ablative	maNitaN-iṭamiruntu	maratt-iliruntu	āRR-iliruntu	pūv-iliruntu

Plural	maNitarkaḷ	maraṅkaḷ	āRukaḷ	pūkkaḷ
Nominative	maNitarkaḷ	maraṅkaḷ	āRukaḷ	pūkkaḷ
Accusative	maNitarkaḷ-ai	maraṅkaḷ-ai	āRukaḷ-ai	pūkkaḷ-ai
Dative	maNitarkaḷ-ukku	maraṅkaḷ-ukku	āRukaḷ-ukku	pūkkaḷ-ukku
Sociative	maNitarkaḷ-ōṭu	maraṅkaḷ-ōṭu	āRukaḷ-ōṭu	pūkkaḷ-ōṭu
Genitive	maNitarkaḷ-uṭaiya	maraṅkaḷ-uṭaiya	āRukaḷ-uṭaiya	pūkkaḷ-uṭaiya
Instrumental	maNitarkaḷ-āl	maraṅkaḷ-āl	āRukaḷ-āl	pūkkaḷ-āl
Locative	maNitarkaḷ-iṭam	maraṅkaḷ-il	āRukaḷ-il	pūkkaḷ-il
Ablative	maNitarkaḷ-iṭamiruntu	maraṅkaḷ-iliruntu	āRukaḷ-iliruntu	pūkkaḷ-iliruntu

Modern standard Tamil has no formal class of articles: other grammatical devices assume their function. The numeral *oru* 'one' often functions as an indefinite article; so, by way of contrast, its absence with a rational noun conveys the meaning of a definite article, e.g. *oru maNitaN* 'a man' but Ø *maNitaN* 'the man'. Irrational direct objects are interpreted as indefinite when inflected for the nominative case, but definite when inflected for the accusative, e.g. *nāN maram pārttēN* 'I₁ saw₃ a tree₂', but *nāN marattaip pārttēN* 'I₁ saw₃ the tree₂'.

A small but significant subset is marked for first or second person. These are the personal pronouns: *nāN* 'I' (obl. *eN(N)-*); *nām* 'we and you' (obl. *nam-*); *nāṅkaḷ* 'we but not you' (obl. *eṅkaḷ-*); *nī* 'thou' (obl. *uN(N)-*); *nīṅkaḷ* 'you' (obl. *uṅkaḷ-*). There are two third person anaphoric pronouns, called reflexives, *tāN* 'self' (obl. *taN(N)-*); and *tāṅkaḷ* 'selves' (obl. *taṅkaḷ*); the antecedent must be a subject, either of the same or a superordinate clause. Modern standard Tamil has deictic pronouns which are formally compound nouns. *avaN* 'that man' consists of *a-* 'that (one)' and *-(v)aN* 'man'. Continental Tamil makes three deictic distinctions, e.g. *ivaN* 'this man', *avaN* 'that man', *evaN* 'which, any man', as opposed to Sri Lanka Tamil which preserves the older, Dravidian system with four. Distal pronouns, marked by *a-*, are less marked than the proximate, marked by *i-*: they appear in contexts of neutralisation and translate English, 'he', 'she', 'it', 'they' etc.

In Ancient and Medieval, but not modern standard Tamil, nouns, often predicate nominals, were inflected for person, e.g. *-ai* marks second person singular in *nī nāṭṭ-ai* 'you₁ (are a) countryman₂'. In Medieval Tamil such nouns could also be inflected for case: in *tēvar-īr-aip pukaẓntu* 'praising₂ you (who are a) god₁' the accusative case marker *-ai* is suffixed to the second person marker *-īr* which in turn is suffixed to the noun *tēvar* 'god'.

Compound nouns are very common. The nouns *maram* 'tree' (obl. *maratt-*), *aṭi* 'base' and *niẓal* 'shadow' combine to form the compound *maratt-aṭi-niẓal* 'shadow at the base of the tree'. Coordinate compounds in which each part refers to a separate entity are also common, e.g. *vīratīracākacaṅkaḷ* 'courage, bravery and valour' consists of *vīram* 'courage', *tīram* 'bravery', *cākacam* 'valour' and the plural suffix *-kaḷ*. Such *dvandvā* compounds contrast with English compounds such as *secretary-treasurer* which refers to a single individual. Some of the so-called adjectives of modern standard Tamil are bound nouns which must occur in compound nouns, but not as their head, e.g. both *nalla nāḷ* 'good$_1$ day$_2$' and *nalla-(v)aN* 'good man' imply a noun *nal* 'goodness' which never occurs by itself. So pervasive are compound nouns that even the Sanskrit privative prefix *a-*, *ava-* 'not, without' has been reanalysed in Tamil as a noun in a compound. Tamil borrowed hundreds of pairs of Sanskrit nouns, one without the privative prefix and one with it, e.g. *mati* 'respect', *ava-mati* 'disrespect'. *ava-mati* is treated like the compound *maratt-aṭi* 'tree-base': the second element is identified with the independent noun *mati* 'respect', while the first element *ava-* is treated as the oblique form of an independent noun *avam* 'void, nothingness, absence'. This reanalysis preserves the strictly suffixal nature of modern standard Tamil morphology.

Verbs are inflected for verbal categories, participating notably in the oppositions of mood and tense. Formally, a verb consists of a verb base and grammatical formative. The base itself consists of a stem and, optionally, two suffixes, one for voice and one for causative. The stem lexically identifies the verb. Sixty per cent of modern standard Tamil verbs participate in the opposition of affective versus effective voice. An affective verb is one the subject of which undergoes the action named by the stem; an effective verb is one the subject of which directs the action named by the stem. The category of effectivity differs from both transitivity and causation. Affective *vilaka* 'separate' and effective *vilakka* 'separate' minimally contrast since both are transitive: *vaṇṭi pātai-(y)ai vilakiNatu* '(the) cart$_1$ left$_3$ (the) path$_2$' vs. *avaN vaṇṭi-(y)ai (pātai-(y)iliruntu) vilakkiNāN* 'he$_1$ drove$_4$ (lit. separated) the cart$_2$ (off the path)$_3$'. Though very productive in Medieval Tamil, the causative suffix *-vi*, *-ppi*, which conveys causation, is lexically ·restricted in modern standard Tamil, having given way to periphrastic causative constructions.

All modern standard Tamil verb forms are inflected for mood, the verbal category which characterises the ontological status of the narrated event either as unreal, possible, potential (modal) or as real, actual (indicative). Mood is implicitly marked in the grammatical formative following the verb base: the past tense, present tense and adverbial participle are indicative; the rest are modal. Modern standard Tamil has three simple tenses, past, present and future, as well as several periphrastic tenses like the perfect series. Some deverbal nouns, such as *pirivu* 'separation' derived from *piriya* 'separate', mark neither tense nor mood.

Modern standard Tamil verbs are finite or non-finite. Finite verbs are inflected for tense and subject-verb agreement, overtly or, in the imperative and optative, covertly. A verb's finiteness has a direct bearing on modern standard Tamil syntax: there can be only one finite verb per sentence. All remaining verbs must be non-finite and belong to one of three classes.

One class of non-finite verbs consists of relative participles, called *peyareccam* '(verbs) deficient in a noun', which are instrumental in the

formation of relative clauses and similar structures. They are verb forms
marked for tense which combine with a following noun: in the following
examples the relative participle *vanta* 'which came' links the preceding
clause to the following nouns, e.g. *nēRRu vanta oru mantiri* 'a₃ minister₄
(who) came₂ yesterday₁', *mantiri nēRRu vanta ceyti* '(the) news₄ (that) (the)
minister₁ came₃ yesterday₂'. The second class of non-finite verbs, called
viNaiyeccam '(verbs) deficient in a verb', includes the infinitive, adverbial
participle, conditional, negative verbal participle and negative conditional.
All are verb forms that combine with a following verb, with or without other
lexical material coming between the two verbs. Given the restriction on
finite verbs, these forms are crucial in the formation of complex sentences.
The infinitive and adverbial participle are instrumental in the formation of
compound verbs, as well. The third class of non-finite verbs includes all
verbal nouns, called *viNaippeyar* 'verbal nouns', forms derived from verbs
but capable of having nominal inflections. Some retain their verbal
characteristics better than others: in the chart showing the conjugation of
piriya 'separate', *piri-nt-atu* 'separation' takes a nominative subject while
pirivu 'separation' takes a genitive. Consult the chart for the simple verb
forms of Tamil, using *piriya* 'separate' as an example. Modern standard
Tamil has seven morphophonemically distinct conjugations, details of which
can be found in most grammars.

The conjugation of *piriya* 'separate'

Finite Verb Forms

	Past	Present	Future	Future Negative
1 sg.	piri-nt-ēN	piri-kiR-ēN	piri-v-ēN	piriya māṭṭ-ēN
2 sg.	piri-nt-āy	piri-kiR-āy	piri-v-āy	piriya māṭṭ-āy
3 sg. hon.	piri-nt-ār	piri-kiR-ār	piri-v-ār	piriya māṭṭ-ār
3 sg. m.	piri-nt-āN	piri-kiR-āN	piri-v-āN	piriya māṭṭ-āN
3 sg. f.	piri-nt-āḷ	piri-kiR-āḷ	piri-v-āḷ	piriya māṭṭ-āḷ
3 sg. irr.	piri-nt-atu	piri-kiR-atu	piri-(y)-um	piri-(y)ātu
1 pl.	piri-nt-ōm	piri-kiR-ōm	piri-v-ōm	piriya māṭṭ-ōm
2 pl.	piri-nt-īrkaḷ	piri-kiR-īrkaḷ	piri-v-īrkaḷ	piriya māṭṭ-īrkaḷ
3 pl. rat.	piri-nt-ārkaḷ	piri-kiR-ārkaḷ	piri-v-ārkaḷ	piriya māṭṭ-ārkaḷ
3 pl. irr.	piri-nt-aNa	piri-kiNR-aNa	piri-(y)um	piri-(y)ātu

Non-Future Negative: *piriya (v)illai* for all persons, numbers and genders.

	Imperative	Negative Imperative	Optative
Sg.	piri	piri-(y)ātē	
Pl., hon.	piri-(y)uṅkaḷ	piri-(y)ātīrkaḷ	piri-ka

Non-Finite Verb Forms

	Past	Present	Future	Negative
Rel. part.	piri-nt-a	piri-kiR-a	piri-(y)um	piri-(y)āta
V.n.	piri-nt-atu	piri-kiR-atu	piri-v-atu	piri-(y)ātatu

Adv. part.: piri-ntu   infin.: piri-(y)a   neg. v. part.: piri-(y)āmal

Cond.: piri-ntāl   neg. cond.: piri-(y)āviṭṭāl

De-v. n.: piri-tal, piri-kai, piri-vu.

Modern standard Tamil has two kinds of compound verb: lexical and auxiliary. Lexical compound verbs are complex morphosyntactic vehicles, made up of two or more simple verbs, that encode those lexical meanings which are not encoded in any single lexeme. *aruka vara* 'approach' consists of the infinitive *aruka* 'near' and an inflected form of *vara* 'come'; *kūrntu kavaNikka* 'peer' consists of the adverbial participle *kūrntu* 'sharpening (i.e. sharply)' and an inflected form of *kavaNikka* 'notice'. By contrast, auxiliary compound verbs are complex morphosyntactic vehicles, made up of two or more simple verbs, that encode those verbal categories which are not encoded in any simple verb form, such as the perfect tense or the causative. *varac ceyya* 'make$_2$ X come$_1$' consists of the modal auxiliary *ceyya* 'make, do' and the infinitive of the main verb *vara* 'come'; *vantu irukka* 'X has$_2$ come$_1$' consists of the indicative auxiliary *irukka* 'be' and the adverbial participle of the main verb *vara* 'come'. The two kinds of compound verbs have different grammatical properties: for example, additional lexical material can separate the components of a lexical compound, but not those of an auxiliary compound, e.g. *kūrntu avaḷaik kavaNikka* 'peer$_{1+3}$ (at) her$_2$', but **vantu vīṭṭukku irukka* 'X has$_3$ to the house$_2$ come$_1$'.

Modern standard Tamil has about fifty auxiliary verbs, half modal and half indicative. It lacks simple adverbs like English *not* and instead uses modal auxiliary verbs to express negation: in *vara māṭṭāN* '(he) won't$_2$ come$_1$' the auxiliary verb *māṭṭa* 'not' signals the future negative of *vara* 'come'. Ancient and Medieval Tamil had a synthetic negative conjugation, remnants of which survive in the third person irrational forms of the future tense.

Modern standard Tamil also compensates for the lack of basic adverbs by a very productive set of noun+verb compounds whose second member is the infinitive *āka* 'become' and which function adverbially. *cikkiramāka* 'quickly, urgently' consists of the noun *cikkiram* 'urgency' and *āka* 'become'.

2.4 A Skeleton Account of Simple and Complex Sentences in Modern Standard Tamil

Simple sentences in modern standard Tamil consist of a subject and a predicate. The subject is a nominal which is inflected for the nominative or, in certain cases, the dative case. The predicate is either a finite verb or a predicate nominal which appears without a copula. From the various combinations of subject and predicate, four basic sentence types emerge: (1) nominative subject and predicate nominal, e.g. *avaN oru maNitaN* 'he$_1$ (is) a$_2$ man$_3$'; (2) nominative subject and finite verb, e.g. *avaN vantāN* 'he$_1$ came$_2$'; (3) dative subject and predicate nominal, e.g. *avaNukku oru makaN* 'he$_1$ (has) a$_2$ son$_3$' (lit. 'to him (is) a son'); and (4) dative subject and finite verb, *avaNukkut tōcai piṭikkum* 'he$_1$ likes$_3$ dosais$_2$'.

While dative subjects do not trigger subject-verb agreement, unlike other datives they possess such subject-like properties as the ability to be the antecedent of a reflexive pronoun. Dative subjects typically combine with stative predicates, favouring particularly those that denote a mental or emotional state, e.g. *ataip paRRi avaNukku cantēkam* 'he$_3$ (has) doubts$_4$ about$_2$ that$_1$', *avaNukkuk kōpam vantatu* 'he$_1$ got$_3$ angry$_2$'. Nominative subjects do trigger subject-verb agreement. Verbs agree with their subjects in person, number and, in the third person, gender.

The four basic sentence types function as templates through which other syntactic structures are fitted. Modern standard Tamil has a rule of clefting, which postposes a nominal phrase to the right of the clause-final verb. Simultaneously, the verb becomes a verbal noun inflected for the nominative case and the oblique case marking on the postposed noun, if any, is optionally deleted. Clefting thus transforms *nāN maturai-(y)il piRantēN* 'I$_1$ was born$_3$ in Madurai$_2$' into *nāN piRantatu maturai* 'Madurai$_3$ (is where) I$_1$ was born$_2$', i.e. 'it is Madurai where I was born'. Observe how the output of clefting conforms to the first basic sentence type above, where a nominative subject, here the verbal noun *piRantatu*, and a predicate nominal, here *maturai*, combine to form a simple sentence.

The basic word order of modern standard Tamil is SOV. As in other rigid SOV languages, genitives precede the nouns they modify, main verbs precede their auxiliaries and complement clauses precede main clauses. Despite the use of cases and postpositions to mark the grammatical relations of noun phrases, modern standard Tamil word order is not entirely free. Although variations do exist, the verb in a simple sentence must remain at the extreme right end of the clause. The unmarked order of *avaN nēRRu avaḷaip pārttāN* 'he$_1$ saw$_4$ her$_3$ yesterday$_2$' can be varied as follows: *avaḷai avaN nēRRu pārttāN; nēRRu avaN avaḷaip pārttāN; avaN avaḷai nēRRu pārttāN*. No semantic difference accompanies these variations, but the verb remains fixed at the end of the clause. A subject may in rhetorically marked contexts be postposed rightwards over a finite verb, typically when its referent is the hero in a narrative whom the speaker wishes to make prominent, e.g. *cītaiyaip pārttāN rāmaN* 'Rama$_3$ saw$_2$ Sita$_1$'.

The structure of complex sentences is a particularly fascinating part of modern standard Tamil syntax. Recall that modern standard Tamil preserves the Proto-Dravidian constraint limiting the number of finite verbs in a sentence to a maximum of one. This necessitates the use of non-finite verbs such as the infinitive, adverbial participle or relative participle in the construction of complex sentences, be they coordinate or subordinate. In *maẓai peytu kuḷam niRaintatu* 'rain$_1$ fell$_2$, (and) the reservoir$_3$ filled$_4$', the adverbial participle *peytu* 'raining' joins two clauses to form a coordinate sentence. By contrast, in *avaḷ nāN colli kēṭka villai* 'she$_1$ didn't$_5$ listen$_4$ (to what) I$_2$ said$_3$', the adverbial participle *colli* 'saying' joins a subordinate clause to its main clause. In *makaN pōka makaḷ vantāḷ* '(as) the son$_1$ went$_2$, the daughter$_3$ came$_4$', the infinitive *pōka* 'go' conjoins two clauses in a coordinate sentence; but in *nāN avaNai varac coNNēN* 'I$_1$ told$_4$ him$_2$ to come$_3$', the infinitive *vara* 'come' joins the subordinate clause to the main clause. In *avaN vantāl avaN-iṭam nāN pēcuvēN* 'if$_2$ he$_1$ comes$_2$, I$_4$ will speak$_5$ with him$_3$', the conditional verb *vantāl* 'if X comes' simultaneously marks the protasis of a conditional sentence and joins it to the apodosis. In all these sentences the single finite verb appears at the extreme right end of the sentence, in the main clause. Non-finite verbs are still used in complex sentences even when the rightmost predicate is a predicate nominal, as in *kavalaippaṭṭu uṅkaḷukku eNNa payaN?* 'what$_3$ use$_4$ (is it) for you$_2$ to worry$_1$?'; the adverbial participle *kavalaippaṭṭu* 'worrying' links two clauses.

Relative participles also serve to build complex sentences. In *nēRRu vanta oru mantiri* 'a$_3$ minister$_4$ (who) came$_2$ yesterday$_1$' the relative participle *vanta* 'which came' joins a relative clause to the head noun *mantiri* 'minister'. Relative participles appear in factive complements, as well: in *mantiri nēRRu vanta ceyti* '(the) news$_4$ (that) the minister$_1$ came$_3$ yesterday$_2$', the relative participle *vanta* 'which came' joins the factive complement to the head noun *ceyti* 'news'.

Despite the ingenuity and dexterity with which non-finite verbs are used to create complex sentences, the restriction against more than one finite verb per sentence raises serious questions. First, how does one represent direct discourse, which requires the preservation of finite verbs in quoted material? Second, how does one embed sentences with predicate nominals? Neither task can be accomplished by recourse to non-finite verbs. Instead, modern standard Tamil employs two special verbs to solve these and other, related syntactic problems: *āka* 'become' and *eNa* 'say'. These verbs take as their direct objects expressions of any category and any complexity, without requiring any morphological change in those expressions (such as requiring the accusative case or a non-finite verb form). They can combine with single words, phrases or entire sentences without disturbing the form of these operands. As verbs, they may subsequently be inflected for non-finite verb morphology and, as described above, function in the construction of complex sentences, bringing their objects with them. The sentence *avaNukku oru makaN* 'he$_1$ (has) a$_2$ son$_3$' can be embedded under the verb of propositional attitude *niNaikka* 'think' using the adverbial participle *eNRu* 'saying' to link the two: *avaNukku oru makaN eNRu nāN niNaikkiRēN* 'I$_5$ think$_6$ that$_4$ (lit. saying) he$_1$ (has) a$_2$ son$_3$'. The conditional form *āNāl* 'if becomes' allows finite verbs to appear in the protasis of conditional sentences: *avaN varuvāN āNāl nāN avaNiṭam pēcuvēN* 'if$_3$ he$_1$ will come$_2$, I$_4$ will speak$_6$ with him$_5$'. These verbs also help to represent direct discourse: in *nāN varuvēN eNRu avaN coNNāN.* 'he$_4$ said$_5$, "I$_1$ will come$_2$"', the adverbial participle *eNRu* 'saying' embeds the direct quotation beneath the verb of quotation *colla* 'tell, say'. To make adverbial expressions, *āka* 'become' embeds individual nouns, while *eNa* 'say' embeds onomatopoeic expressions.

Modern standard Tamil uses the particles -*ē* 'even, and' and -*ō* 'or, whether' to subordinate finite verbs in complex sentences, as well. In *avaN vantāN-ō eNakku cantēkam* 'I$_3$ (have) doubts$_4$ whether (= -*ō*) he$_1$ came$_2$', the clitic -*ō* subordinates one clause to another. In *nēRRu vantān-ē nāN avaNaic cantittēN* 'I$_3$ met$_5$ him$_4$ (who) came$_2$ yesterday$_1$', the clitic -*ē* serves to join the two parts of a correlative relative clause, both of which have finite verbs, i.e. *vantāN* 'he came', *cantittēN* 'I met'.

The constraint against multiple finite verbs in a sentence must be revised in light of these other devices used to construct complex sentences. The number of finite verbs per sentence is limited to a maximum of *n+1*, where *n* equals the number of occurrences of *āka* 'become', *eNa* 'say', -*ē* 'even, and' and -*ō* 'or, whether' that function as complementisers.

This short sketch of Tamil syntax will show, I hope, how much modern standard Tamil syntax relies upon the morphological and lexical resources of the language. The cases of nouns, the distinction between finite and non-finite verbs and the lexemes *āka* 'become' and *eNa* 'say' are indispensable elements of the Tamil sentence.

2.5   The Grammar of Affective Language in Modern Standard Tamil

Like many languages of the world, modern standard Tamil provides its speakers with a variety of grammatical devices which are conventionally used to express the speaker's affective or emotional state. Three such stylistic devices are discussed to give the reader an idea of the rhetorical possibilities of the language.

Onomatopoeic words (*olikuRippu*) are so numerous in modern standard Tamil that they fill an entire dictionary. Such words generally represent a sound and are syntactically joined to a sentence by means of the verb *eNa* 'say', e.g. *kācu ṇaṅ eNRu kīzē vizuntatu* '(the) coin$_1$ fell$_5$ down$_4$ with$_3$ (lit. saying) a clang$_2$', *pustakam top(pu) eNRu kīzē vizuntatu* '(the) book$_1$ fell$_5$ down$_4$ with$_3$ (lit. saying) a thud$_2$'. Many occur reduplicated, e.g. *muṇumuṇu* 'murmur, mutter', *toṇutoṇu* 'sound of beating drums'. Often they acquire an extended meaning so that *toṇutoṇu* comes to mean 'bitching, complaining', while *kuRukuRu* 'scratching, throbbing pulse' comes to mean 'guilt', e.g. *avaN maNacu kuRukuRu eNRu mayaṅkiNatu* 'his$_1$ mind$_2$ was confused$_5$ with$_4$ (lit. saying) guilt$_3$'. Some onomatopoeic stems, but by no means all, can themselves be inflected as verbs, e.g. *avaN ōyāmal toṇutoṇukkiRāN* 'he$_1$ bitches$_3$ ceaselessly$_2$'. The phonological shapes of these words often depart from what the phonotactic rules of modern standard Tamil allow: *ṇaṅ* 'clang' has an initial retroflex and a final velar nasal. But despite that and despite the jaunty air they impart to a sentence, they are still an integral part of modern standard Tamil and cannot be dismissed as quaint and ephemeral slang. Such forms loosely correspond to English onomatopoeic expressions with the prefix *ka-* or *ker-*, e.g. *the bomb went ka-boom, the boy fell ker-splash into the lily pond*.

Like other Dravidian languages, modern standard Tamil has a verbal category called attitude, which characterises the speaker's subjective evaluation of the narrated event. It is grammatically encoded in a subset of the indicative auxiliary verbs. For the most part, these auxiliaries convey the speaker's pejorative opinion of the narrated event and its participants. The auxiliary *tolaiya* 'get lost', which combines with the adverbial participle of the main verb, expresses the speaker's antipathy towards the narrated event, e.g. *avaN vantu tolaintāN* 'he$_1$ came$_2$, damn it$_3$'. The auxiliary *oẓiya* 'purge' expresses the speaker's relief that an unpleasant event has ended, combining aspect and attitude, e.g. *tiruṭaN pōy oẓintāN* '(the) thief$_1$ left$_2$, whew$_3$ (am I glad)!' In *kaṇṇāṭi uṭaintu pōyiRRu* '(the) mirror$_1$ got$_3$ broken$_2$', the auxiliary *pōka* 'go' conveys the speaker's opinion that the event named by the main verb, *uṭaiya* 'break', culminated in an undesirable result. Modern standard Tamil has at least twelve such attitudinal auxiliaries which behave in all respects like other indicative auxiliary verbs, as opposed to modal auxiliaries and lexical compound verbs. Their stylistic impact on a sentence can be compared with the use of *up*, *get* and *go* in the following three English examples: *she upped and left him; he got himself beaten up; the thief went and charged a colour TV on my credit card*. Once again we see how compound verbs compensate for the lack of simple adverbs in modern standard Tamil, here ones that express the speaker's affective state of mind.

Modern standard Tamil has a series of compound words generated through reduplication, e.g. *avaN* 'that man' is reduplicated as *avaNavaN* 'each man, every man' while *vantu* 'coming' is reduplicated as *vantu vantu* 'coming time and again'. As these examples show, reduplicated compounds have a distributive and universal sense. However, modern standard Tamil has a special subset of reduplicated compounds in which the second member of the compound does not exactly duplicate the first. These are called echo-compounds: the second member, the echo-word, partially duplicates the first, the echoed word. The echo-word is the same as the echoed word except that it substitutes *ki-* or *kī-* for the first syllable of the echoed word, depending on whether it is short or long. Thus, from *viyāparam* 'business' we can form the echo compound *viyāparam-kiyāparam* 'business and such'; from *māṭu* 'cattle', *māṭu-kīṭu* 'cattle and such'. However, words which begin with *ki-* or *kī-* cannot themselves be echoed this way: from *kiNaRu* 'well' we cannot form the echo-compound **kiNaRu-kiNaRu* 'wells and such' even though vowel lowering would convert the echoed word, but not the echo-word, into *keNaRu* (echo-compounds can be formed from words whose initial syllable is underlying *ke-* or *kē-*). In such cases, an alternative echo-word with initial *hi-* or *hī-* may be formed, e.g. from *kiḷi* 'parrot' we can form *kiḷi-hiḷi* 'parrots and such'. But since initial *h-* belongs to the phonological periphery, many speakers prefer to form no echo-compound at all rather than to create an echo-word with initial *h-*. Verbs may be echoed as well as nouns (but not pronouns): in *pāttirattai uṭaittāy kiṭaittāy eNRāl uNNai cummāka viṭa māṭṭēN* 'if$_4$ (you) broke$_2$ (the) pots$_1$ or did-any-such-thing$_3$, (I) won't$_8$ let$_7$ you$_5$ alone$_6$', the echo-compound *uṭaittāy-kiṭaittāy* 'break or do some such thing' is based on the finite verb *uṭaittāy* 'you broke'.

Echo-compounds occur in rhetorically marked settings: in grammatical terms this includes modal verb forms such as the future tense and conditional, as well as negative and interrogative contexts, but not indicative forms, e.g. *māṭu kīṭu varum* 'Cows₁ and such₂ will come₃', but *?māṭu kīṭu vantatu* 'Cows₁ and such₂ came₃'. Echo-compounds have two facets of meaning. First, like other reduplicated compounds, they have a distributive meaning so that the compound conveys the idea, 'entities or actions, of which the echoed word refers to a random example from a general range'. According to context, *māṭu-kīṭu* 'cows and such' could refer to a group of domestic animals, the components of a dowry etc. Second, echo-compounds conventionally carry a pejorative nuance to the effect that the speaker neither likes nor cares enough about the entity or action to specify it any further. And, in this respect, modern standard Tamil echo-compounds resemble those in Yiddish English where the echo-word is made with the prefix *shm-*, e.g. *fancy-shmancy*; *cordiality-shmordiality*; *Oedipus-Shmoedipus, at least he loves his mother!*

There are also echo-compounds in modern standard Tamil in which the shape of the echo-word is not predictable and is idiomatically associated with the echoed word, e.g. from *koñcam* 'little' comes the echo-compound *koñcam-nañcam* 'itsy-bitsy'. Most South, South-Central and Central Dravidian languages have both kinds of echo-compound, but as we pass from Central Dravidian into North Dravidian, the second kind comes to predominate.

These and similar grammatical devices, such as the affective lengthening of vowels, exist in other Dravidian languages. The fact that they conventionally encode the speaker's affective state is no reason to consider them anything less than an integral part of the language and its grammar. Since they can reveal as much about the phonological, morphological and syntactic structure of a language as other, more prosaic rules and constructions, they deserve greater recognition in grammatical theory than they have hitherto received.

Bibliography

For a general survey, reference may be made to Zvelebil (1983). Caldwell (1875) is the starting point of modern comparative Dravidian studies. Zvelebil (1970) is an excellent analysis and summary of phonological reconstruction in Dravidian. Bloch (1946) is the standard study of Dravidian comparative grammar, while Andronov (1970) is a good overview of Dravidian morphology. Emeneau (1967) shows, as does Bloch (1946), how much the non-literary languages can reveal about comparative Dravidian. Steever (1981) contains a number of essays concentrating on the analysis of some pressing morphological and syntactic problems in the Dravidian languages. Steever (1987) illustrates how closely Dravidian morphology and syntax are correlated in the property of finiteness.

For Tamil, Arden (1942) is a thorough grammar of modern literary Tamil, beginning with a helpful skeleton grammar, later amplified. Andronov (1969) is a comprehensive grammar, concentrating on morphology. Pope (1979) is a teaching grammar providing an introduction to modern literary Tamil. For the spoken variety of Tamil, Schiffman (1979) is a fine sketch, while Asher (1983) is a detailed grammar following the framework of the Lingua Descriptive Studies series (now Croom Helm Descriptive Grammars). Paramasivam (1983) is an excellent introduction to the linguistic structure of modern Tamil; an English translation is in preparation.

References

Andronov, M.S. 1969. *A Standard Grammar of Modern and Classical Tamil* (New Century Book House, Madras)
—— 1970. *Dravidian Languages* (Nauka, Moscow)
Arden, A.H. 1942. *A Progressive Grammar of the Tamil Language* (Christian Literature Society, Madras)
Asher, R. 1983. *Tamil* (North-Holland, Amsterdam; now distributed by Croom Helm, London)
Bloch, J. 1946. *Structure grammaticale des langues dravidiennes* (Adrien-Maisonneuve, Paris)
Caldwell, R. 1875. *A Comparative Grammar of the Dravidian or South-Indian Family of Languages*, 2nd ed. (University of Madras, Madras)
Emeneau, M.B. 1967. *Collected Papers: Dravidian Linguistics, Ethnology, and Folktales* (Annamalai University Press, Annamalainagar)
Paramasivam, K. 1983. *Ikkālat tamiẓ marapu* (Annam, Sivagangai)
Pope, G.U. 1979. *A Handbook of the Tamil Language* (Asian Educational Services, New Delhi)
Schiffman, H. 1979. *A Grammar of Spoken Tamil* (Christian Literature Society, Madras)
Steever, S.B. 1981. *Selected Papers on Tamil and Dravidian Linguistics* (Muttu Patippakam, Madurai)
—— 1987. *The Serial Verb Formation in the Dravidian Languages* (Motilal Banarsidas, New Delhi)
Zvelebil, K. 1970. *Comparative Dravidian Phonology* (Mouton, The Hague)
—— 1983. 'Dravidian Languages', in *The New Encyclopaedia Britannica, Macropaedia*, vol. 5 (Encyclopaedia Britannica, Chicago), pp. 989–92.

37 TAI LANGUAGES

David Strecker

Tai is the most widespread and best known subgroup of the Kadai or Kam-Tai family. Figure 37.1 shows the distribution of the Kadai languages and figure 37.2 shows, in an approximate and oversimplified way, the distribution of the Tai languages (the actual linguistic geography of Tai is very complex, with much overlapping and interpenetration of languages). The Tai group comprises the following branches:

Southwestern, including Ahom (extinct), Khamti, Tai Nuea (Chinese Shan, Dehong Dai), Tai Long (Shan), Khuen, Tai Lue (Xishuangbanna Dai), Kam Muang (Tai Yuan, Northern Thai), Thai (Siamese, Central Thai), Southern Thai, Lao (Lao dialects in Thailand are also called 'Northeastern Thai'), White Tai, Tai Dam (Black Tai), Red Tai and several other languages which could not be shown in figure 37.2 for lack of space.

Central, an extraordinarily diverse group of dialects known by such names as Tay, Nung and Tho.

Northern, including the languages officially known in China as Bouyei (Buyi) and Zhuang (these actually appear to constitute a dialect continuum, and the name *Zhuang* is also, confusingly, applied to certain Central dialects) and the Yay language in Vietnam.

Saek, generally treated as a Northern Tai language, but showing certain phonological peculiarities that set it apart from all other Tai languages, including Northern.

The total number of native speakers of Tai languages is probably somewhere in the neighbourhood of 60 or 70 million. The largest number of speakers live in Thailand, perhaps somewhere in the neighbourhood of 45 million or more (including speakers both of Thai and of other Tai languages) and the next largest number live in China, about 15 million. Smaller numbers of Tai speakers live in the other countries shown in figure 37.2, perhaps something like five or six million altogether. To this we should add maybe a million or more Tai speakers living in the USA, France and other Western countries, including both many refugees from the Indochinese War and many who emigrated under peaceful circumstances.

Map 37.1: The Kadai Language Family

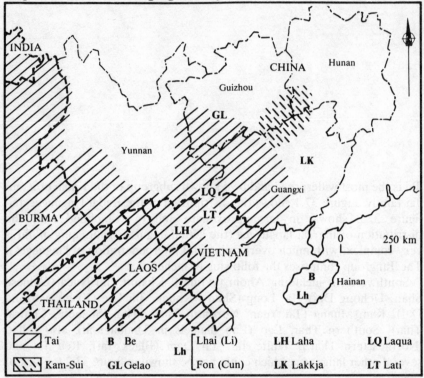

The name *Tai* or *Thai* is the name by which speakers of many, though not all, Southwestern and Central Tai languages call themselves. In accordance with regular rules of sound correspondence, the name is pronounced with either an unaspirated or aspirated *t*, depending on the particular language. Earlier writers on comparative Tai usually called the family *Thai*, but most Tai specialists nowadays call it *Tai*. The form *Thai* nowadays usually refers to one particular Tai language, the national language of Thailand. Some writers, notably A.-G. Haudricourt, restrict the term *Tai* to the Southwestern and Central branches of Tai, but I will follow the usage of F.-K. Li, W. Gedney and others and use *Tai* for the whole group, including the Northern branch.

In phonology and syntax the Tai languages differ from one another about as much as do the Romance languages. The same applies to much of their basic lexicon; for more abstract and technical vocabulary the languages of Vietnam, Guangxi and Guizhou tend to borrow from Chinese whereas those further to the west tend to borrow from Sanskrit and Pali. There is also surprising diversity in grammatical morphemes (e.g. prepositions and aspect and mood particles) and in certain common words such as 'to speak' and 'delicious', which contributes greatly to mutual unintelligibility among Tai

Map 37.2: Approximate General Location of Some Tai Languages

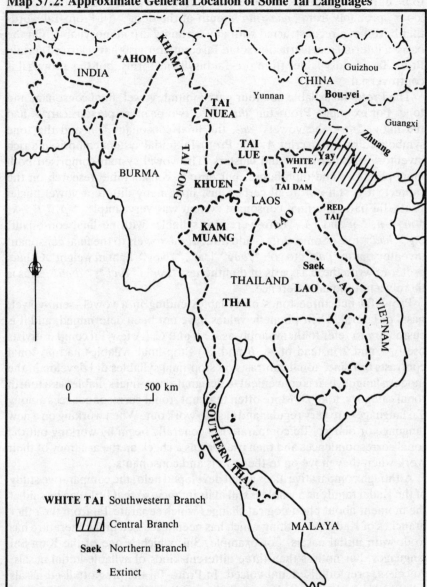

WHITE TAI	Southwestern Branch
/////	Central Branch
Saek	Northern Branch
*	Extinct

languages that in most respects are very close. Certain words serve to identify the different branches of the Tai family. For example *kuk* or *kuuk* is a characteristic Northern Tai word for 'tiger'; Southwestern and Central Tai use a different word, represented by Thai *sǐa* and its cognates.

In Tai languages, as in many other South-East Asian languages, most words are monosyllabic. All the exceptions to this rule in Tai languages seem to be either loanwords or reduced compounds, such as Kam Muang *pàtŭu* 'door', probably from **pàak tŭu* 'mouth of the door'. All Proto-Tai words that have been reconstructed with any certainty are monosyllabic. On the basis of internal reconstruction some Tai comparativists have derived certain Proto-Tai monosyllables from pre-Tai bisyllabic forms, but this proposal is controversial.

The Proto-Tai syllable had four parts: initial, vowel, final consonant and tone. For example, Proto-Tai **thraam*^{A}, 'two or more persons carry', had the initial **thr-*, the vowel **-aa-*, the final consonant **-m* and the tone symbolised by superscript *A*. The Proto-Tai initial system comprised a rich inventory of consonants and clusters. The vowel system comprised both monophthongs and diphthongs, but despite considerable research on the subject, it is still not at all certain just how many different vowel nuclei Proto-Tai had. The final consonant system was very simple: **-p*, **-t*, **-k*, **-m*, **-n*, **-ŋ* and **-l*. There were also syllables with no final consonant, e.g. **haa*^{C} 'five'. Some writers add three semi-vowels to the final consonant inventory, as in **pay*^{A} 'to go', **ʔbaɰ*^{A} 'leaf', **ʔbaw*^{A} 'light in weight'. Others prefer to write these as parts of diphthongs: **pai*^{A}, **ʔbai*^{A}, **ʔbau*^{A}. This is merely a notational difference.

Proto-Tai had three tones on syllables ending in a vowel, semi-vowel, nasal or lateral. Their phonetic values have not been determined, and it is customary to refer to them simply as *A*, *B* and *C*. (A few Tai comparativists use 0, 1 and 2 instead of *A*, *B* and *C*.) Stop-final syllables had no tonal contrasts but since tonal contrasts on stop-final syllables did develop in the modern languages it is convenient to designate stop-final syllables as a fourth tonal category, tone *D*. More often than not, tonal correspondences among Tai languages are very regular and easy to work out. When working on a new language or dialect, Tai comparativists generally begin by working out the tonal correspondences and then use tone as a check on the accuracy of their work when they move on to the vowels and consonants.

Although comparative Tai is a well developed field, the comparative study of the Kadai family as a whole is still in its infancy, so that little can be said at the moment about phonological changes which separate Tai from the other branches of Kadai. One thing which has been discussed in the literature has to do with initial nasals. For example, Sui, which is one of the Kam-Sui languages, has no less than three different kinds of syllable-initial nasals: voiceless, preglottalised and voiced. In Proto-Tai the preglottalised nasals fell together with the voiceless nasals, so that Proto-Tai had only two types of syllable-initial nasals, voiceless and voiced, for example:

	Sui	*Proto-Tai*
'dog'	m̥a^1	**maa*^{A}
'mark'	ʔme^1	**maay*^{A}
'yam'	man^2	**man*^{A}

We may now move on to changes specifically within the Tai group. In the development from Proto-Tai to the modern Tai languages, one change which occurs in all languages is the Great Tone Split. What happened was that in each Tai language, tones developed different allotones conditioned by the manner of articulation of the initial consonant of the syllable. Then certain consonants fell together so that these originally allophonic tonal distinctions became contrastive, as for example in the words for 'face' and 'mother's younger sibling' in Thai:

	Proto-Tai	Thai
'face'	*ŋaa^C	nâa (falling tone)
'mother's younger sibling'	*naa^C	náa (high tone)

Notice that in Proto-Tai, 'face' and 'mother's younger sibling' had the same tone but different initials whereas in modern Thai they have the same initial but different tones. Thus the overall effect of the Great Tone Split has been to cause modern Tai languages to have fewer initials and more tones than Proto-Tai did. The Great Tone Split was a South-East Asian areal change, affecting not only Tai but also most other Kadai languages, most Hmong-Mien languages, Chinese, many Tibeto-Burman languages, Vietnamese and so forth. Some Southwestern Tai languages are written in orthographies that were developed before the Great Tone Split took place, so that in Thai, for example, 'face' and 'mother's younger sibling' are spelled หน้า {hn̊aa} and น้า {n̊aa} respectively, with the same tonal diacritic, ˊ, but different initials: {hn} versus {n}.

The major phonological differences among the different branches of the Tai family include:

(1) differences in tone reflecting an earlier difference between a voiced initial in one group of dialects versus a voiceless initial in others,
(2) differences in vowels.

The examples in the chart given here illustrate the tonal differences.

	Thai (SW)	Longzhou (Central)	Yay (Northern)	Proto-Tai
'to plough'	thăy (rising)	thay^1 (mid level)	say^1 (mid-low level)	*thlay^A
'to reach, arrive'	thǐŋ (rising)	thəŋ^1 (mid level)	taŋ^4 (high rising-falling)	---
'to smear, paint'	thaa (mid)	taa^2 (mid falling)	taa^4 (high rising-falling)	*daa^A

All three words appear to have had tone A in Proto-Tai. After voiceless aspirated stops, tone A became Thai rising tone, Longzhou mid level tone and Yay mid-low level tone, as in 'to plough'. After voiced stops it became Thai mid, Longzhou mid falling and Yay high rising-falling, as in 'to smear'. The problem is determining the initial of 'to reach': in Southwestern and Central Tai this word has the tone which developed after voiceless aspirated stops, as if from Proto-Tai $*thiŋ^A$, whereas in Northern Tai it has the tone which developed after voiced stops, as if from Proto-Tai $*diŋ^A$. One possibility is that the Proto-Tai form was $*dɦiŋ^A$, with a murmured stop which subsequently fell together with $*d$ in the Northern branch but with $*th$ in Southwestern and Central.

The problem with vowels is analogous to the problem with tones. Consider the examples 'year', 'fire' and 'to plough' in the chart.

	Thai (SW)	Longzhou (Central)	Yay (Northern)	Proto-Tai
'year'	pii	pii[1]	pi[1]	$*pii^A$
'fire'	fay	fay[2]	fi[4]	---
'to plough'	thăy	thay[1]	say[1]	$*thlay^A$

It is reasonably certain that 'year' had Proto-Tai $*ii$ and that 'to plough' had Proto-Tai $*ay$, but what about 'fire'? In Southwestern and Central Tai 'fire' regularly rhymes with 'to plough', whereas in Northern Tai it regularly rhymes with 'year'. Some Tai comparativists have proposed a special diphthong in 'fire' and other words showing the same pattern. This diphthong subsequently merged with $*ay$ in Southwestern and Central Tai and with $*ii$ in Northern Tai. Others have suggested that such words as 'fire' were originally bisyllabic. Thus 'fire' might have been something like Proto-Tai $*avii^A$. In Northern Tai the weak pretonic syllable a was simply lost, giving $*vii^A$, whereas in Southwestern and Central Tai it interacted with the vowel of the tonic syllable, giving $*vay^A$. Both suggestions are plausible but difficult to prove. The reconstruction of Proto-Tai vowels is perhaps the most controversial and vexing area in comparative Tai.

Since the Tai languages are uninflected, Tai comparativists have not been able to draw upon comparative morphology in the way that Indo-Europeanists have. This has not been a handicap, since the purely phonological comparisons have been extremely fruitful. Almost no research has been done on comparative Tai syntax. One difference which has been noted involves the order of noun, numeral and classifier. In Tai languages of Vietnam, Guangxi and Guizhou the order is usually numeral + classifier + noun, e.g. Tai Dam

sɔŋ[1]   fin[1]   faa[3]
two   (classifier) cloth
'two pieces of cloth'

It is possible that this is a result of the influence of Chinese, which has the same order. In languages further to the west the order is usually noun + numeral + classifier, e.g. Thai

phâa   sɔ̌ɔŋ   phɨɨn
cloth   two   (classifier)
'two pieces of cloth'

Amost all Tai languages have subject–verb–object word order, but in Khamti and other Tai languages of northeastern India the order is subject–object–verb, possibly as a result of influence from Tibeto-Burman or Indo-Aryan languages.

Finally, I will say a few words about Tai writing systems. Some Tai languages are not written. Speakers of Saek, for example, are literate in Thai or Lao but do not write their own language. But a good many Tai languages do have written forms. Central Tai languages, and Northern Tai languages in Guangxi and Guizhou, are generally written with Chinese characters. The details are complex: some characters represent a Tai word similar in *meaning* to the Chinese word, others represent a Tai word similar in *sound* to the Chinese word and in still other cases Tai-speakers have coined new characters which are not used in Chinese. Southwestern Tai languages are generally written in alphabetic scripts derived from those of India, usually not directly from Indian scripts but rather via other South-East Asian scripts such as that of Cambodian. A great many such Tai alphabets exist; they are often quite different from one another superficially, but systematic study reveals similar patterns in, for example, the representation of vowels and diphthongs and similarities in the shapes of many letters.

Bibliography

The standard handbook is Li (1977). For the relationship of Tai to Kam-Sui, reference may be made to Li (1965). Tai phonology is treated in Harris and Noss (1972) and Haudricourt (1972). Three valuable collections of articles are Harris and Chamberlain (1975), Gething et al. (1976) and Bickner et al. (Forthcoming).

References

Bickner, R.J., J.F. Hartmann, T.J. Hudak and P. Peyasantiwong (eds.) Forthcoming. *Selected Writings in Tai Linguistics by William J. Gedney* (Center for South and Southeast Asian Studies, Ann Arbor)

Gething, T. W., J.G. Harris and P. Kullavanijaya (eds.) 1976. *Tai Linguistics in Honor of Fang-Kuei Li* (Chulalongkorn University Press, Bangkok)

Harris, J.G. and J.R. Chamberlain (eds.) 1975. *Studies in Tai Linguistics in Honor of William J. Gedney* (Central Institute of English Language, Bangkok)

Harris, J.G. and R.B. Noss (eds.) 1972. *Tai Phonetics and Phonology* (Central Institute of English Language, Bangkok)

Haudricourt, A.G. 1972. *Problèmes de phonologie diachronique* (Société pour l'Étude des Langues Africaines, Paris)

Li, F.-K. 1965. 'The Tai and Kam-Sui Languages', *Lingua*, vol. 14, pp. 148–79.

────── 1977. *A Handbook of Comparative Tai* (University Press of Hawaii, Honolulu)

38 Thai

Thomas John Hudak

1 Historical Background

Thai (Siamese, Central Thai) belongs to the Tai language family, a subgroup of the Kadai or Kam-Tai family. A number of linguists now regard Kam-Tai, along with Austronesian, as a branch of Austro-Tai, although this hypothesis remains controversial. All members of the Tai family derive from a single proto-parent designated as Proto-Tai. Linguistic research has shown the area near the border of northern Vietman and southeastern China as the probable place of origin for the Tai languages. Today the Tai family includes languages spoken in Assam, northern Burma, all of Thailand including the peninsula, Laos, northern Vietnam and the Chinese provinces of Yunnan, Guizhou (Kweichow) and Guangxi (Kwangsi). Linguists, notably Fang Kuei Li, divide these languages into a Northern, a Central, and a Southwestern branch. Others, in particular William J. Gedney and A.-G. Haudricourt, view the Central and Southwestern branch as a single group. In the tripartite division, Thai falls into the Southwestern branch.

Sukhothai, established in central Thailand in the early and mid-thirteenth century, represents the first major kingdom of the Thai. Current theories state that the language spoken in Sukhothai resembled Proto-Tai in tonal structure. This early system consisted of three tones on syllables ending in a long vowel, a semi-vowel or a nasal (*kham pen* 'live syllable' in traditional Thai grammatical terms). On syllables ending in *p*, *t*, *k* or in a glottal stop after a short vowel a fourth tone existed, although these syllables showed no tonal differentiation at all (*kham taay* 'dead syllable' in traditional Thai grammatical terms). While the presence of some type of suprasegmental contrasts is considered conclusive at this early stage of the language, the phonetic nature of these contrasts still remains a matter of speculation. This system prevailed at the time of the creation of the writing system by King Ramkhamhaeng (1275–1317) in the latter part of the thirteenth century.

In 1350 the centre of power shifted from Sukhothai to Ayutthaya. Recent theories, which will not be discussed here for lack of space, claim that the Sukhothai and Ayutthaya dialects underwent different sound changes. These theories, furthermore, claim that Southern Thai evolved from the

Sukhothai dialect and Central Thai or Thai from the Ayutthaya dialect (see Brown 1965). The generally accepted theory, however, holds that Thai descended from the Sukhothai dialect with the following sound changes.

The first of the changes, the sound changes known as the tonal splits, affected all of the languages in the Tai family (see the chapter on Tai languages). Because of the splits, sound systems with three contrasting tones, for example, became systems typically with six tones, two different tones from each of the three earlier tones. In some dialects, however, special characteristics of the dialect created more or fewer tones. Thai, for example, now has five tones. In brief, these shifts resulted when the phonetic nature of the initial consonant of each syllable conditioned an allophonic pitch difference. Subsequent changes in the initial consonant, then, caused these allophonic non-contrastive pitches to become contrastive (see section 2 for details of the early tones and the tone split in Thai). Linguists frequently set a date as early as AD 1000 for these sound changes. For the Thai spoken in Ayutthaya, however, the splits seem to have occurred much later.

Several factors suggest a later date for the splits in Thai. First, late thirteenth-century and early fourteenth-century Ayutthayan poetic compositions appear in the three tone language. Second, Khmer loanwords, which probably entered the language after the Thai conquest of Angkor in 1431, also predate the split. In addition, seventeenth-century descriptions of the Thai alphabet demonstrate that the consonant changes involved with the tonal splits had already taken place by that date. Citing this evidence, Gedney proposes a date sometime between the mid-fifteenth and the mid-seventeeth centuries for the tone splits in Thai.

The Ayutthaya period (1350–1767) also saw large numbers of Sanskrit and Pali words borrowed, although this phenomenon was not strictly limited to this period. These Indic loanwords comprise a large portion of the technical vocabularies for science, government, education, religion and literature. Gedney (1947:1) states that these loanwords are as common in spoken Thai as Latin and Greek forms are in spoken English. Sanskrit and, to a much lesser extent, Pali assume the same cultural importance for Thai as Latin does for English. Many of these loanwords exist in both a short and a long form. The shorter form represents the usual Thai pronunciation: *rát* 'state', *thêep* 'god'. The longer alternant usually, but not always, functions as a combining form: *rátthàbaan* 'government' (latter constituent *baan* 'protector, protection'); *thêepphábùt* 'angel' (latter constituent *bùt* 'son'). Most of these compounds seem to have been formed in modern Thai since they do not appear in either Sanskrit or Pali.

During the Ayutthaya period, Thai began to acquire other characteristics that have led the Thai to regard their language as highly complex and stratified, difficult to acquire even for the very educated. In part, this impression grew because of the Indic loanwords. But far more central to the creation of this image was the proliferation of titles, ranks, pronouns, royal vocabulary and royal kin terminology that reflected the growing stratification and complexity of the society. Although much of the complexity applied only to the court, Thai speakers nevertheless interpreted these changes as changes in their own language.

Many of these new terms had their origin in Sanskrit and Pali. Still others came from Khmer. Khmer institutions had always had an influence on the Thai court and this influence increased when the Thai imported Khmer intelligentsia into Thailand after the fall of Angkor. Royal titles provide a good example of this increasing complexity. Originally, during the Sukhothai period, the Khmer title *khŭn* referred to the king. By the Ayutthaya period, this title applied only to officials and the king had acquired far more elaborate ones. Other changes affected the titles for the king's offspring. Newly created titles included those for children by a royal queen, for children by a non-royal queen and for grandchildren. In the nineteenth century titles for great-grandchildren and great-great-grandchildren were also added.

Royalty who assisted the king in the performance of his duties received another set of titles, the *krom* titles, another Khmer institution. Introduced in the seventeenth century, these titles probably first indicated private administrative units, then ministries and finally departments within the ministries. Non-royalty working in the expanding civil service received a different set of titles, also from the Khmer.

This terminology and the emphasis upon its correct use began to be standardised during the reign of King Mongkut (1851–68). Valuing adherence to ancient patterns that produced a 'correctness' in the language, Mongkut issued decrees and proclamations that formalised place names and titles. In addition to these terms, he directed his attention to function words such as prepositions and adverbs. In a letter to Norodom of Cambodia, he listed the rules for correct pronoun usage. Both King Chulalongkorn (1868–1910) and King Vajiravudh (1910–26) added to the regulating of this system. Among other things, Chulalongkorn wrote a lengthy essay explaining the Thai system of royal titles in his reign and Vajiravudh created titles for the ministries and regulated titles for women. In 1932, the revolution abandoned the nobility and granting of titles, other than to the royal offspring. The Thai perceptions of their language, however, were not altered, and Thai is still regarded as a highly complex and difficult language.

In Thailand, Thai serves as the official national language. It is the language taught and used in the schools, the one used by the media and the one used for all government affairs. According to the 1980 census, 47 million people live in Thailand. An estimated 80 per cent of this total or 37,600,000 people speak Thai. Outside of Bangkok and the central plains, other dialects and languages of the Tai family coexist with the standard: Northern Thai (Kam Muang or Yuan) in the north, Southern Thai in the south and Lao or Northeastern Thai in the north-east. Still other Tai languages such as Lue,

Phuthai and Phuan are spoken as small speech islands in various parts of the country. In addition, Thailand has many minority groups who speak languages that do not belong to the Tai family.

2 Phonology

Spoken Thai divides into clearly marked syllables bounded on either side by juncture. Each syllable consists of a vocalic nucleus and a tone. In addition, an initial consonant, a final consonant or an initial and final consonant may or may not occur. Possible syllable shapes include V, VV, VC, VVC, CV, CVV, CCV, CCVV, CVC, CVVC, CCVC and CCVVC, where VV represents a long vowel.

2.1 Consonants

Table 38.1 lists the twenty segmental consonant phonemes in Thai.

Table 38.1: Thai Consonants

	Bilabial	Labio-dental	Alveolar	Palatal	Velar	Glottal
Stops						
Vls. unaspirated	p		t	c	k	
Vls. aspirated	ph		th	ch	kh	
Voiced	b		d			
Fricatives		f	s			h
Sonorants						
Nasals	m		n		ŋ	
Lateral			l			
Trill/Tap			r			
Semi-vowels	w			y		

All twenty consonants may appear in initial position. Permitted initial consonant clusters include labials — *pr*, *pl*, *phr*, *phl*; alveolars — *tr*, *thr*; and velars — *kr*, *kl*, *kw*, *khr*, *khl*, *khw*. Only *p t k m n ŋ w y* occur in final position. No consonant clusters exist in final position.

At this point, some elaboration will help to clarify the status of the glottal stop in this description and the general status of /l/ and /r/ in Thai. Because of its predictability, the glottal stop is not listed as a separate phoneme. It appears initially before a vowel that lacks a syllable-initial consonant or consonant cluster: *ʔaahǎan* 'food'. Finally, it appears with the cessation of a short vowel nucleus followed by no final consonant: *tóʔ* 'table'. Internally, in words of more than one syllable, the glottal stop is frequently omitted, particularly at rapid, conversational speed: *pràʔwàt → pràwàt* 'history'.

The phonemic status of /l/ and /r/ in Thai appears to be in a state of flux; however, all phonemic descriptions of Thai still list the two sounds as separate phonemes. The writing system, moreover, has separate symbols for each of them. Most Thai, especially the educated, claim to distinguish between the two. This seems to be the case for slow and highly conscious speech. In fast speech, however, /r/ freely alternates with /l/, although certain forms occur more often with /l/ than with /r/. Many speakers regard these alternating forms as indicative of 'less correct' or 'substandard' speech. Linguistic hypotheses suggest that this lack of stable contrast may signal a sound change in process.

2.2 Vowels

Table 38.2 lists the nine vowel phonemes.

Table 38.2: Thai Vowels

	Front	Back unrounded	Back rounded
High	i	ɨ	u
Mid	e	ə	o
Low	ɛ	a	ɔ

Each vowel may occur phonemically short or long. When long, the nuclei may be interpreted as two instances of the corresponding short vowel: *ii, ɨɨ, uu, ee, əə, oo, ɛɛ, aa, ɔɔ*, Phonetically, the long vowels average in duration about twice as long as the short vowels. All 18 vocalic nuclei may occur alone, with an initial consonant, with a final consonant or with an initial and final consonant.

2.3 Diphthongs

Each of the three short and long high vowels may be followed by a centring off-glide *a*. The rare short combinations occupy about as much time as the single short vowels and the long combinations about as much time as the long vowels.

Transcriptions of these diphthongs differ. Some studies make no distinction between the long and the short. Others transcribe the short diphthongs as *ia, ɨa, ua* and the long as *iia, ɨɨa, uua*. Still another interprets the short combination as a single short vowel plus *ə*. Because of the relative rarity of the short diphthongs, this description designates both the short and long forms as a sequence of VV.

Gedney notes (1947:14, 20, 21) that for the short diphthongs only *p, t, c, k, ph, th, ch, kh* seem to appear as initials and only *p, t, k*, as finals. The long diphthongs seem to have no restrictions on the permitted initials and finals.

2.4 Tones

Each syllable in Thai carries one of five phonemic tones. These tones, with the symbols used in this transcription placed over the first vowel, include: a mid tone (unmarked, *khaa* 'to be lodged in'); a low tone (*khàa* 'a kind of aromatic root'); a falling tone (*khâa* 'servant, slave'); a high tone (*kháa* 'to do business in'); and a rising tone (*khǎa* 'leg'). Tones in Thai may be described in terms of pitch contour, pitch height and glottalised or non-glottalised voice quality.

Table 38.3: Tones in Thai

Tone	Pitch contour	Pitch height	Voice quality
Mid	Level	Medium	Non-glottalised
Low	Level	Low	Non-glottalised
Falling	Falling	High to low	Glottalised
High	Level	High	Glottalised
Rising	Rising	Low to high	Non-glottalised

Based on tonal occurences, syllables can be divided into three types:

(1) Syllables ending in a long vowel, a semi-vowel or a nasal. All five tones occur on these syllables (see above examples).

(2) Syllables ending with a short vowel and a stop or no final. These syllables have either a low or high tone: *phèt* 'to be peppery, spicy'; *kè* 'sheep'; *rák* 'to love'. Occasionally a falling tone occurs: *kɔ̂* 'then, consequently'. The mid and rising tones do not occur on syllables with this structure.

(3) Syllables with a long vowel followed by a stop. These syllables usually have low and falling tones: *pàak* 'mouth', *châat* 'nation'. Occasionally a high tone appears: *nóot* 'note'; *khwɔ́ɔt* 'quart' (both English borrowings). Mid and rising tones never occur on syllables with this structure.

In addition to these five tones, some linguists analyse a variant of the high tone as a sixth tone. Occurring in emphatic exclamations, this tone, higher in pitch and longer than the normal high tone, may replace any one of the five tones: *dīidii* 'very good' (see section 4, page 766).

The historical development of the Thai tonal system has long been of great interest. Early Thai (pre-fifteenth century) had a system of three tones, A, B, C, on syllables ending in a long vowel, a semi-vowel or a nasal. Syllables with no tone mark had the A tone. Syllables with the *máy èek* (') tone mark had the B tone and those with the *máy thoo* (ʯ) tone mark had the C tone. Checked syllables, i.e. those terminating in *p, t, k* or in a glottal after a short vowel, had a fourth tone D, although these syllables actually showed no tonal differentiation at all. It should be noted that these designated tones and tone markers reveal nothing about the phonetic nature of the ancient tones. Although various theories about the tonal phonetics have been offered, the question remains controversial.

Probably between the fifteenth and seventeenth centuries, the tones in each of the categories split, conditioned by the phonetic nature of the initial consonant of each syllable. In some cases, the presence or absence of friction or aspiration caused the split. In others, the conditioning factor was the presence or absence of voicing. For the checked syllables, both the phonetic nature of the initial and the quantity of the nuclear vowel conditioned the split. Table 38.4 summarises these splits.

Table 38.4: Tone Splits in Thai

Initials at time of split	Tones at time of split A	B (ˋ)	C (ˊ)	D Short vowel nucleus	D Long vowel nucleus
Voiceless friction: h, ph, hm, etc.	Rising tone	Low tone	Falling tone	Low tone	Low tone
Voiceless unaspirated and glottal	Mid tone				
Voiced	Falling tone	High tone	High tone	Falling tone

Note: This chart does not account for words with *máy trii* (ˊ) or *máy càttàwaa* (+) tone marks. Words with these tones must have resulted from other changes in the language after the tone splits. Borrowings from other dialects or languages represent other possible sources for these words. The tone marks were created after the words entered the language.

Following the split, some initial consonants also changed, for example voiced consonants to voiceless ones:

   gaa^B → gâa → khâa 'fee, cost'

Originally, both in sound and in spelling, the initial consonant and tone distinguished *gaa*^{B} from *khaa*^{C} 'slave, servant'. However as a consequence of the tone split and subsequent changes *gaa*^{B} changed to *khâa* while *khaa*^{C} changed to *khâa*. Thus the two forms came to be pronounced exactly alike, but spelled differently. Much of the complication of the spelling system results from these types of sound changes.

2.5 Stress

The question of stress in Thai remains a much debated issue with no consensus whether stress is conditioned by rhythm or rhythm by stress or whether both are phonemic. Most studies agree, however, that the syllable in final position has the greatest prominence or stress. In disyllabic and polysyllabic words, the remaining vowels are reduced, although the reduced vowel may not be as short as a phonemically short vowel. Tone neutralisation may also occur with the vowel reduction.

3   Writing System

The Thai writing system uses as a base an Indic alphabet originally designed to represent the sounds of Sanskrit. King Ramkhamhaeng (1275–1317) of Sukhothai generally receives credit for creating the new alphabet some time prior to AD 1283, the date of the earliest extant inscription written in the alphabet. Borrowing the alphabet then in use by the Khmers, Ramkhamhaeng kept the symbols for the Sanskrit sounds not found in Thai and used them in Indic loanwords to reflect the origin of their pronunciation. For Thai sounds not accommodated by the alphabet, he created new symbols, including those for tones. Because of the redesigning of the

Table 38.5: Consonants (Adapted from Brown vol. 3, 1967: 211)

Mid	*Mid*	*High*	*High*	*Low*	*Low*	*Low*	*Low*	*Low*	*High*	
ก	ข	ฃ	ค	ฅ	ฆ	ง				High ห
k	kh	kh	kh	kh	kh	ŋ				h
จ	ฉ		ช	ซ	ฌ	ญ		ย	ศ	Low ฬ
c	ch		ch	s	ch	y		y	s	l
ฎ	ฏ	ฐ		ฑ	ฒ	ณ		ร	ษ	Mid อ
d	t	th		th	th	n		r	s	?
ด	ต	ถ		ท	ธ	น		ล	ส	Low ฮ
d	t	th		th	th	n		l	s	h
บ	ป	ผ	ฝ	พ	ฟ	ภ	ม	ว		
b	p	ph	f	ph	f	ph	m	w		

symbols to fit Khmer first and then to fit Thai, the eventual system created by Ramkhamhaeng had little resemblance to the Sanskrit originals.

The two types of symbols in the alphabet resulted in a system characterised by several symbols for the same sound. The division of the consonants into three groups (high, mid, low) to indicate tone in spelling further complicated the system. High class consonants represent the original voiceless aspirated sounds, the mid class represent the original voiceless non-aspirated and the preglottalised voiced sounds and the low class represent the original voiced sounds.

Table 38.5 lists the 44 consonants in their alphabetic arrangement and in their consonant classes. To read the chart, proceed from left to right until the solid line, then move to the next line. At the completion of the first section (ม), move up to the beginning of the next section (ย) and continue as before. Table 38.6 lists the symbols for the 18 vowels and the six diphthongs. A ค indicates an initial consonant and a น a non-specific final.

Table 38.6: Vowels (Adapted from Brown vol. 3, 1967: 212)

	Long					*Short*					
	With final		Without		With final					Without final	
	y	Other	final	y		w	m	Other			
a		คา		ไค	ใค	เคา	คำ	คัน		คะ	ค
ə	เคย	เคิน	เคอ							เคอะ	
e		เค				เค็น				เคะ	
o		โค				คน				โคะ	
ua	ควน		คัว			*				คัวะ	
ia		เคีย				*				เคียะ	
ɨa		เคือ				*				เคือะ	
ɛ		แค				แค็น				แคะ	
ɔ		คอ				คอน				เคาะ	
ɨ		คืน		คือ			คึ				
i			คี				คิ				
u			คู				คุ				

*Note: This chart does not include the symbols for the rare short diphthongs plus final consonant.

Table 38.7 shows the five tones as they appear on each of the syllable types in each of the three consonant groups.

Table 38.7: Syllable Types, Consonant Classes and Their Respective Tones (Adapted from Brown vol. 3, 1967: 213)

Syllables with final long vowel, m, n, ŋ, w, y

Tone mark — Consonant class	No mark	Low tone mark '	Falling tone mark ย	High tone mark ๊	Rising tone mark +
High	Rising tone	Low tone	Falling tone		
Mid	Mid tone	Low tone	Falling tone	Low tone	Rising tone
Low		Falling tone	High tone		

Syllables ending with final p, t, k or syllables ending with short vowel and no final

	Short vowel*	Long vowel**
High		
Mid	Low tone	Low tone
Low	High tone	Falling tone

Notes: *In rare instances, a falling tone will appear on a syllable with a short vowel ending in a p, t or k. **In rare instances, a high tone will appear on a syllable with a long vowel ending in p, t or k.

4 Morphology

Thai has no inflections for case, gender, tense or number. Affixing, compounding and reduplicating represent the major derivational processes.

4.1 Affixing

Derivatives may be formed with a few prefixes and suffixes. The more common affixes include:

1. *kaan-* 'the act of, affairs of, matter of' forms abstract nouns from verbs and some nouns: e.g. *lên* 'to play', *kaanlên* 'playing'; *mɯaŋ* 'city', *kaanmɯaŋ* 'politics'.

2. *khwaam-* 'the condition of' forms abstract nouns that express a quality or state: e.g. *rúusìk* 'to feel'; *khwaamrúusìk* 'feeling'.

3. *khîi-* 'characterised by': e.g. *bòn* 'to complain'; *khîibòn* 'given to complaining'.

4. *khrîaŋ-* 'a collection, equipment': e.g. *khĭan* 'to write'; *khrîaŋkhĭan* 'stationery'.

5. *nâa-* 'worthy of': e.g. *rák* 'to love'; *nâarák* 'cute, lovable'.

6. *nák-* 'expert, authority': e.g. *rian* 'to study'; *nákrian* 'student'.

7. *-sàat* 'branch, field of knowledge': e.g. *daaraa* 'star'; *daaraasàat* 'astronomy'.

4.2 Compounding

Compounds in Thai are endocentric constructions in which the first constituent generally determines the syntactic word class. Compounds may be coordinate or attributive. Coordinate nouns include *phɔɔmêɛ* 'parents' (*phɔɔ* 'father' + *mêɛ* 'mother'); *phîinɔɔŋ* 'brothers and sisters' (*phîi* 'older sibling' + *nɔɔŋ* 'younger sibling'). Coordinate verbs include *hŭŋtôm* 'to cook' (*hŭŋ* 'to cook rice' + *tôm* 'to boil food'); *ráprúu* 'to acknowledge, take responsibility' (*ráp* 'to take, accept' + *rúu* 'to know'). Attributive compounds include *námkhĕŋ* 'ice' (*nám* 'water' + *khĕŋ* 'to be hard'); *rótfay* 'train' (*rót* 'vehicle, car' + *fay* 'fire').

4.3 Reduplication

Three general types of reduplication occur in Thai: reduplication of a base form with no changes, ablauting reduplication and reduplication with an accompanying change in tone.

Reduplication of the base conveys several different meanings: softens the base, *dii* 'good' → *diidii* 'rather good'; indicates plurality, *dèk* 'child' → *dèkdèk* 'children'; forms imitatives, *khék* 'to knock' → *khékkhék* 'rapping sound'; intensifies meaning, *ciŋ* 'to be true' → *ciŋciŋ* 'really'.

Examples of ablauting reduplication include: (1) the alternation of a back vowel with its corresponding front vowel, *yûŋ* 'to be confused' → *yûŋyîŋ*; *soosee* 'to stagger'; and (2) the alternation of any vowel with *a*, *chaŋ* 'to hate' → *chiŋchaŋ* 'to hate, detest, loathe'.

Reduplication with an accompanying change in tone generally signifies emphasis in speech. Used more often by women than men, the intensified form consists of the base word with any of the five tones preceded by the reduplication which carries a high tone higher in pitch and longer than the normal high tone: *dii* 'good' → *dīidii* 'really good'.

4.4 Elaborate Expressions

Elaborate expressions, a common South-East Asian areal feature, represent a special type of compounding achieved through the reduplication of part of a compound and the addition of a new part. Usually the expression consists of four syllables, with the repeated elements the first and third syllable or the second and fourth.

> tîin taa tîin cay
> to wake eye to wake heart
> 'to be full of wonder and excitement'

Frequently rhyme occurs as part of the expression, in which case the second and third syllables rhyme.

> hǔu pàa taa thìan
> ear forest eye forest
> 'to be ignorant of what is going on'

The new syllable may be added solely for rhyme and/or it may have some semantic relationship to the original part.

For the Thai, the ability to use elaborate expressions is an essential quality of speaking well and fluently (*phayrɔ́*). Attempts to classify the expressions according to the structure and semantics of the components have largely been unsuccessful.

5 Syntax

Subject–verb–object, in that order, constitutes the most favoured word order in Thai:

> khǎw sɯ́ɯ aahǎan
> he buy food
> 'He buys food.'

Both subject and object may be filled with: (1) a noun phrase consisting of a noun, a pronoun, a demonstrative pronoun or an interrogative-indefinite pronoun; or (2) a noun phrase consisting of noun + attribute in which case the head noun always precedes the attribute. Noun + attribute constructions may be simple or complex. Predicates may be nominal or verbal, simple or complex.

5.1 Noun Phrases

5.1.1 Nouns

Nouns form one of the largest classes of words in the vocabulary, the other being the verbs. Single nouns may occupy the subject or object position (see above example). Typically nouns occur as the head of noun expressions (see noun + attribute).

5.1.2 Pronouns

Like many other South-East Asian languages, Thai exhibits a complex pronoun system. The choice of pronoun used in any one situation depends upon factors such as sex, age, social position and the attitude of the speaker toward the addressee. In those contexts in which the referent is understood, the pronoun is frequently omitted. Common first and second person singular pronouns include those given in table 38.8.

Table 38.8: First and Second Person Singular Pronouns

Situation	First Person	Second Person
1. Polite conversation with strangers and acquaintances	phǒm (used by male) dìchǎn (used by female)	khun
2. Speaking to a superior, showing deference	phǒm (used by male) dìchǎn (used by female)	thân
3. Informal conversation with close friends and family	chǎn	thəə
4. Conversation between intimates of the same sex	kan	kɛɛ
5. Adult to a child	chǎn or kinship term	nǔu or kinship term
6. Child to adult	nǔu	kinship term
7. Child to older sibling	nǔu	phîi

Fewer choices exist for third person singular pronouns. In general, *man* is used for inferiors, for non-humans and for expressing anger. *khǎw* is the general polite form and *thân* the form for superiors. Additional forms not discussed here are employed for the royalty.

raw, which may be inclusive or exclusive, expresses first person plural. It may also be used to mean 'I' when addressing inferiors or oneself.

Second and third person plural forms are generally expressed by the singular forms.

Kinship terms and other nouns referring to relationships may also be used as pronouns. For example, *mɛ̂ɛ* 'mother' may mean 'you, she' when speaking to or about one's mother or 'I, mother' when the mother speaks to her child. Other terms following this pattern include *phɔ̂ɔ* 'father', *lûuk* 'child', *phîi* 'older sibling', *nɔ́ɔŋ* 'younger sibling', *phîan* 'friend'.

5.1.3 Demonstrative Pronouns

Demonstrative pronouns may occupy positions available to nouns, although they never occur with attributes. These pronouns include *nîi* 'this one', *nân* 'that one', and *nôon* 'that one over there'.

nîi   sǔay   mâak
this one beautiful much, many
'This one is very beautiful.'

For some speakers, the demonstrative adjectives, *níi* 'this', *nán* 'that', *nóon* 'that over there', also function as demonstrative pronouns.

5.1.4 Interrogative-indefinite Pronouns
In Thai, the interrogatives and indefinite pronouns have the same form. Occurring in the same positions as nouns, these words make a question or an indefinite statement:

> khray rian phaasǎa thay
> who study language Thai
> 'Who's studying Thai?
> mây mii khray rian phaasǎa thay
> negative have anyone study language Thai
> 'No one's studying Thai.'

Besides *khray* 'who?, anyone', this group includes *àray* 'what?, anything', *nǎy* 'which?' *thîi nǎy* 'where?, anywhere', *day* 'which?, what?, any'.

5.1.5 Noun + Attribute: Simple
Simple attributes consist of single constituents. These constituents may be another noun, a pronoun, a demonstrative adjective or a verb. A noun following the head noun may function as the possessor and the head noun the possessed: *nǎŋsǔ dèk* ('book child') 'child's book'. A complex noun phrase with the preposition *khɔɔ̌ŋ* 'of' frequently replaces this construction: *nǎŋsǔ khɔɔ̌ŋ dèk* 'child's book'. *dèk* may also modify the head noun in which case the expression means 'a book for children'. When a pronoun, the attribute functions as a possessive adjective: *mɛ̂ɛ phǒm* ('mother I') 'my mother'. The three demonstrative adjectives, *níi* 'this, these', *nán* 'that, those', and *nóon* 'that, those over there', may also fill the attribute position.

Words considered to be adjectives in English (*sǔay* 'beautiful', *dii* 'good', *yaaw* 'long') may function as nominal attributes, verbal attributes or as predicates. Because these words behave syntactically as verbs without a copula, they are treated here as verbs. Thus, *bâan sǔay* may be translated as 'the house is beautiful' or 'a beautiful house'.

5.1.6 Noun + Attribute: Complex
Complex attributes consist of more than one constituent. The use of classifiers, one of the most characteristic features of Thai syntax, serves to illustrate a typical complex attribute. With quantifiers, classifiers are obligatory, and the usual word order is noun + quantifier + classifier:

> dèk sǎam khon
> child three classifier
> 'three children'

This regular order changes in two situations. First, when the numeral 'one' is used, the numeral and classifier rearrange to indicate an indefinite meaning: *dèk khon nìŋ* 'a child'. To specify the number of objects, the original order remains: *dèk nìŋ khon* 'one child'. Second, with the verb *hây* 'to give' and an indirect object, the word order following *hây* becomes thing given, person given to, and amount given:

    khruu hây sàmùt   nákrian săam lêm
    teacher give notebook student three classifier
    'The teacher gave the student three notebooks.'

In each noun + classifier construction, the head noun determines the choice of classifier. Examples include *khon* for human beings, *tua* for animals, tables, chairs, clothes, *lêm* for books, carts, sharp pointed instruments and *muan* for cigars and cigarettes. Although unsuccessful, various attempts have been made to link the nouns semantically with their respective classifiers. When referring to a group, more general classifiers such as *fŭuŋ* 'flock, herd' may be used.

Expanding the attribute forms more complex noun phrases:

    Noun   Attribute
    dèk   săam khon   'three boys'
    dèk   lɔɔ săam khon   'three handsome boys'
    dèk   lɔɔ săam khon níi   'these three handsome boys'

In more precise and particularised speech, a classifier is used between the noun and the following verbal attribute or demonstrative adjective: *dèk khon lɔɔ* 'the handsome boy'; *dèk khon níi* 'this very boy'; *dèk khon lɔɔ săam khon níi* 'these three handsome boys'.

5.2 Predicates

Normal word order places the predicate immediately after the subject. Thai verbs have no inflection for tense or number. Context, added time expressions or preverbs generally specify the tense:

    khăw àan năŋsĭi dĭawníi
    he   read book   now
    'He is reading a book now.'

mây 'not' negates the verb:

    khăw mây àan năŋsĭi dĭawníi
    'He isn't reading a book now.'

Predicates may be nominal or verbal, simple or complex.

5.2.1 Nominal Predicate
In predicates of this type, no verb appears, only a noun phrase.

nîi   rooŋrian phǒm
this one school   I
'This is my school.'

Far more frequent are verbal predicates.

5.2.2 Verbal Predicate: Simple
Main verbs, the semantics of which roughly correspond to English verbs, form the nucleus of simple predicates.

5.2.3 Verbal Predicate: Complex
Complex verbal predicates consist of a collocation of verbs generally referred to as serial verbs. In complex collocations, the meaning of the main verb is modified by two classes of secondary verbs, one which precedes the main verb and one which follows. The first class of secondary verbs, those that precede the main verb and follow the subject, often translate as English modals or adverbs:

khǎw tôŋ klàp bâan
he   must return home
'He must return home.'
khǎw yaŋ rian wíchaa nán
he   still study subject that
'He's still studying that subject.'

Other examples of these verbs include *cà* 'shall, will', *mây* 'not', *khuan* 'should, ought to', *khǝǝy* 'ever, to have experienced', *àat* 'capable of', *yàak* 'to want to, wish for'. Verbs in this class may occur together in which case their order is fixed.

phǒm mây yàak cà   rian wíchaa nán
I   not want to will study subject that
'I don't want to study that subject.'

The preverb *dây* frequently indicates the past tense: *mây dây pay* 'did not go'.

The second class of secondary verbs follows both transitive and intransitive main verbs.

khǎw yók nâatàaŋ khîn
he   raise window up   (transitive)
'He raised the window up.'
dɨŋ tàbuu ɔ̀ɔk
pull nail   out   (transitive)
'Pull the nail out'

```
khǎw    nâŋ    loŋ
he      sit    down              (intransitive)
'He sat down'
```

As a class, these verbs have a general meaning of having successfully completed the action begun by the main verb. Other representative examples of this large class include *dây* 'to be able', *pen* 'to know how to, to do from habit', *wǎy* 'to be physically capable of', *pay* 'action away from the speaker', *maa* 'action toward the speaker', *lɛ́ɛw* 'completed action', *yùu* 'ongoing action'. Many of the secondary verbs may also function as main verbs. As a main verb, *khîn* in the above example, means 'to rise, grow, board, climb'.

Frequently, the collocation may consist of all three types of verbs:

```
khun cà  thon    yùu kàp chaawbâan wǎy              rɨɨ
you  will endure live with villagers to be physically question particle
                                    capable of
'Can you stand living with villagers?'
```

5.2.4 Particles

Thai has a large class of particles that end an utterance. These particles can be divided into three broad groups: question particles, polite particles and mood particles.

Question particles form questions that require a yes-no answer. These questions result when the particle is placed at the end of a statement. Two main particles, alone and in combinations with other words, occur: *máy* and *rɨɨ*.

```
(a) khun cà  pay hǎa phîan máy
    you  will go  see friend Q-particle
    'Are you going to see a friend?'
```

In this situation, the speaker has no particular expectation as to what the answer will be.

```
(b) khun cà pay hǎa phîan rɨɨ
    'Are you going to see a friend?'
```

With *rɨɨ*, the speaker has reason to believe his assumption is correct, and the addressee will confirm it.

```
(c) khun cà pay hǎa phîan rɨɨ plàaw
    'Are you going to see a friend or not?'
```

This question is similar to the first question, with no particular expectation for an answer. Literally, *plàaw* means 'to be empty'. In a question, it means 'or not so'.

(d) khun cà pay hǎa phîan chây máy
'You're going to see a friend, aren't you?'

With *chây máy* 'isn't that so', the speaker is quite certain of his statement and expects agreement. This particle is similar to English tag questions.

Polite particles show respect or deference toward the addressee. Marked for gender, these particles include: *khâ* — marks statements by women; *khá* — marks questions by women; *khráp* — marks statements and questions by men.

Mood particles form the third general group of particles. These particles signal the attitude or emotion of the speaker toward the situation at the time of speaking. Representative examples include *nâ* — indicates urging, persuading; *rɔ̀ɔk* — used with negative statements, usually makes a statement milder or corrects a misapprehension; *lǝǝy* — encourages the addressee to do something; *sí* — softens requests or commands.

All of these particles may be used in clusters in which case their order is fixed.

5.3 Complements
Three examples serve to illustrate complements in Thai.

5.3.1 Relative Clauses
The word *thîi* introduces relative clauses. In literary contexts, *sîŋ* replaces *thîi*, although the exact distribution of these two relative pronouns remains unclear.

dèk thîi   rian phaasǎa thay maa lɛ́ɛw
child relative study language Thai come already
     pronoun
'The child who is studying Thai has come already.'

5.3.2 Causatives
The verb *hây* 'to give' forms causatives with the result following *hây*.

phǒm cà   àthíbaay hây   khun khâwcay
I   will explain make, give you   understand
'I'll explain so you understand.'

5.3.3 Comparative-superlative
kwàa 'more' and *thîisùt* 'most' inserted after the verb form the comparative, (a), and the superlative, (b):

(a) nǎŋsǐi níi   yâak kwàa nǎŋsǐi nán
    book this hard more book that
    'This book is harder than that one.'
(b) nǎŋsǐi níi   yâak thîisùt
    book this hard most
    'This book is the hardest.'

Bibliography

Brown (1965) presents a theory of sound change in Tai dialects; this is a difficult, but worthwhile work. Noss (1964) is an excellent descriptive grammar, while Brown (1967) is a standard course book in spoken Thai, including separate volumes for reading (1979) and writing (1979). On individual problems, Cooke (1968) is probably the most comprehensive examination of pronouns in Thai available; Haas (1942) is a basic work on classifiers. Warotamasikkhadit (1972) is a generative approach to Thai syntax. Gedney (1961) is a discussion of royal vocabulary.

References

Brown, J.M. 1965. *From Ancient Thai to Modern Dialects* (Social Science Association Press of Thailand, Bangkok)
—— 1967–79. *A.U.A. Center Thai Course*, 5 vols. (A.U.A. Language Center, Bangkok)
Cooke, J.R. 1968. *Pronominal Reference in Thai, Burmese, and Vietnamese* (University of Calfornia Press, Berkeley)
Gedney, W.J. 1947. 'Indic Loanwords in Spoken Thai', Ph.D. dissertation, Yale University
—— 1961. 'Special Vocabularies in Thai', *Georgetown University Institute of Languages Monograph Series on Languages and Linguistics*, vol. 14, pp. 109–14.
Haas, M.R. 1942. 'The Use of Numeral Classifiers in Thai', *Language*, vol. 18, pp. 201–5
Noss, R.B. 1964. *Thai Reference Grammar* (Foreign Service Institute, Washington, DC)
Warotamasikkhadit, U. 1972. *Thai Syntax* (Mouton, The Hague)

39 VIETNAMESE

Đình-Hoà Nguyễn

1 Background

The language described here, known to its native speakers as *tiếng Việt-nam* or simply *tiếng Việt* (literary appellations: *Việt-ngữ* or *Việt-văn*) is used in daily communication over the whole territory of Vietnam, formerly known as Annam (whence the older name for the language, Annamese or Annamite). It is the mother tongue of the ethnic majority called *người Việt* or *người Kinh* — some 57 million inhabitants who live in the delta lowlands of Vietnam, plus over one million overseas Vietnamese, in France, the USA, Canada, Australia etc. The other ethnic groups (Chinese, Cambodians, Indians and the highlanders called 'Montagnards') know Vietnamese and can use it in their contacts with the Vietnamese.

Although Chinese characters were used in literary texts, in which Chinese loanwords also abound (on account of ten centuries of Chinese political domination), Vietnamese is not at all genetically related to Chinese. It belongs rather to the Mon-Khmer stock, within the Austro-Asiatic family, which comprises several major language groups spoken in a wide area running from Chota Nagpur eastward to Indochina.

In comparing Vietnamese and Mường, a language spoken in the highlands of northern and central Vietnam and considered an archaic form of Vietnamese, the French scholar Jean Przyluski maintained that ancient Vietnamese was at least closely related to the Mon-Khmer group of languages, which have no tones but several prefixes and infixes. Another French linguist, Henri Maspéro, was more inclined to include Vietnamese in the Tai family, whose members are all tonal languages. According to Maspéro, modern Vietnamese seems to result from a mixture of many elements, precisely because it has been successively, at different times in its history, at the northern limit of the Mon-Khmer languages, the eastern limit of the Tai languages and the southern boundary of Chinese. More recently, however, the French botanist-linguist A.-G. Haudricourt pointed out the origin of Vietnamese tones, arguing lucidly in his 1954 article that Vietnamese, a member of the Mon-Khmer phylum, had, as a non-tonal language at the beginning of the Christian era, developed three tones by the sixth century, and that by the twelfth century it had acquired all six tones which characterise it today. This explanation of Vietnamese tonogenesis has thus helped us to point conclusively to the true genetic relationship of Vietnamese: its kinship to Mường, the sister language, with which it forms the Vietnamese-Mường group within the Mon-Khmer phylum.

Up to the late nineteenth century, traditional Vietnamese society comprised the four classes of scholars, farmers, craftsmen and merchants. The French colonial administration, which lasted until 1945, created a small bou:geoisie of functionaries, merchants, physicians, lawyers, importers and exporters, etc. within and around the major urban centres. The language of the class of rural workers retains dialect peculiarities, both in grammar and vocabulary, whereas the language of the city dwellers accepts a large number of loanwords from Chinese and from French, the latter having been the official language for more than eighty years. Since 1945, Vietnamese has replaced French as the medium of instruction in all schools of the land.

The history of Vietnamese has been sketched by Maspéro as follows:

(1) Pre-Vietnamese, common to Vietnamese and Mường before their separation;

(2) Proto-Vietnamese, before the formation of Sino-Vietnamese;

(3) Archaic Vietnamese, characterised by the individualisation of Sino-Vietnamese (towards the tenth century);

(4) Ancient Vietnamese, represented by the Chinese-Vietnamese glossary *Hua-yi Yi-yu* (sixteenth century);

(5) Middle Vietnamese of the Vietnamese-Portuguese-Latin dictionary of Alexandre de Rhodes (seventeenth century); and

(6) Modern Vietnamese, beginning in the nineteenth century.

There are three distinct writing systems: (1) Chinese characters, referred to as *chữ nho* 'scholars' script' or *chữ hán* 'Han script'; (2) the demotic characters called *chữ nôm* (from *nam* 'south') 'southern script'; and finally (3) the Roman script called *chữ quốc-ngữ* 'national script'.

Written Chinese characters, shared by Japanese and Korean, the other two Asian cultures that were also under Chinese influence, for a long time served as the medium of education and official communication, at least among the educated classes of scholars and officials. Indeed, from the early days of Chinese rule (111 BC–AD 939) the Chinese rulers taught the natives not only Chinese calligraphy, but also the texts of Chinese history, philosophy and literature.

The so-called Sino-Vietnamese pronunciation is based on the pronunciation of Ancient Chinese, learned first through the spoken language of the rulers, then later through the scholarly writings of Chinese philosophers and poets. The latter constituted the curriculum of an educational system sanctioned by gruelling literary examinations which were designed to recruit a local scholar-gentry class, thus denying education to the vast majority of illiterate peasants.

While continuing to use Chinese to compose regulated verse as well as prose pieces, some of which were real gems of Vietnamese literature in classical *wen-yen*, Buddhist monks and Confucian scholars, starting in the thirteenth century, proudly used their own language for eight-line stanzas or long narratives in native verse blockprinted in the 'southern characters'. The *chữ nôm* system, whose invention definitely dated from the days when Sino-Vietnamese, or the pronunciation of Chinese graphs *à la vietnamienne*, had been stabilised, i.e. around the eleventh century, was already widely used under the Trần dynasty. Samples of these characters, often undecipherable to the Chinese, have been found on temple bells, on stone inscriptions and in Buddhist-inspired poems and rhymed prose pieces. A fairly extensive number of *nôm* characters appeared in Nguyễn Trãi's *Quốc-âm Thi-tập (Collected Poems in the National Language)*, as the seventh volume in the posthumous works of this scholar-poet-strategist involved in the anti-Ming campaign by his emperor Lê Lợi. The charming 254 poems, long thought lost, yield the earliest evidence of Vietnamese phonology, since many characters, roughly including a semantic element and a phonetic element, shed light on fifteenth-century Vietnamese pronunciation, some features of which were later corroborated in the *Dictionarium Annamiticum-Lusitanum-et-Latinum* and a *Catechism for Eight Days* authored by the gifted Jesuit missionary Alexandre de Rhodes and published in Rome in 1651.

Vietnam owes its Roman script to Catholic missionaries, who at first needed some transcription to help them learn the language of their new converts to Christianity, and some of whom succeeded in learning the tonal language well enough to preach in it in the middle of the seventeenth century. The French colonialists saw in this Romanisation an effective tool for the assimilation of their subjects, who, they thought, would through the intermediary transliteration of Vietnamese in Latin letters make a smooth transition to the process of learning the language of the *métropole*. *Quốc-ngữ* proved to be indeed an adequate system of writing, enabling

Table 39.1: Some Examples of Chữ Nôm

Chữ nôm	Modern Vietnamese	Gloss	Comments
才	tài	talent	Chinese character for Sino-Vietnamese *tài* 'talent'.
符	bùa	written charm	Chinese character for Sino-Vietnamese *phù* 'charm'; the reading *bùa* is earlier than the learned *phù*.
爫	làm	do, make	Part of the Chinese character for Sino-Vietnamese *vi* 'act': 爲
没	một	one	Cf. the homophonous Sino-Vietnamese *một* 'die', for which this is the Chinese character.
別	biết	know	Cf. the nearly homophonous Sino-Vietnamese *biệt* 'separate', for which this is the Chinese character.
買〈	mới	new	Cf. the nearly homophonous Sino-Vietnamese *mãi* 'buy'; the chữ nôm is the Chinese character for this Sino-Vietnamese syllable with the addition of the diacritic: 〈.
巴賴	trái	fruit	A compound of the two Chinese characters, with Sino-Vietnamese readings *ba* and *lại*, respectively, to give a pronunciation with initial *bl-*, as recorded in the 1651 dictionary: 巴賴
委	trời	sky	A semantic compound, using the Chinese characters for, respectively, 'sky' and 'high': 天上
找	quơ	reach for	A combination of, respectively, the Chinese radical for 'hand' (semantic component) and the character with the Sino-Vietnamese reading *qua* (phonetic component): 扌戈
㾺	cỏ	grass	A combination of, respectively, the Chinese character for 'grass' (semantic component) and the character with the Sino-Vietnamese reading *cổ*: 草古

Vietnamese speakers to learn how to read and write their own language in the space of several weeks. Not only did the novel script assist in the literacy campaign, it also helped the spread of education and the dissemination of knowledge, including information about political and social revolutionary movements in Europe and elsewhere in Asia. Nowadays, *quốc-ngữ*, often called *chữ phổ-thông* 'standard script', serves as the medium of instruction at all three levels of education and has been successfully groomed as the official orthography; both before and after reunification in 1976 conferences and seminars have been held to discuss its inconsistencies and to recommend spelling reforms, to be carried out gradually in the future.

Maspéro divided Vietnamese dialects into two main groups: the Upper Annam group, which comprises many local dialects found in villages from the north of Nghệ-an Province to the south of Thừa-thiên Province, and the Tonkin-Cochinchina dialect which covers the remainder.

Phonological structure diverges from the dialect of Hanoi (Hà-Nội), for a long time the political and cultural capital of the Empire of Annam, as one moves towards the south. The second vowel of the three diphthongs *iê*, *uô* and *ươ*, for example, tends towards *â* in the groups written *iêc* [iʌk], *iêng* [iʌŋ], *uôc* [uʌk] and *uông* [uʌŋ]. The Vinh dialect, which should belong to the Upper Annam group, has three retroflexes: affricate *tr* [tʂ], voiceless fricative *s* [ʂ], and voiced fricative *r* [ʐ]. The Hué dialect, considered archaic and difficult, has only five tones, with the hỏi and ngã tones pronounced in the same way with a long rising contour. The initial *z-* is replaced by a semi-vowel *y-*, and the palatal finals *-ch* and *-nh* are replaced by *-t* and *-n*.

In the dialect of Saigon (Sài-Gòn, now renamed Ho Chi Minh City) the phonemes generally are not arranged as shown in the orthography. However, the consonants of the Saigon dialect present the distinction between ordinary and retroflex initials. Also, the groups *iêp*, *iêm*, *uôm*, *ươp* and *ươm* are pronounced *ip*, *im*, *um*, *ưp* and *ưm*, respectively.

Most dialects form part of a continuum from north to south, each of them different to some extent from the neighbouring dialect on either side. Such major urban centres as Hanoi, Hue and Saigon represent rather special dialects marked by the influence of educated speakers and of more frequent contacts with the other regions.

The language described below is typified by the Hanoi dialect, which has served as the basis for the elaboration of the literary language. The spoken style keeps its natural charm in each locality although efforts have been made from the elementary grades up to nationwide conferences and meetings 'to preserve the purity and the clarity' of the standard language, whether spoken or written. The spoken tongue is used for all oral communications except public speeches, whereas the written medium, which one can qualify as literary style, is uniformly used in the press and over the radio and television.

While noting the inconsistencies of the Roman script, French administrators tried several times to recommend spelling reforms. However, efforts at standardisation, begun as early as 1945, started to move ahead only in 1954, when the governments in both zones established spelling norms, a task now facilitated by the spread of literacy to thousands of peasants and workers between 1954 and 1975. There is a very clear tendency to standardise the transliterations of place names and personal names from foreign languages, as well as the transliteration and/or translation of technical terms more and more required by progress in Vietnamese science and technology. Committees responsible for terminological work, i.e. the invention, elaboration and codification of terms in exact sciences as well as in human and social sciences, have contributed considerably to the enrichment of the national lexicon.

Members of the generations that grew up under French rule are bilingual, but later on have added English. The generation of 1945, for whom French ceased to be the medium of instruction, speaks Vietnamese and English. Because of the influence of socialist countries, Chinese, i.e. Mandarin, as well as Russian have become familiar to classes of professors, researchers, cadres and students exposed to various currents of Marxist thought, chiefly in the northern half of the country. In the south, English gained the upper hand over French as a foreign language taught in schools, while French remained and will remain the official language in diplomatic and political contacts. Chinese characters continue to be taught as a classical language needed for studies in Eastern humanities.

2   Phonology and Orthography

The *quốc-ngữ* writing system has the advantage of being close to a phonemic script, to which Portuguese, French and Italian, undoubtedly assisted by Vietnamese priests, contributed. It is fairly consistent, and below Vietnamese orthography is used to represent the phonology, with comments on the few areas of discrepancy.

A syllable has a vocalic nucleus, with a single vowel or two vowels, optionally preceded by an initial consonant and/or followed by a final consonant; this final consonant can only be a voiceless stop or a nasal. There may be an intercalary semi-vowel /w/ (spelled *o* before *a*, *ă*, *e*, otherwise *u*). These possibilities can be summarised by the formula $(C_1) (w) V_1 (V_2) (C_2)$. The syllable carries an obligatory toneme.

The vowels are presented in table 39.2.

Table 39.2: Vietnamese Vowels

| *Front* | *Central* | *Back* | |
		Unrounded	Rounded
i, y		ư	u
ê		ơ	ô
e	ă	â	o
a			

There are some discrepancies between the phonology and orthography of vowels: (1) the letters *i* and *y* are purely orthographic variants representing the phoneme /i/, while *o* and *u* are orthographic variants in representing intercalary /w/ or V_2 (but not V_1). (2) The orthography does not represent the predictable V_2 after a high or high mid vowel not followed by some other V_2, i.e. we find [iị] in *đi* 'go', [êị] in *đê* 'dike', [ưụ] in *đứ dừ* 'exhausted', [ơụ] in *tơ* 'silk', [uṵ] in *mù* 'blind', and [oṵ] in *đổ* 'pour'. (3) Phonemically, there are only four possible V₂s: *i, u, ư, â*, though there are phonetic and orthographic complications in addition to those already noted: (a) /â/ as V₂ is written *a* in open syllables (e.g. *mía* 'sugar cane', *mưa* 'to rain', *mua* 'buy'), but in closed syllables the orthographic representation depends on the V₁: *iê, ươ, uô*, and the pronunciation is with *â* before *ng* (e.g. *miếng* 'morsel', *mương* 'canal', *muống* 'bindweed'), but *ê, ơ* or *ô* (depending on the V₁) before *n* (e.g. *miền* 'region', *vườn* 'garden', *muôn* 'ten thousand'); (b) the spellings *uc, ung, oc, ong, ôc, ông* represent [uṵkᵖ], [uṵngᵐ], [ăṵkᵖ], [ăṵngᵐ], [âṵkᵖ], [âṵngᵐ] respectively, with final labio-velar coarticulation, as in *cúc* 'chrysanthemum', *cốc* 'glass', *cọc* 'stake', *cung* 'arc', *công* 'effort', *cong* 'curve'; (c) syllable-final *ch* and *nh* are orthographic representations of [ik] and [ing] respectively, e.g. *anh* [ăing] 'elder brother'. (4) /ă/ is spelled *a* before *ch, nh, u* and *y*, e.g. *bạch* 'white', *tranh* 'picture', *tàu* 'ship', *vay* 'borrow' (/a/ does not occur before *ch* and *nh*, while /ai/ is written *ai*, e.g. *vai* 'shoulder' and /au/ is written *ao*, e.g. *cao* 'high'). (5) /â/ is spelled *ê* before *ch* and *nh*, e.g. *bênh* 'protect'.

The six tonemes that affect the vocalic nucleus of each syllable are noted by means of diacritics as in table 39.3; when C₂ is a final stop, only tones 2 and 6 are possible.

Table 39.3: Vietnamese Tones

Name	Symbol	Pitch-level	Contour	Other features
1. bằng/ngang	(no mark)	high mid	drawn out, falling	
2. sắc	/´/	high	rising	tense
3. huyền	/`/	low	drawn out	lax
4. hỏi	/ˀ/	mid low	dipping-rising	tense
5. ngã	/˜/	high	rising	glottalised
6. nặng	/./	low	falling	glottalised or tense

Table 39.4: Vietnamese Consonants

	Labial	Labio-dental	Alveolar	Retroflex	Palatal	Velar	Laryngeal
Voiceless stop	p		t	tr	ch	c	
Aspirated stop			th				
Voiced stop	b		đ				
Voiceless fricative		ph	x	s		kh	h
Voiced fricative		v	d	r	gi	g	
Nasal	m		n		nh	ng	
Lateral			l				

The consonant inventory is given in table 39.4. Syllable-finally, the voiceless stops are unexploded. The voiced stops *b*, *d* are preglottalised and often implosive; note that *b*, occurring only syllable-initially, is in fact in complementary distribution with *p*, which occurs only syllable-finally. Word-final *k*, *ng* after *u* have labio-velar articulation (see the examples for point (3b) under vowels). /g/ is a voiced stop after a syllable ending in *ng*, otherwise a voiced fricative, e.g. *gác* 'upper floor' (fricative), but *thang gác* 'staircase' (stop). Word-finally, *ch* is pronounced /ik̟/ and *nh* is pronounced [ing], as already noted in the discussion of vowels.

The voiceless velar plosive is spelled *q* before /w/ (i.e. *qu*), *k* before *i*/*y*, *e*, *ê* and *c* elsewhere. Following the Italian convention, /g/ is spelled *gh* (and /ng/ *ngh*) before *i*, *e*, *ê*. The voiced palatal fricative is spelled *g* before *i* (and *iê*), e.g. *gì* 'what', but *gi* elsewhere, e.g. *giời* 'sky'.

In the Hanoi dialect, *tr* merges in pronunciation with *ch* (palatal), *s* with *x* (alveolar), while all three of *d*, *gi*, *r* merge as a voiced alveolar fricative.

3 Syntax

The noun phrase consists of a head noun, which may be followed by other words (noun, pronoun, place-noun, numeral, classifier, verb, demonstrative or even a relative clause). Examples of different constituents following the head noun follow:

(1) Noun–noun: no function word occurs between the head noun and the second noun; this construction can express (a) measure: *tạ gạo* 'quintal$_1$ of rice$_2$', *lít nước* 'litre$_1$ of water$_2$', *bát cơm* 'bowl$_1$ of rice$_2$', *cốc nước* 'glass$_1$ of water$_2$'; (b) space: *bao thuốc lá* 'pack$_1$ of cigarettes$_{2-3}$', *phòng khách* 'guest$_2$ room$_1$', *chuồng lợn* 'pig$_2$ sty$_1$'; (c) groups: *đàn bò* 'herd$_1$ of cows$_2$', *đoàn sinh-viên* 'group$_1$ of students$_2$', *nải chuối* 'hand$_1$ of bananas$_2$'; (d) images: *tóc mây* 'soft hair' (lit. 'hair cloud'), *cổ cò* 'crane$_2$ neck$_1$', *ngón tay búp măng* 'tapered fingers' (lit. 'bamboo$_4$ shoot$_3$ finger$_{1-2}$'), *tóc rễ tre* 'hair$_1$ stiff as bamboo$_3$ roots$_2$'; (e) characteristics: *gà mẹ* 'mother$_2$ hen$_1$', *máy bay cánh quạt* 'propeller$_{3-4}$-driven aeroplane$_{1-2}$'; (f) identity: *làng Khê-hồi* 'the village$_1$ of Khe-hoi$_2$', *sông Hương* 'the Perfume$_2$ River$_1$', *tuổi Hợi* 'the sign$_1$ of the Pig$_2$'.

(2) Noun–preposition–noun: *vấn-đề của tôi* 'my$_3$ problem$_1$' (note that the second noun may be replaced by a pronoun), *kỳ thi ở Huế* 'the examination$_{1-2}$ in$_3$ Hue$_4$', *cấu-trúc về chi-tiết* 'detailed$_3$ structure$_1$', *bổn-phận đối với cha mẹ* 'duty$_1$ towards$_{2-3}$ one's parents$_{4-5}$'. The preposition may be absent when the idea of kinship, ownership, origin, or utility is obvious: *nhà mày* 'your$_2$ house$_1$', *cha (của) Nguyễn Trãi* 'Nguyen$_3$ Trai's$_4$ father$_1$', *nhà (bằng) gạch* 'brick$_3$ house$_1$', *vải (ở) Tó* 'lychees$_1$ from$_2$ To$_3$', *sách (cho) lớp tám* 'textbook$_1$ for$_2$ the eighth$_4$ grade$_3$'.

(3) Noun–place-noun: *nhà trên* 'main$_2$ building$_1$', *nhà dưới* 'annex$_2$ building$_1$', *ngón giữa* 'middle$_2$ finger$_1$'.

(4) Noun–numeral: *hàng sáu* 'row$_1$ six$_2$, six abreast', *lớp nhất* 'top$_2$ grade$_1$', *tháng ba* 'March' (lit. 'month three'). In cardinal numeral constructions, however, a classifier must be used with the numeral; the usual order is numeral–classifier–noun, though noun–numeral–classifier is also possible: *hai cây nến* 'two$_1$ candles$_3$', *ba quyển sách* 'three$_1$ rolls$_2$ books$_3$', *bốn tờ giấy* 'four$_1$ sheets$_2$ of paper$_3$', *vài chú tiều* 'a few$_1$ woodcutters$_3$', or *tiều vài chú*. Nouns denoting concrete time units do not require a classifier, e.g. *hai năm* 'two years', *ba tuần* 'three weeks'. The choice of classifier is dependent on such features as the animateness, humanness (and social position for humans), and shape (for inanimates) of the noun; e.g. *cây* is used for stick-shaped objects, *quyển* for scrolls and volumes, *tấm* for sheet-like objects. *con* for animals, and *cái* for miscellaneous inanimates.

(5) Noun–verb/adjective (in Vietnamese, there is little reason for setting up distinct classes of verb and adjective — see section 4): *thịt kho* 'meat$_1$ stewed in fish sauce$_2$', *thịt nướng* 'broiled$_2$ meat$_1$', *thịt sống* 'raw$_2$ meat$_1$', *đường về* 'the way$_1$ back$_2$', *con người khổ sở* 'miserable$_{3-4}$ person$_{1-2}$'.

(6) Noun–demonstrative: *cô này* 'this$_2$ young lady$_1$', *ông nọ* 'the other$_2$ gentleman$_1$', *bà kia* 'the other$_2$ lady$_1$'. In such phrases with a demonstrative, a classifier is often used, the order then being classifier–noun–demonstrative: *cái bàn này* 'this$_3$ table$_2$', *con bò ấy* 'that$_3$ cow$_2$'.

(7) Noun–relative clause: *ngôi nhà mà chú tôi vừa tậu năm ngoái* 'the house$_{1-2}$ that$_3$ my$_5$ uncle$_4$ just$_6$ bought$_7$ last$_9$ year$_8$', *voi làm ở Việt-nam* 'the (ceramic) elephants$_1$ made$_2$ in$_3$ Vietnam$_4$'.

The verb phrase consists of a head verb followed by one or two noun phrases, a place-noun, a numeral, another verb, or an adjective (i.e. a stative verb). Likewise, when the head verb is stative ('adjectival'), several different configurations are possible:

(1) Verb–noun (direct object): *xây nhà* 'build$_1$ a house$_2$', *yêu nước* 'love$_1$ one's country$_2$', *ăn đũa* 'eat$_1$ with chopsticks$_2$', *cúi đầu* 'bow$_1$ one's head$_2$', *hết tiền* 'lack$_1$ money$_2$', *nghỉ hè* 'take a summer vacation' (lit. 'rest summer'), *trở nên người hữu-dụng* 'become$_{1-2}$ a useful$_4$ person$_3$'.

(2) Verb–noun–noun (the basic order is for direct object to precede indirect object, but the direct object may also follow if it consists of more than one syllable): *gửi tiền cho bố* 'send$_1$ money$_2$ to$_3$ his father$_4$', *gửi cho bố nhiều tiền* 'send$_1$ to$_2$ his father$_3$ a lot$_4$ of money$_5$', *lấy của ông Giáp hai bộ quần áo* 'steal$_1$ two$_5$ suits$_{6-7}$ from$_2$ Mr$_3$ Giap$_4$', *thọc tay vào túi* 'thrust$_1$ his hand$_2$ into$_3$ his pocket$_4$'.

(3) Verb–noun–verb: *mời sinh-viên ăn tiệc* 'invite$_1$ the students$_2$ to eat$_3$ dinner$_4$', *dạy tôi chữ Hán* 'teach$_1$ me$_2$ Chinese$_4$ characters$_3$'.

(4) Verb–place-noun: *ngồi trên* 'sit$_1$ at a higher position$_2$'.

(5) Verb–numeral: *về nhất* 'finish₁ first₂', *lên tám* 'be eight years old' (lit. 'reach eight').

(6) Verb–verb(–verb): *lo thi* 'worry about examinations' (lit 'worry take-examination'), *liều chết* 'risk death' (lit. 'risk die'), *đi học* 'go to school' (lit. 'go study'), *ngủ ngồi* 'fall asleep in one's chaiι (lit. 'sleep sit'), *chôn sống* 'bury alive' (lit. 'bury live'), *ngủ dậy* 'wake up, get up' (lit. 'sleep wake'), *đi học về* 'come back from school' (lit. 'go study return').

(7) Verb–adjective (there is no separate class of adverbs of manner): *ăn nhanh* 'eat₁ fast₂', *bôi bẩn* 'smear' (lit. 'spread dirty'), *đối-đãi tử-tế* 'treat₁ nicely₂'.

(8) Adjective–noun: *mù mắt* 'blind₁ in the eyes₂', *mỏi tay* 'tired₁ in the arms₂', *đông người* 'crowded₁ with people₂', *giống bố* 'resemble₁ one's father₂', *thạo tiếng Nhật* 'good₁ at Japanese₃ language₂'.

(9) Adjective–verb: *khó nói* 'difficult₁ to say₂'.

(10) Adjective–adjective: *mừng thầm* 'inwardly₂ happy₁'.

A normal message consists of two parts, the subject and the predicate; these two parts are separated by a pause, e.g. *ông ấy / đến rồi* 'he₁₋₂ has already₄ arrived₃', *bà ấy / là người Hành-thiện* 'she₁₋₂ is₃ a native₄ of Hanh-thien₅'. However, the subject can be ellipted, i.e. one can say simply *đến rồi, là người Hành-thiện*.

In addition to the subject and predicate, a sentence may optionally contain supplementary terms; these other phrases manifest complements of time, location, cause, goal, condition, concession etc.: *đêm qua ra đứng bờ ao* 'last₂ night₁ I went₃ to stand₄ on the edge₅ of the pond₆', *ở Việt-nam, chúng tôi học theo lục-cá-nguyệt* 'in₁ Vietnam₂, we₃₋₄ study₅ following₆ the semester₇ system', *tại vợ nó, nó mới chết* 'because of₁ his₃ wife₂, he₄ died₆', *vì tổ-quốc, chúng ta phải hi-sinh tất cả* 'we₃₋₄ must₅ sacrifice₆ everything₇₋₈ for₁ the fatherland₂', *nếu anh bận thì tôi sẽ đi một mình* 'if₁ you₂ are busy₃, then₄ I₅ will₆ go₇ by myself₈₋₉', *tuy nghèo, nhưng anh thích giúp bạn* 'though₁ poor₂, yet₃ he₄ likes₅ to help₆ his friends₇'.

Word order is important, especially given the virtual absence of other overt indicators of grammatical relations, for instance the subject normally precedes its verb while the direct object normally follows. The adverbial of time *bao giờ* or *khi nào* 'when' is placed at the beginning of the sentence to indicate future time reference and at the end to indicate past time reference, e.g. *khi nào cô thư-ký đến?* 'when₁₋₂ will the secretary₃₋₄ arrive₅?', *cô thư-ký đến khi nào?* 'when did the secretary arrive?'.

A noun phrase can be highlighted by placing it at the beginning of the sentence: it then announces a topic ('as for...'), and we have a specific reference to a certain person, a certain thing, a certain concept, an exact location, a given time, a precise quantity or a determined manner, e.g. *chúng tôi thì chúng tôi học theo lục-cá-nguyệt* 'as for us, we follow the semester system', *nước mắm, anh ấy ăn được* 'fish₂ sauce₁ he₃₋₄ can₆ eat₅'.

In the first example, the subject is repeated as topic with the particle *thì*; in the second, the direct object is simply preposed (cf. *anh ấy ăn được nước mắm* 'he can eat fish sauce'). With the particle *cũng* 'even', such preposing can indicate the extent of the scope of the particle: compare *ông ấy mời sinh-viên ăn cơm* 'he invites the students to eat dinner', with *sinh-viên, ông ấy cũng mời ăn cơm* 'he invites even the students to eat dinner' and *ăn cơm, ông ấy cũng mời sinh-viên* 'he invites the students even to eat dinner'. Other examples of topicalisation are *ông ấy tên là Bảng* 'he is named Bang' (lit. 'he$_{1-2}$ name$_3$ is$_4$ Bang$_5$') (cf. *tên ông ấy là Bảng* 'his$_{2-3}$ name$_1$ is$_4$ Bang$_5$'), *bà cụ mắt kém* 'the old lady has poor eyesight' (cf. *mắt bà cụ kém* 'the old$_3$ lady's$_2$ eyes$_1$ are weak$_4$').

A number of verbs denoting existence, appearance or disappearance may have the object whose existence etc. is expressed either before or after the verb; in the latter case, the verb may be preceded by a noun phrase expressing the experiencer of the existence etc., e.g. *đê vỡ* 'the dike$_1$ broke$_2$' or *vỡ đê; tiền mất, tật mang* 'the money$_1$ has gone$_2$, the sickness$_3$ remains$_4$', *(tôi) mất tiền* 'I lost some money'. In such sentences, the noun phrase before the verb is best analysed as a topic.

Passive sentences are found in Vietnamese, e.g. the active *Tám yêu Hiền* 'Tam$_1$ loves$_2$ Hien$_3$' may also appear as *Hiền được Tám yêu* 'Hien is loved by Tam'. However, such passives are best analysed as a subordinate clause *Tám yêu (Hiền)*, dependent on the main verb *được* 'get, enjoy'. If, instead of obtaining a happy result, the party involved suffers from a disadvantage or unpleasant experience, then the main verb *bị* 'suffer' will be used, e.g. *Liên bị Tám ghét* 'Lien is hated by Tam' (cf. *Tám ghét Liên* 'Tam$_1$ hates$_2$ Lien$_3$'). Such passives are not to be confused with instances of topicalisation discussed above, even though the latter are sometimes translatable into English as passives (e.g. *cơm thổi rồi* as 'the rice$_1$ has already$_3$ been cooked$_2$', but cf. *cơm, mẹ thổi rồi* 'the rice$_1$, mother$_2$ has already$_4$ cooked$_3$').

Negation is expressed by means of the negative marker *không*, which literally means 'null, not to be, not to exist', and whose emphatic equivalents are *chẳng* and *chả*, e.g. *ông ấy không/chẳng/chả đến* 'he$_{1-2}$ is not$_3$ coming$_4$'. Either *chưa* or *chửa* means 'not yet', e.g. *ông ấy chưa/chửa đến* 'he hasn't arrived yet'. Before the copula *là*, negation is expressed by *không phải*, literally '(it) is not correct (that) it is...', e.g. *bà ấy không phải là người Hành-thiện* 'she's not a native of Hanh-thien'. Stronger denial may be achieved by means of an interrogative pronoun used as an indefinite pronoun (see page 788), e.g. *ông ấy có đến đâu!* (lit. 'he$_{1-2}$ indeed$_3$ arrive$_4$ where$_5$'), *ông ấy đâu có đến!* 'no, he did *not* show up!', or even *ông ấy không đến đâu!* 'he's not coming, I tell you!, *bà ấy có phải là người Hành-thiện đâu!* or *bà ấy đâu có phải là người Hành-thiện!* 'she's not at all a native of Hanh-thien!'.

Interrogative sentences have three basic structures. The first is used for alternative questions, i.e. the interlocutor has to choose between two terms separated by the conjunction *hay* 'or', e.g. *cô ấy đi hay ông đi?* 'is she$_{1-2}$ going$_3$ or$_4$ are you$_5$ going$_6$?', *nó đi học hay không đi học?* 'is he$_1$ going$_2$ to school$_3$ or$_4$ isn't$_5$ he going$_6$ to school$_7$?'. With the latter example, where the choice is between affirmative and negative alternants, the second clause may be reduced right down to the particle *không*, i.e. *nó có đi học hay không đi học?*, *nó có đi học hay không?*, *nó có đi học không?*, *nó đi học không?* In such examples where the predicate is nominal, the confirmative particle *có* is obligatory in the first clause: *bà ấy có phải là người Hành-thiện không?* 'is she a native of Hanh-thien?'. When the question is about the realisation of an action or process ('yet'), the group *có không* is replaced by *đã chưa*, e.g. *ông ấy (đã) đến chưa?* 'has he$_{1-2}$ arrived$_4$ yet$_{3-5}$?', cf. the fuller version *ông ấy đã đến hay chưa (đến)?* Such questions (lacking an interrogative pronoun) normally have sostenuto intonation, in which the pitch level of each toneme is somewhat higher than in a normal sentence, rather than the more normal diminuendo intonation (in, for instance, statements), in which the intensity gradually diminishes from the beginning of the syllable.

The basic answers to such questions are *có* 'yes' and *không* 'no', e.g. *có, nó có đi học* 'yes, he is going to school', *không, nó không đi học* 'no, he isn't going to school'. But different answers are required with a nominal predicate: *phải, bà ấy là người Hành-thiện* 'yes, she is a native of Hanh-thien', *không phải, bà ấy không phải là người Hành-thiện* 'no, she isn't a native of Hanh-thien', and with 'yet' questions: *rồi, ông ấy đến rồi* 'yes, he has already arrived', *chưa, ông ấy chưa đến* 'no, he hasn't arrived yet'.

The second type of interrogative structure is the content question (*wh*-question), with an interrogative substantive: *ai?* 'who?', *gì?* 'what?', *nào?* 'which?', *đâu?* 'where?', *bao giờ?* 'when?', *bao nhiêu?* 'how much?', *bao lâu?* 'how long?', *sao?* 'why?'. The interrogative substantive normally occurs in the same position in the sentence as would an equivalent ordinary noun phrase, as can be seen in the following question and answer pairs: *ai đến? ông Nam đến?* 'who$_1$ has arrived$_2$? Mr$_3$ Nam$_4$ has arrived$_5$'; *nó bảo ai? nó bảo tôi* 'who$_3$ did he$_1$ tell$_2$? he$_4$ told$_5$ me$_6$'; *người nào đi với anh? ông Nam đi với tôi* 'which$_2$ person$_1$ is going$_3$ with$_4$ you$_5$? Mr$_6$ Nam$_7$ is going$_8$ with$_9$ me$_{10}$'; *anh đi với người nào? tôi đi với sinh-viên* 'which$_5$ people$_4$ are you$_1$ going$_2$ with$_3$? I'm$_6$ going$_7$ with$_8$ the students$_9$'; *nó ăn gì? nó ăn cá* 'what$_3$ does he$_1$ eat$_2$? he$_4$ eats$_5$ fish$_6$'; *ông ấy ở đâu? ông ấy ở Cần-thơ* 'where$_4$ does he$_{1-2}$ live$_3$? he$_{5-6}$ lives in$_7$ Can-tho$_8$'. Content questions usually have crescendo intonation, with the main stress on the interrogative substantive. Incidentally, these same interrogative substantives can also have the function of indefinite pronouns, e.g. *không ai nói* 'no one spoke' (lit. 'not who spoke'); especially in women's speech, they can even have negative indefinite function, provided the interrogative substantive receives very heavy stress, e.g. *ai nói*, with very heavy stress on *ai*, 'no one spoke'.

The confirmation-seeking tag is *phải không*, often reduced to *phỏng*, e.g. *không ăn, phải không? không ăn, phỏng?* 'you're not$_1$ eating$_2$, are you?' A number of final particles serve to mark various nuances of interrogation. Thus *a*, *à* and *ư* are used to express astonishment or to seek confirmation of what is supposed or has been discovered, e.g. *anh chịu à?* 'you₁ gave up₂? I'm surprised!', *ông không mệt ư?* 'aren't₂ you₁ tired₃?'. In the sentence *sao con lại làm thế hử?* 'how₁ did you₂ dare₃ do₄ that₅ my dear?', the particle *hử* expresses a mild reproach while pressing the culprit for a reply. The particle *nhỉ* is used to elicit the confirmation of something just noticed, e.g. *ông Chân có cái nhà to nhỉ?* 'Mr₁ Chan₂ has₃ a big₆ house₄₋₅, hasn't he?'. The dubitative sentence, which expresses doubt or uncertainty, contains the particle *chăng*: *trời sắp sửa mưa chăng?* 'could it be that it's going to rain?' (lit. 'sky about-to rain'), *có lẽ họ không đến chăng?* 'maybe₁₋₂ they₃ are not₄ coming₅'.

Other particles occur at the end of a sentence to lend more movement or force to it: in order to show politeness, the particle *ạ* is used in a social context where the speaker assumes an inferior attitude, expected of children, students, domestic help etc., e.g. *mời Bố xơi cơm ạ* 'please₁ eat₃ the meal₄, Daddy₂', *thưa Thày, hôm nay thứ năm ạ* 'report₁ Teacher₂ today₃₋₄ Thursday₅₋₆', *ông đưa tiền cho tôi rồi ạ* 'you₁ already₆ handed₂ the money₃ to₄ me₅, sir'.

In order to remind someone of something, the final particle *nghe* or *nhé* is used, e.g. *em đứng đây chờ anh nhé!* 'you₁ stand₂ wait for₄ me₅ here₃, O.K.?'.

The particle *chứ* is used to seek confirmation, e.g. *ông uống cà-phê rồi chứ!* 'you₁ already₄ had₂ your coffee₃, I presume', *ông uống cà-phê chứ!* 'you will have some coffee, won't you?'.

Exhortation is expressed by means of *đi*, which marks the imperative or injunctive, e.g. *anh đi ăn đi!* '(you₁) go₂ and eat₃!', *chúng ta đi ăn đi!* 'let us₁₋₂ go₃ and eat₄!', *lấy vợ đi chứ* 'get married₁₋₂! what are you waiting for?'.

The particle *mà*, occurring at the end of a statement, connotes insistence: *tôi biết mà!* 'I₁ know₂ it all', *tôi không biết mà!* 'I told you I₁ didn't₂ know₃ it at all!'.

In addition to the injunctive particle *đi*, which indicates a mild order, a curt intonation makes a statement into a command, e.g. *đứng lại!* 'halt!', *im* 'quiet! shut up!', *nín!* 'shut up! stop crying!', *thôi!* 'enough!'. When inviting or exhorting someone to do something, one uses the particle *hãy* placed before the verb, with or without an expressed subject: *anh hãy ngồi đây* '(you₁) sit₃ here₄', *hãy ăn cơm đi đã* 'go₄ ahead and eat₂₋₃ first₅'. To express prohibition or dissuasion, the particle *đừng* or *chớ* is put before the verb of action: *anh đừng hút thuốc lá nữa* '(you₁) don't₂ smoke₃ cigarettes₄₋₅ any more₆', *chớ nói nhảm* 'don't₁ talk₂ nonsense₃'.

A complex sentence may contain as many clauses as there are action verbs or stative verbs, and under this general heading we may examine both subordination and coordination. The main kinds of subordinate clauses are noun clauses, relative clauses and adverbial clauses.

A noun clause, always placed after the main clause, functions as object of the main clause. It is linked to the main clause either directly, or through the intermediary of the particles *rằng* or *là* 'that', e.g. *đừng cho nó biết (là) tôi trượt* 'don't$_1$ let$_2$ him$_3$ know$_4$ (that$_5$) I$_6$ flunked$_7$', *tôi hi-vọng (rằng) họ sẽ giúp tôi* 'I$_1$ hope$_2$ (that$_3$) they$_4$ will$_5$ help$_6$ me$_7$'.

A relative clause functions as an attribute modifying a noun phrase in the main clause, and is often, though optionally, introduced by the particle *mà*, e.g. *quyển sách (mà) tôi nói hôm nọ bị mất rồi* 'the book$_{1-2}$ (that$_3$) I$_4$ told$_5$ you about the other$_7$ day$_6$ has already$_{10}$ been$_8$ lost$_9$', where the relative clause *(mà) tôi nói hôm nọ* helps specify which book is being spoken of; in *thím tôi đã bán ngôi nhà (mà) chú tôi vừa tậu năm ngoái* 'my$_2$ aunt$_1$ has already$_3$ sold$_4$ the house$_{5-6}$ (that$_7$) my$_9$ uncle$_8$ just$_{10}$ bought$_{11}$ last$_{13}$ year$_{12}$', the clause *(mà) chú tôi vừa tậu năm ngoái* describes further the house that is being discussed. Relative clauses follow their antecedent.

Adverbial clauses serve the same functions as adverbs in the main clause, and express such ideas as purpose, cause, condition, concession etc. Adverbial clauses are introduced by conjunctions, such as *để (cho)* 'so that', *(bởi) vì* 'because', *nếu* 'if', *giá* 'suppose', *dù* 'though'. Examples follow; note that the adverbial clause may either precede or follow the main clause: *tôi xin nói để quí-vị biết* 'I$_1$ beg$_2$ to speak up$_3$ so that$_4$ you$_5$ may know$_6$', *vì anh ấy không có tiền, cho nên chúng tôi cho miễn học-phí* 'because$_1$ he$_{2-3}$ has$_5$ no$_4$ money$_6$, so$_{7-8}$ we$_{9-10}$ gave$_{11}$ him a tuition$_{13}$ waiver$_{12}$', *nếu tôi có tiền, tôi đã mua quyển sách ấy* 'if$_1$ I$_2$ had had$_3$ money$_4$, I$_5$ would already$_6$ have bought$_7$ that$_{10}$ book$_{8-9}$', *giá anh nghe tôi thì việc đó không hỏng* 'suppose$_1$ you$_2$ had listened$_3$ to me$_4$, then$_5$ that$_7$ thing$_6$ would not$_8$ have failed$_9$', *dù phải khó nhọc, nhưng/song họ không nản* 'although$_1$ it was indeed$_2$ tough going$_{3-4}$, yet$_5$ they$_6$ did not$_7$ get discouraged$_8$'.

As for coordination, several independent clauses may either be juxtaposed without any connective, or may be conjoined by means of such conjunctions as *và* 'and', *mà* 'but, yet', *nhưng* 'however', *song* 'nevertheless', e.g. *tôi rửa mặt, chải đầu, đánh răng, ăn sáng* 'I$_1$ washed$_2$ my face$_3$, combed$_4$ my hair$_5$, brushed$_6$ my teeth$_7$ and ate$_8$ breakfast$_9$', *tôi cho hắn vay tiền và giúp hắn tìm con* 'I$_1$ lent$_{2-4}$ him$_3$ money$_5$ and$_6$ helped$_7$ him$_8$ find$_9$ his child$_{10}$', *ông dùng cơm hay dùng bánh mì ạ?* 'would you$_1$ like to eat$_2$ rice$_3$ or$_4$ eat$_5$ bread$_{6-7}$?', *no bụng mà vẫn đói con mắt* 'his belly$_2$ is full$_1$, yet$_3$ he's still$_4$ hungry$_5$ in his eyes$_{6-7}$', *cái bút này rẻ nhưng tốt* 'this$_3$ pen$_{1-2}$ is cheap$_4$, but$_5$ good$_6$'.

4 Word Classes and Grammatical Categories

In the absence of purely morphological criteria, lexico-syntactic criteria are used to distinguish word classes, i.e. the environment of a word and its possible combinations in the spoken chain are examined together with its meaning(s).

A large number of nouns can be identified by means of such prefixed elements as *cái* 'thing, object', *sự* 'fact', *việc* 'action', *niềm* 'sentiment', *chủ-nghīa* 'ideology, -ism'. The classifier *cái* serves to create a noun from an adjective (*cái đẹp* 'beauty') or from a verb (*cái tát* 'a slap'). Likewise, with the classifier *cuộc* 'action, process, game' one can construct such nouns as *cuộc đình-công* 'a strike (industrial)' (from the verb *đình-công* 'be on strike'), *cuộc vui* 'party' (from the adjective *vui* 'merry, fun').

In the southern dialect, such kinship terms as *ông* 'grandfather', *bà* 'grandmother', *cô* 'paternal aunt', *anh* 'elder brother', *chị* 'elder sister' followed by the demonstrative *ấy* 'that' take the dipping-rising *hỏi* tone to function as third person pronouns, e.g. *ổng* 'he', *bả* 'she', *cổ* 'she', *ảnh* 'he', *chỉ* 'she'. The words indicating a given point or position in space or time also display this morphophonemic trait, e.g. *trong ấy* becomes *trỏng* 'in there', *ngoài ấy* becomes *ngoải* 'out there', *trên ấy* becomes *trển* 'up there'. The words designating portions of space have other characteristics of the noun class. This is why it is preferable to put them among nouns instead of considering them prepositions. Predicatives consist of verbs and adjectives. The latter, which are actually stative verbs, or verbs of quality, can be preceded by *rất* 'very', *khá* 'rather', but cannot occur with the exhortative particle *hãy!*: contrast *hãy chăm-chỉ học-hành!* 'study₃ hard₂!' with **hãy đúng!* 'be accurate!'. Moreover, only verbs of action can be followed by a verb of direction ('coverb') (*ra* 'exit', *vào* 'enter', *lên* 'ascend', *xuống* 'descend'), or be used in the frame ...*đi*...*lại* to mark repetition of an action, e.g. *chạy ra* 'run out(side)', *chạy xuống* 'run down', *chạy đi chạy lại* 'run back and forth' (but not, with *mặn* 'salty', **mặn ra*, **mặn xuống*, **mặn đi mặn lại*).

A noun, often defined as a word which denotes a being or thing, can function as predicate only if it is preceded by the copula *là* or its negative *không phải là*. It cannot follow the injunctive particle *hãy* or the prohibitive particles *đừng*, *chớ*. It can constitute a nominal phrase when it is combined with a numeral or plural particle (*những*, *các*) and a classifier, or with a demonstrative (*này* 'this', *ấy* 'that'). Likewise, certain particles can be used to establish the class of verbs, which can be preceded by aspect markers such as *sẽ* 'future', *đã* 'completion', *đều* 'togetherness'. On the other hand, by considering the position of a word in a syntactic group within a sentence, we can confirm its word class: in the noun phrase *khó-khăn của người công-chức* 'the difficulties₁ of₂ an official₃₋₄', the possessive element *của người công-chức* helps us to establish the noun status of *khó-khăn* even when it does not follow a classifier like *nỗi* or a pluraliser like *những*.

Such tests suggest that lexical items in Vietnamese fall into eight broad classes, as follows: nouns, verbs, quantifiers, substitutes, particles, connectors, modals, interjections. The first four classes consist of 'full (content) words', whereas the remaining four represent 'empty (function) words'.

The language does not have paradigms in the classical sense. There are, however, categories, some of which are non-existent in Indo-European languages. Within the class of nouns, it is necessary to mention, besides number, the various features that determine the choice of classifier (see page 785), such as animateness, humanness, shape and social status. Verbs, or more generally predicatives, manifest such categories as tense, result, direction, voice, intensity, orientation. Thus, in addition to the simple sentence *ông ấy đi*, one can specify time reference by means of particles: *ông ấy sẽ đi* 'he will go', *ông ấy sắp đi* 'he is about to go', *ông ấy đã đi rồi* 'he has already gone', *ông ấy vừa/mới đi* 'he has just gone', *ông ấy đang đi* 'he is on his way'. Other categories are illustrated by the following: *tìm thấy* 'find' (lit. 'search find'), *chịu được* 'endure' (lit. 'endure gain'), *bỏ đi* 'abandon' (lit. 'drop go'), *đóng vào* 'close' (lit. 'close enter'), *nhận ra* 'recognise' (lit. 'notice exit'), *phải phạt* 'be punished' (lit. 'suffer punish'), *bị thua* 'be defeated' (lit. 'undergo lose'), *được thưởng* 'be rewarded' (lit. 'gain reward'). Intensity is expressed by repeating the verb, with main stress on the first occurrence, e.g. *'đau đau đau là!* 'oh how it hurts!'.

In the family, kinship terms are used in place of personal pronouns, e.g. *bố cho con tiền ạ!* 'please give me some money, Dad' (lit. 'father give child money please'), *bố không muốn cho con tiền* 'I (lit. 'father') don't want to give you (lit. 'child') money'. Each individual must use appropriate terms of address and reference which place him where he belongs in the clan, and the terms are dictated by the relationship shown in a very precise nomenclature. The term *ông* 'grandfather' is used in formal conversation with a stranger one meets for the first time. The correct first person pronoun is *tôi* 'servant'. Between friends, the term *anh* 'elder brother' is applied to the hearer. Some arrogant pronouns (*tao* 'I', *mày* 'you', etc.) are used only in a familiar or vulgar context. Normally, etiquette recommends an attitude of humility before others, who are addressed in honorific terms (e.g. *cụ* 'great-grandfather', *ngài* 'your excellency', *thày* 'master'), which show respect for the hearer's age, knowledge and social rank.

5 Lexicon

Although the great majority of words have only one syllable (e.g. *nhà* 'house', *có* 'have', *ma* 'ghost', *ăn* 'eat', *cơm* 'rice', *ngon* 'delicious'), one cannot help noticing in modern Vietnamese numerous forms that have two or more syllables. These disyllabic or polysyllabic forms are either native compounds or compounds borrowed from Chinese.

Reduplication, a very frequent derivational process, can be total or partial: *ba-ba* 'river turtle', *chuồn-chuồn* 'dragonfly', *cào-cào* 'grasshopper', *đa-đa* 'partridge', *tùng-tùng* (representation of the sound of a drum); *châu-châu* 'grasshopper', *đom-đóm* 'firebug', *đu-đủ* 'pawpaw, papaya', *đo-đỏ* 'reddish', *trăng-trắng* 'whitish' (note the tonal modifications in this group and the next); *ngấm-ngầm* 'secret(ly)' (cf. *ngầm*), *ngoan-ngoãn* 'well-behaved' (cf. *ngoan*); *mạnh-mē* 'strong(ly)' (cf. *mạnh*), *xấu-xa* 'hideously' (cf. *xấu*), *nhẹ-nhàng* 'gently' (cf. *nhẹ*), *sẵn-sàng* 'all ready' (cf. *sẵn*); *tỉ-mỉ* 'meticulous', *lang-thang* 'wander', *bồi-hồi* 'anxious, nervous', *lầm-bầm* 'mumble'; *học-hiệc* 'to study and the like' (cf. *học*), *xe-xiệc* 'cars and the like' (cf. *xe*); *lơ-tơ-mơ* 'vague, obscure', *sạch-sành-sanh* 'completely (empty)'; *líu-lo líu-lường* 'twitter, jabber', *đủng-đa đủng-đỉnh* 'slowly taking one's time'.

Composition consists in combining two or more lexical bases. Sometimes, the relation among the components is one of coordination, e.g. *nhà cửa* 'house, home' (lit. 'house door'), *bàn ghế* 'furniture' (lit. 'table chair'), *giàu sang* 'rich$_1$ and noble$_2$', *ăn uống* 'eating$_1$ and drinking$_2$', *được thua* 'win$_1$ or lose$_2$', *bờ cõi* 'limits, border' (lit. 'edge region'), *đường sá* 'roads' (lit. 'road street'). In other instances there is a relation of dependency between the two components, e.g. *nước mắt* 'tears' (lit. 'water eye'), *bánh ngọt* 'cake' (lit. 'pastry sweet'), *tháng hai* 'February' (lit. 'month two'), *nhà tắm* 'bathroom' (lit. 'house bathe'), *tàu bò* 'tank' (lit. 'ship crawl'), *đỏ ối* 'scarlet' (lit. 'red dark-red'), *đánh mất* 'lose' (lit. 'hit lose'); *trắng nõn* 'pure white (of skin)' (lit. 'white bud'); *bao-giờ* 'when' (lit. 'what time'), *bây-giờ* 'now' (lit. 'this time'), *bấy-giờ* 'then' (lit. 'that time'). A special case of this dependent relationship is complementation, as in *vâng lời* 'obey' (lit. 'obey words'), *qua đời* 'pass away' (lit. 'pass life'), *khó tính* 'difficult to please' (lit. 'difficult character'); *buồn ngủ* 'sleepy' (lit. 'desire sleep'), *dễ bảo* 'docile' (lit. 'easy tell'). The numerals, which are based on the decimal system, combine dependence and coordination, e.g. *bốn mươi chín* 'forty-nine', literally 'four ten nine', i.e. $(4 \times 10) + 9$.

Within native Vietnamese compounds, the usual order is modified–modifier. Among the numerous Chinese loans, this order applies in cases of complementation (e.g. verb-object), such as *thu-ngân* 'cashier' (lit. 'collect money'), *vệ-sinh* 'hygiene, sanitary' (lit. 'guard life'), but the order is modifier-modified if the head component is a noun, e.g. *giáo-sư* 'teacher' (lit. 'teach master'), *đại-học* 'university' (lit. 'great study'), *ngữ-pháp* 'grammar' (lit. 'language rules'), *Pháp-ngữ* 'French language', *quan-sát-viên* 'observer' (lit. 'observe person'). This parallels the fact that modifiers normally follow the head noun in noun phrases in Vietnamese, but precede in Chinese.

One can even speak of prefixes and suffixes in the Sino-Vietnamese compounds, such as *bất-* (e.g. *bất-hợp-pháp* 'illegal'), *vô-* (e.g. *vô-ích* 'useless'), *khả-* (e.g. *khả-ố* 'loathsome'), *phản-* (e.g. *phản-cách-mạng* 'counter-revolutionary'), *thân-* (e.g. *thân-chính-phủ* 'pro-government'), *đệ-* (ordinal prefix, e.g. *đệ-nhất* 'first'); *-giả* (e.g. *tác-giả* 'author'), *-gia* (e.g. *khoa-học-gia* 'scientist'), *-sư* (e.g. *kiến-trúc-sư* 'architect'), *-sĩ* (e.g. *văn-sĩ* 'writer'), *-viên* (e.g. *đoàn-viên* 'member (of group)'), *-hoá* (e.g. *âu-hoá* 'Europeanise'), *-trưởng* (e.g. *viện-trưởng* 'rector').

Descriptive forms have been created to denote articles of merchandise imported from abroad, e.g. *cái bật lửa* 'cigarette lighter' (lit. 'thing switch fire'), *cái gạt tàn thuốc lá* 'ash tray' (lit. 'thing shake-off ash drug leaf'), *máy thu thanh* 'radio receiver' (lit. 'machine gather sound'), *máy quay phim* 'movie camera' (lit. 'machine turn film'), *máy bay cánh cụp cánh xòe* 'F-111' (lit. 'machine fly wing close wing spread'), *tàu há mồm* 'landing craft' (lit. 'ship open mouth').

The Chinese lexical fund being predominant in literary and scholarly language, an educated speaker often has access to two synonymous terms, a native one used in daily parlance and the other, of Chinese origin, reserved for written texts. For instance, 'train' is either *xe lửa* (lit. 'vehicle fire') or *hoả-xa*, and 'aeroplane' is either *máy bay* (lit. 'machine fly') or *phi-cơ*. Some advocates of standardisation have advocated the exclusive use of native words in place of Sino-Vietnamese loanwords, e.g. *máy bay lên thẳng* (lit. 'machine fly ascend straight') instead of *máy bay trực-thăng* 'helicopter', *Tòa Nhà Trắng* (lit. 'building house white') instead of *Tòa Bạch-ốc* 'White House', *Lầu Năm Góc* (lit. 'palace five angle') instead of *Ngũ-giác-đài* 'Pentagon', *vùng trời* (lit. 'area sky') instead of *không-phận* 'airspace'.

The use of abbreviations to replace entire appellations of administrative units or publications is very widespread, but each syllable (rather than each word) is represented by its initial, e.g. *TCPV* for *Tối-cao Pháp-viện* 'Supreme$_1$ Court$_2$', *DHVK* for *Đại-học Văn-khoa* 'Faculty$_1$ of Letters$_2$', *TCVH* for *Tạp-chí Văn-học* 'Review$_1$ of Literature$_2$'. This practice is, however, limited to the written language, and administrative titles are sometimes very long, e.g. *TGD-TTHBDHV* for *Tổng-giám-đốc Trung, Tiểu-học và Bình-dân Học-vụ* 'Director-General$_1$ of Secondary$_2$, Primary$_3$ and$_4$ Popular$_5$ Education$_6$'.

Since Vietnamese was strongly influenced by Chinese during the ten centuries of Chinese rule, the number of words of Chinese origin is inevitably very large: simple words, disyllables, as well as whole expressions make up the majority of lexical items in any written text of a technical nature. However, this invasion is limited to the large body of content words, while grammatical morphemes ('function words') retain their native identity. 'Suffixes' borrowed from Chinese are sometimes abused, and people say things like *cửa hàng trưởng* for 'store$_{1-2}$ manager$_3$', *đại-khái chủ-nghĩa* 'doctrine$_2$ of approximation$_1$'. A recent convention distinguishes the noun *chủ-nghĩa xã-hội* 'socialism' (lit. 'doctrine society/socialist') from the adjective *xã-hội-chủ-nghĩa* 'socialist'.

Loans from French are relatively less numerous: *ga* 'station', *cà-phê* 'coffee', *xà-phòng* 'soap', *cao-su* 'rubber', *bồ-tạt* 'potash', *xi-măng* 'cement', *bơm* 'pump', *xúc-xích* 'sausage', etc. The spoken language under certain circumstances tolerates such forms, with French bound morphemes, as: *qua-loa-rơ-măng* 'just so and so, not thoroughly' (cf. *qua-loa* 'rough, summary' and the French adverbial suffix *-ment*), *bét-dem* 'the bottom one' (cf. *bét* 'last' and the French ordinal suffix *-ième*), *inchêable* 'impeccable' (with the French negative prefix *in-*, Vietnamese *chê* 'denigrate', and the French adjectival suffix *-able*)!

Bibliography

For the social background to Vietnamese, reference may be made to Nguyễn Đình-Hoà (1980). For the genetic classification, see Haudricourt (1953; 1954); more specific historical topics are covered by Maspéro (1912) and Gregerson (1969), while Nguyễn Đình-Hoà (1982–4) is the state-of-the-art discussion of *chữ nôm*.

In the absence of a single comprehensive and authoritative grammar of Vietnamese, the reader will need to refer to a range of sources, such as Cadière (1958), Emeneau (1951), Lê (1960), Nguyễn Đăng Liêm (1969), Thompson (1965), Trần et al. (1943) and Trương (1970). For special topics, Honey (1959) may be consulted for word classes, and Nguyễn Đình-Hoà (1972a; 1972b; 1979) for various facets of the verb.

A useful collection of articles is Nguyễn Khắc Viện et al. (1976).

References

Cadière, L.M. 1958. *Syntaxe de la langue vietnamienne* (=Publications de l'École Française d'Extrême-Orient, vol. XLII) (Paris)

Emeneau, M.B. 1951. *Studies in Vietnamese (Annamese) Grammar* (University of California Press, Berkeley and Los Angeles)

Gregerson, K.J. 1969. 'A Study of Middle Vietnamese Phonology', *Bulletin de la Société des Études Indochinoises*, vol. 44, no. 2, pp. 131–93

Haudricourt, A.-G. 1953. 'La place du vietnamien dans les langues austroasiatiques', *Bulletin de la Société Linguistique de Paris*, vol. 49, pp. 122–8

―――― 1954. 'De l'origine des tons en vietnamien', *Journal Asiatique*, vol. 242, pp. 69–82

Honey, P.J. 1959. 'Word Classes in Vietnamese', *Bulletin of the School of Oriental and African Studies*, vol. 18, pp. 534–44

Lê Văn Lý. 1960. *Le Parler vietnamien: sa structure phonologique et morphologique functionnelle: esquisse d'une grammaire vietnamienne*, revised ed. (Publications de l'Institut des Recherches Historiques, Saigon)

Maspéro, H. 1912. 'Études sur la phonétique historique de la langue annamite: les initiales', *Bulletin de l'École Française d'Extrême-Orient*, vol. 12, pp. 1–127

Nguyễn Đăng Liêm. 1969. *Vietnamese Grammar: A Combined Tagmemic and Transformational Approach: A Contrastive Analysis of English and Vietnamese*, vol. 2 (Research School of Pacific Studies, Canberra)

Nguyễn Đình-Hoà. 1972a. 'Passivization in Vietnamese', in L. Bernot and J.M.C. Thomas (eds.), *Langues et techniques, nature et société* (Klincksieck, Paris), pp. 179–87

―――― 1972b. 'Vietnamese Categories of Result, Direction and Orientation', in M.E. Smith (ed.), *Studies in Linguistics: Essays in Honor of George L. Trager* (Mouton, The Hague), pp. 395–412

―――― 1979. *201 Vietnamese Verbs* (Barron's Educational Series, Woodbury, NY)

―――― 1980. *Language in Vietnamese Society* (Asia Books, Carbondale, Ill.)

―――― 1982–4. 'Studies in Nôm Characters: The State of the Art'. *Vietnam Culture Journal*, vol. 1, no. 1, pp. 25–36, vol. 2, nos. 1–2 and vol. 3, no. 1, pp. 107–113

Nguyễn Khắc Viện et al. 1976. *Linguistic Essays* (Xunhasaba, Hanoi)

Thompson, L.C. 1965. *A Vietnamese Grammar* (University of Washington Press, Seattle)

Trần Trọng Kim, Phạm Duy Khiêm and Bùi Kỷ. 1943. *Grammaire annamite*, 2nd ed. (Lê Thăng, Hanoi)

Trương Văn Chình. 1970. *Structure de la langue vietnamienne* (Librairie Orientaliste Paul Geuthner, Paris)

40 SINO-TIBETAN LANGUAGES

Scott DeLancey

1 Introduction

The Sino-Tibetan family consists of two branches: Sinitic, consisting of the Chinese languages and possibly the aberrant Bai or Minjia language of Yunnan (although Bai may also be a heavily Sinicised Tibeto-Burman language), and Tibeto-Burman, which includes several hundred languages spoken from the Tibetan plateau in the north to the Malay peninsula in the south and from northern Pakistan in the west to northeastern Vietnam in the east. Earlier classification schemes included Miao-Yao, Tai and Vietnamese in the Sino-Tibetan family on the basis of their remarkable typological resemblance to Chinese, but it is now clear that the structural resemblances and shared vocabulary among these languages are areal features rather than shared inheritance from a common ancestor.

Comparative Tibeto-Burman is a relatively unexplored field and there is not yet a complete and reliable schema for the genetic relationships among the various sub-branches of the family. (Indeed, we cannot say for certain how many Tibeto-Burman languages there are or even whether there may not still be a few — possibly in western Nepal, very probably in northern Burma and southeastern Tibet — that are yet to be discovered.) With the exception of the problematic Rung group, there is general agreement that the groupings listed below constitute genetic units at some level. (Note that many languages are known in the literature by several names, usually including one or more Chinese, Burmese or Indic ethnonyms which sometimes label groups speaking rather diverse languages. A very useful list of language names is given in Hale (1982).)

Bodish: Includes Tibetan; Kanauri, Bunan and other poorly documented languages of the Himalayan frontier of India; Gurung, Tamang, Thakali; probably Newari, the old state language of Nepal; and some (but not all) other Tibeto-Burman languages of Nepal.

East Himalayan: Includes the Kiranti/Rai (Limbu, Thulung, Bahing, Vayu etc.) languages and probably some others in eastern Nepal. Most closely related to Bodish.

Bodo-Garo: Includes Bodo (Boro), Garo and a number of other languages spoken in Assam.

Konyak: A group of languages (Nocte, Chang, Wancho etc.) spoken by tribal peoples in Arunachal Pradesh in India and probably adjacent areas of Burma. The Indian ethnonym 'Naga' is applied to these groups as well as to those speaking 'Naga' languages (see below). The Konyak 'Naga' languages are probably most closely related to the Bodo-Garo group.

Naga: Languages (Angami, Sema, Rengma, Lotha etc.) spoken by tribal peoples in Arunachal Pradesh and adjacent areas of Burma. These 'Naga proper' languages are most closely related to the Kuki-Chin and Mikir-Meithei groups.

Kuki-Chin: Called Kuki in India, Chin in Burma; includes Lushai, Lakher and numerous other languages in western Burma and easternmost India and Bangladesh.

Mikir-Meithei: Two languages of Manipur and Assam states in India; closely related to Naga and Kuki-Chin.

Abor-Miri-Dafla: A group of little known languages of Arunachal Pradesh and adjacent areas of Tibet. Reliable documentation, which is only now beginning to become available, may permit the assignment of some or all of these languages to other groups.

Kachinic: Includes at least the conservative and historically important Jinghpo (Jinghpaw, Chinghpo, often erroneously called 'Kachin', a Burmese ethnonym which refers to speakers of the Burmish Lawng and Zaiwa languages as well as of Jinghpo) dialects of Yunnan, Assam and northern Burma and perhaps the inadequately documented Luish languages.

Lolo-Burmese: The Burmish sub-branch includes Burmese and a few minor languages of Yunnan and northern Burma (notably Lawng or Maru and Zaiwa or Atsi). The Loloish languages are spoken by hill tribes in northern Burma and Thailand, Laos, Yunnan and Vietnam. Important members of Loloish include Yi (Lolo), Lahu, Lisu and Hani (Akha). The Naxi or Moso language of Yunnan is generally considered to be closely linked to Lolo-Burmese and by some scholars to fit in or near the Loloish sub-branch.

Rung: A cover term for several morphologically conservative languages of western China and northern Burma, including the Nung languages (Rawang and Trung), Gyarong, the Qiang languages (Qiang and Primi) and the extinct Tangut. (This corresponds roughly to a grouping called 'Sifan' in early work on Tibeto-Burman.) The relationships of these languages to one another and to the rest of the family are controversial; Nung and Qiang-Tangut show evidence of close relationship to Naxi and Lolo-Burmese, while Nung shows lexical links to Jinghpo, and Gyarong to Tibetan (although this is apparently a result of borrowing) and Kamarupan.

Karen: Several closely related dialects spoken in eastern Burma and adjacent parts of Thailand. Karen is typologically quite divergent from the rest of the family, manifesting fairly consistent SVO syntactic patterns where other Tibeto-Burman languages are resolutely SOV. Largely on this basis there remains some doubt as to whether Karen represents another branch of Tibeto-Burman, coordinate with the others, or one branch of a higher-order Tibeto-Karen family, the other branch of which is Tibeto-Burman. Currently opinion in the field is inclining toward the first alternative, but the problem is not yet settled.

The higher-order grouping of the Tibeto-Burman languages is problematic. The system proposed by Shafer (1966–73) and some tentative suggestions by Benedict (1972) are generally accepted as credible working hypotheses; although several other classification schemes have been proposed, none can be considered reliable. The best known classifications are summarised and compared in Hale (1982). Rather than repeat these readily available schemes here I have represented in figures 40.1 and 40.2 a classification which incorporates several hypotheses being considered in

Figure 40.1: Higher-order Groupings Within Tibeto-Burman

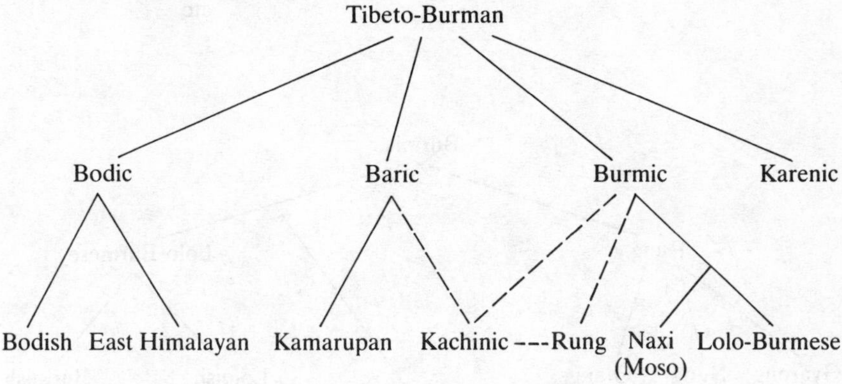

Note: Dotted lines represent uncertain or controversial relationships.

current published and unpublished work by a number of scholars; this should not be taken as necessarily more correct than earlier suggestions of Shafer and Benedict.

Figure 40.2: Middle-level Relationships Within Tibeto-Burman

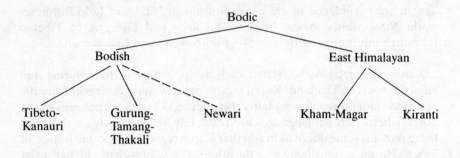

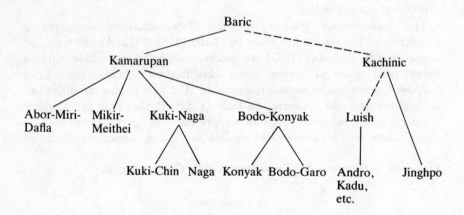

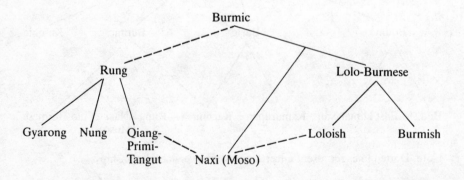

The best known Tibeto-Burman languages are Tibetan and Burmese, the two which have the longest and most extensive literary traditions. Both have a primarily Buddhistic literature written in an Indic script; the Tibetan script dates to the seventh century. The earliest attestations of Burmese are in twelfth-century inscriptions; the earliest Tibetan writings extant were discovered in the caves at Tun-huang and date from the ninth century.

The vast majority of Tibeto-Burman languages are (or were until this century) non-literate, but a few have writing systems of one sort or another. In the sphere of Indian influence, Newari (spoken in Nepal), Lepcha (in Sikkim) and Meithei or Manipuri (Manipur State, India) have independently developed Devanāgarī-based alphabets (although the Lepcha, in particular, is scarcely recognisable as Indic at first glance), in which there exist historical and religious texts which have yet to be investigated linguistically. Apparently all three systems are now considered obsolete and these languages, like others in Nepal and India, are now written in Hindi or Nepali script.

Within the Chinese sphere we find two extremely interesting indigenous writing systems. The better known is that of Tangut or Xixia, the apparently extinct language used in the Tangut kingdom which existed in the north-west of China until 1227. The Tangut script consists of characters reminiscent of and obviously modelled after Chinese, but nevertheless quite distinct. Tangut and its script have been intensively studied in recent decades by scholars in Japan and the Soviet Union. The other system is a basically pictographic script, with a few syllabic phonetic elements, used by priests among the Naxi (Nakhi) or Moso of Yunnan; a very similar system was used among the neighbouring Yi (Lolo). It is generally assumed that the original stimulus for the development of this system was a vague acquaintance with Chinese writing, although there are few recognisably Chinese elements in the system.

2 Comparative Sino-Tibetan Phonology

Our current understanding of Proto-Tibeto-Burman phonology is still uncertain, although considerable progress has been made in the reconstruction of a few sub-branches, in particular Lolo-Burmese. However, the segmental inventory given in table 40.1 is generally accepted by most researchers. Proto-Tibeto-Burman is reconstructed as having two series of stops (the third series found in written Tibetan, Burmese, Jinghpo and several other languages can be shown to be secondary innovations which occurred independently in various languages, usually conditioned by the loss of earlier prefixes) and one of nasals (again, many languages have both voiced and voiceless resonants, but the voiceless series reflect an earlier voiceless prefix, most commonly *s-).

Table 40.1: The Consonants of Proto-Tibeto-Burman

p	t		k
b	d		g
m	n		ŋ
	s		
	z		
	l	r	
w	y		

Proto-Tibeto-Burman certainly had no more than five phonemic vowels, and there remains some question about the Proto-Tibeto-Burman status of the mid vowels.

The relationship of this (or any alternative) Proto-Tibeto-Burman system to that of Proto-Sino-Tibetan is rather difficult to assess, given the considerable uncertainty which remains with respect to the phonological reconstruction of Early Chinese. However, recent work in that area (in particular by F.-K. Li and by N. Bodman and W. Baxter, as well as some less widely accepted proposals by E.G. Pulleyblank and A. Schuessler) present a picture which is much closer to that reconstructed for Proto-Tibeto-Burman than was the earlier and still widely cited system of B. Karlgren.

Historical developments in the Sino-Tibetan sound systems are best described in terms of syllable structure. Like modern East Asian languages, Proto-Tibeto-Burman and Proto-Chinese permitted only a subset of the consonant inventory to occur in syllable-final position; these included one series of stops (presumably voiceless), the nasals, *s, *r, *l, *w and *y. This inventory is greatly reduced in most attested languages; Tibetan orthography preserves all but the semi-vowels, but most languages preserve only the stops and nasals. Modern Central Tibetan allows only /p/ and /m/ in final position, while some Chinese, Loloish and Naga languages have no syllable-final consonants at all. The depletion of the inventory of final consonants typically correlates with a concomitant increase in the number of vowel and tone distinctions in the syllable nucleus.

In syllable-initial position clusters of obstruent or nasal plus medial *y, *w, *r and *l occurred. These are preserved in part in Tibetan and Burmese orthography and some modern languages, but in general they have simplified, typically with *Cl- merging with *Cy- or *Cr-, *Cy- giving either simple *C- or a new palatal series and *Cr- simplifying, merging with *Cy- (as in Burmese), or giving a new retroflex series (as in Central Tibetan). In addition, Benedict and most other scholars reconstruct at least some of the famous Tibetan initial clusters for Proto-Tibeto-Burman. These are probably all etymologically bimorphemic, but it is likely that fossilised, synchronically unanalysable clusters existed in Proto-Tibeto-Burman, if not Proto-Sino-Tibetan. It is, however, extremely common to find the same etymon occurring in different languages with different prefixes, as for example Written Tibetan *rna*, Balti Tibetan *sna*, Tangkhul *khana* < *g-na 'ear', or Balti Tibetan *gwa*, Written Burmese *swa* 'go'. Some such cases may represent lexical alternants at the Proto-Tibeto-Burman level, but others reflect independent secondary compounding in the daughter languages. For example, Balti *gwa* and Burmese *swa* represent independently developed compounds of a Proto-Sino-Tibetan root *wa 'go' with other motion verbs *ga and *sa.

The historical status of tone in Tibeto-Burman and Sino-Tibetan remains a topic of some controversy. Probably a majority of Tibeto-Burman languages have phonemic tone and/or voice register distinctions, as do Chinese and the unrelated Tai, Miao-Yao and Vietnamese languages. In the earliest days of Sino-Tibetan studies, lexical tone was considered a diagnostic Sino-Tibetan feature, an assumption which played a major role in the erroneous assignment of Tai and Vietnamese to the Sino-Tibetan family. It is now clear that the strikingly parallel tone systems of these languages and Chinese represent an areal feature which had diffused across genetic lines; however, the original source of the feature remains unclear.

There is now considerable evidence to suggest that the various tone systems within Sino-Tibetan may not be directly cognate, i.e. that tone systems have developed independently in various branches of the family. Research on the origin of tone systems has demonstrated that phonemic tone can develop in the course of the loss of distinctions between syllable-initial and/or -final consonants. Typically the loss of a voicing contrast in initial consonants results in a phonemic high/low tone distinction, with earlier voiced initial syllables developing low tone and voiceless initial syllables developing high tone, while the depletion of the inventory of possible syllable-final consonants results in a distinction between open syllables and those ending in a glottal stop or constriction, with the latter eventually giving rise to rising or falling tones. Such is the origin, for example, of the secondarily developed tone systems found in the Central Tibetan dialects. Several scholars have presented evidence suggesting that the tones of Chinese may have originated in this way at a date considerably later than the separation of the Chinese and the Tibeto-Burman branches of Sino-Tibetan.

If the tone systems of the Sino-Tibetan languages represent parallel independent developments rather than common inheritance, this would explain the existence of numerous non-tonal Tibeto-Burman languages and the considerable difficulty which has been encountered in attempts to find correspondences among the tones of the various tonal Tibeto-Burman languages. Within major branches tone correspondences can sometimes be found; for example, the tones of the Lolo-Burmese languages correspond regularly and it is clear that a tone system can be reconstructed for Proto-Lolo-Burmese. However, when this system is compared with the tone system of other tone languages such as Jinghpo or Tamang, it frequently turns out that otherwise clearly cognate items do not correspond in tone class, suggesting that the tone systems developed after the separation of the languages being compared.

Nevertheless, the hypothesis of the secondary origin of Sino-Tibetan tone systems is not yet universally accepted. Benedict, in particular, has called attention to some regular correspondences which can be found between the tone classes of cognate morphemes in Chinese and certain Tibeto-Burman languages, particularly Burmese and Karen, on the basis of which he reconstructs a two-tone system for Proto-Sino-Tibetan. This hypothesis entails the wholesale loss of tone in many Tibeto-Burman languages, particularly in the Himalayan branch, subsequently followed by their reemergence in Central Tibetan and a few other Himalayan languages; this consequence has resulted in considerable resistance in the field to Benedict's proposal.

3   Tibeto-Burman Typology and Reconstruction: Morphology and Syntax

With the exception of Karen, all of the Tibeto-Burman languages are postpositional SOV languages with predominantly agglutinative morphology (Burmese, described in a separate chapter in this volume, is in most respects typical) and this must also have been true of Proto-Sino-Tibetan. Several languages retain traces of older inflectional alternations in the verb, and a few show innovative case alternations in pronouns. A number of case marking typologies occur in the family, including consistently ergative marking (Gurung), aspectually split ergative or active/ stative patterns (Newari and various Tibetan dialects), split ergative marking in which third person transitive subjects take ergative case while first and second persons do not (Kiranti, Gyarong) and variations on a more-or-less nominative-accusative topic marking scheme (most Lolo-Burmese languages; see the chapter on Burmese). A detailed examination of an example of this last type can be found in Hope (1974).

Current comparative work on Tibeto-Burman morphological structure presents a picture quite different from what has historically been assumed about Tibeto-Burman languages. Proto-Tibeto-Burman is now reconstructed with a split-ergative case marking and verb agreement system of the sort exemplified by the following Gyarong examples, in which third person but not first and second person transitive subjects are case marked (in the modern languages which retain this system the ergative marker is often identical to the instrumental and/or ablative postposition), while the verb shows pronominal concord with any first or second person argument, regardless of its grammatical role:

ŋa   mə   nasŋo-ŋ
I   s/he   scold-1 sg.
'I scold him/her.'

ŋə-njɔ   mə   nasŋo-č
I-du.   he   scold-1 du.
'We two scold him/her.'

ŋə-ñiɛ   mə   nasŋo-i
I-pl.   s/he   scold-1 pl.
'We (pl.) scold him/her.'

mə-kə   ŋa   u-nasŋo-ŋ
s/he-erg. I   dir.-scold-1 sg.
'S/he scolds me.'

mə-ñiɛ-kə   ŋa   u-nasŋo-ŋ
he-du.-erg. I   dir.-scold.-1 sg.
'They two scold me.'

mə-kə   ŋə-njɔ   u-nasŋo-č
he-erg.   I-du.   dir.-scold-1 du.
'S/he scolds us two.'

Note the ergative postposition -kə marking third but not first person subjects and the fact that both person and number agreement are always with the first person participant, whether it is subject or object.

Both the pronominal and the verb agreement systems probably distinguished dual as well as singular and plural number, as well as an inclusive/exclusive distinction. In a number of modern languages (e.g. Gyarong, Chepang, Nocte) the verb also marks in transitive clauses whether the subject is higher or lower than the object on a 1st > 2nd > 3rd or 1st=2nd > 3rd person hierarchy, and this 'direct/inverse' marking system is probably also to be reconstructed for the Proto-Tibeto-Burman verb. While no modern language preserves this reconstructed system in its entirety, most of these categories are retained at least vestigially in a large number of languages which represent nearly every major division of the family. (The most conservative morphology is found in the East Himalayan, Rung and Jinghpo languages.) Probably the closest attested system to the Proto-

Table 40.3: Intransitive Agreement Affixes in Gyarong (Suomo Dialect)

	Sg.	Du.	Pl.
1st person	V-ŋ	V-č	V-i
2nd person	tə-V-n	tə-V-n-č	tə-V-ñ
3rd person		Ø	

Note: V indicates position of the verb stem.

Tibeto-Burman system is that of Gyarong, spoken in Sichuan; the example sentences above and the paradigms in tables 40.3 and 40.4 (from the work of Jin Peng) exemplify the system.

Table 40.4: Transitive Verb Affixes in Gyarong (Suomo Dialect)

Object	1st person			2nd person			3rd person
	Singular Dual		Plural	Singular Dual		Plural	
Subject Sg. ⎫ 1st Du. ⎬ Pl. ⎭				tə-a-V-n tə-a-V-n-č		tə-a-V-ñ	⎧V-ŋ ⎨V-č ⎩V-i

2nd   Sg. ⎫
       Du. ⎬
       Pl. ⎭
	kə-u-V-ŋ kə-u-V-č kə-u-V-i						⎧tə-V
							⎨tə-V-n-č
							⎩tə-V-ñ

3rd	u-V-ŋ	u-V-č	u-V-i	tə-u-V-n tə-u-V-n-č		tə-u-V-ñ	⎧V-u ⎫ ⎨ ⎬ ⎩ u-V⎭

Note: V indicates position of the verb stem.

The *-ŋ* and *-n* suffixes reflect the Proto-Sino-Tibetan pronouns **ŋa* and **na(ŋ)*, while the dual and plural suffixes *-č* and *-i* are probably reconstructible for Proto-Tibeto-Burman, although their exact form is uncertain. Both series of prefixes are almost certainly reconstructible for Proto-Tibeto-Burman. The *u-* and *a-* are direct/inverse markers; the *tə/kə-* series may also have been part of the direct/inverse system, although their original function is quite unclear. Reflexes of one or the other occur in a great many modern languages as second person agreement indices and in Gyarong one or the other occurs in all and only those verbs with a second person participant, but in the Nung and some other languages a member of the series also occurs on transitive verbs with third person subject and first person object.

Early work on comparative Tibeto-Burman assumed that, since this verbal morphology is not found in Tibetan or Burmese, it must be a secondary innovation in those languages which manifest it; hence all such languages were lumped together in a putatively genetic group of 'pronominalised' languages. Recent research has shown, however, that while the system is apparently completely extinct in Lolo-Burmese, Bodo-Garo and Tibetan proper, it is found in near relatives of each of these and is attested in all other major Tibeto-Burman subgroups except for Karen with a consistency that makes it clear that some version of it must have been a Proto-Tibeto-Burman feature. A good description of a language of this type is Caughley (1982), which also summarises much of the available data on verb paradigms in other Tibeto-Burman languages.

Several other verbal affixes can be reconstructed for Proto-Tibeto-Burman and probably Proto-Sino-Tibetan, although the original functions of most of them remain unclear. A causative *s- prefix is clearly reconstructible for Proto-Sino-Tibetan and an intransitivising *m- definitely for Proto-Tibeto-Burman and probably for Proto-Sino-Tibetan. An *-s suffix is also reconstructed for Proto-Sino-Tibetan; there is good evidence for both perfectivising and nominalising functions for such a suffix and it is possible that these functions reflect two different etyma. There is also phonological evidence for a dental stop suffix with similar functions, which may originally have been a conditioned allomorph of *-s. We also find evidence (particularly from the complex verbal system of Classical Tibetan) for prefixed *g- (or *kV-) and *l- and/or *r- (or *lV-, *rV-) of Proto-Tibeto-Burman provenience, but their original function is not yet recoverable.

There is evidence for a considerable amount of derivational morphology in Tibeto-Burman and Sino-Tibetan, most of which originated in compounding processes. Most if not all of the modern Sino-Tibetan languages and certainly all reconstructible ancestral stages have very productive compounding processes which create bimorphemic two-syllable nouns (and sometimes verbs). In the Tibeto-Burman languages these tend diachronically to reduce one syllable (generally the first), thus eventually creating what appears synchronically and etymologically to be a derivational prefix. The process is illustrated by the following forms from the Yunnan dialect of Jinghpo (for which example I am indebted to L. Diehl): the word *lam* 'road, path' occurs both free and in compounds such as *lamsun* 'narrow path', *lamshe* 'side road', *lamta?* 'level path (along a mountainside)'. But each of these also occurs in one or more reduced forms, e.g. *lamsun~masun~nsun*, *lamshe~mashe*, *lamta?~nta?*; thus there is an identifiable set of forms in which there appears to be a prefix *ma-* or *n-* meaning 'road, path'. The prevalence of this pattern of development has considerably slowed progress in lexical comparison and phonological reconstruction both for Tibeto-Burman and between Tibeto-Burman and Chinese, since these secondary prefixes typically disappear, but before doing so can affect the phonological development of the root initial consonant, thus leaving perturbations in the pattern of regular sound correspondences between attested languages.

Bibliography

Benedict (1972), actually written in the 1940s and out-of-date in some respects, is still the closest the field has come to a handbook of comparative Sino-Tibetan. Volume 1 of Shafer (1966–73) contains his classification scheme for Sino-Tibetan (including Tai); the rest of the work is of limited use. Bibliographical sources are Shafer (1957–63) and Hale (1982), which latter updates Shafer's bibliography to the mid-1970s and includes a valuable synopsis of the various classification schemes for the family, which with the extensive language index makes it possible to deal with the considerable nomenclatural confusion in the field. Wolfenden (1929) is the classic survey of Tibeto-Burman morphology, outdated but not yet supplanted. Matisoff (1978) provides an excellent introduction to the problems of Sino-Tibetan lexical comparison.

The following grammars will give an impression of some of the range of variation found within Tibeto-Burman: Caughley (1982) is a detailed presentation of the verbal system of a conservative 'pronominalised' language and includes a synopsis of verb paradigms from other morphologically conservative languages; Hope (1974) is a detailed presentation of clause organisation in a language which has completely lost the Proto-Tibeto-Burman morphological system; Matisoff (1973) is the most complete grammatical description in existence of any Tibeto-Burman language.

References

Benedict, P.K. 1972. *Sino-Tibetan: A Conspectus* (Cambridge University Press, Cambridge)

Caughley, R. 1982. *The Syntax and Morphology of the Verb in Chepang* (Research School of Pacific Studies, Australian National University, Canberra)

Hale, A. 1982. *Research on Tibeto-Burman Languages* (Mouton, The Hague)

Hope, E. 1974. *The Deep Syntax of Lisu Sentences* (Research School of Pacific Studies, Australian National University, Canberra)

Matisoff, J. 1973. *The Grammar of Lahu* (University of California Press, Berkeley)

—— 1978. *Variational Semantics in Tibeto-Burman: The 'Organic' Approach to Linguistic Comparison* (ISHI Press, Philadelphia)

Shafer, R. 1957–63. *Bibliography of Sino-Tibetan Languages*, 2 parts.

—— 1966–73. *Introduction to Sino-Tibetan* (Otto Harrassowitz, Wiesbaden)

Wolfenden, S. 1929. *Outlines of Tibeto-Burman Linguistic Morphology* (Royal Asiatic Society, London)

41   Chinese

Charles N. Li and Sandra A. Thompson

1   Introduction: The Five Major Dialect Groups of Chinese

It is estimated that more than 1,000,000,000 people, approximately one-fourth of the earth's population, are speakers of some form of Chinese. Genetically, Chinese is an independent branch of the Sino-Tibetan family of languages (see Chapter 40). Within the Chinese branch, there are a number of dialects, which can be classified into a minimum of five groups on the basis of their structural affinities.

Mandarin. This is the major dialect group in China, both in terms of political importance and in terms of number of speakers. The native speakers of this dialect group represent approximately 70 per cent of the total Chinese population. They occupy the North China plain, the middle Yángzǐ plain, the Huái plain, the north-east plain, the Sìchuān basin and most of Guǎngxī, Guèizhōu and Yúnnán provinces. The term 'Mandarin' is an English translation of the old Běijīng expression *guān-huà* 'official language', which was for many centuries the dialect of Běijīng. In modern China, Běijīng dialect was accepted as a standard for the official language in the early part of this century. Since the 1950s, because of political and geographical boundaries, the official language of China, called *pǔtōnghuà* 'common speech', and the official language of Táiwān, called *guóyǔ* 'national language', differ from each other slightly in both vocabulary and grammar, although both are based on the Běijīng dialect. One of the four official languages of Singapore, *huáyǔ*, is also based on the Běijīng dialect. Again, it is somewhat different from both *pǔtōnghuà* and *guóyǔ*.

The other basis for considering Mandarin as the 'major' Chinese dialect group is that, in terms of both vocabulary and structure, the modern written language is closer to Mandarin than to any of the other dialects.

Wú. The Wú dialects are spoken around the lower Yángzǐ River and its tributaries: the provinces of Jiāngsū, Zhèjiāng and Ānhuī, which include the major urban centres of Shànghǎi, Sūzhōu and Wēnzhōu.

811

Map 41.1: Dialect Map of China

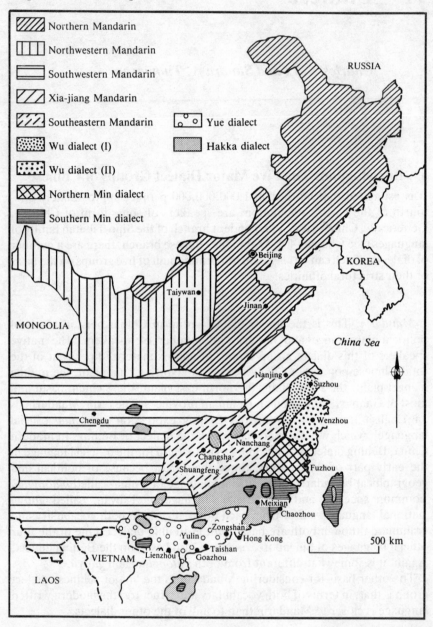

▨ Northern Mandarin	
▥ Northwestern Mandarin	
▤ Southwestern Mandarin	
▧ Xia-jiang Mandarin	
▨ Southeastern Mandarin	⬭ Yue dialect
▦ Wu dialect (I)	▨ Hakka dialect
⠿ Wu dialect (II)	
⬲ Northern Min dialect	
▤ Southern Min dialect	

Mǐn. These dialects are spoken by people living in Táiwān and Fújiàn provinces and Hǎinán Island in the Gulf of Tonkin. In English, these dialects are sometimes referred to as 'Fukkianese', 'Hokkianese', 'Amoy' and

'Taiwanese'. Most of the people of Táiwān are descendants of Mǐn speakers who emigrated from the coastal regions of Fújiàn province. For this reason, 85 per cent of the people in Táiwān still speak a Mǐn dialect as their native language. For the same reason, most of the speakers of Chinese in Singapore are also native speakers of a Mǐn dialect.

Yuè. The Yuè dialects are spoken primarily in the province of Guǎngdōng. Yuè dialects, including the well known Cantonese, the language of Guǎngzhōu (Canton), are spoken in many parts of the Chinese diaspora, particularly Hong Kong and overseas Chinese settlements such as the Chinatowns in the United States, Europe and South-East Asia. For this reason, many of the English words borrowed from Chinese have their origins in Cantonese, such as *kumquat* from Cantonese [kamkwat] and *chop suey* from Cantonese [tsap sui].

Hakka. The Hakka dialects are the least well known outside of China, because few of the Hakka people have emigrated from China. Most of the Hakka are scattered throughout southeastern China in Guǎngxī province and throughout the Mǐn and Yuè regions, as small, tightly-knit agricultural communities. Historically, the Hakka people were northerners who moved south during several waves of migration. Their name Hakka means 'guest', indicating their immigrant status in the southern areas to which they moved.

We have chosen to use the term 'dialect' for these five major groups of languages, even though the differences among them, in terms of both vocabulary and structure, are sufficient to cause mutual unintelligibility. There are two reasons for this choice. First, genetically related languages of one nation are typically considered 'dialects'. Secondly, China has always had a uniform written language which is logographic. People who cannot understand each others' speech can still read the same written language provided that they are educated. This tends to reinforce the idea of 'dialects' as opposed to separate languages.

We adopt this usage of dialect, even though it is based on political and social considerations rather than linguistic ones. In section 5, we will discuss the written language, but first, we will describe some of the structural properties common to Chinese dialects.

2   Phonology

All Chinese dialects, with rare exceptions, share two easily perceptible phonological properties: they are all tone languages, and they have a very highly constrained syllable structure. We will talk about each of these properties in turn.

2.1 Tone

When we speak of a tone language, we mean a language in which every stressed syllable has a significant contrastive pitch. This pitch may be level or contour, but it is an integral part of the pronunciation of the syllable and it serves to distinguish one syllable from another. Běijīng Mandarin serves as a good example, since it has one of the simplest tone systems of the Chinese dialects. As shown in table 41.1, it has four basic tones.

Table 41.1: Běijīng Mandarin Tones

Tone 1:	high level	⌐	55
Tone 2:	high rising	⌐	35
Tone 3:	dipping/falling	⋀	214
Tone 4:	high falling	∨	51

The symbols in the column second from the right are known as tone letters. They provide a simplified time-pitch graph of the voice, where the vertical line on the right serves as a reference line for pitch height. The numbers at the right represent the pitch of the tone according to a scale of five levels, with 1 being the lowest and 5 the highest. Thus, tone 1 is a high level tone pronounced at the same high pitch (level 5) for its duration, while tone 4 is a falling tone which starts with the high pitch at level 5 and ends with the low pitch at level 1.

If we take the syllable [i] in Běijīng Mandarin with each of the four tones, we have four different words, as is shown in table 41.2.

Table 41.2: Four Words in Bějīng Mandarin

[i]^{55}	⌐	'cloth'
[i]^{35}	⌐	'to suspect'
[i]^{214}	⋀	'chair'
[i]^{51}	∨	'meaning'

The Romanisation system officially adopted by the government in Běijīng, called Pīnyīn, represents the tones by means of diacritic marks above the nuclear vowel of the word. The diacritic mark for the high level tone is /⌐/, for the rising tone, /'/, for the curve tone, /ˇ/, and for the falling tone /'/. For example, the four words of table 41.2 written in Pīnyīn are: yī 'cloth', yí 'to suspect', yǐ 'chair', yì 'meaning'.

Tonal variation accounts for the most common differences among the dialects of China. It is often true that the dialects in two villages, just a few miles apart, have different tone systems. As we have stated, Běijīng Mandarin has one of the simplest tone systems of all dialects: it has the second smallest number of tones (only 4) and the rules governing the behaviour of the tones are relatively simple. In contrast, Cantonese has nine tones, six of regular length, and three for so-called 'short' syllables, as shown in table 41.3 (the short syllables are those with short vowels which end in *p*, *t* or *k*). (Tone 1 has a free variant 53).

Table 41.3: The Tones of Cantonese

(1) 55	(4) 21	(7) 5
(2) 35	(5) 23	(8) 3
(3) 33	(6) 22	(9) 2

In many dialects, the complexity of the tone system may be manifested not only in the number of tones, but also in the phenomenon of 'tone sandhi', that is, a change of tones when two or more syllables are pronounced together. The most complicated tone sandhi phenomena can be found in the Wú and Mǐn dialects. For example, in Cháozhōu, a southern Mǐn dialect, there are eight tones for syllables in isolation, including two short tones belonging to syllables with final stops. When a syllable is followed by another syllable, however, tone sandhi occurs: that is, each 'isolation tone' changes to a different tone, called a 'combination tone'. Table 41.4 shows the Cháozhōu isolation tones and their corresponding combination tones.

Table 41.4: Cháozhōu Tones

| Isolation tones | 5 | 2 | 33 | 11 | 35 | 53 | 213 | 55 |
| Combination tones | 3 | 5 | 33 | 11 | 31 | 35 | 53 | 13 |

This means that for each monosyllabic word, speakers of the Cháozhōu dialect learn its isolation tone, the tone it has when it stands by itself, and the rules converting the isolation tone to the combination tone, the tone it has when it is followed by another syllable.

Let us look at an example of how tone sandhi works in Cháozhōu. In table 41.4 we can see that the high short tone in the first column becomes a mid short tone in combination. Thus, if we take the word for 'one' in isolation, we have

[tsek] ⌐ 5 'one'

but if we put it in front of the syllables meaning 'meal', it changes to

[tsek] ⊣ 3

like this:

[tsek] ⊣ 3   [tuʊŋ] ⟍ 53   [puŋ] ⌐ 11   'one meal'

A glance at table 41.4 will reveal that the isolation tone of the second syllable [tuʊŋ], which is a 'classifier' (see page 823), is ⟋ 213.

2.2 Syllable Structure in Chinese

The syllable structure of all the Chinese dialects is relatively simple compared with that of, say, English: no dialect, for example, allows consonant clusters and all dialects allow only a restricted set of consonants in syllable-final position. As with tone, Běijīng Mandarin has a relatively simple syllable structure:

$$(C) (V)V(\begin{smallmatrix}V\\N\end{smallmatrix})$$

Every syllable has a nuclear vowel, which may occur with another vowel to form a diphthong or with two other vowels to form a triphthong. Initial and final consonants are optional and the only final consonants which are permitted are nasals (specifically, [n] and [ŋ]).

To take an example which differs from Mandarin, in Cantonese, a syllable may have a diphthong, but not a triphthong. Also, a Cantonese syllable may have an unreleased stop ([p], [t], [k]) or a nasal ([m], [n], [ŋ]) in the final position. The Cantonese syllable structure may be represented by the following schema:

$$(C)(V)V(C)$$

3 Morphology

Morphology concerns the internal structure of words. When a Chinese dialect is compared to a Slavonic or Romance language, for instance, one of the most obvious features to emerge is the relative simplicity of its word structure. Most Chinese words are made up of just one or two morphemes. In particular, Chinese dialects have few inflectional morphemes. Thus, while many languages, including those in the Indo-European, Semitic, Bantu, Altaic and Tibeto-Burman families, typically have inflectional morphemes indicating categories such as tense/aspect and number/person of the subject or object for verbs or categories such as gender and case for nouns, no such inflectional categories exist for Chinese dialects.

The type of morphological device found in Chinese dialects tends to involve compounds and derivational morphemes rather than inflectional ones. This type of morphological device is especially common in modern Mandarin. Because of this, the traditional characterisation of Mandarin as 'monosyllabic' is no longer accurate. A 'monosyllabic' language would be one in which each word consisted of just one syllable. While no language could be expected to be totally monosyllabic, this characterisation is certainly more applicable to the Yuè and Mǐn dialect groups than it is to Mandarin. According to one popular dictionary, roughly two-thirds of the basic everyday Běijīng Mandarin vocabulary consists of polysyllabic words. Table 41.5 provides a sample of disyllabic words in Běijīng Mandarin whose counterparts in Guǎngzhōu (Yuè) and Shàntóu (Mǐn) are monosyllabic.

Table 41.5: Mandarin Disyllabic Words and Their Corresponding Guǎngzhōu and Shàntóu Monosyllabic Words

	Běijīng Mandarin	Guǎngzhōu (Yuè)	Shàntóu (Mǐn)
'gold'	[tɕin-tsɿ]	[kɐm]	[kim]
'pond'	[tʂʰɿ-tsɿ]/[tʂʰɿ-tʰaŋ]	[tʰɔŋ]	[ti]
'ant'	[ma-i]	[ŋɐi]	[hia]
'tail'	[uei-pa]/[i-pa]	[mei]	[bue]
'clothing'	[i-ʂaŋ]	[sam]	[sã]
Negative existential verb	[mei-iou]	[mou]	[bo]
'good-looking'	[xau-kʰaŋ]	[lɛŋ]	[ŋia]
'to know'	[tsɿ-tau]	[tɕi]	[tsai]
'contemptible'	[tʰau-iɛn]	[tsɐŋ]	[lou]

There is a historical explanation for the fact that Mandarin has the highest proportion of polysyllabic words of all the Chinese dialects. The ancestral language of the modern Chinese dialects was monosyllabic. Because of phonological changes that have taken place, more extensively in Mandarin than in the southern dialects, many formerly distinct syllables in Mandarin have become homophonous. Thus, where Guǎngzhōu, for example, still has a contrastive distinction between syllable-final [m] and [n] as shown in the words: [kɐm] 'gold' and [kɐn] 'tael', Běijīng Mandarin no longer retains that contrastive distinction. The Běijīng counterpart of the two distinct Guǎngzhōu syllables is just the one syllable, [tɕin]. If the Běijīng word for 'gold' (as listed in table 41.5) hadn't become the disyllabic form [tɕīn-tsɿ], the two Běijīng words for 'gold' and 'tael' would have been homophonous in the form [tɕīn]. The threat of too many homophonous words has forced the language to increase dramatically the proportion of polysyllabic words, principally by means of compounding or adding on a derivational suffix. As an example of the latter, the second syllable of the disyllabic Běijīng word, [tɕīn-tsɿ] 'gold', was formerly a diminutive suffix. It has lost its diminutive meaning in the word [tɕīn-tsɿ] and is now merely a part of the word for 'gold'. Let us also look at an example of a disyllabic Běijīng word obtained through compounding: [tʰǎu-ièn] 'contemptible'. This is a compound historically derived from two monosyllabic words, [tʰǎu] 'to beg' and [ièn] 'contempt'. The Guǎngzhōu and the Shàntóu words for 'contemptible' remain monosyllabic, as shown in table 41.5.

3.1   Compounds

3.1.1   Resultative Verb Compound

One important type of verb compound is known as the 'resultative verb compound', where the second part of the compound signals some result of the action or process conveyed by the first part. Here are some examples from Běijīng Mandarin:[1] *dǎ-pò* 'hit-broken = hit (it) with the result that it is broken', *mà-kū* 'scold-cry = scold (someone) with the result that s/he cries'. The following sentences illustrate the use of these two sample resultative verb compounds.

wǒ   bǎ   píngzi   dǎ-pò   le
I   *ba*   bottle   hit-broken crs.
'I broke the bottle.'

tā   bǎ   wǒ   mà-kū   le
s/he *ba*   I   scold-cry crs.
'S/he scolded me so much that I cried.'

One characteristic of all resultative verb compounds is that they may occur in what is known as the 'potential' form, which involves the insertion of -*de*- or -*bu*- between the two parts of the compound. The insertion of -*de*- has the effect of giving the compound an affirmative potential meaning, i.e. 'can', while the insertion of -*bu*- gives the compound the negative potential meaning 'cannot'. Consider one of the examples above, *dǎ-pò* 'hit-break'. Its two potential forms would be:

dǎ -de -pò   dǎ -bu   -pò
hit -can -broken   hit -cannot-broken

---

[1] Most of the examples given from here on will be from Běijīng Mandarin, which has an accepted Romanisation (Pīnyīn) familiar to some readers, rather than from other dialects for which we would have to use a phonetic notation. A table of Pīnyīn symbols and their corresponding IPA values is provided in Appendix 1.

Here they are used in sentences:

tā   *dǎ*   *-de* *-pò*   nèi   -ge   píngzi
s/he   hit   -can -broken that -cl. bottle
'S/he can break that bottle.'

tā   *dǎ*   *-bu*   *-pò*   nèi   -ge   píngzi
s/he   hit   -cannot -broken that -cl. bottle
'S/he cannot break that bottle.'

Another type is the directional resultative verb construction. The first verb in a directional resultative verb construction implies movement and the second, which may itself be a compound, signals the direction in which the person or thing moves as a result. Here is an example and a sample sentence in which it occurs:

pǎo-húi -lái
run-return-come
'run back'

tā   *pǎo-húi* *-lái* le
s/he   run-return-come   crs.
'S/he ran back.'

3.1.2 Parallel Verb Compounds

The two verbs that constitute a parallel verb compound are either synonymous, nearly synonymous or similar in meaning. Here are some examples:

pí-fá	'tired-tired = tired'	jiàn-zhú	'build-build = build'
fáng-shǒu	'defend-defend = defend'	bāng-zhù	'help-help = help'
fàng-qì	'loosen-abandon = to give up'	piāo-liú	'drift-flow = drift'

3.1.3 Nominal Compounds

As in English, Chinese has a wide range of nominal compound types. Here are a few examples, illustrating the different semantic relations between the nominal components of the compound.

(i) N_2 is made of N_1

máo-yī   'wool-clothing = sweater'
tiě-hézi   'iron-box = iron box'

(ii) N_2 is a container of N_1

fàn-wǎn   'rice-bowl = rice bowl'
shǔi-píngzi 'water-bottle = water bottle'

(iii) N₁ and N₂ are parallel

fù-mǔ   'father-mother = parents'
guó-jiā   'country-home = country'

(iv) N₂ denotes a product of N₁

jī-dàn   'chicken-egg = egg'
měiguó-huò   'America-product = American product'

(v) N₂ denotes a malady of N₁

xīngzàng-bìng   'heart-disease = heart disease'
fèi-yán   'lung-inflammation = inflammation of the lung'

(vi) N₂ is used for N₁

qiāng-dàn   'gun-bullet = bullet'
xié-yóu   'shoe-oil = shoe polish'

(vii) N₁ denotes the location of N₂

tián-shǔ   'field-mouse = field mouse'
tái-bù   'table-cloth = tablecloth'

3.1.4 Noun-Verb Compounds

The Chinese dialects also have several types of compounds consisting of a noun and a verb. One type might be called the 'subject-predicate' compound, where the first element historically has a 'subject' relationship to the second element. Here are two examples with sentences illustrating their usage:

dǎn-dà   'gall-big = brave'

tā   hěn   *dǎn-dà*
s/he   very   brave
'S/he is very brave.'

mìng-kǔ   'life-bitter = ill-fated'

wǒ   hěn   *mìng-kǔ*
I   very   ill-fated
'I have a hard life.'

Another type of noun-verb compound is one in which the second element historically bears a 'direct object' relationship to the first element. Here are two examples with sentences illustrating their usage:

xíng-lǐ   'perform-salutation = salute'

wǒ   gěi   tā   *xíng-lǐ*
I   to   s/he salute
'I saluted him/her.'

zhěn-tóu   'rest-head = pillow'

wǒ   yǒu   liǎng -ge   *zhěn-tóu*
I   have two -cl.   pillow
'I have two pillows.'

3.2 Reduplication

As a morphological process, 'reduplication' means that a morpheme is repeated so that the original morpheme together with its repetition form a new word. One way in which reduplication is used in Chinese is to indicate that an action is being done 'a little bit'. Here is an example:

shuō-shuo   'speak-speak = speak a little'

nǐ   *shuō-shuo*   neì -jiàn   shì
you speak a little that -cl.   matter
'Speak a little about that matter!'

Adjectives can also be reduplicated, the semantic effect of which is to intensify their meaning. For example: *hóng* 'red', *hóng-hóng* 'vividly red'.

Manner adverbs can be formed from reduplicated adjectives. For example, *màn* 'slow' is an adjective but *màn-màn-de* 'slowly' is an adverb formed by reduplicating the adjective *màn* and adding on the particle *-de*. The following sentence illustrates the usage of the adverb, *màn-màn-de* 'slowly':

tā   *màn-màn-de*   pǎo
s/he slowly   run
'S/he runs slowly.'

3.3 Affixation

Affixation is the morphological process whereby a bound morpheme is added to another morpheme to form a larger unit. Compared to Indo-European languages, Chinese has few affixation processes and most of them are not inflectional, but derivational.

3.3.1 Prefixes

There are very few prefixes in Chinese. *Kě-* is an example of a prefix which can be added to verbs to form adjectives; its meaning can be described as '-able', as shown in the following examples:

kě-ài   'lovable'   ài   'to love'
kě-xiào 'laughable'   xiào 'to laugh'
kě-kào   'dependable'   kào   'to depend'

Another prefix is *dì-*, which is added to numerals to form ordinals, as in:

dì-liù 'sixth' liù 'six'

3.3.2 Suffixes

There are several categories of suffixes which are very important in Chinese grammar. Foremost among them is the category of verb suffixes serving as aspect markers. Aspect markers vary from dialect to dialect. Here, we will cite two examples from Běijīng Mandarin.

'Aspect' refers to how a situation is viewed with respect to its internal make-up. To take an example, let us first look at an English sentence:

Cheryl **was watching TV** when I **spilled the tea**.

In this English sentence, the first verb phrase, *was watching TV*, differs significantly from the second verb phrase, *spilled the tea*, because the two phrases reflect different ways in which the two situations are viewed. The second verb phrase presents the totality of the situation referred to without reference to its internal make-up: the entire situation is viewed as a single unanalysable whole. When a language has a special verb form to indicate the viewing of an event in its entirety, we say that that form signals the 'perfective' aspect. In Běijīng Mandarin, the suffix *-le* is used for the perfective aspect.

The first verb phrase, *was watching TV*, does not present the situation of Cheryl's watching TV in its entirety. Instead, it makes explicit reference to the internal make-up of 'TV watching', presenting it as ongoing, referring neither to its beginning nor its end, but to its duration. Verbal markers signalling this ongoing/durative aspect can be called 'durative' aspect markers. In Běijīng Mandarin, the durative suffix is *-zhe*, whose occurrence is restricted to certain semantic types of verbs.

Here are some examples of the perfective and the durative suffixes in Běijīng Mandarin:

tā   bǎ   chēzi   mài-*le*
s/he *ba*   car   sell -perf.
'S/he sold the car.'

wǒ   chī-le   sān -wǎn fàn
I   eat-perf.   three-bowl rice
'I ate three bowls of rice.'

tā   chuān-zhe yī -shuāng xīn   xiézi
s/he wear -dur. one-pair   new   shoe
'S/he is wearing a pair of new shoes.'

qiáng-shàng guà -zhe yī -fu   huà
wall -on   hang-dur. one-cl.   painting
'There is a painting hanging on the wall.'

Another important category of suffixes is classifiers. A classifier is a morpheme co-occurring with a noun which is individuated or specified in the discourse, that is, a noun which occurs with a numeral, a quantifier or a demonstrative. Classifiers do not occur with a noun which is non-referential or non-specific. When a noun is individuated, quantified or specified, the classifier occurs as a suffix of the numeral, the quantifier or the demonstrative. Other than the general classifier -*ge* which can occur with most nouns, a noun in Chinese can in general occur with only one classifier and the speaker must learn which classifier goes with which noun. For example, the Běijīng classifier for books is -*běn*, so that 'that book' is:

nèi -*běn* shū
that-cl. book

The classifier for snakes is -*tiáo*, so that 'four snakes' is:

sì   -*tiáo* shé
four-cl. snake

Here are a few other classifiers:

-zhāng   for tables, maps, papers etc.
-jiàn   for garments such as shirts, coats, sweaters, and events, news etc.
-lì   for pearls, marbles, grains of sand, wheat, rice, corn or millet etc.

Earlier we pointed out that classifiers are not used when a noun is non-referential or non-specific. The following sentence contains an example of a non-referential noun, *diànyǐng* 'movie':

wǒ bu   cháng kàn diànyǐng
I   not often see movie
'I don't see movies often.'

A third important category of suffixes in Chinese is that of locative suffixes. These occur with nouns — often marked with a preposition — to specify location with respect to the referent of the noun. Here are some examples:

tā   zài chuáng-*shàng*
s/he at   bed   -on
'S/he is on the bed.'

tā   cóng fángzi-li pǎo-chū-lái   le
s/he from house-in run-exit-come crs.
'S/he came running out from the house.'

Besides the three categories of grammatical suffixes mentioned above, there are the genitive morpheme -*de* and the manner adverbial marker, which also has the form *-de*. Both the genitive morpheme and the adverbial marker occur as suffixes. Examples follow:

wŏ-*de*   qìchē
I -gen. car
'my car'

màn-man-*de*   zŏu
slowly   walk
'Walk slowly!'

Finally we will cite two derivational suffixes. Productive derivational suffixes are not numerous in Chinese, and they do not occupy a very important position in Chinese grammar. One example of a derivational suffix is *-xué* '-ology', as in:

dòngwù-xué	'animal-ology = zoology'
zhíwù -xué	'plant-ology = botany'
shéhuì -xué	'society-ology = sociology'
lìshĭ -xué	'history-ology = history'

Another example of a derivational suffix is *-jiā* '-ist', as in:

lìshĭxué -jiā	'history-ist = historian'
lĭlùn -jiā	'theory-ist = theorist'
xiăoshuō -jiā	'novel-ist = novelist'
dòngwuxué-jiā	'zoology-ist = zoologist'

4 Syntax

4.1 Chinese as an Isolating Language

One of the first things a person familiar with Indo-European languages notices about Chinese is its lack of grammatical inflections. Although there is a morphological category of aspect in Chinese (as discussed above in section 3.3), most words in Chinese have one immutable form, which does not change according to number, case, gender, tense, mood or any of the other inflectional categories familiar from other languages. Languages with very little grammatical inflectional morphology are known as 'isolating' languages. What are some of the concomitant factors of the isolating character of Chinese?

First, there is no case morphology signalling differences between grammatical relations such as subject, direct object or indirect object, nor is there any 'agreement' or cross-indexing on the verb to indicate what is subject and what is object. In Chinese, in fact, there are few grammatical reasons for postulating grammatical relations, although there are, of course, ways of distinguishing who did what to whom, just as there are in all languages. One way to tell who did what to whom is by word order: ordinarily, the noun phrase before the verb is the agent or the experiencer and the noun phrase after the verb is the patient or affected participant, much as in English. Furthermore, in natural discourse, it is usually clear who is the agent and who or what is the patient without any special marking.

A corollary to this de-emphasis of grammatical relations is the fact that Chinese discourse makes extensive use of 'topic-comment' constructions, as shown in the following examples:

> zhèi-ge dìfang zhòng   màizi   hǎo
> this-cl. place plant wheat   good
> 'At this place, it is good to plant wheat.'

> jiāzhōu   qìhou hǎo
> California climate good
> 'California, its climate is good.'

A second factor in the lack of grammatical inflectional morphology is that gender, plurality and tense are either indicated by lexical choice or not indicated at all.

A third factor is the absence of overt markers signalling the relationship of the verbs in the 'serial verb construction'. For instance, consider the following example:

> wǒ   jiào tā   mǎi júzī   chī
> I   tell s/he buy orange eat
> 'I told him/her to buy oranges to eat.'

Notice that the English translation of this sentence contains the morpheme *to*, which signals that *buy* and *eat* are subordinate verbs with unspecified future tense. The Běijīng Mandarin version has no such overt signal; the relationship between the verbs must be inferred from their meanings and from the discourse context in which the combination occurs. In Chinese, there are many different types of such inferred relationships. Here are a few examples where the English translations indicate the various relationships.

> wǒ   yǒu yí -ge píngguǒ hěn hǎo chī
> I   have one-cl. apple   very good eat
> 'I have an apple which is very delicious.'

> tā   tǎng zài chuáng -shang kàn shū
> s/he lie at   bed   -on   see book
> 'S/he lay in bed reading.'

> tā   qù   zhōngguó xué zhōngguó huà
> s/he go   China   learn China   painting
> 'S/he went to China to learn Chinese painting.'

Finally, sentences containing coverbs may be viewed as a type of serial verb construction. The class of coverbs contains words that are partly like verbs and partly like prepositions. They have this mixed status because most of them used to be verbs at earlier stages of the language and many of them still have the properties of verbs and can be used as verbs that have similar meaning. Consider, for example, the following sentences:

    tā   zài   jiā -li   gōngzuò
    s/he at   home -in   work
    'S/he works at home.'

    tā   dào   Běijīng   qù-le
    s/he arrive Běijīng   go-perf.
    'S/he went to Běijīng.'

Zài and *dào* are coverbs. Both may serve as verbs, as in the following:

    nǐ   zài   nǎr?
    you   at   where
    'Where are you?'

    wǒmen   dào -le   Běijīng   le
    we   arrive-perf. Běijīng   crs.
    'We have arrived in Běijīng.'

The Chinese coverb phrase consisting of a coverb and a noun is equivalent to the English prepositional phrase. In English a preposition is normally distinct from a verb. In Chinese, however, the separation of a coverb and a verb is much less clear-cut, and sentences containing coverbs such as those above can be viewed as a type of serial verb construction.

4.2 'Adjectives'

Strictly speaking, there is no class of words in Chinese that we can call 'adjective'. That is, while there are certainly words which denote qualities or properties of entities, from a grammatical point of view it is difficult to distinguish 'adjectives' from 'verbs'. There are at least three ways in which 'adjectives' can be seen to behave like verbs.

First, in Chinese, words denoting qualities and properties do not occur with a copula as they do in Indo-European languages. For example, the English and Běijīng Mandarin versions of a sentence such as *Molly is very intelligent* differ with respect to the presence or absence of the copular verb.

    mǎlì   hěn   cōngming
    Molly   very   intelligent
    'Molly is very intelligent.'

Thus, in English, adjectives have the distinguishing characteristic of occurring with a copula when they are used predicatively. In Chinese, on the other hand, such words appear without any copula, just as verbs do.

Secondly, quality and property words in Chinese are negated by the same particle *bù* as are verbs:

tā   *bù*   kāixīn
s/he   not   happy
'S/he is not happy.'

tā   *bù*   chī   ròu
s/he   not   eat   meat
'S/he does not eat meat.'

Thirdly, when an 'adjective' modifies a noun, it occurs with the same nominalising particle *de* as verb phrases do:

kāixīn   *-de*   rén
happy   noms.   person
'people who are happy'

chī   *ròu*   *de*   rén
eat   meat   noms. person
'people who eat meat'

For these reasons, it is sensible to consider quality and property words in Chinese simply as a subclass of verbs, one which we might call 'adjectival verbs'.

4.3   Questions

4.3.1   Question-word Questions

Question-word questions are formed in Chinese by the use of question words whose position is the same as non-question words having the same function. For example, consider the positions of *shéi?* 'who?' and *shénme?* 'what?' in the following examples:

tā   zhǎo   *shéi?*
s/he   look-for   who
'Who is s/he looking for?'

shéi   zhǎo   tā?
who   look-for   s/he
'Who is looking for him/her?'

nǐ   shuō *shénme?*
you   say what
'What are you saying?'

> *shénme*   guì?
> what   expensive
> 'What is expensive?'

Similarly, *nǎlǐ?* 'where?' can occur wherever a locative noun phrase can occur:

> tā   zài   *nǎlǐ*   yóuyǒng?
> s/he at   where   swim
> 'Where does s/he swim?'

As would be expected, question words which modify nouns occur before the noun, the position in which ordinary noun modifiers are found. The following sentence illustrates the prenominal position of *duōshǎo?* 'how many?':

> nǐ   mǎi-le   *duōshǎo*   rìlì?
> you   buy-perf.   how many   calendar
> 'How many calendars did you buy?'

4.3.2 Yes-no Questions

Chinese has several processes for forming 'yes-no' questions. First, such a question can be signalled by intonation: a rising intonation with a declarative clause has an interrogative force, as in most languages.

Another way to signal yes-no questions is to use a question particle at the end of the sentence. In Běijīng Mandarin the particles *ma* and *ne* are used for this purpose, as in:

> nǐ   xǐhuan   Xīān *ma*?
> you   like   Xīān Q
> 'Do you like Xīān?'

> nǐ   jiějie   shì   gōngchéngshī,   nǐ   mèimei   *ne*?
> you   elder-sister be   engineer   you   younger-sister Q
> 'Your elder sister is an engineer — what about your younger sister?'

Chinese also has another way of forming yes-no questions: an affirmative and a negative version of the same proposition can be combined to make what is known as an 'A-not-A' question. Here are some examples from Běijīng Mandarin:

> nǐ   *xǐhuan-bu -xǐhuan*   tā?
> you   like -not-like   s/he
> 'Do you like him/her?'

> tā   *chī-bu -chī*   píngguǒ?
> s/he eat-not-eat   apple
> 'Does s/he eat apples?'

5   The Writing System

The Chinese writing system is called a logographic or character system, because each symbol is a character/logograph. There are five processes by which the characters are created. We will briefly discuss those five processes in the following:

5.1   Pictographs

Writing in China began over 4,000 years ago with drawings of natural objects. The pictures were gradually simplified and formalised, giving rise to pictorial characters, called pictographs. For example:

Table 41.6: Pictographs in Chinese Writing

Old form	Modern form		Meaning
林林	林	/lín/	'forest'
⧸⧸⧸	川	/chuān/	'river'
⊙	日	/rì/	'sun'

5.2   Ideographs

Ideographs are characters derived from diagrams symbolising ideas or abstract notions. For example, the diagrams ˙— and —˙ were created to symbolise the notions 'above' and 'below'. Today the characters denoting 'above' and 'below' have become 上 /shàng/ and 下 /xià/ respectively.

5.3   Compound Ideographs

A compound ideograph is a character whose meaning is in some way represented by the combination of the meanings of its parts. For example, the character 譶 /tà/, meaning 'loquacious', is formed by combining the character 言 /yán/ 'speak' three times; and the character 明 /míng/ 'bright' is a compound of the character 日 /rì/ 'sun' and the character 月 /yuè/ 'moon', because the sun and the moon are the natural sources of light.

5.4   Loan Characters

Loan characters result from borrowing a character for a word whose pronunciation is the same as that of another word represented by that character. For example, in an earlier stage of the Chinese language, the character 易 /yì/ denoting 'scorpion' was borrowed to stand for the word meaning 'easy' because 'easy' and 'scorpion' had the same pronunciation. In modern Chinese, a new character has been created for the word 'scorpion' and the character, 易 /yì/, denotes 'easy'.

5.5   Phonetic Compounds

A phonetic compound is the combination of two characters, one representing a semantic feature of the word, the other representing the phonetic, i.e. the pronunciation of the word. Consider the character, 鈾 /yóu/ 'uranium', for example. The character is composed of the two characters, 金 /jīn/ and 由 /yóu/. The first, 金 /jīn/, has the meaning 'metal', signifying the metallic nature of uranium. The second character, 由 /yóu/, has a pronunciation which approximates the first syllable of the English word *uranium*, because when the new chemical element, uranium, was discovered, it was decided that the Chinese character should approximate the sound of the first syllable of the English word, *uranium*. Over 90 per cent of all modern Chinese characters are phonetic compounds and the process of forming phonetic compounds remains the standard method for creating new characters.

5.6   Simplification of the Writing System
The movement to simplify the Chinese writing system originated in the 1890s. However, it did not crystallise into an official policy enforced by the government throughout the country until the 1950s. The strategy of simplification involves a reduction in the number of strokes of commonly used characters. This reduction is achieved by eliminating parts of a

Appendix I
The Pīnyīn symbols and their corresponding IPA values

A. Consonants

Pīnyīn symbol	IPA
b	p
p	pʰ
m	m
f	f
d	t
t	tʰ
n	n
l	l
z	ts
c	tsʰ
zh	tʂ
ch	tʂʰ
sh	ʂ
r	r
j	tɕ
q	tɕʰ
x	ç
g	k
k	kʰ
h	x
ng	ŋ
w	w
y	j

character, condensing several strokes into one and replacing a complex character or parts of a complex character with a simpler one. Some examples are provided in table 41.7:

Table 41.7: Simplified Characters

Meaning	Original Version	Simplified version	Pronunciation (Pīnyīn)
'to bid farewell'	辭	辞	cí
'to cross'	過	过	guò
'should'	應	应	yīng
'solid'	實	实	shí
'door'	門	门	mén
'strong'	鞏	巩	gǒng

B. Vowels

Pīnyīn symbol	IPA	Context
a ⟶	[ɛ]	/i___n
	[a]	
o ⟶	[o]	/ $\left\{ \begin{matrix} u\_\_ \\ C\_\# \end{matrix} \right\}$
	[u]	/ $\left\{ \begin{matrix} a\_\_ \\ \_\_ng \end{matrix} \right\}$
e ⟶	[ə]	/___N
	[ɛ]	/ $\left\{ \begin{matrix} i\ \_\_ \\ ü\ \_\_ \end{matrix} \right\}$
	[i]	/___i
	[ɤ]	
	[ɪ]	/ $\left\{ \begin{matrix} zh \\ ch \\ sh \\ r \end{matrix} \right\}\_$
i		
	[ɿ]	/ $\left\{ \begin{matrix} z \\ c \\ s \end{matrix} \right\}\_$
	[ɹ]	
u ⟶	[y]	/y___
	[u]	
ü ⟶	[y]	
er ⟶	[ɚ]	

Bibliography

Newnham (1971) is a popular introduction to the Chinese language. Alleton (1973) is an introductory sketch of Chinese grammar. More thorough reference grammars are Chao (1968), a rich source of insightful observations and data, and Li and Thompson (1981), a major description of the syntactic and morphological structures of Chinese from the viewpoint of the communicative function of language. Rygaloff (1973) contains some interesting descriptive observations on Chinese grammar, while Henne et al. (1977) is pedagogical.

For sociolinguistics, Dil (1976) is a collection of articles on Chinese dialects, the Chinese writing system and issues on language and society by Y.-R. Chao; all are informative and comprehensible. DeFrancis (1967) is an informative article describing in detail the history of and governmental policies concerning the Chinese writing system. For Chinese dialects, Egerod (1967) is an important and valuable survey of the dialects themselves as well as of research into them. Hashimoto (1973) is a modern description of the Hakka dialect with a strong tilt towards historical phonology. Li (1983) offers a glimpse of the complex language-contact situation in western China.

Karlgren (1923) is an introduction to Chinese from the viewpoint of historical phonology. Yang (1974) is a useful source book for research, especially in the area of historical phonology.

Acknowledgement

During the preparation of this paper, Charles N. Li was partially supported by National Science Foundation Grant #BNS 83 08220.

References

Alleton, V. 1973. *Grammaire du chinois* (Presses Universitaires de France, Paris)

Chao, Y.-R. 1968. *A Grammar of Spoken Chinese* (University of California Press, Berkeley and Los Angeles)

DeFrancis, J. 1967. 'Language and Script Reform', in T. Sebeok (ed.), *Current Trends in Linguistics*, vol. 2, *Linguistics in East Asia and South East Asia* (Mouton, The Hague)

Dil, A.S. (ed.) 1976. *Aspects of Chinese Sociolinguistics: Essays by Yuen Ren Chao* (Stanford University Press, Stanford)

Egerod, S. 1967. 'Dialectology', in T. Sebeok (ed.), *Current Trends in Linguistics*, vol. 2, *Linguistics in East Asia and South East Asia* (Mouton, The Hague)

Forrest, R.A.D. 1965. *The Chinese Language* (Faber and Faber, London)

Hashimoto, M.J. 1973. *The Hakka Dialect: A Linguistic Study of its Phonology, Syntax and Lexicon* (Cambridge University Press, Cambridge)

Henne, H., O.B. Rongen and L.J. Hansen. 1977. *A Handbook on Chinese Language Structure* (Universitetsforlaget, Oslo)

Karlgren, B. 1923. *Sound and Symbol in Chinese* (Oxford University Press, London)

Li, C.N. 1983. 'Language in Contact in Western China', *Journal of East Asian Languages*, vol. 1, pp. 31–54

—— and S. Thompson. 1981. *Mandarin Chinese: A Functional Reference Grammar* (University of California Press, Berkeley and Los Angeles)

Newnham, R. 1971. *About Chinese* (Penguin Books, Harmondsworth and Baltimore)

Rygaloff, A. 1973. *Grammaire élémentaire du chinois* (Presses Universitaires de France, Paris)
Yang, P.F.-M. 1974. *Chinese Linguistics: A Selected and Classified Bibliography* (The Chinese University, Hong Kong)

42 Burmese

Julian K. Wheatley

1 Historical Background

Burmese is the official language of the Socialist Republic of the Union of Burma, a nation situated between the Tibetan plateau and the Malay peninsula and sharing borders with Bangladesh and India to the north-west, with China to the north-east and with Thailand to the south-east. Burmese belongs to the Burmish sub-branch of the Lolo-Burmese (or Burmese-Yi) branch of the Tibeto-Burman family and is one of the two languages in that family with an extensive written history (the other being Tibetan).

Standard Burmese has evolved from a 'central' dialect spoken by the Burman population of the lower valleys of the Irrawaddy and Chindwin rivers. Although it is now spoken over a large part of the country, regional variation remains relatively minor; apart from a few localisms, the speech of Mandalay in Upper Burma, for example, is indistinguishable from that of Rangoon, 400 miles to the south. A number of non-standard dialects, showing profound differences in pronunciation and vocabulary, are found in peripheral regions. The best known of these are Arakanese in the south-west, Tavoyan in the south-east and Intha in the east. Despite being heavily influenced in formal registers by the national language, the dialects preserve many features attested in the modern orthography but lost in standard speech.

Burma is a multi-national state. About two thirds of its population are Burmans. The other third is made up of a variety of ethnic groups, including other Tibeto-Burman-speaking peoples such as the Chin, Naga and Karen, Mon-Khmer peoples such as the Mon and Padaung, the Shan, whose language is closely related to Thai, and Chinese and Indians, who live mostly in the towns. The minority languages are partially differentiated from the national language by function, speakers tending to utilise the former in the family and in daily transactions and the latter in school, in dealing with authority and in cross-cultural communication. Most of the population of the country, provisionally put at about 37 million, speaks Burmese as either a first or second language.

The linguistic, as well as the historical evidence, shows that the ancestor of the Burmese language spread westwards from a centre in southwestern China, where its next of kin, the Yi (or Loloish) languages remain to this day. In doing so, it passed from the margins of the Tai and Chinese cultural sphere to a region profoundly influenced by Indian tradition. By the time the Burmese emerge on the historical scene, they have already begun to take on the religious and political features of the Indianised states that flourished in what is now the heart of Burma and from the first inscriptions their language shows the admixture of specialised Indic lexical stock and original Tibeto-Burman roots and grammatical structure that is so salient a feature of the Burmese language today.

It is difficult to be sure of the early history of the Burmese people. They seem to have appeared in central Burma near modern Mandalay in the ninth century AD, possibly in conjunction with raids by Nan Chao, a kingdom that flourished in southwestern China at that time. At any rate, by the tenth century they had established a state with a capital at Pagan and from the beginning of the eleventh to near the end of the thirteenth century, when Pagan was sacked by the Mongols, they were the dominant political power in much of what is now modern Burma. In the course of this rise to power, they apparently absorbed the remnants of the Pyu state. (The Pyu language, thought to have been Tibeto-Burman, is known only through inscriptions.) But their expansion was mainly at the expense of the Indianised Mon state that controlled much of Lower Burma and large parts of (modern) Thailand at that time. The Mon state, whose ruling class spoke the Mon-Khmer language of the same name, was to survive until the middle of the eighteenth century, its political fortunes tending to fluctuate inversely with those of the Burmese. Though the direction of cultural influence was ultimately reversed, the Mons were initially the donors. They were, for example, the source of the Theravada variety of Buddhism that is now dominant in Burma; according to tradition, the Burmese first acquired the Theravada scriptures, written in the old Indian canonical language of Pali, after defeating the Mons in AD 1057, and it is likely that Mon monks, brought to Pagan after that campaign, assisted in adapting their Indic script to the writing of Burmese. The earliest specimens of Burmese writing appear early in the next century. The best known of these is the Rajakumar (or Myazedi) inscription from central Burma, dated AD 1113, which records the offering of a gold Buddha image in four languages, Pali, Mon, Pyu and Burmese. By the end of the twelfth century, Burmese had become the main language of the inscriptions.

As the major substrate language in Lower Burma, Mon is the source of a number of words having to do with the natural and man-made environment; in addition, many Indic loanwords show the effects of transmission by way of Mon. Later we will see that it has also left its mark on the Burmese phonological system.

After the Mongol conquest of Pagan, Burmese rule in the south disintegrated, while political power in Upper Burma passed to a series of Shan rulers. The Shan probably arrived in Burma not long after the Burmans, part of the migration of Tai peoples that peaked in the early thirteenth century. But Shan rule in Upper Burma was nominal; inscriptions continued to be written in Burmese and in fact non-inscriptional literature, mainly poetry, made its appearance during this period. Later the Burmese came into contact with the Thais to the east, close kin of the Shan. Twice they conquered the Thai capital of Ayutthaya and Burmese secular drama owes its beginnings to Thai influence following the last of these invasions. But Shan and Thai influence on the Burmese language — though still inadequately researched — seems to be limited to loanwords for cultural items.

The first notable European presence in Burma was that of the Portuguese in the sixteenth century, followed in the next by small numbers of British, Dutch and French. The nineteenth century brought Burma into conflict with the British in India, who eventually annexed the country in three stages between 1826 and 1886; from 1886 until 1937, it was administered as a province of British India. Independence was restored in 1948.

British rule introduced a large number of words of English origin into Burmese. Many of these were later replaced by Burmese or Indic forms, but large numbers remain and new ones continue to appear, particularly in the fields of science, technology, business and politics. Loanwords tend to be fully adapted to Burmese segmental phonology (though the assignment of tones in the process is unpredictable), but in many cases they remain identifiable by their polysyllabic morphemes and their resistance to internal sandhi processes.

Rather than adapting English or other foreign phonetic material, the Burmese often form neologisms from their own lexical stock or from the highly esteemed classical languages of India, which are to Burmese (and many South-East Asian languages) what Latin and Greek are to European languages. Thus the word for 'spaceship', $?a+ka+\theta\acute{a}yin$ (plusses represent phonological boundaries: see page 841) is composed of $?a+ka+\theta\acute{a}$, a learned term meaning 'space, expanse', originally from Pali ĀKĀSA (transliterations are capitalised) and yin, spelled YĀṄ, derived from Pali YĀNA 'vehicle'. Yin also appears with $y\partial ha?$ 'a reel', originally from Hindi, in the word for 'helicopter', $y\partial ha?yin$, a compound coexisting with the English loan, $h\varepsilon li+k\acute{o}+p\partial ta$. Similar competition between a native formation and a loanword is seen in the two words for 'television', the transparent $yo?myin+\theta anc\grave{a}$, 'image-see sound-hear', and the opaque $t\varepsilon libihy\grave{i}n$.

Pali has been one of the main sources of new lexical material throughout the attested history of Burmese, with the result that the Burmese lexicon has come to have a two-tiered structure not unlike that of English, with its learned Romance and classical elements side by side with older and more colloquial Germanic forms. In Burmese the most common locutions, including grammatical words and formatives, nouns referring to basic cultural material and almost all verbs, tend to be composed of monosyllabic morphemes of Tibeto-Burman stock. Learned or specialised words (many of which must have entered the spoken language by way of the 'literary' language) often contain Pali material, frequently compounded with native stock. Pali is phonotactically quite compatible with Burmese, having no initial clusters and few stem-final consonants. Its morphemes are generally not monosyllabic, however. Disyllabic Pali words ending in a short A are usually rendered as a single syllable in Burmese, e.g.: *kan*, spelled KAM, 'fortune; deeds', from Pali KAMMA; *yoʔ*, spelled RUP, 'image', from Pali RŪPA. But otherwise, Pali loans (like those of English) are set off by the length of their morphemes: cf. *taya* 'constellation (of stars)', from Pali TĀRĀ, versus *cɛ* 'star', a Tibeto-Burman root; *htaná*, spelled ṬHĀNA 'place; department (in a university etc.)', from Pali ṬHĀNA, versus *neya* 'place', a compound of the native morphemes *ne* 'to live; be at' and *(ʔə)ya* 'place; thing'.

It is not uncommon to find two versions of a Pali word in Burmese, one closer to the Pali prototype than the other, e.g.: *man* and *maná*, both 'pride, arrogance' and both from Pali MĀNA, which occur together in the pleonastic expression *man maná hyí-* 'to be haughty, arrogant'.

Often a Pali prototype will be represented in a number of South-East Asian languages, providing a pan-South-East Asian technical lexicon comparable to the 'international' scientific vocabulary based on Latin and Greek: cf. Burmese *seʔ*, Mon *cɒt*, Khmer *cɤt*, Thai *cìt*, all from Pali CITTA 'mind'.

Despite inconsistent spelling and a restricted subject matter, the early inscriptional records probably render the spoken language of the time — Old Burmese — fairly directly. The inscriptional orthography, which can be interpreted in terms of Mon and, ultimately, Indic sound values, reveals a language phonetically very different from the modern spoken standard. It also shows major differences in lexical content, particularly among grammatical words and suffixes. But the grammatical categories and the order of words have remained relatively stable over the intervening 900 years.

The orthography underwent a number of changes after the inscriptional period, apparently reflecting a redistribution of certain vowels and a reduction in the number of medial consonants (see pages 844–5). By the end of the sixteenth century the orthography had assumed more or less its modern form, though there have been modifications in the spelling of individual words since. Pronunciation continued to change though, so there is now a wide gap between the spoken and literal values of the script, e.g.: *cɛʔ* 'chicken' is spelled KRAK; *-θɛ*, an agentive suffix, is spelled -SAÑ.

The modern orthography (sometimes called 'Written Burmese') is often taken as the reflection of an intermediate stage in the history of the language, i.e. Middle Burmese. The construct is a useful one, though the precise nature of the relationship still needs to be worked out.

Along with the orthography, some grammatical and lexical forms from earlier stages of Burmese live on in the language used for literature and most written communication, literary Burmese. Particularly in this century, differences between literary and spoken styles have tended to diminish, so that nowadays, although other 'classical' elements may still appear in literary Burmese, the only feature consistently distinguishing the two is the choice of the textually frequent post-nominal and post-verbal particles and other grammatical words. Literary Burmese retains a set of archaic grammatical morphemes, some reflecting earlier versions of their spoken equivalents, others reflecting forms that have been replaced in the spoken language. For example, instead of the locative postposition -hma 'in, at', literary Burmese uses -NHUIK (read -hnaiʔ) or -TWAṄ (read -twin); instead of the interrogative particles -là and -lè, it has -LO (read -lɔ̀) and -NAÑ: (read -nì), respectively; instead of the possessive marker -yé (-RAIʔ), it has -ʔEʔ (read -ʔì).

Not all the literary particles are functionally homologous with spoken forms. Whereas the spoken language makes use of a single postposition, -ko (-KUI), to mark both objects and goals of motion, the literary language makes use of three: -KUI 'object', -ʔĀ: (read -ʔà) '(usually) second or indirect object', and -SUIʔ (read -θó) 'goal of motion'.

It is possible to write Burmese as it is spoken, i.e. using the standard orthography with the syntax and lexicon of the spoken language. Indeed, in the 1960s an association of writers based in Mandalay advocated the development of such a 'colloquially based' literary style. Despite the appearance of a number of works in the new style, it was not generally adopted. This was partly because it lacked official sanction, but also because no style evolved which could convey the seriousness of purpose connoted by formal literary Burmese.

Particularly in the older and more classical styles of literary Burmese, the influence of Pali grammatical structures can also be seen; for until the nineteenth century, prose writing was mostly translations, adaptations and studies of Pali texts. The extreme case is that of the 'nissaya' texts, which have a history dating from the inscriptional period to the present day (cf. Okell 1965). In these, Burmese forms are inserted after each word or phrase of a Pali text; in many cases the Pali is omitted, resulting in a Burmese 'calque' on the original — Burmese words with Pali grammar. The interesting point is that in addition to mirroring Pali syntax, the nissaya authors developed conventions for representing Pali inflectional categories in Burmese, an uninflected language. For example, the Pali past participle, a category quite alien to Burmese, was sometimes represented periphrastically by placing the 'auxiliary' ʔAP 'be right, proper' after the verb: KHYAK

ʔAP SO CHWAM: 'the food that [should be] cooked, the cooked food'. In the spoken Burmese equivalent no auxiliary is required.

Not surprisingly, given the exalted position of Pali studies in Burmese culture, nissaya forms spread to other kinds of prose, so that Pali can be considered a significant substratum in many and perhaps all styles of literary Burmese.

2 Phonology

In presenting the inventory of phonological oppositions in Burmese, it is necessary to distinguish between full, or 'major' syllables, and reduced, or 'minor' ones. In reduced syllables the functional load is borne by the initial; no medial or final consonants are possible, and there are no tonal contrasts; the vowel is mid central and lax. Minor syllables occur singly or, occasionally, in pairs, always bound to a following major syllable. They can often be related to full syllables, if not synchronically, then historically: the first syllable of *səpwè* 'table' is shown from the spelling to derive from *sà* 'to eat': the word arose as a compound of 'eat' + 'feast'.

The iambic pattern of major preceded by minor syllable is more typical of Mon-Khmer languages than Tibeto-Burman. In fact, in Burmese, where closely bound *major* syllables are involved, it is the first that tends to be more prominent. Burmese probably absorbed the iambic pattern from Mon.

In major syllables, phonological oppositions are concentrated at two points, the initial and the vowel. There are two possible medial consonants, only one final consonant and four tonal contrasts, one of which is partially realised as final consonantism. The inventory of phonological oppositions can be discussed in terms of five syntagmatic positions: initial (C_i), medial (C_m), vowel (V), final (C_f) and tone (T). Of these, C_i, V and T are always present (though the glottal initial is represented by 'zero' in some transcriptions).

There are 34 possible C_i. Three of these are marginal: *r* may be found in learned loanwords; *hw* and *ð* are very rare. In table 42.1, C_i are arranged in three series, labelled 'aspirate', 'plain' and 'voiced'. The aspirates consist of aspirated stops and fricatives and voiceless nasals and resonants; the plain, of voiceless unaspirated stops and fricatives and voiced nasals and resonants; the voiced of voiced stops and fricatives only. The basis of this classification is morphological. First of all, while the plain and aspirate series may appear in absolute initial position (i.e. after pause) in both major word classes, the voiced series is restricted in that position mainly to nouns. The fact that such nouns can often be matched to verbs with plain or aspirate initials (e.g. *bì* 'a comb', *hpì* 'to comb') suggests that deverbative prefixes or other syllables are responsible for the voiced initials; assimilatory processes such as voicing

Table 42.1: Burmese Phonological Oppositions

	Stops and affricates	Fricatives	Nasals	Resonants
C_i Aspirate	hp ht hc hk	hs	hm hn hɲ hŋ	hl hy (hw) h
Plain	p t c k	s θ	m n ɲ ŋ	l y w(r) ʔ
Voiced	b d j g	z(ð)		

V Syllable type

Open	(-∅) i	e	ɛ	a	ɔ		o	u

Closed	(-n) ɪ	eɪ		a		aɪ aʊ oʊ ʊ	
	(-ʔ) ɪ	eɪ	ɛ	a		aɪ aʊ oʊ ʊ	

Transcribed as:

	i	e	ɛ	a	ɔ	ai	au	o	u

C_m -y-, -w- C_f -n, (-ʔ)

T ´ (creaky), ∅ (low), ` (high), -ʔ (checked)

are characteristic of word-internal positions in Burmese (see page 841). The incidence of nouns with C_i in the voiced series has been enlarged by loanwords, but the functional yield of the voiced series remains relatively low.

The aspirate series of C_i is not restricted to a particular class of words like the voiced, but it is associated with one member of derivationally related pairs of verbs such as the following: *pyɛʔ* 'be ruined', *hpyɛʔ* 'destroy'; *myín* 'be high', *hmyín* 'raise, make higher'. In these, the stative or intransitive member has a plain C_i, the causative or transitive, an aspirate. The alternation is represented by over 100 pairs of verbs, but it is not productive. The aspirates in these verbs record the effects of a sibilant causativising prefix, reconstructed at the Proto-Tibeto-Burman level as *s-* (see page 809). The original value of this prefix is reflected in 'irregular' pairs such as *ʔeʔ* 'sleep', *θeʔ* 'put to sleep' (the latter spelled SIP). The process has contributed to the incidence of the typologically rare voiceless nasals (*hm-*, *hn-*, *hɲ-*, *hŋ-*). As in many of the modern transcriptions of Burmese, the members of the aspirate series are consistently transcribed with a prescript 'h'; *hl-* and *hw-*, the latter found only in onomatopoeic words, are voiceless; *hy-* is actually a sibilant, [ʃ] or [ç], linked with *y-* in pairs such as *yɔ́* 'be reduced; be slack', *hyɔ́* [ʃɔ́] 'reduce; slacken'.

The medials are *-y-* and *-w-*. The second co-occurs with most C_i, but the first is only found with labials and occasionally with laterals.

In terms of our transcription there are two C_fs, *-n* and *-ʔ*, but in phonological terms -*?* can be regarded as a fourth tone; it precludes the possibility of any of the other tones and, though it almost always has some segmental realisation, it is also associated with a very short, high and even pitch contour. The reasons for transcribing it as though it were a C_f are partly historical: -*?* derives from an earlier set of final oral stops and is symbolised in the writing system as such.

To discuss the realisation of -*n* and -*?*, it is necessary to begin with the topic of sandhi. The shape of a syllable in Burmese varies according to the degree of syllable juncture. At least two degrees of juncture need to be recognised: open, representing minimal assimilation between syllables, and close, representing maximal. The distinction is realised mainly in terms of the duration, tonal contour and C_f-articulation of the first syllable and the manner of the C_i of the second. Phonetic values vary with tempo but can be generalised as follows: successive major syllables linked in *open* juncture preserve citation values of all variables; for the C_fs -*n* and -*?*, these are nasalisation of the preceding vowel ($\theta\grave{o}n$, [$\theta\widetilde{o\upsilon}$]) and (along with pitch and other features) final glottal stop (*hyi?*, [çɪ?]), respectively. In successive major syllables in *close* juncture, the first is shortened and has a truncated pitch contour, while the C_f of the first and the C_i of the second undergo varying degrees of mutual assimilation, the final tending to adopt the *position* of articulation of the following initial, the initial tending to adopt the *manner* of articulation of the preceding final, e.g.: *lè-hkàn* 'four rooms' is realised [lègã̀], with perseverative voicing on the internal velar stop; $\theta\grave{o}n$-*hkàn* 'three rooms' is realised [$\theta\widetilde{o\upsilon}$ŋgã̀] with the same voicing but, additionally, anticipation of the velar stop by the nasal final; while *hyi?-hkàn* 'eight rooms' is realised [ʃɪkkʰã̀], the aspirate remaining after the checked final, the final taking on the position of the following stop. In this last case, the phonetic final segment associated with -*?* may disappear, leaving only pitch, duration and, in some cases, allophonic vowel quality, to signal the checked tone ([ʃɪkʰã̀]). In the first two cases — those involving smooth (-Ø, -*n*) syllables — these phonological processes result in the neutralisation of manner distinctions for some C_i in favour of the voiced, e.g.: *hk-*, *k-*, and *g-* are all realised [g-].

Sandhi affects combinations of minor and major syllables slightly differently, with interesting results. When the first syllable of two is a minor one, the voicing process does not extend to the aspirates: in *səpwè* 'table', internal -*p-* is voiced, but in *təkhàn* 'one room', the internal -*kh-* remains aspirated. In addition, the initial of a minor syllable often harmonises with the voicing of the following consonant: *səpwè* is most often pronounced [zəbwè], with voicing throughout; but *təkhàn* is realised [təkʰã̀] with both stops voiceless. This sporadic process of consonant harmony reduces even further the number of initial oppositions available for minor syllables.

Close juncture is characteristic of certain grammatical environments, e.g.: noun + classifier, illustrated above, and noun + adjectival verb: (*?en* –

θi? 'new house', is pronounced [ʔẽĩnðĩʔ]). Most particles are also attached to preceding syllables in close juncture: *θwà - hpó* 'in order to go', is pronounced [θwàbó]. But within compounds the degree of juncture between syllables is unpredictable; the constituents of disyllabic compound nouns (other than recent loanwords) tend to be closely linked, but compound verbs vary, some with open, some with close juncture.

In our transcription, syllabic boundaries are shown as follows: open juncture is represented by a space between syllables and open juncture within a compound by a plus (*hkwè+hkwa* 'to separate; leave' is pronounced [kʰwèkʰwa]). Close juncture within a compound is indicated by lack of a space between the syllables (*hkúhkan* 'to resist' is pronounced [kʰúgã]), while close juncture between phrasal constituents is marked with a hyphen (as in the examples of the previous paragraph).

Moving on to the vowels, we find that the number of vocalic contrasts varies according to the type of syllable (see table 42.1): in smooth syllables (-∅, -*n*), there are seven contrasts, in checked (-*ʔ*), eight. In phonetic terms, however, the line of cleavage is not between smooth and checked but between open and closed: vowels in closed syllables (-*n*, -*ʔ*) tend to be noticeably centralised or diphthongised compared to those in open syllables. For purposes of transcription it is of course possible to identify certain elements of the different systems, as in the chart. And it would be possible to reduce the number of symbols even further by identifying the *ɔ* of open syllables with either the *ai* or *au* of closed. Historically (and in the writing system) *ɔ* is connected with *au* (and *o* with *ai*). Such an analysis is not motivated synchronically, nor does it have much practical value, so, like most of the transcriptions in use, we indicate nine vowels (plus the *ə* of reduced syllables).

Four tonal distinctions can be recognised, the 'creaky', the 'low' (or 'level'), the 'high' (or 'heavy') and the 'checked', the last symbolised by -*ʔ*. Tone in Burmese has a complex realisation of which pitch is only one feature. In the case of the checked tone, segmental features of vowel quality and final consonantism as well as suprasegmental features of pitch and duration are involved. The relative presence of these features varies with context. It has been observed, for example, that in disyllabic words such as *zaʔpwè* '(a) play', the pitch of the checked tone (high, in citation) may range from high to low. The same kind of variation is characteristic of creaky tone as well.

In citation form, the three tones that appear in smooth syllables have the following features: the 'creaky', (transcribed ´): tense or creaky phonation (sometimes with final lax glottal stop), medium duration, high intensity and high, often slightly falling pitch; the 'low' (unmarked): normal phonation, medium duration, low intensity and low, often slightly rising pitch; the 'high' (transcribed `): sometimes slightly breathy, relatively long, high intensity and high pitch, often with a fall before a pause.

In citation form, the creaky tone is much less common than the others, a fact accounted for by its relatively late development from affixal elements. The balance is partially restored, however, by the incidence of morphologically conditioned creaky tone (see pages 848–9).

3 The Writing System

The Burmese script is an adaptation of the Mon, which in turn, is derived through uncertain intermediaries from the Brāhmī script, the antecedent of all Indian scripts now in use. Like the Mon, it preserves the main features of its Indian prototype, including signs that originally represented non-Burmese sounds, such as the Indic retroflex and voiced aspirated series. These usually appear only in the spelling of Indic loanwords.

The script is alphabetic in principle, with 'letters' representing phonemes, though the sound values of many of these letters have changed considerably since it was first introduced, as we showed earlier. A few very common literary Burmese grammatical morphemes are represented by logograms — word signs — but these originated as abbreviations of phonographic combinations. Like all Indic scripts, the Burmese differs from European alphabetic scripts in two important respects. First, neither the sequence in

Table 42.2: The Burmese Writing System: Consonants

						Transliteration					Transcription				
	i	ii	iii	iv	v	i	ii	iii	iv	v	i	ii	iii	iv	v
C_I I	က	ခ	ဂ	ဃ	င	K	KH	G	GH	Ṅ	k	hk	g	g	ŋ
II	စ	ဆ	ဇ	ဈ	ဉ/ည	C	CH	J	JH	Ñ	s	hs	z	z	ɲ
III	ဋ	ဌ	ဍ	ဎ	ဏ	Ṭ	ṬH	Ḍ	ḌH	Ṇ	t	ht	d	d	n
IV	တ	ထ	ဒ	ဓ	န	T	TH	D	DH	N	t	ht	d	d	n
V	ပ	ဖ	ဗ	ဘ	မ	P	PH	B	BH	M	p	hp	b	b	m
VI	ယ	ရ	လ	ဝ	သ	Y	R	L	W	S	y	y	l	w	θ
VII		ဟ	ဠ	အ			H	Ḷ	?			h	l	?	

C_M — medials: ျ ြ ွ ှ

-Y- -R- -W- -H-

-y- -y- -w- h -

which the letters appear, nor the order in which they are written, reflects the temporal order of phonemes. Vowel signs appear before, after, above or below C_I signs. (Abbreviations with capitalised subscripts refer to positions in the written syllable.) Secondly, a consonant sign without any vowel sign implies the vowel *a*. It is this use of 'zero' that sometimes leads to Indic writing systems being incorrectly labelled 'syllabic'.

Table 42.2 shows the consonant signs together with a Romanised transliteration based on original Indic values and a transcription of their regular modern pronunciation. The transliteration is a capitalised and otherwise slightly modified version of the widely used Duroiselle system (see Okell 1971). Many of the differences between the transliteration and the transcription reflect changes in the spoken language since the writing system was introduced. Some of these are discussed below.

The 33 consonant signs are given in the traditional Burmese (and Indian) order, which is also the basis of ordering entries in dictionaries. Almost all the consonant signs can appear initially, but only the plain series (K, C, T, P), their nasal counterparts (Ṅ, Ñ, N, M), and Y occur finally in native words. The boxed row (III) representing the Indian retroflex series, is pronounced like the dental series. The boxed columns (iii, iv), representing the Indian voiced and voiced aspirated series, are usually pronounced alike. The *spoken* voiced series, discussed earlier, is often written with the plain or aspirate voiceless consonant signs.

There are four medial consonant signs: Y, R, W, H. The last is subscribed to nasal and resonant C_Is to indicate the aspirates of those series, e.g.: LHA, *hlá* 'beautiful'. In Old Burmese writing, a medial -L- was also found (see below).

The writing system reflects a number of consonantal changes. The development of C_fs will be discussed separately below. As initials, some consonants have undergone phonetic changes, but distinctions have generally been preserved. Row II in table 42.2 shows a shift from palatal affricate to dental sibilant. From the representation of Burmese words in certain Portuguese and English records of the eighteenth and nineteenth centuries, the Burmese scholar, Pe Maung Tin ('Phonetics in a Passport', *Journal of the Burma Research Society*, 1922, vol. 12, pp. 129–31) concluded that this change and the shift from $s > \theta$ (VI,v) began in the late eighteenth century and were followed by the palatalisation of velar stops before medial -*y*- (written -Y- and -R-). The three shifts form a 'drag chain', the first clearing the way for the second, the second for the third ($s>\theta$, $c>s$, $ky>c$, etc.). Two typologically rare consonants arose as a result of these developments: θ, pronounced [t^θ], and *hs*-, an aspirated sibilant ($< c^h$). The functional yield of the latter is very low.

Contrasts among medial consonants have been reduced from four in Old Burmese to three in Middle Burmese (reflected in the standard orthography), to two in the modern spoken language. The medial -*l*-

attested by the inscriptions merged with either -*y*- or -*r*-, according to whether the initial consonant was velar or labial, respectively, i.e.: OBs. *kl-* > MBs. *ky-*, OBs. *pl-* > MBs. *pr-*. MBs. *r* then merged with *y* in all positions, initial as well as medial (so that 'Rangoon' is now transcribed as *Yankon*). Some of the dialects attest to the earlier stages. In Tavoyan, the medial -*l*- of Old Burmese usually survives as such, while earlier -*r*- and -*y*- merge as -*y*-: cf. standard *cá* 'to fall', spelled KYA in the orthography and KLA in the inscriptions, pronounced *klá* in Tavoyan. In Arakanese, on the other hand, earlier -*l*- is distributed between -*r*- and -*y*- with the latter two remaining distinct, e.g. standard *cɛʔ* 'chicken', spelled KRAK, is *kraʔ* in Arakanese, the -*r*- realised as a retroflex continuant.

Whether we are dealing with the script or the spoken language, vowel, final consonant and tone are conveniently treated as a unit, the 'rhyme'. Table 42.3 shows the main (or 'regular') rhymes of Burmese, arranged according to written vowels. (To save space, tonal markings are only indicated where they are incorporated in a vowel sign.) Comparing the transliteration with the transcription reveals both a large reduction in the number of C_fs and a major restructuring of the vowel system.

Consonant signs are marked as final by the superscript hook, or 'killer' stroke. The orthography shows four positions of final oral and nasal stops, and -Y, which — in native words — represents only the rhyme -*ɛ*. ('Little Ñ', the second of the two signs for Ñ, is a modern variant of the first, used to signal the pronunciation -*in* over the otherwise unpredictable alternatives, -*i*, *e* and *ɛ*.) From the table, it can be seen that many combinations of written final and vowel do not occur. Finals -C and -Ñ, for instance, occur only with the 'intrinsic' vowel A. Comparative evidence shows that the 'extra' A-rhymes derive from earlier *-*ik* and *-*iŋ*, respectively, the 'missing' velar rhymes of the high front series (row II). Palatal finals are rare in Tibeto-Burman languages, but common in Mon-Khmer; it is likely that the appearance of these finals in Burmese is another result of Mon influence.

Neither the distributional evidence nor the comparative evidence is clear enough to explain the other gaps in the system of orthographic rhymes.

All positions of final stops have been reduced to just one in the modern language, represented by -*ʔ* for oral stops, -*n* for nasal. The association of high pitch with the former can probably be attributed to the well documented pitch-raising effects of final tense glottal stop. This glottal stop is quite different from the lax glottal stop that sometimes appears in creaky-toned syllables. The latter would be expected to depress pitch.

From table 42.3, vowels can be seen to have split according to the type of syllable they were in, open or closed; thus written I is read *i* or *e*, written U, *u* or *o*, written UI, *o* or *ai*, written O, *ɔ* or *au*, with the first, higher vowel quality found in reflexes of open syllables. (Written UI and O are both digraphs in the script, but only the first is transliterated according to its parts, U + I; the symbol was a Mon invention for representing a mid front rounded

Table 42.3: The Burmese Writing System: Regular Rhymes

	Open		Closed								Open		Closed							
I	I í	I i	X	IN in	IM en	X	AN an	AM un	WAN (win)		Ü u	U u	X	UIN ain	UM on	X	WAN un	WAM un	WAK (we?)	WAT u?	WAP u?
II	I i	I i	IN in	IM en	IT e?	IP e?					U u	UI o	UIŊ ain	UN on	X	X	X	X	X	X	X
III	E e										O ɔ	OW ɔ	OŊ aun	ON X	X	X					
IV	AI ε	AY ε	AÑ in								O ɔ		OK au?	AK ε?	AM an	AN an	AC i?	AT a?	AK ε?	AP a?	UP o?
V	A á	Ā a	AÑ i,(e,ε)/in	AŊ in	AN an	AM an	AC i?	AT a?	AK ε?	AP a?	UI o		UIK ai	OK au?	OW ɔ	O ɔ	UP o?	UT o?	IP e?	IT e?	UK X

Note: Tones not contained in a vowel sign are written as follows: ˳ (originally -ˌ) for *creaky*; -: (*visarga*) for *high*; unmarked for *low*.

vowel and it probably had the same value in Old Burmese.) Written A attests to a three-way split of *a* into *a*, *i* and *ɛ*, conditioned by the final. To an extent, these developments, coupled with the reduction in the number of final consonants, filled the gaps in the pattern of (written) rhymes, so that the only asymmetries in the modern system are the missing nasal rhyme, *-ɛn*, and the uncertain relationship between open *ɔ* and closed *ai* and *au*, discussed above (see table 42.1).

Table 42.3 also shows the relationship between V- and C_f-signs and the representation of tones in Burmese. Much of the complicated system for indicating tone derives from Mon orthographic conventions. Neither Mon nor the Indic languages were tonal. But Old Mon did have short syllables ending in a glottal stop, which must have sounded very similar to the short, creaky-toned syllables of Burmese. In Mon, final *-ʔ* was generally written with the same sign as glottal onset, the 'vowel support'; but with the three vowels I, U and A — the 'short' vowels of the Indian prototype — the symbol for *-ʔ* could be omitted. Both practices were taken over and eventually systematised in the Burmese writing system. From table 42.3, we see that the three 'corner' vowels (II, V) have two written forms; in Indian terms — also the basis of our transliteration — the first is short, the second (with the additional stroke) long ($\bar{V}$). The first indicates a creaky-toned syllable, the second, a low-toned syllable. With all other finals, creaky tone was indicated by the sign for glottal onset, reduced to just a dot in the modern orthography (but, for clarity, still transcribed as *ʔ* herein: UIʔ = *ó*).

There was, apparently, no clear analogue in Mon to the opposition between high and low tones and for some six centuries the two were not consistently distinguished in the orthography. In the modern script, the lower-mid vowel signs (IV) are intrinsically high-toned, with additional strokes ('killed-Y' in one case, the killer alone — originally a superscript killed-W — in the other) changing them to low. Elsewhere, high tone is indicated by two post-scriptal dots ('visarga'): UI: = *ò*. The modern use of visarga (which represents final *-h* in Old Mon) to signal the high tone was occasionally anticipated in the earliest inscriptions, which suggests that breathiness has long been a feature of that tone.

Except in those cases in which the vowel sign is intrinsically creaky or high, the low tone is unmarked: UI = *o*. The checked tone is symbolised by the presence of a final oral stop.

One of the characteristics of Indic alphabets is that vowels are written with special signs when they are in syllable-initial position. Such 'initial-vowel symbols', based on Mon forms, exist for all but three of the Burmese vowels (table 42.4). Nowadays, they are found only in a small number of words — most of them, loanwords. In the modern orthography, 'initial' vowels — actually vowels with glottal onset — are generally written with a combination of the vowel support sign (which represents *ʔ-*) and ordinary vowel signs.

A few other signs also appear in the script; for these and other irregularities, the reader is referred to Roop (1972).

Table 42.4: The Burmese Writing System: Miscellaneous Symbols

Initial vowel signs:

ဣ	ဩ	ʔí	ʔi
ဥ	ဦ	ဦး	ʔú ʔu ʔù
ဧ	(ၔ)	ʔe ʔè
ဪ	ဢ	ʔɔ ʔɔ̀

Numerals:

၁	၂	၃	၄	၅	၆	၇	၈	၉	၀
1	2	3	4	5	6	7	8	9	0

4 Morphology

Morphology in Burmese is primarily derivational morphology and compounding; there is little to discuss under the heading of 'inflection'. Grammatical functions that might be realised as inflections in other languages are mostly carried out by word order or by grammatical particles. There is, however, one phenomenon that can be considered inflectional, and that is the 'induced creaky tone' (Okell's term). Under certain conditions, words with otherwise low tones and sometimes those with high shift to the creaky tone. This shift has a number of apparently disparate functions (cf. Allott 1967). Some of them seem to exploit the sound symbolism of the features of creaky phonation and high intensity: with sentence-final 'appellatives' (kin terms, titles etc. that pick out the audience and convey information about social distance) the induced creaky tone suggests abruptness and urgency. It also appears with the first occurrence of certain repeated words, e.g. ʔinmətan 'very', but ʔinmətán ʔinmətan 'very, very'.

At other times, the induced creaky tone has a specific grammatical function. Usually only with pronouns and nouns of personal reference, it may signal 'possession' or 'attribution': θu 'he; she', θú ʔəmyò+θəmì 'his wife'. In such cases, the creaky tone looks like an allomorph of the creaky-toned possessive particle, -yé (-ké after checked syllables); but although the two often alternate, they may also cooccur, so their relationship is now only historical.

The induced creaky tone also tends to appear — again, mainly with personal referents — before the locative postposition, -hma 'in, at', and the 'accusative' postposition, -*ko* 'object, goal, extent'. With objects in particular, -*ko* is often omitted, leaving the creaky tone to mark the grammatical role: *θú(-ko) mè-lai?-pa* 'ask him!'. The origin of the creaky tone in these contexts is uncertain.

Apart from the regular but non-productive patterns involving aspiration and voicing illustrated earlier, almost all derivational morphology in Burmese involves prefixation of a minor syllable, partial or complete reduplication or combinations of the two. Derivational processes generally act on verbs, turning them into nouns or noun-like expressions that can often function as either nominals or adverbials. Verbs themselves are very rarely derived (just as they are very rarely borrowed). The verbal inventory is expanded through compounding or through the lexicalisation of verb + complement constructions, e.g. *?əyè cì-* 'affair-be big = be important'; the latter retain most of the syntactic properties of phrases. In contrast to verbs, adverbials are almost always derived.

The general function of the productive derivational processes in Burmese is to subordinate verbs. Complete reduplication of stative verbs (with close juncture distinguishing them from iterative repetition) forms manner adverbials: *ca* 'be long (time)', *caca* 'for (some) time'; *θehca* 'be sure, exact', *θeθe+hcahca* 'exactly, definitely'. Prefixation of action verbs by the nominalising prefix *?ə-* creates action nominals: *kai?* 'to bite', but *?əkai? hkan-yá-* 'biting-suffer-get = get bitten' (a 'passive of adversity', see page 853); *hcɛ?* 'to cook', but *?əhcɛ? θin-* 'cooking-learn = learn to cook'. The same process forms adverbials: *myan* 'be fast', but *?əmyan θwà-* 'go in haste, go quickly'; or, with a different prefix, *?əyè+təcì* 'urgently', from the syntactic compound meaning 'be important', mentioned at the end of the last paragraph. Whether reduplicated or prefixed, the verbs may retain nominal complements: *təlá caca nei-* 'one-month-long-stay = to stay for a month'; *hcin (?ə)kai? hkan-yá-* 'get bitten by a mosquito'. In the latter type, the prefix is often deleted and the verbal noun appears in close juncture with the preceding complement as a kind of nonce compound.

Prefixation, but not complete reduplication, is also attested in lexicalised form, e.g. *?əhkwá* 'fork (of a tree)', from the verb *hkwá* 'to fork in two'. In cases involving a prefixed verb and a complement, the lexicalised version becomes a syntactic compound, e.g. *htəmìnhcɛ?* 'a cook', derived from the deverbal *?əhcɛ?* with the generic object, *htəmìn* 'rice; food'. In principle, derived forms such as these can be interpreted literally or idiomatically; *htəminhcɛ?* is also an action nominal with the meaning of 'cooking'.

Other kinds of compounding are well utilised in Burmese as a means of deriving nouns and verbs. Nominal patterns are more varied and several are recursive; compound verbs are usually composed of pairs of verbs. Compounding is a favourite way of coining new technical vocabulary, e.g. *kon+tin+kon+hcá+maùn*, lit. 'an arm (that) loads (and) unloads goods', i.e. 'a crane'; *mainhnòn+pyá+dainkwɛ?* 'a dial (that) shows mile-rate', i.e.

'a speedometer'. *Mainhnòn* and *dainhkwɛ?* are themselves compounds that combine loanwords from English (*main* from 'mile', *dain* from 'dial') with words from Burmese, a practice that is quite common.

Burmese vocabulary also attests to a variety of processes that straddle the line between derivation and compounding. They apparently satisfy an urge, most noticeable in formal and literary styles, to add weight and colour to the monosyllabic root. Nouns and verbs often have pleonastic versions formed by the addition of a near synonym: *yè* and *yè+θà*, both 'write', the latter containing the verb *θà* 'inscribe'; *cí* and *cí+hyú* both 'look at', with *hyú*, a less common verb than *cí*, meaning 'to behold'. The enlarged version may be phonologically as well as semantically matched: *po* and *pomo*, both meaning 'more', the latter with the rhyming and nearly synonymous *mo*. Or it may be phonologically matched but semantically empty: *hkɔ* and *hkɔwɔ* 'call', the latter containing the otherwise meaningless rhyming syllable *-wɔ*; *ɲi* and *ɲiɲa* 'be even', with the meaningless 'chiming' syllable *-ɲa*. In the 'elaborate' adverbial *wòdò+wàdà* 'blurred, unclear', rhyme and chime are intermeshed.

The pattern of four rhythmically or euphonically balanced syllables is prolific. Elaborate nouns are frequently formed by the addition of *?ə-* to both parts of a compound verb: *hnáun+hyɛ?* 'annoy', *?əhnáun+?əhyɛ?* 'annoyance'. Elaborate adverbs may contain any of a variety of minor syllables: *bəyòn+bəyìn* 'tumultuously'; *kəbyàun+kəbyan* 'in an illogical, backwards way'; *təsì+təlòn* 'in unity'. As these examples show, the language has vast resources for expressing fine nuances through the adverbial position. Many adverbials are onomatopoeic or ideophonic, e.g. the pattern *tə-* plus reduplication, as in *təzizi* 'buzzing with noise'; or the pattern of an imitative syllable plus the suffix *-hkənè*, the latter associated with sudden movement: *hyu?hkənè* 'whoosh'; *htwihkənè* 'ptui' (spitting sound, expressing disgust).

5 Syntax

In Burmese the verb and its modifiers occupy the final position in the clause, with nominals and other complements 'freely' ordered before it. There is neither agreement between constituents nor concord within them. The grammatical apparatus consists mainly of postpositional particles — many of them deriving from nouns or verbs — whose relative ordering, though often fixed, tends to accord with their semantic scope: *yu-la-se-hcin-tɛ* 'carry-come-cause-want-realis = (he) wanted to make (him) bring (it)'; *cènaun hsəya-ká-lè-hpè* (*cènaun tì-tɛ*) 'gong-master-contrastive subject-additive-restrictive = and the gong-master, for his part, just (plays the gong)'. The only obligatory grammatical categories involve the verb; with some exceptions, final verb phrases are followed by one of a small set of functionally disparate particles that signal, simultaneously, features of polarity and mood, or polarity, mood and aspect. Thus, *-tɛ*, *-mɛ* and *-pi* carry, in addition to the meanings 'positive' and 'non-imperative', the aspectual distinctions of realis, irrealis, and punctative, respectively. The punctative expresses the realisation of a state (*to-pi* '(that)'s enough') or the initiation of an action (*sà-pi* '(I)'m eating (now)'), different manifestations of the notion 'change of state'. Grammatical categories of voice, tense and definiteness are not found at all; number is an optional category, expressed by a suffix.

The verbal phrase itself, as we saw in the earlier example, often consists of a string of verbs, verb-like morphemes and particles. These exhibit a variety of syntactic and semantic properties. In the phrase *hté θwà* 'put in-go = to take (it) in (it)', two verbs combine in open juncture and retain their lexical meanings; in *hté pè*, 'put (something) in for (someone)', open juncture is still usual, but the second morpheme, *pè*, has its benefactive meaning of 'for the sake of' rather than its literal meaning of 'give'; in *hté-lai?* 'just put (it) in', *hté* is followed in close juncture by a morpheme whose lexical meaning is 'to follow' but which, as a verbal modifier, signals an 'increase in transitivity', and is often translated as 'effective or abrupt action'. The functions of the verbal modifiers are surprisingly diverse: *-hya*, the 'commiserating' particle (with no verbal prototype) conveys 'pity or compassion, usually towards a third person': *la-yá-pyan-hya-tɛ* 'come-had to-again-pity-realis = [she] had to come back, unfortunately'. The directional particle, *-hké* (again, with no obvious lexical prototype), signifies 'displacement in space or time', as in *Pəgan myó-ká wɛ-hké-tɛ* 'Pagan-town-from-buy-there-realis = (we) bought (it) back in Pagan'.

Within the noun phrase, the order of constituents is primarily modifier before modified, with the main exception being stative verb modifiers which follow their head nouns either in close juncture or with the nominalising prefix *ʔə-*. Demonstratives precede their head: *di mìpon* 'this/these lantern(s)'. So do genitive phrases and other nominal modifiers: *ʔəpyó ʔen* 'the young woman's house' (with induced creaky tone on *ʔəpyo* marking possession). So, too, do most relative clauses: *baθa+səkà léla-té lu-te* 'language-study-realis (with induced creaky tone showing subordination)-person-plural = people that study language'. Unlike English, the original semantic role of the relativised noun is not indicated: *θu gàun səpwè-né tai?-mí-tɛ* 'he-head-table-with-hit-inadvertently-realis = he hit (his) head on the table', but *θu gàun tai?-mí-té səpwè* 'the table that he hit (his) head (on)'.

Burmese, like many of the languages spoken on the mainland of South-East Asia, requires classifiers (or 'measures') for the quantification of what in English would be called count nouns. Numeral and classifier follow the quantified noun in an appositional relationship: *θwà lè-hcàun* 'tooth-four-peg = four teeth'; *θəhcìn lè-po?* 'song-four-stanza = four songs'. Some nouns can be self-classifying: *ʔen lè-ʔen* 'four houses'. Classifiers often reflect the shape or some other salient feature of a nominal referent. In many cases, nouns may be classified in several ways, according to the particular aspect of an object the speaker chooses to emphasise; in the case of animate nouns the choice usually reflects status: *lu təyau?* 'one (ordinary) person', *lu tə?ù* 'one (esteemed) person'. But probably as a result of material and cultural change, the semantic or conceptual basis of classification in Burmese is now often obscure, so possible classifiers must be listed with nouns in the dictionary as lexical facts.

Although certain orders of clause elements are much more common than others — agent–beneficiary–patient, for example — order of elements before the verb is, in principle, free. As a result, a sentence such as *Maun Hlá Maun Ŋɛ yai?-tɛ* is ambiguous, each nominal capable of being interpreted as agent or patient: 'Maung Hla struck Maung Nge' or 'Maung Hla was struck by Maung Nge'. Where context is insufficient to ensure the intended interpretation, semantic relations can be marked by postpositional particles. In this case, the agent can be signalled by *-ká*, the patient by *-ko*: Maun Hlá-ko Maun Ŋɛ-ká yai?-tɛ 'Maung Hla was struck by Maung Nge'. These, like many of the other postpositional particles, have several different senses. With locations they mark 'source' and 'goal', respectively: *Yankon-ká Mandəlè-ko θwà-tɛ* '(he) went from Rangoon to Mandalay'. Other functions of *-ko*, such as the marking of beneficiary and extent or degree can be subsumed under the notion of 'goal'. But *-ká* has one other very common function that is not obviously related to the notion of source: where *-ká* does not serve a disambiguating function — in intransitive clauses, for example — it signals 'contrastive topic'; *di-ká təca?, ho-ká ca?-hkwè* 'this-*ká* (costs) one kyat, that-*ká*, one and a half'. *-ká* in this sense may appear with nominals already marked for semantic roles: *?əhtè-htè-hma-ká* 'inside-in-at-*ká*', as in '**inside** it's crowded but outside it's not'.

The last example illustrates the origin of the many of the more specific relational markers. *?əhtè* is a noun meaning 'the inside', which can function as head to a genitive phrase with the meaning 'the inside of': *yehkwe? ?əhtè* 'the inside of the cup'. Without its prefix, and closely bound to the preceding syllable, the morpheme occurs in locative phrases that may be explicitly marked as such by the particle *-hma: yehkwɛ?-htè-hma* 'in the cup'.

Although word order is 'free' in the sense that it does not indicate the grammatical or semantic roles of constituents, it is not without significance. It is conditioned by the pragmatic notions of topic, which establishes a point of departure from previous discourse or from context, and 'comment', which contains the communicative focus of the utterance. It is this pragmatic organisation that leads us to translate the sentence *Maun Hlá-ko Maun Ŋɛ-ká yai?-tɛ* with the English passive, i.e. 'Maung Hla was struck by Maung Nge', rather than the active 'Maung Nge struck Maung Hla'. For, by mentioning Maung Hla first, we take the patient's point of view, just as we do when using the passive in English. But unlike the English, topicalising the patient changes neither the grammatical relations of the nominals (the agent is not demoted) nor the valence of the verb (which keeps the same form), so the term 'passive' does not apply. The closest Burmese gets to a passive construction is a 'passive of adversity', which, as the name suggests, is associated primarily with events that affect a person (or patient) unpleasantly. Thus the unlikely perspective of the sentence, *kà θú-ko tai?-tɛ* 'car-he-obj.-hit-realis = the car hit him', can be reversed by making *tai?* a nominal complement of a verb phrase containing the verbs *hkan* 'suffer; endure', and *yá* 'get; manage to': *θu kàtai? hkan-yá-tɛ* 'he-car hitting-suffer-get-realis = he got hit by a car'. But even this construction is not nearly as frequent as the passive is in English.

A topic, once established, may remain activated over several sentences. Its pragmatic role, in other words, may be 'given'. English typically leaves a pronominal trace in such cases; Burmese generally does not. Nominals, topical or otherwise, whose reference can be recovered from previous discourse or context can be omitted, a process sometimes known as 'zero-pronominalisation'; *pyin pè-mɛ* 'fix-(give)-irrealis = (I)'ll fix (it) for (you)'. Such sentences are grammatically complete like their English counterparts. Pronouns, which almost always have human referents in Burmese, are used either as a hedge against misinterpretation or as a means of making the relative status of the participants explicit.

The primacy of the topic-comment organisation of the sentence in Burmese is also illustrated by sentences of the following type: *di hkəlè θwà cò-θwà-tɛ* 'this-child-teeth-break (intransitive)-(go)-realis = this child has broken (his) teeth'. The verb is intransitive (its corresponding transitive is aspirated) and the two noun phrases are not in a possessive relationship but are clausal constituents; a more literal translation would read 'the child, teeth have been broken'. In such cases, the first topic, *hkəlè*, is a locus for the second topic, *θwà*, and only the second is matched to the selectional requirements of the verb.

Bibliography

Okell (1969) is the most thorough and useful grammatical description of Burmese; part 1 is a structural analysis, part 2 a conspectus of grammatical morphemes. Judson (1888) is still the best English description of formal literary Burmese. For phonology, Bernot (1963) is a functional analysis of standard Burmese phonology, while Allott (1967) deals with grammatical tone. Bernot (1980) is a detailed study of the form and function of the elements of the verb phrase, including data on cooccurrence restrictions.

For the writing system, reference may be made to Roop (1972), a programmed course, and for Romanisation to Okell (1971). Allott (1985) is an important sociolinguistic study. Nissaya Burmese is discussed by Okell (1965).

Acknowledgements

I would like to express my gratitude to the following people: to Anna Allott and John Okell, who, over a number of years, have shared their own materials with me and guided me in my study of Burmese; to them, to Jim Matisoff and to Graham Thurgood, for providing extremely helpful comments on an earlier draft of this paper; to the Social Science Research Council, who supported my research on Burmese in London and Burma from 1978–9; and to the many Burmese people who have looked after me and assisted me in my endeavours to learn their language.

References

Allott, A. 1967. 'Grammatical Tone in Modern Spoken Burmese', *Wissenschaftliche Zeitschrift der Karl-Marx Universität Leipzig, Gesellschafts- und Sprachwissenschaftliche Reihe*, vol. 16, pp. 157–62.

——— 1985. 'Language Policy and Language Planning in Burma', in D. Bradley (ed.) *Papers in South-East Asian Linguistics*, No. 9, *Language Planning and Sociolinguistics in South-East Asia*, pp.131–54. *Pacific Linguistics* A-67, 1985.

Bernot, D. 1963. 'Esquisse d'une description phonologique du birman', *Bulletin de la Société Linguistique de Paris*, vol. 58, pp. 164–224.

——— 1980. *Le Prédicat en birman parlé* (Centre Nationale de la Recherche Scientifique, Paris)

Judson, Rev. A. 1888. *A Grammar of the Burmese Language* (Baptist Board of Publications, Rangoon)

Okell, J. 1965. 'Nissaya Burmese: A Case of Systematic Adaptation to a Foreign Grammar and Syntax', *Lingua*, vol. 15, pp. 186–227.

——— 1969. *A Reference Grammar of Colloquial Burmese*, 2 vols. (Oxford University Press, London)

——— 1971. *A Guide to the Romanization of Burmese* (Luzac and Co., London)

Roop, D.H. 1972. *An Introduction to the Burmese Writing System* (Yale University Press, New Haven)

43 JAPANESE

Masayoshi Shibatani

1 Introduction

Japanese is spoken by virtually the entire population of Japan — some 115 million people as of 1 March 1980. In terms of the number of native speakers, it is thus comparable to German and ranks sixth among the languages of the world. Yet, despite its status as a world's major language and its long literary history, Japanese is surrounded by numerous myths, some of which are perpetuated by Japanese and non-Japanese alike. There are a number of factors which contribute to these myths, e.g. the uncertainty of the genetic relationship of Japanese to other languages, its complex writing system and the relatively small number of non-Japanese (especially Westerners) who speak it.

One of the persistent myths held by the Japanese concerning their language is that it is somehow unique. This myth derives mainly from the superficial comparison between Japanese and closely related Indo-European languages such as English, German and French and the obvious disparities which such work reveals. Another persistent myth is that Japanese, compared to Western languages, notably French, is illogical and/or vague. This belief, remarkable as it may be, is most conspicuously professed by certain Japanese intellectuals well versed in European languages and philosophy. Their conviction is undoubtedly a reflection of the inferiority complex on the part of Japanese intellectuals toward Western

855

civilisation. After all, Japan's modernisation effort started only after the Meiji Restoration (1867). Prior to this, Japan had maintained a feudalistic society and a closed-door policy to the rest of the world for nearly 250 years.

However understandable the historical or cultural causes may be, widespread characterisation of Japanese as a unique and illogical language grossly misrepresents the true nature of the language. In fact, in terms of grammatical structure, Japanese is a rather 'ordinary' human language. Its basic word order — subject–object–verb — is widespread among the world's languages. Also other characteristics associated with an SOV language are consistently exhibited in Japanese (see section 5). In the realm of phonology too, it is a commonplace language, with five hardly exotic vowels, a rather simple set of consonants and the basic CV syllable structure (see section 4).

As for the claim that Japanese is illogical or vague, one can argue that Japanese is in fact structurally superior to Western languages in the domain of discourse organisation. As we shall see in section 6, Japanese enables the speaker to distinguish clearly between the simple description of an event and a judgement about someone or something.

While the notion of uniqueness as applied to the entire domain of a given language is dubious, especially in the case of Japanese as pointed out above, each language does possess certain features that are unique or salient in comparison to other languages. For Japanese, these include honorifics, certain grammatical particles, some of which are distinct for male and female speakers, and the writing system. In this chapter, I shall attempt to include in the discussion those aspects of Japanese that constitute a notable feature of this language which I believe is not shared by many other languages and which makes learning Japanese difficult for many foreigners.

2   Historical Setting

Like Korean, its geographical neighbour, Japanese has long been the target of attempts to establish a genetic relationship between it and other languages and language families. Hypotheses have been presented assigning Japanese to virtually all major language families: Altaic, Austronesian, Sino-Tibetan, Indo-European, and Dravidian. The most persuasive is the Altaic theory, but even here evidence is hardly as firm as that which relates the languages of the Indo-European family, as can be seen in ongoing speculations among both scholars and linguistic amateurs.

With regard to individual languages, Ryūkyūan, Ainu and Korean have been the strongest candidates proposed as possible sister languages. Among these, the Japanese-Ryūkyūan connection has been firmly established. Ryūkyūan, spoken in Okinawa, is, in fact, now considered to be a dialect of Japanese. A Japanese-Ainu relationship has been hypothesised, but evidence is scanty. On the other hand, the Japanese-Korean hypothesis stands on firmer ground and perhaps it is safe to assume that they are related, though remotely.

The earliest written records of the Japanese language date back to the eighth century. The oldest among them, the *Kojiki* ('Record of Ancient Matters') (AD 712) is written in Chinese characters. The preface to this work is written in Chinese syntax as well. What was done is that the characters whose meanings were equivalent to Japanese expressions were arranged according to Chinese syntax. Thus, the document is not readily intelligible to those who do not know how the Chinese ordering of elements corresponds to the Japanese ordering, since Chinese word order is similar to English, e.g. *Mary likes fish*, as opposed to the Japanese order of *Mary fish likes*. Furthermore, it is not clear how such characters were read; they may have been read purely in the Chinese style in imitation of the Chinese pronunciation of the characters used or they may have been read in a Japanese way, i.e. by uttering those Japanese words corresponding in meaning to the written Chinese characters and inverting the order of elements so as to follow the Japanese syntax. Perhaps both methods were used. This means that a character such as 山 'mountain' was read both as *san*, the Chinese reading, and as *yama*, the semantically equivalent Japanese word for the character. This practice of reading Chinese characters both in the Chinese way and in terms of the semantically equivalent Japanese words persists even today.

By the time the *Manyōshū* ('Collection of a Myriad Leaves'), an anthology of Japanese verse, was completed (AD 759), the Japanese had learned to use Chinese characters as phonetic symbols. Thus, the Japanese word *yama* 'mountain' could be written phonetically by using a character with the sound *ya* (e.g. 夜 'evening') and another with the sound *ma* (e.g. 麻 'hemp'), as 夜麻 . In other words, what stands for 'mountain' could be written in two ways. One used the Chinese word 山, as discussed above. The other way was to choose Chinese characters read as *ya* and *ma*. It is this latter phonetic way of writing which gave rise to the two uniquely Japanese syllabary writings known as *kana*.

Since things Chinese were regarded as culturally superior to their native equivalents, the Chinese manner was a formal way of writing. The phonetic representation of Japanese was considered only 'temporary' or mnemonic in nature. Thus, the phonetic writing was called *karina* 'temporary letters' while the Chinese way of writing was called *mana* 'true letters'.

Present-day *karina* (now pronounced as *kana*) have developed as simplified Chinese characters used phonetically. There are two kinds of *kana*. The original *kana* were used as mnemonic symbols in reading characters and were written alongside them; hence they are called *kata-kana* 'side *kana*'. *Hira-gana* 'plain *kana*' have developed by simplifying the grass style (i.e. cursive) writing of characters. These two *kana* syllabaries are set out in table 43.1.

Table 43.1: Japanese *Kana* Syllabaries

Hiragana

A	KA	SA	TA	NA	HA	MA	YA	RA	WA	
あ	か	さ	た	な	は	ま	や	ら	わ	
I	KI	SI	TI	NI	HI	MI		RI		
い	き	し	ち	に	ひ	み		り		
U	KU	SU	TU	NU	HU	MU	YU	RU		
う	く	す	つ	ぬ	ふ	む	ゆ	る		
E	KE	SE	TE	NE	HE	ME		RE		
え	け	せ	て	ね	へ	め		れ		
O	KO	SO	TO	NO	HO	MO	YO	RO	WO	N
お	こ	そ	と	の	ほ	も	よ	ろ	を	ん

Katakana

A	KA	SA	TA	NA	HA	MA	YA	RA	WA	
ア	カ	サ	タ	ナ	ハ	マ	ヤ	ラ	ワ	
I	KI	SI	TI	NI	HI	MI		RI		
イ	キ	シ	チ	ニ	ヒ	ミ		リ		
U	KU	SU	TU	NU	HU	MU	YU	RU		
ウ	ク	ス	ツ	ヌ	フ	ム	ユ	ル		
E	KE	SE	TE	NE	HE	ME		RE		
エ	ケ	セ	テ	ネ	へ	メ		レ		
O	KO	SO	TO	NO	HO	MO	YO	RO	WO	N
オ	コ	ソ	ト	ノ	ホ	モ	ヨ	ロ	ヲ	ン

Note: Voicing oppositions, where applicable, are indicated by the diacritical dots on the upper right hand corner of each *kana*; e.g. *gi* ギ as opposed to *ki* キ.

Katakana were originally used in combination with Chinese characters. *Hiragana*, on the other hand, were mainly used by women and were not mixed with characters. The contemporary practice is to use Chinese characters, called *kanji*, for content words, and *hiragana* for grammatical function words such as particles and inflectional endings. *Katakana* is used to write foreign loanwords, telegrams and in certain onomatopoeic expressions.

In addition, there is *rōmaji*, which is another phonetic writing system using the Roman alphabet. *Rōmaji* is mainly employed in writing station names as an aid for foreigners, in signing documents written in Western languages and in writing foreign acronyms (e.g. *ILO*, *IMF*). It is also used in advertising. Thus the word for 'mountain' can be written as 山 in *kanji*, as ヤマ in *katakana*, as やま in *hiragana* and as *yama* in *rōmaji*. Sometimes all these four ways of writing can be found in one sentence; e.g. the sentence *Hanako is an OL* (< *office lady* i.e. 'office girl') *working in that building* can be written as below:

花子	は	あのビル	で	働いている	OL	です。
Hanako	wa	ano biru	de	hataraite-iru	ooeru	desu.
	top.	that building	at	work-ing	OL	cop.

The traditional way of writing is to write vertically, lines progressing from right to left. Today both vertical writing and horizontal writing, as illustrated above, are practised.

As may be surmised from the above discussion, learning how to write Japanese involves considerable effort. Japanese children must master all four ways of writing by the time they complete nine years of Japan's compulsory education. Of these, the most difficult is the Chinese system. For each *kanji*, at least two ways of reading must be learned: one the *on-yomi*, the Sino-Japanese reading, and the other the *kun-yomi*, the Japanese reading. For the character 山 'mountain', *san* is the Sino-Japanese reading and *yama* the Japanese. Normally, the Sino-Japanese reading is employed in compounds consisting of two or more Chinese characters, while in isolation the Japanese reading is adopted.

An additional complication is the multiplicity of Sino-Japanese readings. This is due to the fact that Chinese characters, or rather their pronunciations, were borrowed from different parts of China as well as at different times. Thus, dialectal differences in pronunciation also had to be learned by the Japanese. One of the two major sources of borrowing was the Wu area of China during the Six Dynasties period. The reading reflecting this dialect is called *go'on*. The other reading called *kan'on* reflects a newer dialect of *Chang-an*, which is believed to be the standard language of the Tang period. The character 米 for 'rice' is pronounced *mai* in *go'on*, *bei* in *kan'on* and *kome* and *yone* in the Japanese reading. Unlike the *on-yomi* versus *kun-yomi*, there is no systematic rule for determining whether a given character is to be read in *kan'on* or in *go'on*; each expression must be learned as to which way it is read. The character 米 for 'rice', for example, will be read in *go'on* in a form like 外米 *gai mai* 'imported rice', but in *kan'on* in a form like 米国 *bei koku* 'America'. That is, the *go'on/kan'on* distinction is purely historical and speakers of Japanese must simply live with the fact that in addition to the Japanese way of reading, most *kanji* have two or more Chinese ways of reading them and that the same *kanji* is likely to be pronounced differently depending on which expression it is used in.

Because of this kind of complexity caused by retaining all these writing methods, there have been movements for abolishing Chinese characters in favour of *kana* writing and even movements for completely Romanising the Japanese language. All these, however, have so far failed and it is safe to say that Chinese characters are here to stay. What has been done instead of abolishing Chinese characters altogether is to limit the number of commonly used characters. In 1946, the Japanese government issued a list of 1,850 characters for this purpose. The list was revised in 1981, and the new list, called *Jōyō Kanji Hyō* ('List of Characters for Daily Use'), contains 1,945 characters recommended for daily use. This is now regarded as the basic list of Chinese characters to be learned during elementary and intermediate education. Also, most newspapers try to limit the use of characters to these

1,945 characters; when those outside the list are used, the reading in *hiragana* accompanies them.

Japan, a mountainous country with many islands, has a setting ideal for fostering language diversification; and, indeed, Japanese is rich in dialectal variation. Many dialects are mutually unintelligible. For example, speakers of the Kagoshima dialect of the southern island of Kyūshū would not be understood by the majority of the speakers on the main island of Honshū. Likewise, northern dialect speakers of Aomori and Akita would not be understood by the people of metropolitan Tōkyō or by anyone from western Japan. Communication among people of different dialects has been made possible through the spread of the so-called *kyootuu-go* 'common language', which consists essentially of versions of local dialects modified according to the 'ideal' form called *hyoozyun-go* 'standard language', which in turn is based on the dialect of the capital Tōkyō.

Hyoozyun-go is used in broadcasting and it is this form of Japanese which elementary education aims at in teaching children. The following description is based on this dialect, sometimes referred to as the standard dialect.

3   Lexicon

The fact that Japan has never been invaded by a foreign force or colonised by a foreign interest causes surprise when one examines the Japanese lexicon, for it shows a characteristic of those languages whose lands have been under foreign control at one time or another. Namely, Japanese vocabulary abounds in foreign words. In this regard, Japanese is similar to Turkish, which has borrowed a large number of Arabic and Persian words without ever being ruled by Arabs or Persians, and contrasts with English and others that have incorporated a large quantity of words from invaders' languages.

In addition to the abundance of foreign words, the Japanese lexicon is characterised by the presence of a large number of onomatopoeic words. This section, still in the spirit of presenting an overall picture of Japanese, surveys these two characteristic aspects of the Japanese lexicon.

Japanese has borrowed words from neighbouring languages such as Ainu and Korean, but by far the most numerous are Chinese loanwords. Traditionally, the Japanese lexicon is characterised in terms of three strata. The terms *wago* 'Japanese words' or *Yamato-kotoba* 'Yamato (Japanese) words' refer to the stratum of the native vocabulary and *kango* 'Chinese words' refers to loanwords of Chinese origin (hereafter called Sino-Japanese words). All other loanwords from European languages are designated by the term *gairaigo* 'foreign words' (lit. 'foreign coming words'). The relative proportions of these loanwords in the *Genkai* dictionary (1859) were: Sino-Japanese words — 60 per cent, foreign words — 1.4 per cent, the rest being native words. Although the proportion of foreign words has been steadily increasing (see below), that of the Sino-Japanese words remains fairly constant.

The effect of loanwords on the Japanese language is not insignificant. In particular, the effects of Sino-Japanese borrowing have been felt in all aspects of the Japanese language, including syntax. Restricting our discussion to the domain of the lexicon, however, Sino-Japanese and foreign loanwords have resulted in a large number of synonymous expressions. This demonstrates that Japanese has borrowed even those words whose equivalents already existed in the language. This may appear at first to be unmotivated and uneconomical. However, synonymous words are often associated with different shades of meaning and stylistic values, thereby enriching the Japanese vocabulary and allowing for a greater range of expression. For example, some interesting observations can be made with regard to the following sets of synonymous triplets:

Gloss	'inn'	'idea'	'acrobat'	'detour'	'cancellation'
Native	yadoya	omoituki	karuwaza	mawarimiti	torikesi
S-J	ryokan	tyakusoo	kyokugei	ukairo	kaiyaku
Foreign	hoteru	aidea	akurobatto	baipasu	kyanseru

In general, the native words have broader meanings than their loan counterparts. For example, *torikesi* can be applied to various kinds of cancellation-type acts, even in taking back one's words. The Sino-Japanese word *kaiyaku* is normally used with reference to the cancellation of contracts and other formal transactions. The foreign word *kyanseru*, on the other hand, is used for the cancellation of appointments or ticket reservations etc. The Sino-Japanese words, which generally convey a more formal impression, tend to be used with reference to higher-quality objects than do the native equivalents. On the other hand, the foreign words have a modern and stylish flavour.

Though various factors can be pointed out to account for the ready acceptance of loanwords in Japanese, the main linguistic reasons have to do with the lack of nominal inflections and the presence of a syllabic writing system. Since Japanese does not mark gender, person or number in nouns and since cases are indicated by separate particles, a loanword can simply be inserted into any position where a native nominal might appear with no morphological readjustment. For the borrowing of verbal expressions, Japanese utilises the verb *suru*, which has the very general meaning 'do'. This useful verb can attach to the nominal forms of loanwords to create verbal expressions; e.g. the Sino-Japanese word *hukusya* 'copy' yields *hukusya-suru* 'to copy' and the English loan *kopii* 'copy' yields *kopii-suru* 'to copy'.

The proportion and the status of the Sino-Japanese words in Japanese are strikingly similar to those of the Latinate words in English. The proportion of Latinate words in English vocabulary is estimated to be around 55 per cent, while that of Germanic (Anglo-Saxon) words and of other foreign loans are 35 per cent and 10 per cent, respectively. Furthermore, the status of the Sino-Japanese words in Japanese is quite similar to that of Latinate words in English. As they tend to express abstract concepts, Sino-Japanese words make up the great majority of learned vocabulary items.

Loanwords other than those belonging to the stratum of Sino-Japanese words are called *gairaigo*. The first Japanese contacts with the western world came about in the middle of the sixteenth century, when a drifting Portuguese merchant ship reached the island of Tanegashima off Kyūshū. The Portuguese were followed by the Spaniards and Dutch. Thus, most of the earliest foreign words were from Portuguese, Spanish and especially Dutch. Toward the latter part of the nineteenth century, English replaced Dutch as the language of foreign studies; and presently, roughly 80 per cent of the foreign vocabulary of Japanese are words of English origin.

English terms were first translated into Japanese semantically using Chinese characters, which resulted in a large number of *kango* 'Chinese words' coined in Japan. This was in keeping with the traditional practice of assigning semantically appropriate Chinese characters to foreign loanwords. In order to represent the original sounds, a *katakana* rendering of the original pronunciation accompanied the translated word. Thus, in the initial phase of loan translation, there were, for each word, both character and *katakana* representations; the former representing the meaning and the latter the sound. These foreign words then had two paths open to them; some retained the character rendering and began to be pronounced according to the readings of the characters, while others preserved the *katakana* rendering. A good number of words took both paths, resulting in the formation of many doublets — the *kango* version and the foreign (phonetic) version; e.g. *kentiku:birudingu* 'building', *sikihu:siitu* 'sheet', *tetyoo:nooto* 'notebook', and more recently *densikeisanki:konpyuutaa* 'computer'.

Contemporary practice now is to borrow by directly representing just the sounds using *katakana*. But when foreign loanwords are rendered in *katakana*, the original pronunciation is most often grossly altered. Since all the *katakana* except ン end in a vowel, consonant clusters and a final consonant of a loanword are altered into sequences consisting of a consonant and a vowel. Thus, a one-syllable word like *strike* becomes the five-mora word *sutoraiku* (see section 4). As a consequence, many Japanese words of English origin are totally incomprehensible to the ears of the native English speaker, much to the chagrin of the Japanese. Japanese-born American historian and former ambassador to Japan, E.O. Reischauer, comments, 'It is pathetic to see the frustration of Japanese in finding that English speakers cannot recognise, much less understand, many of the English words they use.'

In addition to the phonological process, there are three other factors which annoy non-Japanese when encountering Japanised borrowings from their native tongues. They are: (1) change in semantics, e.g. *sutoobu* (< *stove*) exclusively designates a room heater; (2) Japanese coinages, e.g. *bakku miraa* (< *back* + *mirror*) for the rear-view mirror of an automobile; and (3) change in form due to simplification, *pan-suto* (< *panty stockings*) 'panty hose, tights'.

Foreign words are conspicuous not only in number (they abound in commercial messages and inundate Japanese daily life), but also in form, as they are written in *katakana*. The ubiquity and conspicuousness of foreign words in contemporary Japan as well as the fact that they are often used without precise understanding of their original meanings alarm language purists. Occasional public outcries are heard and opinions for curbing the use of foreign words are voiced. However, such purists are fighting a losing battle and, to their dismay, foreign words are gaining a firm footing in the Japanese language.

Foreign loanwords, like slang expressions, are quickly adopted and then abandoned. Only those that are firmly entrenched in the language can be found in dictionaries. The proportion of foreign loanwords in dictionaries is, however, steadily increasing. The ratio of the foreign words in the *Genkai*, published in 1859, was only 1.4 per cent. The rate increased to 3.5 per cent in the *Reikai Kokugojiten* published in 1956. The 1972 version of *Shin Meikai Kokugojiten* has *gairaigo* comprising 7.8 per cent of its entries. It is predicted that foreign words would claim at least a 10 per cent share of the entries in a dictionary compiled today.

Onomatopoeic and other sound symbolic words form another conspicuous group of words in the Japanese lexicon. In a narrow sense, onomatopoeia refers to those conventionalised mimetic expressions of natural sounds. These words are called *giongo* 'phonomimes' in Japanese; e.g. *wan-wan* 'bow-wow', *gata-gata* '(clattering noise)'. In addition to phonomimes, the Japanese lexicon has two other classes of sound symbolic or synaesthetic expressions. They are *gitaigo* 'phenomimes' and *gisyoogo* 'psychomimes'. Phenomimes 'depict' states, conditions or manners of the external world (e.g. *yoboyobo* 'wobbly', *kossori* 'stealthily'), while psychomimes symbolise mental conditions or states (e.g. *ziin* 'poignantly', *tikutiku* 'stingingly'). In the following discussion, all these classes of sound symbolic words will be collectively referred to as onomatopoeic words.

In comparison to English, many Japanese verbs have very general meanings. *Naku*, for example, covers all manners of crying that are expressed in specific English verbs such as *weep* and *sob*. Similarly, *warau* is a general term for laughing. This lack of specificness of the verb meaning is compensated by the presence of onomatopoeic words. Indeed, one may argue that the differences between *weep* and *sob* and between *chuckle* and *smile* etc. are more expressive in Japanese. Some examples follow: 'cry' *waa-waa naku*, 'weep' *meso-meso naku*, 'sob' *kusun-kusun naku*, 'blubber' *oi-oi naku*, 'whimper' *siku-siku naku*, 'howl' *wan-wan naku*, 'pule' *hii-hii naku*, 'mewl' *een-een to naku*; 'laugh' *ha-ha-ha to warau*, 'smile' *niko-niko to warau*, 'chuckle' *kutu-kutu to warau*, 'haw-haw' *wa-ha-ha to warau*, 'giggle' *gera-gera to warau*, 'snigger' *nita-nita warau*, 'simper' *ohoho to warau*, 'grin' *nikori to warau*, 'titter' *kusu-kusu warau*.

Sound qualities and synaesthetic effects are correlated to a certain extent, especially with regard to the voicing opposition and differences in vowel quality. In reference to the voicing opposition, the voiced versions relate to heavier or louder sounds or stronger, bigger, rougher actions or states and the voiceless versions to lighter or softer sounds or crisper or more delicate actions or states.

Differences in vowel quality also correlate with differences in the texture of observed phenomena. High or closed vowels are associated with higher or softer sounds or activities involving smaller objects, with low vowels correlating with the opposite phenomena. The front-back opposition is similarly correlated with loudness and size, as is the high-low opposition. Thus, *kiin* is a shrill metallic sound, while *kaan* is the sound of a fairly large bell and *goon* the sound of a heavy bell of a Buddhist temple. *Boro-boro* symbolises the vertical dropping of relatively small objects such as tear drops, as opposed to *bara-bara*, which depicts the dropping of objects by scattering them. A small whistle sounds *pippii* and a steam whistle goes *poppoo*. A goat bleats *mee*, and a cow lows *moo*. *Gero-gero* is the way a frog croaks, but *goro-goro* is the rumbling of thunder.

Onomatopoeic expressions permeate Japanese life. They occur in animated speech and abound in literary works to the chagrin of the translators of Japanese literature. In baby-talk, many animals are referred to by the words that mimic their cries; *buu-buu* 'pig', *wan-wan* 'dog', *nyan-nyan* 'cat', *moo-moo* 'cow'. Indeed, names of many noise-making insects and certain objects are derived by a similar process; *kakkoo* 'cuckoo', *kirigirisu* '(a type of grass-hopper)', *gatya-gatya* '(a noise-making cricket)'. There are said to be more than thirty kinds of cicadas in Japan and many of them are named after the noises they make: *tuku-tuku-boosi*, *kana-kana*, *min-min-zemi*, *tii-tii-zemi* etc. A hammer is sometimes called *tonkati* and a favourite pastime of the Japanese is *patinko* 'pinball game', which is sometimes referred to by the more expressive form *tinzyara*, mimicking the noise of the *patinko* parlour.

4 Phonology

Although different phonemic interpretations are possible, perhaps the most orthodox inventories of Japanese segmental phonemes are those set out in table 43.2.

The basic vowel phonemes of the standard dialect are rather straightforward. However, a great deal of dialectal variation in the vocalic

Table 43.2: Segmental Phonemes of Japanese

Vowels				
	i		u	
	e		o	
		a		

Consonants				
	p	t	k	
	b	d	g	
		s		h
		z		
		r		
	m	n		
	w		j	
			N	Q

system is observed. Dialectal systems range from a three-vowel system (/i/, /u/, /a/) in the Yonaguni dialect of Okinawa to an eight-vowel system in the Nagoya dialect, which, in addition to the five vowels of the standard dialect, possesses the central vowels /ü/ and /ö/, as well as the low front vowel /æ/. Despite these variations, it is generally believed that the basic vowels of the Japanese language are those five vowels set out in table 43.2, which are observed in the major dialects of Tōkyō, Kyōto, Ōsaka etc., and that the other dialectal systems have evolved from the five-vowel system.

In the standard dialect, there are two characteristics concerning vowels. One is the articulation of /u/; it is unrounded [ɯ]. The other is the devoicing of high vowels /u/ and /i/ in a voiceless environment; [kɯtsɯ] 'shoe', [haʃi] 'chopstick', [sɯsɯki] 'eulalia'. Specifying the notion of voiceless environment precisely is not easy, but the following factors have been identified so far: (1) /i/ and /u/ will only devoice if not contiguous to a voiced sound; (2) the high vowels do not devoice when they are initial even followed by a voiceless sound; and (3) accented high vowels do not devoice even if flanked by voiceless consonants. The phenomenon also depends on speech tempo; in slow, deliberate speech, devoicing is less frequent.

Among the consonants, notable phenomena are two pervasive allophonic rules: the palatalisation and affrication of dental consonants. The former involves /s/, /z/, /t/ and /d/ and the latter /t/, /d/ and /z/.

In the non-Sino-Japanese vocabulary of the Japanese lexicon (cf. section 3), the dental consonants and their palatalised or affricated versions are in complementary distribution:

/s/:	[ʃ]	before *i*
	[s]	elsewhere
/z/:	[dʒ]	before *i*
	[dz]	before *u*
	[z]	elsewhere

/t/:	[tʃ]	before *i*
	[ts]	before *u*
	[t]	elsewhere
/d/:	[dʒ]	before *i*
	[dz]	before *u*
	[d]	elsewhere

In the Sino-Japanese vocabulary, there is a contrast between the dentals and their palatalised versions; e.g. [sa] 'difference': [ʃa] 'diagonal', but these are generally analysed as /sa/ and /sya/, the latter of which undergoes the palatalisation process just like the /si/ sequence seen above. (Except for proper nouns, which are transliterated in *rōmaji*, the Japanese expressions in this text are transliterated according to the phonemic representation; thus what is transliterated as *si*, *ti*, *tu* etc. should be read with appropriate palatalisation and affrication as [ʃi], [tʃi], [tsɯ] etc. according to the above distributional pattern.)

The palatalisation and the affrication described here are very pervasive and cause morphophonemic alternations. Thus, when verb stems that end in a dental consonant are affixed with suffixes beginning in a high vowel, palatalisation or affrication occurs. Observe the alternations: [kas-ɯ] 'lend-pres.': [kas-anai] 'lend-neg.': [kas-e] 'lend-imper.': [kaʃ-imas-ɯ] 'lend-polite-pres.', [kats-ɯ] 'win-pres.': [kat-anai] 'win-neg.': [kat-e] 'win-imper.': [katʃ-imas-ɯ] 'win-polite-pres.'.

The same rules apply to loanwords; e.g. [ʃiidzün] *season*, [tʃiimɯ] *team*, [tsɯaa] *tour*. Many younger speakers have begun to pronounce forms such as *party* and other recent loans with [t]. On the other hand, the pronunciation of [s] before [i] appears to be more difficult, so that words such as *seat* and *system* are almost invariably pronounced with [ʃi].

Other pervasive phonological rules are seen in verb inflection, which involves affixation of various suffixes. The most important consideration here is the distinction between verb stems ending in a consonant (C-stems) and those ending in a vowel (V-stems), for this distinction largely determines the shape of the suffixes. The clearest such case is the choice of an imperative suffix: C-stems take *-e* and V-stems *-ro*; *kak-e* 'write-imper.', *mi-ro* 'look-imper.'.

In other situations, phonological rules intervene to resolve consonant clusters and vowel clusters resulting from the joining of C-stems and consonant-initial suffixes (C-suffixes) and of V-stems and vowel-initial suffixes (V-suffixes). In the former case, the suffix-initial consonants are elided and in the latter, the suffix-initial vowels are elided. For example, the initial consonant of the present tense suffix /-ru/ is elided after a C-stem verb like /kak-/ 'to write', while it is retained after a V-stem verb like /mi-/ 'to see', as seen in the contrast, *kak-u:mi-ru*. As an example of a suffix with an initial vowel, take the negative /-anai/. With /kak-/, it retains the initial vowel, while it is lost after /mi-/: *kak-anai:mi-nai*. The other inflectional categories are exemplified in the chart of verb inflection.

Japanese Verb Inflection

	C-stem 'to cut'	V-stem 'to wear (clothes)'	
Imperative	kir-e	ki-ro	
Present	kir-u	ki-ru	
Past	kit-ta	ki-ta	
Participial	kit-te	ki-te	
Provisional	kir-eba	ki-reba	C-suffixes
Tentative	kir-oo	ki-yoo	
Passive	kir-are-ru	ki-rare-ru*	
Causative	kir-ase-ru	ki-sase-ru	
Negative	kir-ana-i	ki-na-i**	
Polite	kir-imas-u	ki-mas-u	V-suffixes
Desiderative	kir-ita-i	ki-ta-i	
Infinitive	kir-i	ki	

Note:* /-ru/ here and in the causative and /-u/ in the polite form are the present tense suffix. ** /-i/ is the present tense suffix for adjectives.

The basic syllable structure of Japanese is CV and this canonical pattern is also imposed on loanwords. A consonant cluster and a syllable-final consonant will be made into a CV sequence by inserting [ɯ] (or [o] after a dental stop; remember that [tɯ] or [dɯ] do not occur phonetically in Japanese). Thus, a word like *strike* will be turned into [sɯtoraikɯ]. As this word indicates, a vowel by itself forms a syllable — or more precisely a mora (see page 868) — and sequences of vowels occur. This is one deviation from the basic CV pattern. The other deviation has to do with two types of consonants that may close a syllable. They are non-nasal consonants followed by homorganic consonants of the following syllable and a nasal that closes a syllable; e.g. [jappari] 'as expected', [jatto] 'finally', [jɯkkɯri] 'slowly', [hontoo] 'truly', [hampa] 'haphazard', [koŋgari] 'crisply', [hoN] 'book'.

Since the phonetic values of all these syllable-final consonants, except the word-final nasal in [hoN] and other such words, are entirely predictable from the nature of the following consonants, they are assigned to two archiphonemes: /Q/ for the non-nasal consonants and /N/ for the nasal consonants. When /N/ occurs word-finally it assumes the value of the uvular nasal [N] or simply nasalisation of the vowel identical to the preceding vowel. Thus, /hoN/ 'book' will be [hoN] or [hoõ]. (Words such as *pen* and *spoon*, which end in [n], are borrowed with the [N] replacing the final nasal, as [peN] and [sɯpɯɯN], respectively.)

The syllable-final consonants constitute one rhythmic unit, much like the syllabic [n̩] and [l̩] in English. This leads us to a discussion of an important phonological unit of Japanese, namely the *mora*. In Japanese phonology, a distinction needs to be made between the suprasegmental units syllable and mora. A form such as *sinbun* 'newspaper' consists of two syllables *sin* and *bun*, but a Japanese speaker further subdivides the form into four units *si*, *n*, *bu* and *n*, which correspond to the four letters of *kana* in writing the word. A mora in Japanese is a unit which can be represented by one letter of *kana* and which functions as a rhythmic unit in the composition of Japanese *waka* and *haiku*, the Japanese traditional poems. Thus, in poetic compositions, *sinbun* is counted as having four, rather than two, rhythmic units, and would be equivalent in length to *hatimaki* 'headband'.

While ordinary syllables include a vowel, morae need not. In addition to the moraic nasal seen in *sinbun* above, there are consonantal morae. These occur as the first element in geminate consonants discussed above, e.g. *hakkiri* 'clearly', *yappari* 'as expected', *tatta* 'stood up'. Although these geminate consonants have different phonetic values, the first segments, which constitute morae, are written in *hiragana* with a small っ ([tsɯ]). *Hakkiri* is written with four letters and counted as having four morae — *ha-k-ki-ri*. If a native speaker is asked to pronounce this word slowly marking off each mora unit, he would pronounce it according to the way it is written in *hiragana*, namely as, *ha-tu-ki-ri*.

Long vowels, written with two of the same *kana* or with one *kana* followed by a bar indicating length, also count as two morae; e.g. *ookii* 'big' is a two-syllable (*oo-kii*), four-mora (*o-o-ki-i*) word.

Both morae and syllables play an important role in the Japanese accentual system. For one thing, pitch change occurs at the mora level. The one-syllable word *kan* 'completion', for example, has a pitch drop after the first mora as *ka̅n*. This contrasts with another *kan* 'sense', which has the pitch configuration *ka̅n̅*. Moreover, in the standard dialect the initial low pitch can be only one mora in length. Thus, if the first syllable contains two morae, as in *ooi* 'many' or *hantai* 'opposite', only the first mora will have the low pitch: *oo̅i̅*, *ha̅n̅ta̅i̅*. If the initial syllable has just one mora, it of course will have the low pitch (unless it is accented); *ha̅tu̅me̅i̅* 'invention'. (Forms beginning with high pitch can also have high pitch but only for one mora, the second mora and the rest being low pitched.)

The concept of syllable also plays a role in Japanese accentuation. In the standard dialect, it is the syllabic unit which carries accent or the mark of pitch fall. This is seen from the fact that two-mora syllables always have the accent on the first mora. That is, while there are forms like *ko'orogi* 'cricket', which is realised as *ko̅o̅rogi*, there is no form like *koo'rogi*, with an accent on the second mora of the first syllable, which would be pronounced as *koo̅rogi*. This does not mean that there is no form with a high-pitched second mora. Such forms occur in two situations. One case occurs when the word contains no accent, e.g. _kooru_ 'to freeze'. The other case is when the second mora is an independent syllable and carries the accent as in _koga'isya_ (_kogaisya_) 'subsidiary company'. The same applies with other types of mora. There are forms like _ga'nko_ 'stubborn', but none like _gan'ko_, with an accent on the second mora of the first syllable. If a mora were an accentual unit, there should be no reason for such a restriction. Thus, Japanese accentuation rules must refer to both moraic and syllabic units.

Incidentally, not all Japanese dialects have both syllabic and moraic units. Certain dialects in the northern Tohoku region and the southern Kyūshū region do not count forms like _matti_ 'match' and _honya_ 'book-store' as having three rhythmic units. Rather they are separated into only two units, _mat-ti_ and _hon-ya_. A syllable with a long vowel is also counted as one unit in these dialects. Furthermore, in these dialects the syllable is also the unit of pitch assignment.

Since these dialects which recognise only syllabic units occur in the peripheral areas of northern and southern Japan, the Japanese dialectologist Takesi Sibata hypothesises that Japanese was once a syllable language from which the more contemporary mora dialects have developed.

As the preceding discussion indicates, Japanese accentuation involves pitch differences. If a textbook definition were to be applied to Japanese, most Japanese dialects would be called tone languages. In the Kyōto dialect, for example, the segmental form _hasi_ has three pitch patterns each associated with a distinct meaning: _hasi_ with H(igh) H(igh) is 'edge', _hasi_ with L(ow) H is 'chopsticks', and _hasi_ with HL is 'bridge'. In certain dialects not only the level tones H and L, but also a contour tone H-L is observed. Again, in Kyōto, _saru_ 'monkey' is L H-L; that is, the second mora _ru_ begins high and falls to low.

However, the Japanese accentual system is characteristically distinct from the archetypal tone languages of the Chinese type. In this type of language, it is necessary to specify the tone for each syllable. If a word or phrase has two or more syllables, each syllable needs to have a tone specified for it; there is no way of predicting the tone of each syllable of a word or phrase from something else. This is not the case for Japanese. In the majority of Japanese dialects, given diacritic accent markers and a set of rules, the pitch of each syllable of a phrase can be predicted, thereby making the specification of the pitch for each individual syllable unnecessary. In other words, the phonemic nature of the Japanese accentuation is reducible to the abstract accent marker that indicates the location of pitch fall.

Rules that predict actual pitch shapes differ slightly from one dialect to another, but in the standard dialect, the following three ordered rules assign correct pitches (indicated in parentheses) to phonemic representations of such words as /sakura/ (LHH) 'cherry', /za'kuro/ (HLL) 'pomegranate', /koko'ro/ (LHL) 'heart', as well as to those of phrases like /sakura ga/ (LHH H) 'cherry nom.', /miyako' ga/ (LHH L) 'capital nom.' etc.:

(a) Assign high pitch to all morae.

(b) Assign low pitch to all morae following the accent.

(c) Assign low pitch to the first mora if the second is high pitched.

In the standard dialect, one only needs to know the location of pitch fall in predicting the phonetic pitch shape. However, in other dialects additional information may be called for. In some dialects (e.g. Kyōto, Ōsaka) more than the location of pitch change needs be specified in order to assign the pitch contour to a word; specifically, whether a word begins with high pitch or with low pitch must be indicated. The standard dialect has predominant high pitch, as can be noticed from the first of the rules given above, but some dialects (e.g. Kagoshima) have a system with predominant low pitch, in which pitch changes all entail the raising of pitch. Finally, some dialects (e.g. Miyakonojō) have just one accentual pattern, which perforce makes the system non-phonemic.

5 Syntax

The basic word order in Japanese is subject, (indirect object) direct object, verb; e.g.

(a) Taroo ga   Hanako ni   sono hon   o   yatta.
         nom.   dat. that   book acc. gave
'Taro gave that book to Hanako.'

However, emphatic fronting may move a non-subject element to sentence-initial position and therefore variously reordered sentences are possible — an important consideration being that the verb always remains in final position. But there seems to be a restriction: when more than one element is fronted, the resulting sentences are not so well formed as the ones that involve the movement of one element. Thus, the above sentence has the following well formed and less well formed variations:

(b)   Hanako ni Taroo ga sono hon o yatta (fronting of the indirect object).
(c)   Sono hon o Taroo ga Hanako ni yatta (fronting of the direct object).
(d)   ?Hanako ni sono hon o Taroo ga yatta (fronting of both indirect and direct object).
(e)   ?Sono hon o Hanako ni Taroo ga yatta (fronting of both indirect and direct object).
(f)   Taroo ga sono hon o Hanako ni yatta (reversing the order of indirect and direct object).

Related to the basic SOV word order are the following characteristics that are shared by a large number of other SOV languages:

(a) Nominal relations are expressed by postpositional (as opposed to prepositional) particles. (See the above examples.)

(b) The demonstrative, numeral (plus classifier) and descriptive adjective precede the noun in that order; e.g. *sono san-nin no ookii kodomo* (that three person of big child) 'those three big children'. (In this kind of combination, the numeral and adjective expressions may be in reverse order.)

(c) The genitive noun precedes the possessed noun; e.g. *Taroo no hon* (Taro of book) 'Taro's book'.

(d) The relative clause precedes the noun modified; e.g. [*Taroo ga katta*] *hon* ([Taroo nom. bought] book) 'the book which Taro bought'.

(e) The proper noun precedes the common noun; e.g. *Taroo ozisan* (Taro uncle) 'Uncle Taro'.

(f) The adverb precedes the verb; e.g. *hayaku hasiru* (quickly run) 'run quickly'.

(g) Auxiliaries follow the main verb; e.g. *ik-itai* (go-want) 'want to go', *ik-eru* (go can) 'can go'.

(h) The comparative expression takes the order standard–marker of comparison–adjective; e.g. *Taroo yori kasikoi* (Taroo-than-smart) 'smarter than Taro'.

(i) Questions are formed by the addition of the sentence-final particle *ka*; e.g. *Taroo ga kita* 'Taro came' → *Taroo ga kita ka* 'did Taro come?'. Also, unlike English, there is no movement of a *wh*-element in a *wh*-question. Thus, the question word *nani* 'what' remains in object position in the question: *Taroo wa nani o katta ka* (Taroo top. what acc. bought Q) 'What did Taro buy?'

The basic Japanese sentence type exhibits the nominative-accusative case marking pattern, whereby the subjects of both transitive and intransitive sentences are marked by the particle *ga* and the object of a transitive sentence with a distinct particle, *o*. There are, however, three noteworthy deviations from this basic pattern. They are illustrated below along with the basic pattern.

(a) Taroo ga kita.
      nom. came
   'Taro came.'

(b) Taroo ga hebi o korosita.
      nom. snake acc. killed
   'Taro killed the snake.'

(c) Taroo ga Hanako ni atta.
      nom.   dat. met
   'Taro met Hanako.'

(d) Taroo ni eigo ga wakaru.
      dat. English nom. understand
   'Taro understands English.'

(e) Taroo ga Hanako ga suki da.
      nom.   nom. like copula
   'Taro likes Hanako.'

While English consistently exhibits the basic transitive sentence pattern for all these expressions, it is rather exceptional in this regard. Many other languages belonging to different language families show similar deviations along the lines of Japanese. The nominative-dative pattern of (c) is seen in German with verbs like *helfen* 'help' and *danken* 'thank'. The dative-nominative pattern seen in (d) is also very frequently seen in Indo-European languages as well; e.g. Spanish *me gusta la cerveza* 'I like beer', Russian *mne nravitsja kniga* 'I like a book'. In Japanese, predicates like *aru* 'have', *dekiru* 'can do' and *hituyoo da* 'necessary' govern the dative-nominative pattern.

Less frequently seen is the nominative-nominative pattern in (e). As the above examples from Spanish and Russian indicate, the predicate 'like' is normally subsumed under the dative-nominative pattern in those languages that exhibit this pattern. Japanese has a distinct nominative-nominative pattern for predicates such as *suki da* 'like', *zyoozu da* 'good at', *hosii* 'want' etc. Another language that has this pattern regularly with predicates similar to those given here is Korean.

Just as in many other languages, many important syntactic phenomena centre around the subject noun phrase. We will discuss some of them, but since they can be best treated in comparison to the topic noun phrase, we shall now turn to discourse-related phenomena.

6 Discourse Phenomena

One of the most important aspects of Japanese grammar has to do with the construction involving the particle *wa*. This particle, generally regarded as a topic marker, attaches to various nominals and adverbials, as seen below, and those constructions with a *wa*-marked constituent are called the topic construction.

<table>
<tr><td>(a)</td><td colspan="2">Taroo ga</td><td>Hanako ni</td><td>sono hon o</td><td>nitiyoobi ni</td><td>watasita.</td></tr>
<tr><td></td><td></td><td>nom.</td><td>dat.</td><td>that book acc.</td><td>Sunday on</td><td>gave</td></tr>
<tr><td colspan="7">'Taro gave that book to Hanako on Sunday.'</td></tr>
<tr><td>(b)</td><td colspan="6">Taroo wa Hanako ni sono hon o nitiyoobi ni watasita.</td></tr>
<tr><td></td><td colspan="6">(Topicalisation of the subject)</td></tr>
<tr><td>(c)</td><td colspan="6">Hanako ni wa Taroo ga sono hon o nitiyoobi ni watasita.</td></tr>
<tr><td></td><td colspan="6">(Topicalisation of the indirect object)</td></tr>
<tr><td>(d)</td><td colspan="6">Sono hon wa Taroo ga Hanako ni nitiyoobi ni watasita.</td></tr>
<tr><td></td><td colspan="6">(Topicalisation of the direct object)</td></tr>
<tr><td>(e)</td><td colspan="6">Nitiyoobi ni wa Taroo ga sono hon o Hanako ni watasita.</td></tr>
<tr><td></td><td colspan="6">(Topicalisation of the adverbial)</td></tr>
</table>

As seen above, the nominative particle *ga* as well as the accusative *o* drop when *wa* is attached, while other particles tend to be retained (see the dative *ni* in (c), for example).

It is also possible to have two or more *wa*-attached constituents, as in the following example:

(f)   Taroo wa nitiyoobi ni wa Hanako ni sono hon o watasita.
       (Topicalisation of the subject and the adverbial)

In the above examples, the topic has been 'extracted' from clause-internal position. While these are typical topic constructions, there are others whose topics cannot be related to a non-topic structure, i.e. the comment is itself a complete clause structure. For example:

(a)   Sakana wa   tai   ga   ii.
       fish   top. red snapper   nom. good
       'As for fish, red snappers are good.'
(b)   Huro   wa   kimoti   ga   ii.
       bath   top. feeling   nom. good
       'As for the bath, it feels good.'

Recent discussion in the literature of Japanese grammar published in English has concentrated mainly on identifying those factors which determine the attachment of *wa*. What has been explicated are those factors which pertain to the nature of 'topic' or 'theme', namely, that the entity must be old information or given.

What has been lacking in the discussion of *wa* in these treatments is the notion of sentence type, which figures importantly in the tradition of Japanese grammar. The relevant distinction here is the difference between a sentence of description and that of judgement. When one describes an event or a state, no topic construction is used, while when one is to make a certain judgement about an entity, then that entity would be marked by *wa* and the topic construction results. Thus, if someone were just describing the sky, he would say: *sora ga aoi* (sky nom. blue) 'the sky is blue', but if someone were to make a judgement about the sky (in this case that the sky is blue), he would use the topic construction and say: *sora wa aoi*, which would have to be also translated as 'the sky is blue' in English.

In fact, one has a certain degree of freedom as to the use and non-use of the topic construction depending on whether the narration involves making judgement or not. For example, in the following narrative, there is no topic construction involved:

(a)   Hitori   no   kodomo ga   aruite   kita.
       one   of   child   nom. walking   came
       'A child came walking.'
(b)   Soko e   inu   ga   hasitte   kita.
       there at   dog   nom. running   came
       'There came a dog running.'
(c)   Sosite   sono inu   ga   kodomo ni   kamituita.
       and then   that   dog   nom. child   to   bit
       'And then, the dog bit the child.'

In the conventional account, *wa* is attached to an entity referring to old information. *Inu* 'dog' in sentence (c) is expected to be marked *wa*, for it has been previously introduced into the discourse and is hence old information. But the sentences (a)–(c) constitute a perfectly well formed chunk of a narrative. Of course, the *inu* in question can be topicalised, as below, but then there is a slight difference between the two versions of the narrative.

(c′) Sosite   sono inu   wa   kodomo ni   kamituita.
      and then   that dog   top. child   to bit
      'And then, the dog, it bit the child.'

The difference is this: in the (a)–(c) version, each event is described as if witnessed afresh. To seek analogy in cinema, the (a)–(c) version involves three scenes in succession. In the (a)–(c′) version, on the other hand, the first two sentences describe two successive events, presented as two discrete scenes, but the (c′) sentence does not constitute a different scene; it rather dwells on the scene introduced by the (b) sentence by detailing on the dog introduced there. In uttering (c′), the speaker is not simply saying what has happened next; rather he is making a 'judgement' regarding the dog, i.e. what can be said about the dog that came running.

The discussion of the topic construction along these lines accounts naturally for a number of facts. The restriction that only what is identifiable (i.e. old information or given) can be topicalised follows naturally from the notion of making a judgement; one would not make a judgement about something which is not part of the hearer's presumed knowledge. Also, the fact that subordinate clauses do not admit the topic construction is understandable in view of the fact that subordinate clauses normally describe background events and, as seen above, descriptions of events are done in non-topic sentences.

In the tradition of Japanese grammar, the notions of topic and subject are often confused, for, as seen above, they are not clearly separated in languages like English. However, the topic has a status distinct from that of the grammatical subject. That is, the Japanese topic does not participate in any syntactic processes that the subject does. The only exception is the topic that is 'converted' from the subject such as the *sono inu wa* (that dog top.) in (c′) above. We will show this in terms of two grammatical phenomena in which the subject figures importantly, namely reflexivisation and subject honorification.

In Japanese, there is a general constraint that the antecedent of the reflexive form *zibun* 'self' must be the subject at some stage of derivation. Thus, in the following sentence, the reflexive form is coreferential only with the subject Taro.

(a) Taroo ga   Hanako ni   zibun   no   hon   o   watasita.
           nom.   dat.   self   of   book acc. handed
     'Taro handed his own book to Hanako.'

Taroo in (a) functions like a subject even if it is topicalised, but that the subject function is not the property of the topic is seen from the fact that when non-subjects are topicalised, they exhibit no subject properties. In other words, the topicalisation of the indirect object *Hanako* of (a) confers no subject properties on it, as the following sentence cannot be understood to mean that Hanako and *zibun* are coreferential.

(b) Hanako ni wa Taroo ga zibun no hon o watasita.
   'As for Hanako, Taro handed his own book.'

Just as the term 'subject honorification' indicates, there is an honorific phenomenon that is 'triggered' when the subject refers to someone worthy of the speaker's respect. The process essentially involves attaching the prefix *o* to the infinitive form of the verb and then extending the sentence with the verbal form *naru* 'become'. This converts a plain sentence like (a) below into an honorific form as in (b).

(a) Sensei ga waratta.
   teacher nom. laughed
   'The teacher laughed.'
(b) Sensei ga o-warai-ni natta.
   lit. 'The teacher became to be laughing.'

Again, the subject-based topic can trigger subject honorification and the conversion of the *sensei ga* in (b) above into *sensei wa* results in a good sentence. But, the topic 'deriving' from non-subjects cannot trigger this process and (b) below is inappropriate; it expresses deference toward the speaker himself.

(a) Boku ga sensei o tasuketa.
   I nom. teacher acc. helped
   'I helped the teacher.'
(b) #Sensei wa boku ga o-tasuke-ni natta.
   teacher top. I nom. helped (honorific)
   'As for the teacher, I helped him.'

What is called for in a situation like (a)–(b) above is the other honorification process, called 'object honorification', which expresses the speaker's deference toward the referent of a non-subject nominal.

(c) Boku ga sensei o o-tasuke sita.
   I nom. teacher acc. helping did
   lit. 'I did the helping of the teacher.'
(d) Sensei wa boku ga o-tasuke sita.
   lit. 'As for the teacher, I did helping of him.'

The topic and the subject also show an important difference with respect to the scope of discourse domain. Although both subject and topic can function as a reference for a gapped element, the topic has a far larger scope in this function. In an English coordinate expression such as the following, the gap, indicated by Ø, in the second clause is understood to be identical with the subject of the first clause.

(a)　　John came and Ø took off his coat.

When the first clause is a subordinate clause, gapping of the subject of the main clause is not permitted; thus the following are not well formed.

(b)　　*When John came, Ø took off his coat.
(c)　　*As soon as John came, Ø took off his coat.

In Japanese, all of the above sentences are grammatical, for it allows elliptical expressions for a situation where English typically has pronominal expressions. However, note that the coordinate and subordinate clauses are in this respect grammatically distinct. In the case of coordination, as exemplified in (a) below, the gapped subject of the second clause must be interpreted as identical with the subject of the first clause. But in the case of subordination, as exemplified in (b)–(c) below, the gapped subjects of the main clause must be interpreted as different from the subject of the subordinate clause.

(a)　　Taroo ga　　ki-te,　　suguni　　　　Ø　　uwagi　　o　　　nuida.
　　　　　　　　nom. came　　immediately　　　　　coat　　acc.　took off
　　　　'Taro$_i$ came, and immediately Ø$_i$ took off the coat.'
(b)　　Taroo ga　　kuru-to,　　suguni Ø uwagi o nuida.
　　　　　　　　　　come-when
　　　　'When Taro$_i$ came, immediately Ø$_j$ took off the coat.'
(c)　　Taroo ga　　kuru-ya　　inaya,　　　suguni Ø uwagi o nuida.
　　　　　　　　　　come-as　　soon as
　　　　'As soon as Taro$_i$ came, immediately Ø$_j$ took off the coat.'

In the above examples, the subject of the first coordinate clause and the subject of the subordinate clauses are retained. The same situation obtains even in the reverse expressions, where the subject of the second coordinate clause and that of the main clause are retained.

(a)　　Ø kite, suguni Taroo ga uwagi o nuida.
　　　　'Ø$_i$ came, and immediately Taro$_i$ took off the coat.'
(b)　　Ø kuruto, suguni Taroo ga uwagi o nuida.
　　　　'When Ø$_i$ came, immediately Taro$_j$ took off the coat.'
(c)　　Ø kuru-ya ina ya, suguni Taroo ga uwagi o nuida.
　　　　'As soon as Ø$_i$ came, immediately Taro$_j$ took off the coat.'

However, when the topic form is used, the restriction on (b)–(c) does not obtain and the topic can function in reference to both the subject of the subordinate clause and that of the main clause.

(b') Taroo wa,   kuru-to,   suguni   uwagi   o   nuida.
      top. come-when   immediately   coat   acc.   took off
      'As for Taro$_i$, Ø$_i$ immediately took off the coat when Ø$_i$ came.'
(c') Taroo wa, kuru-ya inaya, suguni uwagi o nuida.
      'As for Taro$_i$, Ø$_i$ took off the coat as soon as Ø$_i$ came.'

As the comma after the topic in (b')–(c') above indicates, the structure of these differs from that underlying the non-topic sentences (b)–(c). That is, while the non-topic subordinate structure is like (a) below, the topic version is like (b):

(a)   [Taroo ga kuru]-to suguni Ø uwagi o nuida
(b)   Taroo wa [Ø kuru]-to suguni Ø uwagi o nuida

While the (b) structure above is the normal pattern, the topic can be retained in the subject position of the main clause, but still the topic functions as a reference for the gapped subject of the subordinate clause; e.g.

(c)   [Ø kuru]-to suguni Taroo wa uwagi o nuida

In other words, the topic has the scope over the entire sentence with the role of a reference for the gapped subject of both the subordinate and the main clause. The subject of the subordinate clause or of the main clause, on the other hand, has no such wide scope of reference.

7 Contextual Dependency

Compared to English, Japanese utterances are more context-dependent. This can be seen in assessing the appropriateness of the following two 'equivalent' expressions.

(a)   I'd see him.
(b)   Atasi   kare ni   au   wa.
        I   he   dat.   meet

Aside from semantic and discourse factors that preclude the possibility of (a), it is rather difficult to find a context in which the English sentence (a) is inappropriate. However, this is not the case for (b); there are a number of contextual factors that must be satisfied in order for the sentence to be an appropriate utterance. First, the sex of the speaker must be considered. Only a female speaker can utter this sentence. The first person pronoun *atasi* is a form exclusively used by a female speaker. And the sentence-final particle *wa*, which has the effect of softening the assertion, is also from the repertory of the particles for female speakers. If a comparable expression were to be uttered by a male speaker, it would be something like the following, where the pronoun for a male *boku* and a sex-neutral particle, *yo*, are used:

(c)   Boku kare ni au yo.

Secondly, the (b) sentence is only appropriate when uttered in a very informal setting. The sentence-final particle like *wa* would not be used in a formal setting and the first person pronoun *atasi* is a rather vulgar or coquettish form. Related to this is the status of the addressee. If the addressee is someone superior to the speaker, the addressee honorific ending -*imasu* needs to be employed. Thus, a more appropriate form for a little more formal setting would require the dropping of the sentence-final particle *wa*, the replacement of the pronoun *atasi* by the more formal form *watakusi* and the adjustment of the verbal ending. In other words, (b) would be replaced by the following expression on a little more formal occasion.

(b′)   Watakusi kare ni a-imasu.

The sentence (b′) can still be inappropriate depending on the person being referred to by the third person pronoun *kare* 'he'. If the person referred to is someone to whom the speaker is obliged to be deferential, then it is not quite appropriate to refer to him as *kare*; such a person is better referred to by *sono kata* 'that person' (lit. 'that direction'). Referring to the person by *sono kata* requires the use of the object honorific form of the verb, *o-ai suru* (see section 5). Should one want to make the utterance even politer, the suppletive form of 'to see/meet' *o-me ni kakaru* would be used. These modifications yield the following forms:

(b″)   Watakusi sono kata ni o-ai s-imasu.
(b‴)   Watakusi sono kata ni o-me ni kakar-imasu.

One can still go on elaborating the sentence, but the point should be clear. Japanese has different sets of personal pronouns for male and female speakers and for appropriate levels of politeness. Some of the sentence-final particles, which are used in moderating or strengthening the assertion one way or another, also differ for men and women. Thus, an adequate command of Japanese means both grammatical and sociolinguistic knowledge of the appropriate forms of subject or object honorific address. (Notice that at the elevated level of speech, speech style distinctions according to sex tend to be neutralised; thus, a form such as (b‴) above can be used by both male and female speakers.)

All these considerations mean that there are many synonyms that are differently used in reference to the speaker's sex, the addressee, as well as the referents of the nominals within a sentence. Addressee honorification and subject and object honorification are in general regular, but there are sufficient suppletive forms that are used regularly and so need to be learned separately. Thus, while speech levels are observed in other languages including English, Japanese has a highly grammaticalised system, which entails many synonymous expressions which must be used appropriately according to the context.

We have seen that numerous synonyms have also been created due to borrowing from Chinese and other foreign languages. In addition, one must contend with four kinds of writing systems. It is this multiplicity of coding possibilities which constitutes one unique aspect of Japanese and it is the multitude of synonymous expressions and the complexity of the contextual factors determining the appropriate choice that make the learning of Japanese very difficult for non-Japanese.

Bibliography

Miller (1967) is a comprehensible general account of Japanese with emphasis on the historical development; Miller (1971) presents documentation of the hypothesis relating Japanese to the Altaic family. Sansom (1928) is an excellent account of the grammar of Old Japanese, with a detailed discussion of the development of the writing system.

Martin (1975) is the most comprehensible account of the grammar of modern Japanese written in English, with numerous examples taken from actual published materials. Alfonso (1966) is a useful introduction to the structure of Japanese, while Kuno (1973) is particularly useful on particles and the topic construction. Hinds (1986) is written in a format convenient for looking up specific constructions and phenomena for contrastive and comparative studies. It is also unique among the available reference works for its inclusion of a large amount of actual conversational data. For phonology, McCawley (1968) is a generative treatment, including a useful survey of the accentual systems of Japanese dialects. Shibatani (1976) is a collection of papers dealing with selected topics in Japanese syntax within the framework of generative grammar. Shibatani (1982), another collection of papers, includes papers dealing with Japanese dialectology and sociolinguistics.

Acknowledgement

I am grateful to Charles M. De Wolf of Chiba University for discussing with me a number of topics covered here, as well as providing me with useful suggestions for the improvement of the present essay.

References

Alfonso, A. 1966. *Japanese Language Patterns*, 2 vols. (Sophia University Press, Tokyo)

Hinds, J. 1986. *Japanese* (Croom Helm Descriptive Grammars; Croom Helm, London)

Kuno, S. 1973. *The Structure of the Japanese Language* (MIT Press, Cambridge, Mass.)

McCawley, J.D. 1968. *The Phonological Component of the Grammar of Japanese* (Mouton, The Hague)

Martin, S.E. 1975. *A Reference Grammar of Japanese* (Yale University Press, New Haven)

Miller, R.A. 1967. *The Japanese Language* (University of Chicago Press, Chicago)

—— 1971. *Japanese and the Other Altaic Languages* (University of Chicago Press, Chicago)

Sansom, G. 1928. *An Historical Grammar of Japanese* (Oxford University Press, Oxford)

Shibatani, M. (ed.) 1976. *Japanese Generative Grammar* (Academic Press, New York)

—— (ed.) 1982. *Studies in Japanese Linguistics* (= *Lingua*, vol. 57, nos. 2–4) (North-Holland, Amsterdam)

44 KOREAN

Nam-Kil Kim

1 Historical Background

For a long time scholars have tried to associate the Korean language to one of the major language families but have not been successful in this venture. There have been many theories proposed on the origin of Korean. Based on the views as to where the Korean language first originated, two prominent views, which are called the Southern theory and the Northern theory, have been advocated by some scholars. According to the Southern theory, the Korean people and language originated in the south, namely the South Pacific region. There are two versions of this theory. One is that the Korean language is related to the Dravidian languages of India. This view is not taken seriously by contemporary linguists, but it was strongly advocated by the British scholar Homer B. Hulbert at the end of nineteenth century. Hulbert's argument was based on the syntactic similarities of Korean and the Dravidian languages. For instance, both languages have the same syntactic characteristics: the word order subject–object–verb, postpositions instead of prepositions, no relative pronouns, modifiers in front of the head noun, copula and existential as two distinct grammatical parts of speech etc.

The other version of the Southern theory is the view that Korean may be related to the Austronesian languages. There are some linguistic as well as anthropological and archeological findings which may support this view. The linguistic features of Korean which are shared by some Polynesian languages include the phonological structure of open syllables, the honorific system, numerals and the names of various body parts. The anthropological and archeological elements shared by Koreans and the people in other regions of the South Pacific are rice cultivation, tattooing, a matrilineal family system, the myth of an egg as the birth place of royalty and other recent discoveries in paleolithic or preceramic cultures. Although this Southern theory has been brought to the attention of many linguists, it is not accepted as convincing by linguists.

The Northern theory is the view that Korean is related to the Altaic family. Although this view is not wholly accepted by the linguistic community, the majority of Korean linguists and some western scholars seem inclined towards believing this view. The major language branches which belong to the Altaic family are Turkic, Mongolian and Tungusic. The area in which the Altaic languages are spoken runs from the Balkans to the Kamchatka Peninsula in the North Pacific. The Northern theory stipulates that the Tungusic branch of Altaic tribesmen migrated towards the south and reached the Korean peninsula. The Tungusic languages would include two major languages: Korean and Manchu. The view that Korean is a branch of the Altaic family is supported by anthro-archeological evidence such as comb ceramics (pottery with comb-surface design), bronze-ware, dolmens, menhirs and shamanism. All these findings are similar to those found in Central Asia, Siberia and northern Manchuria. Korean is similar to the Altaic languages with respect to the absence of grammatical elements such as number, genders, articles, fusional morphology, voice, relative pronouns and conjunctions. Vowel harmony and agglutination are also found in Korean as well as in the Altaic languages. Comparing the two theories, it is apparent that the Northern influence in the Korean language is more dominant than the Southern.

It has been discovered in recent archeological excavations that the early race called Paleosiberians lived in the Korean peninsula and Manchuria before the Altaic race migrated to these areas. The Paleosiberians, who include the Chukchi, Koryaks, Kamchadals, Ainu, Eskimos etc., were either driven away to the farther north by the newly arrived race or assimilated by the conquerors when they came to the Korean peninsula. It is believed that the migration of the new race towards the Korean peninsula took place around 4000 BC. Nothing is known about the languages of the earliest settlers. After migration, some ancient Koreans settled down in the regions of Manchuria and northern Korea while others moved farther to the south. Many small tribal states were established in the general region of Manchuria and the Korean peninsula from the first century BC to the first century AD. The ancient Korean language is divided into two dialects: the Puyŏ language and the Han language. The Puyŏ language was spoken by the people of tribal states such as Puyŏ, Kokuryŏ, Okchŏ and Yemaek in

Manchuria and northern Korea. The Han language was spoken by the people of the three Han tribal states of Mahan, Chinhan and Byŏnhan which were created in southern Korea.

Around the fourth century AD the small tribal states were vanquished and three kingdoms with strong central governments appeared in Manchuria and the Korean peninsula. Of these three kingdoms, the biggest kingdom, Kokuryŏ, occupied the territory of Manchuria and the northern portion of the Korean peninsula. The other two kingdoms, Paekche and Silla, established states in the southwestern and the southeastern regions of the Korean peninsula respectively. It is believed that the Kokuryŏ people spoke the Puyŏ language and the Silla people spoke the Han language; however, it is not certain what language the Paekche people spoke because the ruling class of the Paekche kingdom consisted of Puyŏ tribesmen who spoke the Puyŏ language. When the Korea peninsula was unified by Silla in the seventh century, the Han language became the dominant dialect paving the way for the emergence of a homogeneous language. The Han language finally became the sole Korean language through the two succeeding dynasties of Koryŏ (936–1392) and Chosŏn (1392–1910).

Since Silla's unification of the Korean peninsula in the seventh century, it appears that the language spoken in the capital has been the standard dialect. Thus, the Silla capital, Kyŏngju, dialect was the standard dialect during the unified Silla period from the seventh century to the tenth century. When Silla was succeeded by Koryŏ in the tenth century, the capital was moved from Kyŏngju, which was located in the southeastern region of the Korean peninsula, to Kaegyŏng in the central region of Korea and subsequently the dialect spoken in this new capital became the standard language in Koryŏ from the tenth century to the end of the fourteenth century. When the Yi (or Chosŏn) Dynasty succeeded Koryŏ at the end of the fourteenth century, the capital was established at Seoul, the present capital of South Korea, and the language spoken in this area became the standard dialect and has continued as a standard dialect to the present time. Thus, it is obvious that the formation of the standard dialect has been dominated by political decisions. We can find this even in the twentieth century. There are officially two standard dialects existing in Korea; one is the Seoul dialect in South Korea and the other the Phyŏng'yang dialect in North Korea. Each government has established prescriptive criteria for its own standard dialect and made separate policies on language.

Though the dialect distinction of one region from the other is not drastic owing to the relatively small size of the Korean peninsula, each region has its own characteristic dialects. For instance, in the Hamgyŏng dialect of northern Korea the final p of verb bases ending in p is pronounced as [b] before suffixed morphemes starting in a vowel, while in the standard Seoul dialect this final p is pronounced as [w] before a vowel; $təp$- 'hot' is pronounced [təbə] in the Hamgyŏng dialect but [təwə] in the standard dialect. As another example, in the standard dialect palatalisation is normal but in the Pʰyŏng'yang dialect palatalisation does not take place: katʰi 'together' is pronounced as [kacʰi] in the standard dialect but as [katʰi] in the Pʰyŏng'yang dialect. Historically, both Hamgyŏng and Pʰyŏng'yang dialects reflect archaic forms. That is, in the nineteenth-century Yi Dynasty language the words təp- and katʰi were pronounced as they are pronounced in the Hamyŏng and Pʰyŏng'yang dialects; and the pronunciation of these words in the standard dialect reflects this historical change.

The Korean language spoken before the fifteenth century is not well known because there are not many records or documents revealing how the language was used before the fifteenth century. It was in the fifteenth century that the alphabetic script (Han'gŭl) for writing Korean was invented by King Sejong. Before the Korean script was invented, only Chinese characters were used for the purpose of writing. But Chinese characters could not depict the living language spoken by Korean people, since Chinese characters were meaning-based and the grammar of classical Chinese did not have any connection with Korean grammar. Even after the Korean script was invented, Chinese characters were continuously used as the main means of writing until the twentieth century. In traditional Korean society, the learning and study of Chinese characters and classical Chinese were entirely monopolised by a small class of elite aristocrats. For average commoners, the time-consuming learning of Chinese characters was not only a luxury but also useless, because they were busy making a living and knowledge of Chinese characters did not help in improving their lives.

The use of Chinese characters imported a massive quantity of loanwords into the Korean lexicon. More than half of Korean words are Chinese-originated loanwords. Although Chinese loanwords and Korean-originated words have always coexisted, the Chinese loanwords came to dominate the original Korean words and subsequently many native Korean words completely vanished from use. A movement by people who wanted to restore native culture at the end of the nineteenth century tried to stimulate mass interest in the study of the Korean language. When the government proclaimed that the official governmental documents would be written both in Korean script and Chinese characters, the first newspapers and magazines were published in Korean script and the use of the Korean alphabet expanded. In the early twentieth century, more systematic studies on the Korean language were started and a few scholars published Korean grammar books. However, the active study of Korean grammar was discontinued owing to the Japanese colonial policy suppressing the study of Korean.

The study of the Korean language resumed after the end of World War II, but Korea was divided into two countries by the Big Powers. The language policies proposed and implemented by the two governments in the South and the North were different from each other. While both the Korean alphabet and Chinese characters were used in the South, only the Korean alphabet was used in the North. In the North the policy on the use of Chinese characters has been firm; that is, no instruction in Chinese characters has been given to students and Chinese characters are not used in newspapers, magazines or books. This policy has never been changed in the North. Contrary to this, in the South the policy on the instruction of Chinese characters has been inconsistent; whenever a new regime has come to power, both proponents and opponents of the use of Chinese characters have tried to persuade the government to adopt their views. Though the instruction of Chinese characters was abolished a couple of times by the government in the past, this abolition never lasted more than a few years. At the present time in the South, the government has adopted a policy which forces students in secondary schools to learn 1,800 basic Chinese characters.

The South and the North also have different policies on the so-called 'purification' of Korean. The purification of Korean means the sole use of native Korean words in everyday life by discontinuing the use of foreign-originated words. The main targets of this campaign are Sino-Korean words. In the North, the government has been actively involved in this campaign, mobilising newspapers and magazines to spread the newly translated or discovered pure Korean words to a wide audience of readers. In the South, some interested scholars and language study organisations have tried to advocate the purification of Korean through the media and academic journals, but the government has never officially participated in this kind of movement. It will be interesting to see what course each of the two governments will take in future with respect to language policy.

2 Phonology

The sound system of Korean consists of 21 consonants and ten vowels. The vowels can be classified by the three positions formed by the vocal organs. The first is the height of the tongue, the second is the front or the back of the tongue and the third is the shape of the lips. The vowel systems of Korean can be represented as in table 44.1.

Table 44.1: Korean Vowels

	Front		Back	
	Unrounded	Rounded	Unrounded	Rounded
High	i	ü	ŭ	u
Mid	e	ö	ə	o
Low	æ		a	

The vowels /ü/ and /ö/ have free variants [wi] and [we] respectively; thus, /kü/ 'ear' is pronounced either [kü] or [kwi] and /kömul/ 'strange creature' is pronounced either [kömul] or [kwemul]. The vowel *ŭ* is always pronounced [u] after labial sounds; *sŭlpʰŭta* is pronounced as [sŭlpʰuda] and *kamŭm* 'draught' is pronounced as [kamum].

Korean has a large number of morphophonemic alternations. As major examples of Korean morphophonemic processes involving vowels, we can name the following kinds: vowel harmony, glide formation, vowel contraction and vowel deletion. When non-finite endings starting with *ə* are attached to verbal bases, the initial *ə* of the ending is changed to *a* after *a* and *o* as in *nok-əsə* 'melting' → [nokasə], and *mac-əsə* 'be hit' → [macasə]; elsewhere *ə* is not changed as in *mək-əsə* 'eat' → [məkəsə], *kipʰəsə* 'deep' → [kipʰəsə], *kæ-əsə* 'clear' → [kæəsə] and so on.

The vowels *o, i* and *a* undergo vowel contraction with the vowel *i* when the vowels in verbal bases and other morphemes such as the causative and passive are combined with each other. Korean has the following kinds of vowel contraction; *o+i* → *ö*: *po-i-ta* 'be seen' → [pöta]; *ə+i* → *e*: *sə-iu-ta* 'raise' → [seuta]; *a+i* → *æ*: *ca-iu-ta* 'make sleep' → [cæuta]; *u+i* → *ü*: *pak'u-i-ta* 'be changed' → [pak'üta].

The front vowel *i* and the back vowels *u* and *o* of verbal bases undergo glide formation when they are immediately connected to *ə* or *a* of suffixes such as *-ə* and *-əsə*; *i* becomes *y* and *u* and *o* become *w*: *ki-əsə* 'crawl' → [kyəsə], *tu-əsə* 'leave' → [twəsə] and *po-asə* → [pwasə]. As examples of vowel deletion, Korean has two kinds: *ŭ*-deletion and *ə*-deletion. When verbal bases ending in the vowel *ŭ* are attached to an ending starting with the vowel *ə*, the vowel *ŭ* is deleted: *s'ŭ-ə* 'write' → [s'ə] and *k'ŭ-əsə* 'extinguish' → [k'əsə].

Finally, *ə*-deletion occurs when endings starting with the vowel *ə* are combined with verbal bases ending with the vowels *e, æ, ə* and *a*; thus we have the following examples: *se-əs'ta* 'counted' → [ses'ta], *kæ-əsə* 'clear' → [kæsə], *sə-ə* 'stand' → [sə] and *ka-əto* 'even if he goes' → [kato]. Interestingly, the vowels which force *ə*-deletion are those vowels which do not undergo either glide formation or *ŭ*-deletion, i.e. *i, u* and *o* undergo glide formation; *ü* and *ö* have free variant forms [wi] and [we] respectively as in *tü-əs'-ta* 'jumped' → [twiəs'ta] and *k'ö-əs'ta* 'lure' → [kweəs'ta]; *ŭ* is deleted before *ə*. From the above discussion of glide formation and vowel deletion, we can see that all the vowels in the Korean vowel system participate in phonological processes without exception when verbal bases are combined with suffixes starting in *ə*.

Of the 21 consonants, there are 9 stops, 3 affricates, 3 fricatives, 3 nasals, 1 liquid and 2 semi-vowels. The Korean consonants can be illustrated as in table 44.2.

Let us now briefly describe the sound of Korean obstruents (stops, affricates and fricatives). The Korean laxed obstruents are weaker than English voiceless obstruents with respect to the degree of voicelessness. This seems to be due to the fact that Korean obstruents have two other stronger

Table 44.2: Korean Consonants

	Manner	Point	Labial	Dental	Palatal	Velar	Glottal
Stops	voiceless	laxed	p	t		k	
		aspirated	p^h	t^h		k^h	
		tensed	p'	t'		k'	
Affricates	voiceless	laxed			c		
		aspirated			c^h		
		tensed			c'		
Fricatives	voiceless	laxed		s			h
		tensed		s'			
Nasals	voiced		m	n		ŋ	
Liquid	voiced			l			
Semi-vowels			w	y			

voiceless consonants, the tensed and the aspirated. The laxed obstruents are produced without voice and without aspiration and glottal tension. However, the laxed stops and affricates /p,t,k,c/ are pronounced as the voiced obstruents [b,d,g,j] when they occur between two voiced sounds. Even if some voiceless obstruents have voiced allophones, Korean speakers are not aware of this change. For instance, the word /aka/ 'baby' is pronounced [aga] because /k/ occurs between two vowels, which are voiced sounds.

The Korean aspirated obstruents are produced with stronger aspiration than English aspirated sounds. The Korean tensed obstruents are one of the most peculiar sounds among Korean consonants. The tensed obstruents are produced with glottal tension, but these sounds are not glottal sounds or ejectives. For instance, the Korean /t'/ is phonetically similar to the sound [t'] in English which is pronounced after [s] in the word *stop* [stap]; however, the Korean tensed obstruent must be pronounced with more glottal tension.

Liquids and semi-vowels need some explanation. The Korean liquid /l/ has two variants; one is the lateral [l] and the other the flap [r]. The liquid /l/ is pronounced as the lateral [l] in word-final position and in front of another consonant, and as the flap [r] in word-initial position and between two vowels. The Korean semi-vowels, /w/ and /y/, occur only as on-glides, never as off-glides.

In the above, the general qualities of Korean consonants were briefly described. Let us now discuss some of the phonological processes affecting Korean consonants. In pronunciation, consonants are always unreleased in word-final position and before another obstruent. Because of this, consonants belonging to a given phonetic group are pronounced identically in word-final position and before other obstruents. For instance, the labial stops /p/, /p^h/ and /p'/ are all neutralised into /p/ in word-final position; in the same manner, the velar stops /k/, /k^h/ and /k'/ are neutralised to /k/. The largest group of consonants comprises the dental and palatal obstruents, which are pronounced /t/: /t/, /tʰ/, /t'/, /c/, /cʰ/, /c'/, /s/ and /s'/. When examining consonant clusters, it is found that only single consonants occur in both initial and final position of words. Consonant clusters occur only in medial position in words and only clusters of two consonants are permitted to occur there. Some words have final two-consonant clusters in their base forms, but only one consonant is pronounced and the other consonant is deleted; for instance, the word /talk/ 'chicken' has the *lk* cluster in its base, but it is pronounced [tak], losing *l* when it is pronounced alone. However, the cluster *lk* occurs in intervocalic positions: /talk/ + /i/ → [talki]. When the final cluster occurs before a consonant, again one consonant must be deleted as in word-final position to obey the two consonant constraint; e.g. /talk/ 'chicken' + /tali/ 'leg' [taktali] 'chicken leg'.

One of the most interesting characteristics of Korean phonology is its rich consonant assimilation. Korean consonant assimilation comprises nasalisation, labialisation, dentalisation, velarisation, palatalisation and liquid assimilation. Of these, nasalisation is the most productive; for instance, the stops *k*, *t* and *p* (including the neutralised stops) become *ŋ*, *n* and *m* respectively before nasals: /kukmul/ 'soup' → [kuŋmul], /patnŭnta/ 'receive' → [pannŭnda], and /capnŭnta/ 'catch' → [camnŭnda]. As another example of nasalisation, the liquid *l* becomes *n* after the nasals *m* and *ŋ* and the stops *k*, *t*, *p*: e.g. /kamlo/ 'sweet' → [kamno], /pækli/ 'one hundred *li*' → [pækni], /matlyaŋpan/ 'first son' → [matnyaŋpan] and /aplyək/ 'press' → [apnyək]. Interestingly, in the last three examples, the stop sounds which caused *l* to nasalise assimilate to the following new nasals and become nasals themselves: [pækni] → [pæŋni], [matnyaŋban] → [mannyaŋban] and [apnyək] → [amnyək]; thus these three examples undergo two nasalisation processes.

The consonant *h* behaves interestingly in medial positions; when *h* occurs in intervocalic position, it is deleted: /cohŭn/ 'good' → [coŭn]; and when *h* occurs before laxed stops and affricates, metathesis takes place as in the following example: /hayah-ta/ 'white' → [hayatha] → [hayatʰa]. As another example of consonant deletion, we can name *l*-deletion: when the consonant *l* occurs in the initial position, it is deleted: /lyaŋpan/ 'aristocrat' → [yaŋban]. However, *l*-deletion in the initial position is not absolute, because *l* is changed to *n* in the same position depending on the following vowels, as in /lokuk/ 'Russia' → [noguk]. Thus, the right way of explaining the *l* phenomena would be to say that the consonant *l* does not occur in initial position.

Thus far, we have seen the Korean phonemic system and some of its phonological processes. In the remaining portion of this section, the Korean writing system will be briefly presented.

As can be seen from table 44.3, the Korean alphabet, which is called *Han'gŭl*, consists of 40 letters: 10 pure vowels, 11 compound vowels, 14 basic consonants and 5 double consonants. The Korean writing system is

Table 44.3: Korean Alphabet

Letter	Transcription	Letter	Transcription
Pure vowels:			
ㅣ	/i/	ㅡ	/ŭ/
ㅔ	/e/	ㅓ	/ə/
ㅐ	/æ/	ㅏ	/a/
ㅟ	/ü/	ㅜ	/u/
ㅚ	/ö/	ㅗ	/o/
Compound vowels:			
ㅑ	/ya/	ㅘ	/wa/
ㅒ	/yæ/	ㅙ	/wæ/
ㅕ	/yə/	ㅝ	/wə/
ㅖ	/ye/	ㅞ	/we/
ㅛ	/yo/	ㅢ	/ŭi/
ㅠ	/yu/		
Consonants:			
ㄱ	/k/	ㅇ	/ŋ/
ㄴ	/n/	ㅈ	/c/
ㄷ	/t/	ㅊ	/cʰ/
ㄹ	/l/	ㅋ	/kʰ/
ㅁ	/m/	ㅌ	/tʰ/
ㅂ	/p/	ㅍ	/pʰ/
ㅅ	/s/	ㅎ	/h/
Double consonants:			
ㄲ	/k'/	ㅆ	/s'/
ㄸ	/t'/	ㅉ	/c'/
ㅃ	/p'/		

based on the 'one letter per phoneme' principle. However, comparing the number of phonemes with the number of letters, it is found that the writing system has nine more letters. This is because the diphthongs are also represented by their own letters. Thus, the semi-vowels *y* and *w* do not have their own independent letters. They are always represented together with other vowels occurring with them. For instance, the letter ㅑ is a combination of *y* and *a*, and the letter ㅘ is a combination of *w* and *a*.

As a general rule, in writing, Korean letters are formed with strokes from top to bottom and from left to right. The letters forming a syllable have a sequence of CV(C)(C) and they are arranged as a rebus: e.g. *ka* 'go' → 가; *kak* 'each' → 각; *talk* 'chicken' → 닭. One interesting thing about the Korean writing system is that a vowel cannot be written alone; for instance, *a* cannot be written as ㅏ and *i* cannot be written as ㅣ . In the Korean writing system, the absence of a consonant is represented by a Ø consonant, which is shown by the symbol ㅇ and written to the left of the vowel. Thus, *a* is written as 아 and *i* is written as 이 . For instance, a word *ai* 'child' which consists of the two vowels, *a* and *i*, is written as 아이 .

3 Morphology

Korean words can be divided into two classes: inflected and uninflected. The uninflected words are nouns, particles, adverbs and interjections. Inflected words are classed as action verbs, descriptive verbs, copula and existential. The distinction between action and descriptive verbs can be shown by the way in which paradigmatic forms such as propositive and processive are combined with verbal forms. For instance, a descriptive verb lacks propositive and processive forms. Thus, whereas the action verb plus the propositive *ca* or the processive *nŭn* is grammatical, the combinations of descriptive verbs with the same endings are not: *mək-ca* 'let's eat' and *mək-nŭn-ta* 'is eating' but **alŭmtap-ca* 'let's be beautiful' and **alŭmtap-nŭn-ta* 'is being beautiful'. While the copula behaves like a descriptive verb, the existential behaves like an action verb with respect to conjugation; thus, **i-ca* 'let's be' and **i-n-ta* 'is being' are ungrammatical but *is'-ca* 'let's stay' and *is'-nŭn-ta* 'is staying' are grammatical.

As predictable from the above discussion, each inflected form consists of a base plus an ending. Bases and endings can be classed into groups according to the ways in which alternant shapes of bases are combined with endings. There are two kinds of ending: one-shape endings such as *-ko*, *-ta*, *-ci* and *-kes'* and two-shape endings such as *-sŭpnita/-ŭpnita*, *-ŭna/-na* and *-ŭn/-n*. Two-shape endings are phonologically conditioned alternants; thus, for instance, the formal form *-sŭpnita* occurs only with base forms ending in a consonant, but the alternant form of the formal form *-pnita* occurs only with base forms ending in a vowel. Based on these classes of endings, verb bases can be divided into two groups: consonant bases (i.e. bases ending in a consonant) and vowel bases (i.e. bases ending in a vowel). There are, however, some classes of bases whose final sounds are changed when attached to endings. Thus, in addition to regular bases which do not alter when combined with the ending, there are about five classes of consonant bases which alter with the ending: bases ending in *t*, bases ending in *w*, bases ending in *h*, bases ending in sonorants and *s*-dropping bases. Vowel bases have three classes in addition to the regular vowel bases: *l*-extending vowel bases, *l*-doubling bases and *l*-inserting vowel bases.

In order to see how the base form is changed when it is attached to the endings, the partial conjugation of regular and irregular bases ending in *t* is illustrated:

	Irregular	*Regular*
Base	/mut-/ 'ask'	/tat-/ 'close'
Gerund	[muk-ko]	[tak-ko]
Suspective	[muc-ci]	[tac-ci]
Formal Statement	[mus-sŭmnita]	[tas-sŭmnita]
Infinitive	[mul-ə]	[tat-ə]
Adversative	[mul-ŭna]	[tat-ŭna]

When comparing the two base forms, *mut* 'ask' and *tat* 'close', ending in *t*, it is found that both forms undergo morphophonemic changes when combined with endings starting with a consonant. These morphophonemic changes are phonologically conditioned; *t* is changed to *k* before *k*; *t* is changed to *s* before *s* and so on. However, *t* is changed to *l* before vowels only in the base *mut*, but not in the base *tat*.

Below, the partial conjugation of an *l*-inserting vowel base is illustrated together with the conjugation of an ordinary vowel base.

	Irregular	*Regular*
Base	/pʰulŭ-/ 'be blue'	/t'alŭ-/ 'obey'
Gerund	[pʰulŭ-ko]	[t'alŭ-ko]
Suspective	[pʰulŭ-ci]	[t'alŭ-ci]
Formal Statement	[pʰulŭ-mnita]	[t'alŭ-mnita]
Infinitive	[pʰulŭl-ə]	[t'al-ə]
Adversative	[pʰulŭl-ŭna]	[t'al-ŭna]

In regular vowel bases such as *t'alŭ-*, the final vowel is deleted when attached to the endings starting with a vowel, as shown in the conjugation of the infinitive and the adversative. However, in the case of irregular vowel bases such as *pʰulŭ-*, *l* is inserted before the same endings.

The number of endings which can be attached to the base is said to be over 400. In finite verb forms, there are seven sequence positions where different endings can occur: honorific, tense, aspect, modal, formal, aspect and mood. The honorific marker *si* (or *ŭsi*) is attached to the base to show the speaker's intention or behaviour honouring the social status of the subject of the sentence. Tense has marked and unmarked forms; the marked form is past and the unmarked form present. The past marker *əs'/s'* has the meaning of a definite, completed action or state.

Aspect occurs in two different positions because there are two different aspects: experiential-contrastive and retrospective, which are mutually exclusive, i.e. if one occurs, then the other cannot. The experiential-contrastive *əs'/s'*, which has the same form as the past tense marker and only occurs after the past tense, has been called 'the double past'. The two sentences, *John i hakkyo e ka-s'-ta* and *John i hakkyo e ka-s'-əs'-ta*, are usually translated in the same way as 'John went to school'. However, this does not mean that they have the same meaning. To translate them more precisely, the first sentence merely indicates the fact that the subject has gone to school and is there now. But the second sentence has the meaning that the subject has had the experience of being in school or that he had been in school before but has come back to the place where he is now. Thus, the two sentences have quite different meanings. Only the second sentence has an aspectual meaning of experiential-contrastive.

The retrospective *tə* indicates that the speaker recollects what he observed in the past and reports it in the present situation. The sentence *John i cip e ka-tə la* has roughly the meaning 'I observed that John was going home and now I report to you what I observed'.

The modal *kes'* has the meaning indicating the speaker's volition or supposition and is used both for a definite future and a probable present or past. When the modal *kes'* is attached to a verb whose subject is first person, the sentence only has the volitional meaning and is used only with reference to the future: *næ ka næil ka-kes'-ta* 'I will go tomorrow' but **næ ka næil ka-s'-kes-ta*. When the modal *kes'* occurs in a sentence whose subject is second or third person, the sentence has only the suppositional meaning and is used for both a definite future and a probable present or past: *Mary ka næil ka-kes'-ta* 'I suppose that Mary will go tomorrow' and *Mary ka əce ka-s'-kes'-ta* 'I suppose that Mary left yesterday'.

The formal form *sŭpni/pni* is used for the speaker to express politeness or respect to the hearer: *onŭl təp-sŭpni-ta* 'it is hot today' and *onŭl təp-ta* 'it is hot today'. The only difference between the two sentences is the presence or absence of the polite form *sŭpni* in the verbal form. The first sentence could be used for addressing those whose social status is superior to the speaker's but the second sentence would be used for addressing one who is inferior or equal to the speaker in social status (here, social status includes social position, age, sex, job etc.).

Among a large number of mood morphemes, the most typical moods are declarative, interrogative, imperative and propositive. In Korean, sentence types such as declarative, interrogative, imperative and propositive sentences are identified by the mood morphemes: *ta, k'a, la* and *ca*. These mood morphemes occur in the final position of finite verbal forms, e.g. declarative: *ka-pni-ta* 'he is going'; interrogative: *ka-pni-k'a?* 'is he going?'; imperative: *ka-la* 'go'; propositive: *ka-ca* 'let's go'.

Passive and causative verbal forms can be derived by adding suffixes to bases. There are a number of passive and causative suffixes such as *i, hi* and *li* which have common shapes. Generally, causative suffixes can be divided into three groups according to the vowel in the suffix: *i*-theme causatives, *u*-theme causatives and *æ*-theme causatives. Passive suffixes can be grouped with the *i*-theme causative because their theme vowel is only *i*. Because both causative and passive suffixes have identical shapes, homonymous causative and passive verbal forms are frequently produced from the same base: *k'ak'-i* 'cause to cut' and *k'ak'-i* 'be cut' from the base *k'ak'* 'cut'; *anc-hi* 'seat' and *anc-hi* 'be seated' from *anc* 'sit'. Besides the causative morphemes *-i-*

and *-hi-*, there are *-ki-*, *uk^{h}i-*, *-ik^h-*, *-li-*, *-liu-* and *-iu-* morphemes in *i*-theme causatives.

In addition to lexical causatives and passives which are derived from the combination of verb bases with the causative or passive suffixes, Korean has periphrastic causatives and passives. The periphrastic causative is formed by the combination of verb base with the adverbial ending *-ke* followed by the verb *ha* 'do', e.g. *ip-ke-ha-n-ta* 'make (someone) put on'. Some verbs take both lexical and periphrastic causatives, but some other verbs take only periphrastic causatives. Comparing the two types of causative, periphrastic causatives are more productive than lexical causatives in Korean.

In Korean, passives are not so commonly used as in some other languages, such as English or Japanese. There are many transitive verbs which do not undergo passivisation; for instance, the verb *cu* 'give' does not undergo either lexical or periphrastic passivisation. Thus, the number of transitive verbs which undergo passive formation with the passive suffix is limited to a certain group of verbs. There are two kinds of verbs which undergo periphrastic passivisation: one is a group of verbs which take an inchoative verb *ci* and the other a group of verbs which take an inchoative verb *tö* in their passive formation. The passive of the first group is formed by adding the infinitive ending *ə* to the base followed by the inchoative verb *ci*: *pusu-ə ci-ta* 'be broken'. All the transitive verbs which take the inchoative verb *tö* in passive formation are derived from Chinese-originated loan verbs plus the verbaliser *ha*. In the passive formation of these verbs, the verbaliser *ha* is changed to the inchoative verb *tö*; thus, the passive of *sæŋkakha-ta* 'think' is *sæŋkaktö-ta* 'be thought'.

Finally, there are a great number of nouns which are derived from verbs by adding the nominalising morphemes to verbal bases. There are three nominalisers *ki*, *ŭm/m* and *i* which can be added to the base. As examples of derived nouns, we have the following: *ki*-derived nouns: *talliki* 'running', *næki* 'bet', *c^{h}aki* 'kicking' and *poki* 'example'; *ŭm/m*-derived nouns: *əlŭm* 'ice', *cam* 'sleep', *k'um* 'dream' and *c^{h}um* 'dance'; *i*-derived nouns: *kəli* 'hanger', *noli* 'game', *kili* 'length' and *nəlpi* 'width'. Though there is no general rule deciding which nominaliser is attached to which base, more nouns are derived from verbal bases by adding the nominalisers *ŭm/m* and *i* than the nominaliser *ki*.

4 Syntax

In this brief sketch of Korean syntax, the discussion will concentrate on representative examples which make Korean different from many Indo-European languages, especially English. One of the most frequently cited features of Korean syntax is the word order. Korean is a SOV language, meaning that the basic word order of transitive sentences is subject–object–verb. Korean has a relatively free word order compared to

English; here, the phrase 'relatively free' means that Korean is not a completely free word order language. The Korean language obeys a strict grammatical constraint requiring that the sentence end with a verb. As long as the sentence obeys this constraint, a permutation of the major constituents in a sentence is permissible; thus, the sentence *John i Mary eke cʰæk ŭl cu-əs'-ta* 'John gave a book to Mary' can also be said in the following ways: *John i cʰæk ŭl Mary eke cu-əs'-ta*; *Mary eke John i cʰæk ŭl cu-əs'-ta*; *cʰæk ŭl John i Mary eke cu-əs'-ta*; *cʰæk ŭl Mary eke John i cu-əs'-ta*. However, the following sentences are ungrammatical: **John i Mary eke cu-əs'-ta cʰæk ŭl*; **John i cu-əs'-ta cʰæk ŭl Mary eke*. The ungrammaticality of the last two sentences is due to the violation of the verb-final constraint.

In the above examples of Korean sentences, the grammatical elements *i*, *eke* and *ŭl* are postpositional particles corresponding to the cases nominative, dative and accusative. There are other kinds of postpositional particles such as *e* 'to/at', *esə* 'at/in', *to* 'also', *nŭn* 'topic', *putʰə* 'from' and *k'aci* 'to/till'. All these particles must occur after nouns, but some of them can occur after other particles; *ice putʰə to ha-l-su is'-ta* 'we can do it from now, too'; *uli tosəkwan e nŭn cʰæk i manh-ta* 'in our library, there are many books'.

Comparing the Korean example with its English translation, it is found that *cʰæk* 'book' in Korean does not have any number marker, singular or plural, whereas *books* in the English translation has a plural marker *s*. This does not mean that Korean does not have a plural marker. In Korean, the plural marker attachment is not so obligatory as in English. Especially in cases where quantifiers or numerals appear in sentences as in the above example, the plural marker is usually not attached to the noun. Another characteristic of number in Korean is that the plural marker can be attached to adverbs, e.g. *p'alli-tŭl il ŭl ha-n-ta* 'they do work fast'. In the example, the plural marker *tŭl* is attached to the adverb *p'alli* 'fast'. Usually, in this kind of sentence, the subject is deleted, but it is understood that the subject of the sentence is plural instead of singular owing to the presence of the plural marker on the adverb.

When nouns occur with numerals, classifiers are attached to numerals almost obligatorily. Korean has a rich system of classifiers. Each classifier is related to a class of nouns. In other words, a certain classifier occurs only with a certain class of nouns, e.g. *cʰæk han-kwən* 'one volume of a book'; *mækcu tu-pyəŋ* 'two bottles of beer'; *namu han-kŭlu* 'one tree'; *coŋi han-caŋ* 'one piece of paper'. Another interesting thing with respect to numerals is that there is an alternative word order. Thus, the sequence of numeral + classifier, which occurs after nouns in the above examples, can also occur before nouns. When this floating takes place, the genitive particle *ŭi* is inserted between numeral + classifier and the noun: *han-kwən ŭi cʰæk* 'one volume of a book'; *tu-pyəŋ ŭi mækcu* 'two bottles of beer'; *han-kŭlu ŭi namu* 'one tree'; *han-caŋ ŭi coŋi* 'one piece of paper'.

As may have been noticed in some of the examples, deletion of subjects is allowable as long as subjects are recoverable from linguistic or non-linguistic context. Deletion of the first person and second person in Korean is especially free, as in *cʰæk ul sɔ tŭli-kes'-ŭpni-ta* 'I will buy you a book'; *ɔnce t'ɔna-seyo?* 'when do you leave?' In the first sentence, the first person subject is deleted and in the second, the second person subject is deleted because these subjects are recoverable in a discourse context. Although deletion of the third person subject is not so common as deletion of first and second person subjects, it is also possible: *Mary ka cip e kass-ŭlt'æ* **Ø** upʰyɔnpætalpu lŭl manna-s'-ta 'when Mary went home, she met the mailman'. The zero indicates the position where the third person subject is deleted. In the last example, we discover another difference between Korean and English. In the English translation of the last Korean example, the noun *mailman* is preceded by the definite article *the*. This same noun could be preceded by the indefinite article *a*. This means that English has distinct definite and indefinite articles. But Korean does not have articles indicating definiteness or indefiniteness. Although definiteness is indicated by demonstratives in some cases, the distinction between definite and indefinite, in general, is not made in Korean.

Modifiers such as demonstratives, genitives, adjectives and relative clauses precede head nouns in Korean, e.g. *i cʰæk ŭn cæmiis'ta* 'this book is interesting'; **John ŭi** *apɔci nŭn ŭisa-ta* 'John's father is a doctor'; **yep'ŭn** *k'ocʰi is'-ta* 'there is a pretty flower'; **hakkyo e ka-ko is'-nŭn** *haksæŋ ŭn na ŭi cʰinku-ta* 'the student who is going to school is my friend'. All constituents in bold print are located to the left of the head noun. These modifying constituents make Korean a left-branching language. The notion of left-branching becomes clear in the following sentence containing three relative clauses [[[[*næ ka a-nŭn*] *haksæŋ i tani-nŭn*] *hakkyo ka is'-nŭn*] *tosi nŭn kʰŭ-ta*] '[the city [where the school is [where my friend goes [who I know is big]]]]'. One of the characteristics of the relative clause in Korean is that it lacks relative pronouns. Demonstratives can also be classified as one class of modifiers. Korean demonstratives have two distinct characteristics which differ from English demonstratives. First, Korean demonstratives cannot occur independently, i.e. they must occur with nouns. The second difference is that Korean demonstratives have a triple system, unlike that of English. In addition to the demonstratives 'this' and 'that', Korean has a demonstrative which has the meaning 'that over there': *i* 'this', *kŭ* 'that' and *cɔ* 'that over there'. The same triple system is found in demonstrative locative nouns, e.g. *yɔki* 'here', *kɔki* 'there' and *cɔki* 'yonder'.

Korean predicates do not agree in number, person or gender with their subjects. However, predicates show agreement with honorificness and politeness in different styles of speech. Three main levels of speech are distinguished with respect to politeness: plain, polite and deferential. Many other speech levels can also be represented among these three basic speech levels by different endings. The three main speech levels of declarative sentences have the following ending forms: plain: *ta*; polite: *yo*; deferential: *(sŭ)pnita*. Thus, when the speaker expresses his politeness toward the hearer, either the polite or the deferential speech level is used, e.g. *sənsæŋnim i cip e ka-yo* 'the teacher is going home'; *sənsæŋnim i cip e ka-pnita*. In contrast to this, when the speaker does not express any particular politeness toward the hearer, the plain speech level is used; e.g. *sənsæŋnim i cip e ka-n-ta*.

If the speaker wants to express his respect toward the referent of the subject, the honorific marker *si* is inserted between verbal bases and endings: e.g. *sənsæŋnim i cip e ka-si-əyo; sənsæŋnim i cip e ka-si-pnita; sənsæŋnim i cip e ka-si-n-ta*. In the last example, the insertion of the honorific marker *si* is possible in the predicate of a sentence ending in the plain speech level, since the honorificness is expressed to the subject, but not to the hearer. In the above example, if the subject is a student instead of a teacher, then unacceptable sentences are produced: **haksæŋ i hakkyo e ka-si-əyo; *haksæŋ i hakkyo e ka-si-pnita; *haksæŋ i hakkyo e ka-si-nta*. The ungrammaticality of the last examples is due to the violation of agreement between the subject and the predicate with respect to honorificness. In other words, the subject *haksæŋ* 'student' cannot occur with the predicate containing the honorific marker *si*, because *haksæŋ* belongs to the class of nouns which cannot be referred to with the honorific marker *si*.

Let us now turn to negation. Korean has three different negative morphemes: *an*, *ma* and *mos*. The morpheme *an* occurs in declarative and interrogative sentences and the morpheme *ma* occurs in propositive and imperative sentences, e.g. declarative: *cip e an ka-n-ta* 'I do not go home'; interrogative: *cip e an ka-ni?* 'don't you go home?'; propositive: *cip e ka-ci mal-ca* 'let's not go home'; imperative: *cip e ka-ci ma-la* 'don't go home'. The remaining negative morpheme *mos* has the meaning 'cannot', e.g. *cip e mos ka-n-ta* 'I cannot go home'. There are three types of negation in Korean. In the first type, the negative morphemes *an* and *mos* occur immediately before the main verb, as in the declarative and interrogative, as in the last example. The other two types involve more complicated operations. In the second type, the negative behaves like the main predicate and the complementiser *ci* is incorporated, as in the propositive and imperative. The third type of negation involves the main predicate *ha* 'do' in addition to *ci* complementation; *cip e ka-ci ani ha-n-ta* 'I don't go home'; *cip e ka-ci mos ha-n-ta* 'I cannot go home'. From these three types of negation, we can observe different occurrences of negative morphemes. That is, while the negative morpheme *an* appears in all three types of negation, the morpheme *mos* appears in the first and third types of negation. The remaining negative morpheme *ma* appears only in the second type of negation.

As a final example of Korean syntactic characteristics, Korean sentential complements will be briefly discussed. Sentential complements are marked with the nominalisers *kəs*, *ki*, *ŭm* and *ci* and with the complementiser *ko*. Several differences exist between nominalisers and complementisers: first, case particles occur after nominalisers but cannot occur after complementisers: e.g. in the sentence *na nŭn i cʰæk i cæmiis'-nŭn kəs ŭl a-n-ta* 'I know that this book is interesting', the accusative particle *ŭl* occurs right after the nominaliser *kəs*, but in the sentence **na nŭn i cʰæk i cæmiis'ta ko lŭl sæŋkakha-n-ta* 'I think that this book is interesting', the variant accusative particle *lŭl* cannot occur after the complementiser *ko*. Secondly, while the nominaliser is preceded by non-finite modifier forms *-nŭn-* and *-n/ŭn-*, the complementiser is preceded by the finite verbal ending form *-ta*. Thirdly, the nominaliser occurs in both the subject and object positions, but the complementiser occurs only in object position. Sentential complements containing the nominaliser have different syntactic behaviour from sentential complements containing the complementiser. Sentential complements containing the nominaliser behave like regular noun phrases. Thus, whereas sentential complements with the nominaliser undergo syntactic processes such as topicalisation, pseudo-cleft formation, passivisation, noun phrase deletion and pronominalisation, sentential complements with the complementiser do not undergo the same syntactic processes. Of the above nominalisers and complementisers, *ci* is used as a question nominaliser and *ko* is used as quotative complementiser: *na nŭn John i ənce o-nŭn ci molŭ-n-ta* 'I do not know when John will come'; *na nŭn John i næil o-n-ta ko malha-yəs'-ta* 'I said that John would come tomorrow'.

Sentential complements containing *ki* can be differentiated from sentential complements containing *ŭm/m* by syntactic and semantic characteristics. In the majority of cases, *ŭm/m* is used for factive complements (i.e. complements whose truth is presupposed), but *ki* is used for non-factive complements. A given predicate will take only one of these two nominalisers, e.g. *na nŭn John i cip e ka-l-kəs ŭl wənha-n-ta* 'I want John to go home'; **na nŭn John i cip e ka m ŭl wənha-n-ta*; *na nŭn John i cip e ka m ŭl al-as'-ta* 'I knew that John was going home'. **na nŭn John i cip e ka ki lŭl al-as'-ta*. The examples show that the non-factive predicate *wənha* 'want' occurs only with *ki* and the factive predicate *al* 'know' occurs with *ŭm/m*. The nominaliser *kəs* occurs with both factive and non-factive complements: *na nŭn John i cip e ka-nŭn kəs ŭl wənha-n-ta* 'I want John to go home'; *na nŭn John i cip e ka-nŭn kəs ŭl al-as'-ta* 'I knew that John was going home'.

Bibliography

For discussion of the origins and history of Korean, reference may be made to Chin-Wu Kim (1974) and Ki-Moon Lee (1967), the latter also available in a German translation. Ho (1965), a monograph treatment of Korean phonology, is available only in Korean, but two studies are available in English: Martin (1954), a classic treatment of Korean morphophonemics, and B.K. Lee (1977), from the generative viewpoint. Among descriptive grammars, Choi (1954) is available only in Korean and in the absence of a comparable descriptive grammar in English, the most useful sources of general information on Korean grammar are the pedagogical texts by Martin (1969) and Lukoff (1982). Nam-Kil Kim (1984) is a study of Korean sentence complementation from a generative viewpoint.

References

Choi, Hyon Bae. 1954. *Uli Malbon* (Jŏngŭmsa, Seoul)

Ho, Woong. 1965. *Kukŏ Umunhak* (Jŏngŭmsa, Seoul)

Kim, Chin-Wu. 1974. *The Making of the Korean Language* (Center for Korean Studies, University of Hawaii, Honolulu)

Kim, Nam-Kil. 1984. *The Grammar of Korean Complementation* (Center for Korean Studies, University of Hawaii, Honolulu)

Lee, B.K. 1977. *Korean Generative Phonology* (Iljisa, Seoul)

Lee, Ki-Moon. 1967. 'Hankukŏ Hyŏngsŏngsa', in *Hankuk Munhwasa Taekye*, vol. 5 (Korea University Press, Seoul; also available in German translation, *Geschichte der koreanischen Sprache*, translated by B. Lewin, Dr Ludwig Reichert Verlag, Wiesbaden, 1977.)

Lukoff, F. 1982. *An Introductory Course in Korean* (Yonsei University Press, Seoul)

Martin, S. 1954. *Korean Morphophonemics* (Linguistic Society of America, Baltimore)

——— 1969. *Beginning Korean* (Yale University Press, New Haven)

45 AUSTRONESIAN LANGUAGES

Ross Clark

1   Membership, Distribution and Status

The name 'Austronesian' is made up of Greek formatives meaning 'southern islands' and the languages of this family are spoken, with few exceptions, on a range of islands stretching more than halfway around the world from east to west and from the northern fringes of the tropics to the sub-Antarctic south. The number of languages in the family is estimated at somewhere between 500 and 1,000. 'Austronesia' includes Madagascar, Indonesia, the Philippines, Formosa and the Pacific island groups of Melanesia, Micronesia and Polynesia. Apart from recent intrusions, the only non-Austronesian languages in this domain are found on the island of New Guinea (where Austronesian speakers are confined to coastal areas) and some islands near it, including Timor and Halmahera to the west and New Britain, Bougainville and the Santa Cruz group to the east.

It is convenient to divide Austronesia geographically at about 130° east longitude, a line running just to the west of the Caroline Islands and New Guinea. The western area has about 300 languages, with a total of over 170 million speakers. Among these Javanese has pride of place in more than one respect, with the largest number of speakers (over 60 million), the longest written tradition (early inscriptions dating from the eighth century AD) and one of the major literatures of Asia. Malay, with a much smaller number of native speakers, has nevertheless achieved wider currency, as the lingua franca of the Malay Archipelago for several centuries and now as the national language of both Indonesia and Malaysia. Other languages of regional importance in this area include Achinese, Batak and Minangkabau of Sumatra, Sundanese of western Java, Madurese, Balinese and Sasak on islands east of Java, Iban and Ngadju of Borneo and Macassarese and Buginese of Sulawesi.

About 70 Austronesian languages are spoken in the Philippines. Tagalog, with 10 million native speakers in southwestern Luzon, serves as the national language (officially called Pilipino). Other important languages include Ilokano and Bikol, also of Luzon, and Cebuano and Hiligaynon (Ilongo) of the central islands.

The indigenous people of Formosa (Taiwan) spoke a number of Austronesian languages, but as a consequence of continued Chinese settlement since the seventeenth century they are now a small minority of the population, living mainly in the mountainous interior, and subject to cultural and linguistic assimilation to the Chinese. About 20 Formosan languages have been recorded, of which half are now extinct, the remainder having perhaps 200,000 speakers in all.

The Austronesian presence on the Asian continent is confined to Malay (on the Malay Peninsula) and the Chamic group. There are about 10 Chamic languages, spoken by ethnic minorities in southern Vietnam and Cambodia, numbering half a million all together. A small community of Chamic speakers has also been reported on Hainan Island in southern China.

The people of the Malagasy Republic, the far western outpost of Austronesia, speak a group of dialects diverse enough to be considered several different languages, though they are all conventionally referred to as Malagasy. Merina, spoken by about a quarter of the population, is the national standard.

The most striking contrast between the western and eastern regions of Austronesia is in the scale of the speech communities. There are at least 400 languages in the eastern region, but the total number of speakers is not much over two million — a figure exceeded by several individual languages of Indonesia and the Philippines. In Melanesia, one of the world's major foci of linguistic diversity, a typical language has only a few thousand or even a few hundred speakers. Among the larger Austronesian language communities in Melanesia are the Tolai (50,000) at the eastern end of New Britain and the Motu (13,000) on the south coast of New Guinea. Both these languages have acquired greater importance as a result of close contacts with European colonial administration, Tolai being spoken around the old German capital of Rabaul and Motu in the vicinity of Port Moresby, now the capital of Papua New Guinea. A simplified form of Motu (earlier called 'Police Motu' and now 'Hiri Motu') serves as lingua franca in much of the southern half of the country and has been recognised as one of the official languages of the National Parliament — the only Melanesian language to achieve such an official status. Other languages in Melanesia, while not necessarily having large numbers of speakers, have achieved regional importance through missionary use. Examples are Yabem and Gedaged on the north coast of New Guinea, Roviana in the western Solomon Islands and Mota in Vanuatu. The last, while spoken originally by only a few hundred people on one tiny island in the Banks group, has been widely used by Anglicans in both northern Vanuatu and the south-east Solomons.

While the typical pattern in Melanesia is one or more languages per island, in Fiji, Polynesia and Micronesia languages commonly extend over several neighbouring islands and correspondingly larger speech communities are common. Samoan (with over 200,000 speakers), Tongan

(90,000) and Fijian (200,000) are now national languages of independent states. Other Polynesian languages in wide use are Tahitian (70,000), a lingua franca throughout French Polynesia, and Rarotongan or Cook Islands Maori (20,000). Several Polynesian languages are now also spoken by sizable communities of emigrants in New Zealand, the United States and elsewhere.

Hawaii and New Zealand have had a linguistic history very different from that of the rest of Polynesia. Until the end of the eighteenth century both were populated entirely by Polynesians, but over the following hundred years massive intrusion by Europeans (and Asians in the case of Hawaii) reduced the indigenous population to a relatively powerless minority, whose language was largely excluded from public life and actively suppressed in the schools. In the twentieth century, the erosion of Polynesian-speaking rural communities by migration to the cities and the spread of English-language mass communications have accelerated the decline. There are now no more than a few hundred native speakers of Hawaiian and its extinction as a living language seems imminent. The Maori language of New Zealand is in a less desperate situation, with an estimated 70,000 native speakers. But very few of these are children and the number of communities using Maori as an everyday language has declined sharply in the last 40 years. It is unclear whether current programmes being undertaken in support of the language have any chance of reversing this trend. Both Maori and Hawaiian, however, are being studied more widely than ever in schools and universities and even if both should cease to exist as living vernaculars, they would continue to be cultivated as vehicles for the arts of oratory and poetry and as symbols of Polynesian identity in their respective countries.

The small and scattered islands of Micronesia have about a dozen languages among them. Some of these are spread over wide areas, such as the chain of dialects occupying most of the western Caroline Islands, with about 40,000 speakers, which has recently been termed 'Trukic' after its major population centre, Truk Island; Chamorro, spoken on Guam and the Marianas Islands to the north (52,000); and the languages of the Marshall Islands (21,000) and Kiribati (50,000). Others are restricted to single islands or compact groups, such as the languages of Belau (Palau), Yap, Ponape, Kosrae (Kusaie), Nauru and the Polynesian atolls Nukuoro and Kapingamarangi.

2   Comparative Austronesian

The existence of the Austronesian family was first recognised in the early seventeenth century, when the earliest Polynesian word lists collected by Dutch explorers were compared with Malay, which was already known to many Europeans as the lingua franca of the East Indies. These languages are fairly conservative in phonology and lexicon and any basic vocabulary will show many words that are obviously similar and, in some cases, identical:

	Malay	*Futuna (Polynesian)*
'two'	dua	lua
'five; hand'	lima	lima
'eye'	mata	mata
'ear'	telinga	talinga
'stone'	batu	fatu
'fish'	ikan	ika
'louse'	kutu	kutu
'weep'	tangis	tangi
'die'	mati	mate

The connection of Malagasy with Malay was noted at about the same time and the major languages of Indonesia and the Philippines were readily seen to belong to the same family, as were Tongan, Hawaiian, Maori and the other Polynesian languages that became known to Europeans during the eighteenth century. Many Melanesian and Micronesian languages, however, had undergone such extensive phonological and lexical changes that their Austronesian origins were much less apparent and it was not until the early twentieth century that the full extent of the family was understood.

The German scholar Otto Dempwolff, in the 1920s and 30s, laid the foundations of comparative Austronesian linguistics. He demonstrated the regular sound correspondences between many of the better known languages and reconstructed a large number of words of the ancestral language, Proto-Austronesian. Dempwolff also made an important advance in subgrouping (the establishment of the successive stages of differentiation from the ancestral language to the present diversity) by showing that almost all the languages of eastern Austronesia form a single subgroup. Earlier classifications had followed the geographical division into Indonesia, Melanesia, Micronesia and Polynesia and had been strongly influenced by the cultural and racial differences among Austronesian speakers. Dempwolff's group (now known as Oceanic) comprises all the languages of the eastern region with the exception of Palauan and Chamorro in Micronesia (which appear to have their closest connections in the Philippine area) and the languages of the western end of New Guinea, which group with Halmahera in eastern Indonesia.

Research since Dempwolff's time has greatly increased the amount of descriptive information on Austronesian languages from all areas and some consensus has emerged on the general outlines of the subgrouping of the family. Figure 45.1 shows a recent proposal by R. Blust. Atayalic, Tsouic and Paiwanic are three groups of Formosan languages. There is general agreement that the primary division within Austronesian is between Formosan languages and the rest. For the residual, non-Formosan group, Blust has proposed the term Malayo-Polynesian (formerly used as a synonym for Austronesian). Malayo-Polynesian in turn is divided into four subgroups, related as shown in the diagram. Central Malayo-Polynesian consists of about 50 languages of the Lesser Sunda Islands and the Moluccas, while South Halmahera-West New Guinea includes about 45 languages, extending as far east as Cenderawasih Bay. This leaves two very large subgroups: Oceanic, as defined above, and Western Malayo-Polynesian, which comprises all the remaining languages of western Austronesia, along with Chamorro and Palauan. Since these two groups between them account for at least 80 per cent of Austronesian languages, including all the well known ones, the earlier view of Austronesian as divided into an 'eastern' and a 'western' group now appears as an understandable simplification.

Figure 45.1: Subgrouping of Austronesian (after Blust)

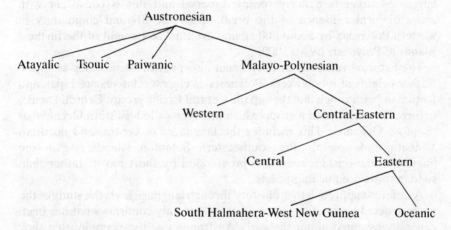

Within Western Malayo-Polynesian and Oceanic, further subgrouping is a matter for much current research and argument. In each case, 30 or so local groupings can be defined, usually geographically coherent and ranging in size from a single language to several dozen. This lowest level of subgrouping seems fairly clear, but what the intermediate units of classification are — or indeed whether there are any — is much less agreed upon.

A great deal of the comparative research on Austronesian languages has been inspired by curiosity as to the origins and migrations of the far-flung Austronesian-speaking peoples. The subgrouping just outlined has certain implications for these questions of prehistory. First, it supports the generally assumed progression of Austronesian speakers from somewhere in the south-east Asian islands, eastward by stages further and further into the Pacific. The view, popular with many nineteenth-century theorists, that particular areas of Oceania were peopled by long-distance migrations from particular islands in Indonesia, finds no support in the linguistic evidence.

Language relationships also shed some light on the remoter fringes of the Austronesian family. In the 1950s, O.C. Dahl showed that the closest relative of Malagasy was the Ma'anyan language of south-east Borneo. This gives a fairly precise homeland for the Austronesian traders who first settled Madagascar, apparently early in the Christian era.

At the other end of Austronesia, the migrations of the Polynesians have been a tempting subject for both science and fantasy. Linguistically, Polynesian is a clearly-defined subgroup consisting of about 20 languages in the triangle defined by Hawaii, New Zealand and Easter Island, plus a further 15 small enclaves in Melanesia and Micronesia. These latter 'outliers' have been shown to be most closely related to Samoan and its near neighbours in western Polynesia, from which they apparently dispersed westward over a long period of time. The close relatedness of all Polynesian languages suggests a fairly recent dispersal and this is consistent with archaeological evidence of the break-up of the original community in western Polynesia by about 500 BC and eventual settlement of the furthest islands of Polynesia by AD 1000.

The external relations of Polynesian also provide some clues as to the further origins of its speakers. Polynesian's closest relatives are Fijian and Rotuman, with which it makes up the Central Pacific group. Central Pacific, in turn, is a member of a group which has been called 'Eastern Oceanic' or 'Remote Oceanic'. This includes the languages of central and northern Vanuatu and possibly the southeastern Solomon Islands. Again the linguistic relationships suggest a progression by short moves rather than sudden trans-oceanic migrations.

A different approach to prehistory through language is via the study of the reconstructed vocabulary. In some cases this only confirms what has been generally assumed about the early Austronesians: for example, that they cultivated crops such as taro and yams and were familiar with sailing outrigger canoes. Recent work by Blust, however, has advanced more controversial hypotheses about material culture (rice cultivation, metal-working) and has combined linguistic with ethnographic data to reconstruct aspects of the social structure of the Proto-Austronesian community.

Is Austronesian related to any other language family? Certainly suggestions have not been wanting, but proposed links with Japanese or Indo-European have not been supported by any significant evidence. The 'Austro-Tai' hypothesis, linking Austronesian with the Kadai languages, has been argued rather more seriously, but still must be considered only a somewhat more promising conjecture.

3   Structural Characteristics

Any generalisation about a large and diverse language family must be taken with caution, but certain structural features are sufficiently widespread to be considered typically Austronesian. These are shared by at least the more conservative languages in all regions, and were probably features of Proto-Austronesian.

The phonemic systems of Austronesian languages range from average complexity to extreme simplicity. Hawaiian, with just 13 phonemes (*p*, *k*, *ʔ*, *h*, *m*, *n*, *l*, *w*, *i*, *e*, *a*, *o*, *u*), was long considered the world's simplest, but it now appears that non-Austronesian Rotokas of Bougainville (North Solomons Province, Papua New Guinea) has only 11. Austronesian languages commonly allow only a restricted range of consonant clusters. Nasal + stop is the most widespread type, though in many Oceanic languages such phonetic sequences are treated as single prenasalised consonants. Final consonants were present in Proto-Austronesian, but have been categorically lost in many of the Oceanic languages. Lexical morphemes are typically bisyllabic.

Morphological complexity is likewise average to low. Nouns are suffixed for pronominal possessor in almost all Austronesian languages, though in Oceanic languages this is restricted to one category of possession. (See the description of Fijian below.) Verbs are prefixed, infixed or suffixed to indicate transitivity, voice and focus and to produce nominalised forms. Reduplication is extensively used to mark such grammatical categories as number and aspect. Pronouns have an 'inclusive' category for groups including both speaker and hearer, contrasting with the first person ('exclusive'), which definitely excludes the hearer.

Word order in Austronesian is predominantly verb-initial or verb-second and prepositional. (A number of languages in the New Guinea area have become verb-final and postpositional under the influence of neighbouring non-Austronesian languages.) Articles, which often distinguish a 'proper' from a 'common' class of nouns, precede the noun; adjectives and relative clauses follow.

Since two representative Western Malayo-Polynesian languages (Malay and Tagalog) are described elsewhere in this volume, I will conclude this chapter with a brief sketch of some features of a typical Oceanic language, Fijian.

The dialects of Fiji, like those of Madagascar, are sufficiently diverse to be considered at least two, if not several, distinct languages. Standard Fijian, the national language, is based on the speech of the southeastern corner of the island of Viti Levu. This area has long been politically powerful and it is likely that its dialect was widely understood even before it was selected as a standard by Protestant missionaries in the 1840s. The examples given here are in the formal type of standard Fijian described in the grammars, which differs in some ways from colloquial usage.

Fijian has the following consonants (given in Fijian orthography, with unexpected phonetic values shown in square brackets):

Voiceless stops: t, k
Voiced (prenasalised) stops: b [mb], d [nd], q [ŋg]
Fricatives: v [β], s, c [ð]
Nasals: m, n, g [ŋ]
Liquids: l, r, dr [nr̃]
Semi-vowels: w, y

The vowels are *i*, *e*, *a*, *o* and *u*, all of which may be either long or short. Vowel length is not normally indicated in writing Fijian, but here it will be shown by doubling the vowel letter. This treatment makes it possible to state the position of the main word stress very simply: it falls on the second-last vowel of the word.

Fijian nouns can be divided into common and proper. Common nouns are preceded by the article *na* (*na vale* 'the house'). Proper nouns, which include names of persons and places as well as personal pronouns, are preceded by the article *ko* (*ko Viti* 'Fiji', *ko ira* 'they'). Certain expressions referring to persons, however, though they involve common nouns, may optionally be preceded by *ko*, sometimes with *na* following: *na ganequ* or *ko na ganequ* 'my sister'. This choice provides for subtle distinctions of intimacy and respect.

The Fijian personal pronouns express four categories of number and four of person. In standard Fijian the independent pronoun forms are as follows:

	Singular	*Dual*	*Paucal*	*Plural*
First Person				
('exclusive')	au	keirau	keitou	keimami
Inclusive	–	kedaru	kedatou	keda
Second Person	iko	kemudrau	kemudou	kemunii
Third Person	koya	rau	iratou	ira

The paucal category refers to a small number, greater than two. (These pronouns are misleadingly termed 'trial' in Fijian grammars.) As explained above, the inclusive category is used when both speaker and hearer are included, whereas first person and second person definitely exclude the other. Thus *kedatou* could be paraphrased 'a small group of people including both you and me', and *keimami* as 'a large group of people including me but not including you'. It will be seen from the definitions that the inclusive singular form is missing because such a combination is logically self-contradictory.

Like most Oceanic languages, Fijian distinguishes more than one relation within what is broadly called 'possession'. In standard Fijian there are four possessive categories. Familiar (inalienable) possession includes the relation between whole and part, including parts of the body, and most kin relations. With a pronominal possessor, familiar possession is indicated by suffixing the possessor directly to the noun: *na yava-qu* 'my leg', *na tama-na* 'her father'. In each of the other three possessive categories, the possessor is suffixed not to the noun but to a distinctive possessive base which precedes it. Edible and drinkable possession, not surprisingly, include the relation of a possessor to something which is eaten or drunk: *na ke-mu dalo* 'your taro', *na me-dra tii* 'their tea'. Eating and drinking are of course culturally defined, so that tobacco counts as edible, whereas various watery foods such as oysters, oranges and sugar cane are drinkable. The edible category also includes certain intrinsic properties and relations of association: *na ke-na balavu* 'its length, his height', *na ke-na tuuraga* 'its (e.g. a village's) chief'. (This appears to be the result of the merger of two historically distinct categories, rather than any conceptual association of such relations with eating.) The fourth category, *neutral*, includes relations not covered by the three more specific types: *na no-qu vale* 'my house', *na no-mu cakacaka* 'your work'.

Certain nouns tend to occur typically with certain possessive types because of their typical relation to possessors in the real world. And there are certain cases of apparently arbitrary assignment: *na yate-na* 'his liver', but *na no-na ivi* 'his kidneys'. Nevertheless, the system cannot be explained as a simple classification of nouns. There are numerous examples of the same noun in two different possessive relations, with the appropriate difference of meaning: *na no-qu yaqona* 'my kava (which I grow or sell)', *na me-qu yaqona* 'my kava (which I drink)'; *na no-na itukutuku* 'her story, the story she tells', *na ke-na itukutuku* 'her story, the story about her'.

The essential elements of the Fijian verb phrase are the verb itself and a preposed pronoun: *daru lako* (incl.-du. go) 'let's go', *e levu* (3 sg. big) 'it's big'. Most verb phrases also include one or more particles preceding or following the verb, which mark such categories as tense, aspect, modality, direction and emphasis: *keimami aa lako tale gaa mai* (1 pl. past go also just hither) 'we also came'; *era dui kanakana tiko* (3 pl. separately eat imperfective) 'they are eating each by himself'.

Transitivity is a highly developed lexical-semantic category in Fijian. A plain verb stem is normally intransitive and can be made transitive by the addition of a suffix: *lutu* 'fall', *lutu-ka* 'fall on (something)'; *gunu* 'drink', *gunu-va* 'drink (something)'; *boko* 'go out (of a fire, etc.)', *boko-ca* 'extinguish (something)'. As the examples show, the subject of the intransitive verb may correspond to the subject of the transitive (as with *lutu* and *gunu*) or to the object (as with *boko*).

The transitive suffixes just illustrated are all of the form -C*a*, where C is a consonant (or zero). Which consonant is used must in general be learned as a property of a particular verb, though there is some correlation with semantic classes. There are also transitive suffixes of the form -C*aka* and many verbs may occur with either type of suffix. In such cases, the two transitive forms generally differ as to which additional participant in the action is treated as the object of the verb. Thus: *vana* 'shoot', *vana-a* 'shoot, shoot at (a person, a target, etc.)', *vana-taka* 'shoot with (a gun, a bow, etc.)'; *masu* 'pray', *masu-ta* 'pray to', *masu-laka* 'pray for'.

When the verb phrase is accompanied by a full noun phrase subject or object, the normal order is verb phrase–object–subject:

era   aa   rai-ca   na yalewa na gone
3 pl. past see-trans.   the woman the child
'The children saw the woman.'

In this sentence the word order identifies *na yalewa* as object and *na gone* as subject. Note also that *na gone* is specified as plural not by marking on the noun phrase itself, but by its coreference with the subject pronoun *era* in the verb phrase.

When the object is proper (in the sense defined above), it occurs within the verb phrase, immediately following the verb, the proper article *ko* is dropped and the final vowel of the transitive suffix changes from *a* to *i*:

era   aa   rai-ci   Viti kece gaa na gone
3 pl. past see-trans.   Fiji all   just the child
'The children all saw Fiji.'

A non-singular human object requires a coreferent object pronoun in this position, which provides another possibility for number marking:

era   aa   rai-ci   rau   na yalewa na gone
3 pl. past see-trans.   3 du. the woman the child
'The children saw the two women.'

The transitive suffix in *-i* also appears in reciprocal and passive constructions:

era   vei-rai-ci   na gone
3 pl. recip.-see-trans.   the child
'The children look at each other.'

e   aa   rai-ci   ko Viti
3 sg. past see-trans.   art. Fiji
'Fiji was seen.'

Note that in the last example the appearance of *ko* indicates that 'Fiji' is subject and not object.

It will be seen that *-Ci* is the more general form of the transitive suffix and that *-Ca* occurs only with third person objects which are either singular or non-human. If we take *-Ca* to be a reduced form of *-Ci-a*, where *-a* is a third person singular/non-human object pronoun, we see that the general rule is that all external object noun phrases must be accompanied by a coreferent object pronoun. This analysis is confirmed by the majority of Fijian dialects and other Oceanic languages.

Finally, Fijian has one verb-object structure where transitive marking does not appear. A generic or non-specific object immediately follows the verb, without suffix or article:

erau rai vale   tiko   na yalewa
3 du. see house imperf. the woman
'The two women are looking at houses.'

Bibliography

Pawley (1974) is a detailed survey article, while Blust (Forthcoming) promises to be a major monograph treatment. For the geographical distribution of Austronesian languages, Wurm and Hattori (1981-4) is an indispensable work, covering all of Austronesia and several neighbouring families; in addition to excellent maps there is much information on subgrouping and numbers of speakers, as well as references to more detailed studies. Sebeok (1971) contains survey articles on all Austronesian areas; some are simply chronicles of research, but others contain considerable linguistic information.

For comparative phonology, Dempwolff (1934-8) is still the fundamental work on comparative Austronesian; Dahl (1973) is a reexamination of Dempwolff's conclusions by one of his students, mainly concerned with comparative phonology. For the linguistic evidence concerning early Austronesian culture history, reference should be made to Blust (1976; 1980).

Grammars of Fijian include Churchward (1941), a concise but perceptive missionary grammar, and Milner (1972), ostensibly pedagogical but usable as reference; however Schütz (1986) is the most comprehensive and systematic description to date, covering not only grammar and phonology but also the history of the study of the language, the development of the writing system, etc. Geraghty (1983) is the definitive study of Fijian linguistic diversity.

References

Blust, R. 1976. 'Austronesian Culture History: Some Linguistic Inferences and Their Relations to the Archaeological Record', *World Archaeology*, vol. 8, pp. 19–43.
—— 1980. 'Early Austronesian Social Organization: The Evidence of Language', *Current Anthropology*, vol. 21, pp. 205–47.
—— Forthcoming. *Austronesian Languages* (Cambridge University Press, Cambridge)
Churchward, M.C. 1941. *A New Fijian Grammar* (reprinted by Government Press, Suva, 1973)
Dahl, O.C. 1973. *Proto-Austronesian* (Studentenlitteratur, Lund)
Dempwolff, O. 1934–8. *Vergleichende Lautlehre des austronesischen Wortschatzes*, 3 vols. (Dietrich Reimer, Berlin)
Geraghty, P.A. 1983. *The History of the Fijian Languages* (University Press of Hawaii, Honolulu)
Milner, G.B. 1972. *Fijian Grammar*, 3rd ed. (Government Press, Suva)

Pawley, A.K. 1974. 'Austronesian Languages', in *The New Encyclopaedia Britannica, Macropaedia* (Encyclopaedia Britannica, Chicago)

Schütz, A.J. 1986. *The Fijian Language* (University Press of Hawaii, Honolulu)

Sebeok, T.A. (ed.) 1971. *Current Trends in Linguistics*, vol. 8: *Linguistics in Oceania* (Mouton, The Hague)

Wurm, S.A. and S. Hattori (eds.) 1981–4. *Language Atlas of the Pacific Area*, 2 parts (Australian Academy of the Humanities, Canberra)

46 Malay (Indonesian and Malaysian)

D.J. Prentice

1 Introduction

A form of the Malay language constitutes the national language in four countries of South-East Asia. In descending order of size of population these are: the Republic of Indonesia (160 million), the Federation of Malaysia (15 million), the Republic of Singapore (three million) and the Sultanate of Brunei (250,000). The variant of Malay used in the first-named state, which is officially termed *Bahasa Indonesia* (Indonesian language), will be referred to here as 'Indonesian'. The second variant, known in Malaysia as *Bahasa Malaysia* (Malaysian language) and in Singapore and Brunei as *Bahasa Melayu* (Malay language) or *Bahasa Kebangsaan* (national language), will be referred to as 'Malaysian'.

As can be seen from the accompanying map, native speakers of Malay are concentrated in the area of the Malacca Straits, a highly strategic location, since the Malacca Straits was the route through which the extensive maritime trade between India and Arabia in the west and China in the east had to pass. Moreover, the monsoon pattern made it impossible to complete the voyage without a pause of some months in the Malay-speaking region, a fact which resulted in Malay eventually acquiring the status of lingua franca throughout the Archipelago. Although this expansion of the language has not been historically documented, it is known that Malay was already in use in eastern Indonesia in the sixteenth century and it was considered quite normal for Francis Xavier to preach in Malay when he was in the Moluccas.

Outside the Malacca Straits area, Malay dialects are also found along the southern and western coasts of Borneo, in the southernmost provinces of Thailand and in the Mergui Archipelago of Burma. Malay-based creoles are found not only among the originally Chinese-speaking inhabitants of the old Straits Settlements of former British Malaya, but also in various ports of eastern Indonesia and on Christmas Island and the Cocos Islands in the Indian Ocean.

Despite this wide geographic distribution, Malay is by no means the mother tongue of the majority of the region's inhabitants. In fact this status is only achieved in Brunei, where it is the language of 60 per cent

913

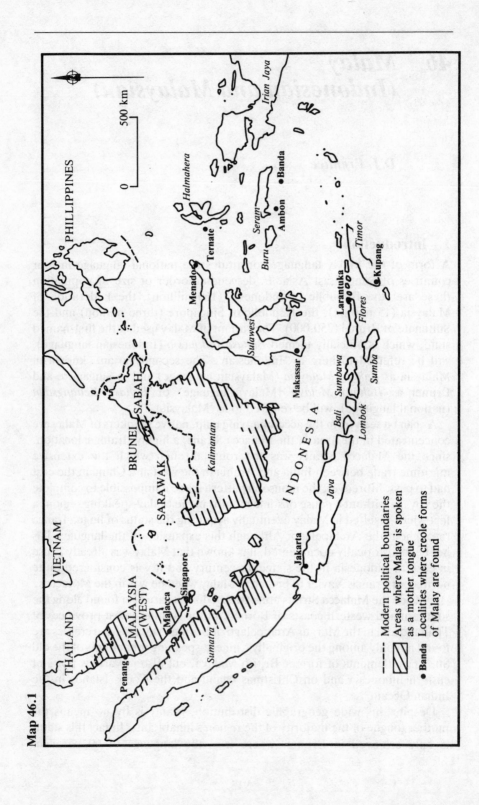

Map 46.1

population (30 per cent speaking Chinese and the remainder non-Malay indigenous languages). In the other three countries the Malay-speaking proportion of the population is as follows: Malaysia 45 per cent (35 per cent speak Chinese languages, 10 per cent Indian languages and 10 per cent non-Malay indigenous languages), Singapore 15 per cent (70 per cent Chinese, 10 per cent Indian languages) and Indonesia 7 per cent (90 per cent non-Malay indigenous languages, 3 per cent Chinese). In terms of native speakers, the most important language of the whole region is Javanese (60 million speakers in central and eastern Java), followed by Sundanese (20 million speakers in western Java). Other important languages spoken in Indonesia (all with more than one million speakers) are Achinese (northernmost Sumatra), Batak (north-central Sumatra), Minangkabau (south-west Sumatra, regarded by many as a dialect of Malay), Buginese, Macassarese (both in southern Celebes), Madurese (Madura and eastern Java) and Balinese (Bali). The exact number of languages in the region is not known but can be safely estimated at around 300, of which the vast majority belong to the Austronesian language family. Non-Austronesian languages are found only in furthest eastern Indonesia and the interior of the Malay Peninsula.

The most important means of inter-ethnic communication in this multi-lingual situation has for centuries been provided by various forms of Malay, a fact which played a decisive role in the choice of Malay as the national language of Indonesia. Except in Singapore, where English is predominant, the language is today the main vehicle of communication for a population of almost 200 million, not only in areas of business and government but also in the mass media and at all levels of education.

The oldest known Malay text is to be found in a stone inscription dating from AD 683. This inscription and a few others of later date originate from the Hindu-Buddhist maritime empire of Srivijaya which had its capital near Palembang (southern Sumatra) and which at the height of its power (ninth to twelfth centuries) ruled over most of what is now Malaysia and western Indonesia. The inscriptions, written in a Pallava script originating from southern India, contain laws and accounts of military expeditions. They show that Malay was the administrative language of the empire, even in areas outside the Malay-speaking region (as shown by a tenth-century Malay inscription from West Java). Since Srivijaya was known far afield as a religious, cultural and commercial centre, it can be assumed that the language was used in these domains too. It was probably in this period that the first form of pidginised Malay (later known as Bazaar Malay) arose as a contact language among traders. Bazaar Malay still exists but is gradually disappearing as more people become familiar with the standard language.

From the late fourteenth to the early sixteenth century, the region was dominated by the powerful sultanate of Malacca, the rulers of which had at an early date been converted to Islam. The courts of this and other Malay sultanates possessed a rich literary tradition which produced many works, the most famous being the *Sejarah Melayu* or 'Malay Annals', a court history probably written in the sixteenth century but known only from a later manuscript. The language used in these literary and religious works, written in an adapted form of the Arabic script, is now termed 'Classical Malay'. It remained the golden standard for written Malay for the next 400 years, i.e. until the first quarter of the twentieth century in Indonesia and until the 1950s in Malaysia.

After the conquest of Malacca by the Portuguese in 1511, the court fled to the south and eventually established a polity which embraced Johore (the southern tip of the Malay Peninsula) and the island groups of Riau and Lingga in modern Indonesia. The literary tradition of the Malacca sultanate survived the upheavals of the colonial period and continued at the court of the Sultans of Riau-Johore. After the Napoleonic wars, the Treaty of London in 1824 regulated the division of the area into spheres of influence for the British and the Dutch (who had previously driven out the Portuguese). The boundary between the two spheres split the Riau-Johore sultanate into two. The literary Malay of the court continued, however, to be regarded as the standard on both sides of the new frontier and served in both areas as the basis for the future national language. Indonesian and Malaysian are therefore much closer to each other than they might have been if the boundary had been set elsewhere. On the other hand, for the whole of the nineteenth and part of the twentieth century the language was exposed to different influences in the two areas: from Dutch and Javanese in the Netherlands East Indies and from English and local Malay dialects in the British-controlled areas. During the crucial period of the Industrial Revolution, with all its new technological developments, advanced education was only available (if at all) through the language of the colonial power, which meant that the few Malay-speaking intellectuals had more contact with their Dutch or British counterparts than with each other. The language therefore lacked a common technical vocabulary. This divergence did not end with the independence of Indonesia and Malaysia: each country plotted its own course in rehabilitating the lexicon of the language to enable it to cope with twentieth-century technology. Not until the late 1970s was a joint Indonesian-Malaysian policy developed for the creation and adaptation of technical terms.

As a result, the major differences between Indonesian and Malaysian are lexical rather than grammatical in nature. The language described in the remainder of this chapter is the majority variant (i.e. Indonesian), although occasional references are made to significant Malaysian differences.

2   Phonology

The segmental phonemes of Indonesian are presented in table 46.1. Most of the symbols used in table 46.1 are also used for the same phonemes in the

Table 46.1: Segmental Phonemes

		Contoids					Vocoids		
		Labial [1]	Dental[2] + Alveolar	Palatal	Velar	Glottal	Front	Central	Back
Consonants	Stops	p b	t d	c j	k g	ʔ			
	Nasals	m	n	ñ	ŋ				
	Fricatives	f[3] v[3]	s z[3]	š[3]	x[3]	h			
	Lateral		l						
	Trill		r[4]						
Vowels	Semi-Vowels						y		w
	High						i		u
	Mid						e	ə	o
	Low							a	

Note: [1] f and v are labio-dental, the remainder bilabial. [2] t (and n preceding t) are dental, the remainder alveolar. [3] $f, v, z, š$ and x occur only in loanwords. [4] In Malaysia r is a uvular fricative word-initially and medially, and is elided word-finally.

standard orthography. The vowels *ə* (frequently called *pəpət*) and *e* are not distinguished, however, both being spelt with 'e'. Dictionaries and grammars generally indicate the difference by using 'é' for *e* and 'e' for *ə*. The same convention will be followed in this chapter. The consonants *š, x, ñ, ŋ* are written 'sy', 'kh', 'ny', 'ng' respectively, while the diphthongs *aw* and *ay* are written 'au' and 'ai'. The phonemic status of *ʔ* is disputed. Some linguists maintain that it is an allophone of *k* in syllable-final position (*kakak* [kakaʔ] 'elder sibling', *rakyat* [raʔyat] 'people') and a predictable, non-phonemic transitional phenomenon between two vowels of which the first is *a* or *e* or between two identical vowels (*seumur* [səʔumur] 'of the same age', *seékor* [səʔekor] 'one (animal)', *keenam* [kəʔənam] 'sixth', *maaf* [maʔaf] 'pardon', *cemooh* [cəmoʔoh] 'mock'). Although this undoubtedly represents the original situation, the picture has changed under the influence of loanwords which do not conform to the pattern just described: *fisik* [fisik] 'physical' versus *bisik* [bisiʔ] 'whisper', *maknit* [maknit] 'magnet' versus *makna* [maʔna] 'meaning'. Summarising, it can be said that orthographic 'k' in word-initial and intervocalic position always represents *k*, while elsewhere (i.e. syllable-finally) it represents either *ʔ* or, less frequently, *k*.

The present orthography, which is used in both Indonesia and Malaysia, dates only from 1972, before which time each country had its own spelling system. Since so much written material is only available in the obsolete orthographies and since many proper names retain their original spellings, the major differences are presented in table 46.2.

A cursory inspection of an Indonesian dictionary reveals a strong predominance of disyllabic lexemes. Monosyllabic forms are without

Table 46.2: Spelling Systems

Post-1972 Common orthography	*Pre-1972* Indonesia	Malaysia
c	tj	ch
j	dj	j
kh	ch	kh
ny	nj	ny
sy	sj	sh
y	j	y
e (ə)	e	e, ĕ
e (e)	e, é	e
i (before word-final h, k)	i	e
i (elsewhere)	i	i
u (before word-final h, k, ng, r)	u, oe*	o
u (elsewhere)	u, oe*	u

Note: *The spelling 'oe' was replaced by 'u' in 1947.

exception (1) bound morphemes, clitics or particles (e.g. *-ku* 'my', *se-* 'one, same', *ke* 'to(wards)', *-kah* (interrogative), *dan* 'and'); (2) loanwords (e.g. *cat* 'paint' from Chinese, *sah* 'authorised' from Arabic, *bom* 'bomb' from Dutch); (3) interjections (e.g. *cih!* 'poo!', *dor!* 'ḅang! (of gunshot)'); or (4) abbreviations of names and terms of address (e.g. *pak* from *bapak* 'father, sir', *bu* from *ibu* 'mother, madam', *Man* from *Suleiman* (male name)). Polysyllabic forms are usually the result of (1) morphological derivation (e.g. *beberapa* 'some, several' from *berapa* 'how many ?' + reduplication, *seumur* 'of the same age' from *se-* 'one, same' + *umur* 'age', *Merapi* (name of two volcanoes, one in Sumatra, the other in Java) from *mer-* (fossilised prefix) + *api* 'fire'); (2) of compounding (e.g. *matahari* 'sun' from *mata* 'eye' + *hari* 'day', *kacamata* 'spectacles' from *kaca* 'glass' + *mata* 'eye'); or (3) of borrowing (e.g. *jendéla* 'window' from Portuguese, *sandiwara* 'play, drama' from Sanskrit, *sintaksis* 'syntax' from Dutch). A small number of polysyllabic forms, however, appear to be inherited and not explicable as the result of one of these processes (e.g. *telinga* 'ear', *belakang* 'back').

Most Indonesian lexemes can be said to conform to the following canonical form:

$$(C_1) \ V_1 \ (C_2) \ V_2 \ (C_3)$$

The minimal free form consists of V_1V_2 (e.g. *ia* 'he, she'). In the inherited vocabulary, the following conditions apply:

C_1 = any consonant except *w* and *y*;
V_1 = any vowel;
C_2 = (1) any consonant; (2) a combination NC, i.e. a consonant preceded by a homorganic nasal (the normal combinations are *mp*, *mb*; *nt*, *nd*; *nc*, *nj*,

where the nasal is palatal despite the spelling; *ngk*, *ngg*; and *ngs*, where the nasal is alveolar for some speakers); or (3) a combination *r*C (only when V$_1$ = *e*);

V$_2$ = any vowel except *e*;

C$_3$ = any consonant except a palatal or a voiced stop (i.e. *c*, *j*, *ny*, *b*, *d* and *g*).

Large numbers of loanwords such as *kompleks* and *struktur* do not of course conform to this pattern.

Stress in Indonesian is non-phonemic and purely a matter of pitch (volume and quantity do not play a role in neutral speech). It regularly falls on the penultimate syllable (e.g. *'barat* 'west', *'tidur* 'sleep', *'péndék* 'short'), except when that syllable contains *e* followed by a single consonant, in which case it falls on the final syllable (e.g. *be'rat* 'heavy', *te'lur* 'egg'). In the case of *e* in the penultimate followed by two consonants, speakers fall into two groups differing in usage: group A, speakers originating from Java and the island to its east and group B, those originating from Sumatra and the Malay Peninsula. Group A displaces the stress to the final syllable while group B retains it on the penultimate *e* (e.g. A:*cer'min*, B:*'cermin* 'mirror', A:*leng'kap*, B:*'lengkap* 'complete'). In the case of suffixation, speakers of group A place the stress on the new penultimate, while those of group B retain it on the original syllable (A:*kepén'dékan*, B:*ke'péndékan* 'shortness, abbreviation', A:*keleng'kapan*, B:*ke'lengkapan* 'completeness').

Evidence from the Srivijayan inscriptions indicates that Malay, like its proto-language, originally had only four vowels: *i*, *u*, *e* and *a*. The phonemes *é* and *o* result from lowering of original *i* and *u*, universally in final closed syllables and unpredictably in non-final syllables. In the former environment, where the distinctions *i/é* and *u/o* are still subphonemic, the choice of an orthographic 'i' and 'u' is arbitrary, as indicated by the pre-1972 spelling systems. However, the existence of a vowel harmony rule (by which a non-central vowel in a non-final syllable may not be followed by a higher vowel in the final syllable) has led to the development not only of doublets (*bungkuk* and *bongkok* 'bow, stoop', *kicuh* and *kécoh* 'cheat, trick') but also of minimal pairs (*burung* 'bird' versus *borong* 'wholesale purchase', *giling* 'crush, grind' versus *géléng* 'shake the head'). Furthermore, the addition to the vocabulary of large numbers of neologisms in which the *i/é* and *u/o* distinctions are maintained in final closed syllables (*palét* 'palette' (from Dutch) versus *palit* 'smear', *kalong* 'fruitbat' (from Javanese) versus *kalung* 'garland, necklace') means that the distinctions have become phonemic in all environments.

3   Morphology

Indonesian has about 25 derivational affixes, but only two inflectional affixes (*meN$_2$*- and *di*-, see page 933). In this respect the standard language is more complex than the Malay dialects and the Malay-based creoles, which have far fewer affixes. In comparison with related Western Austronesian languages such as Javanese or Tagalog, however, the Indonesian affix system can be described as impoverished. The derivational affixes consist of not only prefixes and suffixes but also infixes and simulfixes. The infixes, four in number, are placed between the initial consonant of a base and the following adjective. They are restricted to a limited number of fossilised forms, e.g. -em- (cognate with Tagalog-um- in *gemetar* 'tremble' ← *getar* (idem), *tali-temali* 'rigging, cordage' ← *tali* 'rope'; -el- in *telunjuk* 'index finger' ← *tunjuk* 'point', *jelajah* 'explore' ← *jajah* 'colonise'; -en- in *senantan* '(of fighting cocks) milk-white' ← *santan* 'coconut-milk'; -er- in *seruling* 'flute' ← *suling* (idem). Another quite common fossilised affix is the prefix *mer-* (cognate with the highly productive *mag-* of Tagalog), which survives in *Merapi* (see page 918 above), *mertua* 'parent-in-law' ← *tua* 'old', *mersiul* 'crested wood-quail (bird species)' ← *siul* 'whistle' and other species names of flora and fauna.

Before describing the role of the living affixes, it is necessary to explain the Indonesian word-class system, the classification of which is based on a combination of morphological, syntactic and semantic factors. Indonesian lexical (as opposed to functional) bases are divisible into nominals (including nouns, pronouns and numerals) and verbals. The latter are divided into intransitive verbs and transitive verbs, according as they can cooccur with a grammatical object. The intransitive verbs, finally, can be classified as stative verbs, denoting qualities and states of affairs, or dynamic verbs, denoting changes of state, processes and actions. Examples are:

> nominals: rumah 'house', sapu 'broom', saya 'I', banyak 'many, much';
> stative verbs: bagus 'beautiful', banyak 'numerous', mati 'dead', rusak 'damaged';
> dynamic verbs: pergi 'go', duduk 'sit (down)', mati 'die', tahu 'know';
> transitive verbs: bunuh 'kill', sapu 'sweep', rusak 'damage'.

As shown by the examples *sapu*, *banyak*, *mati* and *rusak*, some bases are members of more than one word class. On the other hand, there are also bases without class membership (termed 'precategorials' and marked with a hyphen before the base) which occur only in derivations, reduplications and compounds (e.g. *-temu* → *bertemu* (d.v.) 'meet'; *-layan* → *layani* (t.v.) 'serve, wait on'; *-tari* → *menari* (d.v.) 'dance' and *tata tari* (nm.) 'choreography'; *-kupu* → *kupu-kupu* (nm.) 'butterfly'). Furthermore, it should be noted that colloquial spoken Indonesian is characterised by (among other things) extensive use of non-affixed forms instead of derivations which results in a greater degree of overlapping between word classes than in the standard (i.e. written, formal) language.

In table 46.3 the inflectional affixes and the most important derivational affixes are presented in the order in which they will be treated in the following pages. Secondary derivation, in which a derived form serves as the basis for a further derivation, is very frequent and is almost invariably

Table 46.3: Inflectional and Derivational Affixes

Derivational	Verb-forming	*ber-*	Stative and dynamic verbs
		meN₁-	Dynamic verbs
		per-	
		-i	Transitive verbs
		-kan	
		ter-	Stative and accidental dynamic verbs
		ke--an₁	
	Noun-forming	*peN-*	
		-an	
		ke--an₂	Deverbal and other nominals
		per--an	
		peN--an	
Inflectional		*meN₂-*	Agent-orientation
		di-	Object-orientation
		∅-	Imperative (*inter alia*)

accompanied by elision of the affix(es) employed in the primary derivation. For instance, the noun *obat* 'medicine', when suffixed with *-i* 'apply [BASE] to', produces *obati* (t.v.) 'treat (medically)'. This transitive verb in turn serves as the basis for derivations with *-kan* 'cause to undergo the action of [BASE]' (producing *obatkan* (t.v.) 'have treated') and with *peN--an* 'act of performing [BASE]' (producing *pengobatan* (nm.) '(medical) treatment'), in which the suffix *-i* of the underlying form is elided.

The prefix *ber-*, which is realised as *be-* when the base begins with *r...* or *CerC...*, forms large numbers of intransitive verbs, many of which occur without the prefix in informal speech. This is indicated by placing the prefix between brackets. Although it occurs with some precategorials to form dynamic verbs (*-main → (ber)main* 'play', *-nyanyi → (ber)nyanyi* 'sing'), it is most productive with nominal bases (including compounds of nominal + numeral and nominal + stative verb), when it forms intransitive verbs with a great variety of meanings: 'possess, wear, use etc. [BASE]'. Examples are: *mobil* 'car' → *bermobil* 'go by car', *sekolah* 'school' → *(ber)sekolah* 'go to school', *bapak* 'father, sir, you' → *berbapak* 'have a father, use *bapak* as a term of address', *ékor* 'tail' + *panjang* 'long' → *berékor panjang* 'long-tailed', *kaki* 'foot, leg' + *empat* 'four' → *berkaki empat* 'four-legged, four-footed'. With verbal bases, *ber-* is less productive. When affixed to a dynamic verb base indicating motion (always in combination with the suffix *-an*), it adds the semantic element 'diffuseness', i.e. plurality of actor, of action or of direction, e.g. *terbang* 'fly' → *beterbangan* 'fly in all directions', *pergi* 'go' → *bepergian* 'go on a journey, go to various places', *keluar* 'come/go out' → *berkeluaran* 'come/go out in large numbers'. When attached to transitive verb bases, *ber-* produces reciprocal verbs. In this case it is frequently accompanied by the suffix *-an* and/or complete reduplication of the base, e.g. *ganti* 'replace' → *berganti(-ganti)* 'succeed each other, take turns', *kejar* 'chase' → *berkejar(-kejar)an* 'chase each other', *kepit* 'squeeze between arm and body' → *berkepit(an)* 'walk/stand arm-in-arm', *tikam* 'stab' → *bertikam-tikaman* 'stab each other'.

In the case of the prefix *meN₁-*, *N* represents a nasal consonant homorganic with the initial phoneme of the base. As can be seen from table 46.4, the general pattern is that the nasals are preposed to voiced initials and substituted for voiceless initials. Nasal substitutions are indicated in the table by the capital letters *M, N, NG, NY*. The similar but more complicated

Table 46.4: Morphophonemics of *meN₁*

Initial phoneme of base	Form of prefix
b	mem-
p	meM-
d, j, c	men-
t	meN-
(vowel), h, g	meng-
k	meNG-
s	meNY-
(other phonemes)	me-

morphophonemics of the functionally distinct *meN₂-* are discussed on page 933 below. Verbs formed with *meN₁-* are always dynamic verbs and are less numerous than those formed with *ber-*. As with the latter, certain *meN₁-* verbs occur without the prefix in informal speech. Affixed to nominals (including compounds) and to precategorials, *meN₁-* has a great variety of meanings: 'behave like, resemble, move towards, collect, produce, consume etc. [BASE]', e.g. *gajah* 'elephant' → *menggajah* 'loom large', *darat* 'mainland' → *mendarat* 'go ashore', *seberang* 'other side (of road, river)' → *menyeberang* or colloquially *seberang* 'cross over', *rumput* 'grass' → *merumput* 'cut grass, (of cattle) graze', *tujuh* 'seven' + *bulan* 'month' → *menujuh bulan* 'hold a ceremony in the seventh month of pregnancy', *-amuk* → *mengamuk* 'run amuck, rage', *-jadi* → *(men)jadi* 'become'. When affixed to a stative verb, *meN₁-* forms a dynamic verb with the meaning '(gradually) become [BASE]' or 'behave in a [BASE] manner', e.g. *jauh* 'far, distant' → *menjauh* 'withdraw', *sombong* 'arrogant' → *menyombong* 'put on airs', *kurang* 'less' → *mengurang* 'diminish'.

The affixes *per-*, *-i* and *-kan* produce transitive verbs both from nominals and from other transitive or intransitive verbs, but are infrequently found with precategorials. Of the three affixes, *per-* was originally an important transitivising and causative prefix (as *pag-*, its cognate in Tagalog, still is — see page 951), but its functions have been usurped by *-kan*, which developed out of the preposition *akan* 'towards, with respect to'. As a result, *per-* as a transitivising prefix no longer has a function that is not also expressed by *-kan* or *-i*. In the formation of transitive verbs in the modern language, the prefix *per-* and the common simulfix *per--kan* always have one of the functions of the suffix *-kan* alone, while the now rare simulfix *per--i* always has one of the functions of *-i*. Accordingly, the following descriptions of *-kan* and *-i* also treat cases of *per-* and *per--kan* and of *per--i* respectively.

The suffix *-kan* is arguably the commonest and most productive of all derivational affixes in Indonesian and is frequently found in neologisms. When the base is a nominal denoting an animate being, a transitive verb derived with *-kan* has the meaning 'cause to become [BASE]' or 'regard, treat as [BASE]': *raja* 'king' → *rajakan* 'crown', *budak* 'slave' → *budakkan*, *perbudak* 'enslave, treat like a slave', *tuhan* 'god' → *pertuhan(kan)* 'deify, treat like a god', *istri* 'wife' → *peristri* 'take as one's wife, marry'. When the base denotes an inanimate object, various semantic patterns are found, the most frequent being 'place in/on [BASE]': *penjara* 'prison' → *penjarakan* 'imprison', *izin* 'permission' → *izinkan* 'permit, allow', *ladang* 'unirrigated field' → *perladang(kan)* 'open up (land) for cultivation', *proklamasi* 'proclamation' → *proklamasikan* 'proclaim'. With a stative verb base, verbs derived with *-kan* have the meaning 'cause to become [BASE]' or 'regard as [BASE]', e.g. *basah* 'wet' → *basahkan* 'wet', *dalam* 'deep' → *dalamkan*, *perdalam* 'deepen', *panjang* 'long' → *panjangkan* 'lengthen, extend' and *perpanjang* (idem) + 'extend the validity of', *kecil* 'small' → *kecilkan* 'reduce (garment, photo)' and *perkecil* 'belittle'. Semantic differentiation between *per-* and *-kan* is not uncommon, as seen in the derivatives of *panjang* and *kecil* above. Some Indonesian speakers, especially those with Javanese as their mother tongue, also maintain a distinction between such pairs as *dalamkan* 'make deep something which is shallow' and *perdalam* 'make deeper something which is already deep'. These distinctions are much less clear-cut in Malaysian, which prefers the simulfix *per--kan* in all the examples just given. Affixation of *-kan* to a dynamic verb produces three categories of transitive verbs: (1) those which mean 'cause to perform the action of [BASE]', e.g. *jatuh* 'fall' → *jatuhkan* 'drop', *berkumpul* 'gather' → *kumpulkan* 'gather, collect', *bekerja* 'work' → *pekerjakan* 'put to work, employ', *menyusu* 'suck at the breast' → *susukan* 'suckle, breast-feed'; (2) those which mean 'produce by the action of [BASE]', e.g. *muntah* 'vomit' → *muntahkan* 'regurgitate', *berkata* 'say, speak' → *katakan* 'say', *menari* 'dance' → *tarikan* 'perform (dance)'; and (3) transitive verbs of emotion, perception or speech which are semantically equivalent to [BASE] + preposition, e.g. *lupa* (± *akan*) 'forget (about)' → *lupakan* 'forget (about)', *mimpi* (+ *tentang*) 'dream (about)' → *mimpikan* 'dream about', *berbicara*

(+ *tentang*) 'talk (about)' → *bicarakan* 'discuss', *berjuang* (+ *untuk*) 'strive, fight (for)' → *perjuangkan* 'strive, fight for'. Derivations with -*kan* based on transitive verbs are divisible into two main groups: those in which object-replacement does not occur (in which case both the base transitive verb and the transitive verb with -*kan* have the direct object or 'goal' of the action as their object) and those in which object-replacement does occur, where a function other than 'goal', i.e. 'beneficiary' or 'instrument', is promoted to object of the verb with -*kan*. The former category can be further divided into causative and non-causative verbs. The non-causative are synonymous (or almost so) with their bases, the only difference being that the form with -*kan* usually connotes a more purposeful or more intense action than the base form. Examples are: *tulis* 'write' → *tuliskan* 'write (down)', *kirim* 'send' → *kirimkan* 'send (off), dispatch', *dengar* 'hear, listen to' → *dengarkan* 'listen to', *antar* 'bring, convey' → *antarkan* (idem). The causative verbs with -*kan* all have the meaning 'cause to undergo the action of [BASE]', e.g. *lihat* 'see' → *(per)lihatkan* 'cause to be seen, show', *dengar* 'hear, listen to' → *perdengarkan* 'cause to be heard, play (tune, record)', *séwa* 'hire' → *séwakan* 'cause to be hired, rent out', *obati* 'treat (medically)' → *obatkan* 'have treated (medically)'. Derivatives with -*kan* which have a beneficiary or instrumental object are more frequent in formal than in colloquial Indonesian. They occasionally give rise to competing forms, e.g. *tulis* 'write' → *tuliskan* 'write for (someone)' and 'write with (something)' (both differing from *tuliskan* 'write (something) down', see above), *beli* 'buy' → *belikan* 'buy for' and 'buy with, spend (money)', *cari* 'look for, seek' → *carikan* 'seek for, find for (someone)', *témbak* 'shoot' → *témbakkan* 'shoot with, fire (gun)'. Use of a derived verb with an instrumental object usually results in the original 'goal' object acquiring a new preposition, as in *témbak babi dengan senapang* 'shoot the pigs with a rifle' versus *témbakkan senapang (ke)pada babi* 'fire the rifle at the pigs', whereas this is usually not the case with verbs with a beneficiary object: *cari rumah untuk Ali* 'look for a house for Ali' versus *carikan Ali rumah* 'find Ali a house'.

The suffix -*i* is much less productive than -*kan*. There is, moreover, one phonologically determined constraint on its occurrence: it cannot be affixed to bases ending with the phonemes *i* or *y*, i.e. bases ending in orthographic 'i'. Combined with a nominal base, -*i* produces transitive verbs with one (or more) of the following meanings: 'apply [BASE] to', 'remove [BASE] from' or 'function as [BASE] of/for', e.g. *obat* 'medicine' → *obati* 'put medicine on, treat medically', *air* 'water' → *airi* 'irrigate', *tanda tangan* 'signature' → *tandatangani* 'sign', *kulit* 'skin' → *kuliti* 'peel (fruit), skin (animal), cover (book)', *bulu* 'fur, feather' → *bului* 'pluck (bird), fletch (arrow)', *ketua* 'chairman' → *ketuai* 'preside over, chair (meeting)', *dalang* 'puppet-master' → *dalangi* 'mastermind (conspiracy)'. In combination with a stative verb denoting a quality, -*i* produces a causative transitive verb with the meaning 'cause to be/become [BASE]'. The few surviving examples of the simulfix *per--i*, all of which have less common variants without *per-*, are confined to this group. Examples: *basah* 'wet' → *basahi* 'wet', *takut* 'afraid' → *takuti* 'frighten', *baik* 'good' → *(per)baiki* 'improve, repair'. Such forms as these can be synonymous with verbs derived with *-kan* from the same stative verb base. Usually, however, there is a subtle semantic distinction: the forms with *-i* imply the application of the quality of [BASE] to the object, an implication which is absent from the *-kan* forms. Thus *basahkan* means 'make wet (by any means, including soaking in liquid)', whereas *basahi* can only mean 'make wet by applying liquid' and not 'by placing in liquid'. When the base is a stative verb denoting emotion or perception or a dynamic verb denoting movement or location, the derivative with *-i* is semantically equivalent to [BASE] + preposition, e.g. *marah* (+ *pada*) 'angry (with)' → *marahi* 'scold', *suka* (± *akan*) 'fond (of something)', and (± *(ke)pada*) 'fond (of someone)' → *sukai* 'like', *hormat* (+ *kepada/terhadap*) 'respectful (towards)' → *hormati* 'respect', *duduk* (+ *di*) 'sit (on)' → *duduki* 'occupy', *berkunjung* (+ *ke(pada)*) 'pay a visit (to)' → *kunjungi* 'visit', *menjauh* (+ *dari*) 'go away, withdraw (from)' → *jauhi* 'avoid'. As with *-kan*, when *-i* is attached to a transitive verb object-replacement may or may not occur. When it does not occur, *-i* denotes plurality of object and/or intensification or repetition of the action: *pukul* 'strike' → *pukuli* 'beat up', *makan* 'eat' → *makani* 'devour', *angkat* 'lift' → *angkati* 'lift many (objects), lift repeatedly'. With object-replacement, the *-i* derivative has the location or direction of the action as its object. The base transitive verb frequently has a synonymous or nearly synonymous form with *-kan*, e.g. *tulis(kan)* 'write (down)' → *tulisi* 'inscribe (with something), write on', *kirim(kan)* 'send (off)' → *kirimi* 'send something to', *tanam(kan)* 'plant (e.g. seed)' → *tanami* 'plant (e.g. field) (with something), plant something in'.

The so-called 'accidental' verbs are formed by the prefix *ter-* or the simulfix *ke--an₁*, of which the former is more common. When affixed to dynamic verb bases, *ter-* indicates sudden or involuntary action: *duduk* 'sit (down)' → *terduduk* 'fall on one's backside', *tidur* 'sleep' → *tertidur* 'fall asleep', *memekik* 'scream' → *terpekik* 'scream involuntarily'. With transitive verb bases, *ter-* yields three kinds of verbs. Firstly it can produce accidental dynamic verbs which in Indonesian (but not in Malaysian) are exclusively object-oriented, i.e. the subject of the *ter-* predicate is the object of the underlying base verb. Examples are: *pukul* 'strike' → *terpukul* 'be struck accidentally', *makan* 'eat' → *termakan* 'be eaten by mistake'. Secondly, and most frequently, *ter-* produces stative verbs indicating the state resulting from the action of the base transitive verb. These verbs are object-oriented in both Indonesian and Malaysian. Examples are: *singgung* 'offend' → *tersinggung* 'offended', *hormat* 'respect' → *terhormat* 'respected', *dapati* 'find, encounter' → *terdapat* 'occur, be found', *letakkan* 'put, place' → *terletak* 'situated, located', *organisasi(kan)* 'organise' → *terorganisasi* 'organised, regimented'. Thirdly, *ter-* can yield object-oriented stative verbs with a semantic element of potentiality. These verbs occur most frequently in negative sentences, preceded by *tidak* 'not', and form an exception to the general rule that in secondary derivations all primary derivational affixes are elided. Examples: *angkat* 'lift' → *tidak terangkat* 'cannot be lifted', *makan* 'eat' → *tidak termakan* 'inedible', *dalami* 'explore in depth' → *tidak terdalami* 'unfathomable', *selesaikan* 'solve' → *tidak terselesaikan* 'insoluble'. The final function of *ter-* is to form superlatives, a function in which it is restricted to occurrence with monomorphemic stative verb bases, e.g. *baik* 'good' → *terbaik* 'best', *tinggi* 'high' → *tertinggi* 'highest'.

Of the much rarer accidental verbs formed with *ke--an₁*, four are object-oriented dynamic verbs or stative verbs based on transitive verbs of perception: *lihat* 'see' → *kelihatan* 'be seen; be visible; appear, seem', *dengar* 'hear' → *kedengaran* 'be heard; be audible; sound', *dapati* 'find, encounter' → *kedapatan* 'be found (doing something)', *ketahui* 'know, find out' → *ketahuan* 'be found out, come to light'. The remainder, which can have bases of any word class, all share the meaning 'be adversely affected by [BASE]': *hujan* (nm.) 'rain' → *kehujanan* 'be caught in the rain', *malam* (nm.) 'night' → *kemalaman* 'be overtaken by nightfall', *takut* (s.v.) 'afraid' → *ketakutan* 'be overcome by fear', *mati* (s.v.) 'dead' and (d.v.) 'die' → *kematian* 'be bereaved', *curi* (t.v.) 'steal' → *kecurian* 'be robbed', *datangi* (t.v.) 'come to, arrive at' → *kedatangan* 'receive (unexpected) visitors'.

The nasal element of the prefix *peN-* combines with the initial phoneme of the base in the same way as that of *meN₁-* (see page 922 above). With a dynamic or transitive verb base *peN-* forms a nominal with the meaning 'person who (customarily) performs [BASE]': *(ber)nyanyi, (me)nyanyi* 'sing' → *penyanyi* 'singer', *menangis* 'weep' → *penangis* 'cry-baby', *duduki* 'occupy' → *penduduk* 'occupant, inhabitant', *kumpulkan* 'collect' → *pengumpul* 'collector'. Less frequently the derived nominal has the meaning 'instrument with which [BASE] is performed': *buka* 'open' → *pembuka botol* 'bottle-opener'. A *peN-* derivative from a stative verb base is both a nominal and a stative verb and has the meaning '(person who is) characterised by [BASE]', e.g. *takut* 'afraid' → *penakut* 'coward(ly)', *marah* 'angry' → *pemarah* 'bad-tempered (person)'.

The suffix *-an*, which occurs either alone or as an element of the simulfixes *ke--an₂*, *per--an* and *peN--an*, is the commonest noun-forming affix. Deverbal nouns formed with *-an*, which (unlike the simulfixes) is no longer productive, refer to the object, instrument, location or action of the base verb, which can be a dynamic or transitive verb: *(ber)nyanyi, (me)nyanyi* 'sing' → *nyanyian* 'song, singing', *makan* 'eat' → *makanan* 'food', *timbang* 'weigh' → *timbangan* 'weighing-scales', *berlabuh* 'drop anchor' → *labuhan* 'anchorage', *pukul* 'strike' → *pukulan* 'blow'. The formation of deverbal nouns through the productive simulfixes is linked to the morphology of the underlying verb: *ke--an₂* occurs with non-derived intransitive verbs, *per--an* with intransitive verbs derived with *ber-* and transitive verbs derived with *per-*, and *peN--an* with all other transitive verbs. All these derived nominals denote 'quality, process or activity of [BASE]': *indah* 'beautiful' → *keindahan* 'beauty', *datang* 'come' → *kedatangan* 'coming, arrival', *bersekutu* 'be allied' → *persekutuan* 'alliance, federation', *perbaiki* 'repair, improve' → *perbaikan* 'repair, improvement', *satu* 'one' → *kesatuan* 'unit, unity', *bersatu* 'united' → *persatuan* 'union, association', *satukan* 'unify' → *penyatuan* 'unification'. The simulfixes *ke--an$_2$* and *per--an* also occur with nominal bases, producing nouns denoting collectivity, e.g. *pulau* 'island' → *kepulauan* 'archipelago', *air* 'water' → *perairan* '(territorial) waters'. They are frequently found in modern Indonesian as the formatives of nouns used almost exclusively in attributive position, as the equivalents of English and Dutch denominal adjectives, e.g. *agama* 'religion' → *keagamaan* '(affairs) pertaining to religion, religious', as in *latar-belakang keagamaannya* 'his/her/its religious background' as opposed to *latar-belakang agamanya* 'the background of his/her/its religion'. Frequently, however, the denominal adjective is borrowed along with the underlying noun, as *géografi* 'geography' and *géografis* 'geographical' from Dutch. Intensive borrowing of foreign derivatives combined with use of indigenous derivational mechanisms often leads to synonymy. From Dutch has been borrowed both the verb *organisir* 'organise' and the noun *organisasi* 'organisation'. As already seen, the latter gives rise to a second verb *organisasi(kan)* 'organise' while both verbs can further serve as bases for nominal derivations: *pengorganisiran* and *pengorganisasian*, both of which mean 'organisation' in the sense of 'the act of organising'.

Another morphological process which is almost as important as affixation and furthermore very characteristic for Indonesian and related languages is reduplication, of which there are three forms. Full reduplication, which involves repetition of the whole lexeme, is used grammatically as one way of indicating plurality with nouns (see page 928 below) but has also numerous lexical uses (e.g. *kuda* 'horse' → *kuda-kuda* 'saw-horse'). In altered reduplication, the whole base is also doubled, but one or more of its phonemes are at the same time replaced (e.g. *balik* 'go back' → *bolak-balik* 'go back and forth'). Partial reduplication can be summarised in the formula $C_1eC_1V_1...$, i.e. repetition of the initial consonant of the base followed by the vowel *e*, e.g. *laki* 'husband' → *lelaki* (also *laki-laki*) 'man, male'. It does not occur with vowel-initial bases and is not very common in Indonesian. In Malaysian on the other hand, not only do all cases of lexical full reduplication have alternatives with partial reduplication (thus *kuda-kuda* and *kekuda* 'saw-horse'), but it is also frequently used for the coinage of new terms: *pasir* 'sand' → *pepasir* 'granule', *bola* 'ball' → *bebola* 'ball-bearing'. Full and altered reduplication are found with bases of all word classes (including precategorials), in combination with various affixes and with diverse functions, of which only a few can be exemplified here: (1) diversity and collectivity, e.g. *daun* 'leaf' → *daun-daunan* or *dedaunan* 'foliage', *sayur* 'vegetable' → *sayur-mayur* 'various vegetables'; (2) similarity, e.g. *anak* 'child' → *anak-anakan* 'doll' (see also *kuda-kuda* above); (3) vagueness, e.g. *mérah* 'red' → *kemérah-mérahan* 'reddish'; (4) aimlessness, e.g. *duduk* 'sit' → *duduk-duduk* 'sit around (doing nothing)', *ikut* 'follow' → *ikut-ikutan* 'follow blindly'; (5) reciprocity, e.g. *hormati* 'respect' → *hormat-menghormati* 'respect each other', see also examples with *ber-(-an)* on page 922 above; (6) continuousness or repetition, e.g. *turun* 'descend' → *turun-temurun* 'from generation to generation' (cf. also *bolak-balik* above); and (7) intensity, e.g. *cabik* 'tear' → *cabik-cabik* 'tear to pieces', *habis* 'finished, used up' → *habis-habisan* 'all-out, total (war, destruction)'.

4 Syntax

Nouns are not marked for number, gender or definiteness, nor are verbs marked for person or tense. A sentence such as *harimau makan babi* 'tiger + eat + pig' has therefore an infinite number of meanings, varying from 'tigers eat pigs' to 'the tigresses have eaten a boar', according to the context. There exist mechanisms for making the distinctions mentioned, but these are only used when the distinction is important and not conveyed by the context. Full reduplication of nouns, for instance, can be used to indicate miscellany, variety or simple plurality: *babi* '(the, a) pig, (the) pigs', *babi-babi* '(the) pigs, various pigs'. Definiteness can be indicated by (among other things) a deictic (*itu* 'the, that') or a personal pronoun (*-nya* 'his/her/its/the') after a noun: *babi itu* 'that/those/the pig(s)', *babi-babinya* 'his/her/its/the (various) pigs'. Gender can be shown by the use of modifiers *lelaki/jantan* 'male' and *perempuan/betina* 'female' (for humans and non-humans respectively) after the noun: *cucu* 'grandchild', *cucu lelaki* 'grandson', *cucu perempuan* 'granddaughter'; *babi* 'pig', *babi jantan* 'boar', *babi betina* 'sow'.

As will be evident from the examples just given, modifiers in noun phrases usually follow the element which they modify. Immediately following the head noun can occur a noun used attributively or possessively (*rumah* 'house', *batu* 'rock, stone', *rumah batu* 'stone house'; *guru* 'teacher', *rumah guru* 'teacher's house') or a monomorphemic stative verb (*baru* 'new', *rumah baru* 'new house'). In second place can occur one or more relative clauses, introduced by the relative linker *yang*, and one or more prepositional phrases (*terbakar* 'burnt', *rumah yang terbakar* 'the house which was burnt down'; *di* 'in, at', *rumah di Jakarta* 'house(s) in Jakarta'). Final position is reserved for the deictics *ini* 'this' and *itu* 'that, the' (*rumah yang terbakar ini* 'this house which has been burnt down', *saya* 'I', *rumah saya di Jakarta yang terbakar itu* 'that house of mine in Jakarta which was burnt down'). When the position immediately following the head noun is occupied, any further attributive modifier must be placed in a *yang*-clause in second position (*rumah batu yang baru* 'new stone house'). This occasionally yields ambiguity: *rumah guru yang baru* can mean 'the teacher's new house' (in which *yang baru* modifies *rumah*) or 'the house of the new teacher' (in which it modifies *guru*). Similarly, an attributive consisting of a qualified or polymorphemic stative verb is placed in a *yang*-clause (*rumah yang terbaru* 'newest house', *rumah yang cukup baru* 'fairly new house').

The most important exception to the general word order rule in noun phrases is the quantifier, which precedes the noun (but can also follow it, especially in lists). The quantifier consists of a numeral (or other quantifying term such as 'several', 'many', etc.) followed by an optional 'classifier'. The numerals from 'one' to 'ten' are: *satu* 'one', *dua* 'two', *tiga* 'three', *empat* 'four', *lima* 'five', *enam* 'six', *tujuh* 'seven', *delapan* 'eight', *sembilan* 'nine' and *sepuluh* 'ten'. The numerals between 'ten' and 'twenty' are formed with *belas*: *sebelas* 'eleven', *dua belas* 'twelve', *tiga belas* 'thirteen' etc. Higher numerals are formed with *puluh* 'tens', *ratus* 'hundreds', *ribu* 'thousands' and *juta* 'millions'. In combination with these forms, as with *belas* and all nouns of measurement, *satu* 'one' takes the form of a prefix *se-*: *sepuluh* 'ten', *seratus tujuh puluh* 'one hundred and seventy', *seribu sembilan ratus delapan puluh lima* '1985', *sejuta* 'one million'. Except for 'first', which is expressed by the Sanskrit loanword *pertama*, ordinals are formed with the prefix *ke-* (e.g. *ketujuh* 'seventh', *kedua puluh lima* 'twenty-fifth'), while fractions are formed with *per-* (e.g. *sepertujuh* 'one seventh', *tiga pertujuh* 'three sevenths').

The classifier is a morpheme-type found in many Asian languages (including non-Austronesian languages such as Vietnamese and Chinese). It occurs between a numeral and a noun and gives information about the form, size or character of the latter. Classical Malay possessed dozens of classifiers, such as *butir* (lit. 'grain') for small round objects and *batang* ('stick') for long, solid cylindrical objects. Although some of these are still in use in fixed expressions, in modern Indonesian membership of this subclass is for all practical purposes reduced to three: *buah* ('fruit') for inanimate nouns, *ékor* ('tail') for animate non-human nouns and *orang* '(person') for human nouns (*tiga buah rumah* 'three houses', *tiga ékor babi* 'three pigs', *tiga orang guru* 'three teachers'). With classifiers, the numeral *satu* is abbreviated to *se-* when it has the meaning 'a, an'; this is the usual way of marking a noun for indefiniteness, thus *sebuah rumah* 'a house' versus *satu (buah) rumah* 'one house'. Similar in their syntactic behaviour to classifiers are metrical nouns, which include not only names for units of measurement such as *jam* 'hour', *méter* 'metre' but also all nouns denoting objects which can be used or regarded as containers, e.g. *sebotol bir* 'a bottle of beer' (as opposed to *sebuah botol bir* 'a beer-bottle'); with *gerobak* 'cart' and *kayu* 'wood', *segerobak kayu* 'a cartload of wood' versus *sebuah gerobak kayu* 'a wooden cart', *tiga gerobak kayu* 'three cartloads of wood' versus *tiga (buah) gerobak kayu* 'three wooden carts'.

Indonesian is particularly rich in pronouns (a subclass of nominals), the majority of which are marked for varying degrees of familiarity or formality. There are only five unmarked pronouns: *saya* 'I', *kami* 'we (exclusive)' (i.e. 'I + he/she/they'), *kita* 'we (inclusive)' (i.e. 'I + you'), *dia* (also *ia* in formal Indonesian) 'he, she' and *meréka* 'they'. For the first person, *aku* 'I' is marked as intimate, while the third person *beliau* 'he, she' is marked as respectful. In the third person, traditionally only the bound form *-nya* can refer to inanimate entities. In recent years, however, the forms *ia* and *dia* are increasingly common in this function. There are no unmarked pronouns for the second person: *(eng)kau* and *kamu*, historically the unmarked singular and plural forms respectively, have not only lost the number distinction but are also marked as intimate. In all non-intimate situations various appellatives are used as second person (and under certain circumstances also first person) pronouns: personal names (to friends and acquaintances of the same age), kinship terms (to blood-relations or people regarded as such) and titles (to strangers, to older or more senior people and to colleagues in formal situations). Indonesian is therefore one of the few languages in the world in which pronouns are an open class, with an infinite membership. In the late 1950s an attempt was made to simplify the situation by propagating the use of *anda* (originally an honorific termination for kinship terms used in letters, e.g. *anakanda* 'dear child', from *anak* 'child') as an unmarked pronoun, intended to be as universal as English *you*. Although in some intellectual circles it is now so used, *anda* has only added to the complexity: it is now commonly used when addressing the general public via the mass media, where the age, status etc. of the reader, listener or viewer is unknown. Three pronouns (*aku*, *(eng)kau/kamu* and *dia/ia*) have inflected (or cliticised) forms for various functions, as shown in table 46.5. All the forms listed in the table for the function 'subject' can also be used for the other functions.

Table 46.5: Inflected (Cliticised) Pronouns

	Free forms Subject	Object	Bound forms Object	Agent	Possessive
1st	aku	*daku	*-ku	ku-	-ku
2nd	(eng)kau kamu	*dikau	*-kau, *-mu	kau-	-kau, -mu
3rd	*ia, dia	dia	-nya	-nya	-nya

Note: * = literary forms

Prepositional phrases consist of a noun phrase or a (nominalised) verb phrase preceded by a relator, which itself can be either simple or compound. A simple relator is either one of the three indigenous clitics (*di* (location), *ke* (movement towards) or *dari* (movement from)) or a word originally belonging to a different word class (nominal or verb), or borrowed from another language. Examples are: *dengan* 'with (accompaniment, instrument)', originally a nominal 'companion'; *melalui* 'through', also an agent-oriented transitive verb 'go/pass through'; *terhadap* 'towards, with regard to', originally a stative verb 'facing, directed towards'; *sebab* 'because of', also a nominal 'cause', borrowed from Arabic; *tanpa* 'without', borrowed from Javanese. A compound relator usually consists of one of the clitics *di/ke/dari*, followed by one of a class of locative words (originally nominals), e.g. *dalam* 'interior', *atas* 'upper surface', *antara* 'interval, space between', as in *di rumah* 'in/at the house, at home', *di dalam rumah* 'in/ inside the house', *ke dalam rumah* 'into the house', *dari dalam rumah* 'from (inside) the house'. Before animate nouns and expressions of time, *di*, *ke* and *dari* are replaced by *pada*, *(ke)pada* and *dari(pada)* respectively: compare *di rumah itu* 'at that house' and *pada waktu itu* 'at that time', *ke Jakarta* 'to Jakarta' and *(ke)pada Ali* 'to Ali'. One or both parts of certain compound relators may be omitted, especially with verbs which contain a notion of direction or location, such as *masuk* 'come/go in': *Ali masuk ke dalam rumah*, *Ali masuk ke rumah*, *Ali masuk dalam rumah* or in colloquial style simply *Ali masuk rumah* 'Ali comes/goes into the house'.

In verb phrases with a dynamic or transitive verb as head, a three-way aspect distinction can be made by the markers *telah* (action completed), *sedang* (action commenced but not completed) and *akan* (action not commenced), which precede the verb: *Ali telah berpindah* 'Ali has (had, will have etc.) moved house', *Ali sedang berpindah* 'Ali is (was etc.) moving house', *Ali akan berpindah* 'Ali will (was going to etc.) move house'. In the spoken language *telah*, *sedang* and *akan* are replaced by *sudah*, *masih* or *lagi* and *mau* respectively, which can also co-occur with stative verbs and (under certain conditions) with nouns and numerals. Other tense-aspect distinctions can be indicated outside the verb phrase by temporal adverbs such as *bésok* 'tomorrow', *ésoknya* 'the next day', *nanti* 'soon', *sekarang* 'now', *tadi* 'just now', *tadinya* 'up to now, until then' etc. Adverbs of degree, which occur mostly but not exclusively with stative verbs, have a fixed position vis-à-vis the head: some occur before the stative verb (*paling* 'most', *terlalu* 'too'), some after the stative verb (*sekali* 'very') and some in either position (*amat* 'very', *benar* 'truly, really'). All verbs can be preceded by modals (e.g. *harus* 'must, have to', *boléh* 'may, be allowed to', *bisa* or *dapat* 'can, be able to', *ingin* 'wish to') and by negatives (e.g. *tidak* 'not', *jangan* (vetative), *bukan* (contrastive negative)). The combination of [negative] + [completed action] is expressed by *belum*: *Ali telah pergi* 'Ali has gone' is negated by *Ali belum pergi* 'Ali hasn't gone (yet)'. Changes in word order reflect semantic differences: *Ali tidak harus hadir* 'Ali doesn't have to be present' versus *Ali harus tidak hadir* 'Ali mustn't be present (must be 'not present')'

The unmarked word order within the sentence is subject–predicate, as seen in all the sentences used as examples above. The order predicate–subject is, however, very frequent and, except when the predicate is an object-oriented transitive verb, indicates focus on the predicate. When the predicate is an agent-oriented transitive verb (see page 933 below) with an object, the latter must always follow the verb; otherwise word order within the sentence is flexible and determined by factors of style and prominence. A copulative verb does not exist: *Ali guru* 'Ali is a teacher', *Ali marah* 'Ali is angry', *Ali di Jakarta* 'Ali is in Jakarta', *Ali (sedang) mendengar radio* 'Ali is listening to the radio'; and with predicate–subject order (with focus on the predicate): *guru Ali* 'Ali is **a teacher**', *marah Ali* 'Ali is **angry**', *di Jakarta Ali* 'Ali is **in Jakarta**', *(sedang) mendengar radio Ali* 'Ali is **listening to the radio**'. Nominal predicates can only be negated by *bukan* (*Ali bukan guru* 'Ali isn't a teacher'), whereas other predicates are negated either by *tidak* 'not (neutral negative)' or by *bukan* 'not (contrastive negative)', e.g. *Ali tidak marah* 'Ali isn't angry' and *Ali bukan marah* 'Ali isn't **angry** (he's **pleased**)'. In the written language an equational sentence, in which both subject and predicate are nominal phrases or nominalised verbal phrases, often has the structure 'subject–*adalah*–predicate'. The marker *adalah* (or *ialah* with third person subjects) is used when structural complexity of subject and/or predicate renders the boundary between the two sentence elements doubtful. In the spoken language this function is performed by intonation (rising intonation on the subject, slight caesura between subject and predicate and falling intonation on the predicate). The following sentences can only be differentiated in written Indonesian by the use of the predicate marker *adalah* in the second:

Subject	Predicate	Object
kerja-nya	menarik	mahasiswa
work-his	attract	student

'His work attracts students.'

Subject		Predicate
kerja-nya	(adalah)	menarik mahasiswa
work-his		attract student

'His work (i.e. job, task) is to attract students.'

The subject of an Indonesian sentence is always definite, i.e. it represents either a unique entity or an entity already known from the linguistic or non-linguistic context or a particularised item or class. Given the general tendency towards limitation of redundancy (see page 928 above), it is not surprising that the subject is frequently not expressed. Thus, when the subject of a subordinate clause is identical to that of the main clause, usually only the latter is expressed, regardless of the order in which the clauses appear:

Ali tinggal di rumah karena (dia) sakit
Ali stay at house because he ill
'Ali stayed at home because he was ill.'

This sentence could also appear as: *karena (dia) sakit, Ali tinggal di rumah* 'because he was ill, Ali stayed at home'. Whenever the subject is an inanimate entity known from the context, it is obligatorily absent, as in:

Jangan masuk rumah itu. Berbahaya.
don't go-in house that dangerous
'Don't go into that house. (It's) dangerous.'

When the predicate is a nominal, a stative verb or a dynamic verb, the subject represents the entity which respectively is equivalent to, is characterised by or performs the action of the predicate. When the predicate is a transitive verb, however, the subject can represent either the entity which performs the action of the predicate or that which undergoes it. This distinction between agent-orientation and object-orientation is marked on the transitive verb by the only inflectional affixes in the Indonesian verb system, *meN₂-* and *di-* respectively. The agent-oriented form is also frequently used as a nominal with the meaning 'the act (or activity) of verb-ing (tr.)', as in the sentence *kerjanya (adalah) menarik mahasiswa* above.

The morphophonemics of *meN₂-* are similar to those of *meN₁-* (see table 46.4). The differences include prenasalisation (rather than nasalisation) of initial voiceless consonants with some bases and the occurrence of an allomorph *menge-* with monosyllabic bases. Thus the initial *p* of the derivational prefix *per-* is never replaced by the nasal of *meN₂-*: *perlihatkan* 'show' → *memperlihatkan*. The same occurs irregularly with verbs which begin with the sequence *per...*, even though this is not a prefix: *percayai* 'trust' (from Sanskrit *pratyaya*) → *mempercayai*. Preservation of initial voiceless consonants is moreover frequent among verbs based on loanwords: *khianati* 'betray' → *mengkhianati*, *takhtakan* 'enthrone' → *mentakhtakan*. Competing forms sometimes arise: *terjemahkan* 'translate' → *menterjemahkan* and *menerjemahkan*. Monosyllabic bases and transitive verbs derived from them take either the regular allomorph of *meN₂-* (with or without deletion of initial voiceless consonants) or the allomorph *menge-* or (in most cases) both: *lém* 'glue' → *mengelém*, *bom* 'bomb' → *mengebom* or *membom*, *sahkan* 'authorise' (from *sah* 'valid') → *mengesahkan* or *mensahkan*.

An object-oriented verb takes the prefix *di-* when the agent is not expressed by a pronoun. The agent often directly follows the verb and is then optionally marked by the preposition *oléh* 'by'. In other positions *oléh* is obligatory: *Ali memukul Zainal kemarin* 'Ali struck Zainal yesterday', *Zainal dipukul (oléh) Ali kemarin* or *Zainal dipukul kemarin oléh Ali* 'Zainal was struck by Ali yesterday'. When the agent is expressed by a pronoun, two constructions are found. With a third person agent the *di*-form of the verb can be suffixed with the clitic pronoun *-nya* 'he, she' or directly followed by the pronoun *meréka* 'they' (in other positions the marker *oléh* must be used: *oléhnya, oléh meréka*): *Zainal dipukulnya kemarin* or *Zainal dipukul kemarin oléhnya* 'he struck Zainal yesterday'. When the agent is first or second person and increasingly in modern usage also when it is third person, the agent pronoun (or a cliticised form thereof, see table 46.5) is placed immediately preceding the zero-form of the verb, i.e. the verb without prefix. In the following examples the agent-oriented sentence is given first: *dia tidak harus membeli buku ini* or *buku ini tidak harus dibelinya* or *buku ini tidak harus dia beli* 'he doesn't have to buy this book', *engkau tidak harus membeli buku ini* or *buku ini tidak harus kaubeli* 'you don't have to buy this book'. The zero-form of a transitive verb is also frequently used in imperative sentences, where it is likewise object-oriented: *Buku ini baik sekali. Beli(lah)!* 'This book's very good. Buy (it)!' (The clitic *-lah* is used with imperatives to soften a command.)

At first glance the distinction between agent-orientation and object-orientation seems comparable to that between active and passive in various Indo-European languages. There are many differences, however. Firstly, as already mentioned, the subject of the sentence is always definite, so that the English sentence 'a dog has bitten Ali's child' would be expressed in Indonesian with an object-oriented construction: *anak Ali digigit anjing*. Secondly, there are numerous grammatical constraints on verb orientation. The relativiser *yang*, for instance, must always be linked to the subject of the verb in the relative clause: *buku yang dibeli Ali mahal sekali* 'the book which Ali bought is very expensive' (**buku yang Ali membeli* is ungrammatical). The same phenomenon is seen in *wh*-questioning and in contrastive focusing, which usually involve relativisation, equationalisation (or clefting) and a predicate–subject word order: *siapa (yang) membeli buku ini?* 'who bought this book?', *apa yang dibeli Ali?* 'what did Ali buy?', *Ali(lah) yang membeli buku ini* 'Ali (not Zainal) was the one who bought this book' or '**Ali** bought this book', *buku ini(lah) yang dibeli Ali* 'this book (not that one) is the one that Ali bought' or 'Ali bought **this** book', *buku(lah) yang dibeli Ali* 'books (not something else) are what Ali bought' or 'Ali bought **books**'. With the subject–predicate order the contrastive element is absent: *yang dibeli Ali (adalah) buku* 'what Ali bought was books'. Finally, choice of verb-orientation can also be governed by stylistic considerations. In written narrative style, for instance, a series of actions is frequently represented by a series of object-oriented constructions with a predicate–subject word order. One example will suffice to bring this chapter to a close: *dia berbaring di tempat tidur, diperbaikinya letak bantalnya, dimatikannya lampu dan dipejamkannya matanya* 'he lay down on the bed, adjusted his pillow, switched off the lamp and closed his eyes'.

Bibliography

Among descriptive grammars of Malay, the following are particularly to be recommended: Lombard (1977), Macdonald and Dardjowidjojo (1967), Alieva et al. (1972) and Kähler (1956). For syntax, reference may be made to Fokker (1951), while Amran Halim (1974) deals with the important question of intonational correlates of syntactic structure. Teeuw (1959) is an important contribution on the history of the language, while Tanner (1967) examines the relations between Bahasa Indonesia and other languages among educated Indonesians. Fuller bibliographical sources are provided by Teeuw (1961) and Uhlenbeck (1971). Adelaar (1985) makes a preliminary reconstruction of the ancestor-language of Standard Malay and five other Malay dialects (or languages very closely related to Malay) and presents information on the history of the language, revealed by the techniques of modern comparative linguistics.

References

Adelaar, K.A. 1985. *Proto-Malayic: the reconstruction of its phonology and parts of its lexicon and morphology*. (Ph.D. thesis, University of Leiden; to appear in the series *Verhandelingen*, Royal Institute of Linguistics and Anthropology (K.I.T.L.V.), Leiden)

Alieva, N.F. et al. 1972. *Grammatika indonezijskogo jazyka* (Nauka, Moscow)

Amran Halim. 1974. *Intonation in Relation to Syntax in Bahasa Indonesia* (Djambatan and Department of Education and Culture, Jakarta)

Fokker, A.A. 1951. *Inleiding tot de studie van de Indonesische syntaxis* (J.B. Wolters, Groningen and Jakarta)

Kähler, H. 1956. *Grammatik der Bahasa Indonesia* (Otto Harrassowitz, Wiesbaden)

Lombard, Denys. 1977. *Introduction à l'indonésien* (S.E.C.M.I., Paris)

Macdonald, R.R. and S. Dardjowidjojo. 1967. *A Student's Reference Grammar of Modern Formal Indonesian* (Georgetown University Press, Washington, DC)

Tanner, N. 1967. 'Speech and Society Among the Indonesian Elite: A Case Study of a Multilingual Community', *Anthropological Linguistics*, vol. 9, no. 3, pp. 15–40.

Teeuw, A. 1959. 'The History of the Malay Language', *Bijdragen tot de Taal-, Land-en Volkenkunde*, vol. 115, no. 2, pp. 138–56.

—— 1961. *A Critical Survey of Studies on Malay and Bahasa Indonesia* (Martinus Nijhoff, The Hague)

Uhlenbeck, E.M. 1971. 'Indonesia and Malaysia', in T.A. Sebeok (ed.) *Current Trends in Linguistics*, vol. 8, *Linguistics in Oceania* (Mouton, The Hague and Paris), pp. 55–111.

47 Tagalog

Paul Schachter

1 Historical Background

Tagalog is a member of the Hesperonesian (West Indonesian) branch of the Austronesian language family. Native to the southern part of the island of Luzon in the Philippines, it has in recent years spread as a second language over virtually the entire Philippine archipelago. Thus, while only about a quarter of the population of the Philippines were Tagalog-speaking in 1940, by 1970 over half were (approximately 20 million out of 35 million), and it has been estimated that by the year 2000 over 98 per cent of all Filipinos will speak Tagalog as either a first or a second language.

The remarkable recent diffusion of Tagalog reflects its selection in 1937 as the Philippine national language. Under the name of Pilipino (or Filipino), Tagalog — with a lexicon enriched by borrowings from other Philippine languages — is now taught in schools throughout the Philippines. The spread of the language has also been favoured by urbanisation — Tagalog is native to the largest city of the Philippines, Manila, and it is used as a lingua franca in many cities with mixed populations — as well as by its prominence in the mass media.

The dialect of Tagalog which is considered standard and which underlies Pilipino is the educated dialect of Manila. Other important regional dialects are those of Bataan, Batangas, Bulacan, Tanay-Paete and Tayabas. The lexicon of educated Manila Tagalog contains many borrowings from Spanish and English, the former reflecting over three centuries of colonial domination of the Philippines by Spain, the latter reflecting the period of American hegemony (1898–1946), as well as the current status of English as both the language of higher education in the Philippines and a lingua franca second in importance only to Pilipino itself. Spanish and English have also had some impact on the phonology of Tagalog (see section 2, below), but little if any on the syntax and morphology. (See section 4, however, for some instances of borrowed Spanish gender distinctions.)

2 Phonology and Orthography

Tagalog phonology has been significantly affected by the incorporation into the language of many loanwords from Spanish, English and other languages. One effect of this incorporation has been an expansion of the phonemic inventory of the language, an expansion that has influenced both the vowel and the consonant systems.

Contemporary Tagalog has the five vowel phonemes shown in table 47.1.

Table 47.1: Tagalog Vowel Phonemes

	Front	*Central*	*Back*
High	i		u
Mid	e		o
Low		a	

This five-vowel system no doubt developed out of a three-vowel system in which [i] and [e] were allophones of a single phoneme and [u] and [o] were allophones of another. Contrasts between /i/ and /e/ and between /u/ and /o/ are, however, well established in contemporary Tagalog, not only in borrowed vocabulary (*misa* /mi:sah/ 'mass' vs. *mesa* /me:sah/ 'table', *bus* /bu:s/ 'bus' vs. *bos* /bo:s/ 'boss') but, albeit less commonly, in native vocabulary as well (*iwan* /ʔi:wan/ 'leave' vs. *aywan* /ʔe:wan/ 'not known', *babuy* /ba:buy/ 'pig-like person' vs. *baboy* /ba:boy/ 'pig'). Vowel length in non-word-final syllables is phonemic, as the following examples illustrate: *aso* /ʔa:soh/ 'dog', *aso* /ʔasoh/ 'smoke', *maglalakbay* /magla:lakbay/ 'will travel', *maglalakbay* /maglalakbay/ 'travel a lot'. In word-final syllables of native words, vowel length is not phonemic: the general rule is that *phrase*-final syllables are long, non-phrase-final syllables short. Thus *sibat* /sibat/ 'spear' is pronounced [siba:t] phrase-finally, but not in *sibat ba?* /sibat bah/ [sibat ba:h] 'is it a spear?'. Word-final syllables of *non*-native words may, however, show phonemic length. For example, borrowed monosyllabic names have a long vowel in any context: e.g. *si Bob ba?* /si ba:b ba/ [si ba:b ba:h] 'is it Bob?'.

There are sixteen consonant phonemes that occur in native words. These are displayed in table 47.2. Probably [d] and [r] were once allophones of a single phoneme, as is evidenced by a good deal of free or morphophonemically-conditioned alternation between them (e.g. *daw* /daw/ ~ *raw* /raw/ 'they say', *dalita* /da:litaʔ/ 'poverty' vs. *maralita* /mara:litaʔ/ 'poor'). There is no doubt, however, that they now contrast, not only in loanwords (*dos* /do:s/ 'two' vs. *Rose* /ro:s/ 'Rose') but in native words as well (*maramdamin* /maramda:min/ 'sensitive' vs. *madamdamin* /madamda:min/ 'moving').

In addition to the consonant phonemes shown in table 47.2, there are two others, the labio-dental fricative /f/ and the alveolar affricate /tʃ/, that occur

Table 47.2: Tagalog Consonant Phonemes

	Labial	Dental	Alveolar	Palatal	Velar	Glottal
Voiceless stop	p	t			k	ʔ
Voiced stop	b	d			g	
Nasal	m	n			ŋ	
Fricative			s			h
Lateral			l			
Tap or trill			r			
Glide				y	w	

in loanwords only: e.g. *Flora* /flo:rah/ 'Flora', *chief* /tʃi:f/ 'chief', *kotse* /ko:tʃeh/ 'car'.

In native words tautosyllabic consonant clusters are restricted to syllable-initial clusters in which the second consonant is a glide: e.g. *diyan* /dyan/ 'there', *buwan* /bwan/ 'month'. In loanwords syllable-initial clusters whose second consonant is /l/ or /r/ are also common: e.g. *plato* /pla:toh/ 'plate', *grado* /gra:doh/ 'grade'; and various syllable-final clusters are found in borrowings from English: e.g. *homework* /ho:mwo:rk/, *dimples* /di:mpols/, *bridge* /bri:ds/.

The most common syllable patterns are CVC, in both final and non-final syllables, and CV(:), in non-final syllables only. When two CVC syllables abut within a word, a very wide range of medial CC clusters is attested. Word-internal geminate clusters do not, however, occur.

Stress is closely tied to vowel length. Syllables with phonemically long vowels are always stressed. Syllables with vowels that are not phonemically long but that are phonetically long as a result of their occurrence in phrase-final position are also stressed if there are no phonemically long vowels in the phrase-final word. Thus the final syllable of *magaling* /magaliŋ/ [magali:ŋ] 'excellent' is stressed in citation, but in *magaling na* /magaliŋ nah/ [magaliŋ na:h] 'it's excellent now', the stress falls on *na* instead. Unstressed vowels are not reduced and the language is syllable-timed rather than stress-timed.

Significant morphophonemic alternations across word boundaries include the deletion of word-final /h/ in non-phrase-final position (*maganda* /magandah/ 'beautiful', *maganda pa* /maganda pah/ 'it's still beautiful', *maganda pa ba?* /maganda pa bah/ 'is it still beautiful?') and the replacement of word-final /ʔ/ by vowel length under the same circumstances (*maputi* /maputiʔ/ 'white', *maputi nga* /maputi: ŋaʔ/ 'it's really white', *maputi nga po* /maputi: ŋa: poʔ/ 'it's really white, sir/madam'. Significant morphophonemic alternations *within* the word include a 'rightward' shift of vowel length — and hence of stress — before the verbal suffixes *-an* and *-in* (*tasa* /ta:sah/ 'assessment' + *-an* → *tasahan* /tasa:han/ 'assess', *pala* /pa:lah/ 'shovel' + *-in* → *palahin* /pala:hin/ '(to) shovel') and a set of assimilations involving prefixes that end in nasals, such as the verbal prefix /maN/ (where /N/ represents an unspecified nasal consonant): e.g. /maN/ + /p/ → /mam/,

/maN/ + /t/ → /man/, /maN/ + /k/ → /maŋ/, as in *mamili* (/maN/ + /pi:li?/ →
/mami:li?/) 'choose', *manakot* (/maN/ + /ta:kot/ → /mana:kot/) 'frighten',
mangailangan (/maN/ + ka?ilaŋan/ → /maŋa?ilaŋan/) 'need'.

Tagalog is not a tone language. It does, however, have a complex
intonational system. As in English, intonation may be used to distinguish
pragmatically different sentence types (e.g. requests for information vs.
requests for repetition), to express speaker attitudes (e.g. cordiality), to
indicate contrast or emphasis etc.

Prior to the Spanish colonisation of the Philippines, a syllabary, probably
of Indian origin, had been used for writing Tagalog, but under the Spanish
this was supplanted by a version of the Roman alphabet. Nowadays Tagalog
uses the same 26 letters that are used for writing English, although the seven
letters *c*, *f*, *j*, *q*, *v*, *x* and *z* are used chiefly in proper names of foreign origin
and in certain other borrowings from English or Spanish. These seven letters
are not included in the conventional Tagalog alphabet, or *abakada*, which
consists of 20 letters (including the digraph *ng*, used for /ŋ/), in the following
order: *a b k d e g h i l m n ng o p r s t u w y*. The writing system does not
indicate vowel length (or stress), marks /h/ only syllable-initially and does
not mark /?/ at all. Thus words that differ from one another only in vowel
length (see examples above) or only in that one ends in /h/ and the other in /?/
(e.g. *bata* /ba:tah/ 'bathrobe' and *bata* /ba:ta?/ 'child') are spelled identically.
There is also some inconsistency — as well as some debate — with regard to
the spelling of loanwords: e.g. *molecule* vs. *molikyul*. And there are two
very common words, the case particle /naŋ/ and the plural particle /maŋah/,
whose conventional spellings, respectively *ng* and *mga*, are non-phonemic.
With these and a few other exceptions, however, there is a fairly good match
between spelling and pronunciation.

3   Syntax

Tagalog is a predicate-initial language. That is, in the most common and
basic type of clause, words or phrases that express predicates precede words
or phrases that express arguments. Predicates belong to one of two classes:
verbal and non-verbal. The structures of basic clauses containing these two
types of predicates are discussed in turn below.

Clauses with verbal predicates consist of a verb followed by one or more
argument expressions (noun phrases, pronouns etc.). These argument
expressions do not in general occur in a fixed order and word order is not
used in distinguishing the roles that are assigned to the various arguments,
e.g. in distinguishing an actor argument (see below) from a patient
argument. Instead these roles are indicated by the form of the verb and/or
the form of the argument expressions themselves.

The verb always contains an affix — which may be a prefix, an infix or a
suffix — that indicates the semantic role of one particular argument

expression. This expression has been variously referred to in descriptions of Tagalog as the subject, the topic or the focus, but all of these terms are misleading in one way or another and it seems better to refer to this argument expression as the *trigger*, a term that reflects the fact that the semantic role of the argument in question triggers the choice of the verbal affix. If, for example, the trigger designates the actor (the participant whose role is presented as central: the agent of an action predicate, the experiencer of an experiential predicate etc.), one affix is used; if the trigger designates the patient, another affix is used. The trigger itself has the same form, whatever the semantic role of its referent: for example, it is preceded by the particle *ang* if it is expressed by a common noun and by the particle *si* if it is expressed by a personal name. The semantic roles of any *other* argument expressions in the clause, however, are indicated by the forms of these expressions themselves: for example, a non-trigger argument that expresses the actor is preceded by the particle *ng* if it is expressed by a common noun, by the particle *ni* if it is expressed by a personal name.

On the basis of what has been said thus far, it might appear that variations in the choice of the trigger could reasonably be described in terms of the familiar grammatical category of *voice*, with actor-trigger clauses being identified as active, patient-trigger clauses as passive and the trigger being identified as the (active or passive) subject. There are, however, important differences between the Tagalog trigger system and familiar voice systems. In the first place, the arguments that can be chosen as trigger show a much wider range of semantic roles than the arguments that can be chosen as subject in typical voice systems and consequently there are many more distinct verb forms than a voice system's typical two. In addition to actor and patient, the trigger argument in a Tagalog clause may have the semantic role of direction (goal or source), beneficiary, instrument, location or reason, among others and each of these choices determines a different choice of verbal affix. Secondly, in voice systems the active can generally be regarded as the unmarked voice by virtue of its frequency, unrestricted distribution and the like. But Tagalog actor-trigger clauses are not unmarked in relation to their non-actor-trigger counterparts. Indeed, the latter turn out to be generally more frequent in texts and to have fewer distributional restrictions. For these reasons, it seems best not to describe the Tagalog trigger system as a voice system.

The following examples illustrate part of the trigger system. In each case the verbal affix that indicates the semantic role of the trigger and the trigger itself are italicised. (All of the verbs in these examples contain a reduplicating aspectual affix — the first *a* of *aalis* — and the actor-, beneficiary- and instrument-trigger verbs also contain certain other affixes whose functions will be explained in section 4.)

As the English translations show, the trigger is normally interpreted as definite, a non-trigger patient as indefinite and other non-trigger arguments

Mag-aalis		*ang*	*tindero*		ng	bigas	sa	sako	para sa	babae.
AT-cont.-take:out		tg.	storekeeper		pat.	rice	drc.	sack	ben.	woman

'The storekeeper will take some rice out of a/the sack for a/the woman.'

Aalis*in*		ng	tindero		*ang*	*bigas*	sa	sako	para sa	babae.
cont.-take:out-PT		acr.	storekeeper		tg.	rice	drc.	sack	ben.	woman

'A/the storekeeper will take the rice out of a/the sack for a/the woman.'

Aalis*an*		ng	tindero		ng	bigas	*ang*	*sako*	para sa	babae.
cont.-take:out-DT		acr.	storekeeper		pat.	rice	tg.	sack	ben.	woman

'A/the storekeeper will take some rice out of the sack for a/the woman.'

*I*pag-aalis		ng	tindero		ng	bigas	sa	sako	*ang*	*babae*.
BT-cont.-take:out		acr.	storekeeper		pat.	rice	drc.	sack	tg.	woman

'A/the storekeeper will take some rice out of a/the sack for the woman.'

*I*pangaalis		ng	tindero		ng	bigas	sa	sako	*ang*	*sandok*.
IT-cont.-take:out		acr.	storekeeper		pat.	rice	drc.	sack	tg.	scoop

'A/the storekeeper will take some rice out of a/the sack with the scoop.'

as either definite or indefinite. Note also that some of the particles have more than one function. Thus *ng* occurs in these examples as both a patient marker and an actor marker, while *sa* occurs as both a direction marker and as part of the beneficiary marker *para sa*.

As noted previously, the order of post-verbal arguments is generally free. Thus in addition to the orderings shown above, any other ordering of the arguments in the examples would also be grammatical (although some would be unusual). There is, however, a general preference for the actor as the first argument in a non-actor-trigger clause and for either the (actor) trigger or the patient as the first argument in an actor-trigger clause.

There is also one set of argument expressions whose order in relation to other argument expressions and to one another is not free. These are the actor and trigger personal pronouns, which are *enclitics*: i.e. they occur in a fixed position immediately after the clause-initial constituent. If there are two enclitic pronouns in the same clause, they observe the rule that monosyllabic pronouns precede disyllabic pronouns. Thus in the following sentence the order of all the words is fixed:

Nakita	mo	siya	kahapon.
PT-perf.-see	you-acr.	he-tg.	yesterday

'You saw him yesterday.'

This contrasts with the variable ordering observable in the following sentences, which show that argument expressions are freely ordered in relation not only to one another but also to adverbs such as *kahapon* 'yesterday':

$$\left\{\begin{array}{l}\text{Nakita} \quad \text{ni Juan si Maria kahapon.}\\ \text{PT-perf.-see acr. Juan tg. Maria yesterday}\\ \text{Nakita ni Juan kahapon si Maria.}\\ \text{Nakita si Maria ni Juan kahapon.}\\ \text{Nakita si Maria kahapon ni Juan.}\\ \text{Nakita kahapon ni Juan si Maria.}\\ \text{Nakita kahapon si Maria ni Juan.}\end{array}\right\}$$

'Juan saw Maria yesterday.'

In addition to enclitic pronouns, Tagalog also has a set of enclitic *particles* that occur in a fixed position in relation to other sentence elements. Note, for example, the position of the interrogative particle *ba* in the following sentence:

Nakita   mo   ba siya   kahapon?
PT-perf.-see   you: acr. Q he:tg. yesterday
'Did you see him yesterday?'

Clauses with non-verbal predicates are in many cases translated into English by sentences with the main verb *be*, which has no Tagalog counterpart. These clauses consist of a predicate expression followed by a trigger expression. The predicate expression may be a noun (phrase), an adjective (phrase) or a prepositional phrase. Some examples are:

Abogado ang   bunso.
lawyer   tg.   youngest:child
'The youngest child is a lawyer.'

Hinog   ang   mga mangga.
ripe   tg.   pl.   mango
'The mangoes are ripe.'

Nasa kusina   si   Nene.
in   kitchen   tg. Nene
'Nene is in the kitchen.'

A construction consisting of a non-verbal predicate and a trigger is also used to express possession, as in:

May trak   si   Ben.
ex.   truck   tg. Ben
'Ben has a truck.'

The same type of non-verbal predicate is also used to express existence. In this case, however, the predicate is not followed by a trigger, but is instead often followed by an adverbial: e.g.

May trak   doon.
ex.   truck   there
'There's a truck over there.'

Although Tagalog is basically predicate-initial, there are certain fairly
common constructions in which some other constituent precedes the
predicate. In one such construction, the clause-initial constituent — which
may be the trigger, an adverbial or one of certain types of non-trigger
arguments — is immediately followed by the particle *ay*. Some examples
are:

Ang sulat   ay tinanggap   ko   kahapon.
tg.   letter inv. PT-perf.-receive I:acr. yesterday
'I received the letter yesterday.'

Doon ay   ipinagbili   niya   ang kalabaw.
there inv. PT-perf.-sell   he:acr. tg. carabao
'There he sold the carabao.'

Saanman   ay   makakaabot   ang   koreyo.
to-any:place   inv. AT-cont.-can-reach   tg.   mail
'The mail can reach any place.'

Ay constructions are more common in writing and in formal speech than
they are in ordinary conversation. It has been suggested that in narratives
the referent of the constituent preceding *ay* is often one that has been
referred to at some earlier point and that *ay* is typically used to reintroduce
such a referent.

In other types of non-predicate-initial constructions, the pre-predicate
constituent may have a special discourse function, such as contrast or
emphasis. Some examples are:

Bukas,   magpapahinga ako. Ngayon, dapat akong   magtrabaho.
tomorrow   AT-cont.-rest I:tg. today   must   I:tg.-lig. AT-work
'Tomorrow, I'll rest. Today, I've got to work.'

Bukas   aalis   si   Pedro
tomorrow   AT-cont.-leave tg. Pedro
'It's tomorrow that Pedro is leaving.'

Just as the ordering of clause constituents shows considerable variability, so
does the ordering of constituents of noun phrases. Although certain
modifiers, such as numbers and other quantifiers, regularly precede the head
noun and others, such as possessive noun phrases, regularly follow it, there
are also several types of modifiers that may either precede or follow the head
noun: e.g. demonstratives, adjectives and possessive pronouns.

A demonstrative or an adjective, whether it precedes or follows the noun, is linked to it by a *ligature*. The ligature has two morphophonemically conditioned alternants: if the citation form of the preceding word ends in /h/, /ʔ/ or /n/, the ligature takes the form of an /ŋ/ (*ng*) replacing the final consonant; in all other cases, the ligature takes the form /na/ (*na*). (Ligatures also occur in certain other constructions, such as constructions involving auxiliary verbs like *dapat* 'must'.) For example, when the demonstrative *ito* /itoh/ 'this' precedes the ligature, the /ŋ/ form occurs and when the noun *galang* /galaŋ/ 'bracelet' precedes, the /na/ form occurs: thus *itong galang* /itoŋ galaŋ/, *galang na ito* /galaŋ na itoh/ 'this bracelet'. Similarly, the noun *bata* /ba:taʔ/ 'child' and the adjective *gutom* /gutom/ 'hungry' respectively require the /ŋ/ and /na/ forms of the ligature in *batang gutom* /ba:taŋ gutom/ 'hungry child' and *gutom na bata* /gutom na ba:taʔ/.

Although a demonstrative and the noun it modifies may occur in either order, the alternative orderings are generally not in free variation, but are, rather, conditioned by discourse factors. The constituent that comes second typically represents the more salient information and may, for example, be contrastive. Thus:

Mahal   itong   galang.   (Pero mura itong   singsing.)
expensive this-lig. bracelet but   cheap this-lig. ring
'This bracelet is expensive. (But this ring is cheap.)'

Mahal   ang galang   na ito. (Pero mura ang galang   na iyan.)
expensive tg. bracelet lig. this but   cheap tg. bracelet lig. that
'This bracelet is expensive. (But that bracelet is cheap.)'

(As the first example illustrates, when a trigger expression begins with a demonstrative, no trigger particle is used.) The alternative orderings of *adjectives* and the nouns they modify, on the other hand, often do appear to be a matter of free variation.

Possessive pronouns, as noted, may also either precede or follow the noun, but in this case a difference in form is associated with the difference in order. When the possessive pronoun precedes, it takes a form that may be called the *sa* form and it is obligatorily linked to the following noun by a ligature. (The *sa* form is so called because it also occurs after the particle *sa*.) When the possessive pronoun follows, it takes a form that may be called the *ng* form, and there is no ligature. (The *ng* form occurs in essentially the same contexts as common-noun phrases introduced by the particle *ng*.) For example, 'my house' may be expressed as either *aking bahay* (the *sa* form first person singular pronoun *akin* + ligature + *bahay* 'house') or *bahay ko* (*bahay* + the *ng* form first person singular pronoun *ko*). The orderings are both very common and there is no obvious difference in usage between them.

Yes-no questions in Tagalog are characterised by rising intonation, as opposed to the characteristic falling intonation of statements. A yes-no question may be distinguished from the corresponding statement by intonation alone or it may, in addition, be marked by the enclitic interrogative particle *ba*. This particle also occurs optionally in question-word questions. The latter, however, have their own distinctive intonation patterns, which differ from those of both yes-no questions and statements. (The most common intonation patterns for both question-word questions and statements are falling patterns, but the patterns differ in detail: the question-word questions start with high pitch and fall steadily throughout; the statements start with mid pitch, rise to high pitch on the last stressed syllable and then fall.)

The questioned constituent normally comes first in a question-word question. If this constituent is an adverbial or a non-trigger argument, any enclitic pronouns and/or particles contained in the clause attach to it and hence precede the predicate, e.g.

> Kailan mo   (ba) siya   nakita?
> when you-acr. Q   he:tg. PT-perf.-see
> 'When did you see him?'

> Sa   aling   parti ka   (ba) pumunta?
> drc. which-lig. party you:tg. Q   AT-perf.-go
> 'Which party did you go to?'

(Role-marking particles and prepositions in general are never 'stranded' in Tagalog. Thus in the last example, *sa* must precede the question word and cannot be left in post-predicate position as *to* is in the English translation.)

If the questioned constituent is a trigger argument, the rest of the clause must be put into the form of a headless relative clause (see below) and preceded by the trigger particle *ang*. Under these circumstances, the enclitic particle *ba* still follows the questioned constituent, but any enclitic actor pronoun follows the predicate. Some examples are:

> Ano (ba) ang ginawa   mo   kahapon?
> what Q   tg. PT-perf.-do you-acr. yesterday
> 'What did you do yesterday?'

> Sino (ba) ang gumawa   ng   sapatos na iyon?
> who Q   tg. AT-perf.-make pat. shoe(s) lig. that
> 'Who made those shoes?'

Imperative sentences of the most common type have a falling intonation pattern like that of question-word questions. Syntactically they are just like statements with verbal predicates and second-person actors (which may but need not be triggers), except that the verb is in the infinitive form, rather than one of the finite forms that are found in statements. Some examples are:

```
Mag-alis      ka    ng    bigas  sa   sako.
AT-take:out   you:tg. pat. rice   drc. sack
'Take some rice out of a/the sack.'
```

```
Basahin   mo    nga     ang    librong   ito.
read-PT   you:acr. please tg.    book-lig. this
'Please read this book.'
```

(*Nga* 'please' in the last example is an enclitic particle.)

Hortative sentences are identical to imperatives, except that the actor is a first person plural inclusive pronoun (see section 4). For example:

```
Mag-alis      tayo         ng    bigas sa   sako.
AT-take:out   we:incl:tg.  pat.  rice  drc. sack
'Let's take some rice out of a/the sack.'
```

```
Basahin   nga    natin         ang    librong   ito.
read-PT   please we:incl.:acr. tg.    book-lig. this
'Please let's read this book.'
```

Tagalog has distinct ways of negating imperative/hortative clauses, existential/possessive clauses and clauses of other types. Imperatives and hortatives are negated with a clause-initial *huwag*, which is immediately followed by any enclitic pronouns and particles, then by a ligature and then by the verb. Examples are:

```
Huwag   kang        mag-alis       ng   bigas sa   sako.
neg.    you:tg.:lig. AT-take:out    pat. rice  drc. sack
'Don't take any rice out of a/the sack.'
```

```
Huwag   nga    nating        basahin ang  librong   ito.
neg.    please we:incl.:lig. read-PT tg.  book-lig. this
'Please, let's not read this book.'
```

Existential and possessive clauses are negated with a clause-initial *wala*. *Wala* replaces the affirmative existential/possessive particle *may(roon)*, and is followed by a ligature. Any enclitics in the clause come between *wala* and the ligature. Examples are:

```
Wala   akong    pera.
neg.   I:tg.-lig. money
'I don't have any money.'
```

```
Walang    bahay   doon.
neg.-lig. house   there
'There isn't a house there.'
```

Clauses of other types are negated with a clause-initial *hindi*. Again, any enclitics immediately follow the negative particle. *Hindi* is not, however, followed by a ligature.

Hindi   ko   nakita   si   Rosa.
neg.   I:acr.   PT-perf.-see   tg.   Rosa
'I didn't see Rosa.'

Hindi   mayaman   si   Rosa.
neg.   rich   tg.   Rosa
'Rosa isn't rich.'

As suggested previously, it does not seem to be appropriate to identify the Tagalog grammatical category trigger with the traditional grammatical category subject. One reason is that there are certain subject-like properties that are associated not with the trigger but, rather, with the actor. For example, as we have already seen, the actor, whether or not it also happens to be the trigger, always represents the addressee of an imperative sentence. It is also the actor that controls the reference of a reflexive (expressed by a possessive pronoun and the nominal *sarili* 'self'), as illustrated by the following sentences:

Mag-aalaala   ang   lolo   sa   kaniyang   sarili.
AT-cont.-worry:about tg.   grandfather   drc.   he-L   self
'Grandfather will worry about himself.'

Aalalahanin   ng lolo   ang   kaniyang   sarili.
cont.-worry:about-DT acr. grandfather tg.   he-L   self
'Grandfather will worry about himself.'

Since the first of these sentences has an actor-trigger verb, the actor, which is the reflexive controller, happens to be the trigger as well. The second sentence, however, has a direction-trigger verb and here we can see clearly that the reflexive controller is the actor and *not* the trigger, since in this case it is the trigger itself that is reflexivised.

On the other hand, there *are* certain subject-like properties that are associated with the trigger. One such property is relativisability. Only trigger arguments (and certain constituents of trigger arguments) may be relativised in Tagalog. Thus if one wishes to relativise an actor, an actor-trigger clause must be used; if one wishes to relativise a patient, a patient-trigger clause must be used; etc. The following examples illustrate this. (As the examples show, relativisation in Tagalog involves the deletion of the relativised argument — the trigger — from the relative clause. The head of the relative clause and the clause itself may occur in either order, but head-first is the more common ordering. A ligature occurs between the head and the relative clause.)

> Iyon ang babaeng magluluto ng isda.
> that tg. woman-lig. AT-cont.-cook pat. fish
> 'That's the woman who will cook some fish.'

> Iyon ang isdang iluluto ng babae.
> that tg. fish-lig. PT-cont.-cook acr. woman
> 'That's the fish that a/the woman will cook.'

In the first sentence the actor is relativised, so the verb in the relative clause must be actor-trigger; in the second sentence the patient is relativised, so the verb in the relative clause must be patient-trigger. Similarly, if a directional argument is relativised, the verb in the relative clause must be direction-trigger, and if a beneficiary is relativised, the verb in the relative clause must be beneficiary-trigger, as in:

> Iyon ang sakong aalisan ko ng bigas.
> that tg. sack-lig. cont.-take:out-DT I:acr. pat. rice
> 'That's the sack that I'll take some rice out of.'

> Iyon ang batang ipagluluto ko ng pagkain.
> that tg. child-lig. BT-cont.-cook I:acr. pat. food
> 'That's the child I'll cook some food for.'

(If one attempts to relativise a *non*-trigger argument, the result is ungrammatical: e.g.:

> *Iyon ang babaeng iluluto ang isda.
> that tg. woman-lig. PT-cont.-cook tg. fish)

Although verbs, adjectives and nouns are clearly distinguished from one another on a *morphological* basis in Tagalog (see section 4), distributionally or syntactically they are all rather similar. We have already seen that all three can serve as predicates. In addition, all three can serve as (heads of) arguments or as modifiers. A verbal or adjectival argument may be analysed as a headless relative clause. For example, compare the following with the last grammatical example cited:

> Iyon ang ipagluluto ko ng pagkain.
> that tg. BT-cont.-cook I:acr. pat. food
> 'That's the one I'll cook some food for.'

Here the phrase headed by the verb *ipagluluto*, which has the form of a relative clause, is functioning as the trigger argument of the sentence. Some relevant examples involving adjectives are:

> Sino ang batang pinakamatalino sa klase?
> who tg. child-lig. most-smart in class
> 'Who is the smartest child in the class?'

Sino   ang   pinakamatalino   sa   klase?
who   tg.   most-smart   in   class
'Who is the smartest one in the class?'

We have already seen both adjectives and verbs (in relative clauses) serving as modifiers, in highly similar constructions involving a ligature between the head and the modifier. Nouns too occur as modifiers in this type of construction: e.g. *gulay na repolyo* 'vegetable dish made from cabbage' (cf. *gulay* 'vegetable (dish)', *repolyo* 'cabbage'), *laruang kalan* 'toy stove' (cf. *laruan* 'toy', *kalan* 'stove'). Thus the syntactic similarities among nouns, verbs and adjectives in Tagalog are quite striking, although, as we shall see, there are clear morphological grounds for distinguishing them.

4   Morphology

Tagalog verb morphology is quite complex. The verb stem may be polymorphemic and there are obligatory trigger-marking and aspectual affixes — which may be prefixes, suffixes or infixes — as well as affixes with a wide range of other functions. The following selective summary of Tagalog verb morphology treats, in order: stem formation, trigger affixation, other non-aspectual affixation and aspectual affixation.

Many Tagalog verb stems consist of a single morpheme: e.g. *abot* (cf. *umabot* 'reach for', which consists of the actor-trigger affix *-um-* plus *abot*), *iyak* (cf. *umiyak* 'cry'), *uwi* (cf. *umuwi* 'go home'). However, there are also a great many verb stems that are analysable as consisting of two or more morphemes. Of these, the most common are those involving the stem-forming prefixes *pag-* and *paN-*.

Pag- combines very productively with nouns to form verb stems that denote characteristic activities involving the referents of the nouns. For example, *pagbus* is the stem of the actor-trigger verb *magbus* 'ride a bus', *pag-Ingles* (cf. *Ingles* 'English') is the stem of *mag-Ingles* 'speak English', *pagtsinelas* (cf. *tsinelas* 'slippers') is the stem of *magtsinelas* 'wear slippers', and *pag-ingat* (cf. *ingat* 'care') is the stem of AT *mag-ingat*/DT *pag-ingatan* 'be careful of '. (In actor-trigger verbs, the initial /p/ of *pag-* and *paN-* is assimilated to the actor-trigger prefix *m-*. For some purposes — see below — it is convenient to refer to the resultant forms, *mag-* and *maN-*, as if they were single affixes rather than composites.)

In addition, *pag-* combines with certain simple verb stems to form the stems of 'intensive' verbs: i.e. verbs that designate intense, frequent or prolonged performance of the activity designated by the simple stem. For example, *pag-* combines with *kain* 'eat' to form the stem of *magkain* 'eat (repeatedly etc.)' and with *lakad* 'walk' to form the stem of *maglakad* 'walk (repeatedly etc.)'. *Pag-* also forms verb stems with adjectives, which may themselves be morphologically complex — e.g. *pagmabait* (cf. *mabait* 'kind', *bait* 'kindness'), which is the stem of AT *magmabait*/*DT pagmabaitan* 'pretend to be kind to' — and even with certain phrases — e.g. *pagmagandang-gabi* (cf. *magandang gabi* 'good evening (the greeting)'), which is the stem of *magmagandang-gabi* 'wish good evening'.

Like *pag-*, but less productively, *paN-* combines with nouns to form stems that denote characteristic activities involving the referents of the nouns. For example, *pamangka* (cf. *bangka* 'boat' — see section 2 for the assimilation of certain morpheme-initial consonants to prefixal /N/) is the stem of the actor-trigger verb *mamangka* 'go boating', and *panganak* (cf. *anak* 'child, offspring') is the stem of AT *manganak*/PT *ipanganak* 'give birth to'. *PaN-* also combines with certain nouns and simple verb stems to form stems that denote destructive or harmful activity and with certain other simple verb stems to form stems that denote activity directed toward multiple objects. For example, *paN-* combines with *walis* 'broom' to form the stem of *mangwalis* 'hit with a broom' and with *kain* 'eat' to form the stem of *mangain* 'devour'; it also combines with *kuha* 'get' to form the stem of *manguha* 'gather' and with *tahi* 'sew' to form the stem of *manahi* 'sew (a number of things, or professionally)'.

There is also a *paN-* stem-forming prefix — distinguishable from the one just discussed on the basis of a different pattern of morphophonemic alternations — that forms the stem of instrument-trigger verbs. This type of stem may occur independently as a noun with instrumental meaning. Examples are *pam(p)unas* 'something to wipe with' (cf. *punas* 'sponge bath'), which is the stem of the instrument-trigger verb *ipam(p)unas* 'wipe with', and *pan(s)ulat* 'something to write with' (cf. *sulat* 'letter'), which is the stem of the instrument-trigger verb *ipan(s)ulat* 'write with'.

Among the other stem-forming affixes that deserve mention are two different reduplicating prefixes, one monosyllabic, the other disyllabic. The monosyllabic reduplicating prefix is in general a copy of the first consonant and vowel of the following simple verb stem (but see the discussion of aspectual reduplication below). In one of its uses it combines with *pag-* to form certain additional intensive verbs: e.g., *pagtatapak* the stem of DT *pagtatapakan* 'step on (repeatedly etc.)' (cf. DT *tapakan* 'step on') and *pagbabagsak*, the stem of PT *ipagbabagsak* 'drop (repeatedly etc.)' (cf. PT *ibagsak* 'drop').

The disyllabic reduplicating prefix generally consists of a copy of the first two (usually the only two) syllables of the following simple stem. One use of the disyllabic reduplicating prefix is to form the stem of 'moderative' verbs, i.e. verbs that designate activities performed in moderation, occasionally, at random etc. Some examples are *hiya-hiya*, the stem of AT *mahiya-hiya* 'be a little ashamed' (cf. AT *mahiya* 'be ashamed') and *linis-linis*, the stem of PT *linis-linisin* 'clean a little' (cf. PT *linisin* 'clean').

As indicated above, trigger affixes mark the semantic role of the trigger phrase. Among the roles that may be affixally marked are: actor, patient, direction, beneficiary and instrument. (Others, which will not be discussed here, include location, reason and referent ('about' object).) The affixes that most commonly mark these roles are shown in table 47.3.

Table 47.3: Trigger-marking Affixes

AT:	-um-, m-, ma-, maka-
PT:	-in, i-, -an, ma-
DT:	-an, -in
BT, IT:	i-

The forms of the affixes given in the table are those that occur in infinitives. Some trigger affixes assume different forms in certain finite (i.e. aspect-marked) verbs. These forms will be presented later, in connection with the discussion of aspectual affixation.

As table 47.3 shows, there are several different actor-, patient- and direction-trigger affixes. The choice among these affixes is lexically determined and to some extent idiosyncratic, although there are certain generalisations that can be made.

The actor-trigger affixes, all of which involve the phoneme /m/, are the infix -um- and the prefixes m-, ma- and maka-. -um- is infixed between the first consonant and first vowel of the stem: e.g. *humingi* 'borrow' (stem: *hingi*), *sumulat* 'write' (stem: *sulat*), *tumakbo* 'run' (stem: *takbo*). (In the written form of verbs whose stem-initial consonant is /ʔ/, -um- appears as a prefix, since /ʔ/ is not represented in the standard orthography: e.g. *umabot* /ʔumabot/ 'reach for' (stem: *abot* /ʔabot/).) -um- is the most common affix in actor-trigger verbs with single-morpheme stems and its occurrence in certain subclasses of actor-trigger verbs is predictable, e.g. in verbs of 'becoming' where the stem also occurs as the stem of a *ma-* adjective — cf. *gumanda* 'become beautiful' – *maganda* 'beautiful', *tumaas* 'become tall' – *mataas* 'tall'.

The prefix *m-* replaces the initial *p-* of the stem-forming prefixes *pag-* and *paN-*, resulting in the forms *mag-* and *maN-* respectively, as in *magbigay* 'give', *magluto* 'cook', *mangisda* 'fish' (cf. *isda* 'fish (noun)'), *mangailangan* 'need' (cf. *kailangan* 'need (noun)'). As indicated above, *mag-* occurs productively in verbs that express a characteristic activity involving the referent of the noun that underlies them (e.g. *mag-Ingles* 'speak English'). There are also certain regular correspondences between -um- and *mag-* verbs formed with the same stem, e.g. cases in which the -um- verb takes two arguments and the *mag-* verb three, such as: *pumasok* 'come/go into' and *magpasok* 'bring/take into', *lumabas* 'come/go outside' and *maglabas* 'bring/take outside'. *MaN-* too has certain characteristic uses — e.g. in verbs indicating destructive activity, such as *mangwalis* 'hit with a broom' (cf. *magwalis* 'sweep') — but it is considerably less common than *mag-*.

AT *ma-* (there is also a PT *ma-*) occurs productively in verbs of 'becoming' whose stems are unaffixed adjectives — e.g. *mabingi* 'become deaf ' (cf. *bingi* 'deaf '), *mamahal* 'become expensive' (cf. *mahal* 'expensive') — and idiosyncratically in a relatively small number of other common verbs: e.g. *matulog* 'sleep', *matuto* 'learn'. *Maka-* occurs idiosyncratically in a few common verbs: e.g., *makakita* 'see', *makarinig* 'hear'. (*Maka-* also occurs productively in ability verbs — see below.)

The most common patient-trigger affixes are *-in* and *i-*. *-in* is the most frequent patient-trigger counterpart of AT *-um-* in corresponding patient- and actor-trigger verbs formed with the same stem (e.g. AT *humuli*/PT *hulihin* 'catch') and *i-* is the most frequent patient-trigger counterpart of AT *m-* (though there are also a good many AT *m-*/PT *-in* correspondences, including some cases where *-in* and *i-* are apparently in free variation, e.g. AT *magluto*/PT *iluto* ~ *lutuin* 'cook'). The stem-forming prefix *pag-* that occurs in AT *m-* verbs is often obligatorily absent — less often optionally absent — from the corresponding patient-trigger verbs. (This is also true of direction-trigger verbs formed with *-in*, and of both patient- and direction-trigger verbs formed with *-an* — see below.) For example, the patient-trigger counterpart of AT *magbigay* 'give' is *ibigay* and the patient-trigger counterpart of AT *magkaila* 'deny' is either *ikaila* or *ipagkaila*. (On the other hand, the patient-trigger counterpart of AT *magbili* 'sell' is *ipagbili*, in which *pag-* is obligatorily retained.) Much less commonly, a stem-forming prefix *paN-* that occurs in an actor-trigger verb is omitted from the patient-trigger counterpart, e.g. the patient-trigger counterpart of AT *mangailangan* 'need' is *kailanganin*.

The suffix *-an*, which is the most common direction-trigger affix, occurs less frequently as a patient-trigger affix, often in verbs that express actions involving surface contact with, or surface effect on, the patient: e.g. *labhan* 'launder', *pintahan* 'paint', *walisan* 'sweep', *hawakan* 'hold'. *Ma-* is the patient-trigger counterpart of AT *maka-* and occurs idiosyncratically in a few verbs: e.g. *makita* 'see', *marinig* 'hear'.

Some examples of DT *-an* are: *puntahan* 'go to', *up(u)an* 'sit on', *masdan* 'look at', *bilhan* 'buy from', *pagbilhan* 'sell to'. The suffix *-in* occurs idiosyncratically as direction-trigger affix in a few verbs — e.g. *pupuin* 'use *po* (sir/madam) in addressing' — and more systematically in certain other cases, among them cases in which DT *-an* is, as it were, preempted. These are cases in which *-an* is used as the direction-trigger affix of a three-argument verb and *-in* as the direction-trigger affix of a two-argument verb formed with the same stem: e.g. *pasukan* 'bring/take into' vs. *pasukin* 'come/go into', *labasan* 'bring/take outside' vs. *labasin* 'come/go outside'.

Beneficiary-trigger verbs are formed with *i-*. Any stem-forming *pag-* or *paN-* in the corresponding actor-trigger verb is retained. Examples are: *ipirma* 'sign for' (cf. AT *pumirma* 'sign'), *ipaglaba* 'launder for' (cf. AT *maglaba* 'launder'), *ipanguha* 'gather for' (cf. *manguha* 'gather').

Instrument-trigger verbs are also formed with *i-*, but in this case the stem must usually be formed with the prefix *paN-*, as in *ipam(p)unas* 'wipe with', *ipan(s)ulat* 'write with'. However, if the simple stem itself designates an instrument, alternative instrument-trigger formations without any stem-forming prefix or with the stem-forming prefix *pag-* also occur. Thus, the stem *suklay* 'comb' occurs in IT *isuklay* and *ipagsuklay* as well as *ipan(s)uklay* 'comb with', and the stem *gunting* 'scissors' occurs in IT *igunting* and *ipaggunting* as well as *ipanggunting* 'cut with'.

Apart from trigger affixes, there are a good many other non-aspectual affixes, among them affixes with ability and causative meanings. The ability affixes are *maka-* and *ma-*. *Maka-* occurs in actor-trigger verbs, in which it replaces *-um-* or *m-*: e.g. AT *makaawit* 'be able to sing' (cf. *umawit* 'sing'), AT *makapagluto* 'be able to cook' (cf. *magluto* 'cook'), AT *makapangisda* 'be able to fish' (cf. *mangisda* 'fish'). *Ma-* occurs with non-actor-trigger verbs. It replaces *-in*, but occurs together with *i-* or *-an*: e.g. PT *magamit* 'be able to use' (cf. *gamitin* 'use'), BT *maibili* 'be able to buy for' (cf. *ibili* 'buy for'), DT *mapuntahan* 'be able to go to' (cf. *puntahan* 'go to').

Causative verbs are all formed with the causative-stem-forming prefix *pa-*, which occurs in addition to a trigger affix. Causative verbs, in a sense, have two actors, one causing the other to act. However, morphologically (as well as syntactically), only the 'causer' is treated as an actor, while the 'causee' is treated as a kind of patient. Thus, when the causer is the trigger, the actor-trigger affix *mag-* (*m-* + *pag-*) is invariably used, but when the causee is the trigger the patient-trigger affix *-in* is invariably used: e.g., A(causer)T *magpapunta*/P(causee)T *papuntahin* 'cause to go' (cf. non-causative AT *pumunta* 'go'), A(causer)T *magpatsinelas*/P(causee)T *papagtsinelasin* 'cause to wear slippers' (cf. AT *magtsinelas* 'wear slippers').

There are also causative verbs in which the trigger is some argument other than the causer or the causee. Under these circumstances, the same trigger affix that occurs in the corresponding non-causative verb is ordinarily used, except that *-in* (which is, as it were, preempted, to mark the causee as trigger) is replaced by *i-* in patient-trigger verbs and by *-an* in direction-trigger verbs. Thus PT *ipalinis* 'cause to clean' (cf. PT *linisin* 'clean') selects as trigger the object cleaned, while P(causee)T *palinisin* selects as trigger the causee, the one caused to do the cleaning. Similarly, DT *papasukan* 'cause to enter' (cf. DT *pasukin* 'enter') selects as trigger the place entered, while P(causee)T *papasukin* selects as trigger the one caused to enter. Some other relevant examples are: PT *papintahan* 'cause to paint' (cf. PT *pintahan* 'paint'), DT *pasulatan* 'cause to write to' (cf. DT *sulatan* 'write to'), BT *ipabili* 'cause to buy for' (cf. BT *ibili* 'buy for').

Turning now to aspectual affixation, let us begin with a brief overview of the Tagalog aspect system. Tagalog, then, makes no true tense distinctions like the English past–non-past distinction, but instead makes a distinction between events viewed as actual and events viewed as hypothetical and, among the actual events, between those viewed as complete and those viewed as incomplete. Events viewed as complete are in the *perfective* aspect, those viewed as incomplete are in the *imperfective* aspect and those viewed as hypothetical are in the *contemplated* aspect. The perfective aspect is often translated into English by the past or the present perfect, the imperfective aspect by the simple present or by the present or past progressive and the contemplated aspect by the future: e.g. perf. *nagwalis* 'swept, has swept', imperf. *nagwawalis* 'sweeps, is/was sweeping', cont. *magwawalis* 'will sweep'. There are, however, other translation equivalents in certain cases. For example, the imperfective rather than the perfective form is used for the equivalent of the English negative perfect: thus 'hasn't swept yet' is expressed by *hindi pa nagwawalis*, not **hindi pa nagwalis*. (*Hindi* is a negator, *pa* an enclitic particle.)

From a morphological point of view, aspect is marked in Tagalog by two patterns of affixation, one of which is common to imperfective and contemplative verbs, the other to imperfective and perfective verbs. The pattern that is common to imperfective and contemplated verbs can be called 'incompleteness' marking (since hypothetical events are necessarily incomplete), while the pattern common to imperfective and perfective verbs can be called 'actuality' marking.

Incompleteness marking involves a monosyllabic reduplicating prefix. This prefix normally consists of a copy of the first consonant and first vowel of the following syllable, except that the vowel of the reduplicating prefix is always long, whatever the length of the vowel in the following syllable. (Vowel length distinguishes this aspectual reduplication from the stem-forming reduplication mentioned above, which always involves a *short* vowel. Compare, for example, the aspectual reduplicating prefix /la:/ in *maglalakbay* /magla:lakbay/ 'will travel' and the stem-forming (intensive) reduplicating prefix /la/ in *maglalakbay* /maglalakbay/ 'travel (repeatedly etc.)'.)

The rules for the placement of the aspectual reduplicating prefix in relation to other prefixes are rather complex. Some other prefixes always precede the reduplicating prefix, but others may either precede or follow it, resulting in the possibility of alternative orderings. For example, in the contemplated and imperfective forms of the verb *maipabili* 'be able to cause to buy', the reduplicating prefix follows the ability prefix *ma-* but may either precede or follow the patient-trigger prefix *i-* and the causative prefix *pa-*; thus cont. *maiipabili*, *maipapabili* and *maipabibili* 'will be able to cause to buy' are all well formed.

Actuality marking, which is common to imperfective and perfective verbs, in most cases involves an affix that contains the phoneme /n/. The sole exceptions to this generalisation are verbs whose infinitives are formed with the actor-trigger infix *-um-*, in which actuality marking consists simply in the retention of this infix. The infix, in other words, is present in imperfective and perfective forms, but absent from contemplated forms. For example, the imperfective and perfective forms of the verb *pumunta* 'go' (stem: *punta*) are, respectively, *pumupunta* and *pumunta*, while the contemplated form is *pupunta*. (As these examples illustrate, the perfective forms of *-um-* verbs are identical with the infinitives.)

There are three actuality-marking affixes that contain /n/: the prefix *n-*, the prefix *ni-* and the infix *-in-*. The prefix *n-* occurs as a replacement of *m-* in all prefixes that begin with the latter in the infinitive. For example, *nagwalis* and *nagwawalis* are the perfective and imperfective forms corresponding to the infinitive *magwalis* 'sweep'. Similarly, *nangisda* is the perfective form of *mangisda* 'fish', and AT *nakakita*/PT *nakita* are the perfective forms of AT *makakita*/PA *makita* 'see'. The prefix *ni-* and the infix *-in-* occur in all other cases as either free or morphophonemically conditioned alternants. For example, the perfective form corresponding to the infinitive *lagyan* 'put on' may be either *nilagyan* or *linagyan*, but the perfective form corresponding to *iabot* 'hand to' must be *iniabot* and that corresponding to *hiraman* 'borrow from' must be *hiniraman*.

If the verb marked by *ni-* or *-in-* contains the prefix *i-*, this always precedes the *ni-* or *-in-*, as in *iniyuko* ~ *iyinuko*, the perfective forms of *iyuko* 'bend', or *ibinigay*, the perfective form of *ibigay* 'give'. Otherwise, *ni-* is always word-initial and *-in-* always follows the first consonant of the word. A special property of verbs whose infinitives are formed with the suffix *-in* is the loss of this suffix in the actuality-marked forms. Thus, corresponding to the infinitive *yayain* 'invite', we find perfective *niyaya* ~ *yinaya* and imperfective *niyayaya* ~ *yinayaya* (cf. the contemplated form *yayayain*, in which the suffix *-in* is retained).

Adjective morphology in Tagalog is also rather complex. Probably the most common adjective formations are those involving the prefix *ma-*: e.g. *mabuti* 'good' (cf. *buti* 'goodness'), *masama* 'bad' (cf. *sama* 'badness'), *malaki* 'big' (cf. *laki* 'bigness'), *maliit* 'small' (cf. *liit* 'smallness'). There are also many unaffixed adjectives — e.g. *mahal* 'expensive', *mura* 'cheap', *hinog* 'ripe', *hilaw* 'raw' — as well as many adjectives formed with various other affixes — e.g. *-an*, as in *putikan* 'virtually covered with mud' (cf. *putik* 'mud'), *-in*, as in *lagnatin* 'susceptible to fever' (cf. *lagnat* 'fever'), and *maka-*, as in *makabayan* 'patriotic' (cf. *bayan* 'country').

In certain cases adjectives may be morphologically marked for number or gender. Many *ma-* adjectives are marked as plural by a monosyllabic reduplicating prefix occurring between *ma-* and the stem: e.g. *mabubuti* 'good (pl.)', *masasama* 'bad (pl.)'. Such plural marking is, however, optional, and the non-pluralised forms may in general be used with plural as well as with singular referents. Gender marking is restricted to certain adjectives borrowed from Spanish, which occur in two gender-marked forms, a feminine form ending in *-a* and a masculine form ending in *-o*: e.g. *komika* (f.)/*komiko* (m.) 'funny', *simpatika* (f.)/*simpatiko* (m.) 'pleasing', *tonta* (f.)/*tonto* (m.) 'stupid'.

Adjectives may also be morphologically marked as intensive or moderative. Intensive formations involve the prefix *napaka-* (which replaces the *ma-* of a *ma-* adjective), while moderative formations involve disyllabic reduplication. Examples are: *napakabuti* 'very good', *napakamahal* 'very expensive', *mabuti-buti* 'rather good', *mahal-mahal* 'rather expensive'.

The comparative of equality is marked by (*ka*)*sing-* — e.g. (*ka*)*singbuti* 'as good as', (*ka*)*singmahal* 'as expensive as' — and the superlative is marked by *pinaka-* — e.g. *pinakamabuti* 'best', *pinakamahal* 'most expensive'. (Note that the *ma-* of a *ma-* adjective such as *mabuti* 'good' is dropped after (*ka*)*sing-* but retained after *pinaka-*.) The comparative of inequality is, however, expressed syntactically (by a preceding *mas*, *lalong* or *higit na* 'more' and a following *kaysa* or (*kaysa*) *sa* 'than').

Tagalog noun morphology is relatively simple. Nouns are not inflected for case or number (there is, however, obligatory *syntactic* role marking involving particles like *ng* and *sa* — see above — as well as optional syntactic pluralisation, involving the particle *mga*), and only certain nouns borrowed from Spanish are marked for gender: e.g. *amiga* (f.)/*amigo* (m.) 'friend', *sekretarya* (f.)/*sekretaryo* (m.) 'secretary'. Nonetheless, a good many morphologically complex nouns occur and some of these reflect quite productive patterns of affixation. Among the latter are: affixation with *-an* to express a place associated with what the stem designates, as in *aklatan* 'library' (cf. *aklat* 'book'), *halamanan* 'garden' (cf. *halaman* 'plant'); affixation with *-in* to express the object of the action expressed by a verb formed with the same stem, as in *awitin* 'song' (cf. *umawit* 'sing'), *bilihin* 'something to buy' (cf. *bumili* 'buy'); and affixation with *taga-* to express the performer of the action of a verb formed with the same stem, as in *tagasulat* 'writer' (cf. *sumulat* 'write'), *tagapagbili* 'seller' (cf. *magbili* 'sell'), *tagapangisda* 'fisherman' (cf. *mangisda* 'fish').

The Tagalog personal pronoun system is summarised in table 47.4. The person-number categories that are distinguished are first, second and third person, singular and plural. There are, however, two distinct types of

Table 47.4: Personal Pronouns

	ng *form*	sa *form*	Unmarked *form*
Singular			
1st person	ko	akin	ako
2nd person	mo	iyo	ka/ikaw
3rd person	niya	kaniya	siya
Plural			
1st person-exclusive	namin	amin	kami
1st person-inclusive	natin	atin	tayo
2nd person	ninyo	inyo	kayo
3rd person	nila	kanila	sila

first person plural. When the addressee is not included in the group being referred to (i.e., when the meaning is 'he/she/they and I'), the *exclusive* forms are used. When, on the other hand, the addressee *is* included in the group being referred to (i.e. when the meaning is 'you (and he/she/they) and I'), the *inclusive* forms are used. Note that no gender distinctions are made: the same third person singular forms are used to refer to males and females. The Tagalog personal pronouns are, however, strictly *personal*, in the sense that they are used to refer only to human beings (and to humanised animals, such as pets or animals in folktales). Where English would use *it* (or *they* with a non-human referent), Tagalog uses either no pronoun at all or a demonstrative.

Each personal pronoun category is associated with three distinct forms, except for the second person singular, which is associated with four. The *ng* form is the form that occurs in the same·contexts as common-noun phrases that are preceded by the particle *ng*: e.g. non-trigger actors. The *sa* form is the form that occurs after the particle *sa* or as a prenominal possessive pronoun. The unmarked form is the form that occurs in most other contexts, e.g. in isolation or when the pronoun functions as the trigger of the clause. In the case of the second person singular pronoun, there are two unmarked forms: *ka*, which functions exclusively as a trigger, and *ikaw*, which occurs in other unmarked contexts.

A similar three-way distinction is made in the demonstrative pronouns, as shown in table 47.5.

Table 47.5: Demonstrative Pronouns

	ng *form*	sa *form*	*Unmarked form*
'this'	nito	dito	ito
'that (near addressee)'	niyan	diyan	iyan
'that (not near addressee)'	niyon, noon	doon	iyon

Three demonstrative categories are distinguished, one equivalent to English 'this' and two that divide the range of English 'that', one of them used when the referent is near the addressee, the other when it is not. Again the *ng* forms are those that occur in the same contexts as *ng* phrases (*niyon* and *noon* are free variants). The *sa* forms of the demonstratives occur in the same contexts as *sa* phrases (including directional and locative *sa* phrases, in which case the demonstratives have the meanings 'here' and 'there'). And the unmarked forms occur in most other contexts.

Finally, it may be mentioned that there are also three contextually distinguished forms of the personal-name marker, i.e. the marker that is used when the head noun is a personal name: the *ng* form *ni*, the *sa* form *kay* and the unmarked form *si*. Such formal distinctions within the nominal system serve to identify the semantic and/or syntactic roles of arguments more or less unambiguously, thus allowing for the freedom of word order which, together with the trigger system and the complex verbal morphology, constitute perhaps the most striking typological features of Tagalog.

Bibliography

Tagalog grammar was first studied by Spanish missionaries in the sixteenth century, but it is only in the present century that the language has been analysed on its own terms, rather than on the basis of often inappropriate European models. Bloomfield's (1917) influential grammar, written from a classic structuralist perspective, served as the basis for the first grammar by a native speaker of the language, Lopez (1940). The most comprehensive grammar of the language written to date is Schachter and Otanes (1972). De Guzman (1978) is an innovative analysis of verbal morphology, so central to the language.

For the history of the diffusion of Tagalog as Pilipino, the Philippine national language, see Gonzales (1977). Constantino (1971) provides a historical survey of the linguistic analysis of Tagalog and seven other Philippine languages.

References

Bloomfield, L. 1917. *Tagalog Texts with Grammatical Analysis* (University of Illinois, Urbana)

Constantino, E. 1971. 'Tagalog and Other Major Languages of the Philippines', in T. A. Sebeok (ed.), *Current Trends in Linguistics*, vol. 8, *Linguistics in Oceania* (Mouton, The Hague)

De Guzman, V. 1978. *Syntactic Derivation of Tagalog Verbs* (= *Oceanic Linguistics*, Special Publication, no. 16)

Gonzales, A. 1977. 'Pilipino in the Year 2000', in B. Sibayan and A. Gonzales (eds.), *Language Planning and the Building of a National Language* (= *Philippine Journal of Linguistics*, Special Monograph, no. 5)

Lopez, C. 1940. *A Manual of the Philippine National Language* (Bureau of Printing, Manila)

Schachter, P. and F. Otanes. 1972. *Tagalog Reference Grammar* (University of California Press, Los Angeles)

48 NIGER-KORDOFANIAN LANGUAGES

Douglas Pulleyblank

Niger-Kordofanian is the family to which the vast majority of the languages of sub-Saharan Africa belong. Hundreds of languages fall into this group and upwards of 100,000,000 people speak Niger-Kordofanian languages. Geographically, this group ranges from Senegal in the west to Kenya in the east and extends as far south as South Africa.

The proposal for the group 'Niger-Kordofanian' dates from Greenberg's (1963) classification of the languages of Africa into four families: Niger-Kordofanian, Nilo-Saharan, Afroasiatic and Khoisan. Greenberg's creation of Niger-Kordofanian differed from earlier work on the classification of the relevant languages with respect to both larger and smaller groupings, as well as in its assignment of certain languages to particular subgroups. For example, at the level of large groupings, he included 'Kordofanian' and 'Niger-Congo' within a single family; at the level of smaller groupings, he argued that Bantu was actually a sub-sub-subgroup of Niger-Congo — not an independent family of its own; with respect to particular languages, he argued (for example) that Fula properly belongs to the West Atlantic subgroup of Niger-Congo. The basic subdivisions for Niger-Kordofanian proposed by Greenberg are as follows: NIGER-CONGO: (1) West Atlantic, (2) Mande, (3) Gur (Voltaic), (4) Kwa, (5) Benue-Congo, (6) Adamawa-Eastern; KORDOFANIAN: (1) Koalib, (2) Tegali, (3) Talodi, (4) Tumtum, (5) Katla.

There are several problems encountered in the classification of the languages of this group. Apart from general problems involved in the classification of any group of languages, one finds a number of specific problems. There are very few historical records of these languages that go back more than a couple of hundred years and yet we are dealing with a very large, very diverse group of languages which has been splitting apart for thousands of years. Obviously the details of larger genetic groupings will ultimately depend on the reconstruction of smaller groups — a task that is a large one given the number of languages involved and the limited amount of knowledge about many of them. To illustrate this point, work by Elugbe and Williamson (1976) on the reconstruction of Proto-Ẹdo and Proto-Ịjọ (two subgroups of Kwa) calls into question the legitimacy of the distinction between Kwa and Benue-Congo. They show that properties considered to be identifying characteristics of Benue-Congo must also be reconstructed for 'Proto-Ẹdo-Ijọ'. Their conclusion is that there is no evidence for separating Kwa from Benue-Congo, and that the two groups really constitute a single 'Benue-Kwa' subfamily of Niger-Congo. It is not within the scope of this short survey to review the work that has been done on the classification of African languages since Greenberg's influential work (although it is worth noting that studies such as that of Elugbe and Williamson serve to refine — not refute — Greenberg's work). Consequently, I will refer to languages and language groups according to their positions within Greenberg's (1963) classification. I stress that this is not intended as a rejection of refinements to the 1963 classification, but simply because that classification is the most familiar.

Because of the large number of languages in the Niger-Kordofanian family, it is probably impossible to make any general statements that hold true of all member languages. And even if one were to have access to a comprehensive reconstruction of Proto-Niger-Kordofanian, this would tell us relatively little about the presently attested characteristics of many (most) of the descendants of that language. For example, while most Niger-Kordofanian languages are tonal (and the proto-language surely was), there are important exceptions in languages like Fula (West Atlantic) and Swahili (Bantu; Benue-Congo). Moreover, even in the 'tonal' languages, the actual properties of the tonal systems vary considerably; languages may employ a fairly restricted system — for example, two tones and a fairly predictable distribution of the tones — or languages may employ highly articulated systems involving several distinct tones, essentially unpredictable lexical placements of the tones, complex realisation rules etc. Languages also differ, for example, as to whether tones are used for lexical and/or grammatical (e.g. tense) contrasts. In the following discussion, I will survey languages and language characteristics of Niger-Congo. Niger-Congo languages will be concentrated on since the Kordofanian group is more limited both in terms of number of speakers and in terms of geographical distribution (all the Kordofanian languages are spoken in the relatively small Kordofan area of Sudan). The languages that will be mentioned were chosen by virtue of being spoken by large numbers of people (although numbers vary from hundreds of thousands to tens of millions); topics to be discussed, however, have been chosen more in terms of anticipated interest than necessarily because they involve pan-Niger-Congo features. For example, perhaps all Niger-Congo languages have dental or alveolar stops while only an important subset of the family has doubly-articulated stops. But in such a case, the doubly-articulated stops will be discussed.

The westernmost branch of Niger-Congo is 'West Atlantic'. The languages of this group are concentrated in the extreme western portion of

West Africa, ranging basically from Senegal to Liberia. This said, the list of languages included in this group will begin with an exception. Fula (Fulani, Fulfulde, Peul, Fulbe etc.), which is perhaps the most well known language of this group, is spoken essentially throughout West Africa in a sub-Saharan belt that extends from Senegal in the west to as far east as Chad. Closely related to Fula is Serer, a language spoken predominantly in Senegal and also in Gambia. Still closely related is Wolof, centred in Senegal but also spoken in Gambia, Mali, Mauritania and Guinea. Other important languages in the West Atlantic group include Dyola (Senegal; also Gambia and Guinea), Balante (Guinea-Bissau; also Senegal), Temne (Sierra Leone), Kissi (Sierra Leone, Guinea; also Liberia), Gola (Liberia; also Sierra Leone) and Limba (Sierra Leone and Guinea).

Despite its not being a very unified group, it is typical for a West Atlantic language to have noun classes and a system of consonant mutations (Sapir 1971). Class systems of the type generally associated with Bantu languages (see for example, the chapter on Swahili and the Bantu languages in this volume) are found in languages of the West Atlantic group. Classes may have phonological, morphological, syntactic and semantic correlates. The morphological indicators of noun class membership generally involve prefixation and/or suffixation (for example, Temne has class prefixes while Fula has suffixes); in a language like Wolof, however, class membership is not morphologically marked and can only be deduced from the effect a noun has on governed elements. The important syntactic effect of noun classes is in determining properties of agreement. The various elements that can occur within a noun phrase will typically be marked to agree in class with the head of the noun phrase. Agreement can extend beyond the noun phrase to include elements such as the verb. The number of noun classes found in a particular language varies considerably within the West Atlantic group. For example, a language like Nalu has only three classes while certain dialects of Fula have up to twenty-five. While classes are generally not definable in terms of their semantics, certain generalisations can often be made. Classes are typically associated with either singular or plural nouns; classes may indicate notions such as 'augmentative' or 'diminutive'. A particularly interesting phonological property that is related to the noun class system is consonant mutation. In Fula, for example, changes in the phonological nature of the initial consonant of a stem accompany the assignment of a particular class suffix. Hence in addition to the suffix marking the appropriate singular or plural class, examples like the following involve changes in the initial stem consonant: *pul-lo* 'a Fula'; *ful-ɓe* 'Fulas'. In the singular class, the initial stem consonant must appear in its 'stop grade'; in the plural class, the initial stem consonant appears in its 'fricative' grade; other classes could require either of the above grades or a third 'nasal grade' (which for the *p/f* series would also be *p*, but which for many other series would be a prenasalised consonant). Although such consonant alternations correlate with noun classes in Fula, this is not always the case. In Serer, for example, the appropriate consonant grade is determined by an interaction between noun class membership and other lexical stem properties. As a final point, consonant mutation is not restricted to nouns; consonants of adjectives, verbs and even (in Fula) certain suffixes may alternate. For example, the following verbs from Fula illustrate the appearance of the fricative grade in the singular and of the nasal grade in the plural: *laamɗo warii* 'the chief came'; *laamɓe ngarii* 'the chiefs came' (*w/ng*).

Mande languages, the second group to be considered here, are spoken as far west as Senegal and as far east as Bourkina Fasso (Upper Volta) and Ivory Coast. The largest languages in this group are Maninka-Bambara-Dyula and Mende. Maninka-Bambara-Dyula refers to a group of very closely related dialects/languages spoken in several countries including Senegal, Gambia, Guinea, Mali, Sierra Leone, Ivory Coast and Bourkina Fasso; Mende is spoken in Sierra Leone. Other languages in the Mande group include Soninke (Mali), Vai (Sierra Leone), Susu-Yalunka (Guinea, Sierre Leone), Loma (Liberia, Guinea), Kpelle (Liberia, Guinea), Mano (Liberia, Guinea), Dan-Kweni (Ivory Coast, Liberia), Samo (Bourkina Fasso, Mali) and Busa (Benin, Nigeria). Note that Busa is exceptional geographically for Mande, occurring as far east as Nigeria.

In contrast with the West Atlantic languages, Mande languages do not have noun classes. Interestingly, however, certain Mande languages do have systems of consonant mutation. Changes in the initial consonant of a word can correlate with properties of definiteness, can occur with particular pronominal elements, can occur in particular syntactic contexts etc. (Welmers 1971: 132). Moreover, there are cases where segmental properties of consonants interact in very interesting ways with tonal properties. While it is not uncommon in general to observe that voiced consonants have a lowering effect on the pitch of an adjacent vowel while voiceless consonants have a raising effect, it is interesting that in a Mande language like Kpelle the presence or absence of a low tone actually correlates with the presence or absence of voicing. Hence a voiceless stop like *p* has a counterpart in Kpelle that is heavily voiced and bears a low tone (Welmers 1962: 71–2).

In general, the tonal properties of Mande languages are of considerable interest and importance. The observation that tone must be assigned in certain cases to morphemes rather than to some smaller phonological unit such as the syllable was first made by Welmers with respect to Kpelle (Welmers 1962: 85–6). Using examples from Mende (Leben 1978) as illustration, it can be shown that words such as the following all involve a single high-low pattern: *mbû* 'owl', *ngílà* 'dog', *félàmà* 'junction'. The high and low tones are realised on a single vowel (the only vowel) in the first example, on the first and second vowels in the second example, and in the third example, the high appears on the first vowel while the low appears on the second and third vowels. Consideration of such cases has been instrumental in determining that phonetic contour tones are best represented as involving sequences of phonologically level tones and that certain vowels that phonetically bear tones are best viewed as receiving their tones by the interaction of general principles with tonal sequences that are assigned underlyingly to morphemes rather than to specific vowels or syllables.

The Gur, or Voltaic, languages are primarily spoken in southeastern Mali, Bourkina Fasso and northern Ghana, although they extend through Togo and Benin as far east as Nigeria. The largest language of this group is Moore (also known as More, Mossi etc.), spoken in Bourkina Fasso, Ghana and Togo. Other languages include Dagari (Ghana, Bourkina Fasso), Dagomba (Ghana, Togo), Dogon (Mali, Bourkina Fasso), Gurma (Bourkina Fasso, Ghana, Togo), Lobiri (Bourkina Fasso, Ivory Coast), Bwamu (Bourkina Fasso), Senari (Ivory Coast) and Suppire-Mianka (Mali) — the two largest 'Senufo' languages —, Tem (Togo, Benin, Ghana) and Bariba (Benin, Togo, Nigeria).

Like the West Atlantic languages (and indeed typical of Niger-Kordofanian in general), Gur languages commonly manifest systems of noun classes (Bendor-Samuel 1971: 164–71). Unlike the most common Niger-Kordofanian pattern of prefixes, however, Gur languages generally have class suffixes. It should be noted, moreover, that the presence of class systems in widely diverse languages is more than simply a typological similarity. For example, it is typical of Gur that there be singular and plural person classes marked by the affixes *a* or *u* (singular) and *ba* or *bi* (plural); there is typically a class not involved in a singular/plural pairing that is used for mass/liquid nouns and generally marked by a nasal affix. Such characteristics, while typical of Gur, are widely attested throughout Niger-Kordofanian.

The morphology of Gur languages presents numerous properties of considerable phonological interest. Consider, for example, the following imperfective forms in Dagara (*ré* 'imperfective'): *dì* + *ré* → *dìré* (*dɪ* 'eat'); *tú* + *ré* → *túúr* (*tú* 'insult'); *cè* + *ré* → *cìér* (*cè* 'construct'). In the first example, the imperfective suffix surfaces basically without modification. In the second example, however, the vowel of the suffix is lost while the stem vowel is lengthened. And in the third example, there is not only loss of the suffix vowel and lengthening of the stem vowel, but, in addition, the stem vowel is diphthongised. Determining the precise conditions under which these types of changes take place involves rather intricate interactions between properties of vowel quality, syllable structure and tone.

Another point concerning the morphology of Gur languages is the high frequency of compounding. For example, it is common for adjective-noun sequences to appear as a compound rather than as a syntactic sequence. In such a case, the noun stem will appear followed by the adjective followed by a single class suffix. When adjectives do appear as a syntactic constituent, there are three basic possibilities: they may be invariant; they may be marked for noun class membership just as nouns — but not participate in agreement; or they may take class affixes that agree with the head noun (Bendor-Samuel 1971: 171–2). It should be noted before leaving the topic of adjectives that this category is a very restricted one throughout Niger-Congo. Typically, the types of meanings that might be expressed by adjectives in a language like English are expressed in Niger-Congo languages by constructions involving either verbs or nouns.

Gur languages manifest some variation with respect to basic word order. For example, although the general order for subject, object and verb in Gur is SVO, certain Gur languages (e.g. Senari) have the basic order SOV. It is worth noting that Gur reflects the overall Niger-Congo patterning in this regard — in general, the Niger-Congo basic order is SVO, although in a group such as Mande it is SOV.

The Kwa languages are found in an area extending basically from Liberia in the west to Nigeria in the east. The four largest languages in the Kwa group are Akan (Ghana), Ewe (Ghana, Togo, Benin), Yoruba (Nigeria, Benin, Togo) (see the chapter on Yoruba in this volume) and Igbo (Nigeria). Other languages in this group include Bassa (Liberia), Kru (Liberia), Baule (Ivory Coast), Bete (Ivory Coast), Gã-Adangme (Ghana), Nupe (Nigeria), Gwari (Nigeria), Ebira (Nigeria), Bini (Nigeria), Igala (Nigeria), Idoma (Nigeria) and Ịjọ (Nigeria). It might be noted that there is some disagreement as to whether Ịjọ really belongs to the Kwa group or to the Benue-Congo group. Of course, such a question ceases to be an issue if it turns out that Kwa and Benue-Congo actually form a single branch of Niger-Congo (as mentioned above as a possibility).

A striking phonetic property of a typical Kwa language is the presence of doubly-articulated 'labial-velar' stops. While such segments appear in numerous non-Kwa languages, in Kwa they are commonplace. Ladefoged (1968: 9) notes that there are at least three ways for a doubly-articulated stop like [k͡p] to be produced: the labial and velar closures may be released on an air-stream that is (1) pulmonic egressive only (e.g. Guang (Ghana)); (2) pulmonic egressive and velaric ingressive (e.g. Yoruba); (3) pulmonic egressive, velaric ingressive and glottalic ingressive (e.g. Idoma).

Another typical phonetic property found in Kwa (although in no way restricted to Kwa) is tonal downstep. Although a language may contrast only two phonological tone levels, it may have a number of phonetic pitch levels that is in principle unlimited. In Igbo, for example, two adjacent high-toned syllables will normally be produced on the same pitch. If, however, a low-toned syllable intervenes between the two high tones, then the second high tone will be produced on a lower pitch than the first one. In an appropriate sequence of alternating tones (e.g. HLHLH ...), a series of gradually lowered high tones will be produced. Such completely transparent examples of phonetic downstepping are often complicated by the presence of 'floating' tones in a language's phonological representations. That is, tones may be phonologically present in certain cases even though there is no vowel available for the tone to be pronounced on. Consider again the type of HLH sequence in a downstepping language where the second high tone will be produced on a slightly lower pitch than the first. If the vowel bearing the low tone were to be deleted for some reason, then in many cases the low tone itself would remain and continue to play a role in the tonal phonology of the sequence in question — for example, by triggering the phonetic lowering of the second high tone. Hence the phonetic sequence of a high tone followed by a slightly lower tone (but not low) is in many cases the phonetic realisation of a H-L'-H sequence (where L' indicates a floating tone). In many other cases, such a slightly lower tone may of course be correctly analysed as a mid tone — phonologically distinct from either high or low. Determining the correct analysis of such non-high tones is often a major problem of tonal phonology.

With respect to syntax, one interesting construction found in a number of Kwa languages is that of the 'predicate cleft'. In this construction a predicate is focused by placing a copy of the verb in a fronted position. The following example is from Yoruba:

rírà   ni   bàbá   ra   bàtà
buying foc. father buy shoe
'Father **bought** shoes.'

In this example, the verb *rà* is focused by placing a nominalised form of the verb in the initial focus position. This construction therefore makes it possible to focus syntactically virtually any constituent of a basic Yoruba sentence — noun phrase subjects, objects etc. being typical focused constituents.

The Benue-Congo languages are distributed throughout east, central and southern Africa, extending as far west as Nigeria. Four sub-branches of Benue-Congo can be distinguished, of which the most important is Bantoid — the branch including the Bantu languages. Since a separate chapter in this volume is devoted to Bantu, the discussion here will concentrate on Benue-Congo languages other than Bantu. With respect to the number of speakers, the Bantu languages stand in marked contrast to the other languages of Benue-Congo. Whereas a large proportion of the speakers of Niger-Kordofanian languages speak Bantu languages, only relatively small groups tend to speak other Benue-Congo languages. Two exceptions to this generalisation are Efik-Ibibio (Nigeria) and Tiv (Nigeria), both spoken by large populations.

When the Bantu group is compared with the rest of the Benue-Congo group, it is striking that there is much more variation within the group not including Bantu than there is within the Bantu group itself. For example, the features that characterise the Bantu group are its systems of noun classes and agglutinative verb morphology and it is generally fairly straightforward to establish correspondences between the particular forms of one language and those of another — or between the forms of one language and the reconstructed forms of Proto-Bantu. Of course, a major reason for including Bantu in the Benue-Congo group is that the typical 'Bantu' properties can be demonstrated to occur in other languages of the Benue-Congo group. But typically, the Benue-Congo languages other than Bantu show considerable diversity in their manifestations of such properties.

Consider, for example, Benue-Congo noun class systems. While noun class systems demonstrably corresponding to Bantu are typical of Benue-Congo, there are Benue-Congo languages that have lost their class systems (e.g. Jukun). And while noun classes are morphologically marked by prefixes in Bantu, in a very closely related language like Tiv, noun classes are marked by both prefixes and suffixes.

The morphology of the Tiv noun class system is quite complex. For example, the singular person class is marked either by the absence of class marking or by a low tone prefix in conjunction with labialisation of the initial stem consonant. An example of the latter possibility is ′kwásé 'wife', where ′ indicates an initial downstep triggered by the low tone prefix, and labialisation of the stem kásé has taken place because of the singular prefix. The plural person class is marked either by a suffix v (e.g. kásév 'wives') or by one of the prefixes ù or mbà. Apart from the phonological properties of the singular affix, an interesting property of the class morphology concerns the appearance of class suffixes on nouns within prepositional phrases (Abraham 1940). One observes that class suffixes cannot occur with a preposition like shá 'on': shá ′kwásé 'on the wife'; shá ùkásé 'on the wives'. In this example, the suffix v that normally appears in the plural of kásé has been replaced by the prefix ù within a prepositional phrase. However, class suffixes can occur within a prepositional phrase if the relevant noun is followed by a demonstrative, possessive pronoun etc. Compare the following examples involving the stem gèrè 'water': ḿgérĕm 'water' (prefix ḿ; suffix ḿ); shím m̀gĕr 'in the water' (prefix ḿ only; final stem vowel is deleted by a regular phonological rule); shím ḿgérĕm mèrá 'in that water' (prefix ḿ; suffix ḿ). Not only is the suffix not present in the form shím m̀gĕr, but the class prefix has lost its normal high tone.

The final branch of Niger-Congo to be considered is Adamawa-Eastern or Adamawa-Ubangian. Geographically, the languages of this group are found as far west as Nigeria (although concentrated groups of Adamawa languages do not begin until Cameroon) and extend as far east as Sudan; the northern and southern extents of Adamawa-Eastern are Chad and the Congo. The largest language of this branch is Gbaya, spoken in the Central African Republic, Cameroon and the Congo. Two other Adamawa-Eastern languages are Banda (Central African Republic, Congo) and Zande (Sudan, Central African Republic, Congo).

Just as most other branches of Niger-Congo, Adamawa-Eastern shows reflexes of a Niger-Congo noun class system. Typically, the class markers in this branch are suffixes, although in some cases they can only be reconstructed through the comparison of 'stem'-final consonants in languages which have ceased to operate a synchronic class system (Boyd 1974: 56–7). Reduplication, in addition to forms of affixation, is a common morphological process in this group (and also common in other groups of Niger-Congo). As a final point concerning morphology in a broad sense (and again actually a more general point than simply relating to Adamawa-Eastern), one should take note of the class of words referred to as 'ideophones'. Although notoriously difficult to define, ideophones form an identifiable class of words in many languages (see pages 981–2 for a discussion of Yoruba ideophones). Typically, they exhibit certain morphological properties such as reduplication; phonological properties such as specific tonal patterns and the occurrence of special phonemes; syntactically, they are often used in adverbial configurations and are often idiomatically restricted to appearing with particular predicates.

With respect to phonology, this branch has a number of interesting properties (where it should be stressed that while such properties may be typical of Adamawa-Eastern, they are not restricted to it). Prenasalised segments are common; in a language like Duru (Cameroon; Boyd 1974: 24), a prenasalised stop series is attested, while in a language like Mbum (Cameroon; Hagège 1970: 54), there are both prenasalised stops and prenasalised fricatives. Evidence that such prenasalised segments belong to a single syllable — even intervocalically in a sequence such as [... aŋga ...] — can be found in the language games of a language like Gbaya (Monino and Roulon 1972: 110–11). Also with respect to nasalisation, one observes in a language like Mbum (Hagège 1970: 62) that if there are two vowels in a word, then either both will be nasal or neither will be nasal — different values for the two vowels are not attested. Also with respect to Mbum, Hagège notes (Hagège 1970: 48, 54) that glides ([y, w]) are in complementary distribution with their corresponding vowels: glides appear initially before a vowel as well as intervocalically, while the vowels appear elsewhere (e.g. *mbòì* 'follow'; *mbóyà* 'to follow'). A final general point can be made about the distribution of consonant phonemes. One typically observes that the full range of contrasts is possible only in initial position; only a restricted inventory may appear in intervocalic positions and an even more limited set is all that is possible in final position.

To close this discussion, a few brief comments will be made about the syntactic possibilities of this group, starting with a construction that is not attested: in the Adamawa-Eastern group, as in certain other groups, there is typically no morphologically marked passive construction. On the other hand, a construction that typically is found is one involving a proximate/obviative distinction between pronouns. That is, a pronoun in an embedded sentence that is coreferential to the matrix subject is distinguished morphologically from a pronoun that is disjoint in reference from the matrix subject (for Yoruba examples, see pages 987–8). Finally, one observes interesting word order properties in a language such as Duru. Boyd (1974: 52) notes that in a morphologically unmarked tense such as the past (perfective), predicates exemplify the more common pattern of this group in placing the object after the verb. But in the present (imperfective) tense, an object in Duru precedes the verb — appearing immediately after a particle that occurs in post-subject position. Hence the basic word order of a sentence depends on its tense.

Bibliography

For the establishment of the Niger-Kordofanian family, reference should be made to Greenberg (1963). Welmers (1973) is an account of a number of recurrent structural properties of sub-Saharan African languages, with emphasis inevitably on Niger-Congo languages. Ladefoged (1968) is a detailed phonetic study of some of the less usual phonetic segments occurring in West African languages. For further bibliography, reference may be made to the contributions to Sebeok (1971) and to Meier (1984).

References

Abraham, R.C. 1940. *A Dictionary of the Tiv Language* (Stephen Austin, Hertford)

Bendor-Samuel, J.T. 1971. 'Niger-Congo, Gur', in Sebeok (1971), pp. 141–78

Boyd, R. 1974. *Étude comparative dans le groupe Adamawa* (SELAF, Paris)

Elugbe, B. and K. Williamson. 1976. 'Reconstructing Nasals in Proto-Benue-Kwa', in A. Juilland (ed.), *Linguistic Studies Offered to Joseph Greenberg*, vol. 2 (Anma Libri, Saratoga, Calif.)

Greenberg, J.H. 1963. *The Languages of Africa* (Indiana University, Bloomington and Mouton, The Hague)

Hagège, C. 1970. *La Langue mbum de Nganha* (SELAF, Paris)

Ladefoged, P. 1968. *A Phonetic Study of West African Languages* (Cambridge University Press, Cambridge)

Leben, W.R. 1978. 'The Representation of Tone', in V.A. Fromkin (ed.), *Tone: A Linguistic Survey* (Academic Press, New York), pp. 177–219

Meier, W. 1984. *Bibliography of African Languages* (Otto Harrassowitz, Wiesbaden)

Monino, Y. and P. Roulon. 1972. *Phonologie du Gbaya Kara 'Bodoe* (SELAF, Paris)

Sapir, J.D. 1971. 'West Atlantic: An Inventory of the Languages, Their Noun Class Systems, and Consonant Alternation', in Sebeok (1971), pp. 45–112

Sebeok, T.A. (ed.) 1971. *Current Trends in Linguistics*, vol. 7, *Linguistics in Sub-Saharan Africa* (Mouton, The Hague)

Welmers, W.E. 1962. 'The Phonology of Kpelle', *Journal of African Languages*, vol. 1, pp. 69–93

—— 1971. 'Niger-Congo, Mande', in Sebeok (1971), pp. 113–40

—— 1973. *African Language Structures* (University of California Press, Berkeley)

49   Yoruba

Douglas Pulleyblank

1   Historical Background

Yorbua belongs to the Yoruboid group of languages, a group belonging to the Kwa branch of Niger-Congo (or belonging to the branch including both Kwa and Benue-Congo, depending on the correct classification of these larger groups see pages 961–2). Other Yoruboid languages include the group of dialects referred to collectively as the Akoko cluster, in addition to Iṣẹkiri and Igala. The vast majority of the speakers of Yoruba are found in Nigeria (upwards of 16 million), located particularly in Ọyọ, Ogun, Ondo and Kwara states — states that essentially make up the southwestern corner of the country. Speakers are also found in southeastern sections of the Republic of Benin, as well as certain sections of Togo.

It is interesting, however, that the study of Yoruba did not begin in any of the places just mentioned. In the early nineteenth century, Yorubas began to form a large percentage of the slaves being exported from West Africa. As this period also marked the beginning of the British suppression of the slave trade, it turned out that many of the freed slaves being resettled in Freetown, Sierra Leone were speakers of Yoruba. When linguistic work undertaken in Freetown was extended to include languages not indigenous to Sierre Leone, Yoruba (or 'Aku' as it was commonly called) was a natural choice for study because of the large number of speakers residing in Freetown. In fact, as early as 1831, Yoruba was selected as one of two African languages to be used as the medium of instruction in a Sierra Leone girls' school. In the 1840s, however, the study of Yoruba began to shift to Yorubaland itself. The sending of the Niger expedition by the British government signalled the beginning of CMS (Church Missionary Society) missionary activity in Yorubaland. One of the central figures in the early study of Yoruba was Samuel Crowther. Crowther was a Yoruba slave who was liberated and settled in Freetown. There he received an education and began his study of Yoruba. After accompanying the Niger expedition to Yorubaland, he both became a priest and published his first work on Yoruba (a grammar and vocabulary). The CMS established itself in Abeokuta; translation of the Bible was undertaken, primers were prepared and a

Yoruba periodical was produced (from 1859 to 1867 — perhaps the earliest such vernacular periodical to be published in West Africa).

One of the particularly important things that happened at this time was a concerted group effort aimed at establishing an efficient orthography for Yoruba. The result, which included digraphs for certain phonemes and diacritically modified letters for others, involved contributions from scholars and missionaries in Europe, Freetown and Abeokuta. Crowther's adoption of the revised orthography in conjunction with his considerable success as a translator did much to establish and promote standard Yoruba. The orthography adopted by Crowther and others in the 1850s remains essentially unmodified up to the present.

But before actually entering into a discussion of issues of Yoruba orthography and grammar, it is appropriate to note the influence that Yoruba language and culture have had in a variety of areas outside Yorubaland. Yoruba slaves were extremely influential in certain areas of Brazil and Cuba. For example, the Nagos (Yorubas) of Bahia in Brazil preserved Yoruba as a ceremonial language at least until very recently. And there are reportedly still small numbers of Yorubas in Sierra Leone. Yoruba has also undergone revivals such as that exhibited in Oyotunji village of the United States. Even where Yoruba has ceased to be spoken, it has often exerted a considerable impact on the languages that have replaced it — such as Krio in Sierra Leone.

In Yorubaland itself, Yoruba has an established and thriving literature, including books, newspapers, pamphlets etc. It is studied up to the university level in several Nigerian universities and serves as the medium of instruction for courses in Yoruba linguistics and literature. It is of course well established as a broadcasting language for both radio and television.

2 Phonology

The segmental phonemes of standard Yoruba are laid out in table 49.1. The oral vowels form a straightforward seven-vowel system. Orthographically, [ε] and [ɔ] are represented as ẹ and ọ respectively, while the other vowels are represented as they appear in the table (that is, *i*, *e*, *a*, *o* and *u*). Although the nasalised vowels appear to represent a fairly symmetrical subset of the oral vowels, the symmetry would perhaps better be represented as deriving from a three-way contrast between high front, high back and low nasalised vowels. This is because the vowel [ε̃] has an extremely limited distribution (appearing in standard Yoruba in only a few lexical items, such as *iyẹn* 'that') and [ɔ̃] and [ã] are variants of a single phoneme. Orthographically, the nasalised vowels are represented as a vowel + *n* sequence when immediately following an oral consonant, and as a simple vowel when immediately following a nasal consonant: *sìn* [sĩ̀] 'accompany', *ìyẹn* [ìyε̃] 'that', *fún* [fṹ] 'give', *pọn* [kpɔ̃] 'draw (water)', *tán* [tɔ́] 'finish', *mọ̀* [mɔ̀̃] 'know'.

Table 49.1: Segmental Phonemes of Yoruba

Oral vowels	i		u
	e		o
	ɛ		ɔ
		a	
Nasalised vowels	ĩ		ũ
	ɛ̃		ɔ̃

	Stop	Fricative	Nasal	Lateral	Tap	Glide
Bilabial	b		m			
Labio-dental		f				
Alveolar	t d	s		l	r	
Palato-alveolar		ʃ				
Palatal	j					y
Velar	k g					w
Labial-velar	kp gb					
Glottal		h				

With respect to the consonant inventory, several comments are in order. Four basic places of articulation are distinguished for Yoruba stops, namely bilabial, alveolar, palatal and velar. While alveolar and velar places of articulation include both voiced and voiceless phonemes, the bilabial and palatal positions allow only voiced ones. In addition to the four places of articulation just referred to, Yoruba has two stops that are doubly articulated — with simultaneous labial and velar closures. These labial-velar stops are orthographically represented as *p* [kp] and *gb* [gb]; the simple letter *p* suffices for the voiceless labial-velar stop since there is no voiceless bilabial stop in the language.

There are four fricatives in Yoruba, all of which are voiceless. Orthographically, the labial, alveolar and glottal fricatives are represented as *f*, *s* and *h*; the palato-alveolar fricative is represented by the dotted consonant *ṣ* [ʃ].

The remaining consonants in table 49.1 are the sonorants, *m, l, r, y* and *w*. Orthographically, these segments are written as just listed and therefore require no special comment. Phonologically, on the other hand, these segments exhibit certain interesting properties that will be discussed shortly. First, however, it is necessary to discuss two types of phonemes not included in table 49.1. The first is the syllabic nasal. Such nasals are orthographically represented as *n* or *m* but their pronunciation depends on the nature of the following segment. If the following segment is a vowel (which occurs in a fairly limited set of circumstances) then the syllabic nasal is pronounced as a velar, as in *n ò lọ* [ŋ̀ ò lɔ́] 'I didn't go'. When the syllabic nasal is followed by a consonant, the nasal is homorganic to the following segment: *ḿbọ̀* [m̀bɔ̀] 'is coming', *ńfọ̀* [m̀ ɱfɔ̀] 'is washing', *ńsùn* [ǹ ṇsũ̀] 'is sleeping', *ńjó* [ɲ̀ ɲjó] 'is dancing', *ńkà* [ŋ̀ ŋkà] 'is reading'. Note that the syllabic nasal is generally only written as 'm' before 'b'. In medial position, there is potential confusion over whether an orthographic *vowel–'n'–consonant* sequence represents a phonetic *nasalised vowel–consonant* sequence or a *vowel–syllabic nasal–consonant* sequence. For example, the phonetic sequence [...ɔŋk...] and [...ɔ̃k...] would both be represented orthographically as '...*ọnk*...'. Where such cases arise, they can be disambiguated by tone-marking the syllabic nasal — which, of course, bears a tone by virtue of being syllabic. This brings us to the second phoneme type not represented in table 49.1, namely tone.

Tone is of major importance in Yoruba. Three tones must be distinguished underlyingly: high, mid and low. High is orthographically represented by an acute accent '´', Low is represented by a grave accent '`' and Mid is generally left unmarked (although if it is necessary to mark it — such as with a syllabic nasal — then a macron '¯' is used). The functional load of tone is considerable in Yoruba. For example, numerous sets of lexical items are distinguished solely by tone: *igbá* 'calabash', *igba* 'two hundred', *ìgbá* 'Locustbean tree', *ìgbà* 'time', *igbà* 'climbing-rope'; *ọbẹ̀* 'soup', *ọ̀bẹ* 'knife'; *ọkọ̀* 'vehicle', *ọkọ́* 'hoe', *ọkọ* 'husband', *ọ̀kọ̀* 'spear'. The functional importance of tone is amplified when one considers how sequences of words are modified by certain phrase-level phonological rules. For example, there is a common process of vowel deletion that affects sequences of adjacent vowels in connected speech. This process takes place in a number of environments, one important one being between a transitive verb and its object. Typically in such cases, the vowel of the verb is lost: *rí aṣọ* → *ráṣọ* 'see cloth', *ra epo* → *repo* 'buy oil'. The vast majority of Yoruba verbs are monosyllabic, of the form CV. Hence if the vowel of the verb deletes, the verb's lexical content is conveyed primarily by its initial consonant and its *tone*.

Turning to matters of phonological organisation, consider first possible syllables in Yoruba. Essentially, a syllable may consist of a vowel nucleus with or without a consonant onset: V-syllable: *a* 'we', *ìwé* 'book'; CV-syllable: *rí* 'see', *gbà* 'take'. Consonant clusters are not permitted (recall that orthographic 'gb' in an example like *gbà* represents not a sequence of phonemes but a single multiply-articulated phoneme). On the other hand, long vowels are attested. Compare, for example, *oògùn* 'medicine' vs. *ògùn* '(name of a river)'; *aago* 'bell' vs. *ago* 'cup'. In many cases, long vowels can be seen to derive from disyllabic sequences that have undergone consonant deletion (for example, *agogo* ~ *aago* 'bell') or to derive from morphological juxtaposition of vowels that do not result in vowel deletion (for example, in the reduplicated form *ọ̀sọ̀ọsẹ̀* 'every week' derived from *ọsẹ̀* 'week'). With respect to the syllabic nasal, several observations should be made. First, when the nucleus of a syllable is a nasal, there can be no onset. That is, a syllabic nasal must constitute a syllable in its entirety. Second, a syllabic nasal may occur initially (*ńlá* 'big') and medially (*aláǹgbá* 'lizard') but not finally. Third, as mentioned above, a syllabic nasal must be homorganic with a following consonant. In fact, even in the cases where a syllabic nasal appears to occur prevocalically (such as *ñ ò lọ* 'I didn't go'), it can be argued that the nasal appears underlyingly in a preconsonantal position since *ò* '(negative)' is derived from *kò* by a rule of *k*-deletion. It is possible therefore to make the general statement that syllabic nasals appear *only* preconsonantally (at least at the relevant stage of their derivation). As a fourth and final point, one observes that in certain types of cases syllabic nasals alternate with a sequence of nasal consonant followed by [i] (for example, *ó wà nílé* ~ *ó wà ńlé* 'she is at home'). All of these observations can be accounted for if syllabic nasals are analysed as deriving from a *nasal–[i]* sequence. The place of articulation of this sequence is derived by assimilation to a following consonant; the nasality of the syllable nucleus is derived by assimilation of the nucleus to the onset. Hence a syllabic nasal cannot have an onset because it actually does have a nasal onset; to allow a phonetic onset to the syllabic nasal would require positing clusters underlyingly — and clusters are not allowed in Yoruba. Similarly, syllabic nasals cannot appear in final position since there is no following consonant to assign a place specification to such a syllable. Hence statements about syllable structure in Yoruba are almost maximally simple: syllables consist of a nucleus with an optional onset.

In the above discussion of syllabic nasals, it was suggested that the nucleus of a syllable assimilates in terms of nasality to a nasal onset. This is in fact due to a widely recognised process that applies irrespective of whether a syllabic nasal is created. Hence a vowel following the nasal consonant [m] will always be nasalised. In fact, the nasalisation process is even more general than even this suggests. As mentioned above, nasalised vowels contrast with oral vowels in Yoruba (for example, *kú* 'die' vs. *kún* [kṹ] 'be full'; *rì* 'drown' vs. *rìn* [r̃ĩ] 'walk'). When a nasalised vowel is preceded in a syllable by a sonorant, the sonorant itself becomes nasalised (hence *rìn* [r̃ĩ] 'walk', *iyán* [iỹɔ̃] 'pounded yam', *wọ́n* [w̃ɔ́] 'they', *hun* [h̃ũ] 'weave'). In general, therefore, a sonorant — whether consonant or vowel — assimilates in nasality to a tautosyllabic nasal segment.

In the above discussion of nasality and syllable structure, I have left untouched the important alternation that one observes in Yoruba between [n] and [l]. These two sounds are in complementary distribution, with [n] occurring only before nasalised vowels and [l] occurring only before oral vowels. Moreover, as a result of vowel deletion, [n] and [l] alternate in various extremely common Yoruba morphemes. Consider the following examples: *ní ọjà* ~ *l'ọ́jà* 'at the market', *ní aṣọ* ~ *l'áṣọ* 'have cloth', *ó ní ó dáa* ~ *ó l'ó dáa* 'he says it's all right'. In all three cases, loss of the nasalised vowel [ĩ] entails complete loss of nasality. Hence the nasality in [n] ~ [l] cases patterns like the nasality in an example like *fún ewúrẹ́* ~ *f'éwúrẹ́* 'give (it to) the goat' in that nasality is completely lost as a result of vowel deletion. It does not pattern like a case such as *mu ẹmu* ~ *m'ẹmu* 'drink palm-wine' where loss of the nasalised vowel [ũ] has no effect on the nasality of the preceding consonant. In other words, the cases with [n] and [l] appear to pattern like the cases involving nasalised vowels — and not like the cases involving nasal consonants. Hence the general consensus has been that [n] is an allophone of the phoneme /l/ — derived when the phoneme /l/ occurs in a syllable with a nasalised vowel (see, for example, Bamgboṣe 1966). In fact, it is possible under such an analysis to assume that the rule changing /l/ into [n] is simply the general rule of syllable-internal nasalisation of sonorants that was described above.

Before leaving this topic, however, a couple of problems should be noted. First, the nasality of a nasalised vowel is sometimes retained even when the vowel itself is deleted: *pín epo* [kpí ekpo] ~ *p'énpo* [kpékpo] 'share the oil'. As far as I know, such a possibility is never observed when the *consonant–nasalised vowel* sequence is /lṼ/. That is, *ní epo* 'have oil' can be realised as *l'épo* [lékpo] but never as *n'epo* [nékpo]. The second problem is that there is a systematic exception to the first one. Whenever /lĩ/ is followed by /i/ — and the sequence undergoes vowel deletion — nasality is retained. For example, *ní ilé* 'at home' can be realised as *n'ílé* but not as *l'ílé*. Finally, the [n] ~ [l] pair patterns quite differently when it comes to certain reduplicated forms than other nasal ~ oral sonorant pairs. In forming a gerundive nominalisation, a CV prefix is attached to a verb stem. The vowel of the verb stem is invariably [í] — and whether or not the stem vowel is nasalised, the prefix vowel is oral: *rà* : *rírà* 'buy : buying', *rán* [rő] : *rírán* [rírő] 'sew : sewing', *wó* : *wíwó* 'pull : pulling', *wón* : *wíwón* 'expensive : expensiveness', *dùn* : *dídùn* 'sweet : sweetness', *pín* : *pípín* 'divide : dividing'. This pattern is broken, however, by the [n] ~ [l] pair. In stems where [n] appears — by hypothesis because the stem vowel is nasalised — [n] also appears in the reduplicative prefix: *ní* : *níní* 'have : having', *ná* : *níná* 'spend : spending'. In one way or another, nasality from the stem is transferred from the stem to the prefix with the sonorant pair [n] ~ [l] but with no others. To conclude, the distribution of [n] and [l] is rule-governed and there is therefore no reason to posit two underlying phonemes. Basically, [n] patterns simply as the nasalised variant of [l] — comparable to the nasalised variants of other sonorants in Yoruba. Nevertheless, the [n] ~ [l] pair behaves somewhat differently from other nasal-oral sonorant pairs.

There are a number of restrictions on the occurrence of vowels in Yoruba. For example, in the standard language, vowel-initial nouns cannot begin with [u] nor can they begin with a nasalised vowel. Moreover, certain vowels cannot cooccur. In three papers in volume 6 of the *Journal of African Languages*, A.O. Awobuluyi and A. Bamgboṣe show that two basic patterns of vowel harmony hold. On the one hand, the mid vowels *e* and *o* do not cooccur with the mid vowels *ẹ* and *ọ* (*ẹsẹ̀* 'foot', *èfó* 'vegetable', *ọṣẹ̀* 'week', *ọkọ* 'husband'; *ètè* 'lips', *epo* 'oil', *òwe* 'proverb', *owó* money'); but **oCọ*, *oCẹ, *eCọ, *eCẹ, *ọCo etc.); on the other hand, front and back vowels do not cooccur in monomorphemic ...CVCV... sequences (ìrókò '(kind of tree)', àbúrò 'younger sibling', ìràwọ̀ 'star', ahéré 'hut', òkìkí 'fame', àtíkè 'make-up powder' etc.). On the whole, these harmonic restrictions operate to define possible morpheme shapes in synchronic Yoruba; there appear to be no productive morphemes manifesting alternate forms depending on the harmonic class of the stem.

It was mentioned above that Yoruba has three contrastive tones: high, mid and low. These tones are modified in a number of ways before reaching their actual phonetic manifestations. For example, although the contrastive tones are all level, phonetic contours occur in certain environments. A high tone immediately following a low tone is realised as a rising tone: ìwé [ìwě] 'book', ọ̀rẹ́ [ɔ̀rɛ̌] 'friend', ìgbá [ìgbǎ] 'Locustbean tree'. A low tone immediately following a high tone is realised as a falling tone: owó wà [ōwó wâ] 'there is money', ó dùn [ó dû] 'it is tasty', ó kéré jù [ó kéré jû] 'it is too small'. Note that there is an asymmetry with respect to a tone's potential to create a contour tone between high and low tones on one hand and mid tones on the other. This asymmetry is also seen in other areas of Yoruba tonal phonology. For example, when a mid-toned vowel is deleted, both vowel and tone disappear. But when a high-toned vowel or a low-toned vowel is deleted, the high or low tone will generally continue to have an effect on adjacent tones (Bamgboṣe 1966, pp. 9–10). For example, in connected speech, the i of ìgbá 'garden egg' is deleted in a phrase such as the following: fẹ́ ìgbá [fɛ́ ìgbǎ] → fẹ́ gbá [fɛ́ gbǎ] 'want a garden egg'. In the phrase that has not undergone vowel deletion, the final high of ìgbá is realised as a rising tone because of the immediately preceding low tone; in the phrase where vowel deletion has taken place, one also observes a rising tone in spite of the apparent deletion of the low-toned vowel. Deletion of a low-toned vowel before a mid-toned vowel can actually derive a level tone that is phonetically distinct from the three basic level tones — namely, a lowered-mid tone (indicated by a vertical accent in the following example): fẹ́ ìwo → fẹ́ wò 'want a horn'. Orthographically, the deletion of a low-toned vowel is often indicated by including a dot where the low-toned vowel had been. A tonal rise, a lowered-mid tone etc. can then be straightforwardly inferred. For example, the two cases just discussed could be represented: fẹ́.gbá and fẹ́.wo. In cases such as these where it is a high-toned vowel that undergoes deletion, one observes that a vowel adjacent to the deleted vowel acquires a high-tone: rí aṣọ → r áṣọ 'see cloth'. As a final general point about tone, it should be noted that there is a distributional restriction for tone that is comparable to one of the restrictions on vowel types. Just as vowel-initial nouns cannot begin with u, so are vowel-initial nouns blocked from beginning with a high tone. Apart from this restriction, however, the co-occurrence of tones is basically free in Yoruba nouns.

3   Morphology

Word formation processes in Yoruba are for the most part derivational and not inflectional. Although certain pronominal forms do vary as a function of tense/aspect (to be discussed below), both nouns and verbs are essentially invariant — for example, nouns are neither declined for case nor inflected for number and verbs are not conjugated for person, number or gender. Word formation in Yoruba involves two basic processes: prefixation and reduplication. In the following discussion, I will begin by looking at these processes and then go on to examine certain morphological properties of pronominal forms and ideophones.

There are several ways of deriving nominal forms from verbs (for some discussion, see Rowlands (1969) pp. 182–93). These processes fall basically into two classes: an 'abstract' class and an 'agentive' class. Prefixes of the 'agentive' class include *a-*, *ò-* and *olù-*. The prefix *a-* productively attaches to verb phrases — that is, a verb plus complements. Consider the following examples: *apànià* 'killer, murderer' (*pa* 'kill', *ènià* 'people'); *apẹja* 'fisherman' (*pa* 'kill', *ẹja* 'fish'), *akọ̀wé* 'clerk' (*kọ* 'write', *ìwé* 'paper, book'), *akọrin* 'one who sings songs' (*kọ* 'sing', *orin* 'song'), *aṣẹgità* 'firewood seller' (*ṣẹ́* 'snap off ', *igi* 'wood', *tà* 'sell'), *abénilórí* 'executioner' (*bẹ́* 'cut off ', *ẹni* 'person', *ní* '(syntactic marker — see discussion in section 4)', *orí* 'head'), *abáolónjẹkú* 'glutton' (*bá* 'accompany', *olónjẹ* 'eater', *kú* 'die'). In all the above examples, one observes a verb with one or two objects, in certain cases with an additional verbal complement. Although the above cases all illustrate derived nouns that denote a *person* who performs the relevant action, nouns derived with *a-* can also indicate the *object* that performs the action: *abẹ* 'razor, penknife' (*bẹ* 'cut, slit'), *ata* 'that which stings' (*ta* 'sting'), *aṣẹ́* 'strainer' (*ṣẹ́* 'strain'), *abọ́máàfọ́* 'enamelled ware' (*bọ́* 'fall', *máà* 'not', *fọ́* 'break'). The last example (*abọ́máàfọ́*) illustrates another property of these derived nouns. In addition to prefixing *a-* to a single phrase, two phrases can be involved in a construction of the form *a+*[X]+*máà+*[Y] with the interpretation 'one who Xes but does not Y' (note that *máà* is the particle used syntactically to negate an imperative). The following are additional examples of this process: *alọmáàdágbére* 'one who leaves without saying goodbye' (*lọ* 'go', *dá gbére* 'bid goodbye'), *alápámáàṣiṣẹ́* 'lazybones (person who has arms but does not work)' (*ní* 'have', *apá* 'arm', *ṣiṣẹ́* 'work'), *alágbáramáàmèrò* 'person who is strong but indecisive' (*ní* 'have', *agbára* 'force, power', *mèrò* 'be sensible').

The prefix *ò-* is comparable to *a-* except that it is less productive. Phonologically, *ò-* harmonises with the base to which it attaches producing the two variants *ò-/ọ̀-* (although this harmony does not appear to be fully productive); in addition, this prefix induces certain tonal changes in the verb. Consider the following examples: *òṣìṣẹ́* 'workman, worker' (*ṣe* 'do', *iṣẹ́* 'work'), *ọ̀mọ̀wé* 'educated person' (*mọ̀* 'know', *ìwé* 'book'), *òjíṣẹ́* 'messenger', (*jẹ́* 'answer', *iṣẹ́* 'message'), *ọ̀mùtí* 'drunkard' (*mu* 'drink', *ọtí* 'spirits'). This prefix appears to be involved in the very large class of nouns derived from a verb phrase headed by the verb *ní* 'have, possess': *oníbàtà* 'shoe-maker' (*bàtà* 'shoes'), *onímọ̀tò* 'car-owner' (*mọ́tò* 'car'), *oníbọ̀tí* 'malt-seller, owner of malt' (*bọ̀tí* 'malt'). These derived nouns have the meanings 'owner of X' or 'person who deals with X' (such as a seller of X or a person who makes X); they can also mean 'thing that has X' (for example, *aṣọ ọlọ́nà* 'cloth which has decorations on it' (*aṣọ* 'cloth', *ọnà* 'decoration'), *ọbẹ̀ ẹlẹ́ran* 'stew with meat in it' (*ọbẹ̀* 'stew', *ẹran* 'meat')). The last two examples illustrate the application of some completely regular phonological processes that affect these words. Recall from the previous section that [n] is actually an allophone of /l/. When the noun following /lí/ ([ní]) begins with a vowel, the vowel of /lí/ deletes: /o+lí+ẹrā/ → *o+l+ẹ́rā*. Since there is no longer a nasalised vowel to trigger nasalisation of /l/, /l/ surfaces in its oral form. In addition, these forms show evidence of a morphophonemic rule of vowel assimilation: the [o] of the agentive prefix completely assimilates to the following vowel when the nasality of *ní* is lost: *o+l+ẹ́rā* → *ẹ+l+ẹ́rā*. The following are some additional examples of these processes: *o+ní+aṣọ* → *aláṣọ* 'cloth-seller' (*aṣọ* 'cloth'), *o+ní+epo* → *elépo* 'oil-seller' (*epo* 'oil'). Note that if the object of *ní* begins with *i*, there is no loss of nasality and no assimilation: *o+ní+igi* → *onígi* 'wood-seller' (*igi* 'wood').

Some examples of the third agentive prefix mentioned above are as follows: *olùkọ́* 'teacher' (*kọ́* 'teach'), *olùfẹ́* 'loved one; lover' (*fẹ́* 'love'), *olùṣọ́* 'guardian' (*ṣọ́* 'watch'), *olùkórè* 'harvester' (*kórè* 'gather in the harvest').

With respect to the prefixes that form abstract nouns from verb phrases, there are basically two: *ì-* and *à-*. Both prefixes may attach to a simple verbal base: *ìmọ̀* 'knowledge' (*mọ̀* 'know'), *àlọ* 'going' (*lọ* 'go'). In such cases, however, the *à-* derivative will tend to be used in wishes and prayers (Rowlands 1969, p. 185), while the *ì-* derivative has a more neutral usage. When the base involves serial verb sequences (see section 4), the tendency is to use *à-*: *àṣejù* 'doing to excess' (*ṣe* 'do', *jù* 'exceed'), *àṣetán* 'doing to completion' (*ṣe* 'do', *tán* 'finish'), *àṣetì* 'attempting to do and failing' (*ṣe* 'do', *tì* 'fail'). Words derived with the prefix *à-* can also have a locative interpretation (for example, *àká* 'granary' (*ká* 'reap')) or a resultative interpretation (for example, *àfimọ́* 'appendix to a book' (*fimọ́* 'add thing to another thing')). Although the first example with the prefix *ì-* was with a simple verb stem, it is much more common to find *ì-* with a verb plus complements: *ìbínú* 'anger' (*bí* 'annoy', *inú* 'stomach'), *ìnáwó* 'expenditure of money' (*ná* 'spend', *owó* 'money'), *ìlọsíwájú* 'progress' (*lọ* 'go', *sí* 'to', *iwájú* 'front'), *ìfẹsẹ̀kọlẹ̀* 'walking away slowly and dejectedly' (*fi* 'put', *ẹsẹ̀* 'foot', *kọ* 'turn towards', *ilẹ̀* 'ground'). In many cases, *ì-* and *à-* can be freely substituted for each other (for example, *ìsọyé*, *àsọyé* 'explanation'). Finally, *ì-* (like *à-*) can have non-abstract interpretations in certain cases: *ìdì* 'bundle' (*dì* 'tie'), *ìránṣẹ́* 'messenger, servant' (*rán* 'send', *iṣẹ́* 'message'). One morphological difference between *ì-* and *à-* lies in their ability to appear in combination with certain other affixes. This question will be returned to below.

The two prefixes *àti-* and *àì-* are used in 'infinitival' or 'gerundive' forms; *àti-* is used in affirmative forms while *àì-* is used in negative forms: *àtilọ* 'act of going, departure' (*lọ* 'go'), *àti pa á* 'to kill him' (*pa á* 'kill him'), *àti raṣọ yẹn* 'to buy that dress' (*rà* 'buy', *aṣọ* 'dress', *yẹn* 'that'), *àtisùn* 'sleeping' (*sùn* 'sleep'); *àìdára* 'not being good' (*dára* 'be good'), *àìlówótó* 'not having enough money' (*ní* 'have', *owó* 'money', *tó* 'be enough'), *àìnínkan púpọ̀* 'not having many things' (*ní* 'have', *nkan* 'thing', *púpọ̀* 'many'), *àìmọ̀* 'ignorance' (*mọ̀* 'know').

It is possible to combine the prefixes *à-* and *àì-* as follows: *à+[X]+àì+[Y]*. Such a word will have the interpretation 'to X without Ying', 'thing that Xes but does not Y', 'thing that is Xed but not Yed', etc. (note that the phonological form of *àì* is modified by certain regular morphophonemic rules): *àjẹìjẹtán* 'eating without finishing' (*à+jẹ+àì+jẹ+tán*: *jẹ* 'eat', *tán* 'finish'), *àbùìbùtán* 'inexhaustibility, endlessness' (*à+bù+àì+bù+tán*: *bù* 'dip out', *tán* 'finish'), *àwíìgbọ́* 'disobedience' (*à+wí+àì+gbọ́*: *wí* 'speak', *gbọ́* 'listen').

Amongst the more interesting word formation processes of Yoruba are a variety of types of reduplication — both partial reduplication and complete reduplication. In some cases, the process involves the addition of affixal material while in other cases reduplication is all that is involved. Complete reduplication can be used to express intensification: *púpọ̀* 'much', *púpọ̀púpọ̀* 'very much'; *díẹ̀* 'little', *díẹ̀díẹ̀* 'very little'. Complete reduplication can also be used with numerals to mean 'a group of X' (where X is a number) or 'all X'. Cardinal numerals in Yoruba have two forms, a morphologically simple form used for counting and a prefixed form used as a noun or adjective. To obtain the 'group' interpretation, the prefix (*má*) is added prior to reduplication: *méjìméjì* 'two by two' (*èjì* 'two'), *mẹ́tàmẹ́tà* 'three by three' (*ẹ̀ta* 'three'), *mẹ́rìndínlógúnmẹ́rìndínlógún* 'sixteen by sixteen' (*ẹẹ́rìndínlógún* 'sixteen'). To obtain the universally quantified form, reduplication takes place prior to prefixation of *má*: *méjèèjì* 'both' (*má+èjì+èjì*: *èjì* 'two'), *mẹ́tẹẹ̀ta* 'all three' (*má+ẹ̀ta+ẹ̀ta*: *ẹ̀ta* 'three'), *mẹ́rẹẹ̀rìndínlógún* 'all sixteen' (*má+ẹ̀rin+ẹ̀rin+dín+ní+ogún*: *ẹẹ́rìndínlógún* 'sixteen'). Related to such cases are reduplications involving nouns of time: *ọdọọdún* 'every year' (*ọdun+ọdún*: *ọdún* 'year'), *oṣooṣù* 'every month' (*oṣu+oṣù*: *oṣù* 'month'), *ọ̀sọ̀ọ̀sẹ̀* 'every week' (*ọsẹ+ọ̀sẹ̀*: *ọ̀sẹ̀* 'week').

In addition to such cases, complete reduplication may involve the addition of a formative in between two reduplicated nouns. One common such process involves the formative *kí*: *[X]+kí+[X]*. The resulting nouns mean 'any kind of X' and often have a derogatory connotation. Consider the following examples: *ẹnikẹ́ni* 'any person' (*ẹni+kí+ẹni*: *ẹni* 'person'), *ewékéwé* 'any leaf at all; useless leaves' (*ewé*+*kí*+*ewé*: *ewé* 'leaf '), *ijókíjó* 'whatever dancing; indecent dancing' (*ijó*+*kí*+*ijó*: *ijó* 'dancing'). This type of reduplication with *kí* is extremely productive with abstract nouns derived with the prefix *ì*-: *ìnákúnă* 'extravagance' (*ì*+*ná*+*kí*+*ì*+*ná*: *ná* 'spend') (note that the change of [i] to [u] in these forms is fairly regular), *ìsọkúsọ* 'nonsense' (*ì*+*sọ*+*kí*+*ì*+*sọ*: *sọ* 'speak').

Apart from such examples of complete reduplication, Yoruba has a productive process of partial reduplication that is used to derive a nominal form from a verb. For this process, the initial consonant of a verb is copied and this copied consonant is followed by a high-toned [í]: *lílọ* 'going' (*lọ* 'go'), *sísọ* 'speaking' (*sọ* 'speak'), *rírí* 'seeing' (*rí* 'see').

It is also possible in Yoruba to derive agentive nominals by reduplicating a sequence of a verb and its object: *jagunjagun* 'warrior' (*jà* 'fight', *ogun* 'war'), *kólékólé* 'burglar' (*kó* 'steal', *ilé* 'house'), *bẹ́ríbẹ́rí* 'executioner' (*bẹ́* 'cut off', *orí* 'head'), *jẹdíjẹdí* 'haemorrhoids' (*jẹ* 'consume', *ìdí* 'bottom').

Before leaving the topic of reduplication, it is appropriate to discuss at least briefly the phenomenon of ideophones. Ideophones are notoriously difficult to define — both in general and with respect to a single language. What is clear, however, is that there is a class of words in Yoruba which have rather distinctive and interesting properties. Reduplication is one of these properties — although as has already been seen above, reduplication is not restricted to ideophones. Consider the following examples: *kẹsẹkẹsẹ* 'of surrounding being dead quiet', *rokírokí* 'of being red', *ròdòrodo* 'of being bright', *rùbùtùrubutu* 'of round object', *kòròbòtòkòròbọtọ* 'of being fat', *pòtòpọ́tọ̀* 'soft mud', *dòdoòdò* 'of coming up brightly', *ramúramù* 'of a loud noise (e.g. lion's)', *gbàlágbàlá* 'of wobbling movement (e.g. of a fish)', *jálajàlajàlàjalà* 'of shabby appearance', *gógórogògòrogògòrògogorò* 'of several things being tall', *súúsùùsúú* 'of perching or assembling in an area'. The above ideophones involve two, three or four repetitions of a sequence. The tonal possibilities for ideophones correlate in many instances with semantic information — for example, the LHLH pattern of *gbàlágbàlá* seen above occurs in forms indicating 'lack of smoothness of activity'. Changes in the tonal pattern of an ideophone can have marked semantic consequences. For example, in the following set of ideophones, a low tone correlates with largeness or heaviness, a high tone correlates with smallness or lightness and a mid tone indicates an average value: *ròrgòdò* 'of a big round object', *rogodo* 'of an average round object', *rógódó* 'of a small round object'. Moreover, the quality of the vowel in such words turns out to be semantically significant in such ideophones as well. While *o* indicates roundness, replacement of *o* by *u* serves to indicate weight (with the same degree distinction possibilities correlated with tone): *rùgùdù* 'large (heavier) object', *rugudu* 'medium (heavy) object', *rúgúdú* 'small (slightly heavy) object'. In some cases, there is no obvious source for an ideophone (or at least, no semantically related source). In other cases, an ideophone can be related both semantically and phonologically to a source morpheme. For example, *kéékèèkéé* 'in small bits' can be seen to derive from *kéré* 'small' with the application of reduplication, *r*-deletion and certain tonal changes. In this respect, it should be noted that rules applying to ideophones can typically be observed to apply elsewhere in the language — to non-ideophones. For example, *r*-deletion applies in the derivation of many ideophones but also applies in many other cases — such as, in deriving the variant *Yoòbá* for *Yorùbá* (vowel assimilation in this example is triggered by *r*-deletion).

Although it was noted at the beginning of this section that Yoruba word-formation processes tend to be derivational, this section will conclude with a short discussion of certain inflectional processes observed in the pronominal system. Yoruba has two classes of pronouns (to be discussed further in section 4). While one class of pronouns is invariant (just like regular nouns), the second class of pronouns varies as a function of grammatical relation and tense/aspect/polarity. For illustration, examples will be given of first and third person singular pronominal forms: subject (for appropriate tense/aspect/polarity): *mo bínú* 'I was angry' (*mo* 'I'), *ó mọ Èkó* 'he/she knows Lagos' (*ó* 'he/she'); subject (before the negative marker *kò*): *n kò mọ* 'I don't know' [ŋ (k)ò mɔ̀] (*n* 'I') or *mi kò mọ* [mi (k)ò mɔ̀] (*mi* 'I'), *kò mọ* 'he/she doesn't know' (Ø 'he/she'); subject (before the future marker *á*): *mà á lọ* 'I will go' (*mà* 'I'), *á á lọ* 'he/she will go' (*á* 'he/she'); object: *ó rí mi* 'he/she saw me' (*mi* 'me'), *mo rí i* 'I saw her/him/it' (*i* 'her/him/it'), *jẹ ẹ́* 'eat it' (*ẹ́* 'it'), *fà á* 'pull it' (*á* 'it'). The last three examples illustrate the fact that the form of the third person singular pronoun object is dependent on the verb that it follows: whatever the quality of the vowel of the verb, the pronoun will have the same quality. Moreover, the tone of object pronouns depends on the tone of the verb: if the verb is mid or low, then the pronoun is high; if the verb is high, then the pronoun is mid. The above examples are not exhaustive — for example, additional forms are required in possessive noun phrases. But they are representative of the morphological changes in both segmental make-up and tone that characterise the various syntactically determined pronominal forms.

4   Syntax

In this section, three basic areas of Yoruba syntax will be discussed: word order properties, clitic pronominals and serial verbs. Consider first properties of word order. Given the paucity of inflectional morphology — in particular, the absence of morphological case marking — it is relatively unsurprising that Yoruba is highly configurational. In the following discussion, word order properties of major constituents will be described and illustrated.

With respect to basic word order, Yoruba is SVO (subject–verb–object):

bàbá   ra   bàtà
father buy shoes
'Father bought shoes.'

If a verb takes more than one object, then both objects follow the verb. The second object in such a case is preceded by a semantically empty preposition *ní*:

Adé fún Tolú ní   owó
Ade give Tolu prep. money
'Ade gave Tolu money.'

In a comparable fashion, when a verb takes a verbal complement, such a complement follows the verb:

Táíwò rò   pé   ó   sanra
Taiwo think that he/she fat
'Taiwo thought that he/she was fat.'

Adverbials generally follow the verb (as in the first example below), but there is a small class of adverbials that precede the verb (as in the second example):

kò   sanra rárá
neg. fat   at all
'He/she is not fat at all.'

ó   sèsè lo
he/she just go
'He/she has just gone.'

Tense and aspect in Yoruba are expressed by particles that appear between the subject and the verb. For example, the following sentences illustrate the placement of the perfective aspect marker *ti* and the future tense marker *á*:

ó   ti   kú
he/she perf. die
'He/she is/was dead.'

òré   mi á   lo
friend my fut. go
'My friend will go.'

To form a yes-no question, a particle can be added at the beginning of the sentence (*sé*, *njé*) or at the end of the sentence (*bí*):

şé   Òjó   lọ?
ǹjẹ́   Òjó   lọ?
Òjó   lọ   bí?
'Did Ojo go?' (lọ 'go')

Turning our attention to the noun phrase, it can be seen that the head of the phrase appears in initial position. Hence, adjectives occur post-nominally:

ajá funfun
dog white
'white dog'

Possessive noun phrases appear after the noun possessed:

fìlà Àkàndé
cap   Akande
'Akande's cap'

Determiners and demonstratives appear after the head noun:

ọmọ náà
child the
'that child' (definite determiner)

Similarly, a relative clause is placed post-nominally:

ẹni   tí ó   wá
person rel. he/she come
'the person who came'

As far as numerals are concerned, the appropriate word order depends on the individual case. For examples below 'one hundred and ninety', numerals that are *not* multiples of ten are placed after the noun:

ajá méjì
dog two
'two dogs'

Numerals that are multiples of ten are placed *before* the noun (starting from 'twenty'):

ogún ajá
twenty dog
'twenty dogs'

But in spite of the prenominal appearance of a numeral like 'twenty', derivatives of such a numeral appear post-nominally:

ajá méjìlélógún
dog twenty-two
'twenty-two dogs' (two over twenty)

As can be seen from the above examples, noun phrases and verb phrases are head-initial. Prepositional phrases are also head-initial (as is obvious from the terminology):

ní ọjà
at market
'at the market'

Hence in general, the head of a phrase in Yoruba comes at the beginning. While a short discussion such as this cannot even attempt to cover all important properties of word order in Yoruba, it would nevertheless be remiss to wind up without at least mentioning the extremely common 'focus' construction. This construction is derived by fronting a constituent which is marked by the morpheme *ni*. The fronted constituent can be an argument of the verb (for example, subject or object); it can be an adjunct (for example, a locative or temporal adjunct); the fronted constituent can even be the verb itself ('predicate cleft'):

èmi ni   Tolú rí
me foc. Tolu see
'It's me that Tolu saw.' (object)

ní ilé   ni   ó ti   bèrè
at house foc. it perf. start
'It was in the house that it started.' (adjunct)

rírà   ni   bàbá   ra   bàtà
buying foc. father buy shoes
'Father BOUGHT shoes.'

As can be seen in the last example, when the emphasised element is the verb, a nominalised form of the verb appears in focus position and the verb itself continues to appear in its appropriate place inside the clause. In a similar way, if the subject is focused, a pronominal form must replace the fronted noun phrase in subject position:

èmi ni   ó   lọ
me foc. 3 sg. go
'It's I that went'

Note that in such constructions, the 'third person singular' pronoun can be used without actually implying any qualities of person or number; in such a sentence, the pronoun serves simply to mark the subject position that the fronted constituent came from. It is possible to focus the possessor of a noun phrase. In such a case (as with subjects), a pronominal form will replace the fronted noun phrase; and as with subjects, the 'third person singular' morphological form may be used with a semantically neutral interpretation in such cases:

bàbá ni ilé   rè wó
father foc. house his collapse
'It was father whose house collapsed.'

As a final point about the focus construction, content questions are formed by placing the appropriate question word in focus position. The properties of such sentences are comparable to those of the non-interrogative focus sentences seen above. Two examples are given below:

ta   ni Tolú rí   òré   rè
who foc. Tolu see friend his/her
'Whose friend did Tolu see?'

ní ibo   ni ó   lo
at where foc. he/she go
'Where has he/she gone?'

At several points in the above discussion, reference has been made to pronominal forms. For example, in the discussion of morphology, it was seen that pronominal forms vary as a function of their syntactic environment and it was noted above that pronominal forms fill in certain positions in focus constructions. As mentioned in the morphology section, however, there are two classes of pronouns in Yoruba — and both properties just mentioned hold of the 'weak' class. In fact, the 'weak' and 'strong' classes turn out to be distinguished on phonological, morphological and syntactic grounds. The strong pronouns behave simply like a true noun phrase. Phonologically, they fit the canonical pattern for Yoruba nouns; morphologically, they are invariant. Syntactically, their distribution parallels that of non-pronominal noun phrases. The weak pronouns, on the other hand, are systematically distinguished from non-pronominal noun phrases. Phonologically, weak pronouns are the only nominal forms that can be of a single syllable. They are also the only forms whose tonal specifications can vary depending on the context — as seen above with weak object pronouns. It has already been shown that the morphological form of weak pronouns varies — unlike regular nominals. Syntactically, the distribution of weak pronouns is quite restricted. For example, weak pronouns cannot be conjoined or modified (although strong pronouns and regular nouns can be). Weak pronouns occur only in a restricted set of syntactic positions; for example, they cannot appear in focus position and they cannot appear with interrogative particles such as dà 'where?' and ńkó 'what about?' (while both strong pronouns and non-pronominal noun phrases can). Such properties suggest that the strong pronouns are indeed pronominal *nouns* — and therefore show the distribution of nouns. Weak pronouns, on the other hand, can be analysed as clitics — with their morphological and phonological shape dependent on the constituent to which they are attached. By analysing them as clitics, their restricted syntactic distribution can be explained.

Apart from the properties just mentioned, there is a particularly interesting set of differences between the two pronominal sets. Consider the following sentences:

Dàda rò   pé ó   sanra
Dada think that he fat
'Dada thought that he (someone else) was fat.' (weak pronoun)

Dàda rò   pé òun sanra
Dada think that he fat
'Dada thought that he himself was fat.' (strong pronoun)

In the sentence with the weak pronoun, the pronoun must refer to someone other than Dada; in the sentence with the strong pronoun, the pronoun must refer to Dada. This difference in interpretation involves reference to the syntactic configuration; it is not due simply to lexical properties of the strong and weak pronouns. Compare, for example, the following sentence including a strong pronoun with the sentence above that also had a strong pronoun:

Tolú sọ pé òun   ni ó   wá
Tolu say that he/she foc. he/she come
'Tolu said that it was he/she who came.'

In this sentence, the pronoun *òun* (a strong pronoun) may either refer to Tolu or to someone else. That is, the pronoun *òun* in the sentence with an embedded focus construction may or may not refer to the preceding subject. But the pronoun *òun* in the sentence with a simple (non-focus) embedded clause must refer to the preceding subject. Comparable syntactic considerations also determine whether a weak pronoun is interpreted as coreferential to a preceding subject. Compare the above example with a weak pronoun to the following sentence:

Dúpé ń   ta aṣọ bí ó ṣe ń   ta ọsàn
Dupe prog. sell cloth as she do prog. sell orange
'Dupe sells cloth the way she sells oranges.'

In this sentence, unlike the previous one, the weak pronoun not only can be interpreted as referring to the preceding subject, but it is normally interpreted in that way. The difference in interpretation is again due to syntactic differences: the weak pronoun in the earlier sentence is contained in a clausal complement to the verb in the main clause; the weak pronoun in the later sentence is contained in a manner adjunct. The correct interpretation of a pronoun in Yoruba therefore depends on two basic factors: (1) whether the pronoun belongs to the strong class or the weak class; and (2) the nature of the syntactic configuration within which the pronoun appears.

Serial verb constructions are the final topic to be discussed in this section. In Yoruba, as in many Kwa languages, one finds sentences in which strings of verb phrases appear consecutively without any intervening conjunction or subordinator. Such sentences are extremely common and exhibit a number of interesting properties. Consider the following examples:

ó   gbé e wá
he/she carry it come
'He/she brought it.'

wón   gbé e lọ
they carry it go
'They took it away.'

In this type of example, the second verb indicates the direction in which the first action took place. In such a case, the subject of the second verb is also the subject of the first verb. It is also possible, however, for the subject of the second verb to be the object of the first verb:

ó   tì   mí ṣubú
he/she push me fall
'He/she pushed me and I fell.'

In such a sentence, it is the object of *tì* 'push' who falls — and not the subject. Two transitive verbs can be combined in a serial verb construction. In some such examples, the serial verb sequence will have two object noun phrases:

ó   pọn omi kún kete
he/she draw water fill pot
'He/she drew water and filled the pot.'

In many examples, however, a single object appears in between the two transitive verbs — and is interpreted as the object of both verbs:

ó   ra   ẹran jẹ
he/she buy meat eat
'He/she bought meat and ate it.'

ó   ra   màlúù tà
he/she buy cow   sell
'He/she bought a cow in order to sell.'

In many examples syntactically comparable to the last two, the meaning of the pair of verbs ranges from being idiomatic but related to the individual verbs' meanings to being completely opaque:

ó   gba   ọ̀rọ̀   náà gbọ́
he/she accept matter the hear
'He/she believed the matter.' (*gbà … gbọ́* 'believe')

ó   ba   kẹ̀kẹ́ mi jẹ́
he/she   bicycle my
'He/she spoiled my bicycle.' (*bà … jẹ́* 'spoil')

Many constructions that might be thought to involve categories other than verbs can be shown to involve serial verb sequences. For example, consider the word *fún* in the following sentence:

ó   tà   á fún mi
he/she sell   it 'to' me
'He/she sold it to me.'

One might think that *fún* in such a sentence is a preposition. In fact, however, the properties of this word are verbal and not prepositional. For example, it can take object clitics such as *mi*; prepositions do not take pronominal clitics. The word *fún* can be nominalised by the process of partial reduplication: *fífún* (just like a verb). In addition, *fún* appears as a main verb meaning 'give':

ó   fún   mi ní   owó
he/she give   me prep. money
'He/she gave me some money.'

Recall that the *ní* that appears in such a sentence is a semantically empty preposition marking a second object to a verb.

The above discussion of serial verbs does not even vaguely attempt to be exhaustive. Serial verb constructions are used in many ways other than those described here — and in many cases the syntactic properties are somewhat different. Without a doubt, what are being called 'serial verb constructions' actually refer to several distinguishable syntactic types. What is probably of most interest is that various syntactic constructions use morphologically indistinguishable verbs and use them in syntactic phrases that themselves do not involve overt markers to distinguish construction types.

Bibliography

Bamgboṣe (1966) is the standard reference grammar. The grammatical notes in Rowlands (1969) are very useful; the volume includes translation exercises. Two pedagogical grammars are Bamgboṣe (1967) and Awobuluyi (1978). For the development of Yoruba orthography, see Ajayi (1960). Hair (1967) is an interesting discussion of early work on Yoruba, including a bibliography up to 1890.

References

Ajayi, J.F.A. 1960. 'How Yoruba was Reduced to Writing', *Odu: A Journal of Yoruba, Edo and Related Studies* (Ministry of Education, Ibadan) pp. 49–58

Awobuluyi, O. 1978. *Essentials of Yoruba Grammar* (Oxford University Press Nigeria, Ibadan)

Bamgboṣe, A. 1966. *A Grammar of Yoruba* (Cambridge University Press, Cambridge)

—— 1967. *A Short Yoruba Grammar* (Heinemann Educational Books (Nigeria), Ibadan)

Hair, P.E.H. 1967. *The Early Study of Nigerian Languages: Essays and Bibliographies* (Cambridge University Press, Cambridge)

Rowlands, E.C. 1969. *Teach Yourself Yoruba* (English Universities Press, London)

50   *Swahili and the Bantu Languages*

Benji Wald

1   Historical and Social Background

The Bantu languages dominate the southern half of the African land mass and were spoken as first languages by an estimated 157 million speakers in the early 1980s, nearly a third of Africa's total population. In their geographical extent, they come into contact with representatives of all the other major African language families: Cushitic (of Afroasiatic superstock) and Nilo-Saharan languages in the north-east, Khoisan in the south (and minimally in the north-east due to the retention of the Khoisan language Sandawe in northeastern Tanzania, surrounded by Bantu languages) and its closest relatives among the Niger-Congo languages in the north-west.

The Bantu languages are thought to have originally spread from the West African transitional area of eastern Nigeria and Cameroon, which now marks the westernmost expansion of Bantu in Africa. From this area Bantu languages were carried eastward and southward in several waves of migration, responsible for the oldest dialect divisions among the languages, and starting no later than the early centuries of the first millennium AD. It was early recognised, for example, that a major dialect division is into West and East Bantu, symptomatised by the distinction between reflexes of the lexical item 'two': Proto-West *bàdé* and Proto-East *bèdé*. West Bantu shows more syntactic diversity than East Bantu, particularly in the north-west, where the morphological richness of the majority of Bantu languages begins to give way to the more isolating syntactic tendencies of the neighbouring Benue-Congo and Kwa languages of Nigeria, e.g. the passive verbal suffix *-o-* is totally replaced by the impersonal construction, i.e. 'they saw me' replaces 'I was seen'.

The vast majority of the speakers of Bantu languages are directly involved in agricultural production. In this they contrast traditionally with the hunters and herders they came into contact with from other language families in much of their present areas, frequently effecting language shift on earlier populations, whether or not the latter maintained their modes of production. More recently, the agricultural majority also contrasts with the growing number of city dwellers involved in distribution and services, as the rapid urbanisation of Bantu Africa continues.

991

Map 50.1: The Bantu-speaking Area

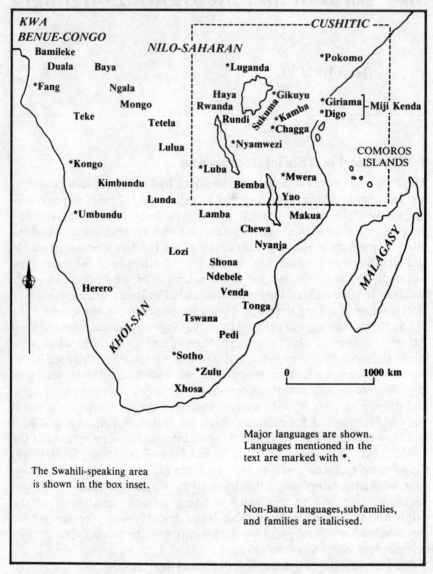

KWA
BENUE-CONGO
Bamileke
Duala   Baya
*Fang   Ngala
Teke   Mongo
Tetela
Lulua
*Kongo
Kimbundu
Lunda
*Umbundu

NILO-SAHARAN

*Luganda

Haya   *Gikuyu
Rwanda
Rundi   Sukuma *Kamba
*Chagga
*Nyamwezi
*Luba
Bemba   *Mwera
Yao
Lamba   Makua
Chewa
Nyanja
Lozi
Shona
Ndebele
Herero   Venda
Tonga
Tswana
Pedi
*Sotho
*Zulu
Xhosa

CUSHITIC

*Pokomo

*Giriama —Miji Kenda
*Digo

COMOROS
ISLANDS

MALAGASY

KHOI-SAN

0   1000 km

Major languages are shown.
Languages mentioned in the
text are marked with *.

The Swahili-speaking area
is shown in the box inset.

Non-Bantu languages, subfamilies,
and families are italicised.

The distinctive typological nature of the Bantu languages and their close genetic relationship were recognised early by scholars. The label Bantu was established by Bleek in 1862 as the reconstructed word for 'people'; the modern Proto-Bantu reconstruction is *ba-ntò*, plural of *mo-ntò* 'person'. Bantu speakers themselves tend to recognise the essential unity of their own and neighbouring Bantu languages with which they are familiar.

Map 50.2: The Swahili-speaking Area

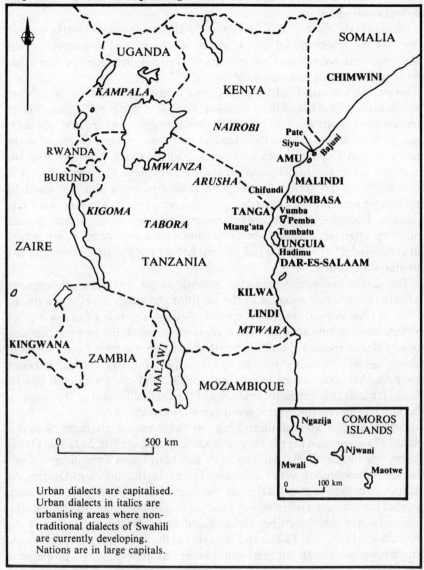

SOMALIA

UGANDA

KENYA

CHIMWINI

KAMPALA

NAIROBI

Pate
Siyu
Bajuni

RWANDA

MWANZA

AMU

BURUNDI

ARUSHA

MALINDI

Chifundi

MOMBASA

KIGOMA

TANGA

Vumba

TABORA

Mtang'ata

Pemba

Tumbatu

ZAIRE

TANZANIA

UNGUIA
Hadimu

DAR-ES-SALAAM

KILWA

LINDI

MTWARA

KINGWANA

ZAMBIA

MALAWI

MOZAMBIQUE

0   500 km

Ngazija   COMOROS
              ISLANDS

Njwani

Mwali

Maotwe

0   100 km

Urban dialects are capitalised.
Urban dialects in italics are
urbanising areas where non-
traditional dialects of Swahili
are currently developing.
Nations are in large capitals.

Consequent to the high degree of structural unity among most Bantu languages, together with the wide area of contact among them, a great deal of mutual influence among Bantu languages in contact renders detailed subclassification according to the tree theory of genetic relations problematic. Usually, broad areas reflecting isogloss bundles clearly circumscribe certain dialect groups despite internal diversity. Between such clear groups transitional areas are often apparent giving the appearance of a dialect continuum.

Swahili is the most widely spoken of the Bantu languages, and is the only one to have international status, as one of the official languages of both Tanzania and Kenya and an important regional language in the urban centres of southern and eastern Zaire.

Swahili is a North-East Coastal Bantu language, extending northward into southern Somalia, where ChiMwini and the northern Bajuni dialects are spoken, southward to northern Mozambique, where the southern coastal dialects are more widely understood than spoken, eastward to the major Indian Ocean islands of Pemba, Zanzibar, the Comoros and the northern tip of the Madagascar subcontinent, where the urban dialect of Zanzibar City has spread amidst numerous distinctive and non-mutually intelligible rural dialects of earlier provenience, and, finally westward into Uganda, Rwanda, Burundi and eastern and southern Zaire, primarily as an auxiliary language, except in the Lubumbashi area of southern Zaire, where an urban dialect of Swahili usually called KiNgwana has arisen since the late nineteenth century.

The distinctive social status of Swahili as an international language reflects the strategic location of the traditional Swahili dialect area on the coast of East Africa, whence it spread, through the role of urban Swahili communities as intermediaries in commerce between the interior peoples, mostly Bantu speaking, and the South Asian communities from Arabia to China. Swahili is thought to have first arisen through contact between southern Arabian entrepreneurs and speakers of closely related coastal Bantu languages in the latter centuries of the first millennium. The origin of the label *Swahili* is the Arabic word *sawa:ḥil* 'coasts'.

Urban Swahili communities grew on the coast of southern Somalia, Kenya, Tanzania and the off-shore islands such as Zanzibar, as Indian Ocean commerce increased. Particularly in its southern forms Swahili spread as a lingua franca among other Bantu speakers in the interior. During the European colonial period of the late nineteenth and early twentieth century, Swahili became even more widely used, as communications and transportation networks developed on an increased scale. British control over the major Swahili areas of Kenya and Tanzania in the twentieth century allowed the development of an international standard Swahili language, propagated through the educational system and mass media, based on the cultivated southern urban dialect of Zanzibar City, a variety close to the basic form of Swahili already used as a lingua franca in precolonial times.

By the mid-1980s the estimated number of speakers of Swahili was nearly 50 million, the majority residing in Tanzania and Kenya. Most speakers use Swahili as an auxiliary language and have a different first language, also Bantu. First-language speakers traditionally tracing their ancestors back to other Swahili speakers number about two million. However, with the rapid urbanisation of East Africa and the prominence of Swahili as a lingua franca among working class East Africans, possibly another four million have come to adopt Swahili as either an only first language or simultaneously with their ethnic language, e.g. in Dar es Salaam, Mombasa, Nairobi, Lubumbashi and smaller urban centres.

Swahili, particularly the standard variety, is currently written in the Roman alphabet, using Latin vowel conventions and simplified English conventions for consonants. A modern Swahili literature has been developing since standardisation in the 1920s. Traditionally Swahili was written in a modified Arabic script, used to commit to paper verse meant to be recited. Manuscripts going back to the early eighteenth century reveal a written poetic tradition originating in the northern area and spreading southward. The literate poetic tradition is strong enough to occasion the reservation of space in standard Swahili newspapers for readers to submit poems.

Among speakers from traditional Swahili communities, Swahili is perceived as a cover term for a series of dialects among people who share a historic cultural as well as linguistic heritage. The dialects themselves are associated with local names reflecting local territoriality and ethnicity. There are three fairly distinct dialect groups:

(1) Northern: includes the sharply distinct urban dialect of ChiMwini in Brava, Somalia (not considered Swahili by its own community or other Swahili speakers); the Bajuni dialects of more southern Somalia and northern coastal Kenya; the urban island dialects of Lamu, Siyu, Pate and the transitional to Central dialect of urban Mombasa, Kenya.

(2) Central: most of these dialects are rural and spoken by relatively small communities on and off the coast of southern Kenya, northern Tanzania and the Comoros. Among these dialects are ChiFundi and Vumba of the Kenyan coast; Mtang'ata of the northern Tanzanian coast; Pemba, Tumbatu and Hadimu of the off-shore Tanzanian islands of Pemba and Zanzibar; Ngazija, Nzwani and Mwali of the Comoro Islands. These dialects are the most distinct and internally varied of the Swahili dialects.

(3) Southern: includes Zanzibar City and the urban districts of coastal Tanzania, e.g. Tanga, Dar es Salaam, Kilwa.

In some respects, the Northern and Southern dialects show more affinity to each other than they do to the Central dialects, particularly in their verbal systems, leading to the impression of a basic distinction between urban and rural dialects overlying the tripartite dialect division.

Among Bantu languages, all Swahili dialects are most striking in the adstratum of Arabic vocabulary in their lexicons while retaining the distinctive Bantu grammatical type, somewhat more extensive than the proportion of Anglo-French loanwords used in English in everyday conversation, e.g. the numerals 'six', 'seven', 'nine' and all higher multiples of 'ten' have replaced Bantu roots with Arabic loans. However, even more extreme than Swahili in its lexical borrowing is the northern Tanzanian language of Mbugu, retaining a Bantu grammar and inventory of grammatical morphemes, but almost totally non-Bantu in its lexicon (mostly of Cushitic origin). The lexical and grammatical effect of non-Bantu languages on Swahili will be discussed separately from its essential Bantu nature.

2 Phonology

The syllabic structure of the reconstructed Common Bantu word is relatively simple, consisting of CV(V) syllables only. However, the transparency of this structure is modified somewhat in various Bantu languages, where non-prominent syllables have been subject to altered glottalic and timing mechanisms which reduce their nuclei to short unvoiced vowels, or completely omit them in some cases. Apocope is most characteristic of certain North-West Bantu languages, where final consonants are found, e.g. in the Cameroonian language Fang.

Most recent reconstructions of the Common Bantu consonantal system display three manners and four points of articulation.

p	t	č	k
b	d	j	g
m	n	ny	ng'
(and		y	in some reconstructions)

Typologically the system is unusual in the absence of a distinctive phoneme /s/, but /s/ is not necessary for reconstructive purposes. This and many other phonemic fricatives exist in most Bantu languages, at least in part due to assimilatory changes caused by adjacent vowels or, through a large part of the area, the shift of the non-nasal palatals to sibilants. Southern Swahili is unusual in its area in retaining the original palatals. The Northern dialects are distinctive in the shift of the original voiceless palatal to a dental stop. Dentalisation of palatals and/or fricatives is characteristic of the Thagicu languages of interior Kenya and adjacent northern Tanzanian languages, e.g. Northern Pare, but not resulting in dental stops, cf. Thagicu [ðeka], Northern Pare [θeka], Northern Swahili [ṭeka] and Southern Swahili [čeka] for Common Bantu *čèka 'laugh'. Alveolar affricates are the reflexes of the palatal stops among the Miji Kenda languages of the north-east coast of Kenya, relatively closely related to the adjacent forms of Swahili, e.g. [tseka] 'laugh', but in Swahili these reflexes of the palatals are only found in the isolated Comoros dialects, possibly a relic of this stage of development among the Northern dialects.

In view of their historical evolution in various Bantu languages, the prenasalised series of Common Bantu should probably be treated phonologically as an independent series rather than as a cluster of nasal + stop.

mp nt nč nk
mb nd nj ng

The voiceless prenasalised series shows considerable instability across many Bantu languages, e.g. with loss of nasalisation among some languages, voicing assimilation to a voiced prenasalised series in others and loss of the stop in still others, cf. *ba-ntò* 'people' > [wa-t'u] in Swahili, [a-ndū] in the Thagicu languages of interior Kenya, [wa-nu] in Luguru (among other central coastal Tanzanian languages). The widespread areal feature of aspiration of the voiceless prenasalised consonants gave rise to a distinct opposition between an aspirated and unaspirated voiceless series upon the denasalisation of the prenasalised voiceless stops in Swahili, e.g. *kaa* 'charcoal' vs. *k'aa* 'crab' < *n-kádá*. This contrast is more typical of traditional Kenyan Swahili communities than of Southern Swahili, where the two series have merged fairly recently through the unconditioned aspiration of the original voiceless stop series.

The prenasalised voiced series is more stable and often shows behaviour parallel to or rotational with the original voiceless stops. Thus, the Common Bantu prenasalised palatal *nj* shifts parallel to *č* to dental in Northern Swahili, e.g. [nḏaa], cf. Southern Swahili [njaa] 'hunger'. Most interesting among the Sotho group of Southern Bantu is the rotational shift of consonants, so that the Common Bantu prenasalised voiced series becomes a voiceless aspirated stop series concomitant with a shift of the Common Bantu voiceless stops to fricatives (the Common Bantu apical series is post-alveolar, resulting in a flap-like liquid *r* or *l* in the lenition processes which have affected the voiced apicals), e.g. Sotho *xo-rutha* from Common Bantu *ko-túnda* 'teach', cf. Swahili *ku-fund-isha*, with a verbal suffix added.

There is a great deal of variety in the glottalic mechanisms by which the Common Bantu stop series is realised across the current Bantu languages. In Swahili, the set of voiced stops is 'implosive' (preglottalised), rather than truly voiced. This set of voiced stops is largely of secondary origin, sometimes due to back-formations based on prenasalised forms, where the stops are truly voiced and not preglottalised. Thus, *ki-ɓovu* 'rotten' (class 7 concord) is a back-formation from *m-bovu* 'rotten' (class 9 concord), cf. *mw-ovu* 'rotten' (class 1 concord) and *-oza* 'rot (v.)' with lenition and loss of initial *b*. Lenition of the voiced non-prenasalised series to corresponding fricatives or sonorants is common in most of the Bantu area, resulting in a series:

[β/w l/r z/ž ɣ/y/Ø]

Swahili shares with a number of North-East Bantu languages a tendency towards further lenition of glides so that Common Bantu *d is lost, primarily in the vicinity of back vowels. However, Swahili is more conservative than many of its North-East relatives in having lost w and y only before high vowels of like fronting, though also variably before a in vernacular speech. The Northern dialects have gone slightly further in loss of y (<*g) before an unlike high vowel as well, e.g. Northern hu-u 'this one (anim.)' < hu-yu, still the Southern and standard form. Glide deletion is most advanced in the Thagicu language Kamba, e.g. -o- 'buy' < *-gòd-, -a- 'divide' < *-gàb-.

In some areas, e.g. in the north-east, lenition also commonly affects some or all of the members of the voiceless series, cf. Giriama henza for earlier North-East Bantu *pɛnja 'love (v.)', cf. Swahili penda; Giriama moho for Common Bantu *mo-yɔ́tɔ 'fire', cf. Swahili moto. Lenition of *p is particularly widespread, while the velar *k is most resistant to lenition.

A widespread tendency toward word-level manner of articulation prosody is shown in some of the more striking consonantal changes affecting large areas in the north-east and extending toward the south-west, e.g. the following dissimilatory changes: Dahl's Law, originally noted in Nyamwezi of interior Tanzania, but of a much wider area, dissimilates the voicing of the first of two consecutive voiceless stops, e.g. -bita < -pita 'pass (v.)'; the Ganda Law, originally noted for LuGanda, dissimilates the first of two consecutive voiced prenasalised stops to the corresponding nasal, e.g. ng'ombe 'cow' (where ng' is the orthographic representation of [ŋ]) < ngɔ̀mbè. Finally, in much of West Bantu a morphophonemic process of nasal harmony is found, changing /d/ to /n/ in verbal suffixes following a root-final nasal, e.g. Luba (southern Zaire) -kwac-ile 'having caught' < *kóát-edɛ, but -dim-ine 'having sown' < *dèm-edɛ.

In contrast to the consonantal system, the vowel system of Common Bantu has remained relatively stable in the various languages. The reconstructed system is a symmetrical seven-vowel system with four degrees of height:

$$i \quad e \quad \varepsilon$$
$$a$$
$$u \quad o \quad \mathbf{\supset}$$

Prosodically, one vowel per word could be distinctively long or short and each vowel of a stem could have a high or low tone. The tonal distinctions are preserved in most of the area, with reduction of the full domain of the original tonal distinctions in large areas of the north-east and south-west. Total loss of lexical tone is unusual and confined to a few languages in the north-east, including all dialects of Swahili. The loss of distinctive vowel length is characteristic of most of the western Bantu area and a large area of the east, including Swahili along with most of the coast. Reduction of the original seven-vowel system to five vowels is characteristic of most Bantu languages, with the exception of an extreme northern band extending from the west coast almost to the east coast and the Sotho group of South-East Bantu. For the most part this five-vowel system is derived from the mergers of the highest two tiers of vowels. Unusual is the merger of Common Bantu *u into *e in part of the southwestern area, e.g. Umbundu o-mbela < *mbúdà 'rain', cf. Swahili mvua.

In most of the five-vowel area, the merger of the highest two tiers of vowels did not occur before influencing the manner of articulation of the preceding consonant, generally through fricativisation of the preceding consonant before the highest original vowels *i and *u. In the largest area of this shift, reduction of point of articulation contrasts accompanied the fricativisation process. In Swahili, all fricatives became labial before *u, e.g. -chofu 'tired' < *-čɔk-u, cf. -choka 'tire', fua 'forge (v.)' < *túda, -ongofu 'deceitful' < *-ɔngɔp-u, cf. -ongopa 'lie (v.)'. However, the situation is much more complicated before *i. Generally, the point of articulation of the resulting fricative is preserved, producing regular morphophonemic alternations such as the following:

-pika 'cook (v.)'   -pish-i 'cook (anim. n.)'
-fuata 'follow (v.)'   -fuas-i 'follower'
-lipa 'pay'   -lif-i 'payer'

In the most northern dialects of Amu and Bajuni, the merger of the labials into the apicals is general, e.g. majority Swahili fimbo > simbo 'walking stick' and vita > zita 'war, battles'. A few lexical items, e.g. mwizi 'thief' where mwivi is expected (and attested, but not common), have become usual in Southern Swahili. The same merger is also characteristic of the Comoros dialects, e.g. Ngazija -zimba 'swell', cf. Southern Swahili -vimba. Otherwise, this merger is general to all urban Swahili dialects only within lexical items where *i is immediately followed by another vowel, reflecting a Common Bantu double vowel, e.g. zaa 'bear children' < *bíada or soma 'read' < *píɔma. Many rural dialects show resistance to merger even under these conditions, as is typical of the North-East coastal Bantu languages outside of Swahili and Giriama, e.g. Vumba vyaa, fyoma.

Bantu vowel harmony consists of lowering *e and *o to *ɛ and *ɔ following a syllable whose nucleus is already at that degree of height. In all the Bantu languages, this is reflected in the use of this type of vowel harmony in the vowel of many verbal extensions, a morphophonemic process, e.g. Swahili pit-i-a 'pass by', pand-i-a 'climb onto', shuk-i-a 'come down to', but tok-e-a 'come from' and end-e-a 'go toward', where the prepositional extension -i/e- < *-e/ɛd- in Common Bantu is determined by the vowel of the preceding syllable. Bantu polysyllabic roots and stems also tend to adhere to this vowel harmony, so that *Cɛ/ɔCɛ/ɔ is much more common than *Cɛ/ɔCe/o.

Generally, the variety of tonal changes that have affected various Bantu languages can be traced back to a two-tone system, e.g. *-bàd- 'count': *-bád- 'shine' (Swahili -waa). The total loss of lexical tone distinctions is confined to a few languages of the north-east. Geographically intermediate are languages like LuGanda which appear to be pitch-stress languages with only one distinctive tone per word. Even among fully tonal languages, especially in the southern Bantu area, there is a tendency for one syllable per word, usually the penultimate, to have special prominence through lengthening. Swahili conforms to the penultimate stress pattern, with regular high pitch and lengthening of the penultimate vowel. Exceptions to this pattern are secondary through borrowing or clipping of reduplicated forms, e.g. kátika 'in' < *kàté-kàté, reduplication of *kàté > Swahili káti 'among'. While traditional Swahili communities maintain the antepenultimate stress of the clipping, second-language speakers tend to regularise stress to penultimate.

3 Morphology

Bantu languages have long been appreciated by scholars for their distinctive morphology, highly agglutinative and allowing great structural complexity to nominal and even more so to verbal forms.

Basic to Bantu nominal morphology is the division of nouns into numerous noun classes, the precise number of which varies from language to language due to syncretism and secondary developments. Traditionally, each reconstructed noun class has been assigned a number. The reconstructed Common Bantu noun classes number nineteen. Each is associated with a different class prefix preceding the noun stem. It is thought that the Bantu noun classes arose in pre-Bantu times from a system of classifiers, probably from nouns even earlier, adding content to the nouns they introduced. The semantic content of many of the classifiers is transparent due to their role in nominal derivation. Some of the noun classes specialise in marking collective or plural nouns and many of the pairings of classes into singular and plural found in the current Bantu languages are traceable to Common Bantu. The list given here presents the reconstructed Bantu noun classes with a rough indication of their semantics. Their semantics is most evident when they are used derivationally. Lexically, there is greater unpredictability for whether a noun of a particular meaning belongs to a certain class, both within and across the various languages.

Class (singular)	Class (plural)
1. *mo- 'human singular'	2. *ba- 'human plural'
3. *mo- 'thin or extended objects, trees, singular'	4. *me- 'plural of class 3'
5. *di/e- 'singular of objects that tend to come in pairs or larger groups, fruits'	6. *ma- 'collective or plural of class 5'

7. *ke- 'instrument, manner'	8. *bi- 'plural of class 7'
9. *ne- 'miscellaneous, animals'	10. *di-ne- 'plural of class 9'
11. *do- 'extended body parts'	'Use class 6/10 plural'
12. *ka- 'diminutive'	13. *to- 'plural of class 12'
14. *bo- 'abstract nouns, qualities'	
15. *ko- 'body parts'	'Use class 6 plural'
16. *pa- 'place where'	
17. *ko- 'place around which, infinitive'	
18. *mo- 'place in which'	
19. *pi- 'diminutive'	'Use class 6/8/10/13 plural'

Exemplifying from Swahili when possible: (1) *m-tu* 'person', pl. (2) *wa-tu*; (3) *m-ti* 'tree', pl. (4) *mi-ti*; (5) *ji-cho* 'eye', pl. (6) *ma-cho* (Swahili also uses this class pair for augmentatives, e.g. (5) *ji-tu* 'giant', pl. (6–5) *ma-ji-tu*); (7) *ki-tu* 'thing', pl. (8) *vi-tu* (Swahili also uses this class for diminutives, e.g. (7–5) *ki-ji-ji* 'village', pl. (8–5) *vi-ji-ji*, cf. (3) *m-ji* 'town', pl. (4) *mi-ji*); (9) *ng'ombe* 'cow', pl. (10) *ng'ombe* (**di*- is not prefixed to plural nouns in most North-East Bantu languages, cf. Zulu (9) *i-n(-)komo* 'cow', pl. (10) *i-zi-n(-)komo*); (11) *u-limi* 'tongue', pl. (10) *n-dimi*; (12) Gikuyu *ka-ana* 'small child', pl. (13) *tw-ana* (the urban Swahili dialects have lost this pair and switched their functions to (7)/(8), as shown above; *ka-* remains lexicalised in *ka-mwe* 'never' < '(not even a) little one'); (14) *u-baya* 'evil' < -*baya* 'bad'; (15) Gikuyu *kū-gūrū* 'leg', pl. (6) *ma-gūrū* (Swahili has shifted this class of nouns to (3) *m-guu*, Southern pl. (4) *mi-guu*, Northern pl. (6) *ma-guu*); the locative classes (16) to (18) can be directly prefixed to nouns in most Bantu languages, cf. coastal southern Tanzanian Mwera (16) *pa-ndu* 'at a place', (17) *ku-ndu* 'around a place', (18) *mu-ndu* 'inside a place', but Swahili uses an associative construction, (16) *p-a nyumba-ni* 'at-of house-loc.', i.e. 'at home', *kw-a nyumba-ni* 'around-of house-loc.', i.e. 'at/around home', *mw-a nyumba-ni* 'in-of home', i.e. 'inside the house'; (19) Kongo (north-west Zaire) *fi-koko-koko* 'little hand', pl. (8) *vi-koko-koko* (this class is largely restricted to West Bantu and does not occur in Swahili).

Regardless of various rearrangements of the noun classes, class concord is a pervasive feature of many grammatical categories in all Bantu languages. All categories modifying a noun have concordial prefixes determined by the noun. In addition, coreferential markers in the verb phrase, such as the subject, object and relative markers, also show class concord. The form taken by the class prefix is determined by the category to which it is prefixed. A secondary set of class prefixes is general for the nasal prefixes, formed by replacing the nasal with *g* (> *y* in Swahili). Which categories take the primary vs. the secondary prefixes varies across the Bantu area. Swahili restricts the nasal class prefixes to adjectives and numerals, except for the retention of nasal class 1 for the object marker, i.e. *m(u)-* rather than *yu-*. The following examples are illustrative of the syntactic extent of class concord in Bantu languages (cp = class prefix, cc = concord):

yu-le	m-tu	*m*-moja	*m*-refu	*a*-li-	*y*-e-	*ki*-soma	*ki*-le	ki-tabu	*ki*-refu
cc-	cp-	cc-	cc-	cc-	cc-	cc-	cc-	cp-	cc-
that	person	one	tall	he past	rel.	it read	that	book	long

'That one tall (1) person who read that long (7) book.'

wa-le	wa-tu	*wa*-wili	*wa*-refu	*wa*-li	*(w)*-o-	*vi*-soma	*vi*-le	vi-tabu	*vi*-refu
cc-	cp-	cc-	cc-	cc-	(cc-)	cc-	cc-	cp-	cc-

'Those two tall (2) people who read those long (8) books.'

An interesting further development of concord has occurred among Swahili and some adjacent North-East coastal Bantu languages: animate concord. This device extends class 1/2 concord to animates, regardless of their lexical noun class. For example, most animals are class 9/10 nouns, e.g. *simba* 'lion', *njovu* 'elephant', *ndege* 'bird'. One result of animate concord is the distinction between *ndege yu-le* 'that bird' with a class 1 animate concord marking the demonstrative and *ndege i-le* 'that aeroplane' with a strictly syntactic class 9 concord on the demonstrative. It must be noted that animate concord is atypical of Bantu languages on the whole. Even in Swahili, when the class of the noun is determined by a semantic rather than a lexical process, class concord overrides animate concord. Thus, *ki-jana yu-le* 'that youth (e.g. teenager)' shows animate concord on the demonstrative, illustrating the perceived lexical arbitrariness of the class 7 prefix on the noun, but *ki-jana ki-le* 'that little-old youth' with class 7, where the class prefix to the noun functions as a diminutive. As a local innovation in North-East coastal Bantu, animate concord serves to illustrate that even though the original semantic motivation for noun class is often obscure for individual lexical items, the syntactic resources of class concord continue to be exploited for semantic purposes.

In addition to the class prefix, it is probable that Common Bantu had a preprefix marking definite and generic nouns and their modifiers. This preprefix survives in various forms and functions in the interior and south-west, usually anticipating at least the vowel of the class prefix, e.g. Zulu *u-mu-ntu* 'the person', *a-ba-ntu* 'the people'. The preprefix has been lost in much of the eastern coastal area. A relic remains in the Northern Bajuni dialects of Swahili in *i-t'i* 'land(s)' < *e-n(e)-čé*, Southern Swahili *nchi*. In most dialects of Swahili, the preprefix was lost earlier than voiceless nasals. With the loss of the preprefix penultimate stress was transferred to the nasal, which prevented the loss of the nasal despite its voicelessness. The opposite chronological sequence is evident for Bajuni. When removed from stress, the voiceless nasal and preprefix are lost in all dialects, cf. Bajuni *t'i-ni*, Southern Swahili *chi-ni* 'below' (i.e. 'on the ground').

The personal pronouns have a variety of specific forms in Bantu, according to the grammatical category to which they are attached. The chart shows the Swahili pattern, indicative of the formal variation, though not the precise shapes, of the personal pronouns in Bantu.

	Independent	*Possessive*	*Subject marker*	*Object marker*
'I'	mimi	-ngu	ni-	ni-
'you'	wewe	-ko	u-	ku-
's/he'	yeye	-ke	a-/yu-	m-
'we'	sisi	-itu	tu-	tu-
'you (pl.)'	ninyi	-inu	m(w)-	wa-
'they'	wao	-(w)o	wa-	wa-

The *k*- forms of the second and third singular are usual in Bantu and also appear as the subject markers *ku*- and *ka*- respectively in a few languages (including the central dialects of Swahili). Some Bantu languages have independent pronouns for the other classes, but Swahili uses demonstratives instead, e.g. for class 7 *hi-ki* 'this thing', *hi-ch-o* (< *hi-ky-o*) 'that thing (proximate)', *ki-le* 'that thing (distal)'.

Nominal derivational processes have already been alluded to above in the discussion of noun classes and class concord. In some Bantu languages these provide sufficient resources to nominalise verb-object predicates, e.g. Swahili *m-fanya-kazi* 'worker' with class 1 animate prefix, < *-fanya kazi* 'do work'. However, all Bantu languages also show extensive use of nominal suffixes, converting verbs to nouns, e.g. **-ɔ*: Swahili *nen-o* 'word' < *-nen-a* 'say', **-i*: Swahili *u-zaz-i* 'parenthood' < *-zaa* 'bear children' via **bo-bíád-i*, **-u*: Swahili *-bov-u* 'rotten' < *-oza* 'rot' via **-bɔd-u*. Note that the suffix *-u* derives stative qualities from process verbs and forms the basis for derived adjectives as well as nouns. Morphologically nouns and adjectives are not distinct in the Bantu languages. Among the noun derivational suffixes is the locative *-ni*, corresponding in function to the locative prefixes. Suffixed to a noun, *-ni* marks the noun as head of a locative phrase, e.g. Swahili *kazi-ni* 'at work', *mto-ni* 'at the river'. Historically, these derivational suffixes are indicative of a syntactic system quite different from the current Bantu systems and well advanced in the process of morphologising by Common Bantu times. This will be further discussed on pages 1010–12.

Bantu verb morphology shows the fullest extent of Bantu agglutinative word structure. Central to the verb is the root, which may be extended to a more complex stem by the addition of derivational suffixes. Final modal suffixes **-a* and **-ε* distinguish the indicative and subjunctive respectively. In the indicative mode this is sufficient complexity for the imperative, e.g. Swahili *fany-a* 'do (it)'. Obligatory elsewhere is a subject marker, referring to and concording with the subject of the clause. Since lexical subjects which are inferrable in the context of discourse need not be expressed, the subject marker is often the only reference to the understood subject in a clause and thus functions as a pronoun. The independent pronouns are not obligatory in the clause. The subject marker is sufficient to form a subjunctive clause in most Bantu languages, e.g. Swahili *a-fany-e* 'he should do (it)'. In the indicative mode, at least one more element is necessary for non-imperatives: the tense/aspect marker. The tense/aspect marker may immediately follow the subject marker, preceding the verb, in which case it is called a tense prefix, or it may be suffixed to the verb stem and its extensions, depending on the particular tense/aspect marker and the language, in which case it is called a tense suffix, e.g. Gikuyu *a-gwat-ire* 'he held (today)' suffixes *-ire* 'an action which has taken place on the day of speaking' to the verb *-gwata* 'catch/hold', but *a-á-gwata* 'he just held' prefixes *-á-* 'an action taking place immediately before the time of speaking'. Most Bantu languages show a richer paradigm of tense prefixes than of tense suffixes, but all show traces of the Common Bantu tense suffix system. Thus, most Swahili dialects and the standard language retain a tense suffix only for the 'present negative' *h-a-fany-i* (neg.-he-do-pres.) 's/he doesn't do/isn't doing (it)'. The Bantu 'tense' suffix *-(n)ga*, marking 'habituality', is found among interior North-East Bantu languages, e.g. Gikuyu *a-ra-gwata-ga* 's/he kept holding' combining the tense prefix *-ra-* 'action took place no earlier than the day before the day of speaking' with the tense suffix *-ga* 'habitual'. It survives in Swahili only as a common suffix for verb nominalisation, e.g. *m-sema-ji* 'speaker' < *sema* 'speak' via **mo-sema-ga-i* (note that the root *sema* is largely restricted to Swahili and is probably not of Bantu origin).

While all of the tense suffixes are traceable to Common Bantu, some tense prefixes are traceable to other grammatical categories. For example, the urban Swahili perfect *-me-*, as in *a-me-fanya* 's/he has done it', is traceable to Bantu **-màda* 'finish' (surviving also in Swahili *mal-iza* 'bring to an end, complete') via **-màd-idɛ* > *-mez-ie* (surviving in Bajuni) with the perfect suffix **-idɛ*. Nevertheless, many of the tense/aspect prefixes are traceable to Common Bantu, showing that at that stage Bantu had already set a precedent for further development of the tense prefix system in the individual languages.

Bantu languages vary in how negation interacts morphologically with particular tenses. In the subjunctive mode the negative marker immediately follows the subject marker, e.g. Swahili *a-si-fany-e* 's/he shouldn't do (it)', where *-si-* < **-ti-* is the negative marker. In the indicative mode, both suffixation and prefixation of the negative to the subject marker are commonly found, e.g. Swahili *h-a-ta-fanya* 's/he won't do (it)' with the negative marker *h(a)-* prefixed to the complex *a-ta-fanya* 's/he will do (it)'. This absolute first position in the verb complex for the negative marker is obligatory with most tenses. With a very few tenses there is dialect division between prefixing and suffixing of a negative, e.g. with the hypothetical marker *-nge-*, Southern *h-a-nge-fanya* and Northern *a-si-nge-fanya* 's/he should/wouldn't do (it)', cf. *a-nge-fanya* 's/he would do (it)'. In a few areas, the negative is an independent particle following the entire verbal word, e.g. among the Chagga dialects (northern Tanzania) *a-le-ca fo* 's/he didn't come' beside *a-le-ca* 'he came', where *-le-* is the tense prefix for 'action took place yesterday or earlier'.

As some of the glosses above suggest, the tense/aspect systems of many

Bantu languages are quite extensive, marking a variety of tenses, aspects and moods. The fine distinction between degrees of pastness is particularly striking as unusual among world languages, e.g. Gikuyu *a-gwat-ire* 's/he held' (current (today) past), *a-ra-gwat-ire* 's/he held' (recent (yesterday) past), *a-à-gwat-ire* 's/he held' (remoter past). Among Bantu languages with such distinctions, some show tense concord between the initial tense and consecutive tense markers, e.g. Giriama *a-dza-fika a-ka-injira* 's/he arrived and entered (today)' vs. *w-a-fika a-ki-injira* 's/he arrived ... (yesterday or earlier)'. The consecutive marker, common in east coast Bantu and extending into the interior, functions as a perfective, necessarily giving a consecutive interpretation to verbs so marked with respect to the preceding verb.

A great many Bantu languages allow concatenation of particular tense/aspect markers, e.g. Gikuyu *ī-ngī-ka-na-endia* 'if I should ever sell (it)' where *-ngī-* is 'hypothetical', *-ka-* is 'future' and *-na-* is 'indeterminate time'. Along the east coast this degree of morphological complexity is largely reduced to a single tense prefix per verb. Thus, in Swahili 'compound tenses' allow two tenses to mark a clause through the device of an auxiliary verb *-ku-wa* 'be(come)' supporting the first tense, e.g. *a-li-ku-wa a-ki-fanya* 's/he used to do it' where *-li-* is the 'past' marker and *-ki-* is 'habitual/progressive'. The construction *a-li-ki-fanya* survives in Northern Swahili with the same meaning.

Both the reduction of some of the paradigmatic complexity and the introduction of new tense-aspect markers in specific contexts have led to extensive asymmetry between affirmative and negative tense/aspect markers among the east coast languages. Swahili provides many examples. Many scholars caution against direct comparison of the semantics of the affirmative and negative tenses. Thus, the chart given here is approximate, in order to indicate differences in the affirmative and negative tenses.

Affirmative		*Negative*
-na/a-	'progressive/general'	-∅-...-i
-me-	'perfect'	-ja- 'not yet'
-li-	'past/anterior'	-ku-
-ta-	'future'	-ta/to-
-nge/ngali-	'hypothetical'	-nge/ngali-
-ki-	'participial, progressive'	-si-po- 'unless'
-ka-	'perfective/consecutive'	(use neg. subjunctive)
		'without then V-ing'

This standard Swahili paradigm is general to most urban Swahili dialects. The rural dialects show various differences, e.g. *-na-* is 'today past/perfect' in the rural coastal dialects, *-∅-...-ie-* < *-ide* serves a similar function in the Bajuni dialects and ChiMwini (*-ire*), Comoros dialects use *nga-...-o* rather than a tense prefix for the 'progressive/general', e.g. *ng-u-som-o* 's/he's reading', cf. standard *a-na-soma*. In addition to the above markers standard Swahili uses *hu-*, usually considered a tense/aspect marker but not admitting a subject marker (< *ni+ku-* = copula + infinitive marker), to mark 'occasional recurrent action' (i.e. 'sometimes'). In the Northern dialects, *hu-* is generally used as the 'progressive/habitual', and *-na-* only occurs in speech to speakers of other varieties of Swahili.

An optional element of the Bantu verb is the object marker, placed immediately before the verb stem. Common to all Bantu languages is the use of an object marker anaphorically to refer to an understood second argument of the clause, not expressed in the clause itself, e.g. Swahili *a-me-vi-ona* 's/he has seen them', where *-vi-* refers to some class 8 object such as *vi-su* 'knives' (pl. of *ki-su*). The invariant reflexive object marker, *-ji-* < **gi* (many Bantu languages use a reflex of **ke-*) marks subject-object coreference, e.g. *a-me-ji-kata* 'he cut himself', *tu-me-ji-kata* 'we cut ourselves' etc.

Many Bantu languages allow multiple object markers, e.g. Umbundu *w-a-u-n-dekisa* 's/he showed him/her to me', where *-u-* is the class 1 object marker 'him/her' and *-n-* is the first person singular object marker 'me'. On the east coast and spreading inland toward the south is the restriction of the object marker to one per verb. In some languages, either of two object arguments may be represented by the object marker, the other being expressed anaphorically by an independent pronoun or demonstrative. Most investigated languages indicate that there are further restrictions on which object may be so represented. Swahili is highly developed in this respect. Animates are selected over inanimates and there is a hierarchy of roles from agent down to direct object. These roles are determined either lexically or by verbal extensions. The verbal extensions will be discussed immediately below. First, however, it is worth mentioning that Swahili is unique in gravitating toward the object marker as an obligatory verbal category, though only for reference to human objects. The use of the object marker with expressed indefinite human objects in the same clause is generally tolerated in Bantu only by those North-East coastal languages which have been in contact with Swahili for several generations (e.g. the Kenyan coastal languages Pokomo and Miji Kenda), but is obligatory in urban dialects of Swahili and the standard language, e.g. *a-li-mw-ona mtu* 's/he saw somebody', where *-m(w)-* class 1 refers to *mtu* 'person' and the referent is not yet known to the addressee. Elsewhere in Bantu the object marker must have an anaphoric reference.

The verbal extensions are verbal suffixes which define the role of one argument of the verb. They are directly suffixed to the verb root or to each other when grammatically possible. All the verbal suffixes are inherited from Common Bantu. The system has undergone little semantic change and a moderate amount of formal change in the current languages. Swahili will serve to illustrate the basic system common to all Bantu languages.

In Swahili the regular causative is *-i/esha* (the vowel determined by the

Causative	-ya, i/esha	< *-ia, *-e/ɛk-ia, respectively
Stative	-(i/e)ka	< *-(e/ɛ)ka
Prepositional	-i/ea	< *-e/ɛda
Reversive	-u/oa	< *-o/ɔda
Reciprocal	-ana	< *-a-na
Passive	-(i/e)wa	< *-(e/ɛd-)oa

vowel harmony rule discussed on page 999), e.g. *pik-isha* 'cause to cook', *chek-esha* 'make laugh'. Its origin appears to be a sequence of stative + causative. The *-ya* causative survives in a few transparent lexical items, e.g. *on-ya* 'warn', cf. *ona* 'see', *on-esha* 'show'. The causative focuses on the agent of the root verb if a specific agent referent is understood. If not, it may focus on the object of the root verb, e.g. *a-li-zi-jeng-esha* 's/he had them built', where 'them' refers to a class 10 noun such as *nyumba* 'houses'.

The stative suffix focuses on the state or potential of the subject. With the perfect *-me-* it focuses on state, e.g. *i-me-vunj-ika* 'it is broken' < *vunja* 'break', *i-me-poto-ka* 'it is twisted' < *potoa* 'twist'. With the general 'present' *-na-*, *-a-* or *hu-* it may focus on a potential, e.g. *i-na-vunj-ika* 'it is breakable' (i.e. 'it can get broken'). With some verbs the stative form is *-i/ekana* as if from stative + reciprocal, e.g. *i-na-pat-ikana* 'it is obtainable' < *pata* 'get'. Sometimes the stative interpretation remains with this tense, e.g. *i-na-jul-ikana* 'it is known' < *jua* 'know'. A number of stative verbs show lexicalisation of the stative marker, e.g. *amka* 'awaken (intr.)', *choka* 'be tired', where no simpler forms of the verb exist.

The prepositional suffix (also called applicative) covers the semantic range of the most common prepositions in English. It may be benefactive, e.g. *ni-li-m-pik-ia* 'I cooked **for** her', directive, e.g. *ni-li-lil-ia kijiko* 'I cried **over** a spoon', directional, e.g. *ni-li-m-j-ia* 'I came **to** him', instrumental, e.g. *ni-li-l-ia kijiko* 'I ate **with** a spoon', affected participant, e.g. *wa-li-m-f-ia* 'they died **on** him'. That is, the prepositional suffix focuses on the role of some argument other than the direct object. The particular role focused on in context is a matter of the lexical meaning of the verb and inference, e.g. *ni-li-mw-ib-ia* may mean either 'I stole **for** him' or 'I stole **from** him'. As with other extensions, in some cases they have lexicalised, e.g. *-ambia* 'say to' < *amb-i-a*, where the verb *-amba* 'say' survives in Swahili elsewhere only as a complementiser, e.g. *nimesikia* **kwamba** *a-me-fika* 'I heard **that** he has arrived'. Double prepositional verbs have a 'persistive' meaning, e.g. *tup-il-ia* 'throw (far) away', *end-el-ea* 'continue' < *end-e-a* 'go in a certain direction' < *enda* 'go'.

The reversive suffix functions to undo the action of the root verb, e.g. *fung-u-a* 'open, untie' < *fung-a* 'close, tie', *chom-o-a* 'pull out' < *chom-a* 'stick in, skewer'.

The reciprocal suffix indicates reciprocal roles for two subjects or a subject and the object of a *na* 'and/with' phrase, e.g. *wa-li-pig-ana* 'they fought (with each other)' < *piga* 'hit', *a-li-pig-ana na-ye* 's/he fought with him/her', where *na-ye* consists of *na* 'with/and' and a cliticised form of the independent pronoun *yeye* 'him/her'.

The passive focuses on the non-agentive status of the subject, e.g. *a-li-shind-wa* 's/he was defeated' < *shinda* 'defeat', *a-li-on-esh-wa* 's/he was shown' (...'see' + causative + passive). Only an object which can be referred to by an object marker with the active verb can be the subject of the passivised verb in Swahili. Thus, the only passive corresponding to the active sentence, *ni-sha-ku-on-esha watu* 'I already showed the people to **you**', is *u-li-on-esh-wa watu* '**you** were shown the people'. The direct object *watu* 'people' cannot be passivised over the indirect object, just as it cannot be represented by an object marker while there is an indirect object in the clause. The passive is always the last verbal extension in the Swahili verb. This appears to be quite general to Eastern Bantu. However, in the south-west the passive may precede the prepositional if the subject has the role of direct object of the active verb, e.g. Umbundu *onjo y-a-tung-iw-ila ina-hé* 'the house was built for his/her mother' < *tunga* 'build', where the subject of *tung-iw-* 'build-passive' is *onjo* 'house' and *ina-hé* 'mother-his/her' is the object of *-ila*, the prepositional suffix. A number of other verbal extensions are extant in Bantu, but are no longer productive, cf. Swahili *kama-ta* 'seize' < *kama* 'squeeze', *nene-pa* 'get fat' < *nene* 'fat (adj.)', *ganda-ma* 'get stuck' < *ganda* 'stick to'. Still further verbal extensions are recognisable through Niger-Congo reconstruction, e.g. **bí-áda* (Swahili *zaa* 'bear children') contains **bi*, a Niger-Congo root for 'child' not common in Bantu.

To complete discussion of the morphological complexity of the verb structure, the relative marker must be mentioned. In most of the Bantu area relativisation is a syntactic process which does not interfere with the verbal complex. However, among the North-East coastal languages, including Swahili, a relative marker may be infixed in the verbal complex by suffixation to the tense prefix. The relative marker in such cases is itself complex, consisting of a secondary class concord marker + the referential morpheme *-o*, e.g. *ni-li-p+o-fika* 'when I arrived'. Here the relative marker *-p+o-* consists of the concord for class 16, a locative used here as a temporal, and the referential *-o*. The form functioning as a relative marker here occurs throughout Bantu in a demonstrative series, e.g. the Swahili proximate 'that' *hu-y+o* (cl. 1), *hi-l+o* (cl. 5) etc. In the languages which have the infixed relative marker it only appears with a few tense prefixes. In all cases these tense prefixes are innovations developing later than the Common Bantu period. The origin of this infixation is postposing of the relative marker to the entire verbal complex. This process survives on the north-east coast and in the south-east, when there is no tense prefix on the verb, e.g. Swahili *mwezi u-Ø-ja-(w+)o* 'the month which is coming', i.e. 'next month', where the *-Ø-* marks the absence of a tense prefix and the relative marker is suffixed to the verb *ja* 'come', or Pokomo *want'u wa-Ø-j-ie-(w+)o* 'the people who came', with the addition of a tense suffix *-ie* to the verb *-ja* 'come'. The tense prefixes which allow the infixed relatives originate in auxiliaries where the relative marker was postposed, e.g. Swahili *-li-* 'past/ anterior' < (*-a-* 'remote past') + *li* 'copula'. The tense prefix *-na-* 'general, progressive' regularly takes infixation in the standard and Southern dialects, but is largely resisted by the Central dialects, e.g. standard Swahili *watu wa-na-(w+)o-sema* 'the people who are speaking', while Central Swahili prefers *watu amba-(w+)o wa-na-sema* 'the people who have spoken', where the relative marker cliticises to a complementiser *amba* introducing the relative clause. This device is used for relativisation in all dialects and is the only option with tense prefixes which do not allow relative infixation.

4 Syntax

Bantu languages have a basic verb-medial word order with a strong tendency toward subject first. Auxiliaries precede the verb (itself usually in infinitive form with **ko-* prefixed). All noun modifiers follow the noun in most of the Bantu area: adjectives, numerals, demonstratives, relative clauses. However, most languages optionally allow demonstratives to precede the noun to mark definiteness. The basic possessive (or 'associative') pattern is *Possessed cc-a Possessor*, where *-a* is the associative marker 'of', and the class concord prefix concords with the possessed noun. As discussed on page 1003, the pronominalised possessor takes a special form, which is suffixed to *-a-*; thus, Swahili *ngoma z-a-mtu* '(the) drums of/for (the) man' with the class concord *z-* (class 10) concording with *ngoma* 'drums' and *ngoma z-a-ke* 'his/ her drums' with the special possessive form of the pronoun suffixed to *-a-*. Most Bantu languages show concord for the class of the pronominalised possessor, but Swahili uses *-ke* for all classes except the animate plural (class 2).

With the exception of **nà* 'and/with', Common Bantu does not appear to have prepositions. Beside the prepositional extension, Swahili uses both verbs and nouns to function like English prepositions, e.g. *a-me-fika toka Dar* 'he has arrived **from** Dar', where *toka* is the verb 'come from'; *a-li-tembea* **mpaka** *Dar* 'he walked **to** Dar', where the noun *mpaka* 'boundary' is used as a vector to mean 'up to, until'. Commonly, the possessive construction is used prepositionally, e.g. *chini y-a nyumba* 'under (of) the house', where *chini* 'down, under' etymologically displays *nchi* 'ground' + *-ni*, the locative suffix. The possessed concord ignores the locative and concords directly with the root noun. The possessive construction is also used with the locative concords prefixed, especially *ku-* (class 17), to express locative, instrumental and manner relations, e.g. *kw-a Fatuma* '**at** Fatuma's (place)', *kw-a nyundo* '**with** (a) hammer', *kw-a nguvu* '**by** force'. In all cases, these preposition-like uses of constructions are noun second. In all respects, then, Swahili and the other Bantu languages are very much like the prototypical SVO language.

However, word order is not invariant. Topicalisation is possible, e.g. *kitabu ni-li-ki-kuta* 'the book, I found it'; note the usual use of the object marker (*-ki-* (class 7) in this case) in the topicalised construction. In Swahili a topicalised possessive construction is optional with animate possessors: *mtu ngoma zake* 'the man, his drums'. Some Bantu languages require a cleft construction for interrogatives, equivalent to Swahili *ni nani uliyemwona?* 'who did you see?' lit. '(it) is who that you saw?', where the interrogative pronoun *nani* 'who' is introduced as the predicate of the copula *ni*, a marker used to focus on noun phrases or entire clauses in the Bantu languages. In Swahili, topicalisation is never obligatory. The usual form of the question leaves an object interrogative in object, i.e. post-verbal, position, e.g. *ulimwona nani?* 'you saw who?'. The widespread use of Bantu interrogative pronouns ending in *-ni*, e.g. Swahili *na-ni* 'who?', *ni-ni* 'what?', *li-ni* 'when?', *ga-ni* 'what kind?' indicates the earlier prevalence of topicalisation in *wh*-questions in Bantu, still found in Bantu's Benue-Congo and Kwa relatives, where cognates of *ni* (< **ne*) are suffixed to topics, whether interrogative or otherwise, e.g. in Yoruba (see page 986).

Beside its predicate-marking function, the particle *ni* (usually called a copula because of its equative function in Bantu languages, e.g. *Fatuma ni m-Swahili* 'Fatuma is a Swahili speaker') functions in some North-East interior languages to mark a main clause, e.g. Gikuyu *nī-a-gwat-ire* 'he held (it)' as main clause, but *mūndū ū-ria a-gwat-ire*, 'the man who held (it)', where *a-gwat-ire* is relativised by means of the demonstrative *ū-ria* (Swahili *yu-le*) introducing the relative clause. Another Bantu 'copula' reflected in Swahili *-li* acts like a verb in taking tense prefixes and is used for both equative and locative purposes in most Bantu languages (replacing *ni* as equative with non-third persons). In Swahili, equative and locative predicates are strictly distinguished, so that *skuli ni hapa* means 'this place is a school' but *skuli i-ko hapa* (*iko* < *i-li-ko*) means 'the/a school is in/around here'.

Despite its typically verb-second syntax, much of the morphology of the Bantu languages indicates a verb-last origin, only sporadically found among the Niger-Congo languages. Signs of verb-last syntax are found in the preposing of the object marker to the verb stem (as if of OV origin), the postposing of the verbal extensions and mode markers (as if of verb–auxiliary origin), the suffixing of the locative marker *-ni* to the affected noun (as if of noun–postposition origin), the class prefix on nouns (as if of modifier–noun origin) and probably the postposing of the relative marker to the non-tense-prefixed verbal complex surviving on the north-east coast and in the south-east (as if of clause–relativiser origin). Otherwise, with its obligatory subject marker and tense prefixes in that order, and its noun–genitive possessive construction, the Bantu languages resemble the majority of their Benue-Congo and Kwa neighbours in the north-west.

The variation in position of some Bantu categories, most characteristic of the north-west, suggests an intermediate stage of evolution between an analytical verb-final syntax and the strict verbal morphology of Swahili and the east coast, with maximally a single tense prefix and object marker per verb. In particular, the morphologisation of auxiliary-like categories, both pre- and post-verbal, does not appear to have occurred uniformly over the Bantu area as the languages assumed their current verb-medial syntax. The slight ordering freedom of verbal extensions, e.g. in the Umbundu example on page 1008, suggests the relatively late survival of pre-Bantu verbal extensions as a separate word class in part of the southwestern area. The prepositional verbal extension *-e/ɛda*, as well as the use of verbs for prepositional direction, e.g. Swahili *(ku)toka* 'come (from)' and *kw-enda* '(go) towards', suggest the serial verb constructions general to Niger-Congo languages, including Bantu's north-west relatives (see pages 988–9). In the process of evolution towards complex verb morphology, the attraction of these auxiliaries to the preceding verb precluded a preverbal position for the object of the 'prepositional' verb and may have precipitated verb-medial syntax. The Bantu languages which still allow multiple object-markers, the interior east and most of the west (in the north-west object markers have been partially lost in favour of post-verbal independent pronouns), indicate the retention of verb-final syntax, allowing two or more preposed objects, but only for a pronominal form of the object. That is, where O is a lexical object and o is a pronominal object, O–V O–aux. appears to have evolved into O-V+aux. O and finally V+aux. O O, but o–V o–aux. evolved into o–o–V+aux. In most contexts, languages like Swahili have gone further in reanalysing the object of the extension as the only object of the main verb. Syntactically, focusing options have been maintained in Swahili through the development of a new prepositional device, using the possessive construction for instrument discussed above, e.g. *a-li-pig-i-a nyundo msumari* 'he hit the nail with a hammer' (i.e. he used a hammer to hit the nail), with the extension focusing on the instrument, and *a-li-piga msumari kwa nyundo*, with the same meaning but use of the possessive construction, reversing the order of lexical objects. Interestingly enough, the instrumental use of the prepositional extension in Swahili still allows an object marker for the direct object despite the presence of the instrument in the clause, e.g. *a-li-u-pig-i-a nyundo msumari* (where *-u-* refers to *msumari* 'nail'). All other uses of all verbal extensions allow the object marker only to refer to the object of the extension when that object is mentioned in the clause. Amidst variation in the position of the negative marker across Bantu languages and according to tense/aspect within the languages, the widespread use of a post-verbal negative marker in the north-west (and in Chagga, as discussed above) suggests an auxiliary origin in verb-final syntax for negation: verb negative (= auxiliary). The preverbal position of the negative marker *ti* (Swahili *si*) appears to be a manifestation of the shift to verb-medial syntax. This *ti* is also the negative copula, e.g. Swahili *mnyama si mtu* 'an animal is not a person'. In the same way that there are traces of a post-predicate position for the currently prepredicate copula *ne (Swahili ni) among the interrogative pronouns, as discussed earlier, the negative 'copula' appears to have shifted to a preverbal auxiliary: negative (= auxiliary) verb. The other forms of negation, which place the negative before the subject marker, appear to be even later developments within the Bantu area, evolving from verbs with inherent negation, e.g. Swahili ha- < nk'a- (still common in the Central dialects) perhaps developing from ni 'copula' + kana 'deny'.

Bantu subordination patterns are relatively consistent across languages. Relativisation is generally introduced by a demonstrative or, among languages with preprefixes, a preprefix when the subject is relativised, e.g. Zulu a-bantu a-ba-funa-yo 'people who want' (note the final relative marker -yo used with no tense prefix). The preprefix itself may derive from an earlier demonstrative in concord with the head noun and subject of the relative clause. Complement clauses and even adverbial clauses are generally introduced by verbs etymologically meaning 'say' (as generally in Niger-Congo), e.g. Swahili kw-amba, Southern and Central Bantu ku-ti, and/or 'be(come)', e.g. Swahili ku-wa. Thus, -amba- in Swahili may introduce reported speech, a relative clause and earlier introduced the protasis of conditional sentences, e.g. na **kwamba** moyo ni chuo ningekupa ukasome 'and **if** the heart were a book, I would give it to you for you to read' (a verse from the early nineteenth-century Mombasan poet, Muyaka). This last use of kwamba has been replaced by kama, of Arabic origin, also used as the preposition 'like'. In the rural dialect of Chifundi ku-wa 'be(come)' retains this function, cf. Zulu u-ku-ba and u-ku-ti which also may function like this. In Swahili ku-wa may also introduce reported speech and other complements of verbs of communication or mental action, e.g. 'think'.

In sum, the syntax of the Bantu languages reflects an SVO language which has evolved out of a language with both SOV characteristics and interclausal relations common to Niger-Congo languages of either basic word order. It is most distinctive among Niger-Congo languages in its noun-class system and its verb morphology. Among Niger-Congo class languages it is specifically distinctive in the complexity of its verb morphology. For example, the distantly related West Atlantic language Fula is also a class language, but the class markers follow rather than precede the noun and there are no tense prefixes or object markers preceding the verb root. Like Bantu, Fula is currently verb-medial showing the prevalence of this type of syntax throughout Niger-Congo.

5   Non-Bantu Influence on Swahili

In view of its general, even extreme, adherence to the Bantu type (extreme, for example, in the extent of its obligatory verb morphology), Swahili is usually viewed as minimally affected in its syntax by non-Bantu influence. In contrast, the Swahili lexicon shows massive borrowing from Arabic and more recently from English. In addition, as the traditional medium of communication between the Indian Ocean commercial network and the Bantu interior, it has accepted words and concepts from numerous other languages, both Bantu and foreign, e.g. Portuguese (in the sixteenth century), Persian and Hindi. Among traditional Swahili communities, words originating in Arabic often maintain some features of their Arabic pronunciation, e.g. *baxt(i)* 'luck' with a consonant cluster and the foreign phoneme /x/. However, as Swahili has spread to non-Arabicised Bantu peoples and everyday usage in traditional Swahili communities, certain Bantu processes of nativisation have taken place, e.g. *bahati* with typical Bantu syllable structure and nativisation of /x/ > /h/. In both the standard language and the traditional dialects the Arabic interdental fricatives have been adopted, e.g. *dhani* 'think', *thelathini* 'thirty'. Among the new urban Swahili communities such as Dar es Salaam in Tanzania, these interdentals are non-standardly replaced by post-alveolars, e.g. *zani, selasini*. The phonological nativisation process for loanwords from languages allowing word-final consonants consists of using the vocalic quality of the final consonant as the nucleus of a final syllable, e.g. *-jibu* 'answer' < Arabic *jib*; *-skwizi* 'hug romantically' < English *squeeze, starehe* 'relax' < Arabic *-stariħ*. An interesting detail concerning loan verbs is that they do not take the modal suffixes. Thus, the subjunctive and indicative are distinguished only by the presence or absence of a tense prefix, i.e. *a-Ø-jibu* 'he should answer' must be subjunctive because there is no tense prefix on the verb.

Bantuisation of loan nouns occurs where the loan is analysable into a class prefix + stem, thus *ki-tabu*, pl. *vi-tabu* 'book' < Arabic *kita:b*. This tendency to metanalyse also occurs within Bantu words when possible, e.g. *chupa* 'bottle' < **ne-čópà* is metanalysed in the newer urban Swahili communities as *ch-upa*, pl. *vy-upa*, by analogy with class 7/8 nouns, e.g. *ch-uma* 'iron' < **ke-ómà*, pl. *vy-uma*. This tendency is not seen in Northern Swahili communities where the reflex *ṭ'upa* is unmistakably class 9, pl. *ṭ'upa* (class 10).

A fuller understanding of the impact of other languages, particularly Arabic through continual contact for a millennium, awaits further examination of the semantics and rhetorical patterns of Swahili and other Bantu languages. Beside the cultural influence of Arabic reflected in Swahili's vocabulary, the use of Arabic adverbials and conjunctions is striking, e.g. *lakini* 'but, however', *au/ama* 'or', *halafu* 'then', *baada* 'after'. As rhetorical style is expressed in art, Swahili poetry has adopted numerous Arabic metres and the use of vocalic rhyme. Vocalic rhyme is unknown in traditional Bantu verse (in contradistinction to tonal rhyme), but Swahili has used the identity of word-final syllables to create a tradition of rhyme schemes far more intricate than in the Arabic source, e.g. the regular form of the Swahili quatrain (four-line stanza) has the rhyme scheme ab/ab/ab/bc, which repeats as de/de/de/ec. Note that only the final rhymes of each stanza are related. This typical pattern of stanza rhyme suggests the refrain pattern of a repeated coda line, marking the end of each stanza, commonly used in Bantu and West African song and often in Swahili song as well. This blending of Bantu and non-Bantu traditions is suggestive of more prosaic adaptations of non-Bantu rhetorical patterns which remain to be described in Swahili.

Bibliography

For Bantu as a whole, Guthrie (1967–70) is the most extensive classification and reconstruction. Nurse and Philippson (1975) presents a classification of Swahili's nearest geographical relatives.

For Swahili, Polomé (1967) is a conveniently arranged introduction to the dialects and the basic structure of the language. Ashton (1944), a pedagogical grammar, is still the most complete introduction to the standard language, while Hinnebusch (1979) presents a descriptive synopsis. Vitale (1981) is a highly comprehensive generative treatment of Swahili syntax; although it offers little in the way of new data, it relates Swahili grammar to issues in generative grammar and organises topics accordingly. Stigand (1915) is still the most extensive English-language discussion of Swahili dialects, excluding most of the Central rural dialects. Whiteley (1969) presents a sociohistorical discussion of the development of standard Swahili.

References

Ashton, E.O. 1944. *Swahili Grammar (Including Intonation)* (Longman, London)
Guthrie, M. 1967–70. *Comparative Bantu*, 4 vols. (Gregg International Publishers)
Hinnebusch, T.J. 1979. 'Swahili', in T. Shopen (ed.), *Languages and Their Status* (Winthrop, Cambridge, Mass.), pp. 204–93
Nurse, D. and G. Philippson. 1975. 'The North-Eastern Bantu Languages of Tanzania and Kenya: A Classification', *Kiswahili*, vol. 45, pp. 1–28
Polomé, E.C. 1967. *Swahili Language Handbook* (Center for Applied Linguistics, Washington DC)
Stigand, C.H. 1915. *A Grammar of Dialectic Changes in the Kiswahili Language* (Cambridge University Press, Cambridge)
Vitale, A.J. 1981. *Swahili Syntax* (Foris, Dordrecht)
Whiteley, W.H. 1969. *Swahili: The Rise of a National Language* (Methuen, London)

Language Index

For language names containing an initial adjective or prefix and not listed as such in the index, consult the entry for the language name minus the adjective or prefix, e.g. *English* for *Old English*, *Romance* for *Ibero-Romance*.

Abor-Miri-Dafla 800, 802
Achinese 901, 915
Adamawa-Eastern 961,968–70
Adare *see* Harari
Afa *see* Pa'a
Afar-Saho 648
Afrikaans 19, 68, 78, 139, 151
Afroasiatic 7, 13, 15, 19, 20, 645–53, 654, 663, 664, 673, 701, 705–8 *passim*, 723, 961, 991
Agaw 648, 651, 652
Ahom 511, 749, 750
Ainu 14, 857, 859
Akan 966
Akha *see* Hani
Akkadian 25, 651, 654–63 *passim*, 516
Akoko 971
Alanic 590
Albanian 10, 34–8 *passim*, 42f., 52, 282, 309, 310, 316, 318, 414, 437
Aleut 20
Algonquian 21
Altaic 7, 9, 13, 16, 622, 649, 673, 817, 856, 879, 882
Amerindian 7, 31, 81, 243
Amharic 9, 11, 15, 655, 662, 663
Amorite 656
Amoy *see* Min
Anatolian (branch of Indo-European) 40, 41, 436
Anatolian (Turkic dialect) 622
Andaman 15
Andean 22
Andro 802
Angami 800
Angas 706, 707, 709

Anglo-Saxon *see* English
Ankwe *see* Goemai
Annamese *see* Vietnamese
Annamite *see* Vietnamese
Apabhraṁśa 441, 442, 445, 471, 490
Arabic 4, 15, 24f., 42, 79, 81, 140, 207, 238–41 *passin*, 276, 415, 454, 471, 475, 478, 480, 523, 524–31 *passim*, 549, 550, 552, 553, 612, 623–5 *passim*, 647, 650, 652, 654, 656–9 *passim*, 661, 662, 664–85, 692, 709, 712, 857, 916, 918, 931, 994–6 *passim*, 1013
Aramaic 15, 523, 656–9 *passim*, 662, 665, 673, 687, 691
Arapaho 21
Arawakan 22, 81
Ardhamāgadhī 441
Argobba 655
Armenian 14, 34–8 *passim*, 42f., 47f., 51, 52, 62, 199, 411, 520
Arumanian 206, 303–5 *passim*, 314, 317, 318
Asamiya *see* Assamese
Ashtiyani 514–16 *passim*
Aśokan 440–2 *passim*
Assamese 440, 490, 491, 493, 500
Atayalic 904
Athapaskan 20f.
Athapaskan-Eyak 20f.
Atsi *see* Zaiwa
Australian 5, 7, 8, 17–19
Austric 21
Austro-Asiatic 21, 29, 511, 725, 777, 795
Austro-Tai 757, 906
Austronesian 7, 11f., 16, 19, 673, 757, 856, 881, 899–912, 915, 920, 936

Avam-Tavgi *see* Nganasan
Avestan 40, 440, 517, 519–21 *passim*
Āwē 725
Awngi 651
Aymara 22
Azerbaidjani 14, 523, 621, 622
Aztecan 21f.

Bachama 706
Bactrian 518f., 548
Badaga 725, 726
Bade 706
Bahing 800
Bai 799
Bakhtiari 514–16 *passim*, 520, 523
Balante 963
Balinese 901, 915
Balkan sprachbund 10, 303, 309, 310, 313,
    315–17 *passim*, 407, 414, 434, 435, 575
Balochi 514–17 *passim*, 520, 521, 523
Balti Tibetan 805
Baltic 40, 42, 51, 52, 61, 64, 70, 325, 519,
    567, 594, 612
Baltic-Finnic 570–6 *passim*, 593, 595, 611,
    617
Balto-Slavonic 40, 42
Bana 706
Banda 968
Bangla *see* Bengali
Bantoid 967
Bantu 19f., 661, 673, 817, 961–3 *passim*,
    967f., 991–1014
Barain 706
Barawa 706
Bariba 965
Baric 801–2
Bartangi 514–16 *passim*, 520, 521
Bashkardi 514–16 *passim*
Basque 7, 13, 19, 238, 239
Bassa 966
Bata 706
Batak 901, 915
Baule 966
Beja 648, 651, 652
Belau *see* Palauan
Bele 706
Beli 751
Bellari 725
Belorussian 322, 323, 329, 331f.
Bengali 12, 24, 443, 445, 446, 470, 490–513
Benue-Congo 961, 962, 966, 967f., 970,
    971, 991, 1010
Benue-Kwa 962
Berber 15, 649–52 *passim*, 707
Bete 966
Bhojpuri 490
Bidiyo 706
Bikol 901
Bini 966

Birgit 706
Biu-Mandara 705, 706, 708
Black Tai *see* Tai Dam
Bodic 801, 802
Bodish 799–802 *passim*
Bodo 800
Bodo-Garo 800, 802, 808
Bodo-Konyak 802
Boghom 706
Bokkos *see* Ron
Bolanci *see* Bole
Bole 706, 709
Boro *see* Bodo
Bouyei 749, 750
Brahui 15, 725, 726
Breton 42
Britannic *see* Brythonic
Brythonic 42
Buduma 706
Buginese 901, 915
Bulgarian 10, 309, 310, 316, 318, 322, 323,
    325, 327, 368, 391, 395, 398, 407, 414
Bunan 799
Bura 706
Burgundi 725
Burmese 16, 800, 803–6 *passim*, 808,
    834–54
Burmic 801–2
Burmish 800, 834
Burushaski 7, 15
Busa 964
Buyi *see* Bouyei
Bwamu 965

Cakchiquel 22
Cambodian *see* Khmer
Canaanite 656–7 *passim*, 665, 691
Cantonese *see* Yue
Carib 22
Cassubian 327, 348
Castilian *see* Spanish
Catalan 203, 205, 206, 208, 211, 239, 244,
    282
Caucasian 7, 9, 14f.
Cebuano 24, 901
Celtic 6, 41f., 43, 51, 56, 57, 75, 83, 86,
    162, 188, 232, 239, 276
Central Iran, dialects of 514–16 *passim*
Central Pacific 906
Chadic 15, 649–52 *passim*, 673, 705–8, 709,
    723
Chaha *see* Ezha-Gumer-Chaha-Gura
Cham 16
Chamic 902
Chamorro 903–5 *passim*
Chang 800
Chepang 807, 810
Cheremis *see* Mari
Cheyenne 21

Chibak 706
ChiMwini 994, 995, 1005f.
Chin *see* Kuki-Chin
Chinese 3, 8, 10f., 14, 15, 23, 25, 53, 77–9
    passim, 81, 82, 98, 140, 276, 751, 752,
    755, 777–80 *passim*, 782, 792–4 *passim*,
    799, 803–6 *passim*, 811–33, 834, 857–62
    passim, 869, 879, 884, 893, 915, 918,
    929
Chinese Shan *see* Tai Nuea
Chinghpo *see* Jinghpo
Chip 706
Chukchi 14
Chukotko-Kamchatkan 28
Chuvash 622
Congo-Kordofanian *see*
    Niger-Kordofanian
Cook Island Maori *see* Rarotongan
Coptic 648, 650
Cornish 42
Corsican 204
Cree 21
Croatian *see* Serbo-Croat
Cuman 590
Curonian 42
Cushitic 10, 15, 648–53 *passim*, 655, 662,
    991, 996
Czech 322–5 *passim*, 342, 348, 367–90
    passim, 396, 398

Daba 706
Dacian 309
Daco-Rumanian *see* Rumanian
Daffo *see* Ron
Dagara 965
Dagari 965
Dagomba 965
Dalmatian 205, 206
Dan-Kweni 964
Dangaléat *see* Dangla
Dangla (Dangaléat) 706, 707
Danish 13, 68, 157–79 *passim*
Dankali *see* Afar-Saho
Dardic 519
Dari *see* Persian
Dass 706
Dehong Dai *see* Tai Nuea
Deno 706
Dera *see* Kanakuru
Dghwede 706
Diri 706
Dizi 651
Djingili 17
Dogon 965
Dravidian 7, 9, 13, 15, 24, 440, 454, 473,
    479, 509, 511, 649, 725–9, 737, 741,
    743, 745, 746, 856, 881
Dullay 648
Duru 969

Dutch 2, 3, 6, 19, 68, 81, 82, 110, 113, 130,
    139–56, 212, 858, 916, 918, 927
Duwai 706
Dyirbal 18f.
Dyola 963

East Gurage 655, 659
East Himalayan 800–2 *passim*, 807
Ebira 966
Ebla 656
Edo 961
Efik-Ibibio 967
Egyptian 15, 25, 648, 650–2 *passim*, 657
Enets 570–2 *passim*, 577
Engadinish 203
English 1, 3f., 5f., 8, 9, 11, 12, 18, 22, 23,
    25, 27f., 50, 51, 60, 61, 64, 68, 69, 71–5
    passim, 77–109, 110, 113, 118–20
    passim, 130, 133–7 *passim*, 140–3
    passim, 145, 146, 149, 151, 153, 158,
    160, 162, 163, 166–70 *passim*, 173–8
    passim, 211, 218, 225, 226, 233f., 240,
    267, 277, 296, 300, 316, 319, 320, 330,
    339, 341, 342, 345–7 *passim*, 386, 437,
    470, 486, 487, 519, 530, 533, 538, 541,
    549, 557, 562f., 565, 573, 578, 606, 612,
    622f., 667f., 676f., 683, 709, 713, 720f.,
    731, 733, 737, 740, 745, 758, 770, 772,
    774, 782, 787, 819, 826, 836, 837, 850–2
    passim, 855, 857–9 *passim*, 862, 872,
    874, 876, 877, 879, 893–5 *passim*, 915,
    916, 927, 930, 936–9 *passim*, 953, 954,
    957, 995, 1007, 1013
Erythraic *see* Afroasiatic
Eskimo 20, 158
Eskimo-Aleut 7, 14, 20
Estonian 13, 569–71 *passim*, 574, 576, 593,
    597
Ethiopian 650, 655–9 *passim*, 662, 663
Etruscan 180, 199, 201
Eurasiatic 7
Ewe 966
Eyak 20
Ezha-Gumer-Chaha-Gura 654f., 657

Faliscan 180, 188
Fang 996
Faroese 68, 125, 157, 159, 160
Fars province, non-Persian dialects of
    514–16 *passim*
Fennic 570
Fijian 903, 906–7 *passim*, 907–11, 911–12
    passim
Filipino *see* Tagalog
Finnish 13, 70, 157f., 569–76 *passim*, 577,
    581, 593–617
Finno-Ugric 569–71 *passim*, 574f., 587,
    590, 593, 608, 611
Formosan 892, 894

Franco-Provençal 211
French 1, 9, 25, 27f., 37, 78, 79, 81, 82,
    84–6 passim, 91, 98, 116, 140, 143, 145,
    147–9 passim, 162, 166, 176–8 passim,
    203–8 passim, 210–35, 237, 239, 242,
    246, 248, 251, 253, 255, 257, 273, 276,
    279, 282, 287, 289, 299, 304–6 passim,
    309, 316, 319, 320, 330, 331, 337, 493,
    536, 573, 588f., 605, 612, 709, 778, 779,
    782, 794f., 855, 995
Frisian 3, 6, 68, 69, 82, 110, 113, 139, 151,
    153, 159
Friulian 204, 206, 282
Fukkianese see Min
Fula 961–4 passim, 1011
Fulani see Fula
Fulbe see Fula
Fulfulde see Fula
Futuna 904
Fyer 706

Gã-Adangme 966
Ga'anda 706, 707
Gabin see Ga'anda
Gabri 706
Gadaba 725, 726
Gadang 706
Gaelic see Goidelic, Scots Gaelic
Gafat 655
Gagauz 622
Galambu 706
Galician 204, 239, 260, 261
Galla see Oromo
Garo 511, 800
Gaulish 232
Gawar 706
Gbaya 968–70 passim
Gedaged 902
Ge'ez 655, 658, 659, 661, 662
Geji 706
Gelao 751
Georgian 9, 14, 678
Gera 706
Gerka 706
German 2, 3, 5f., 8, 11, 24, 26, 27f., 34,
    51, 68, 69, 73, 74, 76, 79, 81, 82, 88,
    97, 100, 110–38, 139–41 passim, 143–9
    passim, 151–5 passim, 158, 162, 163,
    166, 173, 175–8 passim, 184, 201, 212,
    224, 282, 303, 351, 367, 369, 396, 519,
    578, 588, 605, 612, 627, 628, 855, 872
Germanic 6, 9, 37, 42, 47f., 51, 52, 55–7
    passim, 64, 68–76, 81–3 passim, 93, 98,
    110, 116, 122f., 125, 127–30 passim,
    133, 140, 152, 153, 155, 158, 160, 162,
    166, 171, 184, 207, 208, 217, 232, 238,
    239, 241, 253, 276, 324, 574, 594, 599,
    612, 837, 858
Geruma 706

Gidar 706
Gikuyu 1001, 1004f., 1010
Gilaki 514–16, 521
Gilbertese (Kiribati) 78, 903
Gilyak see Nivkh
Giriama 998, 999, 1005
Gisiga 706
Glavda 706
Goemai 706, 707
Goggot 655
Goidelic 41f.
Gola 963
Goṇḍi 725, 726
Gothic 34–9 passim, 45, 47, 54, 56, 58, 59,
    64, 68f., 70–4 passim, 88, 158, 184,
    193, 199
Greek 4, 10, 28, 34–45 passim, 49–52
    passim, 54–9 passim, 61, 72, 81, 162,
    176, 180, 181, 183, 184, 188, 189, 192–4
    passim, 197–201 passim, 232, 233, 239,
    282, 288, 314, 315, 317–19 passim, 322,
    326, 335, 354, 396, 407, 410–39, 440,
    450, 454, 519, 520, 549, 589, 612, 622,
    623, 657, 758, 836, 837
Greenlandic see Eskimo
Guanche 649
Guang 966
Guarani 20, 22
Gude 706
Guduf 706
Gujarati 24, 443, 445, 446
Gur 961, 965
Gurage 656f.
Gurani 514, 520, 521
Gurma 965
Gurung 799, 802, 806
Guruntum 706
Gvoko 706
Gwandara 706, 709
Gwari 966
Gyarong 623, 624, 628–30 passim
Gyeto-Ennemor-Engdegeñ-Ener 656
Gypsy see Romany

Hakka 812, 813, 832
Hamitic 647
Hamito-Semitic see Afroasiatic
Hani 800
Harari 655, 659
Harsusi 655
Hatsa 20
Hausa 15, 24, 667, 673, 705–8 passim,
    708–23
Hawaiian 903, 904, 907
Hebrew 15, 24, 110, 239, 415, 656–60
    passim, 662, 665, 673, 675, 686–704
Hellenic see Greek
Hesperonesian 936
Higi 706

Hiligaynon 901
Hina 706
Hindi *see* Hindi-Urdu
Hindi-Urdu 24, 25, 78, 81, 441, 443, 445,
  446, 470–89, 498, 506, 526, 673, 836,
  1013
Hindustani *see* Hindi-Urdu
Hiri Motu 902
Hitkala *see* Lamang
Hittite 34–9 *passim*, 41, 43, 45, 49, 51, 52,
  54–7 *passim*, 61, 195, 411
Hixkaryana 22
Hmong-Mien 753
Hokan 20
Hokkianese *see* Min
Hona 706
Hungarian 13, 303, 308, 309, 325, 367,
  369, 393, 569–75 *passim*, 577–92, 593,
  595, 597, 609
Hurza-Vame 706

Iban 901
Ibero-Caucasian 21
Icelandic 34, 37, 68, 125, 157, 159, 160,
  162, 565
Idoma 966
Igala 966, 971
Igbo 964f.
Ijo 961f., 966
Illyrian 43, 318
Ilokano 901
Ilongo *see* Hiligaynon
Indic *see* Indo-Aryan
Indo-Aryan (Indic) 15, 24, 40, 415, 440–7,
  448, 453, 469, 470–2 *passim*, 480, 481,
  485, 489, 490, 491, 497, 498–501
  passim, 506–12 *passim*, 519, 520, 549,
  551, 725, 728, 729, 733, 758, 835–7
  passim, 843, 847
Indo-European 5–8 *passim*, 10, 12–15
  passim, 23, 31–67, 70–4 *passim*, 76, 82,
  92, 93, 98, 110, 122f., 149, 166, 180,
  185–9 *passim*, 191–4 *passim*, 196, 197,
  199, 203, 208, 288, 292, 323–5 *passim*,
  337, 340, 398, 410–13 *passim*, 421, 422,
  434, 440, 462–4 *passim*, 466, 470, 471,
  474, 480f., 519, 521, 523, 547, 649, 663,
  725, 754, 792, 817, 821, 824, 826, 855,
  856, 872, 893, 906
Indo-Iranian 40, 48, 56, 64, 188, 411, 440,
  442, 470, 574, 673, 678
Indo-Pacific 7
Indonesian *see* Malay
Indu 725
Ingrian 570–1 *passim*, 593
Iranian 6, 12, 40, 41, 440, 449, 454,
  514–22, 523, 528, 529, 530, 542, 543,
  547–9 *passim*, 554, 559f., 574, 590, 667
Irish 6, 34–8 *passim*, 41, 42, 52, 55, 57, 81,

  188, 189, 193
Iroquoian 21
Irula 725, 726, 730
Işekiri 971
Ishkashmi 514–16 *passim*, 521
Istro-Rumanian 206, 303, 304, 309
Italian 69, 81, 203, 205–8 *passim*, 235, 242,
  276, 279–302, 305–7 *passim*, 309, 316,
  393, 437, 588, 612, 782
Italic 41–3 *passim*, 56, 57, 61, 180–202,
  203, 214, 215
Italo-Celtic 42
Itelmen *see* Kamchadal

Jakun 15
Japanese 7, 8, 9, 11, 14, 16, 25, 79, 81, 99,
  155, 622, 638, 645, 778, 855–80, 893,
  906
Jara 706
Javanese 24, 901, 915, 916, 920, 923, 931
Jegu 706
Jeng *see* Nzangi
Jimbin 706
Jimi 706
Jinghpaw *see* Jinghpo
Jinghpo 800–3 *passim*, 806, 807, 809
Jirrbal *see* Dyirbal
Jonkor of Abu Telfan *see* Migama
Jonkor of Guera *see* Mokulu
Ju 706
Judaeo-German *see* Yiddish
Judaeo-Spanish 205, 236, 258, 259
Jukun 968

Kabalai 706
Kabyle 650, 651
Kachin *see* Jinghpo
Kachinic 800–2 *passim*
Kadai (Kam-Tai) 29, 749, 751–3 *passim*,
  757, 906
Kadu 802
Kafa 651
Kaikudi 725
Kalmyk 13
Kam-Sui 751, 752, 755, 756
Kam-Tai *see* Kadai
Kam Muang 749, 750, 752, 759
Kamarupan 801–2
Kamassian 575
Kamba 998
Kamchadal 14
Kanakuru 706–8 *passim*
Kanauri 799
Kannada 725, 726, 728
Kanuri 709
Kapingamarangi 903
Kapsiki *see* Higi
Karekare 706
Karelian 570–1 *passim*, 593, 595, 612

Karen 801, 806, 808, 834
Karenic 801
Karfa 706
Kariya 706
Kartvelian 14, 649
Kashmiri 440, 443, 447
Kashubian *see* Cassubian
Katla 961
Kazakh 621
Kekchi 22
Kera 706
Ket 7, 14
Khalaj 523
Khalkha 13
Kham-Magar 802
Khamti 749, 750, 755
Khanty 570–4 *passim*, 576, 587
Khmer (Cambodian) 15, 755, 757–9
  passim, 765, 837
Khoisan 7, 20, 961, 991
Khuen 749, 750
Khwarezmian 518, 520, 521, 548
Kilba 706
Kiranti/Rai 800, 802, 806
Kirfi 706
Kirghiz 621
Kiribati *see* Gilbertese
Kissi 963
Koalib 961
Koḍagu 725, 726
Koenoem 706
Kofyar 706
Kola *see* Daba
Kolami 725, 726
Komi 570–4 *passim*, 576
Konda 725, 726
Kongo 1001
Konyak 800, 802
Koraga 725
Korava 725
Kordofanian 961, 962
Korean 7, 9, 14, 16, 25, 81, 622, 778, 856,
  857, 859, 872, 881, 898
Koryak 14
Kosraean 903
Kota 725, 726
Kotoko 706
Kpelle 964, 970
Krio 97, 101, 972
Kru 966
Kubi *see* Deno
Kuchean *see* Tocharian
Kūi 725, 726, 728
Kujarke 706
Kuki-Chin 800, 802, 834
Kuki-Naga 802
Kulere 706
Kumzari 514–16 *passim*
Kupto 706

Kurdish 514–16 *passim*, 520–2 *passim*, 523,
  622, 667
Kuruba 725
Kūṟux 725, 726, 728
Kusaie *see* Kosraean
Kūvi 725, 726
Kwa 961, 962, 966f., 971, 988, 991, 1010
Kwang 706

Ladin 204, 206, 282
Ladino *see* Judaeo-Spanish
Laha 751
Lahnda 549
Lahu 800, 810
Lakher 800
Lakkia 751
Lamang 706
Lame *see* Zime
Lamekhite *see* Afroasiatic
Lao 15, 749, 750, 755, 759
Lapp 13, 158, 569–76 *passim*
Lappic 570, 573
Laqua 751
Lati 751
Latin 1, 4, 9, 24, 25, 27, 28, 34–41 *passim*,
  44, 45, 49–52 *passim*, 71–3 *passim*, 75,
  81, 83, 85, 86, 91, 94, 98, 115, 116, 145,
  159, 162, 176, 177, 180–202, 203–9
  passim, 210, 213–15 *passim*, 217,
  219–22 *passim*, 224, 226, 227, 229, 232,
  233, 235, 237–41 *passim*, 243, 247–9
  passim, 251, 252, 255, 256, 260, 261,
  263, 269, 271, 276, 279, 280, 282, 283,
  286–9 *passim*, 292, 293, 296, 305, 306,
  308–10 *passim*, 312–14 *passim*, 316–20
  passim, 324, 348, 349, 354, 369, 396,
  411, 415, 430, 437, 462, 519, 541, 581,
  588, 612, 657, 675, 758, 836, 837, 858
Latvian 34, 35, 42, 325
Lawng 800
Lechitic 348, 358
Lele 706
Lepcha 803
Lepontic 43
Lettish *see* Latvian
Ligurian 43
Limba 963
Limbu 800
Lisramic *see* Afroasiatic
Lisu 800, 810
Lithuanian 34–8 *passim*, 42, 47, 51, 52,
  323–5 *passim*
Livonian 570–1 *passim*, 575, 593
Lobiri 965
Logone 652, 706
Lolo *see* Yi
Lolo-Burmese 800–2 *passim*, 805, 806,
  808, 834
Loloish 800, 802, 804, 835

Loma 964
Longzhou 753
Lotha 800
Luba 998
Ludian 570–1 *passim*
Lue *see* Tai Lue
Luganda 998–1000
Luguru 997
Luish 800, 802
Luri 514–16 *passim*, 523
Lusatian *see* Sorbian
Lushai 800
Luwian 41
Lycian 41
Lydian 41

Macassarese 901, 915
Macedonian 10, 316, 322, 323, 325, 327,
    368, 391, 395, 407, 414, 434
Mada 706
Madurese 901, 915
Mafa *see* Matakam
Magadhan 490, 491, 493, 499, 500, 506
Māgadhī 442, 490
Magahi 490
Maha 706
Māhārāṣṭrī 441, 442, 444
Mahri 655
Maithili 490, 491
Malagasy 16, 19, 902, 904, 906
Malay 16, 23f., 78, 81, 140, 673, 901–4
    passim, 907, 913–35
Malayāḷam 725, 726, 728, 729f.
Malayo-Polynesian 904f., *see also*
    Austronesian
Maldivian 12
Maltese 13, 647, 664, 671
Malto 511, 725, 726, 729
Mam 22
Manchu 28, 882
Maṇḍa 725, 726
Mandaic 656
Mandara 706, 707
Mandarin *see* Chinese
Mande 709, 961, 964, 966, 970
Mangas 706
Maninka-Bambara-Dyula 964
Manipuri *see* Meithei
Mano 964
Mansi 570–3 *passim*, 575, 587
Manx 24
Maori 903, 904
Mapun 706
Marathi 24, 441, 443, 446, 470, 473, 499
Marba 706
Margi 706–8 *passim*
Mari 569–76 *passim*
Marshallese 903
Maru *see* Lawng

Masa 705, 706
Masqan 655
Matakam 706
Mawa 706
Mayan 22
Mazandarani 514–16 *passim*
Mbabaram 8, 17
Mbara 706
Mbugu 996
Mbum 969, 970
Mburku 706
Median 517
Megleno-Rumanian 303, 304
Meithei 800, 802, 803
Mende 964
Merina 902
Mernyang *see* Kofyar
Mesme 706
Messapic 43, 201
Miao-Yao 16, 799, 805
Migama 706
Miji Kenda 996, 1006
Mikir 800, 802
Miltu 706
Min 276, 812f., 815–18 *passim*
Minangkabau 901, 915
Minjia *see* Bai
Miya 706
Moabite 656
Mod 706
Modgel *see* Kwang
Mofu-Duvangar 706
Mofu-Gudur 706
Moghol 13
Mogum 706
Mokulu 706
Moldavian *see* Rumanian
Moloko 706
Mon 834, 835, 837, 839, 843, 845–7 *passim*
Mon-Khmer 777f., 834, 835, 839, 845
Mongolian 7, 9, 13, 622, 657, 882
Montol 706
Moore 965
Mordva 569–76 *passim*
Mordvinian *see* Mordva
Moso *see* Naxi
Mota 902
Motu 902
Mubi 651, 652, 706
Muher 655
Muktele 706
Mulwi *see* Musgu
Munda 511, 725
Munda-Mon-Khmer *see* Austro-Asiatic
Mundari 511
Mundat 706
Munji 514–16 *passim*, 521, 548
Munjuk *see* Musgu
Musey 706

Musgoi *see* Daba
Musgu 706
Muyang 706
Mwaghavul *see* Sura
Mwera 1001

Na-Dene 7, 20
Nabatean 656, 673
Naga 800, 802, 804, 834
Nahuatl 21f., 81
Naiki 725, 726
Nakhi *see* Naxi
Nalu 963
Nancere 706
Nauruan 903
Navaho 20f.
Navajo *see* Navaho
Naxi 800–3 *passim*
Ndam 706
Negerhollands 139
Nenets 570–1 *passim*, 575
Nepali 441, 473
Newari 799, 802, 803, 806
Ngadju 901
Ngamo 706
Nganasan 570–1 *passim*, 575
Ngizim 706–8 *passim*
Nicobarese 15
Niger-Congo 961, 962–70, 971, 991, 1008, 1010
Niger-Kordofanian 7, 20, 959–70
Nilo-Saharan 7, 20, 961, 991
Nivkh 14
Nocte 800, 807
Northeastern Thai *see* Lao
Northern Pare 996
Northern Thai *see* Kam Muang
Norwegian 3, 68, 157–79 *passim*
Nostratic 649
Nukuoro 903
Nung (Tai) 749
Nung (Tibeto-Burman) 801, 802
Nupe 966
Nyamwezi 998
Nzangi 706

Ob-Ugric 570–6 *passim*, 577
Occitan (Provençal) 203, 205, 206, 211, 279, 282, 588
Oceanic 904, 905, 907, 908
Old Bulgarian *see* Old Church Slavonic
Old Church Slavonic 34–9 *passim*, 52, 56, 305, 314, 318, 322–7 *passim*, 329–31 *passim*, 415, 519
Old Gutnish 159
Old Low Franconian 141, 158
Old Norse 69, 73, 74, *see also* Icelandic
Old Prussian 42, 325
Old Saxon 26, 69, 73, 158

Ollari 725, 726
Omotic 648, 650–1 *passim*, 707
Oriya 490, 491, 493, 500
Ormuri 514–16 *passim*
Oromo 648
Oroshori 514–16 *passim*, 521
Oscan 180–212 *passim*
Osman 622
Osmanli *see* Turkish
Ossete 14, 514–17 *passim*, 520, 521, 590
Ostyak *see* Khanty
Ostyak-Samoyed *see* Selkup

Pa'a 706
Pabir *see* Bura
Padaung 834
Paiwanic 904
Palaic 41
Palauan 903–5 *passim*
Paleoasiatic *see* Paleosiberian
Paleosiberian 14
Pali 441–5 *passim*, 751, 758, 759, 835–9 *passim*
Pamir languages 548
Panjabi 24, 443
Papiamento *see* Papiamentu
Papiamentu 27, 139, 261
Papuan 7, 12, 16f.
Parachi 514–16 *passim*
Parji 725, 726
Parthian 518, 521, 549
Pashto 6, 514, 521, 522, 525, 529, 530, 547–66, 667, 673
Pecheneg 590
Pengo 725, 726, 728
Penutian 20–3 *passim*
Permic 570–4 *passim*, 580
Permyak 570–1 *passim*, 574
Pero 706
Persian 6, 25, 42, 81, 471, 475, 478, 480, 488, 514–22 *passim*, 523–46, 547, 549, 550, 552, 553, 559, 565, 590, 623–5 *passim*, 667, 673, 678f., 857, 1013
Peul *see* Fula
Peve *see* Zime
Phoenician 416, 656f., 673, 839, 840, 843
Phuan 760
Phuthai 760
Pidlimdi *see* Tera
Pilipino *see* Tagalog
Piya 706
Podoko 706
Pokomo 1006, 1008f.
Polabian 322, 348
Polchi 706
Polish 5, 6, 322–7 *passim*, 332, 336, 342, 348–66, 372, 374, 379
Polynesian 882, 902–4 *passim*, 906
Ponapean 903

Portuguese 12, 25, 27, 203–8 *passim*, 239, 242, 244, 260–78, 279, 289, 788, 858, 918, 1013
Prakrit 441–3 *passim*, 445, 471
Primi 623, 624
Provençal *see* Occitan
Putai 706
Pyapun 706
Pyu 835

Qashqa'i 523
Qiang 623, 624
Qïpchaq 623, 624
Quechua 7, 20, 22
Quechumaran 22
Quiché 22

Raetic 43
Rajasthani 24
Rarotongan 903
Rawang 623
Red Tai 749, 750
Rendille 650
Rengma 800
Rhaeto-Romance 203–6 *passim*, 208, 282
Romance 4, 9, 10, 27, 81, 89, 140, 142, 145, 148f., 181, 203–9, 210, 217, 233, 236, 238–42 *passim*, 244, 246, 247, 251, 253, 255, 256, 258, 260, 263, 271, 274, 276, 279, 282, 286, 289, 303–10 *passim*, 315–17 *passim*, 319, 320, 322, 331, 341, 415, 430, 436, 530, 588, 751, 816, 837
Romansh 230f., 206
Romany (Gypsy) 158, 440, 523, 577
Ron 706
Roshani 514–16 *passim*, 521 ·
Rotokas 907
Rotuman 906
Roviana 902
Rumanian 10, 203, 206–8 *passim*, 221, 273, 276, 279, 303–21, 325, 407, 414, 574, 588
Rung 799, 801, 802, 807
Rumelian 622
Russian 5, 6, 22, 79, 81, 82, 91, 100, 113, 319, 322–7 *passim*, 329–47, 351, 352, 361, 362, 372, 374, 375, 382, 383, 385, 392, 396, 399, 400, 403, 404, 581, 612, 628, 782, 872
Ryūkyūan 859

Saam *see* Lappish
Saba 706
Sabine 199
Saek 749, 750, 755
Saka 518, 548, 554
Sakai 15
Samic *see* Lappish

Samo 964
Samoan 78, 902
Samoyedic 569–77 *passim*
Sandawe 20, 991
Sanglechi 514–16 *passim*, 521
Sanskrit 22, 28, 34–40 *passim*, 43–5 *passim*, 47, 50–2 *passim*, 54–9 *passim*, 61–4 *passim*, 72, 188, 189, 192, 199, 201, 323, 410, 411, 415, 440–4 *passim*, 448–69, 471–4 *passim*, 493, 496, 499, 507, 508, 510, 519, 520, 675, 729–31 *passim*, 733, 734, 738, 751, 758, 759, 764, 765, 918
Santali 15, 511
Sardinian 203, 205–9 *passim*
Sarikoli 12, 514–16 *passim*, 521
Sarmatian 517
Sasak 901
Śaurasenī 441, 442, 444
Savara 725, 726
Sayanci *see* Zaar
Scandinavian languages 3, 6, 11, 68, 83f., 86, 94, 130, 151, 155, 157–79, 573
Scots Gaelic 41
Scythian 517
Seljuq 622
Selkup 570–1, 573, 575
Selonian 42
Selti-Wolane-Ulbarag 655
Sema 800
Semang 15
Semigallian 42
Semitic 9f., 15, 416, 436, 647–52 *passim*, 654–63, 664, 665, 673, 693, 695–7 *passim*, 817
Semito-Hamitic *see* Afroasiatic
Semnani 514–16 *passim*
Senari 965, 966
Senufo 965
Serbian *see* Serbo-Croat
Serbo-Croat 282, 304, 322, 323, 325, 327, 342, 368, 374, 383, 391–409, 414, 588
Serer 963, 964
Sha 706
Shagawu 706
Shāhbāzgaṛhī 442
Shahri 655, 662
Shan *see* Tai Long
Shughni 514–16 *passim*, 520, 521
Siamese *see* Thai
Sibine *see* Somrai
Sicilian 203
Sicel 43
Sidamo 648, 652
Sifan 623
Sindhi 443
Sinhala *see* Sinhalese
Sinhalese 12, 440, 731
Sinitic 799

Sino-Tibetan 7, 10f., 15f., 725, 797–810, 811, 856
Siouan 35
Slavonic 4, 6, 10, 40, 42, 51, 52, 56, 61, 110, 162, 207, 305, 306, 308, 309, 312, 314, 316–19 *passim*, 322–8, 329–31 *passim*, 336, 337, 342, 348, 354, 357, 358, 360, 368, 369, 374, 379, 385, 389, 391, 398, 399, 402, 406, 407, 415, 437, 519, 575, 587, 589, 599, 612, 816
Slovak 322, 323, 325, 339, 348, 367–90 *passim*, 398
Slovene 282, 322, 323, 325, 327, 391, 398, 407
Soddo 655
Sogdian 518, 520, 521, 524, 548, 549, 554
Sokoro 706
Somali 15, 648, 651, 652
Somrai 706
Soninke 964
Soqotri 655
Sorbian 322, 323, 327, 346
Sotho 997
South Arabian 650, 655, 657, 658, 662, 665, 673
South Crimean 622
South Halmahera-West New Guinea 905
Southern Thai 749, 750
Spanish 8, 12, 25, 27, 40, 69, 78, 79, 81, 82, 100, 139, 203–8 *passim*, 214, 215, 235, 236–59, 260, 261, 263, 267, 271, 273, 274, 276, 279, 289, 293, 294, 309, 315. 612, 692, 858, 872, 936, 937, 939, 956
Sranan 139, 140
Sui 752
Sukur 706
Sumerian 1, 25
Sundanese 901, 915
Suppire-Mianka 905
Sura 706
Surselvan 203
Sus-Yalinka 964
Swahili 23, 78, 667, 673, 709, 962, 963, 993, 994–1014
Swedish 3, 68, 157–79 *passim*, 593, 595, 612f.
Syriac 42, 656, 657, 673

Tagalog 24, 78, 901, 907, 920, 936–58
Tahitian 903
Tai 7, 15, 511, 747–56, 757–60 *passim*, 775, 778, 799, 805, 809
Tai Dam 749, 750, 754
Tai Long (Shan) 749, 750, 834, 836
Tai Lue 749, 750, 759f.
Tai Nuea 749, 750
Tai Yuan *see* Kam Muang
Taino 81

Taiwanese *see* Min
Tajiki *see* Persian
Tal 706
Talishi 514–16 *passim*
Talodi 961
Tamang 799, 802, 806
Tambas 706
Tamil 24, 78, 454, 509, 725–9 *passim*, 729–46
Tangale 706, 707
Tangkhul 805
Tangut 623–5 *passim*
Tasmanian 7, 19
Tat 514–16 *passim*
Tatar 621
Tati 514–16 *passim*, 521
Tay 749
Teel *see* Montol
Tegali 961
Telugu 24, 725, 726, 728
Tem 965
Temne 963
Tera 706–8 *passim*
Thagicu 996–8 *passim*
Thai 10f., 15, 749–51 *passim*, 753–5 *passim*, 757–75, 834, 836, 837
Thakali 799, 802
Tho 749
Thracian 309, 318
Thraco-Phrygian 43
Thulung 800
Tibetan 11, 16, 799, 801, 803–6 *passim*, 808, 809, 834
Tibeto-Burman 16, 511, 753, 755, 797–810, 817, 834, 835, 837, 840, 845
Tibeto-Kanauri 802
Tibeto-Karen 801
Tigré 655, 657, 663
Tigrinya 655, 657
Tiv 967, 968, 970
Tiwi 17
Tobanga *see* Gabri
Tocharian 34–8 *passim*, 40, 41, 43, 51, 52, 56, 61, 64
Toda 725, 726
Tok Pisin 3, 26, 68
Tolai 902
Tongan 81, 902–4 *passim*
Toram 706
Turkic 903
Trung 623
Tsagu 706
Tsouic 904
Tuareg 709
Tulu 725, 726
Tumak 706
Tumtum 961
Tungusic 7, 9, 13f., 622, 882
Tupi 22, 261, 276

Turfan *see* Tocharian
Turkic 7, 9, 13, 14, 523, 544, 569, 576, 588,
    589f., 619–24, 630, 646, 667, 882
Turkish 13, 24, 38, 81, 140, 309, 319, 396,
    437, 471, 525, 528, 589, 619–22 *passim*,
    622–46, 673, 857
Turkmenian 523, 621, 622–4 *passim*

Ubykh 14
Udmurt 569–71 *passim*, 575, 577
Ugaritic 656, 665, 673
Ugric 570–1 *passim*, 577, 578, 581
Uighur 621, 623
Ukrainian 81, 322f., 323, 329, 331f., 367
Uldeme 706
Umbrian 180–202 *passim*
Umbundu 999, 1006, 1008, 1111
Ural-Altaic 622
Uralic 7, 13, 14, 567–76, 577, 587, 590,
    622, 649
Urdu *see* Hindi-Urdu
Usan 17
Uto-Aztecan 21f.
Uzbek 621

Vafsi 514–16 *passim*.
Vayu 800
Vedic *see* Sanskrit
Venetic 43, 180, 188, 201
Veps 570–1 *passim*, 593
Vietnamese 10f., 15, 25, 753, 777–96, 799,
    805, 929
Vogul *see* Mansi
Volgaic 570
Volscian 188
Voltaic *see* Gur
Votic 570–1 *passim*, 593
Votyak *see* Udmurt
Vumba 999

Wakhi 514–16 *passim*, 520
Wancho 800
Wandala *see* Mandara
Warji 706
Welsh 6, 32
West Atlantic 961, 962–4, 965, 970
West Margi 706
Western Gurage 655f.
Western Panjabi *see* Lahnda
White Russian *see* Belorussian

White Tai 749, 750
Wiyaw 8
Wolof 963
Wu 811, 812, 815
Wurkum *see* Piya

Xamta 652
Xishuangbanna Dai *see* Tai Lue
Xixia *see* Tangut

Yabem 902
Yaghnobi 494–6 *passim*, 518, 520, 521
Yakut 13, 621
Yamaltu 706
Yap 903
Yay 749, 750, 753
Yazgulami 514–16 *passim*, 521
Yedina *see* Buduma
Yenisei-Samoyed *see* Enets
Yerava 725
Yerukula 725
Yi 860, 803
Yiddish 64, 68, 81, 110, 692, 745
Yidgha 514–16 *passim*, 521
Yiwom *see* Gerka
Yoruba 713, 966, 967, 969, 970, 971–90,
    1010
Yoruboid 971
Yotvingian 42
Yucatec 24
Yue (Cantonese) 3, 81, 140, 811, 812,
    815–18 *passim*
Yukaghir 14
Yurak-Samoyed *see* Nenets

Zaar 706
Zaiwa 800
Zakshi *see* Zari
Zanda 968
Zari 706
Zaza 514–16 *passim*, 520, 521
Zebaki 514–16 *passim*, 521
Zeem 706
Zhuang 749, 750
Zime 706
Zulgo 706
Zulu 1001, 1011
Zway 655
Zyrian *see* Komi